Collins
French
Dictionary

HarperCollins Publishers
Westerhill Road
Bishopbriggs
Glasgow
G64 2QT
Great Britain

First Edition 2005

© HarperCollins Publishers 2005

ISBN 0-00-720320-9

Collins® and Bank of English® are
registered trademarks of
HarperCollins Publishers Limited

www.collins.co.uk

A catalogue record for this book is
available from the British Library

HarperCollins Publishers, Inc.
10 East 53rd Street, New York,
NY 10022

ISBN 0-06-074914-8

Library of Congress Cataloging-in-
Publication Data has been applied for

www.harpercollins.com

HarperCollins books may be
purchased for educational, business,
or sales promotional use. For
information, please write to:
Special Markets Department,
HarperCollins Publishers Inc., 10 East
53rd Street, New York, NY 10022

Typeset by Morton Word Processing
Ltd, Scarborough

Printed in Italy by Amadeus S.r.l.

Acknowledgements
We would like to thank those authors
and publishers who kindly gave
permission for copyright material to
be used in the Collins Word Web. We
would also like to thank Times
Newspapers Ltd for providing
valuable data.

editors/rédaction
Pierre-Henri Cousin • Lorna Sinclair Knight
Catherine E. Love • Jean-François Allain • Claude Nimmo
Bob Grossmith • Jean-Benoit Ormal-Grenon
Cécile Aubinière-Robb • Claire Calder • Christine Penman

editorial staff/secrétariat de rédaction
Val McNulty • John Podbielski

series editor/collection dirigée par
Lorna Sinclair Knight

William Collins' dream of knowledge for all began with the publication of his first book in 1819. A self-educated mill worker, he not only enriched millions of lives, but also founded a flourishing publishing house. Today, staying true to this spirit, Collins books are packed with inspiration, innovation, and practical expertise. They place you at the centre of a world of possibility and give you exactly what you need to explore it.

Language is the key to this exploration, and at the heart of Collins Dictionaries, is language as it is really used. New words, phrases, and meanings spring up every day, and all of them are captured and analysed by the Collins Word Web. Constantly updated, and with over 2.5 billion entries, this living language resource is unique to our dictionaries.

Words are tools for life. And a Collins Dictionary makes them work for you.

Collins. Do more.

INTRODUCTION

We are delighted that you have decided to buy this Collins French Dictionary, and hope you will enjoy and benefit from using it at home, at school, on holiday or at work.

The innovative use of colour guides you quickly and efficiently to the word you want, and the comprehensive wordlist provides a wealth of modern and idiomatic phrases not normally found in a dictionary this size.

In addition, the supplement provides you with guidance on using the dictionary, along with entertaining ways of improving your dictionary skills.

We hope that you will enjoy using it and that it will significantly enhance your language studies.

Note on trademarks

COMMENT UTILISER VOTRE ROBERT & COLLINS MINI

Les informations contenues dans ce dictionnaire sont présentées à l'aide de plusieurs polices de caractères, de symboles, abréviations, parenthèses et crochets. Les conventions et symboles utilisés sont expliqués dans les sections qui suivent.

Entrées

Les mots que vous cherchez dans le dictionnaire (les 'entrées') sont classés par ordre alphabétique. Ils sont imprimés en couleur pour pouvoir être repérés rapidement. Les deux entrées figurant en haut de page indiquent le premier et le dernier mot qui apparaissent sur la page en question.

Des informations sur l'emploi ou sur la forme de certaines entrées sont données entre parenthèses, après la transcription phonétique. Ces indications apparaissent sous forme abrégée et en italique (ex: *(fam)*, *(COMM)*).

Plusieurs mots appartenant à la même famille peuvent être regroupés dans un même article (ex: ronger, rongeur). Dans la partie anglais-français et pour les préfixes de la partie français-anglais, la graphie de l'entrée principale est reprise par un tilde: ~ dans les sous-entrées (ex: accept, ~ance). Les sous-entrées apparaissent en caractères rouges, légèrement plus petits que ceux de l'entrée.

Les expressions courantes dans lesquelles apparaît l'entrée sont indiquées par des caractères romains gras (ex **avoir du retard**).

Transcription phonétique

La transcription phonétique symbolisant la prononciation de chaque entrée est indiquée entre crochets immédiatement après l'entrée (ex fumer [fyme]; knead [ni:d]). La liste des symboles phonétiques figure aux pages xiii et xiv.

Traductions

Les traductions interchangeables sont séparées par une virgule; lorsque plusieurs sens coexistent, ces traductions sont séparées par un point-virgule. Vous trouverez souvent entre parenthèses d'autres mots en italique qui précèdent les traductions. Ces mots fournissent certains des contextes dans lesquels l'entrée est susceptible d'être utilisée (ex rough *(voice)* ou *(weather)*) ou offrent des synonymes (ex rough *(violent)*).

'Mots-clés'

Une importance particulière est accordée à certains mots français et anglais qui sont considérés comme des "mots-clés" dans chacune des langues. Cela peut être dû a leur utilisation très fréquente ou au fait qu'ils ont divers types d'usages (ex vouloir, plus; get, that). Une combinaison de losanges et de chiffres vous aident à distinguer différentes catégories grammaticales et différents sens. D'autres renseignements utiles apparaissent en italique et entre parenthèses dans la langue de l'utilisateur.

Données grammaticales

Les catégories grammaticales sont données sous forme abrégée et en italique après la transcription phonétique des entrées (ex *vt, adv, conj*).

Le genre des noms français est indiqué de la manière suivante: *nm* pour un nom masculin et *nf* pour un nom féminin. Le féminin et le pluriel irréguliers sont également indiqués (**directeur, trice; cheval, aux**).

Le masculin et le féminin des adjectifs sont mentionnés lorsque ces deux formes sont différentes (ex **noir, e**). Lorsque l'adjectif a un féminin ou un pluriel irrégulier, ces formes sont clairement indiquées (ex **net, nette**). Les pluriels irréguliers des noms et les formes irrégulières des verbes anglais sont indiqués entre parenthèses, avant la catégorie grammaticale (ex **man** ... (*pl* **men**) *n*; **give** (*pt* **gave**, *pp* **given**) *vt*).

USING YOUR COLLINS FRENCH DICTIONARY

A wealth of information is presented in the dictionary, using various typefaces, sizes of type, symbols, abbreviations and brackets. The conventions and symbols used are explained in the following sections.

Headwords

The words you look up in a dictionary — "headwords" — are listed alphabetically. They are printed in colour for rapid identification. The two headwords appearing at the top of each page indicate the first and last word dealt with on the page in question.

Information about the usage or form of certain headwords is given in brackets after the phonetic spelling. This usually appears in abbreviated form and in italics (e.g. *(fam)*, *(COMM)*).

Where appropriate, words related to headwords are grouped in the same entry (ronger, rongeur; accept, acceptance) in a slightly smaller coloured type than the headword.

Common expressions in which the headword appears are shown in black bold roman type (e.g. **avoir du retard**).

Phonetic spellings

The phonetic spelling of each headword (indicating its pronunciation) is given in square brackets immediately after the headword (e.g. fumer [fyme]; knead [ni:d]). A list of the phonetic symbols is given on pages xiii and xiv.

Translations

Headword translations are given in ordinary type and, where more than one meaning or usage exists, these are separated by a semi-colon. You will often find other words in italics in brackets before the translations. These offer suggested contexts in which the headword might appear (e.g. rough *(voice)* or *(weather)*) or provide synonyms (e.g. rough *(violent)*).

"Key" words

Special status is given to certain French and English words which are considered as "key" words in each language. They may, for example, occur very frequently or have several types of usage (e.g. vouloir, plus; get, that). A combination of lozenges and numbers helps you to distinguish different parts of speech and different meanings. Further helpful information is provided in brackets and in italics in the relevant language for the user.

Grammatical information

Parts of speech are given in abbreviated form in italics after the phonetic spellings of headwords (e.g. *vt, adv, conj*).

Genders of French nouns are indicated as follows: *nm* for a masculine and *nf* for a feminine noun. Feminine and irregular plural forms of nouns are also shown (**directeur, trice; cheval, aux**).

Adjectives are given in both masculine and feminine forms where these forms are different (e.g. **noir, e**). Clear information is provided where adjectives have an irregular feminine or plural form (e.g. **net, nette**).

ABRÉVIATIONS

ABBREVIATIONS

adjectif, locution adjective	adj	adjective, adjectival phrase
abréviation	ab(b)r	abbreviation
adverbe, locution adverbiale	adv	adverb, adverbial phrase
administration	ADMIN	administration
agriculture	AGR	agriculture
anatomie	ANAT	anatomy
architecture	ARCHIT	architecture
article défini	art déf	definite article
article indéfini	art indéf	indefinite article
attribut	attrib	predicative
l'automobile	AUT(O)	the motor car and motoring
auxiliaire	aux	auxiliary
aviation, voyages aériens	AVIAT	flying, air travel
biologie	BIO(L)	biology
botanique	BOT	botany
anglais de Grande-Bretagne	BRIT	British English
commerce, finance, banque	COMM	commerce, finance, banking
comparatif	compar	comparative
informatique	COMPUT	computing
conditionnel	cond	conditional
chimie	CHEM	chemistry
conjonction	conj	conjunction
construction	CONSTR	building
nom utilisé comme adjectif, ne peut s'employer ni comme attribut, ni après le nom qualifié	cpd	compound element: used as an adjective and which cannot follow the noun it qualifies
cuisine, art culinaire	CULIN	cookery
article défini	def art	definite article
déterminant: article démonstratif ou indéfini etc	dét	determiner: article, demonstrative etc
diminutif	dimin	diminutive
économie	ECON	economics
électricité, électronique	ELEC	electricity, electronics
exclamation, interjection	excl	exclamation, interjection
féminin	f	feminine
langue familière (! emploi vulgaire)	fam(!)	informal usage (! very offensive)
emploi figuré	fig	figurative use
(verbe anglais) dont la particule est inséparable du verbe dans la plupart des sens	fus	(phrasal verb) where the particle cannot be separated from main verb in most or all senses
généralement	gén, gen	generally
géographie, géologie	GEO	geography, geology
géométrie	GEOM	geometry
impersonnel	impers	impersonal
article indéfini	indef art	indefinite article
langue familière (! emploi vulgaire)	inf(!)	informal usage (! particularly offensive)
infinitif	infin	infinitive
informatique	INFORM	computing

ABRÉVIATIONS

ABBREVIATIONS

invariable	inv	invariable
irrégulier	irreg	irregular
domaine juridique	JUR	law
grammaire, linguistique	LING	grammar, linguistics
masculin	m	masculine
mathématiques, algèbre	MATH	mathematics, calculus
médecine	MÉD, MED	medical term, medicine
masculin ou féminin, suivant le sexe	m/f	either masculine or feminine depending on sex
domaine militaire, armée	MIL	military matters
musique	MUS	music
nom	n	noun
navigation, nautisme	NAVIG, NAUT	sailing, navigation
nom ou adjectif numéral	num	numeral adjective or noun
	o.s.	oneself
péjoratif	péj, pej	derogatory, pejorative
photographie	PHOT(O)	photography
physiologie	PHYSIOL	physiology
pluriel	pl	plural
politique	POL	politics
participe passé	pp	past participle
préposition	prép, prep	preposition
pronom	pron	pronoun
psychologie, psychiatrie	PSYCH	psychology, psychiatry
temps du passé	pt	past tense
quelque chose	qch	
quelqu'un	qn	
religions, domaine ecclésiastique	REL	religions, church service
	sb	somebody
enseignement, système scolaire et universitaire	SCOL	schooling, schools and universities
singulier	sg	singular
	sth	something
subjonctif	sub	subjunctive
sujet (grammatical)	su(b)j	(grammatical) subject
superlatif	superl	superlative
techniques, technologie	TECH	technical term, technology
télécommunications	TEL	telecommunications
télévision	TV	television
typographie	TYP(O)	typography, printing
anglais des USA	US	American English
verbe	vb	verb
verbe ou groupe verbal à fonction intransitive	vi	verb or phrasal verb used intransitively
verbe ou groupe verbal à fonction transitive	vt	verb or phrasal verb used transitively
zoologie	ZOOL	zoology
marque déposée	®	registered trademark
indique une équivalence culturelle	≈	introduces a cultural equivalent

TRANSCRIPTION PHONÉTIQUE

	CONSONNES		CONSONANTS	

poupée	p	*puppy*	
bombe	b	*baby*	
tente thermal	t	*tent*	
dinde	d	*daddy*	
coq qui képi	k	*cork kiss chord*	
gag bague	g	*gag guess*	
sale ce nation	s	*so rice kiss*	
zéro rose	z	*cousin buzz*	
tache chat	ʃ	*sheep sugar*	
gilet juge	ʒ	*pleasure beige*	
	tʃ	*church*	
	dʒ	*judge general*	
fer phare	f	*farm raffle*	
valve	v	*very rev*	
	θ	*thin maths*	
	ð	*that other*	
lent salle	l	*little ball*	
rare rentrer	ʀ		
	r	*rat rare*	
maman femme	m	*mummy comb*	
non nonne	n	*no ran*	
agneau vigne	ɲ		
	ŋ	*singing bank*	
hop!	h	*hat reheat*	
yeux paille pied	j	*yet*	
nouer oui	w	*wall bewail*	
huile lui	ɥ		
	x	*loch*	

DIVERS

MISCELLANEOUS

PHONETIC TRANSCRIPTION

Voyelles

NB. La mise en équivalence de certains sons n'indique qu'une ressemblance approximative.

Vowels

NB. The pairing of some vowel sounds only indicates approximate equivalence.

ici v*ie* l*y*re	i i:	*hee*l b*ea*d
	ɪ	h*i*t p*i*ty
jou*er* ét*é*	e	s*e*t t*e*nt
la*it* joue*t* m*e*rci	ɛ	
pl*a*t *a*mour	a æ	b*a*t *a*pple
b*a*s p*â*te	ɑ ɑ:	*a*fter c*a*r c*a*lm
	ʌ	f*u*n c*ou*sin
l*e* pr*e*mier	ə	*o*ver *a*bove
b*eu*rre p*eu*r	œ	
p*eu* d*eu*x	ø 3:	*u*rn f*er*n w*or*k
*o*r h*o*mme	ɒ	w*a*sh p*o*t
m*o*t *eau* g*au*che	o ɔ:	b*or*n c*or*k
gen*ou* r*ou*e	u ʊ	f*u*ll s*oo*t
	u:	b*oo*n l*ew*d
r*ue* *u*rne	y	

Diphtongues

Diphthongs

ɪə	b*ee*r t*ie*r
ɛə	t*ea*r f*ai*r th*e*re
eɪ	d*a*te pl*ai*ce d*ay*
aɪ	l*i*fe b*uy* cr*y*
aʊ	*ow*l f*ou*l n*ow*
əʊ	l*ow* n*o*
ɔɪ	b*oi*l b*oy* *oi*ly
ʊə	p*oo*r t*ou*r

Nasales

Nasal Vowels

mat*in* pl*ein*	ɛ̃
br*un*	œ̃
s*an*g *an* d*an*s	ɑ̃
n*on* p*on*t	ɔ̃

xiv

FRANÇAIS – ANGLAIS
FRENCH – ENGLISH

A, a

a [a] *vb voir* **avoir**

MOT-CLÉ

à [a] (*à + le* = **au**, *à + les* = **aux**) *prép* **1** (*endroit, situation*) at, in; **être à Paris/au Portugal** to be in Paris/Portugal; **être à la maison/à l'école** to be at home/at school; **à la campagne** in the country; **c'est à 10 km/à 20 minutes (d'ici)** it's 10 km/20 minutes away

2 (*direction*) to; **aller à Paris/au Portugal** to go to Paris/Portugal; **aller à la maison/à l'école** to go home/to school; **à la campagne** to the country

3 (*temps*): **à 3 heures/minuit** at 3 o'clock/midnight; **au printemps/mois de juin** in the spring/the month of June

4 (*attribution, appartenance*) to; **le livre est à Paul/à lui/à nous** this book is Paul's/his/ours; **donner qch à qn** to give sth to sb

5 (*moyen*) with; **se chauffer au gaz** to have gas heating; **à bicyclette** on a *ou* by bicycle; **à la main/machine** by hand/machine

6 (*provenance*) from; **boire à la bouteille** to drink from the bottle

7 (*caractérisation, manière*): **l'homme aux yeux bleus** the man with the blue eyes; **à la russe** the Russian way

8 (*but, destination*): **tasse à café** coffee cup; **maison à vendre** house for sale

9 (*rapport, évaluation, distribution*): **100 km/unités à l'heure** 100 km/units per *ou* an hour; **payé à l'heure** paid by the hour; **cinq à six** five to six

---

abaisser [abese] *vt* to lower, bring down; (*manette*) to pull down; **s'~** *vi* to go

down; (*fig*) to demean o.s.

abandon [abɑ̃dɔ̃] *nm* abandoning; giving up; withdrawal; **être à l'~** to be in a state of neglect

abandonner [abɑ̃dɔne] *vt* (*personne*) to abandon; (*projet, activité*) to abandon, give up; (*SPORT*) to retire *ou* withdraw from; (*céder*) to surrender; **s'~ à** (*paresse, plaisirs*) to give o.s. up to

abasourdir [abazuʀdiʀ] *vt* to stun, stagger

abat-jour [abaʒuʀ] *nm inv* lampshade

abats [aba] *nmpl* (*de bœuf, porc*) offal *sg*; (*de volaille*) giblets

abattement [abatmɑ̃] *nm*: **~ fiscal** ≈ tax allowance

abattoir [abatwaʀ] *nm* slaughterhouse

abattre [abatʀ] *vt* (*arbre*) to cut down, fell; (*mur, maison*) to pull down; (*avion, personne*) to shoot down; (*animal*) to shoot, kill; (*fig*) to wear out, tire out; to demoralize; **s'~** *vi* to crash down; **ne pas se laisser ~** to keep one's spirits up, not to let things get one down; **s'~ sur** to beat down on; (*fig*) to rain down on

abbaye [abei] *nf* abbey

abbé [abe] *nm* priest; (*d'une abbaye*) abbot

abcès [apsɛ] *nm* abscess

abdiquer [abdike] *vi* to abdicate

abdominaux [abdɔmino] *nmpl*: **faire des ~** to do exercises for one's abdominals, do one's abdominals

abeille [abɛj] *nf* bee

aberrant, e [abeʀɑ̃, ɑ̃t] *adj* absurd

aberration [abeʀasjɔ̃] *nf* aberration

abêtir [abetiʀ] *vt* to make morons of (*ou* a moron of)

abîme [abim] *nm* abyss, gulf

abîmer [abime] *vt* to spoil, damage; **s'~**

vi to get spoilt *ou* damaged

ablation [ablasjɔ̃] *nf* removal

aboiement [abwamã] *nm* bark, barking

abois [abwa] *nmpl*: **aux ~** at bay

abolir [abɔliʀ] *vt* to abolish

abominable [abɔminabl] *adj* abominable

abondance [abɔ̃dãs] *nf* abundance

abondant, e [abɔ̃dã, ãt] *adj* plentiful, abundant, copious; **abonder** *vi* to abound, be plentiful; **abonder dans le sens de qn** to concur with sb

abonné, e [abɔne] *nm/f* subscriber; season ticket holder

abonnement [abɔnmã] *nm* subscription; *(transports, concerts)* season ticket

abonner [abɔne] *vt*: **s'~ à** to subscribe to, take out a subscription to

abord [abɔʀ] *nm*: **au premier ~** at first sight, initially; **~s** *nmpl (environs)* surroundings; **d'~** first

abordable [abɔʀdabl] *adj (prix)* reasonable; *(personne)* approachable

aborder [abɔʀde] *vi* to land ♦ *vt (sujet, difficulté)* to tackle; *(personne)* to approach; *(rivage etc)* to reach

aboutir [abutiʀ] *vi (négociations etc)* to succeed; **~ à** to end up at; **n'~ à rien** to come to nothing

aboyer [abwaje] *vi* to bark

abréger [abʀeʒe] *vt* to shorten

abreuver [abʀœve]: **s'~** *vi* to drink; **abreuvoir** *nm* watering place

abréviation [abʀevjasjɔ̃] *nf* abbreviation

abri [abʀi] *nm* shelter; **être à l'~** to be under cover; **se mettre à l'~** to shelter

abricot [abʀiko] *nm* apricot

abriter [abʀite] *vt* to shelter; **s'~** *vt* to shelter, take cover

abrupt, e [abʀypt] *adj* sheer, steep; *(ton)* abrupt

abruti, e [abʀyti] *adj* stunned, dazed ♦ *nm/f (fam)* idiot, moron; **~ de travail** overworked

absence [apsɑ̃s] *nf* absence; *(MÉD)* blackout; **avoir des ~s** to have mental blanks

absent, e [apsɑ̃, ɑ̃t] *adj* absent ♦ *nm/f* absentee; **absenter: s'absenter** *vi* to take time off work; *(sortir)* to leave, go out

absolu, e [apsɔly] *adj* absolute; **absolument** *adv* absolutely

absorbant, e [apsɔʀbã, ãt] *adj* absorbent

absorber [apsɔʀbe] *vt* to absorb; *(gén MÉD: manger, boire)* to take

abstenir [apstəniʀ] *vb*: **s'~ de qch/de faire** to refrain from sth/from doing

abstraction [apstʀaksjɔ̃] *nf* abstraction

abstrait, e [apstʀɛ, ɛt] *adj* abstract

absurde [apsyʀd] *adj* absurd

abus [aby] *nm* abuse; **~ de confiance** breach of trust; **abuser** *vi* to go too far, overstep the mark; **abuser de** *(duper)* to take advantage of; **abusif, -ive** *adj* exorbitant; *(punition)* excessive

acabit [akabi] *nm*: **de cet ~** of that type

académie [akademi] *nf* academy; *(SCOL: circonscription)* ≈ regional education authority

---

Académie française

i The **Académie française** was founded by Cardinal Richelieu in 1635 during the reign of Louis XIII. It consists of forty elected scholars and writers who are known as "les Quarante" or "les Immortels". One of the Académie's functions is to regulate the development of the French language and its recommendations are frequently the subject of lively public debate. It has produced several editions of its famous dictionary and awards various literary prizes.

---

acajou [akaʒu] *nm* mahogany

acariâtre [akaʀjɑtʀ] *adj* cantankerous

accablant, e [akablã, ãt] *adj (chaleur)* oppressive; *(témoignage, preuve)* overwhelming

accablement [akabləmã] *nm* despondency

accabler [akable] *vt* to overwhelm, overcome; **~ qn d'injures** to heap *ou* shower abuse on sb

accalmie [akalmi] *nf* lull

accaparer [akapaʀe] *vt* to monopolize; (*suj: travail etc*) to take up (all) the time *ou* attention of

accéder [aksede]: **~ à** *vt* (*lieu*) to reach; (*accorder: requête*) to grant, accede to

accélérateur [akseleʀatœʀ] *nm* accelerator

accélération [akseleʀasjɔ̃] *nf* acceleration

accélérer [akseleʀe] *vt* to speed up ♦ *vi* to accelerate

accent [aksɑ̃] *nm* accent; (*PHONÉTIQUE, fig*) stress; **mettre l'~ sur** (*fig*) to stress; **~ aigu/grave/circonflexe** acute/grave/circumflex accent; **accentuer** *vt* (*LING*) to accent; (*fig*) to accentuate, emphasize; **s'accentuer** *vi* to become more marked *ou* pronounced

acceptation [akseptasjɔ̃] *nf* acceptance

accepter [aksepte] *vt* to accept; **~ de faire** to agree to do

accès [akse] *nm* (*à un lieu*) access; (*MÉD: de toux*) fit; (*: de fièvre*) bout; **d'~ facile** easily accessible; **facile d'~** easy to get to; **~ de colère** fit of anger; **accessible** *adj* accessible; (*livre, sujet*): **accessible à qn** within the reach of sb

accessoire [akseswaʀ] *adj* secondary; incidental ♦ *nm* accessory; (*THÉÂTRE*) prop

accident [aksidɑ̃] *nm* accident; **par ~** by chance; **~ de la route** road accident; **~ du travail** industrial injury *ou* accident; **accidenté, e** *adj* damaged; injured; (*relief, terrain*) uneven; hilly; **accidentel, le** *adj* accidental

acclamations [aklamasjɔ̃] *nfpl* cheers

acclamer [aklame] *vt* to cheer, acclaim

acclimater [aklimate]: **s'~** *vi* (*personne*) to adapt (o.s.)

accolade [akɔlad] *nf* (*amicale*) embrace; (*signe*) brace

accommodant, e [akɔmɔdɑ̃, ɑ̃t] *adj* accommodating, easy-going

accommoder [akɔmɔde] *vt* (*CULIN*) to prepare; **s'~ de** *vt* to put up with; (*se contenter de*) to make do with

accompagnateur, -trice [akɔ̃paɲatœʀ, tʀis] *nm/f* (*MUS*) accompanist; (*de voyage: guide*) guide; (*de voyage organisé*) courier

accompagner [akɔ̃paɲe] *vt* to accompany, be *ou* go *ou* come with; (*MUS*) to accompany

accompli, e [akɔ̃pli] *adj* accomplished

accomplir [akɔ̃pliʀ] *vt* (*tâche, projet*) to carry out; (*souhait*) to fulfil; **s'~** *vi* to be fulfilled

accord [akɔʀ] *nm* agreement; (*entre des styles, tons etc*) harmony; (*MUS*) chord; **d'~!** OK!; **se mettre d'~** to come to an agreement; **être d'~ (pour faire qch)** to agree (to do sth)

accordéon [akɔʀdeɔ̃] *nm* (*MUS*) accordion

accorder [akɔʀde] *vt* (*faveur, délai*) to grant; (*harmoniser*) to match; (*MUS*) to tune; **s'~** *vt* to get on together; to agree

accoster [akɔste] *vt* (*NAVIG*) to draw alongside ♦ *vi* to berth

accotement [akɔtmɑ̃] *nm* verge (*BRIT*), shoulder

accouchement [akuʃmɑ̃] *nm* delivery, (child)birth; labour

accoucher [akuʃe] *vi* to give birth, have a baby; **~ d'un garçon** to give birth to a boy; **accoucheur** *nm*: **(médecin) accoucheur** obstetrician

accouder [akude]: **s'~** *vi* to rest one's elbows on/against; **accoudoir** *nm* armrest

accoupler [akuple] *vt* to couple; (*pour la reproduction*) to mate; **s'~** *vt* to mate

accourir [akuʀiʀ] *vi* to rush *ou* run up

accoutrement [akutʀəmɑ̃] (*péj*) *nm* (*tenue*) outfit

accoutumance [akutymɑ̃s] *nf* (*gén*) adaptation; (*MÉD*) addiction

accoutumé, e [akutyme] *adj* (*habituel*) customary, usual

accoutumer [akutyme] *vt*: **s'~ à** to get accustomed *ou* used to

accréditer [akʀedite] *vt* (*nouvelle*) to substantiate

accroc [akʀo] *nm* (*déchirure*) tear; (*fig*) hitch, snag

accrochage [akʁɔʃaʒ] *nm* (*AUTO*) collision; (*dispute*) clash, brush

accrocher [akʁɔʃe] *vt* (*fig*) to catch, attract; **s'~** (*se disputer*) to have a clash *ou* brush; **~ qch à** (*suspendre*) to hang sth (up) on; (*attacher: remorque*) to hitch sth (up) to; **~ qch (à)** (*déchirer*) to catch sth (on); **~ un passant** (*heurter*) to hit a pedestrian; **s'~ à** (*rester pris à*) to catch on; (*agripper, fig*) to hang on *ou* cling to

accroissement [akʁwasmɑ̃] *nm* increase

accroître [akʁwatʁ] **s'~** *vi* to increase

accroupir [akʁupiʁ] **s'~** *vi* to squat, crouch (down)

accru, e [akʁy] *pp de* **accroître**

accueil [akœj] *nm* welcome; **comité d'~** reception committee; **accueillir** *vt* to welcome; (*aller chercher*) to meet, collect

acculer [akyle] *vt*: **~ qn à** *ou* **contre** to drive sb back against

accumuler [akymyle] *vt* to accumulate, amass; **s'~** *vi* to accumulate; to pile up

accusation [akyzasjɔ̃] *nf* (*gén*) accusation; (*JUR*) charge; (*partie*): **l'~** the prosecution

accusé, e [akyze] *nm/f* accused; defendant; **~ de réception** acknowledgement of receipt

accuser [akyze] *vt* to accuse; (*fig*) to emphasize, bring out; to show; **~ qn de** to accuse sb of; (*JUR*) to charge sb with; **~ réception de** to acknowledge receipt of

acerbe [asɛʁb] *adj* caustic, acid

acéré, e [asere] *adj* sharp

acharné, e [aʃaʁne] *adj* (*efforts*) relentless; (*lutte, adversaire*) fierce, bitter

acharner [aʃaʁne] *vb*: **s'~ contre** to set o.s. against; (*suj: malchance*) to dog; **s'~ à faire** to try doggedly to do; (*persister*) to persist in doing

achat [aʃa] *nm* purchase; **faire des ~s** to do some shopping; **faire l'~ de qch** to purchase sth

acheminer [aʃ(ə)mine] *vt* (*courrier*) to forward, dispatch; **s'~ vers** to head for

acheter [aʃ(ə)te] *vt* to buy, purchase; (*soudoyer*) to buy; **~ qch à** (*marchand*) to buy *ou* purchase sth from; (*ami etc: offrir*) to buy sth for; **acheteur, -euse** *nm/f* buyer; shopper; (*COMM*) buyer

achever [aʃ(ə)ve] *vt* to complete, finish; (*blessé*) to finish off; **s'~** *vi* to end

acide [asid] *adj* sour, sharp; (*CHIMIE*) acid(ic) ♦ *nm* (*CHIMIE*) acid; **acidulé, e** *adj* slightly acid

acier [asje] *nm* steel; **aciérie** *nf* steelworks *sg*

acné [akne] *nf* acne

acolyte [akɔlit] (*péj*) *nm* associate

acompte [akɔ̃t] *nm* deposit

à-côté [akote] *nm* side-issue; (*argent*) extra

à-coup [aku] *nm*: **par ~-~s** by fits and starts

acoustique [akustik] *nf* (*d'une salle*) acoustics *pl*

acquéreur [akerœʁ] *nm* buyer, purchaser

acquérir [akeʁiʁ] *vt* to acquire

acquis, e [aki, iz] *pp de* **acquérir** ♦ *nm* (accumulated) experience; **son aide nous est ~e** we can count on his help

acquit [aki] *vb voir* **acquérir** ♦ *nm* (*quittance*) receipt; **par ~ de conscience** to set one's mind at rest

acquitter [akite] *vt* (*JUR*) to acquit; (*facture*) to pay, settle; **s'~ de** *vt* (*devoir*) to discharge; (*promesse*) to fulfil

âcre [ɑkʁ] *adj* acrid, pungent

acrobate [akʁɔbat] *nm/f* acrobat; **acrobatie** *nf* acrobatics *sg*

acte [akt] *nm* act, action; (*THÉÂTRE*) act; **prendre ~ de** to note, take note of; **faire ~ de candidature** to apply; **faire ~ de présence** to put in an appearance; **~ de naissance** birth certificate

acteur [aktœʁ] *nm* actor

actif, -ive [aktif, iv] *adj* active ♦ *nm* (*COMM*) assets *pl*; (*fig*): **avoir à son ~** to have to one's credit; **population active** working population

action [aksjɔ̃] *nf* (*gén*) action; (*COMM*) share; **une bonne ~** a good deed; **actionnaire** *nm/f* shareholder; **actionner** *vt* (*mécanisme*) to activate; (*machine*) to operate

activer [aktive] vt to speed up; **s'~** vi to bustle about; to hurry up

activité [aktivite] nf activity; **en ~** (volcan) active; (fonctionnaire) in active life

actrice [aktʀis] nf actress

actualiser [aktɥalize] vt to bring up to date

actualité [aktɥalite] nf (d'un problème) topicality; (événements): **l'~** current events; **les ~s** nfpl (CINÉMA, TV) the news; **d'~** topical

actuel, le [aktɥɛl] adj (présent) present; (d'actualité) topical; **à l'heure ~le** at the present time; **actuellement** adv at present, at the present time

acuité [akɥite] nf acuteness

acuponcteur [akypɔ̃ktœʀ] nm acupuncturist

acuponcture [akypɔ̃ktyʀ] nf acupuncture

adaptateur [adaptatœʀ] nm (ÉLEC) adapter

adapter [adapte] vt to adapt; **s'~ (à)** (suj: personne) to adapt (to); **~ qch à** (approprier) to adapt sth to (fit); **~ qch sur/dans/à** (fixer) to fit sth on/into/to

additif [aditif] nm additive

addition [adisjɔ̃] nf addition; (au café) bill; **additionner** vt to add (up)

adepte [adɛpt] nm/f follower

adéquat, e [adekwa(t), at] adj appropriate, suitable

adhérent, e [adeʀɑ̃, ɑ̃t] nm/f member

adhérer [adeʀe]: **~ à** vt (coller) to adhere ou stick to; (se rallier à) to join; **adhésif, -ive** adj adhesive, sticky; **ruban adhésif** sticky ou adhesive tape; **adhésion** nf joining; (fait d'être membre) membership; (accord) support

adieu, x [adjø] excl goodbye ♦ nm farewell

adjectif [adʒɛktif] nm adjective

adjoindre [adʒwɛ̃dʀ] vt: **~ qch à** to attach sth to; (ajouter) to add sth to; **s'~** vt (collaborateur etc) to take on, appoint; **adjoint, e** nm/f assistant; **adjoint au maire** deputy mayor; **directeur adjoint** assistant

manager

adjudant [adʒydɑ̃] nm (MIL) warrant officer

adjuger [adʒyʒe] vt (prix, récompense) to award; (lors d'une vente) to auction (off); **s'~** vt to take for o.s.

adjurer [adʒyʀe] vt: **~ qn de faire** to implore ou beg sb to do

admettre [admɛtʀ] vt (laisser entrer) to admit; (candidat: SCOL) to pass; (tolérer) to allow, accept; (reconnaître) to admit, acknowledge

administrateur, -trice [administʀatœʀ, tʀis] nm/f (COMM) director; (ADMIN) administrator

administration [administʀasjɔ̃] nf administration; **l'A~** ≃ the Civil Service

administrer [administʀe] vt (firme) to manage, run; (biens, remède, sacrement etc) to administer

admirable [admiʀabl] adj admirable, wonderful

admirateur, -trice [admiʀatœʀ, tʀis] nm/f admirer

admiration [admiʀasjɔ̃] nf admiration

admirer [admiʀe] vt to admire

admis, e [admi, iz] pp de **admettre**

admissible [admisibl] adj (candidat) eligible; (comportement) admissible, acceptable

admission [admisjɔ̃] nf admission; acknowledgement; **demande d'~** application for membership

ADN sigle m (= acide désoxyribonucléique) DNA

adolescence [adɔlesɑ̃s] nf adolescence

adolescent, e [adɔlesɑ̃, ɑ̃t] nm/f adolescent, teenager

adonner [adɔne]: **s'~ à** vt (sport) to devote o.s. to; (boisson) to give o.s. over to

adopter [adɔpte] vt to adopt; **adoptif, -ive** adj (parents) adoptive; (fils, patrie) adopted

adorable [adɔʀabl] adj delightful, adorable

adorer [adɔʀe] vt to adore; (REL) to worship

adosser [adose] *vt*: **~ qch à** *ou* **contre** to stand sth against; **s'~ à** *ou* **contre** to lean with one's back against

adoucir [adusiʀ] *vt* (*goût, température*) to make milder; (*avec du sucre*) to sweeten; (*peau, voix*) to soften; (*caractère*) to mellow

adresse [adʀɛs] *nf* (*domicile*) address; (*dextérité*) skill, dexterity; **~ électronique** email address

adresser [adʀese] *vt* (*lettre: expédier*) to send; (*: écrire l'adresse sur*) to address; (*injure, compliments*) to address; **s'~ à** (*parler à*) to speak to, address; (*s'informer auprès de*) to go and see; (*: bureau*) to enquire at; (*suj: livre, conseil*) to be aimed at; **~ la parole à** to speak to, address

adroit, e [adʀwa, wat] *adj* skilful, skilled

adulte [adylt] *nm/f* adult, grown-up ♦ *adj* (*chien, arbre*) fully-grown, mature; (*attitude*) adult, grown-up

adultère [adylteʀ] *nm* (*acte*) adultery

advenir [advəniʀ] *vi* to happen

adverbe [advɛʀb] *nm* adverb

adversaire [advɛʀsɛʀ] *nm/f* (*SPORT, gén*) opponent, adversary

adverse [advɛʀs] *adj* opposing

aération [aeʀasjɔ̃] *nf* airing; (*circulation de l'air*) ventilation

aérer [aeʀe] *vt* to air; (*fig*) to lighten; **s'~** *vi* to get some (fresh) air

aérien, ne [aeʀjɛ̃, jɛn] *adj* (*AVIAT*) air *cpd*, aerial; (*câble, métro*) overhead; (*fig*) light; **compagnie ~ne** airline

aéro... [aeʀɔ] *préfixe*: **aérobic** *nm* aerobics *sg*; **aérogare** *nf* airport (buildings); (*en ville*) air terminal; **aéroglisseur** *nm* hovercraft; **Aéronavale** *nf* ≈ Fleet Air Arm (*BRIT*), ≈ Naval Air Force (*US*); **aérophagie** *nf* (*MÉD*) wind, aerophagia (*MÉD*); **aéroport** *nm* airport; **aéroporté, e** *adj* airborne, airlifted; **aérosol** *nm* aerosol

affable [afabl] *adj* affable

affaiblir [afebliʀ]: **s'~** *vi* to weaken

affaire [afɛʀ] *nf* (*problème, question*) matter; (*criminelle, judiciaire*) case; (*scandaleuse etc*) affair; (*entreprise*) business; (*marché, transaction*) deal; business *no pl*; (*occasion intéressante*) bargain; **~s** *nfpl* (*intérêts publics et privés*) affairs; (*activité commerciale*) business *sg*; (*effets personnels*) things, belongings; **ce sont mes ~s** (*cela me concerne*) that's my business; **ça fera l'~** that will do (nicely); **se tirer d'~** to sort it *ou* things out for o.s.; **avoir ~ à** (*être en contact*) to be dealing with; **les A~s étrangères** Foreign Affairs; **affairer: s'affairer** *vi* to busy o.s., bustle about

affaisser [afese]: **s'~** *vi* (*terrain, immeuble*) to subside, sink; (*personne*) to collapse

affaler [afale] *vb*: **s'~ (dans/sur)** to collapse *ou* slump (into/onto)

affamé, e [afame] *adj* starving

affectation [afɛktasjɔ̃] *nf* (*nomination*) appointment; (*manque de naturel*) affectation

affecter [afɛkte] *vt* to affect; **~ qch à** to allocate *ou* allot sth to; **~ qn à** to appoint sb to; (*diplomate*) to post sb to

affectif, -ive [afɛktif, iv] *adj* emotional

affection [afɛksjɔ̃] *nf* affection; (*mal*) ailment; **affectionner** *vt* to be fond of; **affectueux, -euse** *adj* affectionate

affermir [afɛʀmiʀ] *vt* to consolidate, strengthen; (*muscles*) to tone up

affichage [afiʃaʒ] *nm* billposting; (*électronique*) display

affiche [afiʃ] *nf* poster; (*officielle*) notice; (*THÉÂTRE*) bill

afficher [afiʃe] *vt* (*affiche*) to put up; (*réunion*) to put up a notice about; (*électroniquement*) to display; (*fig*) to exhibit, display; **"défense d'~"** "stick no bills"

affilée [afile]: **d'~** *adv* at a stretch

affiler [afile] *vt* to sharpen

affilier [afilje]: **s'~ à** *vt* (*club, société*) to join

affiner [afine] *vt* to refine

affirmatif, -ive [afiʀmatif, iv] *adj* affirmative

affirmation [afiʀmasjɔ̃] *nf* assertion

affirmer [afiʀme] *vt* to assert

affligé, e [afliʒe] *adj* distressed, grieved; **~**

de (*maladie, tare*) afflicted with

affliger [aflize] *vt* (*peiner*) to distress, grieve

affluence [aflyɑ̃s] *nf* crowds *pl*; **heures d'~** rush hours; **jours d'~** busiest days

affluent [aflyɑ̃] *nm* tributary

affluer [aflye] *vi* (*secours, biens*) to flood in, pour in; (*sang*) to rush, flow

affolant, e [afɔlɑ̃, ɑ̃t] *adj* frightening

affolement [afɔlmɑ̃] *nm* panic

affoler [afɔle] *vt* to throw into a panic; **s'~** *vi* to panic

affranchir [afʀɑ̃ʃiʀ] *vt* to put a stamp *ou* stamps on; (*à la machine*) to frank (*BRIT*), meter (*US*); (*fig*) to free, liberate; **affranchissement** *nm* postage

affréter [afʀete] *vt* to charter

affreux, -euse [afʀø, øz] *adj* dreadful, awful

affront [afʀɔ̃] *nm* affront; **affrontement** *nm* clash, confrontation

affronter [afʀɔ̃te] *vt* to confront, face

affubler [afyble] *vt* (*péj*) **~ qn de** to rig *ou* deck sb out in

affût [afy] *nm*: **à l'~ (de)** (*gibier*) lying in wait (for); (*fig*) on the look-out (for)

affûter [afyte] *vt* to sharpen, grind

afin [afɛ̃] **~ que** *conj* so that, in order that; **~ de faire** in order to do, so as to do

africain, e [afʀikɛ̃, ɛn] *adj, nm/f* African

Afrique [afʀik] *nf*: **l'~** Africa; **l'~ du Sud** South Africa

agacer [agase] *vt* to irritate

âge [ɑʒ] *nm* age; **quel ~ as-tu?** how old are you?; **prendre de l'~** to be getting on (in years); **âgé, e** *adj* old, elderly; **âgé de 10 ans** 10 years old

agence [aʒɑ̃s] *nf* agency, office; (*succursale*) branch; **~ de voyages** travel agency; **~ immobilière** estate (*BRIT*) *ou* real estate (*US*) agent's (office)

agencer [aʒɑ̃se] *vt* to put together; (*local*) to arrange, lay out

agenda [aʒɛ̃da] *nm* diary

agenouiller [aʒ(ə)nuje]: **s'~** *vi* to kneel (down)

agent [aʒɑ̃] *nm* (*aussi:* **~ de police**) policeman; (*ADMIN*) official, officer; **~ d'assurances** insurance broker

agglomération [aglɔmeʀasjɔ̃] *nf* town; built-up area; **l'~ parisienne** the urban area of Paris

aggloméré [aglɔmeʀe] *nm* (*bois*) chipboard

aggraver [agʀave]: **s'~** *vi* to worsen

agile [aʒil] *adj* agile, nimble

agir [aʒiʀ] *vi* to act; **il s'agit de** (*ça traite de*) it is about; (*il est important de*) it's a matter *ou* question of

agitation [aʒitasjɔ̃] *nf* (hustle and) bustle; (*trouble*) agitation, excitement; (*politique*) unrest, agitation

agité, e [aʒite] *adj* fidgety, restless; (*troublé*) agitated, perturbed; (*mer*) rough

agiter [aʒite] *vt* (*bouteille, chiffon*) to shake; (*bras, mains*) to wave; (*préoccuper, exciter*) to perturb; **s'~** *vi* (*enfant, élève*) to fidget

agneau, x [aɲo] *nm* lamb

agonie [agɔni] *nf* mortal agony, death pangs *pl*; (*fig*) death throes *pl*

agrafe [agʀaf] *nf* (*de vêtement*) hook, fastener; (*de bureau*) staple; **agrafer** *vt* to fasten; to staple; **agrafeuse** *nf* stapler

agrandir [agʀɑ̃diʀ] *vt* to enlarge; **s'~** *vi* (*ville, famille*) to grow, expand; (*trou, écart*) to get bigger; **agrandissement** *nm* (*PHOTO*) enlargement

agréable [agʀeabl] *adj* pleasant, nice

agréé, e [agʀee] *adj*: **concessionnaire ~** registered dealer

agréer [agʀee] *vt* (*requête*) to accept; **~ à** to please, suit; **veuillez ~ ...** (*formule épistolaire*) yours faithfully

agrégation [agʀegasjɔ̃] *nf* highest teaching diploma in France; **agrégé, e** *nm/f* holder of the *agrégation*

agrément [agʀemɑ̃] *nm* (*accord*) consent, approval; **agrémenter** *vt* to embellish, adorn

agresser [agʀese] *vt* to attack; **agresseur** *nm* aggressor, attacker; (*POL, MIL*) aggressor; **agressif, -ive** *adj* aggressive

agricole [agʀikɔl] *adj* agricultural; **agriculteur** *nm* farmer; **agriculture** *nf* agriculture, farming

agripper [agʀipe] *vt* to grab, clutch; **s'~ à** to cling (on) to, clutch, grip

agroalimentaire [agʀoalimɑ̃tɛʀ] *nm* farm-produce industry

agrumes [agʀym] *nmpl* citrus fruit(s)

aguerrir [ageʀiʀ] *vt* to harden

aguets [age] *nmpl*: **être aux ~** to be on the look out

aguicher [agiʃe] *vt* to entice

ahuri, e [ayʀi] *adj (stupéfait)* flabbergasted

ai [ɛ] *vb voir* **avoir**

aide [ed] *nm/f* assistant; carer ♦ *nf* assistance, help; *(secours financier)* aid; **à l'~ de** *(avec)* with the help *ou* aid of; **appeler (qn) à l'~** to call for help (from sb); **~ familiale** home help, mother's help; **~ judiciaire** ♦ *nf* legal aid; **~ sociale** ♦ *nf (assistance)* state aid; **aide-mémoire** *nm inv* memoranda pages *pl*; *(key facts)* handbook; **aide-soignant, e** *nm/f* auxiliary nurse

aider [ede] *vt* to help; **s'~ de** *(se servir de)* to use, make use of

aie *etc* [ɛ] *vb voir* **avoir**

aïe [aj] *excl* ouch!

aïeul, e [ajœl] *nm/f* grandparent, grandfather(-mother)

aïeux [ajø] *nmpl* grandparents; *(ancêtres)* forebears, forefathers

aigle [egl] *nm* eagle

aigre [egʀ] *adj* sour, sharp; *(fig)* sharp, cutting; **aigre-doux, -ce** *adj (sauce)* sweet and sour; **aigreur** *nf* sourness; sharpness; **aigreurs d'estomac** heartburn *sg*; **aigrir** *vt (personne)* to embitter; *(caractère)* to sour

aigu, ë [egy] *adj (objet, douleur)* sharp; *(son, voix)* high-pitched, shrill; *(note)* high(-pitched)

aiguille [eguij] *nf* needle; *(de montre)* hand; **~ à tricoter** knitting needle

aiguiller [eguije] *vt (orienter)* to direct; **aiguilleur du ciel** *nm* air-traffic controller

aiguillon [eguijɔ̃] *nm (d'abeille)* sting; **aiguillonner** *vt* to spur *ou* goad on

aiguiser [egize] *vt* to sharpen; *(fig)* to stimulate; *(: sens)* to excite

ail [aj, o] *nm* garlic

aile [ɛl] *nf* wing; **aileron** *nm (de requin)* fin; **ailier** *nm* winger

aille *etc* [aj] *vb voir* **aller**

ailleurs [ajœʀ] *adv* elsewhere, somewhere else; **partout/nulle part ~** everywhere/nowhere else; **d'~** *(du reste)* moreover, besides; **par ~** *(d'autre part)* moreover, furthermore

aimable [ɛmabl] *adj* kind, nice

aimant [ɛmɑ̃] *nm* magnet

aimer [eme] *vt* to love; *(d'amitié, affection, par goût)* to like; · *(souhait)*: **j'~ais ...** I would like ...; **bien ~ qn/qch** to like sb/sth; **j'~ais mieux faire** I'd much rather do

aine [ɛn] *nf* groin

aîné, e [ene] *adj* elder, older; *(le plus âgé)* eldest, oldest ♦ *nm/f* oldest child *ou* one, oldest boy *ou* son/girl *ou* daughter

ainsi [ɛ̃si] *adv (de cette façon)* like this, in this way, thus; *(ce faisant)* thus ♦ *conj* thus, so; **~ que** *(comme)* (just) as; *(et aussi)* as well as; **pour ~ dire** so to speak; **et ~ de suite** and so on

aïoli [ajɔli] *nm* garlic mayonnaise

air [ɛʀ] *nm* air; *(mélodie)* tune; *(expression)* look, air; **prendre l'~** to get some (fresh) air; **avoir l'~** *(sembler)* to look, appear; **avoir l'~ de** to look like; **avoir l'~ de faire** to look as though one is doing, appear to be doing; **en l'~** *(promesses)* empty

aisance [ɛzɑ̃s] *nf* ease; *(richesse)* affluence

aise [ɛz] *nf* comfort; **être à l'~** *ou* **à son ~** to be comfortable; *(pas embarrassé)* to be at ease; *(financièrement)* to be comfortably off; **se mettre à l'~** to make o.s. comfortable; **être mal à l'~** to be uncomfortable; *(gêné)* to be ill at ease; **en faire à son ~** to do as one likes; **aisé, e** *adj* easy; *(assez riche)* well-to-do, well-off

aisselle [ɛsɛl] *nf* armpit

ait [ɛ] *vb voir* **avoir**

ajonc [aʒɔ̃] *nm* gorse *no pl*

ajourner [aʒuʀne] *vt* (*réunion*) to adjourn; (*décision*) to defer, postpone

ajouter [aʒute] *vt* to add

ajusté, e [aʒyste] *adj*: **bien ~** (*robe etc*) close-fitting

ajuster [aʒyste] *vt* (*régler*) to adjust; (*vêtement*) to alter; (*coup de fusil*) to aim; (*cible*) to aim at; (*TECH, gén: adapter*): **~ qch à** to fit sth to

alarme [alaʀm] *nf* alarm; **donner l'~** to give *ou* raise the alarm; **alarmer** *vt* to alarm; **s'alarmer** *vi* to become alarmed; **alarmiste** *adj, nm* alarmist

album [albɔm] *nm* album

albumine [albymin] *nf* albumin; **avoir de l'~** to suffer from albuminuria

alcool [alkɔl] *nm*: **l'~** alcohol; **un ~** a spirit, a brandy; **bière sans ~** non-alcoholic *ou* alcohol-free beer; **~ à brûler** methylated spirits (*BRIT*), wood alcohol (*US*); **~ à 90°** surgical spirit; **alcoolique** *adj, nm/f* alcoholic; **alcoolisé, e** *adj* alcoholic; **une boisson non alcoolisée** a soft drink; **alcoolisme** *nm* alcoholism; **alcootest** ® *nm* Breathalyser ®; (*test*) breath-test

aléas [alea] *nmpl* hazards; **aléatoire** *adj* uncertain; (*INFORM*) random

alentour [alɑ̃tuʀ] *adv* around, round about; **~s** *nmpl* (*environs*) surroundings; **aux ~s de** in the vicinity *ou* neighbourhood of, round about; (*temps*) round about

alerte [alɛʀt] *adj* agile, nimble; brisk, lively ♦ *nf* alert; warning; **~ à la bombe** bomb scare; **alerter** *vt* to alert

algèbre [alʒɛbʀ] *nf* algebra

Alger [alʒe] *n* Algiers

Algérie [alʒeʀi] *nf*: **l'~** Algeria; **algérien, ne** *adj* Algerian ♦ *nm/f*: **Algérien, ne** Algerian

algue [alg] *nf* (*gén*) seaweed *no pl*; (*BOT*) alga

alibi [alibi] *nm* alibi

aliéné, e [aljene] *nm/f* insane person, lunatic (*péj*)

aligner [aliɲe] *vt* to align, line up; (*idées, chiffres*) to string together; (*adapter*): **~ qch sur** to bring sth into alignment with; **s'~** (*soldats etc*) to line up; **s'~ sur** (*POL*) to align o.s. on

aliment [alimɑ̃] *nm* food; **alimentaire** *adj*: **denrées alimentaires** foodstuffs; **alimentation** *nf* (*commerce*) food trade; (*magasin*) grocery store; (*régime*) diet; (*en eau etc, de moteur*) supplying; (*INFORM*) feed; **alimenter** *vt* to feed; (*TECH*): **alimenter (en)** to supply (with); to feed (with); (*fig*) to sustain, keep going

alinéa [alinea] *nm* paragraph

aliter [alite]: **s'~** *vi* to take to one's bed

allaiter [alete] *vt* to (breast-)feed, nurse; (*suj: animal*) to suckle

allant [alɑ̃] *nm* drive, go

alléchant, e [aleʃɑ̃, ɑ̃t] *adj* (*odeur*) mouth-watering; (*offre*) enticing

allécher [aleʃe] *vt*: **~ qn** to make sb's mouth water; to tempt *ou* entice sb

allée [ale] *nf* (*de jardin*) path; (*en ville*) avenue, drive; **~s et venues** comings and goings

allégé, e [aleʒe] *adj* (*yaourt etc*) low-fat

alléger [aleʒe] *vt* (*voiture*) to make lighter; (*chargement*) to lighten; (*souffrance*) to alleviate, soothe

allègre [a(l)lɛgʀ] *adj* lively, cheerful

alléguer [a(l)lege] *vt* to put forward (as proof *ou* an excuse)

Allemagne [alman] *nf*: **l'~** Germany; **allemand, e** *adj* German ♦ *nm/f*: **Allemand, e** German ♦ *nm* (*LING*) German

aller [ale] *nm* (*trajet*) outward journey; (*billet: aussi: ~ simple*) single (*BRIT*) *ou* one-way (*US*) ticket ♦ *vi* (*gén*) to go; **~ à** (*convenir*) to suit; (*suj: forme, pointure etc*) to fit; **~ (bien) avec** (*couleurs, style etc*) to go (well) with; **je vais y ~/me fâcher** I'm going to go/to get angry; **~ voir** to go and see, go to see; **allez!** come on!; **allons!** come now!; **comment allez-vous?**

how are you?; **comment ça va?** how are you?; *(affaires etc)* how are things?; **il va bien/mal** he's well/not well, he's fine/ill; **ça va bien/mal** *(affaires etc)* it's going well/not going well; **~ mieux** to be better; **s'en ~** *(partir)* to be off, go, leave; *(disparaître)* to go away; **~ retour** return journey *(BRIT)*, round trip; *(billet)* return (ticket) *(BRIT)*, round trip ticket *(US)*

allergique [alɛʀʒik] *adj*: **~ à** allergic to
alliage [aljaʒ] *nm* alloy
alliance [aljɑ̃s] *nf (MIL, POL)* alliance; *(bague)* wedding ring
allier [alje] *vt (POL, gén)* to ally; *(fig)* to combine; **s'~** to become allies; to combine
allô [alo] *excl* hullo, hallo
allocation [alɔkasjɔ̃] *nf* allowance; **~ (de) chômage** unemployment benefit; **~s familiales** ≃ child benefit
allocution [a(l)lɔkysjɔ̃] *nf* short speech
allonger [alɔ̃ʒe] *vt* to lengthen, make longer; *(étendre: bras, jambe)* to stretch (out); **s'~** *vi* to get longer; *(se coucher)* to lie down, stretch out; **~ le pas** to hasten one's step(s)
allouer [alwe] *vt* to allocate, allot
allumage [alymaʒ] *nm (AUTO)* ignition
allume-cigare [alymsigaʀ] *nm inv* cigar lighter
allumer [alyme] *vt (lampe, phare, radio)* to put *ou* switch on; *(pièce)* to put *ou* switch the light(s) on in; *(feu)* to light; **s'~** *vi* *(lumière, lampe)* to come *ou* go on
allumette [alymɛt] *nf* match
allure [alyʀ] *nf (vitesse)* speed, pace; *(démarche)* walk; *(aspect, air)* look; **avoir de l'~** to have style; **à toute ~** at top speed
allusion [a(l)lyzjɔ̃] *nf* allusion; *(sous-entendu)* hint; **faire ~ à** to allude *ou* refer to; to hint at

MOT-CLÉ

alors [alɔʀ] *adv* **1** *(à ce moment-là)* then, at that time; **il habitait alors à Paris** he lived in Paris at that time

2 *(par conséquent)* then; **tu as fini? alors je m'en vais** have you finished? I'm going then; **et alors?** so what?; **alors que** *conj* **1** *(au moment où)* when, as; **il est arrivé alors que je partais** he arrived as I was leaving

2 *(pendant que)* while, when; **alors qu'il était à Paris, il a visité ...** while *ou* when he was in Paris, he visited ...

3 *(tandis que)* whereas, while; **alors que son frère travaillait dur, lui se reposait** while his brother was working hard, HE would rest

alouette [alwɛt] *nf* (sky)lark
alourdir [aluʀdiʀ] *vt* to weigh down, make heavy
aloyau [alwajo] *nm* sirloin
Alpes [alp] *nfpl*: **les ~** the Alps
alphabet [alfabɛ] *nm* alphabet; *(livre)* ABC (book); **alphabétique** *adj* alphabetical; **alphabétiser** *vt* to teach to read and write; *(pays)* to eliminate illiteracy in
alpinisme [alpinism] *nm* mountaineering, climbing; **alpiniste** *nm/f* mountaineer, climber
Alsace [alzas] *nf* Alsace; **alsacien, ne** *adj* Alsatian ♦ *nm/f*: **Alsacien, ne** Alsatian
altérer [alteʀe] *vt (vérité)* to distort; **s'~** *vi* to deteriorate
alternateur [altɛʀnatœʀ] *nm* alternator
alternatif, -ive [altɛʀnatif, iv] *adj* alternating; **alternative** *nf (choix)* alternative; **alternativement** *adv* alternately; **alterner** *vi* to alternate
Altesse [altɛs] *nf* Highness
altitude [altityd] *nf* altitude, height
alto [alto] *nm (instrument)* viola
aluminium [alyminjɔm] *nm* aluminium *(BRIT)*, aluminum *(US)*
amabilité [amabilite] *nf* kindness
amadouer [amadwe] *vt* to mollify, soothe
amaigrir [amegʀiʀ] *vt* to make thin(ner); **amaigrissant, e** *adj (régime)* slimming
amalgame [amalgam] *nm (péj)* (strange) mixture

amande [amɑ̃d] *nf (de l'amandier)* almond; **amandier** *nm* almond (tree)

amant [amɑ̃] *nm* lover

amarrer [amaʀe] *vt (NAVIG)* to moor; *(gén)* to make fast

amas [amɑ] *nm* heap, pile; **amasser** *vt* to amass; **s'amasser** *vi (foule)* to gather

amateur [amatœʀ] *nm* amateur; **en ~** *(péj)* amateurishly; **~ de musique/sport** *etc* music/sport *etc* lover

amazone [amazon] *nf:* **en ~** sidesaddle

ambassade [ɑ̃basad] *nf* embassy; **l'~ de France** the French Embassy; **ambassadeur, -drice** *nm/f* ambassador(-dress)

ambiance [ɑ̃bjɑ̃s] *nf* atmosphere

ambiant, e [ɑ̃bjɑ̃, jɑ̃t] *adj (air, milieu)* surrounding; *(température)* ambient

ambigu, ë [ɑ̃bigy] *adj* ambiguous

ambitieux, -euse [ɑ̃bisjø, jøz] *adj* ambitious

ambition [ɑ̃bisjɔ̃] *nf* ambition

ambulance [ɑ̃bylɑ̃s] *nf* ambulance; **ambulancier, -ière** *nm/f* ambulance man/woman *(BRIT)*, paramedic *(US)*

ambulant, e [ɑ̃bylɑ̃, ɑ̃t] *adj* travelling, itinerant

âme [ɑm] *nf* soul

amélioration [ameljɔʀasjɔ̃] *nf* improvement

améliorer [ameljɔʀe] *vt* to improve; **s'~** *vi* to improve, get better

aménager [amenaʒe] *vt (agencer, transformer)* to fit out; to lay out; *(: quartier, territoire)* to develop; *(installer)* to fix up, put in; **ferme aménagée** converted farmhouse

amende [amɑ̃d] *nf* fine; **faire ~ honorable** to make amends

amener [am(ə)ne] *vt* to bring; *(causer)* to bring about; **s'~** *vi* to show up *(fam)*, turn up

amenuiser [amənɥize]: **s'~** *vi (chances)* to grow slimmer, lessen

amer, amère [ameʀ] *adj* bitter

américain, e [ameʀikɛ̃, ɛn] *adj* American ♦ *nm/f:* **A~, e** American

Amérique [ameʀik] *nf:* **l'~** America; **l'~ centrale/latine** Central/Latin America; **l'~ du Nord/du Sud** North/South America

amertume [ameʀtym] *nf* bitterness

ameublement [amœbləmɑ̃] *nm* furnishing; *(meubles)* furniture

ameuter [amøte] *vt (peuple)* to rouse

ami, e [ami] *nm/f* friend; *(amant/maîtresse)* boyfriend/girlfriend ♦ *adj:* **pays/groupe ~** friendly country/group

amiable [amjabl]: **à l'~** *adv (JUR)* out of court; *(gén)* amicably

amiante [amjɑ̃t] *nm* asbestos

amical, e, -aux [amikal, o] *adj* friendly; **amicalement** *adv* in a friendly way; *(formule épistolaire)* regards

amidon [amidɔ̃] *nm* starch

amincir [amɛ̃siʀ] *vt:* **~ qn** to make sb thinner *ou* slimmer; *(suj: vêtement)* to make sb look slimmer

amincissant, e [amɛ̃sisɑ̃, ɑ̃t] *adj:* **régime ~** (slimming) diet; **crème ~e** slimming cream

amiral, -aux [amiʀal, o] *nm* admiral

amitié [amitje] *nf* friendship; **prendre en ~** to befriend; **~s, Christèle** best wishes, Christèle; **présenter ses ~s à qn** to send sb one's best wishes

ammoniaque [amɔnjak] *nf* ammonia (water)

amnistie [amnisti] *nf* amnesty

amoindrir [amwɛ̃dʀiʀ] *vt* to reduce

amollir [amɔliʀ] *vt* to soften

amonceler [amɔ̃s(ə)le] *vt* to pile *ou* heap up; **s'~** *vi* to pile *ou* heap up; *(fig)* to accumulate

amont [amɔ̃]: **en ~** *adv* upstream

amorce [amɔʀs] *nf (sur un hameçon)* bait; *(explosif)* cap; primer; priming; *(fig: début)* beginning(s), start; **amorcer** *vt* to start

amorphe [amɔʀf] *adj* passive, lifeless

amortir [amɔʀtiʀ] *vt (atténuer: choc)* to absorb, cushion; *(bruit, douleur)* to deaden; *(COMM: dette)* to pay off; **~ un achat** to make a purchase pay for itself; **amortisseur** *nm* shock absorber

amour [amuʀ] *nm* love; **faire l'~** to make love; **amouracher: s'amouracher de** (*péj*) *vt* to become infatuated with; **amoureux, -euse** *adj* (*regard, tempérament*) amorous; (*vie, problèmes*) love *cpd*; (*personne*): **amoureux (de qn)** in love (with sb) ♦ *nmpl* courting couple(s); **amour-propre** *nm* self-esteem, pride

amovible [amɔvibl] *adj* removable, detachable

ampère [ɑ̃pɛʀ] *nm* amp(ere)

amphithéâtre [ɑ̃fiteatʀ] *nm* amphitheatre; (*d'université*) lecture hall *ou* theatre

ample [ɑ̃pl] *adj* (*vêtement*) roomy, ample; (*gestes, mouvement*) broad; (*ressources*) ample; **amplement** *adv*: **c'est amplement suffisant** that's more than enough; **ampleur** *nf* (*de dégâts, problème*) extent

amplificateur [ɑ̃plifikatœʀ] *nm* amplifier

amplifier [ɑ̃plifje] *vt* (*fig*) to expand, increase

ampoule [ɑ̃pul] *nf* (*électrique*) bulb; (*de médicament*) phial; (*aux mains, pieds*) blister; **ampoulé, e** (*péj*) *adj* pompous, bombastic

amputer [ɑ̃pyte] *vt* (*MÉD*) to amputate; (*fig*) to cut *ou* reduce drastically

amusant, e [amyzɑ̃, ɑ̃t] *adj* (*divertissant, spirituel*) entertaining, amusing; (*comique*) funny, amusing

amuse-gueule [amyzgœl] *nm inv* appetizer, snack

amusement [amyzmɑ̃] *nm* (*divertissement*) amusement; (*jeu etc*) pastime, diversion

amuser [amyze] *vt* (*divertir*) to entertain, amuse; (*égayer, faire rire*) to amuse; **s'~** *vi* (*jouer*) to play; (*se divertir*) to enjoy o.s., have fun; (*fig*) to mess around

amygdale [amidal] *nf* tonsil

an [ɑ̃] *nm* year; **avoir quinze ~s** to be fifteen (years old); **le jour de l'~, le premier de l'~, le nouvel ~** New Year's Day

analogique [analɔʒik] *adj* (*INFORM, montre*) analog

analogue [analɔg] *adj*: **~ (à)** analogous

(to), similar (to)

analphabète [analfabɛt] *nm/f* illiterate

analyse [analiz] *nf* analysis; (*MÉD*) test; **analyser** *vt* to analyse; to test

ananas [anana(s)] *nm* pineapple

anarchie [anaʀʃi] *nf* anarchy

anatomie [anatɔmi] *nf* anatomy

ancêtre [ɑ̃sɛtʀ] *nm/f* ancestor

anchois [ɑ̃ʃwa] *nm* anchovy

ancien, ne [ɑ̃sjɛ̃, jɛn] *adj* old; (*de jadis, de l'antiquité*) ancient; (*précédent, ex-*) former, old; (*par l'expérience*) senior ♦ *nm/f* (*dans une tribu*) elder; **~-combattant** ♦ *nm* war veteran; **anciennement** *adv* formerly; **ancienneté** *nf* (*ADMIN*) (length of) service; (*privilèges obtenus*) seniority

ancre [ɑ̃kʀ] *nf* anchor; **jeter/lever l'~** to cast/weigh anchor; **ancrer** *vt* (*CONSTR: câble etc*) to anchor; (*fig*) to fix firmly

Andorre [ɑ̃dɔʀ] *nf* Andorra

andouille [ɑ̃duj] *nf* (*CULIN*) *sausage made of chitterlings*; (*fam*) clot, nit

âne [ɑn] *nm* donkey, ass; (*péj*) dunce

anéantir [aneɑ̃tiʀ] *vt* to annihilate, wipe out; (*fig*) to obliterate, destroy

anémie [anemi] *nf* anaemia; **anémique** *adj* anaemic

ânerie [ɑnʀi] *nf* stupidity; (*parole etc*) stupid *ou* idiotic comment *etc*

anesthésie [anɛstezi] *nf* anaesthesia; **faire une ~ locale/générale à qn** to give sb a local/general anaesthetic

ange [ɑ̃ʒ] *nm* angel; **être aux ~s** to be over the moon

angélus [ɑ̃ʒelys] *nm* angelus; (*cloches*) evening bells *pl*

angine [ɑ̃ʒin] *nf* throat infection; **~ de poitrine** angina

anglais, e [ɑ̃glɛ, ɛz] *adj* English ♦ *nm/f*: **A~, e** Englishman(-woman) ♦ *nm* (*LING*) English; **les A~** the English; **filer à l'~e** to take French leave

angle [ɑ̃gl] *nm* angle; (*coin*) corner; **~ droit** right angle

Angleterre [ɑ̃glətɛʀ] *nf*: **l'~** England

anglo... [ɑ̃glɔ] *préfixe* Anglo-, anglo(-);

anglophone adj English-speaking

angoisse [ɑ̃gwas] nf anguish, distress; angoissé, e adj (personne) distressed; angoisser vt to harrow, cause anguish to ♦ vi to worry, fret

anguille [ɑ̃gij] nf eel

anicroche [anikʀɔʃ] nf hitch, snag

animal, e, -aux [animal, o] adj, nm animal

animateur, -trice [animatœʀ, tʀis] nm/f (de télévision) host; (de groupe) leader, organizer

animation [animasjɔ̃] nf (voir animé) busyness; liveliness; (CINÉMA: technique) animation; ~s culturelles cultural activities

animé, e [anime] adj (lieu) busy, lively; (conversation, réunion) lively, animated

animer [anime] vt (ville, soirée) to liven up; (mener) to lead; s'~ vi to liven up

anis [ani(s)] nm (CULIN) aniseed; (BOT) anise

ankyloser [ɑ̃kiloze]: s'~ vi to get stiff

anneau, x [ano] nm (de rideau, bague) ring; (de chaîne) link

année [ane] nf year

annexe [anɛks] adj (problème) related; (document) appended; (salle) adjoining ♦ nf (bâtiment) annex(e); (jointe à une lettre) enclosure

anniversaire [anivɛʀsɛʀ] nm birthday; (d'un événement, bâtiment) anniversary

annonce [anɔ̃s] nf announcement; (signe, indice) sign; (aussi: ~ publicitaire) advertisement; les petites ~s the classified advertisements, the small ads

annoncer [anɔ̃se] vt to announce; (être le signe de) to herald; s'~ bien/difficile to look promising/difficult; annonceur, -euse nm/f (publicitaire) advertiser; (TV, RADIO: speaker) announcer

annuaire [anɥɛʀ] nm yearbook, annual; ~ téléphonique (telephone) directory, phone book

annuel, le [anɥɛl] adj annual, yearly

annuité [anɥite] nf annual instalment

annulation [anylasjɔ̃] nf cancellation

annuler [anyle] vt (rendez-vous, voyage) to cancel, call off; (jugement) to quash (BRIT), repeal (US); (MATH, PHYSIQUE) to cancel out

anodin, e [anɔdɛ̃, in] adj (blessure) harmless; (détail) insignificant, trivial

anonymat [anɔnima] nm anonymity

anonyme [anɔnim] adj anonymous; (fig) impersonal

ANPE sigle f (= Agence nationale pour l'emploi) national employment agency

anorexie [anɔʀɛksi] nf anorexia

anormal, e, -aux [anɔʀmal, o] adj abnormal

anse [ɑ̃s] nf (de panier, tasse) handle

antan [ɑ̃tɑ̃]: d'~ adj of long ago

antarctique [ɑ̃taʀktik] adj Antarctic ♦ nm: l'A~ the Antarctic

antécédents [ɑ̃tesedɑ̃] nmpl (MÉD etc) past history sg

antenne [ɑ̃tɛn] nf (de radio) aerial; (d'insecte) antenna, feeler; (poste avancé) outpost; (petite succursale) sub-branch; passer à l'~ to go on the air

antérieur, e [ɑ̃teʀjœʀ] adj (d'avant) previous, earlier; (de devant) front

anti... [ɑ̃ti] préfixe anti...; antialcoolique adj anti-alcohol; antiatomique adj: abri antiatomique fallout shelter; antibiotique nm antibiotic; antibrouillard adj: phare antibrouillard fog lamp (BRIT) ou light (US)

anticipation [ɑ̃tisipasjɔ̃] nf: livre/film d'~ science fiction book/film

anticipé, e [ɑ̃tisipe] adj: avec mes remerciements ~s thanking you in advance ou anticipation

anticiper [ɑ̃tisipe] vt (événement, coup) to anticipate, foresee

anti...: anticonceptionnel, le adj contraceptive; anticorps nm antibody; antidépresseur nm antidepressant; antidote nm antidote; antigel nm antifreeze; antihistaminique nm antihistamine

antillais, e [ɑ̃tije, ɛz] adj West Indian, Caribbean ♦ nm/f: A~, e West Indian, Caribbean

Antilles [ɑ̃tij] nfpl: les ~ the West Indies

antilope [ɑ̃tilɔp] *nf* antelope

anti...: **antimite(s)** *adj*, *nm*: **(produit) antimite(s)** mothproofer; moth repellent; **antipathique** *adj* unpleasant, disagreeable; **antipelliculaire** *adj* anti-dandruff

antipodes [ɑ̃tipɔd] *nmpl* (*fig*): **être aux ~ de** to be the opposite extreme of

antiquaire [ɑ̃tikɛʀ] *nm/f* antique dealer

antique [ɑ̃tik] *adj* antique; (*très vieux*) ancient, antiquated; **antiquité** *nf* (*objet*) antique; **l'Antiquité** Antiquity; **magasin d'antiquités** antique shop

anti...: **antirabique** *adj* rabies *cpd*; **antirouille** *adj inv* anti-rust *cpd*; **antisémite** *adj* anti-Semitic; **antiseptique** *adj*, *nm* antiseptic; **antivol** *adj*, *nm*: **(dispositif) antivol** anti-theft device

antre [ɑ̃tʀ] *nm* den, lair

anxiété [ɑ̃ksjete] *nf* anxiety

anxieux, -euse [ɑ̃ksjø, jøz] *adj* anxious, worried

AOC *sigle f* (= *appellation d'origine contrôlée*) label guaranteeing the quality of wine

┌─────────────┐
│   **AOC**   │
└─────────────┘

i AOC *is the highest French wine classification. It indicates that the wine meets strict requirements concerning the vineyard of origin, the type of vine grown, the method of production, and the volume of alcohol present.*

août [u(t)] *nm* August

apaiser [apeze] *vt* (*colère, douleur*) to soothe; (*personne*) to calm (down), pacify; **s'~** *vi* (*tempête, bruit*) to die down, subside; (*personne*) to calm down

apanage [apanaʒ] *nm*: **être l'~ de** to be the privilege or prerogative of

aparté [aparte] *nm* (*entretien*) private conversation; **en ~** in an aside

apathique [apatik] *adj* apathetic

apatride [apatʀid] *nm/f* stateless person

apercevoir [apɛʀsəvwaʀ] *vt* to see; **s'~ de** *vt* to notice; **s'~ que** to notice that

aperçu [apɛʀsy] *nm* (*vue d'ensemble*) general survey

apéritif [apeʀitif] *nm* (*boisson*) aperitif; (*réunion*) drinks *pl*

à-peu-près [apøpʀɛ] (*péj*) *nm inv* vague approximation

apeuré, e [apœʀe] *adj* frightened, scared

aphte [aft] *nm* mouth ulcer

apiculture [apikyltyʀ] *nf* beekeeping, apiculture

apitoyer [apitwaje] *vt* to move to pity; **s'~ (sur)** to feel pity (for)

aplanir [aplaniʀ] *vt* to level; (*fig*) to smooth away, iron out

aplatir [aplatiʀ] *vt* to flatten; **s'~** *vi* to become flatter; (*écrasé*) to be flattened; **s'~ devant qn** (*fig*: *s'humilier*) to crawl to sb

aplomb [aplɔ̃] *nm* (*équilibre*) balance, equilibrium; (*fig*) self-assurance; nerve; **d'~** steady

apogée [apɔʒe] *nm* (*fig*) peak, apogee

apologie [apɔlɔʒi] *nf* vindication, praise

a posteriori [apɔsteʀjɔʀi] *adv* after the event

apostrophe [apɔstʀɔf] *nf* (*signe*) apostrophe

apostropher [apɔstʀɔfe] *vt* (*interpeller*) to shout at, address sharply

apothéose [apɔteoz] *nf* pinnacle (of achievement); (*MUS*) grand finale

apôtre [apotʀ] *nm* apostle

apparaître [apaʀɛtʀ] *vi* to appear

apparat [apaʀa] *nm*: **tenue d'~** ceremonial dress

appareil [apaʀɛj] *nm* (*outil, machine*) piece of apparatus, device; (*électrique, ménager*) appliance; (*avion*) (aero)plane, aircraft *inv*; (*téléphonique*) phone; (*dentier*) brace (*BRIT*), braces (*US*); **"qui est à l'~?"** "who's speaking?"; **dans le plus simple ~** in one's birthday suit; **appareiller** *vi* (*NAVIG*) to cast off, get under way ♦ *vt* (*assortir*) to match up; **appareil(-photo)** *nm* camera

apparemment [apaʀamɑ̃] *adv* apparently

apparence [apaʀɑ̃s] *nf* appearance; **en ~** apparently

apparent, e [aparɑ̃, ɑ̃t] *adj* visible; *(évident)* obvious; *(superficiel)* apparent

apparenté, e [aparɑ̃te] *adj*: **~ à** related to; *(fig)* similar to

apparition [aparisjɔ̃] *nf* appearance; *(surnaturelle)* apparition

appartement [apartəmɑ̃] *nm* flat *(BRIT)*, apartment *(US)*

appartenir [apartənir]: **~ à** *vt* to belong to; **il lui appartient de** it is his duty to

apparu, e [apary] *pp de* **apparaître**

appât [apɑ] *nm (PÊCHE)* bait; *(fig)* lure, bait; **appâter** *vt* to lure

appauvrir [apovrir] *vt* to impoverish

appel [apɛl] *nm* call; *(nominal)* roll call; *(: SCOL)* register; *(MIL: recrutement)* call-up; **faire ~ à** *(invoquer)* to appeal to; *(avoir recours à)* to call on; *(nécessiter)* to call for, require; **faire ~** *(JUR)* to appeal; **faire l'~** to call the roll; to call the register; **sans ~** *(fig)* final, irrevocable; **~ d'offres** *(COMM)* invitation to tender; **faire un ~ de phares** to flash one's headlights; **~ (téléphonique)** (tele)phone call

appelé [ap(ə)le] *nm (MIL)* conscript

appeler [ap(ə)le] *vt* to call; *(faire venir: médecin etc)* to call, send for; **s'~** *vi*: **elle s'appelle Gabrielle** her name is Gabrielle, she's called Gabrielle; **comment ça s'appelle?** what is it called?; **être appelé à** *(fig)* to be destined to

appendice [apɛ̃dis] *nm* appendix; **appendicite** *nf* appendicitis

appentis [apɑ̃ti] *nm* lean-to

appesantir [apəzɑ̃tir]: **s'~** *vi* to grow heavier; **s'~ sur** *(fig)* to dwell on

appétissant, e [apetisɑ̃, ɑ̃t] *adj* appetizing, mouth-watering

appétit [apeti] *nm* appetite; **bon ~!** enjoy your meal!

applaudir [aplodir] *vt* to applaud ♦ *vi* to applaud, clap; **applaudissements** *nmpl* applause *sg*, clapping *sg*

application [aplikasjɔ̃] *nf* application

applique [aplik] *nf* wall lamp

appliquer [aplike] *vt* to apply; *(loi)* to enforce; **s'~** *vi (élève etc)* to apply o.s.; **s'~ à** to apply to

appoint [apwɛ̃] *nm (extra)* contribution *ou* help; **chauffage d'~** extra heating

appointements [apwɛ̃tmɑ̃] *nmpl* salary *sg*

apport [apɔr] *nm (approvisionnement)* supply; *(contribution)* contribution

apporter [apɔrte] *vt* to bring

apposer [apoze] *vt (signature)* to affix

appréciable [apresjabl] *adj* appreciable

apprécier [apresje] *vt* to appreciate; *(évaluer)* to estimate, assess

appréhender [apreɑ̃de] *vt (craindre)* to dread; *(arrêter)* to apprehend; **appréhension** *nf* apprehension, anxiety

apprendre [aprɑ̃dr] *vt* to learn; *(événement, résultats)* to learn of, hear of; **~ qch à qn** *(informer)* to tell sb (of) sth; *(enseigner)* to teach sb sth; **~ à faire qch** to learn to do sth; **~ à qn à faire qch** to teach sb to do sth; **apprenti, e** *nm/f* apprentice; **apprentissage** *nm* learning; *(COMM, SCOL: période)* apprenticeship

apprêté, e [aprete] *adj (fig)* affected

apprêter [aprete] *vt*: **s'~ à faire qch** to get ready to do sth

appris, e [apri, iz] *pp de* **apprendre**

apprivoiser [aprivwaze] *vt* to tame

approbation [aprɔbasjɔ̃] *nf* approval

approchant, e [aprɔʃɑ̃, ɑ̃t] *adj* similar; **quelque chose d'~** something like that

approche [aprɔʃ] *nf* approach

approcher [aprɔʃe] *vi* to approach, come near ♦ *vt* to approach; *(rapprocher)*: **~ qch (de qch)** to bring *ou* put sth near (to sth); **s'~ de** to approach, go *ou* come near to; **~ de** *(lieu, but)* to draw near to; *(quantité, moment)* to approach

approfondir [aprɔfɔ̃dir] *vt* to deepen; *(question)* to go further into

approprié, e [aprɔprije] *adj*: **~ (à)** appropriate (to), suited to

approprier [aprɔprije]: **s'~** *vt* to appropriate, take over

approuver [apruve] *vt* to agree with;

(*trouver louable*) to approve of

approvisionner [apʀɔvizjɔne] *vt* to supply; (*compte bancaire*) to pay funds into; **s'~ en** to stock up with

approximatif, -ive [apʀɔksimatif, iv] *adj* approximate, rough; (*termes*) vague

appt *abr* = **appartement**

appui [apɥi] *nm* support; **prendre ~ sur** to lean on; (*objet*) to rest on; **l'~ de la fenêtre**, the windowsill, the window ledge; **appui(e)-tête** *nm inv* headrest

appuyer [apɥije] *vt* (*poser*): **~ qch sur/contre** to lean *ou* rest sth on/against; (*soutenir: personne, demande*) to support, back (up) ♦ *vi*: **~ sur** (*bouton, frein*) to press, push; (*mot, détail*) to stress, emphasize; **s'~ sur** to lean on; (*fig: compter sur*) to rely on

âpre [apʀ] *adj* acrid, pungent; **~ au gain** grasping

après [apʀe] *prép* after ♦ *adv* afterwards; **2 heures ~** 2 hours later; **~ qu'il est** *ou* **soit parti** after he left; **~ avoir fait** after having done; **d'~** (*selon*) according to; **~ coup** after the event, afterwards; **~ tout** (*au fond*) after all; **et (puis) ~?** so what?; **après-demain** *adv* the day after tomorrow; **après-guerre** *nm* post-war years *pl*; **après-midi** *nm ou nf inv* afternoon; **après-rasage** *nm inv* aftershave; **après-shampooing** *nm inv* conditioner; **après-ski** *nm inv* snow boot

à-propos [apʀopo] *nm* (*d'une remarque*) aptness; **faire preuve d'~-~** to show presence of mind

apte [apt] *adj* capable; (*MIL*) fit

aquarelle [akwaʀɛl] *nf* watercolour

aquarium [akwaʀjɔm] *nm* aquarium

arabe [aʀab] *adj* Arabic; (*désert, cheval*) Arabian; (*nation, peuple*) Arab ♦ *nm/f*: **A~** Arab ♦ *nm* (*LING*) Arabic

Arabie [aʀabi] *nf*: **l'~ (Saoudite)** Saudi Arabia

arachide [aʀaʃid] *nf* (*plante*) groundnut (plant); (*graine*) peanut, groundnut

araignée [aʀeɲe] *nf* spider

arbitraire [aʀbitʀɛʀ] *adj* arbitrary

arbitre [aʀbitʀ] *nm* (*SPORT*) referee; (: *TENNIS, CRICKET*) umpire; (*fig*) arbiter, judge; (*JUR*) arbitrator; **arbitrer** *vt* to referee; to umpire; to arbitrate

arborer [aʀbɔʀe] *vt* to bear, display

arbre [aʀbʀ] *nm* tree; (*TECH*) shaft; **~ généalogique** family tree

arbuste [aʀbyst] *nm* small shrub

arc [aʀk] *nm* (*arme*) bow; (*GÉOM*) arc; (*ARCHIT*) arch; **en ~ de cercle** semi-circular

arcade [aʀkad] *nf* arch(way); **~s** *nfpl* (*série*) arcade *sg*, arches

arcanes [aʀkan] *nmpl* mysteries

arc-boutant [aʀkbutɑ̃] *nm* flying buttress

arceau, x [aʀso] *nm* (*métallique etc*) hoop

arc-en-ciel [aʀkɑ̃sjɛl] *nm* rainbow

arche [aʀʃ] *nf* arch; **~ de Noé** Noah's Ark

archéologie [aʀkeɔlɔʒi] *nf* arch(a)eology; **archéologue** *nm/f* arch(a)eologist

archet [aʀʃe] *nm* bow

archevêque [aʀʃəvɛk] *nm* archbishop .

archi... [aʀʃi] (*fam*) *préfixe* tremendously; **archicomble** (*fam*) *adj* chock-a-block; **archiconnu, e** (*fam*) *adj* enormously well-known

archipel [aʀʃipɛl] *nm* archipelago

architecte [aʀʃitɛkt] *nm* architect

architecture [aʀʃitɛktyʀ] *nf* architecture

archives [aʀʃiv] *nfpl* (*collection*) archives

arctique [aʀktik] *adj* Arctic ♦ *nm*: **l'A~** the Arctic

ardemment [aʀdamɑ̃] *adv* ardently, fervently

ardent, e [aʀdɑ̃, ɑ̃t] *adj* (*soleil*) blazing; (*amour*) ardent, passionate; (*prière*) fervent

ardeur [aʀdœʀ] *nf* ardour (*BRIT*), ardor (*US*); (*du soleil*) heat

ardoise [aʀdwaz] *nf* slate

ardu, e [aʀdy] *adj* (*travail*) arduous; (*problème*) difficult

arène [aʀɛn] *nf* arena; **~s** *nfpl* (*amphithéâtre*) bull-ring *sg*

arête [aʀɛt] *nf* (*de poisson*) bone; (*d'une montagne*) ridge

argent [aʀʒɑ̃] *nm* (*métal*) silver; (*monnaie*)

money; **~ de poche** pocket money; **~ liquide** ready money, (ready) cash; **argenté, e** *adj* (*couleur*) silver, silvery; **en métal argenté** silver-plated; **argenterie** *nf* silverware

argentin, e [aʀʒɑ̃tɛ̃, in] *adj* Argentinian, Argentine

Argentine [aʀʒɑ̃tin] *nf:* **l'~** Argentina, the Argentine

argile [aʀʒil] *nf* clay

argot [aʀgo] *nm* slang; **argotique** *adj* slang *cpd*; (*très familier*) slangy

argument [aʀgymɑ̃] *nm* argument

argumentaire [aʀgymɑ̃tɛʀ] *nm* sales leaflet

argumenter [aʀgymɑ̃te] *vi* to argue

argus [aʀgys] *nm* guide to second-hand car etc prices

aride [aʀid] *adj* arid

aristocratie [aʀistɔkʀasi] *nf* aristocracy; **aristocratique** *adj* aristocratic

arithmétique [aʀitmetik] *adj* arithmetic(al) ♦ *nf* arithmetic

armateur [aʀmatœʀ] *nm* shipowner

armature [aʀmatyʀ] *nf* framework; (*de tente etc*) frame; **soutien-gorge à/sans ~** underwired/unwired bra

arme [aʀm] *nf* weapon; **~s** *nfpl* (*~ment*) weapons, arms; (*blason*) (coat of) arms; **~ à feu** firearm

armée [aʀme] *nf* army; **~ de l'air** Air Force; **~ de terre** Army

armement [aʀməmɑ̃] *nm* (*matériel*) arms *pl*, weapons *pl*

armer [aʀme] *vt* to arm; (*arme à feu*) to cock; (*appareil-photo*) to wind on; **~ qch de** to reinforce sth with; **s'~ de** to arm o.s. with

armistice [aʀmistis] *nm* armistice; **l'A~** ≃ Remembrance (*BRIT*) *ou* Veterans (*US*) Day

armoire [aʀmwaʀ] *nf* (tall) cupboard; (*penderie*) wardrobe (*BRIT*), closet (*US*)

armoiries [aʀmwaʀi] *nfpl* coat *sg* of arms

armure [aʀmyʀ] *nf* armour *no pl*, suit of armour; **armurier** *nm* gunsmith

arnaque [aʀnak] (*fam*) *nf* swindling; **c'est de l'~** it's a rip-off; **arnaquer** (*fam*) *vt* to swindle

aromates [aʀɔmat] *nmpl* seasoning *sg*, herbs (and spices)

aromathérapie [aʀɔmateʀapi] *nf* aromatherapy

aromatisé, e [aʀɔmatize] *adj* flavoured

arôme [aʀom] *nm* aroma

arpenter [aʀpɑ̃te] *vt* (*salle, couloir*) to pace up and down

arpenteur [aʀpɑ̃tœʀ] *nm* surveyor

arqué, e [aʀke] *adj* arched; (*jambes*) bandy

arrache-pied [aʀaʃpje]: **d'~-~** *adv* relentlessly

arracher [aʀaʃe] *vt* to pull out; (*page etc*) to tear off, tear out; (*légumes, herbe*) to pull up; (*bras etc*) to tear off; **s'~** *vt* (*article recherché*) to fight over; **~ qch à qn** to snatch sth from sb; (*fig*) to wring sth out of sb

arraisonner [aʀezɔne] *vt* (*bateau*) to board and search

arrangeant, e [aʀɑ̃ʒɑ̃, ɑ̃t] *adj* accommodating, obliging

arrangement [aʀɑ̃ʒmɑ̃] *nm* agreement, arrangement

arranger [aʀɑ̃ʒe] *vt* (*gén*) to arrange; (*réparer*) to fix, put right; (*régler: différend*) to settle, sort out; (*convenir à*) to suit, be convenient for; **s'~** *vi* (*se mettre d'accord*) to come to an agreement; **je vais m'~** I'll manage; **ça va s'~** it'll sort itself out

arrestation [aʀestasjɔ̃] *nf* arrest

arrêt [aʀe] *nm* stopping; (*de bus etc*) stop; (*JUR*) judgment, decision; **à l'~** stationary; **tomber en ~ devant** to stop short in front of; **sans ~** (*sans interruption*) nonstop; (*très fréquemment*) continually; **~ de travail** stoppage (of work); **~ maladie** sick leave

arrêté [aʀete] *nm* order, decree

arrêter [aʀete] *vt* to stop; (*chauffage etc*) to turn off, switch off; (*fixer: date etc*) to appoint, decide on; (*criminel, suspect*) to arrest; **s'~** *vi* to stop; **~ de faire** to stop

doing
arrhes [aʀ] *nfpl* deposit *sg*
arrière [aʀjɛʀ] *nm* back; (SPORT) fullback
♦ *adj inv*: **siège/roue ~** back *ou* rear
seat/wheel; **à l'~** behind, at the back; **en
~** behind; (*regarder*) back, behind; (*tomber, aller*) backwards; **arriéré, e** *adj (péj)*
backward ♦ *nm* (*d'argent*) arrears *pl*;
arrière-goût *nm* aftertaste; **arrière-
grand-mère** *nf* great-grandmother;
arrière-grand-père *nm* great-grand-
father; **arrière-pays** *nm inv* hinterland;
arrière-pensée *nf* ulterior motive; mental reservation; **arrière-plan** *nm* background; **arrière-saison** *nf* late autumn;
arrière-train *nm* hindquarters *pl*
arrimer [aʀime] *vt* to secure; (*cargaison*) to
stow
arrivage [aʀivaʒ] *nm* consignment
arrivée [aʀive] *nf* arrival; (*ligne d'~*) finish
arriver [aʀive] *vi* to arrive; (*survenir*) to
happen, occur; **il arrive à Paris à 8h** he
gets to *ou* arrives in Paris at 8; **~ à** (*atteindre*) to reach; **~ à faire qch** to succeed
in doing sth; **en ~ à** (*finir par*) to come to;
il arrive que it happens that; **il lui arrive
de faire** he sometimes does; **arriviste**
nm/f go-getter
arrobase [aʀɔbaz] *nf* (INFORM) @, 'at' sign
arrogance [aʀɔgɑ̃s] *nf* arrogance
arrogant, e [aʀɔgɑ̃, ɑ̃t] *adj* arrogant
arrondir [aʀɔ̃diʀ] *vt* (*forme, objet*) to
round; (*somme*) to round off
arrondissement [aʀɔ̃dismɑ̃] *nm* (ADMIN)
≈ district
arroser [aʀoze] *vt* to water; (*victoire*) to celebrate (over a drink); (CULIN) to baste;
arrosoir *nm* watering can
arsenal, -aux [aʀsənal, o] *nm* (NAVIG) naval dockyard; (MIL) arsenal; (*fig*) gear
art [aʀ] *nm* art
artère [aʀtɛʀ] *nf* (ANAT) artery; (*rue*) main
road
arthrite [aʀtʀit] *nf* arthritis
artichaut [aʀtiʃo] *nm* artichoke
article [aʀtikl] *nm* article; (COMM) item, ar-

ticle; **à l'~ de la mort** at the point of
death; **~s de luxe** luxury goods
articulation [aʀtikylasjɔ̃] *nf* articulation;
(ANAT) joint
articuler [aʀtikyle] *vt* to articulate
artifice [aʀtifis] *nm* device, trick
artificiel, le [aʀtifisjɛl] *adj* artificial
artisan [aʀtizɑ̃] *nm* artisan, (self-employed)
craftsman; **artisanal, e, -aux** *adj* of *ou*
made by craftsmen; (*péj*) cottage industry
cpd; **de fabrication artisanale** homemade; **artisanat** *nm* arts and crafts *pl*
artiste [aʀtist] *nm/f* artist; (*de variétés*) entertainer; (*musicien etc*) performer; **artistique** *adj* artistic
as[1] [a] *vb voir* **avoir**
as[2] [as] *nm* ace
ascendance [asɑ̃dɑ̃s] *nf* (*origine*) ancestry
ascendant, e [asɑ̃dɑ̃, ɑ̃t] *adj* upward
♦ *nm* influence
ascenseur [asɑ̃sœʀ] *nm* lift (BRIT), elevator
(US)
ascension [asɑ̃sjɔ̃] *nf* ascent; (*de montagne*) climb; **l'A~** (REL) the Ascension

---
Ascension

i La fête de l'Ascension *is a French
public holiday, usually in May. As it
falls on a Thursday, many people take Friday off work and enjoy a long weekend;
see also* faire le pont.

---

aseptisé, e (*péj*) *adj* sanitized
aseptiser [asɛptize] *vt* (*ustensile*) to sterilize; (*plaie*) to disinfect
asiatique [azjatik] *adj* Asiatic, Asian
♦ *nm/f*: **A~** Asian
Asie [azi] *nf*: **l'~** Asia
asile [azil] *nm* (*refuge*) refuge, sanctuary;
(POL): **droit d'~** (political) asylum; **~ (de
vieillards)** old people's home
aspect [aspɛ] *nm* appearance, look; (*fig*)
aspect, side; **à l'~ de** at the sight of
asperge [aspɛʀʒ] *nf* asparagus *no pl*
asperger [aspɛʀʒe] *vt* to spray, sprinkle
aspérité [asperite] *nf* bump, protruding

bit (of rock *etc*)

asphalte [asfalt] *nm* asphalt

asphyxier [asfiksje] *vt* to suffocate, asphyxiate; (*fig*) to stifle

aspirateur [aspiratœr] *nm* vacuum cleaner; **passer l'~** to vacuum

aspirer [aspire] *vt* (*air*) to inhale; (*liquide*) to suck (up); (*suj: appareil*) to suck up; **~ à** to aspire to

aspirine [aspirin] *nf* aspirin

assagir [asaʒir]: **s'~** *vi* to quieten down, settle down

assaillir [asajir] *vt* to assail, attack

assainir [asenir] *vt* (*logements*) to clean up; (*eau, air*) to purify

assaisonnement [asɛzɔnmɑ̃] *nм* seasoning

assaisonner [asɛzɔne] *vt* to season

assassin [asasɛ̃] *nm* murderer; assassin; **assassiner** *vt* to murder; (*esp POL*) to assassinate

assaut [aso] *nm* assault, attack; **prendre d'~** to storm, assault; **donner l'~** to attack

assécher [aseʃe] *vt* to drain

assemblage [asɑ̃blaʒ] *nm* (*action*) assembling; (*de couleurs, choses*) collection

assemblée [asɑ̃ble] *nf* (*réunion*) meeting; (*assistance*) gathering; (*POL*) assembly

assembler [asɑ̃ble] *vt* (*joindre, monter*) to assemble, put together; (*amasser*) to gather (together), collect (together); **s'~** *vi* to gather

assener, asséner [asene] *vt*: **~ un coup à qn** to deal sb a blow

assentiment [asɑ̃timɑ̃] *nm* assent, consent

asseoir [aswar] *vt* (*malade, bébé*) to sit up; (*personne debout*) to sit down; (*autorité, réputation*) to establish; **s'~** *vi* to sit (o.s.) down

assermenté, e [asɛrmɑ̃te] *adj* sworn, on oath

asservir [asɛrvir] *vt* to subjugate, enslave

assez [ase] *adv* (*suffisamment*) enough, sufficiently; (*passablement*) rather, quite,

fairly; **~ de pain/livres** enough *ou* sufficient bread/books; **vous en avez ~?** have you got enough?; **j'en ai ~!** I've had enough!

assidu, e [asidy] *adj* (*appliqué*) assiduous, painstaking; (*ponctuel*) regular

assied *etc* [asje] *vb voir* **asseoir**

assiéger [asjeʒe] *vt* to besiege

assiérai *etc* [asjere] *vb voir* **asseoir**

assiette [asjɛt] *nf* plate; (*contenu*) plate(ful); **il n'est pas dans son ~** he's not feeling quite himself; **~ à dessert** dessert plate; **~ anglaise** assorted cold meats; **~ creuse** (soup) dish, soup plate; **~ plate** (dinner) plate

assigner [asiɲe] *vt*: **~ qch à** (*poste, part, travail*) to assign sth to

assimiler [asimile] *vt* to assimilate, absorb; (*comparer*): **~ qch/qn à** to liken *ou* compare sth/sb to

assis, e [asi, iz] *pp de* **asseoir** ♦ *adj* sitting (down), seated; **assise** *nf* (*GÉO*) basis, foundation; **assises** *nfpl* (*JUR*) assizes

assistance [asistɑ̃s] *nf* (*public*) audience; (*aide*) assistance; **enfant de l'A~ publique** child in care

assistant, e [asistɑ̃, ɑ̃t] *nm/f* assistant; (*d'université*) probationary lecturer; **~(e) social(e)** social worker

assisté, e [asiste] *adj* (*AUTO*) power assisted; **~ par ordinateur** computer-assisted

assister [asiste] *vt* (*aider*) to assist; **~ à** (*scène, événement*) to witness; (*conférence, séminaire*) to attend, be at; (*spectacle, match*) to be at, see

association [asɔsjasjɔ̃] *nf* association

associé, e [asɔsje] *nm/f* associate; (*COMM*) partner

associer [asɔsje] *vt* to associate; **s'~** *vi* to join together; **s'~ à qn pour faire** to join (forces) with sb to do; **s'~ à** (*couleurs, qualités*) to be combined with; (*opinions, joie de qn*) to share in; **~ qn à** (*profits*) to give sb a share of; (*affaire*) to make sb a partner in; (*joie, triomphe*) to include sb in;

~ **qch à** (*allier à*) to combine sth with

assoiffé, e [aswafe] *adj* thirsty

assombrir [asɔ̃bRiR] *vt* to darken; (*fig*) to fill with gloom

assommer [asɔme] *vt* (*étourdir, abrutir*) to knock out, stun

Assomption [asɔ̃psjɔ̃] *nf*: **l'~** the Assumption

Assomption

i **La fête de l'Assomption** *on August 15 is a French national holiday. Traditionally, large numbers of holidaymakers set out on this date, frequently causing chaos on the roads; see also* **faire le pont**.

---

assorti, e [asɔRti] *adj* matched, matching; (*varié*) assorted; **~ à** matching; **assortiment** *nm* assortment, selection

assortir [asɔRtiR] *vt* to match; **~ qch à** to match sth with; **~ qch de** to accompany sth with

assoupi, e [asupi] *adj* dozing, sleeping

assoupir [asupiR]: **s'~** *vi* to doze off

assouplir [asupliR] *vt* to make supple; (*fig*) to relax; **assouplissant** *nm* (*fabric*) softener

assourdir [asuRdiR] *vt* (*bruit*) to deaden, muffle; (*suj: bruit*) to deafen

assouvir [asuviR] *vt* to satisfy, appease

assujettir [asyʒetiR] *vt* to subject

assumer [asyme] *vt* (*fonction, emploi*) to assume, take on

assurance [asyRɑ̃s] *nf* (*certitude*) assurance; (*confiance en soi*) (self-)confidence; (*contrat*) insurance (policy); (*secteur commercial*) insurance; **~ maladie** health insurance; **~ tous risques** (*AUTO*) comprehensive insurance; **~s sociales** ≃ National Insurance (*BRIT*), ≃ Social Security (*US*); **assurance-vie** *nf* life assurance *ou* insurance

assuré, e [asyRe] *adj* (*certain: réussite, échec*) certain, sure; (*air*) assured; (*pas*) steady ♦ *nm/f* insured (person); **assurément** *adv* assuredly, most certainly

assurer [asyRe] *vt* (*FIN*) to insure; (*victoire etc*) to ensure; (*frontières, pouvoir*) to make secure; (*service*) to provide, operate; **s'~ (contre)** (*COMM*) to insure o.s. (against); **s'~ de/que** (*vérifier*) to make sure of/that; **s'~ (de)** (*aide de qn*) to secure; **~ à qn que** to assure sb that; **~ qn de** to assure sb of; **assureur** *nm* insurer

asthmatique [asmatik] *adj, nm/f* asthmatic

asthme [asm] *nm* asthma

asticot [astiko] *nm* maggot

astiquer [astike] *vt* to polish, shine

astre [astR] *nm* star

astreignant, e [astRɛɲɑ̃, ɑ̃t] *adj* demanding

astreindre [astRɛ̃dR] *vt*: **~ qn à faire** to compel *ou* force sb to do; **s'~** *vi*: **s'~ à faire** to force o.s. to do

astrologie [astRɔlɔʒi] *nf* astrology

astronaute [astRonot] *nm/f* astronaut

astronomie [astRɔnɔmi] *nf* astronomy

astuce [astys] *nf* shrewdness, astuteness; (*truc*) trick, clever way; **astucieux, -euse** *adj* clever

atelier [atalje] *nm* workshop; (*de peintre*) studio

athée [ate] *adj* atheistic ♦ *nm/f* atheist

Athènes [atɛn] *n* Athens

athlète [atlɛt] *nm/f* (*SPORT*) athlete; **athlétisme** *nm* athletics *sg*

atlantique [atlɑ̃tik] *adj* Atlantic ♦ *nm*: **l'(océan) A~** the Atlantic (Ocean)

atlas [atlɑs] *nm* atlas

atmosphère [atmɔsfɛR] *nf* atmosphere

atome [atom] *nm* atom; **atomique** *adj* atomic, nuclear

atomiseur [atɔmizœR] *nm* atomizer

atout [atu] *nm* trump; (*fig*) asset

âtre [ɑtR] *nm* hearth

atroce [atRɔs] *adj* atrocious

attabler [atable]: **s'~** *vi* to sit down at (the) table

attachant, e [ataʃɑ̃, ɑ̃t] *adj* engaging, lovable, likeable

attache [ataʃ] *nf* clip, fastener; (*fig*) tie

attacher [ataʃe] *vt* to tie up; (*étiquette*) to attach, tie on; (*ceinture*) to fasten ♦ *vi* (*poêle, riz*) to stick; **s'~ à** (*par affection*) to become attached to; **s'~ à faire** to endeavour to do; **~ qch à** to tie *ou* attach sth to

attaque [atak] *nf* attack; (*cérébrale*) stroke; (*d'épilepsie*) fit; **~ à main armée** armed attack

attaquer [atake] *vt* to attack; (*en justice*) to bring an action against, sue ♦ *vi* to attack; **s'~ à** ♦ *vt* (*personne*) to attack; (*problème*) to tackle

attardé, e [ataʀde] *adj* (*enfant*) backward; (*passants*) late

attarder [ataʀde]: **s'~** *vi* to linger

atteindre [atɛ̃dʀ] *vt* to reach; (*blesser*) to hit; (*émouvoir*) to affect; **atteint, e** *adj* (*MÉD*): **être atteint de** to be suffering from; **atteinte** *nf*: **hors d'atteinte** out of reach; **porter atteinte à** to strike a blow at

atteler [at(ə)le] *vt* (*cheval, bœufs*) to hitch up; **s'~ à** (*travail*) to buckle down to

attelle [atɛl] *nf* splint

attenant, e [at(ə)nɑ̃, ɑ̃t] *adj*: **~ (à)** adjoining

attendant [atɑ̃dɑ̃] *adv*: **en ~** meanwhile, in the meantime

attendre [atɑ̃dʀ] *vt* (*gén*) to wait for; (*être destiné ou réservé à*) to await, be in store for ♦ *vi* to wait; **s'~ à (ce que)** to expect (that); **~ un enfant** to be expecting a baby; **~ de faire/d'être** to wait until one does/is; **attendez qu'il vienne** wait until he comes; **~ qch de** to expect sth of

attendrir [atɑ̃dʀiʀ] *vt* to move (to pity); (*viande*) to tenderize; **attendrissant, e** *adj* moving, touching

attendu, e [atɑ̃dy] *adj* (*visiteur*) expected; (*événement*) long-awaited; **~ que** considering that, since

attentat [atɑ̃ta] *nm* assassination attempt; **~ à la bombe** bomb attack; **~ à la pudeur** indecent assault *no pl*

attente [atɑ̃t] *nf* wait; (*espérance*) expecta-

tion

attenter [atɑ̃te]: **~ à** *vt* (*liberté*) to violate; **~ à la vie de qn** to make an attempt on sb's life

attentif, -ive [atɑ̃tif, iv] *adj* (*auditeur*) attentive; (*examen*) careful; **~ à** careful to

attention [atɑ̃sjɔ̃] *nf* attention; (*prévenance*) attention, thoughtfulness *no pl*; **à l'~ de** for the attention of; **faire ~ (à)** to be careful (of); **faire ~ (à ce) que** to be *ou* make sure that; **~!** careful!, watch out!; **attentionné, e** *adj* thoughtful, considerate

atténuer [atenɥe] *vt* (*douleur*) to alleviate, ease; (*couleurs*) to soften

atterrer [ateʀe] *vt* to dismay, appal

atterrir [ateʀiʀ] *vi* to land; **atterrissage** *nm* landing

attestation [atɛstasjɔ̃] *nf* certificate

attester [atɛste] *vt* to testify to

attirail [atiʀaj] (*fam*) *nm* gear; (*péj*) paraphernalia

attirant, e [atiʀɑ̃, ɑ̃t] *adj* attractive, appealing

attirer [atiʀe] *vt* to attract; (*appâter*) to lure, entice; **~ qn dans un coin** to draw sb into a corner; **~ l'attention de qn** to attract sb's attention; **~ l'attention de qn sur** to draw sb's attention to; **s'~ des ennuis** to bring trouble upon o.s., get into trouble

attiser [atize] *vt* (*feu*) to poke (up)

attitré, e [atitʀe] *adj* (*habituel*) regular, usual; (*agréé*) accredited

attitude [atityd] *nf* attitude; (*position du corps*) bearing

attouchements [atuʃmɑ̃] *nmpl* (*sexuels*) fondling *sg*

attraction [atʀaksjɔ̃] *nf* (*gén*) attraction; (*de cabaret, cirque*) number

attrait [atʀɛ] *nm* appeal, attraction

attrape-nigaud [atʀapnigo] (*fam*) *nm* con

attraper [atʀape] *vt* (*gén*) to catch; (*habitude, amende*) to get, pick up; (*fam: duper*) to con; **se faire ~** (*fam*) to be told off

attrayant, e [atʀɛjɑ̃, ɑ̃t] *adj* attractive

attribuer [atʀibɥe] *vt* (*prix*) to award; (*rôle, tâche*) to allocate, assign; (*imputer*): **~ qch à** to attribute sth to; **s'~** *vt* (*s'approprier*) to claim for o.s.; **attribut** *nm* attribute

attrister [atʀiste] *vt* to sadden

attroupement [atʀupmɑ̃] *nm* crowd

attrouper [atʀupe]: **s'~** *vi* to gather

au [o] *prép* +*dét* = **à +le**

aubaine [oben] *nf* godsend

aube [ob] *nf* dawn, daybreak; **à l'~** at dawn *ou* daybreak

aubépine [obepin] *nf* hawthorn

auberge [obeʀʒ] *nf* inn; **~ de jeunesse** youth hostel

aubergine [obeʀʒin] *nf* aubergine

aubergiste [obeʀʒist] *nm/f* inn-keeper, hotel-keeper

aucun, e [okœ̃, yn] *dét* no, *tournure négative* +any; (*positif*) any ♦ *pron* none, *tournure négative* +any; any(one); **sans ~ doute** without any doubt; **plus qu'~ autre** more than any other; **~ des deux** neither of the two; **~ d'entre eux** none of them; **aucunement** *adv* in no way, not in the least

audace [odas] *nf* daring, boldness; (*péj*) audacity; **audacieux, -euse** *adj* daring, bold

au-delà [od(ə)la] *adv* beyond ♦ *nm*: **l'~-~** the hereafter; **~-~ de** beyond

au-dessous [odsu] *adv* underneath; below; **~-~ de** under(neath), below; (*limite, somme etc*) below, under; (*dignité, condition*) below

au-dessus [odsy] *adv* above; **~-~ de** above

au-devant [od(ə)vɑ̃]: **~-~ de** *prép*: **aller ~-~ de** (*personne, danger*) to go (out) and meet; (*souhaits de qn*) to anticipate

audience [odjɑ̃s] *nf* audience; (*JUR*: *séance*) hearing

audimat ® [odimat] *nm* (*taux d'écoute*) ratings *pl*

audio-visuel, le [odjovizɥɛl] *adj* audio-visual

auditeur, -trice [oditœʀ, tʀis] *nm/f* lis-tener

audition [odisjɔ̃] *nf* (*ouïe, écoute*) hearing; (*JUR*: *de témoins*) examination; (*MUS, THÉÂTRE*: *épreuve*) audition

auditoire [oditwaʀ] *nm* audience

auge [oʒ] *nf* trough

augmentation [ɔgmɑ̃tasjɔ̃] *nf* increase; **~ (de salaire)** rise (in salary) (*BRIT*), (pay) raise (*US*)

augmenter [ɔgmɑ̃te] *vt* (*gén*) to increase; (*salaire, prix*) to increase, raise, put up; (*employé*) to increase the salary of ♦ *vi* to increase

augure [ogyʀ] *nm*: **de bon/mauvais ~** of good/ill omen; **augurer** *vt*: **augurer bien de** to augur well for

aujourd'hui [oʒuʀdɥi] *adv* today

aumône [omon] *nf inv* alms *sg*; **aumô-nier** *nm* chaplain

auparavant [oparavɑ̃] *adv* before(hand)

auprès [opʀɛ]: **~ de** *prép* next to, close to; (*recourir, s'adresser*) to; (*en comparaison de*) compared with

auquel [okɛl] *prép* +*pron* = **à +lequel**

aurai *etc* [ɔʀe] *vb voir* **avoir**

auréole [ɔʀeɔl] *nf* halo; (*tache*) ring

aurons *etc* [ɔʀɔ̃] *vb voir* **avoir**

aurore [ɔʀɔʀ] *nf* dawn, daybreak

ausculter [ɔskylte] *vt* to sound (the chest of)

aussi [osi] *adv* (*également*) also, too; (*de comparaison*) as ♦ *conj* therefore, conse-quently; **~ fort que** as strong as; **moi ~** me too

aussitôt [osito] *adv* straight away, im-mediately; **~ que** as soon as

austère [ostɛʀ] *adj* austere

austral, e [ɔstʀal] *adj* southern

Australie [ɔstʀali] *nf*: **l'~** Australia; aus-**tralien, ne** *adj* Australian ♦ *nm/f*: **Aus-tralien, ne** Australian

autant [otɑ̃] *adv* so much; (*comparatif*): **~ (que)** as much (as); (*nombre*) as many (as); **~ (de)** so much (*ou* many); as much (*ou* many); **~ partir** we (*ou* you *etc*) may as well leave; **~ dire que ...** one might as well say that ...; **pour ~** for all that; **d'~ plus/mieux (que)** all the more/the better (since)

autel [otɛl] *nm* altar

auteur [otœʀ] *nm* author

authenticité [otãtisite] *nf* authenticity

authentique [otãtik] *adj* authentic, genuine

auto [oto] *nf* car

auto...: **autobiographie** *nf* autobiography; **autobronzant** *nm* self-tanning cream (*or* lotion *etc*); **autobus** *nm* bus; **autocar** *nm* coach

autochtone [ɔtɔktɔn] *nm/f* native

auto...: **autocollant, e** *adj* self-adhesive; (*enveloppe*) self-seal ♦ *nm* sticker; **auto-couchettes** *adj*: **train auto-couchettes** car sleeper train; **autocuiseur** *nm* pressure cooker; **autodéfense** *nf* self-defence; **autodidacte** *nm/f* self-taught person; **auto-école** *nf* driving school; **autographe** *nm* autograph

automate [ɔtɔmat] *nm* (*machine*) (automatic) machine

automatique [ɔtɔmatik] *adj* automatic ♦ *nm*: **l'~** direct dialling; **automatiquement** *adv* automatically; **automatiser** *vt* to automate

automne [ɔtɔn] *nm* autumn (*BRIT*), fall (*US*)

automobile [ɔtɔmɔbil] *adj* motor *cpd* ♦ *nf* (motor) car; **automobiliste** *nm/f* motorist

autonome [ɔtɔnɔm] *adj* autonomous; **autonomie** *nf* autonomy; (*POL*) self-government, autonomy

autopsie [ɔtɔpsi] *nf* post-mortem (examination), autopsy

autoradio [otoʀadjo] *nm* car radio

autorisation [ɔtɔʀizasjɔ̃] *nf* permission, authorization; (*papiers*) permit

autorisé, e [ɔtɔʀize] *adj* (*opinion, sources*) authoritative

autoriser [ɔtɔʀize] *vt* to give permission for, authorize; (*fig*) to allow (of)

autoritaire [ɔtɔʀitɛʀ] *adj* authoritarian

autorité [ɔtɔʀite] *nf* authority; **faire ~** to be authoritative

autoroute [otoʀut] *nf* motorway (*BRIT*), highway (*US*); **~ de l'information** (*INFORM*) information superhighway

auto-stop [otostɔp] *nm*: **faire de l'~-~** to hitch-hike; **prendre qn en ~-~** to give sb a lift; **auto-stoppeur, -euse** *nm/f* hitch-hiker

autour [otuʀ] *adv* around; **~ de** around; **tout ~** all around

---
MOT-CLÉ
---

autre [otʀ] *adj* **1** (*différent*) other, different; **je préférerais un autre verre** I'd prefer another *ou* a different glass

2 (*supplémentaire*) other; **je voudrais un autre verre d'eau** I'd like another glass of water

3: **autre chose** something else; **autre part** somewhere else; **d'autre part** on the other hand

♦ *pron*: **un autre** another (one); **nous/vous autres** us/you; **d'autres** others; **l'autre** the other (one); **les autres** the others; (*autrui*) others; **l'un et l'autre** both of them; **se détester l'un l'autre/les uns les autres** to hate each other *ou* one another; **d'une semaine à l'autre** from one week to the next; (*incessamment*) any week now; **entre autres** among other things

---

autrefois [otʀəfwa] *adv* in the past

autrement [otʀəmã] *adv* differently; (*d'une manière différente*) in another way; (*sinon*) otherwise; **~ dit** in other words

Autriche [otʀiʃ] *nf*: **l'~** Austria; **autrichien, ne** *adj* Austrian ♦ *nm/f*: **Autrichien, ne** Austrian

autruche [otʀyʃ] *nf* ostrich

autrui [otʀɥi] *pron* others

auvent [ovã] *nm* canopy

aux [o] *prép* +*dét* = **à** +**les**

auxiliaire [ɔksiljɛʀ] *adj, nm/f* auxiliary

auxquelles [okɛl] *prép* +*pron* = **à** +**lesquelles**

auxquels [okɛl] *prép* +*pron* = **à** +**lesquels**

avachi, e [avaʃi] *adj* limp, flabby

aval [aval] *nm*: **en ~** downstream, down-river

avalanche [avalɑ̃ʃ] *nf* avalanche

avaler [avale] *vt* to swallow

avance [avɑ̃s] *nf* (*de troupes etc*) advance; progress; (*d'argent*) advance; (*sur un concurrent*) lead; **~s** *nfpl* (*amoureuses*) advances; **(être) en ~** (to be) early; (*sur un programme*) (to be) ahead of schedule; **à l'~, d'~** in advance

avancé, e [avɑ̃se] *adj* advanced; (*travail*) well on, well under way

avancement [avɑ̃smɑ̃] *nm* (*professionnel*) promotion

avancer [avɑ̃se] *vi* to move forward, advance; (*projet, travail*) to make progress; (*montre, réveil*) to be fast; to gain ♦ *vt* to move forward, advance; (*argent*) to advance; (*montre, pendule*) to put forward; **s'~** *vi* to move forward, advance; (*fig*) to commit o.s.

avant [avɑ̃] *prép, adv* before ♦ *adj inv*: **siège/roue ~** front seat/wheel ♦ *nm* (*d'un véhicule, bâtiment*) front; (*SPORT: joueur*) forward; **~ qu'il (ne) fasse/de faire** before he does/doing; **~ tout** (*surtout*) above all; **à l'~** (*dans un véhicule*) in (the) front; **en ~** forward(s); **en ~ de** in front of

avantage [avɑ̃taʒ] *nm* advantage; **~s sociaux** fringe benefits; **avantager** *vt* (*favoriser*) to favour; (*embellir*) to flatter; **avantageux, -euse** *adj* (*prix*) attractive

avant...: **avant-bras** *nm inv* forearm; **avantcoureur** *adj inv*: **signe avantcoureur** advance indication *ou* sign; **avant-dernier, -ière** *adj, nm/f* next to last, last but one; **avant-goût** *nm* foretaste; **avant-guerre** *nm* pre-war years; **avant-hier** *adv* the day before yesterday; **avant-première** *nf* (*de film*) preview; **avant-projet** *nm* (*preliminary*) draft; **avant-propos** *nm* foreword; **avant-veille** *nf*: **l'avant-veille** two days before

avare [avar] *adj* miserly, avaricious ♦ *nm/f* miser; **~ de** (*compliments etc*) sparing of

avarié, e [avarje] *adj* (*aliment*) rotting

avaries, e [avari] *nfpl* (*NAVIG*) damage *sg*

avec [avɛk] *prép* with; (*à l'égard de*) to(wards), with; **et ~ ça?** (*dans magasin*) anything else?

avenant, e [av(ə)nɑ̃, ɑ̃t] *adj* pleasant; **à l'~** in keeping

avènement [avɛnmɑ̃] *nm* (*d'un changement*) advent, coming

avenir [avnir] *nm* future; **à l'~** in future; **politicien d'~** politician with prospects *ou* a future

aventure [avɑ̃tyr] *nf* adventure; (*amoureuse*) affair; **aventurer: s'aventurer** *vi* to venture; **aventureux, -euse** *adj* adventurous, venturesome; (*projet*) risky, chancy

avenue [avny] *nf* avenue

avérer [avere]: **s'~** *vb* +*attrib* to prove (to be)

averse [avɛrs] *nf* shower

averti, e [avɛrti] *adj* (well-)informed

avertir [avɛrtir] *vt*: **~ qn (de qch/que)** to warn sb (of sth/that); (*renseigner*) to inform sb (of sth/that); **avertissement** *nm* warning; **avertisseur** *nm* horn, siren

aveu, x [avø] *nm* confession

aveugle [avœgl] *adj* blind ♦ *nm/f* blind man/woman; **aveuglément** *adv* blindly; **aveugler** *vt* to blind

aviateur, -trice [avjatœr, tris] *nm/f* aviator, pilot

aviation [avjasjɔ̃] *nf* aviation; (*sport*) flying; (*MIL*) air force

avide [avid] *adj* eager; (*péj*) greedy, grasping

avilir [avilir] *vt* to debase

avion [avjɔ̃] *nm* (aero)plane (*BRIT*), (air)plane (*US*); **aller (quelque part) en ~** to go (somewhere) by plane, fly (somewhere); **par ~** by airmail; **~ à réaction** jet (plane)

aviron [avirɔ̃] *nm* oar; (*sport*): **l'~** rowing

avis [avi] *nm* opinion; (*notification*) notice; **à mon ~** in my opinion; **changer d'~** to change one's mind; **jusqu'à nouvel ~** until further notice

avisé, e [avize] *adj* sensible, wise; **bien/mal ~ de** well-/ill-advised to

aviser [avize] *vt* (*informer*): **~ qn de/que** to advise *ou* inform sb of/that ♦ *vi* to think about things, assess the situation; **nous ~ons sur place** we'll work something out once we're there; **s'~ de qch/que** to become suddenly aware of sth/that; **s'~ de faire** to take it into one's head to do

avocat, e [avɔka, at] *nm/f* (*JUR*) barrister (*BRIT*), lawyer ♦ *nm* (*CULIN*) avocado (pear); **~ de la défense** counsel for the defence; **~ général** assistant public prosecutor

avoine [avwan] *nf* oats *pl*

| MOT-CLÉ |

avoir [avwaʀ] *nm* assets *pl*, resources *pl*; (*COMM*) credit

♦ *vt* **1** (*posséder*) to have; **elle a 2 enfants/une belle maison** she has (got) 2 children/a lovely house; **il a les yeux bleus** he has (got) blue eyes

2 (*âge, dimensions*) to be; **il a 3 ans** he is 3 (years old); **le mur a 3 mètres de haut** the wall is 3 metres high; *voir aussi* **faim**; **peur** *etc*

3 (*fam: duper*) to do, have; **on vous a eu!** you've been done *ou* had!

4: **en avoir contre qn** to have a grudge against sb; **en avoir assez** to be fed up; **j'en ai pour une demi-heure** it'll take me half an hour

♦ *vb aux* **1** to have; **avoir mangé/dormi** to have eaten/slept

2 (*avoir +à +infinitif*): **avoir à faire qch** to have to do sth; **vous n'avez qu'à lui demander** you only have to ask him

♦ *vb impers* **1**: **il y a** (+ *singulier*) there is; (+ *pluriel*) there are; **qu'y-a-t-il?, qu'est-ce qu'il y a?** what's the matter?, what is it?; **il doit y avoir une explication** there must be an explanation; **il n'y a qu'à ...**

we (*ou* you *etc*) will just have to ...

2 (*temporel*): **il y a 10 ans** 10 years ago; **il y a 10 ans/longtemps que je le sais** I've known it for 10 years/a long time; **il y a 10 ans qu'il est arrivé** it's 10 years since he arrived

---

avoisiner [avwazine] *vt* to be near *ou* close to; (*fig*) to border *ou* verge on

avortement [avɔʀtəmɑ̃] *nm* abortion

avorter [avɔʀte] *vi* (*MÉD*) to have an abortion; (*fig*) to fail

avoué, e [avwe] *adj* avowed ♦ *nm* (*JUR*) ≃ solicitor

avouer [avwe] *vt* (*crime, défaut*) to confess (to); **~ avoir fait/que** to admit *ou* confess to having done/that

avril [avʀil] *nm* April

| poisson d'avril |

i The traditional prank on April 1 in France is to stick a cut-out paper fish, known as a *poisson d'avril*, to someone's back without being caught.

---

axe [aks] *nm* axis; (*de roue etc*) axle; (*fig*) main line; **axer** *vt*: **axer qch sur** to centre sth on

ayons *etc* [εjɔ̃] *vb voir* **avoir**

azote [azɔt] *nm* nitrogen

B, b

baba [baba] *nm*: **~ au rhum** rum baba

babines [babin] *nfpl* chops

babiole [babjɔl] *nf* (*bibelot*) trinket; (*vétille*) trifle

bâbord [babɔʀ] *nm*: **à ~** to port, on the port side

baby-foot [babifut] *nm* table football

baby-sitting [babisitiŋ] *nm*: **faire du ~-~** to baby-sit

bac [bak] *abr m* = **baccalauréat** ♦ *nm* (*récipient*) tub

baccalauréat [bakalɔʀea] *nm* high school

diploma

---
baccalauréat
---

i *In France the* **baccalauréat** *or* **bac** *is the school-leaving certificate taken at a lycée at the age of seventeen or eighteen, enabling entry to university. Different subject combinations are available from the broad subject range studied.*

bâche [baʃ] *nf* tarpaulin

bachelier, -ière [baʃəlje, jɛʁ] *nm/f* holder of the baccalauréat

bâcler [bakle] *vt* to botch (up)

badaud, e [bado, od] *nm/f* idle onlooker, stroller

badigeonner [badiʒɔne] *vt* (*barbouiller*) to daub

badiner [badine] *vi*: ~ **avec qch** to treat sth lightly

baffe [baf] (*fam*) *nf* slap, clout

baffle [bafl] *nm* speaker

bafouer [bafwe] *vt* to deride, ridicule

bafouiller [bafuje] *vi, vt* to stammer

bâfrer [bafʁe] (*fam*) *vi* to guzzle

bagages [bagaʒ] *nmpl* luggage *sg*; ~ **à main** hand-luggage

bagarre [bagaʁ] *nf* fight, brawl; **bagarrer: se bagarrer** *vi* to have a fight *ou* scuffle, fight

bagatelle [bagatɛl] *nf* trifle

bagne [baɲ] *nm* penal colony

bagnole [baɲɔl] (*fam*) *nf* car

bagout [bagu] *nm*: **avoir du** ~ to have the gift of the gab

bague [bag] *nf* ring; ~ **de fiançailles** engagement ring

baguette [bagɛt] *nf* stick; (*cuisine chinoise*) chopstick; (*de chef d'orchestre*) baton; (*pain*) stick of (French) bread; ~ **magique** magic wand

baie [bɛ] *nf* (*GÉO*) bay; (*fruit*) berry; ~ (**vitrée**) picture window

baignade [bɛɲad] *nf* bathing; "~ **interdite**" "no bathing"

baigner [bɛɲe] *vt* (*bébé*) to bath; **se** ~ *vi* to have a swim, go swimming *ou* bathing

baignoire [bɛɲwaʁ] *nf* bath(tub)

bail [baj, bo] (*pl* **baux**) *nm* lease

bâillement [bajmɑ̃] *nm* yawn

bâiller [baje] *vi* to yawn; (*être ouvert*) to gape

bâillonner [bajɔne] *vt* to gag

bain [bɛ̃] *nm* bath; **prendre un** ~ to have a bath; **se mettre dans le** ~ (*fig*) to get into it *ou* things; ~ **de soleil: prendre un** ~ **de soleil** to sunbathe; ~**s de mer** sea bathing *sg*; **bain-marie** *nm*: **faire chauffer au bain-marie** (*boîte etc*) to immerse in boiling water

baiser [beze] *nm* kiss ♦ *vt* (*main, front*) to kiss; (*fam!*) to screw (!)

baisse [bɛs] *nf* fall, drop; **être en** ~ to be falling, be declining

baisser [bese] *vt* to lower; (*radio, chauffage*) to turn down ♦ *vi* to fall, drop, go down; (*vue, santé*) to fail, dwindle; **se** ~ *vi* to bend down

bal [bal] *nm* dance; (*grande soirée*) ball; ~ **costumé** fancy-dress ball

balade [balad] (*fam*) *nf* (*à pied*) walk, stroll; (*en voiture*) drive; **balader** (*fam*): **se balader** *vi* to go for a walk *ou* stroll; to go for a drive; **baladeur** *nm* personal stereo, Walkman ®

balafre [balafʁ] *nf* (*cicatrice*) scar

balai [balɛ] *nm* broom, brush; **balai-brosse** *nm* (long-handled) scrubbing brush

balance [balɑ̃s] *nf* scales *pl*; (*signe*): **la B**~ Libra

balancer [balɑ̃se] *vt* to swing; (*fam: lancer*) to fling, chuck; (: *jeter*) to chuck out; **se** ~ *vi* to swing, rock; **se** ~ **de** (*fam*) not to care about

balançoire [balɑ̃swaʁ] *nf* swing; (*sur pivot*) seesaw

balayer [baleje] *vt* (*feuilles etc*) to sweep up, brush up; (*pièce*) to sweep; (*objections*) to sweep aside; (*suj: radar*) to scan; **balayeur, -euse** *nm/f* roadsweeper

balbutier [balbysje] *vi, vt* to stammer

balcon [balkɔ̃] *nm* balcony; (*THÉÂTRE*) dress circle

baleine [balɛn] *nf* whale

balise [baliz] *nf* (*NAVIG*) beacon; (marker) buoy; (*AVIAT*) runway light, beacon; (*AUTO, SKI*) sign, marker; **baliser** *vt* to mark out (with lights *etc*)

balivernes [balivɛRn] *nfpl* nonsense *sg*

ballant, e [balɑ̃, ɑ̃t] *adj* dangling

balle [bal] *nf* (*de fusil*) bullet; (*de sport*) ball; (*fam: franc*) franc

ballerine [bal(ə)Rin] *nf* (*danseuse*) ballet dancer; (*chaussure*) ballet shoe

ballet [balɛ] *nm* ballet

ballon [balɔ̃] *nm* (*de sport*) ball; (*jouet, AVIAT*) balloon; **~ de football** football

ballot [balo] *nm* bundle; (*péj*) nitwit

ballottage [balɔtaʒ] *nm* (*POL*) second ballot

ballotter [balɔte] *vt*: **être ballotté** to be thrown about

balnéaire [balneɛR] *adj* seaside *cpd*; **station ~** seaside resort

balourd, e [baluR, uRd] *adj* clumsy

balustrade [balystRad] *nf* railings *pl*, handrail

bambin [bɑ̃bɛ̃] *nm* little child

bambou [bɑ̃bu] *nm* bamboo

ban [bɑ̃] *nm*: **mettre au ~ de** to outlaw from; **~s** *nmpl* (*de mariage*) banns

banal, e [banal] *adj* banal, commonplace; (*péj*) trite; **banalité** *nf* banality

banane [banan] *nf* banana; (*sac*) waist-bag, bum-bag

banc [bɑ̃] *nm* seat, bench; (*de poissons*) shoal; **~ d'essai** (*fig*) testing ground

bancaire [bɑ̃kɛR] *adj* banking; (*chèque, carte*) bank *cpd*

bancal, e [bɑ̃kal] *adj* wobbly

bandage [bɑ̃daʒ] *nm* bandage

bande [bɑ̃d] *nf* (*de tissu etc*) strip; (*MÉD*) bandage; (*motif*) stripe; (*magnétique etc*) tape; (*groupe*) band; (: *péj*) bunch; **faire ~ à part** to keep to o.s.; **~ dessinée** comic strip; **~ sonore** sound track

---

bande dessinée

i The **bande dessinée** or **BD** enjoys a huge following in France amongst adults as well as children. An international show takes place at Angoulême in January every year. Astérix, Tintin, Lucky Luke and Gaston Lagaffe are among the most famous cartoon characters.

---

bandeau, x [bɑ̃do] *nm* headband; (*sur les yeux*) blindfold

bander [bɑ̃de] *vt* (*blessure*) to bandage; **~ les yeux à qn** to blindfold sb

banderole [bɑ̃dRɔl] *nf* banner, streamer

bandit [bɑ̃di] *nm* bandit; **banditisme** *nm* violent crime, armed robberies *pl*

bandoulière [bɑ̃duljɛR] *nf*: **en ~** (slung *ou* worn) across the shoulder

banlieue [bɑ̃ljø] *nf* suburbs *pl*; **lignes/quartiers de ~** suburban lines/areas; **trains de ~** commuter trains

banlieusard, e [bɑ̃ljøzaR] *nm/f* (suburban) commuter

bannière [banjɛR] *nf* banner

bannir [baniR] *vt* to banish

banque [bɑ̃k] *nf* bank; (*activités*) banking; **~ d'affaires** merchant bank; **banqueroute** *nf* bankruptcy

banquet [bɑ̃kɛ] *nm* dinner; (*d'apparat*) banquet

banquette [bɑ̃kɛt] *nf* seat

banquier [bɑ̃kje] *nm* banker

banquise [bɑ̃kiz] *nf* ice field

baptême [batɛm] *nm* christening; baptism; **~ de l'air** first flight

baptiser [batize] *vt* to baptize, christen

baquet [bakɛ] *nm* tub, bucket

bar [baR] *nm* bar

baraque [baRak] *nf* shed; (*fam*) house; **baraqué, e** (*fam*) *adj* well-built, hefty; **baraquements** *nmpl* (*provisoires*) huts

baratin [baRatɛ̃] (*fam*) *nm* smooth talk, patter; **baratiner** *vt* to chat up

barbare [baRbaR] *adj* barbaric; **barbarie** *nf* barbarity

barbe [baʀb] *nf* beard; **la ~!** (*fam*) damn it!; **quelle ~!** (*fam*) what a drag *ou* bore!; **à la ~ de qn** under sb's nose; **~ à papa** candy-floss (*BRIT*), cotton candy (*US*)

barbelé [baʀbəle] *adj, nm*: **(fil de fer) ~** barbed wire *no pl*

barber [baʀbe] (*fam*) *vt* to bore stiff

barbiturique [baʀbityʀik] *nm* barbiturate

barboter [baʀbɔte] *vi* (*enfant*) to paddle

barbouiller [baʀbuje] *vt* to daub; **avoir l'estomac barbouillé** to feel queasy

barbu, e [baʀby] *adj* bearded

barda [baʀda] (*fam*) *nm* kit, gear

barder [baʀde] (*fam*) *vi*: **ça va ~** sparks will fly, things are going to get hot

barème [baʀɛm] *nm* (*SCOL*) scale; (*table de référence*) table

baril [baʀi(l)] *nm* barrel; (*poudre*) keg

bariolé, e [baʀjɔle] *adj* gaudily-coloured

baromètre [baʀɔmɛtʀ] *nm* barometer

baron, ne [baʀɔ̃] *nm/f* baron(ess)

baroque [baʀɔk] *adj* (*ART*) baroque; (*fig*) weird

barque [baʀk] *nf* small boat

barquette [baʀkɛt] *nf* (*pour repas*) tray; (*pour fruits*) punnet

barrage [baʀaʒ] *nm* dam; (*sur route*) road-block, barricade

barre [baʀ] *nf* bar; (*NAVIG*) helm; (*écrite*) line, stroke

barreau, x [baʀo] *nm* bar; (*JUR*): **le ~** the Bar

barrer [baʀe] *vt* (*route etc*) to block; (*mot*) to cross out; (*chèque*) to cross (*BRIT*); (*NAVIG*) to steer; **se ~** (*fam*) *vi* to clear off

barrette [baʀɛt] *nf* (*pour cheveux*) (hair) slide (*BRIT*) *ou* clip (*US*)

barricader [baʀikade] *vt*: **se ~** *vi* to barricade o.s.

barrière [baʀjɛʀ] *nf* fence; (*obstacle*) barrier; (*porte*) gate

barrique [baʀik] *nf* barrel, cask

bar-tabac [baʀtaba] *nm* bar (*which sells tobacco and stamps*)

bas, basse [ba, bas] *adj* low ♦ *nm* bottom, lower part; (*vêtement*) stocking ♦ *adv* low; (*parler*) softly; **au ~ mot** at the lowest estimate; **en ~** down below; (*d'une liste, d'un mur etc*) at/to the bottom; (*dans une maison*) downstairs; **en ~ de** at the bottom of; **un enfant en ~ âge** a young child; **à ~ ...!** down with ...!; **~ morceaux** *nmpl* (*viande*) cheap cuts

basané, e [bazane] *adj* tanned

bas-côté [bakote] *nm* (*de route*) verge (*BRIT*), shoulder (*US*)

bascule [baskyl] *nf*: **(jeu de) ~** seesaw; **(balance à) ~** scales *pl*; **fauteuil à ~** rocking chair

basculer [baskyle] *vi* to fall over, topple (over); (*benne*) to tip up ♦ *vt* (*contenu*) to tip out; (*benne*) to tip up

base [baz] *nf* base; (*POL*) rank and file; (*fondement, principe*) basis; **de ~** basic; **à ~ de café** *etc* coffee *etc* -based; **~ de données** database; **baser** *vt* to base; **se baser sur** *vt* (*preuves*) to base one's argument on

bas-fond [baf5] *nm* (*NAVIG*) shallow; **~-~s** *nmpl* (*fig*) dregs

basilic [bazilik] *nm* (*CULIN*) basil

basket [baskɛt] *nm* trainer (*BRIT*), sneaker (*US*); (*aussi*: **~-ball**) basketball

basque [bask] *adj, nm/f* Basque

basse [bas] *adj voir* **bas** ♦ *nf* (*MUS*) bass; **basse-cour** *nf* farmyard

bassin [basɛ̃] *nm* (*pièce d'eau*) pond, pool; (*de fontaine, GÉO*) basin; (*ANAT*) pelvis; (*portuaire*) dock

bassine [basin] *nf* (*ustensile*) basin; (*contenu*) bowl(ful)

basson [bas5] *nm* bassoon

bas-ventre [bavɑ̃tʀ] *nm* (lower part of the) stomach

bat [ba] *vb voir* **battre**

bataille [bataj] *nf* (*MIL*) battle; (*rixe*) fight; **batailler** *vi* to fight

bâtard, e [bataʀ, aʀd] *nm/f* illegitimate child, bastard (*péj*)

bateau, x [bato] *nm* boat, ship; **bateau-mouche** *nm* passenger pleasure boat (*on the Seine*)

bâti, e [bɑti] *adj*: **bien ~** well-built
batifoler [batifɔle] *vi* to frolic about
bâtiment [bɑtimɑ̃] *nm* building; (*NAVIG*) ship, vessel; (*industrie*) building trade
bâtir [bɑtiʀ] *vt* to build
bâtisse [bɑtis] *nf* building
bâton [bɑtɔ̃] *nm* stick; **à ~s rompus** informally
bats [ba] *vb voir* **battre**
battage [bataʒ] *nm* (*publicité*) (hard) plugging
battant [batɑ̃, ɑ̃t] *nm*: **porte à double ~** double door
battement [batmɑ̃] *nm* (*de cœur*) beat; (*intervalle*) interval (*between classes, trains*); **10 minutes de ~** 10 minutes to spare
batterie [batʀi] *nf* (*MIL, ÉLEC*) battery; (*MUS*) drums *pl*, drum kit; **~ de cuisine** pots and pans *pl*, kitchen utensils *pl*
batteur [batœʀ] *nm* (*MUS*) drummer; (*appareil*) whisk
battre [batʀ] *vt* to beat; (*blé*) to thresh; (*passer au peigne fin*) to scour; (*cartes*) to shuffle ♦ *vi* (*cœur*) to beat; (*volets etc*) to bang, rattle; **se ~** *vi* to fight; **~ la mesure** to beat time; **~ son plein** to be at its height, be going full swing; **~ des mains** to clap one's hands
battue [baty] *nf* (*chasse*) beat; (*policière etc*) search, hunt
baume [bom] *nm* balm
baux [bo] *nmpl de* **bail**
bavard, e [bavaʀ, aʀd] *adj* (very) talkative; gossipy; **bavarder** *vi* to chatter; (*commérer*) to gossip; (*divulguer un secret*) to blab
bave [bav] *nf* dribble; (*de chien etc*) slobber; (*d'escargot*) slime; **baver** *vi* to dribble; (*chien*) to slobber; **en baver** (*fam*) to have a hard time (of it); **baveux, -euse** *adj* (*omelette*) runny; **bavoir** *nm* bib
bavure [bavyʀ] *nf* smudge; (*fig*) hitch; (*policière etc*) blunder
bayer [baje] *vi*: **~ aux corneilles** to stand gaping
bazar [bazaʀ] *nm* general store; (*fam*) jumble; **bazarder** (*fam*) *vt* to chuck out

BCBG *sigle adj* (= *bon chic bon genre*) preppy, smart and trendy
BCE *sigle f* (= *Banque centrale européenne*) ECB
BD *sigle f* = **bande dessinée**
bd *abr* = **boulevard**
béant, e [beɑ̃, ɑ̃t] *adj* gaping
béat, e [bea, at] *adj*: **~ d'admiration** struck dumb with admiration; **béatitude** *nf* bliss
beau (bel), belle [bo, bɛl] (*mpl* **beaux**) *adj* beautiful, lovely; (*homme*) handsome; (*femme*) beautiful ♦ *adv*: **il fait beau** the weather's fine; **un ~jour** one (fine) day; **de plus belle** more than ever, even more; **on a ~essayer** however hard we try; **bel et bien** well and truly

---

MOT-CLÉ

beaucoup [boku] *adv* **1** a lot; **il boit beaucoup** he drinks a lot; **il ne boit pas beaucoup** he doesn't drink much *ou* a lot
2 (*suivi de plus, trop etc*) much, a lot, far; **il est beaucoup plus grand** he is much *ou* a lot *ou* far taller
3: beaucoup de (*nombre*) many, a lot of; (*quantité*) a lot of; **beaucoup d'étudiants/de touristes** a lot of *ou* many students/tourists; **beaucoup de courage** a lot of courage; **il n'a pas beaucoup d'argent** he hasn't got much *ou* at lot of money
4: de beaucoup by far

---

beau...: beau-fils *nm* son-in-law; (*remariage*) stepson; **beau-frère** *nm* brother-in-law; **beau-père** *nm* father-in-law; (*remariage*) stepfather
beauté [bote] *nf* beauty; **de toute ~** beautiful; **finir qch en ~** to complete sth brilliantly
beaux-arts [bozaʀ] *nmpl* fine arts
beaux-parents [bopaʀɑ̃] *nmpl* wife's/husband's family, in-laws
bébé [bebe] *nm* baby
bec [bɛk] *nm* beak, bill; (*de théière*) spout; (*de casserole*) lip; (*fam*) mouth; **~ de gaz** (street) gaslamp; **~ verseur** pouring lip

bécane [bekan] (*fam*) *nf* bike

bec-de-lièvre [bɛkdəljɛvʀ] *nm* harelip

bêche [bɛʃ] *nf* spade; **bêcher** *vt* to dig

bécoter [bekɔte]: **se ~** *vi* to smooch

becqueter [bekte] (*fam*) *vt* to eat

bedaine [bədɛn] *nf* paunch

bedonnant, e [bədɔnɑ̃, ɑ̃t] *adj* potbellied

bée [be] *adj*: **bouche ~** gaping

beffroi [befʀwa] *nm* belfry

bégayer [begeje] *vt, vi* to stammer

bègue [bɛg] *nm/f*: **être ~** to have a stammer

beige [bɛʒ] *adj* beige

beignet [beɲɛ] *nm* fritter

bel [bɛl] *adj voir* **beau**

bêler [bele] *vi* to bleat

belette [bəlɛt] *nf* weasel

belge [bɛlʒ] *adj* Belgian ♦ *nm/f*: **B~** Belgian

Belgique [bɛlʒik] *nf*: **la ~** Belgium

bélier [belje] *nm* ram; (*signe*): **le B~** Aries

belle [bɛl] *adj voir* **beau** ♦ *nf* (*SPORT*) decider; **belle-fille** *nf* daughter-in-law; (*remariage*) stepdaughter; **belle-mère** *nf* mother-in-law; stepmother; **belle-sœur** *nf* sister-in-law

belliqueux, -euse [belikø, øz] *adj* aggressive, warlike

belvédère [belvedɛʀ] *nm* panoramic viewpoint (*or small building there*)

bémol [bemɔl] *nm* (*MUS*) flat

bénédiction [benediksjɔ̃] *nf* blessing

bénéfice [benefis] *nm* (*COMM*) profit; (*avantage*) benefit; **bénéficier**: **bénéficier de** *vt* to enjoy; (*situation*) to benefit by *ou* from; **bénéfique** *adj* beneficial

bénévole [benevɔl] *adj* voluntary, unpaid

bénin, -igne [benɛ̃, iɲ] *adj* minor, mild; (*tumeur*) benign

bénir [beniʀ] *vt* to bless; **bénit, e** *adj* consecrated; **eau bénite** holy water

benjamin, e [bɛ̃ʒamɛ̃, in] *nm/f* youngest child

benne [bɛn] *nf* skip; (*de téléphérique*) (cable) car; **~ basculante** tipper (*BRIT*), dump truck (*US*)

BEP *sigle m* (= *brevet d'études professionnelles*) *technical school certificate*

béquille [bekij] *nf* crutch; (*de bicyclette*) stand

berceau, x [bɛʀso] *nm* cradle, crib

bercer [bɛʀse] *vt* to rock, cradle; (*suj: musique etc*) to lull; **~ qn de** (*promesses etc*) to delude sb with; **berceuse** *nf* lullaby

béret (basque) [beʀɛ (bask(ə))] *nm* beret

berge [bɛʀʒ] *nf* bank

berger, -ère [bɛʀʒe, ɛʀ] *nm/f* shepherd(-ess); **~ allemand** alsatian (*BRIT*), German shepherd

berlingot [bɛʀlɛ̃go] *nm* (*bonbon*) boiled sweet, humbug (*BRIT*)

berlue [bɛʀly] *nf*: **j'ai la ~** I must be seeing things

berner [bɛʀne] *vt* to fool

besogne [bəzɔɲ] *nf* work *no pl*, job

besoin [bəzwɛ̃] *nm* need; **avoir ~ de qch/faire qch** to need sth/to do sth; **au ~** if need be; **le ~** (*pauvreté*) need, want; **être dans le ~** to be in need *ou* want; **faire ses ~s** to relieve o.s.

bestiaux [bestjo] *nmpl* cattle

bestiole [bestjɔl] *nf* (tiny) creature

bétail [betaj] *nm* livestock, cattle *pl*

bête [bɛt] *nf* animal; (*bestiole*) insect, creature ♦ *adj* stupid, silly; **il cherche la petite ~** he's being pernickety *ou* overfussy; **~ noire** pet hate

bêtement [bɛtmɑ̃] *adv* stupidly

bêtise [betiz] *nf* stupidity; (*action*) stupid thing (to say *ou* do)

béton [betɔ̃] *nm* concrete; **(en) ~** (*alibi, argument*) cast iron; **~ armé** reinforced concrete; **bétonnière** *nf* cement mixer

betterave [betʀav] *nf* beetroot (*BRIT*), beet (*US*); **~ sucrière** sugar beet

beugler [bøgle] *vi* to low; (*radio etc*) to blare ♦ *vt* (*chanson*) to bawl out

Beur [bœʀ] *nm/f* person of North African origin living in France

beurre [bœʀ] *nm* butter; **beurrer** *vt* to butter; **beurrier** *nm* butter dish

beuverie [bøvʀi] *nf* drinking session

bévue [bevy] *nf* blunder
Beyrouth [beʀut] *n* Beirut
bi... [bi] *préfixe* bi..., two-
biais [bjɛ] *nm* (*moyen*) device, expedient; (*aspect*) angle; **en ~, de ~** (*obliquement*) at an angle; **par le ~ de** by means of; **biaiser** *vi* (*fig*) to sidestep the issue
bibelot [biblo] *nm* trinket, curio
biberon [bibʀɔ̃] *nm* (feeding) bottle; **nourrir au ~** to bottle-feed
bible [bibl] *nf* bible
biblio... [bibli] *préfixe*: **bibliobus** *nm* mobile library van; **bibliographie** *nf* bibliography; **bibliothécaire** *nm/f* librarian; **bibliothèque** *nf* library; (*meuble*) bookcase
bic ® [bik] *nm* Biro ®
bicarbonate [bikaʀbɔnat] *nm*: **~ (de soude)** bicarbonate of soda
biceps [bisɛps] *nm* biceps
biche [biʃ] *nf* doe
bichonner [biʃɔne] *vt* to pamper
bicolore [bikɔlɔʀ] *adj* two-coloured
bicoque [bikɔk] (*péj*) *nf* shack
bicyclette [bisiklɛt] *nf* bicycle
bide [bid] (*fam*) *nm* (*ventre*) belly; (THÉÂTRE) flop
bidet [bidɛ] *nm* bidet
bidon [bidɔ̃] *nm* can ♦ *adj inv* (*fam*) phoney
bidonville [bidɔ̃vil] *nm* shanty town
bidule [bidyl] (*fam*) *nm* thingumajig

MOT-CLÉ
---

bien [bjɛ̃] *nm* 1 (*avantage, profit*): **faire du bien à qn** to do sb good; **dire du bien de** to speak well of; **c'est pour son bien** it's for his own good
2 (*possession, patrimoine*) possession, property; **son bien le plus précieux** his most treasured possession; **avoir du bien** to have property; **biens (de consommation** *etc*) (consumer *etc*) goods
3 (*moral*): **le bien** good; **distinguer le bien du mal** to tell good from evil
♦ *adv* 1 (*de façon satisfaisante*) well; **elle travaille/mange bien** she works/eats well; **croyant bien faire, je/il ...** thinking I/he was doing the right thing, I/he ...; **c'est bien fait!** it serves him (*ou* her *etc*) right!
2 (*valeur intensive*) quite; **bien jeune** quite young; **bien assez** quite enough; **bien mieux** (very) much better; **j'espère bien y aller** I do hope to go; **je veux bien le faire** (*concession*) I'm quite willing to do it; **il faut bien le faire** it has to be done
3: **bien du temps/des gens** quite a time/a number of people
♦ *adj inv* 1 (*en bonne forme, à l'aise*): **je me sens bien** I feel fine; **je ne me sens pas bien** I don't feel well; **on est bien dans ce fauteuil** this chair is very comfortable
2 (*joli, beau*) good-looking; **tu es bien dans cette robe** you look good in that dress
3 (*satisfaisant*) good; **elle est bien, cette maison/secrétaire** it's a good house/she's a good secretary
4 (*moralement*) right; (: *personne*) good, nice; (*respectable*) respectable; **ce n'est pas bien de ...** it's not right to ...; **elle est bien, cette femme** she's a nice woman, she's a good sort; **des gens biens** respectable people
5 (*en bons termes*): **être bien avec qn** to be on good terms with sb
♦ *préfixe*: **bien-aimé** *adj, nm/f* beloved; **bien-être** *nm* well-being; **bienfaisance** *nf* charity; **bienfaisant, e** *adj* (*chose*) beneficial; **bienfait** *nm* act of generosity, benefaction; (*de la science etc*) benefit; **bienfaiteur, -trice** *nm/f* benefactor/benefactress; **bien-fondé** *nm* soundness; **bien-fonds** *nm* property; **bienheureux, -euse** *adj* happy; (REL) blessed, blest; **bien que** *conj* (al)though; **bien sûr** *adv* certainly

bienséant, e [bjɛ̃seɑ̃, ɑ̃t] *adj* seemly
bientôt [bjɛ̃to] *adv* soon; **à ~** see you

soon

bienveillant, e [bjɛ̃vɛjɑ̃, ɑ̃t] *adj* kindly

bienvenu, e [bjɛ̃vny] *adj* welcome; **bienvenue** *nf*: **souhaiter la bienvenue à** to welcome; **bienvenue à** welcome to

bière [bjɛʀ] *nf* (*boisson*) beer; (*cercueil*) bier; **~ (à la) pression** draught beer; **~ blonde** lager; **~ brune** brown ale

biffer [bife] *vt* to cross out

bifteck [biftɛk] *nm* steak

bifurquer [bifyʀke] *vi* (*route*) to fork; (*véhicule*) to turn off

bigarré, e [bigaʀe] *adj* multicoloured; (*disparate*) motley

bigorneau, x [bigɔʀno] *nm* winkle

bigot, e [bigo, ɔt] (*péj*) *adj* bigoted

bigoudi [bigudi] *nm* curler

bijou, x [biʒu] *nm* jewel; **bijouterie** *nf* jeweller's (shop); **bijoutier, -ière** *nm/f* jeweller

bikini [bikini] *nm* bikini

bilan [bilɑ̃] *nm* (*fig*) (net) outcome; (: *de victimes*) toll; (*COMM*) balance sheet(s); **un ~ de santé** a (medical) checkup; **faire le ~ de** to assess, review; **déposer son ~** to file a bankruptcy statement

bile [bil] *nf* bile; **se faire de la ~** (*fam*) to worry o.s. sick

bilieux, -euse [biljø, øz] *adj* bilious; (*fig: colérique*) testy

bilingue [bilɛ̃g] *adj* bilingual

billard [bijaʀ] *nm* (*jeu*) billiards *sg*; (*table*) billiard table; **~ américain** pool

bille [bij] *nf* (*gén*) ball; (*du jeu de ~s*) marble

billet [bije] *nm* (*aussi:* **~ de banque**) (bank)note; (*de cinéma, de bus etc*) ticket; (*courte lettre*) note; **~ Bige** cheap rail ticket for under-26s; **billetterie** *nf* ticket office; (*distributeur*) ticket machine; (*BANQUE*) cash dispenser

billion [biljɔ̃] *nm* billion (*BRIT*), trillion (*US*)

billot [bijo] *nm* block

bimensuel, le [bimɑ̃sɥɛl] *adj* bimonthly

binette [binɛt] *nf* hoe

bio... [bjɔ] *préfixe* bio...; **biochimie** *nf* biochemistry; **biodiversité** *nf* biodiversity; **bioéthique** *nf* bioethics *sg*; **biographie** *nf* biography; **biologie** *nf* biology; **biologique** *adj* biological; (*produits, aliments*) organic; **biologiste** *nm/f* biologist

Birmanie [biʀmani] *nf* Burma

bis [bis] *adv*: **12 ~** 12a *ou* A ♦ *excl, nm* encore

bisannuel, le [bizanɥɛl] *adj* biennial

biscornu, e [biskɔʀny] *adj* twisted

biscotte [biskɔt] *nf* toasted bread (*sold in packets*)

biscuit [biskɥi] *nm* biscuit; **~ de savoie** sponge cake

bise [biz] *nf* (*fam: baiser*) kiss; (*vent*) North wind; **grosses ~s (de)** (*sur lettre*) love and kisses (from)

bisou [bizu] (*fam*) *nm* kiss

bissextile [bisɛkstil] *adj*: **année ~** leap year

bistouri [bisturi] *nm* lancet

bistro(t) [bistro] *nm* bistro, café

bitume [bitym] *nm* asphalt

bizarre [bizaʀ] *adj* strange, odd

blafard, e [blafaʀ, aʀd] *adj* wan

blague [blag] *nf* (*propos*) joke; (*farce*) trick; **sans ~!** no kidding!; **blaguer** *vi* to joke

blaireau, x [blɛʀo] *nm* (*ZOOL*) badger; (*brosse*) shaving brush

blairer [blɛʀe] (*fam*) *vt*: **je ne peux pas le ~** I can't bear *ou* stand him

blâme [blɑm] *nm* blame; (*sanction*) reprimand; **blâmer** *vt* to blame

blanc, blanche [blɑ̃, blɑ̃ʃ] *adj* white; (*non imprimé*) blank ♦ *nm/f* white, white man(-woman) ♦ *nm* (*couleur*) white; (*espace non écrit*) blank; (*aussi:* **~ d'œuf**) (egg-)white; (*aussi:* **~ de poulet**) breast, white meat; (*aussi:* **vin ~**) white wine; **~ cassé** off-white; **chèque en ~** blank cheque; **à ~** (*chauffer*) white-hot; (*tirer, charger*) with blanks; **blanc-bec** *nm* greenhorn; **blanche** *nf* (*MUS*) minim (*BRIT*), half-note (*US*); **blancheur** *nf* whiteness

blanchir [blɑ̃ʃiʀ] *vt* (*gén*) to whiten; (*linge*) to launder; (*CULIN*) to blanch; (*fig: discul-*

per) to clear ♦ *vi* to grow white; (*cheveux*) to go white; **blanchisserie** *nf* laundry

blason [blazɔ̃] *nm* coat of arms

blasphème [blasfɛm] *nm* blasphemy

blazer [blazɛʀ] *nm* blazer

blé [ble] *nm* wheat; **~ noir** buckwheat

bled [blɛd] (*péj*) *nm* hole

blême [blɛm] *adj* pale

blessant, e [blesɑ̃, ɑ̃t] *adj* (*offensant*) hurtful

blessé, e [blese] *adj* injured ♦ *nm/f* injured person, casualty

blesser [blese] *vt* to injure; (*délibérément*; *MIL etc*) to wound; (*offenser*) to hurt; **se ~** to injure o.s.; **se ~ au pied etc** to injure one's foot *etc*; **blessure** *nf* (*accidentelle*) injury; (*intentionnelle*) wound

bleu, e [blø] *adj* blue; (*bifteck*) very rare ♦ *nm* (*couleur*) blue; (*contusion*) bruise; (*vêtement: aussi: ~s*) overalls *pl*; **~ marine** navy blue; **bleuet** *nm* cornflower; **bleuté, e** *adj* blue-shaded

blinder [blɛ̃de] *vt* to armour; (*fig*) to harden

bloc [blɔk] *nm* (*de pierre etc*) block; (*de papier à lettres*) pad; (*ensemble*) group, block; **serré à ~** tightened right down; **en ~** as a whole; **~ opératoire** operating *ou* theatre block; **~ sanitaire** toilet block; **blocage** *nm* (*des prix*) freezing; (*PSYCH*) hang-up; **bloc-notes** *nm* note pad

blocus [blɔkys] *nm* blockade

blond, e [blɔ̃, blɔ̃d] *adj* fair, blond; (*sable, blés*) golden; **~ cendré** ash blond; **blonde** *nf* (*femme*) blonde; (*bière*) lager; (*cigarette*) Virginia cigarette

bloquer [blɔke] *vt* (*passage*) to block; (*pièce mobile*) to jam; (*crédits, compte*) to freeze; **se ~** to jam; (*PSYCH*) to have a mental block

blottir [blɔtiʀ]: **se ~** *vi* to huddle up

blouse [bluz] *nf* overall

blouson [bluzɔ̃] *nm* blouson jacket; **~ noir** (*fig*) ≈ rocker

blue-jean [bludʒin] *nm* (pair of) jeans

bluff [blœf] *nm* bluff; **bluffer** *vi* to bluff

bobard [bɔbaʀ] (*fam*) *nm* tall story

bobine [bɔbin] *nf* reel; (*ÉLEC*) coil

bocal, -aux [bɔkal, o] *nm* jar

bock [bɔk] *nm* glass of beer

body [bɔdi] *nm* body(suit); (*SPORT*) leotard

bœuf [bœf] *nm* ox; (*CULIN*) beef

bof! [bɔf] (*fam*) *excl* don't care!; (*pas terrible*) nothing special

bogue [bɔg] *nm*: **le ~ de l'an 2000** the millennium bug

bohème [bɔɛm] *adj* happy-go-lucky, unconventional; **bohémien, ne** *nm/f* gipsy

boire [bwaʀ] *vt* to drink; (*s'imprégner de*) to soak up; **~ un coup** (*fam*) to have a drink

bois [bwa] *nm* wood; **de ~, en ~** wooden; **boisé, e** *adj* woody, wooded

boisson [bwasɔ̃] *nf* drink

boîte [bwat] *nf* box; (*fam: entreprise*) firm; **aliments en ~** canned *ou* tinned (*BRIT*) foods; **~ aux lettres** letter box; **~ d'allumettes** box of matches; (*vide*) matchbox; **~ (de conserve)** can *ou* tin (*BRIT*) (of food); **~ de nuit** night club; **~ de vitesses** gear box; **~ postale** PO Box; **~ vocale** (*TEL*) voice mail

boiter [bwate] *vi* to limp; (*fig: raisonnement*) to be shaky

boîtier [bwatje] *nm* case

boive *etc* [bwav] *vb voir* **boire**

bol [bɔl] *nm* bowl; **un ~ d'air** a breath of fresh air; **j'en ai ras le ~** (*fam*) I'm fed up with this; **avoir du ~** (*fam*) to be lucky

bolide [bɔlid] *nm* racing car; **comme un ~** at top speed, like a rocket

bombardement [bɔ̃baʀdəmɑ̃] *nm* bombing

bombarder [bɔ̃baʀde] *vt* to bomb; **~ qn de** (*cailloux, lettres*) to bombard sb with

bombe [bɔ̃b] *nf* bomb; (*atomiseur*) (aerosol) spray; **bombé, e** *adj* (*forme*) rounded; **bomber** *vt*: **bomber le torse** to swell out one's chest

---

MOT-CLÉ

---

bon, bonne [bɔ̃, bɔn] *adj* 1 (*agréable, satisfaisant*) good; **un bon repas/restaurant** a good meal/restaurant; **être bon en maths** to be good at maths

2 (*charitable*): **être bon (envers)** to be good (to)

3 (*correct*) right; **le bon numéro/moment** the right number/moment

4 (*souhaits*): **bon anniversaire** happy birthday; **bon voyage** have a good trip; **bonne chance** good luck; **bonne année** happy New Year; **bonne nuit** good night

5 (*approprié, apte*): **bon à/pour** fit to/for

6: **bon enfant** *adj inv* accommodating, easy-going; **bonne femme** (*péj*) woman; **de bonne heure** early; **bon marché** *adj inv* cheap ♦ *adv* cheap; **bon mot** witticism; **bon sens** common sense; **bon vivant** jovial chap; **bonnes œuvres** charitable works, charities

♦ *nm* **1** (*billet*) voucher; (*aussi*: **bon cadeau**) gift voucher; **bon d'essence** petrol coupon; **bon du Trésor** Treasury bond

2: **avoir du bon** to have its good points; **pour de bon** for good

♦ *adv*: **il fait bon** it's *ou* the weather is fine; **sentir bon** to smell good; **tenir bon** to stand firm

♦ *excl* good!; **ah bon?** really?; *voir aussi* **bonne**

---

bonbon [bɔ̃bɔ̃] *nm* (boiled) sweet
bonbonne [bɔ̃bɔn] *nf* demijohn
bond [bɔ̃] *nm* leap; **faire un ~** to leap in the air
bondé, e [bɔ̃de] *adj* packed (full)
bondir [bɔ̃diR] *vi* to leap
bonheur [bɔnœR] *nm* happiness; **porter ~ (à qn)** to bring sb luck; **au petit ~** haphazardly; **par ~** fortunately
bonhomie [bɔnɔmi] *nf* goodnaturedness
bonhomme [bɔnɔm] (*pl* **bonshommes**) *nm* fellow; **~ de neige** snowman
bonifier [bɔnifje] *vt* to improve
boniment [bɔnimɑ̃] *nm* patter *no pl*
bonjour [bɔ̃ʒuR] *excl, nm* hello; (*selon l'heure*) good morning/afternoon; **c'est simple comme ~!** it's easy as pie!
bonne [bɔn] *adj voir* **bon** ♦ *nf* (*domestique*)

maid; **bonnement** *adv*: **tout bonnement** quite simply
bonnet [bɔnɛ] *nm* hat; (*de soutien-gorge*) cup; **~ de bain** bathing cap
bonshommes [bɔ̃zɔm] *nmpl de* **bonhomme**
bonsoir [bɔ̃swaR] *excl* good evening
bonté [bɔ̃te] *nf* kindness *no pl*
bonus [bɔnys] *nm* no-claims bonus
bord [bɔR] *nm* (*de table, verre, falaise*) edge; (*de rivière, lac*) bank; (*de route*) side; **(monter) à ~** (to go) on board; **jeter par-dessus ~** to throw overboard; **le commandant de/les hommes du ~** the ship's master/crew; **au ~ de la mer** at the seaside; **être au ~ des larmes** to be on the verge of tears
bordeaux [bɔRdo] *nm* Bordeaux (wine) ♦ *adj inv* maroon
bordel [bɔRdɛl] *nm* brothel; (*fam!*) bloody mess (*!*)
bordelais, e [bɔRdəlɛ, ɛz] *adj* of *ou* from Bordeaux
border [bɔRde] *vt* (*être le long de*) to line; (*qn dans son lit*) to tuck up; (*garnir*): **~ qch de** to edge sth with
bordereau, x [bɔRdəRo] *nm* (*formulaire*) slip
bordure [bɔRdyR] *nf* border; **en ~ de** on the edge of
borgne [bɔRɲ] *adj* one-eyed
borne [bɔRn] *nf* boundary stone; (*aussi*: **~ kilométrique**) kilometre-marker; ≃ milestone; **~s** *nfpl* (*fig*) limits; **dépasser les ~s** to go too far
borné, e [bɔRne] *adj* (*personne*) narrow-minded
borner [bɔRne] *vt*: **se ~ à faire** (*se contenter de*) to content o.s. with doing; (*se limiter à*) to limit o.s. to doing
bosquet [bɔskɛ] *nm* grove
bosse [bɔs] *nf* (*de terrain etc*) bump; (*enflure*) lump; (*du bossu, du chameau*) hump; **avoir la ~ des maths** *etc* (*fam*) to have a gift for maths *etc*; **il a roulé sa ~** (*fam*) he's been around

bosser [bɔse] (*fam*) *vi* (*travailler*) to work; (*travailler dur*) to slave (away)

bossu, e [bɔsy] *nm/f* hunchback

botanique [bɔtanik] *nf* botany ♦ *adj* botanic(al)

botte [bɔt] *nf* (*soulier*) (high) boot; (*gerbe*): ~ **de paille** bundle of straw; ~ **de radis** bunch of radishes; **~s de caoutchouc** wellington boots; **botter** *vt*: **ça me botte** (*fam*) I fancy that

bottin [bɔtɛ̃] *nm* directory

bottine [bɔtin] *nf* ankle boot

bouc [buk] *nm* goat; (*barbe*) goatee; ~ **émissaire** scapegoat

boucan [bukɑ̃] (*fam*) *nm* din, racket

bouche [buʃ] *nf* mouth; **rester ~ bée** to stand open-mouthed; **le ~ à ~** the kiss of life; ~ **d'égout** manhole; ~ **d'incendie** fire hydrant; ~ **de métro** métro entrance

bouché, e [buʃe] *adj* (*temps, ciel*) overcast; **c'est ~** there's no future in it

bouchée [buʃe] *nf* mouthful; **~s à la reine** chicken vol-au-vents

boucher, -ère [buʃe] *nm/f* butcher ♦ *vt* (*trou*) to fill up; (*obstruer*) to block (up); **se ~** *vi* (*tuyau etc*) to block up, get blocked up; **j'ai le nez bouché** my nose is blocked; **se ~ le nez** to hold one's nose; **boucherie** *nf* butcher's (shop); (*fig*) slaughter

bouche-trou [buʃtʀu] *nm* (*fig*) stop-gap

bouchon [buʃɔ̃] *nm* stopper; (*de tube*) top; (*en liège*) cork; (*fig: embouteillage*) holdup; (*PÊCHE*) float

boucle [bukl] *nf* (*forme, figure*) loop; (*objet*) buckle; ~ **(de cheveux)** curl; ~ **d'oreille** earring

bouclé, e [bukle] *adj* (*cheveux*) curly

boucler [bukle] *vt* (*fermer: ceinture etc*) to fasten; (*terminer*) to finish off; (*fam: enfermer*) to shut away; (*quartier*) to seal off ♦ *vi* to curl

bouclier [buklije] *nm* shield

bouddhiste [budist] *nm/f* Buddhist

bouder [bude] *vi* to sulk ♦ *vt* to stay away from

boudin [budɛ̃] *nm*: ~ **(noir)** black pudding; ~ **blanc** white pudding

boue [bu] *nf* mud

bouée [bwe] *nf* buoy; ~ **(de sauvetage)** lifebuoy

boueux, -euse [bwø, øz] *adj* muddy

bouffe [buf] (*fam*) *nf* grub (*fam*), food

bouffée [bufe] *nf* (*de cigarette*) puff; **une ~ d'air pur** a breath of fresh air

bouffer [bufe] (*fam*) *vi* to eat

bouffi, e [bufi] *adj* swollen

bougeoir [buʒwaʀ] *nm* candlestick

bougeotte [buʒɔt] *nf*: **avoir la ~** (*fam*) to have the fidgets

bouger [buʒe] *vi* to move; (*dent etc*) to be loose; (*s'activer*) to get moving ♦ *vt* to move; **les prix/les couleurs n'ont pas bougé** prices/colours haven't changed

bougie [buʒi] *nf* candle; (*AUTO*) spark(ing) plug

bougon, ne [buɡɔ̃, ɔn] *adj* grumpy

bougonner [buɡɔne] *vi, vt* to grumble

bouillabaisse [bujabɛs] *nf* type of fish soup

bouillant, e [bujɑ̃, ɑ̃t] *adj* (*qui bout*) boiling; (*très chaud*) boiling (hot)

bouillie [buji] *nf* (*de bébé*) cereal; **en ~** (*fig*) crushed

bouillir [bujiʀ] *vi, vt* to boil; ~ **d'impatience** to seethe with impatience

bouilloire [bujwaʀ] *nf* kettle

bouillon [bujɔ̃] *nm* (*CULIN*) stock *no pl*; **bouillonner** *vi* to bubble; (*fig: idées*) to bubble up

bouillotte [bujɔt] *nf* hot-water bottle

boulanger, -ère [bulɑ̃ʒe, ɛʀ] *nm/f* baker; **boulangerie** *nf* bakery; **boulangerie-pâtisserie** *nf* baker's and confectioner's (shop)

boule [bul] *nf* (*gén*) ball; **~s** *nfpl* (*jeu*) bowls; **se mettre en ~** (*fig: fam*) to fly off the handle, to blow one's top; **jouer aux ~s** to play bowls; ~ **de neige** snowball

bouleau, x [bulo] *nm* (silver) birch

bouledogue [buldɔg] *nm* bulldog

boulet [bulɛ] *nm* (*aussi:* ~ **de canon**) cannonball

boulette [bulɛt] *nf (de viande)* meatball

boulevard [bulvaʀ] *nm* boulevard

bouleversant, e [bulvɛʀsɑ̃, ɑ̃t] *adj (scène, récit)* deeply moving

bouleversement [bulvɛʀsəmɑ̃] *nm* upheaval

bouleverser [bulvɛʀse] *vt (émouvoir)* to overwhelm; *(causer du chagrin)* to distress; *(pays, vie)* to disrupt; *(papiers, objets)* to turn upside down

boulon [bulɔ̃] *nm* bolt

boulot, te [bulo, ɔt] *adj* plump, tubby ♦ *nm (fam: travail)* work

boum [bum] *nm* bang ♦ *nf (fam)* party

bouquet [bukɛ] *nm (de fleurs)* bunch (of flowers), bouquet; *(de persil etc)* bunch; **c'est le ~!** *(fam)* that takes the biscuit!

bouquin [bukɛ̃] *(fam) nm* book; **bouquiner** *(fam) vi* to read; **bouquiniste** *nm/f* bookseller

bourbeux, -euse [buʀbø, øz] *adj* muddy

bourbier [buʀbje] *nm* (quag)mire

bourde [buʀd] *(fam) nf (erreur)* howler; *(gaffe)* blunder

bourdon [buʀdɔ̃] *nm* bumblebee; **bourdonner** *vi* to buzz

bourg [buʀ] *nm* small market town

bourgeois, e [buʀʒwa, waz] *(péj) adj* ≈ (upper) middle class; **bourgeoisie** *nf* ≈ upper middle classes *pl*

bourgeon [buʀʒɔ̃] *nm* bud

Bourgogne [buʀgɔɲ] *nf*: **la ~** Burgundy ♦ *nm*: **b~** burgundy (wine)

bourguignon, ne [buʀgiɲɔ̃, ɔn] *adj* of *ou* from Burgundy, Burgundian

bourlinguer [buʀlɛ̃ge] *(fam) vi* to knock about a lot, get around a lot

bourrade [buʀad] *nf* shove, thump

bourrage [buʀaʒ] *nm*: **~ de crâne** brainwashing; *(SCOL)* cramming

bourrasque [buʀask] *nf* squall

bourratif, -ive [buʀatif, iv] *(fam) adj* filling, stodgy *(pej)*

bourré, e [buʀe] *adj (fam: ivre)* plastered, tanked up *(BRIT)*; *(rempli)*: **~ de** crammed full of

bourreau, x [buʀo] *nm* executioner; *(fig)* torturer; **~ de travail** workaholic

bourrelet [buʀlɛ] *nm* fold *ou* roll (of flesh)

bourrer [buʀe] *vt (pipe)* to fill; *(poêle)* to pack; *(valise)* to cram (full)

bourrique [buʀik] *nf (âne)* ass

bourru, e [buʀy] *adj* surly, gruff

bourse [buʀs] *nf (subvention)* grant; *(porte-monnaie)* purse; **la B~** the Stock Exchange

boursier, -ière [buʀsje, jɛʀ] *nm/f (étudiant)* grant holder

boursoufler [buʀsufle]: **se ~** *vi* to swell (up)

bous [bu] *vb voir* **bouillir**

bousculade [buskylad] *nf (hâte)* rush; *(cohue)* crush; **bousculer** *vt (heurter)* to knock into; *(fig)* to push, rush

bouse [buz] *nf* dung *no pl*

bousiller [buzije] *(fam) vt (appareil)* to wreck

boussole [busɔl] *nf* compass

bout [bu] *vb voir* **bouillir** ♦ *nm* bit; *(d'un bâton etc)* tip; *(d'une ficelle, table, rue, période)* end; **au ~ de** at the end of, after; **pousser qn à ~** to push sb to the limit; **venir à ~ de** to manage to finish

boutade [butad] *nf* quip, sally

boute-en-train [butɑ̃tʀɛ̃] *nm inv (fig)* live wire

bouteille [butɛj] *nf* bottle; *(de gaz butane)* cylinder

boutique [butik] *nf* shop

bouton [butɔ̃] *nm* button; *(sur la peau)* spot; *(BOT)* bud; **~ d'or** buttercup; **boutonner** *vt* to button up; **boutonnière** *nf* buttonhole; **bouton-pression** *nm* press stud

bouture [butyʀ] *nf* cutting

bovins [bɔvɛ̃] *nmpl* cattle *pl*

bowling [buliŋ] *nm (tenpin)* bowling; *(salle)* bowling alley

box [bɔks] *nm (d'écurie)* loose-box; *(JUR)*: **~ des accusés** dock

boxe [bɔks] *nf* boxing; **boxeur** *nm* boxer

boyaux [bwajo] *nmpl* (*viscères*) entrails, guts

BP *abr* = **boîte postale**

bracelet [bʀaslɛ] *nm* bracelet

braconnier [bʀakɔnje] *nm* poacher

brader [bʀade] *vt* to sell off; **braderie** *nf* cut-price shop/stall

braguette [bʀagɛt] *nf* fly *ou* flies *pl* (*BRIT*), zipper (*US*)

brailler [bʀaje] *vi* to bawl, yell

braire [bʀɛʀ] *vi* to bray

braise [bʀɛz] *nf* embers *pl*

brancard [bʀɑ̃kaʀ] *nm* (*civière*) stretcher; **brancardier** *nm* stretcher-bearer

branchages [bʀɑ̃ʃaʒ] *nmpl* boughs

branche [bʀɑ̃ʃ] *nf* branch

branché, e [bʀɑ̃ʃe] (*fam*) *adj* trendy

brancher [bʀɑ̃ʃe] *vt* to connect (up); (*en mettant la prise*) to plug in

brandir [bʀɑ̃diʀ] *vt* to brandish

branle [bʀɑ̃l] *nm*: **mettre en ~** to set in motion; **branle-bas** *nm inv* commotion

braquer [bʀake] *vi* (*AUTO*) to turn (the wheel) ♦ *vt* (*revolver etc*): **~ qch sur** to aim sth at, point sth at; (*mettre en colère*): **~ qn** to put sb's back up

bras [bʀa] *nm* arm; **~ dessus, ~ dessous** arm in arm; **se retrouver avec qch sur les ~** (*fam*) to be landed with sth; **~ droit** (*fig*) right hand man; **~ de fer** arm wrestling

brasier [bʀazje] *nm* blaze, inferno

bras-le-corps [bʀalkɔʀ] *adv*: **à ~-~-~** (a)round the waist

brassard [bʀasaʀ] *nm* armband

brasse [bʀas] *nf* (*nage*) breast-stroke

brassée [bʀase] *nf* armful

brasser [bʀase] *vt* to mix; **~ l'argent/les affaires** to handle a lot of money/business

brasserie [bʀasʀi] *nf* (*restaurant*) café-restaurant; (*usine*) brewery

brave [bʀav] *adj* (*courageux*) brave; (*bon, gentil*) good, kind

braver [bʀave] *vt* to defy

bravo [bʀavo] *excl* bravo ♦ *nm* cheer

bravoure [bʀavuʀ] *nf* bravery

break [bʀɛk] *nm* (*AUTO*) estate car

brebis [bʀəbi] *nf* ewe; **~ galeuse** black sheep

brèche [bʀɛʃ] *nf* breach, gap; **être toujours sur la ~** (*fig*) to be always on the go

bredouille [bʀəduj] *adj* empty-handed

bredouiller [bʀəduje] *vi*, *vt* to mumble, stammer

bref, brève [bʀɛf, ɛv] *adj* short, brief ♦ *adv* in short; **d'un ton ~** sharply, curtly; **en ~** in short, in brief

Brésil [bʀezil] *nm* Brazil; **brésilien, -ne** *adj* Brazilian ♦ *nm/f*: **Brésilien, ne** Brazilian

Bretagne [bʀətaɲ] *nf* Brittany

bretelle [bʀətɛl] *nf* (*de vêtement, de sac*) strap; (*d'autoroute*) slip road (*BRIT*), entrance/exit ramp (*US*); **~s** *nfpl* (*pour pantalon*) braces (*BRIT*), suspenders (*US*)

breton, ne [bʀətɔ̃, ɔn] *adj* Breton ♦ *nm/f*: **B~, ne** Breton

breuvage [bʀœvaʒ] *nm* beverage, drink

brève [bʀɛv] *adj voir* **bref**

brevet [bʀəvɛ] *nm* diploma, certificate; **~ (d'invention)** patent; **breveté, e** *adj* patented

bribes [bʀib] *nfpl* (*de conversation*) snatches; **par ~** piecemeal

bricolage [bʀikɔlaʒ] *nm*: **le ~** do-it-yourself

bricole [bʀikɔl] *nf* (*babiole*) trifle

bricoler [bʀikɔle] *vi* (*petits travaux*) to do DIY jobs; (*passe-temps*) to potter about ♦ *vt* (*réparer*) to fix up; **bricoleur, -euse** *nm/f* handyman(-woman), DIY enthusiast

bride [bʀid] *nf* bridle; **tenir qn en ~** to keep a tight rein on sb

bridé, e [bʀide] *adj*: **yeux ~s** slit eyes

bridge [bʀidʒ] *nm* (*CARTES*) bridge

brièvement [bʀijɛvmɑ̃] *adv* briefly

brigade [bʀigad] *nf* (*POLICE*) squad; (*MIL*) brigade; **brigadier** *nm* sergeant

brigandage [bʀigɑ̃daʒ] *nm* robbery

briguer [bʀige] *vt* to aspire to

brillamment [bʀijamɑ̃] *adv* brilliantly
brillant, e [bʀijɑ̃, ɑ̃t] *adj* (*remarquable*) bright; (*luisant*) shiny, shining
briller [bʀije] *vi* to shine
brimer [bʀime] *vt* to bully
brin [bʀɛ̃] *nm* (*de laine, ficelle etc*) strand; (*fig*): **un ~ de** a bit of; **~ d'herbe** blade of grass; **~ de muguet** sprig of lily of the valley
brindille [bʀɛ̃dij] *nf* twig
brio [bʀijo] *nm*: **avec ~** with panache
brioche [bʀijɔʃ] *nf* brioche (bun); (*fam*: *ventre*) paunch
brique [bʀik] *nf* brick; (*de lait*) carton
briquer [bʀike] *vt* to polish up
briquet [bʀike] *nm* (cigarette) lighter
brise [bʀiz] *nf* breeze
briser [bʀize] *vt* to break; **se ~** *vi* to break
britannique [bʀitanik] *adj* British ♦ *nm/f*: **B~** British person, Briton; **les B~s** the British
brocante [bʀɔkɑ̃t] *nf* junk, second-hand goods *pl*; **brocanteur, -euse** *nm/f* junk-shop owner; junk dealer
broche [bʀɔʃ] *nf* brooch; (*CULIN*) spit; (*MÉD*) pin; **à la ~** spit-roasted
broché, e [bʀɔʃe] *adj* (*livre*) paper-backed
brochet [bʀɔʃɛ] *nm* pike *inv*
brochette [bʀɔʃɛt] *nf* (*ustensile*) skewer; (*plat*) kebab
brochure [bʀɔʃyʀ] *nf* pamphlet, brochure, booklet
broder [bʀɔde] *vt* to embroider ♦ *vi* to embroider the facts; **broderie** *nf* embroidery
broncher [bʀɔ̃ʃe] *vi*: **sans ~** without flinching, without turning a hair
bronches [bʀɔ̃ʃ] *nfpl* bronchial tubes; **bronchite** *nf* bronchitis
bronze [bʀɔ̃z] *nm* bronze
bronzer [bʀɔ̃ze] *vi* to get a tan; **se ~** to sunbathe
brosse [bʀɔs] *nf* brush; **coiffé en ~** with a crewcut; **~ à cheveux** hairbrush; **~ à dents** toothbrush; **~ à habits** clothesbrush; **brosser** *vt* (*nettoyer*) to brush; (*fig*:

tableau etc) to paint; **se brosser les dents** to brush one's teeth
brouette [bʀuɛt] *nf* wheelbarrow
brouhaha [bʀuaa] *nm* hubbub
brouillard [bʀujaʀ] *nm* fog
brouille [bʀuj] *nf* quarrel
brouiller [bʀuje] *vt* (*œufs, message*) to scramble; (*idées*) to mix up; (*rendre trouble*) to cloud; (*désunir: amis*) to set at odds; **se ~** *vi* (*vue*) to cloud over; (*gens*) to fall out
brouillon, ne [bʀujɔ̃, ɔn] *adj* (*sans soin*) untidy; (*qui manque d'organisation*) disorganized ♦ *nm* draft; (**papier**) **~** rough paper
broussailles [bʀusaj] *nfpl* undergrowth *sg*; **broussailleux, -euse** *adj* bushy
brousse [bʀus] *nf*: **la ~** the bush
brouter [bʀute] *vi* to graze
broutille [bʀutij] *nf* trifle
broyer [bʀwaje] *vt* to crush; **~ du noir** to be down in the dumps
bru [bʀy] *nf* daughter-in-law
brugnon [bʀyɲɔ̃] *nm* (*BOT*) nectarine
bruiner [bʀɥine] *vb impers*: **il bruine** it's drizzling, there's a drizzle
bruire [bʀɥiʀ] *vi* (*feuilles*) to rustle
bruit [bʀɥi] *nm*: **un ~** a noise, a sound; (*fig: rumeur*) a rumour; **le ~** noise; **sans ~** without a sound, noiselessly; **~ de fond** background noise; **bruitage** *nm* sound effects *pl*
brûlant, e [bʀylɑ̃, ɑ̃t] *adj* burning; (*liquide*) boiling (hot)
brûlé, e [bʀyle] *adj* (*fig: démasqué*) blown ♦ *nm*: **odeur de ~** smell of burning
brûle-pourpoint [bʀylpuʀpwɛ̃]: **à ~-~** *adv* point-blank
brûler [bʀyle] *vt* to burn; (*suj: eau bouillante*) to scald; (*consommer: électricité, essence*) to use; (*feu rouge, signal*) to go through ♦ *vi* to burn; (*jeu*): **tu brûles!** you're getting hot!; **se ~** to burn o.s.; (*s'ebouillanter*) to scald o.s.
brûlure [bʀylyʀ] *nf* (*lésion*) burn; **~s d'estomac** heartburn *sg*

brume [bʀym] *nf* mist; **brumisateur** *nm* atomizer

brun, e [bʀœ̃, bʀyn] *adj* (*gén, bière*) brown; (*cheveux, tabac*) dark; **elle est ~e** she's got dark hair

brunch [bʀœntʃ] *nm* brunch

brunir [bʀyniʀ] *vi* to get a tan

brushing [bʀœʃiŋ] *nm* blow-dry

brusque [bʀysk] *adj* abrupt; **brusquer** *vt* to rush

brut, e [bʀyt] *adj* (*minerai, soie*) raw; (*diamant*) rough; (*COMM*) gross; (**pétrole**) **~** crude (oil)

brutal, e, -aux [bʀytal, o] *adj* brutal; **brutaliser** *vt* to handle roughly, manhandle

Bruxelles [bʀysɛl] *n* Brussels

bruyamment [bʀɥijamɑ̃] *adv* noisily

bruyant, e [bʀɥijɑ̃, ɑ̃t] *adj* noisy

bruyère [bʀyjɛʀ] *nf* heather

BTS *sigle m* (= *brevet de technicien supérieur*) *vocational training certificate taken at the end of a higher education course*

bu, e [by] *pp de* **boire**

buccal, e, -aux [bykal, o] *adj*: **par voie ~e** orally

bûche [byʃ] *nf* log; **prendre une ~** (*fig*) to come a cropper; **~ de Noël** Yule log

bûcher [byʃe] *nm* (*funéraire*) pyre; (*supplice*) stake ♦ *vi* (*fam*) to swot (*BRIT*), slave (away) ♦ *vt* (*fam*) to swot up (*BRIT*), slave away at; **bûcheron** *nm* woodcutter; **bûcheur, -euse** (*fam*) *adj* hard-working

budget [bydʒɛ] *nm* budget

buée [bɥe] *nf* (*sur une vitre*) mist

buffet [byfɛ] *nm* (*meuble*) sideboard; (*de réception*) buffet; **~ (de gare)** (station) buffet, snack bar

buffle [byfl] *nm* buffalo

buis [bɥi] *nm* box tree; (*bois*) box(wood)

buisson [bɥisɔ̃] *nm* bush

buissonnière [bɥisɔnjɛʀ] *adj*: **faire l'école ~** to skip school

bulbe [bylb] *nm* (*BOT, ANAT*) bulb

Bulgarie [bylgaʀi] *nf* Bulgaria

bulle [byl] *nf* bubble

bulletin [byltɛ̃] *nm* (*communiqué, journal*) bulletin; (*SCOL*) report; **~ d'informations** news bulletin; **~ de salaire** pay-slip; **~ (de vote)** ballot paper; **~ météorologique** weather report

bureau, x [byʀo] *nm* (*meuble*) desk; (*pièce, service*) office; **~ de change** (foreign) exchange office *ou* bureau; **~ de poste** post office; **~ de tabac** tobacconist's (shop); **~ de vote** polling station; **bureaucratie** [byʀokʀasi] *nf* bureaucracy

burin [byʀɛ̃] *nm* cold chisel; (*ART*) burin

burlesque [byʀlɛsk] *adj* ridiculous; (*LITTÉRATURE*) burlesque

bus¹ [by] *vb voir* **boire**

bus² [bys] *nm* bus

busqué, e [byske] *adj* (*nez*) hook(ed)

buste [byst] *nm* (*torse*) chest; (*seins*) bust

but¹ [by] *vb voir* **boire**

but² [by(t)] *nm* (*cible*) target; (*fig*) goal, aim; (*FOOTBALL etc*) goal; **de ~ en blanc** point-blank; **avoir pour ~ de faire** to aim to do; **dans le ~ de** with the intention of

butane [bytan] *nm* (*camping*) butane; (*usage domestique*) Calor gas ®

buté, e [byte] *adj* stubborn, obstinate

buter [byte] *vi*: **~ contre** (*cogner*) to bump into; (*trébucher*) to stumble against; **se ~** *vi* to get obstinate, dig in one's heels; **~ contre une difficulté** (*fig*) to hit a snag

butin [bytɛ̃] *nm* booty, spoils *pl*; (*d'un vol*) loot

butiner [bytine] *vi* (*abeilles*) to gather nectar

butte [byt] *nf* mound, hillock; **être en ~ à** to be exposed to

buvais *etc* [byvɛ] *vb voir* **boire**

buvard [byvaʀ] *nm* blotter

buvette [byvɛt] *nf* bar

buveur, -euse [byvœʀ, øz] *nm/f* drinker

C, c

c' [s] *dét voir* **ce**

CA *sigle m* = **chiffre d'affaires**

ça [sa] *pron (pour désigner)* this; (: *plus loin*) that; (*comme sujet indéfini*) it; **comment ~ va?** how are you?; **~ va?** (*d'accord?*) OK?, all right?; **où ~?** where's that?; **pourquoi ~?** why's that?; **qui ~?** who's that?; **~ alors!** well really!; **~ fait 10 ans (que)** it's 10 years (since); **c'est ~** that's right; **~ y est** that's it

çà [sa] *adv*: **~ et là** here and there

cabane [kaban] *nf* hut, cabin

cabaret [kabaʀɛ] *nm* night club

cabas [kaba] *nm* shopping bag

cabillaud [kabijo] *nm* cod *inv*

cabine [kabin] *nf (de bateau)* cabin; (*de piscine etc*) cubicle; (*de camion, train*) cab; (*d'avion*) cockpit; **~ d'essayage** fitting room; **~ (téléphonique)** call *ou* (tele)phone box

cabinet [kabinɛ] *nm (petite pièce)* closet; (*de médecin*) surgery (BRIT), office (US); (*de notaire etc*) office; (: *clientèle*) practice; (*POL*) Cabinet; **~s** *nmpl (w.-c.)* toilet *sg*; **~ d'affaires** business consultancy; **~ de toilette** toilet

câble [kɑbl] *nm* cable

cabosser [kabɔse] *vt* to dent

cabrer [kabʀe]: **se ~** *vi (cheval)* to rear up

cabriole [kabʀijɔl] *nf*: **faire des ~s** to caper about

cacahuète [kakaɥɛt] *nf* peanut

cacao [kakao] *nm* cocoa

cache [kaʃ] *nm* mask, card (for masking)

cache-cache [kaʃkaʃ] *nm*: **jouer à ~-~** to play hide-and-seek

cachemire [kaʃmiʀ] *nm* cashmere

cache-nez [kaʃne] *nm inv* scarf, muffler

cacher [kaʃe] *vt* to hide, conceal; **se ~** *vi (volontairement)* to hide; (*être caché*) to be hidden *ou* concealed; **~ qch à qn** to hide *ou* conceal sth from sb

cachet [kaʃɛ] *nm (comprimé)* tablet; (*de la poste*) postmark; (*rétribution*) fee; (*fig*) style, character; **cacheter** *vt* to seal

cachette [kaʃɛt] *nf* hiding place; **en ~** on the sly, secretly

cachot [kaʃo] *nm* dungeon

cachotterie [kaʃɔtʀi] *nf*: **faire des ~s** to be secretive

cactus [kaktys] *nm* cactus

cadavre [kadavʀ] *nm* corpse, (dead) body

Caddie ®, **caddy** [kadi] *nm (supermarket)* trolley

cadeau, x [kado] *nm* present, gift; **faire un ~ à qn** to give sb a present *ou* gift; **faire ~ de qch à qn** to make a present of sth to sb, give sb sth as a present

cadenas [kadna] *nm* padlock

cadence [kadɑ̃s] *nf (tempo)* rhythm; (*de travail etc*) rate; **en ~** rhythmically

cadet, te [kadɛ, ɛt] *adj* younger; (*le plus jeune*) youngest ♦ *nm/f* youngest child *ou* one

cadran [kadʀɑ̃] *nm* dial; **~ solaire** sundial

cadre [kadʀ] *nm* frame; (*environnement*) surroundings *pl* ♦ *nm/f (ADMIN)* managerial employee, executive; **dans le ~ de** (*fig*) in the framework *ou* context of

cadrer [kadʀe] *vi*: **~ avec** to tally *ou* correspond with ♦ *vt* to centre

cafard [kafaʀ] *nm* cockroach; **avoir le ~** (*fam*) to be down in the dumps

café [kafe] *nm* coffee; (*bistro*) café ♦ *adj inv* coffee(-coloured); **~ au lait** white coffee; **~ noir** black coffee; **~ tabac** tobacconist's *or* newsagent's serving coffee and spirits; **cafetière** *nf (pot)* coffee-pot

cafouiller [kafuje] (*fam*) *vi* to get into a shambles

cage [kaʒ] *nf* cage; **~ d'escalier** (stair)well; **~ thoracique** rib cage

cageot [kaʒo] *nm* crate

cagibi [kaʒibi] (*fam*) *nm (débarras)* boxroom

cagnotte [kaɲɔt] *nf* kitty

cagoule [kagul] *nf (passe-montagne)* balaclava

cahier [kaje] *nm* notebook; **~ de brouillons** roughbook, jotter; **~ d'exercices** exercise book

cahot [kao] *nm* jolt, bump

caïd [kaid] *nm* big chief, boss

caille [kaj] *nf* quail

cailler [kaje] *vi* (*lait*) to curdle; **ça caille** (*fam*) it's freezing; **caillot** *nm* (*blood*) clot

caillou, x [kaju] *nm* (little) stone; **caillouteux, -euse** *adj* (*route*) stony

Caire [kɛR] *nm*: **le ~** Cairo

caisse [kɛs] *nf* box; (*tiroir où l'on met la recette*) till; (*où l'on paye*) cash desk (*BRIT*), check-out; (*de banque*) cashier's desk; **~ d'épargne** savings bank; **~ de retraite** pension fund; **~ enregistreuse** cash register; **caissier, -ière** *nm/f* cashier

cajoler [kaʒɔle] *vt* (*câliner*) to cuddle; (*amadouer*) to wheedle, coax

cake [kɛk] *nm* fruit cake

calandre [kalɑ̃dR] *nf* radiator grill

calanque [kalɑ̃k] *nf* rocky inlet

calcaire [kalkɛR] *nm* limestone ♦ *adj* (*eau*) hard; (*GÉO*) limestone *cpd*

calciné, e [kalsine] *adj* burnt to ashes

calcul [kalkyl] *nm* calculation; **le ~** (*SCOL*) arithmetic; **~ (biliaire)** (gall)stone; **calculatrice** *nf* calculator; **calculer** *vt* to calculate, work out; **calculette** *nf* pocket calculator

cale [kal] *nf* (*de bateau*) hold; (*en bois*) wedge; **~ sèche** dry dock

calé, e [kale] (*fam*) *adj* clever, bright

caleçon [kalsɔ̃] *nm* (*d'homme*) boxer shorts; (*de femme*) leggings

calembour [kalɑ̃buR] *nm* pun

calendrier [kalɑ̃dRije] *nm* calendar; (*fig*) timetable

calepin [kalpɛ̃] *nm* notebook

caler [kale] *vt* to wedge ♦ *vi* (*moteur, véhicule*) to stall

calfeutrer [kalføtRe] *vt* to (make) draughtproof; **se ~** *vi* to make o.s. snug and comfortable

calibre [kalibR] *nm* calibre

califourchon [kalifuRʃɔ̃]: **à ~** *adv* astride

câlin, e [kalɛ̃, in] *adj* cuddly, cuddlesome; (*regard, voix*) tender; **câliner** *vt* to cuddle

calmant [kalmɑ̃] *nm* tranquillizer, sedative; (*pour la douleur*) painkiller

calme [kalm] *adj* calm, quiet ♦ *nm* calm(ness), quietness; **calmer** *vt* to calm (down); (*douleur, inquiétude*) to ease, soothe; **se calmer** *vi* to calm down

calomnie [kalɔmni] *nf* slander; (*écrite*) libel; **calomnier** *vt* to slander; to libel

calorie [kalɔRi] *nf* calorie

calotte [kalɔt] *nf* (*coiffure*) skullcap; (*fam: gifle*) slap; **~ glaciaire** (*GÉO*) icecap

calquer [kalke] *vt* to trace; (*fig*) to copy exactly

calvaire [kalvɛR] *nm* (*croix*) wayside cross, calvary; (*souffrances*) suffering

calvitie [kalvisi] *nf* baldness

camarade [kamaRad] *nm/f* friend, pal; (*POL*) comrade; **camaraderie** *nf* friendship

cambouis [kɑ̃bwi] *nm* dirty oil *ou* grease

cambrer [kɑ̃bRe]: **se ~** *vi* to arch one's back

cambriolage [kɑ̃bRijɔlaʒ] *nm* burglary; **cambrioler** *vt* to burgle (*BRIT*), burglarize (*US*); **cambrioleur, -euse** *nm/f* burglar

camelote [kamlɔt] (*fam*) *nf* rubbish, trash, junk

caméra [kameRa] *nf* (*CINÉMA, TV*) camera; (*d'amateur*) cine-camera

caméscope ® [kameskɔp] *nm* camcorder ®

camion [kamjɔ̃] *nm* lorry (*BRIT*), truck; **~ de dépannage** breakdown (*BRIT*) *ou* tow (*US*) truck; **camion-citerne** *nm* tanker; **camionnette** *nf* (small) van; **camionneur** *nm* (*chauffeur*) lorry (*BRIT*) *ou* truck driver; (*entrepreneur*) haulage contractor (*BRIT*), trucker (*US*)

camisole [kamizɔl] *nf*: **~ (de force)** straitjacket

camomille [kamɔmij] *nf* camomile; (*boisson*) camomile tea

camoufler [kamufle] *vt* to camouflage; (*fig*) to conceal, cover up

camp [kɑ̃] *nm* camp; *(fig)* side; **~ de vacances** children's holiday camp *(BRIT)*, summer camp *(US)*

campagnard, e [kɑ̃paɲaʀ, aʀd] *adj* country *cpd*

campagne [kɑ̃paɲ] *nf* country, countryside; *(MIL, POL, COMM)* campaign; **à la ~** in the country

camper [kɑ̃pe] *vi* to camp ♦ *vt* to sketch; **se ~ devant** to plant o.s. in front of; **campeur, -euse** *nm/f* camper

camping [kɑ̃piŋ] *nm* camping; **(terrain de) ~** campsite, camping site; **faire du ~** to go camping; **camping-car** *nm* camper, motorhome *(US)*; **camping-gaz** ® *nm inv* camp(ing) stove

Canada [kanada] *nm*: **le ~** Canada; **canadien, ne** *adj* Canadian ♦ *nm/f*: **Canadien, ne** Canadian; **canadienne** *nf (veste)* fur-lined jacket

canaille [kanɑj] *(péj) nf* scoundrel

canal, -aux [kanal, o] *nm* canal; *(naturel)* channel; **canalisation** *nf (tuyau)* pipe; **canaliser** *vt* to canalize; *(fig)* to channel

canapé [kanape] *nm* settee, sofa

canard [kanaʀ] *nm* duck; *(fam: journal)* rag

canari [kanaʀi] *nm* canary

cancans [kɑ̃kɑ̃] *nmpl (malicious)* gossip *sg*

cancer [kɑ̃sɛʀ] *nm* cancer; *(signe)*: **le C~** Cancer; **~ de la peau** skin cancer

cancre [kɑ̃kʀ] *nm* dunce

candeur [kɑ̃dœʀ] *nf* ingenuousness, guilelessness

candidat, e [kɑ̃dida, at] *nm/f* candidate; *(à un poste)* applicant, candidate; **candidature** *nf (POL)* candidature; *(à poste)* application; **poser sa candidature à un poste** to apply for a job

candide [kɑ̃did] *adj* ingenuous, guileless

cane [kan] *nf (female)* duck

caneton [kantɔ̃] *nm* duckling

canette [kanɛt] *nf (de bière)* (flip-top) bottle

canevas [kanva] *nm (COUTURE)* canvas

caniche [kaniʃ] *nm* poodle

canicule [kanikyl] *nf* scorching heat

canif [kanif] *nm* penknife, pocket knife

canine [kanin] *nf* canine (tooth)

caniveau, x [kanivo] *nm* gutter

canne [kan] *nf (walking)* stick; **~ à pêche** fishing rod; **~ à sucre** sugar cane

cannelle [kanɛl] *nf* cinnamon

canoë [kanɔe] *nm* canoe; *(sport)* canoeing

canon [kanɔ̃] *nm (arme)* gun; *(HISTOIRE)* cannon; *(d'une arme: tube)* barrel; *(fig: norme)* model; *(MUS)* canon

canot [kano] *nm* ding(h)y; **~ de sauvetage** lifeboat; **~ pneumatique** inflatable ding(h)y; **canotier** *nm* boater

cantatrice [kɑ̃tatʀis] *nf (opera)* singer

cantine [kɑ̃tin] *nf* canteen

cantique [kɑ̃tik] *nm* hymn

canton [kɑ̃tɔ̃] *nm district consisting of several communes*; *(en Suisse)* canton

cantonade [kɑ̃tɔnad]: **à la ~** *adv* to everyone in general

cantonner [kɑ̃tɔne]: **se ~ à** *vt* to confine o.s. to

cantonnier [kɑ̃tɔnje] *nm* roadmender

canular [kanylaʀ] *nm* hoax

caoutchouc [kautʃu] *nm* rubber

cap [kap] *nm (GÉO)* cape; *(promontoire)* headland; *(fig: tournant)* watershed; *(NAVIG)*: **changer de ~** to change course; **mettre le ~ sur** to head *ou* steer for

CAP *sigle m (= Certificat d'aptitude professionnelle)* vocational training certificate taken at secondary school

capable [kapabl] *adj* able, capable; **~ de qch/faire** capable of sth/doing

capacité [kapasite] *nf (compétence)* ability; *(JUR, contenance)* capacity

cape [kap] *nf* cape, cloak; **rire sous ~** to laugh up one's sleeve

CAPES [kapɛs] *sigle m (= Certificat d'aptitude pédagogique à l'enseignement secondaire)* teaching diploma

capillaire [kapilɛʀ] *adj (soins, lotion)* hair *cpd*; *(vaisseau etc)* capillary

capitaine [kapitɛn] *nm* captain

capital, e, -aux [kapital, o] *adj (œuvre)* major; *(question, rôle)* fundamental ♦ *nm* capital; (*fig*) stock; **d'une importance ~e** of capital importance; *voir aussi* **capitaux**; **~ (social)** authorized capital; **capitale** *nf* (*ville*) capital; (*lettre*) capital (letter); **capitalisme** *nm* capitalism; **capitaliste** *adj*, *nm/f* capitalist; **capitaux** *nmpl* (*fonds*) capital *sg*

capitonné, e [kapitɔne] *adj* padded

caporal, -aux [kapɔral, o] *nm* lance corporal

capot [kapo] *nm* (*AUTO*) bonnet (*BRIT*), hood (*US*)

capote [kapɔt] *nf* (*de voiture*) hood (*BRIT*), top (*US*); (*fam*) condom

capoter [kapɔte] *vi* (*négociations*) to founder

câpre [kɑpʀ] *nf* caper

caprice [kapʀis] *nm* whim, caprice; **faire des ~s** to make a fuss; **capricieux, -euse** *adj* (*fantasque*) capricious, whimsical; (*enfant*) awkward

Capricorne [kapʀikɔʀn] *nm*: **le ~** Capricorn

capsule [kapsyl] *nf* (*de bouteille*) cap; (*BOT etc, spatiale*) capsule

capter [kapte] *vt* (*ondes radio*) to pick up; (*fig*) to win, capture

captivant, e [kaptivɑ̃, ɑ̃t] *adj* captivating

captivité [kaptivite] *nf* captivity

capturer [kaptyʀe] *vt* to capture

capuche [kapyʃ] *nf* hood

capuchon [kapyʃɔ̃] *nm* hood; (*de stylo*) cap, top

capucine [kapysin] *nf* (*BOT*) nasturtium

caquet [kakɛ] *nm*: **rabattre le ~ à qn** (*fam*) to bring sb down a peg or two

caqueter [kakte] *vi* to cackle

car [kaʀ] *nm* coach ♦ *conj* because, for

carabine [kaʀabin] *nf* rifle

caractère [kaʀaktɛʀ] *nm* (*gén*) character; **avoir bon/mauvais ~** to be good-/ill-natured; **en ~s gras** in bold type; **en petits ~s** in small print; **~s d'imprimerie** (block) capitals; **caractériel, le** *adj* (*traits*) (of) character; (*enfant*) emotionally disturbed

caractérisé, e [kaʀakteʀize] *adj* sheer, downright

caractériser [kaʀakteʀize] *vt* to be characteristic of

caractéristique [kaʀakteʀistik] *adj*, *nf* characteristic

carafe [kaʀaf] *nf* (*pour eau, vin ordinaire*) carafe

caraïbe [kaʀaib] *adj* Caribbean ♦ *n*: **les C~s** the Caribbean (Islands)

carambolage [kaʀɑ̃bɔlaʒ] *nm* multiple crash, pileup

caramel [kaʀamɛl] *nm* (*bonbon*) caramel, toffee; (*substance*) caramel

carapace [kaʀapas] *nf* shell

caravane [kaʀavan] *nf* caravan; **caravaning** *nm* caravanning

carbone [kaʀbɔn] *nm* carbon; (*double*) carbon (copy); **carbonique** *adj*: **gaz carbonique** carbon dioxide; **neige carbonique** dry ice; **carbonisé, e** *adj* charred

carburant [kaʀbyʀɑ̃] *nm* (motor) fuel

carburateur [kaʀbyʀatœʀ] *nm* carburettor

carcan [kaʀkɑ̃] *nm* (*fig*) yoke, shackles *pl*

carcasse [kaʀkas] *nf* carcass; (*de véhicule etc*) shell

cardiaque [kaʀdjak] *adj* cardiac, heart *cpd* ♦ *nm/f* heart patient; **être ~** to have heart trouble

cardigan [kaʀdigɑ̃] *nm* cardigan

cardiologue [kaʀdjɔlɔg] *nm/f* cardiologist, heart specialist

carême [kaʀɛm] *nm*: **le C~** Lent

carence [kaʀɑ̃s] *nf* (*manque*) deficiency

caresse [kaʀɛs] *nf* caress

caresser [kaʀese] *vt* to caress; (*animal*) to stroke

cargaison [kaʀgɛzɔ̃] *nf* cargo, freight

cargo [kaʀgo] *nm* cargo boat, freighter

caricature [kaʀikatyʀ] *nf* caricature

carie [kaʀi] *nf*: **la ~ (dentaire)** tooth decay; **une ~** a bad tooth

carillon [kaʀijɔ̃] *nm* (*air, de pendule*) chimes *pl*

caritatif, -ive [kaʀitatif, iv] *adj*: **organisation caritative** charity

carnassier, -ière [kaʀnasje, jɛʀ] *adj* carnivorous

carnaval [kaʀnaval] *nm* carnival

carnet [kaʀnɛ] *nm* (*calepin*) notebook; (*de tickets, timbres etc*) book; **~ de chèques** cheque book; **~ de notes** school report

carotte [kaʀɔt] *nf* carrot

carpette [kaʀpɛt] *nf* rug

carré, e [kaʀe] *adj* square; (*fig: franc*) straightforward ♦ *nm* (MATH) square; **mètre/kilomètre ~** square metre/kilometre

carreau, x [kaʀo] *nm* (*par terre*) (floor) tile; (*au mur*) (wall) tile; (*de fenêtre*) (window) pane; (*motif*) check, square; (CARTES: *couleur*) diamonds *pl*; **tissu à ~x** checked fabric

carrefour [kaʀfuʀ] *nm* crossroads *sg*

carrelage [kaʀlaʒ] *nm* (*sol*) (tiled) floor

carrelet [kaʀlɛ] *nm* (*poisson*) plaice

carrément [kaʀemɑ̃] *adv* (*franchement*) straight out, bluntly; (*sans hésiter*) straight; (*intensif*) completely; **c'est ~ impossible** it's completely impossible

carrière [kaʀjɛʀ] *nf* (*métier*) career; (*de roches*) quarry; **militaire de ~** professional soldier

carrossable [kaʀɔsabl] *adj* suitable for (motor) vehicles

carrosse [kaʀɔs] *nm* (horse-drawn) coach

carrosserie [kaʀɔsʀi] *nf* body, coachwork *no pl*

carrure [kaʀyʀ] *nf* build; (*fig*) stature, calibre

cartable [kaʀtabl] *nm* satchel, (school)bag

carte [kaʀt] *nf* (*de géographie*) map; (*marine, du ciel*) chart; (*d'abonnement, à jouer*) card; (*au restaurant*) menu; (*aussi:* **~ de visite**) (visiting) card; **à la ~** (*au restaurant*) à la carte; **donner ~ blanche à qn** to give sb a free rein; **~ bancaire** cash card; **~ de crédit** credit card; **~ de fidélité** loyalty card; **~ d'identité** identity card; **~ de séjour** residence permit; **~ grise** (AUTO) ≈ (car) registration book, logbook; **~ postale** postcard; **~ routière** road map; **~ té-**léphonique phonecard

carter [kaʀtɛʀ] *nm* sump

carton [kaʀtɔ̃] *nm* (*matériau*) cardboard; (*boîte*) (cardboard) box; **faire un ~** (*fam*) to score a hit; **~ (à dessin)** portfolio; **carton-pâte** *nm* pasteboard

cartouche [kaʀtuʃ] *nf* cartridge; (*de cigarettes*) carton

cas [kɑ] *nm* case; **ne faire aucun ~ de** to take no notice of; **en aucun ~** on no account; **au ~ où** in case; **en ~ de** in case of, in the event of; **en ~ de besoin** if need be; **en tout ~** in any case, at any rate; **~ de conscience** matter of conscience

casanier, -ière [kazanje, jɛʀ] *adj* stay-at-home

cascade [kaskad] *nf* waterfall, cascade; (*fig*) stream, torrent; **cascadeur, -euse** *nm/f* stuntman(-girl)

case [kɑz] *nf* (*hutte*) hut; (*compartiment*) compartment; (*sur un formulaire, de mots croisés etc*) box

caser [kɑze] (*fam*) *vt* (*placer*) to put (away); (*loger*) to put up; **se ~** *vi* (*se marier*) to settle down; (*trouver un emploi*) to find a (steady) job

caserne [kazɛʀn] *nf* barracks *pl*

cash [kaʃ] *adv*: **payer ~** to pay cash down

casier [kɑzje] *nm* (*pour courrier*) pigeon-hole; (*compartiment*) compartment; (*à clef*) locker; **~ judiciaire** police record

casino [kazino] *nm* casino

casque [kask] *nm* helmet; (*chez le coiffeur*) (hair-)drier; (*pour audition*) (head-)phones *pl*, headset

casquette [kaskɛt] *nf* cap

cassant, e [kɑsɑ̃, ɑ̃t] *adj* brittle; (*fig: ton*) curt, abrupt

cassation [kɑsasjɔ̃] *nf*: **cour de ~** final court of appeal

casse [kɑs] (*fam*) *nf* (*pour voitures*): **mettre à la ~** to scrap; (*dégâts*): **il y a eu de la ~** there were a lot of breakages; **casse-cou** *adj inv* daredevil, reckless; **casse-croûte** *nm inv* snack; **casse-noix** *nm* *inv* nutcrackers *pl*; **casse-pieds** (*fam*) *adj inv*: **il est casse-pieds** he's a pain in the neck

casser [kase] *vt* to break; (*JUR*) to quash; **se ~** *vi* to break; **~ les pieds à qn** (*fam: irriter*) to get on sb's nerves; **se ~ la tête** (*fam*) to go to a lot of trouble

casserole [kasrɔl] *nf* saucepan

casse-tête [kastet] *nm inv* (*difficultés*) headache (*fig*)

cassette [kaset] *nf* (*bande magnétique*) cassette; (*coffret*) casket

casseur [kasœr] *nm* hooligan

cassis [kasis] *nm* blackcurrant

cassoulet [kasulɛ] *nm* bean and sausage hot-pot

cassure [kasyr] *nf* break, crack

castor [kastɔr] *nm* beaver

castrer [kastre] *vt* (*mâle*) to castrate; (: *cheval*) to geld; (*femelle*) to spay

catalogue [katalɔg] *nm* catalogue

cataloguer [katalɔge] *vt* to catalogue, to list; (*péj*) to put a label on

catalyseur [katalizœr] *nm* catalyst; **catalytique** *adj*: **pot catalytique** catalytic convertor

catastrophe [katastrɔf] *nf* catastrophe, disaster; **catastrophé, e** (*fam*) *adj* stunned

catch [katʃ] *nm* (all-in) wrestling

catéchisme [kateʃism] *nm* catechism

catégorie [kategɔri] *nf* category; **catégorique** *adj* categorical

cathédrale [katedral] *nf* cathedral

catholique [katɔlik] *adj, nm/f* (Roman) Catholic; **pas très ~** a bit shady *ou* fishy

catimini [katimini]: **en ~** *adv* on the sly

cauchemar [koʃmar] *nm* nightmare

cause [koz] *nf* cause; (*JUR*) lawsuit, case; **à ~ de** because of, owing to; **pour ~ de** on account of; **(et) pour ~** and for (a very) good reason; **être en ~** (*intérêts*) to be at stake; **remettre en ~** to challenge; **causer** *vt* to cause ♦ *vi* to chat, talk; **causerie** *nf* (*conférence*) talk; **causette** *nf*: **faire la causette** to have a chat

caution [kosjɔ̃] *nf* guarantee, security; (*JUR*) bail (bond); (*fig*) backing, support; **libéré sous ~** released on bail; **cautionner** *vt* (*répondre de*) to guarantee; (*soutenir*) to support

cavalcade [kavalkad] *nf* (*fig*) stampede

cavalier, -ière [kavalje, jer] *adj* (*désinvolte*) offhand ♦ *nm/f* rider; (*au bal*) partner ♦ *nm* (*ÉCHECS*) knight

cave [kav] *nf* cellar

caveau, x [kavo] *nm* vault

caverne [kavern] *nf* cave

CCP *sigle m* = **compte chèques postaux**

CD *sigle m* (= *compact disc*) CD

CD-ROM [sederɔm] *sigle m* CD-ROM

CE *n abr* (= *Communauté Européenne*) EC

MOT-CLÉ

---

ce, cette [sə, sɛt] (*devant nm* **cet** + *voyelle ou h aspiré; pl* **ces**) *dét* (*proximité*) this; these *pl*; (*non-proximité*) that; those *pl*; **cette maison(-ci/là)** this/that house; **cette nuit** (*qui vient*) tonight; (*passée*) last night

♦ *pron* **1**: **c'est** it's *ou* it is; **c'est un peintre** he's *ou* he is a painter; **ce sont des peintres** they're *ou* they are painters; **c'est le facteur** (*à la porte*) it's the postman; **qui est-ce?** who is it?; (*en désignant*) who is he/she?; **qu'est-ce?** what is it?

2: **ce qui, ce que** what; (*chose qui*): **il est bête, ce qui me chagrine** he's stupid, which saddens me; **tout ce qui bouge** everything that *ou* which moves; **tout ce que je sais** all I know; **ce dont j'ai parlé** what I talked about; **ce que c'est grand!** it's so big!; *voir aussi* **-ci**; **est-ce que**; **n'est-ce pas**; **c'est-à-dire**

---

ceci [səsi] *pron* this

cécité [sesite] *nf* blindness

céder [sede] *vt* (*donner*) to give up ♦ *vi* (*chaise, barrage*) to give way; (*personne*) to give in; **~ à** to yield to, give in to

CEDEX [sedɛks] *sigle m* (= *courrier*

d'entreprise à distribution exceptionnelle) post-al service for bulk users

cédille [sedij] *nf* cedilla

cèdre [sedʀ] *nm* cedar

CEI *abr m* (= *Communauté des États Indépendants*) CIS

ceinture [sɛ̃tyʀ] *nf* belt; (*taille*) waist; **~ de sécurité** safety *ou* seat belt

cela [s(ə)la] *pron* that; (*comme sujet indéfini*) it; **quand/où ~?** when/where (was that)?

célèbre [selɛbʀ] *adj* famous; **célébrer** *vt* to celebrate

céleri [sɛlʀi] *nm*: **~-rave** celeriac; **~ (en branche)** celery

célibat [seliba] *nm* (*homme*) bachelorhood; (*femme*) spinsterhood; (*prêtre*) celibacy; **célibataire** *adj* single, unmarried ♦ *nm* bachelor ♦ *nf* unmarried woman

celle(s) [sɛl] *pron voir* **celui**

cellier [selje] *nm* storeroom (*for wine*)

cellule [selyl] *nf* (*gén*) cell

cellulite [selylit] *nf* excess fat, cellulite

MOT-CLÉ

celui, celle [səlɥi, sɛl] (*mpl* **ceux**, *fpl* **celles**) *pron* 1: **celui-ci/là, celle-ci/là** this one/that one; **ceux-ci, celles-ci** these (ones); **ceux-là, celles-là** those (ones); **celui de mon frère** my brother's; **celui du salon/du dessous** the one in (*ou* from) the lounge/below

2: **celui qui bouge** the one which *ou* that moves; (*personne*) the one who moves; **celui que je vois** the one (which *ou* that) I see; the one (whom) I see; **celui dont je parle** the one I'm talking about

3 (*valeur indéfinie*): **celui qui veut** whoever wants

---

cendre [sɑ̃dʀ] *nf* ash; **~s** *nfpl* (*d'un défunt*) ashes; **sous la ~** (*CULIN*) in (the) embers; **cendrier** *nm* ashtray

cène [sɛn] *nf*: **la ~** (Holy) Communion

censé, e [sɑ̃se] *adj*: **être ~ faire** to be supposed to do

censeur [sɑ̃sœʀ] *nm* (*SCOL*) deputy-head

(*BRIT*), vice-principal (*US*); (*CINÉMA, POL*) censor

censure [sɑ̃syʀ] *nf* censorship; **censurer** *vt* (*CINÉMA, PRESSE*) to censor; (*POL*) to censure

cent [sɑ̃] *num* a hundred, one hundred; **centaine** *nf*: **une centaine (de)** about a hundred, a hundred or so; **des centaines (de)** hundreds (of); **centenaire** *adj* hundred-year-old ♦ *nm* (*anniversaire*) centenary; (*monnaie*) cent **centième** *num* hundredth; **centigrade** *nm* centigrade; **centilitre** *nm* centilitre; **centime** *nm* centime; **centimètre** *nm* centimetre; (*ruban*) tape measure, measuring tape

central, e, -aux [sɑ̃tʀal, o] *adj* central ♦ *nm*: **~ (téléphonique)** (telephone) exchange; **centrale** *nf* power station

centre [sɑ̃tʀ] *nm* centre; **~ commercial** shopping centre; **centre-ville** *nm* town centre, downtown (area) (*US*)

centuple [sɑ̃typl] *nm*: **le ~ de qch** a hundred times sth; **au ~** a hundredfold

cep [sɛp] *nm* (vine) stock

cèpe [sɛp] *nm* (edible) boletus

cependant [s(ə)pɑ̃dɑ̃] *adv* however

céramique [seramik] *nf* ceramics *sg*

cercle [sɛʀkl] *nm* circle; **~ vicieux** vicious circle

cercueil [sɛʀkœj] *nm* coffin

céréale [sereal] *nf* cereal; **~s** *nfpl* breakfast cereal

cérémonie [seremɔni] *nf* ceremony; **sans ~** informally

cerf [sɛʀ] *nm* stag

cerfeuil [sɛʀfœj] *nm* chervil

cerf-volant [sɛʀvɔlɑ̃] *nm* kite

cerise [s(ə)ʀiz] *nf* cherry; **cerisier** *nm* cherry (tree)

cerne [sɛʀn] *nm*: **avoir des ~s** to have shadows *ou* dark rings under one's eyes

cerner [sɛʀne] *vt* (*MIL etc*) to surround; (*fig: problème*) to delimit, define

certain, e [sɛʀtɛ̃, ɛn] *adj* certain ♦ *dét* certain; **d'un ~ âge** past one's prime, not so young; **un ~ temps** (quite) some time; **~s**

♦ *pron* some; **certainement** *adv* (*proba-blement*) most probably *ou* likely; (*bien sûr*) certainly, of course

certes [sɛʀt] *adv* (*sans doute*) admittedly; (*bien sûr*) of course

certificat [sɛʀtifika] *nm* certificate

certifier [sɛʀtifje] *vt*: **~ qch à qn** to assure sb of sth; **copie certifiée conforme (à l'original)** certified copy of the original

certitude [sɛʀtityd] *nf* certainty

cerveau, x [sɛʀvo] *nm* brain

cervelas [sɛʀvəla] *nm* saveloy

cervelle [sɛʀvɛl] *nf* (*ANAT*) brain; (*CULIN*) brains

ces [se] *dét voir* **ce**

CES *sigle m* (= *Collège d'enseignement se-condaire*) ≃ (junior) secondary school (*BRIT*)

cesse [sɛs]: **sans ~** *adv* (*tout le temps*) continually, constantly; (*sans interruption*) continuously; **il n'a eu de ~ que** he did not rest until; **cesser** *vt* to stop ♦ *vi* to stop, cease; **cesser de faire** to stop doing; **cessez-le-feu** *nm inv* ceasefire

c'est-à-dire [sɛtadiʀ] *adv* that is (to say)

cet, cette [sɛt] *dét voir* **ce**

ceux [sø] *pron voir* **celui**

CFC *abr* (= *chlorofluorocarbon*) CFC

CFDT *sigle f* (= *Confédération française dé-mocratique du travail*) *French trade union*

CGT *sigle f* (= *Confédération générale du tra-vail*) *French trade union*

chacun, e [ʃakœ̃, yn] *pron* each; (*indéfini*) everyone, everybody

chagrin [ʃagʀɛ̃] *nm* grief, sorrow; **avoir du ~** to be grieved; **chagriner** *vt* to grieve

chahut [ʃay] *nm* uproar; **chahuter** *vt* to rag, bait ♦ *vi* to make an uproar

chaîne [ʃɛn] *nf* chain; (*RADIO, TV: stations*) channel; **~s** *nfpl* (*AUTO*) (snow) chains; **travail à la ~** production line work; **~ (de montage)** production *ou* assembly line; **~ de montagnes** mountain range; **~ (hi-fi)** hi-fi system; **~ laser** CD player; **~ (stéréo)** stereo (system); **chaînette** *nf* (small) chain

chair [ʃɛʀ] *nf* flesh; **avoir la ~ de poule** to

have goosepimples *ou* gooseflesh; **bien en ~** plump, well-padded; **en ~ et en os** in the flesh; **~ à saucisse** sausage meat

chaire [ʃɛʀ] *nf* (*d'église*) pulpit; (*d'université*) chair

chaise [ʃɛz] *nf* chair; **~ longue** deckchair

châle [ʃɑl] *nm* shawl

chaleur [ʃalœʀ] *nf* heat; (*fig: accueil*) warmth; **chaleureux, -euse** *adj* warm

chaloupe [ʃalup] *nf* launch; (*de sauvetage*) lifeboat

chalumeau, x [ʃalymo] *nm* blowlamp, blowtorch

chalutier [ʃalytje] *nm* trawler

chamailler [ʃamaje]: **se ~** *vi* to squabble, bicker

chambouler [ʃɑ̃bule] (*fam*) *vt* to disrupt, turn upside down

chambre [ʃɑ̃bʀ] *nf* bedroom; (*POL, COMM*) chamber; **faire ~ à part** to sleep in sepa-rate rooms; **~ à air** (*de pneu*) (inner) tube; **~ à coucher** bedroom; **~ à un lit/deux lits** (*à l'hôtel*) single-/twin-bedded room; **~ d'amis** spare *ou* guest room; **~ noire** (*PHOTO*) dark room; **chambrer** *vt* (*vin*) to bring to room temperature

chameau, x [ʃamo] *nm* camel

chamois [ʃamwa] *nm* chamois

champ [ʃɑ̃] *nm* field; **~ de bataille** battle-field; **~ de courses** racecourse; **~ de tir** rifle range

champagne [ʃɑ̃paɲ] *nm* champagne

champêtre [ʃɑ̃pɛtʀ] *adj* country *cpd*, rural

champignon [ʃɑ̃piɲɔ̃] *nm* mushroom; (*terme générique*) fungus; **~ de Paris** but-ton mushroom

champion, ne [ʃɑ̃pjɔ̃, jɔn] *adj, nm/f* champion; **championnat** *nm* champion-ship

chance [ʃɑ̃s] *nf*: **la ~** luck; **~s** *nfpl* (*proba-bilités*) chances; **avoir de la ~** to be lucky; **il a des ~s de réussir** he's got a good chance of passing

chanceler [ʃɑ̃s(ə)le] *vi* to totter

chancelier [ʃɑ̃səlje] *nm* (*allemand*) chan-cellor

chanceux, -euse [ʃɑ̃sø, øz] *adj* lucky

chandail [ʃɑ̃daj] *nm* (thick) sweater

Chandeleur [ʃɑ̃dlœʀ] *nf*: **la ~** Candlemas

chandelier [ʃɑ̃dəlje] *nm* candlestick

chandelle [ʃɑ̃dɛl] *nf* (tallow) candle; **dîner aux ~s** candlelight dinner

change [ʃɑ̃ʒ] *nm* (*devises*) exchange

changement [ʃɑ̃ʒmɑ̃] *nm* change; **~ de vitesses** gears *pl*

changer [ʃɑ̃ʒe] *vt* (*modifier*) to change, alter; (*remplacer*, COMM) to change ♦ *vi* to change, alter; **se ~** *vi* to change (o.s.); **~ de** (*remplacer: adresse, nom, voiture etc*) to change one's; (*échanger: place, train etc*) to change; **~ d'avis** to change one's mind; **~ de vitesse** to change gear

chanson [ʃɑ̃sɔ̃] *nf* song

chant [ʃɑ̃] *nm* song; (*art vocal*) singing; (*d'église*) hymn

chantage [ʃɑ̃taʒ] *nm* blackmail; **faire du ~** to use blackmail

chanter [ʃɑ̃te] *vt, vi* to sing; **si cela lui chante** (*fam*) if he feels like it; **chanteur, -euse** *nm/f* singer

chantier [ʃɑ̃tje] *nm* (building) site; (*sur une route*) roadworks *pl*; **mettre en ~** to put in hand; **~ naval** shipyard

chantilly [ʃɑ̃tiji] *nf voir* **crème**

chantonner [ʃɑ̃tɔne] *vi, vt* to sing to oneself, hum

chanvre [ʃɑ̃vʀ] *nm* hemp

chaparder [ʃapaʀde] (*fam*) *vt* to pinch

chapeau, x [ʃapo] *nm* hat; **~!** well done!

chapelet [ʃaplɛ] *nm* (REL) rosary

chapelle [ʃapɛl] *nf* chapel

chapelure [ʃaplyʀ] *nf* (dried) breadcrumbs *pl*

chapiteau, x [ʃapito] *nm* (*de cirque*) marquee, big top

chapitre [ʃapitʀ] *nm* chapter

chaque [ʃak] *dét* each, every; (*indéfini*) every

char [ʃaʀ] *nm* (MIL): **~ (d'assaut)** tank; **~ à voile** sand yacht

charabia [ʃaʀabja] (*péj*) *nm* gibberish

charade [ʃaʀad] *nf* riddle; (*mimée*) charade

charbon [ʃaʀbɔ̃] *nm* coal; **~ de bois** charcoal

charcuterie [ʃaʀkytʀi] *nf* (*magasin*) pork butcher's shop and delicatessen; (*produits*) cooked pork meats *pl*; **charcutier, -ière** *nm/f* pork butcher

chardon [ʃaʀdɔ̃] *nm* thistle

charge [ʃaʀʒ] *nf* (*fardeau*) load, burden; (*explosif, ÉLEC, MIL, JUR*) charge; (*rôle, mission*) responsibility; **~s** *nfpl* (*du loyer*) service charges; **à la ~ de** (*dépendant de*) dependent upon; (*aux frais de*) chargeable to; **prendre en ~** to take charge of; (*suj: véhicule*) to take on; (*dépenses*) to take care of; **~s sociales** social security contributions

chargé, e [ʃaʀʒe] *adj* (*emploi du temps, journée*) full, heavy

chargement [ʃaʀʒəmɑ̃] *nm* (*objets*) load

charger [ʃaʀʒe] *vt* (*voiture, fusil, caméra*) to load; (*batterie*) to charge ♦ *vi* (MIL *etc*) to charge; **se ~ de** *vt* to see to; **~ qn de (faire) qch** to put sb in charge of (doing) sth

chariot [ʃaʀjo] *nm* trolley; (*charrette*) waggon

charité [ʃaʀite] *nf* charity

charmant, e [ʃaʀmɑ̃, ɑ̃t] *adj* charming

charme [ʃaʀm] *nm* charm; **charmer** *vt* to charm

charnel, le [ʃaʀnɛl] *adj* carnal

charnière [ʃaʀnjɛʀ] *nf* hinge; (*fig*) turning-point

charnu, e [ʃaʀny] *adj* fleshy

charpente [ʃaʀpɑ̃t] *nf* frame(work); **charpentier** *nm* carpenter

charpie [ʃaʀpi] *nf*: **en ~** (*fig*) in shreds *ou* ribbons

charrette [ʃaʀɛt] *nf* cart

charrier [ʃaʀje] *vt* (*entraîner: fleuve*) to carry (along); (*transporter*) to cart, carry

charrue [ʃaʀy] *nf* plough (BRIT), plow (US)

charter [ʃaʀtɛʀ] *nm* (*vol*) charter flight

chasse [ʃas] *nf* hunting; (*au fusil*) shooting; (*poursuite*) chase; (*aussi: ~ d'eau*) flush; **~ gardée** private hunting grounds *pl*; **prendre en ~** to give chase to; **tirer la ~ (d'eau)** to flush the toilet, pull the chain; **~ à courre** hunting; **chasse-neige** *nm inv* snowplough (*BRIT*), snowplow (*US*); **chasser** *vt* to hunt; (*expulser*) to chase away *ou* out, drive away *ou* out; **chasseur, -euse** *nm/f* hunter ♦ *nm* (*avion*) fighter

châssis [ʃɑsi] *nm* (*AUTO*) chassis; (*cadre*) frame

chat [ʃa] *nm* cat

châtaigne [ʃatɛɲ] *nf* chestnut; **châtaignier** *nm* chestnut (tree)

châtain [ʃatɛ̃] *adj inv* (*cheveux*) chestnut (brown); (*personne*) chestnut-haired

château, x [ʃato] *nm* (*forteresse*) castle; (*résidence royale*) palace; (*manoir*) mansion; **~ d'eau** water tower; **~ fort** stronghold, fortified castle

châtier [ʃatje] *vt* to punish; **châtiment** *nm* punishment

chaton [ʃatɔ̃] *nm* (*ZOOL*) kitten

chatouiller [ʃatuje] *vt* to tickle; **chatouilleux, -euse** *adj* ticklish; (*fig*) touchy, over-sensitive

chatoyer [ʃatwaje] *vi* to shimmer

châtrer [ʃɑtʀe] *vt* (*mâle*) to castrate; (: *cheval*) to geld; (*femelle*) to spay

chatte [ʃat] *nf* (she-)cat

chaud, e [ʃo, ʃod] *adj* (*gén*) warm; (*très ~*) hot; **il fait ~** it's warm; it's hot; **avoir ~** to be warm; to be hot; **ça me tient ~** it keeps me warm; **rester au ~** to stay in the warm

chaudière [ʃodjɛʀ] *nf* boiler

chaudron [ʃodʀɔ̃] *nm* cauldron

chauffage [ʃofaʒ] *nm* heating; **~ central** central heating

chauffard [ʃofaʀ] *nm* (*péj*) reckless driver

chauffe-eau [ʃofo] *nm inv* water-heater

chauffer [ʃofe] *vt* to heat ♦ *vi* to heat up, warm up; (*trop ~: moteur*) to overheat; **se ~ vi** (*au soleil*) to warm o.s.

chauffeur [ʃofœʀ] *nm* driver; (*privé*) chauffeur

chaume [ʃom] *nm* (*du toit*) thatch; **chau-**

mière *nf* (thatched) cottage

chaussée [ʃose] *nf* road(way)

chausse-pied [ʃospje] *nm* shoe-horn

chausser [ʃose] *vt* (*bottes, skis*) to put on; (*enfant*) to put shoes on; **~ du 38/42** to take size 38/42

chaussette [ʃosɛt] *nf* sock

chausson [ʃosɔ̃] *nm* slipper; (*de bébé*) bootee; **~ (aux pommes)** (apple) turn-over

chaussure [ʃosyʀ] *nf* shoe; **~s à talon** high-heeled shoes; **~s de marche** walking shoes/boots; **~s de ski** ski boots

chauve [ʃov] *adj* bald; **chauve-souris** *nf* bat

chauvin, e [ʃovɛ̃, in] *adj* chauvinistic

chaux [ʃo] *nf* lime; **blanchi à la ~** white-washed

chavirer [ʃaviʀe] *vi* to capsize

chef [ʃɛf] *nm* head, leader; (*de cuisine*) chef; **~ d'accusation** charge; **~ d'entreprise** company head; **~ d'état** head of state; **~ de famille** head of the family; **~ de gare** station master; **~ d'orchestre** conductor; **~ de service** department head; **chef-d'œuvre** *nm* masterpiece; **chef-lieu** *nm* county town

chemin [ʃ(ə)mɛ̃] *nm* path; (*itinéraire, direction, trajet*) way; **en ~** on the way; **~ de fer** railway (*BRIT*), railroad (*US*); **par ~ de fer** by rail

cheminée [ʃ(ə)mine] *nf* chimney; (*à l'intérieur*) chimney piece, fireplace; (*de bateau*) funnel

cheminement [ʃ(ə)minmɑ̃] *nm* progress

cheminot [ʃ(ə)mino] *nm* railwayman

chemise [ʃ(ə)miz] *nf* shirt; (*dossier*) folder; **~ de nuit** nightdress

chemisier [ʃ(ə)mizje, jɛʀ] *nm* blouse

chenal, -aux [ʃanal, o] *nm* channel

chêne [ʃɛn] *nm* oak (tree); (*bois*) oak

chenil [ʃ(ə)nil] *nm* kennels *pl*

chenille [ʃ(ə)nij] *nf* (*ZOOL*) caterpillar

chèque [ʃɛk] *nm* cheque (*BRIT*), check (*US*); **~ sans provision** bad cheque; **~ de**

voyage traveller's cheque; **chéquier** [ʃekje] *nm* cheque book

cher, -ère [ʃɛʀ] *adj* (*aimé*) dear; (*coûteux*) expensive, dear ♦ *adv*: **ça coûte ~** it's expensive

chercher [ʃɛʀʃe] *vt* to look for; (*gloire etc*) to seek; **aller ~** to go for, go and fetch; **~ à faire** to try to do; **chercheur, -euse** *nm/f* researcher, research worker

chère [ʃɛʀ] *adj voir* **cher**

chéri, e [ʃeʀi] *adj* beloved, dear; **(mon) ~** darling

chérir [ʃeʀiʀ] *vt* to cherish

cherté [ʃɛʀte] *nf*: **la ~ de la vie** the high cost of living

chétif, -ive [ʃetif, iv] *adj* (*enfant*) puny

cheval, -aux [ʃ(ə)val, o] *nm* horse; (*AUTO*): **~ (vapeur)** horsepower *no pl*; **faire du ~** to ride; **à ~** on horseback; **à ~ sur** astride; (*fig*) overlapping; **~ de course** racehorse

chevalet [ʃ(ə)valɛ] *nm* easel

chevalier [ʃ(ə)valje] *nm* knight

chevalière [ʃ(ə)valjɛʀ] *nf* signet ring

chevalin, e [ʃ(ə)valɛ̃, in] *adj*: **boucherie ~e** horse-meat butcher's

chevaucher [ʃ(ə)voʃe] *vi* (*aussi*: **se ~**) to overlap (each other) ♦ *vt* to be astride, straddle

chevaux [ʃəvo] *nmpl de* **cheval**

chevelu, e [ʃəv(ə)ly] (*péj*) *adj* long-haired

chevelure [ʃəv(ə)lyʀ] *nf* hair *no pl*

chevet [ʃ(ə)vɛ] *nm*: **au ~ de qn** at sb's bedside; **lampe de ~** bedside lamp

cheveu, x [ʃ(ə)vø] *nm* hair; **~x** *nmpl* (*chevelure*) hair *sg*; **avoir les ~x courts** to have short hair

cheville [ʃ(ə)vij] *nf* (*ANAT*) ankle; (*de bois*) peg; (*pour une vis*) plug

chèvre [ʃɛvʀ] *nf* (she-)goat

chevreau, x [ʃəvʀo] *nm* kid

chèvrefeuille [ʃɛvʀəfœj] *nm* honeysuckle

chevreuil [ʃəvʀœj] *nm* roe deer *inv*; (*CULIN*) venison

chevronné, e [ʃəvʀɔne] *adj* seasoned

MOT-CLÉ

chez [ʃe] *prép* **1** (*à la demeure de*) at; (: *direction*) to; **chez qn** at/to sb's house *ou* place; **chez moi** at home; (*direction*) home

2 (*+profession*) at; (: *direction*) to; **chez le boulanger/dentiste** at *ou* to the baker's/dentist's

3 (*dans le caractère, l'œuvre de*) in; **chez les renards/Racine** in foxes/Racine

---

chez-soi [ʃeswa] *nm inv* home

chic [ʃik] *adj inv* chic, smart; (*fam: généreux*) nice, decent ♦ *nm* stylishness; **~ (alors)!** (*fam*) great!; **avoir le ~ de** to have the knack of

chicane [ʃikan] *nf* (*querelle*) squabble; **chicaner** *vi* (*ergoter*): **chicaner sur** to quibble about

chiche [ʃiʃ] *adj* niggardly, mean ♦ *excl* (*à un défi*) you're on!

chichis [ʃiʃi] (*fam*) *nmpl* fuss *sg*

chicorée [ʃikɔʀe] *nf* (*café*) chicory; (*salade*) endive

chien [ʃjɛ̃] *nm* dog; **~ de garde** guard dog; **chien-loup** *nm* wolfhound

chiendent [ʃjɛ̃dɑ̃] *nm* couch grass

chienne [ʃjɛn] *nf* dog, bitch

chier [ʃje] (*fam!*) *vi* to crap (!)

chiffon [ʃifɔ̃] *nm* (*piece of*) rag; **chiffonner** *vt* to crumple; (*fam: tracasser*) to concern

chiffre [ʃifʀ] *nm* (*représentant un nombre*) figure, numeral; (*montant, total*) total, sum; **en ~s ronds** in round figures; **~ d'affaires** turnover; **chiffrer** *vt* (*dépense*) to put a figure to, assess; (*message*) to (en)code, cipher; **se chiffrer à** to add up to, amount to

chignon [ʃiɲɔ̃] *nm* chignon, bun

Chili [ʃili] *nm*: **le ~** Chile; **chilien, ne** *adj* Chilean ♦ *nm/f*: **Chilien, ne** Chilean

chimie [ʃimi] *nf* chemistry; **chimique** *adj* chemical; **produits chimiques** chemicals

chimpanzé [ʃɛ̃pɑ̃ze] *nm* chimpanzee

Chine [ʃin] *nf*: **la ~** China; **chinois, e** *adj* Chinese ♦ *nm/f*: **Chinois, e** Chinese ♦ *nm* (*LING*) Chinese

chiot [ʃjo] *nm* pup(py)

chiper [ʃipe] (*fam*) *vt* to pinch

chipoter [ʃipɔte] (*fam*) *vi* (*ergoter*) to quibble

chips [ʃips] *nfpl* crisps (*BRIT*), (potato) chips (*US*)

chiquenaude [ʃiknod] *nf* flick, flip

chirurgical, e, -aux [ʃiʀyʀʒikal, o] *adj* surgical

chirurgie [ʃiʀyʀʒi] *nf* surgery; **~ esthétique** plastic surgery; **chirurgien, ne** *nm/f* surgeon

chlore [klɔʀ] *nm* chlorine

choc [ʃɔk] *nm* (*heurt*) impact, shock; (*collision*) crash; (*moral*) shock; (*affrontement*) clash

chocolat [ʃɔkɔla] *nm* chocolate; **~ au lait** milk chocolate; **~ (chaud)** hot chocolate

chœur [kœʀ] *nm* (*chorale*) choir; (*OPÉRA, THÉÂTRE*) chorus; **en ~** in chorus

choisir [ʃwaziʀ] *vt* to choose, select

choix [ʃwa] *nm* choice, selection; **avoir le ~** to have the choice; **premier ~** (*COMM*) class one; **de ~** choice, selected; **au ~** as you wish

chômage [ʃomaʒ] *nm* unemployment; **mettre au ~** to make redundant, put out of work; **être au ~** to be unemployed *ou* out of work; **chômeur, -euse** *nm/f* unemployed person

chope [ʃɔp] *nf* tankard

choper [ʃɔpe] (*fam*) *vt* (*objet, maladie*) to catch

choquer [ʃɔke] *vt* (*offenser*) to shock; (*deuil*) to shake

chorale [kɔʀal] *nf* choir

choriste [kɔʀist] *nm/f* choir member; (*OPÉRA*) chorus member

chose [ʃoz] *nf* thing; **c'est peu de ~** it's nothing (much)

chou, x [ʃu] *nm* cabbage; **mon petit ~** (my) sweetheart; **~ à la crème** choux bun; **~x de Bruxelles** Brussels sprouts;

chouchou, te (*fam*) *nm/f* darling; (*SCOL*) teacher's pet; **choucroute** *nf* sauerkraut

chouette [ʃwet] *nf* owl ♦ *adj* (*fam*) great, smashing

chou-fleur [ʃuflœʀ] *nm* cauliflower

choyer [ʃwaje] *vt* (*dorloter*) to cherish; (: *excessivement*) to pamper

chrétien, ne [kʀetjɛ̃, jɛn] *adj, nm/f* Christian

Christ [kʀist] *nm*: **le ~** Christ; **christianisme** *nm* Christianity

chrome [kʀom] *nm* chromium; **chromé, e** *adj* chromium-plated

chronique [kʀɔnik] *adj* chronic ♦ *nf* (*de journal*) column, page; (*historique*) chronicle; (*RADIO, TV*): **la ~ sportive** the sports review

chronologique [kʀɔnɔlɔʒik] *adj* chronological

chronomètre [kʀɔnɔmetʀ] *nm* stopwatch; **chronométrer** *vt* to time

chrysanthème [kʀizɑ̃tɛm] *nm* chrysanthemum

chuchotement [ʃyʃɔtmɑ̃] *nm* whisper

chuchoter [ʃyʃɔte] *vt, vi* to whisper

chut [ʃyt] *excl* sh!

chute [ʃyt] *nf* fall; (*déchet*) scrap; **faire une ~ (de 10 m)** to fall (10 m); **~ (d'eau)** waterfall; **la ~ des cheveux** hair loss; **~ libre** free fall; **~s de pluie/neige** rain/snowfalls

Chypre [ʃipʀ] *nm/f* Cyprus

-ci [si] *adv voir* **par** ♦ *dét*: **ce garçon-~/-là** this/that boy; **ces femmes-~/-là** these/those women

cible [sibl] *nf* target

ciboulette [sibulet] *nf* (small) chive

cicatrice [sikatʀis] *nf* scar; **cicatriser** *vt* to heal

ci-contre [sikɔ̃tʀ] *adv* opposite

ci-dessous [sidəsu] *adv* below

ci-dessus [sidəsy] *adv* above

cidre [sidʀ] *nm* cider

Cie *abr* (= compagnie) Co.

ciel [sjɛl] *nm* sky; (*REL*) heaven; **cieux** *nmpl* (*REL*) heaven *sg*; **à ~ ouvert** open-air; (*mine*) open-cast

cierge [sjɛʀʒ] nm candle
cieux [sjø] nmpl de **ciel**
cigale [sigal] nf cicada
cigare [sigaʀ] nm cigar
cigarette [sigaʀɛt] nf cigarette
ci-gît [siʒi] adv +vb here lies
cigogne [sigɔɲ] nf stork
ci-inclus, e [siɛ̃kly, yz] adj, adv enclosed
ci-joint, e [siʒwɛ̃, ɛ̃t] adj, adv enclosed
cil [sil] nm (eye)lash
cime [sim] nf top; (*montagne*) peak
ciment [simã] nm cement
cimetière [simtjɛʀ] nm cemetery; (*d'église*) churchyard
cinéaste [sineast] nm/f film-maker
cinéma [sinema] nm cinema; **cinémato-graphique** adj film cpd, cinema cpd
cinglant, e [sɛ̃glã, ãt] adj (*remarque*) biting
cinglé, e [sɛ̃gle] (*fam*) adj crazy
cinq [sɛ̃k] num five; **cinquantaine** nf: **une cinquantaine (de)** about fifty; **avoir la cinquantaine** (*âge*) to be around fifty; **cinquante** num fifty; **cinquantenaire** adj, nm/f fifty-year-old; **cinquième** num fifth
cintre [sɛ̃tʀ] nm coat-hanger
cintré, e [sɛ̃tʀe] adj (*chemise*) fitted
cirage [siʀaʒ] nm (shoe) polish
circonflexe [siʀkɔ̃flɛks] adj: **accent ~** circumflex accent
circonscription [siʀkɔ̃skʀipsjɔ̃] nf district; **~ électorale** (*d'un député*) constituency
circonscrire [siʀkɔ̃skʀiʀ] vt (*sujet*) to define, delimit; (*incendie*) to contain
circonstance [siʀkɔ̃stãs] nf circumstance; (*occasion*) occasion; **~s atténuantes** mitigating circumstances
circuit [siʀkɥi] nm (*ÉLEC, TECH*) circuit; (*trajet*) tour, (round) trip
circulaire [siʀkylɛʀ] adj, nf circular
circulation [siʀkylasjɔ̃] nf circulation; (*AUTO*): **la ~** (the) traffic
circuler [siʀkyle] vi (*sang, devises*) to circulate; (*véhicules*) to drive (along); (*passants*) to walk along; (*train, bus*) to run; **faire ~**

(*nouvelle*) to spread (about), circulate; (*badauds*) to move on
cire [siʀ] nf wax; **ciré** nm oilskin; **cirer** vt to wax, polish
cirque [siʀk] nm circus; (*fig*) chaos, bedlam; **quel ~!** what a carry-on!
cisaille(s) [sizaj] nf(pl) (gardening) shears pl
ciseau, x [sizo] nm: **~ (à bois)** chisel; **~x** nmpl (*paire de ~x*) (pair of) scissors
ciseler [siz(ə)le] vt to chisel, carve
citadin, e [sitadɛ̃, in] nm/f city dweller
citation [sitasjɔ̃] nf (*d'auteur*) quotation; (*JUR*) summons sg
cité [site] nf town; (*plus grande*) city; **~ universitaire** students' residences pl
citer [site] vt (*un auteur*) to quote (from); (*nommer*) to name; (*JUR*) to summon
citerne [sitɛʀn] nf tank
citoyen, ne [sitwajɛ̃, jɛn] nm/f citizen
citron [sitʀɔ̃] nm lemon; **~ vert** lime; **citronnade** nf still lemonade
citrouille [sitʀuj] nf pumpkin
civet [sivɛ] nm: **~ de lapin** rabbit stew
civière [sivjɛʀ] nf stretcher
civil, e [sivil] adj (*mariage, poli*) civil; (*non militaire*) civilian; **en ~** in civilian clothes; **dans le ~** in civilian life
civilisation [sivilizasjɔ̃] nf civilization
clair, e [klɛʀ] adj light; (*pièce*) light, bright; (*eau, son, fig*) clear ♦ adv: **voir ~** to see clearly; **tirer qch au ~** to clear sth up, clarify sth; **mettre au ~** (*notes etc*) to tidy up; **~ de lune** ♦ nm moonlight; **clairement** adv clearly
clairière [klɛʀjɛʀ] nf clearing
clairon [klɛʀɔ̃] nm bugle; **claironner** vt (*fig*) to trumpet, shout from the rooftops
clairsemé, e [klɛʀsəme] adj sparse
clairvoyant, e [klɛʀvwajã, ãt] adj perceptive, clear-sighted
clandestin, e [klãdɛstɛ̃, in] adj clandestine, secret; (*mouvement*) underground; (*travailleur*) illegal; **passager ~** stowaway
clapier [klapje] nm (rabbit) hutch
clapoter [klapɔte] vi to lap

claque [klak] *nf* (*gifle*) slap; **claquer** *vi* (*porte*) to bang, slam; (*fam: mourir*) to snuff it ♦ *vt* (*porte*) to slam, bang; (*doigts*) to snap; (*fam: dépenser*) to blow; **il claquait des dents** his teeth were chattering; **être claqué** (*fam*) to be dead tired; **se claquer un muscle** to pull *ou* strain a muscle; **claquettes** *nfpl* tap-dancing *sg*

clarinette [klarinɛt] *nf* clarinet

clarté [klarte] *nf* (*luminosité*) brightness; (*d'un son, de l'eau*) clearness; (*d'une explication*) clarity

classe [klɑs] *nf* class; (*SCOL: local*) class(room); (: *leçon, élèves*) class; **aller en ~** to go to school; **classement** *nm* (*rang: SCOL*) place; (: *SPORT*) placing; (*liste: SCOL*) class list (in order of merit); (: *SPORT*) placings *pl*

classer [klɑse] *vt* (*idées, livres*) to classify; (*papiers*) to file; (*candidat*) to grade; (*JUR: affaire*) to close; **se ~ premier/dernier** to come first/last; (*SPORT*) to finish first/last; **classeur** *nm* (*cahier*) file

classique [klasik] *adj* classical; (*sobre: coupe etc*) classic(al); (*habituel*) classic

clause [kloz] *nf* clause

clavecin [klav(ə)sɛ̃] *nm* harpsichord

clavicule [klavikyl] *nf* collarbone

clavier [klavje] *nm* keyboard

clé [kle] *nf* key; (*MUS*) clef; (*de mécanicien*) spanner (*BRIT*), wrench (*US*); **prix ~ en main** (*d'une voiture*) on-the-road price; **~ anglaise** (monkey) wrench; **~ de contact** ignition key

clef [kle] *nf* = **clé**

clément, e [klemɑ̃, ɑ̃t] *adj* (*temps*) mild; (*indulgent*) lenient

clerc [klɛr] *nm*: **~ de notaire** solicitor's clerk

clergé [klɛrʒe] *nm* clergy

cliché [kliʃe] *nm* (*fig*) cliché; (*négatif*) negative; (*photo*) print

client, e [klijɑ̃, ɑ̃t] *nm/f* (*acheteur*) customer, client; (*d'hôtel*) guest, patron; (*du docteur*) patient; (*de l'avocat*) client; **clientèle** *nf* (*du magasin*) customers *pl*, clien-tèle; (*du docteur, de l'avocat*) practice

cligner [kliɲe] *vi*: **~ des yeux** to blink (one's eyes); **~ de l'œil** to wink; **clignotant** *nm* (*AUTO*) indicator; **clignoter** *vi* (*étoiles etc*) to twinkle; (*lumière*) to flicker

climat [klima] *nm* climate

climatisation [klimatizasjɔ̃] *nf* air conditioning; **climatisé, e** *adj* air-conditioned

clin d'œil [klɛ̃dœj] *nm* wink; **en un ~** in a flash

clinique [klinik] *nf* private hospital

clinquant, e [klɛ̃kɑ̃, ɑ̃t] *adj* flashy

clip [klip] *nm* (*boucle d'oreille*) clip-on; (**vidéo) ~** (pop) video

cliquer [klike] *vt*: **~ sur** to click on

cliqueter [klik(ə)te] *vi* (*ferraille*) to jangle; (*clés*) to jingle

clochard, e [klɔʃar, ard] *nm/f* tramp

cloche [klɔʃ] *nf* (*d'église*) bell; (*fam*) clot; **cloche-pied: à cloche-pied** *adv* on one leg, hopping (along); **clocher** *nm* church tower; (*en pointe*) steeple ♦ *vi* (*fam*) to be *ou* go wrong; **de clocher** (*péj*) parochial

cloison [klwazɔ̃] *nf* partition (wall)

cloître [klwatr] *nm* cloister; **cloîtrer** *vt*: **se cloîtrer** to shut o.s. up *ou* away

clone [klɔn] *nm* clone ♦ *vt* cloner

cloque [klɔk] *nf* blister

clore [klɔr] *vt* to close; **clos, e** *adj voir* **maison; huis**

clôture [klotyr] *nf* closure; (*barrière*) enclo-sure

clou [klu] *nm* nail; **~s** *nmpl* (*passage ~té*) pedestrian crossing; **pneus à ~s** studded tyres; **le ~ du spectacle** the highlight of the show; **~ de girofle** clove; **clouer** *vt* to nail down *ou* up; **clouer le bec à qn** (*fam*) to shut sb up

clown [klun] *nm* clown

club [klœb] *nm* club

CMU *nf* (= *couverture maladie universelle*) sys-tem of free health care for those on low incomes

CNRS *sigle m* (= *Centre nationale de la re-cherche scientifique*) ≃ SERC (*BRIT*), ≃ NSF (*US*)

coaguler [kɔagyle] *vt, vi* (*aussi: se ~*:

sang) to coagulate

coasser [kɔase] *vi* to croak

cobaye [kɔbaj] *nm* guinea-pig

coca [kɔka] *nm* Coke ®

cocaïne [kɔkain] *nf* cocaine

cocasse [kɔkas] *adj* comical, funny

coccinelle [kɔksinɛl] *nf* ladybird (*BRIT*), ladybug (*US*)

cocher [kɔʃe] *vt* to tick off

cochère [kɔʃɛR] *adj f*: **porte ~** carriage entrance

cochon, ne [kɔʃɔ̃, ɔn] *nm* pig ♦ *adj* (*fam*) dirty, smutty; **~ d'Inde** guinea pig; **cochonnerie** (*fam*) *nf* (*saleté*) filth; (*marchandise*) rubbish, trash

cocktail [kɔktɛl] *nm* cocktail; (*réception*) cocktail party

coco [kɔko] *nm voir* **noix**

cocorico [kɔkɔriko] *excl, nm* cock-a-doodle-do

cocotier [kɔkɔtje] *nm* coconut palm

cocotte [kɔkɔt] *nf* (*en fonte*) casserole; **~ (minute)** pressure cooker; **ma ~** (*fam*) sweetie (pie)

cocu [kɔky] (*fam*) *nm* cuckold

code [kɔd] *nm* code ♦ *adj*: **phares ~s** dipped lights; **se mettre en ~(s)** to dip one's (head)lights; **~ à barres** bar code; **~ civil** Common Law; **~ de la route** highway code; **~ pénal** penal code; **~ postal** (*numéro*) post (*BRIT*) *ou* zip (*US*) code

cœur [kœr] *nm* heart; (*CARTES: couleur*) hearts *pl*; (*: carte*) heart; **avoir bon ~** to be kind-hearted; **avoir mal au ~** to feel sick; **en avoir le ~ net** to be clear in one's own mind (about it); **par ~** by heart; **de bon ~** willingly; **cela lui tient à ~** that's (very) close to his heart

coffre [kɔfR] *nm* (*meuble*) chest; (*d'auto*) boot (*BRIT*), trunk (*US*); **coffre(-fort)** *nm* safe; **coffret** *nm* casket

cognac [kɔɲak] *nm* brandy, cognac

cogner [kɔɲe] *vi* to knock; **se ~ la tête** to bang one's head

cohérent, e [kɔeRɑ̃, ɑ̃t] *adj* coherent, consistent

cohorte [kɔɔRt] *nf* troop

cohue [kɔy] *nf* crowd

coi, coite [kwa, kwat] *adj*: **rester ~** to remain silent

coiffe [kwaf] *nf* headdress

coiffé, e [kwafe] *adj*: **bien/mal ~** with tidy/untidy hair

coiffer [kwafe] *vt* (*fig: surmonter*) to cover, top; **se ~** *vi* to do one's hair; **~ qn** to do sb's hair; **coiffeur, -euse** *nm/f* hairdresser; **coiffeuse** *nf* (*table*) dressing table; **coiffure** *nf* (*cheveux*) hairstyle, hairdo; (*art*): **la coiffure** hairdressing

coin [kwɛ̃] *nm* corner; (*pour ~cer*) wedge; **l'épicerie du ~** the local grocer; **dans le ~** (*aux alentours*) in the area, around about; (*habiter*) locally; **je ne suis pas du ~** I'm not from here; **au ~ du feu** by the fireside; **regard en ~** sideways glance

coincé, e [kwɛ̃se] *adj* stuck, jammed; (*fig: inhibé*) inhibited, hung up (*fam*)

coincer [kwɛ̃se] *vt* to jam; (*fam: attraper*) to pinch

coïncidence [kɔɛ̃sidɑ̃s] *nf* coincidence

coïncider [kɔɛ̃side] *vi* to coincide

coing [kwɛ̃] *nm* quince

col [kɔl] *nm* (*de chemise*) collar; (*encolure, cou*) neck; (*de montagne*) pass; **~ de l'utérus** cervix; **~ roulé** polo-neck

colère [kɔlɛR] *nf* anger; **une ~** a fit of anger; **(se mettre) en ~** (to get) angry; **coléreux, -euse** *adj*, **colérique** *adj* quick-tempered, irascible

colifichet [kɔlifiʃɛ] *nm* trinket

colimaçon [kɔlimasɔ̃] *nm*: **escalier en ~** spiral staircase

colin [kɔlɛ̃] *nm* hake

colique [kɔlik] *nf* diarrhoea

colis [kɔli] *nm* parcel

collaborateur, -trice [kɔ(l)labɔRatœR, tRis] *nm/f* (*aussi POL*) collaborator; (*d'une revue*) contributor

collaborer [kɔ(l)labɔRe] *vi* to collaborate; **~ à** to collaborate on; (*revue*) to contribute to

collant, e [kɔlɑ̃, ɑ̃t] *adj* sticky; (*robe etc*)

clinging, skintight; (péj) clinging ♦ nm (bas) tights pl; (de danseur) leotard

collation [kɔlasjɔ̃] nf light meal

colle [kɔl] nf glue; (à papiers peints) (wallpaper) paste; (fam: devinette) teaser, riddle; (SCOL: fam) detention

collecte [kɔlɛkt] nf collection; **collectif, -ive** adj collective; (visite, billet) group cpd

collection [kɔlɛksjɔ̃] nf collection; (ÉDITION) series; **collectionner** vt to collect; **collectionneur, -euse** nm/f collector

collectivité [kɔlɛktivite] nf group; **~s locales** (ADMIN) local authorities

collège [kɔlɛʒ] nm (école) (secondary) school; (assemblée) body; **collégien** nm schoolboy; **collégienne** nf schoolgirl

> **collège**

🛈 The **collège** is a state secondary school for children aged between eleven and fifteen. Pupils follow a nationally prescribed curriculum consisting of a common core and various options. Schools are free to arrange their own timetable and choose their own teaching methods. Before leaving the collège, pupils are assessed by examination and course work for their **brevet des collèges**.

collègue [kɔ(l)lɛg] nm/f colleague

coller [kɔle] vt (papier, timbre) to stick (on); (affiche) to stick up; (enveloppe) to stick down; (morceaux) to stick ou glue together; (fam: mettre, fourrer) to stick, shove; (SCOL: fam) to keep in ♦ vi (être collant) to be sticky; (adhérer) to stick; **~ à** to stick to; **être collé à un examen** (fam) to fail an exam

collet [kɔlɛ] nm (piège) snare, noose; (cou): **prendre qn au ~** to grab sb by the throat

collier [kɔlje] nm (bijou) necklace; (de chien, TECH) collar

collimateur [kɔlimatœʀ] nm: **avoir qn/qch dans le ~** (fig) to have sb/sth in

one's sights

colline [kɔlin] nf hill

collision [kɔlizjɔ̃] nf collision, crash; **entrer en ~ (avec)** to collide (with)

colloque [kɔ(l)lɔk] nm symposium

collyre [kɔliʀ] nm eye drops

colmater [kɔlmate] vt (fuite) to seal off; (brèche) to plug, fill in

colombe [kɔlɔ̃b] nf dove

Colombie [kɔlɔ̃bi] nf: **la ~** Colombia

colon [kɔlɔ̃] nm settler

colonel [kɔlɔnɛl] nm colonel

colonie [kɔlɔni] nf colony; **~ (de vacances)** holiday camp (for children)

colonne [kɔlɔn] nf column; **se mettre en ~ par deux** to get into twos; **~ (vertébrale)** spine, spinal column

colorant [kɔlɔʀɑ̃, ɑ̃t] nm colouring

colorer [kɔlɔʀe] vt to colour

colorier [kɔlɔʀje] vt to colour (in)

coloris [kɔlɔʀi] nm colour, shade

colporter [kɔlpɔʀte] vt to hawk, peddle

colza [kɔlza] nm rape(seed)

coma [kɔma] nm coma; **être dans le ~** to be in a coma

combat [kɔ̃ba] nm fight, fighting no pl; **~ de boxe** boxing match; **combattant** nm: **ancien combattant** war veteran; **combattre** vt to fight; (épidémie, ignorance) to combat, fight against

combien [kɔ̃bjɛ̃] adv (quantité) how much; (nombre) how many; **~ de** (quantité) how much; (nombre) how many; **~ de temps** how long; **~ ça coûte/pèse?** how much does it cost/weigh?; **on est le ~ aujourd'hui?** (fam) what's the date today?

combinaison [kɔ̃binɛzɔ̃] nf combination; (astuce) device, scheme; (de femme) slip; (de plongée) wetsuit; (bleu de travail) boiler suit (BRIT), coveralls pl (US)

combine [kɔ̃bin] nf trick; (péj) scheme, fiddle (BRIT)

combiné [kɔ̃bine] nm (aussi: **~ téléphonique**) receiver

combiner [kɔ̃bine] vt (grouper) to combine; (plan, horaire) to work out, devise

comble [kɔbl] *adj* (*salle*) packed (full)
♦ *nm* (*du bonheur, plaisir*) height; **~s** *nmpl*
(*CONSTR*) attic *sg*, loft *sg*; **c'est le ~!** that
beats everything!
combler [kɔble] *vt* (*trou*) to fill in; (*besoin,
lacune*) to fill; (*déficit*) to make good; (*satisfaire*) to fulfil
combustible [kɔbystibl] *nm* fuel
comédie [kɔmedi] *nf* comedy; (*fig*) playacting *no pl*; **faire la ~** (*fam*) to make a
fuss; **~ musicale** musical; **comédien, ne**
nm/f actor(-tress)

Comédie française

*Founded in 1680 by Louis XIV, the
Comédie française is the French na-
tional theatre. Subsidized by the state, the
company performs mainly in the Palais
Royal in Paris and stages mainly classical
French plays.*

---

comestible [kɔmestibl] *adj* edible
comique [kɔmik] *adj* (*drôle*) comical;
(*THÉÂTRE*) comic ♦ *nm* (*artiste*) comic, comedian
comité [kɔmite] *nm* committee; **~ d'entreprise** works council
commandant [kɔmãdã] *nm* (*gén*) commander, commandant; (*NAVIG, AVIAT*) captain
commande [kɔmãd] *nf* (*COMM*) order; **~s**
nfpl (*AVIAT etc*) controls; **sur ~** to order;
commandement *nm* command; (*REL*)
commandment; **commander** *vt* (*COMM*)
to order; (*diriger, ordonner*) to command;
commander à qn de faire to command
ou order sb to do
commando [kɔmãdo] *nm* commando
(squad)

MOT-CLÉ

comme [kɔm] *prép* 1 (*comparaison*) like;
tout comme son père just like his father;
fort comme un bœuf as strong as an ox;
joli comme tout ever so pretty
2 (*manière*) like; **faites-le comme ça** do it

like this, do it this way; **comme ci,
comme ça** so-so, middling
3 (*en tant que*) as a; **donner comme prix**
to give as a prize; **travailler comme secrétaire** to work as a secretary
♦ *conj* 1 (*ainsi que*) as; **elle écrit comme
elle parle** she writes as she talks; **comme
si** as if
2 (*au moment où, alors que*) as; **il est parti
comme j'arrivais** he left as I arrived
3 (*parce que, puisque*) as; **comme il était
en retard, il ...** as he was late, he ...
♦ *adv:* **comme il est fort/c'est bon!** he's
so strong/it's so good!

---

commémorer [kɔmemɔre] *vt* to commemorate
commencement [kɔmãsmã] *nm* beginning, start
commencer [kɔmãse] *vt, vi* to begin,
start; **~ à** *ou* **de faire** to begin *ou* start
doing
comment [kɔmã] *adv* how; **~?** (*que dites-
vous*) pardon?
commentaire [kɔmãtɛʀ] *nm* (*remarque*)
comment, remark; (*exposé*) commentary
commenter [kɔmãte] *vt* (*jugement, événement*) to comment (up)on; (*RADIO, TV:
match, manifestation*) to cover
commérages [kɔmeraʒ] *nmpl* gossip *sg*
commerçant, e [kɔmɛʀsã, ãt] *nm/f* shopkeeper, trader
commerce [kɔmɛʀs] *nm* (*activité*) trade,
commerce; (*boutique*) business; **~ électronique** e-commerce; **commercial, e,
-aux** *adj* commercial, trading; (*péj*) commercial; **les commerciaux** the sales
people; **commercialiser** *vt* to market
commère [kɔmɛʀ] *nf* gossip
commettre [kɔmɛtʀ] *vt* to commit
commis [kɔmi] *nm* (*de magasin*) (shop) assistant; (*de banque*) clerk
commissaire [kɔmisɛʀ] *nm* (*de police*) ≃
(police) superintendent; **commissaire-
priseur** *nm* auctioneer; **commissariat**
nm police station

commission [kɔmisjɔ̃] *nf* (*comité, pourcentage*) commission; (*message*) message; (*course*) errand; **~s** *nfpl* (*achats*) shopping *sg*

commode [kɔmɔd] *adj* (*pratique*) convenient, handy; (*facile*) easy; (*personne*): **pas ~** awkward (to deal with) ♦ *nf* chest of drawers; **commodité** *nf* convenience

commotion [kɔmosjɔ̃] *nf*: **~ (cérébrale)** concussion; **commotionné, e** *adj* shocked, shaken

commun, e [kɔmœ̃, yn] *adj* common; (*pièce*) communal, shared; (*effort*) joint; **ça sort du ~** it's out of the ordinary; **le ~ des mortels** the common run of people; **en ~** (*faire*) jointly; **mettre en ~** to pool, share; *voir aussi* **communs**

communauté [kɔmynote] *nf* community

commune [kɔmyn] *nf* (*ADMIN*) commune, ≈ district; (: *urbaine*) ≈ borough

communicatif, -ive [kɔmynikatif, iv] *adj* (*rire*) infectious; (*personne*) communicative

communication [kɔmynikasjɔ̃] *nf* communication; **~ (téléphonique)** (telephone) call

communier [kɔmynje] *vi* (*REL*) to receive communion

communion [kɔmynjɔ̃] *nf* communion

communiquer [kɔmynike] *vt* (*nouvelle, dossier*) to pass on, convey; (*peur etc*) to communicate ♦ *vi* to communicate; **se ~ à** (*se propager*) to spread to

communisme [kɔmynism] *nm* communism; **communiste** *adj, nm/f* communist

communs [kɔmœ̃] *nmpl* (*bâtiments*) outbuildings

commutateur [kɔmytatœʀ] *nm* (*ÉLEC*) (change-over) switch, commutator

compact, e [kɔ̃pakt] *adj* (*dense*) dense; (*appareil*) compact

compagne [kɔ̃paɲ] *nf* companion

compagnie [kɔ̃paɲi] *nf* (*firme, MIL*) company; **tenir ~ à qn** to keep sb company; **fausser ~ à qn** to give sb the slip, slip *ou* sneak away from sb; **~ aérienne** airline (company)

compagnon [kɔ̃paɲɔ̃] *nm* companion

comparable [kɔ̃paʀabl] *adj*: **~ (à)** comparable (to)

comparaison [kɔ̃paʀezɔ̃] *nf* comparison

comparaître [kɔ̃paʀetʀ] *vi*: **~ (devant)** to appear (before)

comparer [kɔ̃paʀe] *vt* to compare; **~ qch/qn à** *ou* **et** (*pour choisir*) to compare sth/sb with *ou* and; (*pour établir une similitude*) to compare sth/sb to

compartiment [kɔ̃paʀtimɑ̃] *nm* compartment

comparution [kɔ̃paʀysjɔ̃] *nf* (*JUR*) appearance

compas [kɔ̃pa] *nm* (*GÉOM*) (pair of) compasses *pl*; (*NAVIG*) compass

compatible [kɔ̃patibl] *adj* compatible

compatir [kɔ̃patiʀ] *vi* to sympathize

compatriote [kɔ̃patʀijɔt] *nm/f* compatriot

compensation [kɔ̃pɑ̃sasjɔ̃] *nf* compensation

compenser [kɔ̃pɑ̃se] *vt* to compensate for, make up for

compère [kɔ̃peʀ] *nm* accomplice

compétence [kɔ̃petɑ̃s] *nf* competence

compétent, e [kɔ̃petɑ̃, ɑ̃t] *adj* (*apte*) competent, capable

compétition [kɔ̃petisjɔ̃] *nf* (*gén*) competition; (*SPORT: épreuve*) event; **la ~ automobile** motor racing

complainte [kɔ̃plɛ̃t] *nf* lament

complaire [kɔ̃plɛʀ]: **se ~** *vi*: **se ~ dans** to take pleasure in

complaisance [kɔ̃plɛzɑ̃s] *nf* kindness; **pavillon de ~** flag of convenience

complaisant, e [kɔ̃plɛzɑ̃, ɑ̃t] *adj* (*aimable*) kind, obliging

complément [kɔ̃plemɑ̃] *nm* complement; (*reste*) remainder; **~ d'information** (*ADMIN*) supplementary *ou* further information; **complémentaire** *adj* complementary; (*additionnel*) supplementary

complet, -ète [kɔ̃ple, et] *adj* complete; (*plein: hôtel etc*) full ♦ *nm* (*aussi:* **~-veston**) suit; **pain ~** wholemeal bread; **complètement** *adv* completely;

compléter *vt* (*porter à la quantité voulue*) to complete; (*augmenter: connaissances, études*) to complement, supplement; (*: garde-robe*) to add to; **se compléter** (*caractères*) to complement one another

complexe [kɔ̃plɛks] *adj, nm* complex; complexé, e *adj* mixed-up, hung-up

complication [kɔ̃plikasjɔ̃] *nf* complexity, intricacy; (*difficulté, ennui*) complication

complice [kɔ̃plis] *nm* accomplice; complicité *nf* complicity

compliment [kɔ̃plimɑ̃] *nm* (*louange*) compliment; **~s** *nmpl* (*félicitations*) congratulations

compliqué, e [kɔ̃plike] *adj* complicated, complex; (*personne*) complicated

compliquer [kɔ̃plike] *vt* to complicate; **se ~** to become complicated

complot [kɔ̃plo] *nm* plot

comportement [kɔ̃pɔrtəmɑ̃] *nm* behaviour

comporter [kɔ̃pɔrte] *vt* (*consister en*) to consist of, comprise; (*inclure*) to have; **se ~** *vi* to behave

composant [kɔ̃pozɑ̃] *nm*, **composante** [kɔ̃pozɑ̃t] *nf* component

composé [kɔ̃poze] *nm* compound

composer [kɔ̃poze] *vt* (*musique, texte*) to compose; (*mélange, équipe*) to make up; (*numéro*) to dial; (*constituer*) to make up, form ♦ *vi* (*transiger*) to come to terms; **se ~ de** to be composed of, be made up of; compositeur, -trice *nm/f* (*MUS*) composer; composition *nf* composition; (*SCOL*) test

composter [kɔ̃pɔste] *vt* (*billet*) to punch

compote [kɔ̃pɔt] *nf* stewed fruit *no pl*; **~ de pommes** stewed apples

compréhensible [kɔ̃preɑ̃sibl] *adj* comprehensible; (*attitude*) understandable

compréhensif, -ive [kɔ̃preɑ̃sif, iv] *adj* understanding

comprendre [kɔ̃prɑ̃dr] *vt* to understand; (*se composer de*) to comprise, consist of

compresse [kɔ̃prɛs] *nf* compress

compression [kɔ̃presjɔ̃] *nf* compression;

(*de personnes*) reduction

comprimé [kɔ̃prime] *nm* tablet

comprimer [kɔ̃prime] *vt* to compress; (*fig: crédit etc*) to reduce, cut down

compris, e [kɔ̃pri, iz] *pp de* **comprendre** ♦ *adj* (*inclus*) included; **~ entre** (*situé*) contained between; **l'électricité ~e/non ~e, y/non ~ l'électricité** including/excluding electricity; **10 euros tout ~** 10 euros all inclusive *ou* all-in

compromettre [kɔ̃prɔmetr] *vt* to compromise; compromis *nm* compromise

comptabilité [kɔ̃tabilite] *nf* (*activité*) accounting, accountancy; (*comptes*) accounts *pl*, books *pl*; (*service*) accounts office

comptable [kɔ̃tabl] *nm/f* accountant

comptant [kɔ̃tɑ̃] *adv*: **payer ~** to pay cash; **acheter ~** to buy for cash

compte [kɔ̃t] *nm* count; (*total, montant*) count, (right) number; (*bancaire, facture*) account; **~s** *nmpl* (*FINANCE*) accounts, books; (*fig*) explanation *sg*; **en fin de ~** all things considered; **s'en tirer à bon ~** to get off lightly; **pour le ~ de** on behalf of; **pour son propre ~** for one's own benefit; **tenir ~ de** to take account of; **travailler à son ~** to work for oneself; **rendre ~ (à qn) de qch** to give (sb) an account of sth; *voir aussi* **rendre** ♦ **~ à rebours** countdown; **~ chèques postaux** Post Office account; **~ courant** current account; **~ rendu** account, report; (*de film, livre*) review; compte-gouttes *nm inv* dropper

compter [kɔ̃te] *vt* to count; (*facturer*) to charge for; (*avoir à son actif, comporter*) to have; (*prévoir*) to allow, reckon; (*penser, espérer*): **~ réussir** to expect to succeed ♦ *vi* to count; (*être économe*) to economize; (*figurer*): **~ parmi** to be *ou* rank among; **~ sur** to count (up)on; **~ avec qch/qn** to reckon with *ou* take account of sth/sb; **sans ~ que** besides which

compteur [kɔ̃tœr] *nm* meter; **~ de vitesse** speedometer

comptine [kɔ̃tin] *nf* nursery rhyme

comptoir [kɔ̃twaʀ] *nm* (*de magasin*) counter; (*bar*) bar

compulser [kɔ̃pylse] *vt* to consult

comte [kɔ̃t] *nm* count; **comtesse** *nf* countess

con, ne [kɔ̃, kɔn] (*fam!*) *adj* damned *ou* bloody (*BRIT*) stupid (*!*)

concéder [kɔ̃sede] *vt* to grant; (*défaite, point*) to concede

concentré, e [kɔ̃sɑ̃tre] *adj* (*lait*) condensed ♦ *nm*: **~ de tomates** tomato purée

concentrer [kɔ̃sɑ̃tre] *vt* to concentrate; **se ~** *vi* to concentrate

concept [kɔ̃sɛpt] *nm* concept

conception [kɔ̃sɛpsjɔ̃] *nf* conception; (*d'une machine etc*) design; (*d'un problème, de la vie*) approach

concerner [kɔ̃sɛʀne] *vt* to concern; **en ce qui me concerne** as far as I am concerned

concert [kɔ̃sɛʀ] *nm* concert; **de ~** (*décider*) unanimously; **concerter: se concerter** *vi* to put their *etc* heads together

concession [kɔ̃sesjɔ̃] *nf* concession; **concessionnaire** *nm/f* agent, dealer

concevoir [kɔ̃s(ə)vwaʀ] *vt* (*idée, projet*) to conceive (of); (*comprendre*) to understand; (*enfant*) to conceive; **bien/mal conçu** well-/badly-designed

concierge [kɔ̃sjɛʀʒ] *nm/f* caretaker

conciliabules [kɔ̃siljabyl] *nmpl* (private) discussions, confabulations

concilier [kɔ̃silje] *vt* to reconcile; **se ~** *vt* to win over

concis, e [kɔ̃si, iz] *adj* concise

concitoyen, ne [kɔ̃sitwajɛ̃, jɛn] *nm/f* fellow citizen

concluant, e [kɔ̃klyɑ̃, ɑ̃t] *adj* conclusive

conclure [kɔ̃klyʀ] *vt* to conclude; **conclusion** *nf* conclusion

conçois *etc* [kɔ̃swa] *vb voir* **concevoir**

concombre [kɔ̃kɔ̃bʀ] *nm* cucumber

concorder [kɔ̃kɔʀde] *vi* to tally, agree

concourir [kɔ̃kuʀiʀ] *vi* (*SPORT*) to compete; **~ à** (*effet etc*) to work towards

concours [kɔ̃kuʀ] *nm* competition; (*SCOL*) competitive examination; (*assistance*) aid, help; **~ de circonstances** combination of circumstances; **~ hippique** horse show

concret, -ète [kɔ̃kʀɛ, ɛt] *adj* concrete

concrétiser [kɔ̃kʀetize] *se ~* *vi* to materialize

conçu, e [kɔ̃sy] *pp de* **concevoir**

concubinage [kɔ̃kybinaʒ] *nm* (*JUR*) cohabitation

concurrence [kɔ̃kyʀɑ̃s] *nf* competition; **faire ~ à** to be in competition with; **jusqu'à ~ de** up to

concurrent, e [kɔ̃kyʀɑ̃, ɑ̃t] *nm/f* (*SPORT, ÉCON etc*) competitor; (*SCOL*) candidate

condamner [kɔ̃dane] *vt* (*blâmer*) to condemn; (*JUR*) to sentence; (*porte, ouverture*) to fill in, block up; **~ qn à 2 ans de prison** to sentence sb to 2 years' imprisonment

condensation [kɔ̃dɑ̃sasjɔ̃] *nf* condensation

condenser [kɔ̃dɑ̃se] *vt* to condense; **se ~** *vi* to condense

condisciple [kɔ̃disipl] *nm/f* fellow student

condition [kɔ̃disjɔ̃] *nf* condition; **~s** *nfpl* (*tarif, prix*) terms; (*circonstances*) conditions; **à ~ de** *ou* **que** provided that; **conditionnel, le** *nm* conditional (tense)

conditionnement [kɔ̃disjɔnmɑ̃] *nm* (*emballage*) packaging

conditionner [kɔ̃disjɔne] *vt* (*déterminer*) to determine; (*COMM: produit*) to package; **air conditionné** air conditioning

condoléances [kɔ̃dɔleɑ̃s] *nfpl* condolences

conducteur, -trice [kɔ̃dyktœʀ, tʀis] *nm/f* driver ♦ *nm* (*ÉLEC etc*) conductor

conduire [kɔ̃dɥiʀ] *vt* to drive; (*délégation, troupeau*) to lead; **se ~** *vi* to behave; **~ à** to lead to; **~ qn quelque part** to take sb somewhere; to drive sb somewhere

conduite [kɔ̃dɥit] *nf* (*comportement*) behaviour; (*d'eau, de gaz*) pipe; **sous la ~ de** led by; **~ à gauche** left-hand drive

cône [kon] nm cone
confection [kɔ̃fɛksjɔ̃] nf (fabrication) making; (COUTURE): la ~ the clothing industry
confectionner [kɔ̃fɛksjɔne] vt to make
conférence [kɔ̃feʀɑ̃s] nf conference; (exposé) lecture; ~ de presse press conference; conférencier, -ière nm/f speaker, lecturer
confesser [kɔ̃fese] vt to confess; se ~ vi (REL) to go to confession; confession nf confession; (culte: catholique etc) denomination
confiance [kɔ̃fjɑ̃s] nf (en l'honnêteté de qn) confidence, trust; (en la valeur de qch) faith; avoir ~ en to have confidence ou faith in, trust; faire ~ à qn to trust sb; mettre qn en ~ to win sb's trust; ~ en soi self-confidence
confiant, e [kɔ̃fjɑ̃, jɑ̃t] adj confident; trusting
confidence [kɔ̃fidɑ̃s] nf confidence; confidentiel, le adj confidential
confier [kɔ̃fje] vt: ~ à qn (objet, travail) to entrust to sb; (secret, pensée) to confide to sb; se ~ à qn to confide in sb
confins [kɔ̃fɛ̃] nmpl: aux ~ de on the borders of
confirmation [kɔ̃fiʀmasjɔ̃] nf confirmation
confirmer [kɔ̃fiʀme] vt to confirm
confiserie [kɔ̃fizʀi] nf (magasin) confectioner's ou sweet shop; ~s nfpl (bonbons) confectionery sg
confisquer [kɔ̃fiske] vt to confiscate
confit, e [kɔ̃fi, it] adj: fruits ~s crystallized fruits ♦ nm: ~ d'oie conserve of goose
confiture [kɔ̃fityʀ] nf jam; ~ d'oranges (orange) marmalade
conflit [kɔ̃fli] nm conflict
confondre [kɔ̃fɔ̃dʀ] vt (jumeaux, faits) to confuse, mix up; (témoin, menteur) to confound; se ~ vi to merge; se ~ en excuses to apologize profusely; confondu, e adj (stupéfait) speechless; overcome
conforme [kɔ̃fɔʀm] adj: ~ à (loi, règle) in accordance with; conformément adv: conformément à in accordance with;

conformer vt: se conformer à to conform to
confort [kɔ̃fɔʀ] nm comfort; tout ~ (COMM) with all modern conveniences; confortable adj comfortable
confrère [kɔ̃fʀɛʀ] nm colleague
confronter [kɔ̃fʀɔ̃te] vt to confront
confus, e [kɔ̃fy, yz] adj (vague) confused; (embarrassé) embarrassed; confusion nf (voir confus) confusion; embarrassment; (voir confondre) confusion, mixing up
congé [kɔ̃ʒe] nm (vacances) holiday; en ~ on holiday; semaine de ~ week off; prendre ~ de qn to take one's leave of sb; donner son ~ à to give in one's notice to; ~ de maladie sick leave; ~ de maternité maternity leave; ~s payés paid holiday
congédier [kɔ̃ʒedje] vt to dismiss
congélateur [kɔ̃ʒelatœʀ] nm freezer
congeler [kɔ̃ʒ(ə)le] vt to freeze; les produits congelés frozen foods
congestion [kɔ̃ʒɛstjɔ̃] nf congestion; ~ cérébrale stroke; congestionner vt (rue) to congest; (visage) to flush
congrès [kɔ̃gʀɛ] nm congress
conifère [kɔnifɛʀ] nm conifer
conjecture [kɔ̃ʒɛktyʀ] nf conjecture
conjoint, e [kɔ̃ʒwɛ̃, wɛ̃t] adj joint ♦ nm/f spouse
conjonction [kɔ̃ʒɔ̃ksjɔ̃] nf (LING) conjunction
conjonctivite [kɔ̃ʒɔ̃ktivit] nf conjunctivitis
conjoncture [kɔ̃ʒɔ̃ktyʀ] nf circumstances pl; la ~ actuelle the present (economic) situation
conjugaison [kɔ̃ʒygɛzɔ̃] nf (LING) conjugation
conjuguer [kɔ̃ʒyge] vt (LING) to conjugate; (efforts etc) to combine
conjuration [kɔ̃ʒyʀasjɔ̃] nf conspiracy
conjurer [kɔ̃ʒyʀe] vt (sort, maladie) to avert; (implorer) to beseech, entreat
connaissance [kɔnɛsɑ̃s] nf (savoir) knowledge no pl; (personne connue) acquaintance; être sans ~ to be unconscious;

perdre/reprendre ~ to lose/regain consciousness; **à ma** ~ to (the best of) my knowledge; **faire la** ~ **de qn** to meet sb

connaisseur [kɔnɛsœʀ, øz] *nm* connoisseur

connaître [kɔnɛtʀ] *vt* to know; (*éprouver*) to experience; (*avoir: succès*) to have, enjoy; ~ **de nom/vue** to know by name/sight; **ils se sont connus à Genève** they (first) met in Geneva; **s'y** ~ **en qch** to know a lot about sth

connecter [kɔnɛkte] *vt* to connect; **se** ~ (*INFORM*) to log on

connerie [kɔnʀi] (*fam!*) *nf* stupid thing (to do/say)

connu, e [kɔny] *adj* (*célèbre*) well-known

conquérir [kɔ̃keʀiʀ] *vt* to conquer

consacrer [kɔ̃sakʀe] *vt* (*employer*) to devote, dedicate; (*REL*) to consecrate

conscience [kɔ̃sjɑ̃s] *nf* conscience; **avoir/prendre** ~ **de** to be/become aware of; **perdre** ~ to lose consciousness; **avoir mauvaise** ~ to have a guilty conscience; **consciencieux, -euse** *adj* conscientious; **conscient, e** *adj* conscious

conscrit [kɔ̃skʀi] *nm* conscript

consécutif, -ive [kɔ̃sekytif, iv] *adj* consecutive; ~ **à** following upon

conseil [kɔ̃sɛj] *nm* (*avis*) piece of advice; (*assemblée*) council; **des** ~**s** advice; **prendre** ~ **(auprès de qn)** to take advice (from sb); ~ **d'administration** board (of directors); **le** ~ **des ministres** ≃ the Cabinet; ~ **municipal** town council

conseiller, -ère [kɔ̃seje, ɛʀ] *nm/f* adviser ♦ *vt* (*personne*) to advise; (*méthode, action*) to recommend, advise; ~ **à qn de** to advise sb to; ~ **municipal** town councillor

consentement [kɔ̃sɑ̃tmɑ̃] *nm* consent

consentir [kɔ̃sɑ̃tiʀ] *vt* to agree, consent

conséquence [kɔ̃sekɑ̃s] *nf* consequence; **en** ~ (*donc*) consequently; (*de façon appropriée*) accordingly; **conséquent, e** *adj* logical, rational; (*fam: important*) substantial; **par conséquent** consequently

conservateur, -trice [kɔ̃sɛʀvatœʀ, tʀis]

nm/f (*POL*) conservative; (*de musée*) curator ♦ *nm* (*pour aliments*) preservative

conservatoire [kɔ̃sɛʀvatwaʀ] *nm* academy

conserve [kɔ̃sɛʀv] *nf* (*gén pl*) canned *ou* tinned (*BRIT*) food; **en** ~ canned, tinned (*BRIT*)

conserver [kɔ̃sɛʀve] *vt* (*faculté*) to retain, keep; (*amis, livres*) to keep; (*préserver, aussi CULIN*) to preserve

considérable [kɔ̃sideʀabl] *adj* considerable, significant, extensive

considération [kɔ̃sideʀasjɔ̃] *nf* consideration; (*estime*) esteem

considérer [kɔ̃sideʀe] *vt* to consider; ~ **qch comme** to regard sth as

consigne [kɔ̃siɲ] *nf* (*de gare*) left luggage (office) (*BRIT*), checkroom (*US*); (*ordre, instruction*) instructions *pl*; ~ **(automatique)** left-luggage locker; **consigner** *vt* (*note, pensée*) to record; (*punir: élève*) to put in detention; (*COMM*) to put a deposit on

consistant, e [kɔ̃sistɑ̃, ɑ̃t] *adj* (*mélange*) thick; (*repas*) solid

consister [kɔ̃siste] *vi*: ~ **en/à faire** to consist of/in doing

consœur [kɔ̃sœʀ] *nf* (lady) colleague

console [kɔ̃sɔl] *nf*: ~ **de jeux** games console

consoler [kɔ̃sɔle] *vt* to console

consolider [kɔ̃sɔlide] *vt* to strengthen; (*fig*) to consolidate

consommateur, -trice [kɔ̃sɔmatœʀ, tʀis] *nm/f* (*ÉCON*) consumer; (*dans un café*) customer

consommation [kɔ̃sɔmasjɔ̃] *nf* (*boisson*) drink; (*ÉCON*) consumption

consommer [kɔ̃sɔme] *vt* (*suj: personne*) to eat *ou* drink, consume; (*: voiture, machine*) to use, consume; (*mariage*) to consummate ♦ *vi* (*dans un café*) to (have a) drink

consonne [kɔ̃sɔn] *nf* consonant

conspirer [kɔ̃spiʀe] *vi* to conspire

constamment [kɔ̃stamɑ̃] *adv* constantly

constant, e [kɔ̃stɑ̃, ɑ̃t] *adj* constant; (*personne*) steadfast

constat [kɔ̃sta] *nm* (*de police, d'accident*) report; **~ (à l')amiable** *jointly-agreed statement for insurance purposes*; **~ d'échec** acknowledgement of failure

constatation [kɔ̃statasjɔ̃] *nf* (*observation*) (observed) fact, observation

constater [kɔ̃state] *vt* (*remarquer*) to note; (*ADMIN, JUR: attester*) to certify

consterner [kɔ̃stɛrne] *vt* to dismay

constipé, e [kɔ̃stipe] *adj* constipated

constitué, e [kɔ̃stitɥe] *adj*: **~ de** made up *ou* composed of

constituer [kɔ̃stitɥe] *vt* (*équipe*) to set up; (*dossier, collection*) to put together; (*suj: éléments: composer*) to make up, constitute; (*représenter, être*) to constitute; **se ~ prisonnier** to give o.s. up; **constitution** *nf* (*composition*) composition, make-up; (*santé, POL*) constitution

constructeur [kɔ̃stryktœr] *nm* manufacturer, builder

constructif, -ive [kɔ̃stryktif, iv] *adj* constructive

construction [kɔ̃stryksjɔ̃] *nf* construction, building

construire [kɔ̃strɥir] *vt* to build, construct

consul [kɔ̃syl] *nm* consul; **consulat** *nm* consulate

consultant, e [kɔ̃syltɑ̃, ɑ̃t] *adj, nm* consultant

consultation [kɔ̃syltasjɔ̃] *nf* consultation; **~s** *nfpl* (*POL*) talks; **heures de ~** (*MÉD*) surgery (*BRIT*) *ou* office (*US*) hours

consulter [kɔ̃sylte] *vt* to consult ♦ *vi* (*médecin*) to hold surgery (*BRIT*), be in (the office) (*US*); **se ~** *vi* to confer

consumer [kɔ̃syme] *vt* to consume; **se ~** *vi* to burn

contact [kɔ̃takt] *nm* contact; **au ~ de** (*air, peau*) on contact with; (*gens*) through contact with; **mettre/couper le ~** (*AUTO*) to switch on/off the ignition; **entrer en** *ou* **prendre ~ avec** to get in touch *ou* contact with; **contacter** *vt* to contact, get in touch with

contagieux, -euse [kɔ̃taʒjø, jøz] *adj* infectious; (*par le contact*) contagious

contaminer [kɔ̃tamine] *vt* to contaminate

conte [kɔ̃t] *nm* tale; **~ de fées** fairy tale

contempler [kɔ̃tɑ̃ple] *vt* to contemplate, gaze at

contemporain, e [kɔ̃tɑ̃pɔrɛ̃, ɛn] *adj, nm/f* contemporary

contenance [kɔ̃t(ə)nɑ̃s] *nf* (*d'un récipient*) capacity; (*attitude*) bearing, attitude; **perdre ~** to lose one's composure

conteneur [kɔ̃t(ə)nœr] *nm* container

contenir [kɔ̃t(ə)nir] *vt* to contain; (*avoir une capacité de*) to hold; **se ~** *vi* to contain o.s.

content, e [kɔ̃tɑ̃, ɑ̃t] *adj* pleased, glad; **~ de** pleased with; **contenter** *vt* to satisfy, please; **se contenter de** to content o.s. with

contentieux [kɔ̃tɑ̃sjø] *nm* (*COMM*) litigation; (*service*) litigation department

contenu [kɔ̃t(ə)ny] *nm* (*d'un récipient*) contents *pl*; (*d'un texte*) content

conter [kɔ̃te] *vt* to recount, relate

contestable [kɔ̃tɛstabl] *adj* questionable

contestation [kɔ̃tɛstasjɔ̃] *nf* (*POL*) protest

conteste [kɔ̃tɛst]: **sans ~** *adv* unquestionably, indisputably; **contester** *vt* to question, contest ♦ *vi* (*POL, gén*) to protest, rebel (against established authority)

contexte [kɔ̃tɛkst] *nm* context

contigu, ë [kɔ̃tigy] *adj*: **~ (à)** adjacent (to)

continent [kɔ̃tinɑ̃] *nm* continent

continu, e [kɔ̃tiny] *adj* continuous; **faire la journée ~e** to work without taking a full lunch break; **(courant) ~** direct current, DC

continuel, le [kɔ̃tinɥɛl] *adj* (*qui se répète*) constant, continual; (*continu*) continuous

continuer [kɔ̃tinɥe] *vt* (*travail, voyage etc*) to continue (with), carry on (with), go on (with); (*prolonger: alignement, rue*) to continue ♦ *vi* (*vie, bruit*) to continue, go on; **~ à** *ou* **de faire** to go on *ou* continue doing

contorsionner [kɔ̃tɔrsjɔne]: **se ~** *vi* to

contort o.s., writhe about

contour [kɔ̃tuʀ] *nm* outline, contour; **contourner** *vt* to go round; (*difficulté*) to get round

contraceptif, -ive [kɔ̃tʀaseptif, iv] *adj, nm* contraceptive; **contraception** *nf* contraception

contracté, e [kɔ̃tʀakte] *adj* tense

contracter [kɔ̃tʀakte] *vt* (*muscle etc*) to tense, contract; (*maladie, dette*) to contract; (*assurance*) to take out; **se ~** *vi* (*muscles*) to contract

contractuel, le [kɔ̃tʀaktɥɛl] *nm/f* (*agent*) traffic warden

contradiction [kɔ̃tʀadiksjɔ̃] *nf* contradiction; **contradictoire** *adj* contradictory, conflicting

contraignant, e [kɔ̃tʀɛɲɑ̃, ɑ̃t] *adj* restricting

contraindre [kɔ̃tʀɛ̃dʀ] *vt*: **~ qn à faire** to compel sb to do; **contrainte** *nf* constraint

contraire [kɔ̃tʀɛʀ] *adj, nm* opposite; **~ à** contrary to; **au ~** on the contrary

contrarier [kɔ̃tʀaʀje] *vt* (*personne: irriter*) to annoy; (*fig: projets*) to thwart, frustrate; **contrariété** *nf* annoyance

contraste [kɔ̃tʀast] *nm* contrast

contrat [kɔ̃tʀa] *nm* contract; **~ de travail** employment contract

contravention [kɔ̃tʀavɑ̃sjɔ̃] *nf* parking ticket

contre [kɔ̃tʀ] *prép* against; (*en échange*) (in exchange) for; **par ~** on the other hand

contrebande [kɔ̃tʀəbɑ̃d] *nf* (*trafic*) contraband, smuggling; (*marchandise*) contraband, smuggled goods *pl*; **faire la ~ de** to smuggle; **contrebandier, -ière** *nm/f* smuggler

contrebas [kɔ̃tʀəba]: **en ~** *adv* (down) below

contrebasse [kɔ̃tʀəbas] *nf* (double) bass

contre...: **contrecarrer** *vt* to thwart; **contrecœur**: **à contrecœur** *adv* (be)grudgingly, reluctantly; **contrecoup** *nm* repercussions *pl*; **contredire** *vt* (*per-*

sonne) to contradict; (*faits*) to refute

contrée [kɔ̃tʀe] *nf* (*région*) region; (*pays*) land

contrefaçon [kɔ̃tʀəfasɔ̃] *nf* forgery

contrefaire [kɔ̃tʀəfɛʀ] *vt* (*document, signature*) to forge, counterfeit

contre...: **contre-indication** (*pl* **contre-indications**) *nf* (MÉD) contraindication; **"contre-indication en cas d'eczéma"** "should not be used by people with eczema"; **contre-indiqué, e** *adj* (MÉD) contraindicated; (*déconseillé*) unadvisable, ill-advised; **contre-jour**: **à contre-jour** *adv* against the sunlight

contremaître [kɔ̃tʀəmɛtʀ] *nm* foreman

contrepartie [kɔ̃tʀəparti] *nf*: **en ~** in return

contre-pied [kɔ̃tʀəpje] *nm*: **prendre le ~-~ de** (*opinion*) to take the opposing view of; (*action*) to take the opposite course to

contre-plaqué [kɔ̃tʀəplake] *nm* plywood

contrepoids [kɔ̃tʀəpwa] *nm* counterweight, counterbalance

contrepoison [kɔ̃tʀəpwazɔ̃] *nm* antidote

contrer [kɔ̃tʀe] *vt* to counter

contresens [kɔ̃tʀəsɑ̃s] *nm* (*erreur*) misinterpretation; (*de traduction*) mistranslation; **à ~** the wrong way

contretemps [kɔ̃tʀətɑ̃] *nm* hitch; **à ~** (*fig*) at an inopportune moment

contrevenir [kɔ̃tʀəv(ə)niʀ] *vt*: **~ à** to contravene

contribuable [kɔ̃tʀibɥabl] *nm/f* taxpayer

contribuer [kɔ̃tʀibɥe]: **~ à** *vt* to contribute towards; **contribution** *nf* contribution; **contributions directes/indirectes** direct/indirect taxation; **mettre à contribution** to call upon

contrôle [kɔ̃tʀol] *nm* checking *no pl*, check; (*des prix*) monitoring, control; (*test*) test, examination; **perdre le ~ de** (*véhicule*) to lose control of; **~ continu** (SCOL) continuous assessment; **~ d'identité** identity check

contrôler [kɔ̃tʀole] *vt* (*vérifier*) to check;

(*surveiller: opérations*) to supervise; (*: prix*) to monitor, control; (*maîtriser, COMM: firme*) to control; **se ~** *vi* to control o.s.; **contrôleur, -euse** *nm/f* (*de train*) (ticket) inspector; (*de bus*) (bus) conductor(-tress)

contrordre [kɔ̃trɔrdr] *nm*: **sauf ~** unless otherwise directed

controversé, e [kɔ̃trɔverse] *adj* (*personnage, question*) controversial

contusion [kɔ̃tyzjɔ̃] *nf* bruise, contusion

convaincre [kɔ̃vɛ̃kr] *vt*: **~ qn (de qch)** to convince sb (of sth); **~ qn (de faire)** to persuade sb (to do)

convalescence [kɔ̃valesɑ̃s] *nf* convalescence

convenable [kɔ̃vnabl] *adj* suitable; (*assez bon, respectable*) decent

convenance [kɔ̃vnɑ̃s] *nf*: **à ma/votre ~** to my/your liking; **~s** *nfpl* (*normes sociales*) proprieties

convenir [kɔ̃vnir] *vi* to be suitable; **~ à** to suit; **~ de** (*bien-fondé de qch*) to admit (to), acknowledge; (*date, somme etc*) to agree upon; **~ que** (*admettre*) to admit that; **~ de faire** to agree to do

convention [kɔ̃vɑ̃sjɔ̃] *nf* convention; **~s** *nfpl* (*convenances*) convention *sg*; **~ collective** (*ÉCON*) collective agreement; **conventionné, e** *adj* (*ADMIN*) applying charges laid down by the state

convenu, e [kɔ̃vny] *pp de* **convenir ♦** *adj* agreed

conversation [kɔ̃vɛrsasjɔ̃] *nf* conversation

convertir [kɔ̃vertir] *vt*: **~ qn (à)** to convert sb (to); **se ~ (à)** to be converted (to); **~ qch en** to convert sth into

conviction [kɔ̃viksjɔ̃] *nf* conviction

convienne *etc* [kɔ̃vjɛn] *vb voir* **convenir**

convier [kɔ̃vje] *vt*: **~ qn à** (*dîner etc*) to (cordially) invite sb to

convive [kɔ̃viv] *nm/f* guest (*at table*)

convivial, e, -aux [kɔ̃vivjal, jo] *adj* (*INFORM*) user-friendly

convocation [kɔ̃vɔkasjɔ̃] *nf* (*document*) notification to attend; (*: JUR*) summons *sg*

convoi [kɔ̃vwa] *nm* convoy; (*train*) train

convoiter [kɔ̃vwate] *vt* to covet

convoquer [kɔ̃vɔke] *vt* (*assemblée*) to convene; (*subordonné*) to summon; (*candidat*) to ask to attend

convoyeur [kɔ̃vwajœr] *nm*: **~ de fonds** security guard

coopération [kɔɔperasjɔ̃] *nf* co-operation; (*ADMIN*): **la C~** ≈ Voluntary Service Overseas (*BRIT*), ≈ Peace Corps (*US*)

coopérer [kɔɔpere] *vi*: **~ (à)** to co-operate (in)

coordonnées [kɔɔrdɔne] *nfpl*: **donnez-moi vos ~** (*fam*) can I have your details please?

coordonner [kɔɔrdɔne] *vt* to coordinate

copain [kɔpɛ̃] (*fam*) *nm* mate, pal; (*petit ami*) boyfriend

copeau, x [kɔpo] *nm* shaving

copie [kɔpi] *nf* copy; (*SCOL*) script, paper; **copier** *vt*, *vi* to copy; **copier sur** to copy from; **copieur** *nm* (photo)copier

copieux, -euse [kɔpjø, jøz] *adj* copious

copine [kɔpin] (*fam*) *nf* mate, pal; (*petite amie*) girlfriend

copropriété [kɔprɔprijete] *nf* co-ownership, joint ownership

coq [kɔk] *nm* cock, rooster; **coq-à-l'âne** *nm inv* abrupt change of subject

coque [kɔk] *nf* (*de noix, mollusque*) shell; (*de bateau*) hull; **à la ~** (*CULIN*) (soft-) boiled

coquelicot [kɔkliko] *nm* poppy

coqueluche [kɔklyʃ] *nf* whooping-cough

coquet, te [kɔkɛ, ɛt] *adj* appearance-conscious; (*logement*) smart, charming

coquetier [kɔk(ə)tje] *nm* egg-cup

coquillage [kɔkijaʒ] *nm* (*mollusque*) shellfish *inv*; (*coquille*) shell

coquille [kɔkij] *nf* shell; (*TYPO*) misprint; **~ St Jacques** scallop

coquin, e [kɔkɛ̃, in] *adj* mischievous, roguish; (*polisson*) naughty

cor [kɔr] *nm* (*MUS*) horn; (*MÉD*): **~ (au pied)** corn

corail, -aux [kɔraj, o] *nm* coral *no pl*

Coran [kɔrɑ̃] *nm*: **le ~** the Koran

corbeau, x [kɔʀbo] *nm* crow

corbeille [kɔʀbɛj] *nf* basket; **~ à papier** waste paper basket *ou* bin

corbillard [kɔʀbijaʀ] *nm* hearse

corde [kɔʀd] *nf* rope; *(de violon, raquette)* string; **usé jusqu'à la ~** threadbare; **~ à linge** washing *ou* clothes line; **~ à sauter** skipping rope; **~s vocales** vocal cords

cordée *nf (d'alpinistes)* rope, roped party

cordialement [kɔʀdjalmɑ̃] *adv (formule épistolaire)* (kind) regards

cordon [kɔʀdɔ̃] *nm* cord, string; **~ ombilical** umbilical cord; **~ sanitaire/de police** sanitary/police cordon

cordonnerie [kɔʀdɔnʀi] *nf* shoe repairer's (shop); **cordonnier** *nm* shoe repairer

Corée [kɔʀe] *nf*: **la ~ du Sud/du Nord** South/North Korea

coriace [kɔʀjas] *adj* tough

corne [kɔʀn] *nf* horn; *(de cerf)* antler

cornée [kɔʀne] *nf* cornea

corneille [kɔʀnɛj] *nf* crow

cornemuse [kɔʀnəmyz] *nf* bagpipes *pl*

cornet [kɔʀnɛ] *nm* (paper) cone; *(de glace)* cornet, cone

corniche [kɔʀniʃ] *nf (route)* coast road

cornichon [kɔʀniʃɔ̃] *nm* gherkin

Cornouailles [kɔʀnwaj] *nf* Cornwall

corporation [kɔʀpɔʀasjɔ̃] *nf* corporate body

corporel, le [kɔʀpɔʀɛl] *adj* bodily; *(punition)* corporal

corps [kɔʀ] *nm* body; **à ~ perdu** headlong; **prendre ~** to take shape; **~ à ~** ♦ *adv* hand-to-hand ♦ *nm* clinch; **le ~ électoral** the electorate; **le ~ enseignant** the teaching profession

corpulent, e [kɔʀpylɑ̃, ɑ̃t] *adj* stout

correct, e [kɔʀɛkt] *adj* correct; *(fam: acceptable: salaire, hôtel)* reasonable, decent; **correcteur, -trice** *nm/f (SCOL)* examiner; **correction** *nf (voir corriger)* correction; *(voir correct)* correctness; *(coups)* thrashing; **correctionnel, le** *adj (JUR)*: **tribunal correctionnel** ≃ criminal court

correspondance [kɔʀɛspɔ̃dɑ̃s] *nf* correspondence; *(de train, d'avion)* connection; **cours par ~** correspondence course; **vente par ~** mail-order business

correspondant, e [kɔʀɛspɔ̃dɑ̃, ɑ̃t] *nm/f* correspondent; *(TÉL)* person phoning *(ou* being phoned)

correspondre [kɔʀɛspɔ̃dʀ] *vi* to correspond, tally; **~ à** to correspond to; **~ avec qn** to correspond with sb

corrida [kɔʀida] *nf* bullfight

corridor [kɔʀidɔʀ] *nm* corridor

corrigé [kɔʀiʒe] *nm (SCOL: d'exercice)* correct version

corriger [kɔʀiʒe] *vt (devoir)* to correct; *(punir)* to thrash; **~ qn de** *(défaut)* to cure sb of

corroborer [kɔʀɔbɔʀe] *vt* to corroborate

corrompre [kɔʀɔ̃pʀ] *vt* to corrupt; *(acheter: témoin etc)* to bribe

corruption [kɔʀypsjɔ̃] *nf* corruption; *(de témoins)* bribery

corsage [kɔʀsaʒ] *nm* bodice; *(chemisier)* blouse

corsaire [kɔʀsɛʀ] *nm* pirate

corse [kɔʀs] *adj, nm/f* Corsican ♦ *nf*: **la C~** Corsica

corsé, e [kɔʀse] *adj (café)* full-flavoured; *(sauce)* spicy; *(problème)* tough

corset [kɔʀsɛ] *nm* corset

cortège [kɔʀtɛʒ] *nm* procession

cortisone [kɔʀtizɔn] *nf* cortisone

corvée [kɔʀve] *nf* chore, drudgery *no pl*

cosmétique [kɔsmetik] *nm* beauty care product

cosmopolite [kɔsmɔpɔlit] *adj* cosmopolitan

cossu, e [kɔsy] *adj (maison)* opulent(-looking)

costaud, e [kɔsto, od] *(fam) adj* strong, sturdy

costume [kɔstym] *nm (d'homme)* suit; *(de théâtre)* costume; **costumé, e** *adj* dressed up; **bal costumé** fancy dress ball

cote [kɔt] *nf (en Bourse)* quotation; **~ d'alerte** danger *ou* flood level

côte [kot] *nf (rivage)* coast(line); *(pente)*

hill; (*ANAT*) rib; (*d'un tricot, tissu*) rib, ribbing *ou* pl; **~ à ~** side by side; **la C~ (d'Azur)** the (French) Riviera

coté, e [kɔte] *adj*: **être bien ~** to be highly rated

côté [kote] *nm* (*gén*) side; (*direction*) way, direction; **de chaque ~ (de)** on each side (of); **de tous les ~s** from all directions; **de quel ~ est-il parti?** which way did he go?; **de ce/de l'autre ~** this/the other way; **du ~ de** (*provenance*) from; (*direction*) towards; (*proximité*) near; **de ~** (*regarder*) sideways; (*mettre*) aside; **mettre de l'argent de ~** to save some money; **à ~** (right) nearby; (*voisins*) next door; **à ~ de** beside, next to; (*en comparaison*) compared to; **être aux ~s de** to be by the side of

coteau, x [kɔto] *nm* hill

côtelette [kotlɛt] *nf* chop

côtier, -ière [kotje, jɛʀ] *adj* coastal

cotisation [kɔtizasjɔ̃] *nf* subscription, dues *pl*; (*pour une pension*) contributions *pl*

cotiser [kɔtize] *vi*: **~ (à)** to pay contributions (to); **se ~** *vi* to club together

coton [kɔtɔ̃] *nm* cotton; **~ hydrophile** cotton wool (*BRIT*), absorbent cotton (*US*); **Coton-Tige** ® *nm* cotton bud

côtoyer [kotwaje] *vt* (*fréquenter*) to rub shoulders with

cou [ku] *nm* neck

couchant [kuʃɑ̃] *adj*: **soleil ~** setting sun

couche [kuʃ] *nf* layer; (*de peinture, vernis*) coat; (*de bébé*) nappy (*BRIT*), diaper (*US*); **~ d'ozone** ozone layer; **~s sociales** social levels *ou* strata

couché, e [kuʃe] *adj* lying down; (*au lit*) in bed

coucher [kuʃe] *nm* (*du soleil*) setting ♦ *vt* (*personne*) to put to bed; (: *loger*) to put up; (*objet*) to lay on its side ♦ *vi* to sleep; **se ~** *vi* (*pour dormir*) to go to bed; (*pour se reposer*) to lie down; (*soleil*) to set; **~ de soleil** sunset

couchette [kuʃɛt] *nf* couchette; (*pour voyageur, sur bateau*) berth

coucou [kuku] *nm* cuckoo

coude [kud] *nm* (*ANAT*) elbow; (*de tuyau, de la route*) bend; **~ à ~** shoulder to shoulder, side by side

coudre [kudʀ] *vt* (*bouton*) to sew on ♦ *vi* to sew

couenne [kwan] *nf* (*de lard*) rind

couette [kwɛt] *nf* duvet, quilt; **~s** *nfpl* (*cheveux*) bunches

couffin [kufɛ̃] *nm* Moses basket

couler [kule] *vi* to flow, run; (*fuir: stylo, récipient*) to leak; (*nez*) to run; (*sombrer: bateau*) to sink ♦ *vt* (*cloche, sculpture*) to cast; (*bateau*) to sink; (*faire échouer: personne*) to bring down

couleur [kulœʀ] *nf* colour (*BRIT*), color (*US*); (*CARTES*) suit; **film/télévision en ~s** colo(u)r film/television

couleuvre [kulœvʀ] *nf* grass snake

coulisse [kulis] *nf*: **~s** *nfpl* (*THÉÂTRE*) wings; (*fig*): **dans les ~s** behind the scenes; **coulisser** *vi* to slide, run

couloir [kulwaʀ] *nm* corridor, passage; (*d'avion*) aisle; (*de bus*) gangway; **~ aérien/de navigation** air/shipping lane

coup [ku] *nm* (*heurt, choc*) knock; (*affectif*) blow, shock; (*agressif*) blow; (*avec arme à feu*) shot; (*de l'horloge*) stroke; (*tennis, golf*) stroke; (*boxe*) blow; (*fam: fois*) time; **~ de coude** nudge (with the elbow); **~ de tonnerre** clap of thunder; **~ de sonnette** ring of the bell; **donner un ~ de balai** to give the floor a sweep; **boire un ~** (*fam*) to have a drink; **être dans le ~** to be in on it; **du ~ ...** as a result; **d'un seul ~** (*subitement*) suddenly; (*à la fois*) at one go; **du premier ~** first time; **du même ~** at the same time; **à tous les ~s** (*fam*) every time; **tenir le ~** to hold out; **après ~** afterwards; **à ~ sûr** definitely, without fail; **~ sur ~** in quick succession; **sur le ~** outright; **sous le ~ de** (*surprise etc*) under the influence of; **en ~ de vent** in a tearing hurry; **~ de chance** stroke of luck; **~ de couteau** stab (of a knife); **~ d'État** coup; **~ de feu** shot; **~ de fil** (*fam*) phone call; **~ de frein** (sharp) braking *no pl*; **~ de main: donner un ~ de main à qn** to give sb a (helping) hand; **~ d'œil** glance; **~ de pied** kick; **~ de poing** punch; **~ de soleil** sunburn *no pl*; **~ de téléphone** phone call; **~ de tête** (*fig*) (sudden) impulse

coupable [kupabl] *adj* guilty ♦ *nm/f* (*gén*) culprit; (*JUR*) guilty party

coupe [kup] *nf* (*verre*) goblet; (*à fruits*) dish; (*SPORT*) cup; (*de cheveux, de vêtement*) cut; (*graphique, plan*) (cross) section

coupe-papier [kuppapje] *nm inv* paper knife

couper [kupe] *vt* to cut; (*retrancher*) to cut (out); (*route, courant*) to cut off; (*appétit*) to take away; (*vin à table*) to dilute ♦ *vi* to cut; (*prendre un raccourci*) to take a short-cut; **se ~** *vi* (*se blesser*) to cut o.s.; **~ la parole à qn** to cut sb short

couple [kupl] *nm* couple

couplet [kuple] *nm* verse

coupole [kupɔl] *nf* dome

coupon [kupɔ̃] *nm* (*ticket*) coupon; (*reste de tissu*) remnant; **coupon-réponse** *nm* reply coupon

coupure [kupyʀ] *nf* cut; (*billet de banque*) note; (*de journal*) cutting; **~ de courant** power cut

cour [kuʀ] *nf* (*de ferme, jardin*) (court)yard; (*d'immeuble*) back yard; (*JUR, royale*) court; **faire la ~ à qn** to court sb; **~ d'assises** court of assizes; **~ de récréation** playground; **~ martiale** court-martial

courage [kuʀaʒ] *nm* courage, bravery; **courageux, -euse** *adj* brave, courageous

couramment [kuʀamɑ̃] *adv* commonly; (*parler*) fluently

courant, e [kuʀɑ̃, ɑ̃t] *adj* (*fréquent*) common; (*COMM, gén: normal*) standard; (*en cours*) current ♦ *nm* current; (*fig*) movement; (*: d'opinion*) trend; **être au ~ (de)** (*fait, nouvelle*) to know (about); **mettre qn au ~ (de)** to tell sb (about); (*nouveau travail etc*) to teach sb the basics (of); **se te-**

nir au ~ (de) (*techniques etc*) to keep o.s. up-to-date (on); **dans le ~ de** (*pendant*) in the course of; **le 10 ~** (*COMM*) the 10th inst.; **~ d'air** draught; **~ électrique** (electric) current, power

courbature [kuʀbatyʀ] *nf* ache

courbe [kuʀb] *adj* curved ♦ *nf* curve; **courber** *vt* to bend; **se courber** *vi* (*personne*) to bend (down), stoop

coureur, -euse [kuʀœʀ, øz] *nm/f* (*SPORT*) runner (*ou* driver); (*péj*) womanizer; man-hunter; **~ automobile** racing driver

courge [kuʀʒ] *nf* (*CULIN*) marrow; **courgette** *nf* courgette (*BRIT*), zucchini (*US*)

courir [kuʀiʀ] *vi* to run ♦ *vt* (*SPORT: épreuve*) to compete in; (*risque*) to run; (*danger*) to face; **~ les magasins** to go round the shops; **le bruit court que** the rumour is going round that

couronne [kuʀɔn] *nf* crown; (*de fleurs*) wreath, circlet

courons *etc* [kuʀɔ̃] *vb voir* **courir**

courrier [kuʀje] *nm* mail, post; (*lettres à écrire*) letters *pl*; **~ électronique** E-mail

courroie [kuʀwa] *nf* strap; (*TECH*) belt

courrons *etc* [kuʀɔ̃] *vb voir* **courir**

cours [kuʀ] *nm* (*leçon*) class; (*: particulier*) lesson; (*série de leçons, cheminement*) course; (*écoulement*) flow; (*COMM: de devises*) rate; (*: de denrées*) price; **donner libre ~ à** to give free expression to; **avoir ~** (*SCOL*) to have a class *ou* lecture; **en ~** (*année*) current; (*travaux*) in progress; **en ~ de route** on the way; **au ~ de** in the course of, during; **~ d'eau** waterway; **~ du soir** night school; **~ intensif** crash course

course [kuʀs] *nf* running; (*SPORT: épreuve*) race; (*d'un taxi*) journey, trip; (*commission*) errand; **~s** *nfpl* (*achats*) shopping *sg*; **faire des ~s** to do some shopping

court, e [kuʀ, kuʀt(ə)] *adj* short ♦ *adv* short ♦ *nm*: **~ (de tennis)** (tennis) court; **à ~ de** short of; **prendre qn de ~** to catch sb unawares; **court-circuit** *nm* short-circuit

courtier, -ère [kuʀtje, jɛʀ] *nm/f* broker

courtiser [kuʀtize] *vt* to court, woo

courtois, e [kuʀtwa, waz] *adj* courteous; **courtoisie** *nf* courtesy

couru, e [kuʀy] *pp de* **courir**

cousais *etc* [kuze] *vb voir* **coudre**

couscous [kuskus] *nm* couscous

cousin, e [kuzɛ̃, in] *nm/f* cousin

coussin [kusɛ̃] *nm* cushion

cousu, e [kuzy] *pp de* **coudre**

coût [ku] *nm* cost; **le ~ de la vie** the cost of living; **coûtant** *adj m*: **au prix coûtant** at cost price

couteau, x [kuto] *nm* knife

coûter [kute] *vt, vi* to cost; **combien ça coûte?** how much is it?, what does it cost?; **coûte que coûte** at all costs; **coûteux, -euse** *adj* costly, expensive

coutume [kutym] *nf* custom

couture [kutyʀ] *nf* sewing; (*profession*) dressmaking; (*points*) seam; **couturier** *nm* fashion designer; **couturière** *nf* dressmaker

couvée [kuve] *nf* brood, clutch

couvent [kuvɑ̃] *nm* (*de sœurs*) convent; (*de frères*) monastery

couver [kuve] *vt* to hatch; (*maladie*) to be coming down with ♦ *vi* (*feu*) to smoulder; (*révolte*) to be brewing

couvercle [kuvɛʀkl] *nm* lid; (*de bombe aérosol etc, qui se visse*) cap, top

couvert, e [kuvɛʀ, ɛʀt] *pp de* **couvrir** ♦ *adj* (*ciel*) overcast ♦ *nm* place setting; (*place à table*) place; **~s** *nmpl* (*ustensiles*) cutlery *sg*; **~ de** covered with *ou* in; **mettre le ~** to lay the table

couverture [kuvɛʀtyʀ] *nf* blanket; (*de livre, assurance, fig*) cover; (*presse*) coverage; **~ chauffante** electric blanket

couveuse [kuvøz] *nf* (*de maternité*) incubator

couvre-feu [kuvʀəfø] *nm* curfew

couvre-lit [kuvʀəli] *nm* bedspread

couvreur [kuvʀœʀ] *nm* roofer

couvrir [kuvʀiʀ] *vt* to cover; **se ~** *vi* (*s'habiller*) to cover up; (*se coiffer*) to put on one's hat; (*ciel*) to cloud over

cow-boy [kobɔj] *nm* cowboy

crabe [kʀab] *nm* crab

cracher [kʀaʃe] *vi, vt* to spit

crachin [kʀaʃɛ̃] *nm* drizzle

crack [kʀak] *nm* (*fam: as*) ace

craie [kʀɛ] *nf* chalk

craindre [kʀɛ̃dʀ] *vt* to fear, be afraid of; (*être sensible à: chaleur, froid*) to be easily damaged by

crainte [kʀɛ̃t] *nf* fear; **de ~ de/que** for fear of/that; **craintif, -ive** *adj* timid

cramoisi, e [kʀamwazi] *adj* crimson

crampe [kʀɑ̃p] *nf* cramp

crampon [kʀɑ̃pɔ̃] *nm* (*de chaussure de football*) stud; (*de chaussure de course*) spike; (*d'alpinisme*) crampon; **cramponner** *vb*: **se cramponner (à)** to hang *ou* cling on (to)

cran [kʀɑ̃] *nm* (*entaille*) notch; (*de courroie*) hole; (*fam: courage*) guts *pl*; **~ d'arrêt** safety catch

crâne [kʀɑn] *nm* skull

crâner [kʀane] (*fam*) *vi* to show off

crapaud [kʀapo] *nm* toad

crapule [kʀapyl] *nf* villain

craquement [kʀakmɑ̃] *nm* crack, snap; (*du plancher*) creak, creaking *no pl*

craquer [kʀake] *vi* (*bois, plancher*) to creak; (*fil, branche*) to snap; (*couture*) to come apart; (*fig: accusé*) to break down; (: *fam*) to crack up ♦ *vt* (*allumette*) to strike; **j'ai craqué** (*fam*) I couldn't resist it

crasse [kʀas] *nf* grime, filth; **crasseux, -euse** *adj* grimy, filthy

cravache [kʀavaʃ] *nf* (*riding*) crop

cravate [kʀavat] *nf* tie

crawl [kʀol] *nm* crawl; **dos ~é** backstroke

crayon [kʀɛjɔ̃] *nm* pencil; **~ à bille** ballpoint pen; **~ de couleur** crayon, colouring pencil; **crayon-feutre** (*pl* **crayons-feutres**) *nm* felt(-tip) pen

créancier, -ière [kʀeɑ̃sje, jɛʀ] *nm/f* creditor

création [kʀeasjɔ̃] *nf* creation

créature [kʀeatyʀ] *nf* creature

crèche [kʀɛʃ] nf (de Noël) crib; (garderie) crèche, day nursery

crédit [kʀedi] nm (gén) credit; **~s** nmpl (fonds) funds; **payer/acheter à ~** to pay/buy on credit ou on easy terms; **faire ~ à qn** to give sb credit; **créditer** vt: **créditer un compte (de)** to credit an account (with)

crédule [kʀedyl] adj credulous, gullible

créer [kʀee] vt to create

crémaillère [kʀemajɛʀ] nf: **pendre la ~** to have a house-warming party

crématoire [kʀematwaʀ] adj: **four ~** crematorium

crème [kʀɛm] nf cream; (entremets) cream dessert ♦ adj inv cream(-coloured); **un (café) ~** ≃ a white coffee; **~ anglaise** (egg) custard; **~ chantilly** whipped cream; **~ fouettée = crème chantilly**; **crémerie** nf dairy; **crémeux, -euse** adj creamy

créneau, x [kʀeno] nm (de fortification) crenel(le); (dans marché) gap, niche; (AUTO): **faire un ~** to reverse into a parking space (between two cars alongside the kerb)

crêpe [kʀɛp] nf (galette) pancake ♦ nm (tissu) crêpe; **crêpé, e** adj (cheveux) backcombed; **crêperie** nf pancake shop ou restaurant

crépiter [kʀepite] vi (friture) to sputter, splutter; (fire) to crackle

crépu, e [kʀepy] adj frizzy, fuzzy

crépuscule [kʀepyskyl] nm twilight, dusk

cresson [kʀesɔ̃] nm watercress

crête [kʀɛt] nf (de coq) comb; (de vague, montagne) crest

creuser [kʀøze] vt (trou, tunnel) to dig; (sol) to dig a hole in; (fig) to go (deeply) into; **ça creuse** that gives you a real appetite; **se ~ la cervelle** (fam) to rack one's brains

creux, -euse [kʀø, kʀøz] adj hollow ♦ nm hollow; **heures creuses** slack periods; (électricité, téléphone) off-peak periods; **avoir un ~** (fam) to be hungry

crevaison [kʀəvezɔ̃] nf puncture

crevasse [kʀəvas] nf (dans le sol, la peau) crack; (de glacier) crevasse

crevé, e [kʀəve] (fam) adj (fatigué) all in, exhausted

crever [kʀəve] vt (ballon) to burst ♦ vi (pneu) to burst; (automobiliste) to have a puncture (BRIT) ou a flat (tire) (US); (fam) to die

crevette [kʀəvɛt] nf: **~ (rose)** prawn; **~ grise** shrimp

cri [kʀi] nm cry, shout; (d'animal: spécifique) cry, call; **c'est le dernier ~** (fig) it's the latest fashion

criant, e [kʀijɑ̃, kʀijɑ̃t] adj (injustice) glaring

criard, e [kʀijaʀ, kʀijaʀd] adj (couleur) garish, loud; (voix) yelling

crible [kʀibl] nm riddle; **passer qch au ~** (fig) to go over sth with a fine-tooth comb; **criblé, e** adj: **criblé de** riddled with; (de dettes) crippled with

cric [kʀik] nm (AUTO) jack

crier [kʀije] vi (pour appeler) to shout, cry (out); (de douleur etc) to scream, yell ♦ vt (injure) to shout (out), yell (out)

crime [kʀim] nm crime; (meurtre) murder; **criminel, le** nm/f criminal; (assassin) murderer

crin [kʀɛ̃] nm (de cheval) hair no pl

crinière [kʀinjɛʀ] nf mane

crique [kʀik] nf creek, inlet

criquet [kʀike] nm grasshopper

crise [kʀiz] nf crisis; (MÉD) attack; (: d'épilepsie) fit; **piquer une ~ de nerfs** to go hysterical; **~ cardiaque** heart attack; **~ de foie** bilious attack

crisper [kʀispe] vt (poings) to clench; **se ~** vi (visage) to tense; (personne) to get tense

crisser [kʀise] vi (neige) to crunch; (pneu) to screech

cristal, -aux [kʀistal, o] nm crystal; **cristallin, e** adj crystal-clear

critère [kʀitɛʀ] nm criterion

critiquable [kʀitikabl] adj open to criticism

critique [kʀitik] *adj* critical ♦ *nm/f (de théâtre, musique)* critic ♦ *nf* criticism; *(THÉÂTRE etc: article)* review

critiquer [kʀitike] *vt (dénigrer)* to criticize; *(évaluer)* to assess, examine (critically)

croasser [kʀɔase] *vi* to caw

Croatie [kʀɔasi] *nf* Croatia

croc [kʀo] *nm (dent)* fang; *(de boucher)* hook; **croc-en-jambe** *nm*: **faire un croc-en-jambe à qn** to trip sb up

croche [kʀɔʃ] *nf (MUS)* quaver *(BRIT)*, eighth note *(US)*; **croche-pied** *nm* = **croc-en-jambe**

crochet [kʀɔʃɛ] *nm* hook; *(détour)* detour; *(TRICOT: aiguille)* crochet hook; *(: technique)* crochet; **vivre aux ~s de qn** to live *ou* sponge off sb

crochu, e [kʀɔʃy] *adj (nez)* hooked; *(doigts)* claw-like

crocodile [kʀɔkɔdil] *nm* crocodile

croire [kʀwaʀ] *vt* to believe; **se ~ fort** to think one is strong; **~ que** to believe *ou* think that; **~ à, ~ en** to believe in

croîs [kʀwa] *vb voir* **croître**

croisade [kʀwazad] *nf* crusade

croisé, e [kʀwaze] *adj (veste)* double-breasted

croisement [kʀwazmɑ̃] *nm (carrefour)* crossroads *sg*; *(BIO)* crossing; *(: résultat)* crossbreed

croiser [kʀwaze] *vt (personne, voiture)* to pass; *(route)* to cross, cut across; *(BIO)* to cross; **se ~** *vi (personnes, véhicules)* to pass each other; *(routes, lettres)* to cross; *(regards)* to meet; **~ les jambes/bras** to cross one's legs/fold one's arms

croisière [kʀwazjɛʀ] *nf* cruise

croissance [kʀwasɑ̃s] *nf* growth

croissant [kʀwasɑ̃] *nm (à manger)* croissant; *(motif)* crescent

croître [kʀwatʀ] *vi* to grow

croix [kʀwa] *nf* cross; **~ gammée** swastika; **la C~ Rouge** the Red Cross

croque-monsieur [kʀɔkməsjø] *nm inv* toasted ham and cheese sandwich

croquer [kʀɔke] *vt (manger)* to crunch; *(: fruit)* to munch; *(dessiner)* to sketch; **chocolat à ~** plain dessert chocolate

croquis [kʀɔki] *nm* sketch

cross [kʀɔs] *nm*: **faire du ~ (à pied)** to do cross-country running

crosse [kʀɔs] *nf (de fusil)* butt; *(de revolver)* grip

crotte [kʀɔt] *nf* droppings *pl*; **crotté, e** *adj* muddy, mucky; **crottin** *nm* dung, manure; *(fromage)* (small round) cheese *(made of goat's milk)*

crouler [kʀule] *vi (s'effondrer)* to collapse; *(être délabré)* to be crumbling

croupe [kʀup] *nf* rump; **en ~** pillion

croupir [kʀupiʀ] *vi* to stagnate

croustillant, e [kʀustijɑ̃, ɑ̃t] *adj* crisp

croûte [kʀut] *nf* crust; *(du fromage)* rind; *(MÉD)* scab; **en ~** *(CULIN)* in pastry

croûton [kʀutɔ̃] *nm (CULIN)* crouton; *(bout du pain)* crust, heel

croyable [kʀwajabl] *adj* credible

croyant, e [kʀwajɑ̃, ɑ̃t] *nm/f* believer

CRS *sigle fpl* (= *Compagnies républicaines de sécurité*) state security police force ♦ *sigle m* member of the CRS

cru, e [kʀy] *pp de* **croire** ♦ *adj (non cuit)* raw; *(lumière, couleur)* harsh; *(paroles)* crude ♦ *nm (vignoble)* vineyard; *(vin)* wine; **un grand ~** a great vintage; **jambon ~** Parma ham

crû [kʀy] *pp de* **croître**

cruauté [kʀyote] *nf* cruelty

cruche [kʀyʃ] *nf* pitcher, jug

crucifix [kʀysifi] *nm* crucifix; **crucifixion** *nf* crucifixion

crudités [kʀydite] *nfpl (CULIN)* salads

crue [kʀy] *nf (inondation)* flood

cruel, le [kʀyɛl] *adj* cruel

crus *etc* [kʀy] *vb voir* **croire**; **croître**

crûs *etc* [kʀy] *vb voir* **croître**

crustacés [kʀystase] *nmpl* shellfish

Cuba [kyba] *nf* Cuba; **cubain, e** *adj* Cuban ♦ *nm/f*: **Cubain, e** Cuban

cube [kyb] *nm* cube; *(jouet)* brick; **mètre ~** cubic metre; **2 au ~** 2 cubed

cueillette [kœjɛt] *nf* picking; *(quantité)* crop, harvest

cueillir [kœjiʀ] *vt (fruits, fleurs)* to pick, gather; *(fig)* to catch

cuiller [kɥijɛʀ], **cuillère** [kɥijɛʀ] *nf* spoon; **~ à café** coffee spoon; *(CULIN)* teaspoonful; **~ à soupe** soup-spoon; *(CULIN)* tablespoonful; **cuillerée** *nf* spoonful

cuir [kɥiʀ] *nm* leather; **~ chevelu** scalp

cuire [kɥiʀ] *vt (aliments)* to cook; *(au four)* to bake ♦ *vi* to cook; **bien cuit** *(viande)* well done; **trop cuit** overdone

cuisant, e [kɥizɑ̃, ɑ̃t] *adj (douleur)* stinging; *(fig: souvenir, échec)* bitter

cuisine [kɥizin] *nf (pièce)* kitchen; *(art culinaire)* cookery, cooking; *(nourriture)* cooking, food; **faire la ~** to cook; **cuisiné, e** *adj*: **plat cuisiné** ready-made meal *ou* dish; **cuisiner** *vt* to cook; *(fam)* to grill ♦ *vi* to cook; **cuisinier, -ière** *nm/f* cook; **cuisinière** *nf (poêle)* cooker

cuisse [kɥis] *nf* thigh; *(CULIN)* leg

cuisson [kɥisɔ̃] *nf* cooking

cuit, e [kɥi, kɥit] *pp de* **cuire**

cuivre [kɥivʀ] *nm* copper; **les ~s** *(MUS)* the brass

cul [ky] *(fam!) nm* arse (!)

culbute [kylbyt] *nf* somersault; *(accidentelle)* tumble, fall

culminant, e [kylminɑ̃, ɑ̃t] *adj*: **point ~** highest point

culminer [kylmine] *vi* to reach its highest point

culot [kylo] *(fam) nm (effronterie)* cheek

culotte [kylɔt] *nf (de femme)* knickers *pl* *(BRIT)*, panties *pl*

culpabilité [kylpabilite] *nf* guilt

culte [kylt] *nm (religion)* religion; *(hommage, vénération)* worship; *(protestant)* service

cultivateur, -trice [kyltivatœʀ, tʀis] *nm/f* farmer

cultivé, e [kyltive] *adj (personne)* cultured, cultivated

cultiver [kyltive] *vt* to cultivate; *(légumes)* to grow, cultivate

culture [kyltyʀ] *nf* cultivation; *(connaissances etc)* culture; **les ~s intensives** intensive farming; **~ physique** physical training; **culturel, le** *adj* cultural; **culturisme** *nm* body-building

cumin [kymɛ̃] *nm* cumin

cumuler [kymyle] *vt (emplois)* to hold concurrently; *(salaires)* to draw concurrently

cupide [kypid] *adj* greedy, grasping

cure [kyʀ] *nf (MÉD)* course of treatment

curé [kyʀe] *nm* parish priest

cure-dent [kyʀdɑ̃] *nm* toothpick

cure-pipe [kyʀpip] *nm* pipe cleaner

curer [kyʀe] *vt* to clean out

curieusement [kyʀjøzmɑ̃] *adv* curiously

curieux, -euse [kyʀjø, jøz] *adj (indiscret)* curious, inquisitive; *(étrange)* strange, curious ♦ *nmpl (badauds)* onlookers; **curiosité** *nf* curiosity; *(site)* unusual feature

curriculum vitae [kyʀikylɔmvite] *nm inv* curriculum vitae

curseur [kyʀsœʀ] *nm (INFORM)* cursor

cutané, e [kytane] *adj* skin

cuti-réaction [kytiʀeaksjɔ̃] *nf (MÉD)* skin-test

cuve [kyv] *nf* vat; *(à mazout etc)* tank

cuvée [kyve] *nf* vintage

cuvette [kyvet] *nf (récipient)* bowl, basin; *(GÉO)* basin

CV *sigle m (AUTO)* = **cheval vapeur**; *(COMM)* = **curriculum vitae**

cyanure [sjanyʀ] *nm* cyanide

cybercafé [sibɛʀkafe] *nm* cybercafé

cyclable [siklabl] *adj*: **piste ~** cycle track

cyclable [siklabl] *adj*: **piste ~** cycle track

cycle [sikl] *nm* cycle; **cyclisme** *nm* cycling; **cycliste** *nm/f* cyclist ♦ *adj* cycle *cpd*; **coureur cycliste** racing cyclist

cyclomoteur [siklɔmɔtœʀ] *nm* moped

cyclone [siklon] *nm* hurricane

cygne [siɲ] *nm* swan

cylindre [silɛ̃dʀ] *nm* cylinder; **cylindrée** *nf (AUTO)* (cubic) capacity

cymbale [sɛ̃bal] *nf* cymbal

cynique [sinik] *adj* cynical

cystite [sistit] *nf* cystitis

D, d

d' [d] *prép voir* **de**

dactylo [daktilo] *nf* (*aussi:* **~graphe**) typist; (*aussi:* **~graphie**) typing; **dactylographier** *vt* to type (out)

dada [dada] *nm* hobby-horse

daigner [deɲe] *vt* to deign

daim [dɛ̃] *nm* (fallow) deer *inv*; (*cuir suédé*) suede

dalle [dal] *nf* paving stone, slab

daltonien, ne [daltɔnjɛ̃, jɛn] *adj* colour-blind

dam [dɑ̃] *nm*: **au grand ~ de** much to the detriment (*ou* annoyance) of

dame [dam] *nf* lady; (*CARTES, ÉCHECS*) queen; **~s** *nfpl* (*jeu*) draughts *sg* (*BRIT*), checkers *sg* (*US*)

damner [dɑne] *vt* to damn

dancing [dɑ̃siŋ] *nm* dance hall

Danemark [danmark] *nm* Denmark

danger [dɑ̃ʒe] *nm* danger; **dangereux, -euse** *adj* dangerous

danois, e [danwa, waz] *adj* Danish ♦ *nm/f*: **D~, e** Dane ♦ *nm* (*LING*) Danish

MOT-CLÉ

dans [dɑ̃] *prép* **1** (*position*) in; (*à l'intérieur de*) inside; **c'est dans le tiroir/le salon** it's in the drawer/lounge; **dans la boîte** in *ou* inside the box; **marcher dans la ville** to walk about the town

2 (*direction*) into; **elle a couru dans le salon** she ran into the lounge

3 (*provenance*) out of, from; **je l'ai pris dans le tiroir/salon** I took it out of *ou* from the drawer/lounge; **boire dans un verre** to drink out of *ou* from a glass

4 (*temps*) in; **dans 2 mois** in 2 months, in 2 months' time

5 (*approximation*) about; **dans les 20 F** about 20F

danse [dɑ̃s] *nf*: **la ~** dancing; **une ~** a

dance; **la ~ classique** ballet; **danser** *vi, vt* to dance; **danseur, -euse** *nm/f* ballet dancer; (*au bal etc*) dancer; (: *cavalier*) partner

dard [daʀ] *nm* (*d'animal*) sting

date [dat] *nf* date; **de longue ~** long-standing; **~ de naissance** date of birth; **~ de péremption** expiry date; **~ limite** deadline; **dater** *vt, vi* to date; **dater de** to date from; **à dater de** (as) from

datte [dat] *nf* date

dauphin [dofɛ̃] *nm* (*ZOOL*) dolphin

davantage [davɑ̃taʒ] *adv* more; (*plus long-temps*) longer; **~ de** more

MOT-CLÉ

de, d' [də] (*de + le* = **du**, *de + les* = **des**) *prép* **1** (*appartenance*) of; **le toit de la maison** the roof of the house; **la voiture d'Elisabeth/de mes parents** Elisabeth's/my parents' car

2 (*provenance*) from; **il vient de Londres** he comes from London; **elle est sortie du cinéma** she came out of the cinema

3 (*caractérisation, mesure*): **un mur de brique/bureau d'acajou** a brick wall/mahogany desk; **un billet de 50 F** a 50F note; **une pièce de 2 m de large** *ou* **large de 2 m** a room 2m wide, a 2m-wide room; **un bébé de 10 mois** a 10-month-old baby; **12 mois de crédit/travail** 12 months' credit/work; **augmenter de 10 F** to increase by 10F; **de 14 à 18** from 14 to 18

♦ *dét* **1** (*phrases affirmatives*) some (*souvent omis*); **du vin, de l'eau, des pommes** (some) wine, (some) water, (some) apples; **des enfants sont venus** some children came; **pendant des mois** for months

2 (*phrases interrogatives et négatives*) any; **a-t-il du vin?** has he got any wine?; **il n'a pas de pommes/d'enfants** he hasn't (got) any apples/children, he has no apples/children

dé |de| *nm* (*à jouer*) die *ou* dice; (*aussi:* ~ **à coudre**) thimble

dealer |dilœr| (*fam*) *nm* (drug) pusher

déambuler |deãbyle| *vi* to stroll about

débâcle |debakl| *nf* rout

déballer |debale| *vt* to unpack

débandade |debãdad| *nf* (*dispersion*) scattering

débarbouiller |debarbuje| *vt* to wash; **se ~** *vi* to wash (one's face)

débarcadère |debarkader| *nm* wharf

débardeur |debardœr| *nm* (*maillot*) tank top

débarquer |debarke| *vt* to unload, land ♦ *vi* to disembark; (*fig: fam*) to turn up

débarras |debara| *nm* (*pièce*) lumber room; (*placard*) junk cupboard; **bon ~!** good riddance!; **débarrasser** *vt* to clear; **se débarrasser de** *vt* to get rid of; **débarrasser qn de** (*vêtements, paquets*) to relieve sb of

débat |deba| *nm* discussion, debate; **débattre** *vt* to discuss, debate; **se débattre** *vi* to struggle

débaucher |deboʃe| *vt* (*licencier*) to lay off, dismiss; (*entraîner*) to lead astray, debauch

débile |debil| (*fam*) *adj* (*idiot*) dim-witted

débit |debi| *nm* (*d'un liquide, fleuve*) flow; (*d'un magasin*) turnover (of goods); (*élocution*) delivery; (*bancaire*) debit; **~ de boissons** drinking establishment; **~ de tabac** tobacconist's; **haut ~** (*Internet*) ≈ broadband; **débiter** *vt* (*compte*) to debit; (*couper: bois, viande*) to cut up; (*péj: dire*) to churn out; **débiteur, -trice** *nm/f* debtor ♦ *adj* in debit; (*compte*) debit *cpd*

déblayer |debleje| *vt* to clear

débloquer |debloke| *vt* (*prix, crédits*) to free

déboires |debwar| *nmpl* setbacks

déboiser |debwaze| *vt* to deforest

déboîter |debwate| *vt* (*AUTO*) to pull out; **se ~ le genou** *etc* to dislocate one's knee *etc*

débonnaire |deboner| *adj* easy-going, good-natured

débordé, e |deborde| *adj*: **être ~ (de)** (*travail, demandes*) to be snowed under (with)

déborder |deborde| *vi* to overflow; (*lait etc*) to boil over; **~ (de) qch** (*dépasser*) to extend beyond sth

débouché |debuʃe| *nm* (*pour vendre*) outlet; (*perspective d'emploi*) opening

déboucher |debuʃe| *vt* (*évier, tuyau etc*) to unblock; (*bouteille*) to uncork ♦ *vi*: **~ de** to emerge from; **~ sur** (*études*) to lead on to

débourser |deburse| *vt* to pay out

déboussolé, e |debusole| (*fam*) *adj* disorientated

debout |d(ə)bu| *adv*: **être ~** (*personne*) to be standing, stand; (: *levé, éveillé*) to be up; **se mettre ~** to stand up; **se tenir ~** to stand; **~!** stand up!; (*du lit*) get up!; **cette histoire ne tient pas ~** this story doesn't hold water

déboutonner |debutone| *vt* to undo, unbutton

débraillé, e |debraje| *adj* slovenly, untidy

débrancher |debrãʃe| *vt* to disconnect; (*appareil électrique*) to unplug

débrayage |debrejaʒ| *nm* (*AUTO*) clutch; **débrayer** *vi* (*AUTO*) to declutch; (*cesser le travail*) to stop work

débris |debri| *nmpl* fragments

débrouillard, e |debrujar, ard| (*fam*) *adj* smart, resourceful

débrouiller |debruje| *vt* to disentangle, untangle; **se ~** *vi* to manage; **débrouillez-vous** you'll have to sort things out yourself

début |deby| *nm* beginning, start; **~s** *nmpl* (*de carrière*) début *sg*; **~ juin** in early June; **débutant, e** *nm/f* beginner, novice; **débuter** *vi* to begin, start; (*faire ses débuts*) to start out

deçà |dəsa|: **en ~ de** *prép* this side of

décadence |dekadãs| *nf* decline

décaféiné, e |dekafeine| *adj* decaffeinated

décalage |dekalaʒ| *nm* gap; **~ horaire** time difference

décaler [dekale] *vt* to shift

décalquer [dekalke] *vt* to trace

décamper [dekɑ̃pe] (*fam*) *vi* to clear out *ou* off

décaper [dekape] *vt* (*surface peinte*) to strip

décapiter [dekapite] *vt* (*par accident*) to behead; (*par accident*) to decapitate

décapotable [dekapɔtabl] *adj* convertible

décapsuleur [dekapsylœʁ] *nm* bottle-opener

décarcasser [dekaʁkase]: **se ~** (*fam*) *vi* to flog o.s. to death

décédé, e [desede] *adj* deceased

décéder [desede] *vi* to die

déceler [des(ə)le] *vt* (*trouver*) to discover, detect

décembre [desɑ̃bʁ] *nm* December

décemment [desamɑ̃] *adv* decently

décennie [deseni] *nf* decade

décent, e [desɑ̃, ɑ̃t] *adj* decent

déception [desɛpsjɔ̃] *nf* disappointment

décerner [desɛʁne] *vt* to award

décès [desɛ] *nm* death

décevant, e [des(ə)vɑ̃, ɑ̃t] *adj* disappointing

décevoir [des(ə)vwaʁ] *vt* to disappoint

déchaîner [deʃene] *vt* (*violence*) to unleash; (*enthousiasme*) to arouse; **se ~** (*tempête*) to rage; (*personne*) to fly into a rage

déchanter [deʃɑ̃te] *vi* to become disillusioned

décharge [deʃaʁʒ] *nf* (*dépôt d'ordures*) rubbish tip *ou* dump; (*électrique*) electrical discharge; **décharger** *vt* (*marchandise, véhicule*) to unload; (*tirer*) to discharge; **se décharger** *vi* (*batterie*) to go flat; **décharger qn de** (*responsabilité*) to release sb from

décharné, e [deʃaʁne] *adj* emaciated

déchausser [deʃose] *vt* (*skis*) to take off; **se ~** *vi* to take off one's shoes; (*dent*) to come *ou* work loose

déchéance [deʃeɑ̃s] *nf* (*physique*) degeneration; (*morale*) decay

déchet [deʃɛ] *nm* (*reste*) scrap; **~s** *nmpl* (*ordures*) refuse *sg*, rubbish *sg*; **~s nucléaires** nuclear waste

déchiffrer [deʃifʁe] *vt* to decipher

déchiqueter [deʃik(ə)te] *vt* to tear *ou* pull to pieces

déchirant, e [deʃiʁɑ̃, ɑ̃t] *adj* heart-rending

déchirement [deʃiʁmɑ̃] *nm* (*chagrin*) wrench, heartbreak; (*gén pl*: *conflit*) rift, split

déchirer [deʃiʁe] *vt* to tear; (*en morceaux*) to tear up; (*arracher*) to tear out; (*fig*: *conflit*) to tear (apart); **se ~** *vi* to tear, rip; **se ~ un muscle** to tear a muscle

déchirure [deʃiʁyʁ] *nf* (*accroc*) tear, rip; **~ musculaire** torn muscle

déchoir [deʃwaʁ] *vi* (*personne*) to lower o.s., demean o.s.

déchu, e [deʃy] *adj* (*roi*) deposed

décidé, e [deside] *adj* (*personne, air*) determined; **c'est ~** it's decided; **décidément** *adv* really

décider [deside] *vt*: **~ qch** to decide on sth; **se ~ (à faire)** to decide (to do), make up one's mind (to do); **se ~ pour** to decide on *ou* in favour of; **~ de faire/que** to decide to do/that; **~ qn (à faire qch)** to persuade sb (to do sth)

décimal, e, -aux [desimal, o] *adj* decimal; **décimale** *nf* decimal

décimètre [desimɛtʁ] *nm* decimetre

décisif, -ive [desizif, iv] *adj* decisive

décision [desizjɔ̃] *nf* decision

déclaration [deklaʁasjɔ̃] *nf* declaration; (*discours*: POL *etc*) statement; **~ (d'impôts)** ≈ tax return

déclarer [deklaʁe] *vt* to declare; (*décès, naissance*) to register; **se ~** *vi* (*feu*) to break out

déclencher [deklɑ̃ʃe] *vt* (*mécanisme etc*) to release; (*sonnerie*) to set off; (*attaque, grève*) to launch; (*provoquer*) to trigger off; **se ~** *vi* to go off

déclic [deklik] *nm* (*bruit*) click

décliner [dekline] *vi* to decline ♦ *vt* (*invitation*) to decline; (*nom, adresse*) to state

décocher [dekɔʃe] vt (coup de poing) to throw; (flèche, regard) to shoot

décoiffer [dekwafe] vt: ~ **qn** to mess up sb's hair; **je suis toute décoiffée** my hair is in a real mess

déçois etc [deswa] vb voir **décevoir**

décollage [dekɔlaʒ] nm (AVIAT) takeoff

décoller [dekɔle] vt to unstick ♦ vi (avion) to take off; **se ~** vi to come unstick

décolleté, e [dekɔlte] adj low-cut ♦ nm low neck(line); (plongeant) cleavage

décolorer [dekɔlɔʀe]: **se ~** vi to fade; **se faire ~ les cheveux** to have one's hair bleached

décombres [dekɔ̃bʀ] nmpl rubble sg, debris sg

décommander [dekɔmɑ̃de] vt to cancel; **se ~** to cry off

décomposé, e [dekɔ̃poze] adj (pourri) decomposed; (visage) haggard, distorted

décompte [dekɔ̃t] nm deduction; (facture) detailed account

déconcerter [dekɔ̃sɛʀte] vt to disconcert, confound

déconfit, e [dekɔ̃fi, it] adj crestfallen

décongeler [dekɔ̃ʒ(ə)le] vt to thaw

déconner [dekɔne] (fam) vi to talk rubbish

déconseiller [dekɔ̃seje] vt: ~ **qch (à qn)** to advise (sb) against sth; **c'est déconseillé** it's not recommended

décontracté, e [dekɔ̃tʀakte] adj relaxed, laid-back (fam)

décontracter [dekɔ̃tʀakte]: **se ~** vi to relax

déconvenue [dekɔ̃v(ə)ny] nf disappointment

décor [dekɔʀ] nm décor; (paysage) scenery; **~s** nmpl (THÉÂTRE) scenery sg, décor sg; (CINÉMA) set sg; **décorateur** nm (interior) decorator; **décoration** nf decoration; **décorer** vt to decorate

décortiquer [dekɔʀtike] vt to shell; (fig: texte) to dissect

découcher [dekuʃe] vi to spend the night away from home

découdre [dekudʀ]: **se ~** vi to come un-

stitched

découler [dekule] vi: ~ **de** to ensue ou follow from

découper [dekupe] vt (papier, tissu etc) to cut up; (viande) to carve; (article) to cut out; **se ~ sur** to stand out against

décourager [dekuʀaʒe] vt to discourage; **se ~** vi to lose heart, become discouraged

décousu, e [dekuzy] adj unstitched; (fig) disjointed, disconnected

découvert, e [dekuvɛʀ, ɛʀt] adj (tête) bare, uncovered; (lieu) open, exposed ♦ nm (bancaire) overdraft; **découverte** nf discovery; **faire la découverte de** to discover

découvrir [dekuvʀiʀ] vt to discover; (enlever ce qui couvre) to uncover; (dévoiler) to reveal; **se ~** vi (chapeau) to take off one's hat; (vêtement) to take something off; (ciel) to clear

décret [dekʀɛ] nm decree; **décréter** vt to decree

décrié, e [dekʀije] adj disparaged

décrire [dekʀiʀ] vt to describe

décrocher [dekʀɔʃe] vt (détacher) to take down; (téléphone) to take off the hook; (: pour répondre) to lift the receiver; (fam: contrat etc) to get, land ♦ vi (fam: abandonner) to drop out; (: cesser d'écouter) to switch off

décroître [dekʀwɑtʀ] vi to decrease, decline

décrypter [dekʀipte] vt to decipher

déçu, e [desy] pp de **décevoir**

décupler [dekyple] vt, vi to increase tenfold

dédaigner [dedeɲe] vt to despise, scorn; (négliger) to disregard, spurn; **dédaigneux, -euse** adj scornful, disdainful; **dédain** nm scorn, disdain

dédale [dedal] nm maze

dedans [dədɑ̃] adv inside; (pas en plein air) indoors, inside ♦ nm inside; **au ~** inside

dédicacer [dedikase] vt: ~ **(à qn)** to sign (for sb), autograph (for sb)

dédier [dedje] vt to dedicate

dédire [dediʀ]: **se ~** vi to go back on one's word, retract

dédommagement [dedɔmaʒmɑ̃] nm compensation

dédommager [dedɔmaʒe] vt: **~ qn (de)** to compensate sb (for)

dédouaner [dedwane] vt to clear through customs

dédoubler [deduble] vt (*classe, effectifs*) to split (into two)

déduire [dedɥiʀ] vt: **~ qch (de)** (*ôter*) to deduct sth (from); (*conclure*) to deduce *ou* infer sth (from)

déesse [deɛs] nf goddess

défaillance [defajɑ̃s] nf (*syncope*) blackout; (*fatigue*) (sudden) weakness *no pl*; (*technique*) fault, failure; **~ cardiaque** heart failure

défaillir [defajiʀ] vi to feel faint; (*mémoire etc*) to fail

défaire [defɛʀ] vt to undo; (*installation*) to take down, dismantle; **se ~** vi to come undone; **se ~ de** to get rid of

défait, e [defɛ, ɛt] adj (*visage*) haggard, ravaged; **défaite** nf defeat

défalquer [defalke] vt to deduct

défaut [defo] nm (*moral*) fault, failing, defect; (*tissus*) fault, flaw; (*manque, carence*): **~ de** shortage of; **prendre qn en ~** to catch sb out; **faire ~** (*manquer*) to be lacking; **à ~** for lack *ou* want of

défavorable [defavɔʀabl] adj unfavourable (*BRIT*), unfavorable (*US*)

défavoriser [defavɔʀize] vt to put at a disadvantage

défection [defɛksjɔ̃] nf defection, failure to give support

défectueux, -euse [defɛktɥø, øz] adj faulty, defective

défendre [defɑ̃dʀ] vt to defend; (*interdire*) to forbid; **se ~** vi to defend o.s.; **~ à qn qch/de faire** to forbid sb sth/to do; **il se défend** (*fam: se débrouille*) he can hold his own; **se ~ de/contre** (*se protéger*) to protect o.s. from/against; **se ~ de** (*se garder de*) to refrain from

défense [defɑ̃s] nf defence; (*d'éléphant etc*) tusk; **"~ de fumer"** "no smoking"

déférer [defeʀe] vt (*JUR*) to refer; **~ à** (*requête, décision*) to defer to

déferler [defeʀle] vi (*vagues*) to break; (*fig: foule*) to surge

défi [defi] nm challenge; **lancer un ~ à qn** to challenge sb; **sur un ton de ~** defiantly

déficit [defisit] nm (*COMM*) deficit; **déficitaire** adj in deficit

défier [defje] vt (*provoquer*) to challenge; (*mort, autorité*) to defy

défigurer [defigyʀe] vt to disfigure

défilé [defile] nm (*GÉO*) (narrow) gorge *ou* pass; (*soldats*) parade; (*manifestants*) procession, march; **~ de mode** fashion parade

défiler [defile] vi (*troupes*) to march past; (*sportifs*) to parade; (*manifestants*) to march; (*visiteurs*) to pour, stream; **se ~** vi: **il s'est défilé** (*fam*) he wriggled out of it

définir [definiʀ] vt to define

définitif, -ive [definitif, iv] adj (*final*) final, definitive; (*pour longtemps*) permanent, definitive; (*refus*) definite; **définitive** nf: **en définitive** eventually; (*somme toute*) in fact; **définitivement** adv (*partir, s'installer*) for good

défoncer [defɔ̃se] vt (*porte*) to smash in *ou* down; **se ~** (*fam*) vi (*travailler*) to work like a dog; (*drogué*) to get high

déformer [defɔʀme] vt to put out of shape; (*pensée, fait*) to distort; **se ~** vi to lose its shape

défouler [defule]: **se ~** vi to unwind, let off steam

défraîchir [defʀeʃiʀ]: **se ~** vi to fade

défricher [defʀiʃe] vt to clear (for cultivation)

défunt, e [defœ̃, œ̃t] nm/f deceased

dégagé, e [degaʒe] adj (*route, ciel*) clear; **sur un ton ~** casually

dégagement [degaʒmɑ̃] nm: **voie de ~**

slip road

dégager [degaʒe] vt (exhaler) to give off; (délivrer) to free, extricate; (désencombrer) to clear; (isoler: idée, aspect) to bring out; **se ~** vi (passage, ciel) to clear

dégarnir [degaʀniʀ] vt (vider) to empty, clear; **se ~** vi (tempes, crâne) to go bald

dégâts [dega] nmpl damage sg

dégel [deʒɛl] nm thaw; **dégeler** vt to thaw (out)

dégénérer [deʒeneʀe] vi to degenerate

dégingandé, e [deʒɛ̃gɑ̃de] adj gangling

dégivrer [deʒivʀe] vt (frigo) to defrost; (vitres) to de-ice

dégonflé, e [degɔ̃fle] adj (pneu) flat

dégonfler [degɔ̃fle] vt (pneu, ballon) to let down, deflate; **se ~** vi (fam) to chicken out

dégouliner [deguline] vi to trickle, drip

dégourdi, e [deguʀdi] adj smart, resourceful

dégourdir [deguʀdiʀ] vt: **se ~ les jambes** to stretch one's legs (fig)

dégoût [degu] nm disgust, distaste; **dégoûtant, e** adj disgusting; **dégoûté, e** adj disgusted; **dégoûté de** sick of; **dégoûter** vt to disgust; **dégoûter qn de qch** to put sb off sth

dégrader [degʀade] vt (MIL: officier) to degrade; (abîmer) to damage, deface; **se ~** vi (relations, situation) to deteriorate

dégrafer [degʀafe] vt to unclip, unhook

degré [dəgʀe] nm degree

dégressif, -ive [degʀesif, iv] adj on a decreasing scale

dégringoler [degʀɛ̃gɔle] vi to tumble (down)

dégrossir [degʀosiʀ] vt (fig: projet) to work out roughly

déguenillé, e [deg(ə)nije] adj ragged, tattered

déguerpir [degɛʀpiʀ] vi to clear off

dégueulasse [degœlas] (fam) adj disgusting

dégueuler [degœle] (fam) vi to throw up

déguisement [degizmɑ̃] nm (pour s'amuser) fancy dress

déguiser [degize]: **se ~** vi (se costumer) to dress up; (pour tromper) to disguise o.s.

dégustation [degystasjɔ̃] nf (de fromages etc) sampling; **~ de vins** wine-tasting session

déguster [degyste] vt (vins) to taste; (fromages etc) to sample; (savourer) to enjoy, savour

dehors [dəɔʀ] adv outside; (en plein air) outdoors ♦ nm outside ♦ nmpl (apparences) appearances; **mettre** ou **jeter ~** (expulser) to throw out; **au ~** outside; **au ~ de** outside; **en ~ de** (hormis) apart from

déjà [deʒa] adv already; (auparavant) before, already

déjeuner [deʒœne] vi to (have) lunch; (le matin) to have breakfast ♦ nm lunch

déjouer [deʒwe] vt (complot) to foil

delà [dəla] adv: **en ~ (de), au ~ (de)** beyond

délabrer [delabʀe]: **se ~** vi to fall into decay, become dilapidated

délacer [delase] vt (chaussures) to undo

délai [delɛ] nm (attente) waiting period; (sursis) extension of time; (temps accordé) time limit; **sans ~** without delay; **dans les ~s** within the time limit

délaisser [delese] vt to abandon, desert

délasser [delase] vt to relax; **se ~** vi to relax

délavé, e [delave] adj faded

délayer [deleje] vt (CULIN) to mix (with water etc); (peinture) to thin down

delco [dɛlko] nm (AUTO) distributor

délecter [delɛkte]: **se ~** vi to revel ou delight in

délégué, e [delege] nm/f representative

déléguer [delege] vt to delegate

délibéré, e [delibere] adj (conscient) deliberate

délibérer [delibere] vi to deliberate

délicat, e [delika, at] adj delicate; (plein de tact) tactful; (attention) thoughtful; **délicatement** adv delicately; (avec douceur) gently

délice [delis] *nm* delight

délicieux, -euse [delisjø, jøz] *adj (au goût)* delicious; *(sensation)* delightful

délimiter [delimite] *vt (terrain)* to delimit, demarcate

délinquance [delɛ̃kɑ̃s] *nf* criminality

délirant, e [deliʀɑ̃, ɑ̃t] *(fam) adj* wild

délirer [deliʀe] *vi* to be delirious; **tu délires!** *(fam)* you're crazy!

délit [deli] *nm* (criminal) offence

délivrer [delivʀe] *vt (prisonnier)* to (set) free, release; *(passeport)* to issue

déloger [delɔʒe] *vt (objet coincé)* to dislodge

déloyal, e, -aux [delwajal, o] *adj (ami)* disloyal; *(procédé)* unfair

deltaplane [dɛltaplan] *nm* hang-glider

déluge [delyʒ] *nm (pluie)* downpour; *(biblique)* Flood

déluré, e [delyʀe] *(péj) adj* forward, pert

demain [d(ə)mɛ̃] *adv* tomorrow

demande [d(ə)mɑ̃d] *nf (requête)* request; *(revendication)* demand; *(d'emploi)* application; *(ÉCON:* **la ~** demand; **"~s d'emploi"** *(annonces)* "situations wanted"; **~ en mariage** proposal (of marriage)

demandé, e [d(ə)mɑ̃de] *adj (article etc)*: **très ~** (very) much in demand

demander [d(ə)mɑ̃de] *vt* to ask for; *(chemin, heure etc)* to ask; *(nécessiter)* to require, demand; **se ~ si/pourquoi** *etc* to wonder whether/why *etc*; **~ qch à qn** to ask sb for sth; **~ un service à qn** to ask sb a favour; **~ à qn de faire** to ask sb to do; **demandeur, -euse** *nm/f*: **demandeur d'emploi** job-seeker; **~ d'asile** asylum-seeker

démangeaison [demɑ̃ʒɛzɔ̃] *nf* itching; **avoir des ~s** to be itching

démanger [demɑ̃ʒe] *vi* to itch

démanteler [demɑ̃t(ə)le] *vt* to break up

démaquillant [demakijɑ̃] *nm* make-up remover

démaquiller [demakije] *vt*: **se ~** to remove one's make-up

démarche [demaʀʃ] *nf (allure)* gait, walk;

(intervention) step; *(fig: intellectuelle)* thought processes *pl*; **faire les ~s nécessaires (pour obtenir qch)** to take the necessary steps (to obtain sth)

démarcheur, -euse [demaʀʃœʀ, øz] *nm/f (COMM)* door-to-door salesman(-woman)

démarque [demaʀk] *nf (article)* markdown

démarrage [demaʀaʒ] *nm* start

démarrer [demaʀe] *vi (conducteur)* to start (up); *(véhicule)* to move off; *(travaux)* to get moving; **démarreur** *nm (AUTO)* starter

démêlant [demɛlɑ̃] *nm* conditioner

démêler [demɛle] *vt* to untangle; **démêlés** *nmpl* problems

déménagement [demenaʒmɑ̃] *nm* move; **camion de ~** removal van

déménager [demenaʒe] *vt (meubles)* to (re)move ♦ *vi* to move (house); **déménageur** *nm* removal man

démener [dem(ə)ne]: **se ~** *vi (se dépenser)* to exert o.s.; *(pour obtenir qch)* to go to great lengths

dément, e [demɑ̃, ɑ̃t] *adj (fou)* mad, crazy; *(fam)* brilliant, fantastic

démentiel, le [demɑ̃sjɛl] *adj* insane

démentir [demɑ̃tiʀ] *vt* to refute; **~ que** to deny that

démerder [demɛʀde] *(fam)*: **se ~** *vi* to sort things out for o.s.

démesuré, e [dem(ə)zyʀe] *adj* immoderate

démettre [demɛtʀ] *vt*: **~ qn de** *(fonction, poste)* to dismiss sb from; **se ~ l'épaule** *etc* to dislocate one's shoulder *etc*

demeurant [d(ə)mœʀɑ̃]: **au ~** *adv* for all that

demeure [d(ə)mœʀ] *nf* residence; **demeurer** *vi (habiter)* to live; *(rester)* to remain

demi, e [dəmi] *adj* half ♦ *nm (bière)* ≈ half-pint *(0,25 litres)* ♦ *préfixe*: **~...** half-, semi..., demi-; **trois heures/bouteilles et ~es** three and a half hours/bottles, three hours/bottles and a half; **il est 2 heures**

et ~e/midi et ~ it's half past 2/half past 12; **à ~** half-; **à la ~e** (*heure*) on the half-hour; **demi-cercle** *nm* semicircle; **en demi-cercle ♦** *adj* semicircular **♦** *adv* in a half circle; **demi-douzaine** *nf* half-dozen, half a dozen; **demi-finale** *nf* semifinal; **demi-frère** *nm* half-brother; **demi-heure** *nf* half-hour, half an hour; **demi-journée** *nf* half-day, half a day; **demi-litre** *nm* half-litre, half a litre; **demi-livre** *nf* half-pound, half a pound; **demi-mot** *adv*: **à demi-mot** without having to spell things out; **demi-pension** *nf* (*à l'hôtel*) half-board; **demi-pensionnaire** *nm/f*: **être demi-pensionnaire** to take school lunches; **demi-place** *nf* half-fare

démis, e [demi, iz] *adj* (*épaule etc*) dislocated

demi-sel [dəmisɛl] *adj inv* (*beurre, fromage*) slightly salted

demi-sœur [dəmisœʀ] *nf* half-sister

démission [demisjɔ̃] *nf* resignation; **donner sa ~** to give ou hand in one's notice; **démissionner** *vi* to resign

demi-tarif [dəmitaʀif] *nm* half-price; **voyager à ~-~** to travel half-fare

demi-tour [dəmituʀ] *nm* about-turn; **faire ~-~** to turn (and go) back

démocratie [demɔkʀasi] *nf* democracy; **démocratique** *adj* democratic

démodé, e [demɔde] *adj* old-fashioned

demoiselle [d(ə)mwazɛl] *nf* (*jeune fille*) young lady; (*célibataire*) single lady, maiden lady; **~ d'honneur** bridesmaid

démolir [demɔliʀ] *vt* to demolish

démon [demɔ̃] *nm* (*enfant turbulent*) devil, demon; **le D~** the Devil

démonstration [demɔ̃stʀasjɔ̃] *nf* demonstration

démonté, e [demɔ̃te] *adj* (*mer*) raging, wild

démonter [demɔ̃te] *vt* (*machine etc*) to take down, dismantle

démontrer [demɔ̃tʀe] *vt* to demonstrate

démordre [demɔʀdʀ] *vi*: **ne pas ~ de** to refuse to give up, stick to

démouler [demule] *vt* to turn out

démuni, e [demyni] *adj* (*sans argent*) impoverished; **~ de** without

démunir [demyniʀ] *vt*: **~ qn de** to deprive sb of; **se ~ de** to part with, give up

dénaturer [denatyʀe] *vt* (*goût*) to alter; (*pensée, fait*) to distort

dénicher [deniʃe] (*fam*) *vt* (*objet*) to unearth; (*restaurant etc*) to discover

dénier [denje] *vt* to deny

dénigrer [denigʀe] *vt* to denigrate, run down

dénivellation [denivelasjɔ̃] *nf* (*pente*) slope

dénombrer [denɔ̃bʀe] *vt* to count

dénomination [denɔminasjɔ̃] *nf* designation, appellation

dénommé, e [denɔme] *adj*: **un ~ Dupont** a certain Mr Dupont

dénoncer [denɔ̃se] *vt* to denounce

dénouement [denumɑ̃] *nm* outcome

dénouer [denwe] *vt* to unknot, undo; **se ~** *vi* (*nœud*) to come undone

dénoyauter [denwajote] *vt* to stone

denrée [dɑ̃ʀe] *nf*: **~s (alimentaires)** foodstuffs

dense [dɑ̃s] *adj* dense; **densité** *nf* density

dent [dɑ̃] *nf* tooth; **~ de lait/sagesse** milk/wisdom tooth; **dentaire** *adj* dental

dentelé, e [dɑ̃t(ə)le] *adj* jagged, indented

dentelle [dɑ̃tɛl] *nf* lace *no pl*

dentier [dɑ̃tje] *nm* denture

dentifrice [dɑ̃tifʀis] *nm* toothpaste

dentiste [dɑ̃tist] *nm/f* dentist

dentition [dɑ̃tisjɔ̃] *nf* teeth

dénuder [denyde] *vt* to bare

dénué, e [denɥe] *adj*: **~ de** devoid of; **dénuement** *nm* destitution

déodorant [deɔdɔʀɑ̃] *nm* deodorant

déontologie [deɔtɔlɔʒi] *nf* code of practice

dépannage [depanaʒ] *nm*: **service de ~** (*AUTO*) breakdown service

dépanner [depane] *vt* (*voiture, télévision*) to fix, repair; (*fig*) to bail out, help out; **dépanneuse** *nf* breakdown lorry (*BRIT*), tow truck (*US*)

dépareillé, e [depaʀeje] *adj* (*collection, service*) incomplete; (*objet*) odd

départ [depaʀ] *nm* departure; (*SPORT*) start; **au ~** at the start; **la veille de son ~** the day before he leaves/left

départager [depaʀtaʒe] *vt* to decide between

département [depaʀtəmɑ̃] *nm* department

---

département

i France is divided into 96 administrative units called **départements**. These local government divisions are headed by a state-appointed **préfet**, and administered by an elected **Conseil général**. Départements are usually named after prominent geographical features such as rivers or mountain ranges; see also **DOM-TOM**.

---

dépassé, e [depɑse] *adj* superseded, outmoded; **il est complètement ~** he's completely out of his depth, he can't cope

dépasser [depɑse] *vt* (*véhicule, concurrent*) to overtake; (*endroit*) to pass, go past; (*somme, limite*) to exceed; (*fig: en beauté etc*) to surpass, outshine ♦ *vi* (*jupon etc*) to show

dépaysé, e [depeize] *adj* disoriented

dépaysement [depeizmɑ̃] *nm* (*changement*) change of scenery

dépecer [depəse] *vt* to joint, cut up

dépêche [depɛʃ] *nf* dispatch

dépêcher [depeʃe]: **se ~** *vi* to hurry

dépeindre [depɛ̃dʀ] *vt* to depict

dépendance [depɑ̃dɑ̃s] *nf* dependence; (*bâtiment*) outbuilding

dépendre [depɑ̃dʀ]: **~ de** *vt* to depend on; (*financièrement etc*) to be dependent on

dépens [depɑ̃] *nmpl*: **aux ~ de** at the expense of

dépense [depɑ̃s] *nf* spending *no pl*, expense, expenditure *no pl*; **dépenser** *vt*

to spend; (*énergie*) to expend, use up; **se dépenser** *vi* to exert o.s.; **dépensier, -ière** *adj*: **il est dépensier** he's a spendthrift

dépérir [depeʀiʀ] *vi* (*personne*) to waste away; (*plante*) to wither

dépêtrer [depetʀe] *vt*: **se ~ de** to extricate o.s. from

dépeupler [depœple]: **se ~** *vi* to become depopulated

dépilatoire [depilatwaʀ] *adj* depilatory, hair-removing

dépister [depiste] *vt* to detect; (*voleur*) to track down

dépit [depi] *nm* vexation, frustration; **en ~ de** in spite of; **en ~ du bon sens** contrary to all good sense; **dépité, e** *adj* vexed, frustrated

déplacé, e [deplase] *adj* (*propos*) out of place, uncalled-for

déplacement [deplasmɑ̃] *nm* (*voyage*) trip, travelling *no pl*

déplacer [deplase] *vt* (*table, voiture*) to move, shift; **se ~** *vi* to move; (*voyager*) to travel; **se ~ une vertèbre** to slip a disc

déplaire [deplɛʀ] *vt*: **ça me déplaît** I don't like this, I dislike this; **se ~** *vi* to be unhappy; **déplaisant, e** *adj* disagreeable

dépliant [deplijɑ̃] *nm* leaflet

déplier [deplije] *vt* to unfold

déplorer [deplɔʀe] *vt* to deplore

déployer [deplwaje] *vt* (*carte*) to open out; (*ailes*) to spread; (*troupes*) to deploy

déporter [depɔʀte] *vt* (*exiler*) to deport; (*dévier*) to carry off course

déposer [depoze] *vt* (*gén: mettre, poser*) to lay *ou* put down; (*à la banque, à la consigne*) to deposit; (*passager*) to drop (off), set down; (*roi*) to depose; (*plainte*) to lodge; (*marque*) to register; **se ~** *vi* to settle; **dépositaire** *nm/f* (*COMM*) agent; **déposition** *nf* statement

dépôt [depo] *nm* (*à la banque, sédiment*) deposit; (*entrepôt*) warehouse, store

dépotoir [depɔtwaʀ] *nm* dumping ground, rubbish dump

dépouiller [depuje] *vt* (*documents*) to go through, peruse; **~ qn/qch de** to strip sb/sth of; **~ le scrutin** to count the votes

dépourvu, e [depuʀvy] *adj*: **~ de** lacking in, without; **prendre qn au ~** to catch sb unprepared

déprécier [depʀesje]: **se ~** *vi* to depreciate

dépression [depʀesjɔ̃] *nf* depression; **~ (nerveuse)** (nervous) breakdown

déprimant, e [depʀimɑ̃, ɑ̃t] *adj* depressing

déprimer [depʀime] *vi* to be/get depressed

MOT-CLÉ
---

depuis [dəpɥi] *prép* **1** (*point de départ dans le temps*) since; **il habite Paris depuis 1983/l'an dernier** he has been living in Paris since 1983/last year; **depuis quand le connaissez-vous?** how long have you known him?

2 (*temps écoulé*) for; **il habite Paris depuis 5 ans** he has been living in Paris for 5 years; **je le connais depuis 3 ans** I've known him for 3 years

3 (*lieu*): **il a plu depuis Metz** it's been raining since Metz; **elle a téléphoné depuis Valence** she rang from Valence

4 (*quantité, rang*) from; **depuis les plus petits jusqu'aux plus grands** from the youngest to the oldest

♦ *adv* (*temps*) since (then); **je ne lui ai pas parlé depuis** I haven't spoken to him since (then)

depuis que *conj* (ever) since; **depuis qu'il m'a dit ça** (ever) since he said that to me

---

député, e [depyte] *nm/f* (*POL*) ≃ Member of Parliament (*BRIT*), ≃ Member of Congress (*US*)

députer [depyte] *vt* to delegate

déraciner [deʀasine] *vt* to uproot

dérailler [deʀaje] *vi* (*train*) to be derailed; **faire ~** to derail

déraisonner [deʀezɔne] *vi* to talk nonsense, rave

dérangement [deʀɑ̃ʒmɑ̃] *nm* (*gêne*) trouble; (*gastrique etc*) disorder; **en ~** (*téléphone, machine*) out of order

déranger [deʀɑ̃ʒe] *vt* (*personne*) to trouble, bother; (*projets*) to disrupt, upset; (*objets, vêtements*) to disarrange; **se ~** *vi*: **surtout ne vous dérangez pas pour moi** please don't put yourself out on my account; **est-ce que cela vous dérange si ...?** do you mind if ...?

déraper [deʀape] *vi* (*voiture*) to skid; (*personne, semelles*) to slip

dérégler [deʀegle] *vt* (*mécanisme*) to put out of order; (*estomac*) to upset

dérider [deʀide]: **se ~** *vi* to brighten up

dérision [deʀizjɔ̃] *nf*: **tourner en ~** to deride; **dérisoire** *adj* derisory

dérive [deʀiv] *nf*: **aller à la ~** (*NAVIG, fig*) to drift

dérivé, e [deʀive] *nm* (*TECH*) by-product

dériver [deʀive] *vt* (*MATH*) to derive; (*cours d'eau etc*) to divert ♦ *vi* (*bateau*) to drift; **~ de** to derive from

dermatologue [deʀmatɔlɔg] *nm/f* dermatologist

dernier, -ière [deʀnje, jeʀ] *adj* last; (*le plus récent*) latest, last; **lundi/le mois ~** last Monday/month; **c'est le ~ cri** it's the very latest thing; **en ~** last; **ce ~** the latter; **dernièrement** *adv* recently

dérobé, e [deʀɔbe] *adj*: **à la ~e** surreptitiously

dérober [deʀɔbe] *vt* to steal; **se ~** *vi* (*s'esquiver*) to slip away; **se ~ à** (*justice, regards*) to hide from; (*obligation*) to shirk

dérogation [deʀɔgasjɔ̃] *nf* (special) dispensation

déroger [deʀɔʒe]: **~ à** *vt* to go against, depart from

dérouiller [deʀuje] *vt*: **se ~ les jambes** to stretch one's legs (*fig*)

déroulement [deʀulmɑ̃] *nm* (*d'une opération etc*) progress

dérouler [deʀule] *vt* (*ficelle*) to unwind; **se**

~ *vi* (*avoir lieu*) to take place; (*se passer*) to go (off); **tout s'est déroulé comme prévu** everything went as planned

dérouter [deʀute] *vt* (*avion, train*) to re-route, divert; (*étonner*) to disconcert, throw (out)

derrière [dɛʀjɛʀ] *adv, prép* behind ♦ *nm* (*d'une maison*) back; (*postérieur*) behind, bottom; **les pattes de** ~ the back *ou* hind legs; **par** ~ from behind; (*fig*) behind one's back

des [de] *dét voir* **de** ♦ *prép* +*des* = **de** +**les**

dès [dɛ] *prép* from; ~ **que** as soon as; ~ **son retour** as soon as he was (*ou* is) back

désabusé, e [dezabyze] *adj* disillusioned

désaccord [dezakɔʀ] *nm* disagreement; **désaccordé, e** *adj* (*MUS*) out of tune

désaffecté, e [dezafɛkte] *adj* disused

désagréable [dezagʀeabl] *adj* unpleasant

désagréger [dezagʀeʒe]: **se** ~ *vi* to disintegrate, break up

désagrément [dezagʀemɑ̃] *nm* annoyance, trouble *no pl*

désaltérer [dezalteʀe] *vt*: **se** ~ to quench one's thirst

désapprobateur, -trice [dezapʀɔbatœʀ, tʀis] *adj* disapproving

désapprouver [dezapʀuve] *vt* to disapprove of

désarmant, e [dezaʀmɑ̃, ɑ̃t] *adj* disarming

désarroi [dezaʀwa] *nm* disarray

désastre [dezastʀ] *nm* disaster; **désastreux, -euse** *adj* disastrous

désavantage [dezavɑ̃taʒ] *nm* disadvantage; **désavantager** *vt* to put at a disadvantage

descendre [desɑ̃dʀ] *vt* (*escalier, montagne*) to go (*ou* come) down; (*valise, paquet*) to take *ou* get down; (*étagère etc*) to lower; (*fam: abattre*) to shoot down ♦ *vi* to go (*ou* come) down; (*passager: s'arrêter*) to get out, alight; ~ **à pied/en voiture** to walk/drive down; ~ **du train** to get out of *ou* get off the train; ~ **de cheval** to dismount; ~ **à l'hôtel** to stay at a hotel

descente [desɑ̃t] *nf* descent, going down; (*chemin*) way down; (*SKI*) downhill (race); ~ **de lit** bedside rug; ~ (**de police**) (police) raid

description [dɛskʀipsjɔ̃] *nf* description

désemparé, e [dezɑ̃paʀe] *adj* bewildered, distraught

désemplir [dezɑ̃pliʀ] *vi*: **ne pas** ~ to be always full

déséquilibre [dezekilibʀ] *nm* (*position*): **en** ~ unsteady; (*fig: des forces, du budget*) imbalance; **déséquilibré, e** *nm/f* (*PSYCH*) unbalanced person; **déséquilibrer** *vt* to throw off balance

désert, e [dezɛʀ, ɛʀt] *adj* deserted ♦ *nm* desert; **déserter** *vi, vt* to desert; **désertique** *adj* desert *cpd*

désespéré, e [dezɛspeʀe] *adj* desperate

désespérer [dezɛspeʀe] *vi*: ~ (**de**) to despair (of); **désespoir** *nm* despair; **en désespoir de cause** in desperation

déshabiller [dezabije] *vt* to undress; **se** ~ *vi* to undress (o.s.)

déshériter [dezeʀite] *vt* to disinherit; **déshérités** *nmpl*: **les déshérités** the underprivileged

déshonneur [dezɔnœʀ] *nm* dishonour

déshydraté, e [dezidʀate] *adj* dehydrated

desiderata [dezideʀata] *nmpl* requirements

désigner [dezine] *vt* (*montrer*) to point out, indicate; (*dénommer*) to denote; (*candidat etc*) to name

désinfectant, e [dezɛ̃fɛktɑ̃, ɑ̃t] *adj, nm* disinfectant

désinfecter [dezɛ̃fɛkte] *vt* to disinfect

désintégrer [dezɛ̃tegʀe]: **se** ~ *vi* to disintegrate

désintéressé, e [dezɛ̃teʀese] *adj* disinterested, unselfish

désintéresser [dezɛ̃teʀese] *vt*: **se** ~ (**de**) to lose interest (in)

désintoxication [dezɛ̃tɔksikasjɔ̃] *nf*: **faire une cure de** ~ to undergo treatment for alcoholism (*ou* drug addiction)

désinvolte [dezɛ̃vɔlt] *adj* casual, off-hand; **désinvolture** *nf* casualness

désir [deziʀ] *nm* wish; (*sensuel*) desire; **désirer** *vt* to want, wish for; (*sexuellement*) to desire; **je désire ...** (*formule de politesse*) I would like ...

désister [deziste]: **se ~** *vi* to stand down, withdraw

désobéir [dezɔbeiʀ] *vi*: **~ (à qn/qch)** to disobey (sb/sth); **désobéissant, e** *adj* disobedient

désobligeant, e [dezɔbliʒɑ̃, ɑ̃t] *adj* disagreeable

désodorisant [dezɔdɔʀizɑ̃] *nm* air freshener, deodorizer

désœuvré, e [dezœvʀe] *adj* idle

désolé, e [dezɔle] *adj* (*paysage*) desolate; **je suis ~** I'm sorry

désoler [dezɔle] *vt* to distress, grieve

désopilant, e [dezɔpilɑ̃, ɑ̃t] *adj* hilarious

désordonné, e [dezɔʀdɔne] *adj* untidy

désordre [dezɔʀdʀ] *nm* disorder(liness), untidiness; (*anarchie*) disorder; **en ~** in a mess, untidy

désorienté, e [dezɔʀjɑ̃te] *adj* disorientated

désormais [dezɔʀmɛ] *adv* from now on

désossé, e [dezɔse] *adj* (*viande*) boned

desquelles [dekɛl] *prép* +*pron* = **de +lesquelles**

desquels [dekɛl] *prép* +*pron* = **de +lesquels**

desséché, e [deseʃe] *adj* dried up

dessécher [deseʃe]: **se ~** *vi* to dry out

dessein [desɛ̃] *nm*: **à ~** intentionally, deliberately

desserrer [deseʀe] *vt* to loosen; (*frein*) to release

dessert [desɛʀ] *nm* dessert, pudding

desserte [desɛʀt] *nf* (*table*) side table; (*transport*): **la ~ du village est assurée par autocar** there is a coach service to the village

desservir [desɛʀviʀ] *vt* (*ville, quartier*) to serve; (*débarrasser*): **~ (la table)** to clear the table

dessin [desɛ̃] *nm* (*œuvre, art*) drawing; (*motif*) pattern, design; **~ animé** cartoon (film); **~ humoristique** cartoon; **dessinateur, -trice** *nm/f* drawer; (*de bandes dessinées*) cartoonist; (*industriel*) draughtsman(-woman) (*BRIT*), draftsman(-woman) (*US*); **dessiner** *vt* to draw; (*concevoir*) to design

dessous [d(ə)su] *adv* underneath, beneath ♦ *nm* underside ♦ *nmpl* (*sous-vêtements*) underwear *sg*; **en ~, par ~** underneath; **au-~ (de)** below; (*peu digne de*) beneath; **avoir le ~** to get the worst of it; **les voisins du ~** the downstairs neighbours; **dessous-de-plat** *nm inv* tablemat

dessus [d(ə)sy] *adv* on top; (*collé, écrit*) on it ♦ *nm* top; **en ~** above; **par ~** ♦ *adv* over it ♦ *prép* over; **au-~ (de)** above; **avoir le ~** to get the upper hand; **dessus-de-lit** *nm inv* bedspread

destin [destɛ̃] *nm* fate; (*avenir*) destiny

destinataire [destinatɛʀ] *nm/f* (*POSTES*) addressee; (*d'un colis*) consignee

destination [destinasjɔ̃] *nf* (*lieu*) destination; (*usage*) purpose; **à ~ de** bound for, travelling to

destinée [destine] *nf* fate; (*existence, avenir*) destiny

destiner [destine] *vt*: **~ qch à qn** (*envisager de donner*) to intend sb to have sth; (*adresser*) to intend sth for sb; **être destiné à** (*usage*) to be meant for

désuet, -ète [dezɥɛ, ɛt] *adj* outdated, outmoded

détachant [detaʃɑ̃] *nm* stain remover

détachement [detaʃmɑ̃] *nm* detachment

détacher [detaʃe] *vt* (*enlever*) to detach, remove; (*délier*) to untie; (*ADMIN*): **~ qn (auprès de** *ou* **à)** to post sb (to); **se ~** *vi* (*se séparer*) to come off; (: *page*) to come out; (*se défaire*) to come undone; **se ~ sur** to stand out against; **se ~ de** (*se désintéresser*) to grow away from

détail [detaj] *nm* detail; (*COMM*): **le ~** retail; **en ~** in detail; **au ~** (*COMM*) retail; **détaillant** *nm* retailer; **détaillé, e** *adj* (*plan, explications*) detailed; (*facture*) itemized; **détailler** vt (*expliquer*) to explain in detail

détaler [detale] (*fam*) vi (*personne*) to take off

détartrant [detartrɑ̃] nm scale remover

détaxé, e [detakse] adj: **produits ~s** tax-free goods

détecter [detɛkte] vt to detect

détective [detɛktiv] nm: **~ (privé)** private detective

déteindre [detɛ̃dʀ] vi (*au lavage*) to run, lose its colour

détendre [detɑ̃dʀ] vt (*corps, esprit*) to relax; **se ~** vi (*ressort*) to lose its tension; (*personne*) to relax

détenir [det(ə)niʀ] vt (*record, pouvoir, secret*) to hold; (*prisonnier*) to detain, hold

détente [detɑ̃t] nf relaxation

détention [detɑ̃sjɔ̃] nf (*d'armes*) possession; (*captivité*) detention; **~ préventive** custody

détenu, e [det(ə)ny] nm/f prisoner

détergent [detɛʀʒɑ̃] nm detergent

détériorer [deteʀjɔʀe] vt to damage; **se ~** vi to deteriorate

déterminé, e [detɛʀmine] adj (*résolu*) determined; (*précis*) specific, definite

déterminer [detɛʀmine] vt (*fixer*) to determine; **se ~ à faire qch** to make up one's mind to do sth

déterrer [detɛʀe] vt to dig up

détestable [detɛstabl] adj foul, detestable

détester [detɛste] vt to hate, detest

détonner [detɔne] vi (*fig*) to clash

détour [detuʀ] nm detour; (*tournant*) bend, curve; **ça vaut le ~** it's worth the trip; **sans ~** (*fig*) plainly

détourné, e [detuʀne] adj (*moyen*) roundabout

détournement [detuʀnəmɑ̃] nm: **~ d'avion** hijacking

détourner [detuʀne] vt to divert; (*par la force*) to hijack; (*yeux, tête*) to turn away; (*de l'argent*) to embezzle; **se ~** vi to turn away

détracteur, -trice [detʀaktœʀ, tʀis] nm/f disparager, critic

détraquer [detʀake] vt to put out of order; (*estomac*) to upset; **se ~** vi (*machine*) to go wrong

détrempé, e [detʀɑ̃pe] adj (*sol*) sodden, waterlogged

détresse [detʀɛs] nf distress

détriment [detʀimɑ̃] nm: **au ~ de** to the detriment of

détritus [detʀity(s)] nmpl rubbish *sg*, refuse *sg*

détroit [detʀwa] nm strait

détromper [detʀɔ̃pe] vt to disabuse

détruire [detʀɥiʀ] vt to destroy

dette [dɛt] nf debt

DEUG *sigle m* (= *diplôme d'études universitaires générales*) *diploma taken after 2 years at university*

deuil [dœj] nm (*perte*) bereavement; (*période*) mourning; **être en ~** to be in mourning

deux [dø] num two; **tous les ~** both; **ses ~ mains** both his hands, his two hands; **~ fois** twice; **deuxième** num second; **deuxièmement** adv secondly; **deux-pièces** nm inv (*tailleur*) two-piece suit; (*de bain*) two-piece (swimsuit); (*appartement*) two-roomed flat (*BRIT*) ou apartment (*US*); **deux-points** nm inv colon *sg*; **deux-roues** nm inv two-wheeled vehicle

devais etc [dəvɛ] vb voir **devoir**

dévaler [devale] vt to hurtle down

dévaliser [devalize] vt to rob, burgle

dévaloriser [devalɔʀize] vt to depreciate; **se ~** vi to depreciate

dévaluation [devaluasjɔ̃] nf devaluation

devancer [d(ə)vɑ̃se] vt (*coureur, rival*) to get ahead of; (*arriver*) to arrive before; (*prévenir: questions, désirs*) to anticipate

devant [d(ə)vɑ̃] adv in front; (*à distance: en avant*) ahead ♦ prép in front of; (*en avant*) ahead of; (*avec mouvement: passer*) past; (*en présence de*) before, in front of; (*étant donné*) in view of ♦ nm front; **prendre les ~s** to make the first move; **les pattes de**

~ the front legs, the forelegs; **par ~** (*boutonner*) at the front; (*entrer*) the front way; **aller au-~ de qn** to go out to meet sb; **aller au-~ de** (*désirs de qn*) to anticipate

devanture [d(ə)vɑ̃tyʀ] *nf* (*étalage*) display; (*vitrine*) (shop) window

déveine [devɛn] (*fam*) *nf* rotten luck *no pl*

développement [dev(ə)lɔpmɑ̃] *nm* development; **pays en voie de ~** developing countries

développer [dev(ə)lɔpe] *vt* to develop; **se ~** *vi* to develop

devenir [dəv(ə)niʀ] *vb* +attrib to become; **que sont-ils devenus?** what has become of them?

dévergondé, e [deveʀgɔ̃de] *adj* wild, shameless

déverser [devɛʀse] *vt* (*liquide*) to pour (out); (*ordures*) to tip (out); **se ~ dans** (*fleuve*) to flow into

dévêtir [devetiʀ]: **se ~** *vi* to undress

devez *etc* [dəve] *vb voir* **devoir**

déviation [devjasjɔ̃] *nf* (AUTO) diversion (BRIT), detour (US)

devienne *etc* [dəvjɛn] *vb voir* **devenir**

dévier [devje] *vt* (*fleuve, circulation*) to divert; (*coup*) to deflect ♦ *vi* to veer (off course)

devin [dəvɛ̃] *nm* soothsayer, seer

deviner [d(ə)vine] *vt* to guess; (*apercevoir*) to distinguish; **devinette** *nf* riddle

devins *etc* [dəvɛ̃] *vb voir* **devenir**

devis [d(ə)vi] *nm* estimate, quotation

dévisager [devizaʒe] *vt* to stare at

devise [dəviz] *nf* (*formule*) motto, watchword; **~s** *nfpl* (*argent*) currency *sg*

deviser [dəvize] *vi* to converse

dévisser [devise] *vt* to unscrew, undo

dévoiler [devwale] *vt* to unveil

devoir [d(ə)vwaʀ] *nm* duty; (SCOL) homework *no pl*; (: *en classe*) exercise ♦ *vt* (*argent, respect*): **~ qch (à qn)** to owe (sb) sth; (+*infin*: *obligation*): **il doit le faire** he has to do it, he must do it; (: *intention*): **le nouveau centre commercial doit**

ouvrir en mai the new shopping centre is due to open in May; (: *probabilité*): **il doit être tard** it must be late

dévolu [devɔly] *nm*: **jeter son ~ sur** to fix one's choice on

dévorer [devɔʀe] *vt* to devour

dévot, e [devo, ɔt] *adj* devout, pious; **dévotion** *nf* devoutness

dévoué, e [devwe] *adj* devoted

dévouement [devumɑ̃] *nm* devotion

dévouer [devwe]: **se ~** *vi* (*se sacrifier*): **se ~ (pour)** to sacrifice o.s. (for); (*se consacrer*): **se ~ à** to devote *ou* dedicate o.s. to

dévoyé, e [devwaje] *adj* delinquent

devrai *etc* [dəvʀe] *vb voir* **devoir**

diabète [djabɛt] *nm* diabetes *sg*; **diabétique** *nm/f* diabetic

diable [djabl] *nm* devil

diabolo [djabɔlo] *nm* (*boisson*) lemonade with fruit cordial

diagnostic [djagnɔstik] *nm* diagnosis *sg*; **diagnostiquer** *vt* to diagnose

diagonal, e, -aux [djagɔnal, o] *adj* diagonal; **diagonale** *nf* diagonal; **en diagonale** diagonally

diagramme [djagʀam] *nm* chart, graph

dialecte [djalɛkt] *nm* dialect

dialogue [djalɔg] *nm* dialogue

diamant [djamɑ̃] *nm* diamond

diamètre [djamɛtʀ] *nm* diameter

diapason [djapazɔ̃] *nm* tuning fork

diaphragme [djafʀagm] *nm* diaphragm

diapo [djapo] (*fam*) *nf* slide

diapositive [djapozitiv] *nf* transparency, slide

diarrhée [djaʀe] *nf* diarrhoea

dictateur [diktatœʀ] *nm* dictator; **dictature** *nf* dictatorship

dictée [dikte] *nf* dictation

dicter [dikte] *vt* to dictate

dictionnaire [diksjɔnɛʀ] *nm* dictionary

dicton [diktɔ̃] *nm* saying, dictum

dièse [djɛz] *nm* sharp

diesel [djezɛl] *nm* diesel ♦ *adj inv* diesel

diète [djɛt] *nf* (*jeûne*) starvation diet; (*régime*) diet; **diététique** *adj*: **magasin dié-**

tétique health food shop

dieu, x [djø] *nm* god; **D~** God; **mon D~!** good heavens!

diffamation [difamasjɔ̃] *nf* slander; (*écrite*) libel

différé [difeʀe] *nm* (*TV*): **en ~** (pre-) recorded

différemment [difeʀamɑ̃] *adv* differently

différence [difeʀɑ̃s] *nf* difference; **à la ~ de** unlike; **différencier** *vt* to differentiate; **différend** *nm* difference (of opinion), disagreement

différent, e [difeʀɑ̃, ɑ̃t] *adj* (*dissemblable*) different; **~ de** different from; (*divers*) different, various

différer [difeʀe] *vt* to postpone, put off ♦ *vi:* **~ (de)** to differ (from)

difficile [difisil] *adj* difficult; (*exigeant*) hard to please; **difficilement** *adv* with difficulty

difficulté [difikylte] *nf* difficulty; **en ~** (*bateau, alpiniste*) in difficulties

difforme [difɔʀm] *adj* deformed, misshapen

diffuser [difyze] *vt* (*chaleur*) to diffuse; (*émission, musique*) to broadcast; (*nouvelle*) to circulate; (*COMM*) to distribute

digérer [diʒeʀe] *vt* to digest; (*fam: accepter*) to stomach, put up with; **digestif** *nm* (after-dinner) liqueur; **digestion** *nf* digestion

digne [diɲ] *adj* dignified; **~ de** worthy of; **~ de foi** trustworthy; **dignité** *nf* dignity

digue [dig] *nf* dike, dyke

dilapider [dilapide] *vt* to squander

dilemme [dilɛm] *nm* dilemma

dilettante [diletɑ̃t] *nm/f:* **faire qch en ~** to dabble in sth

diligence [diliʒɑ̃s] *nf* stagecoach

diluer [dilɥe] *vt* to dilute

diluvien, ne [dilyvjɛ̃, jɛn] *adj:* **pluie ~ne** torrential rain

dimanche [dimɑ̃ʃ] *nm* Sunday

dimension [dimɑ̃sjɔ̃] *nf* (*grandeur*) size; (~s) dimensions

diminué, e [diminɥe] *adj:* **il est très ~**

depuis son accident he's not at all the man he was since his accident

diminuer [diminɥe] *vt* to reduce, decrease; (*ardeur etc*) to lessen; (*dénigrer*) to belittle ♦ *vi* to decrease, diminish; **diminutif** *nm* (*surnom*) pet name; **diminution** *nf* decreasing, diminishing

dinde [dɛ̃d] *nf* turkey

dindon [dɛ̃dɔ̃] *nm* turkey

dîner [dine] *nm* dinner ♦ *vi* to have dinner

dingue [dɛ̃g] (*fam*) *adj* crazy

dinosaure [dinɔzɔʀ] *nm* dinosaur

diplomate [diplɔmat] *adj* diplomatic ♦ *nm* diplomat; (*fig*) diplomatist; **diplomatie** *nf* diplomacy

diplôme [diplom] *nm* diploma; **avoir des ~s** to have qualifications; **diplômé, e** *adj* qualified

dire [diʀ] *nm:* **au ~ de** according to ♦ *vt* to say; (*secret, mensonge, heure*) to tell; **~ qch à qn** to tell sb sth; **~ à qn qu'il fasse** *ou* **de faire** to tell sb to do; **on dit que** they say that; **ceci dit** that being said; **si cela lui dit** (*plaire*) if he fancies it; **que dites-vous de** (*penser*) what do you think of; **on dirait que** it looks (*ou* sounds *etc*) as if; **dis/dites (donc)!** I say!

direct, e [diʀɛkt] *adj* direct ♦ *nm* (*TV*): **en ~** live; **directement** *adv* directly

directeur, -trice [diʀɛktœʀ, tʀis] *nm/f* (*d'entreprise*) director; (*de service*) manager(-eress); (*d'école*) head(teacher) (*BRIT*), principal (*US*)

direction [diʀɛksjɔ̃] *nf* (*sens*) direction; (*d'entreprise*) management; (*AUTO*) steering; **"toutes ~s"** "all routes"

dirent [diʀ] *vb voir* **dire**

dirigeant, e [diʀiʒɑ̃, ɑ̃t] *adj* (*classe*) ruling ♦ *nm/f* (*d'un parti etc*) leader

diriger [diʀiʒe] *vt* (*entreprise*) to manage, run; (*véhicule*) to steer; (*orchestre*) to conduct; (*recherches, travaux*) to supervise; **se ~** (*s'orienter*) to find one's way; **se ~ vers** *ou* **sur** to make *ou* head for

dis *etc* [di] *vb voir* **dire**

discernement [disɛʀnəmɑ̃] *nm* (*bon sens*)

discernment, judgement

discerner [diserne] *vt* to discern, make out

discipline [disiplin] *nf* discipline; **discipliner** *vt* to discipline

discontinu, e [diskɔ̃tiny] *adj* intermittent

discontinuer [diskɔ̃tinɥe] *vi*: **sans ~** without stopping, without a break

discordant, e [diskɔrdɑ̃, ɑ̃t] *adj* discordant

discothèque [diskɔtɛk] *nf* (*boîte de nuit*) disco(thèque)

discours [diskur] *nm* speech

discret, -ète [diskrɛ, ɛt] *adj* discreet; (*parfum, maquillage*) unobtrusive; **discrétion** *nf* discretion; **à discrétion** as much as one wants

discrimination [diskriminasjɔ̃] *nf* discrimination; **sans ~** indiscriminately

disculper [diskylpe] *vt* to exonerate

discussion [diskysjɔ̃] *nf* discussion

discutable [diskytabl] *adj* debatable

discuté, e [diskyte] *adj* controversial

discuter [diskyte] *vt* (*débattre*) to discuss; (*contester*) to question, dispute ♦ *vi* to talk; (*protester*) to argue; **~ de** to discuss

dise *etc* [diz] *vb voir* **dire**

diseuse [dizøz] *nf*: **~ de bonne aventure** fortuneteller

disgracieux, -euse [disgrasjø, jøz] *adj* ungainly, awkward

disjoindre [disʒwɛ̃dr] *vt* to take apart; **se ~** *vi* to come apart

disjoncteur [disʒɔ̃ktœr] *nm* (ÉLEC) circuit breaker

disloquer [dislɔke] *vt*: **se ~** *vi* (*parti, empire*) to break up

disons [dizɔ̃] *vb voir* **dire**

disparaître [disparɛtr] *vi* to disappear; (*se perdre: traditions etc*) to die out; **faire ~** (*tache*) to remove; (*douleur*) to get rid of

disparition [disparisjɔ̃] *nf* disappearance; **espèce en voie de ~** endangered species

disparu, e [dispary] *nm/f* missing person ♦ *adj*: **être porté ~** to be reported missing

dispensaire [dispɑ̃sɛr] *nm* community clinic

dispenser [dispɑ̃se] *vt*: **~ qn de** to exempt sb from; **se ~ de** *vt* (*corvée*) to get out of

disperser [disperse] *vt* to scatter; **se ~** *vi* to break up

disponibilité [dispɔnibilite] *nf* availability; **disponible** *adj* available

dispos [dispo] *adj m*: **(frais et) ~** fresh (as a daisy)

disposé, e [dispoze] *adj*: **bien/mal ~** (*humeur*) in a good/bad mood; **~ à** (*prêt à*) willing *ou* prepared to

disposer [dispoze] *vt* to arrange ♦ *vi*: **vous pouvez ~** you may leave; **~ de** to have (at one's disposal); **se ~ à faire** to prepare to do, be about to do

dispositif [dispozitif] *nm* device; (*fig*) system, plan of action

disposition [dispozisjɔ̃] *nf* (*arrangement*) arrangement, layout; (*humeur*) mood; **prendre ses ~s** to make arrangements; **avoir des ~s pour la musique** *etc* to have a special aptitude for music *etc*; **à la ~ de qn** at sb's disposal; **je suis à votre ~** I am at your service

disproportionné, e [disprɔpɔrsjɔne] *adj* disproportionate, out of all proportion

dispute [dispyt] *nf* quarrel, argument; **disputer** *vt* (*match*) to play; (*combat*) to fight; **se disputer** *vi* to quarrel

disquaire [diskɛr] *nm/f* record dealer

disqualifier [diskalifje] *vt* to disqualify

disque [disk] *nm* (MUS) record; (*forme, pièce*) disc; (SPORT) discus; **~ compact** compact disc; **~ dur** hard disk; **disquette** *nf* floppy disk, diskette

disséminer [disemine] *vt* to scatter

disséquer [diseke] *vt* to dissect

dissertation [disɛrtasjɔ̃] *nf* (SCOL) essay

dissimuler [disimyle] *vt* to conceal

dissipé, e [disipe] *adj* (*élève*) undisciplined, unruly

dissiper [disipe] *vt* to dissipate; (*fortune*)

to squander; **se ~** *vi* (*brouillard*) to clear, disperse

dissolvant [disɔlvã] *nm* nail polish remover

dissonant, e [disɔnã, ãt] *adj* discordant

dissoudre [disudʀ] *vt* to dissolve; **se ~** *vi* to dissolve

dissuader [disɥade] *vt*: **~ qn de faire** to dissuade sb from doing; **dissuasion** *nf*: **force de dissuasion** deterrent power

distance [distãs] *nf* distance; (*fig: écart*) gap; **à ~** at *ou* from a distance; **distancer** *vt* to outdistance

distant, e [distã, ãt] *adj* (*réservé*) distant; **~ de** (*lieu*) far away from

distendre [distãdʀ]: **se ~** *vi* to distend

distillerie [distilʀi] *nf* distillery

distinct, e [distɛ̃(kt), ɛ̃kt] *adj* distinct; **distinctement** *adv* distinctly, clearly; **distinctif, -ive** *adj* distinctive

distingué, e [distɛ̃ge] *adj* distinguished

distinguer [distɛ̃ge] *vt* to distinguish

distraction [distʀaksjɔ̃] *nf* (*inattention*) absent-mindedness; (*passe-temps*) distraction, entertainment

distraire [distʀɛʀ] *vt* (*divertir*) to entertain, divert; (*déranger*) to distract; **se ~** *vi* to amuse *ou* enjoy o.s.; **distrait, e** *adj* absent-minded

distrayant, e [distʀɛjã, ãt] *adj* entertaining

distribuer [distʀibɥe] *vt* to distribute, hand out; (*CARTES*) to deal (out); (*courrier*) to deliver; **distributeur** *nm* (*COMM*) distributor; (*automatique*) (vending) machine; (: *de billets*) (cash) dispenser; **distribution** *nf* distribution; (*postale*) delivery; (*choix d'acteurs*) casting, cast

dit, e [di, dit] *pp de* **dire** ♦ *adj* (*fixé*): **le jour ~** the arranged day; (*surnommé*): **X, ~ Pierrot** X, known as Pierrot

dites [dit] *vb voir* **dire**

divaguer [divage] *vi* to ramble; (*fam*) to rave

divan [divã] *nm* divan

diverger [divɛʀʒe] *vi* to diverge

divers, e [divɛʀ, ɛʀs] *adj* (*varié*) diverse, varied; (*différent*) different, various; **~es personnes** various *ou* several people

diversifier [divɛʀsifje] *vt* to vary

diversité [divɛʀsite] *nf* (*variété*) diversity

divertir [divɛʀtiʀ]: **se ~** *vi* to amuse *ou* enjoy o.s.; **divertissement** *nm* distraction, entertainment

divin, e [divɛ̃, in] *adj* divine

diviser [divize] *vt* to divide; **division** *nf* division

divorce [divɔʀs] *nm* divorce; **divorcé, e** *nm/f* divorcee; **divorcer** *vi* to get a divorce, get divorced

divulguer [divylge] *vt* to divulge, disclose

dix [dis] *num* ten; **dixième** *num* tenth

dizaine [dizɛn] *nf*: **une ~ (de)** about ten, ten or so

do [do] *nm* (*note*) C; (*en chantant la gamme*) do(h)

docile [dɔsil] *adj* docile

dock [dɔk] *nm* dock; **docker** *nm* docker

docteur [dɔktœʀ] *nm* doctor; **doctorat** *nm* doctorate; **doctoresse** *nf* lady doctor

doctrine [dɔktʀin] *nf* doctrine

document [dɔkymã] *nm* document; **documentaire** *adj, nm* documentary; **documentaliste** *nm/f* (*SCOL*) librarian; **documentation** *nf* documentation, literature; **documenter** *vt*: **se documenter (sur)** to gather information (on)

dodo [dodo] *nm* (*langage enfantin*): **aller faire ~** to go to beddy-byes

dodu, e [dɔdy] *adj* plump

dogue [dɔg] *nm* mastiff

doigt [dwa] *nm* finger; **à deux ~s de** within an inch of; **~ de pied** toe; **doigté** *nm* (*MUS*) fingering; (*fig: habileté*) diplomacy, tact

doit *etc* [dwa] *vb voir* **devoir**

doléances [dɔleãs] *nfpl* grievances

dollar [dɔlaʀ] *nm* dollar

domaine [dɔmɛn] *nm* estate, property; (*fig*) domain, field

domestique [dɔmɛstik] *adj* domestic

♦ *nm/f* servant, domestic; **domestiquer**
vt to domesticate
domicile [dɔmisil] *nm* home, place of residence; **à ~** at home; **livrer à ~** to deliver; **domicilié, e** *adj*: **"domicilié à ..."**
"address ..."
dominant, e [dɔminɑ̃, ɑ̃t] *adj* (*opinion*)
predominant
dominer [dɔmine] *vt* to dominate; (*sujet*)
to master; (*surpasser*) to outclass, surpass;
(*surplomber*) to tower above, dominate
♦ *vi* to be in the dominant position; **se ~**
vi to control o.s.
domino [dɔmino] *nm* domino
dommage [dɔmaʒ] *nm*: **~s** (*dégâts*) damage *no pl*; **c'est ~!** what a shame!; **c'est
~ que** it's a shame *ou* pity that;
dommages-intérêts *nmpl* damages
dompter [dɔ̃(p)te] *vt* to tame; **dompteur,
-euse** *nm/f* trainer
DOM-TOM [dɔmtɔm] *sigle m* (= *départements et territoires d'outre-mer*) French overseas departments and territories
don [dɔ̃] *nm* gift; (*charité*) donation; **avoir
des ~s pour** to have a gift *ou* talent for;
elle a le ~ de m'énerver she's got a
knack of getting on my nerves
donc [dɔ̃k] *conj* therefore, so; (*après une digression*) so, then
donjon [dɔ̃ʒɔ̃] *nm* keep
donné, e [dɔne] *adj* (*convenu: lieu, heure*)
given; (*pas cher: fam*): **c'est ~** it's a gift;
étant ~ ... given ...; **données** *nfpl* data
donner [dɔne] *vt* to give; (*vieux habits etc*)
to give away; (*spectacle*) to put on; **~ qch
à qn** to give sb sth, give sth to sb; **~ sur**
(*suj: fenêtre, chambre*) to look (out) onto;
ça donne soif/faim it makes you (feel)
thirsty/hungry; (*spectacle*) to give one's
all; **se ~ à fond** to give one's
all; **se ~ du mal** to take (great) trouble;
s'en ~ à cœur joie (*fam*) to have a great
time

MOT-CLÉ

dont [dɔ̃] *pron relatif* **1** (*appartenance: objets*) whose, of which; (*appartenance: êtres*

animés) whose; **la maison dont le toit est
rouge** the house the roof of which is red,
the house whose roof is red; **l'homme
dont je connais la sœur** the man whose
sister I know
2 (*parmi lesquel(le)s*): **2 livres, dont l'un
est ...** 2 books, one of which is ...; **il y
avait plusieurs personnes, dont Gabrielle** there were several people, among
them Gabrielle; **10 blessés, dont 2
grièvement** 10 injured, 2 of them seriously
3 (*complément d'adjectif, de verbe*): **le fils
dont il est si fier** the son he's so proud
of; **ce dont je parle** what I'm talking
about

doré, e [dɔre] *adj* golden; (*avec dorure*)
gilt, gilded
dorénavant [dɔrenavɑ̃] *adv* henceforth
dorer [dɔre] *vt* to gild; **(faire) ~** (*CULIN*) to
brown
dorloter [dɔrlɔte] *vt* to pamper
dormir [dɔrmir] *vi* to sleep; (*être endormi*)
to be asleep
dortoir [dɔrtwar] *nm* dormitory
dorure [dɔryr] *nf* gilding
dos [do] *nm* back; (*de livre*) spine; **"voir au
~"** "see over"; **de ~** from the back
dosage [dozaʒ] *nm* mixture
dose [doz] *nf* dose; **doser** *vt* to measure
out; **il faut savoir doser ses efforts** you
have to be able to pace yourself
dossard [dosar] *nm* number (*worn by
competitor*)
dossier [dosje] *nm* (*documents*) file; (*de
chaise*) back; (*PRESSE*) feature; **un ~ scolaire** a school report
dot [dɔt] *nf* dowry
doter [dɔte] *vt*: **~ de** to equip with
douane [dwan] *nf* customs *pl*; **(droits de)
~** (customs) duty; **douanier, -ière** *adj*
customs *cpd* ♦ *nm* customs officer
double [dubl] *adj, adv* double ♦ *nm* (*2 fois
plus*): **le ~ (de)** twice as much (*ou* many)
(as); (*autre exemplaire*) duplicate, copy;

(*sosie*) double; (*TENNIS*) doubles *sg*; **en ~ (exemplaire)** in duplicate; **faire ~ emploi** to be redundant

double-cliquer [dublklike] *vi* (*INFORM*) to double-click

doubler [duble] *vt* (*multiplier par 2*) to double; (*vêtement*) to line; (*dépasser*) to overtake, pass; (*film*) to dub; (*acteur*) to stand in for ♦ *vi* to double

doublure [dublyʀ] *nf* lining; (*CINÉMA*) stand-in

douce [dus] *adj voir* **doux**; **douceâtre** *adj* sickly sweet; **doucement** *adv* gently; (*lentement*) slowly; **doucereux, -euse** (*péj*) *adj* sugary; **douceur** *nf* softness; (*de quelqu'un*) gentleness; (*de climat*) mildness

douche [duʃ] *nf* shower; **doucher: se doucher** *vi* to have *ou* take a shower

doudoune [dudun] *nf* padded jacket

doué, e [dwe] *adj* gifted, talented; **être ~ pour** to have a gift for

douille [duj] *nf* (*ÉLEC*) socket

douillet, te [dujɛ, ɛt] *adj* cosy; (*péj: à la douleur*) soft

douleur [dulœʀ] *nf* pain; (*chagrin*) grief, distress; **douloureux, -euse** *adj* painful

doute [dut] *nm* doubt; **sans ~** no doubt; (*probablement*) probably; **sans aucun ~** without a doubt; **douter** *vt* to doubt; **douter de** (*sincérité de qn*) to have (one's) doubts about; (*réussite*) to be doubtful of; **se douter de qch/que** to suspect sth/that; **je m'en doutais** I suspected as much; **douteux, -euse** *adj* (*incertain*) doubtful; (*péj*) dubious-looking

Douvres [duvʀ] *n* Dover

doux, douce [du, dus] *adj* soft; (*sucré*) sweet; (*peu fort: moutarde, clément: climat*) mild; (*pas brusque*) gentle

douzaine [duzɛn] *nf* (*12*) dozen; (*environ 12*): **une ~ (de)** a dozen or so

douze [duz] *num* twelve; **douzième** *num* twelfth

doyen, ne [dwajɛ̃, jɛn] *nm/f* (*en âge*) most senior member; (*de faculté*) dean

dragée [dʀaʒe] *nf* sugared almond

draguer [dʀage] *vt* (*rivière*) to dredge; (*fam*) to try to pick up

dramatique [dʀamatik] *adj* dramatic; (*tragique*) tragic ♦ *nf* (*TV*) (television) drama

dramaturge [dʀamatyʀʒ] *nm* dramatist, playwright

drame [dʀam] *nm* drama

drap [dʀa] *nm* (*de lit*) sheet; (*tissu*) woollen fabric

drapeau, x [dʀapo] *nm* flag

drap-housse [dʀaus] *nm* fitted sheet

dresser [dʀese] *vt* (*mettre vertical, monter*) to put up, erect; (*liste*) to draw up; (*animal*) to train; **se ~** *vi* (*obstacle*) to stand; (*personne*) to draw o.s. up; **~ qn contre qn** to set sb against sb; **~ l'oreille** to prick up one's ears

drogue [dʀɔg] *nf* drug; **la ~** drugs *pl*; **drogué, e** *nm/f* drug addict; **droguer** *vt* (*victime*) to drug; **se droguer** *vi* (*aux stupéfiants*) to take drugs; (*péj: de médicaments*) to dose o.s. up; **droguerie** *nf* hardware shop; **droguiste** *nm* keeper/owner of a hardware shop

droit, e [dʀwa, dʀwat] *adj* (*non courbe*) straight; (*vertical*) upright, straight; (*fig: loyal*) upright, straight(forward); (*opposé à gauche*) right, right-hand ♦ *adv* straight ♦ *nm* (*prérogative*) right; (*taxe*) duty, tax; (: *d'inscription*) fee; (*JUR*) **le ~** law; **avoir le ~ de** to be allowed to; **avoir ~ à** to be entitled to; **être dans son ~** to be within one's rights; **à ~e** on the right; (*direction*) (to the) right; **~s d'auteur** royalties; **~s de l'homme** human rights; **~s d'inscription** enrolment fee; **droite** *nf* (*POL*): **la droite** the right (wing); **droitier, -ière** *nm/f* right-handed person; **droiture** *nf* uprightness, straightness

drôle [dʀol] *adj* funny; **une ~ d'idée** a funny idea; **drôlement** (*fam*) *adv* (*très*) terribly, awfully

dromadaire [dʀɔmadɛʀ] *nm* dromedary

dru, e [dʀy] *adj* (*cheveux*) thick, bushy; (*pluie*) heavy

du [dy] *dét voir* **de** ♦ *prép* +*dét* = **de + le**

dû, due [dy] *vb voir* **devoir** ♦ *adj (somme)* owing, owed; *(causé par):* ~ **à** due to ♦ *nm* due

duc [dyk] *nm* duke; **duchesse** *nf* duchess

dûment [dymɑ̃] *adv* duly

dune [dyn] *nf* dune

Dunkerque [dœ̃kɛʀk] *n* Dunkirk

duo [dyo] *nm (MUS)* duet

dupe [dyp] *nf* dupe ♦ *adj:* **(ne pas) être ~ de** (not) to be taken in by

duplex [dyplɛks] *nm (appartement)* split-level apartment, duplex

duplicata [dyplikata] *nm* duplicate

duquel [dykɛl] *prép +pron* = **de +lequel**

dur, e [dyʀ] *adj (pierre, siège, travail, problème)* hard; *(voix, climat)* harsh; *(sévère)* hard, harsh; *(cruel)* hard(-hearted); *(porte, col)* stiff; *(viande)* tough ♦ *adv* hard ♦ *nm (fam: meneur)* tough nut; ~ **d'oreille** hard of hearing

durant [dyʀɑ̃] *prép (au cours de)* during; *(pendant)* for; **des mois ~** for months

durcir [dyʀsiʀ] *vt, vi* to harden; **se ~** *vi* to harden

durée [dyʀe] *nf* length; *(d'une pile etc)* life; **de courte ~** *(séjour)* short

durement [dyʀmɑ̃] *adv* harshly

durer [dyʀe] *vi* to last

dureté [dyʀte] *nf* hardness; harshness; stiffness; toughness

durit ® [dyʀit] *nf (car radiator)* hose

dus *etc* [dy] *vb voir* **devoir**

duvet [dyvɛ] *nm* down; *(sac de couchage)* down-filled sleeping bag

DVD *sigle m* (= *digital versatile disc*) DVD

dynamique [dinamik] *adj* dynamic; **dynamisme** *nm* dynamism

dynamite [dinamit] *nf* dynamite

dynamo [dinamo] *nf* dynamo

dysenterie [disɑ̃tʀi] *nf* dysentery

dyslexie [dislɛksi] *nf* dyslexia, word-blindness

E, e

eau, x [o] *nf* water; **~x** *nfpl (MÉD)* waters; **prendre l'~** to leak, let in water; **tomber à l'~** *(fig)* to fall through; ~ **courante** running water; ~ **de Javel** bleach; ~ **de toilette** toilet water; ~ **douce** fresh water; ~ **gazeuse** sparkling (mineral) water; ~ **minérale** mineral water; ~ **plate** still water; ~ **potable** drinking water; **eau-de-vie** *nf* brandy; **eau-forte** *nf* etching

ébahi, e [ebai] *adj* dumbfounded

ébattre [ebatʀ]: **s'~** *vi* to frolic

ébaucher [eboʃe] *vt* to sketch out, outline; **s'~** *vi* to take shape

ébène [ebɛn] *nf* ebony; **ébéniste** *nm* cabinetmaker

éberlué, e [ebɛʀlɥe] *adj* astounded

éblouir [ebluiʀ] *vt* to dazzle

éborgner [ebɔʀɲe] *vt* to blind in one eye

éboueur [ebwœʀ] *nm* dustman *(BRIT)*, garbageman *(US)*

ébouillanter [ebujɑ̃te] *vt* to scald; *(CULIN)* to blanch

éboulement [ebulmɑ̃] *nm* rock fall

ébouler [ebule]: **s'~** *vi* to crumble, collapse; **éboulis** *nmpl* fallen rocks

ébouriffé, e [ebuʀife] *adj* tousled

ébranler [ebʀɑ̃le] *vt* to shake; *(affaiblir)* to weaken; **s'~** *vi (partir)* to move off

ébrécher [ebʀeʃe] *vt* to chip

ébriété [ebʀijete] *nf:* **en état d'~** in a state of intoxication

ébrouer [ebʀue]: **s'~** *vi* to shake o.s.

ébruiter [ebʀɥite] *vt* to spread, disclose

ébullition [ebylisjɔ̃] *nf* boiling point

écaille [ekɑj] *nf (de poisson)* scale; *(matière)* tortoiseshell; **écailler** *vt (poisson)* to scale; **s'écailler** *vi* to flake *ou* peel (off)

écarlate [ekaʀlat] *adj* scarlet

écarquiller [ekaʀkije] *vt:* ~ **les yeux** to stare wide-eyed

écart [ekaʀ] *nm* gap; **à l'~** out of the way; **à l'~ de** away from; **faire un ~** *(voi-*

ture) to swerve; **~ de conduite** misdemeanour

écarté, e [ekaʀte] *adj* (*lieu*) out-of-theway, remote; (*ouvert*): **les jambes ~es** legs apart; **les bras ~s** arms outstretched

écarter [ekaʀte] *vt* (*séparer*) to move apart, separate; (*éloigner*) to push back, move away; (*ouvrir: bras, jambes*) to spread, open; (: *rideau*) to draw (back); (*éliminer: candidat, possibilité*) to dismiss; **s'~** *vi* to part; (*s'éloigner*) to move away; **s'~ de** to wander from

écervelé, e [esɛʀvəle] *adj* scatterbrained, featherbrained

échafaud [eʃafo] *nm* scaffold

échafaudage [eʃafodaʒ] *nm* scaffolding

échafauder [eʃafode] *vt* (*plan*) to construct

échalote [eʃalɔt] *nf* shallot

échancrure [eʃɑ̃kʀyʀ] *nf* (*de robe*) scoop neckline

échange [eʃɑ̃ʒ] *nm* exchange; **en ~ de** in exchange for; **échanger** *vt*: **échanger qch (contre)** to exchange sth (for); **échangeur** *nm* (AUTO) interchange

échantillon [eʃɑ̃tijɔ̃] *nm* sample

échappement [eʃapmɑ̃] *nm* (AUTO) exhaust

échapper [eʃape]: **~ à** *vt* (*gardien*) to escape (from); (*punition, péril*) to escape; **s'~** *vi* to escape; **~ à qn** (*détail, sens*) to escape sb; (*objet qu'on tient*) to slip out of sb's hands; **laisser ~** (*cri etc*) to let out; **l'~ belle** to have a narrow escape

écharde [eʃaʀd] *nf* splinter (of wood)

écharpe [eʃaʀp] *nf* scarf; **avoir le bras en ~** to have one's arm in a sling

échasse [eʃas] *nf* stilt

échassier [eʃasje] *nm* wader

échauffer [eʃofe] *vt* (*moteur*) to overheat; **s'~** *vi* (SPORT) to warm up; (*dans la discussion*) to become heated

échéance [eʃeɑ̃s] *nf* (*d'un paiement: date*) settlement date; (*fig*) deadline; **à brève ~** in the short term; **à longue ~** in the long run

échéant [eʃeɑ̃]: **le cas ~** *adv* if the case arises

échec [eʃɛk] *nm* failure; (ÉCHECS): **~ et mat/au roi** checkmate/check; **~s** *nmpl* (*jeu*) chess *sg*; **tenir en ~** to hold in check

échelle [eʃɛl] *nf* ladder; (*fig, d'une carte*) scale

échelon [eʃ(ə)lɔ̃] *nm* (*d'échelle*) rung; (ADMIN) grade; **échelonner** *vt* to space out

échevelé, e [eʃəv(ə)le] *adj* tousled, dishevelled

échine [eʃin] *nf* backbone, spine

échiquier [eʃikje] *nm* chessboard

écho [eko] *nm* echo; **échographie** *nf*: **passer une échographie** to have a scan

échoir [eʃwaʀ] *vi* (*dette*) to fall due; (*délais*) to expire; **~ à** to fall to

échouer [eʃwe] *vi* to fail; **s'~** *vi* to run aground

échu, e [eʃy] *pp de* **échoir**

éclabousser [eklabuse] *vt* to splash

éclair [eklɛʀ] *nm* (*d'orage*) flash of lightning, lightning *no pl*; (*gâteau*) éclair

éclairage [eklɛʀaʒ] *nm* lighting

éclaircie [eklɛʀsi] *nf* bright interval

éclaircir [eklɛʀsiʀ] *vt* to lighten; (*fig: mystère*) to clear up; (: *point*) to clarify; **s'~** *vi* (*ciel*) to clear; **s'~ la voix** to clear one's throat; **éclaircissement** *nm* (*sur un point*) clarification

éclairer [eklɛʀe] *vt* (*lieu*) to light (up); (*personne: avec une lampe etc*) to light the way for; (*fig: problème*) to shed light on ♦ *vi*: **~ mal/bien** to give a poor/good light; **s'~ à la bougie** to use candlelight

éclaireur, -euse [eklɛʀœʀ, øz] *nm/f* (*scout*) (boy) scout/(girl) guide ♦ *nm* (MIL) scout

éclat [ekla] *nm* (*de bombe, de verre*) fragment; (*du soleil, d'une couleur etc*) brightness, brilliance; (*d'une cérémonie*) splendour; (*scandale*): **faire un ~** to cause a commotion; **~s de voix** shouts; **~ de rire** roar of laughter

éclatant, e [eklatɑ̃, ɑ̃t] *adj* brilliant

éclater [eklate] *vi* (*pneu*) to burst; (*bombe*) to explode; (*guerre*) to break out; (*groupe*, *parti*) to break up; **~ en sanglots/de rire** to burst out sobbing/laughing

éclipser [eklipse]: **s'~** *vi* to slip away

éclore [eklɔʀ] *vi* (*œuf*) to hatch; (*fleur*) to open (out)

écluse [eklyz] *nf* lock

écœurant, e [ekœʀɑ̃, ɑ̃t] *adj* (*gâteau etc*) sickly; (*fig*) sickening

écœurer [ekœʀe] *vt*: **~ qn** (*nourriture*) to make sb feel sick; (*conduite, personne*) to disgust sb

école [ekɔl] *nf* school; **aller à l'~** to go to school; **~ maternelle/primaire** nursery/ primary school; **~ publique** state school; **écolier, -ière** *nm/f* schoolboy(-girl)

école maternelle

i Nursery school (*l'école maternelle*) *is publicly funded in France and, though not compulsory, is attended by most children between the ages of two and six. Statutory education begins with primary school (*l'école primaire*) from the age of six to ten or eleven.*

écologie [ekɔlɔʒi] *nf* ecology; **écologique** *adj* environment-friendly; **écologiste** *nm/f* ecologist

éconduire [ekɔ̃dɥiʀ] *vt* to dismiss

économe [ekɔnɔm] *adj* thrifty ♦ *nm/f* (*de lycée etc*) bursar (*BRIT*), treasurer (*US*)

économie [ekɔnɔmi] *nf* economy; (*gain: d'argent, de temps etc*) saving; (*science*) economics *sg*; **~s** *nfpl* (*pécule*) savings; **économique** *adj* (*avantageux*) economical; (*ÉCON*) economic; **économiser** *vt, vi* to save; **économiseur** *nm* (*INFORM*): **~ d'écran** screensaver

écoper [ekɔpe] *vi* to bale out; **~ de 3 ans de prison** (*fig: fam*) to get sentenced to 3 years

écorce [ekɔʀs] *nf* bark; (*de fruit*) peel

écorcher [ekɔʀʃe] *vt*: **s'~ le genou/la main** to graze one's knee/one's hand;

écorchure [ekɔʀʃyʀ] *nf* graze

écossais, e [ekɔsɛ, ɛz] *adj* Scottish ♦ *nm/ f*: **É~, e** Scot

Écosse [ekɔs] *nf*: **l'~** Scotland

écosser [ekɔse] *vt* to shell

écoulement [ekulmɑ̃] *nm* (*d'eau*) flow

écouler [ekule] *vt* (*objet*) to sell; **s'~** *vi* (*eau*) to flow (out); (*temps*) to pass (by)

écourter [ekuʀte] *vt* to curtail, cut short

écoute [ekut] *nf* (*RADIO, TV*): **temps/heure d'~** listening (*ou* viewing) time/hour; **rester à l'~ (de)** to stay tuned in (to); **~s téléphoniques** phone tapping *sg*

écouter [ekute] *vt* to listen to; **écouteur** *nm* (*TÉL*) receiver; (*RADIO*) headphones *pl*, headset

écoutille [ekutij] *nf* hatch

écran [ekʀɑ̃] *nm* screen; **petit ~** television; **~ total** sunblock

écrasant, e [ekʀazɑ̃, ɑ̃t] *adj* overwhelming

écraser [ekʀaze] *vt* to crush; (*piéton*) to run over; **s'~** *vi* to crash; **s'~ contre** to crash into

écrémé, e [ekʀeme] *adj* (*lait*) skimmed

écrevisse [ekʀəvis] *nf* crayfish *inv*

écrier [ekʀije]: **s'~** *vi* to exclaim

écrin [ekʀɛ̃] *nm* case, box

écrire [ekʀiʀ] *vt* to write; **s'~** to write to each other; **ça s'écrit comment?** how is it spelt?; **écrit** *nm* (*examen*) written paper; **par écrit** in writing

écriteau, x [ekʀito] *nm* notice, sign

écriture [ekʀityʀ] *nf* writing; **l'É~, les É~s** the Scriptures

écrivain [ekʀivɛ̃] *nm* writer

écrou [ekʀu] *nm* nut

écrouer [ekʀue] *vt* to imprison

écrouler [ekʀule]: **s'~** *vi* to collapse

écru, e [ekʀy] *adj* (*couleur*) off-white, écru

ECU [eky] *sigle m* ECU

écueil [ekœj] *nm* reef; (*fig*) pitfall

éculé, e [ekyle] *adj* (*chaussure*) down-at-heel; (*fig: péj*) hackneyed

écume [ekym] *nf* foam; **écumer** *vt* (*CULIN*) to skim; **écumoire** *nf* skimmer

écureuil [ekyʀœj] *nm* squirrel

écurie [ekyʀi] *nf* stable

écusson [ekysɔ̃] *nm* badge

écuyer, -ère [ekɥije, jɛʀ] *nm/f* rider

eczéma [egzema] *nm* eczema

édenté, e [edɑ̃te] *adj* toothless

EDF *sigle f* (= *Électricité de France*) *national electricity company*

édifice [edifis] *nm* edifice, building

édifier [edifje] *vt* to build, erect; (*fig*) to edify

Édimbourg [edɛ̃buʀ] *n* Edinburgh

éditer [edite] *vt* (*publier*) to publish; (*annoter*) to edit; **éditeur, -trice** *nm/f* publisher; **édition** *nf* edition; (*industrie du livre*) publishing

édredon [edʀədɔ̃] *nm* eiderdown

éducateur, -trice [edykatœʀ, tʀis] *nm/f* teacher; (*in special school*) instructor

éducatif, -ive [edykatif, iv] *adj* educational

éducation [edykasjɔ̃] *nf* education; (*familiale*) upbringing; (*manières*) (good) manners *pl*; **~ physique** physical education

édulcorant [edylkɔʀɑ̃] *nm* sweetener

éduquer [edyke] *vt* to educate; (*élever*) to bring up

effacé, e [efase] *adj* unassuming

effacer [efase] *vt* to erase, rub out; **s'~** *vi* (*inscription etc*) to wear off; (*pour laisser passer*) to step aside

effarant, e [efaʀɑ̃, ɑ̃t] *adj* alarming

effarer [efaʀe] *vt* to alarm

effaroucher [efaʀuʃe] *vt* to frighten *ou* scare away

effectif, -ive [efɛktif, iv] *adj* real ♦ *nm* (*SCOL*) (pupil) numbers *pl*; (*entreprise*) staff, workforce; **effectivement** *adv* (*réellement*) actually, really; (*en effet*) indeed

effectuer [efɛktɥe] *vt* (*opération*) to carry out; (*trajet*) to make

efféminé, e [efemine] *adj* effeminate

effervescent, e [efɛʀvesɑ̃, ɑ̃t] *adj* effervescent

effet [efɛ] *nm* effect; (*impression*) impression; **~s** *nmpl* (*vêtements etc*) things; **faire**

~ (*médicament*) to take effect; **faire bon/mauvais ~ sur qn** to make a good/bad impression on sb; **en ~** indeed; **~ de serre** greenhouse effect

efficace [efikas] *adj* (*personne*) efficient; (*action, médicament*) effective; **efficacité** *nf* efficiency; effectiveness

effilocher [efilɔʃe]: **s'~** *vi* to fray

efflanqué, e [eflɑ̃ke] *adj* emaciated

effleurer [eflœʀe] *vt* to brush (against); (*sujet*) to touch upon; (*suj: idée, pensée*): **ça ne m'a pas effleuré** it didn't cross my mind

effluves [eflyv] *nmpl* exhalation(s)

effondrer [efɔ̃dʀe]: **s'~** *vi* to collapse

efforcer [efɔʀse]: **s'~ de** *vt*: **s'~ de faire** to try hard to do

effort [efɔʀ] *nm* effort

effraction [efʀaksjɔ̃] *nf*: **s'introduire par ~ dans** to break into

effrayant, e [efʀɛjɑ̃, ɑ̃t] *adj* frightening

effrayer [efʀeje] *vt* to frighten, scare

effréné, e [efʀene] *adj* wild

effriter [efʀite]: **s'~** *vi* to crumble

effroi [efʀwa] *nm* terror, dread *no pl*

effronté, e [efʀɔ̃te] *adj* cheeky

effroyable [efʀwajabl] *adj* horrifying, appalling

effusion [efyzjɔ̃] *nf* effusion; **sans ~ de sang** without bloodshed

égal, e, -aux [egal, o] *adj* equal; (*constant: vitesse*) steady ♦ *nm/f* equal; **être ~ à** (*prix, nombre*) to be equal to; **ça lui est ~** it's all the same to him, he doesn't mind; **sans ~** matchless, unequalled; **d'~ à ~** as equals; **également** *adv* equally; (*aussi*) too, as well; **égaler** *vt* to equal; **égaliser** *vt* (*sol, salaires*) to level (out); (*chances*) to equalize ♦ *vi* (*SPORT*) to equalize; **égalité** *nf* equality; **être à égalité** to be level

égard [egaʀ] *nm*: **~s** consideration *sg*; **à cet ~** in this respect; **par ~ pour** out of consideration for; **à l'~ de** towards

égarement [egaʀmɑ̃] *nm* distraction

égarer [egaʀe] *vt* to mislay; **s'~** *vi* to get

lost, lose one's way; (*objet*) to go astray

égayer [egeje] *vt* to cheer up; (*pièce*) to brighten up

églantine [eglɑ̃tin] *nf* wild *ou* dog rose

églefin [egləfɛ̃] *nm* haddock

église [egliz] *nf* church; **aller à l'~** to go to church

égoïsme [egɔism] *nm* selfishness; **égoïste** *adj* selfish

égorger [egɔrʒe] *vt* to cut the throat of

égosiller [egozije]: **s'~** *vi* to shout o.s. hoarse⋅

égout [egu] *nm* sewer

égoutter [egute] *vi* to drip; **s'~** *vi* to drip; **égouttoir** *nm* draining board; (*mobile*) draining rack

égratigner [egratiɲe] *vt* to scratch; **égratignure** *nf* scratch

Égypte [eʒipt] *nf*: **l'~** Egypt; **égyptien, ne** *adj* ⋅Egyptian ♦ *nm/f*: **Égyptien, ne** Egyptian

eh [e] *excl* hey!; **~ bien** well

éhonté, e [eɔ̃te] *adj* shameless, brazen

éjecter [eʒɛkte] *vt* (*TECH*) to eject; (*fam*) to kick *ou* chuck out

élaborer [elabɔre] *vt* to elaborate; (*projet, stratégie*) to work out; (*rapport*) to draft

élan [elɑ̃] *nm* (*ZOOL*) elk, moose; (*SPORT*) run up; (*fig: de tendresse etc*) surge; **prendre de l'~** to gather speed

élancé, e [elɑ̃se] *adj* slender

élancement [elɑ̃smɑ̃] *nm* shooting pain

élancer [elɑ̃se]: **s'~** *vi* to dash, hurl o.s.

élargir [elarʒir] *vt* to widen; **s'~** *vi* to widen; (*vêtement*) to stretch

élastique [elastik] *adj* elastic ♦ *nm* (*de bureau*) rubber band; (*pour la couture*) elastic *no pl*

électeur, -trice [elɛktœr, tris] *nm/f* elector, voter

élection [elɛksjɔ̃] *nf* election

électorat [elɛktɔra] *nm* electorate

électricien, ne [elɛktrisjɛ̃, jɛn] *nm/f* electrician

électricité [elɛktrisite] *nf* electricity; **allumer/éteindre l'~** to put on/off the light

électrique [elɛktrik] *adj* electric(al)

électrocuter [elɛktrɔkyte] *vt* to electrocute

électroménager [elɛktrɔmenaʒe] *adj, nm*: **appareils ~s, l'~** domestic (electrical) appliances

électronique [elɛktrɔnik] *adj* electronic ♦ *nf* electronics *sg*

électrophone [elɛktrɔfɔn] *nm* record player

élégance [elegɑ̃s] *nf* elegance

élégant, e [elegɑ̃, ɑ̃t] *adj* elegant

élément [elemɑ̃] *nm* element; (*pièce*) component, part; **~s de cuisine** kitchen units; **élémentaire** *adj* elementary

éléphant [elefɑ̃] *nm* elephant

élevage [el(ə)vaʒ] *nm* breeding; (*de bovins*) cattle rearing; **truite d'~** farmed trout

élévation [elevasjɔ̃] *nf* (*hausse*) rise

élevé, e [el(ə)ve] *adj* high; **bien/mal ~** well-/ill-mannered

élève [elɛv] *nm/f* pupil

élever [el(ə)ve] *vt* (*enfant*) to bring up, raise; (*animaux*) to breed; (*hausser: taux, niveau*) to raise; (*édifier: monument*) to put up, erect; **s'~** *vi* (*avion*) to go up; (*niveau, température*) to rise; **s'~ à** (*suj: frais, dégâts*) to amount to, add up to; **s'~ contre qch** to rise up against sth; **~ la voix** to raise one's voice; **éleveur, -euse** *nm/f* breeder

élimé, e [elime] *adj* threadbare

éliminatoire [eliminatwar] *nf* (*SPORT*) heat

éliminer [elimine] *vt* to eliminate

élire [elir] *vt* to elect

elle [ɛl] *pron* (*sujet*) she; (: *chose*) it; (*complément*) her; it; **~s** (*sujet*) they; (*complément*) them; **~-même** herself; itself; **~s-mêmes** themselves; *voir aussi* **il**

élocution [elɔkysjɔ̃] *nf* delivery; **défaut d'~** speech impediment

éloge [elɔʒ] *nm* (*gén no pl*) praise; **faire l'~ de** to praise; **élogieux, -euse** *adj* laudatory, full of praise

éloigné, e [elwaɲe] *adj* distant, far-off;

(parent) distant; **éloignement** *nm (distance, aussi fig)* distance

éloigner [elwaɲe] *vt (échéance)* to put off, postpone; *(soupçons, danger)* to ward off; *(objet):* **~ qch (de)** to move *ou* take sth away (from); *(personne):* **~ qn (de)** to take sb away *ou* remove sb (from); **s'~ (de)** *(personne)* to go away (from); *(véhicule)* to move away (from); *(affectivement)* to become estranged (from); **ne vous éloignez pas!** don't go far away!

élu, e [ely] *pp de* **élire** ♦ *nm/f (POL)* elected representative

éluder [elyde] *vt* to evade

Élysée [elize] *nm:* **(le palais de) l'~** the Élysée Palace *(the French president's residence)*

émacié, e [emasje] *adj* emaciated

émail, -aux [emaj, o] *nm* enamel

émaillé, e [emaje] *adj (fig):* **~ de** dotted with

émanciper [emɑ̃sipe]: **s'~** *vi (fig)* to become emancipated *ou* liberated

émaner [emane]: **~ de** *vt* to come from

emballage [ɑ̃balaʒ] *nm (papier)* wrapping; *(boîte)* packaging

emballer [ɑ̃bale] *vt* to wrap (up); *(dans un carton)* to pack (up); *(fig: fam)* to thrill (to bits); **s'~** *vi (moteur)* to race; *(cheval)* to bolt; *(fig: personne)* to get carried away

embarcadère [ɑ̃barkadɛr] *nm* wharf, pier

embarcation [ɑ̃barkasjɔ̃] *nf* (small) boat, (small) craft *inv*

embardée [ɑ̃barde] *nf:* **faire une ~** to swerve

embarquement [ɑ̃barkəmɑ̃] *nm (de passagers)* boarding; *(de marchandises)* loading

embarquer [ɑ̃barke] *vt (personne)* to embark; *(marchandise)* to load; *(fam)* to cart off ♦ *vi (passager)* to board; **s'~** *vi* to board; **s'~ dans** *(affaire, aventure)* to embark upon

embarras [ɑ̃bara] *nm (gêne)* embarrassment; **mettre qn dans l'~** to put sb in

an awkward position; **vous n'avez que l'~ du choix** the only problem is choosing

embarrassant, e [ɑ̃barasɑ̃, ɑ̃t] *adj* embarrassing

embarrasser [ɑ̃barase] *vt (encombrer)* to clutter (up); *(gêner)* to hinder, hamper; **~ qn** to put sb in an awkward position; **s'~ de** to burden o.s. with

embauche [ɑ̃boʃ] *nf* hiring; **embaucher** *vt* to take on, hire

embaumer [ɑ̃bome] *vt:* **~ la lavande** *etc* to be fragrant with (the scent of) lavender *etc*

embellie [ɑ̃beli] *nf* brighter period

embellir [ɑ̃belir] *vt* to make more attractive; *(une histoire)* to embellish ♦ *vi* to grow lovelier *ou* more attractive

embêtements [ɑ̃bɛtmɑ̃] *nmpl* trouble *sg*

embêter [ɑ̃bete] *vt* to bother; **s'~** *vi* *(s'ennuyer)* to be bored

emblée [ɑ̃ble]: **d'~** *adv* straightaway

embobiner [ɑ̃bɔbine] *vt (fam)* to get round

emboîter [ɑ̃bwate] *vt* to fit together; **s'~ (dans)** to fit (into); **~ le pas à qn** to follow in sb's footsteps

embonpoint [ɑ̃bɔ̃pwɛ̃] *nm* stoutness

embouchure [ɑ̃buʃyr] *nf (GÉO)* mouth

embourber [ɑ̃burbe]: **s'~** *vi* to get stuck in the mud

embourgeoiser [ɑ̃burʒwaze]: **s'~** *vi* to become middle-class

embouteillage [ɑ̃butɛjaʒ] *nm* traffic jam

emboutir [ɑ̃butir] *vt (heurter)* to crash into, ram

embranchement [ɑ̃brɑ̃ʃmɑ̃] *nm (routier)* junction

embraser [ɑ̃braze]: **s'~** *vi* to flare up

embrassades [ɑ̃brasad] *nfpl* hugging and kissing

embrasser [ɑ̃brase] *vt* to kiss; *(sujet, période)* to embrace, encompass; **s'~** to kiss (each other)

embrasure [ɑ̃brazyr] *nf:* **dans l'~ de la porte** in the door(way)

embrayage [ãbʀejaʒ] *nm* clutch
embrayer [ãbʀeje] *vi* (AUTO) to let in the clutch
embrocher [ãbʀɔʃe] *vt* to put on a spit
embrouiller [ãbʀuje] *vt* to muddle up; (*fils*) to tangle (up); **s'~** *vi* (*personne*) to get in a muddle
embruns [ãbʀœ̃] *nmpl* sea spray *sg*
embryon [ãbʀijɔ̃] *nm* embryo
embûches [ãbyʃ] *nfpl* pitfalls, traps
embué, e [ãbɥe] *adj* misted up
embuscade [ãbyskad] *nf* ambush
éméché, e [emeʃe] *adj* tipsy, merry
émeraude [em(ə)ʀod] *nf* emerald
émerger [emɛʀʒe] *vi* to emerge; (*faire saillie, aussi fig*) to stand out
émeri [em(ə)ʀi] *nm*: **toile** *ou* **papier ~** emery paper
émerveillement [emɛʀvejmã] *nm* wonder
émerveiller [emɛʀveje] *vt* to fill with wonder; **s'~ de** to marvel at
émettre [emɛtʀ] *vt* (*son, lumière*) to give out, emit;˙(*message etc*: RADIO) to transmit; (*billet, timbre, emprunt*) to issue; (*hypothèse, avis*) to voice, put forward ♦ *vi* to broadcast
émeus *etc* [emø] *vb voir* **émouvoir**
émeute [emøt] *nf* riot
émietter [emjete] *vt* to crumble
émigrer [emigʀe] *vi* to emigrate
émincer [emɛ̃se] *vt* to cut into thin slices
éminent, e [eminã, ãt] *adj* distinguished
émission [emisjɔ̃] *nf* (RADIO, TV) programme, broadcast; (*d'un message*) transmission; (*de timbre*) issue
emmagasiner [ãmagazine] *vt* (*amasser*) to store up
emmanchure [ãmãʃyʀ] *nf* armhole
emmêler [ãmele] *vt* to tangle (up); (*fig*) to muddle up; **s'~** *vi* to get in a tangle
emménager [ãmenaʒe] *vi* to move in; **~ dans** to move into
emmener [ãm(ə)ne] *vt* to take (with one); (*comme otage, capture*) to take away; **~ qn au cinéma** to take sb to the cinema

emmerder [ãmɛʀde] (*fam!*) *vt* to bug, bother; **s'~** *vi* to be bored stiff
emmitoufler [ãmitufle]: **s'~** *vi* to wrap up (warmly)
émoi [emwa] *nm* commotion
émotif, -ive [emɔtif, iv] *adj* emotional
émotion [emosjɔ̃] *nf* emotion
émousser [emuse] *vt* to blunt; (*fig*) to dull
émouvoir [emuvwaʀ] *vt* to move; **s'~** *vi* to be moved; (*s'indigner*) to be roused
empailler [ãpaje] *vt* to stuff
empaqueter [ãpakte] *vt* to parcel up
emparer [ãpaʀe]: **s'~ de** *vt* (*objet*) to seize, grab; (*comme otage, MIL*) to seize; (*suj: peur etc*) to take hold of
empâter [ãpate]: **s'~** *vi* to thicken out
empêchement [ãpɛʃmã] *nm* (unexpected) obstacle, hitch
empêcher [ãpeʃe] *vt* to prevent; **~ qn de faire** to prevent *ou* stop sb (from) doing; **il n'empêche que** nevertheless; **il n'a pas pu s'~ de rire** he couldn't help laughing
empereur [ãpʀœʀ] *nm* emperor
empester [ãpeste] *vi* to stink, reek
empêtrer [ãpetʀe] *vt*: **s'~ dans** (*fils etc*) to get tangled up in
emphase [ãfaz] *nf* pomposity, bombast
empiéter [ãpjete] *vi*: **~ sur** to encroach upon
empiffrer [ãpifʀe]: **s'~** (*fam*) *vi* to stuff o.s.
empiler [ãpile] *vt* to pile (up)
empire [ãpiʀ] *nm* empire; (*fig*) influence
empirer [ãpiʀe] *vi* to worsen, deteriorate
emplacement [ãplasmã] *nm* site
emplettes [ãplet] *nfpl* shopping *sg*
emplir [ãpliʀ] *vt* to fill; **s'~ (de)** to fill (with)
emploi [ãplwa] *nm* use; (COMM, ÉCON) employment; (*poste*) job, situation; **mode d'~** directions for use; **~ du temps** timetable, schedule
employé, e [ãplwaje] *nm/f* employee; **~ de bureau** office employee *ou* clerk

employer [ɑ̃plwaje] *vt* to use; (*ouvrier, main-d'œuvre*) to employ; **s'~ à faire** to apply *ou* devote o.s. to doing; **employeur, -euse** *nm/f* employer

empocher [ɑ̃pɔʃe] *vt* to pocket

empoigner [ɑ̃pwaɲe] *vt* to grab

empoisonner [ɑ̃pwazɔne] *vt* to poison; (*empester: air, pièce*) to stink out; (*fam*): **~ qn** to drive sb mad

emporté, e [ɑ̃pɔrte] *adj* quick-tempered

emporter [ɑ̃pɔrte] *vt* to take (with one); (*en dérobant ou enlevant, emmener: blessés, voyageurs*) to take away; (*entraîner*) to carry away; **s'~** *vi* (*de colère*) to lose one's temper; **l'~ (sur)** to get the upper hand (of); **plats à ~** take-away meals

empreint, e [ɑ̃prɛ̃, ɛ̃t] *adj*: **~ de** (*regret, jalousie*) marked with; **empreinte** *nf*: **empreinte (de pas)** footprint; **empreinte (digitale)** fingerprint

empressé, e [ɑ̃prese] *adj* attentive

empressement [ɑ̃prɛsmɑ̃] *nm* (*hâte*) eagerness

empresser [ɑ̃prese]: **s'~** *vi*: **s'~ auprès de qn** to surround sb with attentions; **s'~ de faire** (*se hâter*) to hasten to do

emprise [ɑ̃priz] *nf* hold, ascendancy

emprisonnement [ɑ̃prizɔnmɑ̃] *nm* imprisonment

emprisonner [ɑ̃prizɔne] *vt* to imprison

emprunt [ɑ̃prœ̃] *nm* loan

emprunté, e [ɑ̃prœ̃te] *adj* (*fig*) ill-at-ease, awkward

emprunter [ɑ̃prœ̃te] *vt* to borrow; (*itinéraire*) to take, follow

ému, e [emy] *pp de* **émouvoir** ♦ *adj* (*gratitude*) touched; (*compassion*) moved

---

MOT-CLÉ

en [ɑ̃] *prép* **1** (*endroit, pays*) in; (*direction*) to; **habiter en France/ville** to live in France/town; **aller en France/ville** to go to France/town

2 (*moment, temps*) in; **en été/juin** in summer/June

3 (*moyen*) by; **en avion/taxi** by plane/taxi

4 (*composition*) made of; **c'est en verre** it's (made of) glass; **un collier en argent** a silver necklace

5 (*description, état*): **une femme (habillée) en rouge** a woman (dressed) in red; **peindre qch en rouge** to paint sth red; **en T/étoile** T/star-shaped; **en chemise/chaussettes** in one's shirt-sleeves/socks; **en soldat** as a soldier; **cassé en plusieurs morceaux** broken into several pieces; **en réparation** being repaired, under repair; **en vacances** on holiday; **en deuil** in mourning; **le même en plus grand** the same but *ou* only bigger

6 (*avec gérondif*) while, on, by; **en dormant** while sleeping, as one sleeps; **en sortant** on going out, as he *etc* went out; **sortir en courant** to run out

♦ *pron* **1** (*indéfini*): **j'en ai/veux** I have/want some; **en as-tu?** have you got any?; **je n'en veux pas** I don't want any; **j'en ai 2** I've got 2; **combien y en a-t-il?** how many (of them) are there?; **j'en ai assez** I've got enough (of it *ou* them); (*j'en ai marre*) I've had enough

2 (*provenance*) from there; **j'en viens** I've come from there

3 (*cause*): **il en est malade/perd le sommeil** he is ill/can't sleep because of it

4 (*complément de nom, d'adjectif, de verbe*): **j'en connais les dangers** I know its *ou* the dangers; **j'en suis fier/ai besoin** I am proud of it/need it

---

ENA *sigle f* (= *École Nationale d'Administration*) one of the *Grandes Écoles*

encadrement [ɑ̃kadramɑ̃] *nm* (*cadres*) managerial staff

encadrer [ɑ̃kadre] *vt* (*tableau, image*) to frame; (*fig: entourer*) to surround; (*personnel, soldats etc*) to train

encaissé, e [ɑ̃kese] *adj* (*vallée*) steep-sided; (*rivière*) with steep banks

encaisser [ɑ̃kese] *vt* (*chèque*) to cash; (*argent*) to collect; (*fam: coup, défaite*) to take

encart [ɑ̃kar] *nm* insert

en-cas [ãka] *nm* snack

encastré, e [ãkastʀe] *adj*: **four ~** built-in oven

enceinte [ãsɛ̃t] *adj f*: **~ (de 6 mois)** (6 months) pregnant ♦ *nf* (*mur*) wall; (*espace*) enclosure; (*aussi*: **~ acoustique**) (loud)speaker

encens [ãsã] *nm* incense

encercler [ãseʀkle] *vt* to surround

enchaîner [ãʃene] *vt* to chain up; (*mouvements, séquences*) to link (together) ♦ *vi* to carry on

enchanté, e [ãʃãte] *adj* (*ravi*) delighted; (*magique*) enchanted; **~ (de faire votre connaissance)** pleased to meet you

enchantement [ãʃãtmã] *nm* delight; (*magie*) enchantment

enchère [ãʃɛʀ] *nf* bid; **mettre/vendre aux ~s** to put up for (sale by)/sell by auction

enchevêtrer [ãʃ(ə)vetʀe]: **s'~** *vi* to get in a tangle

enclencher [ãklãʃe] *vt* (*mécanisme*) to engage; **s'~** *vi* to engage

enclin, e [ãklɛ̃, in] *adj*: **~ à** inclined *ou* prone to

enclos [ãklo] *nm* enclosure

enclume [ãklym] *nf* anvil

encoche [ãkɔʃ] *nf* notch

encoignure [ãkɔɲyʀ] *nf* corner

encolure [ãkɔlyʀ] *nf* (*cou*) neck

encombrant, e [ãkɔ̃bʀã, ãt] *adj* cumbersome, bulky

encombre [ãkɔ̃bʀ]: **sans ~** *adv* without mishap *ou* incident; **encombrement** *nm*: **être pris dans un encombrement** to be stuck in a traffic jam

encombrer [ãkɔ̃bʀe] *vt* to clutter (up); (*gêner*) to hamper; **s'~ de** (*bagages etc*) to load *ou* burden o.s. with

encontre [ãkɔ̃tʀ]: **à l'~ de** *prép* against, counter to

MOT-CLÉ

---

encore [ãkɔʀ] *adv* **1** (*continuation*) still; **il y travaille encore** he's still working on it;

pas encore not yet

2 (*de nouveau*) again; **j'irai encore demain** I'll go again tomorrow; **encore une fois** (once) again; **encore deux jours** two more days

3 (*intensif*) even, still; **encore plus fort/mieux** even louder/better, louder/better still

4 (*restriction*) even so *ou* then, only; **encore pourrais-je le faire si ...** even so, I might be able to do it if ...; **si encore** if only; **encore que** *conj* although

---

encouragement [ãkuʀaʒmã] *nm* encouragement

encourager [ãkuʀaʒe] *vt* to encourage

encourir [ãkuʀiʀ] *vt* to incur

encrasser [ãkʀase] *vt* to make filthy

encre [ãkʀ] *nf* ink; **encrier** *nm* inkwell

encroûter [ãkʀute]: **s'~** (*fam*) *vi* (*fig*) to get into a rut, get set in one's ways

encyclopédie [ãsiklɔpedi] *nf* encyclopaedia

endetter [ãdete]: **s'~** *vi* to get into debt

endiablé, e [ãdjable] *adj* (*danse*) furious

endimanché, e [ãdimãʃe] *adj* in one's Sunday best

endive [ãdiv] *nf* chicory *no pl*

endoctriner [ãdɔktʀine] *vt* to indoctrinate

endommager [ãdɔmaʒe] *vt* to damage

endormi, e [ãdɔʀmi] *adj* asleep

endormir [ãdɔʀmiʀ] *vt* to put to sleep; (*suj: chaleur etc*) to send to sleep; (*MÉD: dent, nerf*) to anaesthetize; (*fig: soupçons*) to allay; **s'~** *vi* to fall asleep, go to sleep

endosser [ãdose] *vt* (*responsabilité*) to take, shoulder; (*chèque*) to endorse; (*uniforme, tenue*) to put on, don

endroit [ãdʀwa] *nm* place; (*opposé à l'envers*) right side; **à l'~** (*vêtement*) the right way out; (*objet posé*) the right way round

enduire [ãdɥiʀ] *vt* to coat

enduit [ãdɥi] *nm* coating

endurance [ãdyʀãs] *nf* endurance

endurant, e [ãdyʀã, ãt] *adj* tough, hardy

endurcir [ɑ̃dyʀsiʀ]: **s'~** *vi* (*physiquement*) to become tougher; (*moralement*) to become hardened

endurer [ɑ̃dyʀe] *vt* to endure, bear

énergétique [enɛʀʒetik] *adj* (*aliment*) energy-giving

énergie [enɛʀʒi] *nf* (PHYSIQUE) energy; (TECH) power; (*morale*) vigour, spirit; **énergique** *adj* energetic, vigorous; (*mesures*) drastic, stringent

énervant, e [enɛʀvɑ̃, ɑ̃t] *adj* irritating, annoying

énerver [enɛʀve] *vt* to irritate, annoy; **s'~** *vi* to get excited, get worked up

enfance [ɑ̃fɑ̃s] *nf* childhood

enfant [ɑ̃fɑ̃] *nm/f* child; **~ de chœur** *nm* (REL) altar boy; **enfantillage** (*péj*) *nm* childish behaviour *no pl*; **enfantin, e** *adj* (*puéril*) childlike; (*langage, jeu etc*) children's *cpd*

enfer [ɑ̃fɛʀ] *nm* hell

enfermer [ɑ̃fɛʀme] *vt* to shut up; (*à clef, interner*) to lock up

enfiévré, e [ɑ̃fjevʀe] *adj* feverish

enfiler [ɑ̃file] *vt* (*vêtement*) to slip on, slip into; (*perles*) to string; (*aiguille*) to thread

enfin [ɑ̃fɛ̃] *adv* at last; (*en énumérant*) lastly; (*toutefois*) still; (*pour conclure*) in a word; (*somme toute*) after all

enflammer [ɑ̃flame]: **s'~** *vi* to catch fire; (MÉD) to become inflamed

enflé, e [ɑ̃fle] *adj* swollen

enfler [ɑ̃fle] *vi* to swell (up)

enfoncer [ɑ̃fɔ̃se] *vt* (*clou*) to drive in; (*faire pénétrer*): **~ qch dans** to push (*ou* drive) sth into; (*forcer: porte*) to break open; **s'~** *vi* to sink; **s'~ dans** to sink into; (*forêt, ville*) to disappear into

enfouir [ɑ̃fwiʀ] *vt* (*dans le sol*) to bury; (*dans un tiroir etc*) to tuck away

enfourcher [ɑ̃fuʀʃe] *vt* to mount

enfreindre [ɑ̃fʀɛ̃dʀ] *vt* to infringe, break

enfuir [ɑ̃fɥiʀ]: **s'~** *vi* to run away *ou* off

enfumer [ɑ̃fyme] *vt* (*pièce*) to fill with smoke

engageant, e [ɑ̃gaʒɑ̃, ɑ̃t] *adj* attractive, appealing

engagement [ɑ̃gaʒmɑ̃] *nm* commitment

engager [ɑ̃gaʒe] *vt* (*embaucher*) to take on; (: *artiste*) to engage; (*commencer*) to start; (*lier*) to bind, commit; (*impliquer*) to involve; (*investir*) to invest, lay out; (*inciter*) to urge; (*introduire: clé*) to insert; **s'~** *vi* (*promettre*) to commit o.s.; (MIL) to enlist; (*débuter: conversation etc*) to start (up); **s'~ à faire** to undertake to do; **s'~ dans** (*rue, passage*) to turn into; (*fig: affaire, discussion*) to enter into, embark on

engelures [ɑ̃ʒlyʀ] *nfpl* chilblains

engendrer [ɑ̃ʒɑ̃dʀe] *vt* to breed, create

engin [ɑ̃ʒɛ̃] *nm* machine; (*outil*) instrument; (AUT) vehicle; (AVIAT) aircraft *inv*

englober [ɑ̃glɔbe] *vt* to include

engloutir [ɑ̃glutiʀ] *vt* to swallow up

engoncé, e [ɑ̃gɔ̃se] *adj*: **~ dans** cramped in

engorger [ɑ̃gɔʀʒe] *vt* to obstruct, block

engouement [ɑ̃gumɑ̃] *nm* (sudden) passion

engouffrer [ɑ̃gufʀe] *vt* to swallow up, devour; **s'~ dans** to rush into

engourdir [ɑ̃guʀdiʀ] *vt* to numb; (*fig*) to dull, blunt; **s'~** *vi* to go numb

engrais [ɑ̃gʀɛ] *nm* manure; **~ (chimique)** (chemical) fertilizer

engraisser [ɑ̃gʀese] *vt* to fatten (up)

engrenage [ɑ̃gʀənaʒ] *nm* gears *pl*, gearing; (*fig*) chain

engueuler [ɑ̃gœle] (*fam*) *vt* to bawl at

enhardir [ɑ̃aʀdiʀ]: **s'~** *vi* to grow bolder

énigme [enigm] *nf* riddle

enivrer [ɑ̃nivʀe] *vt*: **s'~** to get drunk

enjambée [ɑ̃ʒɑ̃be] *nf* stride

enjamber [ɑ̃ʒɑ̃be] *vt* to stride over

enjeu, x [ɑ̃ʒø] *nm* stakes *pl*

enjôler [ɑ̃ʒole] *vt* to coax, wheedle

enjoliver [ɑ̃ʒɔlive] *vt* to embellish; **enjoliveur** *nm* (AUTO) hub cap

enjoué, e [ɑ̃ʒwe] *adj* playful

enlacer [ɑ̃lase] *vt* (*étreindre*) to embrace, hug

enlaidir [ɑ̃lediʀ] *vt* to make ugly ♦ *vi* to

become ugly

enlèvement [ɑ̃lɛvmɑ̃] *nm* (*rapt*) abduction, kidnapping

enlever [ɑ̃l(ə)ve] *vt* (*ôter: gén*) to remove; (: *vêtement, lunettes*) to take off; (*emporter: ordures etc*) to take away; (*kidnapper*) to abduct, kidnap; (*obtenir: prix, contrat*) to win; (*prendre*): ~ **qch à qn** to take sth (away) from sb

enliser [ɑ̃lize]: **s'~** *vi* to sink, get stuck

enneigé, e [ɑ̃neʒe] *adj* (*route, maison*) snowed-up; (*paysage*) snowy

ennemi, e [ɛnmi] *adj* hostile; (*MIL*) enemy *cpd* ♦ *nm/f* enemy

ennui [ɑ̃nɥi] *nm* (*lassitude*) boredom; (*difficulté*) trouble *no pl*; **avoir des ~s** to have problems; **ennuyer** *vt* to bother; (*lasser*) to bore; **s'ennuyer** *vi* to be bored; **ennuyeux, -euse** *adj* boring, tedious; (*embêtant*) annoying

énoncé [enɔ̃se] *nm* (*de problème*) terms *pl*

énoncer [enɔ̃se] *vt* (*faits*) to set out, state

enorgueillir [ɑ̃nɔʀɡœjiʀ]: **s'~ de** *vt* to pride o.s. on

énorme [enɔʀm] *adj* enormous, huge; **énormément** *adv* enormously; **énormément de neige/gens** an enormous amount of snow/number of people; **énormité** *nf* (*propos*) outrageous remark

enquérir [ɑ̃keʀiʀ]: **s'~ de** *vt* to inquire about

enquête [ɑ̃kɛt] *nf* (*de journaliste, de police*) investigation; (*judiciaire, administrative*) inquiry; (*sondage d'opinion*) survey; **enquêter** *vi* to investigate

enquiers *etc* [ɑ̃kje] *vb voir* **enquérir**

enquiquiner [ɑ̃kikine] (*fam*) *vt* to annoy, irritate, bother

enraciné, e [ɑ̃ʀasine] *adj* deep-rooted

enragé, e [ɑ̃ʀaʒe] *adj* (*MÉD*) rabid, with rabies; (*fig*) fanatical

enrageant, e [ɑ̃ʀaʒɑ̃, ɑ̃t] *adj* infuriating

enrager [ɑ̃ʀaʒe] *vi* to be in a rage

enrayer [ɑ̃ʀeje] *vt* to check, stop

enregistrement [ɑ̃ʀ(ə)ʒistʀəmɑ̃] *nm* recording; ~ **des bagages** (*à l'aéroport*) baggage check-in

enregistrer [ɑ̃ʀ(ə)ʒistʀe] *vt* (*MUS etc*) to record; (*fig: mémoriser*) to make a mental note of; (*bagages: à l'aéroport*) to check in

enrhumer [ɑ̃ʀyme] *vt*: **s'~, être enrhumé** to catch a cold

enrichir [ɑ̃ʀiʃiʀ] *vt* to make rich(er); (*fig*) to enrich; **s'~** *vi* to get rich(er)

enrober [ɑ̃ʀɔbe] *vt*: ~ **qch de** to coat sth with

enrôler [ɑ̃ʀole] *vt* to enlist; **s'~ (dans)** to enlist (in)

enrouer [ɑ̃ʀwe]: **s'~** *vi* to go hoarse

enrouler [ɑ̃ʀule] *vt* (*fil, corde*) to wind (up)

ensanglanté, e [ɑ̃sɑ̃ɡlɑ̃te] *adj* covered with blood

enseignant, e [ɑ̃sɛɲɑ̃, ɑ̃t] *nm/f* teacher

enseigne [ɑ̃sɛɲ] *nf* sign; ~ **lumineuse** neon sign

enseignement [ɑ̃sɛɲ(ə)mɑ̃] *nm* teaching; (*ADMIN*) education

enseigner [ɑ̃seɲe] *vt, vi* to teach; ~ **qch à qn** to teach sb sth

ensemble [ɑ̃sɑ̃bl] *adv* together ♦ *nm* (*groupement*) set; (*vêtements*) outfit; (*totalité*): **l'~ du/de la** the whole *ou* entire; (*unité, harmonie*) unity; **impression/idée d'~** overall *ou* general impression/idea; **dans l'~** (*en gros*) on the whole

ensemencer [ɑ̃s(ə)mɑ̃se] *vt* to sow

ensevelir [ɑ̃səv(ə)liʀ] *vt* to bury

ensoleillé, e [ɑ̃sɔleje] *adj* sunny

ensommeillé, e [ɑ̃sɔmeje] *adj* drowsy

ensorceler [ɑ̃sɔʀsəle] *vt* to enchant, bewitch

ensuite [ɑ̃sɥit] *adv* then, next; (*plus tard*) afterwards, later

ensuivre [ɑ̃sɥivʀ]: **s'~** *vi* to follow, ensue; **et tout ce qui s'ensuit** and all that goes with it

entaille [ɑ̃taj] *nf* cut; (*sur un objet*) notch

entamer [ɑ̃tame] *vt* (*pain, bouteille*) to start; (*hostilités, pourparlers*) to start

entasser [ɑ̃tase] *vt* (*empiler*) to pile up, heap up; **s'~** *vi* (*s'amonceler*) to pile up; **s'~ dans** (*personnes*) to cram into

entendre [ɑ̃tɑ̃dʀ] *vt* to hear; (*comprendre*) to understand; (*vouloir dire*) to mean; **s'~** *vi* (*sympathiser*) to get on; (*se mettre d'accord*) to agree; **j'ai entendu dire que** I've heard (it said) that

entendu, e [ɑ̃tɑ̃dy] *adj* (*réglé*) agreed; (*au courant: air*) knowing; **(c'est) ~** all right, agreed; **bien ~** of course

entente [ɑ̃tɑ̃t] *nf* understanding; (*accord, traité*) agreement; **à double ~** (*sens*) with a double meaning

entériner [ɑ̃teʀine] *vt* to ratify, confirm

enterrement [ɑ̃teʀmɑ̃] *nm* (*cérémonie*) funeral, burial

enterrer [ɑ̃teʀe] *vt* to bury

entêtant, e [ɑ̃tetɑ̃, ɑ̃t] *adj* heady

entêté, e [ɑ̃tete] *adj* stubborn

en-tête [ɑ̃tɛt] *nm* heading; **papier à ~-~** headed notepaper

entêter [ɑ̃tete]: **s'~** *vi*: **s'~ (à faire)** to persist (in doing)

enthousiasme [ɑ̃tuzjasm] *nm* enthusiasm; **enthousiasmer** *vt* to fill with enthusiasm; **s'enthousiasmer (pour qch)** to get enthusiastic (about sth); **enthousiaste** *adj* enthusiastic

enticher [ɑ̃tiʃe]: **s'~ de** *vt* to become infatuated with

entier, -ère [ɑ̃tje, jɛʀ] *adj* whole; (*total: satisfaction etc*) complete; (*fig: caractère*) unbending ♦ *nm* (*MATH*) whole; **en ~** totally; **lait ~** full-cream milk; **entièrement** *adv* entirely, wholly

entonner [ɑ̃tɔne] *vt* (*chanson*) to strike up

entonnoir [ɑ̃tɔnwaʀ] *nm* funnel

entorse [ɑ̃tɔʀs] *nf* (*MÉD*) sprain; (*fig*): **~ au règlement** infringement of the rule

entortiller [ɑ̃tɔʀtije] *vt* (*enrouler*) to twist, wind; (*fam: cajoler*) to get round

entourage [ɑ̃tuʀaʒ] *nm* circle; (*famille*) circle of family/friends; (*ce qui enclôt*) surround

entourer [ɑ̃tuʀe] *vt* to surround; (*apporter son soutien à*) to rally round; **~ de** to surround with

entracte [ɑ̃tʀakt] *nm* interval

entraide [ɑ̃tʀɛd] *nf* mutual aid; **s'~r** *vi* to help each other

entrain [ɑ̃tʀɛ̃] *nm* spirit; **avec/sans ~** spiritedly/half-heartedly

entraînement [ɑ̃tʀɛnmɑ̃] *nm* training

entraîner [ɑ̃tʀene] *vt* (*charrier*) to carry *ou* drag along; (*TECH*) to drive; (*emmener: personne*) to take (off); (*influencer*) to lead; (*SPORT*) to train; (*impliquer*) to entail; **s'~** *vi* (*SPORT*) to train; **s'~ à qch/à faire** to train o.s. for sth/to do; **~ qn à faire** (*inciter*) to lead sb to do; **entraîneur, -euse** *nm/f* (*SPORT*) coach, trainer ♦ *nm* (*HIPPISME*) trainer

entraver [ɑ̃tʀave] *vt* (*action, progrès*) to hinder

entre [ɑ̃tʀ] *prép* between; (*parmi*) among(st); **l'un d'~ eux/nous** one of them/us; **~ eux** among(st) themselves; **entrebâillé, e** *adj* half-open, ajar; **entrechoquer: s'entrechoquer** *vi* to knock *ou* bang together; **entrecôte** *nf* entrecôte *ou* rib steak; **entrecouper** *vt*: **entrecouper qch de** to intersperse sth with; **entrecroiser: s'entrecroiser** *vi* to intertwine

entrée [ɑ̃tʀe] *nf* entrance; (*accès: au cinéma etc*) admission; (*billet*) (admission) ticket; (*CULIN*) first course

entre...: **entrefaites: sur ces entrefaites** *adv* at this juncture; **entrefilet** *nm* paragraph (*short article*); **entrejambes** *nm* crotch; **entrelacer** *vt* to intertwine; **entremêler: s'entremêler** *vi* to become entangled; **entremets** *nm* (cream) dessert; **entremise** *nf* intervention; **par l'entremise de** through

entreposer [ɑ̃tʀəpoze] *vt* to store, put into storage

entrepôt [ɑ̃tʀəpo] *nm* warehouse

entreprenant, e [ɑ̃tʀəpʀənɑ̃, ɑ̃t] *adj* (*actif*) enterprising; (*trop galant*) forward

entreprendre [ɑ̃tʀəpʀɑ̃dʀ] *vt* (*se lancer dans*) to undertake; (*commencer*) to begin *ou* start (upon)

entrepreneur [ɑ̃tʀəpʀənœʀ, øz] *nm*: **~**

(en bâtiment) (building) contractor

entreprise [ɑ̃tʀəpʀiz] nf (société) firm, concern; (action) undertaking, venture

entrer [ɑ̃tʀe] vi to go (ou come) in, enter ♦ vt (INFORM) to enter, input; **(faire)** ~ **qch dans** to get sth into; ~ **dans** (gén) to enter; (pièce) to come in; (club) to join; (heurter) to run into; ~ **à l'hôpital** to go into hospital; **faire** ~ (visiteur) to show in

entresol [ɑ̃tʀəsɔl] nm mezzanine

entre-temps [ɑ̃tʀətɑ̃] adv meanwhile

entretenir [ɑ̃tʀət(ə)niʀ] vt to maintain; (famille, maîtresse) to support, keep; ~ **qn (de)** to speak to sb (about)

entretien [ɑ̃tʀətjɛ̃] nm maintenance; (discussion) discussion, talk; (pour un emploi) interview

entrevoir [ɑ̃tʀəvwaʀ] vt (à peine) to make out; (brièvement) to catch a glimpse of

entrevue [ɑ̃tʀəvy] nf (audience) interview

entrouvert, e [ɑ̃tʀuvɛʀ, ɛʀt] adj half-open

énumérer [enymeʀe] vt to list, enumerate

envahir [ɑ̃vaiʀ] vt to invade; (suj: inquiétude, peur) to come over; **envahissant, e** (péj) adj (personne) interfering, intrusive

enveloppe [ɑ̃v(ə)lɔp] nf (de lettre) envelope; (crédits) budget; **envelopper** vt to wrap; (fig) to envelop, shroud

envenimer [ɑ̃v(ə)nime] vt to aggravate

envergure [ɑ̃vɛʀgyʀ] nf (fig) scope; (personne) calibre

enverrai etc [ɑ̃veʀe] vb voir **envoyer**

envers [ɑ̃vɛʀ] prép towards, to ♦ nm other side; (d'une étoffe) wrong side; **à l'~** (verticalement) upside down; (pull) back to front; (chaussettes) inside out

envie [ɑ̃vi] nf (sentiment) envy; (souhait) desire, wish; **avoir** ~ **de (faire)** to feel like (doing); (plus fort) to want (to do); **avoir** ~ **que** to wish that; **cette glace me fait** ~ I fancy some of that ice cream; **envier** vt to envy; **envieux, -euse** adj envious

environ [ɑ̃viʀɔ̃] adv: ~ **3 h/2 km** (around) about 3 o'clock/2 km; voir aussi **environs**

environnant, e [ɑ̃viʀɔnɑ̃, ɑ̃t] adj surrounding

environnement [ɑ̃viʀɔnmɑ̃] nm environment

environs [ɑ̃viʀɔ̃] nmpl surroundings; **aux** ~ **de** (round) about

envisager [ɑ̃vizaʒe] vt to contemplate, envisage; ~ **de faire** to consider doing

envoi [ɑ̃vwa] nm (paquet) parcel, consignment; **coup d'~** (SPORT) kick-off

envoler [ɑ̃vɔle]: **s'~** vi (oiseau) to fly away; (avion) to take off; (papier, feuille) to blow away; (fig) to vanish (into thin air)

envoûter [ɑ̃vute] vt to bewitch

envoyé, e [ɑ̃vwaje] nm/f (POL) envoy; (PRESSE) correspondent

envoyer [ɑ̃vwaje] vt to send; (lancer) to hurl, throw; ~ **chercher** to send for; ~ **promener qn** (fam) to send sb packing

Éole [eɔl] sigle m (= est-ouest-liaison-express) Paris high-speed, east-west subway service

épagneul, e [epaɲœl] nm/f spaniel

épais, se [epɛ, ɛs] adj thick; **épaisseur** nf thickness

épancher [epɑ̃ʃe]: **s'~** vi to open one's heart

épanouir [epanwiʀ]: **s'~** vi (fleur) to bloom, open out; (visage) to light up; (personne) to blossom

épargne [epaʀɲ] nf saving

épargner [epaʀɲe] vt to save; (ne pas tuer ou endommager) to spare ♦ vi to save; ~ **qch à qn** to spare sb sth

éparpiller [epaʀpije] vt to scatter; **s'~** vi to scatter; (fig) to dissipate one's efforts

épars, e [epaʀ, aʀs] adj scattered

épatant, e [epatɑ̃, ɑ̃t] (fam) adj super

épater [epate] (fam) vt (étonner) to amaze; (impressionner) to impress

épaule [epol] nf shoulder

épauler [epole] vt (aider) to back up, support; (arme) to raise (to one's shoulder) ♦ vi to (take) aim

épaulette [epolɛt] nf (MIL) epaulette; (rembourrage) shoulder pad

épave [epav] nf wreck

épée [epe] nf sword

épeler [ep(ə)le] vt to spell

éperdu, e [epɛʀdy] *adj* distraught, overcome; (*amour*) passionate

éperon [epʀɔ̃] *nm* spur

épervier [epɛʀvje] *nm* sparrowhawk

épi [epi] *nm* (*de blé, d'orge*) ear; (*de maïs*) cob

épice [epis] *nf* spice

épicé, e [epise] *adj* spicy

épicer [epise] *vt* to spice

épicerie [episʀi] *nf* grocer's shop; (*denrées*) groceries *pl*; **~ fine** delicatessen; **épicier, -ière** *nm/f* grocer

épidémie [epidemi] *nf* epidemic

épiderme [epidɛʀm] *nm* skin

épier [epje] *vt* to spy on, watch closely

épilepsie [epilɛpsi] *nf* epilepsy

épiler [epile] *vt* (*jambes*) to remove the hair from; (*sourcils*) to pluck

épilogue [epilɔg] *nm* (*fig*) conclusion, dénouement; **épiloguer** *vi*: **épiloguer sur** to hold forth on

épinards [epinaʀ] *nmpl* spinach *sg*

épine [epin] *nf* thorn, prickle; (*d'oursin etc*) spine; **~ dorsale** backbone; **épineux, -euse** *adj* thorny

épingle [epɛ̃gl] *nf* pin; **~ à cheveux** hairpin; **~ de nourrice** *ou* **de sûreté** safety pin; **épingler** *vt* (*badge, décoration*): **épingler qch sur** to pin sth on(to); (*fam*) to catch, nick

épique [epik] *adj* epic

épisode [epizɔd] *nm* episode; **film/roman à ~s** serial; **épisodique** *adj* occasional

éploré, e [eplɔʀe] *adj* tearful

épluche-légumes [eplyʃlegym] *nm inv* (potato) peeler

éplucher [eplyʃe] *vt* (*fruit, légumes*) to peel; (*fig*) to go over with a fine-tooth comb; **épluchures** *nfpl* peelings

éponge [epɔ̃ʒ] *nf* sponge; **éponger** *vt* (*liquide*) to mop up; (*surface*) to sponge; (*fig: déficit*) to soak up

épopée [epɔpe] *nf* epic

époque [epɔk] *nf* (*de l'histoire*) age, era; (*de l'année, la vie*) time; **d'~** (*meuble*) period *cpd*

époumoner [epumɔne]: **s'~** *vi* to shout o.s. hoarse

épouse [epuz] *nf* wife; **épouser** *vt* to marry

épousseter [epuste] *vt* to dust

époustouflant, e [epustuflɑ̃, ɑ̃t] (*fam*) *adj* staggering, mind-boggling

épouvantable [epuvɑ̃tabl] *adj* appalling, dreadful

épouvantail [epuvɑ̃taj] *nm* scarecrow

épouvante [epuvɑ̃t] *nf* terror; **film d'~** horror film; **épouvanter** *vt* to terrify

époux [epu] *nm* husband ♦ *nmpl* (married) couple

éprendre [epʀɑ̃dʀ]: **s'~ de** *vt* to fall in love with

épreuve [epʀœv] *nf* (*d'examen*) test; (*malheur, difficulté*) trial, ordeal; (*PHOTO*) print; (*TYPO*) proof; (*SPORT*) event; **à toute ~** unfailing; **mettre à l'~** to put to the test

épris, e [epʀi, iz] *pp* de **éprendre**

éprouvant, e [epʀuvɑ̃, ɑ̃t] *adj* trying, testing

éprouver [epʀuve] *vt* (*tester*) to test; (*marquer, faire souffrir*) to afflict, distress; (*ressentir*) to experience

éprouvette [epʀuvɛt] *nf* test tube

épuisé, e [epɥize] *adj* exhausted; (*livre*) out of print; **épuisement** *nm* exhaustion

épuiser [epɥize] *vt* (*fatiguer*) to exhaust, wear *ou* tire out; (*stock, sujet*) to exhaust; **s'~** *vi* to wear *ou* tire o.s. out, exhaust o.s.

épuisette [epɥizɛt] *nf* shrimping net

épurer [epyʀe] *vt* (*liquide*) to purify; (*parti etc*) to purge

équateur [ekwatœʀ] *nm* equator; **(la république de) l'É~** Ecuador

équation [ekwasjɔ̃] *nf* equation

équerre [ekɛʀ] *nf* (*à dessin*) (set) square

équilibre [ekilibʀ] *nm* balance; **garder/ perdre l'~** to keep/lose one's balance; **être en ~** to be balanced; **équilibré, e** *adj* well-balanced; **équilibrer** *vt* to balance; **s'équilibrer** *vi* (*poids*) to balance; (*fig: défauts etc*) to balance each other out

équipage [ekipaʒ] *nm* crew

équipe [ekip] *nf* team

équipé, e [ekipe] *adj*: **bien/mal ~** well-/poorly-equipped; **équipée** *nf* escapade

équipement [ekipmã] *nm* equipment; **~s** *nmpl* (*installations*) amenities, facilities

équiper [ekipe] *vt* to equip; **~ qn/qch de** to equip sb/sth with

équipier, -ière [ekipje, jɛʀ] *nm/f* team member

équitable [ekitabl] *adj* fair

équitation [ekitasjɔ̃] *nf* (horse-)riding; **faire de l'~** to go riding

équivalent, e [ekivalã, ãt] *adj, nm* equivalent

équivaloir [ekivalwaʀ]: **~ à** *vt* to be equivalent to

équivoque [ekivɔk] *adj* equivocal, ambiguous; (*louche*) dubious ♦ *nf* (*incertitude*) doubt

érable [eʀabl] *nm* maple

érafler [eʀafle] *vt* to scratch; **éraflure** *nf* scratch

éraillé, e [eʀaje] *adj* (*voix*) rasping

ère [ɛʀ] *nf* era; **en l'an 1050 de notre ~** in the year 1050 A.D.

érection [eʀɛksjɔ̃] *nf* erection

éreinter [eʀɛ̃te] *vt* to exhaust, wear out; (*critiquer*) to pull to pieces

ériger [eʀiʒe] *vt* (*monument*) to erect

ermite [ɛʀmit] *nm* hermit

éroder [eʀɔde] *vt* to erode

érotique [eʀɔtik] *adj* erotic

errer [eʀe] *vi* to wander

erreur [eʀœʀ] *nf* mistake, error; **faire ~** to be mistaken; **par ~** by mistake; **~ judiciaire** miscarriage of justice

érudit, e [eʀydi, it] *adj* erudite, learned

éruption [eʀypsjɔ̃] *nf* eruption; (*MÉD*) rash

es [ɛ] *vb voir* **être**

ès [ɛs] *prép*: **licencié ~ lettres/sciences** ≈ Bachelor of Arts/Science

escabeau, x [ɛskabo] *nm* (*tabouret*) stool; (*échelle*) stepladder

escadron [ɛskadʀɔ̃] *nm* squadron

escalade [ɛskalad] *nf* climbing *no pl*; (*POL*

etc) escalation; **escalader** *vt* to climb

escale [ɛskal] *nf* (*NAVIG: durée*) call; (*endroit*) port of call; (*AVIAT*) stop(over); **faire ~ à** (*NAVIG*) to put in at; (*AVIAT*) to stop over at; **vol sans ~** nonstop flight

escalier [ɛskalje] *nm* stairs *pl*; **dans l'~** on the stairs; **~ roulant** escalator

escamoter [ɛskamɔte] *vt* (*esquiver*) to get round, evade; (*faire disparaître*) to conjure away

escapade [ɛskapad] *nf*: **faire une ~** to go on a jaunt; (*s'enfuir*) to run away *ou* off

escargot [ɛskaʀgo] *nm* snail

escarpé, e [ɛskaʀpe] *adj* steep

escarpin [ɛskaʀpɛ̃] *nm* low-fronted shoe, court shoe (*BRIT*)

escient [ɛsjã] *nm*: **à bon ~** advisedly

esclaffer [ɛsklafe]: **s'~** *vi* to guffaw

esclandre [ɛsklãdʀ] *nm* scene, fracas

esclavage [ɛsklavaʒ] *nm* slavery

esclave [ɛsklav] *nm/f* slave

escompte [ɛskɔ̃t] *nm* discount; **escompter** *vt* (*fig*) to expect

escorte [ɛskɔʀt] *nf* escort; **escorter** *vt* to escort

escrime [ɛskʀim] *nf* fencing

escrimer [ɛskʀime]: **s'~** *vi*: **s'~ à faire** to wear o.s. out doing

escroc [ɛskʀo] *nm* swindler, conman; **escroquer** [ɛskʀɔke] *vt*: **escroquer qch (à qn)** to swindle sth (out of sb); **escroquerie** *nf* swindle

espace [ɛspas] *nm* space

espacer [ɛspase] *vt* to space out; **s'~** *vi* (*visites etc*) to become less frequent

espadon [ɛspadɔ̃] *nm* swordfish *inv*

espadrille [ɛspadʀij] *nf* rope-soled sandal

Espagne [ɛspaɲ] *nf*: **l'~** Spain; **espagnol, e** *adj* Spanish ♦ *nm/f*: **Espagnol, e** Spaniard ♦ *nm* (*LING*) Spanish

escouade [ɛskwad] *nf* squad

espèce [ɛspɛs] *nf* (*BIO, BOT, ZOOL*) species *inv*; (*gén: sorte*) sort, kind, type; (*péj*): **~ de maladroit!** you clumsy oaf!; **~s** *nfpl* (*COMM*) cash *sg*; **en ~** in cash

espérance [ɛspeʀãs] *nf* hope; **~ de vie**

life expectancy

espérer [espeRe] *vt* to hope for; **j'espère (bien)** I hope so; **~ que/faire** to hope that/to do

espiègle [espjɛgl] *adj* mischievous

espion, ne [espjɔ̃, jɔn] *nm/f* spy; **espionnage** *nm* espionage, spying; **espionner** *vt* to spy (up)on

esplanade [esplanad] *nf* esplanade

espoir [espwaʀ] *nm* hope

esprit [espʀi] *nm* (*intellect*) mind; (*humour*) wit; (*mentalité, d'une loi etc, fantôme etc*) spirit; **faire de l'~** to try to be witty; **reprendre ses ~s** to come to; **perdre l'~** to lose one's mind

esquimau, de, x [ɛskimo, od] *adj* Eskimo ♦ *nm/f*: **E~, de** Eskimo ♦ *nm*: **E~** ® ice lolly (*BRIT*), popsicle (*US*)

esquinter [ɛskɛ̃te] (*fam*) *vt* to mess up

esquisse [ɛskis] *nf* sketch; **esquisser** *vt* to sketch; **esquisser un sourire** to give a vague smile

esquiver [ɛskive] *vt* to dodge; **s'~** *vi* to slip away

essai [ese] *nm* (*tentative*) attempt, try; (*de produit*) testing; (*RUGBY*) try; (*LITTÉRATURE*) essay; **~s** *nmpl* (*AUTO*) trials; **~ gratuit** (*COMM*) free trial; **à l'~** on a trial basis

essaim [esɛ̃] *nm* swarm

essayer [eseje] *vt* to try; (*vêtement, chaussures*) to try (on); (*méthode, voiture*) to try (out) ♦ *vi* to try; **~ de faire** to try *ou* attempt to do

essence [esɑ̃s] *nf* (*de voiture*) petrol (*BRIT*), gas(oline) (*US*); (*extrait de plante*) essence; (*espèce: d'arbre*) species *inv*

essentiel, le [esɑ̃sjɛl] *adj* essential; **c'est l'~** (*ce qui importe*) that's the main thing; **l'~ de** the main part of

essieu, x [esjø] *nm* axle

essor [esɔʀ] *nm* (*de l'économie etc*) rapid expansion

essorer [esɔʀe] *vt* (*en tordant*) to wring (out); (*par la force centrifuge*) to spin-dry; **essoreuse** *nf* spin-dryer

essouffler [esufle]: **s'~** *vi* to get out of breath

essuie-glace [esɥiglas] *nm inv* windscreen (*BRIT*) *ou* windshield (*US*) wiper

essuyer [esɥije] *vt* to wipe; (*fig: échec*) to suffer; **s'~** *vi* (*après le bain*) to dry o.s.; **~ la vaisselle** to dry up

est¹ [ɛ] *vb voir* **être**

est² [ɛst] *nm* east ♦ *adj inv* east; (*région*) east(ern); **à l'~** in the east; (*direction*) to the east, east(wards); **à l'~ de** (to the) east of

estampe [ɛstɑ̃p] *nf* print, engraving

est-ce que [ɛskə] *adv*: **~ c'est cher/c'était bon?** is it expensive/was it good?; **quand est-ce qu'il part?** when does he leave?, when is he leaving?; *voir aussi* **que**

esthéticienne [ɛstetisjɛn] *nf* beautician

esthétique [ɛstetik] *adj* attractive

estimation [ɛstimasjɔ̃] *nf* valuation; (*chiffre*) estimate

estime [ɛstim] *nf* esteem, regard; **estimer** *vt* (*respecter*) to esteem; (*expertiser: bijou etc*) to value; (*évaluer: coût etc*) to assess, estimate; (*penser*): **estimer que/être** to consider that/o.s. to be

estival, e, -aux [ɛstival, o] *adj* summer *cpd*

estivant, e [ɛstivɑ̃, ɑ̃t] *nm/f* (summer) holiday-maker

estomac [ɛstɔma] *nm* stomach

estomaqué, e [ɛstɔmake] (*fam*) *adj* flabbergasted

estomper [ɛstɔ̃pe]: **s'~** *vi* (*sentiments*) to soften; (*contour*) to become blurred

estrade [ɛstʀad] *nf* platform, rostrum

estragon [ɛstʀagɔ̃] *nm* tarragon

estuaire [ɛstɥɛʀ] *nm* estuary

et [e] *conj* and; **~ lui?** what about him?; **~ alors!** so what!

étable [etabl] *nf* cowshed

établi [etabli] *nm* (work)bench

établir [etabliʀ] *vt* (*papiers d'identité, facture*) to make out; (*liste, programme*) to draw up; (*entreprise*) to set up; (*réputation, usage, fait, culpabilité*) to establish; **s'~** *vi* to be established; **s'~ (à son compte)** to set up in business; **s'~ à/près de** to settle in/near

établissement [etablismɑ̃] *nm* (*entreprise, institution*) establishment; **~ scolaire** school, educational establishment

étage [etaʒ] *nm* (*d'immeuble*) storey, floor; **à l'~** upstairs; **au 2ème ~** on the 2nd (*BRIT*) *ou* 3rd (*US*) floor

étagère [etaʒɛʀ] *nf* (*rayon*) shelf; (*meuble*) shelves *pl*

étai [etɛ] *nm* stay, prop

étain [etɛ̃] *nm* pewter *no pl*

étais *etc* [etɛ] *vb voir* **être**

étal [etal] *nm* stall

étalage [etalaʒ] *nm* display; (*devanture*) display window; **faire ~ de** to show off, parade

étaler [etale] *vt* (*carte, nappe*) to spread (out); (*peinture*) to spread; (*échelonner: paiements, vacances*) to spread, stagger; (*marchandises*) to display; (*connaissances*) to parade; **s'~** *vi* (*liquide*) to spread out; (*fam*) to fall flat on one's face; **s'~ sur** (*suj: paiements etc*) to be spread out over

étalon [etalɔ̃] *nm* (*cheval*) stallion

étanche [etɑ̃ʃ] *adj* (*récipient*) watertight; (*montre, vêtement*) waterproof; **étancher** *vt*: **étancher sa soif** to quench one's thirst

étang [etɑ̃] *nm* pond

étant [etɑ̃] *vb voir* **être**; **donné**

étape [etap] *nf* stage; (*lieu d'arrivée*) stopping place; (: *CYCLISME*) staging point

état [eta] *nm* (*POL, condition*) state; **en mauvais ~** in poor condition; **en ~ (de marche)** in (working) order; **remettre en ~** to repair; **hors d'~** out of order; **être en ~/hors d'~ de faire** to be in a/in no fit state to do; **être dans tous ses ~s** to be in a state; **faire ~ de** (*alléguer*) to put forward; **l'É~** the State; **~ civil** civil status; **~ des lieux** inventory of fixtures; **étatiser** *vt* to bring under state control; **état-major** *nm* (*MIL*) staff; **États-Unis** *nmpl*: **les États-Unis** the United States

étau, x [eto] *nm* vice (*BRIT*), vise (*US*)

étayer [eteje] *vt* to prop *ou* shore up

etc. [ɛtseteʀa] *adv* etc

et c(a)etera [ɛtseteʀa] *adv* et cetera, and so on

été [ete] *pp de* **être** ♦ *nm* summer

éteindre [etɛ̃dʀ] *vt* (*lampe, lumière, radio*) to turn *ou* switch off; (*cigarette, feu*) to put out, extinguish; **s'~** *vi* (*feu, lumière*) to go out; (*mourir*) to pass away; **éteint, e** *adj* (*fig*) lacklustre, dull; (*volcan*) extinct

étendard [etɑ̃daʀ] *nm* standard

étendre [etɑ̃dʀ] *vt* (*pâte, liquide*) to spread; (*carte etc*) to spread out; (*linge*) to hang up; (*bras, jambes*) to stretch out; (*fig: agrandir*) to extend; **s'~** *vi* (*augmenter, se propager*) to spread; (*terrain, forêt etc*) to stretch; (*s'allonger*) to stretch out; (*se coucher*) to lie down; (*fig: expliquer*) to elaborate

étendu, e [etɑ̃dy] *adj* extensive; **étendue** *nf* (*d'eau, de sable*) stretch, expanse; (*importance*) extent

éternel, le [etɛʀnɛl] *adj* eternal

éterniser [etɛʀnize]: **s'~** *vi* to last for ages; (*visiteur*) to stay for ages

éternité [etɛʀnite] *nf* eternity; **ça a duré une ~** it lasted for ages

éternuement [etɛʀnymɑ̃] *nm* sneeze

éternuer [etɛʀnɥe] *vi* to sneeze

êtes [ɛt(z)] *vb voir* **être**

éthique [etik] *adj* ethical

ethnie [etni] *nf* ethnic group

éthylisme [etilism] *nm* alcoholism

étiez [etje] *vb voir* **être**

étinceler [etɛ̃s(ə)le] *vi* to sparkle

étincelle [etɛ̃sɛl] *nf* spark

étiqueter [etik(ə)te] *vt* to label

étiquette [etikɛt] *nf* label; (*protocole*): **l'~** etiquette

étirer [etiʀe]: **s'~** *vi* (*personne*) to stretch; (*convoi, route*): **s'~ sur** to stretch out over

étoffe [etɔf] *nf* material, fabric

étoffer [etɔfe] *vt* to fill out; **s'~** *vi* to fill out

étoile [etwal] *nf* star; **à la belle ~** in the open; **~ de mer** starfish; **~ filante** shooting star; **étoilé, e** *adj* starry

étonnant, e [etɔnɑ̃, ɑ̃t] *adj* amazing

étonnement [etɔnmɑ̃] *nm* surprise, amazement

étonner [etɔne] *vt* to surprise, amaze; **s'~ que/de** to be amazed that/at; **cela m'~ait (que)** (*j'en doute*) I'd be very surprised (if)

étouffant, e [etufɑ̃, ɑ̃t] *adj* stifling

étouffée [etufe] **à l'~** *adv* (CULIN: *légumes*) steamed; (: *viande*) braised

étouffer [etufe] *vt* to suffocate; (*bruit*) to muffle; (*scandale*) to hush up ♦ *vi* to suffocate; **s'~** *vi* (*en mangeant etc*) to choke; **on étouffe** it's stifling

étourderie [eturdəri] *nf* (*caractère*) absent-mindedness *no pl*; (*faute*) thoughtless blunder

étourdi, e [eturdi] *adj* (*distrait*) scatterbrained, heedless

étourdir [eturdir] *vt* (*assommer*) to stun, daze; (*griser*) to make dizzy *ou* giddy; **étourdissement** *nm* dizzy spell

étourneau, x [eturno] *nm* starling

étrange [etrɑ̃ʒ] *adj* strange

étranger, -ère [etrɑ̃ʒe, ɛr] *adj* foreign; (*pas de la famille, non familier*) strange ♦ *nm/f* foreigner; stranger ♦ *nm*: **à l'~** abroad

étrangler [etrɑ̃gle] *vt* to strangle; **s'~** *vi* (*en mangeant etc*) to choke

---

MOT-CLÉ

être [etr] *nm* being; **être humain** human being

♦ *vb +attrib* **1** (*état, description*) to be; **il est instituteur** he is *ou* he's a teacher; **vous êtes grand/intelligent/fatigué** you are *ou* you're tall/clever/tired

2 (+**à**: *appartenir*) to be; **le livre est à Paul** the book is Paul's *ou* belongs to Paul; **c'est à moi/eux** it is *ou* it's mine/theirs

3 (+**de**: *provenance*): **il est de Paris** he is from Paris; (: *appartenance*): **il est des nôtres** he is one of us

4 (*date*): **nous sommes le 10 janvier** it's the 10th of January (today)

♦ *vi* to be; **je ne serai pas ici demain** I won't be here tomorrow

♦ *vb aux* **1** to have; to be; **être arrivé/ allé** to have arrived/gone; **il est parti** he has left, he has gone

2 (*forme passive*) to be; **être fait par** to be made by; **il a été promu** he has been promoted

3 (+**à**: *obligation*): **c'est à réparer** it needs repairing; **c'est à essayer** it should be tried

♦ *vb impers* **1**: **il est** +*adjectif* it is +*adjective*; **il est impossible de le faire** it's impossible to do it

2 (*heure, date*): **il est 10 heures, c'est 10 heures** it is *ou* it's 10 o'clock

3 (*emphatique*): **c'est moi** it's me; **c'est lui de le faire** it's up to him to do it

---

étreindre [etrɛ̃dr] *vt* to clutch, grip; (*amoureusement, amicalement*) to embrace; **s'~** *vi* to embrace

étrenner [etrene] *vt* to use (*ou* wear) for the first time; **étrennes** *nfpl* Christmas box *sg*

étrier [etrije] *nm* stirrup

étriqué, e [etrike] *adj* skimpy

étroit, e [etrwa, wat] *adj* narrow; (*vêtement*) tight; (*fig: liens, collaboration*) close; **à l'~** cramped; **~ d'esprit** narrowminded

étude [etyd] *nf* studying; (*ouvrage, rapport*) study; (SCOL: *salle de travail*) study room; **~s** *nfpl* (SCOL) studies; **être à l'~** (*projet etc*) to be under consideration; **faire des ~s (de droit/médecine)** to study (law/medicine)

étudiant, e [etydjɑ̃, ɑ̃t] *nm/f* student

étudier [etydje] *vt, vi* to study

étui [etɥi] *nm* case

étuve [etyv] *nf* steamroom

étuvée [etyve]: **à l'~** *adv* braised

eu, eue [y] *pp de* **avoir**

euh [ø] *excl* er

euro [øʀo] *nm* euro

Euroland [øʀɔlɑ̃d] *nm* Euroland

Europe [øʀɔp] *nf*: **l'~** Europe; **européen,
ne** *adj* European ♦ *nm/f*: **Européen, ne**
European

eus *etc* [y] *vb voir* **avoir**

eux [ø] *pron* (*sujet*) they; (*objet*) them

évacuer [evakɥe] *vt* to evacuate

évader [evade]: **s'~** *vi* to escape

évaluer [evalɥe] *vt* (*expertiser*) to appraise,
evaluate; (*juger approximativement*) to estimate

évangile [evɑ̃ʒil] *nm* gospel

évanouir [evanwiʀ]: **s'~** *vi* to faint; (*disparaître*) to vanish, disappear; **évanouissement** *nm* (*syncope*) fainting fit

évaporer [evapɔʀe]: **s'~** *vi* to evaporate

évasé, e [evɑze] *adj* (*manches, jupe*) flared

évasif, -ive [evazif, iv] *adj* evasive

évasion [evazjɔ̃] *nf* escape

évêché [eveʃe] *nm* bishop's palace

éveil [evɛj] *nm* awakening; **être en ~** to
be alert; **éveillé, e** *adj* awake; (*vif*) alert,
sharp; **éveiller** *vt* to (a)waken; (*soupçons
etc*) to arouse; **s'éveiller** *vi* to (a)waken;
(*fig*) to be aroused

événement [evɛnmɑ̃] *nm* event

éventail [evɑ̃taj] *nm* fan; (*choix*) range

éventaire [evɑ̃tɛʀ] *nm* stall, stand

éventer [evɑ̃te] *vt* (*secret*) to uncover; **s'~**
vi (*parfum*) to go stale

éventualité [evɑ̃tɥalite] *nf* eventuality;
possibility; **dans l'~ de** in the event of

éventuel, le [evɑ̃tɥɛl] *adj* possible; **éven-
tuellement** *adv* possibly

évêque [evɛk] *nm* bishop

évertuer [evɛʀtɥe]: **s'~** *vi*: **s'~ à faire** to
try ever hard to do

éviction [eviksjɔ̃] *nf* (*de locataire*) eviction

évidemment [evidamɑ̃] *adv* (*bien sûr*) of
course; (*certainement*) obviously

évidence [evidɑ̃s] *nf* obviousness; (*fait*)
obvious fact; **de toute ~** quite obviously
ou evidently; **être en ~** to be clearly visible; **mettre en ~** (*fait*) to highlight; **évident, e** *adj* obvious, evident; **ce n'est**

pas évident! (*fam*) it's not that easy!

évider [evide] *vt* to scoop out

évier [evje] *nm* (kitchen) sink

évincer [evɛ̃se] *vt* to oust

éviter [evite] *vt* to avoid; **~ de faire** to
avoid doing; **~ qch à qn** to spare sb sth

évolué, e [evɔlɥe] *adj* advanced

évoluer [evɔlɥe] *vi* (*enfant, maladie*) to develop; (*situation, moralement*) to evolve,
develop; (*aller et venir*) to move about;
évolution *nf* development, evolution

évoquer [evɔke] *vt* to call to mind, evoke;
(*mentionner*) to mention

ex... [ɛks] *préfixe* ex-

exact, e [ɛgza(kt), ɛgzakt] *adj* exact; (*correct*) correct; (*ponctuel*) punctual; **l'heure
~e** the right *ou* exact time; **exactement**
adv exactly

ex aequo [ɛgzeko] *adj* equally placed; **arriver ~** to finish neck and neck

exagéré, e [ɛgzaʒeʀe] *adj* (*prix etc*) excessive

exagérer [ɛgzaʒeʀe] *vt* to exaggerate ♦ *vi*
to exaggerate; (*abuser*) to go too far

exalter [ɛgzalte] *vt* (*enthousiasmer*) to excite, elate

examen [ɛgzamɛ̃] *nm* examination; (*SCOL*)
exam(ination); **à l'~** under consideration

examinateur, -trice [ɛgzaminatœʀ, tʀis]
nm/f examiner

examiner [ɛgzamine] *vt* to examine

exaspérant, e [ɛgzaspeʀɑ̃, ɑ̃t] *adj* ex-
asperating

exaspérer [ɛgzaspeʀe] *vt* to exasperate

exaucer [ɛgzose] *vt* (*vœu*) to grant

excédent [ɛksedɑ̃] *nm* surplus; **en ~** surplus; **~ de bagages** excess luggage

excéder [ɛksede] *vt* (*dépasser*) to exceed;
(*agacer*) to exasperate

excellent, e [ɛksɛlɑ̃, ɑ̃t] *adj* excellent

excentrique [ɛksɑ̃tʀik] *adj* eccentric

excepté, e [ɛksɛpte] *adj, prép*: **les élèves
~s, les élèves** except for the pupils

exception [ɛksɛpsjɔ̃] *nf* exception; **à l'~
de** except for, with the exception of; **d'~**
(*mesure, loi*) special, exceptional; **excep-**

tionnel, le *adj* exceptional; **exceptionnellement** *adv* exceptionally

excès [ɛksɛ] *nm* surplus ♦ *nmpl* excesses; **faire des ~** to overindulge; **~ de vitesse** speeding *no pl*; **excessif, -ive** *adj* excessive

excitant, e [ɛksitɑ̃, ɑ̃t] *adj* exciting ♦ *nm* stimulant; **excitation** *nf* (*état*) excitement

exciter [ɛksite] *vt* to excite; (*suj: café etc*) to stimulate; **s'~** *vi* to get excited

exclamation [ɛksklamasjɔ̃] *nf* exclamation

exclamer [ɛksklame]: **s'~** *vi* to exclaim

exclure [ɛksklyʀ] *vt* (*faire sortir*) to expel; (*ne pas compter*) to exclude, leave out; (*rendre impossible*) to exclude, rule out; **il est exclu que** it's out of the question that ...; **il n'est pas exclu que ...** it's not impossible that ...; **exclusif, -ive** *adj* exclusive; **exclusion** *nf* exclusion; **à l'exclusion de** with the exclusion *ou* exception of; **exclusivité** *nf* (*COMM*) exclusive rights *pl*; **film passant en exclusivité à** film showing only at

excursion [ɛkskyʀsjɔ̃] *nf* (*en autocar*) excursion, trip; (*à pied*) walk, hike

excuse [ɛkskyz] *nf* excuse; **~s** *nfpl* (*regret*) apology *sg*, apologies; **excuser** *vt* to excuse; **s'excuser (de)** to apologize (for); **"excusez-moi"** "I'm sorry"; (*pour attirer l'attention*) "excuse me"

exécrable [ɛgzekʀabl] *adj* atrocious

exécuter [ɛgzekyte] *vt* (*tuer*) to execute; (*tâche etc*) to execute, carry out; (*MUS: jouer*) to perform, execute; **s'~** *vi* to comply; **exécutif, -ive** *adj, nm* (*POL*) executive; **exécution** *nf* execution; **mettre à exécution** to carry out

exemplaire [ɛgzɑ̃plɛʀ] *nm* copy

exemple [ɛgzɑ̃pl] *nm* example; **par ~** for instance, for example; **donner l'~** to set an example

exempt, e [ɛgzɑ̃, ɑ̃(p)t] *adj*: **~ de** (*dispensé de*) exempt from; (*sans*) free from

exercer [ɛgzɛʀse] *vt* (*pratiquer*) to exercise, practise; (*influence, contrôle*) to exert; (*former*) to exercise, train; **s'~** *vi* (*sportif, musicien*) to practise

exercice [ɛgzɛʀsis] *nm* exercise

exhaustif, -ive [ɛgzostif, iv] *adj* exhaustive

exhiber [ɛgzibe] *vt* (*montrer: papiers, certificat*) to present, produce; (*péj*) to display, flaunt; **s'~** *vi* to parade; (*suj: exhibitionniste*) to expose o.s; **exhibitionniste** [ɛgzibisjɔnist] *nm/f* flasher

exhorter [ɛgzɔʀte] *vt* to urge

exigeant, e [ɛgziʒɑ̃, ɑ̃t] *adj* demanding; (*péj*) hard to please

exigence [ɛgziʒɑ̃s] *nf* demand, requirement

exiger [ɛgziʒe] *vt* to demand, require

exigu, ë [ɛgzigy] *adj* cramped, tiny

exil [ɛgzil] *nm* exile; **exiler** *vt* to exile; **s'exiler** *vi* to go into exile

existence [ɛgzistɑ̃s] *nf* existence

exister [ɛgziste] *vi* to exist; **il existe un/ des** there is a/are (some)

exonérer [ɛgzɔneʀe] *vt*: **~ de** to exempt from

exorbitant, e [ɛgzɔʀbitɑ̃, ɑ̃t] *adj* exorbitant

exorbité, e [ɛgzɔʀbite] *adj*: **yeux ~s** bulging eyes

exotique [ɛgzɔtik] *adj* exotic; **yaourt aux fruits ~s** tropical fruit yoghurt

expatrier [ɛkspatʀije] *vt*: **s'~** to leave one's country

expectative [ɛkspɛktativ] *nf*: **être dans l'~** to be still waiting

expédient [ɛkspedjɑ̃, jɑ̃t] (*péj*) *nm*: **vivre d'~s** to live by one's wits

expédier [ɛkspedje] *vt* (*lettre, paquet*) to send; (*troupes*) to dispatch; (*fam: travail etc*) to dispose of, dispatch; **expéditeur, -trice** *nm/f* sender; **expédition** *nf* sending; (*scientifique, sportive, MIL*) expedition

expérience [ɛkspeʀjɑ̃s] *nf* (*de la vie*) experience; (*scientifique*) experiment

expérimenté, e [ɛkspeʀimɑ̃te] *adj* experienced

expérimenter [ɛkspeʀimɑ̃te] *vt* to test out, experiment with

expert, e [ɛkspɛʀ, ɛʀt] *adj, nm* expert; **expert-comptable** *nm* ≃ chartered accountant (*BRIT*), ≃ certified public accountant (*US*)

expertise [ɛkspɛʀtiz] *nf* (*évaluation*) expert evaluation

expertiser [ɛkspɛʀtize] *vt* (*objet de valeur*) to value; (*voiture accidentée etc*) to assess damage to

expier [ɛkspje] *vt* to expiate, atone for

expirer [ɛkspiʀe] *vi* (*prendre fin, mourir*) to expire; (*respirer*) to breathe out

explicatif, -ive [ɛksplikatif, iv] *adj* explanatory

explication [ɛksplikasjɔ̃] *nf* explanation; (*discussion*) discussion; (*dispute*) argument; **~ de texte** (*SCOL*) critical analysis

explicite [ɛksplisit] *adj* explicit

expliquer [ɛksplike] *vt* to explain; **s'~** to explain (o.s.); **s'~ avec qn** (*discuter*) to explain o.s. to sb; **son erreur s'explique** one can understand his mistake

exploit [ɛksplwa] *nm* exploit, feat; **exploitant, e** *nm/f*: **exploitant (agricole)** farmer

exploitation *nf* exploitation; (*d'une entreprise*) running; **~ agricole** farming concern; **exploiter** *vt* (*personne, don*) to exploit; (*entreprise, ferme*) to run, operate; (*mine*) to exploit, work

explorer [ɛksplɔʀe] *vt* to explore

exploser [ɛksploze] *vi* to explode, blow up; (*engin explosif*) to go off; (*personne: de colère*) to flare up; **explosif, -ive** *adj, nm* explosive; **explosion** *nf* explosion

exportateur, -trice [ɛkspɔʀtatœʀ, tʀis] *adj* export *cpd*, exporting ♦ *nm* exporter

exportation [ɛkspɔʀtasjɔ̃] *nf* (*action*) exportation; (*produit*) export

exporter [ɛkspɔʀte] *vt* to export

exposant [ɛkspozɑ̃] *nm* exhibitor

exposé, e [ɛkspoze] *nm* talk ♦ *adj*: **~ au sud** facing south

exposer [ɛkspoze] *vt* (*marchandise*) to display; (*peinture*) to exhibit, show; (*parler de*) to explain, set out; (*mettre en danger*, orienter, *PHOTO*) to expose; **exposition** *nf* (*manifestation*) exhibition; (*PHOTO*) exposure

exprès¹ [ɛkspʀɛ] *adv* (*délibérément*) on purpose; (*spécialement*) specially

exprès², -esse [ɛkspʀɛs] *adj* (*ordre, défense*) express, formal ♦ *adj inv* (*PTT*) express ♦ *adv* express

express [ɛkspʀɛs] *adj, nm*: **(café) ~** espresso (coffee); **(train) ~** fast train

expressément [ɛkspʀesemɑ̃] *adv* (*spécialement*) specifically

expressif, -ive [ɛkspʀesif, iv] *adj* expressive

expression [ɛkspʀesjɔ̃] *nf* expression

exprimer [ɛkspʀime] *vt* (*sentiment, idée*) to express; (*jus, liquide*) to press out; **s'~** *vi* (*personne*) to express o.s

exproprier [ɛkspʀɔpʀije] *vt* to buy up by compulsory purchase, expropriate

expulser [ɛkspylse] *vt* to expel; (*locataire*) to evict; (*SPORT*) to send off

exquis [ɛkski, iz] *adj* exquisite

extase [ɛkstaz] *nf* ecstasy; **extasier: s'extasier sur** *vt* to go into raptures over

extension [ɛkstɑ̃sjɔ̃] *nf* (*fig*) extension

exténuer [ɛkstenɥe] *vt* to exhaust

extérieur, e [ɛksteʀjœʀ] *adj* (*porte, mur etc*) outer, outside; (*au dehors: escalier, w.-c.*) outside; (*commerce*) foreign; (*influences*) external; (*apparent: calme, gaieté etc*) surface *cpd* ♦ *nm* (*d'une maison, d'un récipient etc*) outside, exterior; (*apparence*) exterior; **à l'~** outside; (*à l'étranger*) abroad; **extérieurement** *adv* on the outside; (*en apparence*) on the surface

exterminer [ɛkstɛʀmine] *vt* to exterminate, wipe out

externat [ɛkstɛʀna] *nm* day school

externe [ɛkstɛʀn] *adj* external, outer ♦ *nm/f* (*MÉD*) non-resident medical student (*BRIT*), extern (*US*); (*SCOL*) day pupil

extincteur [ɛkstɛ̃ktœʀ] *nm* (fire) extinguisher

extinction [ɛkstɛ̃ksjɔ̃] *nf*: **~ de voix** loss of voice

extorquer [ɛkstɔʀke] *vt* to extort
extra [ɛkstʀa] *adj inv* first-rate; *(fam)* fantastic ♦ *nm inv* extra help
extrader [ɛkstʀade] *vt* to extradite
extraire [ɛkstʀɛʀ] *vt* to extract; **extrait** *nm* extract
extraordinaire [ɛkstʀaɔʀdinɛʀ] *adj* extraordinary; *(POL: mesures etc)* special
extravagant, e [ɛkstʀavagã, ãt] *adj* extravagant
extraverti, e [ɛkstʀavɛʀti] *adj* extrovert
extrême [ɛkstʀɛm] *adj, nm* extreme; **extrêmement** *adv* extremely; **extrême-onction** *nf* last rites *pl*; **Extrême-Orient** *nm* Far East
extrémité [ɛkstʀemite] *nf* end; *(situation)* straits *pl*, plight; *(geste désespéré)* extreme action; **~s** *nfpl (pieds et mains)* extremities
exubérant, e [ɛgzybeʀã, ãt] *adj* exuberant
exutoire [ɛgzytwaʀ] *nm* outlet, release

F, f

F *abr* = **franc**
fa [fa] *nm inv (MUS)* F; *(en chantant la gamme)* fa
fable [fabl] *nf* fable
fabricant [fabʀikã, ãt] *nm* manufacturer
fabrication [fabʀikasjɔ̃] *nf* manufacture
fabrique [fabʀik] *nf* factory; **fabriquer** *vt* to make; *(industriellement)* to manufacture; *(fig)*: **qu'est-ce qu'il fabrique?** *(fam)* what is he doing?
fabulation [fabylasjɔ̃] *nf* fantasizing
fac [fak] *(fam) abr f (SCOL)* = **faculté**
façade [fasad] *nf* front, façade
face [fas] *nf* face; *(fig: aspect)* side ♦ *adj*: **le côté ~** heads; **en ~ de** opposite; *(fig)* in front of; **de ~** *(voir)* face on; **~ à** facing; *(fig)* faced with, in the face of; **faire ~ à** to face; **~ à ~** *adv* facing each other ♦ *nm inv* encounter
fâché, e [faʃe] *adj* angry; *(désolé)* sorry
fâcher [faʃe] *vt* to anger; **se ~** *vi* to get

angry; **se ~ avec** *(se brouiller)* to fall out with
fâcheux, -euse [faʃø, øz] *adj* unfortunate, regrettable
facile [fasil] *adj* easy; *(caractère)* easy-going; **facilement** *adv* easily
facilité *nf* easiness; *(disposition, don)* aptitude; **facilités de paiement** easy terms; **faciliter** *vt* to make easier
façon [fasɔ̃] *nf (manière)* way; *(d'une robe etc)* making-up, cut; **~s** *nfpl (péj)* fuss *sg*; **de ~ à/à ce que** so as to/that; **de toute ~** anyway, in any case
façonner [fasɔne] *vt (travailler: matière)* to shape, fashion
facteur, -trice [faktœʀ] *nm/f* postman(-woman) *(BRIT)*, mailman(-woman) *(US)* ♦ *nm (MATH, fig: élément)* factor
factice [faktis] *adj* artificial
faction [faksjɔ̃] *nf* faction; **être de ~** to be on guard (duty)
facture [faktyʀ] *nf (à payer: gén)* bill; invoice
facturer [faktyʀe] *vt* to invoice
facultatif, -ive [fakyltatif, iv] *adj* optional
faculté [fakylte] *nf (intellectuelle, d'université)* faculty; *(pouvoir, possibilité)* power
fade [fad] *adj* insipid
fagot [fago] *nm* bundle of sticks
faible [fɛbl] *adj* weak; *(voix, lumière, vent)* faint; *(rendement, revenu)* low ♦ *nm (pour quelqu'un)* weakness, soft spot; **faiblesse** *nf* weakness; **faiblir** *vi* to weaken; *(lumière)* to dim; *(vent)* to drop
faïence [fajãs] *nf* earthenware *no pl*
faignant, e [fɛɲã, ãt] *nm/f* = **fainéant, e**
faille [faj] *vb voir* **falloir** ♦ *nf (GÉO)* fault; *(fig)* flaw, weakness
faillir [fajiʀ] *vi*: **j'ai failli tomber** I almost *ou* very nearly fell
faillite [fajit] *nf* bankruptcy
faim [fɛ̃] *nf* hunger; **avoir ~** to be hungry; **rester sur sa ~** *(aussi fig)* to be left wanting more
fainéant, e [feneã, ãt] *nm/f* idler, loafer

MOT-CLÉ

faire [fɛʀ] *vt* **1** (*fabriquer, être l'auteur de*) to make; **faire du vin/une offre/un film** to make wine/an offer/a film; **faire du bruit** to make a noise

2 (*effectuer: travail, opération*) to do; **que faites-vous?** (*quel métier etc*) what do you do?; (*quelle activité: au moment de la question*) what are you doing?; **faire la lessive** to do the washing

3 (*études*) to do; (*sport, musique*) to play; **faire du droit/du français** to do law/French; **faire du rugby/piano** to play rugby/the piano

4 (*simuler*): **faire le malade/l'ignorant** to act the invalid/the fool

5 (*transformer, avoir un effet sur*): **faire de qn un frustré/avocat** to make sb frustrated/a lawyer; **ça ne me fait rien** (*m'est égal*) I don't care *ou* mind; (*me laisse froid*) it has no effect on me; **ça ne me fait rien** it doesn't matter; **faire que** (*impliquer*) to mean that

6 (*calculs, prix, mesures*): **2 et 2 font 4** 2 and 2 are *ou* make 4; **ça fait 10 m/15 F** it's 10 m/15F; **je vous le fais 10 F** I'll let you have it for 10F

7: **qu'a-t-il fait de sa valise?** what has he done with his case?

8: **ne faire que**: **il ne fait que critiquer** (*sans cesse*) all he (ever) does is criticize; (*seulement*) he's only criticizing

9 (*dire*) to say; **"vraiment?" fit-il** "really?" he said

10 (*maladie*) to have; **faire du diabète** to have diabetes *sg*

♦ *vi* **1** (*agir, s'y prendre*) to act, do; **il faut faire vite** we (*ou* you *etc*) must act quickly; **comment a-t-il fait pour?** how did he manage to?; **faites comme chez vous** make yourself at home

2 (*paraître*) to look; **faire vieux/démodé** to look old/old-fashioned; **ça fait bien** it looks good

♦ *vb substitut* to do; **ne le casse pas comme je l'ai fait** don't break it as I did; **je peux le voir? - faites!** can I see it? - please do!

♦ *vb impers* **1**: **il fait beau** *etc* the weather is fine *etc*; *voir aussi* **jour**; **froid** *etc*

2 (*temps écoulé, durée*): **ça fait 2 ans qu'il est parti** it's 2 years since he left; **ça fait 2 ans qu'il y est** he's been there for 2 years

♦ *vb semi-aux* **1**: **faire** +*infinitif* (*action directe*) to make; **faire tomber/bouger qch** to make sth fall/move; **faire démarrer un moteur/chauffer de l'eau** to start up an engine/heat some water; **cela fait dormir** it makes you sleep; **faire travailler les enfants** to make the children work *ou* get the children to work

2 (*indirectement, par un intermédiaire*): **faire réparer qch** to get *ou* have sth repaired; **faire punir les enfants** to have the children punished

se faire *vi* **1** (*vin, fromage*) to mature

2: **cela se fait beaucoup/ne se fait pas** it's done a lot/not done

3: **se faire** +*nom ou pron*: **se faire une jupe** to make o.s. a skirt; **se faire des amis** to make friends; **se faire du souci** to worry; **il ne s'en fait pas** he doesn't worry

4: **se faire** +*adj* (*devenir*): **se faire vieux** to be getting old; (*délibérément*): **se faire beau** to do o.s. up

5: **se faire à** (*s'habituer*) to get used to; **je n'arrive pas à me faire à la nourriture/au climat** I can't get used to the food/climate

6: **se faire** +*infinitif*: **se faire examiner la vue/opérer** to have one's eyes tested/to have an operation; **se faire couper les cheveux** to get one's hair cut; **il va se faire tuer/punir** he's going to get himself killed/get (himself) punished; **il s'est fait aider** he got somebody to help him; **il s'est fait aider par Simon** he got Simon to help him; **se faire faire un vêtement** to get a garment made for o.s.

7 (*impersonnel*): **comment se fait-il/faisait-il que?** how is it/was it that?

faire-part [fɛʀpaʀ] *nm inv* announcement (*of birth, marriage etc*)

faisable [fəzabl] *adj* feasible

faisan, e [fəzɑ̃, an] *nm/f* pheasant; **faisandé, e** *adj* high (*bad*)

faisceau, x [fɛso] *nm* (*de lumière etc*) beam

faisons [fəzɔ̃] *vb voir* **faire**

fait, e [fɛ, fɛt] *adj* (*mûr: fromage, melon*) ripe ♦ *nm* (*événement*) event, occurrence; (*réalité, donnée*) fact; **être au ~ (de)** to be informed (of); **au ~** (*à propos*) by the way; **en venir au ~** to get to the point; **du ~ de ceci/qu'il a menti** because of *ou* on account of this/his having lied; **de ce ~** for this reason; **en ~** in fact; **prendre qn sur le ~** to catch sb in the act; **~ divers** news item

faîte [fɛt] *nm* top; (*fig*) pinnacle, height

faites [fɛt] *vb voir* **faire**

faitout [fɛtu] *nm*, **fait-tout** [fɛtu] *nm inv* stewpot

falaise [falɛz] *nf* cliff

falloir [falwaʀ] *vb impers*: **il faut qu'il parte/a fallu qu'il parte** (*obligation*) he has to *ou* must leave/had to leave; **il a fallu le faire** it had to be done; **il faut faire attention** you have to be careful; **il me faudrait 100 F** I would need 100 F; **il vous faut tourner à gauche après l'église** you have to turn left past the church; **nous avons ce qu'il (nous) faut** we have what we need; **s'en ~**: **il s'en est fallu de 100 F/5 minutes** we/they *etc* were 100 F short/5 minutes late (*ou* early); **il s'en faut de beaucoup qu'il soit** he is far from being; **il s'en est fallu de peu que cela n'arrive** it very nearly happened

falsifier [falsifje] *vt* to falsify, doctor

famé, e [fame] *adj*: **mal ~** disreputable, of ill repute

famélique [famelik] *adj* half-starved

fameux, -euse [famø, øz] *adj* (*illustre*) famous; (*bon: repas, plat etc*) first-rate, first-class; (*valeur intensive*) real, downright

familial, e, -aux [familjal, jo] *adj* family *cpd*

familiarité [familjaʀite] *nf* familiarity; **~s** *nfpl* (*privautés*) familiarities

familier, -ère [familje, jɛʀ] *adj* (*connu*) familiar; (*atmosphère*) informal, friendly; (*LING*) informal, colloquial ♦ *nm* regular (visitor)

famille [famij] *nf* family; **il a de la ~ à Paris** he has relatives in Paris

famine [famin] *nf* famine

fanatique [fanatik] *adj* fanatical ♦ *nm/f* fanatic; **fanatisme** *nm* fanaticism

faner [fane]: **se ~** *vi* to fade

fanfare [fɑ̃faʀ] *nf* (*orchestre*) brass band; (*musique*) fanfare

fanfaron, ne [fɑ̃faʀɔ̃, ɔn] *nm/f* braggart

fantaisie [fɑ̃tezi] *nf* (*spontanéité*) fancy, imagination; (*caprice*) whim ♦ *adj*: **bijou ~** costume jewellery; **fantaisiste** (*péj*) *adj* unorthodox, eccentric

fantasme [fɑ̃tasm] *nm* fantasy

fantasque [fɑ̃task] *adj* whimsical, capricious

fantastique [fɑ̃tastik] *adj* fantastic

fantôme [fɑ̃tom] *nm* ghost, phantom

faon [fɑ̃] *nm* fawn

farce [faʀs] *nf* (*viande*) stuffing; (*blague*) (practical) joke; (*THÉÂTRE*) farce; **farcir** *vt* (*viande*) to stuff

fardeau, x [faʀdo] *nm* burden

farder [faʀde]: **se ~** *vi* to make (o.s.) up

farfelu, e [faʀfəly] *adj* hare-brained

farine [faʀin] *nf* flour; **farineux, -euse** *adj* (*sauce, pomme*) floury

farouche [faʀuʃ] *adj* (*timide*) shy, timid

fart [faʀt] *nm* (ski) wax

fascicule [fasikyl] *nm* volume

fascination [fasinasjɔ̃] *nf* fascination

fasciner [fasine] *vt* to fascinate

fascisme [faʃism] *nm* fascism

fasse *etc* [fas] *vb voir* **faire**

faste [fast] *nm* splendour

fastidieux, -euse [fastidjø, jøz] *adj* tedious, tiresome

fastueux, -euse [fastɥø, øz] *adj* sumptuous, luxurious

fatal, e [fatal] *adj* fatal; (*inévitable*) inevitable; **fatalité** *nf* (*destin*) fate; (*coïncidence*) fateful coincidence

fatidique [fatidik] *adj* fateful

fatigant, e [fatigɑ̃, ɑ̃t] *adj* tiring; (*agaçant*) tiresome

fatigue [fatig] *nf* tiredness, fatigue; **fatigué, e** *adj* tired; **fatiguer** *vt* to tire, make tired; (*fig: agacer*) to annoy ♦ *vi* (*moteur*) to labour, strain; **se fatiguer** to get tired

fatras [fatrɑ] *nm* jumble, hotchpotch

faubourg [fobur] *nm* suburb

fauché, e [foʃe] (*fam*) *adj* broke

faucher [foʃe] *vt* (*herbe*) to cut; (*champs, blés*) to reap; (*fig: véhicule*) to mow down; (*fam: voler*) to pinch

faucille [fosij] *nf* sickle

faucon [fokɔ̃] *nm* falcon, hawk

faudra [fodra] *vb voir* **falloir**

faufiler [fofile] *vt*: **se ~** *vi*: **se ~ dans** to edge one's way into; **se ~ parmi/entre** to thread one's way among/between

faune [fon] *nf* (*ZOOL*) wildlife, fauna

faussaire [foser] *nm* forger

fausse [fos] *adj voir* **faux**; **faussement** *adv* (*accuser*) wrongly, wrongfully; (*croire*) falsely

fausser [fose] *vt* (*objet*) to bend, buckle; (*fig*) to distort; **~ compagnie à qn** to give sb the slip

faut [fo] *vb voir* **falloir**

faute [fot] *nf* (*erreur*) mistake, error; (*mauvaise action*) misdemeanour; (*FOOTBALL etc*) offence; (*TENNIS*) fault; **c'est de sa/ma ~** it's his/my fault; **être en ~** to be in the wrong; **~ de** (*temps, argent*) for *ou* through lack of; **sans ~** without fail; **~ de frappe** typing error; **~ de goût** error of taste; **~ professionnelle** professional misconduct *no pl*

fauteuil [fotœj] *nm* armchair; **~ roulant** wheelchair

fauteur [fotœr] *nm*: **~ de troubles** trouble-maker

fautif, -ive [fotif, iv] *adj* (*responsable*) at fault, in the wrong; (*incorrect*) incorrect, inaccurate; **il se sentait ~** he felt guilty

fauve [fov] *nm* wildcat ♦ *adj* (*couleur*) fawn

faux¹ [fo] *nf* scythe

faux², fausse [fo, fos] *adj* (*inexact*) wrong; (*voix*) out of tune; (*billet*) fake, forged; (*sournois, postiche*) false ♦ *adv* (*MUS*) out of tune ♦ *nm* (*copie*) fake, forgery; (*opposé au vrai*): **le ~** falsehood; **faire ~ bond à qn** to stand sb up; **fausse alerte** false alarm; **fausse couche** miscarriage; **~ frais** ♦ *nmpl* extras, incidental expenses; **~ pas** tripping *no pl*; (*fig*) faux pas; **~ témoignage** (*délit*) perjury; **faux-filet** *nm* sirloin; **faux-monnayeur** *nm* counterfeiter, forger

faveur [favœr] *nf* favour; **traitement de ~** preferential treatment; **en ~ de** in favour of

favorable [favɔrabl] *adj* favourable

favori, te [favɔri, it] *adj, nm/f* favourite

favoriser [favɔrize] *vt* to favour

fax [faks] *nm* fax; **faxer** *vt* to fax

FB *abr* (= *franc belge*) BF

fébrile [febril] *adj* feverish, febrile

fécond, e [fekɔ̃, ɔ̃d] *adj* fertile; **féconder** *vt* to fertilize; **fécondité** *nf* fertility

fécule [fekyl] *nf* potato flour; **féculent** *nm* starchy food

fédéral, e, -aux [federal, o] *adj* federal

fée [fe] *nf* fairy; **féerique** *adj* magical, fairytale *cpd*

feignant, e [fɛɲɑ̃, ɑ̃t] *nm/f* = **fainéant, e**

feindre [fɛ̃dr] *vt* to feign; **~ de faire** to pretend to do

feinte [fɛ̃t] *nf* (*SPORT*) dummy

fêler [fele] *vt* to crack

félicitations [felisitasjɔ̃] *nfpl* congratulations

féliciter [felisite] *vt*: **~ qn (de)** to congratulate sb (on)

félin, e [felɛ̃, in] *nm* (big) cat

fêlure [felyʀ] *nf* crack

femelle [fəmɛl] *adj, nf* female

féminin, e [feminɛ̃, in] *adj* feminine; *(sexe)* female; *(équipe, vêtements etc)* women's ♦ *nm* (LING) feminine; **féministe** [feminist] *adj* feminist

femme [fam] *nf* woman; *(épouse)* wife; **~ au foyer** housewife; **~ de chambre** chambermaid; **~ de ménage** cleaning lady

fémur [femyʀ] *nm* femur, thighbone

fendre [fɑ̃dʀ] *vt (couper en deux)* to split; *(fissurer)* to crack; *(traverser: foule, air)* to cleave through; **se ~** *vi* to crack

fenêtre [f(ə)nɛtʀ] *nf* window

fenouil [fənuj] *nm* fennel

fente [fɑ̃t] *nf (fissure)* crack; *(de boîte à lettres etc)* slit

féodal, e, -aux [feɔdal, o] *adj* feudal

fer [fɛʀ] *nm* iron; **~ à cheval** horseshoe; **~ (à repasser)** iron; **~ forgé** wrought iron

ferai *etc* [fəʀe] *vb voir* **faire**

fer-blanc [fɛʀblɑ̃] *nm* tin(plate)

férié, e [feʀje] *adj*: **jour ~** public holiday

ferions *etc* [fəʀjɔ̃] *vb voir* **faire**

ferme [fɛʀm] *adj* firm ♦ *adv (travailler etc)* hard ♦ *nf (exploitation)* farm; *(maison)* farmhouse

fermé, e [fɛʀme] *adj* closed, shut; *(gaz, eau etc)* off; *(fig: milieu)* exclusive

fermenter [fɛʀmɑ̃te] *vi* to ferment

fermer [fɛʀme] *vt* to close, shut; *(cesser l'exploitation de)* to close down, shut down; *(eau, électricité, robinet)* to put off, turn off; *(aéroport, route)* to close ♦ *vi* to close, shut; *(magasin: definitivement)* to close down, shut down; **se ~** *vi* to close, shut

fermeté [fɛʀməte] *nf* firmness

fermeture [fɛʀmətyʀ] *nf* closing; *(dispositif)* catch; **heures de ~** closing times; **~ éclair** ® zip (fastener) (BRIT), zipper (US)

fermier [fɛʀmje, jɛʀ] *nm* farmer; **fermière** *nf* woman farmer; *(épouse)* farmer's wife

fermoir [fɛʀmwaʀ] *nm* clasp

féroce [feʀɔs] *adj* ferocious, fierce

ferons [fəʀɔ̃] *vb voir* **faire**

ferraille [feʀaj] *nf* scrap iron; **mettre à la ~** to scrap

ferrer [feʀe] *vt (cheval)* to shoe

ferronnerie [feʀɔnʀi] *nf* ironwork

ferroviaire [feʀɔvjɛʀ] *adj* rail(way) *cpd* (BRIT), rail(road) *cpd* (US)

ferry(boat) [feʀe(bot)] *nm* ferry

fertile [fɛʀtil] *adj* fertile; **~ en incidents** eventful, packed with incidents

féru, e [feʀy] *adj*: **~ de** with a keen interest in

fervent, e [fɛʀvɑ̃, ɑ̃t] *adj* fervent

fesse [fɛs] *nf* buttock; **fessée** *nf* spanking

festin [fɛstɛ̃] *nm* feast

festival [festival] *nm* festival

festivités [festivite] *nfpl* festivities

festoyer [fɛstwaje] *vi* to feast

fêtard [fetaʀ, aʀd] *(fam) nm* high liver, merry-maker

fête [fɛt] *nf (religieuse)* feast; *(publique)* holiday; *(réception)* party; *(kermesse)* fête, fair; *(du nom)* feast day, name day; **faire la ~** to live it up; **faire ~ à qn** to give sb a warm welcome; **les ~s (de fin d'année)** the festive season; **la salle des ~s** the village hall; **~ foraine** (fun) fair; **fêter** *vt* to celebrate; *(personne)* to have a celebration for

feu, x [fø] *nm (gén)* fire; *(signal lumineux)* light; *(de cuisinière)* ring; **~x** *nmpl* (AUTO) (traffic) lights; **au ~!** *(incendie)* fire!; **à doux/vif** over a slow/brisk heat; **à petit ~** (CULIN) over a gentle heat; *(fig)* slowly; **faire ~** to fire; **prendre ~** to catch fire; **mettre le ~ à** to set fire to; **faire du ~** to make a fire; **avez-vous du ~?** *(pour cigarette)* have you (got) a light?; **~ arrière** rear light; **~ d'artifice** *(spectacle)* fireworks *pl*; **~ de joie** bonfire; **~ rouge/vert/orange** red/green/amber (BRIT) *ou* yellow (US) light; **~x de brouillard** fog-lamps; **~x de croisement** dipped (BRIT) *ou* dimmed (US) headlights; **~x de position** sidelights; **~x de route** headlights

feuillage [fœjaʒ] *nm* foliage, leaves *pl*

feuille [fœj] nf (d'arbre) leaf; (de papier) sheet; (de maladie medical expenses claim form; ~ **de paie** pay slip

feuillet [fœjɛ] nm leaf

feuilleté, e [fœjte] adj: **pâte ~** flaky pastry

feuilleter [fœjte] vt (livre) to leaf through

feuilleton [fœjtɔ̃] nm serial

feutre [føtʀ] nm felt; (chapeau) felt hat; (aussi: **stylo-~**) felt-tip pen; **feutré, e** adj (atmosphère) muffled

fève [fɛv] nf broad bean

février [fevʀije] nm February

FF abr (= franc français) FF

fiable [fjabl] adj reliable

fiançailles [fjɑ̃saj] nfpl engagement sg

fiancé, e [fjɑ̃se] nm/f fiancé(e) ♦ adj: **être ~ (à)** to be engaged (to)

fiancer [fjɑ̃se]: **se ~** vi to become engaged

fibre [fibʀ] nf fibre; ~ **de verre** fibreglass, glass fibre

ficeler [fis(ə)le] vt to tie up

ficelle [fisɛl] nf string no pl; (morceau) piece ou length of string

fiche [fiʃ] nf (pour fichier) (index) card; (formulaire) form; (ÉLEC) plug

ficher [fiʃe] vt (dans un fichier) to file; (PO-LICE) to put on file; (fam: faire) to do; (: donner) to give; (: mettre) to stick ou shove; **se ~ de** (fam: se gausser) to make fun of; **fiche-(moi) le camp** (fam) clear off; **fiche-moi la paix** (fam) leave me alone; **je m'en fiche!** (fam) I don't care!

fichier [fiʃje] nm file

fichu, e [fiʃy] pp de **ficher** (fam) ♦ adj (fam: fini, inutilisable) bust, done for; (: intensif) wretched, darned ♦ nm (foulard) (head)scarf; **mal ~** (fam) feeling lousy

fictif, -ive [fiktif, iv] adj fictitious

fiction [fiksjɔ̃] nf fiction; (fait imaginé) invention

fidèle [fidɛl] adj faithful ♦ nm/f (REL): **les ~s** (à l'église) the congregation sg; **fidélité** nf fidelity

fier¹ [fje]: **se ~ à** vt to trust

fier², fière [fjɛʀ] adj proud; **fierté** nf pride

fièvre [fjɛvʀ] nf fever; **avoir de la ~/39 de ~** to have a high temperature/a temperature of 39°C; **fiévreux, -euse** adj feverish

figé, e [fiʒe] adj (manières) stiff; (société) rigid; (sourire) set

figer [fiʒe]: **se ~** vi (huile) to congeal; (personne) to freeze

fignoler [fiɲɔle] (fam) vt to polish up

figue [fig] nf fig; **figuier** nm fig tree

figurant, e [figyʀɑ̃, ɑ̃t] nm/f (THÉÂTRE) walk-on; (CINÉMA) extra

figure [figyʀ] nf (visage) face; (forme, personnage) figure; (illustration) picture, diagram

figuré, e [figyʀe] adj (sens) figurative

figurer [figyʀe] vi to appear ♦ vt to represent; **se ~ que** to imagine that

fil [fil] nm (brin, fig: d'une histoire) thread; (électrique) wire; (d'un couteau) edge; **au ~ des années** with the passing of the years; **au ~ de l'eau** with the stream ou current; **coup de ~** (fam) phone call; ~ **à coudre** (sewing) thread; ~ **de fer** wire; ~ **de fer barbelé** barbed wire

filament [filamɑ̃] nm (ÉLEC) filament

filandreux, -euse [filɑ̃dʀø, øz] adj stringy

filature [filatyʀ] nf (fabrique) mill; (policière) shadowing no pl, tailing no pl

file [fil] nf line; (AUTO) lane; **en ~ indienne** in single file; **à la ~** (d'affilée) in succession; ~ **(d'attente)** queue (BRIT), line (US)

filer [file] vt (tissu, toile) to spin; (prendre en filature) to shadow, tail; (fam: donner): ~ **qch à qn** to slip sb sth ♦ vi (bas) to run; (aller vite) to fly past; (fam: partir) to make ou be off; ~ **doux** to toe the line

filet [filɛ] nm net; (CULIN) fillet; (d'eau, de sang) trickle; ~ **(à provisions)** string bag

filiale [filjal] nf (COMM) subsidiary

filière [filjɛʀ] nf (carrière) path; **suivre la ~** (dans sa carrière) to work one's way up (through the hierarchy)

filiforme [filifɔʀm] *adj* spindly

filigrane [filigʀan] *nm* (*d'un billet, timbre*) watermark

fille [fij] *nf* girl; (*opposé à fils*) daughter; **vieille ~** old maid; **fillette** *nf* (little) girl

filleul, e [fijœl] *nm/f* godchild, godson/ daughter

film [film] *nm* (*pour photo*) (roll of) film; (*œuvre*) film, picture, movie; **~ d'épouvante** horror film; **~ policier** thriller

filon [filɔ̃] *nm* vein, lode; (*fig*) lucrative line, money spinner

fils [fis] *nm* son; **~ à papa** daddy's boy

filtre [filtʀ] *nm* filter; **filtrer** *vt* to filter; (*fig: candidats, visiteurs*) to screen

fin[1] [fɛ̃] *nf* end; **~s** *nfpl* (*but*) ends; **prendre ~** to come to an end; **mettre ~ à** to put an end to; **à la ~** in the end, eventually; **en ~ de compte** in the end; **sans ~** endless; **~ juin** at the end of June

fin[2]**, e** [fɛ̃, fin] *adj* (*papier, couche, fil*) thin; (*cheveux, visage*) fine; (*taille*) neat, slim; (*esprit, remarque*) subtle ♦ *adv* (*couper*) finely; **~ prêt** quite ready; **~es herbes** mixed herbs

final, e [final, o] *adj* final ♦ *nm* (*MUS*) finale; **finale** *nf* final; **quarts de finale** quarter finals; **finalement** *adv* finally, in the end; (*après tout*) after all

finance [finɑ̃s] *nf*: **~s** *nfpl* (*situation*) finances; (*activités*) finance *sg*; **moyennant ~** for a fee; **financer** *vt* to finance; **financier, -ière** *adj* financial

finaud, e [fino, od] *adj* wily

finesse [fines] *nf* thinness; (*raffinement*) fineness; (*subtilité*) subtlety

fini, e [fini] *adj* finished; (*MATH*) finite ♦ *nm* (*d'un objet manufacturé*) finish

finir [finiʀ] *vt* to finish ♦ *vi* to finish, end; **~ par faire** to end up *ou* finish up doing; **~ de faire** to finish doing; (*cesser*) to stop doing; **il finit par m'agacer** he's beginning to get on my nerves; **en ~ avec** to be *ou* have done with; **il va mal ~** he will come to a bad end

finition [finisjɔ̃] *nf* (*résultat*) finish

finlandais, e [fɛ̃lɑ̃dɛ, ɛz] *adj* Finnish ♦ *nm/f*: **F~, e** Finn

Finlande [fɛ̃lɑ̃d] *nf*: **la ~** Finland

fiole [fjɔl] *nf* phial

firme [firm] *nf* firm

fis [fi] *vb voir* **faire**

fisc [fisk] *nm* tax authorities *pl*; **fiscal, e, -aux** *adj* tax *cpd*, fiscal; **fiscalité** *nf* tax system

fissure [fisyʀ] *nf* crack; **fissurer** *vt* to crack; **se fissurer** *vi* to crack

fiston [fistɔ̃] (*fam*) *nm* son, lad

fit [fi] *vb voir* **faire**

fixation [fiksasjɔ̃] *nf* (*attache*) fastening; (*PSYCH*) fixation

fixe [fiks] *adj* fixed; (*emploi*) steady, regular ♦ *nm* (*salaire*) basic salary; **à heure ~** at a set time; **menu à prix ~** set menu

fixé, e [fikse] *adj*: **être ~ (sur)** (*savoir à quoi s'en tenir*) to have made up one's mind (about)

fixer [fikse] *vt* (*attacher*): **~ qch (à/sur)** to fix *ou* fasten sth (to/onto); (*déterminer*) to fix, set; (*regarder*) to stare at; **se ~** *vi* (*s'établir*) to settle down; **se ~ sur** (*suj: attention*) to focus on

flacon [flakɔ̃] *nm* bottle

flageoler [flaʒɔle] *vi* (*jambes*) to sag

flageolet [flaʒɔle] *nm* (*CULIN*) dwarf kidney bean

flagrant, e [flagʀɑ̃, ɑ̃t] *adj* flagrant, blatant; **en ~ délit** in the act

flair [flɛʀ] *nm* sense of smell; (*fig*) intuition; **flairer** *vt* (*humer*) to sniff (at); (*détecter*) to scent

flamand, e [flamɑ̃, ɑ̃d] *adj* Flemish ♦ *nm* (*LING*) Flemish ♦ *nm/f*: **F~, e** Fleming; **les F~s** the Flemish

flamant [flamɑ̃] *nm* flamingo

flambant [flɑ̃bɑ̃, ɑ̃t] *adv*: **~ neuf** brand new

flambé, e [flɑ̃be] *adj* (*CULIN*) flambé

flambeau, x [flɑ̃bo] *nm* (flaming) torch

flambée [flɑ̃be] *nf* blaze; (*fig: des prix*) explosion

flamber [flɑ̃be] *vi* to blaze (up)

flamboyer [flɑ̃bwaje] *vi* to blaze (up)

flamme [flɑm] *nf* flame; (*fig*) fire, fervour; **en ~s** on fire, ablaze

flan [flɑ̃] *nm* (*CULIN*) custard tart *ou* pie

flanc [flɑ̃] *nm* side; (*MIL*) flank

flancher [flɑ̃ʃe] (*fam*) *vi* to fail, pack up

flanelle [flanɛl] *nf* flannel

flâner [flɑne] *vi* to stroll; **flânerie** *nf* stroll

flanquer [flɑ̃ke] *vt* to flank; (*fam: mettre*) to chuck, shove; (: *jeter*): **~ par terre/à la porte** to fling to the ground/chuck out

flaque [flak] *nf* (*d'eau*) puddle; (*d'huile, de sang etc*) pool

flash [flaʃ] (*pl* **~es**) *nm* (*PHOTO*) flash; **~ (d'information)** newsflash

flasque [flask] *adj* flabby

flatter [flate] *vt* to flatter; **se ~ de qch** to pride o.s. on sth; **flatterie** *nf* flattery *no pl*; **flatteur, -euse** *adj* flattering

fléau, x [fleo] *nm* scourge

flèche [flɛʃ] *nf* arrow; (*de clocher*) spire; **monter en ~** (*fig*) to soar, rocket; **partir en ~** to be off like a shot; **fléchette** *nf* dart

fléchir [fleʃiʀ] *vt* (*corps, genou*) to bend; (*fig*) to sway, weaken ♦ *vi* (*fig*) to weaken, flag

flemmard, e [flemaʀ, aʀd] (*fam*) *nm/f* lazybones *sg*, loafer

flemme [flɛm] *nf* (*fam*) laziness; **j'ai la ~ de le faire** I can't be bothered doing it

flétrir [fletʀiʀ]: **se ~** *vi* to wither

fleur [flœʀ] *nf* flower; (*d'un arbre*) blossom; **en ~** (*arbre*) in blossom; **à ~s** flowery

fleuri, e [flœʀi] *adj* (*jardin*) in flower *ou* bloom; (*tissu, papier*) flowery

fleurir [flœʀiʀ] *vi* (*rose*) to flower; (*arbre*) to blossom; (*fig*) to flourish ♦ *vt* (*tombe*) to put flowers on; (*chambre*) to decorate with flowers

fleuriste [flœʀist] *nm/f* florist

fleuve [flœv] *nm* river

flexible [fleksibl] *adj* flexible

flic [flik] *nm* (*fam: péj*) cop

flipper [flipœʀ] *nm* pinball (machine)

flirter [flœʀte] *vi* to flirt

flocon [flɔkɔ̃] *nm* flake

flopée [flɔpe] (*fam*) *nf*: **une ~ de** loads of, masses of

floraison [flɔʀɛzɔ̃] *nf* flowering

flore [flɔʀ] *nf* flora

florissant, e [flɔʀisɑ̃, ɑ̃t] *adj* (*économie*) flourishing

flot [flo] *nm* flood, stream; **~s** *nmpl* (*de la mer*) waves; **être à ~** (*NAVIG*) to be afloat; **entrer à ~s** to stream *ou* pour in

flottant, e [flɔtɑ̃, ɑ̃t] *adj* (*vêtement*) loose

flotte [flɔt] *nf* (*NAVIG*) fleet; (*fam: eau*) water; (: *pluie*) rain

flottement [flɔtmɑ̃] *nm* (*fig*) wavering, hesitation

flotter [flɔte] *vi* to float; (*nuage, odeur*) to drift; (*drapeau*) to fly; (*vêtements*) to hang loose; (*fam: pleuvoir*) to rain; **faire ~** to float; **flotteur** *nm* float

flou, e [flu] *adj* fuzzy, blurred; (*fig*) woolly, vague

fluctuation [flyktɥasjɔ̃] *nf* fluctuation

fluet, te [flɥɛ, ɛt] *adj* thin, slight

fluide [flɥid] *adj* fluid; (*circulation etc*) flowing freely ♦ *nm* fluid

fluor [flyɔʀ] *nm*: **dentifrice au ~** fluoride toothpaste

fluorescent, e [flyɔʀesɑ̃, ɑ̃t] *adj* fluorescent

flûte [flyt] *nf* flute; (*verre*) flute glass; (*pain*) long loaf; **~! drat it!; ~ à bec** recorder

flux [fly] *nm* incoming tide; (*écoulement*) flow; **le ~ et le reflux** the ebb and flow

FM *sigle f* (= *fréquence modulée*) FM

foc [fɔk] *nm* jib

foi [fwa] *nf* faith; **digne de ~** reliable; **être de bonne/mauvaise ~** to be sincere/insincere; **ma ~ ...** well ...

foie [fwa] *nm* liver; **crise de ~** stomach upset

foin [fwɛ̃] *nm* hay; **faire du ~** (*fig: fam*) to kick up a row

foire [fwaʀ] *nf* fair; (*fête foraine*) (fun) fair; **faire la ~** (*fig: fam*) to whoop it up; **~ (exposition)** trade fair

fois [fwa] *nf* time; **une/deux ~** once/

twice; **2 ~ 2** 2 times 2; **une ~** *(passé)* once; *(futur)* sometime; **une ~ pour toutes** once and for all; **une ~ que** once; **des ~** *(parfois)* sometimes; **à la ~** *(ensemble)* at once

foison [fwazɔ̃] *nf*: **à ~** in plenty; **foisonner** *vi* to abound

fol [fɔl] *adj voir* **fou**

folie [fɔli] *nf (d'une décision, d'un acte)* madness, folly; *(état)* madness, insanity; **la ~ des grandeurs** delusions of grandeur; **faire des ~s** *(en dépenses)* to be extravagant

folklorique [fɔlklɔʀik] *adj* folk *cpd*; *(fam)* weird

folle [fɔl] *adj, nf voir* **fou**; **follement** *adv* *(très)* madly, wildly

foncé, e [fɔ̃se] *adj* dark

foncer [fɔ̃se] *vi* to go darker; *(fam: aller vite)* to tear *ou* belt along; **~ sur** to charge at

foncier, -ère [fɔ̃sje, jɛʀ] *adj (honnêteté etc)* basic, fundamental; *(COMM)* real estate *cpd*

fonction [fɔ̃ksjɔ̃] *nf* function; *(emploi, poste)* post, position; **~s** *nfpl (professionnelles)* duties; **voiture de ~** company car; **en ~ de** *(par rapport à)* according to; **faire ~ de** to serve as; **la ~ publique** the state *ou* civil *(BRIT)* service; **fonctionnaire** *nm/f* state employee, local authority employee; *(dans l'administration)* ≃ civil servant; **fonctionner** *vi* to work, function

fond [fɔ̃] *nm (d'un récipient, trou)* bottom; *(d'une salle, scène)* back; *(d'un tableau, décor)* background; *(opposé à la forme)* content; *(SPORT)*: **le ~** long distance (running); **au ~ de** at the bottom of; at the back of; **à ~** *(connaître, soutenir)* thoroughly; *(appuyer, visser)* right down *ou* home; **à ~ (de train)** *(fam)* full tilt; **dans le ~, au ~** *(en somme)* basically, really; **de ~ en comble** from top to bottom; *voir aussi* **fonds**; **~ de teint** foundation (cream)

fondamental, e, -aux [fɔ̃damɑ̃tal, o] *adj* fundamental

fondant, e [fɔ̃dɑ̃, ɑ̃t] *adj (neige)* melting; *(poire)* that melts in the mouth

fondateur, -trice [fɔ̃datœʀ, tʀis] *nm/f* founder

fondation [fɔ̃dasjɔ̃] *nf* founding; *(établissement)* foundation; **~s** *nfpl (d'une maison)* foundations

fondé, e [fɔ̃de] *adj (accusation etc)* well-founded; **être ~ à** to have grounds for *ou* good reason to

fondement [fɔ̃dmɑ̃] *nm*: **sans ~** *(rumeur etc)* groundless, unfounded

fonder [fɔ̃de] *vt* to found; *(fig)* to base; **se ~ sur** *(suj: personne)* to base o.s. on

fonderie [fɔ̃dʀi] *nf* smelting works *sg*

fondre [fɔ̃dʀ] *vt (aussi:* **faire ~**) to melt; *(dans l'eau)* to dissolve; *(fig: mélanger)* to merge, blend ♦ *vi (à la chaleur)* to melt; *(dans l'eau)* to dissolve; *(fig)* to melt away; *(se précipiter)*: **~ sur** to swoop down on; **~ en larmes** to burst into tears

fonds [fɔ̃] *nm (COMM)*: **~ (de commerce)** business ♦ *nmpl (argent)* funds

fondu, e [fɔ̃dy] *adj (beurre, neige)* melted; *(métal)* molten; **fondue** *nf (CULIN)* fondue

font [fɔ̃] *vb voir* **faire**

fontaine [fɔ̃tɛn] *nf* fountain; *(source)* spring

fonte [fɔ̃t] *nf* melting; *(métal)* cast iron; **la ~ des neiges** (the spring) thaw

foot [fut] *(fam) nm* football

football [futbol] *nm* football, soccer; **footballeur** *nm* footballer

footing [futiŋ] *nm* jogging; **faire du ~** to go jogging

for [fɔʀ] *nm*: **dans son ~ intérieur** in one's heart of hearts

forain, e [fɔʀɛ̃, ɛn] *adj* fairground *cpd* ♦ *nm (marchand)* stallholder; *(acteur)* fairground entertainer

forçat [fɔʀsa] *nm* convict

force [fɔʀs] *nf* strength; *(PHYSIQUE, MÉCANIQUE)* force; **~s** *nfpl (physiques)* strength *sg*; *(MIL)* forces; **à ~ d'insister** by dint of insisting; as he *(ou* I *etc)* kept on insisting; **de ~** forcibly, by force; **les ~s de l'ordre** the police

forcé, e [fɔʀse] *adj* forced; **c'est ~** *(fam)* it's inevitable; **forcément** *adv* inevitably; **pas forcément** not necessarily

forcené, e [fɔʀsəne] *nm/f* maniac

forcer [fɔʀse] *vt* to force; *(voix)* to strain ♦ *vi (SPORT)* to overtax o.s.; **~ la dose** *(fam)* to overdo it; **se ~ (à faire)** to force o.s. (to do)

forcir [fɔʀsiʀ] *vi (grossir)* to broaden out

forer [fɔʀe] *vt* to drill, bore

forestier, -ère [fɔʀestje, jɛʀ] *adj* forest *cpd*

forêt [fɔʀɛ] *nf* forest

forfait [fɔʀfɛ] *nm (COMM)* all-in deal *ou* price; **forfaitaire** *adj* inclusive

forge [fɔʀʒ] *nf* forge, smithy; **forger** *vt* to forge; *(fig: prétexte)* to contrive, make up; **forgeron** *nm* (black)smith

formaliser [fɔʀmalize]: **se ~** *vi*: **se ~ (de)** to take offence (at)

formalité [fɔʀmalite] *nf* formality; **simple ~** mere formality

format [fɔʀma] *nm* size; **formater** *vt (disque)* to format

formation [fɔʀmasjɔ̃] *nf (développement)* forming; *(apprentissage)* training; **~ permanente** continuing education; **~ professionnelle** vocational training

forme [fɔʀm] *nf (gén)* form; *(d'un objet)* shape, form; **~s** *nfpl (bonnes manières)* proprieties; *(d'une femme)* figure *sg*; **être en ~** *(SPORT etc)* to be on form; **en bonne et due ~** in due form

formel, le [fɔʀmɛl] *adj (catégorique)* definite, positive; **formellement** *adv (absolument)* positively; **formellement interdit** strictly forbidden

former [fɔʀme] *vt* to form; *(éduquer)* to train; **se ~** *vi* to form

formidable [fɔʀmidabl] *adj* tremendous

formulaire [fɔʀmylɛʀ] *nm* form

formule [fɔʀmyl] *nf (gén)* formula; *(expression)* phrase; **~ de politesse** polite phrase; *(en fin de lettre)* letter ending; for-

muler *vt (émettre: désir)* to formulate

fort, e [fɔʀ, fɔʀt] *adj* strong; *(intensité, rendement)* high, great; *(corpulent)* stout; *(doué)* good, able ♦ *adv (serrer, frapper)* hard; *(parler)* loud(ly); *(beaucoup)* greatly, very much; *(très)* very ♦ *nm (édifice)* fort; *(point ~)* strong point, forte; **~e tête** rebel; **forteresse** *nf* stronghold

fortifiant [fɔʀtifjã, jãt] *nm* tonic

fortifier [fɔʀtifje] *vt* to strengthen, fortify

fortiori [fɔʀsjɔʀi]: **à ~** *adv* all the more so

fortuit, e [fɔʀtɥi, it] *adj* fortuitous, chance *cpd*

fortune [fɔʀtyn] *nf* fortune; **faire ~** to make one's fortune; **de ~** makeshift; **fortuné, e** *adj* wealthy

fosse [fos] *nf (grand trou)* pit; *(tombe)* grave

fossé [fose] *nm* ditch; *(fig)* gulf, gap

fossette [fosɛt] *nf* dimple

fossile [fosil] *nm* fossil

fossoyeur [foswajœʀ] *nm* gravedigger

fou, (fol), folle [fu, fɔl] *adj* mad; *(déréglé etc)* wild, erratic; *(fam: extrême, très grand)* terrific, tremendous ♦ *nm/f* madman(-woman) ♦ *nm (du roi)* jester; **être ~de** to be mad *ou* crazy about; **avoir le ~rire** to have the giggles

foudre [fudʀ] *nf*: **la ~** lightning

foudroyant, e [fudʀwajã, ãt] *adj (progrès)* lightning *cpd*; *(succès)* stunning; *(maladie, poison)* violent

foudroyer [fudʀwaje] *vt* to strike down; **être foudroyé** to be struck by lightning; **~ qn du regard** to glare at sb

fouet [fwɛ] *nm* whip; *(CULIN)* whisk; **de plein ~** *(se heurter)* head on; **fouetter** *vt* to whip; *(crème)* to whisk

fougère [fuʒɛʀ] *nf* fern

fougue [fug] *nf* ardour, spirit; **fougueux, -euse** *adj* fiery

fouille [fuj] *nf* search; **~s** *nfpl (archéologiques)* excavations; **fouiller** *vt* to search; *(creuser)* to dig ♦ *vi* to rummage; **fouillis** *nm* jumble, muddle

fouiner [fwine] *(péj) vi*: **~ dans** to nose

around *ou* about in

foulard [fulaʀ] *nm* scarf

foule [ful] *nf* crowd; **la ~** crowds *pl*; **une ~ de** masses of

foulée [fule] *nf* stride

fouler [fule] *vt* to press; (*sol*) to tread upon; **se ~ la cheville** to sprain one's ankle; **ne pas se ~** not to overexert o.s.; **il ne se foule pas** he doesn't put himself out; **foulure** *nf* sprain

four [fuʀ] *nm* oven; (*de potier*) kiln; (*THÉÂTRE: échec*) flop

fourbe [fuʀb] *adj* deceitful

fourbu, e [fuʀby] *adj* exhausted

fourche [fuʀʃ] *nf* pitchfork

fourchette [fuʀʃɛt] *nf* fork; (*STATISTIQUE*) bracket, margin

fourgon [fuʀgɔ̃] *nm* van; (*RAIL*) wag(g)on; **fourgonnette** *nf* (small) van

fourmi [fuʀmi] *nf* ant; **~s** *nfpl* (*fig*) pins and needles; **fourmilière** *nf* ant-hill; **fourmiller** *vi* to swarm

fournaise [fuʀnɛz] *nf* blaze; (*fig*) furnace, oven

fourneau, x [fuʀno] *nm* stove

fournée [fuʀne] *nf* batch

fourni, e [fuʀni] *adj* (*barbe, cheveux*) thick; (*magasin*) **bien ~ (en)** well stocked (with)

fournir [fuʀniʀ] *vt* to supply; (*preuve, exemple*) to provide, supply; (*effort*) to put in; **fournisseur, -euse** *nm/f* supplier; **fournisseur** *m* **d'accès** service provider; **fourniture** *nf* supply(ing); **fournitures scolaires** school stationery

fourrage [fuʀaʒ] *nm* fodder

fourré, e [fuʀe] *adj* (*bonbon etc*) filled; (*manteau etc*) fur-lined ♦ *nm* thicket

fourrer [fuʀe] (*fam*) *vt* to stick, shove; **se ~ dans/sous** to get into/under; **fourre-tout** *nm inv* (*sac*) holdall; (*fig*) rag-bag

fourrière [fuʀjɛʀ] *nf* pound

fourrure [fuʀyʀ] *nf* fur; (*sur l'animal*) coat

fourvoyer [fuʀvwaje]: **se ~** *vi* to go astray, stray

foutre [futʀ] (*fam!*) *vt* = **ficher**; **foutu, e** (*fam!*) *adj* = **fichu, e**

foyer [fwaje] *nm* (*maison*) home; (*famille*) family; (*de cheminée*) hearth; (*de jeunes etc*) (social) club; (*résidence*) hostel; (*salon*) foyer; **lunettes à double ~** bi-focals

fracas [fʀaka] *nm* (*d'objet qui tombe*) crash; **fracassant, e** *adj* (*succès*) thundering; **fracasser** *vt* to smash

fraction [fʀaksjɔ̃] *nf* fraction; **fractionner** *vt* to divide (up), split (up)

fracture [fʀaktyʀ] *nf* fracture; **~ du crâne** fractured skull; **fracturer** *vt* (*coffre, serrure*) to break open; (*os, membre*) to fracture

fragile [fʀaʒil] *adj* fragile, delicate; (*fig*) frail; **fragilité** *nf* fragility

fragment [fʀagmɑ̃] *nm* (*d'un objet*) fragment, piece

fraîche [fʀɛʃ] *adj voir* **frais**; **fraîcheur** *nf* coolness; (*d'un aliment*) freshness; **fraîchir** *vi* to get cooler; (*vent*) to freshen

frais, fraîche [fʀɛ, fʀɛʃ] *adj* fresh; (*froid*) cool ♦ *adv* (*récemment*) newly, fresh(ly) ♦ *nm*: **mettre au ~** to put in a cool place ♦ *nmpl* (*gén*) expenses; (*COMM*) costs; **il fait ~** it's cool; **servir ~** serve chilled; **prendre le ~** to take a breath of cool air; **faire de ~** to go to a lot of expense; **~ de scolarité** school fees (*BRIT*), tuition (*US*); **~ généraux** overheads

fraise [fʀɛz] *nf* strawberry; **~ des bois** wild strawberry

framboise [fʀɑ̃bwaz] *nf* raspberry

franc, franche [fʀɑ̃, fʀɑ̃ʃ] *adj* (*personne*) frank, straightforward; (*visage*) open; (*net: refus*) clear; (*: coupure*) clean; (*intensif*) downright ♦ *nm* (*HIST*) franc

français, e [fʀɑ̃sɛ, ɛz] *adj* French ♦ *nm/f*: **F~, e** Frenchman(-woman) ♦ *nm* (*LING*) French; **les F~** the French

France [fʀɑ̃s] *nf*: **la ~** France

franche [fʀɑ̃ʃ] *adj voir* **franc**; **franchement** *adv* frankly; (*nettement*) definitely; (*tout à fait etc*) downright

franchir [fʀɑ̃ʃiʀ] *vt* (*obstacle*) to clear, get over; (*seuil, ligne, rivière*) to cross; (*distance*) to cover

franchise [frɑ̃ʃiz] *nf* frankness; (*douanière*) exemption; (*ASSURANCES*) excess

franc-maçon [frɑ̃masɔ̃] *nm* freemason

franco [frɑ̃ko] *adv* (*COMM*): **~ (de port)** postage paid

francophone [frɑ̃kɔfɔn] *adj* French-speaking

franc-parler [frɑ̃parle] *nm inv* outspokenness; **avoir son ~-~** to speak one's mind

frange [frɑ̃ʒ] *nf* fringe

frangipane [frɑ̃ʒipan] *nf* almond paste

franquette [frɑ̃kɛt]: **à la bonne ~** *adv* without any fuss

frappant, e [frapɑ̃, ɑ̃t] *adj* striking

frappé, e [frape] *adj* iced

frapper [frape] *vt* to hit, strike; (*étonner*) to strike; **~ dans ses mains** to clap one's hands; **frappé de stupeur** dumbfounded

frasques [frask] *nfpl* escapades

fraternel, le [fratɛrnɛl] *adj* brotherly, fraternal; **fraternité** *nf* brotherhood

fraude [frod] *nf* fraud; (*SCOL*) cheating; **passer qch en ~** to smuggle sth in (*ou* out); **~ fiscale** tax evasion; **frauder** *vi, vt* to cheat; **frauduleux, -euse** *adj* fraudulent

frayer [freje] *vt* to open up, clear ♦ *vi* to spawn; **se ~ un chemin dans la foule** to force one's way through the crowd

frayeur [frejœr] *nf* fright

fredonner [frədɔne] *vt* to hum

freezer [frizœr] *nm* freezing compartment

frein [frɛ̃] *nm* brake; **mettre un ~ à** (*fig*) to curb, check; **~ à main** handbrake; **freiner** *vi* to brake ♦ *vt* (*progrès etc*) to check

frêle [frɛl] *adj* frail, fragile

frelon [frəlɔ̃] *nm* hornet

frémir [fremir] *vi* (*de peur, d'horreur*) to shudder; (*de colère*) to shake; (*feuillage*) to quiver

frêne [frɛn] *nm* ash

frénétique [frenetik] *adj* frenzied, frenetic

fréquemment [frekamɑ̃] *adv* frequently

fréquent, e [frekɑ̃, ɑ̃t] *adj* frequent

fréquentation [frekɑ̃tasjɔ̃] *nf* frequenting; **~s** *nfpl* (*relations*) company *sg*

fréquenté, e [frekɑ̃te] *adj*: **très ~** (very) busy; **mal ~** patronized by disreputable elements

fréquenter [frekɑ̃te] *vt* (*lieu*) to frequent; (*personne*) to see; **se ~** to see each other

frère [frɛr] *nm* brother

fresque [frɛsk] *nf* (*ART*) fresco

fret [frɛ(t)] *nm* freight

frétiller [fretije] *vi* (*poisson*) to wriggle

fretin [frətɛ̃] *nm*: **menu ~** small fry

friable [frijabl] *adj* crumbly

friand, e [frijɑ̃, frijɑ̃d] *adj*: **~ de** very fond of ♦ *nm*: **~ au fromage** cheese puff

friandise [frijɑ̃diz] *nf* sweet

fric [frik] (*fam*) *nm* cash, bread

friche [friʃ]: **en ~** *adj, adv* (lying) fallow

friction [friksjɔ̃] *nf* (*massage*) rub, rub-down; (*TECH, fig*) friction; **frictionner** *vt* to rub (down)

frigidaire ® [friʒidɛr] *nm* refrigerator

frigide [friʒid] *adj* frigid

frigo [frigo] (*fam*) *nm* fridge

frigorifié, e [frigɔrifje] (*fam*) *adj*: **être ~** to be frozen stiff

frigorifique [frigɔrifik] *adj* refrigerating

frileux, -euse [frilø, øz] *adj* sensitive to (the) cold

frime [frim] (*fam*) *nf*: **c'est de la ~** it's a lot of eyewash, it's all put on; **frimer** (*fam*) *vi* to show off

frimousse [frimus] *nf* (sweet) little face

fringale [frɛ̃gal] (*fam*) *nf*: **avoir la ~** to be ravenous

fringant, e [frɛ̃gɑ̃, ɑ̃t] *adj* dashing

fringues [frɛ̃g] (*fam*) *nfpl* clothes

fripé, e [fripe] *adj* crumpled

fripon, ne [fripɔ̃, ɔn] *adj* roguish, mischievous ♦ *nm/f* rascal, rogue

fripouille [fripuj] *nf* scoundrel

frire [frir] *vt, vi*: **faire ~** to fry

frisé, e [frize] *adj* (*cheveux*) curly; (*personne*) curly-haired

frisson [frisɔ̃] *nm* (*de froid*) shiver; (*de peur*) shudder; **frissonner** *vi* (*de fièvre, froid*) to shiver; (*d'horreur*) to shudder

frit, e [fʀi, fʀit] *pp de* **frire**; **frite** *nf*: **(pommes) frites** chips (*BRIT*), French fries; **friteuse** *nf* chip pan; **friture** *nf* (*huile*) (deep) fat; (*plat*): **friture (de poissons)** fried fish

frivole [fʀivɔl] *adj* frivolous

froid, e [fʀwa, fʀwad] *adj, nm* cold; **il fait ~** it's cold; **avoir/prendre ~** to be/catch cold; **être en ~ avec** to be on bad terms with; **froidement** *adv* (*accueillir*) coldly; (*décider*) coolly

froideur [fʀwadœʀ] *nf* coldness

froisser [fʀwase] *vt* to crumple (up), crease; (*fig*) to hurt, offend; **se ~** *vi* to crumple, crease; (*personne*) to take offence; **se ~ un muscle** to strain a muscle

frôler [fʀole] *vt* to brush against; (*suj: projectile*) to skim past; (*fig*) to come very close to

fromage [fʀɔmaʒ] *nm* cheese; **~ blanc** soft white cheese

froment [fʀɔmã] *nm* wheat

froncer [fʀɔ̃se] *vt* to gather; **~ les sourcils** to frown

frondaisons [fʀɔ̃dɛzɔ̃] *nfpl* foliage *sg*

front [fʀɔ̃] *nm* forehead, brow; (*MIL*) front; **de ~** (*se heurter*) head-on; (*rouler*) together (*i.e. 2 or 3 abreast*); (*simultanément*) at once; **faire ~ à** to face up to

frontalier, -ère [fʀɔ̃talje, jɛʀ] *adj* border *cpd*, frontier *cpd*

frontière [fʀɔ̃tjɛʀ] *nf* frontier, border

frotter [fʀɔte] *vi* to rub, scrape ♦ *vt* to rub; (*pommes de terre, plancher*) to scrub; **~ une allumette** to strike a match

fructifier [fʀyktifje] *vi* to yield a profit

fructueux, -euse [fʀyktɥø, øz] *adj* fruitful

frugal, e, -aux [fʀygal, o] *adj* frugal

fruit [fʀɥi] *nm* fruit *gen no pl*; **~ de la passion** passion fruit; **~s de mer** seafood(s); **~s secs** dried fruit *sg*; **fruité, e** *adj* fruity; **fruitier, -ère** *adj*: **arbre fruitier** fruit tree

fruste [fʀyst] *adj* unpolished, uncultivated

frustrer [fʀystʀe] *vt* to frustrate

FS *abr* (= *franc suisse*) SF

fuel(-oil) [fjul(ɔjl)] *nm* fuel oil; (*domestique*) heating oil

fugace [fygas] *adj* fleeting

fugitif, -ive [fyʒitif, iv] *adj* (*fugace*) fleeting ♦ *nm/f* fugitive

fugue [fyg] *nf*: **faire une ~** to run away, abscond

fuir [fɥiʀ] *vt* to flee from; (*éviter*) to shun ♦ *vi* to run away; (*gaz, robinet*) to leak

fuite [fɥit] *nf* flight; (*écoulement, divulgation*) leak; **être en ~** to be on the run; **mettre en ~** to put to flight

fulgurant, e [fylgyʀã, ãt] *adj* lightning *cpd*, dazzling

fulminer [fylmine] *vi* to thunder forth

fumé, e [fyme] *adj* (*CULIN*) smoked; (*verre*) tinted; **fumée** *nf* smoke

fumer [fyme] *vi* to smoke; (*soupe*) to steam ♦ *vt* to smoke

fûmes *etc* [fym] *vb voir* **être**

fumet [fyme] *nm* aroma

fumeur, -euse [fymœʀ, øz] *nm/f* smoker

fumeux, -euse [fymø, øz] (*péj*) *adj* woolly, hazy

fumier [fymje] *nm* manure

fumiste [fymist] *nm/f* (*péj: paresseux*) shirker

funèbre [fynɛbʀ] *adj* funeral *cpd*; (*fig: atmosphère*) gloomy

funérailles [fyneʀaj] *nfpl* funeral *sg*

funeste [fynɛst] *adj* (*erreur*) disastrous

fur [fyʀ]: **au ~ et à mesure** *adv* as one goes along; **au ~ et à mesure que** as

furet [fyʀe] *nm* ferret

fureter [fyʀ(ə)te] (*péj*) *vi* to nose about

fureur [fyʀœʀ] *nf* fury; **être en ~** to be infuriated; **faire ~** to be all the rage

furibond, e [fyʀibɔ̃, ɔ̃d] *adj* furious

furie [fyʀi] *nf* fury; (*femme*) shrew, vixen; **en ~** (*mer*) raging; **furieux, -euse** *adj* furious

furoncle [fyʀɔ̃kl] *nm* boil

furtif, -ive [fyʀtif, iv] *adj* furtive

fus [fy] *vb voir* **être**

fusain [fyzɛ̃] *nm* (*ART*) charcoal

fuseau, x [fyzo] *nm* (*pour filer*) spindle;

(pantalon) (ski) pants; ~ **horaire** time zone

fusée [fyze] *nf* rocket; ~ **éclairante** flare

fuser [fyze] *vi (rires etc)* to burst forth

fusible [fyzibl] *nm (ÉLEC: fil)* fuse wire; *(: fiche)* fuse

fusil [fyzi] *nm (de guerre, à canon rayé)* rifle, gun; *(de chasse, à canon lisse)* shotgun, gun; **fusillade** *nf* gunfire *no pl*, shooting *no pl*; **fusiller** *vt* to shoot; **fusil-mitrailleur** *nm* machine gun

fusionner [fyzjɔne] *vi* to merge.

fut [fy] *vb voir* **être**

fût [fy] *vb voir* **être** ♦ *nm (tonneau)* barrel, cask

futé, e [fyte] *adj* crafty; **Bison** ~ ® *TV and radio traffic monitoring service*

futile [fytil] *adj* futile; frivolous

futur, e [fytyʀ] *adj, nm* future ·

fuyant, e [fɥijã, ãt] *vb voir* **fuir** ♦ *adj (regard etc)* evasive; *(lignes etc)* receding

fuyard, e [fɥijaʀ, aʀd] *nm/f* runaway

G, g

gâcher [gɑʃe] *vt (gâter)* to spoil; *(gaspiller)* to waste; **gâchis** *nm* waste *no pl*

gadoue [gadu] *nf* sludge

gaffe [gaf] *nf* blunder; **faire** ~ *(fam)* to be careful

gage [gaʒ] *nm (dans un jeu)* forfeit; *(fig: de fidélité, d'amour)* token

gageure [gaʒyʀ] *nf:* **c'est une** ~ it's attempting the impossible

gagnant, e [gaɲã, ãt] *nm/f* winner

gagne-pain [gaɲpɛ̃] *nm inv* job

gagner [gaɲe] *vt* to win; *(somme d'argent, revenu)* to earn; *(aller vers, atteindre)* to reach; *(envahir: sommeil, peur)* to overcome; *(: mal)* to spread to ♦ *vi* to win; *(fig)* to gain; ~ **du temps/de la place** to gain time/save space; ~ **sa vie** to earn one's living

gai, e [ge] *adj* cheerful; *(un peu ivre)* merry; **gaiement** *adv* cheerfully; **gaieté** *nf* cheerfulness; **de gaieté de cœur** with a

light heart

gaillard [gajaʀ, aʀd] *nm (strapping)* fellow

gain [gɛ̃] *nm (revenu)* earnings *pl*; *(bénéfice: gén pl)* profits *pl*

gaine [gɛn] *nf (corset)* girdle; *(fourreau)* sheath

gala [gala] *nm* official reception; **de** ~ *(soirée etc)* gala

galant, e [galã, ãt] *adj (courtois)* courteous, gentlemanly; *(entreprenant)* flirtatious, gallant; *(scène, rendez-vous)* romantic

galère [galɛʀ] *nf* galley; **quelle** ~! *(fam)* it's a real grind!; **galérer** *(fam)* *vi* to slog away, work hard; *(rencontrer les difficultés)* to have a hassle

galerie [galʀi] *nf* gallery; *(THÉÂTRE)* circle; *(de voiture)* roof rack; *(fig: spectateurs)* audience; ~ **de peinture** (private) art gallery; ~ **marchande** shopping arcade

galet [galɛ] *nm* pebble

galette [galɛt] *nf* flat cake; ~ **des Rois** *cake eaten on Twelfth Night*

galipette [galipɛt] *nf* somersault

Galles [gal] *nfpl:* **le pays de** ~ Wales; **gallois, e** *adj* Welsh ♦ *nm/f:* **Gallois, e** Welshman(-woman) ♦ *nm (LING)* Welsh

galon [galɔ̃] *nm (MIL)* stripe; *(décoratif)* piece of braid

galop [galo] *nm* gallop; **galoper** *vi* to gallop

galopin [galɔpɛ̃] *nm* urchin, ragamuffin

gambader [gɑ̃bade] *vi (animal, enfant)* to leap about

gambas [gɑ̃bas] *nfpl* Mediterranean prawns

gamin, e [gamɛ̃, in] *nm/f* kid ♦ *adj* childish

gamme [gam] *nf (MUS)* scale; *(fig)* range

gammé, e [game] *adj:* **croix** ~**e** swastika

gang [gɑ̃g] *nm (de criminels)* gang

gant [gɑ̃] *nm* glove; ~ **de toilette** face flannel *(BRIT)*, face cloth

garage [gaʀaʒ] *nm* garage; **garagiste** *nm/f* garage owner; *(employé)* garage mechanic

garantie [gaʀɑ̃ti] *nf* guarantee; **(bon de)** ~

guarantee *ou* warranty slip

garantir [garɑ̃tiʀ] *vt* to guarantee

garce [gaʀs] *(fam) nf* bitch

garçon [gaʀsɔ̃] *nm* boy; *(célibataire):* **vieux ~** bachelor; *(serveur):* **~ (de café)** waiter; **~ de courses** messenger; **~ d'honneur** best man; **garçonnière** *nf* bachelor flat

garde [gaʀd(ə)] *nm (de prisonnier)* guard; *(de domaine etc)* warden; *(soldat, sentinelle)* guardsman ♦ *nf (soldats)* guard; **de ~** on duty; **monter la ~** to stand guard; **mettre en ~** to warn; **prendre ~ (à)** to be careful (of); **~ champêtre** ♦ *nm* rural policeman; **~ du corps** ♦ *nm* bodyguard; **~ des enfants** ♦ *nf (après divorce)* custody of the children; **~ à vue** ♦ *nf (JUR)* ≃ police custody; **garde-à-vous** *nm:* **être/se mettre au garde-à-vous** to be at/stand to attention; **garde-barrière** *nm/f* level-crossing keeper; **garde-boue** *nm inv* mudguard; **garde-chasse** *nm* gamekeeper; **garde-malade** *nf* home nurse; **garde-manger** *nm inv (armoire)* meat safe; *(pièce)* pantry, larder

garder [gaʀde] *vt (conserver)* to keep; *(surveiller: enfants)* to look after; *(: immeuble, lieu, prisonnier)* to guard; **se ~** *vi (aliment: se conserver)* to keep; **se ~ de faire** to be careful not to do; **~ le lit/la chambre** to stay in bed/indoors; **pêche/chasse gardée** private fishing/hunting (ground)

garderie [gaʀdəʀi] *nf* day nursery, crèche

garde-robe [gaʀdəʀɔb] *nf* wardrobe

gardien, ne [gaʀdjɛ̃, jɛn] *nm/f (garde)* guard; *(de prison)* warder; *(de domaine, réserve)* warden; *(de musée etc)* attendant; *(de phare, cimetière)* keeper; *(d'immeuble)* caretaker; *(fig)* guardian; **~ de but** goalkeeper; **~ de la paix** policeman; **~ de nuit** night watchman

gare [gaʀ] *nf* station; **~ routière** bus station

garer [gaʀe] *vt* to park; **se ~** *vi* to park

gargariser [gaʀgaʀize]: **se ~** *vi* to gargle

gargote [gaʀgɔt] *nf* cheap restaurant

gargouille [gaʀguj] *nf* gargoyle

gargouiller [gaʀguje] *vi* to gurgle

garnement [gaʀnəmɑ̃] *nm* rascal, scallywag

garni, e [gaʀni] *adj (plat)* served with vegetables *(and chips or rice etc)*

garnison [gaʀnizɔ̃] *nf* garrison

garniture [gaʀnityʀ] *nf (CULIN)* vegetables *pl*; **~ de frein** brake lining

gars [ga] *(fam) nm* guy

Gascogne [gaskɔɲ] *nf* Gascony; **le golfe de ~** the Bay of Biscay

gas-oil [gazɔjl] *nm* diesel (oil)

gaspiller [gaspije] *vt* to waste

gastronome [gastʀɔnɔm] *nm/f* gourmet; **gastronomie** *nf* gastronomy; **gastronomique** *adj* gastronomic

gâteau, x [gato] *nm* cake; **~ sec** biscuit

gâter [gate] *vt* to spoil; **se ~** *vi (dent, fruit)* to go bad; *(temps, situation)* to change for the worse

gâterie [gatʀi] *nf* little treat

gâteux, -euse [gatø, øz] *adj* senile

gauche [goʃ] *adj* left, left-hand; *(maladroit)* awkward, clumsy ♦ *nf (POL)* left; *(wing)* **le bras ~** the left arm; **le côté ~** the left-hand side; **à ~** on the left; *(direction)* (to the) left; **gaucher, -ère** *adj* left-handed; **gauchiste** *nm/f* leftist

gaufre [gofʀ] *nf* waffle

gaufrette [gofʀɛt] *nf* wafer

gaulois, e [golwa, waz] *adj* Gallic ♦ *nm/f:* **G~, e** Gaul

gaver [gave] *vt* to force-feed; **se ~ de** to stuff o.s. with

gaz [gaz] *nm inv* gas

gaze [gaz] *nf* gauze

gazer [gaze] *(fam) vi:* **ça gaze?** how's things?

gazette [gazɛt] *nf* news sheet

gazeux, -euse [gazø, øz] *adj (boisson)* fizzy; *(eau)* sparkling

gazoduc [gazodyk] *nm* gas pipeline

gazon [gazɔ̃] *nm (herbe)* grass; *(pelouse)* lawn

gazouiller [gazuje] *vi* to chirp; *(enfant)* to babble

geai [ʒɛ] *nm* jay

géant, e [ʒeɑ̃, ɑ̃t] *adj* gigantic; (*COMM*) giant-size ♦ *nm/f* giant

geindre [ʒɛ̃dʀ] *vi* to groan, moan

gel [ʒɛl] *nm* frost

gélatine [ʒelatin] *nf* gelatine

gelée [ʒ(ə)le] *nf* jelly; (*gel*) frost

geler [ʒ(ə)le] *vt, vi* to freeze; **il gèle** it's freezing

gélule [ʒelyl] *nf* (*MÉD*) capsule

gelures [ʒəlyʀ] *nfpl* frostbite *sg*

Gémeaux [ʒemo] *nmpl*: **les ~** Gemini

gémir [ʒemiʀ] *vi* to groan, moan

gênant, e [ʒɛnɑ̃, ɑ̃t] *adj* (*irritant*) annoying; (*embarrassant*) embarrassing

gencive [ʒɑ̃siv] *nf* gum

gendarme [ʒɑ̃daʀm] *nm* gendarme; **gendarmerie** *nf* military police force in countryside and small towns; their police station or barracks

gendre [ʒɑ̃dʀ] *nm* son-in-law

gêné, e [ʒene] *adj* embarrassed

gêner [ʒene] *vt* (*incommoder*) to bother; (*encombrer*) to be in the way; (*embarrasser*): **~ qn** to make sb feel ill-at-ease

général, e, -aux [ʒeneʀal, o] *adj, nm* general; **en ~** usually, in general; **générale** *nf*: (*répétition*) **générale** final dress rehearsal; **généralement** *adv* generally; **généraliser** *vt, vi* to generalize; **se généraliser** *vi* to become widespread; **généraliste** *nm/f* general practitioner, G.P.

génération [ʒeneʀasjɔ̃] *nf* generation

généreux, -euse [ʒeneʀø, øz] *adj* generous

générique [ʒeneʀik] *nm* (*CINÉMA*) credits *pl*

générosité [ʒeneʀozite] *nf* generosity

genêt [ʒ(ə)nɛ] *nm* broom *no pl* (*shrub*)

génétique [ʒenetik] *adj* genetic; **génétiquement** *adv*: **génétiquement modifié** genetically-modified

Genève [ʒ(ə)nɛv] *n* Geneva

génial, e, -aux [ʒenjal, jo] *adj* of genius; (*fam: formidable*) fantastic, brilliant

génie [ʒeni] *nm* genius; (*MIL*): **le ~** the Engineers *pl*; **~ civil** civil engineering

genièvre [ʒənjɛvʀ] *nm* juniper

génisse [ʒenis] *nf* heifer

génital, e, -aux [ʒenital, o] *adj* genital; **les parties ~es** the genitals

génoise [ʒenwaz] *nf* sponge cake

genou, x [ʒ(ə)nu] *nm* knee; **à ~x** on one's knees; **se mettre à ~x** to kneel down

genre [ʒɑ̃ʀ] *nm* kind, type, sort; (*LING*) gender; **avoir bon ~** to look a nice sort; **avoir mauvais ~** to be coarse-looking; **ce n'est pas son ~** it's not like him

gens [ʒɑ̃] *nmpl* (f in some phrases) people *pl*

gentil, le [ʒɑ̃ti, ij] *adj* kind; (*enfant: sage*) good; (*endroit etc*) nice; **gentillesse** *nf* kindness; **gentiment** *adv* kindly

géographie [ʒeɔgʀafi] *nf* geography

geôlier [ʒolje, jɛʀ] *nm* jailer

géologie [ʒeɔlɔʒi] *nf* geology

géomètre [ʒeɔmɛtʀ] *nm/f* (*arpenteur*) (land) surveyor

géométrie [ʒeɔmetʀi] *nf* geometry; **géométrique** *adj* geometric

géranium [ʒeʀanjɔm] *nm* geranium

gérant, e [ʒeʀɑ̃, ɑ̃t] *nm/f* manager(-eress)

gerbe [ʒɛʀb] *nf* (*de fleurs*) spray; (*de blé*) sheaf

gercé, e [ʒɛʀse] *adj* chapped

gerçure [ʒɛʀsyʀ] *nf* crack

gérer [ʒeʀe] *vt* to manage

germain, e [ʒɛʀmɛ̃, ɛn] *adj*: **cousin ~** first cousin

germe [ʒɛʀm] *nm* germ; **germer** *vi* to sprout; (*semence*) to germinate

geste [ʒɛst] *nm* gesture

gestion [ʒɛstjɔ̃] *nf* management

gibier [ʒibje] *nm* (*animaux*) game

giboulée [ʒibule] *nf* sudden shower

gicler [ʒikle] *vi* to spurt, squirt

gifle [ʒifl] *nf* slap (in the face); **gifler** *vt* to slap (in the face)

gigantesque [ʒigɑ̃tɛsk] *adj* gigantic

gigogne [ʒigɔɲ] *adj*: **lits ~s** truckle (*BRIT*) *ou* trundle beds

gigot [ʒigo] *nm* leg (of mutton *ou* lamb)

gigoter [ʒigɔte] *vi* to wriggle (about)

gilet [ʒilɛ] *nm* waistcoat; (*pull*) cardigan; ~ **de sauvetage** life jacket

gin [dʒin] *nm* gin; **~-tonic** gin and tonic

gingembre [ʒɛ̃ʒɑ̃bʀ] *nm* ginger

girafe [ʒiʀaf] *nf* giraffe

giratoire [ʒiʀatwaʀ] *adj*: **sens ~** roundabout

girofle [ʒiʀɔfl] *nf*: **clou de ~** clove

girouette [ʒiʀwɛt] *nf* weather vane *ou* cock

gitan, e [ʒitɑ̃, an] *nm/f* gipsy

gîte [ʒit] *nm* (*maison*) home; (*abri*) shelter; **~ rural** holiday cottage *ou* apartment

givre [ʒivʀ] *nm* (hoar) frost; **givré, e** *adj* covered in frost; (*fam: fou*) nuts; **orange givrée** orange sorbet (*served in peel*)

glace [glas] *nf* ice; (*crème glacée*) ice cream; (*miroir*) mirror; (*de voiture*) window

glacé, e [glase] *adj* (*mains, vent, pluie*) freezing; (*lac*) frozen; (*boisson*) iced

glacer [glase] *vt* to freeze; (*gâteau*) to ice; (*fig*): **~ qn** (*intimider*) to chill sb; (*paralyser*) to make sb's blood run cold

glacial, e [glasjal, jo] *adj* icy

glacier [glasje] *nm* (*GÉO*) glacier; (*marchand*) ice-cream maker

glacière [glasjɛʀ] *nf* icebox

glaçon [glasɔ̃] *nm* icicle; (*pour boisson*) ice cube

glaïeul [glajœl] *nm* gladiolus

glaise [glɛz] *nf* clay

gland [glɑ̃] *nm* acorn; (*décoration*) tassel

glande [glɑ̃d] *nf* gland

glander [glɑ̃de] (*fam*) *vi* to fart around (!)

glauque [glok] *adj* dull blue-green

glissade [glisad] *nf* (*par jeu*) slide; (*chute*) slip; **faire des ~s sur la glace** to slide on the ice

glissant, e [glisɑ̃, ɑ̃t] *adj* slippery

glissement [glismɑ̃] *nm*: **~ de terrain** landslide

glisser [glise] *vi* (*avancer*) to glide *ou* slide along; (*coulisser, tomber*) to slide; (*déraper*) to slip; (*être glissant*) to be slippery ♦ *vt* to slip; **se ~ dans** to slip into

global, e, -aux [glɔbal, o] *adj* overall

globe [glɔb] *nm* globe

globule [glɔbyl] *nm* (*du sang*) corpuscle

globuleux, -euse [glɔbylø, øz] *adj*: **yeux ~** protruding eyes

gloire [glwaʀ] *nf* glory; **glorieux, -euse** *adj* glorious

glousser [gluse] *vi* to cluck; (*rire*) to chuckle; **gloussement** *nm* cluck; chuckle

glouton, ne [glutɔ̃, ɔn] *adj* gluttonous

gluant, e [glyɑ̃, ɑ̃t] *adj* sticky, gummy

glucose [glykoz] *nm* glucose

glycine [glisin] *nf* wisteria

goal [gol] *nm* goalkeeper

GO *sigle* (= **grandes ondes**) LW

gobelet [gɔblɛ] *nm* (*en étain, verre, argent*) tumbler; (*d'enfant, de pique-nique*) beaker; (*à dés*) cup

gober [gɔbe] *vt* to swallow (whole)

godasse [gɔdas] (*fam*) *nf* shoe

godet [gɔdɛ] *nm* pot

goéland [gɔelɑ̃] *nm* (sea)gull

goélette [gɔelɛt] *nf* schooner

gogo [gɔgo]: **à ~** *adv* galore

goguenard, e [gɔg(ə)naʀ, aʀd] *adj* mocking

goinfre [gwɛ̃fʀ] *nm* glutton

golf [gɔlf] *nm* golf; (*terrain*) golf course

golfe [gɔlf] *nm* gulf; (*petit*) bay

gomme [gɔm] *nf* (*à effacer*) rubber (BRIT), eraser; **gommer** *vt* to rub out (BRIT), erase

gond [gɔ̃] *nm* hinge; **sortir de ses ~s** (*fig*) to fly off the handle

gondoler [gɔ̃dɔle]: **se ~** *vi* (*planche*) to warp; (*métal*) to buckle

gonflé, e [gɔ̃fle] *adj* swollen; **il est ~** (*fam: courageux*) he's got some nerve; (*impertinent*) he's got a nerve

gonfler [gɔ̃fle] *vt* (*pneu, ballon: en soufflant*) to blow up; (: *avec une pompe*) to pump up; (*nombre, importance*) to inflate ♦ *vi* to swell (up); (*CULIN: pâte*) to rise; **gonfleur** *nm* pump

gonzesse [gɔ̃zɛs] (*fam*) *nf* chick, bird (BRIT)

goret [gɔʀɛ] *nm* piglet

gorge [gɔʀʒ] *nf* (ANAT) throat; (vallée) gorge

gorgé, e [gɔʀʒe] *adj*: ~ **de** filled with; (eau) saturated with; **gorgée** *nf* (petite) sip; (grande) gulp

gorille [gɔʀij] *nm* gorilla; (fam) bodyguard

gosier [gozje] *nm* throat

gosse [gɔs] (fam) *nm/f* kid

goudron [gudʀɔ̃] *nm* tar; **goudronner** *vt* to tar(mac) (BRIT), asphalt (US)

gouffre [gufʀ] *nm* abyss, gulf

goujat [guʒa] *nm* boor

goulot [gulo] *nm* neck; **boire au** ~ to drink from the bottle

goulu, e [guly] *adj* greedy

gourd, e [guʀ, guʀd] *adj* numb (with cold)

gourde [guʀd] *nf* (récipient) flask; (fam) (clumsy) clot *ou* oaf ♦ *adj* oafish

gourdin [guʀdɛ̃] *nm* club, bludgeon

gourer [guʀe] (fam): **se** ~ *vi* to boob

gourmand, e [guʀmɑ̃, ɑ̃d] *adj* greedy; **gourmandise** [guʀmɑ̃diz] *nf* greed; (bonbon) sweet

gourmet [guʀmɛ] *nm* gourmet

gourmette [guʀmɛt] *nf* chain bracelet

gousse [gus] *nf*: ~ **d'ail** clove of garlic

goût [gu] *nm* taste; **avoir bon** ~ to taste good; **de bon** ~ tasteful; **de mauvais** ~ tasteless; **prendre** ~ **à** to develop a taste *ou* a liking for

goûter [gute] *vt* (essayer) to taste; (apprécier) to enjoy ♦ *vi* to have (afternoon) tea ♦ *nm* (afternoon) tea

goutte [gut] *nf* drop; (MÉD) gout; (alcool) brandy; **tomber** ~ **à** ~ to drip; **goutte-à-goutte** *nm* (MÉD) drip

gouttelette [gut(ə)lɛt] *nf* droplet

gouttière [gutjɛʀ] *nf* gutter

gouvernail [guvɛʀnaj] *nm* rudder; (barre) helm, tiller

gouvernante [guvɛʀnɑ̃t] *nf* governess

gouvernement [guvɛʀnəmɑ̃] *nm* government

gouverner [guvɛʀne] *vt* to govern

grabuge [gʀabyʒ] (fam) *nm* mayhem

grâce [gʀɑs] *nf* (charme) grace; (faveur) favour; (JUR) pardon; ~**s** *nfpl* (REL) grace *sg*; **faire** ~ **à qn de qch** to spare sb sth; **rendre** ~(**s**) **à** to give thanks to; **demander** ~ to beg for mercy; ~ **à** thanks to; **gracier** *vt* to pardon; **gracieux, -euse** *adj* graceful

grade [gʀad] *nm* rank; **monter en** ~ to be promoted

gradin [gʀadɛ̃] *nm* tier; step; ~**s** *nmpl* (de stade) terracing *sg*

gradué, e [gʀadɥe] *adj*: **verre** ~ measuring jug

graduel, le [gʀadɥɛl] *adj* gradual

graduer [gʀadɥe] *vt* (effort etc) to increase gradually; (règle, verre) to graduate

graffiti [gʀafiti] *nmpl* graffiti

grain [gʀɛ̃] *nm* (gén) grain; (NAVIG) squall; ~ **de beauté** beauty spot; ~ **de café** coffee bean; ~ **de poivre** peppercorn; ~ **de poussière** speck of dust; ~ **de raisin** grape

graine [gʀɛn] *nf* seed

graissage [gʀesaʒ] *nm* lubrication, greasing

graisse [gʀɛs] *nf* fat; (lubrifiant) grease; **graisser** *vt* to lubricate, grease; (tacher) to make greasy; **graisseux, -euse** *adj* greasy

grammaire [gʀa(m)mɛʀ] *nf* grammar; **grammatical, e, -aux** *adj* grammatical

gramme [gʀam] *nm* gramme

grand, e [gʀɑ̃, gʀɑ̃d] *adj* (haut) tall; (gros, vaste, large) big, large; (long) long; (plus âgé) big; (adulte) grown-up; (sens abstraits) great ♦ *adv*: ~ **ouvert** wide open; **au** ~ **air** in the open (air); **les** ~**s blessés** the severely injured; ~ **ensemble** housing scheme; ~ **magasin** department store; ~**e personne** grown-up; ~**e surface** hypermarket; ~**es écoles** prestige schools of university level; ~**es lignes** (RAIL) main lines; ~**es vacances** summer holidays; **grand-chose** [gʀɑ̃ʃoz] *nm/f inv*: **pas grand-chose** not much; **Grande-**

Bretagne *nf* (Great) Britain; **grandeur** *nf* (dimension) size; **grandeur nature** life-size; **grandiose** *adj* imposing; **grandir** *vi* to grow ♦ *vt*: **grandir qn** (*suj: vêtement, chaussure*) to make sb look taller; **grand-mère** *nf* grandmother; **grand-messe** *nf* high mass; **grand-peine: à grand-peine** *adv* with difficulty; **grand-père** *nm* grandfather; **grand-route** *nf* main road; **grands-parents** *nmpl* grandparents

grange [grãʒ] *nf* barn

granit(e) [granit] *nm* granite

graphique [grafik] *adj* graphic ♦ *nm* graph

grappe [grap] *nf* cluster; **~ de raisin** bunch of grapes

gras, se [gra, gras] *adj* (*viande, soupe*) fatty; (*personne*) fat; (*surface, main*) greasy; (*plaisanterie*) coarse; (*TYPO*) bold ♦ *nm* (*CULIN*) fat; **faire la ~se matinée** to have a lie-in (*BRIT*), sleep late (*US*); **grassement** *adv*: **grassement payé** handsomely paid; **grassouillet, te** *adj* podgy, plump

gratifiant, e [gratifjã, jãt] *adj* gratifying

gratin [gratẽ] *nm* (*plat*) cheese-topped dish; (*croûte*) cheese topping; **gratiné, e** *adj* (*CULIN*) au gratin

gratis [gratis] *adv* free

gratitude [gratityd] *nf* gratitude

gratte-ciel [gratsjɛl] *nm inv* skyscraper

gratte-papier [gratpapje] (*péj*) *nm inv* penpusher

gratter [grate] *vt* (*avec un outil*) to scrape; (*enlever: avec un outil*) to scrape off; (: *avec un ongle*) to scratch; (*enlever avec un ongle*) to scratch off ♦ *vi* (*irriter*) to be scratchy; (*démanger*) to itch; **se ~** to scratch (o.s.)

gratuit, e [gratyi, ɥit] *adj* (*entrée, billet*) free; (*fig*) gratuitous

gravats [grava] *nmpl* rubble *sg*

grave [grav] *adj* (*maladie, accident*) serious, bad; (*sujet, problème*) serious, grave; (*air*) grave, solemn; (*voix, son*) deep, low-pitched; **gravement** *adv* seriously; (*parler, regarder*) gravely

graver [grave] *vt* to engrave

graveur [gravœr] *nm*: **~ de CD/DVD** CD/DVD burner

gravier [gravje] *nm* gravel *no pl*; **gravillons** *nmpl* loose chippings *ou* gravel *sg*

gravir [gravir] *vt* to climb (up)

gravité [gravite] *nf* (*de maladie, d'accident*) seriousness; (*de sujet, problème*) gravity

graviter [gravite] *vi* to revolve

gravure [gravyr] *nf* engraving; (*reproduction*) print

gré [gre] *nm*: **de bon ~** willingly; **contre le ~ de qn** against sb's will; **de son (plein) ~** of one's own free will; **bon ~ mal ~** like it or not; **de ~ ou de force** whether one likes it or not; **savoir ~ à qn de qch** to be grateful to sb for sth

grec, grecque [grɛk] *adj* Greek; (*classique: vase etc*) Grecian ♦ *nm/f*: **G~, Grecque** Greek ♦ *nm* (*LING*) Greek

Grèce [grɛs] *nf*: **la ~** Greece

greffe [grɛf] *nf* (*BOT, MÉD: de tissu*) graft; (*MÉD: d'organe*) transplant; **greffer** *vt* (*BOT, MÉD: tissu*) to graft; (*MÉD: organe*) to transplant

greffier [grefje, jɛr] *nm* clerk of the court

grêle [grɛl] *adj* (very) thin ♦ *nf* hail; **grêler** *vb impers*: **il grêle** it's hailing; **grêlon** *nm* hailstone

grelot [grəlo] *nm* little bell

grelotter [grəlɔte] *vi* to shiver

grenade [grənad] *nf* (*explosive*) grenade; (*BOT*) pomegranate

grenat [grəna] *adj inv* dark red

grenier [grənje] *nm* attic; (*de ferme*) loft

grenouille [grənuj] *nf* frog

grès [grɛ] *nm* sandstone; (*poterie*) stoneware

grésiller [grezije] *vi* to sizzle; (*RADIO*) to crackle

grève [grɛv] *nf* (*d'ouvriers*) strike; (*plage*) shore; **se mettre en/faire ~** to go on/be on strike; **~ de la faim** hunger strike; **~ du zèle** work-to-rule (*BRIT*), slowdown (*US*); **~ sauvage** wildcat strike

gréviste [grevist] *nm/f* striker

gribouiller [gribuje] *vt* to scribble, scrawl

grièvement [gʀijɛvmɑ̃] *adv* seriously

griffe [gʀif] *nf* claw; (*de couturier*) label; **griffer** *vt* to scratch

griffonner [gʀifɔne] *vt* to scribble

grignoter [gʀiɲɔte] *vt* (*personne*) to nibble at; (*souris*) to gnaw at ♦ *vi* to nibble

gril [gʀil] *nm* steak *ou* grill pan; **faire cuire au ~** to grill; **grillade** *nf* (*viande etc*) grill

grillage [gʀijaʒ] *nm* (*treillis*) wire netting; (*clôture*) wire fencing

grille [gʀij] *nf* (*clôture*) wire fence; (*portail*) (metal) gate; (*d'égout*) (metal) grate; (*fig*) grid

grille-pain [gʀijpɛ̃] *nm inv* toaster

griller [gʀije] *vt* (*pain*) to toast; (*viande*) to grill; (*fig: ampoule etc*) to blow; **faire ~** to toast; to grill; (*châtaignes*) to roast; **~ un feu rouge** to jump the lights

grillon [gʀijɔ̃] *nm* cricket

grimace [gʀimas] *nf* grimace; (*pour faire rire*): **faire des ~s** to pull *ou* make faces

grimper [gʀɛ̃pe] *vi, vt* to climb

grincer [gʀɛ̃se] *vi* (*objet métallique*) to grate; (*plancher, porte*) to creak; **~ des dents** to grind one's teeth

grincheux, -euse [gʀɛ̃ʃø, øz] *adj* grumpy

grippe [gʀip] *nf* flu, influenza; **grippé, e** *adj*: **être grippé** to have flu

gris, e [gʀi, gʀiz] *adj* grey; (*ivre*) tipsy

grisaille [gʀizaj] *nf* greyness, dullness

griser [gʀize] *vt* to intoxicate

grisonner [gʀizɔne] *vi* to be going grey

grisou [gʀizu] *nm* firedamp

grive [gʀiv] *nf* thrush

grivois, e [gʀivwa, waz] *adj* saucy

Groenland [gʀɔɛnlɑ̃d] *nm* Greenland

grogner [gʀɔɲe] *vi* to growl; (*fig*) to grumble; **grognon, ne** *adj* grumpy

groin [gʀwɛ̃] *nm* snout

grommeler [gʀɔm(ə)le] *vi* to mutter to o.s.

gronder [gʀɔ̃de] *vi* to rumble; (*fig: révolte*) to be brewing ♦ *vt* to scold; **se faire ~** to get a telling-off

groom [gʀum] *nm* bellboy

gros, se [gʀo, gʀos] *adj* big, large; (*obèse*) fat; (*travaux, dégâts*) extensive; (*épais*) thick; (*rhume, averse*) heavy ♦ *adv*: **risquer/gagner ~** to risk/win a lot ♦ *nm/f* fat man/woman ♦ *nm* (COMM): **le ~** the wholesale business; **prix de ~** wholesale price; **par ~ temps/grosse mer** in rough weather/heavy seas; **en ~** roughly; (COMM) wholesale; **~ lot** jackpot; **~ mot** coarse word; **~ plan** (PHOTO) close-up; **~ sel** cooking salt; **~ titre** headline; **~se caisse** big drum

groseille [gʀozɛj] *nf*: **~ (rouge/blanche)** red/white currant; **~ à maquereau** gooseberry

grosse [gʀos] *adj voir* **gros**; **grossesse** *nf* pregnancy; **grosseur** *nf* size; (*tumeur*) lump

grossier, -ière [gʀosje, jɛʀ] *adj* coarse; (*insolent*) rude; (*dessin*) rough; (*travail*) roughly done; (*imitation, instrument*) crude; (*évident: erreur*) gross; **grossièrement** *adv* (*sommairement*) roughly; (*vulgairement*) coarsely; **grossièretés** *nfpl*: **dire des grossièretés** to use coarse language

grossir [gʀosiʀ] *vi* (*personne*) to put on weight ♦ *vt* (*exagérer*) to exaggerate; (*au microscope*) to magnify; (*suj: vêtement*): **~ qn** to make sb look fatter

grossiste [gʀosist] *nm/f* wholesaler

grosso modo [gʀosomɔdo] *adv* roughly

grotesque [gʀɔtɛsk] *adj* (*extravagant*) grotesque; (*ridicule*) ludicrous

grotte [gʀɔt] *nf* cave

grouiller [gʀuje] *vi*: **~ de** to be swarming with; **se ~** (*fam*) ♦ *vi* to get a move on; **grouillant, e** *adj* swarming

groupe [gʀup] *nm* group; **le ~ des 7** Group of 7; **~ sanguin** blood group; **groupement** *nm* (*action*) grouping; (*groupe*) group; **grouper** *vt* to group; **se grouper** *vi* to gather

grue [gʀy] *nf* crane

grumeaux [gʀymo] *nmpl* lumps

guenilles [gənij] *nfpl* rags

guenon [gənɔ̃] *nf* female monkey

guépard [gepaʀ] *nm* cheetah

guêpe [gɛp] *nf* wasp

guêpier [gepje] *nm* (*fig*) trap

guère [gɛʀ] *adv* (*avec adjectif, adverbe*): **ne ... ~** hardly; (*avec verbe*): **ne ... ~** (*pas beaucoup*) *tournure négative +much*; (*pas souvent*) hardly ever; (*pas longtemps*) *tournure négative +(very)* long; **il n'y a ~ que/de** there's hardly anybody (*ou* anything) but/hardly any; **ce n'est ~ difficile** it's hardly difficult; **nous n'avons ~ de temps** we have hardly any time

guéridon [geʀidɔ̃] *nm* pedestal table

guérilla [geʀija] *nf* guerrilla warfare

guérillero [geʀijeʀo] *nm* guerrilla

guérir [geʀiʀ] *vt* (*personne, maladie*) to cure; (*membre, plaie*) to heal ♦ *vi* (*malade, maladie*) to be cured; (*blessure*) to heal; **guérison** *nf* (*de maladie*) curing; (*de membre, plaie*) healing; (*de malade*) recovery; **guérisseur, -euse** *nm/f* healer

guerre [gɛʀ] *nf* war; **~ civile** civil war; **en ~** at war; **faire la ~ à** to wage war against; **guerrier, -ière** *adj* warlike ♦ *nm/f* warrior

guet [gɛ] *nm*: **faire le ~** to be on the watch *ou* look-out; **guet-apens** [gɛtapɑ̃] *nm* ambush; **guetter** *vt* (*épier*) to watch (intently); (*attendre*) to watch (out) for; (*hostilement*) to be lying in wait for

gueule [gœl] *nf* (*d'animal*) mouth; (*: figure*) face; (*: bouche*) mouth; **ta ~!** (*fam*) shut up!; **~ de bois** (*fam*) hangover; **gueuler** (*fam*) *vi* to bawl; **gueuleton** (*fam*) *nm* blow-out

gui [gi] *nm* mistletoe

guichet [giʃɛ] *nm* (*de bureau, banque*) counter; **les ~s** (*à la gare, au théâtre*) the ticket office *sg*; **~ automatique** cash dispenser (*BRIT*), automatic telling machine (*US*)

guide [gid] *nm* guide ♦ *nf* (*éclaireuse*) girl guide; **guider** *vt* to guide

guidon [gidɔ̃] *nm* handlebars *pl*

guignol [giɲɔl] *nm* ≃ Punch and Judy show; (*fig*) clown

guillemets [gijmɛ] *nmpl*: **entre ~** in inverted commas

guillotiner [gijɔtine] *vt* to guillotine

guindé, e [gɛ̃de] *adj* (*personne, air*) stiff, starchy; (*style*) stilted

guirlande [giʀlɑ̃d] *nf* (*fleurs*) garland; **~ de Noël** tinsel garland; **~ lumineuse** string of fairy lights; **~ de papier** paper chain

guise [giz] *nf*: **à votre ~** as you wish *ou* please; **en ~ de** by way of

guitare [gitaʀ] *nf* guitar

gym [ʒim] *nf* (*exercices*) gym; **gymnase** *nm* gym(nasium); **gymnaste** *nm/f* gymnast; **gymnastique** *nf* gymnastics *sg*; (*au réveil etc*) keep-fit exercises *pl*

gynécologie [ʒinekɔlɔʒi] *nf* gynaecology; **gynécologique** *adj* gynaecological; **gynécologue** *nm/f* gynaecologist

H, h

habile [abil] *adj* skilful; (*malin*) clever; **habileté** [abilte] *nf* skill, skilfulness; cleverness

habillé, e [abije] *adj* dressed; (*chic*) dressy

habillement [abijmɑ̃] *nm* clothes *pl*

habiller [abije] *vt* to dress; (*fournir en vêtements*) to clothe; **s'~** *vi* to dress (o.s.); (*se déguiser, mettre des vêtements chic*) to dress up

habit [abi] *nm* outfit; **~s** *nmpl* (*vêtements*) clothes; **~ (de soirée)** evening dress; (*pour homme*) tails *pl*

habitant, e [abitɑ̃, ɑ̃t] *nm/f* inhabitant; (*d'une maison*) occupant; **loger chez l'~** to stay with the locals

habitation [abitasjɔ̃] *nf* house; **~s à loyer modéré** (block of) council flats

habiter [abite] *vt* to live in ♦ *vi*: **~ à/dans** to live in

habitude [abityd] *nf* habit; **avoir l'~ de faire** to be in the habit of doing; (*expérience*) to be used to doing; **d'~** usually; **comme d'~** as usual

habitué, e [abitɥe] *nm/f* (*de maison*) regular visitor; (*de café*) regular (customer)

habituel, le [abityɛl] *adj* usual

habituer [abitɥe] *vt*: **~ qn à** to get sb used to; **s'~ à** to get used to

'**hache** [ˈaʃ] *nf* axe

'**hacher** [ˈaʃe] *vt* (*viande*) to mince; (*persil*) to chop; '**hachis** *nm* mince *no pl*; **hachis Parmentier** ≃ shepherd's pie

'**hachisch** [ˈaʃiʃ] *nm* hashish

'**hachoir** [ˈaʃwaʀ] *nm* (*couteau*) chopper; (*appareil*) (meat) mincer; (*planche*) chopping board

'**hagard, e** [ˈagaʀ, aʀd] *adj* wild, distraught

'**haie** [ˈɛ] *nf* hedge; (*SPORT*) hurdle

'**haillons** [ˈajɔ̃] *nmpl* rags

'**haine** [ˈɛn] *nf* hatred

'**haïr** [ˈaiʀ] *vt* to detest, hate

'**hâlé, e** [ˈɑle] *adj* (sun)tanned, sunburnt

haleine [alɛn] *nf* breath; **hors d'~** out of breath; **tenir en ~** (*attention*) to hold spellbound; (*incertitude*) to keep in suspense; **de longue ~** long-term

'**haleter** [ˈalte] *vt* to pant

'**hall** [ˈol] *nm* hall

'**halle** [ˈal] *nf* (covered) market; **~s** *nfpl* (*d'une grande ville*) central food market *sg*

hallucinant, e [alysinɑ̃, ɑ̃t] *adj* staggering

hallucination [alysinasjɔ̃] *nf* hallucination

'**halte** [ˈalt] *nf* stop, break; (*endroit*) stopping place ♦ *excl* stop!; **faire ~** to stop

haltère [altɛʀ] *nm* dumbbell, barbell; **~s** *nmpl*: (**poids et**) **~s** (*activité*) weightlifting *sg*; **haltérophilie** *nf* weightlifting

'**hamac** [ˈamak] *nm* hammock

'**hamburger** [ˈɑ̃buʀgœʀ] *nm* hamburger

'**hameau, x** [ˈamo] *nm* hamlet

hameçon [amsɔ̃] *nm* (fish) hook

'**hanche** [ˈɑ̃ʃ] *nf* hip

'**hand-ball** [ˈɑ̃dbal] *nm* handball

'**handicapé, e** [ˈɑ̃dikape] *nm/f* physically (*ou* mentally) handicapped person; **~ moteur** spastic

'**hangar** [ˈɑ̃gaʀ] *nm* shed; (*AVIAT*) hangar

'**hanneton** [ˈantɔ̃] *nm* cockchafer

'**hanter** [ˈɑ̃te] *vt* to haunt

'**hantise** [ˈɑ̃tiz] *nf* obsessive fear

'**happer** [ˈape] *vt* to snatch; (*suj: train etc*) to hit

'**haras** [ˈaʀa] *nm* stud farm

'**harassant, e** [ˈaʀasɑ̃, ɑ̃t] *adj* exhausting

'**harcèlement** [ˈaʀsɛlmɑ̃] *nm* harassment; **~ sexuel** sexual harassment

'**harceler** [ˈaʀsəle] *vt* to harass; **~ qn de questions** to plague sb with questions

'**hardi, e** [ˈaʀdi] *adj* bold, daring

'**hareng** [ˈaʀɑ̃] *nm* herring

'**hargne** [ˈaʀɲ] *nf* aggressiveness; '**hargneux, -euse** *adj* aggressive

'**haricot** [ˈaʀiko] *nm* bean; **~ blanc** haricot bean; **~ vert** green bean; **~ rouge** kidney bean

harmonica [aʀmɔnika] *nm* mouth organ

harmonie [aʀmɔni] *nf* harmony; **harmonieux, -euse** *adj* harmonious; (*couleurs, couple*) well-matched

'**harnacher** [ˈaʀnaʃe] *vt* to harness

'**harnais** [ˈaʀnɛ] *nm* harness

'**harpe** [ˈaʀp] *nf* harp

'**harponner** [ˈaʀpɔne] *vt* to harpoon; (*fam*) to collar

'**hasard** [ˈazaʀ] *nm*: **le ~** chance, fate; **un ~** a coincidence; **au ~** (*aller*) aimlessly; (*choisir*) at random; **par ~** by chance; **à tout ~** (*en cas de besoin*) just in case; (*en espérant trouver ce qu'on cherche*) on the off chance (*BRIT*); '**hasarder** *vt* (*mot*) to venture; **se hasarder à faire** to risk doing

'**hâte** [ˈɑt] *nf* haste; **à la ~** hurriedly, hastily; **en ~** posthaste, with all possible speed; **avoir ~ de** to be eager *ou* anxious to; '**hâter** *vt* to hasten; **se hâter** *vi* to hurry; '**hâtif, -ive** *adj* (*travail*) hurried; (*décision, jugement*) hasty

'**hausse** [ˈos] *nf* rise, increase; **être en ~** to be going up; '**hausser** *vt* to raise; **hausser les épaules** to shrug (one's shoulders)

'**haut, e** [ˈo, ˈot] *adj* high; (*grand*) tall ♦ *adv* high ♦ *nm* top (part); **de 3 m de ~** 3 m high, 3 m in height; **des ~s et des bas** ups and downs; **en ~ lieu** in high places; **à ~e voix, (tout) ~** aloud, out loud; **du ~ de** from the top of; **de ~ en bas** from top to bottom; **plus ~** higher up, further up; (*dans un texte*) above; (*parler*) louder; **en ~** (*être/aller*) at/to the top; (*dans une maison*) upstairs; **en ~ de** at the top of

'**hautain, e** ['otɛ̃, ɛn] *adj* haughty

'**hautbois** ['obwa] *nm* oboe

'**haut-de-forme** ['odfɔrm] *nm* top hat

'**hauteur** ['otœr] *nf* height; **à la ~ de** (*accident*) near; (*fig: tâche, situation*) equal to; **à la ~** (*fig*) up to it

'**haut...:** '**haut-fourneau** *nm* blast *ou* smelting furnace; '**haut-le-cœur** *nm inv* retch, heave; '**haut-parleur** *nm* (loud)speaker

'**havre** ['ɑvr] *nm* haven

'**Haye** ['ɛ] *n*: **la ~** the Hague

'**hayon** ['ɛjɔ̃] *nm* hatchback

hebdo [ɛbdo] (*fam*) *nm* weekly

hebdomadaire [ɛbdɔmadɛr] *adj, nm* weekly

hébergement [ebɛrʒəmɑ̃] *nm* accommodation

héberger [ebɛrʒe] *vt* (*touristes*) to accommodate, lodge; (*amis*) to put up; (*réfugiés*) to take in

hébété, e [ebete] *adj* dazed

hébreu, x [ebrø] *adj m, nm* Hebrew

hécatombe [ekatɔ̃b] *nf* slaughter

hectare [ɛktar] *nm* hectare

'**hein** ['ɛ̃] *excl* eh?

'**hélas** ['elas] *excl* alas! ♦ *adv* unfortunately

'**héler** ['ele] *vt* to hail

hélice [elis] *nf* propeller

hélicoptère [elikɔptɛr] *nm* helicopter

helvétique [ɛlvetik] *adj* Swiss

hématome [ematɔm] *nm* nasty bruise

hémicycle [emisikl] *nm* (*POL*): **l'~** ≃ the benches (of the Commons) (*BRIT*), ≃ the floor (of the House of Representatives) (*US*)

hémisphère [emisfɛr] *nm*: **l'~ nord/sud** the northern/southern hemisphere

hémorragie [emɔraʒi] *nf* bleeding *no pl*, haemorrhage

hémorroïdes [emɔrɔid] *nfpl* piles, haemorrhoids

'**hennir** ['enir] *vi* to neigh, whinny; '**hennissement** *nm* neigh, whinny

hépatite [epatit] *nf* hepatitis

herbe [ɛrb] *nf* grass; (*CULIN, MÉD*) herb; **~s de Provence** mixed herbs; **en ~** unripe; (*fig*) budding; **herbicide** *nm* weed-killer; **herboriste** *nm/f* herbalist

'**hère** ['ɛr] *nm*: **pauvre ~** poor wretch

héréditaire [erediter] *adj* hereditary

'**hérisser** ['erise] *vt*: **~ qn** (*fig*) to ruffle sb; **se ~** *vi* to bristle, bristle up; '**hérisson** *nm* hedgehog

héritage [eritaʒ] *nm* inheritance; (*coutumes, système*) heritage, legacy

hériter [erite] *vi*: **~ de qch (de qn)** to inherit sth (from sb); **héritier, -ière** [eritje, jɛr] *nm/f* heir(-ess)

hermétique [ɛrmetik] *adj* airtight; watertight; (*fig: obscur*) abstruse; (: *impénétrable*) impenetrable

hermine [ɛrmin] *nf* ermine

'**hernie** ['ɛrni] *nf* hernia

héroïne [erɔin] *nf* heroine; (*drogue*) heroin

héroïque [erɔik] *adj* heroic

'**héron** ['erɔ̃] *nm* heron

'**héros** ['ero] *nm* hero

hésitant, e [ezitɑ̃, ɑ̃t] *adj* hesitant

hésitation [ezitasjɔ̃] *nf* hesitation

hésiter [ezite] *vi*: **~ (à faire)** to hesitate (to do)

hétéroclite [eterɔklit] *adj* heterogeneous; (*objets*) sundry

hétérogène [eterɔʒɛn] *adj* heterogeneous

hétérosexuel, le [eterɔsɛkɥɛl] *adj* heterosexual

'**hêtre** ['ɛtr] *nm* beech

heure [œr] *nf* hour; (*SCOL*) period; (*moment*) time; **c'est l'~** it's time; **quelle ~ est-il?** what time is it?; **2 ~s (du matin)** 2 o'clock (in the morning); **être à l'~** to be on time; (*montre*) to be right; **mettre à l'~** to set right; **à une ~ avancée (de la nuit)** at a late hour of the night; **à toute ~** at any time; **24 ~s sur 24** round the clock, 24 hours a day; **à l'~ qu'il est** at this time (of day); by now; **sur l'~** at once; ~ **de pointe** rush hour; (*téléphone*) peak period; ~ **d'affluence** rush hour; **~s creuses** slack periods; (*pour électricité, téléphone etc*) off-peak periods; **~s supplémentaires** overtime *sg*

heureusement [œʀøzmɑ̃] *adv* (*par bonheur*) fortunately, luckily

heureux, -euse [œʀø, øz] *adj* happy; (*chanceux*) lucky, fortunate

'**heurter** ['œʀte] *vt* (*mur*) to strike, hit; (*personne*) to collide with; **se ~ à** *vt* (*fig*) to come up against

'**heurts** ['œʀ] *nmpl* (*fig*) clashes

hexagone [ɛgzagɔn] *nm* hexagon; (*la France*) France (*because of its shape*)

hiberner [ibɛʀne] *vi* to hibernate

'**hibou, x** ['ibu] *nm* owl

'**hideux, -euse** ['idø, øz] *adj* hideous

hier [jɛʀ] *adv* yesterday; ~ **soir** last night, yesterday evening; **toute la journée d'~** all day yesterday; **toute la matinée d'~** all yesterday morning

'**hiérarchie** ['jeʀaʀʃi] *nf* hierarchy

'**hi-fi** ['ifi] *adj inv* hi-fi ♦ *nf* hi-fi

hilare [ilaʀ] *adj* mirthful

hindou, e [ɛ̃du] *adj* Hindu ♦ *nm/f*: **H~, e** Hindu

hippique [ipik] *adj* equestrian, horse *cpd*; **un club ~** a riding centre; **un concours ~** a horse show; **hippisme** *nm* (horse)riding

hippodrome [ipɔdʀom] *nm* racecourse

hippopotame [ipɔpɔtam] *nm* hippopotamus

hirondelle [iʀɔ̃dɛl] *nf* swallow

hirsute [iʀsyt] *adj* (*personne*) shaggy-haired; (*barbe*) shaggy; (*tête*) tousled

'**hisser** ['ise] *vt* to hoist, haul up; **se ~** *vi* to heave o.s. up

histoire [istwaʀ] *nf* (*science, événements*) history; (*anecdote, récit, mensonge*) story; (*affaire*) business *no pl*; **~s** *nfpl* (*chichis*) fuss *no pl*; (*ennuis*) trouble *sg*; **historique** *adj* historical; (*important*) historic

'**hit-parade** ['itpaʀad] *nm*: **le ~-~** the charts

hiver [ivɛʀ] *nm* winter; **hivernal, e, -aux** *adj* winter *cpd*; (*glacial*) wintry; **hiverner** *vi* to winter

HLM *nm ou f* (= habitation à loyer modéré) council flat; **des HLM** council housing

'**hobby** ['ɔbi] *nm* hobby

'**hocher** ['ɔʃe] *vt*: ~ **la tête** to nod; (*signe négatif ou dubitatif*) to shake one's head

'**hochet** ['ɔʃɛ] *nm* rattle

'**hockey** ['ɔkɛ] *nm*: ~ **(sur glace / gazon)** (ice/field) hockey

'**hold-up** ['ɔldœp] *nm inv* hold-up

'**hollandais, e** ['ɔlɑ̃dɛ, ɛz] *adj* Dutch ♦ *nm* (*LING*) Dutch ♦ *nm/f*: **H~, e** Dutchman(-woman); **les H~** the Dutch

'**Hollande** ['ɔlɑ̃d] *nf*: **la ~** Holland

'**homard** ['ɔmaʀ] *nm* lobster

homéopathique [ɔmeɔpatik] *adj* homoeopathic

homicide [ɔmisid] *nm* murder; ~ **involontaire** manslaughter

hommage [ɔmaʒ] *nm* tribute; **~s** *nmpl*: **présenter ses ~s** to pay one's respects; **rendre ~ à** to pay tribute *ou* homage to

homme [ɔm] *nm* man; ~ **d'affaires** businessman; ~ **d'État** statesman; ~ **de main** hired man; ~ **de paille** stooge; ~ **politique** politician; **homme-grenouille** *nm* frogman

homo...: **homogène** *adj* homogeneous; **homologue** *nm/f* counterpart; **homologué, e** *adj* (*SPORT*) ratified; (*tarif*) authorized; **homonyme** *nm* (*LING*) homonym; (*d'une personne*) namesake; **homosexuel, le** *adj* homosexual

'**Hongrie** ['ɔ̃gʀi] *nf*: **la ~** Hungary; '**hongrois, e** *adj* Hungarian ♦ *nm/f*: **Hongrois, e** Hungarian ♦ *nm* (*LING*) Hungarian

honnête [ɔnɛt] *adj* (*intègre*) honest; (*juste, satisfaisant*) fair; **honnêtement** *adv* honestly; **honnêteté** *nf* honesty

honneur [ɔnœʀ] *nm* honour; (*mérite*) credit; **en l'~ de** in honour of; (*événement*) on the occasion of; **faire ~ à** *(engagements)* to honour; *(famille)* to be a credit to; *(fig: repas etc)* to do justice to

honorable [ɔnɔʀabl] *adj* worthy, honourable; *(suffisant)* decent

honoraire [ɔnɔʀɛʀ] *adj* honorary; **professeur ~** professor emeritus; **honoraires** [ɔnɔʀɛʀ] *nmpl* fees *pl*

honorer [ɔnɔʀe] *vt* to honour; *(estimer)* to hold in high regard; *(faire honneur à)* to do credit to; **honorifique** [ɔnɔʀifik] *adj* honorary

'honte ['ɔt] *nf* shame; **avoir ~ de** to be ashamed of; **faire ~ à qn** to make sb (feel) ashamed; **'honteux, -euse** *adj* ashamed; *(conduite, acte)* shameful

hôpital, -aux [ɔpital, o] *nm* hospital

'hoquet ['ɔkɛ] *nm*: **avoir le ~** to have (the) hiccoughs; **'hoqueter** *vi* to hiccough

horaire [ɔʀɛʀ] *adj* hourly ♦ *nm* timetable, schedule; **~s** *nmpl (d'employé)* hours; **~ souple** flexitime

horizon [ɔʀizɔ] *nm* horizon

horizontal, e, -aux [ɔʀizɔtal, o] *adj* horizontal

horloge [ɔʀlɔʒ] *nf* clock; **l'~ parlante** the speaking clock; **horloger, -ère** *nm/f* watchmaker; clockmaker

'hormis ['ɔʀmi] *prép* save

horoscope [ɔʀɔskɔp] *nm* horoscope

horreur [ɔʀœʀ] *nf* horror; **quelle ~!** how awful!; **avoir ~ de** to loathe *ou* detest; **horrible** *adj* horrible; **horrifier** *vt* to horrify

horripiler [ɔʀipile] *vt* to exasperate

'hors ['ɔʀ] *prép*: **~ de** out of; **~ pair** outstanding; **~ de propos** inopportune; **être ~ de soi** to be beside o.s.; **~ d'usage** out of service; **'hors-bord** *nm inv* speedboat *(with outboard motor)*; **'hors-d'œuvre** *nm inv* hors d'œuvre; **'hors-jeu** *nm inv* offside; **'hors-la-loi** *nm inv* outlaw; **'hors-taxe** *adj (boutique, articles)* duty-free

hortensia [ɔʀtɑsja] *nm* hydrangea

hospice [ɔspis] *nm (de vieillards)* home

hospitalier, -ière [ɔspitalje, jɛʀ] *adj (accueillant)* hospitable; *(MÉD: service, centre)* hospital *cpd*

hospitaliser [ɔspitalize] *vt* to take/send to hospital, hospitalize

hospitalité [ɔspitalite] *nf* hospitality

hostie [ɔsti] *nf* host *(REL)*

hostile [ɔstil] *adj* hostile; **hostilité** *nf* hostility

hosto [ɔsto] *(fam) nm* hospital

hôte [ot] *nm (maître de maison)* host; *(invité)* guest

hôtel [otel] *nm* hotel; **aller à l'~** to stay in a hotel; **~ de ville** town hall; **~ (particulier)** (private) mansion; **hôtelier, -ière** *adj* hotel *cpd* ♦ *nm/f* hotelier; **hôtellerie** *nf* hotel business

hôtesse [otes] *nf* hostess; **~ de l'air** air stewardess; **~ (d'accueil)** receptionist

'hotte ['ɔt] *nf (panier)* basket *(carried on the back)*; **~ aspirante** cooker hood

'houblon ['ubl] *nm (BOT)* hop; *(pour la bière)* hops *pl*

'houille ['uj] *nf* coal; **~ blanche** hydro-electric power

'houle ['ul] *nf* swell; **'houleux, -euse** *adj* stormy

'houligan ['uligɑ] *nm* hooligan

'hourra ['uʀa] *excl* hurrah!

'houspiller ['uspije] *vt* to scold

'housse ['us] *nf* cover

'houx ['u] *nm* holly

HTML *sigle m* HTML

'hublot ['yblo] *nm* porthole

'huche ['yʃ] *nf*: **~ à pain** bread bin

'huer ['ɥe] *vt* to boo

huile [ɥil] *nf* oil; **~ solaire** suntan oil; **huiler** *vt* to oil; **huileux, -euse** *adj* oily

huis [ɥi] *nm*: **à ~ clos** in camera

huissier [ɥisje] *nm* usher; *(JUR)* ≈ bailiff

'huit ['ɥi(t)] *num* eight; **samedi en ~** a week on Saturday; **dans ~ jours** in a week; **'huitaine** *nf*: **une huitaine (de jours)** a week or so; **'huitième** *num* eighth

huître [ɥitʀ] *nf* oyster

humain, e [ymɛ̃, ɛn] *adj* human; *(compatissant)* humane ♦ *nm* human (being); **humanitaire** *adj* humanitarian; **humanité** *nf* humanity

humble [œbl] *adj* humble

humecter [ymɛkte] *vt* to dampen

'humer ['yme] *vt (plat)* to smell; *(parfum)* to inhale

humeur [ymœR] *nf* mood; **de bonne/mauvaise ~** in a good/bad mood

humide [ymid] *adj* damp; *(main, yeux)* moist; *(climat, chaleur)* humid; *(saison, route)* wet

humilier [ymilje] *vt* to humiliate

humilité [ymilite] *nf* humility, humbleness

humoristique [ymɔristik] *adj* humorous

humour [ymuR] *nm* humour; **avoir de l'~** to have a sense of humour; **~ noir** black humour

'huppé, e ['ype] *(fam) adj* posh

'hurlement ['yRləmɑ̃] *nm* howling *no pl*, howl, yelling *no pl*, yell

'hurler ['yRle] *vi* to howl, yell

hurluberlu [yRlybɛRly] *(péj) nm* crank

'hutte ['yt] *nf* hut

hybride [ibRid] *adj, nm* hybrid

hydratant, e [idRatɑ̃, ɑ̃t] *adj (crème)* moisturizing

hydraulique [idRolik] *adj* hydraulic

hydravion [idRavjɔ̃] *nm* seaplane

hydrogène [idRɔʒen] *nm* hydrogen

hydroglisseur [idRɔglisœR] *nm* hydroplane

hyène [jɛn] *nf* hyena

hygiénique [iʒenik] *adj* hygienic

hymne [imn] *nm* hymn; **~ national** national anthem

hypermarché [ipɛRmaRʃe] *nm* hypermarket

hypermétrope [ipɛRmetRɔp] *adj* longsighted

hypertension [ipɛRtɑ̃sjɔ̃] *nf* high blood pressure

hypnose [ipnoz] *nf* hypnosis; **hypnotiser** *vt* to hypnotize; **hypnotiseur** *nm* hypnotist

hypocrisie [ipɔkRizi] *nf* hypocrisy; **hypocrite** *adj* hypocritical

hypothèque [ipɔtek] *nf* mortgage

hypothèse [ipɔtez] *nf* hypothesis

hystérique [isteRik] *adj* hysterical

I, i

iceberg [ajsbɛRg] *nm* iceberg

ici [isi] *adv* here; **jusqu'~** as far as this; *(temps)* so far; **d'~ demain** by tomorrow; **d'~ là** by then, in the meantime; **d'~ peu** before long

icône [ikon] *nf* icon

idéal, e, -aux [ideal, o] *adj* ideal ♦ *nm* ideal; **idéaliste** *adj* idealistic ♦ *nm/f* idealist

idée [ide] *nf* idea; **avoir dans l'~ que** to have an idea that; **~ fixe** obsession; **~ reçue** generally accepted idea; **~s noires** black *ou* dark thoughts

identifier [idɑ̃tifje] *vt* to identify; **s'~ à** *(héros etc)* to identify with

identique [idɑ̃tik] *adj*: **~ (à)** identical (to)

identité [idɑ̃tite] *nf* identity

idiot, e [idjo, idjɔt] *adj* idiotic ♦ *nm/f* idiot; **idiotie** *nf* idiotic thing

idole [idɔl] *nf* idol

if [if] *nm* yew

igloo [iglu] *nm* igloo

ignare [iɲaR] *adj* ignorant

ignifugé, e [iɲifyʒe] *adj* fireproof

ignoble [iɲɔbl] *adj* vile

ignorant, e [iɲɔRɑ̃, ɑ̃t] *adj* ignorant

ignorer [iɲɔRe] *vt* not to know; *(personne)* to ignore

il [il] *pron* he; *(animal, chose, en tournure impersonnelle)* it; **~s** they; *voir aussi* **avoir**

île [il] *nf* island; **l'~ Maurice** Mauritius; **les ~s anglo-normandes** the Channel Islands; **les ~s Britanniques** the British Isles

illégal, e, -aux [i(l)legal, o] *adj* illegal

illégitime [i(l)leʒitim] *adj* illegitimate

illettré, e [i(l)letRe] *adj, nm/f* illiterate

illimité, e [i(l)limite] *adj* unlimited

illisible [i(l)lizibl] *adj* illegible; (*roman*) unreadable

illogique [i(l)lɔʒik] *adj* illogical

illumination [i(l)lyminasjɔ̃] *nf* illumination; (*idée*) flash of inspiration

illuminer [i(l)lymine] *vt* to light up; (*monument, rue: pour une fête*) to illuminate; (*: au moyen de projecteurs*) to floodlight

illusion [i(l)lyzjɔ̃] *nf* illusion; **se faire des ~s** to delude o.s.; **faire ~** to delude *ou* fool people; **illusionniste** *nm/f* conjuror

illustration [i(l)lystʀasjɔ̃] *nf* illustration

illustre [i(l)lystʀ] *adj* illustrious

illustré, e [i(l)lystʀe] *adj* illustrated ♦ *nm* comic

illustrer [i(l)lystʀe] *vt* to illustrate; **s'~** to become famous, win fame

îlot [ilo] *nm* small island, islet

ils [il] *pron voir* **il**

image [imaʒ] *nf* (*gén*) picture; (*métaphore*) image; **~ de marque** brand image; (*fig*) public image; **imagé, e** *adj* (*texte*) full of imagery; (*langage*) colourful

imaginaire [imaʒinɛʀ] *adj* imaginary

imagination [imaʒinasjɔ̃] *nf* imagination; **avoir de l'~** to be imaginative

imaginer [imaʒine] *vt* to imagine; (*inventer: expédient*) to devise, think up; **s'~** *vt* (*se figurer: scène etc*) to imagine, picture; **s'~ que** to imagine that

imbattable [ɛ̃batabl] *adj* unbeatable

imbécile [ɛ̃besil] *adj* idiotic ♦ *nm/f* idiot; **imbécillité** *nf* idiocy; (*action*) idiotic thing; (*film, livre, propos*) rubbish

imbiber [ɛ̃bibe] *vt* to soak; **s'~ de** to become saturated with

imbu, e [ɛ̃by] *adj*: **~ de** full of

imbuvable [ɛ̃byvabl] *adj* undrinkable; (*personne: fam*) unbearable

imitateur, -trice [imitatœʀ, tʀis] *nm/f* (*gén*) imitator; (*MUSIC-HALL*) impersonator

imitation [imitasjɔ̃] *nf* imitation; (*de personnalité*) impersonation

imiter [imite] *vt* to imitate; (*contrefaire*) to forge; (*ressembler à*) to look like

immaculé, e [imakyle] *adj* (*linge, surface, réputation*) spotless; (*blancheur*) immaculate

immangeable [ɛ̃mɑ̃ʒabl] *adj* inedible

immatriculation [imatʀikylasjɔ̃] *nf* registration

immatriculer [imatʀikyle] *vt* to register; **faire/se faire ~** to register

immédiat, e [imedja, jat] *adj* immediate ♦ *nm*: **dans l'~** for the time being; **immédiatement** *adv* immediately

immense [i(m)mɑ̃s] *adj* immense

immerger [imɛʀʒe] *vt* to immerse, submerge

immeuble [imœbl] *nm* building; (*à usage d'habitation*) block of flats

immigration [imigʀasjɔ̃] *nf* immigration

immigré, e [imigʀe] *nm/f* immigrant

imminent, e [iminɑ̃, ɑ̃t] *adj* imminent

immiscer [imise]: **s'~** *vi*: **s'~ dans** to interfere in *ou* with

immobile [i(m)mɔbil] *adj* still, motionless

immobilier, -ière [imɔbilje, jɛʀ] *adj* property *cpd* ♦ *nm*: **l'~** the property business

immobiliser [imɔbilize] *vt* (*gén*) to immobilize; (*circulation, véhicule, affaires*) to bring to a standstill; **s'~** (*personne*) to stand still; (*machine, véhicule*) to come to a halt

immonde [i(m)mɔ̃d] *adj* foul

immoral, e, -aux [i(m)mɔʀal, o] *adj* immoral

immortel, le [imɔʀtɛl] *adj* immortal

immuable [imɥabl] *adj* unchanging

immunisé, e [im(m)ynize] *adj*: **~ contre** immune to

immunité [imynite] *nf* immunity

impact [ɛ̃pakt] *nm* impact

impair, e [ɛ̃pɛʀ] *adj* odd ♦ *nm* faux pas, blunder

impardonnable [ɛ̃paʀdɔnabl] *adj* unpardonable, unforgivable

imparfait, e [ɛ̃paʀfɛ, ɛt] *adj* imperfect

impartial, e, -aux [ɛ̃paʀsjal, jo] *adj* impartial, unbiased

impasse [ɛ̃pɑs] *nf* dead end, cul-de-sac;

(*fig*) deadlock

impassible [ɛ̃pasibl] *adj* impassive

impatience [ɛ̃pasjɑ̃s] *nf* impatience

impatient, e [ɛ̃pasjɑ̃, jɑ̃t] *adj* impatient; **impatienter: s'impatienter** *vi* to get impatient

impeccable [ɛ̃pekabl] *adj* (*parfait*) perfect; (*propre*) impeccable; (*fam*) smashing

impensable [ɛ̃pɑ̃sabl] *adj* (*événement hypothétique*) unthinkable; (*événement qui a eu lieu*) unbelievable

imper [ɛ̃pɛʀ] (*fam*) *nm* raincoat

impératif, -ive [ɛ̃peʀatif, iv] *adj* imperative ♦ *nm* (*LING*) imperative; **~s** *nmpl* (*exigences: d'une fonction, d'une charge*) requirements; (*: de la mode*) demands

impératrice [ɛ̃peʀatʀis] *nf* empress

imperceptible [ɛ̃pɛʀsɛptibl] *adj* imperceptible

impérial, e, -aux [ɛ̃peʀjal, jo] *adj* imperial; **impériale** *nf* top deck

impérieux, -euse [ɛ̃peʀjø, jøz] *adj* (*caractère, ton*) imperious; (*obligation, besoin*) pressing, urgent

impérissable [ɛ̃peʀisabl] *adj* undying

imperméable [ɛ̃pɛʀmeabl] *adj* waterproof; (*fig*): **~ à** impervious to ♦ *nm* raincoat

impertinent, e [ɛ̃pɛʀtinɑ̃, ɑ̃t] *adj* impertinent

imperturbable [ɛ̃pɛʀtyʀbabl] *adj* (*personne, caractère*) unperturbable; (*sang-froid, gaieté, sérieux*) unshakeable

impétueux, -euse [ɛ̃petɥø, øz] *adj* impetuous

impitoyable [ɛ̃pitwajabl] *adj* pitiless, merciless

implanter [ɛ̃plɑ̃te]: **s'~** *vi* to be set up

impliquer [ɛ̃plike] *vt* to imply; **~ qn (dans)** to implicate sb (in)

impoli, e [ɛ̃pɔli] *adj* impolite, rude

impopulaire [ɛ̃pɔpylɛʀ] *adj* unpopular

importance [ɛ̃pɔʀtɑ̃s] *nf* importance; **sans ~** unimportant

important, e [ɛ̃pɔʀtɑ̃, ɑ̃t] *adj* important; (*en quantité: somme, retard*) considerable,

sizeable; (*: dégâts*) extensive; (*péj: airs, ton*) self-important ♦ *nm*: **l'~** the important thing

importateur, -trice [ɛ̃pɔʀtatœʀ, tʀis] *nm/f* importer

importation [ɛ̃pɔʀtasjɔ̃] *nf* importation; (*produit*) import

importer [ɛ̃pɔʀte] *vt* (*COMM*) to import; (*maladies, plantes*) to introduce ♦ *vi* (*être important*) to matter; **il importe qu'il fasse** it is important that he should do; **peu m'importe** (*je n'ai pas de préférence*) I don't mind; (*je m'en moque*) I don't care; **peu importe (que)** it doesn't matter (if); *voir aussi* **n'importe**

importun, e [ɛ̃pɔʀtœ̃, yn] *adj* irksome, importunate; (*arrivée, visite*) inopportune, ill-timed ♦ *nm* intruder; **importuner** *vt* to bother

imposable [ɛ̃pozabl] *adj* taxable

imposant, e [ɛ̃pozɑ̃, ɑ̃t] *adj* imposing

imposer [ɛ̃poze] *vt* (*taxer*) to tax; **s'~** (*être nécessaire*) to be imperative; **~ qch à qn** to impose sth on sb; **en ~ à** to impress; **s'~ comme** to emerge as; **s'~ par** to win recognition through

impossibilité [ɛ̃pɔsibilite] *nf* impossibility; **être dans l'~ de faire qch** to be unable to do sth

impossible [ɛ̃pɔsibl] *adj* impossible; **il m'est ~ de le faire** it is impossible for me to do it, I can't possibly do it; **faire l'~** to do one's utmost

imposteur [ɛ̃pɔstœʀ] *nm* impostor

impôt [ɛ̃po] *nm* tax; **~s** *nmpl* (*contributions*) (income) tax *sg*; **payer 100 euros d'~s** to pay 100 euros in tax; **~ foncier** land tax; **~ sur le chiffre d'affaires** corporation (*BRIT*) *ou* corporate (*US*) tax; **~ sur le revenu** income tax

impotent, e [ɛ̃pɔtɑ̃, ɑ̃t] *adj* disabled

impraticable [ɛ̃pʀatikabl] *adj* (*projet*) impracticable, unworkable; (*piste*) impassable

imprécis, e [ɛ̃pʀesi, iz] *adj* imprecise

imprégner [ɛ̃pʀeɲe] *vt* (*tissu*) to impregnate; (*lieu, air*) to fill; **s'~ de** (*fig*) to absorb

imprenable [ɛpʀənabl] *adj* (*forteresse*) impregnable; **vue ~** unimpeded outlook

imprésario [ɛpʀesaʀjo] *nm* manager

impression [ɛpʀesjɔ̃] *nf* impression; (*d'un ouvrage, tissu*) printing; **faire bonne ~** to make a good impression; **impressionnant, e** *adj* (*imposant*) impressive; (*bouleversant*) upsetting; **impressionner** *vt* (*frapper*) to impress; (*bouleverser*) to upset

imprévisible [ɛpʀevizibl] *adj* unforeseeable

imprévoyant, e [ɛpʀevwajɑ̃, ɑ̃t] *adj* lacking in foresight; (*en matière d'argent*) improvident

imprévu, e [ɛpʀevy] *adj* unforeseen, unexpected ♦ *nm* (*incident*) unexpected incident; **des vacances pleines d'~** holidays full of surprises; **en cas d'~** if anything unexpected happens; **sauf ~** unless anything unexpected crops up

imprimante [ɛpʀimɑ̃t] *nf* printer

imprimé [ɛpʀime] *nm* (*formulaire*) printed form; (*POSTES*) printed matter *no pl*; (*tissu*) printed fabric; **~ à fleur** floral print

imprimer [ɛpʀime] *vt* to print; (*publier*) to publish; **imprimerie** *nf* printing; (*établissement*) printing works *sg*; **imprimeur** *nm* printer

impromptu, e [ɛpʀɔ̃pty] *adj* (*repas, discours*) impromptu; (*départ*) sudden; (*visite*) surprise

impropre [ɛpʀɔpʀ] *adj* inappropriate; **~ à** unfit for

improviser [ɛpʀɔvize] *vt, vi* to improvise

improviste [ɛpʀɔvist]: **à l'~** *adv* unexpectedly, without warning

imprudence [ɛpʀydɑ̃s] *nf* (*d'une personne, d'une action*) carelessness *no pl*; (*d'une remarque*) imprudence *no pl*; **commettre une ~** to do something foolish

imprudent, e [ɛpʀydɑ̃, ɑ̃t] *adj* (*conducteur, geste, action*) careless; (*remarque*) unwise, imprudent; (*projet*) foolhardy

impudent, e [ɛpydɑ̃, ɑ̃t] *adj* impudent

impudique [ɛpydik] *adj* shameless

impuissant, e [ɛpɥisɑ̃, ɑ̃t] *adj* helpless; (*sans effet*) ineffectual; (*sexuellement*) impotent

impulsif, -ive [ɛpylsif, iv] *adj* impulsive

impulsion [ɛpylsjɔ̃] *nf* (*ÉLEC, instinct*) impulse; (*élan, influence*) impetus

impunément [ɛpynemɑ̃] *adv* with impunity

inabordable [inabɔʀdabl] *adj* (*cher*) prohibitive

inacceptable [inaksɛptabl] *adj* unacceptable

inaccessible [inaksesibl] *adj* inaccessible

inachevé, e [inaʃ(ə)ve] *adj* unfinished

inactif, -ive [inaktif, iv] *adj* inactive; (*remède*) ineffective; (*BOURSE: marché*) slack ♦ *nm*: **les ~s** the non-working population

inadapté, e [inadapte] *adj* (*gén*): **~ à** not adapted to, unsuited to; (*PSYCH*) maladjusted

inadéquat, e [inadekwa(t), kwat] *adj* inadequate

inadmissible [inadmisibl] *adj* inadmissible

inadvertance [inadvɛʀtɑ̃s]: **par ~** *adv* inadvertently

inaltérable [inalteʀabl] *adj* (*matière*) stable; (*fig*) unfailing; **~ à** unaffected by

inanimé, e [inanime] *adj* (*matière*) inanimate; (*évanoui*) unconscious; (*sans vie*) lifeless

inanition [inanisjɔ̃] *nf*: **tomber d'~** to faint with hunger (and exhaustion)

inaperçu, e [inapɛʀsy] *adj*: **passer ~** to go unnoticed

inapte [inapt] *adj*: **~ à** incapable of; (*MIL*) unfit for

inattaquable [inatakabl] *adj* (*texte, preuve*) irrefutable

inattendu, e [inatɑ̃dy] *adj* unexpected

inattentif, -ive [inatɑ̃tif, iv] *adj* inattentive; **~ à** (*dangers, détails*) heedless of; **inattention** *nf*: **faute d'inattention** careless mistake

inauguration [inogyʀasjɔ̃] *nf* inauguration

inaugurer [inogyʀe] *vt* (*monument*) to unveil; (exposition, usine) to open; (fig) to inaugurate

inavouable [inavwabl] adj shameful; (bénéfices) undisclosable

incalculable [ɛ̃kalkylabl] adj incalculable

incandescence [ɛ̃kɑ̃desɑ̃s] nf: **porter à ~** to heat white-hot

incapable [ɛ̃kapabl] adj incapable; **~ de faire** incapable of doing; (empêché) unable to do

incapacité [ɛ̃kapasite] nf (incompétence) incapability; (impossibilité) incapacity; **dans l'~ de faire** unable to do

incarcérer [ɛ̃karsere] vt to incarcerate, imprison

incarné, e [ɛ̃karne] adj (ongle) ingrown

incarner [ɛ̃karne] vt to embody, personify; (THÉÂTRE) to play

incassable [ɛ̃kasabl] adj unbreakable

incendiaire [ɛ̃sɑ̃djɛr] adj incendiary; (fig: discours) inflammatory

incendie [ɛ̃sɑ̃di] nm fire; **~ criminel** arson no pl; **~ de forêt** forest fire; **incendier** vt (mettre le feu à) to set fire to, set alight; (brûler complètement) to burn down; **se faire incendier** (fam) to get a rocket

incertain, e [ɛ̃sɛrtɛ̃, ɛn] adj uncertain; (temps) unsettled; (imprécis: contours) indistinct, blurred; **incertitude** nf uncertainty

incessamment [ɛ̃sesamɑ̃] adv very shortly

incident [ɛ̃sidɑ̃, ɑ̃t] nm incident; **~ de parcours** minor hitch ou setback; **~ technique** technical difficulties pl

incinérer [ɛ̃sinere] vt (ordures) to incinerate; (mort) to cremate

incisive [ɛ̃siziv] nf incisor

inciter [ɛ̃site] vt: **~ qn à (faire) qch** to encourage sb to do sth; (à la révolte etc) to incite sb to do sth

inclinable [ɛ̃klinabl] adj: **siège à dossier ~** reclining seat

inclinaison [ɛ̃klinɛzɔ̃] nf (déclivité: d'une route etc) incline; (: d'un toit) slope; (état penché) tilt

inclination [ɛ̃klinasjɔ̃] nf (penchant) inclination; **~ de (la) tête** nod (of the head); **~ (de buste)** bow

incliner [ɛ̃kline] vt (pencher) to tilt ♦ vi: **~ à qch/à faire** to incline towards sth/doing; **s'~ (devant)** to bow (before); (céder) to give in ou yield (to); **~ la tête** to give a slight bow

inclure [ɛ̃klyr] vt to include; (joindre à un envoi) to enclose; **jusqu'au 10 mars inclus** until 10th March inclusive

incognito [ɛ̃kɔɲito] adv incognito ♦ nm: **garder l'~** to remain incognito

incohérent, e [ɛ̃kɔerɑ̃, ɑ̃t] adj (comportement) inconsistent; (geste, langage, texte) incoherent

incollable [ɛ̃kɔlabl] adj (riz) non-stick; **il est ~** (fam) he's got all the answers

incolore [ɛ̃kɔlɔr] adj colourless

incommoder [ɛ̃kɔmɔde] vt (chaleur, odeur): **~ qn** to bother sb

incomparable [ɛ̃kɔ̃parabl] adj incomparable

incompatible [ɛ̃kɔ̃patibl] adj incompatible

incompétent, e [ɛ̃kɔ̃petɑ̃, ɑ̃t] adj incompetent

incomplet, -ète [ɛ̃kɔ̃plɛ, ɛt] adj incomplete

incompréhensible [ɛ̃kɔ̃preɑ̃sibl] adj incomprehensible

incompris, e [ɛ̃kɔ̃pri, iz] adj misunderstood

inconcevable [ɛ̃kɔ̃s(ə)vabl] adj inconceivable

inconciliable [ɛ̃kɔ̃siljabl] adj irreconcilable

inconditionnel, le [ɛ̃kɔ̃disjɔnɛl] adj unconditional; (partisan) unquestioning ♦ nm/f (d'un homme politique) ardent supporter; (d'un écrivain, d'un chanteur) ardent admirer; (d'une activité) fanatic

inconfort [ɛ̃kɔ̃fɔr] nm discomfort; **inconfortable** adj uncomfortable

incongru, e [ɛ̃kɔ̃gry] adj unseemly

inconnu, e [ɛ̃kɔny] adj unknown ♦ nm/f stranger ♦ nm: **l'~** the unknown; **inconnue** nf unknown factor

inconsciemment [ɛ̃kɔ̃sjamɑ̃] adv unconsciously

inconscient, e [ɛ̃kɔ̃sjɑ̃, jɑ̃t] *adj* unconscious; (*irréfléchi*) thoughtless, reckless; (*sentiment*) subconscious ♦ *nm* (*PSYCH*): **l'~** the unconscious; **~ de** unaware of

inconsidéré, e [ɛ̃kɔ̃sidere] *adj* ill-considered

inconsistant, e [ɛ̃kɔ̃sistɑ̃, ɑ̃t] *adj* (*fig*) flimsy, weak

inconsolable [ɛ̃kɔ̃sɔlabl] *adj* inconsolable

incontestable [ɛ̃kɔ̃tɛstabl] *adj* indisputable

incontinent, e [ɛ̃kɔ̃tinɑ̃, ɑ̃t] *adj* incontinent

incontournable [ɛ̃kɔ̃turnabl] *adj* unavoidable

incontrôlable [ɛ̃kɔ̃trolabl] *adj* unverifiable; (*irrépressible*) uncontrollable

inconvenant, e [ɛ̃kɔ̃v(ə)nɑ̃, ɑ̃t] *adj* unseemly, improper

inconvénient [ɛ̃kɔ̃venjɑ̃] *nm* disadvantage, drawback; **si vous n'y voyez pas d'~** if you have no objections

incorporer [ɛ̃kɔrpɔre] *vt*: **~ (à)** to mix in (with); **~ (dans)** (*paragraphe etc*) to incorporate (in); (*MIL*: *appeler*) to recruit (into); **il a très bien su s'~ à notre groupe** he was very easily incorporated into our group

incorrect, e [ɛ̃kɔrɛkt] *adj* (*impropre, inconvenant*) improper; (*défectueux*) faulty; (*inexact*) incorrect; (*impoli*) impolite; (*déloyal*) underhand

incorrigible [ɛ̃kɔriʒibl] *adj* incorrigible

incrédule [ɛ̃kredyl] *adj* incredulous; (*REL*) unbelieving

increvable [ɛ̃krəvabl] (*fam*) *adj* tireless

incriminer [ɛ̃krimine] *vt* (*personne*) to incriminate; (*action, conduite*) to bring under attack; (*bonne foi, honnêteté*) to call into question

incroyable [ɛ̃krwajabl] *adj* incredible

incruster [ɛ̃kryste] *vt* (*ART*) to inlay; **s'~** *vi* (*invité*) to take root

inculpé, e [ɛ̃kylpe] *nm/f* accused

inculper [ɛ̃kylpe] *vt*: **~ (de)** to charge

(with)

inculquer [ɛ̃kylke] *vt*: **~ qch à** to inculcate sth in *ou* instil sth into

inculte [ɛ̃kylt] *adj* uncultivated; (*esprit, peuple*) uncultured

Inde [ɛ̃d] *nf*: **l'~** India

indécent, e [ɛ̃desɑ̃, ɑ̃t] *adj* indecent

indéchiffrable [ɛ̃deʃifrabl] *adj* indecipherable

indécis, e [ɛ̃desi, iz] *adj* (*par nature*) indecisive; (*temporairement*) undecided

indéfendable [ɛ̃defɑ̃dabl] *adj* indefensible

indéfini, e [ɛ̃defini] *adj* (*imprécis, incertain*) undefined; (*illimité, LING*) indefinite; **indéfiniment** *adv* indefinitely; **indéfinissable** *adj* indefinable

indélébile [ɛ̃delebil] *adj* indelible

indélicat, e [ɛ̃delika, at] *adj* tactless

indemne [ɛ̃dɛmn] *adj* unharmed; **indemniser** *vt*: **indemniser qn (de)** to compensate sb (for)

indemnité [ɛ̃dɛmnite] *nf* (*dédommagement*) compensation *no pl*; (*allocation*) allowance; **indemnité de licenciement** redundancy payment

indépendamment [ɛ̃depɑ̃damɑ̃] *adv* independently; **~ de** (*abstraction faite de*) irrespective of; (*en plus de*) over and above

indépendance [ɛ̃depɑ̃dɑ̃s] *nf* independence

indépendant, e [ɛ̃depɑ̃dɑ̃, ɑ̃t] *adj* independent; **~ de** independent of

indescriptible [ɛ̃dɛskriptibl] *adj* indescribable

indésirable [ɛ̃dezirabl] *adj* undesirable

indestructible [ɛ̃dɛstryktibl] *adj* indestructible

indétermination [ɛ̃detɛrminasjɔ̃] *nf* (*irrésolution*: *chronique*) indecision; (: *temporaire*) indecisiveness

indéterminé, e [ɛ̃detɛrmine] *adj* (*date, cause, nature*) unspecified; (*forme, longueur, quantité*) indeterminate

index [ɛ̃dɛks] *nm* (*doigt*) index finger; (*d'un livre etc*) index; **mettre à l'~** to blacklist; **indexé,** e *adj* (*ÉCON*): **indexé (sur)**

index-linked (to)

indic [ɛ̃dik] (*fam*) *nm* (*POLICE*) grass

indicateur [ɛ̃dikatœʀ] *nm* (*POLICE*) informer; (*TECH*) gauge, indicator

indicatif, -ive [ɛ̃dikatif, iv] *adj*: **à titre ~** for (your) information ♦ *nm* (*LING*) indicative; (*RADIO*) theme *ou* signature tune; (*TÉL*) dialling code

indication [ɛ̃dikasjɔ̃] *nf* indication; (*renseignement*) information *no pl*; **~s** *nfpl* (*directives*) instructions

indice [ɛ̃dis] *nm* (*marque, signe*) indication, sign; (*POLICE: lors d'une enquête*) clue; (*JUR: présomption*) piece of evidence; (*SCIENCE, ÉCON, TECH*) index

indicible [ɛ̃disibl] *adj* inexpressible

indien, ne [ɛ̃djɛ̃, jɛn] *adj* Indian ♦ *nm/f*: **I~, ne** Indian

indifféremment [ɛ̃diferamɑ̃] *adv* (*sans distinction*) equally (well)

indifférence [ɛ̃diferɑ̃s] *nf* indifference

indifférent, e [ɛ̃diferɑ̃, ɑ̃t] *adj* (*peu intéressé*) indifferent; **ça m'est ~** it doesn't matter to me; **elle m'est ~e** I am indifferent to her

indigence [ɛ̃diʒɑ̃s] *nf* poverty

indigène [ɛ̃diʒɛn] *adj* native, indigenous; (*des gens du pays*) local ♦ *nm/f* native

indigeste [ɛ̃diʒɛst] *adj* indigestible

indigestion [ɛ̃diʒɛstjɔ̃] *nf* indigestion *no pl*

indigne [ɛ̃diɲ] *adj* unworthy

indigner [ɛ̃diɲe] *vt*: **s'~ (de** *ou* **contre)** to get indignant (at)

indiqué, e [ɛ̃dike] *adj* (*date, lieu*) agreed; (*traitement*) appropriate; (*conseillé*) advisable

indiquer [ɛ̃dike] *vt* (*suj: pendule, aiguille*) to show; (: *étiquette, panneau*) to show, indicate; (*renseigner sur*) to point out, tell; (*déterminer: date, lieu*) to give, state; (*signaler, dénoter*) to indicate, point to; **~ qch/qn à qn** (*montrer du doigt*) to point sth/sb out to sb; (*faire connaître: médecin, restaurant*) to tell sb of sth/sb

indirect, e [ɛ̃diʀɛkt] *adj* indirect

indiscipliné, e [ɛ̃disipline] *adj* undisciplined

indiscret, -ète [ɛ̃diskʀɛ, ɛt] *adj* indiscreet

indiscutable [ɛ̃diskytabl] *adj* indisputable

indispensable [ɛ̃dispɑ̃sabl] *adj* indispensable, essential

indisposé, e [ɛ̃dispoze] *adj* indisposed

indisposer [ɛ̃dispoze] *vt* (*incommoder*) to upset; (*déplaire à*) to antagonize; (*énerver*) to irritate

indistinct, e [ɛ̃distɛ̃(kt), ɛ̃kt] *adj* indistinct; **indistinctement** *adv* (*voir, prononcer*) indistinctly; (*sans distinction*) indiscriminately

individu [ɛ̃dividy] *nm* individual; **individuel, le** *adj* (*gén*) individual; (*responsabilité, propriété, liberté*) personal; **chambre individuelle** single room; **maison individuelle** detached house

indolore [ɛ̃dɔlɔʀ] *adj* painless

indomptable [ɛ̃dɔ̃(p)tabl] *adj* untameable; (*fig*) invincible

Indonésie [ɛ̃dɔnezi] *nf* Indonesia

indu, e [ɛ̃dy] *adj*: **à une heure ~e** at some ungodly hour

induire [ɛ̃dɥiʀ] *vt*: **~ qn en erreur** to lead sb astray, mislead sb

indulgent, e [ɛ̃dylʒɑ̃, ɑ̃t] *adj* (*parent, regard*) indulgent; (*juge, examinateur*) lenient

industrialisé, e [ɛ̃dystʀijalize] *adj* industrialized

industrie [ɛ̃dystʀi] *nf* industry; **industriel, le** *adj* industrial ♦ *nm* industrialist

inébranlable [inebʀɑ̃labl] *adj* (*masse, colonne*) solid; (*personne, certitude, foi*) unshakeable

inédit, e [inedi, it] *adj* (*correspondance, livre*) hitherto unpublished; (*spectacle, moyen*) novel, original; (*film*) unreleased

ineffaçable [inefasabl] *adj* indelible

inefficace [inefikas] *adj* (*remède, moyen*) ineffective; (*machine, employé*) inefficient

inégal, e, -aux [inegal, o] *adj* unequal; (*irrégulier*) uneven; **inégalable** *adj* matchless; **inégalé, e** *adj* (*record*) unequalled; (*beauté*) unrivalled; **inégalité** *nf* inequality

inépuisable [inepɥizabl] *adj* inexhaustible

inerte [inɛʀt] *adj* (*immobile*) lifeless; (*sans réaction*) passive

inespéré, e [inɛspeʀe] *adj* unexpected, unhoped-for

inestimable [inɛstimabl] *adj* priceless; (*fig: bienfait*) invaluable

inévitable [inevitabl] *adj* unavoidable; (*fatal, habituel*) inevitable

inexact, e [inɛgza(kt), akt] *adj* inaccurate

inexcusable [inɛkskyzabl] *adj* unforgivable

inexplicable [inɛksplikabl] *adj* inexplicable

in extremis [inɛkstʀemis] *adv* at the last minute ♦ *adj* last-minute

infaillible [ɛ̃fajibl] *adj* infallible

infâme [ɛ̃fɑm] *adj* vile

infarctus [ɛ̃faʀktys] *nm*: ~ **(du myocarde)** coronary (thrombosis)

infatigable [ɛ̃fatigabl] *adj* tireless

infect, e [ɛ̃fɛkt] *adj* revolting; (*personne*) obnoxious; (*temps*) foul

infecter [ɛ̃fɛkte] *vt* (*atmosphère, eau*) to contaminate; (*MÉD*) to infect; **s'~** to become infected *ou* septic; **infection** *nf* infection; (*puanteur*) stench

inférieur, e [ɛ̃feʀjœʀ] *adj* lower; (*en qualité, intelligence*) inferior; ~ **à** (*somme, quantité*) less *ou* smaller than; (*moins bon que*) inferior to

infernal, e, -aux [ɛ̃fɛʀnal, o] *adj* (*insupportable: chaleur, rythme*) infernal; (: *enfant*) horrid; (*satanique, effrayant*) diabolical

infidèle [ɛ̃fidɛl] *adj* unfaithful

infiltrer [ɛ̃filtʀe] *vb*: **s'~ dans** to get into; (*liquide*) to seep through; (*fig: groupe, ennemi*) to infiltrate

infime [ɛ̃fim] *adj* minute, tiny

infini, e [ɛ̃fini] *adj* infinite ♦ *nm* infinity; **à l'~** endlessly; **infiniment** *adv* infinitely; **infinité** *nf*: **une infinité de** an infinite number of

infinitif [ɛ̃finitif, iv] *nm* infinitive

infirme [ɛ̃fiʀm] *adj* disabled ♦ *nm/f* disabled person

infirmerie [ɛ̃fiʀməʀi] *nf* medical room

infirmier, -ière [ɛ̃fiʀmje] *nm/f* nurse; **infirmière chef** sister

infirmité [ɛ̃fiʀmite] *nf* disability

inflammable [ɛ̃flamabl] *adj* (in)flammable

inflation [ɛ̃flasjɔ̃] *nf* inflation

infliger [ɛ̃fliʒe] *vt*: ~ **qch (à qn)** to inflict sth (on sb); (*amende, sanction*) to impose sth (on sb)

influençable [ɛ̃flyɑ̃sabl] *adj* easily influenced

influence [ɛ̃flyɑ̃s] *nf* influence; **influencer** *vt* to influence; **influent, e** *adj* influential

informateur, -trice [ɛ̃fɔʀmatœʀ, tʀis] *nm/f* (*POLICE*) informer

informaticien, ne [ɛ̃fɔʀmatisjɛ̃, jɛn] *nm/f* computer scientist

information [ɛ̃fɔʀmasjɔ̃] *nf* (*renseignement*) piece of information; (*PRESSE, TV: nouvelle*) item of news; (*diffusion de renseignements, INFORM*) information; (*JUR*) inquiry, investigation; **~s** *nfpl* (*TV*) news *sg*

informatique [ɛ̃fɔʀmatik] *nf* (*technique*) data processing; (*science*) computer science ♦ *adj* computer *cpd*; **informatiser** *vt* to computerize

informe [ɛ̃fɔʀm] *adj* shapeless

informer [ɛ̃fɔʀme] *vt*: ~ **qn (de)** to inform sb (of); **s'~ (de/si)** to inquire *ou* find out (about/whether *ou* if)

infos [ɛ̃fo] *nfpl*: **les ~** the news *sg*

infraction [ɛ̃fʀaksjɔ̃] *nf* offence; ~ **à** violation *ou* breach of; **être en ~** to be in breach of the law

infranchissable [ɛ̃fʀɑ̃fisabl] *adj* impassable; (*fig*) insuperable

infrarouge [ɛ̃fʀaʀuʒ] *adj* infrared

infrastructure [ɛ̃fʀastʀyktyʀ] *nf* (*AVIAT, MIL*) ground installations *pl*; (*ÉCON: touristique etc*) infrastructure

infuser [ɛ̃fyze] *vt, vi* (*thé*) to brew; (*tisane*) to infuse; **infusion** *nf* (*tisane*) herb tea

ingénier [ɛ̃ʒenje]: **s'~** *vi*: **s'~ à faire** to strive to do

ingénierie [ɛ̃ʒeniʀi] *nf* engineering; ~ **génétique** genetic engineering

ingénieur [ɛ̃ʒenjœʀ] *nm* engineer; **ingénieur du son** sound engineer

ingénieux, -euse [ɛ̃ʒenjø, jøz] *adj* ingenious, clever

ingénu, e [ɛ̃ʒeny] *adj* ingenuous, artless

ingérer [ɛ̃ʒeʀe] *vb*: **s'~ dans** to interfere in

ingrat, e [ɛ̃gʀa, at] *adj* (*personne*) ungrateful; (*travail, sujet*) thankless; (*visage*) unprepossessing

ingrédient [ɛ̃gʀedjɑ̃] *nm* ingredient

ingurgiter [ɛ̃gyʀʒite] *vt* to swallow

inhabitable [inabitabl] *adj* uninhabitable

inhabité, e [inabite] *adj* uninhabited

inhabituel, le [inabituɛl] *adj* unusual

inhibition [inibisjɔ̃] *nf* inhibition

inhumain, e [inymɛ̃, ɛn] *adj* inhuman

inhumation [inymasjɔ̃] *nf* burial

inhumer [inyme] *vt* to inter, bury

inimaginable [inimaʒinabl] *adj* unimaginable

ininterrompu, e [inɛ̃teʀɔ̃py] *adj* (*file, série*) unbroken; (*flot, vacarme*) uninterrupted, non-stop; (*effort*) unremitting, continuous; (*suite, ligne*) unbroken

initial, e, -aux [inisjal, jo] *adj* initial; **initiale** *nf* initial; **initialiser** *vt* to initialize

initiation [inisjasjɔ̃] *nf*: **~ à** introduction to

initiative [inisjativ] *nf* initiative

initier [inisje] *vt*: **~ qn à** to initiate sb into; (*faire découvrir: art, jeu*) to introduce sb to

injecté, e [ɛ̃ʒekte] *adj*: **yeux ~s de sang** bloodshot eyes

injecter [ɛ̃ʒekte] *vt* to inject; **injection** *nf* injection; **à injection** (*AUTO*) fuel injection *cpd*

injure [ɛ̃ʒyʀ] *nf* insult, abuse *no pl*; **injurier** *vt* to insult, abuse; **injurieux, -euse** *adj* abusive, insulting

injuste [ɛ̃ʒyst] *adj* unjust, unfair; **injustice** *nf* injustice

inlassable [ɛ̃lɑsabl] *adj* tireless

inné, e [i(n)ne] *adj* innate, inborn

innocent, e [inɔsɑ̃, ɑ̃t] *adj* innocent; **innocenter** *vt* to clear, prove innocent

innombrable [i(n)nɔ̃bʀabl] *adj* innumerable

innommable [i(n)nɔmabl] *adj* unspeakable

innover [inɔve] *vi* to break new ground

inoccupé, e [inɔkype] *adj* unoccupied

inodore [inɔdɔʀ] *adj* (*gaz*) odourless; (*fleur*) scentless

inoffensif, -ive [inɔfɑ̃sif, iv] *adj* harmless, innocuous

inondation [inɔ̃dasjɔ̃] *nf* flood

inonder [inɔ̃de] *vt* to flood; **~ de** to flood with

inopiné, e [inɔpine] *adj* unexpected; (*mort*) sudden

inopportun, e [inɔpɔʀtœ̃, yn] *adj* illtimed, untimely

inoubliable [inublijabl] *adj* unforgettable

inouï, e [inwi] *adj* unheard-of, extraordinary

inox [inɔks] *nm* stainless steel

inqualifiable [ɛ̃kalifjabl] *adj* unspeakable

inquiet, -ète [ɛ̃kjɛ, ɛ̃kjɛt] *adj* anxious; **inquiétant, e** *adj* worrying, disturbing; **inquiéter** *vt* to worry; **s'inquiéter** to worry; **s'inquiéter de** to worry about; (*s'enquérir de*) to inquire about; **inquiétude** *nf* anxiety

insaisissable [ɛ̃sezisabl] *adj* (*fugitif, ennemi*) elusive; (*différence, nuance*) imperceptible

insalubre [ɛ̃salybʀ] *adj* insalubrious

insatisfaisant, e [ɛ̃satisfəzɑ̃, ɑ̃t] *adj* unsatisfactory

insatisfait, e [ɛ̃satisfɛ, ɛt] *adj* (*non comblé*) unsatisfied; (*mécontent*) dissatisfied

inscription [ɛ̃skʀipsjɔ̃] *nf* inscription; (*immatriculation*) enrolment

inscrire [ɛ̃skʀiʀ] *vt* (*marquer: sur son calepin etc*) to note *ou* write down; (: *sur un mur, une affiche etc*) to write; (: *dans la pierre, le métal*) to inscribe; (*mettre: sur une liste, un budget etc*) to put down; **s'~** (*pour une excursion etc*) to put one's name down; **s'~ (à)** (*club, parti*) to join; (*université*) to register *ou* enrol (at); (*examen, concours*) to register (for); **~ qn à** (*club, parti*) to enrol sb at

insecte [ɛ̃sɛkt] *nm* insect; **insecticide** *nm* insecticide

insensé, e [ɛ̃sɑ̃se] *adj* mad

insensibiliser [ɛ̃sɑ̃sibilize] *vt* to anaesthetize

insensible [ɛ̃sɑ̃sibl] *adj* (*nerf, membre*) numb; (*dur, indifférent*) insensitive

inséparable [ɛ̃separabl] *adj* inseparable ♦ *nm*: **~s** (*oiseaux*) lovebirds

insigne [ɛ̃siɲ] *nm* (*d'un parti, club*) badge; (*d'une fonction*) insignia ♦ *adj* distinguished

insignifiant, e [ɛ̃siɲifjɑ̃, jɑ̃t] *adj* insignificant; trivial

insinuer [ɛ̃sinɥe] *vt* to insinuate; **s'~ dans** (*fig*) to worm one's way into

insipide [ɛ̃sipid] *adj* insipid

insister [ɛ̃siste] *vi* to insist; (*continuer à sonner*) to keep on trying; **~ sur** (*détail, sujet*) to lay stress on

insolation [ɛ̃sɔlasjɔ̃] *nf* (*MÉD*) sunstroke *no pl*

insolent, e [ɛ̃sɔlɑ̃, ɑ̃t] *adj* insolent

insolite [ɛ̃sɔlit] *adj* strange, unusual

insomnie [ɛ̃sɔmni] *nf* insomnia *no pl*

insonoriser [ɛ̃sɔnɔrize] *vt* to soundproof

insouciant, e [ɛ̃susjɑ̃, jɑ̃t] *adj* carefree; **~ du danger** heedless of (the) danger

insoumis, e [ɛ̃sumi, iz] *adj* (*caractère, enfant*) rebellious, refractory; (*contrée, tribu*) unsubdued

insoupçonnable [ɛ̃supsɔnabl] *adj* unsuspected; (*personne*) above suspicion

insoupçonné, e [ɛ̃supsɔne] *adj* unsuspected

insoutenable [ɛ̃sut(ə)nabl] *adj* (*argument*) untenable; (*chaleur*) unbearable

inspecter [ɛ̃spɛkte] *vt* to inspect; **inspecteur, -trice** *nm/f* inspector; **inspecteur d'Académie** (regional) director of education; **inspecteur des finances** ≈ tax inspector (*BRIT*), ≈ Internal Revenue Service agent (*US*); **inspection** *nf* inspection

inspirer [ɛ̃spire] *vt* (*gén*) to inspire ♦ *vi* (*aspirer*) to breathe in; **s'~ de** (*suj: artiste*) to draw one's inspiration from

instable [ɛ̃stabl] *adj* unstable; (*meuble, équilibre*) unsteady; (*temps*) unsettled

installation [ɛ̃stalasjɔ̃] *nf* installation; **~s** *nfpl* facilities

installer [ɛ̃stale] *vt* (*loger, placer*) to put; (*meuble, gaz, électricité*) to put in; (*rideau, étagère, tente*) to put up; (*appartement*) to fit out; **s'~** (*s'établir: artisan, dentiste etc*) to set o.s. up; (*se loger*) to settle; (*emménager*) to settle in; (*sur un siège, à un emplacement*) to settle (down); (*fig: maladie, grève*) to take a firm hold

instance [ɛ̃stɑ̃s] *nf* (*ADMIN: autorité*) authority; **affaire en ~** matter pending; **être en ~ de divorce** to be awaiting a divorce

instant [ɛ̃stɑ̃] *nm* moment, instant; **dans un ~** in a moment; **à l'~** this instant; **pour l'~** for the moment, for the time being

instantané, e [ɛ̃stɑ̃tane] *adj* (*lait, café*) instant; (*explosion, mort*) instantaneous ♦ *nm* snapshot

instar [ɛ̃star]: **à l'~ de** *prép* following the example of, like

instaurer [ɛ̃stɔre] *vt* to institute; (*couvre-feu*) to impose

instinct [ɛ̃stɛ̃] *nm* instinct; **instinctivement** *adv* instinctively

instit [ɛ̃stit] (*fam*) *nm/f* (primary school) teacher

instituer [ɛ̃stitɥe] *vt* to establish

institut [ɛ̃stity] *nm* institute; **~ de beauté** beauty salon; **Institut universitaire de technologie** ≈ polytechnic

instituteur, -trice [ɛ̃stitytœr, tris] *nm/f* (primary school) teacher

institution [ɛ̃stitysjɔ̃] *nf* institution; (*collège*) private school

instructif, -ive [ɛ̃stryktif, iv] *adj* instructive

instruction [ɛ̃stryksjɔ̃] *nf* (*enseignement, savoir*) education; (*JUR*) (preliminary) investigation and hearing; **~s** *nfpl* (*ordres, mode d'emploi*) instructions; **~ civique** civics *sg*

instruire [ɛ̃stʀɥiʀ] *vt* (*élèves*) to teach; (*recrues*) to train; (*JUR: affaire*) to conduct the investigation for; **s'~** to educate o.s.; **instruit, e** *adj* educated

instrument [ɛ̃stʀymɑ̃] *nm* instrument; **~ à cordes/vent** stringed/wind instrument; **~ de mesure** measuring instrument; **~ de musique** musical instrument; **~ de travail** (working) tool

insu [ɛ̃sy] *nm*: **à l'~ de qn** without sb knowing (it)

insubmersible [ɛ̃sybmɛʀsibl] *adj* unsinkable

insuffisant, e [ɛ̃syfizɑ̃, ɑ̃t] *adj* (*en quantité*) insufficient; (*en qualité*) inadequate; (*sur une copie*) poor

insulaire [ɛ̃sylɛʀ] *adj* island *cpd*; (*attitude*) insular

insuline [ɛ̃sylin] *nf* insulin

insulte [ɛ̃sylt] *nf* insult; **insulter** *vt* to insult

insupportable [ɛ̃sypɔʀtabl] *adj* unbearable

insurger [ɛ̃syʀʒe] *vb*: **s'~ (contre)** to rise up *ou* rebel (against)

insurmontable [ɛ̃syʀmɔ̃tabl] *adj* (*difficulté*) insuperable; (*aversion*) unconquerable

insurrection [ɛ̃syʀɛksjɔ̃] *nf* insurrection

intact, e [ɛ̃takt] *adj* intact

intangible [ɛ̃tɑ̃ʒibl] *adj* intangible; (*principe*) inviolable

intarissable [ɛ̃taʀisabl] *adj* inexhaustible

intégral, e, -aux [ɛ̃tegʀal, o] *adj* complete; **texte ~** unabridged version; **bronzage ~** all-over suntan; **intégralement** *adv* in full; **intégralité** *nf* whole; **dans son intégralité** in full; **intégrant, e** *adj*: **faire partie intégrante de** to be an integral part of

intègre [ɛ̃tegʀ] *adj* upright

intégrer [ɛ̃tegʀe] *vt*: **bien s'~** to integrate well

intégrisme [ɛ̃tegʀism] *nm* fundamentalism

intellectuel, le [ɛ̃telɛktɥɛl] *adj* intellectual

♦ *nm/f* intellectual; (*péj*) highbrow

intelligence [ɛ̃teliʒɑ̃s] *nf* intelligence; (*compréhension*): **l'~ de** the understanding of; (*complicité*): **regard d'~** glance of complicity; (*accord*): **vivre en bonne ~ avec qn** to be on good terms with sb

intelligent, e [ɛ̃teliʒɑ̃, ɑ̃t] *adj* intelligent

intelligible [ɛ̃teliʒibl] *adj* intelligible

intempéries [ɛ̃tɑ̃peʀi] *nfpl* bad weather *sg*

intempestif, -ive [ɛ̃tɑ̃pɛstif, iv] *adj* untimely

intenable [ɛ̃t(ə)nabl] *adj* (*chaleur*) unbearable

intendant, e [ɛ̃tɑ̃dɑ̃] *nm/f* (*MIL*) quartermaster; (*SCOL*) bursar

intense [ɛ̃tɑ̃s] *adj* intense; **intensif, -ive** *adj* intensive; **un cours intensif** a crash course

intenter [ɛ̃tɑ̃te] *vt*: **~ un procès contre** *ou* **à** to start proceedings against

intention [ɛ̃tɑ̃sjɔ̃] *nf* intention; (*JUR*) intent; **avoir l'~ de faire** to intend to do; **à l'~ de** for; (*renseignement*) for the benefit of; (*film, ouvrage*) aimed at; **à cette ~** with this aim in view; **intentionné, e** *adj*: **bien intentionné** well-meaning *ou* -intentioned; **mal intentionné** ill-intentioned

interactif, -ive [ɛ̃teʀaktif, iv] *adj* (*COMPUT*) interactive

intercalaire [ɛ̃teʀkalɛʀ] *nm* divider

intercaler [ɛ̃teʀkale] *vt* to insert

intercepter [ɛ̃teʀsɛpte] *vt* to intercept; (*lumière, chaleur*) to cut off

interchangeable [ɛ̃teʀʃɑ̃ʒabl] *adj* interchangeable

interclasse [ɛ̃teʀklɑs] *nm* (*SCOL*) break (between classes)

interdiction [ɛ̃teʀdiksjɔ̃] *nf* ban; **~ de stationner** no parking; **~ de fumer** no smoking

interdire [ɛ̃teʀdiʀ] *vt* to forbid; (*ADMIN*) to ban, prohibit; (: *journal, livre*) to ban; **~ à qn de faire** to forbid sb to do; (*suj: empêchement*) to prevent sb from doing

interdit, e [ɛ̃tɛʀdi, it] *adj (stupéfait)* taken aback

intéressant, e [ɛ̃teʀesɑ̃, ɑ̃t] *adj* interesting; *(avantageux)* attractive

intéressé, e [ɛ̃teʀese] *adj (parties)* involved, concerned; *(amitié, motifs)* self-interested

intéresser [ɛ̃teʀese] *vt (captiver)* to interest; *(toucher)* to be of interest to; *(ADMIN: concerner)* to affect, concern; **s'~ à** to be interested in

intérêt [ɛ̃teʀe] *nm* interest; *(égoïsme)* self-interest; **tu as ~ à accepter** it's in your interest to accept; **tu as ~ à te dépêcher** you'd better hurry

intérieur, e [ɛ̃teʀjœʀ] *adj (mur, escalier, poche)* inside; *(commerce, politique)* domestic; *(cour, calme, vie)* inner; *(navigation)* inland ♦ *nm (d'une maison, d'un récipient etc)* inside; *(d'un pays, aussi décor, mobilier)* interior; **à l'~ (de)** inside; **intérieurement** *adv* inwardly

intérim [ɛ̃teʀim] *nm* interim period; **faire de l'~** to temp; **assurer l'~ (de)** to deputize (for); **par ~** interim

intérimaire [ɛ̃teʀimɛʀ] *adj (directeur, ministre)* acting; *(secrétaire, personnel)* temporary ♦ *nm/f (secrétaire)* temporary secretary, temp *(BRIT)*

interlocuteur, -trice [ɛ̃tɛʀlɔkytœʀ, tʀis] *nm/f* speaker; **son ~** the person he was speaking to

interloquer [ɛ̃tɛʀlɔke] *vt* to take aback

intermède [ɛ̃tɛʀmɛd] *nm* interlude

intermédiaire [ɛ̃tɛʀmedjɛʀ] *adj* intermediate; *(solution)* temporary ♦ *nm/f* intermediary; *(COMM)* middleman; **sans ~** directly; **par l'~ de** through

interminable [ɛ̃tɛʀminabl] *adj* endless

intermittence [ɛ̃tɛʀmitɑ̃s] *nf:* **par ~** sporadically, intermittently

internat [ɛ̃tɛʀna] *nm (SCOL)* boarding school

international, e, -aux [ɛ̃tɛʀnasjɔnal, o] *adj, nm/f* international

interne [ɛ̃tɛʀn] *adj* internal ♦ *nm/f (SCOL)* boarder; *(MÉD)* houseman

interner [ɛ̃tɛʀne] *vt (POL)* to intern; *(MÉD)* to confine to a mental institution

Internet [ɛ̃tɛʀnɛt] *nm* Internet

interpeller [ɛ̃tɛʀpəle] *vt (appeler)* to call out to; *(apostropher)* to shout at; *(POLICE, POL)* to question; *(concerner)* to concern

interphone [ɛ̃tɛʀfɔn] *nm* intercom; *(d'immeuble)* entry phone

interposer [ɛ̃tɛʀpoze] *vt:* **s'~** to intervene; **par personnes interposées** through a third party

interprétation [ɛ̃tɛʀpʀetasjɔ̃] *nf* interpretation

interprète [ɛ̃tɛʀpʀɛt] *nm/f* interpreter; *(porte-parole)* spokesperson

interpréter [ɛ̃tɛʀpʀete] *vt* to interpret; *(jouer)* to play; *(chanter)* to sing

interrogateur, -trice [ɛ̃teʀɔgatœʀ, tʀis] *adj* questioning, inquiring

interrogatif, -ive [ɛ̃teʀɔgatif, iv] *adj (LING)* interrogative

interrogation [ɛ̃teʀɔgasjɔ̃] *nf* question; *(action)* questioning; *(SCOL)* (written *ou* oral) test

interrogatoire [ɛ̃teʀɔgatwaʀ] *nm (POLICE)* questioning *no pl; (JUR, aussi fig)* cross-examination

interroger [ɛ̃teʀɔʒe] *vt* to question; *(INFORM)* to consult; *(SCOL)* to test

interrompre [ɛ̃teʀɔ̃pʀ] *vt (gén)* to interrupt; *(négociations)* to break off; *(match)* to stop; **s'~** to break off; **interrupteur** *nm* switch; **interruption** *nf* interruption; *(pause)* break; **sans interruption** without stopping

intersection [ɛ̃tɛʀsɛksjɔ̃] *nf* intersection

interstice [ɛ̃tɛʀstis] *nm* crack; *(de volet)* slit

interurbain, e [ɛ̃teʀyʀbɛ̃, ɛn] *adj (TÉL)* long-distance

intervalle [ɛ̃tɛʀval] *nm (espace)* space; *(de temps)* interval; **à deux jours d'~** two days apart

intervenir [ɛ̃tɛʀvəniʀ] *vi (gén)* to intervene; **~ auprès de qn** to intervene with sb

intervention [ɛ̃tɛʀvɑ̃sjɔ̃] *nf* intervention; (*discours*) speech; **~ chirurgicale** (surgical) operation

intervertir [ɛ̃tɛʀvɛʀtiʀ] *vt* to invert (the order of), reverse

interview [ɛ̃tɛʀvju] *nf* interview

intestin [ɛ̃tɛstɛ̃, in] *nm* intestine

intime [ɛ̃tim] *adj* intimate; (*vie*) private; (*conviction*) inmost; (*dîner, cérémonie*) quiet ♦ *nm/f* close friend; **un journal ~** a diary

intimider [ɛ̃timide] *vt* to intimidate

intimité [ɛ̃timite] *nf*: **dans l'~** in private; (*sans formalités*) with only a few friends, quietly

intitulé, e [ɛ̃tityle] *adj* entitled

intolérable [ɛ̃tɔleʀabl] *adj* intolerable

intox [ɛ̃tɔks] (*fam*) *nf* brainwashing

intoxication [ɛ̃tɔksikasjɔ̃] *nf*: **~ alimentaire** food poisoning

intoxiquer [ɛ̃tɔksike] *vt* to poison; (*fig*) to brainwash

intraduisible [ɛ̃tʀadɥizibl] *adj* untranslatable; (*fig*) inexpressible

intraitable [ɛ̃tʀɛtabl] *adj* inflexible, uncompromising

intranet [ɛ̃tʀanɛt] *nm* intranet

intransigeant, e [ɛ̃tʀɑ̃ziʒɑ̃, ɑ̃t] *adj* intransigent

intransitif, -ive [ɛ̃tʀɑ̃zitif, iv] *adj* (*LING*) intransitive

intrépide [ɛ̃tʀepid] *adj* dauntless

intrigue [ɛ̃tʀig] *nf* (*scénario*) plot; **intriguer** *vt* to puzzle, intrigue

intrinsèque [ɛ̃tʀɛ̃sɛk] *adj* intrinsic

introduction [ɛ̃tʀɔdyksjɔ̃] *nf* introduction

introduire [ɛ̃tʀɔdɥiʀ] *vt* to introduce; (*visiteur*) to show in; (*aiguille, clef*) **~ qch dans** to insert *ou* introduce sth into; **s'~ (dans)** to get in(to); (*dans un groupe*) to get o.s. accepted (into)

introuvable [ɛ̃tʀuvabl] *adj* which cannot be found; (*COMM*) unobtainable

introverti, e [ɛ̃tʀɔvɛʀti] *nm/f* introvert

intrus, e [ɛ̃tʀy, yz] *nm/f* intruder

intrusion [ɛ̃tʀyzjɔ̃] *nf* intrusion

intuition [ɛ̃tɥisjɔ̃] *nf* intuition

inusable [inyzabl] *adj* hard-wearing

inusité, e [inyzite] *adj* rarely used

inutile [inytil] *adj* useless; (*superflu*) unnecessary; **inutilement** *adv* unnecessarily; **inutilisable** *adj* unusable

invalide [ɛ̃valid] *adj* disabled ♦ *nm*: **~ de guerre** disabled ex-serviceman

invasion [ɛ̃vazjɔ̃] *nf* invasion

invectiver [ɛ̃vɛktive] *vt* to hurl abuse at

invendable [ɛ̃vɑ̃dabl] *adj* unsaleable; (*COMM*) unmarketable; **invendus** *nmpl* unsold goods

inventaire [ɛ̃vɑ̃tɛʀ] *nm* inventory; (*COMM: liste*) stocklist; (: *opération*) stocktaking *no pl*

inventer [ɛ̃vɑ̃te] *vt* to invent; (*subterfuge*) to devise, invent; (*histoire, excuse*) to make up, invent; **inventeur** *nm* inventor; **inventif, -ive** *adj* inventive; **invention** *nf* invention

inverse [ɛ̃vɛʀs] *adj* opposite ♦ *nm* opposite; **dans l'ordre ~** in the reverse order; **en sens ~** in (*ou* from) the opposite direction; **dans le sens ~ des aiguilles d'une montre** anticlockwise; **tu t'es trompé, c'est l'~** you've got it wrong, it's the other way round; **inversement** *adv* conversely; **inverser** *vt* to invert, reverse; (*ÉLEC*) to reverse

investigation [ɛ̃vɛstigasjɔ̃] *nf* investigation

investir [ɛ̃vɛstiʀ] *vt* to invest; **investissement** *nm* investment; **investiture** *nf* nomination

invétéré, e [ɛ̃vetere] *adj* inveterate

invisible [ɛ̃vizibl] *adj* invisible

invitation [ɛ̃vitasjɔ̃] *nf* invitation

invité, e [ɛ̃vite] *nm/f* guest

inviter [ɛ̃vite] *vt* to invite

invivable [ɛ̃vivabl] *adj* unbearable

involontaire [ɛ̃vɔlɔ̃tɛʀ] *adj* (*mouvement*) involuntary; (*insulte*) unintentional; (*complice*) unwitting

invoquer [ɛ̃vɔke] *vt* (*Dieu, muse*) to call upon, invoke; (*prétexte*) to put forward (as an excuse); (*loi, texte*) to refer to

invraisemblable [ɛ̃vʀɛsɑ̃blabl] *adj* (*fait,*

nouvelle) unlikely, improbable; (*insolence, habit*) incredible

iode [jɔd] *nm* iodine

irai *etc* [iʀe] *vb voir* **aller**

Irak [iʀak] *nm* Iraq; **irakien, ne** *adj* Iraqi ♦ *nm/f*: **Irakien, ne** Iraqi

Iran [iʀɑ̃] *nm* Iran; **iranien, ne** *adj* Iranian ♦ *nm/f*: **Iranien, ne** Iranian

irascible [iʀasibl] *adj* short-tempered

irions *etc* [iʀjɔ̃] *vb voir* **aller**

iris [iʀis] *nm* iris

irlandais, e [iʀlɑ̃dɛ, ɛz] *adj* Irish ♦ *nm/f*: **Irlandais, e** Irishman(-woman); **les Irlandais** the Irish

Irlande [iʀlɑ̃d] *nf* Ireland; **~ du Nord** Northern Ireland; **la République d'~** the Irish Republic

ironie [iʀɔni] *nf* irony; **ironique** *adj* ironical; **ironiser** *vi* to be ironical

irons *etc* [iʀɔ̃] *vb voir* **aller**

irradier [iʀadje] *vt* to irradiate

irraisonné, e [iʀezɔne] *adj* irrational

irrationnel, le [iʀasjɔnɛl] *adj* irrational

irréalisable [iʀealizabl] *adj* unrealizable; (*projet*) impracticable

irrécupérable [iʀekypeʀabl] *adj* beyond repair; (*personne*) beyond redemption

irréductible [iʀedyktibl] *adj* (*volonté*) indomitable; (*ennemi*) implacable

irréel, le [iʀeɛl] *adj* unreal

irréfléchi, e [iʀefleʃi] *adj* thoughtless

irrégularité [iʀegylaʀite] *nf* irregularity; (*de travail, d'effort, de qualité*) unevenness *no pl*

irrégulier, -ière [iʀegylje, jɛʀ] *adj* irregular; (*travail, effort, qualité*) uneven; (*élève, athlète*) erratic

irrémédiable [iʀemedjabl] *adj* irreparable

irremplaçable [iʀɑ̃plasabl] *adj* irreplaceable

irréparable [iʀepaʀabl] *adj* (*objet*) beyond repair; (*dommage etc*) irreparable

irréprochable [iʀepʀɔʃabl] *adj* irreproachable, beyond reproach; (*tenue*) impeccable

irrésistible [iʀezistibl] *adj* irresistible; (*be-*

soin, désir, preuve, logique) compelling; (*amusant*) hilarious

irrésolu, e [iʀezɔly] *adj* (*personne*) irresolute; (*problème*) unresolved

irrespectueux, -euse [iʀespektɥø, øz] *adj* disrespectful

irrespirable [iʀespiʀabl] *adj* unbreathable; (*fig*) oppressive

irresponsable [iʀespɔ̃sabl] *adj* irresponsible

irriguer [iʀige] *vt* to irrigate

irritable [iʀitabl] *adj* irritable

irriter [iʀite] *vt* to irritate

irruption [iʀypsjɔ̃] *nf*: **faire ~ (chez qn)** to burst in (on sb)

Islam [islam] *nm* Islam; **islamique** *adj* Islamic; **islamiste** *adj* (*militant*) Islamic; (*mouvement*) Islamic fundamentalist ♦ *nm/f* Islamic fundamentalist

Islande [islɑ̃d] *nf* Iceland

isolant, e [izɔlɑ̃, ɑ̃t] *adj* insulating; (*insonorisant*) soundproofing

isolation [izɔlasjɔ̃] *nf* insulation

isolé, e [izɔle] *adj* isolated; (*contre le froid*) insulated

isoler [izɔle] *vt* to isolate; (*prisonnier*) to put in solitary confinement; (*ville*) to cut off, isolate; (*contre le froid*) to insulate; **s'~** *vi* to isolate o.s.; **isoloir** [izɔlwaʀ] *nm* polling booth

Israël [israɛl] *nm* Israel; **israélien, ne** *adj* Israeli ♦ *nm/f*: **Israélien, ne** Israeli; **israélite** *adj* Jewish ♦ *nm/f*: **Israélite** Jew (Jewess)

issu, e [isy] *adj*: **~ de** (*né de*) descended from; (*résultant de*) stemming from; **issue** *nf* (*ouverture, sortie*) exit; (*solution*) way out, solution; (*dénouement*) outcome; **à l'issue de** at the conclusion *ou* close of; **voie sans issue** dead end; **issue de secours** emergency exit

Italie [itali] *nf* Italy; **italien, ne** *adj* Italian ♦ *nm/f*: **Italien, ne** Italian ♦ *nm* (*LING*) Italian

italique [italik] *nm*: **en ~** in italics

itinéraire [itineʀɛʀ] *nm* itinerary, route; **~**

bis diversion

IUT *sigle m* = **Institut universitaire de technologie**

IVG *sigle f* (= *interruption volontaire de grossesse*) abortion

ivoire [ivwaʀ] *nm* ivory

ivre [ivʀ] *adj* drunk; **~ de** (*colère, bonheur*) wild with; **ivresse** *nf* drunkenness; **ivrogne** *nm/f* drunkard

J, j

j' [ʒ] *pron voir* **je**

jacasser [ʒakase] *vi* to chatter

jacinthe [ʒasɛ̃t] *nf* hyacinth

jadis [ʒadis] *adv* long ago

jaillir [ʒajiʀ] *vi* (*liquide*) to spurt out; (*cris, responses*) to burst forth

jais [ʒɛ] *nm* jet; **(d'un noir) de ~** jet-black

jalousie [ʒaluzi] *nf* jealousy; (*store*) slatted blind

jaloux, -ouse [ʒalu, uz] *adj* jealous

jamais [ʒamɛ] *adv* never; (*sans négation*) ever; **ne ... ~** never; **à ~** for ever

jambe [ʒɑ̃b] *nf* leg

jambon [ʒɑ̃bɔ̃] *nm* ham; **~ blanc** boiled *ou* cooked ham; **jambonneau, x** *nm* knuckle of ham

jante [ʒɑ̃t] *nf* (*wheel*) rim

janvier [ʒɑ̃vje] *nm* January

Japon [ʒapɔ̃] *nm* Japan; **japonais, e** *adj* Japanese ♦ *nm/f*: **Japonais, e** Japanese ♦ *nm* (*LING*) Japanese

japper [ʒape] *vi* to yap, yelp

jaquette [ʒakɛt] *nf* (*de cérémonie*) morning coat

jardin [ʒaʀdɛ̃] *nm* garden; **~ d'enfants** nursery school; **jardinage** *nm* gardening; **jardiner** *vi* to do some gardening; **jardinier, -ière** *nm/f* gardener; **jardinière** *nf* planter; (*de fenêtre*) window box; **jardinière de légumes** mixed vegetables

jargon [ʒaʀgɔ̃] *nm* (*baragouin*) gibberish; (*langue professionnelle*) jargon

jarret [ʒaʀɛ] *nm* back of knee; (*CULIN*)

knuckle, shin

jarretelle [ʒaʀtɛl] *nf* suspender (*BRIT*), garter (*US*)

jarretière [ʒaʀtjɛʀ] *nf* garter

jaser [ʒaze] *vi* (*médire*) to gossip

jatte [ʒat] *nf* basin, bowl

jauge [ʒoʒ] *nf* (*instrument*) gauge; **~ d'essence** petrol gauge; **~ d'huile** (oil) dipstick

jaune [ʒon] *adj, nm* yellow ♦ *adv* (*fam*): **rire ~** to laugh on the other side of one's face; **~ d'œuf** (egg) yolk; **jaunir** *vi, vt* to turn yellow; **jaunisse** *nf* jaundice

Javel [ʒavɛl] *nf voir* **eau**

javelot [ʒavlo] *nm* javelin

J.-C. *abr* = **Jésus-Christ**

je, j' [ʒə] *pron* I

jean [dʒin] *nm* jeans *pl*

Jésus-Christ [ʒezykʀi(st)] *n* Jesus Christ; **600 avant/après ~-~** *ou* **J.-C.** 600 B.C./A.D.

jet[1] [ʒɛ] *nm* (*lancer: action*) throwing *no pl*; (*: résultat*) throw; (*jaillissement: d'eaux*) jet; (*: de sang*) spurt; **~ d'eau** spray

jet[2] [dʒɛt] *nm* (*avion*) jet

jetable [ʒ(ə)tabl] *adj* disposable

jetée [ʒ(ə)te] *nf* jetty; (*grande*) pier

jeter [ʒ(ə)te] *vt* (*gén*) to throw; (*se défaire de*) to throw away *ou* out; **se ~ dans** to flow into; **~ qch à qn** to throw sth to sb; (*de façon agressive*) to throw sth at sb; **~ un coup d'œil (à)** to take a look (at); **~ un sort à qn** to cast a spell on sb; **se ~ sur qn** to rush at sb

jeton [ʒ(ə)tɔ̃] *nm* (*au jeu*) counter; (*de téléphone*) token

jette *etc* [ʒɛt] *vb voir* **jeter**

jeu, x [ʒø] *nm* (*divertissement, TECH: d'une pièce*) play; (*TENNIS: partie, FOOTBALL etc: façon de jouer*) game; (*THÉÂTRE etc*) acting; (*série d'objets, jouet*) set; (*CARTES*) hand; (*au casino*): **le ~** gambling; **être en ~** to be at stake; **entrer/mettre en ~** to come/bring into play; **~ de cartes** pack of cards; **~ d'échecs** chess set; **~ de hasard** game of chance; **~ de mots** pun; **~ de**

société parlour game; ~ **télévisé** television quiz; ~ **vidéo** video game

jeudi [ʒødi] *nm* Thursday

jeun [ʒœ̃]: **à** ~ *adv* on an empty stomach; **être à** ~ to have eaten nothing; **rester à** ~ not to eat anything

jeune [ʒœn] *adj* young; **les** ~**s** young people; ~ **fille** girl; ~ **homme** young man; ~**s mariés** newly-weds

jeûne [ʒøn] *nm* fast

jeunesse [ʒœnɛs] *nf* youth; *(aspect)* youthfulness

joaillerie [ʒɔajri] *nf* jewellery; *(magasin)* jeweller's; **joaillier, -ière** *nm/f* jeweller

jogging [dʒɔgin] *nm* jogging; *(survêtement)* tracksuit; **faire du** ~ to go jogging

joie [ʒwa] *nf* joy

joindre [ʒwɛ̃dʀ] *vt* to join; *(à une lettre)*: ~ **qch à** to enclose sth with; *(contacter)* to contact, get in touch with; **se** ~ **à** to join; ~ **les mains** to put one's hands together

joint, e [ʒwɛ̃, ɛt] *adj*: **pièce** ~**e** enclosure ♦ *nm* joint; *(ligne)* join; ~ **de culasse** cylinder head gasket; ~ **de robinet** washer

joli, e [ʒɔli] *adj* pretty, attractive; **c'est du** ~! *(ironique)* that's very nice!; **c'est bien** ~, **mais** ... that's all very well but ...

jonc [ʒɔ̃] *nm* (bul)rush

jonction [ʒɔ̃ksjɔ̃] *nf* junction

jongleur, -euse [ʒɔ̃glœʀ, øz] *nm/f* juggler

jonquille [ʒɔ̃kij] *nf* daffodil

Jordanie [ʒɔʀdani] *nf*: **la** ~ Jordan

joue [ʒu] *nf* cheek

jouer [ʒwe] *vt* to play; *(somme d'argent, réputation)* to stake, wager; *(simuler: sentiment)* to affect, feign ♦ *vi* to play; *(THÉÂTRE, CINÉMA)* to act; *(au casino)* to gamble; *(bois, porte: se voiler)* to warp; *(clef, pièce: avoir du jeu)* to be loose; ~ **sur** *(miser)* to gamble on; ~ **de** *(MUS)* to play; ~ **à** *(jeu, sport, roulette)* to play; ~ **un tour à qn** to play a trick on sb; ~ **serré** to play a close game; ~ **la comédie** to put on an act; **bien joué!** well done!; **on joue Hamlet au théâtre X** Hamlet is on at the X theatre

jouet [ʒwɛ] *nm* toy; **être le** ~ **de** *(illusion etc)* to be the victim of

joueur, -euse [ʒwœʀ, øz] *nm/f* player; **être beau** ~ to be a good loser

joufflu, e [ʒufly] *adj* chubby-cheeked

joug [ʒu] *nm* yoke

jouir [ʒwiʀ] *vi* *(sexe: fam)* to come ♦ *vt*: ~ **de** to enjoy; **jouissance** *nf* pleasure; *(JUR)* use

joujou [ʒuʒu] *(fam) nm* toy

jour [ʒuʀ] *nm* day; *(opposé à la nuit)* day, daytime; *(clarté)* daylight; *(fig: aspect)* light; *(ouverture)* gap; **au** ~ **le** ~ from day to day; **de nos** ~**s** these days; **du** ~ **au lendemain** overnight; **il fait** ~ it's daylight; **au grand** ~ *(fig)* in the open; **mettre au** ~ to disclose; **mettre à** ~ to update; **donner le** ~ **à** to give birth to; **voir le** ~ to be born; ~ **férié** public holiday; ~ **de fête** holiday; ~ **ouvrable** week-day, working day

journal, -aux [ʒuʀnal, o] *nm* (news)paper; *(spécialisé)* journal; *(intime)* diary; ~ **de bord** log; ~ **télévisé** television news *sg*

journalier, -ière [ʒuʀnalje, jɛʀ] *adj* daily; *(banal)* everyday

journalisme [ʒuʀnalism] *nm* journalism; **journaliste** *nm/f* journalist

journée [ʒuʀne] *nf* day; **faire la** ~ **continue** to work over lunch

journellement [ʒuʀnɛlmɑ̃] *adv* daily

joyau, x [ʒwajo] *nm* gem, jewel

joyeux, -euse [ʒwajø, øz] *adj* joyful, merry; ~ **Noël!** merry Christmas!; ~ **anniversaire!** happy birthday!

jubiler [ʒybile] *vi* to be jubilant, exult

jucher [ʒyʃe] *vt, vi* to perch

judas [ʒyda] *nm (trou)* spy-hole

judiciaire [ʒydisjɛʀ] *adj* judicial

judicieux, -euse [ʒydisjø, øz] *adj* judicious

judo [ʒydo] *nm* judo

juge [ʒyʒ] *nm* judge; ~ **d'instruction** examining *(BRIT)* ou committing *(US)* magistrate; **~ de paix** justice of the peace; **~ de touche** linesman

jugé [ʒyʒe]: **au ~** *adv* by guesswork

jugement [ʒyʒmɑ̃] *nm* judgment; (*JUR: au pénal*) sentence; (: *au civil*) decision

jugeote [ʒyʒɔt] (*fam*) *nf* commonsense

juger [ʒyʒe] *vt* to judge; (*estimer*) to consider; **~ qn/qch satisfaisant** to consider sb/sth (to be) satisfactory; **~ bon de faire** to see fit to do; **~ de** to appreciate

juif, -ive [ʒɥif, ʒɥiv] *adj* Jewish ♦ *nm/f*: **J~, ive** Jew (Jewess)

juillet [ʒɥije] *nm* July

┌─────────────┐
│ **14 juillet** │
└─────────────┘

i *In France,* **le 14 juillet** *is a national holiday commemorating the storming of the Bastille during the French Revolution, celebrated by parades, music, dancing and firework displays. In Paris, there is a military parade along the Champs-Élysées, attended by the President.*

juin [ʒɥɛ̃] *nm* June

jumeau, -elle, x [ʒymo, ɛl] *adj, nm/f* twin

jumeler [ʒym(ə)le] *vt* to twin

jumelle [ʒymɛl] *adj, nf voir* **jumeau**; **~s** *nfpl* (*appareil*) binoculars

jument [ʒymɑ̃] *nf* mare

jungle [ʒœ̃gl] *nf* jungle

jupe [ʒyp] *nf* skirt

jupon [ʒypɔ̃] *nm* waist slip

juré, e [ʒyʀe] *nm/f* juror

jurer [ʒyʀe] *vt* (*obéissance etc*) to swear, vow ♦ *vi* (*dire des jurons*) to swear, curse; (*dissoner*): **~ (avec)** to clash (with); **~ de faire/que** to swear to do/that; **~ de qch** (*s'en porter garant*) to swear to sth

juridique [ʒyʀidik] *adj* legal

juron [ʒyʀɔ̃] *nm* curse, swearword

jury [ʒyʀi] *nm* jury; (*ART, SPORT*) panel of judges; (*SCOL*) board of examiners

jus [ʒy] *nm* juice; (*de viande*) gravy, (meat) juice; **~ de fruit** fruit juice

jusque [ʒysk]: **jusqu'à** *prép* (*endroit*) as far as, (up) to; (*moment*) until, till; (*limite*) up to; **~ sur/dans** up to; (*y compris*) even on/in; **jusqu'à ce que** until; **jusqu'à présent** so far; **jusqu'où?** how far?

justaucorps [ʒystokɔʀ] *nm* leotard

juste [ʒyst] *adj* (*équitable*) just, fair; (*légitime*) just; (*exact*) right; (*pertinent*) apt; (*étroit*) tight; (*insuffisant*) on the short side ♦ *adv* rightly, correctly; (*chanter*) in tune; (*exactement, seulement*) just; **~ assez/au-dessus** just enough/above; **au ~** exactly; **le ~ milieu** the happy medium; **c'était ~** it was a close thing; **justement** *adv* justly; (*précisément*) just, precisely; **justesse** *nf* (*précision*) accuracy; (*d'une remarque*) aptness; (*d'une opinion*) soundness; **de justesse** only just

justice [ʒystis] *nf* (*équité*) fairness, justice; (*ADMIN*) justice; **rendre ~ à qn** to do sb justice; **justicier, -ière** *nm/f* righter of wrongs

justificatif, -ive [ʒystifikatif, iv] *adj* (*document*) supporting; **pièce justificative** written proof

justifier [ʒystifje] *vt* to justify; **~ de** to prove

juteux, -euse [ʒytø, øz] *adj* juicy

juvénile [ʒyvenil] *adj* youthful

K, k

K [ka] *nm* (*INFORM*) K

kaki [kaki] *adj inv* khaki

kangourou [kɑ̃guʀu] *nm* kangaroo

karaté [kaʀate] *nm* karate

karting [kaʀtiŋ] *nm* go-carting, karting

kascher [kaʃɛʀ] *adj* kosher

kayak [kajak] *nm* canoe, kayak; **faire du ~** to go canoeing

képi [kepi] *nm* kepi

kermesse [kɛʀmɛs] *nf* fair; (*fête de charité*) bazaar, (charity) fête

kidnapper [kidnape] *vt* to kidnap

kilo [kilo] *nm* = **kilogramme**

kilo...: **kilogramme** *nm* kilogramme; **ki-**

lométrage nm number of kilometres travelled, ≃ mileage; **kilomètre** nm kilometre; **kilométrique** adj (distance) in kilometres

kinésithérapeute [kineziteʀapøt] nm/f physiotherapist

kiosque [kjɔsk] nm kiosk, stall; **~ à musique** bandstand

kir [kiʀ] nm kir (white wine with blackcurrant liqueur)

kit [kit] nm: **en ~** in kit form

klaxon [klaksɔn] nm horn; **klaxonner** vi, vt to hoot (BRIT), honk (US)

km abr = **kilomètre**

km/h abr (= kilomètres/heure) ≃ mph

K.-O. (fam) adj inv shattered, knackered

Kosovo [kɔsɔvo] nm Kosovo

k-way ® [kawɛ] nm (lightweight nylon) cagoule

kyste [kist] nm cyst

L, l

l' [l] art déf voir **le**

la [la] art déf voir **le ♦** nm (MUS) A; (en chantant la gamme) la

là [la] adv there; (ici) here; (dans le temps) then; **elle n'est pas ~** she isn't here; **c'est ~ que** this is where; **~ où** where; **de ~** (fig) hence; **par ~** (fig) by that; voir aussi **-ci; ce; celui; là-bas** adv there

label [label] nm stamp, seal

labeur [labœʀ] nm toil no pl, toiling no pl

labo [labo] (fam) nm (= laboratoire) lab

laboratoire [labɔʀatwaʀ] nm laboratory; **~ de langues** language laboratory

laborieux, -euse [labɔʀjø, jøz] adj (tâche) laborious

labour [labuʀ] nm ploughing no pl; **~s** nmpl (champs) ploughed fields; **cheval de ~** plough- ou cart-horse; **labourer** vt to plough

labyrinthe [labiʀɛ̃t] nm labyrinth, maze

lac [lak] nm lake

lacer [lase] vt to lace ou do up

lacérer [laseʀe] vt to tear to shreds

lacet [lasɛ] nm (de chaussure) lace; (de route) sharp bend; (piège) snare

lâche [lɑʃ] adj (poltron) cowardly; (desserré) loose, slack ♦ nm/f coward

lâcher [lɑʃe] vt to let go of; (ce qui tombe, abandonner) to drop; (oiseau, animal: libérer) to release, set free; (fig: mot, remarque) to let slip, come out with ♦ vi (freins) to fail; **~ les amarres** (NAVIG) to cast off (the moorings); **~ prise** to let go

lâcheté [lɑʃte] nf cowardice

lacrymogène [lakʀimɔʒɛn] adj: **gaz ~** teargas

lacté, e [lakte] adj (produit, régime) milk cpd

lacune [lakyn] nf gap

là-dedans [ladədɑ̃] adv inside (there), in it; (fig) in that

là-dessous [ladsu] adv underneath, under there; (fig) behind that

là-dessus [ladsy] adv on there; (fig: sur ces mots) at that point; (: à ce sujet) about that

ladite [ladit] dét voir **ledit**

lagune [lagyn] nf lagoon

là-haut [lao] adv up there

laïc [laik] adj, nm/f = **laïque**

laid, e [lɛ, lɛd] adj ugly; **laideur** nf ugliness no pl

lainage [lɛnaʒ] nm (vêtement) woollen garment; (étoffe) woollen material

laine [lɛn] nf wool

laïque [laik] adj lay, civil; (SCOL) state cpd ♦ nm/f layman(-woman)

laisse [lɛs] nf (de chien) lead, leash; **tenir en ~** to keep on a lead ou leash

laisser [lese] vt to leave ♦ vb aux: **~ qn faire** to let sb do; **se ~ aller** to let o.s. go; **laisse-toi faire** let me (ou him etc) do it; **laisser-aller** nm carelessness, slovenliness; **laissez-passer** nm inv pass

lait [lɛ] nm milk; **frère/sœur de ~** foster brother/sister; **~ condensé/concentré** evaporated/condensed milk; **~ démaquillant** cleansing milk; **laitage** nm dairy product; **laiterie** *nf* dairy; **laitier, -ière** *adj* dairy *cpd* ♦ *nm/f* milkman (dairywoman)

laiton [lɛtɔ̃] *nm* brass

laitue [lety] *nf* lettuce

laïus [lajys] (*péj*) *nm* spiel

lambeau, x [lɑ̃bo] *nm* scrap; **en ~x** in tatters, tattered

lambris [lɑ̃bʀi] *nm* panelling *no pl*

lame [lam] *nf* blade; (*vague*) wave; (*lamelle*) strip; **~ de fond** ground swell *no pl*; **~ de rasoir** razor blade; **lamelle** *nf* thin strip *ou* blade

lamentable [lamɑ̃tabl] *adj* appalling

lamenter [lamɑ̃te] *vb*: **se ~ (sur)** to moan (over)

lampadaire [lɑ̃padɛʀ] *nm* (*de salon*) standard lamp; (*dans la rue*) street lamp

lampe [lɑ̃p] *nf* lamp; (*TECH*) valve; **~ à souder** blowlamp; **~ de chevet** bedside lamp; **~ de poche** torch (*BRIT*), flashlight (*US*)

lampion [lɑ̃pjɔ̃] *nm* Chinese lantern

lance [lɑ̃s] *nf* spear; **~ d'incendie** fire hose

lancée [lɑ̃se] *nf*: **être/continuer sur sa ~** to be under way/keep going

lancement [lɑ̃smɑ̃] *nm* launching

lance-pierres [lɑ̃spjɛʀ] *nm inv* catapult

lancer [lɑ̃se] *nm* (*SPORT*) throwing *no pl*, throw ♦ *vt* to throw; (*émettre, projeter*) to throw out, send out; (*produit, fusée, bateau, artiste*) to launch; (*injure*) to hurl, fling; **se ~** *vi* (*prendre de l'élan*) to build up speed; (*se précipiter*): **se ~ sur** *ou* **contre** to rush at; **se ~ dans** (*discussion*) to launch into; (*aventure*) to embark on; **~ qch à qn** to throw sth to sb; (*de façon agressive*) to throw sth at sb; **~ du poids** putting the shot

lancinant, e [lɑ̃sinɑ̃, ɑ̃t] *adj* (*douleur*) shooting

landau [lɑ̃do] *nm* pram (*BRIT*), baby carriage (*US*)

lande [lɑ̃d] *nf* moor

langage [lɑ̃gaʒ] *nm* language

langouste [lɑ̃gust] *nf* crayfish *inv*; **lan-**

goustine *nf* Dublin Bay prawn

langue [lɑ̃g] *nf* (*ANAT, CULIN*) tongue; (*LING*) language; **tirer la ~ (à)** to stick out one's tongue (at); **de ~ française** French-speaking; **~ maternelle** native language, mother tongue; **~ vivante/ étrangère** modern/foreign language

langueur [lɑ̃gœʀ] *nf* languidness

languir [lɑ̃giʀ] *vi* to languish; (*conversation*) to flag; **faire ~ qn** to keep sb waiting

lanière [lanjɛʀ] *nf* (*de fouet*) lash; (*de sac, bretelle*) strap

lanterne [lɑ̃tɛʀn] *nf* (*portable*) lantern; (*électrique*) light, lamp; (*de voiture*) (side)light

laper [lape] *vt* to lap up

lapidaire [lapidɛʀ] *adj* (*fig*) terse

lapin [lapɛ̃] *nm* rabbit; (*peau*) rabbitskin; (*fourrure*) cony; **poser un ~ à qn** (*fam*) to stand sb up

Laponie [lapɔni] *nf* Lapland

laps [laps] *nm*: **~ de temps** space of time, time *no pl*

laque [lak] *nf* (*vernis*) lacquer; (*pour cheveux*) hair spray

laquelle [lakɛl] *pron voir* **lequel**

larcin [laʀsɛ̃] *nm* theft

lard [laʀ] *nm* (*bacon*) (streaky) bacon; (*graisse*) fat

lardon [laʀdɔ̃] *nm*: **~s** chopped bacon

large [laʀʒ] *adj* wide, broad; (*fig*) generous ♦ *adv*: **calculer/voir ~** to allow extra/ think big ♦ *nm* (*largeur*): **5 m de ~** 5 m wide *ou* in width; (*mer*): **le ~** the open sea; **au ~ de** off; **~ d'esprit** broadminded; **largement** *adv* widely; (*de loin*) greatly; (*au moins*) easily; (*généreusement*) generously; **c'est largement suffisant** that's ample; **largesse** *nf* generosity; **largesses** *nfpl* (*dons*) liberalities; **largeur** *nf* (*qu'on mesure*) width; (*impression visuelle*) wideness, width; (*d'esprit*) broadness

larguer [laʀge] *vt* to drop; **~ les amarres** to cast off (the moorings)

larme [laʀm] *nf* tear; (*fam: goutte*) drop; **en ~s** in tears; **larmoyer** *vi* (*yeux*) to water; (*se plaindre*) to whimper

larvé, e [laʀve] *adj* (*fig*) latent

laryngite [laʀɛ̃ʒit] *nf* laryngitis

las, lasse [lɑ, lɑs] *adj* weary

laser [lazɛʀ] *nm*: **(rayon)** ~ laser (beam);
chaîne ~ compact disc (player); **disque**
~ compact disc

lasse [lɑs] *adj voir* **las**

lasser [lɑse] *vt* to weary, tire; **se** ~ **de** *vt*
to grow weary *ou* tired of

latéral, e, -aux [lateʀal, o] *adj* side *cpd*,
lateral

latin, e [latɛ̃, in] *adj* Latin ♦ *nm/f*: **L**~, **e**
Latin ♦ *nm* (*LING*) Latin

latitude [latityd] *nf* latitude

latte [lat] *nf* lath, slat; (*de plancher*) board

lauréat, e [lɔʀea, at] *nm/f* winner

laurier [lɔʀje] *nm* (*BOT*) laurel; (*CULIN*) bay
leaves *pl*

lavable [lavabl] *adj* washable

lavabo [lavabo] *nm* washbasin; ~**s** *nmpl*
(*toilettes*) toilet *sg*

lavage [lavaʒ] *nm* washing *no pl*, wash; ~
de cerveau brainwashing *no pl*

lavande [lavɑ̃d] *nf* lavender

lave [lav] *nf* lava *no pl*

lave-linge [lavlɛ̃ʒ] *nm inv* washing
machine

laver [lave] *vt* to wash; (*tache*) to wash off;
se ~ *vi* to have a wash, wash; **se** ~ **les
mains/dents** to wash one's hands/clean
one's teeth; ~ **qn** (*accusation*) to clear
sb of; **laverie** *nf*: **laverie (automatique)**
launderette; **lavette** *nf* dish cloth; (*fam*)
drip; **laveur, -euse** *nm/f* cleaner; **lave-
vaisselle** *nm inv* dishwasher; **lavoir** *nm*
wash house; (*évier*) sink

laxatif, -ive [laksatif, iv] *adj, nm* laxative

layette [lejɛt] *nf* baby clothes

MOT-CLÉ

le [lə], **la, l'** (*pl* **les**) *art déf* **1** the; **le
livre/la pomme/l'arbre** the book/the
apple/the tree; **les étudiants** the students
2 (*noms abstraits*): **le courage/l'amour/la
jeunesse** courage/love/youth

3 (*indiquant la possession*): **se casser la
jambe** *etc* to break one's leg *etc*; **levez la
main** put your hand up; **avoir les yeux
gris/le nez rouge** to have grey eyes/a
red nose

4 (*temps*): **le matin/soir** in the morning/
evening; mornings/evenings; **le jeudi**
(*d'habitude*) on Thursdays *etc*; (*ce jeudi-là
etc*) on (the) Thursday

5 (*distribution, évaluation*) a, an; **10 F le
mètre/kilo** 10F a *ou* per metre/kilo; **le
tiers/quart de** a third/quarter of

♦ *pron* **1** (*personne: mâle*) him; (*personne:
femelle*) her; (: *pluriel*) them; **je le/la/les
vois** I can see him/her/them

2 (*animal, chose: singulier*) it; (: *pluriel*)
them; **je le** (*ou* **la**) **vois** I can see it; **je les
vois** I can see them

3 (*remplaçant une phrase*): **je ne le savais
pas** I didn't know (about it); **il était riche
et ne l'est plus** he was once rich but no
longer is

---

lécher [leʃe] *vt* to lick; (*laper: lait, eau*) to
lick *ou* lap up; **lèche-vitrines** *nm*: **faire
du lèche-vitrines** to go window-
shopping

leçon [l(ə)sɔ̃] *nf* lesson; **faire la** ~ **à** (*fig*)
to give a lecture to; ~**s de conduite** driv-
ing lessons

lecteur, -trice [lektœʀ, tʀis] *nm/f* reader;
(*d'université*) foreign language assistant
♦ *nm* (*TECH*): ~ **de cassettes/CD** cas-
sette/CD player; ~ **de disquette** disk drive

lecture [lektyʀ] *nf* reading

ledit [lədi], **ladite** (*mpl* **lesdits**, *fpl* **lesdites**) *dét* the aforesaid

légal, e, -aux [legal, o] *adj* legal; **légali-
ser** *vt* to legalize; **légalité** *nf* law

légendaire [leʒɑ̃dɛʀ] *adj* legendary

légende [leʒɑ̃d] *nf* (*mythe*) legend; (*de
carte, plan*) key; (*de dessin*) caption

léger, -ère [leʒe, ɛʀ] *adj* light; (*bruit, retard*) slight; (*personne: superficiel*) thoughtless; (: *volage*) free and easy; **à la légère**
(*parler, agir*) rashly, thoughtlessly; **lé-**

gèrement *adv* (*s'habiller*, *bouger*) lightly; (*un peu*) slightly; **manger légèrement** to eat a light meal; **légèreté** *nf* lightness; (*d'une remarque*) flippancy

Légion d'honneur

i *Created by Napoleon in 1802 to reward service to the state,* **la Légion d'honneur** *is a prestigious French order headed by the President of the Republic, the Grand Maître. Members receive an annual tax-free payment.*

législatif, -ive [leʒislatif, iv] *adj* legislative; **législatives** *nfpl* general election *sg*

légitime [leʒitim] *adj* (*JUR*) lawful, legitimate; (*fig*) rightful, legitimate; **en état de ~ défense** in self-defence

legs [leg] *nm* legacy

léguer [lege] *vt*: **~ qch à qn** (*JUR*) to bequeath sth to sb

légume [legym] *nm* vegetable

lendemain [lɑ̃dmɛ̃] *nm*: **le ~** the next *ou* following day; **le ~ matin/soir** the next *ou* following morning/evening; **le ~ de** the day after

lent, e [lɑ̃, lɑ̃t] *adj* slow; **lentement** *adv* slowly; **lenteur** *nf* slowness *no pl*

lentille [lɑ̃tij] *nf* (*OPTIQUE*) lens *sg*; (*CULIN*) lentil

léopard [leɔpaʀ] *nm* leopard

lèpre [lɛpʀ] *nf* leprosy

MOT-CLÉ

lequel, laquelle [ləkɛl, lakɛl] (*mpl* **lesquels**, *fpl* **lesquelles**) (*à* + *lequel* = **auquel**, *de* + *lequel* = **duquel** *etc*) *pron* 1 (*interrogatif*) which, which one

2 (*relatif: personne: sujet*) who; (*: objet, après préposition*) whom; (*: chose*) which

♦ *adj*: **auquel cas** in which case

les [le] *dét voir* **le**

lesbienne [lɛsbjɛn] *nf* lesbian

lesdites [ledit], **lesdits** [ledi] *dét pl voir* **ledit**

léser [leze] *vt* to wrong

lésiner [lezine] *vi*: **ne pas ~ sur les moyens** (*pour mariage etc*) to push the boat out

lésion [lezjɔ̃] *nf* lesion, damage *no pl*

lesquelles, lesquels [lekɛl] *pron pl voir* **lequel**

lessive [lesiv] *nf* (*poudre*) washing powder; (*linge*) washing *no pl*, wash; **lessiver** *vt* to wash; (*fam: fatiguer*) to tire out, exhaust

lest [lɛst] *nm* ballast

leste [lɛst] *adj* sprightly, nimble

lettre [lɛtʀ] *nf* letter; **~s** *nfpl* (*littérature*) literature *sg*; (*SCOL*) arts (subjects); **à la ~** literally; **en toutes ~s** in full

leucémie [løsemi] *nf* leukaemia

MOT-CLÉ

leur [lœʀ] *adj possessif* their; **leur maison** their house; **leurs amis** their friends

♦ *pron* 1 (*objet indirect*) (to) them; **je leur ai dit la vérité** I told them the truth; **je le leur ai donné** I gave it to them, I gave them it

2 (*possessif*): **le(la) leur, les leurs** theirs

leurre [lœʀ] *nm* (*fig: illusion*) delusion; (*: duperie*) deception; **leurrer** *vt* to delude, deceive

leurs [lœʀ] *adj voir* **leur**

levain [ləvɛ̃] *nm* leaven

levé, e [ləve] *adj*: **être ~** to be up; **levée** *nf* (*POSTES*) collection

lever [l(ə)ve] *vt* (*vitre, bras etc*) to raise; (*soulever de terre, supprimer: interdiction, siège*) to lift; (*impôts, armée*) to levy ♦ *vi* to rise ♦ *nm*: **au ~** on getting up; **se ~** *vi* to get up; (*soleil*) to rise; (*jour*) to break; (*brouillard*) to lift; **~ de soleil** sunrise; **~ du jour** daybreak

levier [ləvje] *nm* lever

lèvre [lɛvʀ] *nf* lip

lévrier [levʀije] *nm* greyhound

levure [l(ə)vyʀ] *nf* yeast; **~ chimique** baking powder

lexique [lɛksik] *nm* vocabulary; (*glossaire*) lexicon

lézard [lezaʀ] *nm* lizard

lézarde [lezaʀd] *nf* crack

liaison [ljɛzɔ̃] *nf* (*rapport*) connection; (*transport*) link; (*amoureuse*) affair; (*PHONÉTIQUE*) liaison; **entrer/être en ~ avec** to get/be in contact with

liane [ljan] *nf* creeper

liant, e [ljɑ̃, ljɑ̃t] *adj* sociable

liasse [ljas] *nf* wad, bundle

Liban [libɑ̃] *nm*: **le ~** (the) Lebanon; **libanais, e** *adj* Lebanese ♦ *nm/f*: **Libanais, e** Lebanese

libeller [libele] *vt* (*chèque, mandat*): **~ (au nom de)** to make out (to); (*lettre*) to word

libellule [libelyl] *nf* dragonfly

libéral, e, -aux [liberal, o] *adj, nm/f* liberal; **profession ~** (liberal) profession

libérer [libere] *vt* (*délivrer*) to free, liberate; (*relâcher: prisonnier*) to discharge, release; (: *d'inhibitions*) to liberate; (*gaz*) to release; **se ~** *vi* (*de rendez-vous*) to get out of previous engagements

liberté [liberte] *nf* freedom; (*loisir*) free time; **~s** *nfpl* (*privautés*) liberties; **mettre/être en ~** to set/be free; **en ~ provisoire/surveillée/conditionnelle** on bail/probation/parole

libraire [libʀɛʀ] *nm/f* bookseller

librairie [libʀɛʀi] *nf* bookshop

libre [libʀ] *adj* free; (*route, voie*) clear; (*place, salle*) free; (*ligne*) not engaged; (*SCOL*) non-state; **~ de qch/de faire** free from sth/to do; **~ arbitre** free will; **libre-échange** *nm* free trade; **libre-service** *nm* self-service store

Libye [libi] *nf*: **la ~** Libya

licence [lisɑ̃s] *nf* (*permis*) permit; (*diplôme*) degree; (*liberté*) liberty; **licencié, e** *nm/f* (*SCOL*): **licencié ès lettres/en droit** ≃ Bachelor of Arts/Law

licenciement [lisɑ̃simɑ̃] *nm* redundancy

licencier [lisɑ̃sje] *vt* (*débaucher*) to make redundant, lay off; (*renvoyer*) to dismiss

licite [lisit] *adj* lawful

lie [li] *nf* dregs *pl*, sediment

lié, e [lje] *adj*: **très ~ avec** very friendly with *ou* close to

liège [ljɛʒ] *nm* cork

lien [ljɛ̃] *nm* (*corde, fig: affectif*) bond; (*rapport*) link, connection; **~ de parenté** family tie

lier [lje] *vt* (*attacher*) to tie up; (*joindre*) to link up; (*fig: unir, engager*) to bind; **se ~ avec** to make friends with; **~ qch à** to tie *ou* link sth to; **~ conversation avec** to strike up a conversation with

lierre [ljɛʀ] *nm* ivy

liesse [ljɛs] *nf*: **être en ~** to be celebrating *ou* jubilant

lieu, x [ljø] *nm* place; **~x** *nmpl* (*locaux*) premises; (*endroit: d'un accident etc*) scene *sg*; **en ~ sûr** in a safe place; **en premier ~** in the first place; **en dernier ~** lastly; **avoir ~** to take place; **tenir ~ de** to serve as; **donner ~ à** to give rise to; **au ~ de** instead of; **lieu-dit** (*pl* **lieux-dits**) *nm* locality

lieutenant [ljøt(ə)nɑ̃] *nm* lieutenant

lièvre [ljɛvʀ] *nm* hare

ligament [ligamɑ̃] *nm* ligament

ligne [liɲ] *nf* (*gén*) line; (*TRANSPORTS: liaison*) service; (: *trajet*) route; (*silhouette*) figure; **entrer en ~ de compte** to come into it

lignée [liɲe] *nf* line, lineage

ligoter [ligɔte] *vt* to tie up

ligue [lig] *nf* league; **liguer** *vt*: **se liguer contre** (*fig*) to combine against

lilas [lila] *nm* lilac

limace [limas] *nf* slug

limande [limɑ̃d] *nf* dab

lime [lim] *nf* file; **~ à ongles** nail file; **limer** *vt* to file

limier [limje] *nm* bloodhound; (*détective*) sleuth

limitation [limitasjɔ̃] *nf*: **~ de vitesse** speed limit

limite [limit] *nf* (*de terrain*) boundary; (*partie ou point extrême*) limit; **vitesse/charge**

~ maximum speed/load; **cas** ~ border-line case; **date** ~ deadline; **limiter** *vt* (*restreindre*) to limit, restrict; (*délimiter*) to border; **limitrophe** *adj* border *cpd*

limoger [limɔʒe] *vt* to dismiss

limon [limɔ̃] *nm* silt

limonade [limɔnad] *nf* lemonade

lin [lɛ̃] *nm* (*tissu*) linen

linceul [lɛ̃sœl] *nm* shroud

linge [lɛ̃ʒ] *nm* (*serviettes etc*) linen; (*lessive*) washing; (*aussi*: ~ **de corps**) underwear; **lingerie** *nf* lingerie, underwear

lingot [lɛ̃go] *nm* ingot

linguistique [lɛ̃gɥistik] *adj* linguistic ♦ *nf* linguistics *sg*

lion, ne [ljɔ̃, ljɔn] *nm/f* lion (lioness); (*signe*): **le L~** Leo; **lionceau, x** *nm* lion cub

liqueur [likœʀ] *nf* liqueur

liquidation [likidasjɔ̃] *nf* (*vente*) sale

liquide [likid] *adj* liquid ♦ *nm* liquid; (*COMM*): **en** ~ in ready money *ou* cash; **liquider** *vt* to liquidate; (*COMM*: *articles*) to clear, sell off; **liquidités** *nfpl* (*COMM*) liquid assets

lire [liʀ] *nf* (*monnaie*) lira ♦ *vt, vi* to read

lis [lis] *nm* = **lys**

lisible [lizibl] *adj* legible

lisière [lizjɛʀ] *nf* (*de forêt*) edge

lisons [lizɔ̃] *vb voir* **lire**

lisse [lis] *adj* smooth

liste [list] *nf* list; **faire la** ~ **de** to list; ~ **électorale** electoral roll; **listing** *nm* (*INFORM*) printout

lit [li] *nm* bed; **petit** ~, **lit à une place** single bed; **grand** ~, **lit à deux places** double bed; **faire son** ~ to make one's bed; **aller/se mettre au** ~ to go to/get into bed; ~ **de camp** campbed; ~ **d'enfant** cot (*BRIT*), crib (*US*)

literie [litʀi] *nf* bedding, bedclothes *pl*

litière [litjɛʀ] *nf* litter

litige [litiʒ] *nm* dispute

litre [litʀ] *nm* litre

littéraire [liteʀɛʀ] *adj* literary ♦ *nm/f* arts student; **elle est très** ~ (she's very literary)

littéral, e, -aux [liteʀal, o] *adj* literal

littérature [liteʀatyʀ] *nf* literature

littoral, -aux [litɔʀal, o] *nm* coast

liturgie [lityʀʒi] *nf* liturgy

livide [livid] *adj* livid, pallid

livraison [livʀɛzɔ̃] *nf* delivery

livre [livʀ] *nm* book ♦ *nf* (*poids, monnaie*) pound; ~ **de bord** logbook; ~ **de poche** paperback

livré, e [livʀe] *adj*: ~ **à soi-même** left to o.s. *ou* one's own devices; **livrée** *nf* livery

livrer [livʀe] *vt* (*COMM*) to deliver; (*otage, coupable*) to hand over; (*secret, information*) to give away; **se** ~ **à** (*se confier*) to confide in; (*se rendre, s'abandonner*) to give o.s. up to; (*faire: pratiques, actes*) to indulge in; (*enquête*) to carry out

livret [livʀɛ] *nm* booklet; (*d'opéra*) libretto; ~ **de caisse d'épargne** (savings) bank-book; ~ **de famille** (official) family record book; ~ **scolaire** (school) report book

livreur, -euse [livʀœʀ, øz] *nm/f* delivery boy *ou* man/girl *ou* woman

local, e, -aux [lɔkal, o] *adj* local ♦ *nm* (*salle*) premises *pl*; *voir aussi* **locaux**; **localiser** *vt* (*repérer*) to locate, place; (*limiter*) to confine; **localité** *nf* locality

locataire [lɔkatɛʀ] *nm/f* tenant; (*de chambre*) lodger

location [lɔkasjɔ̃] *nf* (*par le locataire, le loueur*) renting; (*par le propriétaire*) renting out, letting; (*THÉÂTRE*) booking office; **"~ de voitures"** "car rental"; **habiter en** ~ to live in rented accommodation; **prendre une** ~ (**pour les vacances**) to rent a house *etc* (for the holidays)

locaux [lɔko] *nmpl* premises

locomotive [lɔkɔmɔtiv] *nf* locomotive, engine

locution [lɔkysjɔ̃] *nf* phrase

loge [lɔʒ] *nf* (*THÉÂTRE: d'artiste*) dressing room; (: *de spectateurs*) box; (*de concierge, franc-maçon*) lodge

logement [lɔʒmɑ̃] *nm* accommodation *no pl* (*BRIT*), accommodations *pl* (*US*); (*appartement*) flat (*BRIT*), apartment (*US*); (*héber-*

gement) housing *no pl*

loger [lɔʒe] *vt* to accommodate ♦ *vi* to live; **se ~ dans** *(suj: balle, flèche)* to lodge itself in; **trouver à se ~** to find accommodation; **logeur, -euse** *nm/f* landlord(-lady)

logiciel [lɔʒisjɛl] *nm* software

logique [lɔʒik] *adj* logical ♦ *nf* logic

logis [lɔʒi] *nm* abode, dwelling

logo [lɔgo] *nm* logo

loi [lwa] *nf* law; **faire la ~** to lay down the law

loin [lwɛ̃] *adv* far; *(dans le temps: futur)* a long way off; *(: passé)* a long time ago; **plus ~** further; **~ de** far from; **au ~** far off; **de ~** from a distance; *(fig: de beaucoup)* by far

lointain, e [lwɛ̃tɛ̃, ɛn] *adj* faraway, distant; *(dans le futur, passé)* distant; *(cause, parent)* remote, distant ♦ *nm*: **dans le ~** in the distance

loir [lwaʀ] *nm* dormouse

loisir [lwaziʀ] *nm*: **heures de ~** spare time; **~s** *nmpl (temps libre)* leisure *sg*; *(activités)* leisure activities; **avoir le ~ de faire** to have the time *ou* opportunity to do; **à ~** at leisure

londonien, ne [lɔ̃dɔnjɛ̃, jɛn] *adj* London *cpd*, of London ♦ *nm/f*: **L~, ne** Londoner

Londres [lɔ̃dʀ] *n* London

long, longue [lɔ̃, lɔ̃g] *adj* long ♦ *adv*: **en savoir ~** to know a great deal ♦ *nm*: **de 3 m de ~** 3 m long, 3 m in length; **ne pas faire ~ feu** not to last long; **(tout) le ~ de** (all) along; **tout au ~ de** *(année, vie)* throughout; **de ~ en large** *(marcher)* to and fro, up and down; *voir aussi* **longue**

longer [lɔ̃ʒe] *vt* to go *(ou* walk *ou* drive) along(side); *(suj: mur, route)* to border

longiligne [lɔ̃ʒiliɲ] *adj* long-limbed

longitude [lɔ̃ʒityd] *nf* longitude

longtemps [lɔ̃tɑ̃] *adv* (for) a long time, (for) long; **avant ~** before long; **pour** *ou* **pendant ~** for a long time; **mettre ~ à faire** to take a long time to do

longue [lɔ̃g] *adj voir* **long** ♦ *nf*: **à la ~** in

the end; **longuement** *adv (longtemps)* for a long time; *(en détail)* at length

longueur [lɔ̃gœʀ] *nf* length; **~s** *nfpl (fig: d'un film etc)* tedious parts; **en ~** lengthwise; **tirer en ~** to drag on; **à ~ de journée** all day long; **~ d'onde** wavelength

longue-vue [lɔ̃gvy] *nf* telescope

look [luk] *(fam) nm* look, image

lopin [lɔpɛ̃] *nm*: **~ de terre** patch of land

loque [lɔk] *nf (personne)* wreck; **~s** *nfpl (habits)* rags

loquet [lɔkɛ] *nm* latch

lorgner [lɔʀɲe] *vt* to eye; *(fig)* to have one's eye on

lors [lɔʀ]: **~ de** *prép* at the time of; during

lorsque [lɔʀsk] *conj* when, as

losange [lɔzɑ̃ʒ] *nm* diamond

lot [lo] *nm (part)* share; *(de ~erie)* prize; *(fig: destin)* fate, lot; *(COMM, INFORM)* batch; **le gros ~** the jackpot

loterie [lɔtʀi] *nf* lottery

loti, e [lɔti] *adj*: **bien / mal ~** well-/badly off

lotion [losjɔ̃] *nf* lotion

lotissement [lɔtismɑ̃] *nm* housing development; *(parcelle)* plot, lot

loto [lɔto] *nm* lotto

Loto

i **Le Loto** is a state-run national lottery with large cash prizes. Participants select 7 numbers out of 49. The more correct numbers, the greater the prize. The draw is televised twice weekly.

---

lotte [lɔt] *nf* monkfish

louable [lwabl] *adj* commendable

louanges [lwɑ̃ʒ] *nfpl* praise *sg*

loubard [lubaʀ] *(fam) nm* lout

louche [luʃ] *adj* shady, fishy, dubious ♦ *nf* ladle; **loucher** *vi* to squint

louer [lwe] *vt (maison: suj: propriétaire)* to let, rent (out); *(: locataire)* to rent; *(voiture etc: entreprise)* to hire out *(BRIT)*, rent (out); *(: locataire)* to hire, rent; *(réserver)* to book; *(faire l'éloge de)* to praise; **"à ~"**

"to let" (BRIT), "for rent" (US)

loup [lu] nm wolf

loupe [lup] nf magnifying glass

louper [lupe] (fam) vt (manquer) to miss; (examen) to flunk

lourd, e [luʀ, luʀd] adj, adv heavy; **~ de** (conséquences, menaces) charged with; **il fait ~** the weather is close, it's sultry; **lourdaud, e** (péj) adj clumsy; **lourdement** adv heavily; **lourdeur** nf weight; **lourdeurs d'estomac** indigestion

loutre [lutʀ] nf otter

louveteau, x [luv(ə)to] nm wolf-cub; (scout) cub (scout)

louvoyer [luvwaje] vi (fig) to hedge, evade the issue

loyal, e, -aux [lwajal, o] adj (fidèle) loyal, faithful; (fair-play) fair; **loyauté** nf loyalty, faithfulness; fairness

loyer [lwaje] nm rent

lu, e [ly] pp de **lire**

lubie [lybi] nf whim, craze

lubrifiant [lybʀifjɑ̃, jɑ̃t] nm lubricant

lubrifier [lybʀifje] vt to lubricate

lubrique [lybʀik] adj lecherous

lucarne [lykaʀn] nf skylight

lucide [lysid] adj lucid; (accidenté) conscious

lucratif, -ive [lykʀatif, iv] adj lucrative, profitable; **à but non ~** non profit-making

lueur [lɥœʀ] nf (pâle) (faint) light; (chatoyante) glimmer no pl; (fig) glimmer; gleam

luge [lyʒ] nf sledge (BRIT), sled (US)

lugubre [lygybʀ] adj gloomy, dismal

MOT-CLÉ

lui [lɥi] pron 1 (objet indirect: mâle) (to) him; (: femelle) (to) her; (: chose, animal) (to) it; **je lui ai parlé** I have spoken to him (ou to her); **il lui a offert un cadeau** he gave him (ou her) a present

2 (après préposition, comparatif: personne) him; (: chose, animal) it; **elle est contente de lui** she is pleased with him; **je la connais mieux que lui** I know her better than he does; I know her better than him

3 (sujet, forme emphatique) he; **lui, il est à Paris** HE is in Paris

4: **lui-même** himself; itself

luire [lɥiʀ] vi to shine; (en rougeoyant) to glow

lumière [lymjɛʀ] nf light; **mettre en ~** (fig) to highlight; **~ du jour** daylight

luminaire [lyminɛʀ] nm lamp, light

lumineux, -euse [lyminø, øz] adj luminous; (éclairé) illuminated; (ciel, couleur) bright; (rayon) of light, light cpd; (fig: regard) radiant

lunatique [lynatik] adj whimsical, temperamental

lundi [lœdi] nm Monday; **~ de Pâques** Easter Monday

lune [lyn] nf moon; **~ de miel** honeymoon

lunette [lynɛt] nf: **~s ♦** nfpl glasses, spectacles; (protectrices) goggles; **~ arrière** (AUTO) rear window; **~s de soleil** sunglasses

lus etc [ly] vb voir **lire**

lustre [lystʀ] nm (de plafond) chandelier; (fig: éclat) lustre; **lustrer** vt to shine

lut [ly] vb voir **lire**

luth [lyt] nm lute

lutin [lytɛ̃] nm imp, goblin

lutte [lyt] nf (conflit) struggle; (sport) wrestling; **lutter** vi to fight, struggle

luxe [lyks] nm luxury; **de ~** luxury cpd

Luxembourg [lyksɑ̃buʀ] nm: **le ~** Luxembourg

luxer [lykse] vt: **se ~ l'épaule** to dislocate one's shoulder

luxueux, -euse [lyksɥø, øz] adj luxurious

luxure [lyksyʀ] nf lust

luxuriant, e [lyksyʀjɑ̃, jɑ̃t] adj luxuriant

lycée [lise] nm secondary school; **lycéen, ne** nm/f secondary school pupil

lyophilisé, e [ljɔfilize] adj (café) freeze-dried

lyrique [liʀik] adj lyrical; (OPÉRA) lyric; **artiste ~** opera singer

lys [lis] *nm* lily

M, m

M *abr* = **Monsieur**

m' [m] *pron voir* **me**

ma [ma] *adj voir* **mon**

macaron [makaʀɔ̃] *nm* (*gâteau*) macaroon; (*insigne*) (round) badge

macaronis [makaʀɔni] *nmpl* macaroni *sg*

macédoine [masedwan] *nf*: **~ de fruits** fruit salad; **~ de légumes** mixed vegetables

macérer [maseʀe] *vi, vt* to macerate; (*dans du vinaigre*) to pickle

mâcher [mɑʃe] *vt* to chew; **ne pas ~ ses mots** not to mince one's words

machin [maʃɛ̃] (*fam*) *nm* thing(umajig)

machinal, e, -aux [maʃinal, o] *adj* mechanical, automatic; **machinalement** *adv* mechanically, automatically

machination [maʃinasjɔ̃] *nf* frame-up

machine [maʃin] *nf* machine; (*locomotive*) engine; **~ à écrire** typewriter; **~ à laver/ coudre** washing/sewing machine; **~ à sous** fruit machine

macho [matʃo] (*fam*) *nm* male chauvinist

mâchoire [mɑʃwaʀ] *nf* jaw

mâchonner [mɑʃɔne] *vt* to chew (at)

maçon [masɔ̃] *nm* builder; (*poseur de briques*) bricklayer; **maçonnerie** *nf* (*murs*) brickwork; (*pierres*) masonry, stonework

maculer [makyle] *vt* to stain

Madame [madam] (*pl* **Mesdames**) *nf*: **~ X** Mrs X; **occupez-vous de ~/ Monsieur/Mademoiselle** please serve this lady/gentleman/(young) lady; **bonjour ~/Monsieur/Mademoiselle** good morning; (*ton déférent*) good morning Madam/Sir/Madam; (*le nom est connu*) good morning Mrs/Mr/Miss X; **~/Monsieur/Mademoiselle!** (*pour appeler*) Madam/Sir/Miss!; **~/Monsieur/Mademoiselle** (*sur lettre*) Dear Madam/Sir/ Madam; **chère ~/cher Monsieur/chère**

Mademoiselle Dear Mrs/Mr/Miss X; **Mesdames** Ladies

madeleine [madlɛn] *nf* madeleine; *small sponge cake*

Mademoiselle [madmwazɛl] (*pl* **Mesdemoiselles**) *nf* Miss; *voir aussi* **Madame**

madère [madɛʀ] *nm* Madeira (wine)

magasin [magazɛ̃] *nm* (*boutique*) shop; (*entrepôt*) warehouse; **en ~** (*COMM*) in stock

magazine [magazin] *nm* magazine

Maghreb [magʀɛb] *nm*: **le ~** North Africa; **maghrébin, e** *adj* North African ♦ *nm/f*: **Maghrébin, e** North African

magicien, ne [maʒisjɛ̃, jɛn] *nm/f* magician

magie [maʒi] *nf* magic; **magique** *adj* magic; (*enchanteur*) magical

magistral, e, -aux [maʒistʀal, o] *adj* (*œuvre, adresse*) masterly; (*ton*) authoritative; **cours ~** lecture

magistrat [maʒistʀa] *nm* magistrate

magnat [magna] *nm* tycoon

magnétique [maɲetik] *adj* magnetic

magnétiser [maɲetize] *vt* to magnetize; (*fig*) to mesmerize, hypnotize

magnétophone [maɲetɔfɔn] *nm* tape recorder; **~ à cassettes** cassette recorder

magnétoscope [maɲetɔskɔp] *nm* videotape recorder

magnifique [maɲifik] *adj* magnificent

magot [mago] (*fam*) *nm* (*argent*) pile (of money); (*économies*) nest egg

magouille [maguj] (*fam*) *nf* scheming; **magouiller** (*fam*) *vi* to scheme

magret [magʀɛ] *nm*: **~ de canard** duck steaklet

mai [mɛ] *nm* May

mai

i **Le premier mai** *is a public holiday in France marking union demonstrations in the United States in 1886 to secure the eight-hour working day. It is traditional to exchange and wear sprigs of lily of the valley.* **Le 8 mai** *is a public holiday in*

France commemorating the surrender of the German army to Eisenhower on May 7, 1945. There are parades of ex-servicemen in most towns. The social upheavals of May and June 1968, marked by student demonstrations, strikes and rioting, are generally referred to as "les événements de **mai 68"***. De Gaulle's government survived, but reforms in education and a move towards decentralization ensued.*

---

maigre [mɛgʀ] *adj* (very) thin, skinny; (*viande*) lean; (*fromage*) low-fat; (*végétation*) thin, sparse; (*fig*) poor, meagre, skimpy; **jours ~s** days of abstinence, fish days; **maigreur** *nf* thinness; **maigrir** *vi* to get thinner, lose weight; **maigrir de 2 kilos** to lose 2 kilos

maille [maj] *nf* stitch; **avoir ~ à partir avec qn** to have a brush with sb; **~ à l'endroit/à l'envers** plain/purl stitch

maillet [majɛ] *nm* mallet

maillon [majɔ̃] *nm* link

maillot [majo] *nm* (*aussi: ~* **de corps**) vest; (*de sportif*) jersey; **~ de bain** swimsuit; (*d'homme*) bathing trunks *pl*

main [mɛ̃] *nf* hand; **à la ~** in one's hand; **se donner la ~** to hold hands; **donner** *ou* **tendre la ~ à qn** to hold out one's hand to sb; **serrer la ~ à qn** to shake hands with sb; **sous la ~** to *ou* at hand; **à remettre en ~s propres** to be delivered personally; **mettre la dernière ~ à** to put the finishing touches to; **se faire/ perdre la ~** to get one's hand in/lose one's touch; **avoir qch bien en ~** to have (got) the hang of sth; **main-d'œuvre** *nf* manpower, labour; **main-forte** *nf*: **prêter main-forte à qn** to come to sb's assistance; **mainmise** *nf* (*fig*): **mainmise sur** complete hold on

maint, e [mɛ̃, mɛ̃t] *adj* many a; **~s** many; **à ~es reprises** time and (time) again

maintenant [mɛ̃t(ə)nɑ̃] *adv* now; (*actuellement*) nowadays

maintenir [mɛ̃t(ə)niʀ] *vt* (*retenir, soutenir*) to support; (*contenir: foule etc*) to hold back; (*conserver, affirmer*) to maintain; **se ~** *vi* (*prix*) to keep steady; (*amélioration*) to persist

maintien [mɛ̃tjɛ̃] *nm* (*sauvegarde*) maintenance; (*attitude*) bearing

maire [mɛʀ] *nm* mayor; **mairie** *nf* (*bâtiment*) town hall; (*administration*) town council

mais [mɛ] *conj* but; **~ non!** of course not!; **~ enfin** but after all; (*indignation*) look here!

maïs [mais] *nm* maize (*BRIT*), corn (*US*)

maison [mɛzɔ̃] *nf* house; (*chez-soi*) home; (*COMM*) firm ♦ *adj inv* (*CULIN*) homemade; (*fig*) in-house, own; **à la ~** at home; (*direction*) home; **~ close** *ou* **de passe** brothel; **~ de repos** convalescent home; **~ de santé** mental home; **~ des jeunes** ≈ youth club; **~ mère** parent company; **maisonnée** *nf* household, family; **maisonnette** *nf* small house, cottage

---

maisons des jeunes et de la culture

(i) **Maisons des jeunes et de la culture** are centres for young people which organize a wide range of sporting and cultural activities, and are also engaged in welfare work. The centres are, in part, publicly financed.

---

maître, -esse [mɛtʀ, mɛtʀɛs] *nm/f* master (mistress); (*SCOL*) teacher, schoolmaster(-mistress) ♦ *nm* (*peintre etc*) master; (*titre*): **M~** Maître, *term of address gen for a barrister* ♦ *adj* (*principal, essentiel*) main; **être ~ de** (*soi, situation*) to be in control of; **une maîtresse femme** a managing woman; **~ chanteur** blackmailer; **~ d'école** schoolmaster; **~ d'hôtel** (*domestique*) butler; (*d'hôtel*) head waiter; **~ nageur** lifeguard; **maîtresse** *nf* (*amante*) mistress; **maîtresse (d'école)** teacher, (school)mistress; **maîtresse de maison**

hostess; (*ménagère*) housewife

maîtrise [metʀiz] *nf* (*aussi:* ~ **de soi**) self-control, self-possession; (*habileté*) skill, mastery; (*suprématie*) mastery, command; (*diplôme*) ≈ master's degree; **maîtriser** *vt* (*cheval, incendie*) to (bring under) control; (*sujet*) to master; (*émotion*) to control, master; **se maîtriser** to control o.s.

maïzena ® [maizena] *nf* cornflour

majestueux, -euse [maʒɛstɥø, øz] *adj* majestic

majeur, e [maʒœʀ] *adj* (*important*) major; (*JUR*) of age ♦ *nm* (*doigt*) middle finger; **en ~e partie** for the most part; **la ~e partie de** most of

majoration [maʒɔʀasjɔ̃] *nf* rise, increase

majorer [maʒɔʀe] *vt* to increase

majoritaire [maʒɔʀitɛʀ] *adj* majority *cpd*

majorité [maʒɔʀite] *nf* (*gén*) majority; (*parti*) party in power; **en ~** mainly

majuscule [maʒyskyl] *adj, nf*: **(lettre) ~** capital (letter)

mal [mal, mo] (*pl* **maux**) *nm* (*opposé au bien*) evil; (*tort, dommage*) harm; (*douleur physique*) pain, ache; (*~adie*) illness, sickness *no pl* ♦ *adv* badly ♦ *adj* bad, wrong; **être ~ à l'aise** to be uncomfortable; **être ~ avec qn** to be on bad terms with sb; **il a ~ compris** he misunderstood; **dire/penser du ~ de** to speak/think ill of; **ne voir aucun ~ à** to see no harm in, see nothing wrong in; **faire ~ à qn** to hurt sb; **se faire ~** to hurt o.s.; **se donner du ~ pour faire qch** to go to a lot of trouble to do sth; **ça fait ~** it hurts; **j'ai ~ au dos** my back hurts; **avoir ~ à la tête/à la gorge/aux dents** to have a headache/a sore throat/toothache; **avoir le ~ du pays** to be homesick; *voir aussi* **cœur; maux;** ~ **de mer** seasickness; ~ **en point** in a bad state

malade [malad] *adj* ill, sick; (*poitrine, jambe*) bad; (*plante*) diseased ♦ *nm/f* invalid, sick person; (*à l'hôpital etc*) patient; **tomber ~** to fall ill; **être ~ du cœur** to have heart trouble *ou* a bad heart; ~

mental mentally sick *ou* ill person; **maladie** *nf* (*spécifique*) disease, illness; (*mauvaise santé*) illness, sickness; **maladif, -ive** *adj* sickly; (*curiosité, besoin*) pathological

maladresse [maladʀɛs] *nf* clumsiness *no pl*; (*gaffe*) blunder

maladroit, e [maladʀwa, wat] *adj* clumsy

malaise [malɛz] *nm* (*MÉD*) feeling of faintness; (*fig*) uneasiness, malaise; **avoir un ~** to feel faint

malaisé, e [maleze] *adj* difficult

malaria [malaʀja] *nf* malaria

malaxer [malakse] *vt* (*pétrir*) to knead; (*mélanger*) to mix

malchance [malʃɑ̃s] *nf* misfortune, ill luck *no pl*; **par ~** unfortunately; **malchanceux, -euse** *adj* unlucky

mâle [mɑl] *adj* (*aussi ÉLEC, TECH*) male; (*viril: voix, traits*) manly ♦ *nm* male

malédiction [malediksjɔ̃] *nf* curse

mal...: malencontreux, -euse *adj* unfortunate, untoward; **mal-en-point** *adj inv* in a sorry state; **malentendant, e** *nm/f*: **les malentendants** the hard of hearing; **malentendu** *nm* misunderstanding; **malfaçon** *nf* fault; **malfaisant, e** *adj* evil, harmful; **malfaiteur** *nm* lawbreaker, criminal; (*voleur*) burglar, thief; **malfamé, e** *adj* disreputable

malgache [malgaʃ] *adj* Madagascan, Malagasy ♦ *nm/f*: **M~** Madagascan, Malagasy ♦ *nm* (*LING*) Malagasy

malgré [malgʀe] *prép* in spite of, despite; ~ **tout** all the same

malhabile [malabil] *adj* clumsy, awkward

malheur [malœʀ] *nm* (*situation*) adversity, misfortune; (*événement*) misfortune; (*: très grave*) disaster, tragedy; **faire un ~** to be a smash hit; **malheureusement** *adv* unfortunately; **malheureux, -euse** *adj* (*triste*) unhappy, miserable; (*infortuné, regrettable*) unfortunate; (*malchanceux*) unlucky; (*insignifiant*) wretched ♦ *nm/f* poor soul; **les malheureux** the destitute

malhonnête [malɔnɛt] *adj* dishonest; **malhonnêteté** *nf* dishonesty

malice [malis] *nf* mischievousness; *(mé-chanceté)*: **par ~** out of malice *ou* spite; **sans ~** guileless; **malicieux, -euse** *adj* mischievous

malin, -igne [malɛ̃, maliɲ] *adj* *(futé: f gén: maline)* smart, shrewd; *(MÉD)* malignant

malingre [malɛ̃gr] *adj* puny

malle [mal] *nf* trunk; **mallette** *nf* (small) suitcase; *(porte-documents)* attaché case

malmener [malməne] *vt* to manhandle; *(fig)* to give a rough handling to

malodorant, e [malɔdɔrɑ̃, ɑ̃t] *adj* foul- *ou* ill-smelling

malotru [malɔtry] *nm* lout, boor

malpoli, e [malpɔli] *adj* impolite

malpropre [malprɔpr] *adj* dirty

malsain, e [malsɛ̃, ɛn] *adj* unhealthy

malt [malt] *nm* malt

Malte [malt] *nf* Malta

maltraiter [maltrete] *vt* to manhandle, ill-treat

malveillance [malvejɑ̃s] *nf* *(animosité)* ill will; *(intention de nuire)* malevolence

malversation [malvɛrsasjɔ̃] *nf* embezzlement

maman [mamɑ̃] *nf* mum(my), mother

mamelle [mamɛl] *nf* teat

mamelon [mam(ə)lɔ̃] *nm* *(ANAT)* nipple

mamie [mami] *(fam) nf* granny

mammifère [mamifɛr] *nm* mammal

mammouth [mamut] *nm* mammoth

manche [mɑ̃ʃ] *nf* *(de vêtement)* sleeve; *(d'un jeu, tournoi)* round; *(GÉO)*: **la M~** the Channel ♦ *nm* *(d'outil, casserole)* handle; *(de pelle, pioche etc)* shaft; **à ~s courtes/ longues** short-/long-sleeved

manchette [mɑ̃ʃɛt] *nf* *(de chemise)* cuff; *(coup)* forearm blow; *(titre)* headline

manchot [mɑ̃ʃo, ɔt] *nm* one-armed man; armless man; *(ZOOL)* penguin

mandarine [mɑ̃darin] *nf* mandarin (orange), tangerine

mandat [mɑ̃da] *nm* *(postal)* postal *ou* money order; *(d'un député etc)* mandate; *(procuration)* power of attorney, proxy; *(POLICE)* warrant; **~ d'arrêt** warrant for ar-

rest; **mandataire** *nm/f* *(représentant)* representative; *(JUR)* proxy

manège [manɛʒ] *nm* riding school; *(à la foire)* roundabout, merry-go-round; *(fig)* game, ploy

manette [manɛt] *nf* lever, tap; **~ de jeu** joystick

mangeable [mɑ̃ʒabl] *adj* edible, eatable

mangeoire [mɑ̃ʒwar] *nf* trough, manger

manger [mɑ̃ʒe] *vt* to eat; *(ronger: suj: rouille etc)* to eat into *ou* away ♦ *vi* to eat; **donner à ~ à** *(enfant)* to feed; **mangeur, -euse** *nm/f* eater; **gros mangeur** big eater

mangue [mɑ̃g] *nf* mango

maniable [manjabl] *adj* *(outil)* handy; *(voiture, voilier)* easy to handle

maniaque [manjak] *adj* finicky, fussy ♦ *nm/f* *(méticuleux)* fusspot; *(fou)* maniac

manie [mani] *nf* *(tic)* odd habit; *(obsession)* mania; **avoir la ~ de** to be obsessive about

manier [manje] *vt* to handle

manière [manjɛr] *nf* *(façon)* way, manner; **~s** *nfpl* *(attitude)* manners; *(chichis)* fuss *sg*; **de ~ à** so as to; **de cette ~** in this way *ou* manner; **d'une certaine ~** in a way; **de toute ~** in any case

maniéré, e [manjere] *adj* affected

manif [manif] *(fam) nf* demo

manifestant, e [manifɛstɑ̃, ɑ̃t] *nm/f* demonstrator

manifestation [manifɛstasjɔ̃] *nf* *(de joie, mécontentement)* expression, demonstration; *(symptôme)* outward sign; *(culturelle etc)* event; *(POL)* demonstration

manifeste [manifɛst] *adj* obvious, evident ♦ *nm* manifesto; **manifester** *vt* *(volonté, intentions)* to show, indicate; *(joie, peur)* to express, show ♦ *vi* to demonstrate; **se manifester** *vi* *(émotion)* to show *ou* express itself; *(difficultés)* to arise; *(symptômes)* to appear

manigance [manigɑ̃s] *nf* scheme; **manigancer** *vt* to plot

manipulation [manipylasjɔ̃] *nf* handling;

(POL, génétique) manipulation

manipuler [manipyle] vt to handle; (fig) to manipulate

manivelle [manivɛl] nf crank

mannequin [mankɛ̃] nm (COUTURE) dummy; (MODE) model

manœuvre [manœvʀ] nf (gén) manoeuvre (BRIT), maneuver (US) ♦ nm labourer; **manœuvrer** vt to manoeuvre (BRIT), maneuver (US); (levier, machine) to operate ♦ vi to manoeuvre

manoir [manwaʀ] nm manor ou country house

manque [mãk] nm (insuffisance): ~ **de** lack of; (vide) emptiness, gap; (MÉD) withdrawal; **être en état de** ~ to suffer withdrawal symptoms

manqué, e [mãke] adj failed; **garçon** ~ tomboy

manquer [mãke] vi (faire défaut) to be lacking; (être absent) to be missing; (échouer) to fail ♦ vt to miss ♦ vb impers: **il (nous) manque encore 10 euros** we are still 10 euros short; **il manque des pages (au livre)** there are some pages missing (from the book); **il/cela me manque** I miss him/this; ~ **à** (règles etc) to be in breach of, fail to observe; ~ **de** to lack; **je ne ~ai pas de le lui dire** I'll be sure to tell him; **il a manqué (de) se tuer** he very nearly got killed

mansarde [mãsaʀd] nf attic; **mansardé, e** adj: **chambre mansardée** attic room

manteau, x [mãto] nm coat

manucure [manykyʀ] nf manicurist

manuel, le [manɥɛl] adj manual ♦ nm (ouvrage) manual, handbook

manufacture [manyfaktyʀ] nf factory; **manufacturé, e** adj manufactured

manuscrit, e [manyskʀi, it] adj handwritten ♦ nm manuscript

manutention [manytãsjɔ̃] nf (COMM) handling

mappemonde [mapmɔ̃d] nf (plane) map of the world; (sphère) globe

maquereau, x [makʀo] nm (ZOOL) mackerel inv; (fam) pimp

maquette [makɛt] nf (à échelle réduite) (scale) model; (d'une page illustrée) paste-up

maquillage [makijaʒ] nm making up; (crème etc) make-up

maquiller [makije] vt (personne, visage) to make up; (truquer: passeport, statistique) to fake; (: voiture volée) to do over (respray etc); **se** ~ vi to make up (one's face)

maquis [maki] nm (GÉO) scrub; (MIL) maquis, underground fighting no pl

maraîcher, -ère [maʀeʃe, ɛʀ] adj: **cultures maraîchères** market gardening sg ♦ nm/f market gardener

marais [maʀɛ] nm marsh, swamp

marasme [maʀasm] nm stagnation, slump

marathon [maʀatɔ̃] nm marathon

maraudeur [maʀodœʀ, øz] nm prowler

marbre [maʀbʀ] nm marble

marc [maʀ] nm (de raisin, pommes) marc; ~ **de café** coffee grounds pl ou dregs pl

marchand, e [maʀʃã, ãd] nm/f shopkeeper, tradesman(-woman); (au marché) stallholder; (de vins, charbon) merchant ♦ adj: **prix/valeur ~(e)** market price/value; **~(e) de fruits** fruiterer (BRIT), fruit seller (US); **~(e) de journaux** newsagent; **~(e) de légumes** greengrocer (BRIT), produce dealer (US); **~(e) de poissons** fishmonger; **marchander** vi to bargain, haggle; **marchandise** nf goods pl, merchandise no pl

marche [maʀʃ] nf (d'escalier) step; (activité) walking; (promenade, trajet, allure) walk; (démarche) walk, gait; (MIL etc) march; (fonctionnement) running; (des événements) course; **dans le sens de la** ~ (RAIL) facing the engine; **en** ~ (monter etc) while the vehicle is moving ou in motion; **mettre en** ~ to start; **se mettre en** ~ (personne) to get moving; (machine) to start; **être en état de** ~ to be in working order; ~ **à suivre** (correct) procedure; ~ **arrière** reverse (gear); **faire** ~ **arrière** to reverse; (fig) to backtrack, back-pedal

marché [maʀʃe] *nm* market; (*transaction*) bargain, deal; **faire du ~ noir** to buy and sell on the black market; **~ aux puces** flea market; **M~ commun** Common Market

marchepied [maʀʃəpje] *nm* (*RAIL*) step

marcher [maʀʃe] *vi* to walk; (*MIL*) to march; (*aller: voiture, train, affaires*) to go; (*prospérer*) to go well; (*fonctionner*) to work, run; (*fam: consentir*) to go along, agree; (: *croire naïvement*) to be taken in; **faire ~ qn** (*taquiner*) to pull sb's leg; (*tromper*) to lead sb up the garden path; **marcheur, -euse** *nm/f* walker

mardi [maʀdi] *nm* Tuesday; **M~ gras** Shrove Tuesday

mare [maʀ] *nf* pond; (*flaque*) pool

marécage [maʀekaʒ] *nm* marsh, swamp; **marécageux, -euse** *adj* marshy

maréchal, -aux [maʀeʃal, o] *nm* marshal; **maréchal-ferrant** [maʀeʃalfɛʀɑ̃, maʀeʃo-] (*pl* **maréchaux-ferrants**) *nm* blacksmith, farrier

marée [maʀe] *nf* tide; (*poissons*) fresh (sea) fish; **~ haute/basse** high/low tide; **~ montante/descendante** rising/ebb tide; **~ noire** oil slick

marelle [maʀɛl] *nf* hopscotch

margarine [maʀɡaʀin] *nf* margarine

marge [maʀʒ] *nf* margin; **en ~ de** (*fig*) on the fringe of; **~ bénéficiaire** profit margin

marginal, e, -aux [maʀʒinal, o] *nm/f* (*original*) eccentric; (*déshérité*) dropout

marguerite [maʀɡəʀit] *nf* marguerite, (oxeye) daisy; (*d'imprimante*) daisy-wheel

mari [maʀi] *nm* husband

mariage [maʀjaʒ] *nm* marriage; (*noce*) wedding; **~ civil/religieux** registry office (*BRIT*) *ou* civil/church wedding

marié, e [maʀje] *adj* married ♦ *nm* (bride)groom; **les ~s** the bride and groom; **les (jeunes) ~s** the newly-weds; **mariée** *nf* bride

marier [maʀje] *vt* to marry; (*fig*) to blend; **se ~** *vr* to get married; **se ~ (avec)** to marry

marin, e [maʀɛ̃, in] *adj* sea *cpd*, marine ♦ *nm* sailor

marine [maʀin] *adj* voir **marin** ♦ *adj inv* navy (blue) ♦ *nm* (*MIL*) marine ♦ *nf* navy; **~ de guerre** navy; **~ marchande** merchant navy

mariner [maʀine] *vt*: **faire ~** to marinade

marionnette [maʀjɔnɛt] *nf* puppet

maritalement [maʀitalmɑ̃] *adv*: **vivre ~** to live as husband and wife

maritime [maʀitim] *adj* sea *cpd*, maritime

mark [maʀk] *nm* mark

marmelade [maʀməlad] *nf* stewed fruit, compote; **~ d'oranges** marmalade

marmite [maʀmit] *nf* (cooking-)pot

marmonner [maʀmɔne] *vt, vi* to mumble, mutter

marmot [maʀmo] (*fam*) *nm* kid

marmotter [maʀmɔte] *vt* to mumble

Maroc [maʀɔk] *nm*: **le ~** Morocco; **marocain, e** [maʀɔkɛ̃, ɛn] *adj* Moroccan ♦ *nm/f*: **Marocain, e** Moroccan

maroquinerie [maʀɔkinʀi] *nf* (*articles*) fine leather goods *pl*; (*boutique*) shop selling fine leather goods

marquant, e [maʀkɑ̃, ɑ̃t] *adj* outstanding

marque [maʀk] *nf* mark; (*COMM: de nourriture*) brand; (: *de voiture, produits manufacturés*) make; (*de disques*) label; **de ~** (*produits*) high-class; (*visiteur etc*) distinguished, well-known; **une grande ~ de vin** a well-known brand of wine; **~ de fabrique** trademark; **~ déposée** registered trademark

marquer [maʀke] *vt* to mark; (*inscrire*) to write down; (*bétail*) to brand; (*SPORT: but etc*) to score; (: *joueur*) to mark; (*accentuer: taille etc*) to emphasize; (*manifester: refus, intérêt*) to show ♦ *vi* (*événement*) to stand out, to be outstanding; (*SPORT*) to score

marqueterie [maʀkɛtʀi] *nf* inlaid work, marquetry

marquis [maʀki] *nm* marquis, marquess; **marquise** *nf* marchioness; (*auvent*) glass canopy *ou* awning

marraine [maʀɛn] *nf* godmother

marrant, e [maʀɑ̃, ɑ̃t] *(fam) adj* funny

marre [maʀ] *(fam) adv*: **en avoir ~ de** to be fed up with

marrer [maʀe]: **se ~** *(fam) vi* to have a (good) laugh

marron [maʀɔ̃] *nm (fruit)* chestnut ♦ *adj inv* brown; **~s glacés** candied chestnuts; **marronnier** *nm* chestnut (tree)

mars [maʀs] *nm* March

Marseille [maʀsɛj] *n* Marseilles

Marseillaise

i **La Marseillaise** has been France's national anthem since 1879. The words of the "Chant de guerre de l'armée du Rhin", as the song was originally called, were written to an anonymous tune by the army captain Rouget de Lisle in 1792. Adopted as a marching song by the battalion of Marseilles, it was finally popularized as the Marseillaise.

---

marsouin [maʀswɛ̃] *nm* porpoise

marteau, x [maʀto] *nm* hammer; **être ~** *(fam)* to be nuts; **marteau-piqueur** *nm* pneumatic drill

marteler [maʀtəle] *vt* to hammer

martien, ne [maʀsjɛ̃, jɛn] *adj* Martian, of *ou* from Mars

martyr, e [maʀtiʀ] *nm/f* martyr; **martyre** *nm* martyrdom; *(fig: sens affaibli)* agony, torture; **martyriser** *vt (REL)* to martyr; *(fig)* to bully; *(enfant)* to batter, beat

marxiste [maʀksist] *adj, nm/f* Marxist

mascara [maskaʀa] *nm* mascara

masculin, e [maskylɛ̃, in] *adj* masculine; *(sexe, population)* male; *(équipe, vêtements)* men's; *(viril)* manly ♦ *nm* masculine; **masculinité** *nf* masculinity

masochiste [mazɔʃist] *adj* masochistic

masque [mask] *nm* mask; **masquer** *vt (cacher: paysage, porte)* to hide, conceal; *(dissimuler: vérité, projet)* to mask, obscure

massacre [masakʀ] *nm* massacre, slaughter; **massacrer** *vt* to massacre, slaughter; *(fam: texte etc)* to murder

massage [masaʒ] *nm* massage

masse [mas] *nf* mass; *(ÉLEC)* earth; *(maillet)* sledgehammer; *(péj)*: **la ~** 'the masses *pl*; **une ~ de** *(fam)* masses *ou* loads of; **en ~** ♦ *adv (acheter)* in bulk; *(en foule)* en masse ♦ *adj (exécutions, production)* mass *cpd*

masser [mase] *vt (assembler: gens)* to gather; *(pétrir)* to massage; **se ~** *vi (foule)* to gather; **masseur, -euse** *nm/f* masseur(-euse)

massif, -ive [masif, iv] *adj (porte)* solid, massive; *(visage)* heavy, large; *(bois, or)* solid; *(dose)* massive; *(déportations etc)* mass *cpd* ♦ *nm (montagneux)* massif; *(de fleurs)* clump, bank

massue [masy] *nf* club, bludgeon

mastic [mastik] *nm (pour vitres)* putty; *(pour fentes)* filler

mastiquer [mastike] *vt (aliment)* to chew, masticate

mat, e [mat] *adj (couleur, métal)* mat(t); *(bruit, son)* dull ♦ *adj inv (ÉCHECS)*: **être ~** to be checkmate

mât [mɑ] *nm (NAVIG)* mast; *(poteau)* pole, post

match [matʃ] *nm* match; **faire ~ nul** to draw; **~ aller** first leg; **~ retour** second leg, return match

matelas [mat(ə)la] *nm* mattress; **~ pneumatique** air bed *ou* mattress; **matelassé, e** *adj (vêtement)* padded; *(tissu)* quilted

matelot [mat(ə)lo] *nm* sailor, seaman

mater [mate] *vt (personne)* to bring to heel, subdue; *(révolte)* to put down

matérialiser [mateʀjalize]: **se ~** *vi* to materialize

matérialiste [mateʀjalist] *adj* materialistic

matériaux [mateʀjo] *nmpl* material(s)

matériel, le [mateʀjɛl] *adj* material ♦ *nm* equipment *no pl*; *(de camping etc)* gear *no pl*; *(INFORM)* hardware

maternel, le [mateʀnɛl] *adj (amour, geste)* motherly, maternal; *(grand-père, oncle)* maternal; **maternelle** *nf (aussi:* **école maternelle)** (state) nursery school

maternité [matɛʀnite] nf (établissement) maternity hospital; (état de mère) motherhood, maternity; (grossesse) pregnancy; **congé de ~** maternity leave

mathématique [matematik] adj mathematical; **mathématiques** nfpl (science) mathematics sg

maths [mat] (fam) nfpl maths

matière [matjɛʀ] nf matter; (COMM, TECH) material, matter no pl; (fig: d'un livre etc) subject matter, material; (SCOL) subject; **en ~ de** as regards; **~s grasses** fat content sg; **~s premières** raw materials

---
hôtel Matignon

ⓘ L'hôtel Matignon is the Paris office and residence of the French Prime Minister. By extension, the term "Matignon" is often used to refer to the Prime Minister or his staff.

---

matin [matɛ̃] nm, adv morning; **du ~ au soir** from morning till night; **de bon ou grand ~** early in the morning; **matinal, e, -aux** adj (toilette, gymnastique) morning cpd; **être matinal** (personne) to be up early; to be an early riser; **matinée** nf morning; (spectacle) matinée

matou [matu] nm tom(cat)

matraque [matʀak] nf (de policier) truncheon (BRIT), billy (US)

matricule [matʀikyl] nm (MIL) regimental number; (ADMIN) reference number

matrimonial, e, -aux [matʀimɔnjal, jo] adj marital, marriage cpd

maudire [modiʀ] vt to curse; **maudit, e** (fam) adj (satané) blasted, confounded

maugréer [mogʀee] vi to grumble

maussade [mosad] adj sullen; (temps) gloomy

mauvais, e [mɔvɛ, ɛz] adj bad; (faux): **le ~ numéro/moment** the wrong number/moment; (méchant, malveillant) malicious, spiteful; **il fait ~** the weather is bad; **la mer est ~e** the sea is rough; **~ plaisant** hoaxer; **~e herbe** weed; **~e langue** gossip, scandalmonger (BRIT); **~e passe** bad patch

mauve [mov] adj mauve

maux [mo] nmpl de **mal**; **~ de ventre** stomachache sg

maximum [maksimɔm] adj, nm maximum; **au ~** (le plus possible) as much as one can; (tout au plus) at the (very) most ou maximum; **faire le ~** to do one's level best

mayonnaise [majɔnɛz] nf mayonnaise

mazout [mazut] nm (fuel) oil

Me abr = **Maître**

me, m' [m(ə)] pron (direct: téléphoner, attendre etc) me; (indirect: parler, donner etc) (to) me; (réfléchi) myself

mec [mɛk] (fam) nm bloke, guy

mécanicien, ne [mekanisjɛ̃, jɛn] nm/f mechanic; (RAIL) (train ou engine) driver

mécanique [mekanik] adj mechanical ♦ nf (science) mechanics sg; (mécanisme) mechanism; **ennui ~** engine trouble no pl

mécanisme [mekanism] nm mechanism

méchamment [meʃamɑ̃] adv nastily, maliciously, spitefully

méchanceté [meʃɑ̃ste] nf nastiness, maliciousness; **dire des ~s à qn** to say spiteful things to sb

méchant, e [meʃɑ̃, ɑ̃t] adj nasty, malicious, spiteful; (enfant: pas sage) naughty; (animal) vicious

mèche [mɛʃ] nf (de cheveux) lock; (de lampe, bougie) wick; (d'un explosif) fuse; **de ~ avec** in league with

méchoui [meʃwi] nm barbecue of a whole roast sheep

méconnaissable [mekɔnɛsabl] adj unrecognizable

méconnaître [mekɔnɛtʀ] vt (ignorer) to be unaware of; (mésestimer) to misjudge

mécontent, e [mekɔ̃tɑ̃, ɑ̃t] adj: **~ (de)** discontented ou dissatisfied ou displeased (with); (contrarié) annoyed (at); **mécontentement** nm dissatisfaction, discontent, displeasure; (irritation) annoyance

médaille [medaj] nf medal
médaillon [medajɔ̃] nm (bijou) locket
médecin [med(ə)sɛ̃] nm doctor; ~ **légiste** forensic surgeon
médecine [med(ə)sin] nf medicine
média [medja] nmpl: **les** ~ the media; **médiatique** adj media cpd; **médiatisé, e** adj reported in the media; **ce procès a été très médiatisé** (péj) this trial was turned into a media event
médical, e, -aux [medikal, o] adj medical; **passer une visite** ~**e** to have a medical
médicament [medikamɑ̃] nm medicine, drug
médiéval, e, -aux [medjeval, o] adj medieval
médiocre [medjɔkʀ] adj mediocre, poor
médire [mediʀ] vi: ~ **de** to speak ill of; **médisance** nf scandalmongering (BRIT)
méditer [medite] vi to meditate
Méditerranée [mediteʀane] nf: **la (mer)** ~ the Mediterranean (Sea); **méditerranéen, ne** adj Mediterranean ♦ nm/f: **Méditerranéen, ne** native ou inhabitant of a Mediterranean country
méduse [medyz] nf jellyfish
meeting [mitiŋ] nm (POL, SPORT) rally
méfait [mefɛ] nm (faute) misdemeanour, wrongdoing; ~**s** nmpl (ravages) ravages, damage sg
méfiance [mefjɑ̃s] nf mistrust, distrust
méfiant, e [mefjɑ̃, jɑ̃t] adj mistrustful, distrustful
méfier [mefje]: **se** ~ vi to be wary; to be careful; **se** ~ **de** to mistrust, distrust, be wary of
mégarde [megaʀd] nf: **par** ~ (accidentellement) accidentally; (par erreur) by mistake
mégère [meʒɛʀ] nf shrew
mégot [mego] (fam) nm cigarette end
meilleur, e [mɛjœʀ] adj, adv better ♦ nm: **le** ~ the best; **le** ~ **des deux** the better of the two; ~ **marché** (inv) cheaper; **meilleure** nf: **la meilleure** the best (one)

mélancolie [melɑ̃kɔli] nf melancholy, gloom; **mélancolique** adj melancholic, melancholy
mélange [melɑ̃ʒ] nm mixture; **mélanger** vt to mix; (vins, couleurs) to blend; (mettre en désordre) to mix up, muddle (up)
mélasse [melas] nf treacle, molasses sg
mêlée [mele] nf mêlée, scramble; (RUGBY) scrum(mage)
mêler [mele] vt (unir) to mix; (embrouiller) to muddle (up), mix up; **se** ~ vi to mix, mingle; **se** ~ **à** (personne: se joindre) to join; (: s'associer à) to mix with; **se** ~ **de** (suj: personne) to meddle with, interfere in; **mêle-toi de ce qui te regarde!** mind your own business!
mélodie [melɔdi] nf melody; **mélodieux, -euse** adj melodious
melon [m(ə)lɔ̃] nm (BOT) (honeydew) melon; (aussi: **chapeau** ~) bowler (hat)
membre [mɑ̃bʀ] nm (ANAT) limb; (personne, pays, élément) member ♦ adj member cpd
mémé [meme] (fam) nf granny

| MOT-CLÉ |
---

même [mɛm] adj **1** (avant le nom) same; **en même temps** at the same time
2 (après le nom: renforcement): **il est la loyauté même** he is loyalty itself; **ce sont ses paroles/celles-là mêmes** they are his very words/the very ones
♦ pron: **le(la) même** the same one
♦ adv **1** (renforcement): **il n'a même pas pleuré** he didn't even cry; **même lui l'a dit** even HE said it; **ici même** at this very place
2: **à même**: **à même la bouteille** straight from the bottle; **à même la peau** next to the skin; **être à même de faire** to be in a position to do, be able to do
3: **de même**: **faire de même** to do likewise; **lui de même** so does (ou did ou is) he; **de même que** just as; **il en va de même pour** the same goes for

mémo [memo] *(fam) nm* memo

mémoire [memwaʀ] *nf* memory ♦ *nm* (*SCOL*) dissertation, paper; **~s** *nmpl* (*souvenirs*) memoirs; **à la ~ de** to the *ou* in memory of; **de ~** from memory; **~ morte/vive** (*INFORM*) ROM/RAM

mémorable [memɔʀabl] *adj* memorable, unforgettable

menace [mənas] *nf* threat; **menacer** *vt* to threaten

ménage [menaʒ] *nm* (*travail*) housekeeping, housework; (*couple*) (married) couple; (*famille*, *ADMIN*) household; **faire le ~** to do the housework; **ménagement** *nm* care and attention; **ménager, -ère** *adj* household *cpd*, domestic ♦ *vt* (*traiter: personne*) to handle with tact; (*utiliser*) to use sparingly; (*prendre soin de*) to take (great) care of, look after; (*organiser*) to arrange; **ménager qch à qn** (*réserver*) to have sth in store for sb; **ménagère** *nf* housewife

mendiant, e [mɑ̃djɑ̃, jɑ̃t] *nm/f* beggar

mendier [mɑ̃dje] *vi* to beg ♦ *vt* to beg (for)

mener [m(ə)ne] *vt* to lead; (*enquête*) to conduct; (*affaires*) to manage ♦ *vi*: **~ à/dans** (*emmener*) to take to/into; **~ qch à bien** to see sth through (to a successful conclusion), complete sth successfully

meneur, -euse [mənœʀ, øz] *nm/f* leader; (*péj*) agitator

méningite [menɛ̃ʒit] *nf* meningitis *no pl*

ménopause [menopoz] *nf* menopause

menottes [mənɔt] *nfpl* handcuffs

mensonge [mɑ̃sɔ̃ʒ] *nm* lie; (*action*) lying *no pl*; **mensonger, -ère** *adj* false

mensualité [mɑ̃sɥalite] *nf* (*traite*) monthly payment

mensuel, le [mɑ̃sɥɛl] *adj* monthly

mensurations [mɑ̃syʀasjɔ̃] *nfpl* measurements

mental, e, -aux [mɑ̃tal, o] *adj* mental; **mentalité** *nf* mentality

menteur, -euse [mɑ̃tœʀ, øz] *nm/f* liar

menthe [mɑ̃t] *nf* mint

mention [mɑ̃sjɔ̃] *nf* (*annotation*) note, comment; (*SCOL*) grade; **~ bien** *etc* ≃ grade B *etc* (*ou* upper 2nd class *etc*) pass (*BRIT*), ≃ pass with (high) honors (*US*); (*ADMIN*): **"rayer les ~s inutiles"** "delete as appropriate"; **mentionner** *vt* to mention

mentir [mɑ̃tiʀ] *vi* to lie

menton [mɑ̃tɔ̃] *nm* chin

menu, e [məny] *adj* (*personne*) slim, slight; (*frais, difficulté*) minor ♦ *adv* (*couper, hacher*) very fine ♦ *nm* menu; **~ touristique/gastronomique** economy/gourmet's menu

menuiserie [mənɥizʀi] *nf* (*métier*) joinery, carpentry; (*passe-temps*) woodwork; **menuisier** *nm* joiner, carpenter

méprendre [mepʀɑ̃dʀ]: **se ~** *vi*: **se ~ sur** to be mistaken (about)

mépris [mepʀi] *nm* (*dédain*) contempt, scorn; **au ~ de** regardless of, in defiance of; **méprisable** *adj* contemptible, despicable; **méprisant, e** *adj* scornful; **méprise** *nf* mistake, error; **mépriser** *vt* to scorn, despise; (*gloire, danger*) to scorn, spurn

mer [mɛʀ] *nf* sea; (*marée*) tide; **en ~** at sea; **en haute** *ou* **pleine ~** off shore, on the open sea; **la ~ du Nord/Rouge** the North/Red Sea

mercenaire [mɛʀsənɛʀ] *nm* mercenary, hired soldier

mercerie [mɛʀsəʀi] *nf* (*boutique*) haberdasher's shop (*BRIT*), notions store (*US*)

merci [mɛʀsi] *excl* thank you ♦ *nf*: **à la ~ de qn/qch** at sb's mercy/the mercy of sth; **~ beaucoup** thank you very much; **~ de** thank you for; **sans ~** merciless(ly)

mercredi [mɛʀkʀədi] *nm* Wednesday

mercure [mɛʀkyʀ] *nm* mercury

merde [mɛʀd] (*fam!*) *nf* shit (!) ♦ *excl* (bloody) hell (!)

mère [mɛʀ] *nf* mother; **~ célibataire** unmarried mother

merguez [mɛʀgɛz] *nf* merguez sausage (*type of spicy sausage from N Africa*)

méridional, e, -aux [meʀidjɔnal, o] *adj*

southern ♦ *nm/f* Southerner

meringue [mərɛ̃g] *nf* meringue

mérite [meʀit] *nm* merit; **avoir du ~ (à faire qch)** to deserve credit (for doing sth); **mériter** *vt* to deserve

merlan [mɛʀlɑ̃] *nm* whiting

merle [mɛʀl] *nm* blackbird

merveille [mɛʀvɛj] *nf* marvel, wonder; **faire ~** to work wonders; **à ~** perfectly, wonderfully; **merveilleux, -euse** *adj* marvellous, wonderful

mes [me] *adj voir* **mon**

mésange [mezɑ̃ʒ] *nf* tit(mouse)

mésaventure [mezavɑ̃tyʀ] *nf* misadventure, misfortune

Mesdames [medam] *nfpl de* **Madame**

Mesdemoiselles [medmwazɛl] *nfpl de* **Mademoiselle**

mesquin, e [mɛskɛ̃, in] *adj* mean, petty; **mesquinerie** *nf* meanness; (*procédé*) mean trick

message [mesaʒ] *nm* message; **messager, -ère** *nm/f* messenger; **messagerie** *nf* (*INTERNET*): **messagerie électronique** bulletin board

messe [mɛs] *nf* mass

Messieurs [mesjø] *nmpl de* **Monsieur**

mesure [m(ə)zyʀ] *nf* (*évaluation, dimension*) measurement; (*récipient*) measure; (*MUS: cadence*) time, tempo; (: *division*) bar; (*retenue*) moderation; (*disposition*) measure, step; **sur ~** (*costume*) made-to-measure; **dans la ~ où** insofar as, inasmuch as; **à ~ que** as; **être en ~ de** to be in a position to; **dans une certaine ~** to a certain extent

mesurer [məzyʀe] *vt* to measure; (*juger*) to weigh up, assess; (*modérer: ses paroles etc*) to moderate; **se ~ avec** to have a confrontation with; **il mesure 1 m 80** he's 1 m 80 tall

met [mɛ] *vb voir* **mettre**

métal, -aux [metal, o] *nm* metal; **métallique** *adj* metallic

météo [meteo] *nf* (*bulletin*) weather report

météorologie [meteɔʀɔlɔʒi] *nf* meteorology

méthode [metɔd] *nf* method; (*livre, ouvrage*) manual, tutor

méticuleux, -euse [metikylø, øz] *adj* meticulous

métier [metje] *nm* (*profession: gén*) job; (: *manuel*) trade; (*artisanal*) craft; (*technique, expérience*) (acquired) skill *ou* technique; (*aussi: ~ à tisser*) (weaving) loom; **avoir du ~** to have practical experience

métis, se [metis] *adj, nm/f* half-caste, half-breed

métrage [metʀaʒ] *nm*: **long/moyen/court ~** full-length/medium-length/short film

mètre [mɛtʀ] *nm* metre; (*règle*) (metre) rule; (*ruban*) tape measure; **métrique** *adj* metric

métro [metʀo] *nm* underground (*BRIT*), subway

métropole [metʀɔpɔl] *nf* (*capitale*) metropolis; (*pays*) home country

mets [mɛ] *nm* dish

metteur [metœʀ] *nm*: **~ en scène** (*THÉÂTRE*) producer; (*CINÉMA*) director

---

MOT-CLÉ

---

mettre [mɛtʀ] *vt* 1 (*placer*) to put; **mettre en bouteille/en sac** to bottle/put in bags *ou* sacks; **mettre en charge (pour)** to charge (with), indict (for)

2 (*vêtements: revêtir*) to put on; (: *porter*) to wear; **mets ton gilet** put your cardigan on; **je ne mets plus mon manteau** I no longer wear my coat

3 (*faire fonctionner: chauffage, électricité*) to put on; (: *reveil, minuteur*) to set; (*installer: gaz, eau*) to put in, lay on; **mettre en marche** to start up

4 (*consacrer*): **mettre du temps à faire qch** to take time to do sth *ou* over sth

5 (*noter, écrire*) to say, put (down); **qu'est-ce qu'il a mis sur la carte?** what did he say *ou* write on the card?; **mettez au pluriel ...** put ... into the plural

6 (*supposer*): **mettons que ...** let's suppose *ou* say that ...

7: **y mettre du sien** to pull one's weight

se mettre *vi* **1** (*se placer*): **vous pouvez vous mettre là** you can sit (*ou* stand) there; **où ça se met?** where does it go?; **se mettre au lit** to get into bed; **se mettre au piano** to sit down at the piano; **se mettre de l'encre sur les doigts** to get ink on one's fingers

2 (*s'habiller*): **se mettre en maillot de bain** to get into *ou* put on a swimsuit; **n'avoir rien à se mettre** to have nothing to wear

3: **se mettre à** to begin, start; **se mettre à faire** to begin *ou* start doing *ou* to do; **se mettre au piano** to start learning the piano; **se mettre au travail/à l'étude** to get down to work/one's studies

meuble [mœbl] *nm* piece of furniture; **des ~s** furniture; **meublé** *nm* furnished flatlet (*BRIT*) *ou* room; **meubler** *vt* to furnish

meugler [møgle] *vi* to low, moo

meule [møl] *nf* (*de foin, blé*) stack; (*de fromage*) round; (*à broyer*) millstone

meunier [mønje, jɛʀ] *nm* miller; **meunière** *nf* miller's wife

meure *etc* [mœʀ] *vb voir* **mourir**

meurtre [mœʀtʀ] *nm* murder; **meurtrier, -ière** *adj* (*arme etc*) deadly; (*fureur, instincts*) murderous ♦ *nm/f* murderer(-eress)

meurtrir [mœʀtʀiʀ] *vt* to bruise; (*fig*) to wound; **meurtrissure** *nf* bruise

meus *etc* [mœ] *vb voir* **mouvoir**

meute [møt] *nf* pack

mexicain, e [mɛksikɛ̃, ɛn] *adj* Mexican ♦ *nm/f*: **M~, e** Mexican

Mexico [mɛksiko] *n* Mexico City

Mexique [mɛksik] *nm*: **le ~** Mexico

Mgr *abr* = **Monseigneur**

mi [mi] *nm* (*MUS*) E; (*en chantant la gamme*) mi ♦ *préfixe*: **~...** half(-); mid-; **à la ~-janvier** in mid-January; **à ~-hauteur** halfway up; **mi-bas** *nm inv* knee sock

miauler [mjole] *vi* to mew

miche [miʃ] *nf* round *ou* cob loaf

mi-chemin [miʃmɛ̃]: **à ~-~** *adv* halfway, midway

mi-clos, e [miklo, kloz] *adj* half-closed

micro [mikʀo] *nm* mike, microphone; (*INFORM*) micro

microbe [mikʀɔb] *nm* germ, microbe

micro...: **micro-onde** *nf*: **four à micro-ondes** microwave oven; **micro-ordinateur** *nm* microcomputer; **microscope** *nm* microscope; **microscopique** *adj* microscopic

midi [midi] *nm* midday, noon; (*moment du déjeuner*) lunchtime; (*sud*) south; **à ~** at 12 (o'clock) *ou* midday *ou* noon; **le M~** the South (of France), the Midi

mie [mi] *nf* crumb (of the loaf)

miel [mjɛl] *nm* honey; **mielleux, -euse** *adj* (*personne*) unctuous, syrupy

mien, ne [mjɛ̃, mjɛn] *pron*: **le(la) ~(ne), les ~(ne)s** mine; **les ~s** my family

miette [mjɛt] *nf* (*de pain, gâteau*) crumb; (*fig: de la conversation etc*) scrap; **en ~s** in pieces *ou* bits

---

MOT-CLÉ

mieux [mjø] *adv* **1** (*d'une meilleure façon*): **mieux (que)** better (than); **elle travaille/mange mieux** she works/eats better; **elle va mieux** she is better

2 (*de la meilleure façon*) best; **ce que je sais le mieux** what I know best; **les livres les mieux faits** the best made books

3: **de mieux en mieux** better and better

♦ *adj* **1** (*plus à l'aise, en meilleure forme*) better; **se sentir mieux** to feel better

2 (*plus satisfaisant*) better; **c'est mieux ainsi** it's better like this; **c'est le mieux des deux** it's the better of the two; **le(la) mieux, les mieux** the best; **demandez-lui, c'est le mieux** ask him, it's the best thing

3 (*plus joli*) better-looking

4: **au mieux** at best; **au mieux avec** on the best of terms with; **pour le mieux** for the best

♦ *nm* **1** (*progrès*) improvement

2: **de mon/ton mieux** as best I/you can (*ou* could); **faire de son mieux** to do one's best

mièvre [mjɛvʀ] *adj* mawkish (*BRIT*), sickly sentimental

mignon, ne [miɲɔ̃, ɔn] *adj* sweet, cute

migraine [migʀɛn] *nf* headache; (*MÉD*) migraine

mijoter [miʒɔte] *vt* to simmer; (*préparer avec soin*) to cook lovingly; (*fam: tramer*) to plot, cook up ♦ *vi* to simmer

mil [mil] *num* = **mille**

milieu, x [miljø] *nm* (*centre*) middle; (*BIO, GÉO*) environment; (*entourage social*) milieu; (*provenance*) background; (*pègre*): **le ~** the underworld; **au ~ de** in the middle of; **au beau** *ou* **en plein ~ (de)** right in the middle (of); **un juste ~** a happy medium

militaire [militɛʀ] *adj* military, army *cpd* ♦ *nm* serviceman

militant, e [militɑ̃, ɑ̃t] *adj, nm/f* militant

militer [milite] *vi* to be a militant

mille [mil] *num* a *ou* one thousand ♦ *nm* (*mesure*): **~ (marin)** nautical mile; **mettre dans le ~** (*fig*) to be bang on target; **millefeuille** *nm* cream *ou* vanilla slice; **millénaire** *nm* millennium ♦ *adj* thousand-year-old; (*fig*) ancient; **mille-pattes** *nm inv* centipede

millésimé, e [milezime] *adj* vintage *cpd*

millet [mijɛ] *nm* millet

milliard [miljaʀ] *nm* milliard, thousand million (*BRIT*), billion (*US*); **milliardaire** *nm/f* multimillionaire (*BRIT*), billionaire (*US*)

millier [milje] *nm* thousand; **un ~ (de)** a thousand or so, about a thousand; **par ~s** in (their) thousands, by the thousand

milligramme [miligʀam] *nm* milligramme

millimètre [milimɛtʀ] *nm* millimetre

million [miljɔ̃] *nm* million; **deux ~s de** two million; **millionnaire** *nm/f* millionaire

mime [mim] *nm/f* (*acteur*) mime(r) ♦ *nm* (*art*) mime, miming; **mimer** *vt* to mime; (*singer*) to mimic, take off

mimique [mimik] *nf* (*grimace*) (funny) face; (*signes*) gesticulations *pl*, sign language *no pl*

minable [minabl] *adj* (*décrépit*) shabby(-looking); (*médiocre*) pathetic

mince [mɛ̃s] *adj* thin; (*personne, taille*) slim, slender; (*fig: profit, connaissances*) slight, small, weak ♦ *excl*: **~ alors!** drat it!, darn it! (*US*); **minceur** *nf* thinness; (*d'une personne*) slimness, slenderness; **mincir** *vi* to get slimmer

mine [min] *nf* (*physionomie*) expression, look; (*allure*) exterior, appearance; (*de crayon*) lead; (*gisement, explosif, fig: source*) mine; **avoir bonne ~** (*personne*) to look well; (*ironique*) to look an utter idiot; **avoir mauvaise ~** to look unwell *ou* poorly; **faire ~ de faire** to make a pretence of doing; **~ de rien** although you wouldn't think so

miner [mine] *vt* (*saper*) to undermine, erode; (*MIL*) to mine

minerai [minʀɛ] *nm* ore

minéral, e, -aux [mineʀal, o] *adj, nm* mineral

minéralogique [mineʀalɔʒik] *adj*: **numéro ~** registration number

minet, te [minɛ, ɛt] *nm/f* (*chat*) pussy-cat; (*péj*) young trendy

mineur, e [minœʀ] *adj* minor ♦ *nm/f* (*JUR*) minor, person under age ♦ *nm* (*travailleur*) miner

miniature [minjatyʀ] *adj, nf* miniature

minibus [minibys] *nm* minibus

mini-cassette [minikaset] *nf* cassette (recorder)

minier, -ière [minje, jɛʀ] *adj* mining

mini-jupe [miniʒyp] *nf* mini-skirt

minime [minim] *adj* minor, minimal

minimiser [minimize] *vt* to minimize; (*fig*) to play down

minimum [minimɔm] *adj, nm* minimum; **au ~** (*au moins*) at the very least

ministère [ministɛʀ] *nm* (*aussi REL*) ministry; (*cabinet*) government

ministre [ministʀ] *nm* (*aussi REL*) minister
Minitel ® [minitɛl] *nm* videotext terminal
and service

Minitel

ⓘ **Minitel** *is a personal computer terminal supplied free of change by France-
Télécom to telephone subscribers. It serves
as a computerized telephone directory as
well as giving access to various services,
including information on train timetables,
the stock market and situations vacant.
Services are accessed by phoning the relevant number and charged to the subscriber's phone bill.*

---

minoritaire [minɔʀitɛʀ] *adj* minority
minorité [minɔʀite] *nf* minority; **être en ~**
to be in the *ou* a minority
minuit [minɥi] *nm* midnight
minuscule [minyskyl] *adj* minute, tiny
♦ *nf*: (**lettre**) **~** small letter
minute [minyt] *nf* minute; **à la ~** (just)
this instant; (*faire*) there and then; **minuter** *vt* to time; **minuterie** *nf* time switch
minutieux, -euse [minysjø, jøz] *adj* (*personne*) meticulous; (*travail*) minutely detailed
mirabelle [miʀabɛl] *nf* (cherry) plum
miracle [miʀakl] *nm* miracle
mirage [miʀaʒ] *nm* mirage
mire [miʀ] *nf*: **point de ~** (*fig*) focal point
miroir [miʀwaʀ] *nm* mirror
miroiter [miʀwate] *vi* to sparkle, shimmer;
faire ~ qch à qn to paint sth in glowing
colours for sb, dangle sth in front of sb's
eyes
mis, e [mi, miz] *pp de* **mettre** ♦ *adj*: **bien
~** well-dressed
mise [miz] *nf* (*argent: au jeu*) stake; (*tenue*)
clothing, attire; **être de ~** to be acceptable *ou* in season; **~ au point** (*fig*) clarification; **~ de fonds** capital outlay; **~ en
examen** charging, indictment; **~ en plis**
set; **~ en scène** production
miser [mize] *vt* (*enjeu*) to stake, bet; **~ sur**

(*cheval, numéro*) to bet on; (*fig*) to bank
ou count on
misérable [mizeʀabl] *adj* (*lamentable, malheureux*) pitiful, wretched; (*pauvre*)
poverty-stricken; (*insignifiant, mesquin*) miserable ♦ *nm/f* wretch
misère [mizɛʀ] *nf* (extreme) poverty, destitution; **~s** *nfpl* (*malheurs*) woes, miseries;
(*ennuis*) little troubles; **salaire de ~** starvation wage
missile [misil] *nm* missile
mission [misjɔ̃] *nf* mission; **partir en ~**
(*ADMIN, POL*) to go on an assignment;
missionnaire *nm/f* missionary
mit [mi] *vb voir* **mettre**
mité, e [mite] *adj* moth-eaten
mi-temps [mitɑ̃] *nf inv* (*SPORT: période*)
half; (*: pause*) half-time; **à ~-** part-time
miteux, -euse [mitø, øz] *adj* (*lieu*) seedy
mitigé, e [mitiʒe] *adj*: **sentiments ~s**
mixed feelings
mitonner [mitɔne] *vt* to cook with loving
care; (*fig*) to cook up quietly
mitoyen, ne [mitwajɛ̃, jɛn] *adj* (*mur*) common, party *cpd*
mitrailler [mitʀaje] *vt* to machine-gun;
(*fig*) to pelt, bombard; (*: photographier*) to
take shot after shot of; **mitraillette** *nf*
submachine gun; **mitrailleuse** *nf*
machine gun
mi-voix [mivwa]: **à ~-** *adv* in a low *ou*
hushed voice
mixage [miksaʒ] *nm* (*CINÉMA*) (sound) mixing
mixer [miksœʀ] *nm* (food) mixer
mixte [mikst] *adj* (*gén*) mixed; (*SCOL*)
mixed, coeducational
mixture [mikstyʀ] *nf* mixture; (*fig*) concoc-
tion
Mlle (*pl* **Mlles**) *abr* = **Mademoiselle**
MM *abr* = **Messieurs**
Mme (*pl* **Mmes**) *abr* = **Madame**
mobile [mɔbil] *adj* mobile; (*pièce de
machine*) moving ♦ *nm* (*motif*) motive;
(*œuvre d'art*) mobile
mobilier, -ière [mɔbilje, jɛʀ] *nm* furniture

mobiliser [mɔbilize] *vt* to mobilize

mocassin [mɔkasē] *nm* moccasin

moche [mɔʃ] (*fam*) *adj* (*laid*) ugly; (*mauvais*) rotten

modalité [mɔdalite] *nf* form, mode; **~s de paiement** methods of payment

mode [mɔd] *nf* fashion ♦ *nm* (*manière*) form, mode; **à la ~** fashionable, in fashion; **~ d'emploi** directions *pl* (for use)

modèle [mɔdɛl] *adj, nm* model; (*qui pose: de peintre*) sitter; **~ déposé** registered design; **~ réduit** small-scale model; **modeler** *vt* to model

modem [mɔdɛm] *nm* modem

modéré, e [mɔdeʀe] *adj, nm/f* moderate

modérer [mɔdeʀe] *vt* to moderate; **se ~** *vi* to restrain o.s.

moderne [mɔdɛʀn] *adj* modern ♦ *nm* (*style*) modern style; (*meubles*) modern furniture; **moderniser** *vt* to modernize

modeste [mɔdɛst] *adj* modest; **modestie** *nf* modesty

modifier [mɔdifje] *vt* to modify, alter; **se ~** *vi* to alter

modique [mɔdik] *adj* modest

modiste [mɔdist] *nf* milliner

module [mɔdyl] *nm* module

moelle [mwal] *nf* marrow; **~ épinière** spinal cord

moelleux, -euse [mwalø, øz] *adj* soft; (*gâteau*) light and moist

mœurs [mœʀ] *nfpl* (*conduite*) morals; (*manières*) manners; (*pratiques sociales, mode de vie*) habits

mohair [mɔɛʀ] *nm* mohair

moi [mwa] *pron* me; (*emphatique*): **~, je ...** for my part, I ..., I myself ...; **à ~** mine; **moi-même** *pron* myself; (*emphatique*) I myself

moindre [mwɛdʀ] *adj* lesser; lower; **le(la) ~, les ~s** the least, the slightest; **merci – c'est la ~ des choses!** thank you – it's a pleasure!

moine [mwan] *nm* monk, friar

moineau, x [mwano] *nm* sparrow

MOT-CLÉ

moins [mwɛ̃] *adv* **1** (*comparatif*): **moins (que)** less (than); **moins grand que** less tall than, not as tall as; **moins je travaille, mieux je me porte** the less I work, the better I feel

2 (*superlatif*): **le moins** (the) least; **c'est ce que j'aime le moins** it's what I like (the) least; **le(la) moins doué(e)** the least gifted; **au moins, du moins** at least; **pour le moins** at the very least

3: **moins de** (*quantité*) less (than); (*nombre*) fewer (than); **moins de sable/ d'eau** less sand/water; **moins de livres/ gens** fewer books/people; **moins de 2 ans** less than 2 years; **moins de midi** not yet midday

4: **de moins, en moins**: **100 F/3 jours de moins** 100F/3 days less; **3 livres en moins** 3 books fewer; 3 books too few; **de l'argent en moins** less money; **le soleil en moins** but for the sun, minus the sun; **de moins en moins** less and less

5: **à moins de, à moins que** unless; **à moins de faire** unless we do (*ou* he does *etc*); **à moins que tu ne fasses** unless you do; **à moins d'un accident** barring any accident

♦ *prép*: **4 moins 2** 4 minus 2; **il est moins 5** it's 5 to; **il fait moins 5** it's 5 (degrees) below (freezing), it's minus 5

---

mois [mwa] *nm* month

moisi [mwazi] *nm* mould, mildew; **odeur de ~** musty smell; **moisir** *vi* to go mouldy; **moisissure** *nf* mould *no pl*

moisson [mwasɔ̃] *nf* harvest; **moissonner** *vt* to harvest, reap; **moissonneuse** *nf* (*machine*) harvester

moite [mwat] *adj* sweaty, sticky

moitié [mwatje] *nf* half; **la ~** half; **la ~ de** half (of); **la ~ du temps** half the time; **à la ~ de** halfway through; **à ~** (*avant le verbe*) half; (*avant l'adjectif*) half-; **à ~ prix** (at) half-price; **~ moitié** half-and-half

moka [mɔka] *nm* coffee gateau

mol [mɔl] *adj voir* **mou**

molaire [mɔlɛʀ] *nf* molar

molester [mɔlɛste] *vt* to manhandle, maul (about)

molle [mɔl] *adj voir* **mou**; **mollement** *adv* (*péj: travailler*) sluggishly; (*protester*) feebly

mollet [mɔlɛ] *nm* calf ♦ *adj m*: **œuf ~** soft-boiled egg

molletonné, e [mɔltɔne] *adj* fleece-lined

mollir [mɔliʀ] *vi* (*fléchir*) to relent; (*substance*) to go soft

mollusque [mɔlysk] *nm* mollusc

môme [mom] (*fam*) *nm/f* (*enfant*) brat

moment [mɔmã] *nm* moment; **ce n'est pas le ~** this is not the (right) time; **pour un bon ~** for a good while; **pour le ~** for the moment, for the time being; **au ~ de** at the time of; **au ~ où** just as; **à tout ~** (*peut arriver etc*) at any time *ou* moment; (*constamment*) constantly, continually; **en ce ~** at the moment; at present; **sur le ~** at the time; **par ~s** now and then, at times; **du ~ où** *ou* **que** seeing that, since; **momentané, e** *adj* temporary, momentary; **momentanément** *adv* (*court instant*) for a short while

momie [mɔmi] *nf* mummy

mon, ma [mɔ̃, ma] (*pl* **mes**) *adj* my

Monaco [mɔnako] *nm* Monaco

monarchie [mɔnaʀʃi] *nf* monarchy

monastère [mɔnastɛʀ] *nm* monastery

monceau, x [mɔ̃so] *nm* heap

mondain, e [mɔ̃dɛ̃, ɛn] *adj* (*vie*) society *cpd*

monde [mɔ̃d] *nm* world; (*haute société*): **le ~** (high) society; **il y a du ~** (*beaucoup de gens*) there are a lot of people; (*quelques personnes*) there are some people; **beaucoup/peu de ~** many/few people; **mettre au ~** to bring into the world; **pas le moins du ~** not in the least; **se faire un ~ de qch** to make a great deal of fuss about sth; **mondial, e, -aux** *adj* (*population*) world *cpd*; (*influence*) world-wide; **mondialement** *adv* throughout the world

monégasque [mɔnegask] *adj* Monegasque, *ou* from Monaco

monétaire [mɔnetɛʀ] *adj* monetary

moniteur, -trice [mɔnitœʀ, tʀis] *nm/f* (*SPORT*) instructor(-tress); (*de colonie de vacances*) supervisor ♦ *nm* (*écran*) monitor

monnaie [mɔnɛ] *nf* (*ÉCON, gén: moyen d'échange*) currency; (*petites pièces*): **avoir de la ~** to have (some) change; **une pièce de ~** a coin; **faire de la ~** to get (some) change; **avoir/faire la ~ de 20 F** to have change of/get change for 20 F; **rendre à qn la ~ (sur 20 F)** to give sb the change (out of *ou* from 20 F); **monnayer** *vt* to convert into cash; (*talent*) to capitalize on

monologue [mɔnɔlɔg] *nm* monologue, soliloquy; **monologuer** *vi* to soliloquize

monopole [mɔnɔpɔl] *nm* monopoly

monotone [mɔnɔtɔn] *adj* monotonous

Monsieur [məsjø] (*pl* **Messieurs**) *titre* Mr ♦ *nm* (*homme quelconque*): **un/le m~** a/ the gentleman; **~, ...** (*en tête de lettre*) Dear Sir, ...; *voir aussi* **Madame**

monstre [mɔ̃stʀ] *nm* monster ♦ *adj* (*fam: colossal*) monstrous; **un travail ~** a fantastic amount of work; **monstrueux, -euse** *adj* monstrous

mont [mɔ̃] *nm*: **par ~s et par vaux** up hill and down dale; **le M~ Blanc** Mont Blanc

montage [mɔ̃taʒ] *nm* (*assemblage: d'appareil*) assembly; (*PHOTO*) photomontage; (*CINÉMA*) editing

montagnard, e [mɔ̃taɲaʀ, aʀd] *adj* mountain *cpd* ♦ *nm/f* mountain-dweller

montagne [mɔ̃taɲ] *nf* (*cime*) mountain; (*région*): **la ~** the mountains *pl*; **~s russes** big dipper *sg*, switchback *sg*; **montagneux, -euse** *adj* mountainous; (*basse montagne*) hilly

montant, e [mɔ̃tã, ãt] *adj* rising; **pull à col ~** high-necked jumper ♦ *nm* (*somme, total*) (sum) total, (total) amount; (*de fenêtre*) upright; (*de lit*) post

monte-charge [mɔ̃tʃaʀʒ] *nm inv* goods

lift, hoist

montée [mɔ̃te] *nf* (*des prix, hostilités*) rise; (*escalade*) climb; (*côte*) hill; **au milieu de la ~** halfway up

monter [mɔ̃te] *vt* (*escalier, côte*) to go (*ou* come) up; (*valise, paquet*) to take (*ou* bring) up; (*étagère*) to put up; (*tente, échafaudage*) to put up; (*machine*) to assemble; (*CINÉMA*) to edit; (*THÉÂTRE*) to put on, stage; (*société etc*) to set up ♦ *vi* to go (*ou* come) up; (*prix, niveau, température*) to go up, rise; (*passager*) to get on; **se ~ à** (*frais etc*) to add up to, come to; **~ à pied** to walk up, go up on foot; **~ dans le train/l'avion** to get into the train/plane, board the train/plane; **~ sur** to climb up onto; **à cheval** (*faire du cheval*) to ride, go riding

montre [mɔ̃tʀ] *nf* watch; **contre la ~** (*SPORT*) against the clock; **montre-bracelet** *nf* wristwatch

montrer [mɔ̃tʀe] *vt* to show; **~ qch à qn** to show sb sth

monture [mɔ̃tyʀ] *nf* (*cheval*) mount; (*de lunettes*) frame; (*d'une bague*) setting

monument [mɔnymɑ̃] *nm* monument; **~ aux morts** war memorial

moquer [mɔke]: **se ~ de** *vt* to make fun of, laugh at; (*fam: se désintéresser de*) not to care about; (*tromper*): **se ~ de qn** to take sb for a ride; **moquerie** *nf* mockery

moquette [mɔkɛt] *nf* fitted carpet

moqueur, -euse [mɔkœʀ, øz] *adj* mocking

moral, e, -aux [mɔʀal, o] *adj* moral ♦ *nm* morale; **avoir le ~** (*fam*) to be in good spirits; **avoir le ~ à zéro** (*fam*) to be really down; **morale** *nf* (*mœurs*) morals *pl*; (*valeurs*) moral standards *pl*, morality; (*d'une fable etc*) moral; **faire la morale à** to lecture, preach at; **moralité** *nf* morality; (*de fable*) moral

morceau, x [mɔʀso] *nm* piece, bit; (*d'une œuvre*) passage, extract; (*MUS*) piece; (*CULIN: de viande*) cut; (*de sucre*) lump; **mettre en ~x** to pull to pieces *ou* bits; **manger**

un ~ to have a bite (to eat)

morceler [mɔʀsəle] *vt* to break up, divide up

mordant, e [mɔʀdɑ̃, ɑ̃t] *adj* (*ton, remarque*) scathing, cutting; (*ironie, froid*) biting ♦ *nm* (*style*) bite, punch

mordiller [mɔʀdije] *vt* to nibble at, chew at

mordre [mɔʀdʀ] *vt* to bite ♦ *vi* (*poisson*) to bite; **~ sur** (*fig*) to go over into, overlap into; **~ à l'hameçon** to bite, rise to the bait

mordu, e [mɔʀdy] (*fam*) *nm/f* enthusiast; **un ~ de jazz** a jazz fanatic

morfondre [mɔʀfɔ̃dʀ]: **se ~** *vi* to mope

morgue [mɔʀg] *nf* (*arrogance*) haughtiness; (*lieu: de la police*) morgue; (: *à l'hôpital*) mortuary

morne [mɔʀn] *adj* dismal, dreary

morose [mɔʀoz] *adj* sullen, morose

mors [mɔʀ] *nm* bit

morse [mɔʀs] *nm* (*ZOOL*) walrus; (*TÉL*) Morse (code)

morsure [mɔʀsyʀ] *nf* bite

mort¹ [mɔʀ] *nf* death

mort², e [mɔʀ, mɔʀt] *pp de* **mourir** ♦ *adj* dead ♦ *nm/f* (*défunt*) dead man/woman; (*victime*): **il y a eu plusieurs ~s** several people were killed, there were several killed; **~ de peur/fatigue** frightened to death/dead tired

mortalité [mɔʀtalite] *nf* mortality, death rate

mortel, le [mɔʀtɛl] *adj* (*poison etc*) deadly, lethal; (*accident, blessure*) fatal; (*silence, ennemi*) deadly; (*péché*) mortal; (*fam: ennuyeux*) deadly boring

mortier [mɔʀtje] *nm* (*gén*) mortar

mort-né, e [mɔʀne] *adj* (*enfant*) stillborn

mortuaire [mɔʀtɥɛʀ] *adj*: **avis ~** death announcement

morue [mɔʀy] *nf* (*ZOOL*) cod *inv*

mosaïque [mɔzaik] *nf* mosaic

Moscou [mɔsku] *n* Moscow

mosquée [mɔske] *nf* mosque

mot [mo] *nm* word; (*message*) line, note; **~**

à ~ word for word; ~ **d'ordre** watchword; ~ **de passe** password; **~s croisés** crossword (puzzle) *sg*

motard [mɔtaʀ, aʀd] *nm* biker; (*policier*) motorcycle cop

motel [mɔtɛl] *nm* motel

moteur, -trice [mɔtœʀ, tʀis] *adj* (*ANAT, PHYSIOL*) motor; (*TECH*) driving; (*AUTO*): **à 4 roues motrices** 4-wheel drive ♦ *nm* engine, motor; **à** ~ power-driven, motor *cpd*; ~ **de recherche** search engine

motif [mɔtif] *nm* (*cause*) motive; (*décoratif*) design, pattern, motif; **sans** ~ groundless

motivation [mɔtivasjɔ̃] *nf* motivation

motiver [mɔtive] *vt* to motivate; (*justifier*) to justify, account for

moto [mɔto] *nf* (*motor*)bike; **motocycliste** *nm/f* motorcyclist

motorisé, e [mɔtɔʀize] *adj* (*personne*) having transport *ou* a car

motrice [mɔtʀis] *adj voir* **moteur**

motte [mɔt] *nf*: ~ **de terre** lump of earth, clod (of earth); ~ **de beurre** lump of butter

mou (mol), molle [mu, mɔl] *adj* soft; (*personne*) lethargic; (*protestations*) weak ♦ *nm*: **avoir du mou** to be slack

moucharder [muʃaʀde] (*fam*) *vt* (*SCOL*) to sneak on; (*POLICE*) to grass on

mouche [muʃ] *nf* fly

moucher [muʃe]: **se** ~ *vi* to blow one's nose

moucheron [muʃʀɔ̃] *nm* midge

mouchoir [muʃwaʀ] *nm* handkerchief, hanky; ~ **en papier** tissue, paper hanky

moudre [mudʀ] *vt* to grind

moue [mu] *nf* pout; **faire la** ~ to pout; (*fig*) to pull a face

mouette [mwɛt] *nf* (*sea*)gull

moufle [mufl] *nf* (*gant*) mitt(en)

mouillé, e [muje] *adj* wet

mouiller [muje] *vt* (*humecter*) to wet, moisten; (*tremper*): ~ **qn/qch** to make sb/sth wet ♦ *vi* (*NAVIG*) to lie *ou* be at anchor; **se** ~ to get wet; (*fam: prendre des risques*) to commit o.s.

moulant, e [mulɑ̃, ɑ̃t] *adj* figure-hugging

moule [mul] *nf* mussel ♦ *nm* (*CULIN*) mould; ~ **à gâteaux** ♦ *nm* cake tin (*BRIT*) *ou* pan (*US*)

moulent [mul] *vb voir* **moudre; mouler**

mouler [mule] *vt* (*suj: vêtement*) to hug, fit closely round

moulin [mulɛ̃] *nm* mill; ~ **à café/à poivre** coffee/pepper mill; ~ **à légumes** (vegetable) shredder; ~ **à paroles** (*fig*) chatterbox; ~ **à vent** windmill

moulinet [mulinɛ] *nm* (*de canne à pêche*) reel; (*mouvement*): **faire des ~s avec qch** to whirl sth around

moulinette ® [mulinɛt] *nf* (vegetable) shredder

moulu, e [muly] *pp de* **moudre**

mourant, e [muʀɑ̃, ɑ̃t] *adj* dying

mourir [muʀiʀ] *vi* to die; (*civilisation*) to die out; ~ **de froid/faim** to die of exposure/hunger; ~ **de faim/d'ennui** (*fig*) to be starving/be bored to death; ~ **d'envie de faire** to be dying to do

mousse [mus] *nf* (*BOT*) moss; (*de savon*) lather; (*écume: sur eau, bière*) froth, foam; (*CULIN*) mousse ♦ *nm* (*NAVIG*) ship's boy; ~ **à raser** shaving foam

mousseline [muslin] *nf* muslin; **pommes** ~ mashed potatoes

mousser [muse] *vi* (*bière, détergent*) to foam; (*savon*) to lather; **mousseux, -euse** *adj* frothy ♦ *nm*: **(vin) mousseux** sparkling wine

mousson [musɔ̃] *nf* monsoon

moustache [mustaʃ] *nf* moustache; **~s** *nfpl* (*du chat*) whiskers *pl*; **moustachu, e** *adj* with a moustache

moustiquaire [mustikɛʀ] *nf* mosquito net

moustique [mustik] *nm* mosquito

moutarde [mutaʀd] *nf* mustard

mouton [mutɔ̃] *nm* sheep *inv*; (*peau*) sheepskin; (*CULIN*) mutton

mouvement [muvmɑ̃] *nm* movement; (*fig: impulsion*) gesture; **avoir un bon** ~ to make a nice gesture; **en** ~ in motion; on the move; **mouvementé, e** *adj* (*vie,* *poursuite)* eventful; *(réunion)* turbulent

mouvoir [muvwaʀ]: **se ~** *vi* to move

moyen, ne [mwajɛ̃, jɛn] *adj* average; *(tailles, prix)* medium; *(de grandeur moyenne)* medium-sized ♦ *nm (façon)* means *sg*, way; **~s** *nmpl (capacités)* means; **très ~** *(résultats)* pretty poor; **je n'en ai pas les ~s** I can't afford it; **au ~ de** by means of; **par tous les ~s** by every possible means, every possible way; **par ses propres ~s** all by oneself; **~ âge** Middle Ages; **~ de transport** means of transport

moyennant [mwajɛnɑ̃] *prép (somme)* for; *(service, conditions)* in return for; *(travail, effort)* with

moyenne [mwajɛn] *nf* average; *(MATH)* mean; *(SCOL: à l'examen)* pass mark; **en ~** on (an) average; **~ d'âge** average age

Moyen-Orient [mwajɛnɔʀjɑ̃] *nm*: **le ~-~** the Middle East

moyeu, x [mwajø] *nm* hub

MST *sigle f (= maladie sexuellement transmissible)* STD

MTC *sigle m (= mécanisme du taux de change)* ERM

mû, mue [my] *pp de* **mouvoir**

muer [mɥe] *vi (oiseau, mammifère)* to moult; *(serpent)* to slough; *(jeune garçon)*: **il mue** his voice is breaking; **se ~ en** to transform into

muet, te [mɥɛ, mɥɛt] *adj* dumb; *(fig)*: **~ d'admiration** *etc* speechless with admiration *etc*; *(CINÉMA)* silent ♦ *nm/f* mute

mufle [myfl] *nm* muzzle; *(fam: goujat)* boor

mugir [myʒiʀ] *vi (taureau)* to bellow; *(vache)* to low; *(fig)* to howl

muguet [mygɛ] *nm* lily of the valley

mule [myl] *nf (ZOOL)* (she-)mule

mulet [mylɛ] *nm (ZOOL)* (he-)mule

multinationale [myltinasjɔnal] *nf* multinational

multiple [myltipl] *adj* multiple, numerous; *(varié)* many, manifold; **multiplier** *vt* to multiply; **se multiplier** *vi* to multiply

municipal, e, -aux [mynisipal, o] *adj* *(élections, stade)* municipal; *(conseil)* town *cpd*; **piscine / bibliothèque ~e** public swimming pool/library; **municipalité** *nf* *(ville)* municipality; *(conseil)* town council

munir [myniʀ] *vt*: **~ qch de** to equip sth with; **se ~ de** to arm o.s. with

munitions [mynisjɔ̃] *nfpl* ammunition *sg*

mur [myʀ] *nm* wall; **~ du son** sound barrier

mûr, e [myʀ] *adj* ripe; *(personne)* mature

muraille [myʀaj] *nf* (high) wall

mural, e, -aux [myʀal, o] *adj* wall *cpd*; *(art)* mural

mûre [myʀ] *nf* blackberry

muret [myʀɛ] *nm* low wall

mûrir [myʀiʀ] *vi (fruit, blé)* to ripen; *(abcès)* to come to a head; *(fig: idée, personne)* to mature ♦ *vt (projet)* to nurture; *(personne)* to (make) mature

murmure [myʀmyʀ] *nm* murmur; **murmurer** *vi* to murmur

muscade [myskad] *nf (aussi:* **noix (de) ~)** nutmeg

muscat [myska] *nm (raisins)* muscat grape; *(vin)* muscatel (wine)

muscle [myskl] *nm* muscle; **musclé, e** *adj* muscular; *(fig)* strong-arm

museau, x [myzo] *nm* muzzle; *(CULIN)* brawn

musée [myze] *nm* museum; *(de peinture)* art gallery

museler [myz(ə)le] *vt* to muzzle

musette [myzɛt] *nf (sac)* lunchbag

musical, e, -aux [myzikal, o] *adj* musical

music-hall [myzikol] *nm (salle)* variety theatre; *(genre)* variety

musicien, ne [myzisjɛ̃, jɛn] *adj* musical ♦ *nm/f* musician

musique [myzik] *nf* music; **~ d'ambiance** background music

musulman, e [myzylmɑ̃, an] *adj, nm/f* Moslem, Muslim

mutation [mytasjɔ̃] *nf (ADMIN)* transfer

muter [myte] *vt* to transfer, move

mutilé, e [mytile] *nm/f* disabled person *(through loss of limbs)*

mutiler [mytile] *vt* to mutilate, maim

mutin, e [mytɛ̃, in] *adj* (*air, ton*) mischievous, impish ♦ *nm/f* (MIL, NAVIG) mutineer; **mutinerie** *nf* mutiny

mutisme [mytism] *nm* silence

mutuel, le [mytɥɛl] *adj* mutual; **mutuelle** *nf* voluntary insurance premiums for back-up health cover

myope [mjɔp] *adj* short-sighted

myosotis [mjozɔtis] *nm* forget-me-not

myrtille [miʀtij] *nf* bilberry

mystère [mistɛʀ] *nm* mystery; **mystérieux, -euse** *adj* mysterious

mystifier [mistifje] *vt* to fool

mythe [mit] *nm* myth

mythologie [mitɔlɔʒi] *nf* mythology

N, n

n' [n] *adv voir* **ne**

nacre [nakʀ] *nf* mother of pearl

nage [naʒ] *nf* swimming; (*manière*) style of swimming, stroke; **traverser à la ~** to swim across; **en ~** bathed in sweat; **nageoire** *nf* fin; **nager** *vi* to swim; **nageur, -euse** *nm/f* swimmer

naguère [nagɛʀ] *adv* formerly

naïf, -ïve [naif, naiv] *adj* naïve

nain, e [nɛ̃, nɛn] *nm/f* dwarf

naissance [nesɑ̃s] *nf* birth; **donner ~ à** to give birth to; (*fig*) to give rise to

naître [netʀ] *vi* to be born; (*fig*): **~ de** to arise from, be born out of; **il est né en 1960** he was born in 1960; **faire ~** (*fig*) to give rise to, arouse

naïve [naiv] *adj voir* **naïf**

naïveté [naivte] *nf* naïvety

nana [nana] (*fam*) *nf* (*fille*) chick, bird (BRIT)

nantir [nɑ̃tiʀ] *vt*: **~ qn de** to provide sb with; **les nantis** (*péj*) the well-to-do

nappe [nap] *nf* tablecloth; (*de pétrole, gaz*) layer; **~ phréatique** ground water; **napperon** *nm* table-mat

naquit *etc* [naki] *vb voir* **naître**

narcodollars [naʀkodɔlaʀ] *nmpl* drug money *sg*

narguer [naʀge] *vt* to taunt

narine [naʀin] *nf* nostril

narquois, e [naʀkwa, waz] *adj* mocking

natal, e [natal] *adj* native; **natalité** *nf* birth rate

natation [natasjɔ̃] *nf* swimming

natif, -ive [natif, iv] *adj* native

nation [nasjɔ̃] *nf* nation; **national, e, -aux** *adj* national; **nationale** *nf*: (**route**) **nationale** ≃ A road (BRIT), ≃ state highway (US); **nationaliser** *vt* to nationalize; **nationalisme** *nm* nationalism; **nationalité** *nf* nationality

natte [nat] *nf* (*cheveux*) plait; (*tapis*) mat

naturaliser [natyralize] *vt* to naturalize

nature [natyʀ] *nf* nature ♦ *adj, adv* (CULIN) plain, without seasoning *ou* sweetening; (*café, thé*) black, without sugar; (*yaourt*) natural; **payer en ~** to pay in kind; **~ morte** still-life; **naturel, le** *adj* (*gén, aussi enfant*) natural ♦ *nm* (*absence d'affectation*) naturalness; (*caractère*) disposition, nature; **naturellement** *adv* naturally; (*bien sûr*) of course

naufrage [nofʀaʒ] *nm* (ship)wreck; **faire ~** to be shipwrecked

nauséabond, e [nozeabɔ̃, ɔd] *adj* foul

nausée [noze] *nf* nausea

nautique [notik] *adj* nautical, water *cpd*; **sports ~s** water sports

naval, e [naval] *adj* naval; (*industrie*) shipbuilding

navet [navɛ] *nm* turnip; (*péj: film*) rubbishy film

navette [navɛt] *nf* shuttle; **faire la ~ (entre)** to go to and fro *ou* shuttle (between)

navigateur [navigatœʀ, tʀis] *nm* (NAVIG) seafarer; (INFORM) browser

navigation [navigasjɔ̃] *nf* navigation, sailing

naviguer [navige] *vi* to navigate, sail; **~ sur Internet** to surf the net

navire [naviʀ] *nm* ship

navrer [navʀe] *vt* to upset, distress; **je suis navré** I'm so sorry

ne, **n'** [n(ə)] *adv voir* **pas**; **plus**; **jamais** *etc*; *(sans valeur négative: non traduit)*: **c'est plus loin que je ~ le croyais** it's further than I thought

né, e [ne] *pp (voir* **naître***)*: **~ en 1960** born in 1960; **~e Scott** née Scott

néanmoins [neãmwɛ̃] *adv* nevertheless

néant [neã] *nm* nothingness; **réduire à ~** to bring to nought; *(espoir)* to dash

nécessaire [nesesɛʀ] *adj* necessary ♦ *nm* necessary; *(sac)* kit; **je vais faire le ~** I'll see to it; **~ de couture** sewing kit; **nécessité** *nf* necessity; **nécessiter** *vt* to require

nécrologique [nekʀɔlɔʒik] *adj*: **rubrique ~** obituary column

nectar [nektaʀ] *nm* nectar

néerlandais, e [neɛʀlɑ̃dɛ, ɛz] *adj* Dutch

nef [nɛf] *nf (d'église)* nave

néfaste [nefast] *adj (nuisible)* harmful; *(funeste)* ill-fated

négatif, -ive [negatif, iv] *adj* negative ♦ *nm (PHOTO)* negative

négligé, e [negliʒe] *adj (en désordre)* slovenly ♦ *nm (tenue)* negligee

négligeable [negliʒabl] *adj* negligible

négligent, e [negliʒɑ̃, ɑ̃t] *adj* careless, negligent

négliger [negliʒe] *vt (tenue)* to be careless about; *(avis, précautions)* to disregard; *(épouse, jardin)* to neglect; **~ de faire** to fail to do, not bother to do

négoce [negɔs] *nm* trade

négociant [negɔsjɑ̃, jɑ̃t] *nm* merchant

négociation [negɔsjasjɔ̃] *nf* negotiation

négocier [negɔsje] *vi, vt* to negotiate

nègre [negʀ] *(péj) nm (écrivain)* ghost (writer)

neige [nɛʒ] *nf* snow; **neiger** *vi* to snow

nénuphar [nenyfaʀ] *nm* water-lily

néon [neɔ̃] *nm* neon

néo-zélandais, e [neozelɑ̃dɛ, ɛz] *adj* New Zealand *cpd* ♦ *nm/f*: **N~-Z~, e** New Zealander

nerf [nɛʀ] *nm* nerve; **être sur les ~s** to be all keyed up; **allons, du ~!** come on, buck up!; **nerveux, -euse** *adj* nervous; *(irritable)* touchy, nervy; *(voiture)* nippy, responsive; **nervosité** *nf* excitability, tenseness; *(irritabilité passagère)* irritability

nervure [nɛʀvyʀ] *nf* vein

n'est-ce pas [nɛspa] *adv* isn't it?, won't you? *etc, selon le verbe qui précède*

Net [nɛt] *nm (Internet)*: **le ~** the Net

net, nette [nɛt] *adj (sans équivoque, distinct)* clear; *(évident: amélioration, différence)* marked, distinct; *(propre)* neat, clean; *(COMM: prix, salaire)* net ♦ *adv (refuser)* flatly ♦ *nm*: **mettre au ~** to copy out; **s'arrêter ~** to stop dead; **nettement** *adv* clearly, distinctly; *(incontestablement)* decidedly, distinctly; **netteté** *nf* clearness

nettoyage [netwajaʒ] *nm* cleaning; **~ à sec** dry cleaning

nettoyer [netwaje] *vt* to clean

neuf[1] [nœf] *num* nine

neuf[2], neuve [nœf, nœv] *adj* new ♦ *nm*: **remettre à ~** to do up (as good as new), refurbish; **quoi de ~?** what's new?

neutre [nøtʀ] *adj* neutral; *(LING)* neuter

neuve [nœv] *adj voir* **neuf[2]**

neuvième [nœvjɛm] *num* ninth

neveu, x [n(ə)vø] *nm* nephew

névrosé, e [nevʀoze] *adj, nm/f* neurotic

nez [ne] *nm* nose; **~ à ~ avec** face to face with; **avoir du ~** to have flair

ni [ni] *conj*: **~ ... ~** neither ... nor; **je n'aime ~ les lentilles ~ les épinards** I like neither lentils nor spinach; **il n'a dit ~ oui ~ non** he didn't say either yes or no; **elles ne sont venues ~ l'une ~ l'autre** neither of them came

niais, e [njɛ, njɛz] *adj* silly, thick

niche [niʃ] *nf (du chien)* kennel; *(de mur)* recess, niche; **nicher** *vi* to nest

nid [ni] *nm* nest; **~ de poule** pothole

nièce [njɛs] *nf* niece

nier [nje] *vt* to deny

nigaud, e [nigo, od] *nm/f* booby, fool

Nil [nil] *nm*: **le ~** the Nile

n'importe [nɛ̃pɔʀt] *adv*: **~ qui/quoi/où** anybody/anything/anywhere; **~ quand**

any time; **~ quel/quelle** any; **~ lequel/ laquelle** any (one); **~ comment** (*sans soin*) carelessly

niveau, x [nivo] *nm* level; (*des élèves, études*) standard; **~ de vie** standard of living

niveler [niv(ə)le] *vt* to level

NN *abr* (= *nouvelle norme*) revised standard of hotel classification

noble [nɔbl] *adj* noble; **noblesse** *nf* nobility; (*d'une action etc*) nobleness

noce [nɔs] *nf* wedding; (*gens*) wedding party (*ou* guests *pl*); **faire la ~** (*fam*) to go on a binge

nocif, -ive [nɔsif, iv] *adj* harmful, noxious

nocturne [nɔktyrn] *adj* nocturnal ♦ *nf* late-night opening

Noël [nɔel] *nm* Christmas

nœud [nø] *nm* knot; (*ruban*) bow; **~ papillon** bow tie

noir, e [nwar] *adj* black; (*obscur, sombre*) dark ♦ *nm/f* black man/woman ♦ *nm*: **dans le ~** in the dark; **travail au ~** moonlighting; **travailler au ~** to work on the side; **noircir** *vt, vi* to blacken; **noire** *nf* (*MUS*) crotchet (*BRIT*), quarter note (*US*)

noisette [nwazet] *nf* hazelnut

noix [nwa] *nf* walnut; (*CULIN*): **une ~ de beurre** a knob of butter; **~ de cajou** cashew nut; **~ de coco** coconut; **à la ~** (*fam*) worthless

nom [nɔ̃] *nm* name; (*LING*) noun; **~ de famille** surname; **~ de jeune fille** maiden name; **~ déposé** trade name; **~ propre** proper noun

nomade [nɔmad] *nm/f* nomad

nombre [nɔ̃br] *nm* number; **venir en ~** to come in large numbers; **depuis ~ d'années** for many years; **au ~ de mes amis** among my friends; **nombreux, -euse** *adj* many, numerous; (*avec nom sg: foule etc*) large; **peu nombreux** few

nombril [nɔ̃bri(l)] *nm* navel

nommer [nɔme] *vt* to name; (*élire*) to appoint, nominate; **se ~: il se nomme Pascal** his name's Pascal, he's called Pascal

non [nɔ̃] *adv* (*réponse*) no; (*avec loin, sans, seulement*) not; **~ (pas) que** not that; **moi ~ plus** neither do I, I don't either; **c'est bon ~?** (*exprimant le doute*) it's good, isn't it?

non-alcoolisé, e [nɔ̃alkɔlize] *adj* nonalcoholic

nonante [nɔnɑ̃t] (*BELGIQUE, SUISSE*) *num* ninety

non-fumeur [nɔ̃fymœr, øz] *nm* nonsmoker

non-sens [nɔ̃sɑ̃s] *nm* absurdity

nonchalant, e [nɔ̃ʃalɑ̃, ɑ̃t] *adj* nonchalant

nord [nɔr] *nm* North ♦ *adj* northern; north; **au ~** (*situation*) in the north; (*direction*) to the north; **au ~ de** (to the) north of; **nord-est** *nm* North-East; **nord-ouest** *nm* North-West

normal, e, -aux [nɔrmal, o] *adj* normal; **c'est tout à fait ~** it's perfectly natural; **vous trouvez ça ~?** does it seem right to you?; **normale** *nf*: **la normale** the norm, the average; **normalement** *adv* (*en général*) normally

normand, e [nɔrmɑ̃, ɑ̃d] *adj* of Normandy

Normandie [nɔrmɑ̃di] *nf* Normandy

norme [nɔrm] *nf* norm; (*TECH*) standard

Norvège [nɔrvɛʒ] *nf* Norway; **norvégien, ne** *adj* Norwegian ♦ *nm/f*: **Norvégien, ne** Norwegian ♦ *nm* (*LING*) Norwegian

nos [no] *adj voir* **notre**

nostalgie [nɔstalʒi] *nf* nostalgia; **nostalgique** *adj* nostalgic

notable [nɔtabl] *adj* (*fait*) notable, noteworthy; (*marqué*) noticeable, marked ♦ *nm* prominent citizen

notaire [nɔtɛr] *nm* solicitor

notamment [nɔtamɑ̃] *adv* in particular, among others

note [nɔt] *nf* (*écrite, MUS*) note; (*SCOL*) mark (*BRIT*), grade; (*facture*) bill; **~ de service** memorandum

noté, e [nɔte] *adj*: **être bien/mal ~** (*employé etc*) to have a good/bad record

noter [nɔte] *vt* (*écrire*) to write down; (*re-*

marquer) to note, notice; *(devoir)* to mark, grade

notice [nɔtis] *nf* summary, short article; *(brochure)* leaflet, instruction book

notifier [nɔtifje] *vt*: **~ qch à qn** to notify sb of sth, notify sth to sb

notion [nosjɔ̃] *nf* notion, idea

notoire [nɔtwaʀ] *adj* widely known; *(en mal)* notorious

notre [nɔtʀ] *(pl* **nos)** *adj* our

nôtre [notʀ] *pron*: **le ~, la ~, les ~s** ours ♦ *adj* ours; **les ~s** ours; *(alliés etc)* our own people; **soyez des ~s** join us

nouer [nwe] *vt* to tie, knot; *(fig: alliance etc)* to strike up

noueux, -euse [nwø, øz] *adj* gnarled

nouilles [nuj] *nfpl* noodles

nourrice [nuʀis] *nf (gardienne)* child-minder

nourrir [nuʀiʀ] *vt* to feed; *(fig: espoir)* to harbour, nurse; **se ~** to eat; **se ~ de** to feed (o.s.) on; **nourrissant, e** *adj* nourishing, nutritious; **nourrisson** *nm* (un-weaned) infant; **nourriture** *nf* food

nous [nu] *pron (sujet)* we; *(objet)* us; **nous-mêmes** *pron* ourselves

nouveau (nouvel), -elle, x [nuvo, nuvɛl] *adj* new ♦ *nm*: **y a-t-il du ~?** is there anything new on this? ♦ *nm/f* new pupil *(ou* employee); **de ~, à ~** again; **~ venu, nouvelle venue** newcomer; **~x mariés** newly-weds; **nouveau-né, e** *nm/f* newborn baby; **nouveauté** *nf* novelty; *(objet)* new thing *ou* article

nouvel [nuvɛl] *adj voir* **nouveau**; **N~ An** New Year

nouvelle [nuvɛl] *adj voir* **nouveau** ♦ *nf* (piece of) news *sg*; *(LITTÉRATURE)* short story; **les ~s** the news; **je suis sans ~s de lui** I haven't heard from him; **Nouvelle-Calédonie** *nf* New Caledonia; **nouvellement** *adv* recently, newly; **Nouvelle-Zélande** *nf* New Zealand

novembre [nɔvɑ̃bʀ] *nm* November

novice [nɔvis] *adj* inexperienced

noyade [nwajad] *nf* drowning *no pl*

noyau, x [nwajo] *nm (de fruit)* stone; *(BIO, PHYSIQUE)* nucleus; *(fig: centre)* core; **noyauter** *vt (POL)* to infiltrate

noyer [nwaje] *nm* walnut (tree); *(bois)* walnut ♦ *vt* to drown; *(moteur)* to flood; **se ~** *vi* to be drowned, drown; *(suicide)* to drown o.s.

nu, e [ny] *adj* naked; *(membres)* naked, bare; *(pieds, mains, chambre, fil électrique)* bare ♦ *nm (ART)* nude; **tout ~** stark naked; **se mettre ~** to strip; **mettre à ~** to bare

nuage [nɥaʒ] *nm* cloud; **nuageux, -euse** *adj* cloudy

nuance [nɥɑ̃s] *nf (de couleur, sens)* shade; **il y a une ~ (entre)** there's a slight difference (between); **nuancer** *vt (opinion)* to bring some reservations *ou* qualifications to

nucléaire [nykleɛʀ] *adj* nuclear ♦ *nm*: **le ~** nuclear energy

nudiste [nydist] *nm/f* nudist

nuée [nɥe] *nf*: **une ~ de** a cloud *ou* host *ou* swarm of

nues [ny] *nfpl*: **tomber des ~** to be taken aback; **porter qn aux ~** to praise sb to the skies

nuire [nɥiʀ] *vi* to be harmful; **~ à** to harm, do damage to; **nuisible** *adj* harmful; **animal nuisible** *nm* pest

nuit [nɥi] *nf* night; **il fait ~** it's dark; **cette ~ (hier)** last night; *(aujourd'hui)* tonight; **~ blanche** sleepless night

nul, nulle [nyl] *adj (aucun)* no; *(minime)* nil, non-existent; *(non valable)* null; *(péj)* useless, hopeless ♦ *pron* none, no one; **match** *ou* **résultat ~** draw; **~le part** nowhere; **nullement** *adv* by no means; **nullité** *nf (personne)* nonentity

numérique [nymeʀik] *adj* numerical; *(affichage)* digital

numéro [nymeʀo] *nm* number; *(spectacle)* act, turn; *(PRESSE)* issue, number; **~ de téléphone** (tele)phone number; **~ vert** ≃ freefone ® number *(BRIT)*, ≃ toll-free number *(US)*; **numéroter** *vt* to number

nu-pieds [nypje] *adj inv, adv* barefoot
nuque [nyk] *nf* nape of the neck
nu-tête [nytet] *adj inv, adv* bareheaded
nutritif, -ive [nytʀitif, iv] *adj* (*besoins, valeur*) nutritional; (*nourrissant*) nutritious
nylon [nilɔ̃] *nm* nylon

O, o

oasis [ɔazis] *nf* oasis
obéir [ɔbeiʀ] *vi* to obey; ~ **à** to obey; **obéissance** *nf* obedience; **obéissant, e** *adj* obedient
obèse [ɔbɛz] *adj* obese; **obésité** *nf* obesity
objecter [ɔbʒɛkte] *vt* (*prétexter*) to plead, put forward as an excuse; ~ **(à qn) que** to object (to sb) that; **objecteur** *nm*: **objecteur de conscience** conscientious objector
objectif, -ive [ɔbʒɛktif, iv] *adj* objective ♦ *nm* objective; (*PHOTO*) lens *sg*, objective; **objectivité** *nf* objectivity
objection [ɔbʒɛksjɔ̃] *nf* objection
objet [ɔbʒɛ] *nm* object; (*d'une discussion, recherche*) subject; **être** *ou* **faire l'~ de** (*discussion*) to be the subject of; (*soins*) to be given *ou* shown; **sans ~** purposeless; groundless; ~ **d'art** object of art; **~s trouvés** lost property *sg* (*BRIT*), lost-and-found *sg* (*US*); **~s de valeur** valuables
obligation [ɔbligasjɔ̃] *nf* obligation; (*COMM*) bond, debenture; **obligatoire** *adj* compulsory, obligatory; **obligatoirement** *adv* necessarily; (*fam: sans aucun doute*) inevitably
obligé, e [ɔbliʒe] *adj* (*redevable*): **être très ~ à qn** to be most obliged to sb
obligeance [ɔbliʒɑ̃s] *nf*: **avoir l'~ de ...** to be kind *ou* good enough to ...; **obligeant, e** *adj* (*personne*) obliging, kind
obliger [ɔbliʒe] *vt* (*contraindre*): ~ **qn à faire** to force *ou* oblige sb to do; **je suis bien obligé** I have to
oblique [ɔblik] *adj* oblique; **en ~** diagon-

ally; **obliquer** *vi*: **obliquer vers** to turn off towards
oblitérer [ɔblitere] *vt* (*timbre-poste*) to cancel
obnubiler [ɔbnybile] *vt* to obsess
obscène [ɔpsɛn] *adj* obscene
obscur, e [ɔpskyʀ] *adj* dark; (*méconnu*) obscure; **obscurcir** *vt* to darken; (*fig*) to obscure; **s'obscurcir** *vi* to grow dark; **obscurité** *nf* darkness; **dans l'obscurité** in the dark, in darkness
obsédé, e [ɔpsede] *nm/f*: **un ~ (sexuel)** a sex maniac
obséder [ɔpsede] *vt* to obsess, haunt
obsèques [ɔpsɛk] *nfpl* funeral *sg*
observateur, -trice [ɔpsɛʀvatœʀ, tʀis] *adj* observant, perceptive ♦ *nm/f* observer
observation [ɔpsɛʀvasjɔ̃] *nf* observation; (*d'un règlement etc*) observance; (*reproche*) reproof; **être en ~** (*MÉD*) to be under observation
observatoire [ɔpsɛʀvatwaʀ] *nm* observatory
observer [ɔpsɛʀve] *vt* (*regarder*) to observe, watch; (*scientifiquement; aussi règlement etc*) to observe; (*surveiller*) to watch; (*remarquer*) to observe, notice; **faire ~ qch à qn** (*dire*) to point out sth to sb
obsession [ɔpsesjɔ̃] *nf* obsession
obstacle [ɔpstakl] *nm* obstacle; (*ÉQUITATION*) jump, hurdle; **faire ~ à** (*projet*) to hinder, put obstacles in the path of
obstiné, e [ɔpstine] *adj* obstinate
obstiner [ɔpstine]: **s'~** *vi* to insist, dig one's heels in; **s'~ à faire** to persist (obstinately) in doing
obstruer [ɔpstʀye] *vt* to block, obstruct
obtenir [ɔptəniʀ] *vt* to obtain, get; (*résultat*) to achieve, obtain; ~ **de pouvoir faire** to obtain permission to do
obturateur [ɔptyʀatœʀ, tʀis] *nm* (*PHOTO*) shutter
obus [ɔby] *nm* shell
occasion [ɔkazjɔ̃] *nf* (*aubaine, possibilité*) opportunity; (*circonstance*) occasion;

(*COMM: article non neuf*) secondhand buy; (: *acquisition avantageuse*) bargain; **à plusieurs ~s** on several occasions; **à l'~** sometimes, on occasions; **d'~** secondhand; **occasionnel, le** *adj* (*non régulier*) occasional; **occasionnellement** *adv* occasionally, from time to time

occasionner [ɔkazjɔne] *vt* to cause

occident [ɔksidɑ̃] *nm:* **l'O~** the West; **occidental, e, -aux** *adj* western; (*POL*) Western ♦ *nm/f* Westerner

occupation [ɔkypasjɔ̃] *nf* occupation

occupé, e [ɔkype] *adj* (*personne*) busy; (*place*) taken; (*toilettes*) engaged; (*ligne*) engaged (*BRIT*), busy (*US*); (*MIL, POL*) occupied

occuper [ɔkype] *vt* to occupy; (*poste*) to hold; **s'~ de** (*être responsable de*) to be in charge of; (*se charger de: affaire*) to take charge of, deal with; (: *clients etc*) to attend to; **s'~ (à qch)** to occupy o.s. *ou* keep o.s. busy (with sth)

occurrence [ɔkyrɑ̃s] *nf:* **en l'~** in this case

océan [ɔseɑ̃] *nm* ocean

octante [ɔktɑ̃t] *adj* (*regional*) eighty

octet [ɔktɛ] *nm* byte

octobre [ɔktɔbr] *nm* October

octroyer [ɔktrwaje] *vt:* **s'~** *vt* (*vacances etc*) to treat o.s. to

oculiste [ɔkylist] *nm/f* eye specialist

odeur [ɔdœr] *nf* smell

odieux, -euse [ɔdjø, jøz] *adj* hateful

odorant, e [ɔdɔrɑ̃, ɑ̃t] *adj* fragrant

odorat [ɔdɔra] *nm* (sense of) smell

œil [œj] (*pl* **yeux**) *nm* eye; **à l'~** (*fam*) for free; **à l'~ nu** with the naked eye; **tenir qn à l'~** to keep an eye *ou* a watch on sb; **avoir l'~ à** to keep an eye on; **fermer les yeux (sur)** (*fig*) to turn a blind eye (to); **voir qch d'un bon/mauvais ~** to look on sth favourably/unfavourably

œillères [œjɛr] *nfpl* blinkers (*BRIT*), blinders (*US*)

œillet [œjɛ] *nm* (*BOT*) carnation

œuf [œf, *pl* ø] *nm* egg; **~ à la coque/sur le plat/dur** boiled/fried/hard-boiled egg;

~ de Pâques Easter egg; **~s brouillés** scrambled eggs

œuvre [œvr] *nf* (*tâche*) task, undertaking; (*livre, tableau etc*) work; (*ensemble de la production artistique*) works *pl* ♦ *nm* (*CONSTR*): **le gros ~** the shell; **~ (de bienfaisance)** charity; **mettre en ~** (*moyens*) to make use of; **~ d'art** work of art

offense [ɔfɑ̃s] *nf* insult; **offenser** *vt* to offend, hurt

offert, e [ɔfɛr, ɛrt] *pp de* **offrir**

office [ɔfis] *nm* (*agence*) bureau, agency; (*REL*) service ♦ *nm ou nf* (*pièce*) pantry; **faire ~ de** to act as; **d'~** automatically; **~ du tourisme** tourist bureau

officiel, le [ɔfisjɛl] *adj, nm/f* official

officier [ɔfisje] *nm* officer

officieux, -euse [ɔfisjø, jøz] *adj* unofficial

offrande [ɔfrɑ̃d] *nf* offering

offre [ɔfr] *nf* offer; (*aux enchères*) bid; (*ADMIN: soumission*) tender; (*ÉCON*): **l'~ et la demande** supply and demand; **"~s d'emploi"** "situations vacant"; **~ d'emploi** job advertised

offrir [ɔfrir] *vt:* **~ (à qn)** to offer (to sb); (*faire cadeau de*) to give (to sb); **s'~** *vt* (*vacances, voiture*) to treat o.s. to; **~ (à qn) de faire qch** to offer to do sth (for sb); **~ à boire à qn** (*chez soi*) to offer sb a drink

offusquer [ɔfyske] *vt* to offend

OGM *sigle m* (= *organisme génétiquement modifié*) GMO

oie [wa] *nf* (*ZOOL*) goose

oignon [ɔɲɔ̃] *nm* onion; (*de tulipe etc*) bulb

oiseau, x [wazo] *nm* bird; **~ de proie** bird of prey

oisif, -ive [wazif, iv] *adj* idle

oléoduc [ɔleɔdyk] *nm* (oil) pipeline

olive [ɔliv] *nf* (*BOT*) olive; **olivier** *nm* olive (tree)

OLP *sigle f* (= *Organisation de libération de la Palestine*) PLO

olympique [ɔlɛ̃pik] *adj* Olympic

ombragé, e [ɔbraʒe] *adj* shaded, shady; **ombrageux, -euse** *adj* (*personne*) touchy, easily offended

ombre [ɔ̃bʀ] nf (*espace non ensoleillé*) shade; (~ *portée, tache*) shadow; **à l'~** in the shade; **dans l'~** (*fig*) in the dark; **~ à paupières** eyeshadow; **ombrelle** nf parasol, sunshade

omelette [ɔmlɛt] nf omelette; **~ norvégienne** baked Alaska

omettre [ɔmɛtʀ] vt to omit, leave out

omnibus [ɔmnibys] nm slow ou stopping train

omoplate [ɔmɔplat] nf shoulder blade

MOT-CLÉ

on [ɔ̃] pron 1 (*indéterminé*) you, one; **on peut le faire ainsi** you ou one can do it like this, it can be done like this

2 (*quelqu'un*): **on les a attaqués** they were attacked; **on vous demande au téléphone** there's a phone call for you, you're wanted on the phone

3 (*nous*) we; **on va y aller demain** we're going tomorrow

4 (*les gens*) they; **autrefois, on croyait ...** they used to believe ...

5: **on ne peut plus**

♦ adv: **on ne peut plus stupide** as stupid as can be

---

oncle [ɔ̃kl] nm uncle

onctueux, -euse [ɔ̃ktɥø, øz] adj creamy, smooth

onde [ɔ̃d] nf wave; **sur les ~s** on the radio; **sur ~s courtes** on short wave sg; **moyennes/longues ~s** medium/long wave sg

ondée [ɔ̃de] nf shower

on-dit [ɔ̃di] nm inv rumour

onduler [ɔ̃dyle] vi to undulate; (*cheveux*) to wave

onéreux, -euse [ɔneʀø, øz] adj costly

ongle [ɔ̃gl] nm nail

ont [ɔ̃] vb voir **avoir**

ONU sigle f (= *Organisation des Nations Unies*) UN

onze ['ɔ̃z] num eleven; **onzième** num eleventh

OPA sigle f = **offre publique d'achat**

opaque [ɔpak] adj opaque

opéra [ɔpeʀa] nm opera; (*édifice*) opera house

opérateur, -trice [ɔpeʀatœʀ, tʀis] nm/f operator; **~ (de prise de vues)** cameraman

opération [ɔpeʀasjɔ̃] nf operation; (*COMM*) dealing

opératoire [ɔpeʀatwaʀ] adj (*choc etc*) post-operative

opérer [ɔpeʀe] vt (*personne*) to operate on; (*faire, exécuter*) to carry out, make ♦ vi (*remède: faire effet*) to act, work; (*MÉD*) to operate; **s'~** vi (*avoir lieu*) to occur, take place; **se faire ~** to have an operation

opérette [ɔpeʀɛt] nf operetta, light opera

ophtalmologiste [ɔftalmɔlɔʒist] nm/f ophthalmologist, optician

opiner [ɔpine] vi: **~ de la tête** to nod assent

opinion [ɔpinjɔ̃] nf opinion; **l'~ (publique)** public opinion

opportun, e [ɔpɔʀtœ̃, yn] adj timely, opportune; **opportuniste** nm/f opportunist

opposant, e [ɔpozɑ̃, ɑ̃t] nm/f opponent

opposé, e [ɔpoze] adj (*direction*) opposite; (*faction*) opposing; (*opinions, intérêts*) conflicting; (*contre*): **~ à** opposed to, against ♦ nm: **l'~** the other ou opposite side (ou direction); (*contraire*) the opposite; **à l'~** (*fig*) on the other hand; **à l'~ de** (*fig*) contrary to, unlike

opposer [ɔpoze] vt (*personnes, équipes*) to oppose; (*couleurs*) to contrast; **s'~** vi (*équipes*) to confront each other; (*opinions*) to conflict; (*couleurs, styles*) to contrast; **s'~ à** (*interdire*) to oppose; **~ qch à** (*comme obstacle, défense*) to set sth against; (*comme objection*) to put sth forward against

opposition [ɔpozisjɔ̃] nf opposition; **par ~ à** as opposed to, in contrast with; **entrer en ~ avec** to come into conflict with; **faire ~ à un chèque** to stop a cheque

oppressant, e [ɔprɛsɑ̃, ɑ̃t] *adj* oppressive

oppresser [ɔprese] *vt* to oppress; **oppression** *nf* oppression

opprimer [ɔprime] *vt* to oppress

opter [ɔpte] *vi*: **~ pour** to opt for

opticien, ne [ɔptisjɛ̃, jɛn] *nm/f* optician

optimisme [ɔptimism] *nm* optimism; **optimiste** *nm/f* optimist ♦ *adj* optimistic

option [ɔpsjɔ̃] *nf* option; **matière à ~** (*SCOL*) optional subject

optique [ɔptik] *adj* (*nerf*) optic; (*verres*) optical ♦ *nf* (*fig: manière de voir*) perspective

opulent, e [ɔpylɑ̃, ɑ̃t] *adj* wealthy, opulent; (*formes, poitrine*) ample, generous

or [ɔʀ] *nm* gold ♦ *conj* now, but; **en ~** (*objet*) gold *cpd*; **une affaire en ~** a real bargain; **il croyait gagner ~ il a perdu** he was sure he would win and yet he lost

orage [ɔʀaʒ] *nm* (thunder)storm; **orageux, -euse** *adj* stormy

oral, e, -aux [ɔʀal, o] *adj, nm* oral; **par voie ~e** (*MÉD*) orally

orange [ɔʀɑ̃ʒ] *nf* orange ♦ *adj inv* orange; **orangeade** *nf* orangeade; **orangé, e** *adj* orangey, orange-coloured; **oranger** *nm* orange tree

orateur [ɔʀatœʀ, tʀis] *nm* speaker

orbite [ɔʀbit] *nf* (*ANAT*) (eye-)socket; (*PHYSIQUE*) orbit

orchestre [ɔʀkɛstʀ] *nm* orchestra; (*de jazz*) band; (*places*) stalls *pl* (*BRIT*), orchestra (*US*); **orchestrer** *vt* to orchestrate

orchidée [ɔʀkide] *nf* orchid

ordinaire [ɔʀdinɛʀ] *adj* ordinary; (*qualité*) standard; (*péj: commun*) common ♦ *nm* ordinary; (*menus*) everyday fare ♦ *nf* (*essence*) ≈ two-star (petrol) (*BRIT*), ≈ regular gas (*US*); **d'~** usually, normally; **comme à l'~** as usual

ordinateur [ɔʀdinatœʀ] *nm* computer

ordonnance [ɔʀdɔnɑ̃s] *nf* (*MÉD*) prescription; (*MIL*) orderly, batman (*BRIT*)

ordonné, e [ɔʀdɔne] *adj* tidy, orderly

ordonner [ɔʀdɔne] *vt* (*agencer*) to organize, arrange; (*donner un ordre*): **~ à qn de faire** to order sb to do; (*REL*) to ordain;

(*MÉD*) to prescribe

ordre [ɔʀdʀ] *nm* order; (*propreté et soin*) orderliness, tidiness; (*nature*): **d'~ pratique** of a practical nature; **~s** *nmpl* (*REL*) holy orders; **mettre en ~** to tidy (up), put in order; **à l'~ de qn** payable to sb; **être aux ~s de qn/sous les ~s de qn** to be at sb's disposal/under sb's command; **jusqu'à nouvel ~** until further notice; **de premier ~** first-rate; **~ du jour** (*d'une réunion*) agenda; **à l'~ du jour** (*fig*) topical

ordure [ɔʀdyʀ] *nf* filth *no pl*; **~s** *nfpl* (*balayures, déchets*) rubbish *sg*, refuse *sg*; **~s ménagères** household refuse

oreille [ɔʀɛj] *nf* ear; **avoir de l'~** to have a good ear (for music)

oreiller [ɔʀeje] *nm* pillow

oreillons [ɔʀejɔ̃] *nmpl* mumps *sg*

ores [ɔʀ]: **d'~ et déjà** *adv* already

orfèvrerie [ɔʀfɛvʀəʀi] *nf* goldsmith's (*ou* silversmith's) trade; (*ouvrage*) gold (*ou* silver) plate

organe [ɔʀgan] *nm* organ; (*porte-parole*) representative, mouthpiece

organigramme [ɔʀganigʀam] *nm* (*tableau hiérarchique*) organization chart; (*schéma*) flow chart

organique [ɔʀganik] *adj* organic

organisateur, -trice [ɔʀganizatœʀ, tʀis] *nm/f* organizer

organisation [ɔʀganizasjɔ̃] *nf* organization

organiser [ɔʀganize] *vt* to organize; (*mettre sur pied: service etc*) to set up; **s'~** to get organized

organisme [ɔʀganism] *nm* (*BIO*) organism; (*corps, ADMIN*) body

organiste [ɔʀganist] *nm/f* organist

orgasme [ɔʀgasm] *nm* orgasm, climax

orge [ɔʀʒ] *nf* barley

orgue [ɔʀg] *nm* organ; **~s** *nfpl* (*MUS*) organ *sg*

orgueil [ɔʀgœj] *nm* pride; **orgueilleux, -euse** *adj* proud

Orient [ɔʀjɑ̃] *nm*: **l'~** the East, the Orient; **oriental, e, -aux** *adj* (*langue, produit*) oriental; (*frontière*) eastern

orientation [ɔRjɑ̃tasjɔ̃] nf (de recherches) orientation; (d'une maison etc) aspect; (d'un journal) leanings pl; **avoir le sens de l'~** to have a (good) sense of direction; **~ professionnelle** careers advisory service

orienté, e [ɔRjɑ̃te] adj (fig: article, journal) slanted; **bien/mal ~** (appartement) well/badly positioned; **~ au sud** facing south, with a southern aspect

orienter [ɔRjɑ̃te] vt (tourner: antenne) to direct, turn; (personne, recherches) to direct; (fig: élève) to orientate; **s'~** (se repérer) to find one's bearings; **s'~ vers** (fig) to turn towards

origan [ɔRigɑ̃] nm oregano

originaire [ɔRiʒinɛR] adj: **être ~ de** to be a native of

original, e, -aux [ɔRiʒinal, o] adj original; (bizarre) eccentric ♦ nm/f eccentric ♦ nm (document etc, ART) original

origine [ɔRiʒin] nf origin; **dès l'~** at ou from the outset; **à l'~** originally; **originel, le** adj original

orme [ɔRm] nm elm

ornement [ɔRnəmɑ̃] nm ornament

orner [ɔRne] vt to decorate, adorn

ornière [ɔRnjɛR] nf rut

orphelin, e [ɔRfəlɛ̃, in] adj orphan(ed) ♦ nm/f orphan; **~ de père/mère** fatherless/motherless; **orphelinat** nm orphanage

orteil [ɔRtɛj] nm toe; **gros ~** big toe

orthographe [ɔRtɔgRaf] nf spelling

ortie [ɔRti] nf (stinging) nettle

os [ɔs] nm bone; **tomber sur un ~** (fam) to hit a snag

osciller [ɔsile] vi (au vent etc) to rock; (fig): **~ entre** to waver ou fluctuate between

osé, e [oze] adj daring, bold

oseille [ozɛj] nf sorrel

oser [oze] vi, vt to dare; **~ faire** to dare (to) do

osier [ozje] nm willow; **d'~, en ~** wicker(work)

ossature [ɔsatyR] nf (ANAT) frame, skeletal

structure; (fig) framework

osseux, -euse [ɔsø, øz] adj bony; (tissu, maladie, greffe) bone cpd

ostensible [ɔstɑ̃sibl] adj conspicuous

otage [ɔtaʒ] nm hostage; **prendre qn comme ~** to take sb hostage

OTAN sigle f (= Organisation du traité de l'Atlantique Nord) NATO

otarie [ɔtaRi] nf sea-lion

ôter [ote] vt to remove; (soustraire) to take away; **~ qch à qn** to take sth (away) from sb; **~ qch de** to remove sth from

otite [ɔtit] nf ear infection

ou [u] conj or; **~ ... ~** either ... or; **~ bien** or (else)

MOT-CLÉ
---

où [u] pron relatif **1** (position, situation) where, that (souvent omis); **la chambre où il était** the room (that) he was in, the room where he was; **la ville où je l'ai rencontré** the town where I met him; **la pièce d'où il est sorti** the room he came out of; **le village d'où je viens** the village I come from; **les villes par où il est passé** the towns he went through

2 (temps, état) that (souvent omis); **le jour où il est parti** the day (that) he left; **au prix où c'est** at the price it is

♦ adv **1** (interrogation) where; **où est-il/va-t-il?** where is he/is he going?; **par où?** which way?; **d'où vient que ...?** how come ...?

2 (position) where; **je sais où il est** I know where he is; **où que l'on aille** wherever you go

---

ouate ['wat] nf cotton wool (BRIT), cotton (US)

oubli [ubli] nm (acte): **l'~ de** forgetting; (trou de mémoire) lapse of memory; (négligence) omission, oversight; **tomber dans l'~** to sink into oblivion

oublier [ublije] vt to forget; (laisser quelque part: chapeau etc) to leave behind; (ne pas voir: erreurs etc) to miss

oubliettes [ublijɛt] *nfpl* dungeon *sg*
ouest [wɛst] *nm* west ♦ *adj inv* west; (*région*) western; **à l'~** in the west; (*direction*) (to the) west, westwards; **à l'~ de** (to the) west of
ouf [uf] *excl* phew!
oui [wi] *adv* yes
ouï-dire ['widiʀ]: **par ~-~** *adv* by hearsay
ouïe [wi] *nf* hearing; **~s** *nfpl* (*de poisson*) gills
ouille ['uj] *excl* ouch!
ouragan [uʀagɑ̃] *nm* hurricane
ourlet [uʀlɛ] *nm* hem
ours [uʀs] *nm* bear; **~ brun/blanc** brown/polar bear; **~ (en peluche)** teddy (bear)
oursin [uʀsɛ̃] *nm* sea urchin
ourson [uʀsɔ̃] *nm* (bear-)cub
ouste [ust] *excl* hop it!
outil [uti] *nm* tool; **outiller** *vt* to equip
outrage [utʀaʒ] *nm* insult; **~ à la pudeur** indecent conduct *no pl*; **outrager** *vt* to offend gravely
outrance [utʀɑ̃s]: **à ~** *adv* excessively, to excess
outre [utʀ] *prép* besides ♦ *adv*: **passer ~ à** to disregard, take no notice of; **en ~** besides, moreover; **~ mesure** to excess; (*manger, boire*) immoderately; **outre-Atlantique** *adv* across the Atlantic; **outre-Manche** *adv* across the Channel; **outre-mer** *adv* overseas; **outrepasser** *vt* to go beyond, exceed
ouvert, e [uvɛʀ, ɛʀt] *pp de* **ouvrir** ♦ *adj* open; (*robinet, gaz etc*) on; **ouvertement** *adv* openly; **ouverture** *nf* opening; (*MUS*) overture; **ouverture d'esprit** open-mindedness
ouvrable [uvʀabl] *adj*: **jour ~** working day, weekday
ouvrage [uvʀaʒ] *nm* (*tâche, de tricot etc*) work *no pl*; (*texte, livre*) work; **ouvragé, e** *adj* finely embroidered (*ou* worked *ou* carved)
ouvre-boîte(s) [uvʀəbwat] *nm inv* tin (*BRIT*) *ou* can opener
ouvre-bouteille(s) [uvʀəbutɛj] *nm inv*

bottle-opener
ouvreuse [uvʀøz] *nf* usherette
ouvrier, -ière [uvʀije, ijɛʀ] *nm/f* worker ♦ *adj* working-class; (*conflit*) industrial; (*mouvement*) labour *cpd*; **classe ouvrière** working class
ouvrir [uvʀiʀ] *vt* (*gén*) to open; (*brèche, passage, MÉD: abcès*) to open up; (*commencer l'exploitation de, créer*) to open (up); (*eau, électricité, chauffage, robinet*) to turn on ♦ *vi* to open; to open up; **s'~** *vi* to open; **s'~ à qn** to open one's heart to sb; **~ l'appétit à qn** to whet sb's appetite
ovaire [ovɛʀ] *nf* ovary
ovale [oval] *adj* oval
ovni [ovni] *sigle m* (= *objet volant non identifié*) UFO
oxyder [ɔkside]: **s'~** *vi* to become oxidized
oxygène [ɔksiʒɛn] *nm* oxygen
oxygéné, e [ɔksiʒene] *adj*: **eau ~e** hydrogen peroxide
oxygéner [ɔksiʒene]: **s'~** (*fam*) *vi* to get some fresh air
ozone [ozon] *nf* ozone; **la couche d'~** the ozone layer

P, p

pacifique [pasifik] *adj* peaceful ♦ *nm*: **le P~, l'océan P~** the Pacific (Ocean)
pacotille [pakɔtij] *nf* cheap junk
pack [pak] *nm* pack
pacte [pakt] *nm* pact, treaty
pagaie [pagɛ] *nf* paddle
pagaille [pagaj] *nf* mess, shambles *sg*
pagayer [pageje] *vi* to paddle
page [paʒ] *nf* page ♦ *nm* page (boy); **à la ~** (*fig*) up-to-date; **~ d'accueil** (*INFORM*) home page
paiement [pɛmɑ̃] *nm* payment
païen, ne [pajɛ̃, pajɛn] *adj, nm/f* pagan, heathen
paillasson [pajasɔ̃] *nm* doormat
paille [pɑj] *nf* straw

paillettes [pajɛt] *nfpl* (*décoratives*) sequins, spangles

pain [pɛ̃] *nm* (*substance*) bread; (*unité*) loaf (of bread); (*morceau*) **~ de savon** *etc* bar of soap *etc*; **~ au chocolat** chocolate-filled pastry; **~ aux raisins** currant bun; **~ bis/complet** brown/wholemeal (*BRIT*) *ou* wholewheat (*US*) bread; **~ d'épice** gingerbread; **~ de mie** sandwich loaf; **~ grillé** toast

pair, e [pɛʀ] *adj* (*nombre*) even ♦ *nm* peer; **aller de ~** to go hand in hand *ou* together; **jeune fille au ~** au pair; **paire** *nf* pair

paisible [pezibl] *adj* peaceful, quiet

paître [pɛtʀ] *vi* to graze

paix [pɛ] *nf* peace; **faire/avoir la ~** to make/have peace; **fiche-lui la ~!** (*fam*) leave him alone!

Pakistan [pakistɑ̃] *nm*: **le ~** Pakistan

palace [palas] *nm* luxury hotel

palais [palɛ] *nm* palace; (*ANAT*) palate

pâle [pɑl] *adj* pale; **bleu ~** pale blue

Palestine [palɛstin] *nf*: **la ~** Palestine

palet [palɛ] *nm* disc; (*HOCKEY*) puck

paletot [palto] *nm* (thick) cardigan

palette [palɛt] *nf* (*de peintre*) palette; (*produits*) range

pâleur [palœʀ] *nf* paleness

palier [palje] *nm* (*d'escalier*) landing; (*fig*) level, plateau; **par ~s** in stages

pâlir [paliʀ] *vi* to turn *ou* go pale; (*couleur*) to fade

palissade [palisad] *nf* fence

pallier [palje] *nm*: **~ à** *vt* to offset, make up for

palmarès [palmaʀɛs] *nm* record (of achievements); (*SPORT*) list of winners

palme [palm] *nf* (*de plongeur*) flipper; **palmé, e** *adj* (*pattes*) webbed

palmier [palmje] *nm* palm tree; (*gâteau*) *heart-shaped biscuit made of flaky pastry*

pâlot, te [palo, ɔt] *adj* pale, peaky

palourde [paluʀd] *nf* clam

palper [palpe] *vt* to feel, finger

palpitant, e [palpitɑ̃, ɑ̃t] *adj* thrilling

palpiter [palpite] *vi* (*cœur, pouls*) to beat; (: *plus fort*) to pound, throb

paludisme [palydism] *nm* malaria

pamphlet [pɑ̃flɛ] *nm* lampoon, satirical tract

pamplemousse [pɑ̃pləmus] *nm* grapefruit

pan [pɑ̃] *nm* section, piece ♦ *excl* bang!

panache [panaʃ] *nm* plume; (*fig*) spirit, panache

panaché, e [panaʃe] *adj*: **glace ~e** mixed-flavour ice cream ♦ *nm* (*bière*) shandy

pancarte [pɑ̃kaʀt] *nf* sign, notice

pancréas [pɑ̃kʀeas] *nm* pancreas

pané, e [pane] *adj* fried in breadcrumbs

panier [panje] *nm* basket; **mettre au ~** to chuck away; **~ à provisions** shopping basket; **panier-repas** *nm* packed lunch

panique [panik] *nf, adj* panic; **paniquer** *vi* to panic

panne [pan] *nf* breakdown; **être/tomber en ~** to have broken down/break down; **être en ~ d'essence** *ou* **sèche** to have run out of petrol (*BRIT*) *ou* gas (*US*); **~ d'électricité** *ou* **de courant** power *ou* electrical failure

panneau, x [pano] *nm* (*écriteau*) sign, notice; **~ d'affichage** notice board; **~ de signalisation** roadsign

panoplie [panɔpli] *nf* (*jouet*) outfit; (*fig*) array

panorama [panɔʀama] *nm* panorama

panse [pɑ̃s] *nf* paunch

pansement [pɑ̃smɑ̃] *nm* dressing, bandage; **~ adhésif** sticking plaster

panser [pɑ̃se] *vt* (*plaie*) to dress, bandage; (*bras*) to put a dressing on, bandage; (*cheval*) to groom

pantalon [pɑ̃talɔ̃] *nm* trousers *pl*, pair of trousers; **~ de ski** ski pants *pl*

panthère [pɑ̃tɛʀ] *nf* panther

pantin [pɑ̃tɛ̃] *nm* puppet

pantois [pɑ̃twa] *adj m*: **rester ~** to be flabbergasted

pantoufle [pɑ̃tufl] *nf* slipper

paon [pɑ̃] *nm* peacock

papa [papa] *nm* dad(dy)

pape [pap] *nm* pope

paperasse [papʀas] (*péj*) *nf* bumf *no pl*, papers *pl*; **paperasserie** (*péj*) *nf* paperwork *no pl*; (*tracasserie*) red tape *no pl*

papeterie [papɛtʀi] *nf* (*magasin*) stationer's (shop)

papi *nm* (*fam*) granddad

papier [papje] *nm* paper; (*article*) article; **~s** *nmpl* (*aussi*: **~s d'identité**) (identity) papers; **~ à lettres** writing paper, notepaper; **~ carbone** carbon paper; **~ (d')aluminium** aluminium (*BRIT*) *ou* aluminum (*US*) foil, tinfoil; **~ de verre** sandpaper; **~ hygiénique** *ou* **de toilette** toilet paper; **~ journal** newspaper; **~ peint** wallpaper

papillon [papijɔ̃] *nm* butterfly; (*fam: contravention*) (parking) ticket; **~ de nuit** moth

papillote [papijɔt] *nf*: **en ~** cooked in tinfoil

papoter [papɔte] *vi* to chatter

paquebot [pak(ə)bo] *nm* liner

pâquerette [pɑkʀɛt] *nf* daisy

Pâques [pɑk] *nm*, *nfpl* Easter

paquet [pakɛ] *nm* packet; (*colis*) parcel; (*fig: tas*): **~ de** pile *ou* heap of; **paquet-cadeau** *nm*: **faites-moi un paquet-cadeau** gift-wrap it for me

par [paʀ] *prép* by; **finir** *etc* **~** to end *etc* with; **~ amour** out of love; **passer ~ Lyon/la côte** to go via *ou* through Lyons/along by the coast; **~ la fenêtre** (*jeter, regarder*) out of the window; **3 ~ jour/personne** 3 a *ou* per day/head; **2 ~ 2** in twos; **~ ici** this way; (*dans le coin*) round here; **~-ci, ~-là** here and there; **~ temps de pluie** in wet weather

parabolique [paʀabɔlik] *adj*: **antenne ~** parabolic *ou* dish aerial

parachever [paʀaʃ(ə)ve] *vt* to perfect

parachute [paʀaʃyt] *nm* parachute; **parachutiste** *nm/f* parachutist; (*MIL*) paratrooper

parade [paʀad] *nf* (*spectacle, défilé*) parade; (*ESCRIME, BOXE*) parry

paradis [paʀadi] *nm* heaven, paradise

paradoxe [paʀadɔks] *nm* paradox

paraffine [paʀafin] *nf* paraffin

parages [paʀaʒ] *nmpl*: **dans les ~ (de)** in the area *ou* vicinity (of)

paragraphe [paʀagʀaf] *nm* paragraph

paraître [paʀɛtʀ] *vb +attrib* to seem, look, appear ♦ *vi* to appear; (*être visible*) to show; (*PRESSE, ÉDITION*) to be published, come out, appear ♦ *vb impers*: **il paraît que** it seems *ou* appears that, they say that; **chercher à ~** to show off

parallèle [paʀalɛl] *adj* parallel; (*non officiel*) unofficial ♦ *nm* (*comparaison*): **faire un ~ entre** to draw a parallel between ♦ *nf* parallel (line)

paralyser [paʀalize] *vt* to paralyse

paramédical, e, -aux [paʀamedikal, o] *adj*: **personnel ~** paramedics *pl*, paramedical workers *pl*

paraphrase [paʀafʀaz] *nf* paraphrase

parapluie [paʀaplyi] *nm* umbrella

parasite [paʀazit] *nm* parasite; **~s** *nmpl* (*TÉL*) interference *sg*

parasol [paʀasɔl] *nm* parasol, sunshade

paratonnerre [paʀatɔnɛʀ] *nm* lightning conductor

paravent [paʀavɑ̃] *nm* folding screen

parc [paʀk] *nm* (*public*) park, gardens *pl*; (*de château etc*) grounds *pl*; (*d'enfant*) playpen; (*ensemble d'unités*) stock; (*de voitures etc*) fleet; **~ d'attractions** theme park; **~ de stationnement** car park

parcelle [paʀsɛl] *nf* fragment, scrap; (*de terrain*) plot, parcel

parce que [paʀsk(ə)] *conj* because

parchemin [paʀʃəmɛ̃] *nm* parchment

parcmètre [paʀkmɛtʀ] *nm* parking meter

parcourir [paʀkuʀiʀ] *vt* (*trajet, distance*) to cover; (*article, livre*) to skim *ou* glance through; (*lieu*) to go all over, travel up and down; (*suj: frisson*) to run through

parcours [paʀkuʀ] *nm* (*trajet*) journey; (*itinéraire*) route

par-derrière [paʀdɛʀjɛʀ] *adv* round the back; **dire du mal de qn ~-~** to speak ill of sb behind his back

par-dessous [paʀd(ə)su] *prép, adv* under(neath)

pardessus [paʀdəsy] *nm* overcoat

par-dessus [paʀd(ə)sy] *prép* over (the top of) ♦ *adv* over (the top); **~-~ le marché** on top of all that; **~-~ tout** above all; **en avoir ~-~ la tête** to have had enough

par-devant [paʀd(ə)vɑ̃] *adv* (*passer*) round the front

pardon [paʀdɔ̃] *nm* forgiveness *no pl* ♦ *excl* sorry!; (*pour interpeller etc*) excuse me!; **demander ~ à qn (de)** to apologize to sb (for); **je vous demande ~** I'm sorry; (*pour interpeller*) excuse me; **pardonner** *vt* to forgive; **pardonner qch à qn** to forgive sb for sth

pare...: **pare-balles** *adj inv* bulletproof; **pare-brise** *nm inv* windscreen (*BRIT*), windshield (*US*); **pare-chocs** *nm inv* bumper

paré, e [paʀe] *adj* ready, all set

pareil, le [paʀɛj] *adj* (*identique*) the same, alike; (*similaire*) similar; (*tel*): **un courage/livre ~** such courage/a book, courage/a book like this; **de ~s livres** such books; **ne pas avoir son(sa) ~(le)** to be second to none; **~ à** the same as; (*similaire*) similar to; **sans ~** unparalleled, unequalled

parent, e [paʀɑ̃, ɑ̃t] *nm/f*: **un(e) ~(e)** a relative *ou* relation; **~s** *nmpl* (*père et mère*) parents; **parenté** *nf* (*lien*) relationship

parenthèse [paʀɑ̃tɛz] *nf* (*ponctuation*) bracket, parenthesis; (*digression*) parenthesis, digression; **entre ~s** in brackets; (*fig*) incidentally

parer [paʀe] *vt* to adorn; (*éviter*) to ward off; **~ au plus pressé** to attend to the most urgent things first

paresse [paʀɛs] *nf* laziness; **paresseux, -euse** *adj* lazy

parfaire [paʀfɛʀ] *vt* to perfect

parfait, e [paʀfɛ, ɛt] *adj* perfect ♦ *nm* (*LING*) perfect (tense); **parfaitement** *adv* perfectly ♦ *excl* (most) certainly

parfois [paʀfwa] *adv* sometimes

parfum [paʀfœ̃] *nm* (*produit*) perfume, scent; (*odeur: de fleur*) scent, fragrance; (*goût*) flavour; **parfumé, e** *adj* (*fleur, fruit*) fragrant; (*femme*) perfumed; **parfumé au café** coffee-flavoured; **parfumer** *vt* (*suj: odeur, bouquet*) to perfume; (*crème, gâteau*) to flavour; **parfumerie** *nf* (*produits*) perfumes *pl*; (*boutique*) perfume shop

pari [paʀi] *nm* bet; **parier** *vt* to bet

Paris [paʀi] *n* Paris; **parisien, ne** *adj* Parisian; (*GÉO, ADMIN*) Paris *cpd* ♦ *nm/f*: **Parisien, ne** Parisian

parjure [paʀʒyʀ] *nm* perjury

parking [paʀkiŋ] *nm* (*lieu*) car park

parlant, e [paʀlɑ̃, ɑ̃t] *adj* (*regard*) eloquent; (*CINÉMA*) talking; **les chiffres sont ~s** the figures speak for themselves

parlement [paʀləmɑ̃] *nm* parliament; **parlementaire** *adj* parliamentary ♦ *nm/f* member of parliament; **parlementer** *vi* to negotiate, parley

parler [paʀle] *vi* to speak, talk; (*avouer*) to talk; **~ (à qn) de** to talk *ou* speak (to sb) about; **le/en français** to speak French/in French; **~ affaires** to talk business; **sans ~ de** (*fig*) not to mention, to say nothing of; **tu parles!** (*fam: bien sûr*) you bet!

parloir [paʀlwaʀ] *nm* (*de prison, d'hôpital*) visiting room

parmi [paʀmi] *prép* among(st)

paroi [paʀwa] *nf* wall; (*cloison*) partition; **~ rocheuse** rock face

paroisse [paʀwas] *nf* parish

parole [paʀɔl] *nf* (*faculté*): **la ~** speech; (*mot, promesse*) word; **~s** *nfpl* (*MUS*) words, lyrics; **tenir ~** to keep one's word; **prendre la ~** to speak; **demander la ~** to ask for permission to speak; **je te crois sur ~** I'll take your word for it

parquer [paʀke] *vt* (*voiture, matériel*) to park; (*bestiaux*) to pen (in *ou* up)

parquet [paʀke] *nm* (*parquet*) floor; (*JUR*):

le ~ the Public Prosecutor's department

parrain [paʀɛ̃] *nm* godfather; **parrainer** *vt* (*suj: entreprise*) to sponsor

pars [paʀ] *vb voir* **partir**

parsemer [paʀsəme] *vt* (*suj: feuilles, papiers*) to be scattered over; **~ qch de** to scatter sth with

part [paʀ] *nf* (*qui revient à qn*) share; (*fraction, partie*) part; **prendre ~ à** (*débat etc*) to take part in; (*soucis, douleur de qn*) to share in; **faire ~ de qch à qn** to announce sth to sb, inform sb of sth; **pour ma ~** as for me, as far as I'm concerned; **à ~ entière** full; **de la ~ de** (*au nom de*) on behalf of; (*donné par*) from; **de toute(s) ~(s)** from all sides *ou* quarters; **de ~ et d'autre** on both sides, on either side; **d'une ~ ... d'autre ~** on the one hand ... on the other hand; **d'autre ~** (*de plus*) moreover; **à ~** *adv* (*séparément*) separately; (*de côté*) aside ♦ *prép* apart from, except for; **faire la ~ des choses** to make allowances

partage [paʀtaʒ] *nm* (*fractionnement*) dividing up; (*répartition*) sharing (out) *no pl*, share-out

partager [paʀtaʒe] *vt* to share; (*distribuer, répartir*) to share (out); (*morceler, diviser*) to divide (up); **se ~** *vt* (*héritage etc*) to share between themselves (*ou* ourselves)

partance [paʀtɑ̃s] **en ~** *adv*: **en ~ pour** (bound) for

partenaire [paʀtənɛʀ] *nm/f* partner

parterre [paʀtɛʀ] *nm* (*de fleurs*) (flower) bed; (*THÉÂTRE*) stalls *pl*

parti [paʀti] *nm* (*POL*) party; (*décision*) course of action; (*personne à marier*) match; **tirer ~ de** to take advantage of, turn to good account; **prendre ~ (pour/contre)** to take sides *ou* a stand (for/against); **~ pris** bias

partial, e, -aux [paʀsjal, jo] *adj* biased, partial

participant, e [paʀtisipɑ̃, ɑ̃t] *nm/f* participant; (*à un concours*) entrant

participation [paʀtisipasjɔ̃] *nf* participation; (*financière*) contribution

participer [paʀtisipe]: **~ à** *vt* (*course, réunion*) to take part in; (*frais etc*) to contribute to; (*chagrin, succès de qn*) to share (in)

particularité [paʀtikylaʀite] *nf* (distinctive) characteristic

particulier, -ière [paʀtikylje, jɛʀ] *adj* (*spécifique*) particular; (*spécial*) special, particular; (*personnel, privé*) private; (*étrange*) peculiar, odd ♦ *nm* (*individu: ADMIN*) private individual; **~ à** peculiar to; **en ~** (*surtout*) in particular, particularly; (*en privé*) in private; **particulièrement** *adv* particularly

partie [paʀti] *nf* (*gén*) part; (*JUR etc: protagonistes*) party; (*de cartes, tennis etc*) game; **une ~ de pêche** a fishing party *ou* trip; **en ~** partly, in part; **faire ~ de** (*suj: chose*) to be part of; **prendre qn à ~** to take sb to task; **en grande ~** largely, in the main; **~ civile** (*JUR*) party claiming damages in a criminal case

partiel, le [paʀsjɛl] *adj* partial ♦ *nm* (*SCOL*) class exam

partir [paʀtiʀ] *vi* (*gén*) to go; (*quitter*) to go, leave; (*tache*) to go, come out; **~ de** (*lieu: quitter*) to leave; (: *commencer à*) to start from; **à ~ de** from

partisan, e [paʀtizɑ̃, an] *nm/f* partisan ♦ *adj*: **être ~ de qch/de faire** to be in favour of sth/doing

partition [paʀtisjɔ̃] *nf* (*MUS*) score

partout [paʀtu] *adv* everywhere; **~ où il allait** everywhere *ou* wherever he went

paru [paʀy] *pp de* **paraître**

parure [paʀyʀ] *nf* (*bijoux etc*) finery *no pl*; jewellery *no pl*; (*assortiment*) set

parution [paʀysjɔ̃] *nf* publication

parvenir [paʀvəniʀ]: **~ à** *vt* (*atteindre*) to reach; (*réussir*): **~ à faire** to manage to do, succeed in doing; **~ à ses fins** to achieve one's ends

pas¹ [pɑ] *nm* (*enjambée, DANSE*) step; (*allure, mesure*) pace; (*bruit*) (foot)step; (*trace*) footprint; **~ à ~** step by step; **au ~** at walking pace; **faire les cent ~** to pace up and down; **faire les premiers ~** to make the first move; **sur le ~ de la porte** on the doorstep

---

MOT-CLÉ

---

pas² [pɑ] *adv* 1 (*en corrélation avec ne, non etc*) not; **il ne pleure pas** he does not *ou* doesn't cry; he's not *ou* isn't crying; **il n'a pas pleuré/ne pleurera pas** he did not *ou* didn't/will not *ou* won't cry; **ils n'ont pas de voiture/d'enfants** they haven't got a car/any children, they have no car/ children; **il m'a dit de ne pas le faire** he told me not to do it; **non pas que ...** not that ...

2 (*employé sans ne etc*): **pas moi** not me; not I, I don't (*ou* can't *etc*); **une pomme pas mûre** an apple which isn't ripe; **pas plus tard qu'hier** only yesterday; **pas du tout** not at all

3: **pas mal** not bad; not badly; **pas mal de** quite a lot of

---

passage [pɑsaʒ] *nm* (*fait de passer*) *voir* **passer**; (*lieu, prix de la traversée, extrait*) passage; (*chemin*) way; **de ~** (*touristes*) passing through; **~ à niveau** level crossing; **~ clouté** pedestrian crossing; **"~ interdit"** "no entry"; **~ souterrain** subway (*BRIT*), underpass

passager, -ère [pɑsaʒe, ɛʀ] *adj* passing ♦ *nm/f* passenger; **~ clandestin** stowaway

passant, e [pɑsɑ̃, ɑ̃t] *adj* (*rue, endroit*) busy ♦ *nm/f* passer-by; **en ~** in passing

passe¹ [pɑs] *nf* (*SPORT, NAVIG*) pass; **être en ~ de faire** to be on the way to doing; **être dans une mauvaise ~** to be going through a rough patch

passe² [pɑs] *nm* (~-partout) master *ou* skeleton key

passé, e [pɑse] *adj* (*révolu*) past; (*dernier: semaine etc*) last; (*couleur*) faded ♦ *prép* after ♦ *nm* past; (*LING*) past (tense); **~ de mode** out of fashion; **~ composé** perfect (tense); **~ simple** past historic

passe-partout [pɑspaʀtu] *nm inv* master *ou* skeleton key ♦ *adj inv* all-purpose

passeport [pɑspɔʀ] *nm* passport

passer [pɑse] *vi* (*aller*) to go; (*voiture, piétons: défiler*) to pass (by), go by; (*facteur, laitier etc*) to come, call; (*pour rendre visite*) to call *ou* drop in; (*film, émission*) to be on; (*temps, jours*) to pass, go by; (*couleur*) to fade; (*mode*) to die out; (*douleur*) to pass, go away; (*SCOL*) to go up (to the next class) ♦ *vt* (*frontière, rivière etc*) to cross; (*douane*) to go through; (*examen*) to sit, take; (*visite médicale etc*) to have; (*journée, temps*) to spend; (*enfiler: vêtement*) to slip on; (*film, pièce*) to show, put on; (*disque*) to play, put on; (*marché, accord*) to agree on; **se ~** *vi* (*avoir lieu: scène, action*) to take place; (*se dérouler: entretien etc*) to go; (*s'écouler: semaine etc*) to pass, go by; (*arriver*): **que s'est-il passé?** what happened?; **~ qch à qn** (*sel etc*) to pass sth to sb; (*prêter*) to lend sb sth; (*lettre, message*) to pass sth on to sb; (*tolérer*) to let sb get away with sth; **~ par** to go through; **~ avant qch/qn** (*fig*) to come before sth/sb; **~ un coup de fil à qn** (*fam*) to give sb a ring; **laisser ~** (*air, lumière, personne*) to let through; (*occasion*) to let slip, miss; (*erreur*) to overlook; **~ la seconde** (*AUTO*) to change into second; **~ le balai/l'aspirateur** to sweep up/ hoover; **je vous passe M. X** (*je vous mets en communication avec lui*) I'm putting you through to Mr X; (*je lui passe l'appareil*) here is Mr X, I'll hand you over to Mr X; **se ~ de** to go *ou* do without

passerelle [pɑsʀɛl] *nf* footbridge; (*de navire, avion*) gangway

passe-temps [pɑstɑ̃] *nm inv* pastime

passible [pɑsibl] *adj*: **~ de** liable to

passif, -ive [pasif, iv] *adj* passive

passion [pɑsjɔ̃] *nf* passion; **passionnant, e** *adj* fascinating; **passionné, e** *adj* (*personne*) passionate; (*récit*) impassioned; **être passionné de** to have a passion for; **passionner** *vt* (*personne*) to fascinate, grip; **se passionner pour** (*sport*) to have a passion for

passoire [paswar] *nf* sieve; (*à légumes*) colander; (*à thé*) strainer

pastèque [pastɛk] *nf* watermelon

pasteur [pastœr] *nm* (*protestant*) minister, pastor

pasteurisé, e [pastœrize] *adj* pasteurized

pastille [pastij] *nf* (*à sucer*) lozenge, pastille

patate [patat] *nf* (*fam: pomme de terre*) spud; ~ **douce** sweet potato

patauger [patoʒe] *vi* to splash about

pâte [pat] *nf* (*à tarte*) pastry; (*à pain*) dough; (*à frire*) batter; ~**s** *nfpl* (*macaroni etc*) pasta *sg*; ~ **à modeler** modelling clay, Plasticine ® (*BRIT*); ~ **brisée** shortcrust pastry; ~ **d'amandes** almond paste; ~ **de fruits** crystallized fruit *no pl*; ~ **feuilletée** puff *ou* flaky pastry

pâté [pate] *nm* (*charcuterie*) pâté; (*tache*) ink blot; (*de sable*) sandpie; ~ **de maisons** block (of houses); ~ **en croûte** ≃ pork pie

pâtée [pate] *nf* mash, feed

patente [patɑ̃t] *nf* (*COMM*) trading licence

paternel, le [patɛrnɛl] *adj* (*amour, soins*) fatherly; (*ligne, autorité*) paternal

pâteux, -euse [patø, øz] *adj* pasty; (*langue*) coated

pathétique [patetik] *adj* moving

patience [pasjɑ̃s] *nf* patience

patient, e [pasjɑ̃, ɑ̃t] *adj, nm/f* patient; **patienter** *vi* to wait

patin [patɛ̃] *nm* skate; (*sport*) skating; ~**s (à glace)** (ice) skates; ~**s à roulettes** roller skates

patinage [patinaʒ] *nm* skating

patiner [patine] *vi* to skate; (*roue, voiture*) to spin; **se** ~ *vi* (*meuble, cuir*) to acquire a sheen; **patineur, -euse** *nm/f* skater; **patinoire** *nf* skating rink, (ice) rink

pâtir [patir]: ~ **de** *vt* to suffer because of

pâtisserie [patisri] *nf* (*boutique*) cake shop; (*gâteau*) cake, pastry; (*à la maison*) pastry- *ou* cake-making, baking; **pâtissier, -ière** *nm/f* pastrycook

patois [patwa, waz] *nm* dialect, patois

patraque [patrak] (*fam*) *adj* peaky, off-colour

patrie [patri] *nf* homeland

patrimoine [patrimwan] *nm* (*culture*) heritage

patriotique [patrijɔtik] *adj* patriotic

patron, ne [patrɔ̃, ɔn] *nm/f* boss; (*REL*) patron saint ♦ *nm* (*COUTURE*) pattern; **patronat** *nm* employers *pl*; **patronner** *vt* to sponsor, support

patrouille [patruj] *nf* patrol

patte [pat] *nf* (*jambe*) leg; (*pied: de chien, chat*) paw; (: *d'oiseau*) foot

pâturage [patyraʒ] *nm* pasture

paume [pom] *nf* palm

paumé, e [pome] (*fam*) *nm/f* drop-out

paumer [pome] (*fam*) *vt* to lose

paupière [popjɛr] *nf* eyelid

pause [poz] *nf* (*arrêt*) break; (*en parlant, MUS*) pause

pauvre [povr] *adj* poor; **pauvreté** *nf* (*état*) poverty

pavaner [pavane]: **se** ~ *vi* to strut about

pavé, e [pave] *adj* (*cour*) paved; (*chaussée*) cobbled ♦ *nm* (*bloc*) paving stone; cobblestone

pavillon [pavijɔ̃] *nm* (*de banlieue*) small (detached) house; pavilion; (*drapeau*) flag

pavoiser [pavwaze] *vi* (*fig*) to rejoice, exult

pavot [pavo] *nm* poppy

payant, e [pejɑ̃, ɑ̃t] *adj* (*spectateurs etc*) paying; (*fig: entreprise*) profitable; (*effort*) which pays off; **c'est** ~ you have to pay, there is a charge

paye [pɛj] *nf* pay, wages *pl*

payer [peje] *vt* (*créancier, employé, loyer*) to pay; (*achat, réparations, fig: faute*) to pay for ♦ *vi* to pay; (*métier*) to be well-paid; (*tactique etc*) to pay off; **il me l'a fait ~ 10 euros** he charged me 10 euros for it; ~ **qch à qn** to buy sth for sb, buy sb sth; **se ~ la tête de qn** (*fam*) to take the mickey out of sb

pays [pei] *nm* country; (*région*) region; **du** ~ local

paysage [peizaʒ] *nm* landscape

paysan, ne [peizɑ̃, an] *nm/f* farmer; (*péj*) peasant ♦ *adj* (*agricole*) farming; (*rural*) country

Pays-Bas [peiba] *nmpl*: **les ~-~** the Netherlands

PC *nm* (*INFORM*) PC ♦ *sigle m* = **parti communiste**

P.D.G. *sigle m* = **président directeur général**

péage [peaʒ] *nm* toll; (*endroit*) tollgate

peau, x [po] *nf* skin; **gants de ~** fine leather gloves; **être bien/mal dans sa ~** to be quite at ease/ill-at-ease; **~ de chamois** (*chiffon*) chamois leather, shammy; **Peau-Rouge** *nm/f* Red Indian, redskin

pêche [pɛʃ] *nf* (*sport, activité*) fishing; (*poissons pêchés*) catch; (*fruit*) peach; **~ à la ligne** (*en rivière*) angling

péché [peʃe] *nm* sin

pécher [peʃe] *vi* (*REL*) to sin

pêcher [peʃe] *nm* peach tree ♦ *vi* to go fishing ♦ *vt* (*attraper*) to catch; (*être pêcheur de*) to fish for

pécheur, -eresse [peʃœʀ, peʃʀɛs] *nm/f* sinner

pêcheur [pɛʃœʀ] *nm* fisherman; (*à la ligne*) angler

pécule [pekyl] *nm* savings *pl*, nest egg

pédagogie [pedagɔʒi] *nf* educational methods *pl*, pedagogy; **pédagogique** *adj* educational

pédale [pedal] *nf* pedal

pédalo [pedalo] *nm* pedal-boat

pédant, e [pedɑ̃, ɑ̃t] (*péj*) *adj* pedantic

pédestre [pedɛstʀ] *adj*: **randonnée ~** ramble; **sentier ~** pedestrian footpath

pédiatre [pedjatʀ] *nm/f* paediatrician, child specialist

pédicure [pedikyʀ] *nm/f* chiropodist

pègre [pɛgʀ] *nf* underworld

peignais *etc* [peɲɛ] *vb voir* **peindre; peigner**

peigne [pɛɲ] *nm* comb; **peigner** *vt* to comb (the hair of); **se peigner** *vi* to comb one's hair

peignoir *nm* dressing gown; **peignoir de bain** bathrobe

peindre [pɛ̃dʀ] *vt* to paint; (*fig*) to portray, depict

peine [pɛn] *nf* (*affliction*) sorrow, sadness *no pl*; (*mal, effort*) trouble *no pl*, effort; (*difficulté*) difficulty; (*JUR*) sentence; **avoir de la ~** to be sad; **faire de la ~ à qn** to distress *ou* upset sb; **prendre la ~ de faire** to go to the trouble of doing; **se donner de la ~** to make an effort; **ce n'est pas la ~ de faire** there's no point in doing, it's not worth doing; **à ~** scarcely, hardly, barely; **à ~ ... que** hardly ... than; **~ capitale** *ou* **de mort** capital punishment, death sentence; **peiner** *vi* (*personne*) to work hard; (*moteur, voiture*) to labour ♦ *vt* to grieve, sadden

peintre [pɛ̃tʀ] *nm* painter; **~ en bâtiment** house painter

peinture [pɛ̃tyʀ] *nf* painting; (*matière*) paint; (*surfaces peintes: aussi:* **~s**) paintwork; **"~ fraîche"** "wet paint"

péjoratif, -ive [peʒɔʀatif, iv] *adj* pejorative, derogatory

pelage [pəlaʒ] *nm* coat, fur

pêle-mêle [pɛlmɛl] *adv* higgledy-piggledy

peler [pəle] *vt, vi* to peel

pèlerin [pɛlʀɛ̃] *nm* pilgrim

pèlerinage [pɛlʀinaʒ] *nm* pilgrimage

pelle [pɛl] *nf* shovel; (*d'enfant, de terrassier*) spade

pellicule [pelikyl] *nf* film; **~s** *nfpl* (*MÉD*) dandruff *sg*

pelote [p(ə)lɔt] *nf* (*de fil, laine*) ball

peloton [p(ə)lɔtɔ̃] *nm* group, squad; (*CYCLISME*) pack; **~ d'exécution** firing squad

pelotonner [p(ə)lɔtɔne]: **se ~** *vi* to curl (o.s.) up

pelouse [p(ə)luz] *nf* lawn

peluche [p(ə)lyʃ] *nf*: **(animal en) ~** fluffy animal, soft toy; **chien/lapin en ~** fluffy dog/rabbit

pelure [p(ə)lyʀ] *nf* peeling, peel *no pl*

pénal, e, -aux [penal, o] *adj* penal; **pénalité** *nf* penalty

penaud, e [pəno, od] *adj* sheepish, contrite

penchant [pɑ̃ʃɑ̃] *nm* (*tendance*) tendency, propensity; (*faible*) liking, fondness

pencher [pɑ̃ʃe] *vi* to tilt, lean over ♦ *vt* to tilt; **se ~** *vi* to lean over; (*se baisser*) to bend down; **se ~ sur** *vt fig: problème*) to look into; **~ pour** to be inclined to favour

pendaison [pɑ̃dɛzɔ̃] *nf* hanging

pendant [pɑ̃dɑ̃] *prép* (*au cours de*) during; (*indique la durée*) for; **~ que** while

pendentif [pɑ̃dɑ̃tif] *nm* pendant

penderie [pɑ̃dʀi] *nf* wardrobe

pendre [pɑ̃dʀ] *vt, vi* to hang; **se ~** (*se suicider*) to hang o.s.; **~ la crémaillère** to have a house-warming party

pendule [pɑ̃dyl] *nf* clock ♦ *nm* pendulum

pénétrer [penetʀe] *vi, vt* to penetrate; **~ dans** to enter

pénible [penibl] *adj* (*travail*) hard; (*sujet*) painful; (*personne*) tiresome; **péniblement** *adv* with difficulty

péniche [peniʃ] *nf* barge

pénicilline [penisilin] *nf* penicillin

péninsule [penɛ̃syl] *nf* peninsula

pénis [penis] *nm* penis

pénitence [penitɑ̃s] *nf* (*peine*) penance; (*repentir*) penitence; **pénitencier** *nm* penitentiary

pénombre [penɔ̃bʀ] *nf* (*faible clarté*) half-light; (*obscurité*) darkness

pensée [pɑ̃se] *nf* thought; (*démarche, doctrine*) thinking *no pl*; (*fleur*) pansy; **en ~** in one's mind

penser [pɑ̃se] *vi, vt* to think; **~ à** (*ami, vacances*) to think of *ou* about; (*réfléchir à: problème, offre*) to think *ou* over; (*prévoir*) to think of; **faire ~ à** to remind one of; **~ faire qch** to be thinking of doing sth, intend to do sth; **pensif, -ive** *adj* pensive, thoughtful

pension [pɑ̃sjɔ̃] *nf* (*allocation*) pension; (*prix du logement*) board and lodgings, bed and board; (*école*) boarding school; **~ alimentaire** (*de divorcée*) maintenance allowance, alimony; **~ complète** full board; **~ (de famille)** boarding house, guest-house; **pensionnaire** *nm/f* (SCOL) boarder; **pensionnat** *nm* boarding school

pente [pɑ̃t] *nf* slope; **en ~** sloping

Pentecôte [pɑ̃tkot] *nf*: **la ~** Whitsun (BRIT), Pentecost

pénurie [penyʀi] *nf* shortage

pépé [pepe] (*fam*) *nm* grandad

pépin [pepɛ̃] *nm* (BOT: *graine*) pip; (*ennui*) snag, hitch

pépinière [pepinjɛʀ] *nf* nursery

perçant, e [pɛʀsɑ̃, ɑ̃t] *adj* (*cri*) piercing, shrill; (*regard*) piercing

percée [pɛʀse] *nf* (*trouée*) opening; (MIL, *technologique*) breakthrough

perce-neige [pɛʀsənɛʒ] *nf inv* snowdrop

percepteur [pɛʀsɛptœʀ, tʀis] *nm* tax collector

perception [pɛʀsɛpsjɔ̃] *nf* perception; (*bureau*) tax office

percer [pɛʀse] *vt* to pierce; (*ouverture etc*) to make; (*mystère, énigme*) to penetrate ♦ *vi* to break through; **perceuse** *nf* drill

percevoir [pɛʀsəvwaʀ] *vt* (*distinguer*) to perceive, detect; (*taxe, impôt*) to collect; (*revenu, indemnité*) to receive

perche [pɛʀʃ] *nf* (*bâton*) pole

percher [pɛʀʃe] *vt, vi* to perch; **se ~** *vi* to perch; **perchoir** *nm* perch

perçois etc [pɛʀswa] *vb voir* **percevoir**

percolateur [pɛʀkɔlatœʀ] *nm* percolator

perçu, e [pɛʀsy] *pp de* **percevoir**

percussion [pɛʀkysjɔ̃] *nf* percussion

percuter [pɛʀkyte] *vt* to strike; (*suj: véhicule*) to crash into

perdant, e [pɛʀdɑ̃, ɑ̃t] *nm/f* loser

perdre [pɛʀdʀ] *vt* to lose; (*gaspiller: temps, argent*) to waste; (*personne: moralement etc*) to ruin ♦ *vi* to lose; (*sur une vente etc*) to lose out; **se ~** *vi* (*s'égarer*) to get lost, lose one's way; (*denrées*) to go to waste

perdrix [pɛʀdʀi] *nf* partridge

perdu, e [pɛʀdy] *pp de* **perdre** ♦ *adj* (*isolé*) out-of-the-way; (COMM: *emballage*) non-returnable; (*malade*): **il est ~** there's no hope left for him; **à vos moments ~s** in your spare time

père [pɛʀ] *nm* father; ~ **de famille** father; **le** ~ **Noël** Father Christmas

perfection [pɛʀfɛksjɔ̃] *nf* perfection; **à la** ~ to perfection; **perfectionné, e** *adj* sophisticated; **perfectionner** *vt* to improve, perfect

perforatrice [pɛʀfɔʀatʀis] *nf* (*de bureau*) punch

perforer [pɛʀfɔʀe] *vt* (*poinçonner*) to punch

performant, e [pɛʀfɔʀmɑ̃, ɑ̃t] *adj*: **très** ~ high-performance *cpd*

perfusion [pɛʀfyzjɔ̃] *nf*: **faire une** ~ **à qn** to put sb on a drip

péricliter [peʀiklite] *vi* to collapse

péril [peʀil] *nm* peril

périmé, e [peʀime] *adj* (*ADMIN*) out-of-date, expired

périmètre [peʀimɛtʀ] *nm* perimeter

période [peʀjɔd] *nf* period; **périodique** *adj* periodic ♦ *nm* periodical

péripéties [peʀipesi] *nfpl* events, episodes

périphérique [peʀifeʀik] *adj* (*quartiers*) outlying ♦ *nm* (*AUTO*) ring road

périple [peʀipl] *nm* journey

périr [peʀiʀ] *vi* to die, perish

périssable [peʀisabl] *adj* perishable

perle [pɛʀl] *nf* pearl; (*de plastique, métal, sueur*) bead

permanence [pɛʀmanɑ̃s] *nf* permanence; (*local*) (duty) office; **assurer une** ~ (*service public, bureaux*) to operate *ou* maintain a basic service; **être de** ~ to be on call *ou* duty; **en** ~ continuously

permanent, e [pɛʀmanɑ̃, ɑ̃t] *adj* permanent; (*spectacle*) continuous; **permanente** *nf* perm

perméable [pɛʀmeabl] *adj* (*terrain*) permeable; ~ **à** (*fig*) receptive *ou* open to

permettre [pɛʀmɛtʀ] *vt* to allow, permit; ~ **à qn de faire/qch** to allow sb to do/sth; **se** ~ **de faire** to take the liberty of doing

permis [pɛʀmi, iz] *nm* permit, licence; ~ **de chasse** hunting permit; ~ **(de conduire)** (driving) licence (*BRIT*), (driver's) license (*US*); ~ **de construire** planning permission (*BRIT*), building permit (*US*); ~ **de séjour** residence permit; ~ **de travail** work permit

permission [pɛʀmisjɔ̃] *nf* permission; (*MIL*) leave; **avoir la** ~ **de faire** to have permission to do; **en** ~ on leave

permuter [pɛʀmyte] *vt* to change around, permutate ♦ *vi* to change, swap

Pérou [peʀu] *nm* Peru

perpétuel, le [pɛʀpetɥɛl] *adj* perpetual; **perpétuité** *nf*: **à perpétuité** for life; **être condamné à perpétuité** to receive a life sentence

perplexe [pɛʀplɛks] *adj* perplexed, puzzled

perquisitionner [pɛʀkizisjɔne] *vi* to carry out a search

perron [pɛʀɔ̃] *nm* steps *pl* (*leading to entrance*)

perroquet [pɛʀɔkɛ] *nm* parrot

perruche [pɛʀyʃ] *nf* budgerigar (*BRIT*), budgie (*BRIT*), parakeet (*US*)

perruque [pɛʀyk] *nf* wig

persan, e [pɛʀsɑ̃, an] *adj* Persian

persécuter [pɛʀsekyte] *vt* to persecute

persévérer [pɛʀsevere] *vi* to persevere

persiennes [pɛʀsjɛn] *nfpl* shutters

persil [pɛʀsi] *nm* parsley

Persique [pɛʀsik] *adj*: **le golfe** ~ the (Persian) Gulf

persistant, e [pɛʀsistɑ̃, ɑ̃t] *adj* persistent

persister [pɛʀsiste] *vi* to persist; ~ **à faire qch** to persist in doing sth

personnage [pɛʀsɔnaʒ] *nm* (*individu*) character, individual; (*célébrité*) important person; (*de roman, film*) character; (*PEINTURE*) figure

personnalité [pɛʀsɔnalite] *nf* personality; (*personnage*) prominent figure

personne [pɛʀsɔn] *nf* person ♦ *pron* nobody, no one; (*avec négation en anglais*) anybody, anyone; ~**s** *nfpl* (*gens*) people *pl*; **il n'y a** ~ there's nobody there, there isn't anybody there; ~ **âgée** elderly person; **personnel, le** *adj* personal; (*égoïste*) selfish ♦ *nm* staff, personnel; **personnel-**

lement *adv* personally

perspective [pɛʀspɛktiv] *nf* (*ART*) perspective; (*vue*) view; (*point de vue*) viewpoint, angle; (*chose envisagée*) prospect; **en ~** in prospect

perspicace [pɛʀspikas] *adj* clear-sighted, gifted with (*ou* showing) insight; **perspicacité** *nf* clear-sightedness

persuader [pɛʀsɥade] *vt*: **~ qn (de faire)** to persuade sb (to do)

persuasif, -ive [pɛʀsɥazif, iv] *adj* persuasive

perte [pɛʀt] *nf* loss; (*de temps*) waste; (*fig: morale*) ruin; **à ~ de vue** as far as the eye can (*ou* could) see; **~s blanches** (vaginal) discharge *sg*

pertinemment [pɛʀtinamɑ̃] *adv* (*savoir*) full well

pertinent, e [pɛʀtinɑ̃, ɑ̃t] *adj* apt, relevant

perturbation [pɛʀtyʀbasjɔ̃] *nf*: **~ (atmosphérique)** atmospheric disturbance

perturber [pɛʀtyʀbe] *vt* to disrupt; (*PSYCH*) to perturb, disturb

pervers, e [pɛʀvɛʀ, ɛʀs] *adj* perverted

pervertir [pɛʀvɛʀtiʀ] *vt* to pervert

pesant, e [pəzɑ̃, ɑ̃t] *adj* heavy; (*fig: présence*) burdensome

pèse-personne [pɛzpɛʀsɔn] *nm* (bathroom) scales *pl*

peser [pəze] *vt* to weigh ♦ *vi* to weigh; (*fig: avoir de l'importance*) to carry weight; **~ lourd** to be heavy

pessimisme [pesimism] *nm* pessimism

pessimiste [pesimist] *adj* pessimistic ♦ *nm/f* pessimist

peste [pɛst] *nf* plague

pester [pɛste] *vi*: **~ contre** to curse

pétale [petal] *nm* petal

pétanque [petɑ̃k] *nf* type of bowls

pétanque

i **Pétanque**, which originated in the south of France, is a version of the game of **boules** played on a variety of hard surfaces. Standing with their feet to-

gether, players throw steel bowls towards a wooden jack.

pétarader [petaʀade] *vi* to backfire

pétard [petaʀ] *nm* banger (*BRIT*), firecracker

péter [pete] *vi* (*fam: casser*) to bust; (*fam!*) to fart (*!*)

pétillant, e [petijɑ̃, ɑ̃t] *adj* sparkling

pétiller [petije] *vi* (*feu*) to crackle; (*champagne*) to bubble; (*yeux*) to sparkle

petit, e [p(ə)ti, it] *adj* small; (*avec nuance affective*) little; (*voyage*) short, little; (*bruit etc*) faint, slight; **~s** *nmpl* (*d'un animal*) young *pl*; **les tout-~s** the little ones, the tiny tots; **~ à ~** bit by bit, gradually; **~(e) ami(e)** boyfriend/girlfriend; **~ déjeuner** breakfast; **~ pain** (bread) roll; **les ~es annonces** the small ads; **~s pois** garden peas; **petite-fille** *nf* granddaughter; **petit-fils** *nm* grandson

pétition [petisjɔ̃] *nf* petition

petits-enfants [pətizɑ̃fɑ̃] *nmpl* grandchildren

petit-suisse [pətisɥis] (*pl* **~s-~s**) *nm* small individual pot of cream cheese

pétrin [petʀɛ̃] *nm* (*fig*): **dans le ~** (*fam*) in a jam *ou* fix

pétrir [petʀiʀ] *vt* to knead

pétrole [petʀɔl] *nm* oil; (*pour lampe, réchaud etc*) paraffin (oil); **pétrolier, -ière** *nm* oil tanker

---

MOT-CLÉ

peu [pø] *adv* **1** (*modifiant verbe, adjectif, adverbe*): **il boit peu** he doesn't drink (very) much; **il est peu bavard** he's not very talkative; **peu avant/après** shortly before/afterwards

2 (*modifiant nom*): **peu de**: **peu de gens/d'arbres** few *ou* not (very) many people/trees; **il a peu d'espoir** he hasn't (got) much hope, he has little hope; **pour peu de temps** for (only) a short while

3: **peu à peu** little by little; **à peu près** just about, more or less; **à peu près 10**

kg/10 F approximately 10 kg/10F
♦ *nm* 1: **le peu de gens qui** the few people who; **le peu de sable qui** what little sand, the little sand which
2: **un peu** a little; **un petit peu** a little bit; **un peu d'espoir** a little hope
♦ *pron*: **peu le savent** few know (it); **avant** *ou* **sous peu** shortly, before long; **de peu** (only) just

peuple [pœpl] *nm* people; **peupler** *vt* (*pays, région*) to populate; (*étang*) to stock; (*suj: hommes, poissons*) to inhabit

peuplier [pøplije] *nm* poplar (tree)

peur [pœʀ] *nf* fear; **avoir ~ (de/de faire/ que)** to be frightened *ou* afraid (of/of doing/that); **faire ~ à** to frighten; **de ~ de/que** for fear of/that; **peureux, -euse** *adj* fearful, timorous

peut [pø] *vb voir* **pouvoir**

peut-être [pøtɛtʀ] *adv* perhaps, maybe; **~-~ que** perhaps, maybe; **~-~ bien qu'il fera/est** he may well do/be

peux *etc* [pø] *vb voir* **pouvoir**

phare [faʀ] *nm* lighthouse; (*de véhicule*) headlight; **~s de recul** reversing lights

pharmacie [faʀmasi] *nf* (*magasin*) chemist's (*BRIT*), pharmacy; (*de salle de bain*) medicine cabinet; **pharmacien, ne** *nm/f* pharmacist, chemist (*BRIT*)

phénomène [fenɔmɛn] *nm* phenomenon

philatélie [filateli] *nf* philately, stamp collecting

philosophe [filɔzɔf] *nm/f* philosopher ♦ *adj* philosophical

philosophie [filɔzɔfi] *nf* philosophy

phobie [fɔbi] *nf* phobia

phonétique [fɔnetik] *nf* phonetics *sg*

phoque [fɔk] *nm* seal

phosphorescent, e [fɔsfɔʀesɑ̃, ɑ̃t] *adj* luminous

photo [fɔto] *nf* photo(graph); **prendre en ~** to take a photo of; **faire de la ~** to take photos; **~ d'identité** passport photograph; **photocopie** *nf* photocopy; **photocopier** *vt* to photocopy; **photoco-**

pieuse *nf* photocopier; **photographe** *nm/f* photographer; **photographie** *nf* (*technique*) photography; (*cliché*) photograph; **photographier** *vt* to photograph

phrase [fʀaz] *nf* sentence

physicien, ne [fizisjɛ̃, jɛn] *nm/f* physicist

physionomie [fizjɔnɔmi] *nf* face

physique [fizik] *adj* physical ♦ *nm* physique ♦ *nf* physics *sg*; **au ~** physically; **physiquement** *adv* physically

piailler [pjaje] *vi* to squawk

pianiste [pjanist] *nm/f* pianist

piano [pjano] *nm* piano; **pianoter** *vi* to tinkle away (at the piano)

pic [pik] *nm* (*instrument*) pick(axe); (*montagne*) peak; (*ZOOL*) woodpecker; **à ~** vertically; (*fig: tomber, arriver*) just at the right time

pichet [piʃɛ] *nm* jug

picorer [pikɔʀe] *vt* to peck

picoter [pikɔte] *vt* (*suj: oiseau*) to peck ♦ *vi* (*irriter*) to smart, prickle

pie [pi] *nf* magpie

pièce [pjɛs] *nf* (*d'un logement*) room; (*THÉÂTRE*) play; (*de machine*) part; (*de monnaie*) coin; (*document*) document; (*fragment, de collection*) piece; **dix francs ~** ten francs each; **vendre à la ~** to sell separately; **travailler à la ~** to do piecework; **un maillot une ~** a one-piece swimsuit; **un deux-~s cuisine** a two-room(ed) flat (*BRIT*) *ou* apartment (*US*) with kitchen; **~ à conviction** exhibit; **~ d'identité: avez-vous une ~ d'identité?** have you got any (means of) identification?; **~ montée** tiered cake; **~s détachées** spares, (spare) parts; **~s justificatives** supporting documents

pied [pje] *nm* foot; (*de table*) leg; (*de lampe*) base; **à ~** on foot; **au ~ de la lettre** literally; **avoir ~** to be able to touch the bottom, not to be out of one's depth; **avoir le ~ marin** to be a good sailor; **sur ~** (*debout, rétabli*) up and about; **mettre sur ~** (*entreprise*) to set up; **c'est le ~** (*fam*) it's brilliant; **mettre les ~s dans le**

plat (*fam*) to put one's foot in it; **il se débrouille comme un ~** (*fam*) he's completely useless; **pied-noir** *nm* Algerian-born Frenchman

piège [pjɛʒ] *nm* trap; **prendre au ~** to trap; **piéger** *vt* (*avec une bombe*) to booby-trap; **lettre/voiture piégée** letter-/car-bomb

pierre [pjɛʀ] *nf* stone; **~ précieuse** precious stone, gem; **~ tombale** tombstone; **pierreries** *nfpl* gems, precious stones

piétiner [pjetine] *vi* (*trépigner*) to stamp (one's foot); (*fig*) to be at a standstill ♦ *vt* to trample on

piéton, ne [pjetɔ̃, ɔn] *nm/f* pedestrian; **piétonnier, -ière** *adj*: **rue** *ou* **zone piétonnière** pedestrian precinct

pieu, x [pjø] *nm* post; (*pointu*) stake

pieuvre [pjœvʀ] *nf* octopus

pieux, -euse [pjø, pjøz] *adj* pious

piffer [pife] (*fam*) *vt*: **je ne peux pas le ~** I can't stand him

pigeon [piʒɔ̃] *nm* pigeon

piger [piʒe] (*fam*) *vi*, *vt* to understand

pigiste [piʒist] *nm/f* freelance(r)

pignon [piɲɔ̃] *nm* (*de mur*) gable

pile [pil] *nf* (*tas*) pile; (*ÉLEC*) battery ♦ *adv* (*fam: s'arrêter etc*) dead; **à deux heures ~** at two on the dot; **jouer à ~ ou face** to toss up (for it); **~ ou face?** heads or tails?

piler [pile] *vt* to crush, pound

pilier [pilje] *nm* pillar

piller [pije] *vt* to pillage, plunder, loot

pilote [pilɔt] *nm* pilot; (*de voiture*) driver ♦ *adj* pilot *cpd*; **~ de course** racing driver; **~ de ligne/d'essai/de chasse** airline/test/fighter pilot; **piloter** *vt* (*avion*) to pilot, fly; (*voiture*) to drive

pilule [pilyl] *nf* pill; **prendre la ~** to be on the pill

piment [pimɑ̃] *nm* (*aussi: ~ rouge*) chilli; (*fig*) spice, piquancy; **~ doux** pepper, capsicum; **pimenté, e** *adj* (*plat*) hot, spicy

pimpant, e [pɛ̃pɑ̃, ɑ̃t] *adj* spruce

pin [pɛ̃] *nm* pine

pinard [pinaʀ] (*fam*) *nm* (cheap) wine,

plonk (*BRIT*)

pince [pɛ̃s] *nf* (*outil*) pliers *pl*; (*de homard, crabe*) pincer, claw; (*COUTURE: pli*) dart; **~ à épiler** tweezers *pl*; **~ à linge** clothes peg (*BRIT*) *ou* pin (*US*)

pincé, e [pɛ̃se] *adj* (*air*) stiff

pinceau, x [pɛ̃so] *nm* (paint)brush

pincée [pɛ̃se] *nf*: **une ~ de** a pinch of

pincer [pɛ̃se] *vt* to pinch; (*fam*) to nab

pinède [pined] *nf* pinewood, pine forest

pingouin [pɛ̃gwɛ̃] *nm* penguin

ping-pong ® [piŋpɔ̃g] *nm* table tennis

pingre [pɛ̃gʀ] *adj* niggardly

pinson [pɛ̃sɔ̃] *nm* chaffinch

pintade [pɛ̃tad] *nf* guinea-fowl

pioche [pjɔʃ] *nf* pickaxe; **piocher** *vt* to dig up (with a pickaxe); **piocher dans** (*le tas, ses économies*) to dig into

pion [pjɔ̃] *nm* (*ÉCHECS*) pawn; (*DAMES*) piece; (*SCOL*) supervisor

pionnier [pjɔnje] *nm* pioneer

pipe [pip] *nf* pipe; **fumer la ~** to smoke a pipe

pipeau, x [pipo] *nm* (reed-)pipe

piquant, e [pikɑ̃, ɑ̃t] *adj* (*barbe, rosier etc*) prickly; (*saveur, sauce*) hot, pungent; (*détail*) titillating; (*froid*) biting ♦ *nm* (*épine*) thorn, prickle; (*fig*) spiciness, spice

pique [pik] *nf* pike; (*fig*) cutting remark ♦ *nm* (*CARTES*) spades *pl*

pique-nique [piknik] *nm* picnic; **pique-niquer** *vi* to have a picnic

piquer [pike] *vt* (*suj: guêpe, fumée, orties*) to sting; (: *moustique*) to bite; (: *barbe*) to prick; (: *froid*) to bite; (*MÉD*) to give a jab to; (: *chien, chat*) to put to sleep; (*intérêt*) to arouse; (*fam: voler*) to pinch ♦ *vi* (*avion*) to go into a dive; **se ~** (*avec une aiguille*) to prick o.s.; (*dans les orties*) to get stung; (*suj: toxicomane*) to shoot up; **~ une colère** to fly into a rage

piquet [pike] *nm* (*pieu*) post, stake; (*de tente*) peg; **~ de grève** (strike-)picket

piqûre [pikyʀ] *nf* (*d'épingle*) prick; (*d'ortie*) sting; (*de moustique*) bite; (*MÉD*) injection, shot (*US*); **faire une ~ à qn** to give sb an injection

pirate [piʀat] *nm, adj* pirate; **~ de l'air** hijacker

pire [piʀ] *adj* worse; *(superlatif)*: **le(la) ~ ...** the worst ... ♦ *nm*: **le ~ (de)** the worst (of); **au ~** at (the very) worst

pis [pi] *nm (de vache)* udder; *(pire)*: **le ~** the worst ♦ *adj, adv* worse; **de mal en ~** from bad to worse

piscine [pisin] *nf* (swimming) pool; **~ couverte** indoor (swimming) pool

pissenlit [pisɑ̃li] *nm* dandelion

pistache [pistaʃ] *nf* pistachio (nut)

piste [pist] *nf (d'un animal, sentier)* track, trail; *(indice)* lead; *(de stade)* track; *(de cirque)* ring; *(de danse)* floor; *(de patinage)* rink; *(de ski)* run; *(AVIAT)* runway; **~ cyclable** cycle track

pistolet [pistɔlɛ] *nm (arme)* pistol, gun; *(à peinture)* spray gun; **pistolet-mitrailleur** *nm* submachine gun

piston [pistɔ̃] *nm (TECH)* piston; **avoir du ~** *(fam)* to have friends in the right places; **pistonner** *vt (candidat)* to pull strings for

piteux, -euse [pitø, øz] *adj* pitiful, sorry *(avant le nom)*

pitié [pitje] *nf* pity; **il me fait ~** I feel sorry for him; **avoir ~ de** *(compassion)* to pity, feel sorry for; *(merci)* to have pity *ou* mercy on sb

pitoyable [pitwajabl] *adj* pitiful

pitre [pitʀ] *nm* clown; **pitrerie** *nf* tomfoolery *no pl*

pittoresque [pitɔʀɛsk] *adj* picturesque

pivot [pivo] *nm* pivot; **pivoter** *vi* to revolve; *(fauteuil)* to swivel

P.J. *sigle f (= police judiciaire)* ≈ CID *(BRIT)*, ≈ FBI *(US)*

placard [plakaʀ] *nm (armoire)* cupboard; *(affiche)* poster, notice

place [plas] *nf (emplacement, classement)* place; *(de ville, village)* square; *(espace libre)* room, space; *(de parking)* space; *(siège: de train, cinéma, voiture)* seat; *(emploi)* job; **en ~** *(mettre)* in its place; **sur ~** on the spot; **faire ~ à** to give way to; **ça prend de la**

~ it takes up a lot of room *ou* space; **à la ~ de** in place of, instead of; **à ta ~ ...** if I were you ...; **se mettre à la ~ de qn** to put o.s. in sb's place *ou* in sb's shoes

placé, e [plase] *adj*: **être bien/mal ~** *(spectateur)* to have a good/a poor seat; *(concurrent)* to be in a good/bad position; **il est bien ~ pour le savoir** he is in a position to know

placement [plasmɑ̃] *nm (FINANCE)* investment; **bureau de ~** employment agency

placer [plase] *vt* to place; *(convive, spectateur)* to seat; *(argent)* to place, invest; **il n'a pas pu ~ un mot** he couldn't get a word in; **se ~ au premier rang** to go and stand *(ou* sit) in the first row

plafond [plafɔ̃] *nm* ceiling

plage [plaʒ] *nf* beach

plagiat [plaʒja] *nm* plagiarism

plaid [plɛd] *nm* (tartan) car rug

plaider [plede] *vi (avocat)* to plead ♦ *vt* to plead; **~ pour** *(fig)* to speak for; **plaidoyer** *nm (JUR)* speech for the defence; *(fig)* plea

plaie [plɛ] *nf* wound

plaignant, e [plɛɲɑ̃, ɑ̃t] *nm/f* plaintiff

plaindre [plɛ̃dʀ] *vt* to pity, feel sorry for; **se ~** *vi (gémir)* to moan; *(protester)*: **se ~ (à qn) (de)** to complain (to sb) (about); *(souffrir)*: **se ~ de** to complain of

plaine [plɛn] *nf* plain

plain-pied [plɛ̃pje] *adv*: **de ~-~ (avec)** on the same level (as)

plainte [plɛ̃t] *nf (gémissement)* moan, groan; *(doléance)* complaint; **porter ~** to lodge a complaint

plaire [plɛʀ] *vi* to be a success, be successful; **ça plaît beaucoup aux jeunes** it's very popular with young people; **~ à:** **cela me plaît** I like it; **se ~ quelque part** to like being somewhere *ou* like it somewhere; **j'irai si ça me plaît** I'll go if I feel like it; **s'il vous plaît** please

plaisance [plɛzɑ̃s] *nf (aussi:* **navigation de ~)** (pleasure) sailing, yachting

plaisant, e [plɛzɑ̃, ɑ̃t] *adj* pleasant; *(his-*

toire, anecdote) amusing

plaisanter [plɛzɑ̃te] *vi* to joke; **plaisanterie** *nf* joke

plaise *etc* [plez] *vb voir* **plaire**

plaisir [pleziʀ] *nm* pleasure; **faire ~ à qn** (*délibérément*) to be nice to sb, please sb; **ça me fait ~** I like (doing) it; **j'espère que ça te fera ~** I hope you'll like it; **pour le ~** for pleasure

plaît [plɛ] *vb voir* **plaire**

plan, e [plɑ̃, an] *adj* flat ♦ *nm* plan; (*fig*) level, plane; (*CINÉMA*) shot; **au premier/ second ~** in the foreground/middle distance; **à l'arrière ~** in the background; **rester en ~** (*fam*) to be left stranded; **laisser en ~** (*fam: travail*) to drop, abandon; **~ d'eau** lake

planche [plɑ̃ʃ] *nf* (*pièce de bois*) plank, (wooden) board; (*illustration*) plate; **~ à repasser** ironing board; **~ à roulettes** skateboard; **~ à voile** (*sport*) windsurfing

plancher [plɑ̃ʃe] *nm* floor; floorboards *pl* ♦ *vi* (*fam*) to work hard

planer [plane] *vi* to glide; (*fam: rêveur*) to have one's head in the clouds; **~ sur** (*fig: danger*) to hang over

planète [planɛt] *nf* planet

planeur [planœʀ] *nm* glider

planification [planifikasjɔ̃] *nf* (economic) planning

planifier [planifje] *vt* to plan

planning [planiŋ] *nm* programme, schedule

planque [plɑ̃k] (*fam*) *nf* (*emploi peu fatigant*) cushy (*BRIT*) *ou* easy number; (*cachette*) hiding place

plant [plɑ̃] *nm* seedling, young plant

plante [plɑ̃t] *nf* plant; **~ d'appartement** house *ou* pot plant; **~ des pieds** sole (of the foot)

planter [plɑ̃te] *vt* (*plante*) to plant; (*enfoncer*) to hammer *ou* drive in; (*tente*) to put up, pitch; (*fam: personne*) to dump; **se ~** (*fam: se tromper*) to get it wrong

plantureux, -euse [plɑ̃tyʀø, øz] *adj* copious, lavish; (*femme*) buxom

plaque [plak] *nf* plate; (*de verglas, d'eczéma*) patch; (*avec inscription*) plaque; **~ chauffante** hotplate; **~ de chocolat** bar of chocolate; **~ (minéralogique** *ou* **d'immatriculation)** number (*BRIT*) *ou* license (*US*) plate; **~ tournante** (*fig*) centre

plaqué, e [plake] *adj*: **~ or/argent** gold-/ silver-plated

plaquer [plake] *vt* (*aplatir*): **~ qch sur** *ou* **contre** to make sth stick *ou* cling to; (*RUGBY*) to bring down; (*fam: laisser tomber*) to drop

plaquette [plakɛt] *nf* (*de chocolat*) bar; (*beurre*) pack(et); **~ de frein** brake pad

plastique [plastik] *adj, nm* plastic; **plastiquer** *vt* to blow up (with a plastic bomb)

plat, e [pla, -at] *adj* flat; (*cheveux*) straight; (*style*) flat, dull ♦ *nm* (*récipient, CULIN*) dish; (*d'un repas*) course; **à ~ ventre** face down; **à ~** (*pneu, batterie*) flat; (*fam: personne*) dead beat; **~ cuisiné** pre-cooked meal; **~ de résistance** main course; **~ du jour** dish of the day

platane [platan] *nm* plane tree

plateau, x [plato] *nm* (*support*) tray; (*GÉO*) plateau; (*CINÉMA*) set; **~ de fromages** cheeseboard

plate-bande [platbɑ̃d] *nf* flower bed

plate-forme [platfɔʀm] *nf* platform; **~-~ de forage/pétrolière** drilling/oil rig

platine [platin] *nm* platinum ♦ *nf* (*d'un tourne-disque*) turntable

plâtre [plɑtʀ] *nm* (*matériau*) plaster; (*statue*) plaster statue; (*MÉD*) (plaster) cast; **avoir un bras dans le ~** to have an arm in plaster

plein, e [plɛ̃, plɛn] *adj* full ♦ *nm*: **faire le ~ (d'essence)** to fill up (with petrol); **à ~es mains** (*ramasser*) in handfuls; **à ~ temps** full-time; **en ~ air** in the open air; **en ~ soleil** in direct sunlight; **en ~e nuit/rue** in the middle of the night/street; **en ~ jour** in broad daylight

pleurer [plœʀe] *vi* to cry; (*yeux*) to water ♦ *vt* to mourn (for); **~ sur** to lament (over), to bemoan

pleurnicher [plœʀniʃe] *vi* to snivel, whine

pleurs [plœʀ] *nmpl*: **en ~** in tears

pleut [plø] *vb voir* **pleuvoir**

pleuvoir [pløvwaʀ] *vb impers* to rain ♦ *vi* (*coups*) to rain down; (*critiques, invitations*) to shower down; **il pleut** it's raining

pli [pli] *nm* fold; (*de jupe*) pleat; (*de pantalon*) crease; **prendre le ~ de faire** to get into the habit of doing; **un mauvais ~** a bad habit

pliant, e [plijɑ̃, plijɑ̃t] *adj* folding

plier [plije] *vt* to fold; (*pour ranger*) to fold up; (*genou, bras*) to bend ♦ *vi* to bend; (*fig*) to yield; **se ~** *vi* to fold; **se ~ à** to submit to

plinthe [plɛ̃t] *nf* skirting board

plisser [plise] *vt* (*jupe*) to put pleats in; (*yeux*) to screw up; (*front*) to crease

plomb [plɔ̃] *nm* (*métal*) lead; (*d'une cartouche*) (lead) shot; (*PÊCHE*) sinker; (*ÉLEC*) fuse; **sans ~** (*essence etc*) unleaded

plombage [plɔ̃baʒ] *nm* (*de dent*) filling

plomberie [plɔ̃bʀi] *nf* plumbing

plombier [plɔ̃bje] *nm* plumber

plonge [plɔ̃ʒ] *nf* washing-up

plongeant, e [plɔ̃ʒɑ̃, ɑ̃t] *adj* (*vue*) from above; (*décolleté*) plunging

plongée [plɔ̃ʒe] *nf* (*SPORT*) diving *no pl*; (*sans scaphandre*) skin diving; **~ sousmarine** diving

plongeoir [plɔ̃ʒwaʀ] *nm* diving board

plongeon [plɔ̃ʒɔ̃] *nm* dive

plonger [plɔ̃ʒe] *vi* to dive ♦ *vt*: **~ qch dans** to plunge sth into; **se ~ dans** (*études, lecture*) to bury *ou* immerse o.s. in; **plongeur** *nm* diver

ployer [plwaje] *vt, vi* to bend

plu [ply] *pp de* **plaire; pleuvoir**

pluie [plɥi] *nf* rain

plume [plym] *nf* feather; (*pour écrire*) (pen) nib; (*fig*) pen

plupart [plypaʀ]: **la ~** *pron* the majority, most (of them); **la ~ des** most, the majority of; **la ~ du temps/d'entre nous** most of the time/of us; **pour la ~** for the most part, mostly

pluriel [plyʀjɛl] *nm* plural

plus¹ [ply] *vb voir* **plaire**

MOT-CLÉ
---

plus² [ply] *adv* **1** (*forme négative*): **ne ... plus** no more, no longer; **je n'ai plus d'argent** I've got no more money *ou* no money left; **il ne travaille plus** he's no longer working, he doesn't work any more

2 (*comparatif*) more, ...+er; (*superlatif*): **le plus** the most, the ...+est; **plus grand/ intelligent (que)** bigger/more intelligent (than); **le plus grand/intelligent** the biggest/most intelligent; **tout au plus** at the very most

3 (*davantage*) more; **il travaille plus (que)** he works more (than); **plus il travaille, plus il est heureux** the more he works, the happier he is; **plus de pain** more bread; **plus de 10 personnes** more than 10 people, over 10 people; **3 heures de plus que** 3 hours more than; **de plus** what's more, moreover; **3 kilos en plus** 3 kilos more; **en plus de** in addition to; **de plus en plus** more and more; **plus ou moins** more or less; **ni plus ni moins** no more, no less

♦ *prép*: **4 plus 2** 4 plus 2

---

plusieurs [plyzjœʀ] *dét, pron* several; **ils sont ~** there are several of them

plus-value [plyvaly] *nf* (*bénéfice*) surplus

plut [ply] *vb voir* **plaire**

plutôt [plyto] *adv* rather; **je préfère ~ celui-ci** I'd rather have this one; **~ que (de) faire** rather than *ou* instead of doing

pluvieux, -euse [plyvjø, jøz] *adj* rainy, wet

PME *sigle f* (= *petite(s) et moyenne(s) entreprise(s)*) small business(es)

PMU *sigle m* (= *Pari mutuel urbain*) system of betting on horses; (*café*) betting agency

PNB *sigle m* (= *produit national brut*) GNP

pneu [pnø] *nm* tyre (*BRIT*), tire (*US*)

pneumonie [pnømɔni] *nf* pneumonia

poche [pɔʃ] *nf* pocket; (*sous les yeux*) bag, pouch; **argent de ~** pocket money

pocher [pɔʃe] *vt* (CULIN) to poach

pochette [pɔʃɛt] *nf* (*d'aiguilles etc*) case; (*mouchoir*) breast pocket handkerchief; (*sac à main*) clutch bag; **~ de disque** record sleeve

poêle [pwal] *nm* stove ♦ *nf*: **~ (à frire)** frying pan

poème [pɔɛm] *nm* poem

poésie [pɔezi] *nf* (*poème*) poem; (*art*): **la ~** poetry

poète [pɔɛt] *nm* poet

poids [pwa] *nm* weight; (SPORT) shot; **vendre au ~** to sell by weight; **prendre du ~** to put on weight; **~ lourd** (*camion*) lorry (BRIT), truck (US)

poignant, e [pwaɲɑ̃, ɑ̃t] *adj* poignant

poignard [pwaɲaR] *nm* dagger; **poignarder** *vt* to stab, knife

poigne [pwaɲ] *nf* grip; **avoir de la ~** (*fig*) to rule with a firm hand

poignée [pwaɲe] *nf* (*de sel etc, fig*) handful; (*de couvercle, porte*) handle; **~ de main** handshake

poignet [pwaɲɛ] *nm* (ANAT) wrist; (*de chemise*) cuff

poil [pwal] *nm* (ANAT) hair; (*de pinceau, brosse*) bristle; (*de tapis*) strand; (*pelage*) coat; **à ~** (*fam*) starkers; **au ~** (*fam*) hunky-dory; **poilu, e** *adj* hairy

poinçon [pwɛ̃sɔ̃] *nm* (*marque*) hallmark; **poinçonner** *vt* (*bijou*) to hallmark; (*billet*) to punch

poing [pwɛ̃] *nm* fist; **coup de ~** punch

point [pwɛ̃] *nm* point; (*endroit*) spot; (*marque, signe*) dot; (: *de ponctuation*) full stop, period (US); (COUTURE, TRICOT) stitch ♦ *adv* = **pas²**; **faire le ~** (*fig*) to take stock (of the situation); **sur le ~ de faire** (just) about to do; **à tel ~ que** so much so that; **mettre au ~** (*procédé*) to develop; (*affaire*) to settle; **à ~** (CULIN: *viande*) medium; **à ~ (nommé)** just at the right time; **deux ~s** colon; **~ (de côté)** stitch (*pain*); **~ d'exclamation/d'interrogation**

exclamation/question mark; **~ de repère** landmark; (*dans le temps*) point of reference; **~ de suture** (MÉD) stitch; **~ de vente** retail outlet; **~ de vue** viewpoint; (*fig: opinion*) point of view; **~ d'honneur: mettre un ~ d'honneur à faire qch** to make it a point of honour to do sth; **~ faible/fort** weak/strong point; **~ noir** blackhead; **~s de suspension** suspension points

pointe [pwɛ̃t] *nf* point; (*clou*) tack; (*fig*): **une ~ de** a hint of; **être à la ~ de** (*fig*) to be in the forefront of; **sur la ~ des pieds** on tiptoe; **en ~** pointed, tapered; **de ~** (*technique etc*) leading; **heures de ~** peak hours

pointer [pwɛ̃te] *vt* (*diriger: canon, doigt*): **~ sur qch** to point at sth ♦ *vi* (*employé*) to clock in

pointillé [pwɛ̃tije] *nm* (*trait*) dotted line

pointilleux, -euse [pwɛ̃tijø, øz] *adj* particular, pernickety

pointu, e [pwɛ̃ty] *adj* pointed; (*voix*) shrill; (*analyse*) precise

pointure [pwɛ̃tyR] *nf* size

point-virgule [pwɛ̃viRgyl] *nm* semi-colon

poire [pwaR] *nf* pear; (*fam: péj*) mug

poireau, x [pwaRo] *nm* leek

poireauter [pwaRote] *vi* (*fam*) to be left kicking one's heels

poirier [pwaRje] *nm* pear tree

pois [pwa] *nm* (BOT) pea; (*sur une étoffe*) dot, spot; **~ chiche** chickpea; **à ~** (*cravate etc*) spotted, polka-dot *cpd*

poison [pwazɔ̃] *nm* poison

poisse [pwas] *nf* (*fam*) rotten luck

poisseux, -euse [pwasø, øz] *adj* sticky

poisson [pwasɔ̃] *nm* fish *gén inv*; **les P~s** (*signe*) Pisces; **~ d'avril!** April fool!; **~ rouge** goldfish; **poissonnerie** *nf* fish-shop; **poissonnier, -ière** *nm/f* fishmonger (BRIT), fish merchant (US)

poitrine [pwatRin] *nf* chest; (*seins*) bust, bosom; (CULIN) breast

poivre [pwavR] *nm* pepper

poivron [pwavRɔ̃] *nm* pepper, capsicum

polaire [pɔlɛR] *adj* polar

polar [pɔlaʀ] (fam) nm detective novel

pôle [pol] nm (GÉO, ÉLEC) pole

poli, e [pɔli] adj polite; (lisse) smooth

police [pɔlis] nf police; ~ **d'assurance** insurance policy; ~ **judiciaire** ≃ Criminal Investigation Department (BRIT), ≃ Federal Bureau of Investigation (US); ~ **secours** ≃ emergency services pl (BRIT), ≃ paramedics pl (US); **policier, -ière** adj police cpd ♦ nm policeman; (aussi: **roman policier**) detective novel

polio [pɔljo] nf polio

polir [pɔliʀ] vt to polish

polisson, ne [pɔlisɔ̃, ɔn] nm/f (enfant) (little) rascal

politesse [pɔlites] nf politeness

politicien, ne [pɔlitisjɛ̃, jɛn] (péj) nm/f politician

politique [pɔlitik] adj political ♦ nf politics sg; (mesures, méthode) policies pl

pollen [pɔlɛn] nm pollen

polluant, e [pɔlɥɑ̃, ɑ̃t] adj polluting; **produit ~** pollutant

polluer [pɔlɥe] vt to pollute; **pollution** nf pollution

polo [pɔlo] nm (chemise) polo shirt

Pologne [pɔlɔɲ] nf: **la ~** Poland; **polonais, e** adj Polish ♦ nm/f: **Polonais, e** Pole ♦ nm (LING) Polish

poltron, ne [pɔltʀɔ̃, ɔn] adj cowardly

polycopier [pɔlikɔpje] vt to duplicate

Polynésie [pɔlinezi] nf: **la ~** Polynesia

polyvalent, e [pɔlivalɑ̃, ɑ̃t] adj (rôle) varied; (salle) multi-purpose

pommade [pɔmad] nf ointment, cream

pomme [pɔm] nf apple; **tomber dans les ~s** (fam) to pass out; ~ **d'Adam** Adam's apple; ~ **de pin** pine ou fir cone; ~ **de terre** potato

pommeau, x [pɔmo] nm (boule) knob; (de selle) pommel

pommette [pɔmɛt] nf cheekbone

pommier [pɔmje] nm apple tree

pompe [pɔ̃p] nf pump; (faste) pomp (and ceremony); ~ **à essence** petrol pump; ~**s funèbres** funeral parlour sg, undertaker's

sg; **pomper** vt to pump; (aspirer) to pump up; (absorber) to soak up

pompeux, -euse [pɔ̃pø, øz] adj pompous

pompier [pɔ̃pje] nm fireman

pompiste [pɔ̃pist] nm/f petrol (BRIT) ou gas (US) pump attendant

poncer [pɔ̃se] vt to sand (down)

ponctuation [pɔ̃ktɥasjɔ̃] nf punctuation

ponctuel, le [pɔ̃ktɥel] adj punctual

pondéré, e [pɔ̃deʀe] adj level-headed, composed

pondre [pɔ̃dʀ] vt to lay

poney [pɔnɛ] nm pony

pont [pɔ̃] nm bridge; (NAVIG) deck; **faire le ~** to take the extra day off; ~ **suspendu** suspension bridge; **pont-levis** nm drawbridge

---

faire le pont

ⓘ *The expression "faire le pont" refers to the practice of taking a Monday or Friday off to make a long weekend if a public holiday falls on a Tuesday or Thursday. The French often do this at l'Ascension, l'Assomption and le 14 juillet.*

---

pop [pɔp] adj inv pop

populace [pɔpylas] (péj) nf rabble

populaire [pɔpylɛʀ] adj popular; (manifestation) mass cpd; (milieux, quartier) working-class; (expression) vernacular

popularité [pɔpylaʀite] nf popularity

population [pɔpylasjɔ̃] nf population; ~ **active** working population

populeux, -euse [pɔpylø, øz] adj densely populated

porc [pɔʀ] nm pig; (CULIN) pork

porcelaine [pɔʀsəlɛn] nf porcelain, china; piece of china(ware)

porc-épic [pɔʀkepik] nm porcupine

porche [pɔʀʃ] nm porch

porcherie [pɔʀʃəʀi] nf pigsty

pore [pɔʀ] nm pore

porno [pɔʀno] adj porno ♦ nm porn

port [pɔʀ] *nm* harbour, port; (*ville*) port; (*de l'uniforme etc*) wearing; (*pour lettre*) postage; (*pour colis, aussi: posture*) carriage; **~ de pêche/de plaisance** fishing/ sailing harbour

portable [pɔʀtabl] *nm* (COMPUT) laptop (computer); (*téléphone*) mobile

portail [pɔʀtaj] *nm* gate

portant, e [pɔʀtɑ̃, ɑ̃t] *adj*: **bien/mal ~** in good/poor health

portatif, -ive [pɔʀtatif, iv] *adj* portable

porte [pɔʀt] *nf* door; (*de ville, jardin*) gate; **mettre à la ~** to throw out; **~ à ~** ♦ *nm* door-to-door selling; **~ d'entrée** front door; **porte-avions** *nm inv* aircraft carrier; **porte-bagages** *nm inv* luggage rack; **porte-bonheur** *nm inv* lucky charm; **porte-clefs** *nm inv* key ring; **porte-documents** *nm inv* attaché *ou* document case

porté, e [pɔʀte] *adj*: **être ~ à faire** to be inclined to do; **être ~ sur qch** to be keen on sth; **portée** *nf* (*d'une arme*) range; (*fig: effet*) impact, import; (*: capacité*) scope, capability; (*de chatte etc*) litter; (MUS) stave, staff; **à/hors de portée (de)** within/out of reach (of); **à portée de (la) main** within (arm's) reach; **à la portée de qn** (*fig*) at sb's level, within sb's capabilities

porte...: **porte-fenêtre** *nf* French window; **portefeuille** *nm* wallet; **portemanteau, x** *nm* (*cintre*) coat hanger; (*au mur*) coat rack; **porte-monnaie** *nm inv* purse; **porte-parole** *nm inv* spokesman

porter [pɔʀte] *vt* to carry; (*sur soi: vêtement, barbe, bague*) to wear; (*fig: responsabilité etc*) to bear, carry; (*inscription, nom, fruits*) to bear; (*coup*) to deal; (*attention*) to turn; (*apporter*): **~ qch à qn** to take sth to sb ♦ *vi* (*voix*) to carry; (*coup, argument*) to hit home; **se ~** *vi* (*se sentir*): **se ~ bien/mal** to be well/unwell; **se ~** (*recherches*) to be concerned with; **se faire ~ malade** to report sick

porteur [pɔʀtœʀ, øz] *nm* (*de bagages*) por-

ter; (*de chèque*) bearer

porte-voix [pɔʀtəvwa] *nm inv* megaphone

portier [pɔʀtje] *nm* doorman

portière [pɔʀtjɛʀ] *nf* door

portillon [pɔʀtijɔ̃] *nm* gate

portion [pɔʀsjɔ̃] *nf* (*part*) portion, share; (*partie*) portion, section

porto [pɔʀto] *nm* port (wine)

portrait [pɔʀtʀɛ] *nm* (*peinture*) portrait; (*photo*) photograph; **portrait-robot** *nm* Identikit ® *ou* photo-fit ® picture

portuaire [pɔʀtɥɛʀ] *adj* port *cpd*, harbour *cpd*

portugais, e [pɔʀtygɛ, ɛz] *adj* Portuguese ♦ *nm/f*: **P~, e** Portuguese ♦ *nm* (LING) Portuguese

Portugal [pɔʀtygal] *nm*: **le ~** Portugal

pose [poz] *nf* (*de moquette*) laying; (*attitude, d'un modèle*) pose; (PHOTO) exposure

posé, e [poze] *adj* serious

poser [poze] *vt* to put; (*installer: moquette, carrelage*) to lay; (*rideaux, papier peint*) to hang; (*question*) to ask; (*principe, conditions*) to lay *ou* set down; (*problème*) to formulate; (*difficulté*) to pose ♦ *vi* (*modèle*) to pose; **se ~** *vi* (*oiseau, avion*) to land; (*question*) to arise; **~ qch (sur)** (*déposer*) to put sth down (on); **~ qch sur/quelque part** (*placer*) to put sth on/somewhere; **~ sa candidature à un poste** to apply for a post

positif, -ive [pozitif, iv] *adj* positive

position [pozisjɔ̃] *nf* position; **prendre ~** (*fig*) to take a stand

posologie [pozɔlɔʒi] *nf* dosage

posséder [posede] *vt* to own, possess; (*qualité, talent*) to have, possess; (*sexuellement*) to possess; **possession** *nf* ownership *no pl*, possession

possibilité [posibilite] *nf* possibility; **~s** *nfpl* (*potentiel*) potential *sg*

possible [posibl] *adj* possible; (*projet, entreprise*) feasible ♦ *nm*: **faire son ~** to do all one can, do one's utmost; **le plus/ moins de livres ~** as many/few books as possible; **le plus vite ~** as quickly as possible; **dès que ~** as soon as possible

postal, e, -aux [pɔstal, o] *adj* postal

poste [pɔst] *nf* (*service*) post, postal service; (*administration, bureau*) post office ♦ *nm* (*fonction, MIL*) post; (*TÉL*) extension; (*de radio etc*) set; **mettre à la ~** to post; **~ (de police)** nm police station; **~ de secours** nm first-aid post; **~ restante** nf poste restante (*BRIT*), general delivery (*US*)

poster¹ [pɔste] *vt* to post

poster² [pɔstɛʀ] *nm* poster

postérieur, e [pɔsteʀjœʀ] *adj* (*date*) later; (*partie*) back ♦ *nm* (*fam*) behind

posthume [pɔstym] *adj* posthumous

postulant, e [pɔstylɑ̃, ɑ̃t] *nm/f* applicant

postuler [pɔstyle] *vi*: **~ à** *ou* **pour un emploi** to apply for a job

posture [pɔstyʀ] *nf* position

pot [po] *nm* (*en verre*) jar; (*en terre*) pot; (*en plastique, carton*) carton; (*en métal*) tin; (*fam: chance*) luck; **avoir du ~** (*fam*) to be lucky; **boire** *ou* **prendre un ~** (*fam*) to have a drink; **petit ~ (pour bébé)** (jar of) baby food; **~ catalytique** catalytic converter; **~ d'échappement** exhaust pipe; **~ de fleurs** plant pot, flowerpot; (*plante*) pot plant

potable [pɔtabl] *adj*: **eau (non) ~** (non-) drinking water

potage [pɔtaʒ] *nm* soup; **potager, -ère** *adj*: **(jardin) potager** kitchen *ou* vegetable garden

pot-au-feu [pɔtofø] *nm inv* (beef) stew

pot-de-vin [pɔdvɛ̃] *nm* bribe

pote [pɔt] (*fam*) *nm* pal

poteau, x [pɔto] *nm* post; **~ indicateur** signpost

potelé, e [pɔt(ə)le] *adj* plump, chubby

potence [pɔtɑ̃s] *nf* gallows *sg*

potentiel, le [pɔtɑ̃sjɛl] *adj, nm* potential

poterie [pɔtʀi] *nf* pottery; (*objet*) piece of pottery

potier [pɔtje, jɛʀ] *nm* potter

potins [pɔtɛ̃] (*fam*) *nmpl* gossip *sg*

potiron [pɔtiʀɔ̃] *nm* pumpkin

pou, x [pu] *nm* louse

poubelle [pubɛl] *nf* (dust)bin

pouce [pus] *nm* thumb

poudre [pudʀ] *nf* powder; (*fard*) (face) powder; (*explosif*) gunpowder; **en ~: café en ~** instant coffee; **lait en ~** dried *ou* powdered milk; **poudreuse** nf powder snow; **poudrier** nm (powder) compact

pouffer [pufe] *vi*: **~ (de rire)** to burst out laughing

poulailler [pulaje] *nm* henhouse

poulain [pulɛ̃] *nm* foal; (*fig*) protégé

poule [pul] *nf* hen; (*CULIN*) (boiling) fowl

poulet [pulɛ] *nm* chicken; (*fam*) cop

poulie [puli] *nf* pulley

pouls [pu] *nm* pulse; **prendre le ~ de qn** to feel sb's pulse

poumon [pumɔ̃] *nm* lung

poupe [pup] *nf* stern; **en ~** astern

poupée [pupe] *nf* doll

pouponnière [puponjɛʀ] *nf* crèche, day nursery

pour [puʀ] *prép* for ♦ *nm*: **le ~ et le contre** the pros and cons; **~ faire** (so as) to do, in order to do; **~ avoir fait** for having done; **~ que** so that, in order that; **~ 100 francs d'essence** 100 francs' worth of petrol; **~ cent** per cent; **~ ce qui est de** as for

pourboire [puʀbwaʀ] *nm* tip

pourcentage [puʀsɑ̃taʒ] *nm* percentage

pourchasser [puʀʃase] *vt* to pursue

pourparlers [puʀpaʀle] *nmpl* talks, negotiations

pourpre [puʀpʀ] *adj* crimson

pourquoi [puʀkwa] *adv, conj* why ♦ *nm inv*: **le ~ (de)** the reason (for)

pourrai *etc* [puʀe] *vb voir* **pouvoir**

pourri, e [puʀi] *adj* rotten

pourrir [puʀiʀ] *vi* to rot; (*fruit*) to go rotten *ou* bad ♦ *vt* to rot; (*fig*) to spoil thoroughly; **pourriture** nf rot

pourrons *etc* [puʀɔ̃] *vb voir* **pouvoir**

poursuite [puʀsɥit] *nf* pursuit, chase; **~s** *nfpl* (*JUR*) legal proceedings

poursuivre [puʀsɥivʀ] *vt* to pursue, chase (after); (*obséder*) to haunt; (*JUR*) to bring proceedings against, prosecute; (: *au civil*) to sue; (*but*) to strive towards; (*continuer: études etc*) to carry on with, continue; **se ~** *vi* to go on, continue

pourtant [puʀtɑ̃] *adv* yet; **c'est ~ facile** (and) yet it's easy

pourtour [puʀtuʀ] *nm* perimeter

pourvoir [puʀvwaʀ] *vt*: **~ qch/qn de** to equip sth/sb with ♦ *vi*: **~ à** to provide for; **pourvoyeur** *nm* supplier; **pourvu, e** *adj*: **pourvu de** equipped with; **pourvu que** (*si*) provided that, so long as; (*espérons que*) let's hope (that)

pousse [pus] *nf* growth; (*bourgeon*) shoot

poussé, e [puse] *adj* (*enquête*) exhaustive; (*études*) advanced; **poussée** *nf* thrust; (*d'acné*) eruption; (*fig: prix*) upsurge

pousser [puse] *vt* to push; (*émettre: cri, soupir*) to give; (*stimuler: élève*) to urge on; (*poursuivre: études, discussion*) to carry on (further) ♦ *vi* to push; (*croître*) to grow; **se ~** *vi* to move over; **~ qn à** (*inciter*) to urge ou press sb to; (*acculer*) to drive sb to; **faire ~** (*plante*) to grow

poussette [puset] *nf* push chair (*BRIT*), stroller (*US*)

poussière [pusjɛʀ] *nf* dust; **poussiéreux, -euse** *adj* dusty

poussin [pusɛ̃] *nm* chick

poutre [putʀ] *nf* beam

MOT-CLÉ

pouvoir [puvwaʀ] *nm* power; (*POL: dirigeants*): **le pouvoir** those in power; **les pouvoirs publics** the authorities; **pouvoir d'achat** purchasing power

♦ *vb semi-aux* 1 (*être en état de*) can, be able to; **je ne peux pas le réparer** I can't ou I am not able to repair it; **déçu de ne pas pouvoir le faire** disappointed not to be able to do it

2 (*avoir la permission*) can, may, be allowed to; **vous pouvez aller au cinéma** you can ou may go to the pictures

3 (*probabilité, hypothèse*) may, might, could; **il a pu avoir un accident** he may ou might ou could have had an accident; **il aurait pu le dire!** he might ou could have said (so)!

♦ *vb impers* may, might, could; **il peut arriver que** it may ou might ou could happen that

♦ *vt* can, be able to; **j'ai fait tout ce que j'ai pu** I did all I could; **je n'en peux plus** (*épuisé*) I'm exhausted; (*à bout*) I can't take any more; **se pouvoir** *vi*: **il se peut que** it may ou might be that; **cela se pourrait** that's quite possible

prairie [pʀeʀi] *nf* meadow

praline [pʀalin] *nf* sugared almond

praticable [pʀatikabl] *adj* passable, practicable

pratiquant, e [pʀatikɑ̃, ɑ̃t] *nm/f* (regular) churchgoer

pratique [pʀatik] *nf* practice ♦ *adj* practical; **pratiquement** *adv* (*pour ainsi dire*) practically, virtually; **pratiquer** *vt* to practise; (*l'équitation, la pêche*) to go in for; (*le golf, football*) to play; (*intervention, opération*) to carry out

pré [pʀe] *nm* meadow

préalable [pʀealabl] *adj* preliminary; **au ~** beforehand

préambule [pʀeɑ̃byl] *nm* preamble; (*fig*) prelude; **sans ~** straight away

préau [pʀeo] *nm* (*SCOL*) covered playground

préavis [pʀeavi] *nm* notice

précaution [pʀekosjɔ̃] *nf* precaution; **avec ~** cautiously; **par ~** as a precaution

précédemment [pʀesedamɑ̃] *adv* before, previously

précédent, e [pʀesedɑ̃, ɑ̃t] *adj* previous ♦ *nm* precedent

précéder [pʀesede] *vt* to precede

précepteur, -trice [pʀeseptœʀ, tʀis] *nm/f* (private) tutor

prêcher [pʀeʃe] *vt* to preach

précieux, -euse [pʀesjø, jøz] *adj* precious; (*aide, conseil*) invaluable

précipice [pʀesipis] *nm* drop, chasm

précipitamment [pʀesipitamɑ̃] *adv* hurriedly, hastily

précipitation [pʀesipitasjɔ̃] *nf* (*hâte*) haste; **~s** *nfpl* (*pluie*) rain *sg*

précipité, e [pʀesipite] *adj* hurried, hasty

précipiter [pʀesipite] *vt* (*hâter: départ*) to hasten; (*faire tomber*): **~ qn/qch du haut de** to throw *ou* hurl sb/sth off *ou* from; **se ~** *vi* to speed up; **se ~ sur/vers** to rush at/towards

précis, e [pʀesi, iz] *adj* precise; (*mesures*) accurate, precise; **à 4 heures ~es** at 4 o'clock sharp; **précisément** *adv* precisely; **préciser** *vt* (*expliquer*) to be more specific about, clarify; (*spécifier*) to state, specify; **se préciser** *vi* to become clear(er); **précision** *nf* precision; (*détail*) point *ou* detail; **demander des précisions** to ask for further explanation

précoce [pʀekɔs] *adj* early; (*enfant*) precocious

préconçu, e [pʀekɔ̃sy] *adj* preconceived

préconiser [pʀekɔnize] *vt* to advocate

prédécesseur [pʀedesesœʀ] *nm* predecessor

prédilection [pʀedileksjɔ̃] *nf:* **avoir une ~ pour** to be partial to

prédire [pʀediʀ] *vt* to predict

prédominer [pʀedɔmine] *vi* to predominate

préface [pʀefas] *nf* preface

préfecture [pʀefektyʀ] *nf* prefecture; **~ de police** police headquarters pl

préférable [pʀefeʀabl] *adj* preferable

préféré, e [pʀefeʀe] *adj, nm/f* favourite

préférence [pʀefeʀɑ̃s] *nf* preference; **de ~** preferably

préférer [pʀefeʀe] *vt:* **~ qn/qch (à)** to prefer sb/sth (to), like sb/sth better (than); **~ faire** to prefer to do; **je ~ais du thé** I would rather have tea, I'd prefer tea

préfet [pʀefɛ] *nm* prefect

préhistorique [pʀeistɔʀik] *adj* prehistoric

préjudice [pʀeʒydis] *nm* (*matériel*) loss; (*moral*) harm *no pl*; **porter ~ à** to harm, be detrimental to; **au ~ de** at the expense of

préjugé [pʀeʒyʒe] *nm* prejudice; **avoir un ~ contre** to be prejudiced *ou* biased against

préjuger [pʀeʒyʒe]: **~ de** *vt* to prejudge

prélasser [pʀelɑse]: **se ~** *vi* to lounge

prélèvement [pʀelɛvmɑ̃] *nm* (*montant*) deduction; **faire un ~ de sang** to take a blood sample

prélever [pʀel(ə)ve] *vt* (*échantillon*) to take; **~ (sur)** (*montant*) to deduct (from); (*argent: sur son compte*) to withdraw (from)

prématuré, e [pʀematyʀe] *adj* premature ♦ *nm* premature baby

premier, -ière [pʀəmje, jɛʀ] *adj* first; (*rang*) front; (*fig: objectif*) basic; **le ~ venu** the first person to come along; **de ~ ordre** first-rate; **P~ Ministre** Prime Minister; **première** *nf* (*SCOL*) lower sixth form; (*THÉÂTRE*) first night; (*AUTO*) first (gear); (*AVIAT, RAIL etc*) first class; (*CINÉMA*) première; (*exploit*) first; **premièrement** *adv* firstly

prémonition [pʀemɔnisjɔ̃] *nf* premonition

prémunir [pʀemyniʀ]: **se ~** *vi:* **se ~ contre** to guard against

prenant, e [pʀənɑ̃, ɑ̃t] *adj* absorbing, engrossing

prénatal, e [pʀenatal] *adj* (*MÉD*) antenatal

prendre [pʀɑ̃dʀ] *vt* to take; (*repas*) to have; (*se procurer*) to get; (*malfaiteur, poisson*) to catch; (*passager*) to pick up; (*personnel*) to take on; (*traiter: personne*) to handle; (*voix, ton*) to put on; (*ôter*): **~ qch à** to take sth from; (*coincer*): **se ~ les doigts dans** to get one's fingers caught in ♦ *vi* (*liquide, ciment*) to set; (*greffe, vaccin*) to take; (*feu: foyer*) to go; (*se diriger*): **~ à gauche** to turn (to the) left; **~ froid** to catch cold; **se ~ pour** to think one is; **s'en ~ à** to attack; **se ~ d'amitié pour** to befriend; **s'y ~** (*procéder*) to set about it

preneur [pʀənœʀ, øz] *nm:* **être/trouver ~** to be willing to buy/find a buyer

preniez [pʀənje] *vb voir* **prendre**

prenne *etc* [pʀɛn] *vb voir* **prendre**

prénom [pʀenɔ̃] _nm_ first _ou_ Christian name

préoccupation [pʀeɔkypasjɔ̃] _nf_ (_souci_) concern; (_idée fixe_) preoccupation

préoccuper [pʀeɔkype] _vt_ (_inquiéter_) to worry; (_absorber_) to preoccupy; **se ~ de** to be concerned with

préparatifs [pʀepaʀatif] _nmpl_ preparations

préparation [pʀepaʀasjɔ̃] _nf_ preparation

préparer [pʀepaʀe] _vt_ to prepare; (_café, thé_) to make; (_examen_) to prepare for; (_voyage, entreprise_) to plan; **se ~** _vi_ (_orage, tragédie_) to brew, be in the air; **~ qch à qn** (_surprise etc_) to have sth in store for sb; **se ~ (à qch/faire)** to prepare (o.s.) _ou_ get ready (for sth/to do)

prépondérant, e [pʀepɔ̃deʀɑ̃, ɑ̃t] _adj_ major, dominating

préposé, e [pʀepoze] _nm/f_ employee; (_facteur_) postman

préposition [pʀepozisjɔ̃] _nf_ preposition

près [pʀɛ] _adv_ near, close; **~ de** near (to), close to; (_environ_) nearly, almost; **de ~** closely; **à 5 kg ~** to within about 5 kg; **à cela ~ que** apart from the fact that; **il n'est pas à 10 minutes ~** he can spare 10 minutes

présage [pʀezaʒ] _nm_ omen; **présager** _vt_ to foresee

presbyte [pʀɛsbit] _adj_ long-sighted

presbytère [pʀɛsbitɛʀ] _nm_ presbytery

prescription [pʀɛskʀipsjɔ̃] _nf_ prescription

prescrire [pʀɛskʀiʀ] _vt_ to prescribe

présence [pʀezɑ̃s] _nf_ presence; (_au bureau, à l'école_) attendance

présent, e [pʀezɑ̃, ɑ̃t] _adj, nm_ present; **à ~ (que)** now (that)

présentation [pʀezɑ̃tasjɔ̃] _nf_ presentation; (_de nouveau venu_) introduction; (_allure_) appearance; **faire les ~s** to do the introductions

présenter [pʀezɑ̃te] _vt_ to present; (_excuses, condoléances_) to offer; (_invité, conférencier_): **~ qn (à)** to introduce sb (to) ♦ _vi_: **~ bien** to have a pleasing appearance; **se**

~ _vi_ (_occasion_) to arise; **se ~ à** (_examen_) to sit; (_élection_) to stand at, run for

préservatif [pʀezɛʀvatif, iv] _nm_ sheath, condom

préserver [pʀezɛʀve] _vt_: **~ de** (_protéger_) to protect from

président [pʀezidɑ̃] _nm_ (_POL_) president; (_d'une assemblée, COMM_) chairman; **~ directeur général** chairman and managing director; **présidentielles** _nfpl_ presidential elections

présider [pʀezide] _vt_ to preside over; (_dîner_) to be the guest of honour at

présomptueux, -euse [pʀezɔ̃ptɥø, øz] _adj_ presumptuous

presque [pʀɛsk] _adv_ almost, nearly; **~ personne** hardly anyone; **~ rien** hardly anything; **~ pas** hardly (at all); **~ pas (de)** hardly any

presqu'île [pʀɛskil] _nf_ peninsula

pressant, e [pʀesɑ̃, ɑ̃t] _adj_ urgent

presse [pʀɛs] _nf_ press; (_affluence_): **heures de ~** busy times

pressé, e [pʀese] _adj_ in a hurry; (_travail_) urgent; **orange ~e** freshly-squeezed orange juice

pressentiment [pʀesɑ̃timɑ̃] _nm_ foreboding, premonition

pressentir [pʀesɑ̃tiʀ] _vt_ to sense

presse-papiers [pʀɛspapje] _nm inv_ paperweight

presser [pʀese] _vt_ (_fruit, éponge_) to squeeze; (_bouton_) to press; (_allure_) to speed up; (_inciter_): **~ qn de faire** to urge _ou_ press sb to do ♦ _vi_ to be urgent; **se ~** _vi_ (_se hâter_) to hurry (up); **se ~ contre qn** to squeeze up against sb; **rien ne presse** there's no hurry

pressing [pʀesiŋ] _nm_ (_magasin_) drycleaner's

pression [pʀesjɔ̃] _nf_ pressure; (_bouton_) press stud; (_fam: bière_) draught beer; **faire ~ sur** to put pressure on; **~ artérielle** blood pressure

prestance [pʀɛstɑ̃s] _nf_ presence, imposing bearing

prestataire [pʀɛstatɛʀ] *nm/f* supplier

prestation [pʀɛstasjɔ̃] *nf* (*allocation*) benefit; (*d'une entreprise*) service provided; (*d'un artiste*) performance

prestidigitateur, -trice [pʀɛstidiʒitatœʀ, tʀis] *nm/f* conjurer

prestige [pʀɛstiʒ] *nm* prestige; **prestigieux, -euse** *adj* prestigious

présumer [pʀezyme] *vt*: **~ que** to presume *ou* assume that

prêt, e [pʀɛ, pʀɛt] *adj* ready ♦ *nm* (*somme*) loan; **prêt-à-porter** *nm* ready-to-wear *ou* off-the-peg (*BRIT*) clothes *pl*

prétendre [pʀetɑ̃dʀ] *vt* (*affirmer*): **~ que** to claim that; (*avoir l'intention de*): **~ faire qch** to mean *ou* intend to do sth; **prétendu, e** *adj* (*supposé*) so-called

prétentieux, -euse [pʀetɑ̃sjø, jøz] *adj* pretentious

prétention [pʀetɑ̃sjɔ̃] *nf* claim; (*vanité*) pretentiousness; **~s** *nfpl* (*salaire*) expected salary

prêter [pʀete] *vt* (*livres, argent*): **~ qch (à)** to lend sth (to); (*supposer*): **~ à qn** (*caractère, propos*) to attribute to sb; **se ~ à** to lend o.s. (*ou* itself) to; (*manigances etc*) to go along with; **~ à** (*critique, commentaires etc*) to be open to, give rise to; **~ attention à** to pay attention to; **~ serment** to take the oath

prétexte [pʀetɛkst] *nm* pretext, excuse; **sous aucun ~** on no account; **prétexter** *vt* to give as a pretext *ou* an excuse

prêtre [pʀɛtʀ] *nm* priest

preuve [pʀœv] *nf* proof; (*indice*) proof, evidence *no pl*; **faire ~ de** to show; **faire ses ~s** to prove o.s. (*ou* itself)

prévaloir [pʀevalwaʀ] *vi* to prevail

prévenant, e [pʀev(ə)nɑ̃, ɑ̃t] *adj* thoughtful, kind

prévenir [pʀev(ə)niʀ] *vt* (*éviter: catastrophe etc*) to avoid, prevent; (*anticiper: désirs, besoins*) to anticipate; **~ qn (de)** (*avertir*) to warn sb (about); (*informer*) to tell *ou* inform sb (about)

préventif, -ive [pʀevɑ̃tif, iv] *adj* preven-

tive

prévention [pʀevɑ̃sjɔ̃] *nf* prevention; **~ routière** road safety

prévenu, e [pʀev(ə)ny] *nm/f* (*JUR*) defendant, accused

prévision [pʀevizjɔ̃] *nf*: **~s** predictions; (*ÉCON*) forecast *sg*; **en ~ de** in anticipation of; **~s météorologiques** weather forecast *sg*

prévoir [pʀevwaʀ] *vt* (*anticiper*) to foresee; (*s'attendre à*) to expect, reckon on; (*organiser: voyage etc*) to plan; (*envisager*) to allow; **comme prévu** as planned; **prévoyant, e** *adj* (*showing*) foresight; **prévu, e** *pp de* **prévoir**

prier [pʀije] *vi* to pray ♦ *vt* (*Dieu*) to pray to; (*implorer*) to beg; (*demander*): **~ qn de faire** to ask sb to do; **se faire ~** to need coaxing *ou* persuading; **je vous en prie** (*allez-y*) please do; (*de rien*) don't mention it; **prière** *nf* prayer; **"prière de ..."** "please ..."

primaire [pʀimɛʀ] *adj* primary ♦ *nm* (*SCOL*) primary education

prime [pʀim] *nf* (*bonus*) bonus; (*subvention*) premium; (*COMM: cadeau*) free gift; (*ASSURANCES, BOURSE*) premium ♦ *adj*: **de ~ abord** at first glance; **primer** *vt* (*récompenser*) to award a prize to ♦ *vi* to dominate; to be most important

primeurs [pʀimœʀ] *nfpl* early fruits and vegetables

primevère [pʀimvɛʀ] *nf* primrose

primitif, -ive [pʀimitif, iv] *adj* primitive; (*originel*) original

primordial, e, -iaux [pʀimɔʀdjal, jo] *adj* essential

prince [pʀɛ̃s] *nm* prince; **princesse** *nf* princess

principal, e, -aux [pʀɛ̃sipal, o] *adj* principal, main ♦ *nm* (*SCOL*) principal, head(master); (*essentiel*) main thing

principe [pʀɛ̃sip] *nm* principle; **par ~** on principle; **en ~** (*habituellement*) as a rule; (*théoriquement*) in principle

printemps [pʀɛ̃tɑ̃] *nm* spring

priorité [prijɔrite] *nf* priority; (*AUTO*) right of way; **~ à droite** right of way to vehicles coming from the right

pris, e [pri, priz] *pp de* **prendre** ♦ *adj* (*place*) taken; (*mains*) full; (*personne*) busy; **avoir le nez/la gorge ~(e)** to have a stuffy nose/a hoarse throat; **être ~ de panique** to be panic-stricken

prise [priz] *nf* (*d'une ville*) capture; (*PÊCHE, CHASSE*) catch; (*point d'appui ou pour empoigner*) hold; (*ÉLEC: fiche*) plug; (: *femelle*) socket; **être aux ~s avec** to be grappling with; **~ de conscience** awareness, realization; **~ de contact** (*rencontre*) initial meeting, first contact; **~ de courant** power point; **~ de sang** blood test; **~ de vue** (*photo*) shot; **~ multiple** adaptor

priser [prize] *vt* (*estimer*) to prize, value

prison [prizɔ̃] *nf* prison; **aller/être en ~** to go to/be in prison *ou* jail; **prisonnier, -ière** *nm/f* prisoner ♦ *adj* captive

prit [pri] *vb voir* **prendre**

privé, e [prive] *adj* private ♦ *nm* (*COMM*) private sector; **en ~** in private

priver [prive] *vt*: **~ qn de** to deprive sb of; **se ~ de** to go *ou* do without

privilège [privilɛʒ] *nm* privilege

prix [pri] *nm* price; (*récompense, SCOL*) prize; **hors de ~** exorbitantly priced; **à aucun ~** not at any price; **à tout ~** at all costs; **~ d'achat/de vente/de revient** purchasing/selling/cost price

probable [prɔbabl] *adj* likely, probable; **probablement** *adv* probably

probant, e [prɔbɑ̃, ɑ̃t] *adj* convincing

problème [prɔblɛm] *nm* problem

procédé [prɔsede] *nm* (*méthode*) process; (*comportement*) behaviour *no pl*

procéder [prɔsede] *vi* to proceed; (*moralement*) to behave; **~ à** to carry out

procès [prɔsɛ] *nm* trial; (*poursuites*) proceedings *pl*; **être en ~ avec** to be involved in a lawsuit with

processus [prɔsesys] *nm* process

procès-verbal, -aux [prɔsɛverbal, o] *nm* (*de réunion*) minutes *pl*; (*aussi:* **P.V.**) parking ticket

prochain, e [prɔʃɛ̃, ɛn] *adj* next; (*proche: départ, arrivée*) impending ♦ *nm* fellow man; **la ~e fois/semaine ~e** next time/week; **prochainement** *adv* soon, shortly

proche [prɔʃ] *adj* nearby; (*dans le temps*) imminent; (*parent, ami*) close; **~s** *nmpl* (*parents*) close relatives; **être ~ (de)** to be near, be close (to); **le P~ Orient** the Middle East

proclamer [prɔklame] *vt* to proclaim

procuration [prɔkyrasjɔ̃] *nf* proxy

procurer [prɔkyre] *vt*: **~ qch à qn** (*fournir*) to obtain sth for sb; (*causer: plaisir etc*) to bring sb sth; **se ~** *vt* to get; **procureur** *nm* public prosecutor

prodige [prɔdiʒ] *nm* marvel, wonder; (*personne*) prodigy; **prodiguer** *vt* (*soins, attentions*): **prodiguer qch à qn** to give sb sth

producteur, -trice [prɔdyktœr, tris] *nm/f* producer

productif, -ive [prɔdyktif, iv] *adj* productive

production [prɔdyksjɔ̃] *nf* production; (*rendement*) output

productivité [prɔdyktivite] *nf* productivity

produire [prɔdɥir] *vt* to produce; **se ~** *vi* (*événement*) to happen, occur; (*acteur*) to perform, appear

produit [prɔdɥi] *nm* product; **~ chimique** chemical; **~ d'entretien** cleaning product; **~ national brut** gross national product; **~s alimentaires** foodstuffs

prof [prɔf] (*fam*) *nm* teacher

profane [prɔfan] *adj* (*REL*) secular ♦ *nm/f* layman(-woman)

proférer [prɔfere] *vt* to utter

professeur [prɔfesœr] *nm* teacher; (*de faculté*) (university) lecturer; (: *titulaire d'une chaire*) professor

profession [prɔfesjɔ̃] *nf* occupation; **~ libérale** (liberal) profession; **sans ~** unemployed; **professionnel, le** *adj, nm/f* professional

profil [prɔfil] *nm* profile; **de ~** in profile

profit [pʀɔfi] *nm* (*avantage*) benefit, advantage; (*COMM, FINANCE*) profit; **au ~ de** in aid of; **tirer ~ de** to profit from; **profitable** *adj* (*utile*) beneficial; (*lucratif*) profitable; **profiter** *vi*: **profiter de** (*situation, occasion*) to take advantage of; (*vacances, jeunesse etc*) to make the most of

profond, e [pʀɔfɔ̃, ɔ̃d] *adj* deep; (*sentiment, intérêt*) profound; **profondément** *adv* deeply; **il dort profondément** he is sound asleep; **profondeur** *nf* depth

progéniture [pʀɔʒenityʀ] *nf* offspring *inv*

programme [pʀɔgʀam] *nm* programme; (*SCOL*) syllabus, curriculum; (*INFORM*) program; **programmer** *vt* (*émission*) to schedule; (*INFORM*) to program; **programmeur, -euse** *nm/f* programmer

progrès [pʀɔgʀɛ] *nm* progress *no pl*; **faire des ~** to make progress; **progresser** *vi* to progress; **progressif, -ive** *adj* progressive

prohiber [pʀɔibe] *vt* to prohibit, ban

proie [pʀwa] *nf* prey *no pl*

projecteur [pʀɔʒɛktœʀ] *nm* (*pour film*) projector; (*de théâtre, cirque*) spotlight

projectile [pʀɔʒɛktil] *nm* missile

projection [pʀɔʒɛksjɔ̃] *nf* projection; (*séance*) showing

projet [pʀɔʒɛ] *nm* plan; (*ébauche*) draft; **~ de loi** bill; **projeter** *vt* (*envisager*) to plan; (*film, photos*) to project; (*ombre, lueur*) to throw, cast; (*jeter*) to throw up (*ou* off *ou* out)

prolétaire [pʀɔletɛʀ] *adj, nmf* proletarian

prolongement [pʀɔlɔ̃ʒmɑ̃] *nm* extension; **dans le ~ de** running on from

prolonger [pʀɔlɔ̃ʒe] *vt* (*débat, séjour*) to prolong; (*délai, billet, rue*) to extend; **se ~** *vi* to go on

promenade [pʀɔm(ə)nad] *nf* walk (*ou* drive *ou* ride); **faire une ~** to go for a walk; **une ~ en voiture/à vélo** a drive/ (bicycle) ride

promener [pʀɔm(ə)ne] *vt* (*chien*) to take out for a walk; (*doigts, regard*): **~ qch sur** to run sth over; **se ~** *vi* to go for (*ou* be

out for) a walk

promesse [pʀɔmɛs] *nf* promise

promettre [pʀɔmɛtʀ] *vt* to promise ♦ *vi* to be *ou* look promising; **~ à qn de faire** to promise sb that one will do

promiscuité [pʀɔmiskɥite] *nf* (*chambre*) lack of privacy

promontoire [pʀɔmɔ̃twaʀ] *nm* headland

promoteur, -trice [pʀɔmɔtœʀ, tʀis] *nm/f*: **~ (immobilier)** property developer (*BRIT*), real estate promoter (*US*)

promotion [pʀɔmosjɔ̃] *nf* promotion; **en ~** on special offer

promouvoir [pʀɔmuvwaʀ] *vt* to promote

prompt, e [pʀɔ̃(pt), pʀɔ̃(p)t] *adj* swift, rapid

prôner [pʀone] *vt* (*préconiser*) to advocate

pronom [pʀɔnɔ̃] *nm* pronoun

prononcer [pʀɔnɔ̃se] *vt* to pronounce; (*dire*) to utter; (*discours*) to deliver; **se ~** *vi* to be pronounced; **se ~ (sur)** (*se décider*) to reach a decision (on *ou* about), give a verdict (on); **prononciation** *nf* pronunciation

pronostic [pʀɔnɔstik] *nm* (*MÉD*) prognosis; (*fig: aussi:* **~s**) forecast

propagande [pʀɔpagɑ̃d] *nf* propaganda

propager [pʀɔpaʒe] *vt* to spread; **se ~** *vi* to spread

prophète [pʀɔfɛt] *nm* prophet

prophétie [pʀɔfesi] *nf* prophecy

propice [pʀɔpis] *adj* favourable

proportion [pʀɔpɔʀsjɔ̃] *nf* proportion; **toute(s) ~(s) gardée(s)** making due allowance(s)

propos [pʀɔpo] *nm* (*intention*) intention, aim; (*sujet*): **à quel ~?** what about? ♦ *nmpl* (*paroles*) talk *no pl*, remarks; **à ~ de** about, regarding; **à tout ~** for the slightest thing *ou* reason; **à ~** by the way; (*opportunément*) at the right moment

proposer [pʀɔpoze] *vt* to propose; **~ qch (à qn)** (*suggérer*) to suggest sth (to sb), propose sth (to sb); (*offrir*) to offer (sb) sth; **se ~** to offer one's services; **se ~ de faire** to intend *ou* propose to do; **propo-**

sition (*suggestion*) *nf* proposal, suggestion; (*LING*) clause

propre [pʀɔpʀ] *adj* clean; (*net*) neat, tidy; (*possessif*) own; (*sens*) literal; (*particulier*): ~ **à** peculiar to; (*approprié*): ~ **à** suitable for ♦ *nm*: **recopier au ~** to make a fair copy of; **proprement** *adv* (*avec propreté*) cleanly; **le village proprement dit** the village itself; **à proprement parler** strictly speaking; **propreté** *nf* cleanliness

propriétaire [pʀɔpʀijetɛʀ] *nm/f* owner; (*pour le locataire*) landlord(-lady)

propriété [pʀɔpʀijete] *nf* property; (*droit*) ownership

propulser [pʀɔpylse] *vt* to propel

proroger [pʀɔʀɔʒe] *vt* (*prolonger*) to extend

proscrire [pʀɔskʀiʀ] *vt* (*interdire*) to ban, prohibit

prose [pʀoz] *nf* (*style*) prose

prospecter [pʀɔspɛkte] *vt* to prospect; (*COMM*) to canvass

prospectus [pʀɔspɛktys] *nm* leaflet

prospère [pʀɔspɛʀ] *adj* prosperous; **prospérer** *vi* to prosper

prosterner [pʀɔstɛʀne]: **se ~** *vi* to bow low, prostrate o.s.

prostituée [pʀɔstitɥe] *nf* prostitute

prostitution [pʀɔstitysjɔ̃] *nf* prostitution

protecteur, -trice [pʀɔtɛktœʀ, tʀis] *adj* protective; (*air, ton*: *péj*) patronizing ♦ *nm/f* protector

protection [pʀɔtɛksjɔ̃] *nf* protection; (*d'un personnage influent*: *aide*) patronage

protéger [pʀɔteʒe] *vt* to protect; **se ~ de** *ou* **contre** to protect o.s. from

protéine [pʀɔtein] *nf* protein

protestant, e [pʀɔtɛstɑ̃, ɑ̃t] *adj, nm/f* Protestant

protestation [pʀɔtɛstasjɔ̃] *nf* (*plainte*) protest

protester [pʀɔtɛste] *vi*: ~ **(contre)** to protest (against *ou* about); ~ **de** (*son innocence*) to protest

prothèse [pʀɔtɛz] *nf*: ~ **dentaire** denture

protocole [pʀɔtɔkɔl] *nm* (*fig*) etiquette

proue [pʀu] *nf* bow(s *pl*), prow

prouesse [pʀues] *nf* feat

prouver [pʀuve] *vt* to prove

provenance [pʀɔv(ə)nɑ̃s] *nf* origin; **avion en ~ de** plane (arriving) from

provenir [pʀɔv(ə)niʀ]: ~ **de** *vt* to come from

proverbe [pʀɔvɛʀb] *nm* proverb

province [pʀɔvɛ̃s] *nf* province

proviseur [pʀɔvizœʀ] *nm* ≈ head(teacher) (*BRIT*), ≈ principal (*US*)

provision [pʀɔvizjɔ̃] *nf* (*réserve*) stock, supply; **~s** *nfpl* (*vivres*) provisions, food *no pl*

provisoire [pʀɔvizwaʀ] *adj* temporary; **provisoirement** *adv* temporarily

provocant, e [pʀɔvɔkɑ̃, ɑ̃t] *adj* provocative

provoquer [pʀɔvɔke] *vt* (*défier*) to provoke; (*causer*) to cause, bring about; (*inciter*): ~ **qn à** to incite sb to

proxénète [pʀɔksenɛt] *nm* procurer

proximité [pʀɔksimite] *nf* nearness, closeness; (*dans le temps*) imminence, closeness; **à ~** near *ou* close by; **à ~ de** near (to), close to

prudemment [pʀydamɑ̃] *adv* carefully, wisely, sensibly

prudence [pʀydɑ̃s] *nf* carefulness; **avec ~** carefully; **par ~** as a precaution

prudent, e [pʀydɑ̃, ɑ̃t] *adj* (*pas téméraire*) careful; (: *en général*) safety-conscious; (*sage, conseillé*) wise, sensible; **c'est plus ~** it's wiser

prune [pʀyn] *nf* plum

pruneau, x [pʀyno] *nm* prune

prunelle [pʀynɛl] *nf* (*BOT*) sloe; **il y tient comme à la ~ de ses yeux** he treasures *ou* cherishes it

prunier [pʀynje] *nm* plum tree

PS *sigle m* = **parti socialiste**

psaume [psom] *nm* psalm

pseudonyme [psødɔnim] *nm* (*gén*) fictitious name; (*d'écrivain*) pseudonym, pen name

psychanalyse [psikanaliz] *nf* psychoanalysis

psychiatre [psikjatʀ] nm/f psychiatrist; **psychiatrique** adj psychiatric

psychique [psiʃik] adj psychological

psychologie [psikɔlɔʒi] nf psychology; **psychologique** adj psychological; **psychologue** nm/f psychologist

P.T.T. sigle fpl = **Postes, Télécommunications et Télédiffusion**

pu [py] pp de **pouvoir**

puanteur [pɥɑ̃tœʀ] nf stink, stench

pub [pyb] nf (fam: annonce) ad, advert; (pratique) advertising

public, -ique [pyblik] adj public; (école, instruction) state cpd ♦ nm public; (assistance) audience; **en ~** in public

publicitaire [pyblisitɛʀ] adj advertising cpd; (film) publicity cpd

publicité [pyblisite] nf (méthode, profession) advertising; (annonce) advertisement; (révélations) publicity

publier [pyblije] vt to publish

publique [pyblik] adj voir **public**

puce [pys] nf flea; (INFORM) chip; **carte à ~** smart card; **~s** nfpl (marché) flea market sg

pudeur [pydœʀ] nf modesty

pudique [pydik] adj (chaste) modest; (discret) discreet

puer [pɥe] (péj) vi to stink

puéricultrice [pɥeʀikyltʀis] nf p(a)ediatric nurse

puéril, e [pɥeʀil] adj childish

puis [pɥi] vb voir **pouvoir** ♦ adv then

puiser [pɥize] vt: ~ **(dans)** to draw (from)

puisque [pɥisk] conj since

puissance [pɥisɑ̃s] nf power; **en ~** ♦ adj potential

puissant, e [pɥisɑ̃, ɑ̃t] adj powerful

puisse etc [pɥis] vb voir **pouvoir**

puits [pɥi] nm well

pull(-over) [pyl(ɔvɛʀ)] nm sweater

pulluler [pylyle] vi to swarm

pulpe [pylp] nf pulp

pulvérisateur [pylveʀizatœʀ] nm spray

pulvériser [pylveʀize] vt to pulverize; (liquide) to spray

punaise [pynɛz] nf (ZOOL) bug; (clou) drawing pin (BRIT), thumbtack (US)

punch¹ [pɔ̃ʃ] nm (boisson) punch

punch² [pœnʃ] nm (BOXE, fig) punch

punir [pyniʀ] vt to punish; **punition** nf punishment

pupille [pypij] nf (ANAT) pupil ♦ nm/f (enfant) ward

pupitre [pypitʀ] nm (SCOL) desk

pur, e [pyʀ] adj pure; (vin) undiluted; (whisky) neat; **en ~e perte** to no avail; **c'est de la folie ~e** it's sheer madness; **purement** adv purely

purée [pyʀe] nf: ~ **(de pommes de terre)** mashed potatoes pl; ~ **de marrons** chestnut purée

purgatoire [pyʀgatwaʀ] nm purgatory

purger [pyʀʒe] vt (MÉD, POL) to purge; (JUR: peine) to serve

purin [pyʀɛ̃] nm liquid manure

pur-sang [pyʀsɑ̃] nm inv thoroughbred

pus [py] nm pus

putain [pytɛ̃] nf (fam!) whore (!)

puzzle [pœzl] nm jigsaw (puzzle)

P.-V. sigle m = **procès-verbal**

pyjama [piʒama] nm pyjamas pl (BRIT), pajamas pl (US)

pyramide [piʀamid] nf pyramid

Pyrénées [piʀene] nfpl: **les ~** the Pyrenees

Q, q

QI sigle m (= quotient intellectuel) IQ

quadragénaire [k(w)adʀaʒenɛʀ] nm/f man/woman in his/her forties

quadriller [kadʀije] vt (POLICE) to keep under tight control

quadruple [k(w)adʀypl] nm: **le ~ de** four times as much as; **quadruplés, -ées** nm/fpl quadruplets, quads

quai [ke] nm (de port) quay; (de gare) platform; **être à ~** (navire) to be alongside

qualification [kalifikasjɔ̃] nf (aptitude)

qualification

qualifié, e [kalifje] *adj* qualified; (*main d'œuvre*) skilled

qualifier [kalifje] *vt* to qualify; **se ~** *vi* to qualify; **~ qch/qn de** to describe sth/sb as

qualité [kalite] *nf* quality

quand [kɑ̃] *conj, adv* when; **~ je serai riche** when I'm rich; **~ même** all the same; **~ même, il exagère!** really, he overdoes it!; **~ bien même** even though

quant [kɑ̃]: **~ à** *prép* (*pour ce qui est de*) as for, as to; (*au sujet de*) regarding; **quant-à-soi** *nm*: **rester sur son quant-à-soi** to remain aloof

quantité [kɑ̃tite] *nf* quantity, amount; (*grand nombre*): **une** *ou* **des ~(s) de** a great deal of

quarantaine [karɑ̃tɛn] *nf* (*MÉD*) quarantine; **avoir la ~** (*âge*) to be around forty; **une ~ (de)** forty or so, about forty

quarante [karɑ̃t] *num* forty

quart [kaʀ] *nm* (*fraction*) quarter; (*surveillance*) watch; **un ~ de vin** a quarter litre of wine; **le ~ de** a quarter of; **~ d'heure** quarter of an hour; **~s de finale** quarter finals

quartier [kaʀtje] *nm* (*de ville*) district, area; (*de bœuf*) quarter; (*de fruit*) piece; **cinéma de ~** local cinema; **avoir ~ libre** (*fig*) to be free; **~ général** headquarters *pl*

quartz [kwaʀts] *nm* quartz

quasi [kazi] *adv* almost, nearly; **quasiment** *adv* almost, nearly; **quasiment jamais** hardly ever

quatorze [katɔʀz] *num* fourteen

quatre [katʀ] *num* four; **à ~ pattes** on all fours; **se mettre en ~ pour qn** to go out of one's way for sb; **~ à ~** (*monter, descendre*) four at a time; **quatre-quarts** *nm inv* pound cake; **quatre-vingt-dix** *num* ninety; **quatre-vingts** *num* eighty; **quatre-vingt-un** *num* eighty-one; **quatrième** *num* fourth ♦ *nf* (*SCOL*) third form *ou* year

quatuor [kwatɥɔʀ] *nm* quartet(te)

MOT-CLÉ

que [kə] *conj* **1** (*introduisant complétive*) that; **il sait que tu es là** he knows (that) you're here; **je veux que tu acceptes** I want you to accept; **il a dit que oui** he said he would (*ou* it was *etc*)

2 (*reprise d'autres conjonctions*): **quand il rentrera et qu'il aura mangé** when he gets back and (when) he has eaten; **si vous y allez ou que vous ...** if you go there or if you ...

3 (*en tête de phrase: hypothèse, souhait etc*): **qu'il la veuille ou non** whether he likes it or not; **qu'il fasse ce qu'il voudra** let him do as he pleases!

4 (*après comparatif*) than, as; *voir aussi* **plus**; **aussi**; **autant** *etc*

5 (*seulement*): **ne ... que** only; **il ne boit que de l'eau** he only drinks water

♦ *adv* (*exclamation*): **qu'il** *ou* **qu'est-ce qu'il est bête/court vite!** he's so silly!/he runs so fast!; **que de livres!** what a lot of books!

♦ *pron* **1** (*relatif: personne*) whom; (: *chose*) that, which; **l'homme que je vois** the man (whom) I see; **le livre que tu vois** the book (that *ou* which) you see; **un jour que j'étais ...** a day when I was ...

2 (*interrogatif*) what; **que fais-tu?**, **qu'est-ce que tu fais?** what are you doing?; **qu'est-ce que c'est?** what is it?, what's that?; **que faire?** what can one do?

Québec [kebɛk] *n*: **le ~** Quebec; **québecois, e** *adj* Quebec ♦ *nm/f*: **Québecois, e** Quebecker ♦ *nm* (*LING*) Quebec French

MOT-CLÉ

quel, quelle [kɛl] *adj* **1** (*interrogatif: personne*) who; (: *chose*) what; which; **quel est cet homme?** who is this man?; **quel est ce livre?** what is this book?; **quel livre/homme?** what book/man?; (*parmi un certain choix*) which book/man?; **quels**

acteurs préférez-vous? which actors do you prefer?; **dans quels pays êtes-vous allé?** which *ou* what countries did you go to?

2 (*exclamatif*): **quelle surprise!** what a surprise!

3: **quel que soit le coupable** whoever is guilty; **quel que soit votre avis** whatever your opinion

quelconque [kɛlkɔ̃k] *adj* (*indéfini*): **un ami/prétexte ~** some friend/pretext or other; (*médiocre: repas*) indifferent, poor; (*laid: personne*) plain-looking

---
MOT-CLÉ
---

quelque [kɛlk] *adj* 1 some; a few; (*tournure interrogative*) any; **quelque espoir** some hope; **il a quelques amis** he has a few *ou* some friends; **a-t-il quelques amis?** has he any *ou* some friends?; **les quelques livres qui** the few books which; **20 kg et quelque(s)** a bit over 20 kg

2: **quelque ... que: quelque livre qu'il choisisse** whatever (*ou* whichever) book he chooses

3: **quelque chose** something; (*tournure interrogative*) anything; **quelque chose d'autre** something else; anything else; **quelque part** somewhere; anywhere; **en quelque sorte** as it were

♦ *adv* 1 (*environ*): **quelque 100 mètres** some 100 metres

2: **quelque peu** rather, somewhat

---

quelquefois [kɛlkəfwa] *adv* sometimes

quelques-uns, -unes [kɛlkəzœ̃, yn] *pron* a few, some

quelqu'un [kɛlkœ̃] *pron* someone, somebody; (*+tournure interrogative*) anyone, anybody; **~ d'autre** someone *ou* somebody else; (*+ tournure interrogative*) anybody else

quémander [kemɑ̃de] *vt* to beg for

qu'en dira-t-on [kɑ̃diratɔ̃] *nm inv*: **le ~ ~-~-~** gossip, what people say

querelle [kəʀɛl] *nf* quarrel; **quereller: se quereller** *vi* to quarrel

qu'est-ce que [kɛskə] *voir* **que**

qu'est-ce qui [kɛski] *voir* **qui**

question [kɛstjɔ̃] *nf* question; (*fig*) matter, issue; **il a été ~ de** we (*ou* they) spoke about; **de quoi est-il ~?** what is it about?; **il n'en est pas ~** there's no question of it; **hors de ~** out of the question; **remettre en ~** to question; **questionnaire** *nm* questionnaire; **questionner** *vt* to question

quête [kɛt] *nf* collection; (*recherche*) quest, search; **faire la ~** (*à l'église*) to take the collection; (*artiste*) to pass the hat round

quetsche [kwɛtʃ] *nf* kind of dark-red plum

queue [kø] *nf* tail; (*fig: du classement*) bottom; (: *de poêle*) handle; (: *de fruit, feuille*) stalk; (: *de train, colonne, file*) rear; **faire la ~** to queue (up) (*BRIT*), line up (*US*); **~ de cheval** ponytail; **~ de poisson** (*AUT*): **faire une ~ de poisson à qn** to cut in front of sb

qui [ki] *pron* (*personne*) who; (+*prép*) whom; (*chose, animal*) which, that; **qu'est-ce ~ est sur la table?** what's on the table?; **~ est-ce ~?** who?; **~ est-ce que?** who?; **à ~ est ce sac?** whose bag is this?; **à ~ parlais-tu?** who were you talking to?, to whom were you talking?; **amenez ~ vous voulez** bring who you like; **~ que ce soit** whoever it may be

quiconque [kikɔ̃k] *pron* (*celui qui*) whoever, anyone who; (*n'importe qui*) anyone, anybody

quiétude [kjetyd] *nf*: **en toute ~** in complete peace

quille [kij] *nf*: **(jeu de) ~s** skittles *sg* (*BRIT*), bowling (*US*)

quincaillerie [kɛ̃kajri] *nf* (*ustensiles*) hardware; (*magasin*) hardware shop; **quincaillier, -ière** *nm/f* hardware dealer

quinquagénaire [kɛ̃kazenɛr] *nm/f* man/woman in his/her fifties

quintal, -aux [kɛ̃tal, o] *nm* quintal (*100 kg*)

quinte [kɛ̃t] *nf*: ~ **(de toux)** coughing fit

quintuple [kɛ̃typl] *nm*: **le ~ de** five times as much as; **quintuplés, -ées** *nm/fpl* quintuplets, quins

quinzaine [kɛ̃zɛn] *nf*: **une ~ (de)** about fifteen, fifteen or so; **une ~ (de jours)** a fortnight (*BRIT*), two weeks

quinze [kɛ̃z] *num* fifteen; **dans ~ jours** in a fortnight('s time), in two weeks(' time)

quiproquo [kiprɔko] *nm* misunderstanding

quittance [kitɑ̃s] *nf* (*reçu*) receipt

quitte [kit] *adj*: **être ~ envers qn** to be no longer in sb's debt; (*fig*) to be quits with sb; **~ à faire** even if it means doing

quitter [kite] *vt* to leave; (*vêtement*) to take off; **se ~** *vi* (*couples, interlocuteurs*) to part; **ne quittez pas** (*au téléphone*) hold the line

qui-vive [kiviv] *nm*: **être sur le ~-~** to be on the alert

quoi [kwa] *pron* (*interrogatif*) what; **~ de neuf?** what's the news?; **as-tu de ~ écrire?** have you anything to write with?; **~ qu'il arrive** whatever happens; **~ qu'il en soit** be that as it may; **~ que ce soit** anything at all; **"il n'y a pas de ~"** "(please) don't mention it"; **il n'y a pas de ~ rire** there's nothing to laugh about; **à ~ bon?** what's the use?; **en ~ puis-je vous aider?** how can I help you?

quoique [kwak] *conj* (al)though

quote-part [kɔtpar] *nf* share

quotidien, ne [kɔtidjɛ̃, jɛn] *adj* daily; (*banal*) everyday ♦ *nm* (*journal*) daily (paper); **quotidiennement** *adv* daily

R, r

r. *abr* = **route**; **rue**

rab [Rab] (*fam*) *nm* (*nourriture*) extra; **est-ce qu'il y a du ~?** is there any extra (left)?

rabâcher [Rabaʃe] *vt* to keep on repeating

rabais [Rabɛ] *nm* reduction, discount; **rabaisser** *vt* (*dénigrer*) to belittle; (*rabattre:*

prix) to reduce

rabat-joie [Rabaʒwa] *nm inv* killjoy

rabattre [RabatR] *vt* (*couvercle, siège*) to pull down; (*déduire*) to reduce; **se ~** *vi* (*se refermer: couvercle*) to fall shut; (*véhicule, coureur*) to cut in; **se ~ sur** to fall back on

rabbin [Rabɛ̃] *nm* rabbi

râblé, e [Rable] *adj* stocky

rabot [Rabo] *nm* plane

rabougri, e [Rabugri] *adj* stunted

rabrouer [RabRue] *vt* to snub

racaille [Rakaj] (*péj*) *nf* rabble, riffraff

raccommoder [Rakɔmɔde] *vt* to mend, repair; **se ~** *vi* (*fam*) to make it up

raccompagner [Rakɔ̃paɲe] *vt* to take *ou* see back

raccord [RakɔR] *nm* link; (*retouche*) touch up; **raccorder** *vt* to join (up), link up; (*suj: pont etc*) to connect, link

raccourci [Rakursi] *nm* short cut

raccourcir [Rakursir] *vt* to shorten ♦ *vi* (*jours*) to grow shorter, draw in

raccrocher [RakRɔʃe] *vt* (*tableau*) to hang back up; (*récepteur*) to put down ♦ *vi* (*TÉL*) to hang up, ring off; **se ~ à** *vt* to cling to, hang on to

race [Ras] *nf* race; (*d'animaux, fig*) breed; **de ~** purebred, pedigree

rachat [Raʃa] *nm* buying; (*du même objet*) buying back

racheter [Raʃ(ə)te] *vt* (*article perdu*) to buy another; (*après avoir vendu*) to buy back; (*d'occasion*) to buy; (*COMM: part, firme*) to buy up; (*davantage*): **~ du lait/3 œufs** to buy more milk/another 3 eggs *ou* 3 more eggs; **se ~** *vi* (*fig*) to make amends

racial, e, -aux [Rasjal, jo] *adj* racial

racine [Rasin] *nf* root; **~ carrée/cubique** square/cube root

raciste [Rasist] *adj, nm/f* raci(al)ist

racket [Raket] *nm* racketeering *no pl*

raclée [Rakle] (*fam*) *nf* hiding, thrashing

racler [Rakle] *vt* (*surface*) to scrape; **se ~ la gorge** to clear one's throat

racoler [Rakɔle] *vt* (*suj: prostituée*) to solicit;

(: *parti, marchand*) to tout for

racontars [ʀakɔ̃taʀ] *nmpl* story, lie

raconter [ʀakɔ̃te] *vt*: ~ **(à qn)** (*décrire*) to relate (to sb), tell (sb) about; (*dire de mauvaise foi*) to tell (sb); ~ **une histoire** to tell a story

racorni, e [ʀakɔʀni] *adj* hard(ened)

radar [ʀadaʀ] *nm* radar

rade [ʀad] *nf* (natural) harbour; **rester en ~** (*fig*) to be left stranded

radeau, x [ʀado] *nm* raft

radiateur [ʀadjatœʀ] *nm* radiator, heater; (*AUTO*) radiator; ~ **électrique/à gaz** electric/gas heater *ou* fire

radiation [ʀadjasjɔ̃] *nf* (*PHYSIQUE*) radiation

radical, e, -aux [ʀadikal, o] *adj* radical

radier [ʀadje] *vt* to strike off

radieux, -euse [ʀadjø, jøz] *adj* radiant

radin, e [ʀadɛ̃, in] (*fam*) *adj* stingy

radio [ʀadjo] *nf* radio; (*MÉD*) X-ray ♦ *nm* radio operator; **à la ~** on the radio; **radioactif, -ive** *adj* radioactive; **radiocassette** *nm* cassette radio, radio cassette player; **radiodiffuser** *vt* to broadcast; **radiographie** *nf* radiography; (*photo*) X-ray photograph; **radiophonique** *adj* radio *cpd*; **radio-réveil** (*pl* **radios-réveils**) *nm* radio alarm clock

radis [ʀadi] *nm* radish

radoter [ʀadɔte] *vi* to ramble on

radoucir [ʀadusiʀ]: **se ~** *vi* (*temps*) to become milder; (*se calmer*) to calm down

rafale [ʀafal] *nf* (*vent*) gust (of wind); (*tir*) burst of gunfire

raffermir [ʀafɛʀmiʀ] *vt* to firm up; **se ~** *vi* (*fig: autorité, prix*) to strengthen

raffiner [ʀafine] *vt* to refine; **raffinerie** *nf* refinery

raffoler [ʀafɔle]: ~ **de** *vt* to be very keen on

rafistoler [ʀafistɔle] (*fam*) *vt* to patch up

rafle [ʀɑfl] *nf* (*de police*) raid; **rafler** (*fam*) *vt* to swipe, nick

rafraîchir [ʀafʀeʃiʀ] *vt* (*atmosphère, température*) to cool (down); (*aussi:* **mettre à ~**) to chill; (*fig: rénover*) to brighten up; **se**

~ *vi* (*temps*) to grow cooler; (*en se lavant*) to freshen up; (*en buvant*) to refresh o.s.; **rafraîchissant, e** *adj* refreshing; **rafraîchissement** *nm* (*boisson*) cool drink; **rafraîchissements** *nmpl* (*boissons, fruits etc*) refreshments

rage [ʀaʒ] *nf* (*MÉD*): **la ~** rabies; (*fureur*) rage, fury; **faire ~** to rage; ~ **de dents** (raging) toothache

ragot [ʀago] (*fam*) *nm* malicious gossip *no pl*

ragoût [ʀagu] *nm* stew

raide [ʀɛd] *adj* stiff; (*câble*) taut, tight; (*escarpé*) steep; (*droit: cheveux*) straight; (*fam: sans argent*) flat broke; (*osé*) daring, bold ♦ *adv* (*en pente*) steeply; ~ **mort** stone dead; **raidir** *vt* (*muscles*) to stiffen; **se raidir** *vi* (*tissu*) to stiffen; (*personne*) to tense up; (: *se préparer moralement*) to brace o.s.; (*fig: position*) to harden; **raideur** *nf* (*rigidité*) stiffness; **avec raideur** (*répondre*) stiffly, abruptly

raie [ʀɛ] *nf* (*ZOOL*) skate, ray; (*rayure*) stripe; (*des cheveux*) parting

raifort [ʀefɔʀ] *nm* horseradish

rail [ʀɑj] *nm* rail; (*chemins de fer*) railways *pl*; **par ~** by rail

railler [ʀɑje] *vt* to scoff at, jeer at

rainure [ʀenyʀ] *nf* groove

raisin [ʀezɛ̃] *nm* (*aussi:* ~**s**) grapes *pl*; ~**s secs** raisins

raison [ʀezɔ̃] *nf* reason; **avoir ~** to be right; **donner ~ à qn** to agree with sb; (*événement*) to prove sb right; **perdre la ~** to become insane; ~ **de plus** all the more reason; **à plus forte ~** all the more so; **en ~ de** because of; **à ~ de** at the rate of; **sans ~** for no reason; **raisonnable** *adj* reasonable, sensible

raisonnement [ʀezɔnmɑ̃] *nm* (*façon de réfléchir*) reasoning; (*argumentation*) argument

raisonner [ʀezɔne] *vi* (*penser*) to reason; (*argumenter, discuter*) to argue ♦ *vt* (*personne*) to reason with

rajeunir [ʀaʒœniʀ] *vt* (*suj: coiffure, robe*): ~

qn to make sb look younger; *(fig: personnel)* to inject new blood into ♦ *vi* to become *(ou* look) younger

rajouter [ʀaʒute] *vt* to add

rajuster [ʀaʒyste] *vt (vêtement)* to straighten, tidy; *(salaires)* to adjust

ralenti [ʀalɑ̃ti] *nm:* **au ~** *(fig)* at a slower pace; **tourner au ~** *(AUTO)* to tick over *(AUTO)*, idle

ralentir [ʀalɑ̃tiʀ] *vt* to slow down

râler [ʀale] *vi* to groan; *(fam)* to grouse, moan (and groan)

rallier [ʀalje] *vt (rejoindre)* to rejoin; *(gagner à sa cause)* to win over; **se ~ à** *(avis)* to come over *ou* round to

rallonge [ʀalɔ̃ʒ] *nf (de table)* (extra) leaf

rallonger [ʀalɔ̃ʒe] *vt* to lengthen

rallye [ʀali] *nm* rally; *(POL)* march

ramadan [ʀamadɑ̃] *nm* Ramadan

ramassage [ʀamasaʒ] *nm:* **~ scolaire** school bus service

ramassé, e [ʀamase] *adj (trapu)* squat

ramasser [ʀamase] *vt (objet tombé ou par terre, fam)* to pick up; *(recueillir: copies, ordures)* to collect; *(récolter)* to gather; **se ~** *vi (sur soi-même)* to huddle up; **ramassis** *(péj) nm (de voyous)* bunch; *(d'objets)* jumble

rambarde [ʀɑ̃baʀd] *nf* guardrail

rame [ʀam] *nf (aviron)* oar; *(de métro)* train; *(de papier)* ream

rameau, x [ʀamo] *nm* (small) branch; **les R~x** *(REL)* Palm Sunday *sg*

ramener [ʀam(ə)ne] *vt* to bring back; *(reconduire)* to take back; **~ qch à** *(réduire à)* to reduce sth to

ramer [ʀame] *vi* to row

ramollir [ʀamɔliʀ] *vt* to soften; **se ~** *vi* to go soft

ramoner [ʀamɔne] *vt* to sweep

rampe [ʀɑ̃p] *nf (d'escalier)* banister(s *pl*); *(dans un garage)* ramp; *(THÉÂTRE):* **la ~** the footlights *pl*

ramper [ʀɑ̃pe] *vi* to crawl

rancard [ʀɑ̃kaʀ] *(fam) nm (rendez-vous)* date

rancart [ʀɑ̃kaʀ] *nm:* **mettre au ~** *(fam)* to scrap

rance [ʀɑ̃s] *adj* rancid

rancœur [ʀɑ̃kœʀ] *nf* rancour

rançon [ʀɑ̃sɔ̃] *nf* ransom

rancune [ʀɑ̃kyn] *nf* grudge, rancour; **garder ~ à qn (de qch)** to bear sb a grudge (for sth); **sans ~!** no hard feelings!; **rancunier, -ière** *adj* vindictive, spiteful

randonnée [ʀɑ̃dɔne] *nf* ride; *(pédestre)* walk, ramble; *(: en montagne)* hike, hiking *no pl*

rang [ʀɑ̃] *nm (rangée)* row; *(grade, classement)* rank; **~s** *nmpl (MIL)* ranks; **se mettre en ~s** to get into *ou* form rows; **au premier ~** in the first row; *(fig)* ranking first

rangé, e [ʀɑ̃ʒe] *adj (vie)* well-ordered; *(personne)* steady

rangée [ʀɑ̃ʒe] *nf* row

ranger [ʀɑ̃ʒe] *vt (mettre de l'ordre dans)* to tidy up; *(classer, grouper)* to order, arrange; *(mettre à sa place)* to put away; *(fig: classer):* **~ qn/qch parmi** to rank sb/sth among; **se ~** *vi (véhicule, conducteur)* to pull over *ou* in; *(piéton)* to step aside; *(s'assagir)* to settle down; **se ~ à** *(avis)* to come round to

ranimer [ʀanime] *vt (personne)* to bring round; *(douleur, souvenir)* to revive; *(feu)* to rekindle

rap [ʀap] *nm* rap (music)

rapace [ʀapas] *nm* bird of prey

râpe [ʀɑp] *nf (CULIN)* grater; **râper** *vt (CULIN)* to grate

rapetisser [ʀap(ə)tise] *vt* to shorten

rapide [ʀapid] *adj* fast; *(prompt: coup d'œil, mouvement)* quick ♦ *nm* express (train); *(de cours d'eau)* rapid; **rapidement** *adv* fast; quickly

rapiécer [ʀapjese] *vt* to patch

rappel [ʀapel] *nm (THÉÂTRE)* curtain call; *(MÉD: vaccination)* booster; *(deuxième avis)* reminder; **rappeler** *vt* to call back; *(ambassadeur, MIL)* to recall; *(faire se souvenir):* **rappeler qch à qn** to remind sb of sth;

se rappeler vt (*se souvenir de*) to remember, recall

rapport [Rapɔʀ] nm (*lien, analogie*) connection; (*compte rendu*) report; (*profit*) yield, return; **~s** nmpl (*entre personnes, pays*) relations; **avoir ~ à** to have something to do with; **être/se mettre en ~ avec qn** to be/get in touch with sb; **par ~ à** in relation to; **~s (sexuels)** (sexual) intercourse *sg*

rapporter [Rapɔʀte] vt (*rendre, ramener*) to bring back; (*bénéfice*) to yield, bring in; (*mentionner, répéter*) to report ♦ vi (*investissement*) to give a good return *ou* yield; (: *activité*) to be very profitable; **se ~ à** vt (*correspondre à*) to relate to; **rapporteur, -euse** nm/f (*péj*) telltale ♦ nm (*GÉOM*) protractor

rapprochement [Rapʀɔʃmɑ̃] nm (*de nations*) reconciliation; (*rapport*) parallel

rapprocher [Rapʀɔʃe] vt (*deux objets*) to bring closer together; (*fig: ennemis, partis etc*) to bring together; (*comparer*) to establish a parallel between; (*chaise d'une table*): **~ qch (de)** to bring sth closer (to); **se ~** vi to draw closer *ou* nearer; **se ~ de** to come closer to; (*présenter une analogie avec*) to be close to

rapt [Rapt] nm abduction

raquette [Raket] nf (*de tennis*) racket; (*de ping-pong*) bat

rare [RɑR] adj rare; **se faire ~** to become scarce; **rarement** adv rarely, seldom

ras, e [Rɑ, Rɑz] adj (*poil, herbe*) short; (*tête*) close-cropped ♦ adv short; **en ~e campagne** in open country; **à ~ bords** to the brim; **en avoir ~ le bol** (*fam*) to be fed up; **~ du cou** ♦ adj (*pull, robe*) crew-neck

rasade [Rɑzad] nf glassful

raser [Rɑze] vt (*barbe, cheveux*) to shave off; (*menton, personne*) to shave; (*fam: ennuyer*) to bore; (*démolir*) to raze (to the ground); (*frôler*) to graze, skim; **se ~** vi to shave; (*fam*) to be bored (to tears); **rasoir** nm razor

rassasier [Rɑsazje] vt: **être rassasié** to have eaten one's fill

rassemblement [Rɑsɑ̃bləmɑ̃] nm (*groupe*) gathering; (*POL*) union

rassembler [Rɑsɑ̃ble] vt (*réunir*) to assemble, gather; (*documents, notes*) to gather together, collect; **se ~** vi to gather

rassis, e [Rasi, iz] adj (*pain*) stale

rassurer [RasyRe] vt to reassure; **se ~** vi to reassure o.s.; **rassure-toi** don't worry

rat [Ra] nm rat

rate [Rat] nf spleen

raté, e [Rate] adj (*tentative*) unsuccessful, failed ♦ nm/f (*fam: personne*) failure

râteau, x [Rɑto] nm rake

rater [Rate] vi (*affaire, projet etc*) to go wrong, fail ♦ vt (*fam: cible, train, occasion*) to miss; (*plat*) to spoil; (*fam: examen*) to fail

ration [Rasjɔ̃] nf ration

ratisser [Ratise] vt (*allée*) to rake; (*feuilles*) to rake up; (*suj: armée, police*) to comb

RATP sigle f (= *Régie autonome des transports parisiens*) *Paris transport authority*

rattacher [Rataʃe] vt (*animal, cheveux*) to tie up again; (*fig: relier*): **~ qch à** to link sth with

rattrapage [RatRapaʒ] nm: **cours de ~** remedial class

rattraper [RatRape] vt (*fugitif*) to recapture; (*empêcher de tomber*) to catch (hold of); (*atteindre, rejoindre*) to catch up with; (*réparer: erreur*) to make up for; **se ~** vi to make up for it; **se ~ (à)** (*se raccrocher*) to stop o.s. falling (by catching hold of)

rature [RatyR] nf deletion, erasure

rauque [Rok] adj (*voix*) hoarse

ravages [Ravaʒ] nmpl: **faire des ~** to wreak havoc

ravaler [Ravale] vt (*mur, façade*) to restore; (*déprécier*) to lower

ravi, e [Ravi] adj: **être ~ de/que** to be delighted with/that

ravigoter [Ravigɔte] (*fam*) vt to buck up

ravin [Ravɛ̃] nm gully, ravine

ravir [RaviR] vt (*enchanter*) to delight; **à ~** adv beautifully

raviser [ʀavize]: **se ~** *vi* to change one's mind

ravissant, e [ʀavisɑ̃, ɑ̃t] *adj* delightful

ravisseur, -euse [ʀavisœʀ, øz] *nm/f* abductor, kidnapper

ravitaillement [ʀavitajmɑ̃] *nm* (*réserves*) supplies *pl*

ravitailler [ʀavitaje] *vt* (*en vivres, ammunitions*) to provide with fresh supplies; (*avion*) to refuel; **se ~** *vi* to get fresh supplies; (*avion*) to refuel

raviver [ʀavive] *vt* (*feu, douleur*) to revive; (*couleurs*) to brighten up

rayé, e [ʀeje] *adj* (*à rayures*) striped

rayer [ʀeje] *vt* (*érafler*) to scratch; (*barrer*) to cross out; (*d'une liste*) to cross off

rayon [ʀejɔ̃] *nm* (*de soleil etc*) ray; (*GÉOM*) radius; (*de roue*) spoke; (*étagère*) shelf; (*de grand magasin*) department; **dans un ~ de** within a radius of; **~ de soleil** sunbeam; **~s X** X-rays

rayonnement [ʀejɔnmɑ̃] *nm* (*fig: d'une culture*) influence

rayonner [ʀejɔne] *vi* (*fig*) to shine forth; (*personne: de joie, de beauté*) to be radiant; (*touriste*) to go touring (*from one base*)

rayure [ʀejyʀ] *nf* (*motif*) stripe; (*éraflure*) scratch; **à ~s** striped

raz-de-marée [ʀɑdmaʀe] *nm inv* tidal wave

ré [ʀe] *nm* (*MUS*) D; (*en chantant la gamme*) re

réacteur [ʀeaktœʀ] *nm* (*d'avion*) jet engine; (*nucléaire*) reactor

réaction [ʀeaksjɔ̃] *nf* reaction

réadapter [ʀeadapte]: **se ~ (à)** *vi* to readjust (to)

réagir [ʀeaʒiʀ] *vi* to react

réalisateur, -trice [ʀealizatœʀ, tʀis] *nm/f* (*TV, CINÉMA*) director

réalisation [ʀealizasjɔ̃] *nf* realization; (*cinéma*) production; **en cours de ~** under way

réaliser [ʀealize] *vt* (*projet, opération*) to carry out, realize; (*rêve, souhait*) to realize, fulfil; (*exploit*) to achieve; (*film*) to produce; (*se rendre compte de*) to realize; **se ~** *vi* to be realized

réaliste [ʀealist] *adj* realistic

réalité [ʀealite] *nf* reality; **en ~** in (actual) fact; **dans la ~** in reality

réanimation [ʀeanimasjɔ̃] *nf* resuscitation; **service de ~** intensive care unit

rébarbatif, -ive [ʀebaʀbatif, iv] *adj* forbidding

rebattu, e [ʀ(ə)baty] *adj* hackneyed

rebelle [ʀəbɛl] *nm/f* rebel ♦ *adj* (*troupes*) rebel; (*enfant*) rebellious; (*mèche etc*) unruly

rebeller [ʀ(ə)bele]: **se ~** *vi* to rebel

rebondi, e [ʀ(ə)bɔ̃di] *adj* (*joues*) chubby

rebondir [ʀ(ə)bɔ̃diʀ] *vi* (*ballon: au sol*) to bounce; (: *contre un mur*) to rebound; (*fig*) to get moving again; **rebondissement** *nm* new development

rebord [ʀ(ə)bɔʀ] *nm* edge; **le ~ de la fenêtre** the windowsill

rebours [ʀ(ə)buʀ]: **à ~** *adv* the wrong way

rebrousser [ʀ(ə)bʀuse] *vt*: **~ chemin** to turn back

rebut [ʀəby] *nm*: **mettre au ~** to scrap; **rebutant, e** *adj* off-putting; **rebuter** *vt* to put off

récalcitrant, e [ʀekalsitʀɑ̃, ɑ̃t] *adj* refractory

recaler [ʀ(ə)kale] *vt* (*SCOL*) to fail; **se faire ~** to fail

récapituler [ʀekapityle] *vt* to recapitulate, sum up

receler [ʀ(ə)səle] *vt* (*produit d'un vol*) to receive; (*fig*) to conceal; **receleur, -euse** *nm/f* receiver

récemment [ʀesamɑ̃] *adv* recently

recensement [ʀ(ə)sɑ̃smɑ̃] *nm* (*population*) census

recenser [ʀ(ə)sɑ̃se] *vt* (*population*) to take a census of; (*inventorier*) to list

récent, e [ʀesɑ̃, ɑ̃t] *adj* recent

récépissé [ʀesepise] *nm* receipt

récepteur [ʀeseptœʀ, tʀis] *nm* receiver

réception [ʀesɛpsjɔ̃] *nf* receiving *no pl*;

(*accueil*) reception, welcome; (*bureau*) reception desk; (*réunion mondaine*) reception, party; **réceptionniste** *nm/f* receptionist

recette [R(ə)sɛt] *nf* recipe; (*COMM*) takings *pl*; **~s** *nfpl* (*COMM: rentrées*) receipts

receveur, -euse [R(ə)səvœR, øz] *nm/f* (*des contributions*) tax collector; (*des postes*) postmaster(-mistress)

recevoir [R(ə)səvwaR] *vt* to receive; (*client, patient*) to see; **être reçu** (*à un examen*) to pass

rechange [R(ə)ʃɑ̃ʒ]: **de ~** *adj* (*pièces, roue*) spare; (*fig: solution*) alternative; **des vêtements de ~** a change of clothes

réchapper [Reʃape]: **~ de** *ou* **à** *vt* (*accident, maladie*) to come through

recharge [R(ə)ʃaRʒ] *nf* refill; **rechargeable** *adj* (*stylo etc*) refillable; **recharger** *vt* (*stylo*) to refill; (*batterie*) to recharge

réchaud [Reʃo] *nm* (portable) stove

réchauffer [Reʃofe] *vt* (*plat*) to reheat; (*mains, personne*) to warm; **se ~** *vi* (*température*) to get warmer; (*personne*) to warm o.s. (up)

rêche [Rɛʃ] *adj* rough

recherche [R(ə)ʃɛRʃ] *nf* (*action*) search; (*raffinement*) studied elegance; (*scientifique etc*): **la ~** research; **~s** *nfpl* (*de la police*) investigations; (*scientifiques*) research.*sg*; **la ~ de** the search for; **être à la ~ de qch** to be looking for sth

recherché, e [R(ə)ʃɛRʃe] *adj* (*rare, demandé*) much sought-after; (*raffiné: style*) mannered; (*: tenue*) elegant

rechercher [R(ə)ʃɛRʃe] *vt* (*objet égaré, personne*) to look for; (*causes, nouveau procédé*) to try to find; (*bonheur, compliments*) to seek

rechigner [R(ə)ʃiɲe] *vi*: **~ à faire qch** to balk *ou* jib at doing sth

rechute [R(ə)ʃyt] *nf* (*MÉD*) relapse

récidiver [Residive] *vi* to commit a subsequent offence; (*fig*) to do it again

récif [Resif] *nm* reef

récipient [Resipjɑ̃] *nm* container

réciproque [ResipRɔk] *adj* reciprocal

récit [Resi] *nm* story; **récital** *nm* recital; **réciter** *vt* to recite

réclamation [Reklamasjɔ̃] *nf* complaint; **~s** *nfpl* (*bureau*) complaints department *sg*

réclame [Reklam] *nf* ad, advert(isement); **en ~** on special offer; **réclamer** *vt* to ask for; (*revendiquer*) to claim, demand ♦ *vi* to complain

réclusion [Reklyzjɔ̃] *nf* imprisonment

recoin [Rəkwɛ̃] *nm* nook, corner

reçois *etc* [Rəswa] *vb voir* **recevoir**

récolte [Rekɔlt] *nf* harvesting, gathering; (*produits*) harvest, crop; **récolter** *vt* to harvest, gather (in); (*fig*) to collect

recommandé [R(ə)kɔmɑ̃de] *nm* (*POSTES*): **en ~** by registered mail

recommander [R(ə)kɔmɑ̃de] *vt* to recommend; (*POSTES*) to register

recommencer [R(ə)kɔmɑ̃se] *vt* (*reprendre: lutte, séance*) to resume, start again; (*refaire: travail, explications*) to start afresh, start (over) again ♦ *vi* to start again; (*récidiver*) to do it again

récompense [Rekɔ̃pɑ̃s] *nf* reward; (*prix*) award; **récompenser** *vt*: **récompenser qn (de** *ou* **pour)** to reward sb (for)

réconcilier [Rekɔ̃silje] *vt* to reconcile; **se ~ (avec)** to be reconciled (with)

reconduire [R(ə)kɔ̃dɥiR] *vt* (*raccompagner*) to take *ou* see back; (*renouveler*) to renew

réconfort [Rekɔ̃fɔR] *nm* comfort; **réconforter** *vt* (*consoler*) to comfort

reconnaissance [R(ə)kɔnɛsɑ̃s] *nf* (*gratitude*) gratitude, gratefulness; (*action de reconnaître*) recognition; (*MIL*) reconnaissance, recce; **reconnaissant, e** *adj* grateful

reconnaître [R(ə)kɔnɛtR] *vt* to recognize; (*MIL: lieu*) to reconnoitre; (*JUR: enfant, torts*) to acknowledge; **~ que** to admit *ou* acknowledge that; **reconnu, e** *adj* (*indiscuté, connu*) recognized

reconstituant, e [R(ə)kɔ̃stitɥɑ̃, ɑ̃t] *adj* (*aliment, régime*) strength-building

reconstituer [ʀ(ə)kɔ̃stitɥe] *vt* (*événement, accident*) to reconstruct; (*fresque, vase brisé*) to piece together, reconstitute

reconstruction [ʀ(ə)kɔ̃stʀyksjɔ̃] *nf* rebuilding

reconstruire [ʀ(ə)kɔ̃stʀɥiʀ] *vt* to rebuild

reconvertir [ʀ(ə)kɔ̃vɛʀtiʀ]: **se ~ dans** *vr* (*un métier, une branche*) to go into

record [ʀ(ə)kɔʀ] *nm, adj* record

recoupement [ʀ(ə)kupmɑ̃] *nm*: **par ~** by cross-checking

recouper [ʀ(ə)kupe]: **se ~** *vi* (*témoignages*) to tie *ou* match up

recourber [ʀ(ə)kuʀbe]: **se ~** *vi* to curve (up), bend (up)

recourir [ʀ(ə)kuʀiʀ]: **~ à** *vt* (*ami, agence*) to turn *ou* appeal to; (*force, ruse, emprunt*) to resort to

recours [ʀ(ə)kuʀ] *nm*: **avoir ~ à = recourir à; en dernier ~** as a last resort

recouvrer [ʀ(ə)kuvʀe] *vt* (*vue, santé etc*) to recover, regain

recouvrir [ʀ(ə)kuvʀiʀ] *vt* (*couvrir à nouveau*) to re-cover; (*couvrir entièrement, aussi fig*) to cover

récréation [ʀekʀeasjɔ̃] *nf* (SCOL) break

récrier [ʀekʀije]: **se ~** *vi* to exclaim

récriminations [ʀekʀiminasjɔ̃] *nfpl* remonstrations, complaints

recroqueviller [ʀ(ə)kʀɔk(ə)vije]: **se ~** *vi* (*personne*) to huddle up

recrudescence [ʀ(ə)kʀydesɑ̃s] *nf* fresh outbreak

recrue [ʀəkʀy] *nf* recruit

recruter [ʀ(ə)kʀyte] *vt* to recruit

rectangle [ʀɛktɑ̃gl] *nm* rectangle; **rectangulaire** *adj* rectangular

rectificatif, iv [ʀɛktifikatif, iv] *nm* correction

rectifier [ʀɛktifje] *vt* (*calcul, adresse, paroles*) to correct; (*erreur*) to rectify

rectiligne [ʀɛktiliɲ] *adj* straight

recto [ʀɛkto] *nm* front (of a page); **~ verso** on both sides (of the page)

reçu, e [ʀ(ə)sy] *pp de* **recevoir** ♦ *adj* (*candidat*) successful; (*admis, consacré*) accepted ♦ *nm* (COMM) receipt

recueil [ʀəkœj] *nm* collection; **recueillir** *vt* to collect; (*voix, suffrages*) to win; (*accueillir: réfugiés, chat*) to take in; **se recueillir** *vi* to gather one's thoughts, meditate

recul [ʀ(ə)kyl] *nm* (*éloignement*) distance; (*déclin*) decline; **être en ~** to be on the decline; **avec du ~** with hindsight; **avoir un mouvement de ~** to recoil; **prendre du ~** to stand back; **reculé, e** *adj* remote; **reculer** *vi* to move back, back away; (AUTO) to reverse, back (up); (*fig*) to (be on the) decline ♦ *vt* to move back; (*véhicule*) to reverse, back (up); (*date, décision*) to postpone; **reculons: à reculons** *adv* backwards

récupérer [ʀekypeʀe] *vt* to recover, get back; (*heures de travail*) to make up; (*déchets*) to salvage ♦ *vi* to recover

récurer [ʀekyʀe] *vt* to scour

récuser [ʀekyze] *vt* to challenge; **se ~** *vi* to decline to give an opinion

reçut [ʀəsy] *vb voir* **recevoir**

recycler [ʀ(ə)sikle] *vt* (TECH) to recycle; **se ~** *vi* to retrain

rédacteur, -trice [ʀedaktœʀ, tʀis] *nm/f* (*journaliste*) writer; subeditor; (*d'ouvrage de référence*) editor, compiler; **~ en chef** chief editor

rédaction [ʀedaksjɔ̃] *nf* writing; (*rédacteurs*) editorial staff; (SCOL: *devoir*) essay, composition

redemander [ʀədmɑ̃de] *vt* (*une nouvelle fois*) to ask again for; (*davantage*) to ask for more of

redescendre [ʀ(ə)desɑ̃dʀ] *vi* to go back down ♦ *vt* (*pente etc*) to go down

redevance [ʀ(ə)dəvɑ̃s] *nf* (TÉL) rental charge; (TV) licence fee

rédiger [ʀediʒe] *vt* to write; (*contrat*) to draw up

redire [ʀ(ə)diʀ] *vt* to repeat; **trouver à ~ à** to find fault with

redonner [ʀ(ə)dɔne] *vt* (*rendre*) to give back; (*resservir: nourriture*) to give more

redoubler [ʀ(ə)duble] *vi* (*tempête, violence*)

to intensify; (SCOL) to repeat a year; **~ de patience/prudence** to be doubly patient/careful

redoutable [R(ə)dutabl] *adj* formidable, fearsome

redouter [R(ə)dute] *vt* to dread

redressement [R(ə)dRɛsmɑ̃] *nm* (économique) recovery

redresser [R(ə)dRɛse] *vt* (relever) to set upright; (pièce tordue) to straighten out; (situation, économie) to put right; **se ~** *vi* (personne) to sit (ou stand) up (straight); (économie) to recover

réduction [Redyksjɔ̃] *nf* reduction

réduire [Redɥiʀ] *vt* to reduce; (prix, dépenses) to cut, reduce; **se ~ à** (revenir à) to boil down to; **réduit** *nm* (pièce) tiny room

rééducation [Reedykasjɔ̃] *nf* (d'un membre) re-education; (de délinquants, d'un blessé) rehabilitation

réel, le [Reɛl] *adj* real; **réellement** *adv* really

réexpédier [Reɛkspedje] *vt* (à l'envoyeur) to return, send back; (au destinataire) to send on, forward

refaire [R(ə)fɛR] *vt* to do again; (faire de nouveau: sport) to take up again; (réparer, restaurer) to do up

réfection [Refɛksjɔ̃] *nf* repair

réfectoire [RefɛktwaR] *nm* refectory

référence [Referɑ̃s] *nf* reference; **~s** *nfpl* (recommandations) reference *sg*

référer [Refere] : **se ~ à** *vt* to refer to

refermer [R(ə)fɛRme] *vt* to close *ou* shut again; **se ~** *vi* (porte) to close *ou* shut (again)

refiler [R(ə)file] *vi* (fam) to palm off

réfléchi, e [Refleʃi] *adj* (caractère) thoughtful; (action) well-thought-out; (LING) reflexive; **c'est tout ~** my mind's made up

réfléchir [RefleʃiR] *vt* to reflect ♦ *vi* to think; **~ à** to think about

reflet [R(ə)flɛ] *nm* reflection; (sur l'eau etc) sheen *no pl*, glint; **refléter** *vt* to reflect;

se refléter *vi* to be reflected

réflexe [Reflɛks] *nm, adj* reflex

réflexion [Reflɛksjɔ̃] *nf* (de la lumière etc) reflection; (fait de penser) thought; (remarque) remark; **~ faite, à la ~** on reflection

refluer [R(ə)flye] *vi* to flow back; (foule) to surge back

reflux [Rəfly] *nm* (de la mer) ebb

réforme [RefɔRm] *nf* reform; (REL): **la R~** the Reformation; **réformer** *vt* to reform; (MIL) to declare unfit for service

refouler [R(ə)fule] *vt* (envahisseurs) to drive back; (larmes) to force back; (désir, colère) to repress

refrain [R(ə)fRɛ̃] *nm* refrain, chorus

refréner [Rəfrene] *vt*, **réfréner** [Refrene] *vt* to curb, check

réfrigérateur [RefRiʒeRatœR] *nm* refrigerator, fridge

refroidir [R(ə)fRwadiR] *vt* to cool; (fig: personne) to put off ♦ *vi* to cool (down); **se ~** *vi* (temps) to get cooler *ou* colder; (fig: ardeur) to cool (off); **refroidissement** *nm* (grippe etc) chill

refuge [R(ə)fyʒ] *nm* refuge; **réfugié, e** *adj, nm/f* refugee; **réfugier** : **se réfugier** *vi* to take refuge

refus [R(ə)fy] *nm* refusal; **ce n'est pas de ~** I won't say no, it's welcome; **refuser** *vt* to refuse; (SCOL: candidat) to fail; **refuser qch à qn** to refuse sb sth; **se refuser à faire** to refuse to do

réfuter [Refyte] *yt* to refute

regagner [R(ə)gaɲe] *vt* (faveur) to win back; (lieu) to get back to

regain [Rəgɛ̃] *nm* (renouveau): **un ~ de** renewed +*nom*

régal [Regal] *nm* treat; **régaler** : **se régaler** *vi* to have a delicious meal; (fig) to enjoy o.s.

regard [R(ə)gaR] *nm* (coup d'œil) look, glance; (expression) look (in one's eye); **au ~ de** (loi, morale) from the point of view of; **en ~ de** in comparison with

regardant, e [R(ə)gaRdɑ̃, ɑ̃t] *adj* (économe) tight-fisted; **peu ~ (sur)** very free (about)

regarder [R(ə)gaRde] *vt* to look at; (*film, télévision, match*) to watch; (*concerner*) to concern ♦ *vi* to look; **ne pas ~ à la dépense** to spare no expense; **~ qn/qch comme** to regard sb/sth as

régie [Reʒi] *nf* (*COMM, INDUSTRIE*) state-owned company; (*THÉÂTRE, CINÉMA*) production; (*RADIO, TV*) control room

regimber [R(ə)ʒɛ̃be] *vi* to balk, jib

régime [Reʒim] *nm* (*POL*) régime; (*MÉD*) diet; (*ADMIN: carcéral, fiscal etc*) system; (*de bananes, dattes*) bunch; **se mettre au/suivre un ~** to go on/be on a diet

régiment [Reʒimã] *nm* regiment

région [Reʒjɔ̃] *nf* region; **régional, e, -aux** *adj* regional

régir [Reʒir] *vt* to govern

régisseur [Reʒisœr] *nm* (*d'un domaine*) steward; (*CINÉMA, TV*) assistant director; (*THÉÂTRE*) stage manager

registre [RəʒistR] *nm* register

réglage [Reglaʒ] *nm* adjustment

règle [Regl] *nf* (*instrument*) ruler; (*loi*) rule; **~s** *nfpl* (*menstruation*) period *sg*; **en ~** (*papiers d'identité*) in order; **en ~ générale** as a (general) rule

réglé, e [Regle] *adj* (*vie*) well-ordered; (*arrangé*) settled

règlement [Regləmã] *nm* (*paiement*) settlement; (*arrêté*) regulation; (*règles, statuts*) regulations *pl*, rules *pl*; **~ de compte(s)** settling of old scores; **réglementaire** *adj* conforming to the regulations; (*tenue*) regulation *cpd*; **réglementation** *nf* (*règles*) regulations; **réglementer** *vt* to regulate

régler [Regle] *vt* (*conflit, facture*) to settle; (*personne*) to settle up with; (*mécanisme, machine*) to regulate, adjust; (*thermostat etc*) to set, adjust

réglisse [Reglis] *nf* liquorice

règne [Rɛɲ] *nm* (*d'un roi etc, fig*) reign; **régner** *vi* (*roi*) to rule, reign; (*fig*) to reign

regorger [R(ə)gɔRʒe] *vi*: **~ de** to overflow with, be bursting with

regret [R(ə)gRɛ] *nm* regret; **à ~** with re-

gret; **sans ~** with no regrets; **regrettable** *adj* regrettable; **regretter** *vt* to regret; (*personne*) to miss; **je regrette mais ...** I'm sorry but ...

regrouper [R(ə)gRupe] *vt* (*grouper*) to group together; (*contenir*) to include, comprise; **se ~** *vi* to gather (together)

régulier, -ière [Regylje, jɛR] *adj* (*gén*) regular; (*vitesse, qualité*) steady; (*égal: couche, ligne*) even, (*TRANSPORTS: ligne, service*), scheduled, regular; (*légal*) lawful, in order; (*honnête*) straight, on the level; **régulièrement** *adv* regularly, (*uniformément*) evenly

rehausser [Rəose] *vt* (*relever*) to heighten, raise; (*fig: souligner*) to set off, enhance

rein [Rɛ̃] *nm* kidney; **~s** *nmpl* (*dos*) back *sg*

reine [Rɛn] *nf* queen

reine-claude [Rɛnklod] *nf* greengage

réinsertion [Reɛ̃sɛRsjɔ̃] *nf* (*de délinquant*) reintegration, rehabilitation

réintégrer [Reɛ̃tegRe] *vt* (*lieu*) to return to; (*fonctionnaire*) to reinstate

rejaillir [R(ə)ʒajiR] *vi* to splash up; **~ sur** (*fig: scandale*) to rebound on; (: *gloire*) to be reflected on

rejet [Raʒɛ] *nm* rejection; **rejeter** *vt* (*relancer*) to throw back; (*écarter*) to reject; (*déverser*) to throw out, discharge; (*vomir*) to bring *ou* throw up; **rejeter la responsabilité de qch sur qn** to lay the responsibility for sth at sb's door

rejoindre [R(ə)ʒwɛ̃dR] *vt* (*famille, régiment*) to rejoin, return to; (*lieu*) to get (back) to; (*suj: route etc*) to meet, join; (*rattraper*) to catch up (with); **se ~** *vi* to meet; **je te rejoins à la gare** I'll see *ou* meet you at the station

réjouir [ReʒwiR] *vt* to delight; **se ~ (de)** *vi* to be delighted (about); **réjouissances** *nfpl* (*fête*) festivities

relâche [Rəlaʃ] *nm ou nf*: **sans ~** without respite *ou* a break; **relâché, e** *adj* loose, lax; **relâcher** *vt* (*libérer*) to release; (*desserrer*) to loosen; **se relâcher** *vi* (*discipline*) to become slack *ou* lax; (*élève etc*) to slacken off

relais [R(ə)lɛ] *nm* (*SPORT*): **(course de)** ~ relay (race); **prendre le ~ (de)** to take over (from); **~ routier** ≃ transport café (*BRIT*), ≃ truck stop (*US*)

relancer [R(ə)lɑ̃se] *vt* (*balle*) to throw back; (*moteur*) to restart; (*fig*) to boost, revive; (*harceler*): **~ qn** to pester sb

relatif, -ive [R(ə)latif, iv] *adj* relative

relation [R(ə)lasjɔ̃] *nf* (*rapport*) relation(ship); (*connaissance*) acquaintance; **~s** *nfpl* (*rapports*) relations; (*connaissances*) connections; **être/entrer en ~(s) avec** to be/get in contact with

relaxe [Rəlaks] (*fam*) *adj* (*tenue*) informal; (*personne*) relaxed; **relaxer: se relaxer** *vi* to relax

relayer [R(ə)leje] *vt* (*collaborateur, coureur etc*) to relieve; **se ~** *vi* (*dans une activité*) to take it in turns

reléguer [R(ə)lege] *vt* to relegate

relent(s) [Rəlɑ̃] *nm(pl)* (foul) smell

relevé, e [Rəl(ə)ve] *adj* (*manches*) rolled-up; (*sauce*) highly-seasoned ♦ *nm* (*de compteur*) reading; (*bancaire*) statement

relève [Rəlɛv] *nf* (*personne*) relief; **prendre la ~** to take over

relever [Rəl(ə)ve] *vt* (*meuble*) to stand up again; (*personne tombée*) to help up; (*vitre, niveau de vie*) to raise; (*col*) to turn up; (*style*) to elevate; (*plat, sauce*) to season; (*sentinelle, équipe*) to relieve; (*fautes*) to pick out; (*défi*) to accept, take up; (*noter: adresse etc*) to take down, note; (: *plan*) to sketch; (*compteur*) to read; (*ramasser: cahiers*) to collect, take in; **se ~** *vi* (*se remettre debout*) to get up; **~ de** (*maladie*) to be recovering from; (*être du ressort de*) to be a matter for; (*fig*) to pertain to; **~ qn de** (*fonctions*) to relieve sb of

relief [Rəljɛf] *nm* relief; **mettre en ~** (*fig*) to bring out, highlight

relier [Rəlje] *vt* to link up; (*livre*) to bind; **~ qch à** to link sth to

religieuse [R(ə)liʒjøz] *nf* nun; (*gâteau*) cream bun

religieux, -euse [R(ə)liʒjø, jøz] *adj* religious ♦ *nm* monk

religion [R(ə)liʒjɔ̃] *nf* religion

relire [R(ə)liR] *vt* (*à nouveau*) to reread, read again; (*vérifier*) to read over

reliure [RəljyR] *nf* binding

reluire [R(ə)lɥiR] *vi* to gleam

remanier [R(ə)manje] *vt* to reshape, recast; (*POL*) to reshuffle

remarquable [R(ə)maRkabl] *adj* remarkable

remarque [R(ə)maRk] *nf* remark; (*écrite*) note

remarquer [R(ə)maRke] *vt* (*voir*) to notice; **se ~** *vi* to be noticeable; **faire ~ (à qn) que** to point out (to sb) that; **faire ~ qch (à qn)** to point sth out (to sb); **remarquez, ...** mind you ...; **se faire ~** to draw attention to o.s.

rembourrer [Rɑ̃buRe] *vt* to stuff

remboursement [Rɑ̃buRsəmɑ̃] *nm* (*de dette, d'emprunt*) repayment; (*de frais*) refund; **rembourser** *vt* to pay back, repay; (*frais, billet etc*) to refund; **se faire rembourser** to get a refund

remède [R(ə)mɛd] *nm* (*médicament*) medicine; (*traitement, fig*) remedy, cure

remémorer [R(ə)memɔRe]: **se ~** *vt* to recall, recollect

remerciements [RəmɛRsimɑ̃] *nmpl* thanks

remercier [R(ə)mɛRsje] *vt* to thank; (*congédier*) to dismiss; **~ qn de/d'avoir fait** to thank sb for/for having done

remettre [R(ə)mɛtR] *vt* (*replacer*) to put back; (*vêtement*) to put back on; (*ajouter*) to add; (*ajourner*): **~ qch (à)** to postpone sth (until); **se ~ vi** to recover (from); **~ qch à qn** (*donner: lettre, clé etc*) to hand over sth to sb; (: *prix, décoration*) to present sb with sth; **se ~ à faire qch** to start doing sth again

remise [R(ə)miz] *nf* (*rabais*) discount; (*local*) shed; **~ de peine** reduction of sentence; **~ en jeu** (*FOOTBALL*) throw-in

remontant [R(ə)mɔ̃tɑ̃, ɑ̃t] *nm* tonic, pickme-up

remonte-pente [ʀ(ə)mɔ̃tpɑ̃t] *nm* ski-lift

remonter [ʀ(ə)mɔ̃te] *vi* to go back up; (*prix, température*) to go up again ♦ *vt* (*pente*) to go back up; (*fleuve*) to sail (*ou* swim *etc*) up; (*manches, pantalon*) to roll up; (*col*) to turn up; (*niveau, limite*) to raise; (*fig: personne*) to buck up; (*qch de démonté*) to put back together, reassemble; (*montre*) to wind up; **~ le moral à qn** to raise sb's spirits; **~ à** (*dater de*) to date *ou* go back to

remontrance [ʀ(ə)mɔ̃trɑ̃s] *nf* reproof, reprimand

remontrer [ʀ(ə)mɔ̃tre] *vt* (*fig*): **en ~ à** to prove one's superiority over

remords [ʀ(ə)mɔr] *nm* remorse *no pl*; **avoir des ~** to feel remorse

remorque [ʀ(ə)mɔrk] *nf* trailer; **remorquer** *vt* to tow; **remorqueur** *nm* tug(boat)

remous [ʀəmu] *nm* (*d'un navire*) (back)wash *no pl*; (*de rivière*) swirl, eddy ♦ *nmpl* (*fig*) stir *sg*

remparts [ʀɑ̃par] *nmpl* walls, ramparts

remplaçant, e [ʀɑ̃plasɑ̃, ɑ̃t] *nm/f* replacement, stand-in; (*SCOL*) supply teacher

remplacement [ʀɑ̃plasmɑ̃] *nm* replacement; **faire des ~s** (*professeur*) to do supply teaching; (*secrétaire*) to temp

remplacer [ʀɑ̃plase] *vt* to replace; **~ qch/qn par** to replace sth/sb with

rempli, e [ʀɑ̃pli] *adj* (*emploi du temps*) full, busy; **~ de** full of, filled with

remplir [ʀɑ̃plir] *vt* to fill (up); (*questionnaire*) to fill out *ou* up; (*obligations, fonction, condition*) to fulfil; **se ~** *vi* to fill up

remporter [ʀɑ̃pɔrte] *vt* (*marchandise*) to take away; (*fig*) to win, achieve

remuant, e [ʀəmɥɑ̃, ɑ̃t] *adj* restless

remue-ménage [ʀ(ə)mymenaʒ] *nm inv* commotion

remuer [ʀəmɥe] *vt* to move; (*café, sauce*) to stir ♦ *vi* to move; **se ~** *vi* to move; (*fam: s'activer*) to get a move on

rémunérer [remynere] *vt* to remunerate

renard [ʀ(ə)nar] *nm* fox

renchérir [ʀɑ̃feʀir] *vi* (*fig*): **~ (sur)** (*en paroles*) to add something (to)

rencontre [ʀɑ̃kɔ̃tr] *nf* meeting; (*imprévue*) encounter; **aller à la ~ de qn** to go and meet sb; **rencontrer** *vt* to meet; (*mot, expression*) to come across; (*difficultés*) to meet with; **se rencontrer** *vi* to meet

rendement [ʀɑ̃dmɑ̃] *nm* (*d'un travailleur, d'une machine*) output; (*d'un champ*) yield

rendez-vous [ʀɑ̃devu] *nm* appointment; (*d'amoureux*) date; (*lieu*) meeting place; **donner ~-~ à qn** to arrange to meet sb; **avoir/prendre ~-~ (avec)** to have/make an appointment (with)

rendre [ʀɑ̃dr] *vt* (*restituer*) to give back, return; (*invitation*) to return, repay; (*vomir*) to bring up; (*exprimer, traduire*) to render; (*faire devenir*): **~ qn célèbre/qch possible** to make sb famous/sth possible; **se ~** *vi* (*capituler*) to surrender, give o.s. up; (*aller*): **se ~ quelque part** to go somewhere; **~ la monnaie à qn** to give sb his change; **se ~ compte de qch** to realize sth

rênes [ʀɛn] *nfpl* reins

renfermé, e [ʀɑ̃ferme] *adj* (*fig*) withdrawn ♦ *nm*: **sentir le ~** to smell stuffy

renfermer [ʀɑ̃ferme] *vt* to contain

renflouer [ʀɑ̃flue] *vt* to refloat; (*fig*) to set back on its (*ou* his/her *etc*) feet

renfoncement [ʀɑ̃fɔ̃smɑ̃] *nm* recess

renforcer [ʀɑ̃fɔrse] *vt* to reinforce; **renfort: renforts** *nmpl* reinforcements; **à grand renfort de** with a great deal of

renfrogné, e [ʀɑ̃frɔɲe] *adj* sullen

rengaine [ʀɑ̃gɛn] (*péj*) *nf* old tune

renier [ʀənje] *vt* (*personne*) to disown, repudiate; (*foi*) to renounce

renifler [ʀ(ə)nifle] *vi, vt* to sniff

renne [ʀɛn] *nm* reindeer *inv*

renom [ʀənɔ̃] *nm* reputation; (*célébrité*) renown; **renommé, e** *adj* celebrated, renowned; **renommée** *nf* fame

renoncer [ʀ(ə)nɔ̃se] *vt*: **~ à** *vt* to give up; **~ à faire** to give up the idea of doing

renouer [ʀənwe] *vt*: **~ avec** (*habitude*) to

take up again

renouvelable [R(ə)nuv(ə)labl] *adj* (*énergie etc*) renewable

renouveler [R(ə)nuv(ə)le] *vt* to renew; (*exploit, méfait*) to repeat; **se ~** *vi* (*incident*) to recur, happen again; **renouvellement** *nm* (*remplacement*) renewal

rénover [Renɔve] *vt* (*immeuble*) to renovate, do up; (*quartier*) to redevelop

renseignement [Rɑ̃seɲmɑ̃] *nm* information *no pl*, piece of information; **(bureau des) ~s** information office

renseigner [Rɑ̃seɲe] *vt:* **~ qn (sur)** to give information to sb (about); **se ~** *vi* to ask for information, make inquiries

rentabilité [Rɑ̃tabilite] *nf* profitability

rentable [Rɑ̃tabl] *adj* profitable

rente [Rɑ̃t] *nf* private income; (*pension*) pension

rentrée [Rɑ̃tre] *nf:* **~ (d'argent)** cash *no pl* coming in; **la ~ (des classes)** the start of the new school year

---

rentrée (des classes)

---

i La rentrée (des classes) *in September marks an important point in the French year. Children and teachers return to school, and political and social life begin again after the long summer break.*

---

rentrer [Rɑ̃tre] *vi* (*revenir chez soi*) to go (*ou* come) (back) home; (*entrer de nouveau*) to go (*ou* come) back in; (*entrer*) to go (*ou* come) in; (*air, clou: pénétrer*) to go in; (*revenu*) to come in ♦ *vt* to bring in; (*mettre à l'abri: animaux etc*) to bring in; (: *véhicule*) to put away; (*chemise dans pantalon etc*) to tuck in; (*griffes*) to draw in; **~ le ventre** to pull in one's stomach; **~ dans** (*heurter*) to crash into; **~ dans l'ordre** to be back to normal; **~ dans ses frais** to recover one's expenses

renverse [Rɑ̃vɛʀs]: **à la ~** *adv* backwards

renverser [Rɑ̃vɛʀse] *vt* (*faire tomber: chaise, verre*) to knock over, overturn; (*liquide, contenu*) to spill, upset; (*piéton*) to knock down; (*retourner*) to turn upside down; (: *ordre des mots etc*) to reverse; (*fig: gouvernement etc*) to overthrow; (*fam: stupéfier*) to bowl over; **se ~** *vi* (*verre, vase*) to fall over; (*contenu*) to spill

renvoi [Rɑ̃vwa] *nm* (*d'employé*) dismissal; (*d'élève*) expulsion; (*référence*) cross-reference; (*éructation*) belch; **renvoyer** *vt* to send back; (*congédier*) to dismiss; (*élève: définitivement*) to expel; (*lumière*) to reflect; (*ajourner*): **renvoyer qch (à)** to put sth off *ou* postpone sth (until)

repaire [R(ə)pɛʀ] *nm* den

répandre [Repɑ̃dʀ] *vt* (*renverser*) to spill; (*étaler, diffuser*) to spread; (*odeur*) to give off; **se ~** *vi* to spill; (*se propager*) to spread; **répandu, e** *adj* (*opinion, usage*) widespread

réparation [Repaʀasjɔ̃] *nf* repair

réparer [Repaʀe] *vt* to repair; (*fig: offense*) to make up for, atone for; (: *oubli, erreur*) to put right

repartie [Repaʀti] *nf* retort; **avoir de la ~** to be quick at repartee

repartir [R(ə)paʀtiʀ] *vi* to leave again; (*voyageur*) to set off again; (*fig*) to get going again; **~ à zéro** to start from scratch (again)

répartir [Repaʀtiʀ] *vt* (*pour attribuer*) to share out; (*pour disperser, disposer*) to divide up; (*poids*) to distribute; **se ~** *vt* (*travail, rôles*) to share out between themselves; **répartition** *nf* (*des richesses etc*) distribution

repas [R(ə)pa] *nm* meal

repassage [R(ə)pasaʒ] *nm* ironing

repasser [R(ə)pase] *vi* to come (*ou* go) back ♦ *vt* (*vêtement, tissu*) to iron; (*examen*) to retake, resit; (*film*) to show again; (*leçon: revoir*) to go over (again)

repêcher [R(ə)peʃe] *vt* to fish out; (*candidat*) to pass (*by inflating marks*)

repentir [Rəpɑ̃tiʀ] *nm* repentance; **se ~** *vi* to repent; **se ~ d'avoir fait qch** (*regretter*) to regret having done sth

répercussions [RepɛRkysjɔ̃] *nfpl* (*fig*) repercussions

répercuter [RepeRkyte]: **se ~** *vi* (*bruit*) to reverberate; (*fig*): **se ~ sur** to have repercussions on

repère [R(ə)pER] *nm* mark; (*monument, événement*) landmark

repérer [R(ə)peRe] *vt* (*fam: erreur, personne*) to spot; (: *endroit*) to locate; **se ~** *vi* to find one's way about

répertoire [RepeRtwaR] *nm* (*liste*) (alphabetical) list; (*carnet*) index notebook; (*INFORM*) folder, directory; (*d'un artiste*) repertoire

répéter [Repete] *vt* to repeat; (*préparer: leçon*) to learn, go over; (*THÉÂTRE*) to rehearse; **se ~** *vi* (*redire*) to repeat o.s.; (*se reproduire*) to be repeated, recur

répétition [Repetisjɔ̃] *nf* repetition; (*THÉÂTRE*) rehearsal

répit [Repi] *nm* respite

replier [R(ə)plije] *vt* (*rabattre*) to fold down *ou* over; **se ~** *vi* (*troupes, armée*) to withdraw, fall back; (*sur soi-même*) to withdraw into o.s.

réplique [Replik] *nf* (*repartie, fig*) reply; (*THÉÂTRE*) line; (*copie*) replica; **répliquer** *vi* to reply; (*riposter*) to retaliate

répondeur [Repɔ̃dœR, øz] *nm*: **~ automatique** (*TÉL*) answering machine

répondre [Repɔ̃dR] *vi* to answer, reply; (*freins*) to respond; **~ à** to reply to, answer; (*affection, salut*) to return; (*provocation*) to respond to; (*correspondre à: besoin*) to answer; (: *conditions*) to meet; (: *description*) to match; (*avec impertinence*): **~ à qn** to answer sb back; **~ de** to answer for

réponse [Repɔ̃s] *nf* answer, reply; **en ~ à** in reply to

reportage [R(ə)pɔRtaʒ] *nm* report; **~ en direct** (live) commentary

reporter[1] [RəpɔRtER] *nm* reporter

reporter[2] [RəpɔRte] *vt* (*ajourner*): **~ qch (à)** to postpone sth (until); (*transférer*): **~ qch sur** to transfer sth to; **se ~ à** (*époque*) to think back to; (*document*) to refer to

repos [R(ə)po] *nm* rest; (*tranquillité*) peace (and quiet); (*MIL*): **~!** stand at ease!; **ce**

n'est pas de tout ~! it's no picnic!

reposant, e [R(ə)pozɑ̃, ɑ̃t] *adj* restful

reposer [R(ə)poze] *vt* (*verre, livre*) to put down; (*délasser*) to rest ♦ *vi*: **laisser ~** (*pâte*) to leave to stand; **se ~** *vi* to rest; **se ~ sur qn** to rely on sb; **~ sur** (*fig*) to rest on

repoussant, e [R(ə)pusɑ̃, ɑ̃t] *adj* repulsive

repousser [R(ə)puse] *vi* to grow again ♦ *vt* to repel, repulse; (*offre*) to turn down, reject; (*personne*) to push back; (*différer*) to put back

reprendre [R(ə)pRɑ̃dR] *vt* (*objet prêté, donné*) to take back; (*prisonnier, ville*) to recapture; (*firme, entreprise*) to take over; (*le travail*) to resume; (*emprunter: argument, idée*) to take up, use; (*refaire: article etc*) to go over again; (*vêtement*) to alter; (*réprimander*) to tell off; (*corriger*) to correct; (*chercher*): **je viendrai te ~ à 4 h** I'll come and fetch you at 4; (*se resservir de*): **~ du pain/un œuf** to take (*ou* eat) more bread/another egg ♦ *vi* (*classes, pluie*) to start (up) again; (*activités, travaux, combats*) to resume, start (up) again; (*affaires*) to pick up; (*dire*): **reprit-il** he went on; **se ~** *vi* (*se ressaisir*) to recover; **~ des forces** to recover one's strength; **~ courage** to take new heart; **~ la route** to set off again; **~ haleine** *ou* **son souffle** to get one's breath back

représailles [R(ə)pRezaj] *nfpl* reprisals

représentant, e [R(ə)pRezɑ̃tɑ̃, ɑ̃t] *nm/f* representative

représentation [R(ə)pRezɑ̃tasjɔ̃] *nf* (*symbole, image*) representation; (*spectacle*) performance

représenter [R(ə)pRezɑ̃te] *vt* to represent; (*donner: pièce, opéra*) to perform; **se ~** *vt* (*se figurer*) to imagine

répression [Represjɔ̃] *nf* repression

réprimer [RepRime] *vt* (*émotions*) to suppress; (*peuple etc*) to repress

repris [R(ə)pRi, iz] *nm*: **~ de justice** ex-prisoner, ex-convict

reprise [R(ə)pRiz] *nf* (*recommencement*) resumption; (*économique*) recovery; (*TV*) repeat; (*COMM*) trade-in, part exchange; (*raccommodage*) mend; **à plusieurs ~s** on several occasions

repriser [R(ə)pRize] *vt* (*chaussette, lainage*) to darn; (*tissu*) to mend

reproche [R(ə)pRɔʃ] *nm* (*remontrance*) reproach; **faire des ~s à qn** to reproach sb; **sans ~(s)** beyond reproach; **reprocher** *vt*: **reprocher qch à qn** to reproach *ou* blame sb for sth; **reprocher qch à** (*critiquer*) to have sth against

reproduction [R(ə)pRɔdyksjɔ̃] *nf* reproduction

reproduire [R(ə)pRɔdɥiR] *vt* to reproduce; **se ~** *vi* (*BIO*) to reproduce; (*recommencer*) to recur, re-occur

réprouver [RepRuve] *vt* to reprove

reptile [Reptil] *nm* reptile

repu, e [Rəpy] *adj* satisfied, sated

république [Repyblik] *nf* republic

répugnant, e [Repyɲɑ̃, ɑ̃t] *adj* disgusting

répugner [Repyɲe]: **~ à** *vt*: **~ à qn** to repel *ou* disgust sb; **~ à faire** to be loath *ou* reluctant to do

réputation [Repytasjɔ̃] *nf* reputation; **réputé, e** *adj* renowned

requérir [RəkeRiR] *vt* (*nécessiter*) to require, call for

requête [Rəkɛt] *nf* request

requin [Rəkɛ̃] *nm* shark

requis, e [Rəki, iz] *adj* required

RER *sigle m* (= *réseau express régional*) Greater Paris high-speed train service

rescapé, e [Reskape] *nm/f* survivor

rescousse [Reskus] *nf*: **aller à la ~ de qn** to go to sb's aid *ou* rescue

réseau, x [Rezo] *nm* network

réservation [RezeRvasjɔ̃] *nf* booking, reservation

réserve [RezeRv] *nf* (*retenue*) reserve; (*entrepôt*) storeroom; (*restriction, d'Indiens*) reservation; (*de pêche, chasse*) preserve; **de ~** (*provisions etc*) in reserve

réservé, e [RezeRve] *adj* reserved; **chasse/pêche ~e** private hunting/fishing

réserver [RezeRve] *vt* to reserve; (*chambre, billet etc*) to book, reserve; (*fig: destiner*) to have in store; (*garder*): **~ qch pour/à** to keep *ou* save sth for

réservoir [RezeRvwaR] *nm* tank

résidence [Rezidɑ̃s] *nf* residence; **~ secondaire** second home; **résidentiel, le** *adj* residential; **résider** *vi*: **résider à/dans/en** to reside in; **résider dans** (*fig*) to lie in

résidu [Rezidy] *nm* residue *no pl*

résigner [Rezine]: **se ~** *vi*: **se ~ (à qch/à faire)** to resign o.s. (to sth/to doing)

résilier [Rezilje] *vt* to terminate

résistance [Rezistɑ̃s] *nf* resistance; (*de réchaud, bouilloire: fil*) element

résistant, e [Rezistɑ̃, ɑ̃t] *adj* (*personne*) robust, tough; (*matériau*) strong, hard-wearing

résister [Reziste] *vi* to resist; **~ à** (*assaut, tentation*) to resist; (*supporter: gel etc*) to withstand; (*désobéir à*) to stand up to, oppose

résolu, e [Rezɔly] *pp de* **résoudre** ♦ *adj*: **être ~ à qch/faire** to be set upon sth/doing

résolution [Rezɔlysjɔ̃] *nf* (*fermeté, décision*) resolution; (*d'un problème*) solution

résolve *etc* [Rezɔlv] *vb voir* **résoudre**

résonner [Rezɔne] *vi* (*cloche, pas*) to reverberate, resound; (*salle*) to be resonant

résorber [RezɔRbe]: **se ~** *vi* (*fig: chômage*) to be reduced; (: *déficit*) to be absorbed

résoudre [RezudR] *vt* to solve; **se ~ à faire** to bring o.s. to do

respect [Rɛspɛ] *nm* respect; **tenir en ~** to keep at bay; **respecter** *vt* to respect; **respectueux, -euse** *adj* respectful

respiration [RɛspiRasjɔ̃] *nf* breathing *no pl*

respirer [RɛspiRe] *vi* to breathe; (*fig: se détendre*) to get one's breath; (: *se rassurer*) to breathe again ♦ *vt* to breathe (in), inhale; (*manifester: santé, calme etc*) to exude

resplendir [Rɛsplɑ̃diR] *vi* to shine; (*fig*): **~ (de)** to be radiant (with)

responsabilité [Rɛspɔ̃sabilite] *nf* responsibility; (*légale*) liability

responsable [rɛspɔ̃sabl] *adj* responsible ♦ *nm/f* (*coupable*) person responsible; (*personne compétente*) person in charge; (*de parti, syndicat*) official; **~ de** responsible for

resquiller [rɛskije] (*fam*) *vi* to get in without paying; (*ne pas faire la queue*) to jump the queue

ressaisir [R(ə)seziR]: **se ~** *vi* to regain one's self-control

ressasser [R(ə)sase] *vt* to keep going over

ressemblance [R(ə)sɑ̃blɑ̃s] *nf* resemblance, similarity, likeness

ressemblant, e [R(ə)sɑ̃blɑ̃, ɑ̃t] *adj* (*portrait*) lifelike, true to life

ressembler [R(ə)sɑ̃ble]: **~ à** *vt* to be like, resemble; (*visuellement*) to look like; **se ~** *vi* to be (*ou* look) alike

ressemeler [R(ə)sɑ̃m(ə)le] *vt* to (re)sole

ressentiment [R(ə)sɑ̃timɑ̃] *nm* resentment

ressentir [R(ə)sɑ̃tiR] *vt* to feel

resserrer [R(ə)sɛʀe] *vt* (*nœud, boulon*) to tighten (up); (*fig: liens*) to strengthen

resservir [R(ə)sɛʀviʀ] *vi* to do *ou* serve again; **se ~ (de)** *vt* to help o.s. again

ressort [RəsɔR] *nm* (*pièce*) spring; (*énergie*) spirit; (*recours*): **en dernier ~** as a last resort; (*compétence*): **être du ~ de** to fall within the competence of

ressortir [RəsɔRtiR] *vi* to go (*ou* come) out (again); (*contraster*) to stand out; **~ de** to emerge from; **faire ~** (*fig: souligner*) to bring out

ressortissant, e [R(ə)sɔRtisɑ̃, ɑ̃t] *nm/f* national

ressources [R(ə)suRs] *nfpl* (*moyens*) resources

ressusciter [Resysite] *vt* (*fig*) to revive, bring back ♦ *vi* to rise (from the dead)

restant, e [Rɛstɑ̃, ɑ̃t] *adj* remaining ♦ *nm*: **le ~ (de)** the remainder (of); **un ~ de** (*de trop*) some left-over

restaurant [Rɛstɔʀɑ̃] *nm* restaurant

restauration [Rɛstɔʀasjɔ̃] *nf* restoration; (*hôtellerie*) catering; **~ rapide** fast food

restaurer [Rɛstɔʀe] *vt* to restore; **se ~** *vi* to have something to eat

reste [Rɛst] *nm* (*restant*): **le ~ (de)** the rest (of); (*de trop*): **un ~ (de)** some left-over; **~s** *nmpl* (*nourriture*) left-overs; (*d'une cité etc, dépouille mortelle*) remains; **du ~, au ~** besides, moreover

rester [Rɛste] *vi* to stay, remain; (*subsister*) to remain, be left; (*durer*) to last, live on ♦ *vb impers*: **il reste du pain/2 œufs** there's some bread/there are 2 eggs left (over); **restons-en là** let's leave it at that; **il me reste assez de temps** I have enough time left; **il ne me reste plus qu'à ...** I've just got to ...

restituer [Rɛstitɥe] *vt* (*objet, somme*): **~ qch (à qn)** to return sth (to sb)

restreindre [RɛstRɛ̃dR] *vt* to restrict, limit

restriction [Rɛstriksjɔ̃] *nf* restriction

résultat [Rezylta] *nm* result; (*d'examen, d'élection*) results *pl*

résulter [Rezylte]: **~ de** *vt* to result from, be the result of

résumé [Rezyme] *nm* summary, résumé

résumer [Rezyme] *vt* (*texte*) to summarize; (*récapituler*) to sum up

résurrection [RezyRɛksjɔ̃] *nf* resurrection

rétablir [Retablir] *vt* to restore, re-establish; **se ~** *vi* (*guérir*) to recover; (*silence, calme*) to return, be restored; **rétablissement** *nmm* restoring; (*guérison*) recovery

retaper [R(ə)tape] (*fam*) *vt* (*maison, voiture etc*) to do up; (*revigorer*) to buck up

retard [R(ə)taR] *nm* (*d'une personne attendue*) lateness *no pl*; (*sur l'horaire, un programme*) delay; (*fig: scolaire, mental etc*) backwardness; **en ~ (de 2 heures)** (2 hours) late; **avoir du ~** to be late; (*sur un programme*) to be behind (schedule); **prendre du ~** (*train, avion*) to be delayed; **sans ~** without delay

retardataire [R(ə)taRdatɛR] *nmf* latecomer

retardement [R(ə)taRdəmɑ̃]: **à ~** *adj* delayed action *cpd*; **bombe à ~** time bomb

retarder [R(ə)taRde] *vt* to delay; (*montre*)

to put back ♦ *vi (montre)* to be slow; ~ **qn (d'une heure)** *(sur un horaire)* to delay sb (an hour); ~ **qch (de 2 jours)** *(départ, date)* to put sth back (2 days)

retenir [Rət(ə)niR] *vt (garder, retarder)* to keep, detain; *(maintenir: objet qui glisse, fig: colère, larmes)* to hold back; *(se rappeler)* to retain; *(réserver)* to reserve; *(accepter: proposition etc)* to accept; *(fig: empêcher d'agir):* ~ **qn (de faire)** to hold sb back (from doing); *(prélever):* ~ **qch (sur)** to deduct sth (from); **se** ~ *vi (se raccrocher):* **se** ~ **à** to hold onto; *(se contenir):* **se** ~ **de faire** to restrain o.s. from doing; ~ **son souffle** to hold one's breath

retentir [R(ə)tãtiR] *vi* to ring out; *(salle):* ~ **de** to ring *ou* resound with; **retentissant, e** *adj* resounding; **retentissement** *nm* repercussion

retenu, e [Rət(ə)ny] *adj (place)* reserved; *(personne: empêché)* held up; **retenue** *nf (prélèvement)* deduction; *(SCOL)* detention; *(modération)* (self-)restraint

réticence [Retisãs] *nf* hesitation, reluctance *no pl*; **réticent, e** *adj* hesitant, reluctant

rétine [Retin] *nf* retina

retiré, e [R(ə)tiRe] *adj (vie)* secluded; *(lieu)* remote

retirer [R(ə)tiRe] *vt (vêtement, lunettes)* to take off, remove; *(argent, plainte)* to withdraw; *(reprendre: bagages, billets)* to collect, pick up; *(extraire):* ~ **qch de** to take sth out of, remove sth from

retombées [Rət5be] *nfpl (radioactives)* fallout *sg; (fig: répercussions)* effects

retomber [R(ə)t5be] *vi (à nouveau)* to fall again; *(atterrir: après un saut etc)* to land; *(échoir):* ~ **sur qn** to fall on sb

rétorquer [RetɔRke] *vt:* ~ **(à qn) que** to retort (to sb) that

retouche [R(ə)tuʃ] *nf (sur vêtement)* alteration; **retoucher** *vt (photographie)* to touch up; *(texte, vêtement)* to alter

retour [R(ə)tuR] *nm* return; **au** ~ *(en route)* on the way back; **à mon** ~ when I get/

got back; **être de** ~ **(de)** to be back (from); **par** ~ **du courrier** by return of post

retourner [R(ə)tuRne] *vt (dans l'autre sens: matelas, crêpe etc)* to turn (over); *(: sac, vêtement)* to turn inside out; *(fam: bouleverser)* to shake; *(renvoyer, restituer):* ~ **qch à qn** to return sth to sb ♦ *vi (aller, revenir):* ~ **quelque part/à** to go back *ou* return somewhere/to; **se** ~ *vi (tourner la tête)* to turn round; ~ **à** *(état, activité)* to return to, go back to; **se** ~ **contre** *(fig)* to turn against

retrait [R(ə)tRɛ] *nm (d'argent)* withdrawal; **en** ~ set back; ~ **du permis (de conduire)** disqualification from driving *(BRIT)*, revocation of driver's license *(US)*

retraite [R(ə)tRɛt] *nf (d'un employé)* retirement; *(revenu)* pension; *(d'une armée, REL)* retreat; **prendre sa** ~ to retire; ~ **anticipée** early retirement; **retraité, e** *adj* retired ♦ *nm/f* pensioner

retrancher [R(ə)tRãʃe] *vt (nombre, somme):* ~ **qch de** to take *ou* deduct sth from; **se** ~ **derrière/dans** to take refuge behind/in

retransmettre [R(ə)tRãsmɛtR] *vt (RADIO)* to broadcast; *(TV)* to show

rétrécir [RetResiR] *vt (vêtement)* to take in ♦ *vi* to shrink

rétribution [RetRibysj5] *nf* payment

rétro [RetRo] *adj inv:* **la mode** ~ the nostalgia vogue

rétrograde [RetRɔgRad] *adj* reactionary, backward-looking

rétroprojecteur [RetRopRɔʒɛktœR] *nm* overhead projector

rétrospective [RetRɔspɛktiv] *nf* retrospective exhibition/season; **rétrospectivement** *adv* in retrospect

retrousser [R(ə)tRuse] *vt* to roll up

retrouvailles [R(ə)tRuvaj] *nfpl* reunion *sg*

retrouver [R(ə)tRuve] *vt (fugitif, objet perdu)* to find; *(calme, santé)* to regain; *(revoir)* to see again; *(rejoindre)* to meet (again), join; **se** ~ *vi* to meet; *(s'orienter)* to find one's way; **se** ~ **quelque part** to find o.s.

somewhere; **s'y ~** (*y voir clair*) to make sense of it; (*rentrer dans ses frais*) to break even

rétroviseur [RetRɔvizœR] *nm* (rear-view) mirror

réunion [Reynjɔ̃] *nf* (*séance*) meeting

réunir [ReyniR] *vt* (*rassembler*) to gather together; (*inviter: amis, famille*) to have round, have in; (*cumuler: qualités etc*) to combine; (*rapprocher: ennemis*) to bring together (again), reunite; (*rattacher: parties*) to join (together); **se ~** *vi* (*se rencontrer*) to meet

réussi, e [Reysi] *adj* successful

réussir [ReysiR] *vi* to succeed, be successful; (*à un examen*) to pass ♦ *vt* to make a success of; **~ à faire** to succeed in doing; **~ à qn** (*être bénéfique à*) to agree with sb; **réussite** *nf* success; (*CARTES*) patience

revaloir [R(ə)valwaR] *vt*: **je vous revaudrai cela** I'll repay you some day; (*en mal*) I'll pay you back for this

revanche [R(ə)vɑ̃ʃ] *nf* revenge; (*sport*) revenge match; **en ~** on the other hand

rêve [Rɛv] *nm* dream; **de ~** dream *cpd*; **faire un ~** to have a dream

revêche [Rəvɛʃ] *adj* surly, sour-tempered

réveil [Revɛj] *nm* waking up *no pl*; (*fig*) awakening; (*pendule*) alarm (clock); **au ~** on waking (up); **réveille-matin** *nm inv* alarm clock; **réveiller** *vt* (*personne*) to wake up; (*fig*) to awaken, revive; **se réveiller** *vi* to wake up

réveillon [Revɛjɔ̃] *nm* Christmas Eve; (*de la Saint-Sylvestre*) New Year's Eve; **réveillonner** *vi* to celebrate Christmas Eve (*ou* New Year's Eve)

révélateur, -trice [RevelatœR, tRis] *adj*: **~ (de qch)** revealing (sth)

révéler [Revele] *vt* to reveal; **se ~** *vi* to be revealed, reveal itself ♦ *vb +attrib*: **se ~ difficile/aisé** to prove difficult/easy

revenant, e [R(ə)vənɑ̃, ɑ̃t] *nm/f* ghost

revendeur, -euse [R(ə)vɑ̃dœR, øz] *nm/f* (*détaillant*) retailer; (*de drogue*) (drug-) dealer

revendication [R(ə)vɑ̃dikasjɔ̃] *nf* claim, demand

revendiquer [R(ə)vɑ̃dike] *vt* to claim, demand; (*responsabilité*) to claim

revendre [R(ə)vɑ̃dR] *vt* (*d'occasion*) to resell; (*détailler*) to sell; **à ~** (*en abondance*) to spare

revenir [Rəv(ə)niR] *vi* to come back; (*coûter*): **~ cher/à 10 euros (à qn)** to cost (sb) a lot/10 euros; **~ à** (*reprendre: études, projet*) to return to, go back to; (*équivaloir à*) to amount to; **~ à qn** (*part, honneur*) to go to sb, be sb's; (*souvenir, nom*) to come back to sb; **~ sur** (*question, sujet*) to go back over; (*engagement*) to go back on; **~ à soi** to come round; **n'en pas ~: je n'en reviens pas** I can't get over it; **~ sur ses pas** to retrace one's steps; **cela revient à dire que/au même** it amounts to saying that/the same thing; **faire ~** (*CULIN*) to brown

revenu [Rəv(ə)ny] *nm* income; **~s** *nmpl* income *sg*

rêver [Reve] *vi, vt* to dream; **~ de/à** to dream of

réverbère [RevɛRbɛR] *nm* street lamp *ou* light; **réverbérer** *vt* to reflect

révérence [RevɛRɑ̃s] *nf* (*salut*) bow; (: *de femme*) curtsey

rêverie [Rɛ vRi] *nf* daydreaming *no pl*, daydream

revers [R(ə)vɛR] *nm* (*de feuille, main*) back; (*d'étoffe*) wrong side; (*de pièce, médaille*) back, reverse; (*TENNIS, PING-PONG*) backhand; (*de veste*) lapel; (*fig: échec*) setback

revêtement [R(ə)vɛtmɑ̃] *nm* (*des sols*) flooring; (*de chaussée*) surface

revêtir [R(ə)vetiR] *vt* (*habit*) to don, put on; (*prendre: importance, apparence*) to take on; **~ qch de** to cover sth with

rêveur, -euse [RevœR, øz] *adj* dreamy ♦ *nm/f* dreamer

revient [Rəvjɛ̃] *vb voir* **revenir**

revigorer [R(ə)vigɔRe] *vt* (*air frais*) to invigorate, brace up; (*repas, boisson*) to revive, buck up

revirement [R(ə)viʀmɑ̃] *nm* change of mind; (*d'une situation*) reversal

réviser [Revize] *vt* to revise; (*machine*) to overhaul, service

révision [Reviʒjɔ̃] *nf* revision; (*de voiture*) servicing *no pl*

revivre [R(ə)vivʀ] *vi* (*reprendre des forces*) to come alive again ♦ *vt* (*épreuve, moment*) to relive

revoir [Rəvwaʀ] *vt* to see again; (*réviser*) to revise ♦ *nm*: **au ~** goodbye

révoltant, e [Revɔltɑ̃, ɑ̃t] *adj* revolting, appalling

révolte [Revɔlt] *nf* rebellion, revolt

révolter [Revɔlte] *vt* to revolt; **se ~ (contre)** to rebel (against); **ça me révolte (de voir que ...)** I'm revolted *ou* appalled (to see that ...)

révolu, e [Revɔly] *adj* past; (*ADMIN*): **âgé de 18 ans ~s** over 18 years of age

révolution [Revɔlysjɔ̃] *nf* revolution; **révolutionnaire** *adj, nm/f* revolutionary

revolver [Revɔlvɛʀ] *nm* gun; (*à barillet*) revolver

révoquer [Revɔke] *vt* (*fonctionnaire*) to dismiss; (*arrêt, contrat*) to revoke

revue [R(ə)vy] *nf* review; (*périodique*) review, magazine; (*de music-hall*) variety show; **passer en ~** (*mentalement*) to go through

rez-de-chaussée [Red(ə)ʃose] *nm inv* ground floor

RF *sigle f* = **République française**

Rhin [Rɛ̃] *nm* Rhine

rhinocéros [RinɔseRɔs] *nm* rhinoceros

Rhône [Ron] *nm* Rhone

rhubarbe [RybaRb] *nf* rhubarb

rhum [Rɔm] *nm* rum

rhumatisme [Rymatism] *nm* rheumatism *no pl*

rhume [Rym] *nm* cold; **~ de cerveau** head cold; **le ~ des foins** hay fever

ri [Ri] *pp de* **rire**

riant, e [R(i)jɑ̃, R(i)jɑ̃t] *adj* smiling, cheerful

ricaner [Rikane] *vi* (*avec méchanceté*) to snigger; (*bêtement*) to giggle

riche [Riʃ] *adj* rich; (*personne, pays*) rich, wealthy; **~ en** rich in; **richesse** *nf* wealth; (*fig: de sol, musée etc*) richness; **richesses** *nfpl* (*ressources, argent*) wealth *sg*; (*fig: trésors*) treasures

ricochet [Rikɔʃɛ] *nm*: **faire des ~s** to skip stones; **par ~** (*fig*) as an indirect result

rictus [Riktys] *nm* grin

ride [Rid] *nf* wrinkle

rideau, x [Rido] *nm* curtain; **~ de fer** (*boutique*) metal shutter(s)

rider [Ride] *vt* to wrinkle; **se ~** *vi* to become wrinkled

ridicule [Ridikyl] *adj* ridiculous ♦ *nm*: **le ~** ridicule; **ridiculiser**: **se ridiculiser** *vi* to make a fool of o.s.

MOT-CLÉ

rien [Rjɛ̃] *pron* **1**: **(ne) ... rien** nothing; *tournure negative + anything*; **qu'est-ce que vous avez? – rien** what have you got? – nothing; **il n'a rien dit/fait** he said/did nothing, he hasn't said/done anything; **il n'a rien** (*n'est pas blessé*) he's all right; **de rien!** not at all!

2 (*quelque chose*): **a-t-il jamais rien fait pour nous?** has he ever done anything for us?

3: **rien de**: **rien d'intéressant** nothing interesting; **rien d'autre** nothing else; **rien du tout** nothing at all

4: **rien que** just, only; nothing but; **rien que pour lui faire plaisir** only *ou* just to please him; **rien que la vérité** nothing but the truth; **rien que cela** that alone

♦ *nm*: **un petit rien** (*cadeau*) a little something; **des riens** trivia *pl*; **un rien de** a hint of; **en un rien de temps** in no time at all

---

rieur, -euse [R(i)jœR, R(i)jøz] *adj* cheerful

rigide [Riʒid] *adj* stiff; (*fig*) rigid; strict

rigole [Rigɔl] *nf* (*conduit*) channel

rigoler [Rigɔle] *vi* (*fam: rire*) to laugh; (*s'amuser*) to have (some) fun; (*plaisanter*) to be joking *ou* kidding; **rigolo, -ote**

(*fam*) *adj* funny ♦ *nm/f* comic; (*péj*) fraud, phoney

rigoureusement [RiguRøzmɑ̃] *adv* (*vrai*) absolutely; (*interdit*) strictly

rigoureux, -euse [RiguRø, øz] *adj* rigorous; (*hiver*) hard, harsh

rigueur [RigœR] *nf* rigour; **être de ~** to be the rule; **à la ~** at a pinch; **tenir ~ à qn de qch** to hold sth against sb

rillettes [Rijɛt] *nfpl* potted meat (*made from pork or goose*)

rime [Rim] *nf* rhyme

rinçage [Rɛ̃saʒ] *nm* rinsing (out); (*opération*) rinse

rincer [Rɛ̃se] *vt* to rinse; (*récipient*) to rinse out

ring [Riŋ] *nm* (boxing) ring

ringard, e [Rɛ̃gaR, aRd] (*fam*) *adj* old-fashioned

rions [Ri5] *vb voir* **rire**

riposter [Riposte] *vi* to retaliate ♦ *vt*: **~ que** to retort that

rire [RiR] *vi* to laugh; (*se divertir*) to have fun ♦ *nm* laugh; **le ~** laughter; **~ de** to laugh at; **pour ~** (*pas sérieusement*) for a joke *ou* a laugh

risée [Rize] *nf*: **être la ~ de** to be the laughing stock of

risible [Rizibl] *adj* laughable

risque [Risk] *nm* risk; **le ~** danger; **à ses ~s et périls** at his own risk; **risqué, e** *adj* risky; (*plaisanterie*) risqué, daring; **risquer** *vt* to risk; (*allusion, question*) to venture, hazard; **ça ne risque rien** it's quite safe; **risquer de: il risque de se tuer** he could get himself killed; **ce qui risque de se produire** what might *ou* could well happen; **il ne risque pas de recommencer** there's no chance of him doing that again; **se risquer à faire** (*tenter*) to venture *ou* dare to do

rissoler [Risole] *vt, vi*: **(faire) ~** to brown

ristourne [RistuRn] *nf* discount

rite [Rit] *nm* rite; (*fig*) ritual

rivage [Rivaʒ] *nm* shore

rival, e, -aux [Rival, o] *adj, nm/f* rival; ri-

valiser *vi*: **rivaliser avec** (*personne*) to rival, vie with; **rivalité** *nf* rivalry

rive [Riv] *nf* shore; (*de fleuve*) bank; **riverain, e** *nm/f* riverside (*ou* lakeside) resident; (*d'une route*) local resident

rivet [Rivɛ] *nm* rivet

rivière [RivjɛR] *nf* river

rixe [Riks] *nf* brawl, scuffle

riz [Ri] *nm* rice; **rizière** *nf* paddy-field, rice-field

RMI *sigle m* (= *revenu minimum d'insertion*) ≃ income support (*BRIT*), welfare (*US*)

RN *sigle f* = **route nationale**

robe [Rɔb] *nf* dress; (*de juge*) robe; (*pelage*) coat; **~ de chambre** dressing gown; **~ de soirée/de mariée** evening/wedding dress

robinet [Rɔbinɛ] *nm* tap

robot [Rɔbo] *nm* robot

robuste [Rɔbyst] *adj* robust, sturdy; **robustesse** *nf* robustness, sturdiness

roc [Rɔk] *nm* rock

rocade [Rɔkad] *nf* bypass

rocaille [Rɔkaj] *nf* loose stones *pl*; (*jardin*) rockery, rock garden

roche [Rɔʃ] *nf* rock

rocher [Rɔʃe] *nm* rock

rocheux, -euse [Rɔʃø, øz] *adj* rocky

rodage [Rɔdaʒ] *nm*: **en ~** running in

roder [Rɔde] *vt* (*AUTO*) to run in

rôder [Rode] *vi* to roam about; (*de façon suspecte*) to lurk (about *ou* around); **rôdeur, -euse** *nm/f* prowler

rogne [Rɔɲ] (*fam*) *nf*: **être en ~** to be in a temper

rogner [Rɔɲe] *vt* to clip; **~ sur** (*fig*) to cut down *ou* back on

rognons [Rɔɲ5] *nmpl* (*CULIN*) kidneys

roi [Rwa] *nm* king; **la fête des R~s, les R~s** Twelfth Night

fête des Rois

i La **fête des Rois** *is celebrated on January 6. Figurines representing the magi are traditionally added to the Christmas crib and people eat* **la galette des**

Rois, *a plain, flat cake in which a porcelain charm (**la fève**) is hidden. Whoever finds the charm is king or queen for the day and chooses a partner.*

rôle [Rol] *nm* role, part

rollers [RɔlɛR] *mpl* Rollerblades ®

romain, e [Rɔmɛ̃, ɛn] *adj* Roman ♦ *nm/f*: **R~, e** Roman

roman, e [Rɔmɑ̃, an] *adj* (ARCHIT) Romanesque ♦ *nm* novel; **~ d'espionnage** spy novel *ou* story; **~ policier** detective story

romance [Rɔmɑ̃s] *nf* ballad

romancer [Rɔmɑ̃se] *vt* (agrémenter) to romanticize; **romancier, -ière** *nm/f* novelist; **romanesque** *adj* (amours, aventures) storybook *cpd*; (sentimental) romantic

roman-feuilleton [Rɔmɑ̃fœjtɔ̃] *nm* serialized novel

romanichel, le [Rɔmaniʃɛl] (péj) *nm/f* gipsy

romantique [Rɔmɑ̃tik] *adj* romantic

romarin [RɔmaRɛ̃] *nm* rosemary

rompre [Rɔ̃pR] *vt* to break; (entretien, fiançailles) to break off ♦ *vi* (fiancés) to break it off; **se ~** *vi* to break; **rompu, e** *adj* (fourbu) exhausted

ronces [Rɔ̃s] *nfpl* brambles

ronchonner [Rɔ̃ʃɔne] (fam) *vi* to grouse, grouch

rond, e [Rɔ̃, Rɔ̃d] *adj* round; (joues, mollets) well-rounded; (fam: ivre) tight ♦ *nm* (cercle) ring; (fam: sou): **je n'ai plus un ~** I haven't a penny left; **en ~** (s'asseoir, danser) in a ring; **ronde** *nf* (gén: de surveillance) rounds *pl*, patrol; (danse) round (dance); (MUS) semibreve (BRIT), whole note (US); **à la ronde** (alentour): **à 10 km à la ronde** for 10 km round; **rondelet, te** *adj* plump

rondelle [Rɔ̃dɛl] *nf* (tranche) slice, round; (TECH) washer

rondement [Rɔ̃dmɑ̃] *adv* (efficacement) briskly

rondin [Rɔ̃dɛ̃] *nm* log

rond-point [Rɔ̃pwɛ̃] *nm* roundabout

ronflant, e [Rɔ̃flɑ̃, ɑ̃t] (péj) *adj* high-flown, grand

ronflement [Rɔ̃flǝmɑ̃] *nm* snore, snoring

ronfler [Rɔ̃fle] *vi* to snore; (moteur, poêle) to hum

ronger [Rɔ̃ʒe] *vt* to gnaw (at); (suj: vers, rouille) to eat into; **se ~ les ongles** to bite one's nails; **se ~ les sangs** to worry o.s. sick; **rongeur** *nm* rodent

ronronner [Rɔ̃Rɔne] *vi* to purr

rosace [Rozas] *nf* (vitrail) rose window

rosbif [Rɔsbif] *nm*: **du ~** roasting beef; (cuit) roast beef

rose [Roz] *nf* rose ♦ *adj* pink

rosé, e [Roze] *adj* pinkish; **(vin) ~** rosé

roseau, x [Rozo] *nm* reed

rosée [Roze] *nf* dew

rosette [Rozɛt] *nf* (nœud) bow

rosier [Rozje] *nm* rosebush, rose tree

rosse [Rɔs] (fam) *adj* nasty, vicious

rossignol [Rɔsiɲɔl] *nm* (ZOOL) nightingale

rot [Ro] *nm* belch; (de bébé) burp

rotatif, -ive [Rɔtatif, iv] *adj* rotary

rotation [Rɔtasjɔ̃] *nf* rotation

roter [Rɔte] (fam) *vi* to burp, belch

rôti [Roti] *nm*: **du ~** roasting meat; (cuit) roast meat; **~ de bœuf/porc** joint of beef/pork

rotin [Rɔtɛ̃] *nm* rattan (cane); **fauteuil en ~** cane (arm)chair

rôtir [RotiR] *vi, vt* (aussi: **faire ~**) to roast; **rôtisserie** *nf* (restaurant) steakhouse; (traiteur) roast meat shop; **rôtissoire** *nf* (roasting) spit

rotule [Rɔtyl] *nf* kneecap

roturier, -ière [Rɔtyrje, jɛR] *nm/f* commoner

rouage [Rwaʒ] *nm* cog(wheel), gearwheel; **les ~s de l'État** the wheels of State

roucouler [Rukule] *vi* to coo

roue [Ru] *nf* wheel; **~ de secours** spare wheel

roué, e [Rwe] *adj* wily

rouer [Rwe] *vt*: **~ qn de coups** to give sb a thrashing

rouge [Ruʒ] *adj, nm/f* red ♦ *nm* red; **(vin)**

~ red wine; **sur la liste** ~ ex-directory (*BRIT*), unlisted (*US*); **passer au** ~ (*signal*) to go red; (*automobiliste*) to go through a red light; ~ **(à lèvres)** lipstick; **rouge-gorge** *nm* robin (redbreast)

rougeole [ʀuʒɔl] *nf* measles *sg*

rougeoyer [ʀuʒwaje] *vi* to glow red

rouget [ʀuʒɛ] *nm* mullet

rougeur [ʀuʒœʀ] *nf* redness; (*MÉD: tache*) red blotch

rougir [ʀuʒiʀ] *vi* to turn red; (*de honte, timidité*) to blush, flush; (*de plaisir, colère*) to flush

rouille [ʀuj] *nf* rust; **rouillé, e** *adj* rusty; **rouiller** *vt* to rust ♦ *vi* to rust, go rusty; **se rouiller** *vi* to rust

roulant, e [ʀulɑ̃, ɑ̃t] *adj* (*meuble*) on wheels; (*tapis etc*) moving; **escalier** ~ escalator

rouleau, x [ʀulo] *nm* roll; (*à mise en plis, à peinture, vague*) roller; ~ **à pâtisserie** rolling pin

roulement [ʀulmɑ̃] *nm* (*rotation*) rotation; (*bruit*) rumbling *no pl*, rumble; **travailler par** ~ to work on a rota (*BRIT*) *ou* rotation (*US*) basis; ~ **(à billes)** ball bearings *pl*; ~ **de tambour** drum roll

rouler [ʀule] *vt* (*papier, tapis*) to roll up; (*CULIN: pâte*) to roll out; (*fam: duper*) to do, con ♦ *vi* (*bille, boule*) to roll; (*voiture, train*) to go, run; (*automobiliste*) to drive; (*bateau*) to roll; **se ~ dans** (*boue*) to roll in; (*couverture*) to roll o.s. (up) in

roulette [ʀulɛt] *nf* (*de table, fauteuil*) castor; (*de dentiste*) drill; (*jeu*) roulette; **à ~s** on castors; **ça a marché comme sur des ~s** (*fam*) it went off very smoothly

roulis [ʀuli] *nm* roll(ing)

roulotte [ʀulɔt] *nf* caravan

roumain, e [ʀumɛ̃, ɛn] *adj* Rumanian ♦ *nm/f:* **R~, e** Rumanian

Roumanie [ʀumani] *nf* Rumania

rouquin, e [ʀukɛ̃, in] (*péj*) *nm/f* redhead

rouspéter [ʀuspete] (*fam*) *vi* to moan

rousse [ʀus] *adj voir* **roux**

roussir [ʀusiʀ] *vt* to scorch ♦ *vi* (*CULIN*): **faire** ~ to brown

route [ʀut] *nf* road; (*fig: chemin*) way; (*itinéraire, parcours*) route; (*fig: voie*) road, path; **il y a 3h de** ~ it's a 3-hour ride *ou* journey; **en** ~ on the way; **mettre en** ~ to start up; **se mettre en** ~ to set off; ~ **nationale** ≈ A road (*BRIT*), ≈ state highway (*US*); **routier, -ière** *adj* road *cpd* ♦ *nm* (*camionneur*) (long-distance) lorry (*BRIT*) *ou* truck (*US*) driver; (*restaurant*) ≈ transport café (*BRIT*), ≈ truck stop (*US*)

routine [ʀutin] *nf* routine; **routinier, -ière** (*péj*) *adj* (*activité*) humdrum; (*personne*) addicted to routine

rouvrir [ʀuvʀiʀ] *vt, vi* to reopen, open again; **se** ~ *vi* to reopen, open again

roux, rousse [ʀu, ʀus] *adj* red; (*personne*) red-haired ♦ *nm/f* redhead

royal, e, -aux [ʀwajal, o] *adj* royal; (*cadeau etc*) fit for a king

royaume [ʀwajom] *nm* kingdom; (*fig*) realm; **le R~-Uni** the United Kingdom

royauté [ʀwajote] *nf* (*régime*) monarchy

RPR *sigle m:* **Rassemblement pour la République** *French right-wing political party*

ruban [ʀybɑ̃] *nm* ribbon; ~ **adhésif** adhesive tape

rubéole [ʀybeɔl] *nf* German measles *sg*, rubella

rubis [ʀybi] *nm* ruby

rubrique [ʀybʀik] *nf* (*titre, catégorie*) heading; (*PRESSE: article*) column

ruche [ʀyʃ] *nf* hive

rude [ʀyd] *adj* (*au toucher*) rough; (*métier, tâche*) hard, tough; (*climat*) severe, harsh; (*bourru*) harsh, rough; (*fruste: manières*) rugged, tough; (*fam: fameux*) jolly good; **rudement** (*fam*) *adv* (*très*) terribly

rudimentaire [ʀydimɑ̃tɛʀ] *adj* rudimentary, basic

rudiments [ʀydimɑ̃] *nmpl:* **avoir des** ~ **d'anglais** to have a smattering of English

rudoyer [ʀydwaje] *vt* to treat harshly

rue [ʀy] *nf* street

ruée [ʀɥe] *nf* rush

ruelle [ʀɥɛl] *nf* alley(-way)

ruer [ʀɥe] *vi* (*cheval*) to kick out; **se ~** *vi*: **se ~ sur** to pounce on; **se ~ vers/dans/hors de** to rush *ou* dash towards/into/out of

rugby [ʀygbi] *nm* rugby (football)

rugir [ʀyʒiʀ] *vi* to roar

rugueux, -euse [ʀygø, øz] *adj* rough

ruine [ʀɥin] *nf* ruin; **ruiner** *vt* to ruin; **ruineux, -euse** *adj* ruinous

ruisseau, x [ʀɥiso] *nm* stream, brook

ruisseler [ʀɥis(ə)le] *vi* to stream

rumeur [ʀymœʀ] *nf* (*nouvelle*) rumour; (*bruit confus*) rumbling

ruminer [ʀymine] *vt* (*herbe*) to ruminate; (*fig*) to ruminate on *ou* over, chew over

rupture [ʀyptyʀ] *nf* (*séparation, désunion*) break-up, split; (*de négociations etc*) breakdown; (*de contrat*) breach; (*dans continuité*) break

rural, e, -aux [ʀyʀal, o] *adj* rural, country *cpd*

ruse [ʀyz] *nf*: **la ~** cunning, craftiness; (*pour tromper*) trickery; **une ~** a trick, a ruse; **rusé, e** *adj* cunning, crafty

russe [ʀys] *adj* Russian ♦ *nm/f*: **R~** Russian ♦ *nm* (*LING*) Russian

Russie [ʀysi] *nf*: **la ~** Russia

rustine ® [ʀystin] *nf* rubber repair patch (*for bicycle tyre*)

rustique [ʀystik] *adj* rustic

rustre [ʀystʀ] *nm* boor

rutilant, e [ʀytilɑ̃, ɑ̃t] *adj* gleaming

rythme [ʀitm] *nm* rhythm; (*vitesse*) rate; (: *de la vie*) pace, tempo; **rythmé, e** *adj* rhythmic(al)

S, s

s' [s] *pron voir* **se**

sa [sa] *adj voir* **son**[1]

SA *sigle* (= *société anonyme*) ≃ Ltd (*BRIT*), ≃ Inc. (*US*)

sable [sɑbl] *nm* sand; **~s mouvants** quicksand(s)

sablé [sɑble] *nm* shortbread biscuit

sabler [sɑble] *vt* (*contre le verglas*) to grit; **~ le champagne** to drink champagne

sablier [sɑblije] *nm* hourglass; (*de cuisine*) egg timer

sablonneux, -euse [sɑblɔnø, øz] *adj* sandy

saborder [sabɔʀde] *vt* (*navire*) to scuttle; (*fig: projet*) to put paid to, scupper

sabot [sabo] *nm* clog; (*de cheval*) hoof; **~ de frein** brake shoe

saboter [sabɔte] *vt* to sabotage; (*bâcler*) to make a mess of, botch

sac [sak] *nm* bag; (*à charbon etc*) sack; **~ à dos** rucksack; **~ à main** handbag; **~ de couchage** sleeping bag; **~ de voyage** travelling bag; **~ poubelle** bin liner

saccadé, e [sakade] *adj* jerky; (*respiration*) spasmodic

saccager [sakaʒe] *vt* (*piller*) to sack; (*dévaster*) to create havoc in

saccharine [sakaʀin] *nf* saccharin

sacerdoce [sasɛʀdɔs] *nm* priesthood; (*fig*) calling, vocation

sache *etc* [saʃ] *vb voir* **savoir**

sachet [saʃɛ] *nm* (small) bag; (*de sucre, café*) sachet; **du potage en ~** packet soup; **~ de thé** tea bag

sacoche [sakɔʃ] *nf* (*gén*) bag; (*de bicyclette*) saddlebag

sacquer [sake] (*fam*) *vt* (*employé*) to fire; (*détester*): **je ne peux pas le ~** I can't stand him

sacre [sakʀ] *nm* (*roi*) coronation

sacré, e [sakʀe] *adj* sacred; (*fam: satané*) blasted; (: *fameux*): **un ~ toupet** a heck of a cheek

sacrement [sakʀəmɑ̃] *nm* sacrament

sacrifice [sakʀifis] *nm* sacrifice; **sacrifier** *vt* to sacrifice

sacristie [sakʀisti] *nf* (*catholique*) sacristy; (*protestante*) vestry

sadique [sadik] *adj* sadistic

safran [safʀɑ̃] *nm* saffron

sage [saʒ] *adj* wise; (*enfant*) good

sage-femme [saʒfam] *nf* midwife

sagesse [saʒɛs] *nf* wisdom

Sagittaire [saʒitɛʀ] *nm*: **le ~** Sagittarius

Sahara [saaʀa] *nm*: **le ~** the Sahara (desert)

saignant, e [seɲɑ̃, ɑ̃t] *adj* (*viande*) rare

saignée [seɲe] *nf* (*fig*) heavy losses *pl*

saigner [seɲe] *vi* to bleed ♦ *vt* to bleed; (*animal*) to kill (by bleeding); **~ du nez** to have a nosebleed

saillie [saji] *nf* (*sur un mur etc*) projection

saillir [sajiʀ] *vi* to project, stick out; (*veine, muscle*) to bulge

sain, e [sɛ̃, sɛn] *adj* healthy; **~ d'esprit** sound in mind, sane; **~ et sauf** safe and sound, unharmed

saindoux [sɛ̃du] *nm* lard

saint, e [sɛ̃, sɛ̃t] *adj* holy ♦ *nm/f* saint; **le S~ Esprit** the Holy Spirit *ou* Ghost; **la S~e Vierge** The Blessed Virgin; **la S~ Sylvestre** New Year's Eve; **sainteté** *nf* holiness

sais *etc* [sɛ] *vb voir* **savoir**

saisi, e [sezi] *adj*: **~ de panique** panic-stricken; **être ~ (par le froid)** to be struck by the sudden cold

saisie *nf* seizure; **~e (de données)** (data) capture

saisir [seziʀ] *vt* to take hold of, grab; (*fig: occasion*) to seize; (*comprendre*) to grasp; (*entendre*) to get, catch; (*données*) to capture; (*CULIN*) to fry quickly; (*JUR: biens, publication*) to seize; **se ~ de** *vt* to seize; **saisissant, e** *adj* startling, striking

saison [sezɔ̃] *nf* season; **morte ~** slack season; **saisonnier, -ière** *adj* seasonal

sait [sɛ] *vb voir* **savoir**

salade [salad] *nf* (*BOT*) lettuce *etc*; (*CULIN*) (green) salad; (*fam: confusion*) tangle, muddle; **~ composée** mixed salad; **~ de fruits** fruit salad; **saladier** *nm* (salad) bowl

salaire [salɛʀ] *nm* (*annuel, mensuel*) salary; (*hebdomadaire, journalier*) pay, wages *pl*; **~ minimum interprofessionnel de croissance** index-linked guaranteed minimum wage

salarié, e [salaʀje] *nm/f* salaried employee; wage-earner

salaud [salo] (*fam!*) *nm* sod (!), bastard (!)

sale [sal] *adj* dirty, filthy; (*fam: mauvais*) nasty

salé, e [sale] *adj* (*mer, goût*) salty; (*CULIN: amandes, beurre etc*) salted; (: *gâteaux*) savoury; (*fam: grivois*) spicy; (: *facture*) steep

saler [sale] *vt* to salt

saleté [salte] *nf* (*état*) dirtiness; (*crasse*) dirt, filth; (*tache etc*) dirt *no pl*; (*fam: méchanceté*) dirty trick; (: *camelote*) rubbish *no pl*; (: *obscénité*) filthy thing (to say)

salière [saljɛʀ] *nf* saltcellar

salin, e [salɛ̃, in] *adj* saline

salir [saliʀ] *vt* to (make) dirty; (*fig: quelqu'un*) to soil the reputation of; **se ~** *vi* to get dirty; **salissant, e** *adj* (*tissu*) which shows the dirt; (*travail*) dirty, messy

salle [sal] *nf* room; (*d'hôpital*) ward; (*de restaurant*) dining room; (*d'un cinéma*) auditorium; (: *public*) audience; **~ à manger** dining room; **~ d'attente** waiting room; **~ de bain(s)** bathroom; **~ de classe** classroom; **~ de concert** concert hall; **~ d'eau** shower-room; **~ d'embarquement** (*à l'aéroport*) departure lounge; **~ de jeux** (*pour enfants*) playroom; **~ d'opération** (*d'hôpital*) operating theatre; **~ de séjour** living room; **~ des ventes** saleroom

salon [salɔ̃] *nm* lounge, sitting room; (*mobilier*) lounge suite; (*exposition*) exhibition, show; **~ de coiffure** hairdressing salon; **~ de thé** tearoom

salope [salɔp] (*fam!*) *nf* bitch (!); **saloperie** (*fam!*) *nf* (*action*) dirty trick; (*chose sans valeur*) rubbish *no pl*

salopette [salɔpɛt] *nf* dungarees *pl*; (*d'ouvrier*) overall(s)

salsifis [salsifi] *nm* salsify

salubre [salybʀ] *adj* healthy, salubrious

saluer [salɥe] *vt* (*pour dire bonjour, fig*) to greet; (*pour dire au revoir*) to take one's leave; (*MIL*) to salute

salut [saly] *nm* (*geste*) wave; (*parole*) greeting; (*MIL*) salute; (*sauvegarde*) safety; (*REL*) salvation ♦ *excl* (*fam: bonjour*) hi (there);

(: *au revoir*) see you, bye

salutations [salytasjɔ̃] *nfpl* greetings; **Veuillez agréer, Monsieur, mes ~ distinguées** yours faithfully

samedi [samdi] *nm* Saturday

SAMU [samy] *sigle m* (= *service d'assistance médicale d'urgence*) ≈ ambulance (service) (*BRIT*), ≈ paramedics *pl* (*US*)

sanction [sɑ̃ksjɔ̃] *nf* sanction; **sanctionner** *vt* (*loi, usage*) to sanction; (*punir*) to punish

sandale [sɑ̃dal] *nf* sandal

sandwich [sɑ̃dwi(t)ʃ] *nm* sandwich

sang [sɑ̃] *nm* blood; **en ~** covered in blood; **se faire du mauvais ~** to fret, get in a state; **sang-froid** *nm* calm, sangfroid; **de sang-froid** in cold blood; **sanglant, e** *adj* bloody

sangle [sɑ̃gl] *nf* strap

sanglier [sɑ̃glije] *nm* (wild) boar

sanglot [sɑ̃glo] *nm* sob; **sangloter** *vi* to sob

sangsue [sɑ̃sy] *nf* leech

sanguin, e [sɑ̃gɛ̃, in] *adj* blood *cpd*; **sanguinaire** *adj* bloodthirsty

sanitaire [saniteʀ] *adj* health *cpd*; **~s** *nmpl* (*lieu*) bathroom *sg*

sans [sɑ̃] *prép* without; **un pull ~ manches** a sleeveless jumper; **~ faute** without fail; **~ arrêt** without a break; **~ ça** (*fam*) otherwise; **~ qu'il s'en aperçoive** without him *ou* his noticing; **sans-abri** *nmpl* homeless; **sans-emploi** *nm/f inv* unemployed person; **les sans-emploi** the unemployed; **sans-gêne** *adj inv* inconsiderate

santé [sɑ̃te] *nf* health; **en bonne ~** in good health; **boire à la ~ de qn** to drink (to) sb's health; **à ta/votre ~!** cheers!

saoudien, ne [saudjɛ̃, jɛn] *adj* Saudi Arabian ♦ *nm/f*: **S~, ne** Saudi Arabian

saoul, e [su, sul] *adj* = **soûl**

saper [sape] *vt* to undermine, sap

sapeur-pompier [sapœʀpɔ̃pje] *nm* fireman

saphir [safiʀ] *nm* sapphire

sapin [sapɛ̃] *nm* fir (tree); (*bois*) fir; **~ de Noël** Christmas tree

sarcastique [saʀkastik] *adj* sarcastic

sarcler [saʀkle] *vt* to weed

Sardaigne [saʀdɛɲ] *nf*: **la ~** Sardinia

sardine [saʀdin] *nf* sardine

sarrasin [saʀazɛ̃] *nm* buckwheat

SARL *sigle f* (= *société à responsabilité limitée*) ≈ plc (*BRIT*), ≈ Inc. (*US*)

sas [sas] *nm* (*de sous-marin, d'engin spatial*) airlock; (*d'écluse*) lock

satané, e [satane] (*fam*) *adj* confounded

satellite [satelit] *nm* satellite

satin [satɛ̃] *nm* satin

satire [satiʀ] *nf* satire; **satirique** *adj* satirical

satisfaction [satisfaksjɔ̃] *nf* satisfaction

satisfaire [satisfɛʀ] *vt* to satisfy; **~ à** (*conditions*) to meet; **satisfaisant, e** *adj* (*acceptable*) satisfactory; **satisfait, e** *adj* satisfied; **satisfait de** happy *ou* satisfied with

saturer [satyʀe] *vt* to saturate

sauce [sos] *nf* sauce; (*avec un rôti*) gravy; **saucière** *nf* sauceboat

saucisse [sosis] *nf* sausage

saucisson [sosisɔ̃] *nm* (slicing) sausage

sauf, sauve [sof, sov] *adj* unharmed, unhurt; (*fig: honneur*) intact, saved ♦ *prép* except; **laisser la vie sauve à qn** to spare sb's life; **~ si** (*à moins que*) unless; **~ erreur** if I'm not mistaken; **~ avis contraire** unless you hear to the contrary

sauge [soʒ] *nf* sage

saugrenu, e [sogʀany] *adj* preposterous

saule [sol] *nm* willow (tree)

saumon [somɔ̃] *nm* salmon *inv*

saumure [somyʀ] *nf* brine

saupoudrer [sopudʀe] *vt*: **~ qch de** to sprinkle sth with

saur [sɔʀ] *adj m*: **hareng ~** smoked *ou* red herring, kipper

saurai [sɔʀe] *vb voir* **savoir**

saut [so] *nm* jump; (*discipline sportive*) jumping; **faire un ~ chez qn** to pop over to sb's (place); **~ à l'élastique** bungee jumping; **~ à la perche** pole vaulting; **~ en hauteur/longueur** high/long jump; **~ périlleux** somersault

saute [sot] *nf*: **~ d'humeur** sudden change of mood

sauter [sote] *vi* to jump, leap; (*exploser*) to blow up, explode; (: *fusibles*) to blow; (*se détacher*) to pop out (*ou* off) ♦ *vt* to jump (over), leap (over); (*fig: omettre*) to skip, miss (out); **faire ~** to blow up; (*CULIN*) to sauté; **~ au cou de qn** to fly into sb's arms; **~ sur une occasion** to jump at an opportunity; **~ aux yeux** to be (quite) obvious

sauterelle [sotʀɛl] *nf* grasshopper

sautiller [sotije] *vi* (*oiseau*) to hop; (*enfant*) to skip

sauvage [sovaʒ] *adj* (*gén*) wild; (*peuplade*) savage; (*farouche: personne*) unsociable; (*barbare*) wild, savage; (*non officiel*) unauthorized, unofficial; **faire du camping ~** to camp in the wild ♦ *nm/f* savage; (*timide*) unsociable type

sauve [sov] *adj f voir* **sauf**

sauvegarde [sovgaʀd] *nf* safeguard; (*INFORM*) backup; **sauvegarder** *vt* to safeguard; (*INFORM: enregistrer*) to save; (: *copier*) to back up

sauve-qui-peut [sovkipø] *excl* run for your life!

sauver [sove] *vt* to save; (*porter secours à*) to rescue; (*récupérer*) to salvage, rescue; **se ~** *vi* (*s'enfuir*) to run away; (*fam: partir*) to be off; **sauvetage** *nm* rescue; **sauveteur** *nm* rescuer; **sauvette**: **à la sauvette** *adv* (*se marier etc*) hastily, hurriedly; **sauveur** *nm* saviour (*BRIT*), savior (*US*)

savais *etc* [save] *vb voir* **savoir**

savamment [savamā] *adv* (*avec érudition*) learnedly; (*habilement*) skilfully, cleverly

savant, e [savā, āt] *adj* scholarly, learned ♦ *nm* scientist

saveur [savœʀ] *nf* flavour; (*fig*) savour

savoir [savwaʀ] *vt* to know; (*être capable de*): **il sait nager** he can swim ♦ *nm* knowledge; **se ~** *vi* (*être connu*) to be

known; **à ~** that is, namely; **faire ~ qch à qn** to let sb know sth; **pas que je sache** not as far as I know

savon [savɔ̃] *nm* (*produit*) soap; (*morceau*) bar of soap; (*fam*): **passer un ~ à qn** to give sb a good dressing-down; **savonner** *vt* to soap; **savonnette** *nf* bar of soap

savons [savɔ̃] *vb voir* **savoir**

savourer [savuʀe] *vt* to savour; **savoureux, -euse** *adj* tasty; (*fig: anecdote*) spicy, juicy

saxo(phone) [saksɔ(fɔn)] *nm* sax(ophone)

scabreux, -euse [skabʀø, øz] *adj* risky; (*indécent*) improper, shocking

scandale [skādal] *nm* scandal; (*tapage*): **faire un ~** to make a scene, create a disturbance; **faire ~** to scandalize people; **scandaleux, -euse** *adj* scandalous, outrageous

scandinave [skādinav] *adj* Scandinavian ♦ *nm/f*: **S~** Scandinavian

Scandinavie [skādinavi] *nf* Scandinavia

scaphandre [skafādʀ] *nm* (*de plongeur*) diving suit

scarabée [skaʀabe] *nm* beetle

scarlatine [skaʀlatin] *nf* scarlet fever

scarole [skaʀɔl] *nf* endive

sceau, x [so] *nm* seal

scélérat, e [selera, at] *nm/f* villain

sceller [sele] *vt* to seal

scénario [senaʀjo] *nm* scenario

scène [sɛn] *nf* (*gén*) scene; (*estrade, fig: théâtre*) stage; **entrer en ~** to come on stage; **mettre en ~** (*THÉÂTRE*) to stage; (*CINÉMA*) to direct; **~ de ménage** domestic scene

sceptique [sɛptik] *adj* sceptical

schéma [ʃema] *nm* (*diagramme*) diagram, sketch; **schématique** *adj* diagrammatic(al), schematic; (*fig*) oversimplified

sciatique [sjatik] *nf* sciatica

scie [si] *nf* saw; **~ à métaux** hacksaw

sciemment [sjamā] *adv* knowingly

science [sjās] *nf* science; (*savoir*) knowledge; **~s naturelles** (*SCOL*) natural science *sg*, biology *sg*; **~s po** political science *ou* studies *pl*; **science-fiction** *nf* science fiction; **scientifique** *adj* scientific ♦ *nm/f* scientist; (*étudiant*) science student

scier [sje] *vt* to saw; (*retrancher*) to saw off; **scierie** *nf* sawmill

scinder [sɛ̃de] *vt* to split up; **se ~** *vi* to split up

scintiller [sɛ̃tije] *vi* to sparkle; (*étoile*) to twinkle

scission [sisjɔ̃] *nf* split

sciure [sjyʀ] *nf*: **~ (de bois)** sawdust

sclérose [skleʀoz] *nf*: **~ en plaques** multiple sclerosis

scolaire [skɔlɛʀ] *adj* school *cpd*; **scolariser** *vt* to provide with schooling/schools; **scolarité** *nf* schooling

scooter [skutœʀ] *nm* (motor) scooter

score [skɔʀ] *nm* score

scorpion [skɔʀpjɔ̃] *nm* (*signe*): **le S~** Scorpio

Scotch ® [skɔtʃ] *nm* adhesive tape

scout, e [skut] *adj, nm* scout

script [skʀipt] *nm* (*écriture*) printing; (*CINÉMA*) (shooting) script

scrupule [skʀypyl] *nm* scruple

scruter [skʀyte] *vt* to scrutinize; (*l'obscurité*) to peer into

scrutin [skʀytɛ̃] *nm* (*vote*) ballot; (*ensemble des opérations*) poll

sculpter [skylte] *vt* to sculpt; (*bois*) to carve; **sculpteur** *nm* sculptor; **sculpture** *nf* sculpture; **sculpture sur bois** wood carving

SDF *sigle m* (= *sans domicile fixe*) homeless person; **les SDF** the homeless

MOT-CLÉ

se [sə], **s'** *pron* 1 (*emploi réfléchi*) oneself; (*: masc*) himself; (*: fém*) herself; (*: sujet non humain*) itself; (*: pl*) themselves; **se voir comme l'on est** to see o.s. as one is

2 (*réciproque*) one another, each other; **ils s'aiment** they love one another *ou* each other

3 (*passif*): **cela se répare facilement** it is easily repaired

4 (*possessif*): **se casser la jambe/laver les mains** to break one's leg/wash one's hands

séance [seɑ̃s] *nf* (*d'assemblée*) meeting, session; (*de tribunal*) sitting, session; (*musicale, CINÉMA, THÉÂTRE*) performance; **~ tenante** forthwith

seau, x [so] *nm* bucket, pail

sec, sèche [sɛk, sɛʃ] *adj* dry; (*raisins, figues*) dried; (*cœur: insensible*) hard, cold ♦ *nm*: **tenir au ~** to keep in a dry place ♦ *adv* hard; **je le bois ~** I drink it straight *ou* neat; **à ~** (*puits*) dried up

sécateur [sekatœʀ] *nm* secateurs *pl* (*BRIT*), shears *pl*

sèche [sɛʃ] *adj f voir* **sec**; **sèche-cheveux** *nm inv* hair-drier; **sèche-linge** *nm inv* tumble dryer; **sèchement** *adv* (*répondre*) drily

sécher [seʃe] *vt* to dry; (*dessécher: peau, blé*) to dry (out); (*: étang*) to dry up; (*fam: cours*) to skip ♦ *vi* to dry; to dry out; to dry up; (*fam: candidat*) to be stumped; **se ~** (*après le bain*) to dry o.s.; **sécheresse** *nf* dryness; (*absence de pluie*) drought; **séchoir** *nm* drier

second, e [s(ə)gɔ̃, ɔ̃d] *adj* second ♦ *nm* (*assistant*) second in command; (*NAVIG*) first mate; **voyager en ~e** to travel second-class; **secondaire** *adj* secondary; **seconde** *nf* second; **seconder** *vt* to assist

secouer [s(ə)kwe] *vt* to shake; (*passagers*) to rock; (*traumatiser*) to shake (up); **se ~** *vi* (*fam: faire un effort*) to shake o.s. up; (*: se dépêcher*) to get a move on

secourir [s(ə)kuʀiʀ] *vt* (*venir en aide à*) to assist, aid; **secourisme** *nm* first aid; **secouriste** *nmf* first-aid worker

secours [s(ə)kuʀ] *nm* help, aid, assistance ♦ *nmpl* aid *sg*; **au ~!** help!; **appeler au ~** to shout *ou* call for help; **porter ~ à qn** to give sb assistance, help sb; **les premiers ~** first aid *sg*

secousse [s(ə)kus] *nf* jolt, bump; (*électri-*

que) shock; (*fig: psychologique*) jolt, shock; ~ **sismique** earth tremor

secret, -ète [sǝkrɛ, ɛt] *adj* secret; (*fig: renfermé*) reticent, reserved ♦ *nm* secret; (*discrétion absolue*): **le** ~ secrecy

secrétaire [s(ǝ)krɛtɛr] *nm/f* secretary ♦ *nm* (*meuble*) writing desk; ~ **de direction** private *ou* personal secretary; ~ **d'État** junior minister; ~ **général** (*COMM*) company secretary; **secrétariat** *nm* (*profession*) secretarial work; (*bureau*) office; (: *d'organisation internationale*) secretariat

secteur [sɛktœr] *nm* sector; (*zone*) area; (*ÉLEC*): **branché sur** ~ plugged into the mains (supply)

section [sɛksjɔ̃] *nf* section; (*de parcours d'autobus*) fare stage; (*MIL: unité*) platoon; **sectionner** *vt* to sever

Sécu [seky] *abr f* = **sécurité sociale**

séculaire [sekylɛr] *adj* (*très vieux*) age-old

sécuriser [sekyrize] *vt* to give (a feeling of) security to

sécurité [sekyrite] *nf* (*absence de danger*) safety; (*absence de troubles*) security; **système de** ~ security system; **être en** ~ to be safe; **la** ~ **routière** road safety; **la** ~ **sociale** ≃ (the) Social Security (*BRIT*), ≃ Welfare (*US*)

sédentaire [sedɑ̃tɛr] *adj* sedentary

séduction [sedyksjɔ̃] *nf* seduction; (*charme, attrait*) charm

séduire [sedɥir] *vt* to charm; (*femme: abuser de*) to seduce; **séduisant, e** *adj* (*femme*) seductive; (*homme, offre*) very attractive

ségrégation [segregasjɔ̃] *nf* segregation

seigle [sɛgl] *nm* rye

seigneur [sɛɲœr] *nm* lord

sein [sɛ̃] *nm* breast; (*entrailles*) womb; **au** ~ **de** (*équipe, institution*) within

séisme [seism] *nm* earthquake

seize [sɛz] *num* sixteen; **seizième** *num* sixteenth

séjour [seʒur] *nm* stay; (*pièce*) living room; **séjourner** *vi* to stay

sel [sɛl] *nm* salt; (*fig: piquant*) spice

sélection [selɛksjɔ̃] *nf* selection; **sélectionner** *vt* to select

self-service [sɛlfsɛrvis] *adj, nm* self-service

selle [sɛl] *nf* saddle; ~**s** *nfpl* (*MÉD*) stools; **seller** *vt* to saddle

sellette [sɛlɛt] *nf*: **être sur la** ~ to be in the hot seat

selon [s(ǝ)lɔ̃] *prép* according to; (*en se conformant à*) in accordance with; ~ **que** according to whether; ~ **moi** as I see it

semaine [s(ǝ)mɛn] *nf* week; **en** ~ during the week, on weekdays

semblable [sɑ̃blabl] *adj* similar; (*de ce genre*): **de** ~**s mésaventures** such mishaps ♦ *nm* fellow creature *ou* man; ~ **à** similar to, like

semblant [sɑ̃blɑ̃] *nm*: **un** ~ **de ...** a semblance of ...; **faire** ~ **(de faire)** to pretend (to do)

sembler [sɑ̃ble] *vb +attrib* to seem ♦ *vb impers*: **il semble (bien) que/inutile de** it (really) seems *ou* appears that/useless to; **il me semble que** it seems to me that; **comme bon lui semble** as he sees fit

semelle [s(ǝ)mɛl] *nf* sole; (*intérieure*) insole, inner sole

semence [s(ǝ)mɑ̃s] *nf* (*graine*) seed

semer [s(ǝ)me] *vt* to sow; (*fig: éparpiller*) to scatter; (: *confusion*) to spread; (*fam: poursuivants*) to lose, shake off; **semé de** (*difficultés*) riddled with

semestre [s(ǝ)mɛstr] *nm* half-year; (*SCOL*) semester

séminaire [seminɛr] *nm* seminar

semi-remorque [sǝmirǝmɔrk] *nm* articulated lorry (*BRIT*), semi(trailer) (*US*)

semoule [s(ǝ)mul] *nf* semolina

sempiternel, le [sɑ̃pitɛrnɛl] *adj* eternal, never-ending

sénat [sena] *nm* senate; **sénateur** *nm* senator

sens [sɑ̃s] *nm* (*PHYSIOL, instinct*) sense; (*signification*) meaning, sense; (*direction*) direction; **à mon** ~ to my mind; **dans le** ~ **des aiguilles d'une montre** clockwise; ~

dessus dessous upside down; ~ **interdit** one-way street; ~ **unique** one-way street

sensation [sɑ̃sasjɔ̃] *nf* sensation; **à** ~ (*péj*) sensational; **faire** ~ to cause *ou* create a sensation; **sensationnel, le** *adj* (*fam*) fantastic, terrific

sensé, e [sɑ̃se] *adj* sensible

sensibiliser [sɑ̃sibilize] *vt:* ~ **qn à** to make sb sensitive to

sensibilité [sɑ̃sibilite] *nf* sensitivity

sensible [sɑ̃sibl] *adj* sensitive; (*aux sens*) perceptible; (*appréciable: différence, progrès*) appreciable, noticeable; **sensiblement** *adv* (*à peu près*): **ils sont sensiblement du même âge** they are approximately the same age; **sensiblerie** *nf* sentimentality

sensuel, le [sɑ̃sɥɛl] *adj* (*personne*) sensual; (*musique*) sensuous

sentence [sɑ̃tɑ̃s] *nf* (*jugement*) sentence

sentier [sɑ̃tje] *nm* path

sentiment [sɑ̃timɑ̃] *nm* feeling; **sentimental, e, -aux** *adj* sentimental; (*vie, aventure*) love *cpd*

sentinelle [sɑ̃tinɛl] *nf* sentry

sentir [sɑ̃tiʀ] *vt* (*par l'odorat*) to smell; (*par le goût*) to taste; (*au toucher, fig*) to feel; (*répandre une odeur de*) to smell of; (: *ressemblance*) to smell like ♦ *vi* to smell; ~ **mauvais** to smell bad; **se** ~ **bien** to feel good; **se** ~ **mal** (*être indisposé*) to feel unwell *ou* ill; **se** ~ **le courage/la force de faire** to feel brave/strong enough to do; **il ne peut pas le** ~ (*fam*) he can't stand him

séparation [separasjɔ̃] *nf* separation; (*cloison*) division, partition

séparé, e [separe] *adj* (*distinct*) separate; (*époux*) separated; **séparément** *adv* separately

séparer [separe] *vt* to separate; (*désunir*) to drive apart; (*détacher*): ~ **qch de** to pull sth (off) from; (*se diviser: route etc*) to divide; **se** ~ **de** (*époux*) to separate *ou* part from; (*employé, objet personnel*) to part with

sept [sɛt] *num* seven; **septante** (*BELGIQUE, SUISSE*) *adj inv* seventy

septembre [sɛptɑ̃bʀ] *nm* September

septennat [sɛptena] *nm* seven year term of office (of French President)

septentrional, e, -aux [sɛptɑ̃tʀijɔnal, o] *adj* northern

septicémie [sɛptisemi] *nf* blood poisoning, septicaemia

septième [sɛtjɛm] *num* seventh

septique [sɛptik] *adj:* **fosse** ~ septic tank

sépulture [sepyltyʀ] *nf* (*tombeau*) burial place, grave

séquelles [sekɛl] *nfpl* after-effects; (*fig*) aftermath *sg*

séquestrer [sekɛstʀe] *vt* (*personne*) to confine illegally; (*biens*) to impound

serai *etc* [səʀe] *vb voir* **être**

serein, e [səʀɛ̃, ɛn] *adj* serene

serez [səʀe] *vb voir* **être**

sergent [sɛʀʒɑ̃] *nm* sergeant

série [seʀi] *nf* series *inv*; (*de clés, casseroles, outils*) set; (*catégorie: SPORT*) rank; **en** ~ in quick succession; (*COMM*) mass *cpd*; **hors** ~ (*COMM*) custom-built

sérieusement [seʀjøzmɑ̃] *adv* seriously

sérieux, -euse [seʀjø, jøz] *adj* serious; (*élève, employé*) reliable, responsible; (*client, maison*) reliable, dependable ♦ *nm* seriousness; (*d'une entreprise etc*) reliability; **garder son** ~ to keep a straight face; **prendre qch/qn au** ~ to take sth/sb seriously

serin [s(ə)ʀɛ̃] *nm* canary

seringue [s(ə)ʀɛ̃g] *nf* syringe

serions [səʀjɔ̃] *vb voir* **être**

serment [sɛʀmɑ̃] *nm* (*juré*) oath; (*promesse*) pledge, vow

sermon [sɛʀmɔ̃] *nm* sermon

séronégatif, -ive [seʀonegatif, iv] *adj* (*MÉD*) HIV negative

séropositif, -ive [seʀopozitif, iv] *adj* (*MÉD*) HIV positive

serpent [sɛʀpɑ̃] *nm* snake; **serpenter** *vi* to wind

serpillière [sɛʀpijɛʀ] *nf* floorcloth

serre [sɛʀ] *nf* (*AGR*) greenhouse; **~s** *nfpl* (*griffes*) claws, talons

serré, e [sɛʀe] *adj* (*habits*) tight; (*fig: lutte, match*) tight, close-fought; (*passagers etc*) (tightly) packed; (*réseau*) dense; **avoir le cœur ~** to have a heavy heart

serrer [sɛʀe] *vt* (*tenir*) to grip *ou* hold tight; (*comprimer, coincer*) to squeeze; (*poings, mâchoires*) to clench; (*suj: vêtement*) to be too tight for; (*ceinture, nœud, vis*) to tighten ♦ *vi*: **~ à droite** to keep *ou* get over to the right; **se ~** *vi* (*se rapprocher*) to squeeze up; **se ~ contre qn** to huddle up to sb; **~ la main à qn** to shake sb's hand; **~ qn dans ses bras** to hug sb, clasp sb in one's arms

serrure [sɛʀyʀ] *nf* lock; **serrurier** *nm* locksmith

sert *etc* [sɛʀ] *vb voir* **servir**

servante [sɛʀvɑ̃t] *nf* (maid)servant

serveur, -euse [sɛʀvœʀ, øz] *nm/f* waiter (waitress)

serviable [sɛʀvjabl] *adj* obliging, willing to help

service [sɛʀvis] *nm* service; (*assortiment de vaisselle*) set, service; (*bureau: de la vente etc*) department, section; (*travail*) duty; **premier ~** (*série de repas*) first sitting; **être de ~** to be on duty; **faire le ~** to serve; **rendre un ~ à qn** to do sb a favour; (*objet: s'avérer utile*) to come in useful *ou* handy for sb; **mettre en ~** to put into service *ou* operation; **~ compris/non compris** service included/not included; **hors ~** out of order; **~ après-vente** after-sales service; **~ d'ordre** police (*ou* stewards) in charge of maintaining order; **~ militaire** military service; **~s secrets** secret service *sg*

┌──────────────────────┐
│ **service militaire** │
└──────────────────────┘

i French men over eighteen are required to do to ten months' **service militaire** if pronounced fit. The call-up can be delayed if the conscript is in full-time higher education. Conscientious objectors are required

to do two years' public service. Since 1970, women have been able to do military service, though few do.

──────────────────────

serviette [sɛʀvjɛt] *nf* (*de table*) (table) napkin, serviette; (*de toilette*) towel; (*porte-documents*) briefcase; **~ hygiénique** sanitary towel

servir [sɛʀviʀ] *vt* to serve; (*au restaurant*) to wait on; (*au magasin*) to serve, attend to ♦ *vi* (*TENNIS*) to serve; (*CARTES*) to deal; **se ~** *vi* (*prendre d'un plat*) to help o.s.; **vous êtes servi?** are you being served?; **~ qn** (*diplôme, livre*) to be of use to sb; **~ à qch/faire** (*outil etc*) to be used for sth/doing; **ça ne sert à rien** it's no use; **~ (à qn) de** to serve as (for sb); **se ~ de** (*plat*) to help o.s. to; (*voiture, outil, relations*) to use

serviteur [sɛʀvitœʀ] *nm* servant

ses [se] *adj voir* **son**[1]

set [sɛt] *nm*: **~ (de table)** tablemat, place mat

seuil [sœj] *nm* doorstep; (*fig*) threshold

seul, e [sœl] *adj* (*sans compagnie*) alone; (*unique*): **un ~ livre** only one book, a single book ♦ *adv* (*vivre*) alone, on one's own ♦ *nm, nf*: **il en reste un(e) ~(e)** there's only one left; **le ~ livre** the only book; **parler tout ~** to talk to oneself; **faire qch (tout) ~** to do sth (all) on one's own *ou* (all) by oneself; **à lui (tout) ~** single-handed, on his own; **se sentir ~** to feel lonely; **seulement** *adv* only; **non seulement ... mais aussi** *ou* **encore** not only ... but also

sève [sɛv] *nf* sap

sévère [sevɛʀ] *adj* severe

sévices [sevis] *nmpl* (physical) cruelty *sg*, ill treatment *sg*

sévir [seviʀ] *vi* (*punir*) to use harsh measures, crack down; (*suj: fléau*) to rage, be rampant

sevrer [savʀe] *vt* (*enfant etc*) to wean

sexe [sɛks] *nm* sex; (*organes génitaux*) genitals, sex organs; **sexuel, le** *adj* sexual

seyant, e [sɛjɑ̃, ɑ̃t] *adj* becoming
shampooing [ʃɑ̃pwɛ̃] *nm* shampoo
short [ʃɔʀt] *nm* (pair of) shorts *pl*

MOT-CLÉ

si [si] *nm* (MUS) B; (*en chantant la gamme*) ti
♦ *adv* **1** (*oui*) yes
2 (*tellement*) so; **si gentil/rapidement** so
kind/fast; **(tant et) si bien que** so much
so that; **si rapide qu'il soit** however fast
he may be
♦ *conj* if; **si tu veux** if you want; **je me**
demande si I wonder if *ou* whether; **si**
seulement if only

Sicile [sisil] *nf*: **la ~** Sicily
SIDA [sida] *sigle m* (= *syndrome immuno-*
déficitaire acquis) AIDS *sg*
sidéré, e [sideʀe] *adj* staggered
sidérurgie [sideʀyʀʒi] *nf* steel industry
siècle [sjɛkl] *nm* century
siège [sjɛʒ] *nm* seat; (*d'entreprise*) head
office; (*d'organisation*) headquarters *pl*;
(MIL) siege; **~ social** registered office; **sié-**
ger *vi* to sit
sien, ne [sjɛ̃, sjɛn] *pron*: **le(la) ~(ne), les**
~(ne)s (*homme*) his; (*femme*) hers; (*chose,*
animal) its; **les ~s** (*sa famille*) one's family;
faire des ~nes (*fam*) to be up to one's
(usual) tricks
sieste [sjɛst] *nf* (afternoon) snooze *ou* nap;
faire la ~ to have a snooze *ou* nap
sifflement [sifləmɑ̃] *nm*: **un ~** a whistle
siffler [sifle] *vi* (*gén*) to whistle; (*en respi-*
rant) to wheeze; (*serpent, vapeur*) to hiss ♦ *vt*
(*chanson*) to whistle; (*chien etc*) to whistle
for; (*fille*) to whistle at; (*pièce, orateur*) to hiss,
boo; (*fin du match, départ*) to blow one's
whistle for; (*fam: verre*) to guzzle
sifflet [siflɛ] *nm* whistle; **coup de ~** whistle
siffloter [siflɔte] *vi, vt* to whistle
sigle [sigl] *nm* acronym
signal, -aux [siɲal, o] *nm* signal; (*indice,*
écriteau) sign; **donner le ~ de** to give the
signal for; **~ d'alarme** alarm signal; **si-**

gnaux (lumineux) (AUTO) traffic signals;
signalement *nm* description, particulars
pl
signaler [siɲale] *vt* to indicate; (*personne:*
faire un signe) to signal; (*vol, perte*) to report; (*faire remarquer*): **~ qch à qn/(à qn)**
que to point out sth to sb/(to sb) that;
se ~ (par) to distinguish o.s. (by)
signature [siɲatyʀ] *nf* signature; (*action*)
signing
signe [siɲ] *nm* sign; (TYPO) mark; **faire un**
~ de la main to give a sign with one's
hand; **faire ~ à qn** (*fig: contacter*) to get
in touch with sb; **faire ~ à qn d'entrer** to
motion (to) sb to come in; **signer** *vt* to
sign; **se signer** *vi* to cross o.s.
significatif, -ive [siɲifikatif, iv] *adj* significant
signification [siɲifikasjɔ̃] *nf* meaning
signifier [siɲifje] *vt* (*vouloir dire*) to mean;
(*faire connaître*): **~ qch (à qn)** to make sth
known (to sb)
silence [silɑ̃s] *nm* silence; (MUS) rest; **gar-**
der le ~ to keep silent, say nothing; **si-**
lencieux, -euse *adj* quiet, silent ♦ *nm*
silencer
silex [silɛks] *nm* flint
silhouette [silwɛt] *nf* outline, silhouette;
(*lignes, contour*) outline; (*allure*) figure
silicium [silisjɔm] *nm* silicon
sillage [sijaʒ] *nm* wake
sillon [sijɔ̃] *nm* furrow; (*de disque*) groove;
sillonner *vt* to criss-cross
simagrées [simagʀe] *nfpl* fuss *sg*
similaire [similɛʀ] *adj* similar; **similicuir**
nm imitation leather; **similitude** *nf* similarity
simple [sɛ̃pl] *adj* simple; (*non multiple*) single; **~ messieurs** (TENNIS) men's sin-
gles *sg*; **~ soldat** private
simplicité [sɛ̃plisite] *nf* simplicity
simplifier [sɛ̃plifje] *vt* to simplify
simulacre [simylakʀ] *nm* (*péj*): **un ~ de** a
pretence of
simuler [simyle] *vt* to sham, simulate
simultané, e [simyltane] *adj* simulta-

neous

sincère [sɛ̃sɛʀ] *adj* sincere; **sincèrement** *adv* sincerely; *(pour parler franchement)* honestly, really; **sincérité***nf* sincerity

sine qua non [sinekwanɔn] *adj:* **condition ~** indispensable condition

singe [sɛ̃ʒ] *nm* monkey; *(de grande taille)* ape; **singer***vt* to ape, mimic; **singeries** *nfpl* antics

singulariser [sɛ̃gylaʀize]: **se ~** *vi* to call attention to o.s.

singularité [sɛ̃gylaʀite] *nf* peculiarity

singulier, -ière [sɛ̃gylje, jɛʀ] *adj* remarkable, singular ♦ *nm* singular

sinistre [sinistʀ] *adj* sinister ♦ *nm (incendie)* blaze; *(catastrophe)* disaster; *(ASSURANCES)* damage *(giving rise to a claim)*; **sinistré, e***adj* disaster-stricken ♦ *nm/f* disaster victim

sinon [sinɔ̃] *conj (autrement, sans quoi)* otherwise, or else; *(sauf)* except, other than; *(si ce n'est)* if not

sinueux, -euse [sinɥø, øz] *adj* winding

sinus [sinys] *nm (ANAT)* sinus; *(GÉOM)* sine; **sinusite***nf* sinusitis

siphon [sifɔ̃] *nm (tube, d'eau gazeuse)* siphon; *(d'évier etc)* U-bend

sirène [siʀɛn] *nf* siren; **~ d'alarme** fire alarm; *(en temps de guerre)* air-raid siren

sirop [siʀo] *nm (à diluer: de fruit etc)* syrup; *(pharmaceutique)* syrup, mixture; **~ pour la toux** cough mixture

siroter [siʀɔte] *vt* to sip

sismique [sismik] *adj* seismic

site [sit] *nm (paysage, environnement)* setting; *(d'une ville etc: emplacement)* site; **~ (pittoresque)** beauty spot; **~s touristiques** places of interest; **~ Web** *(INFORM)* website

sitôt [sito] *adv:* **~ parti** as soon as he *etc* had left; **~ que** as soon as; **pas de ~** not for a long time

situation [sitɥasjɔ̃] *nf* situation; *(d'un édifice, d'une ville)* position, location; **~ de famille** marital status

situé, e [sitɥe] *adj* situated

situer [sitɥe] *vt* to site, situate; *(en pensée)* to set, place; **se ~** *vi* to be situated

six [sis] *num* six; **sixième***num* sixth ♦ *nf (SCOL)* first form

Skaï ® [skaj] *nm* Leatherette ®

ski [ski] *nm (objet)* ski; *(sport)* skiing; **faire du ~** to ski; **~ de fond** cross-country skiing; **~ nautique** water-skiing; **~ de piste** downhill skiing; **~ de randonnée** cross-country skiing; **skier** *vi* to ski; **skieur, -euse***nm/f* skier

slip [slip] *nm (sous-vêtement)* pants *pl*, briefs *pl*; *(de bain: d'homme)* trunks *pl*; *(: du bikini)* (bikini) briefs *pl*

SMIC [smik] *sigle m* = **salaire minimum interprofessionnel de croissance**

SMIC

ⓘ In France, the **SMIC** is the minimum legal hourly rate for workers over eighteen. It is index-linked and is raised each time the cost of living rises by 2%.

---

smicard, e [smikaʀ, aʀd] *(fam) nm/f* minimum wage earner

smoking [smɔkiŋ] *nm* dinner suit

SMS *abr m* (= *Short Message Service*) SMS

SNCF *sigle f* (= *Société nationale des chemins de fer français*) French railways

snob [snɔb] *adj* snobbish ♦ *nm/f* snob; **snobisme***nm* snobbery, snobbishness

sobre [sɔbʀ] *adj (personne)* temperate, abstemious; *(élégance, style)* sober

sobriquet [sɔbʀikɛ] *nm* nickname

social, e, -aux [sɔsjal, jo] *adj* social

socialisme [sɔsjalism] *nm* socialism; **socialiste***nm/f* socialist

société [sɔsjete] *nf* society; *(sportive)* club; *(COMM)* company; **la ~ de consommation** the consumer society; **~ anonyme** ≃ limited *(BRIT) ou* incorporated *(US)* company

sociologie [sɔsjɔlɔʒi] *nf* sociology

socle [sɔkl] *nm (de colonne, statue)* plinth, pedestal; *(de lampe)* base

socquette [sɔkɛt] *nf* ankle sock

sœur [sœʀ] *nf* sister; (*religieuse*) nun, sister

soi [swa] *pron* oneself; **en ~** (*intrinsèquement*) in itself; **cela va de ~** that *ou* it goes without saying; **soi-disant** *adj inv* so-called ♦ *adv* supposedly

soie [swa] *nf* silk; **soierie** *nf* (*tissu*) silk

soif [swaf] *nf* thirst; **avoir ~** to be thirsty; **donner ~ à qn** to make sb thirsty

soigné, e [swaɲe] *adj* (*tenue*) well-groomed, neat; (*travail*) careful, meticulous

soigner [swaɲe] *vt* (*malade, maladie: suj: docteur*) to treat; (*suj: infirmière, mère*) to nurse over, look after; (*travail, détails*) to take care over; (*jardin, invités*) to look after; **soigneux, -euse** *adj* (*propre*) tidy, neat; (*appliqué*) painstaking, careful

soi-même [swamɛm] *pron* oneself

soin [swɛ̃] *nm* (*application*) care; (*propreté, ordre*) tidiness, neatness; **~s** *nmpl* (*à un malade, blessé*) treatment *sg*, medical attention *sg*; (*hygiène*) care *sg*; **prendre ~ de** to take care of, look after; **prendre ~ de faire** to take care to do; **les premiers ~s** first aid *sg*

soir [swaʀ] *nm* evening; **ce ~** this evening, tonight; **demain ~** tomorrow evening, tomorrow night; **soirée** *nf* evening; (*réception*) party

soit [swa] *vb voir* **être** ♦ *conj* (*à savoir*) namely; (*ou*): **~ ... ~** either ... or ♦ *adv* so be it, very well; **~ que ... ~ que** *ou* **ou que** whether ... or whether

soixantaine [swasɑ̃tɛn] *nf*: **une ~ (de)** sixty or so, about sixty; **avoir la ~** (*âge*) to be around sixty

soixante [swasɑ̃t] *num* sixty; **soixante-dix** *num* seventy

soja [sɔʒa] *nm* soya; (*graines*) soya beans *pl*; **germes de ~** beansprouts

sol [sɔl] *nm* ground; (*de logement*) floor; (*AGR*) soil; (*MUS*) G; (: *en chantant la gamme*) so(h)

solaire [sɔlɛʀ] *adj* (*énergie etc*) solar; (*crème etc*) sun *cpd*

soldat [sɔlda] *nm* soldier

solde [sɔld] *nf* pay ♦ *nm* (*COMM*) balance; **~s** *nm ou f pl* (*articles*) sale goods; (*vente*) sales; **en ~** at sale price; **solder** *vt* (*marchandise*) to sell at sale price, sell off; **se solder par** (*fig*) to end in; **article soldé (à) 10 F** item reduced to 10 F

sole [sɔl] *nf* sole *inv* (*fish*)

soleil [sɔlɛj] *nm* sun; (*lumière*) sun(light); (*temps ensoleillé*) sun(shine); **il fait du ~** it's sunny; **au ~** in the sun

solennel, le [sɔlanɛl] *adj* solemn

solfège [sɔlfɛʒ] *nm* musical theory

solidaire [sɔlidɛʀ] *adj*: **être ~s** to show solidarity, stand *ou* stick together; **être ~ de** (*collègues*) to stand by; **solidarité** *nf* solidarity; **par solidarité (avec)** in sympathy (with)

solide [sɔlid] *adj* solid; (*mur, maison, meuble*) solid, sturdy; (*connaissances, argument*) sound; (*personne, estomac*) robust, sturdy ♦ *nm* solid

soliste [sɔlist] *nm/f* soloist

solitaire [sɔlitɛʀ] *adj* (*sans compagnie*) solitary, lonely; (*lieu*) lonely ♦ *nm/f* (*ermite*) recluse; (*fig: ours*) loner

solitude [sɔlityd] *nf* loneliness; (*tranquillité*) solitude

solive [sɔliv] *nf* joist

solliciter [sɔlisite] *vt* (*personne*) to appeal to; (*emploi, faveur*) to seek

sollicitude [sɔlisityd] *nf* concern

soluble [sɔlybl] *adj* soluble

solution [sɔlysjɔ̃] *nf* solution; **~ de facilité** easy way out

solvable [sɔlvabl] *adj* solvent

sombre [sɔ̃bʀ] *adj* dark; (*fig*) gloomy; **sombrer** *vi* (*bateau*) to sink; **sombrer dans** (*misère, désespoir*) to sink into

sommaire [sɔmɛʀ] *adj* (*simple*) basic; (*expéditif*) summary ♦ *nm* summary

sommation [sɔmasjɔ̃] *nf* (*JUR*) summons *sg*; (*avant de faire feu*) warning

somme [sɔm] *nf* (*MATH*) sum; (*quantité*) amount; (*argent*) sum, amount ♦ *nm*: **faire un ~** to have a (short) nap; **en ~** all in all; **~ toute** all in all

sommeil [sɔmɛj] *nm* sleep; **avoir ~** to be sleepy; **sommeiller** *vi* to doze

sommer [sɔme] *vt*: **~ qn de faire** to command *ou* order sb to do

sommes [sɔm] *vb voir* **être**

sommet [sɔmɛ] *nm* top; (*d'une montagne*) summit, top; (*fig: de la perfection, gloire*) height

sommier [sɔmje] *nm* (bed) base

somnambule [sɔmnãbyl] *nm/f* sleepwalker

somnifère [sɔmnifɛʀ] *nm* sleeping drug *no pl* (*ou* pill)

somnoler [sɔmnɔle] *vi* to doze

somptueux, -euse [sɔ̃ptɥø, øz] *adj* sumptuous

son¹, sa [sɔ̃, sa] (*pl* **ses**) *adj* (*antécédent humain: mâle*) his; (: *femelle*) her; (: *valeur indéfinie*) one's, his/her; (*antécédent non humain*) its

son² [sɔ̃] *nm* sound; (*de blé*) bran

sondage [sɔ̃daʒ] *nm*: **~ (d'opinion)** (opinion) poll

sonde [sɔ̃d] *nf* (*NAVIG*) lead *ou* sounding line; (*MÉD*) probe; (*TECH: de forage*) borer, driller

sonder [sɔ̃de] *vt* (*NAVIG*) to sound; (*TECH*) to bore, drill; (*fig: personne*) to sound out; **~ le terrain** (*fig*) to test the ground

songe [sɔ̃ʒ] *nm* dream; **songer** *vi*: **songer à** (*penser à*) to think over; (*envisager*) to consider, think of; **songer que** to think that; **songeur, -euse** *adj* pensive

sonnant, e [sɔnɑ̃, ɑ̃t] *adj*: **à 8 heures ~es** on the stroke of 8

sonné, e [sɔne] *adj* (*fam*) cracked; **il est midi ~** it's gone twelve

sonner [sɔne] *vi* to ring ♦ *vt* (*cloche*) to ring; (*glas, tocsin*) to sound; (*portier, infirmière*) to ring for; **~ faux** (*instrument*) to sound out of tune; (*rire*) to ring false

sonnerie [sɔnʀi] *nf* (*son*) ringing; (*sonnette*) bell; **~ d'alarme** alarm bell

sonnette [sɔnɛt] *nf* bell; **~ d'alarme** alarm bell

sono [sɔno] *abr f* = **sonorisation**

sonore [sɔnɔʀ] *adj* (*voix*) sonorous, ringing; (*salle*) resonant; (*film, signal*) sound *cpd*; **sonorisation** *nf* (*équipement: de salle de conférences*) public address system, P.A. system; (: *de discothèque*) sound system; **sonorité** *nf* (*de piano, violon*) tone; (*d'une salle*) acoustics *pl*

sont [sɔ̃] *vb voir* **être**

sophistiqué, e [sɔfistike] *adj* sophisticated

sorbet [sɔʀbɛ] *nm* water ice, sorbet

sorcellerie [sɔʀsɛlʀi] *nf* witchcraft *no pl*

sorcier [sɔʀsje] *nm* sorcerer; **sorcière** *nf* witch *ou* sorceress

sordide [sɔʀdid] *adj* (*lieu*) squalid; (*action*) sordid

sornettes [sɔʀnɛt] *nfpl* twaddle *sg*

sort [sɔʀ] *nm* (*destinée*) fate; (*condition*) lot; (*magique*) curse, spell; **tirer au ~** to draw lots

sorte [sɔʀt] *nf* sort, kind; **de la ~** in that way; **de (telle) ~ que** so that; **en quelque ~** in a way; **faire en ~ que** to see to it that

sortie [sɔʀti] *nf* (*issue*) way out, exit; (*remarque drôle*) sally; (*promenade*) outing; (*le soir: au restaurant etc*) night out; (*COMM: d'un disque*) release; (: *d'un livre*) publication; (: *d'un modèle*) launching; **~s** *nfpl* (*COMM: somme*) items of expenditure, outgoings; **~ de bain** (*vêtement*) bathrobe; **~ de secours** emergency exit

sortilège [sɔʀtilɛʒ] *nm* (magic) spell

sortir [sɔʀtiʀ] *vi* (*gén*) to come out; (*partir, se promener, aller au spectacle*) to go out; (*numéro gagnant*) to come up ♦ *vt* (*gén*) to take out; (*produit, modèle*) to bring out; (*fam: dire*) to come out with; **~ avec qn** to be going out with sb; **s'en ~** (*malade*) to pull through; (*d'une difficulté etc*) to get through; **~ de** (*endroit*) to go (*ou* come) out of, leave; (*provenir de*) to come from; (*compétence*) to be outside

sosie [sɔzi] *nm* double

sot, sotte [so, sɔt] *adj* silly, foolish ♦ *nm/f* fool; **sottise** *nf* (*caractère*) silliness, foolishness; *(action)* silly *ou* foolish thing

sou [su] *nm*: **près de ses ~s** tight-fisted; **sans le ~** penniless

soubresaut [subʀəso] *nm* start; *(cahot)* jolt

souche [suʃ] *nf (d'arbre)* stump; *(de carnet)* counterfoil *(BRIT)*, stub

souci [susi] *nm (inquiétude)* worry; *(préoccupation)* concern; *(BOT)* marigold; **se faire du ~** to worry; **soucier: se soucier de** *vt* to care about; **soucieux, -euse** *adj* concerned, worried

soucoupe [sukup] *nf* saucer; **~ volante** flying saucer

soudain, e [sudɛ̃, ɛn] *adj (douleur, mort)* sudden ♦ *adv* suddenly, all of a sudden

soude [sud] *nf* soda

souder [sude] *vt (avec fil à ~)* to solder; *(par soudure autogène)* to weld; *(fig)* to bind together

soudoyer [sudwaje] *(péj) vt* to bribe

soudure [sudyʀ] *nf* soldering; welding; *(joint)* soldered joint; weld

souffert, e [sufɛʀ, ɛʀt] *pp de* **souffrir**

souffle [sufl] *nm (en expirant)* breath; *(en soufflant)* puff, blow; *(respiration)* breathing; *(d'explosion, de ventilateur)* blast; *(du vent)* blowing; **être à bout de ~** to be out of breath; **un ~ d'air** a breath of air

soufflé, e [sufle] *adj (fam: stupéfié)* staggered ♦ *nm (CULIN)* soufflé

souffler [sufle] *vi (gén)* to blow; *(haleter)* to puff (and blow) ♦ *vt (feu, bougie)* to blow out; *(chasser: poussière etc)* to blow away; *(TECH: verre)* to blow; *(dire)*: **~ qch à qn** to whisper sth to sb; **soufflet** *nm (instrument)* bellows *pl*; *(gifle)* slap (in the face); **souffleur** *nm (THÉÂTRE)* prompter

souffrance [sufʀɑ̃s] *nf* suffering; **en ~** *(affaire)* pending

souffrant, e [sufʀɑ̃, ɑ̃t] *adj* unwell

souffre-douleur [sufʀədulœʀ] *nm inv* butt, underdog

souffrir [sufʀiʀ] *vi* to suffer, be in pain ♦ *vt* to suffer, endure; *(supporter)* to bear, stand; **~ de** *(maladie, froid)* to suffer from;

elle ne peut pas le ~ she can't stand *ou* bear him

soufre [sufʀ] *nm* sulphur

souhait [swɛ] *nm* wish; **tous nos ~s de** good wishes *ou* our best wishes for; **à vos ~s!** bless you!; **souhaitable** *adj* desirable

souhaiter [swete] *vt* to wish for; **~ la bonne année à qn** to wish sb a happy New Year; **~ que** to hope that

souiller [suje] *vt* to dirty, soil; *(fig: réputation etc)* to sully, tarnish

soûl, e [su, sul] *adj* drunk ♦ *nm*: **tout son ~** to one's heart's content

soulagement [sulaʒmɑ̃] *nm* relief

soulager [sulaʒe] *vt* to relieve

soûler [sule] *vt*: **~ qn** to get sb drunk; *(suj: boisson)* to make sb drunk; *(fig)* to make sb's head spin *ou* reel; **se ~** *vi* to get drunk

soulever [sul(ə)ve] *vt* to lift; *(poussière)* to send up; *(enthousiasme)* to arouse; *(question, débat)* to raise; **se ~** *vi (peuple)* to rise up; *(personne couchée)* to lift o.s. up

soulier [sulje] *nm* shoe

souligner [suliɲe] *vt* to underline; *(fig)* to emphasize, stress

soumettre [sumetʀ] *vt (pays)* to subject, subjugate; *(rebelle)* to put down, subdue; **se ~ (à)** to submit (to); **~ qch à qn** *(projet etc)* to submit sth to sb

soumis, e [sumi, iz] *adj* submissive; **soumission** *nf* submission

soupape [supap] *nf* valve

soupçon [supsɔ̃] *nm* suspicion; *(petite quantité)*: **un ~ de** a hint *ou* touch of; **soupçonner** *vt* to suspect; **soupçonneux, -euse** *adj* suspicious

soupe [sup] *nf* soup

souper [supe] *vi* to have supper ♦ *nm* supper

soupeser [supəze] *vt* to weigh in one's hand(s); *(fig)* to weigh up

soupière [supjɛʀ] *nf* (soup) tureen

soupir [supiʀ] *nm* sigh; **pousser un ~ de soulagement** to heave a sigh of relief

soupirail, -aux [supiʀaj, o] *nm* (small) basement window

soupirer [supiʀe] *vi* to sigh

souple [supl] *adj* supple; (*fig: règlement, caractère*) flexible; (: *démarche, taille*) lithe, supple; **souplesse** *nf* suppleness; (*de caractère*) flexibility

source [suʀs] *nf* (*point d'eau*) spring; (*d'un cours d'eau, fig*) source; **de bonne ~** on good authority

sourcil [suʀsi] *nm* (eye)brow; **sourciller** *vi*: **sans sourciller** without turning a hair *ou* batting an eyelid

sourd, e [suʀ, suʀd] *adj* deaf; (*bruit*) muffled; (*douleur*) dull ♦ *nm/f* deaf person; **faire la ~e oreille** to turn a deaf ear; **sourdine** *nf* (*MUS*) mute; **en sourdine** softly, quietly; **sourd-muet, sourde-muette** *adj* deaf-and-dumb ♦ *nm/f* deaf-mute

souriant, e [suʀjɑ̃, jɑ̃t] *adj* cheerful

souricière [suʀisjɛʀ] *nf* mousetrap; (*fig*) trap

sourire [suʀiʀ] *nm* smile ♦ *vi* to smile; **~ à qn** to smile at sb; (*fig: plaire à*) to appeal to sb; (*suj: chance*) to smile on sb; **garder le ~** to keep smiling

souris [suʀi] *nf* mouse

sournois, e [suʀnwa, waz] *adj* deceitful, underhand

sous [su] *prép* under; **~ la pluie** in the rain; **~ terre** underground; **~ peu** shortly, before long; **sous-bois** *nm inv* undergrowth

souscrire [suskʀiʀ]: **~ à** *vt* to subscribe to

sous...: **sous-directeur, -trice** *nm/f* assistant manager(-manageress); **sous-entendre** *vt* to understand, infer; **sous-entendu, e** *adj* implied ♦ *nm* innuendo, insinuation; **sous-estimer** *vt* to underestimate; **sous-jacent, e** *adj* underlying; **sous-louer** *vt* to sublet; **sous-marin, e** *adj* (*flore, faune*) submarine; (*pêche*) underwater ♦ *nm* submarine; **sous-officier** *nm* ≈ non-commissioned officer (N.C.O.);

sous-produit *nm* by-product; **sous-pull** *nm* thin poloneck jersey; **soussigné, e** *adj*: **je soussigné** I the undersigned; **sous-sol** *nm* basement; **sous-titre** *nm* subtitle

soustraction [sustʀaksjɔ̃] *nf* subtraction

soustraire [sustʀeʀ] *vt* to subtract, take away; (*dérober*) **~ qch à qn** to remove sth from sb; **se ~ à** (*autorité etc*) to elude, escape from

sous...: **sous-traitant** *nm* subcontractor; **sous-traiter** *vt* to subcontract; **sous-vêtements** *nmpl* underwear *sg*

soutane [sutan] *nf* cassock, soutane

soute [sut] *nf* hold

soutenir [sut(ə)niʀ] *vt* to support; (*assaut, choc*) to stand up to, withstand; (*intérêt, effort*) to keep up; (*assurer*) **~ que** to maintain that; **soutenu, e** *adj* (*efforts*) sustained, unflagging; (*style*) elevated

souterrain, e [suteʀɛ̃, ɛn] *adj* underground ♦ *nm* underground passage

soutien [sutjɛ̃] *nm* support; **soutien-gorge** *nm* bra

soutirer [sutiʀe] *vt*: **~ qch à qn** to squeeze *ou* get sth out of sb

souvenir [suv(ə)niʀ] *nm* (*réminiscence*) memory; (*objet*) souvenir ♦ *vb*: **se ~ de** ♦ *vt* to remember; **se ~ que** to remember that; **en ~ de** in memory *ou* remembrance of

souvent [suvɑ̃] *adv* often; **peu ~** seldom, infrequently

souverain, e [suv(ə)ʀɛ̃, ɛn] *nm/f* sovereign, monarch

soyeux, -euse [swajø, øz] *adj* silky

soyons *etc* [swajɔ̃] *vb voir* **être**

spacieux, -euse [spasjø, jøz] *adj* spacious, roomy

spaghettis [spageti] *nmpl* spaghetti *sg*

sparadrap [spaʀadʀa] *nm* sticking plaster (*BRIT*), Bandaid ® (*US*)

spatial, e, -aux [spasjal, jo] *adj* (*AVIAT*) space *cpd*

speaker, ine [spikœʀ, kʀin] *nm/f* announcer

spécial, e, -aux [spesjal, jo] *adj* special; (*bizarre*) peculiar; **spécialement** *adv* especially, particularly; (*tout exprès*) specially; **spécialiser: se spécialiser** *vi* to specialize; **spécialiste** *nm/f* specialist; **spécialité** *nf* speciality; (*branche*) special field

spécifier [spesifje] *vt* to specify, state

spécimen [spesimɛn] *nm* specimen

spectacle [spɛktakl] *nm* (*scène*) sight; (*représentation*) show; (*industrie*) show business; **spectaculaire** *adj* spectacular

spectateur, -trice [spɛktatœr, tris] *nm/f* (*CINÉMA etc*) member of the audience; (*SPORT*) spectator; (*d'un événement*) onlooker, witness

spéculer [spekyle] *vi* to speculate

spéléologie [speleɔlɔʒi] *nf* potholing

sperme [spɛrm] *nm* semen, sperm

sphère [sfɛr] *nf* sphere

spirale [spiral] *nf* spiral

spirituel, le [spirityɛl] *adj* spiritual; (*fin, piquant*) witty

splendide [splɑ̃did] *adj* splendid

sponsoriser [spɔ̃sɔrize] *vt* to sponsor

spontané, e [spɔ̃tane] *adj* spontaneous; **spontanéité** *nf* spontaneity

sport [spɔr] *nm* sport ♦ *adj inv* (*vêtement*) casual; **faire du ~** to do sport; **~s d'hiver** winter sports; **sportif, -ive** *adj* (*journal, association, épreuve*) sports *cpd*; (*allure, démarche*) athletic; (*attitude, esprit*) sporting

spot [spɔt] *nm* (*lampe*) spot(light); (*annonce*): **~ (publicitaire)** commercial (break)

square [skwar] *nm* public garden(s)

squelette [skəlɛt] *nm* skeleton; **squelettique** *adj* scrawny

stabiliser [stabilize] *vt* to stabilize

stable [stabl] *adj* stable, steady

stade [stad] *nm* (*SPORT*) stadium; (*phase, niveau*) stage

stage [staʒ] *nm* (*cours*) training course; **~ de formation (professionnelle)** voca-

tional (training) course; **~ de perfectionnement** advanced training course; **stagiaire** *nm/f, adj* trainee

stagner [stagne] *vi* to stagnate

stalle [stal] *nf* stall, box

stand [stɑ̃d] *nm* (*d'exposition*) stand; (*de foire*) stall; **~ de tir** (*à la foire, SPORT*) shooting range

standard [stɑ̃dar] *adj inv* standard ♦ *nm* switchboard; **standardiste** *nm/f* switchboard operator

standing [stɑ̃diŋ] *nm* standing; **de grand ~** luxury

starter [starter] *nm* (*AUTO*) choke

station [stasjɔ̃] *nf* station; (*de bus*) stop; (*de villégiature*) resort; **~ balnéaire** seaside resort; **~ de ski** ski resort; **~ de taxis** taxi rank (*BRIT*) *ou* stand (*US*); **stationnement** *nm* parking; **stationner** *vi* to park; **station-service** *nf* service station

statistique [statistik] *nf* (*science*) statistics *sg*; (*rapport, étude*) statistic ♦ *adj* statistical

statue [staty] *nf* statue

statu quo [statykwo] *nm* status quo

statut [staty] *nm* status; **~s** *nmpl* (*JUR, ADMIN*) statutes; **statutaire** *adj* statutory

Sté *abr* = **société**

steak [stɛk] *nm* steak; **~ haché** hamburger

sténo(dactylo) [steno(daktilo)] *nf* shorthand typist (*BRIT*), stenographer (*US*)

sténo(graphie) [stenɔ(grafi)] *nf* shorthand

stéréo [stereo] *adj* stereo

stérile [steril] *adj* sterile

stérilet [sterilɛ] *nm* coil, loop

stériliser [sterilize] *vt* to sterilize

stigmates [stigmat] *nmpl* scars, marks

stimulant [stimylɑ̃] *nm* (*fig*) stimulus, incentive; (*physique*) stimulant

stimuler [stimyle] *vt* to stimulate

stipuler [stipyle] *vt* to stipulate

stock [stɔk] *nm* stock; **stocker** *vt* to stock

stop [stɔp] *nm* (*AUTO: écriteau*) stop sign; (: *feu arrière*) brake-light; **faire du ~** (*fam*) to hitch(hike); **stopper** *vt, vi* to stop, halt

store [stɔr] *nm* blind; (*de magasin*) shade,

awning

strabisme [stʀabism] *nm* squinting

strapontin [stʀapɔ̃tɛ̃] *nm* jump *ou* fold-away seat

stratégie [stʀateʒi] *nf* strategy; **stratégique** *adj* strategic

stress [stʀɛs] *nm* stress; **stressant, e** *adj* stressful; **stresser** *vt*: **stresser qn** to make sb (feel) tense

strict, e [stʀikt] *adj* strict; (*tenue, décor*) severe, plain; **le ~ nécessaire/minimum** the bare essentials/minimum

strident, e [stʀidɑ̃, ɑ̃t] *adj* shrill, strident

strophe [stʀɔf] *nf* verse, stanza

structure [stʀyktyʀ] *nf* structure

studieux, -euse [stydjø, jøz] *adj* studious

studio [stydjo] *nm* (*logement*) (one-roomed) flatlet (*BRIT*) *ou* apartment (*US*); (*d'artiste, TV etc*) studio

stupéfait, e [stypefɛ, ɛt] *adj* astonished

stupéfiant, e [stypefjɑ̃, jɑ̃t] *adj* (*étonnant*) stunning, astounding ♦ *nm* (*MÉD*) drug, narcotic

stupéfier [stypefje] *vt* (*étonner*) to stun, astonish

stupeur [stypœʀ] *nf* astonishment

stupide [stypid] *adj* stupid; **stupidité** *nf* stupidity; (*parole, acte*) stupid thing (to do *ou* say)

style [stil] *nm* style

stylé, e [stile] *adj* well-trained

styliste [stilist] *nm/f* designer

stylo [stilo] *nm*: **~ (à encre)** (fountain) pen; **~ (à) bille** ball-point pen; **~-feutre** felt-tip pen

su, e [sy] *pp de* **savoir** ♦ *nm*: **au ~ de** with the knowledge of

suave [sɥav] *adj* sweet

subalterne [sybaltɛʀn] *adj* (*employé, officier*) junior; (*rôle*) subordinate, subsidiary ♦ *nm/f* subordinate

subconscient [sypkɔ̃sjɑ̃] *nm* subconscious

subir [sybiʀ] *vt* (*affront, dégâts*) to suffer; (*opération, châtiment*) to undergo

subit, e [sybi, it] *adj* sudden; **subitement**

adv suddenly, all of a sudden

subjectif, -ive [sybʒɛktif, iv] *adj* subjective

subjonctif [sybʒɔ̃ktif] *nm* subjunctive

subjuguer [sybʒyge] *vt* to captivate

submerger [sybmɛʀʒe] *vt* to submerge; (*fig*) to overwhelm

subordonné, e [sybɔʀdɔne] *adj, nm/f* subordinate

subrepticement [sybʀɛptismɑ̃] *adv* surreptitiously

subside [sybzid] *nm* grant

subsidiaire [sybzidjɛʀ] *adj*: **question ~** deciding question

subsister [sybziste] *vi* (*rester*) to remain, subsist; (*survivre*) to live on

substance [sypstɑ̃s] *nf* substance

substituer [sypstitɥe] *vt*: **~ qn/qch à** to substitute sb/sth for; **se ~ à qn** (*évincer*) to substitute o.s. for sb

substitut [sypstity] *nm* (*succédané*) substitute

subterfuge [syptɛʀfyʒ] *nm* subterfuge

subtil, e [syptil] *adj* subtle

subtiliser [syptilize] *vt*: **~ qch (à qn)** to spirit sth away (from sb)

subvenir [sybvəniʀ]: **~ à** *vt* to meet

subvention [sybvɑ̃sjɔ̃] *nf* subsidy, grant; **subventionner** *vt* to subsidize

suc [syk] *nm* (*BOT*) sap; (*de viande, fruit*) juice

succédané [syksedane] *nm* substitute

succéder [syksede]: **~ à** *vt* to succeed; **se ~** *vi* (*accidents, années*) to follow one another

succès [syksɛ] *nm* success; **avoir du ~** to be a success, be successful; **à ~** successful; **~ de librairie** bestseller; **~ (féminins)** conquests

successif, -ive [syksesif, iv] *adj* successive

successeur [syksesœʀ] *nm* successor

succession [syksesjɔ̃] *nf* (*série, POL*) succession; (*JUR: patrimoine*) estate, inheritance

succomber [sykɔ̃be] *vi* to die, succumb;

(*fig*): ~ **à** to succumb to

succulent, e [sykylã, ãt] *adj* (*repas, mets*) delicious

succursale [sykyʀsal] *nf* branch

sucer [syse] *vt* to suck; **sucette** *nf* (*bonbon*) lollipop; (*de bébé*) dummy (*BRIT*), pacifier (*US*)

sucre [sykʀ] *nm* (*substance*) sugar; (*morceau*) lump of sugar, sugar lump *ou* cube; ~ **d'orge** barley sugar; ~ **en morceaux/ en poudre** lump/caster sugar; ~ **glace/ roux** icing/brown sugar; **sucré, e** *adj* (*produit alimentaire*) sweetened; (*au goût*) sweet; **sucrer** *vt* (*thé, café*) to sweeten, put sugar in; **sucreries** *nfpl* (*bonbons*) sweets, sweet things; **sucrier** *nm* (*récipient*) sugar bowl

sud [syd] *nm*: **le** ~ the south ♦ *adj inv* south; (*côte*) south, southern; **au** ~ (*situation*) in the south; (*direction*) to the south; **au** ~ **de** (to the) south of; **sud-africain, e** *adj* South African ♦ *nm/f*: **Sud-Africain, e** South African; **sud-américain, e** *adj* South American ♦ *nm/f*: **Sud-Américain, e** South American; **sud-est** *nm, adj inv* south-east; **sud-ouest** ~ *nm, adj inv* south-west

Suède [sɥɛd] *nf*: **la** ~ Sweden; **suédois, e** *adj* Swedish ♦ *nm/f*: **Suédois, e** Swede ♦ *nm* (*LING*) Swedish

suer [sɥe] *vi* to sweat; (*suinter*) to ooze; **sueur** *nf* sweat; **en sueur** sweating, in a sweat; **donner des sueurs froids à qn** to put sb in(to) a cold sweat

suffire [syfiʀ] *vi* (*être assez*): ~ (**à qn/pour qch/pour faire**) to be enough *ou* sufficient (for sb/for sth/to do); **il suffit d'une négligence ...** it only takes one act of carelessness ...; **il suffit qu'on oublie pour que ...** one only needs to forget for ...; **ça suffit!** that's enough!

suffisamment [syfizamã] *adv* sufficiently, enough; ~ **de** sufficient, enough

suffisant, e [syfizã, ãt] *adj* sufficient; (*résultats*) satisfactory; (*vaniteux*) self-important, bumptious

suffixe [syfiks] *nm* suffix

suffoquer [syfɔke] *vt* to choke, suffocate; (*stupéfier*) to stagger, astound ♦ *vi* to choke, suffocate

suffrage [syfʀaʒ] *nm* (*POL: voix*) vote

suggérer [syɡʒeʀe] *vt* to suggest; **suggestion** *nf* suggestion

suicide [sɥisid] *nm* suicide; **suicider: se suicider** *vi* to commit suicide

suie [sɥi] *nf* soot

suinter [sɥɛte] *vi* to ooze

suis [sɥi] *vb voir* **être**; **suivre**

suisse [sɥis] *adj* Swiss ♦ *nm*: **S**~ Swiss *pl inv* ♦ *nf*: **la S**~ Switzerland; **la S**~ **romande/allemande** French-speaking/ German-speaking Switzerland; **Suissesse** *nf* Swiss (woman *ou* girl)

suite [sɥit] *nf* (*continuation: d'énumération etc*) rest, remainder; (: *de feuilleton*) continuation; (: *film etc sur le même thème*) sequel; (*série*) series, succession; (*conséquence*) result; (*ordre, liaison logique*) coherence; (*appartement, MUS*) suite; (*escorte*) retinue, suite; ~**s** *nfpl* (*d'une maladie etc*) effects; **prendre la** ~ **de** (*directeur etc*) to succeed, take over from; **donner** ~ **à** (*requête, projet*) to follow up; **faire** ~ **à** to follow; **(faisant)** ~ **à votre lettre du ...** further to your letter of the ...; **de** ~ (*d'affilée*) in succession; (*immédiatement*) at once; **par la** ~ afterwards, subsequently; **à la** ~ one after the other; **à la** ~ **de** (*derrière*) behind; (*en conséquence de*) following

suivant, e [sɥivã, ãt] *adj* next, following ♦ *prép* (*selon*) according to; **au** ~! next!

suivi, e [sɥivi] *adj* (*effort, qualité*) consistent; (*cohérent*) coherent; **très/peu** ~ (*cours*) well-/poorly-attended

suivre [sɥivʀ] *vt* (*gén*) to follow; (*SCOL: cours*) to attend; (*comprendre*) to keep up with; (*COMM: article*) to continue to stock ♦ *vi* to follow; (*élève: assimiler*) to keep up; **se** ~ *vi* (*accidents etc*) to follow one after the other; **faire** ~ (*lettre*) to forward; **"à** ~**"** "to be continued"

sujet, te [syʒɛ, ɛt] *adj*: **être ~ à** (*vertige etc*) to be liable *ou* subject to ♦ *nm/f* (*d'un souverain*) subject ♦ *nm* subject; **au ~ de** about; **~ de conversation** topic *ou* subject of conversation; **~ d'examen** (*SCOL*) examination question

summum [sɔ(m)mɔm] *nm*: **le ~ de** the height of

super [sypɛʀ] (*fam*) *adj inv* terrific, great, fantastic, super

superbe [sypɛʀb] *adj* magnificent, superb

super(carburant) [sypɛʀ(kaʀbyʀɑ̃)] *nm* ≃ 4-star petrol (*BRIT*), ≃ high-octane gasoline (*US*)

supercherie [sypɛʀʃəʀi] *nf* trick

supérette [sypeʀɛt] *nf* (*COMM*) minimarket, superette (*US*)

superficie [sypɛʀfisi] *nf* (*surface*) area

superficiel, le [sypɛʀfisjɛl] *adj* superficial

superflu, e [sypɛʀfly] *adj* superfluous

supérieur, e [sypeʀjœʀ] *adj* (*lèvre, étages, classes*) upper; (*plus élevé: température, niveau, enseignement*): **~ (à)** higher (than); (*meilleur: qualité, produit*): **~ (à)** superior (to); (*excellent, hautain*) superior ♦ *nm, nf* superior; **supériorité** *nf* superiority

superlatif [sypɛʀlatif] *nm* superlative

supermarché [sypɛʀmaʀʃe] *nm* supermarket

superposer [sypɛʀpoze] *vt* (*faire chevaucher*) to superimpose; **lits superposés** bunk beds

superproduction [sypɛʀpʀɔdyksjɔ̃] *nf* (*film*) spectacular

superpuissance [sypɛʀpɥisɑ̃s] *nf* superpower

superstitieux, -euse [sypɛʀstisjø, jøz] *adj* superstitious

superviser [sypɛʀvize] *vt* to supervise

supplanter [syplɑ̃te] *vt* to supplant

suppléance [sypleɑ̃s] *nf*: **faire des ~s** (*professeur*) to do supply teaching; **suppléant, e** *adj* (*professeur*) supply *cpd*; (*juge, fonctionnaire*) deputy *cpd* ♦ *nm/f* (*professeur*) supply teacher

suppléer [syplee] *vt* (*ajouter: mot man-* *quant etc*) to supply, provide; (*compenser: lacune*) to fill in; **~ à** to make up for

supplément [syplemɑ̃] *nm* supplement; (*de frites etc*) extra portion; **un ~ de travail** extra *ou* additional work; **payer un ~** to pay an additional charge; **le vin est en ~** wine is extra; **supplémentaire** *adj* additional, further; (*train, bus*) relief *cpd*, extra

supplications [syplikasjɔ̃] *nfpl* pleas, entreaties

supplice [syplis] *nm* torture *no pl*

supplier [syplije] *vt* to implore, beseech

support [sypɔʀ] *nm* support; (*publicitaire*) medium; (*audio-visuel*) aid

supportable [sypɔʀtabl] *adj* (*douleur*) bearable

supporter¹ [sypɔʀtɛʀ] *nm* supporter, fan

supporter² [sypɔʀte] *vt* (*conséquences, épreuve*) to bear, endure; (*défauts, personne*) to put up with; (*suj: chose: chaleur etc*) to withstand; (*: personne: chaleur, vin*) to be able to take

supposer [sypoze] *vt* to suppose; (*impliquer*) to presuppose; **à ~ que** supposing (that)

suppositoire [sypozitwaʀ] *nm* suppository

suppression [sypʀesjɔ̃] *nf* (*voir supprimer*) cancellation; removal; deletion

supprimer [sypʀime] *vt* (*congés, service d'autobus etc*) to cancel; (*emplois, privilèges, témoin gênant*) to do away with; (*cloison, cause, anxiété*) to remove; (*clause, mot*) to delete

suprême [sypʀɛm] *adj* supreme

MOT-CLÉ

sur [syʀ] *prép* **1** (*position*) on; (*par-dessus*) over; (*au-dessus*) above; **pose-le sur la table** put it on the table; **je n'ai pas d'argent sur moi** I haven't any money on me **2** (*direction*) towards; **en allant sur Paris** going towards Paris; **sur votre droite** on *ou* to your right **3** (*à propos de*) on, about; **un livre/une conférence sur Balzac** a book/lecture on *ou* about Balzac

4 (*proportion, mesures*) out of, by; **un sur 10** one in 10; (*SCOL*) one out of 10; **4 m sur 2** 4 m by 2

sur ce *adv* hereupon

---

sûr, e [syr] *adj* sure, certain; (*digne de confiance*) reliable; (*sans danger*) safe; (*diagnostic, goût*) reliable; **le plus ~ est de** the safest thing is to; **~ de soi** self-confident; **~ et certain** absolutely certain

surcharge [syrʃarʒ] *nf* (*de passagers etc*) excess load; **surcharger** *vt* to overload

surchoix [syrʃwa] *adj inv* top-quality

surclasser [syrklase] *vt* to outclass

surcroît [syrkrwa] *nm*: **un ~ de** additional +*nom*; **par** *ou* **de ~** moreover; **en ~** in addition

surdité [syrdite] *nf* deafness

surélever [syrel(ə)ve] *vt* to raise, heighten

sûrement [syrmɑ̃] *adv* (*certainement*) certainly; (*sans risques*) safely

surenchère [syrɑ̃ʃɛr] *nf* (*aux enchères*) higher bid; **surenchérir** *vi* to bid higher; (*fig*) to try and outbid each other

surent [syr] *vb voir* **savoir**

surestimer [syrɛstime] *vt* to overestimate

sûreté [syrte] *nf* (*sécurité*) safety; (*exactitude: de renseignements etc*) reliability; (*d'un geste*) steadiness; **mettre en ~** to put in a safe place; **pour plus de ~** as an extra precaution, to be on the safe side

surf [sœrf] *nm* surfing

surface [syrfas] *nf* surface; (*superficie*) surface area; **une grande ~** a supermarket; **faire ~** to surface; **en ~** near the surface; (*fig*) superficially

surfait, e [syrfɛ, ɛt] *adj* overrated

surfer [syrfe] *vi* to surf; **~ sur Internet** to surf the net

surgelé, e [syrʒəle] *adj* (deep-)frozen ♦ *nm*: **les ~s** (deep-)frozen food

surgir [syrʒir] *vi* to appear suddenly; (*fig: problème, conflit*) to arise

sur...: **surhumain, e** *adj* superhuman; **sur-le-champ** *adv* immediately; **surlen-**

demain *nm*: **le surlendemain (soir)** two days later (in the evening); **le surlendemain de** two days after; **surmenage** *nm* overwork(ing); **surmener: se surmener** *vi* to overwork

surmonter [syrmɔ̃te] *vt* (*vaincre*) to overcome; (*être au-dessus de*) to top

surnaturel, le [syrnatyrɛl] *adj, nm* supernatural

surnom [syrnɔ̃] *nm* nickname

surnombre [syrnɔ̃br] *nm*: **être en ~** to be too many (*ou* one too many)

surpeuplé, e [syrpœple] *adj* overpopulated

sur-place [syrplas] *nm*: **faire du ~-~** to mark time

surplomber [syrplɔ̃be] *vt, vi* to overhang

surplus [syrply] *nm* (*COMM*) surplus; (*reste*): **~ de bois** wood left over

surprenant, e [syrprənɑ̃, ɑ̃t] *adj* amazing

surprendre [syrprɑ̃dr] *vt* (*étonner*) to surprise; (*tomber sur: intrus etc*) to catch; (*entendre*) to overhear

surpris, e [syrpri, iz] *adj*: **~ (de/que)** surprised (at/that); **surprise** *nf* surprise; **faire une surprise à qn** to give sb a surprise; **surprise-partie** *nf* party

surréservation [syrrezɛrvasjɔ̃] *nf* double booking, overbooking

sursaut [syrso] *nm* start, jump; **~ de** (*énergie, indignation*) sudden fit *ou* burst of; **en ~** with a start; **sursauter** *vi* to (give a) start, jump

sursis [syrsi] *nm* (*JUR: gén*) suspended sentence; (*fig*) reprieve

surtaxe [syrtaks] *nf* surcharge

surtout [syrtu] *adv* (*avant tout*) above all; (*spécialement*) especially; **~, ne dites rien!** whatever you do don't say anything!; **~ pas!** certainly *ou* definitely not!; **~ que ...** especially as ...

surveillance [syrvejɑ̃s] *nf* watch; (*POLICE, MIL*) surveillance; **sous ~ médicale** under medical supervision

surveillant, e [syrvejɑ̃, ɑ̃t] *nm/f* (*de pri-*

son) warder; (*SCOL*) monitor

surveiller [syʀveje] *vt* (*enfant, élèves, bagages*) to watch, keep an eye on; (*prisonnier, suspect*) to keep (a) watch on; (*territoire, bâtiment*) to (keep) watch over; (*travaux, cuisson*) to supervise; (*SCOL: examen*) to invigilate; **~ son langage/sa ligne** to watch one's language/figure

survenir [syʀvəniʀ] *vi* (*incident, retards*) to occur, arise; (*événement*) to take place

survêt(ement) [syʀvɛt(mɑ̃)] *nm* tracksuit

survie [syʀvi] *nf* survival; **survivant, e** *nm/f* survivor; **survivre** *vi* to survive; **survivre à** (*accident etc*) to survive

survoler [syʀvɔle] *vt* to fly over; (*fig: livre*) to skim through

survolté, e [syʀvɔlte] *adj* (*fig*) worked up

sus [sy(s)]: **en ~ de** *prép* in addition to, over and above; **en ~** in addition

susceptible [syseptibl] *adj* touchy, sensitive; **~ de faire** (*hypothèse*) liable to do

susciter [sysite] *vt* (*admiration*) to arouse; (*ennuis*) to create (for sb)

suspect, e [syspɛ(kt), ɛkt] *adj* suspicious; (*témoignage, opinions*) suspect ♦ *nm/f* suspect; **suspecter** *vt* to suspect; (*honnêteté de qn*) to question, have one's suspicions about

suspendre [syspɑ̃dʀ] *vt* (*accrocher: vêtement*): **~ qch (à)** to hang sth up (on); (*interrompre, démettre*) to suspend; **se ~ à** to hang from

suspendu, e [syspɑ̃dy] *adj* (*accroché*): **~ à** hanging on (*ou* from); (*perché*): **~ au-dessus de** suspended over

suspens [syspɑ̃]: **en ~** *adv* (*affaire*) in abeyance; **tenir en ~** to keep in suspense

suspense [syspɛns, syspɑ̃s] *nm* suspense

suspension [syspɑ̃sjɔ̃] *nf* suspension; (*lustre*) light fitting *ou* fitment

sut [sy] *vb voir* **savoir**

suture [sytyʀ] *nf* (*MÉD*): **point de ~** stitch

svelte [svɛlt] *adj* slender, svelte

SVP *abr* (= *s'il vous plaît*) please

sweat-shirt [switʃœʀt] (*pl* **~-~s**) *nm* sweatshirt

syllabe [si(l)lab] *nf* syllable

symbole [sɛ̃bɔl] *nm* symbol; **symbolique** *adj* symbolic(al); (*geste, offrande*) token *cpd*; **symboliser** *vt* to symbolize

symétrique [simetʀik] *adj* symmetrical

sympa [sɛ̃pa] (*fam*) *adj inv* nice; **sois ~, prête-le moi** be a pal and lend it to me

sympathie [sɛ̃pati] *nf* (*inclination*) liking; (*affinité*) friendship; (*condoléances*) sympathy; **j'ai beaucoup de ~ pour lui** I like him a lot; **sympathique** *adj* nice, friendly

sympathisant, e [sɛ̃patizɑ̃, ɑ̃t] *nm/f* sympathizer

sympathiser [sɛ̃patize] *vi* (*voisins etc: s'entendre*) to get on (*BRIT*) *ou* along (*US*) (well)

symphonie [sɛ̃fɔni] *nf* symphony

symptôme [sɛ̃ptom] *nm* symptom

synagogue [sinagɔg] *nf* synagogue

syncope [sɛ̃kɔp] *nf* (*MÉD*) blackout; **tomber en ~** to faint, pass out

syndic [sɛ̃dik] *nm* (*d'immeuble*) managing agent

syndical, e, -aux [sɛ̃dikal, o] *adj* (trade) union *cpd*; **syndicaliste** *nm/f* trade unionist

syndicat [sɛ̃dika] *nm* (*d'ouvriers, employés*) (trade) union; **~ d'initiative** tourist office; **syndiqué, e** *adj* belonging to a (trade) union; **syndiquer: se syndiquer** *vi* to form a trade union; (*adhérer*) to join a trade union

synonyme [sinɔnim] *adj* synonymous ♦ *nm* synonym; **~ de** synonymous with

syntaxe [sɛ̃taks] *nf* syntax

synthèse [sɛ̃tez] *nf* synthesis

synthétique [sɛ̃tetik] *adj* synthetic

Syrie [siʀi] *nf*: **la ~** Syria

systématique [sistematik] *adj* systematic

système [sistɛm] *nm* system; **~ D** (*fam*) resourcefulness

T, t

t' [t] *pron voir* **te**

ta [ta] *adj voir* **ton**[1]

tabac [taba] *nm* tobacco; (*magasin*) tobacconist's (shop); **~ blond/brun** light/dark tobacco

tabagisme [tabaʒism] *nm*: **~ passif** passive smoking

tabasser [tabase] (*fam*) *vt* to beat up

table [tabl] *nf* table; **à ~!** dinner *etc* is ready!; **se mettre à ~** to sit down to eat; **mettre la ~** to lay the table; **faire ~ rase de** to make a clean sweep of; **~ à repasser** ironing board; **~ de cuisson** (*à l'électricité*) hotplate; (*au gaz*) gas ring; **~ de nuit** *ou* **de chevet** bedside table; **~ des matières** (table of) contents *pl*; **~ d'orientation** viewpoint indicator; **~ roulante** trolley

tableau, x [tablo] *nm* (*peinture*) painting; (*reproduction, fig*) picture; (*panneau*) board; (*schéma*) table, chart; **~ d'affichage** notice board; **~ de bord** dashboard; (*AVIAT*) instrument panel; **~ noir** blackboard

tabler [table] *vi*: **~ sur** to bank on

tablette [tablet] *nf* (*planche*) shelf; **~ de chocolat** bar of chocolate

tableur [tablœʀ] *nm* spreadsheet

tablier [tablije] *nm* apron

tabou [tabu] *nm* taboo

tabouret [tabuʀɛ] *nm* stool

tac [tak] *nm*: **il m'a répondu du ~ au ~** he answered me right back

tache [taʃ] *nf* (*saleté*) stain, mark; (*ART, de couleur, lumière*) spot; **~ de rousseur** freckle

tâche [taʃ] *nf* task

tacher [taʃe] *vt* to stain, mark

tâcher [taʃe] *vi*: **~ de faire** to try *ou* endeavour to do

tacheté, e [taʃte] *adj* spotted

tacot [tako] (*péj*) *nm* banger (*BRIT*), (old) heap

tact [takt] *nm* tact; **avoir du ~** to be tactful

tactique [taktik] *adj* tactical ♦ *nf* (*technique*) tactics *sg*; (*plan*) tactic

taie [tɛ] *nf*: **~ (d'oreiller)** pillowslip, pillowcase

taille [taj] *nf* cutting; (*d'arbre etc*) pruning; (*milieu du corps*) waist; (*hauteur*) height; (*grandeur*) size; **de ~ à faire** capable of doing; **de ~** sizeable; **taille-crayon(s)** *nm* pencil sharpener

tailler [taje] *vt* (*pierre, diamant*) to cut; (*arbre, plante*) to prune; (*vêtement*) to cut out; (*crayon*) to sharpen

tailleur [tajœʀ] *nm* (*couturier*) tailor; (*vêtement*) suit; **en ~** (*assis*) cross-legged

taillis [taji] *nm* copse

taire [tɛʀ] *vi*: **faire ~ qn** to make sb be quiet; **se ~** *vi* to be silent *ou* quiet

talc [talk] *nm* talc, talcum powder

talent [talɑ̃] *nm* talent

talkie-walkie [tokiwoki] *nm* walkie-talkie

taloche [talɔʃ] (*fam*) *nf* clout, cuff

talon [talɔ̃] *nm* heel; (*de chèque, billet*) stub, counterfoil (*BRIT*); **~s plats/aiguilles** flat/stiletto heels

talonner [talɔne] *vt* (*suivre*) to follow hot on the heels of; (*harceler*) to hound

talus [taly] *nm* embankment

tambour [tɑ̃buʀ] *nm* (*MUS, aussi*) drum; (*musicien*) drummer; (*porte*) revolving door(s *pl*); **tambourin** *nm* tambourine; **tambouriner** *vi* to drum; **tambouriner à/sur** to drum on

tamis [tami] *nm* sieve

Tamise [tamiz] *nf*: **la ~** the Thames

tamisé, e [tamize] *adj* (*fig*) subdued, soft

tampon [tɑ̃pɔ̃] *nm* (*de coton, d'ouate*) wad, pad; (*amortisseur*) buffer; (*bouchon*) plug, stopper; (*cachet, timbre*) stamp; **(mémoire) ~** (*INFORM*) buffer; **~ (hygiénique)** tampon; **tamponner** *vt* (*timbres*) to stamp; (*heurter*) to crash *ou* ram into; **tamponneuse** *adj f*: **autos tamponneuses** dodgems

tandem [tɑ̃dɛm] *nm* tandem

tandis [tɑ̃di]: ~ **que** *conj* while

tanguer [tɑ̃ge] *vi* to pitch (and toss)

tanière [tanjɛʀ] *nf* lair, den

tanné, e [tane] *adj* weather-beaten

tanner [tane] *vt* to tan; (*fam: harceler*) to badger

tant [tɑ̃] *adv* so much; ~ **de** (*sable, eau*) so much; (*gens, livres*) so many; ~ **que** as long as; (*autant que*) as much as; ~ **mieux** that's great; (*avec une certaine réserve*) so much the better; ~ **pis** too bad; (*conciliant*) never mind

tante [tɑ̃t] *nf* aunt

tantôt [tɑ̃to] *adv* (*parfois*): ~ **...** ~ now ... now; (*cet après-midi*) this afternoon

taon [tɑ̃] *nm* horsefly

tapage [tapaʒ] *nm* uproar, din

tapageur, -euse [tapaʒœʀ, øz] *adj* noisy; (*voyant*) loud, flashy

tape [tap] *nf* slap

tape-à-l'œil [tapalœj] *adj inv* flashy, showy

taper [tape] *vt* (*porte*) to bang, slam; (*enfant*) to slap; (*dactylographier*) to type (out); (*fam: emprunter*): ~ **qn de 10 F** to touch sb for 10 F ♦ *vi* (*soleil*) to beat down; **se** ~ *vt* (*repas*) to put away; (*fam: corvée*) to get landed with; ~ **sur qn** to thump sb; (*fig*) to run sb down; ~ **sur un clou** to hit a nail; ~ **à** (*porte etc*) to knock on; ~ **dans** (*se servir*) to dig into; ~ **des mains/pieds** to clap one's hands/stamp one's feet; ~ **(à la machine)** to type; **se** ~ **un travail** (*fam*) to land o.s. a job

tapi, e [tapi] *adj* (*blotti*) crouching; (*caché*) hidden away

tapis [tapi] *nm* carpet; (*petit*) rug; **mettre sur le** ~ (*fig*) to bring up for discussion; ~ **de bain** bath mat; ~ **de sol** (*de tente*) groundsheet; ~ **de souris** mouse mat; ~ **roulant** (*pour piétons*) moving walkway; (*pour bagages*) carousel

tapisser [tapise] *vt* (*avec du papier peint*) to paper; (*recouvrir*): ~ **qch (de)** to cover sth (with); **tapisserie** *nf* (*tenture, broderie*) tapestry; (*papier peint*) wallpaper; **tapissier,**

-ière *nm/f*: **tapissier-décorateur** interior decorator

tapoter [tapɔte] *vt* (*joue, main*) to pat; (*objet*) to tap

taquin, e [takɛ̃, in] *adj* teasing; **taquiner** *vt* to tease

tarabiscoté, e [taʀabiskɔte] *adj* overornate, fussy

tard [taʀ] *adv* late; **plus** ~ later (on); **au plus** ~ at the latest; **sur le** ~ late in life

tarder [taʀde] *vi* (*chose*) to be a long time coming; (*personne*): ~ **à faire** to delay doing; **il me tarde d'être** I am longing to be; **sans (plus)** ~ without (further) delay

tardif, -ive [taʀdif, iv] *adj* late

taré, e [taʀe] *nm/f* cretin

tarif [taʀif] *nm*: ~ **des consommations** price list; ~**s postaux/douaniers** postal/customs rates; ~ **des taxis** taxi fares; ~ **plein/réduit** (*train*) full/reduced fare; (*téléphone*) peak/off-peak rate

tarir [taʀiʀ] *vi* to dry up, run dry

tarte [taʀt] *nf* tart; ~ **aux fraises** strawberry tart; ~ **Tatin** ≃ apple upside-down tart

tartine [taʀtin] *nf* slice of bread; ~ **de miel** slice of bread and honey; **tartiner** *vt* to spread; **fromage à tartiner** cheese spread

tartre [taʀtʀ] *nm* (*des dents*) tartar; (*de bouilloire*) fur, scale

tas [tɑ] *nm* heap, pile; (*fig*): **un** ~ **de** heaps of, lots of; **en** ~ in a heap *ou* pile; **formé sur le** ~ trained on the job

tasse [tɑs] *nf* cup; ~ **à café** coffee cup

tassé, e [tɑse] *adj*: **bien** ~ (*café etc*) strong

tasser [tɑse] *vt* (*terre, neige*) to pack down; (*entasser*): ~ **qch dans** to cram sth into; **se** ~ *vi* (*se serrer*) to squeeze up; (*s'affaisser*) to settle; (*fig*) to settle down

tata [tata] *nf* auntie

tâter [tɑte] *vt* to feel; (*fig*) to try out; **se** ~ (*hésiter*) to be in two minds; ~ **de** (*prison etc*) to have a taste of

tatillon, ne [tatijɔ̃, ɔn] *adj* pernickety

tâtonnement [tɑtɔnmɑ̃] *nm*: **par** ~**s** (*fig*)

by trial and error

tâtonner [tatɔne] *vi* to grope one's way along

tâtons [tatɔ̃]: **à ~** *adv*: **chercher à ~** to grope around for

tatouage [tatwaʒ] *nm* tattoo

tatouer [tatwe] *vt* to tattoo

taudis [todi] *nm* hovel, slum

taule [tol] *(fam) nf* nick *(fam)*, prison

taupe [top] *nf* mole

taureau, x [tɔʀo] *nm* bull; *(signe):* **le T~** Taurus

tauromachie [tɔʀɔmaʃi] *nf* bullfighting

taux [to] *nm* rate; *(d'alcool)* level; **~ de change** exchange rate; **~ d'intérêt** interest rate

taxe [taks] *nf* tax; *(douanière)* duty; **toutes ~s comprises** inclusive of tax; **la boutique hors ~s** the duty free shop; **~ à la valeur ajoutée** value added tax

taxer [takse] *vt (personne)* to tax; *(produit)* to put a tax on, tax

taxi [taksi] *nm* taxi; *(fam)* taxi driver

Tchécoslovaquie [tʃekɔslɔvaki] *nf* Czechoslovakia; **tchèque** *adj* Czech ♦ *nm/f:* **Tchèque** Czech ♦ *nm (LING)* Czech; **la République tchèque** the Czech Republic

te, t' [tə] *pron* you; *(réfléchi)* yourself

technicien, ne [tɛknisjɛ̃, jɛn] *nm/f* technician

technico-commercial, e, -aux [tɛknikɔkɔmɛʀsjal, jo] *adj:* **agent ~-~** sales technician

technique [tɛknik] *adj* technical ♦ *nf* technique; **techniquement** *adv* technically

technologie [tɛknɔlɔʒi] *nf* technology; **technologique** *adj* technological

teck [tɛk] *nm* teak

tee-shirt [tiʃœʀt] *nm* T-shirt, tee-shirt

teignais *etc* [tɛɲɛ] *vb voir* **teindre**

teindre [tɛ̃dʀ] *vt* to dye; **se ~ les cheveux** to dye one's hair; **teint, e** *adj* dyed ♦ *nm (du visage)* complexion; *(momentané)* colour ♦ *nf* shade; **grand teint** colourfast

teinté, e [tɛ̃te] *adj:* **~ de** *(fig)* tinged with

teinter [tɛ̃te] *vt (verre, papier)* to tint; *(bois)* to stain

teinture [tɛ̃tyʀ] *nf* dye; **~ d'iode** tincture of iodine; **teinturerie** *nf* dry cleaner's; **teinturier** *nm* dry cleaner

tel, telle [tɛl] *adj (pareil)* such; *(comme):* **~ un/des ...** like a/like ...; *(indéfini)* such-and-such a; *(intensif):* **un ~/de tels ...** such (a)/such ...; **rien de ~** nothing like it; **~ que** like, such as; **~ quel** as it is *ou* stands *(ou* was *etc)*; **venez ~ jour** come on such-and-such a day

télé [tele] *(fam) nf* TV

télé...: **télécabine** *nf (benne)* cable car; **télécarte** *nf* phonecard; **télécharger** *vt* to download; **télécommande** *nf* remote control; **télécopie** *nf* fax; **envoyer qch par télécopie** to fax sth; **télécopieur** *nm* fax machine; **télédistribution** *nf* cable TV; **téléférique** *nm* = **téléphérique**; **télégramme** *nm* telegram; **télégraphier** *vt* to telegraph, cable; **téléguider** *vt* to radio-control; **télématique** *nf* telematics *sg*; **téléobjectif** *nm* telephoto lens *sg*; **télépathie** *nf* telepathy; **téléphérique** *nm* cable car

téléphone [telefɔn] *nm* telephone; **avoir le ~** to be on the (tele)phone; **au ~** on the phone; **~ mobile** mobile phone; **~ rouge** hot line; **~ sans fil** cordless (tele)phone; **~ de voiture** car phone; **téléphoner** *vi* to make a phone call; **téléphoner à** to phone, call up; **téléphonique** *adj* (tele)phone *cpd*

téléréalité [teleʀealite] *nf* reality TV

télescope [teleskɔp] *nm* telescope

télescoper [teleskɔpe] *vt* to smash up; **se ~** *(véhicules)* to concertina

télé...: **téléscripteur** *nm* teleprinter; **télésiège** *nm* chairlift; **téléski** *nm* ski-tow; **téléspectateur, -trice** *nm/f* (television) viewer; **télévente** *nf* telesales; **téléviseur** *nm* television set; **télévision** *nf* television; **à la télévision** on television; **télévision numérique** digital TV

telle [tɛl] *adj voir* **tel**; **tellement** *adv* (*tant*) so much; (*si*) so; **tellement de** (*sable, eau*) so much; (*gens, livres*) so many; **il s'est endormi tellement il était fatigué** he was so tired (that) he fell asleep; **pas tellement** not (all) that much; not (all) that +*adjectif*

téméraire [temerɛR] *adj* reckless, rash; **témérité** *nf* recklessness, rashness

témoignage [temwaɲaʒ] *nm* (*JUR: déclaration*) testimony *no pl*, evidence *no pl*; (*rapport, récit*) account; (*fig: d'affection etc: cadeau*) token, mark; (: *geste*) expression

témoigner [temwaɲe] *vt* (*intérêt, gratitude*) to show ♦ *vi* (*JUR*) to testify, give evidence; **~ de** to bear witness to, testify to

témoin [temwɛ̃] *nm* witness ♦ *adj*: **appartement ~** show flat (*BRIT*); **être ~ de** to witness; **~ oculaire** eyewitness

tempe [tɑ̃p] *nf* temple

tempérament [tɑ̃peRamɑ̃] *nm* temperament, disposition; **à ~** (*vente*) on deferred (payment) terms; (*achat*) by instalments, hire purchase *cpd*

température [tɑ̃peRatyR] *nf* temperature; **avoir** *ou* **faire de la ~** to be running *ou* have a temperature

tempéré, e [tɑ̃peRe] *adj* temperate

tempête [tɑ̃pɛt] *nf* storm; **~ de sable/ neige** sand/snowstorm

temple [tɑ̃pl] *nm* temple; (*protestant*) church

temporaire [tɑ̃pɔRɛR] *adj* temporary

temps [tɑ̃] *nm* (*atmosphérique*) weather; (*durée*) time; (*époque*) time, times *pl*; (*LING*) tense; (*MUS*) beat; (*TECH*) stroke; **un ~ de chien** (*fam*) rotten weather; **quel ~ fait-il?** what's the weather like?; **il fait beau/mauvais** the weather is fine/ bad; **avoir le ~/tout son ~** to have time/plenty of time; **en ~ de paix/guerre** in peacetime/wartime; **en ~ utile** *ou* **voulu** in due time *ou* course; **ces derniers ~** lately; **dans quelque ~** in a (little) while; **de ~ en ~, de ~ à autre** from time to time; **à ~** (*partir, arriver*) in time; **à ~**

complet, à plein ~ full-time; **à ~ partiel** part-time; **dans le ~** at one time; **~ d'arrêt** pause, halt; **~ mort** (*COMM*) slack period

tenable [t(ə)nabl] *adj* bearable

tenace [tənas] *adj* persistent

tenailler [tənaje] *vt* (*fig*) to torment

tenailles [tənaj] *nfpl* pincers

tenais *etc* [t(ə)nɛ] *vb voir* **tenir**

tenancier, -ière [tənɑ̃sje] *nm/f* manager/manageress

tenant, e [tənɑ̃, ɑ̃t] *nm/f* (*SPORT*): **~ du titre** title-holder

tendance [tɑ̃dɑ̃s] *nf* tendency; (*opinions*) leanings *pl*, sympathies *pl*; (*évolution*) trend; **avoir ~ à** to have a tendency to, tend to

tendeur [tɑ̃dœR] *nm* (*attache*) elastic strap

tendre [tɑ̃dR] *adj* tender; (*bois, roche, couleur*) soft ♦ *vt* (*élastique, peau*) to stretch; (*corde*) to tighten; (*muscle*) to tense; (*fig: piège*) to set, lay; (*donner*): **~ qch à qn** to hold sth out to sb; (*offrir*) to offer sb sth; **se ~** *vi* (*corde*) to tighten; (*relations*) to become strained; **~ à qch/à faire** to tend towards sth/to do; **~ l'oreille** to prick up one's ears; **~ la main/le bras** to hold out one's hand/stretch out one's arm; **tendrement** *adv* tenderly; **tendresse** *nf* tenderness

tendu, e [tɑ̃dy] *pp de* **tendre** ♦ *adj* (*corde*) tight; (*muscles*) tensed; (*relations*) strained

ténèbres [tenɛbR] *nfpl* darkness *sg*

teneur [tənœR] *nf* content; (*d'une lettre*) terms *pl*, content

tenir [t(ə)niR] *vt* to hold; (*magasin, hôtel*) to run; (*promesse*) to keep ♦ *vi* to hold; (*neige, gel*) to last; **se ~** *vi* (*avoir lieu*) to be held, take place; (*être: personne*) to stand; **~ à** (*personne, objet*) to be attached to; (*réputation*) to care about; **~ à faire** to be determined to do; **~ de** (*ressembler à*) to take after; **ça ne tient qu'à lui** it is entirely up to him; **~ qn pour** to regard sb as; **~ qch de qn** (*histoire*) to have heard *ou* learnt sth from sb; (*qualité,* *défaut*) to have inherited *ou* got sth from sb; **~ dans** to fit into; **~ compte de qch** to take sth into account; **~ les comptes** to keep the books; **~ bon** to stand fast; **~ le coup** to hold out; **~ au chaud** to keep hot; **tiens/tenez, voilà le stylo** there's the pen!; **tiens, voilà Alain!** look, here's Alain!; **tiens?** (*surprise*) really?; **se ~ droit** to stand (*ou* sit) up straight; **bien se ~** to behave well; **se ~ à qch** to hold on to sth; **s'en ~ à qch** to confine o.s. to sth

tennis [tenis] *nm* tennis; (*court*) tennis court ♦ *nm ou f pl* (*aussi:* **chaussures de ~**) tennis *ou* gym shoes; **~ de table** table tennis; **tennisman** *nm* tennis player

tension [tɑ̃sjɔ̃] *nf* tension; (*MÉD*) blood pressure; **avoir de la ~** to have high blood pressure

tentation [tɑ̃tasjɔ̃] *nf* temptation

tentative [tɑ̃tativ] *nf* attempt

tente [tɑ̃t] *nf* tent

tenter [tɑ̃te] *vt* (*éprouver, attirer*) to tempt; (*essayer*): **~ qch/de faire** to attempt *ou* try sth/to do; **~ sa chance** to try one's luck

tenture [tɑ̃tyʀ] *nf* hanging

tenu, e [t(ə)ny] *pp de* **tenir** ♦ *adj* (*maison, comptes*): **bien ~** well-kept; (*obligé*): **~ de faire** obliged to do ♦ *nf* (*vêtements*) clothes *pl*; (*comportement*) (good) manners *pl*, good behaviour; (*d'une maison*) upkeep; **en petite ~e** scantily dressed *ou* clad; **~e de route** (*AUTO*) road-holding; **~e de soirée** evening dress

ter [tɛʀ] *adj:* **16 ~ 16b** *ou* B

térébenthine [teʀebɑ̃tin] *nf:* (**essence de**) **~** (oil of) turpentine

Tergal ® [tɛʀɡal] *nm* Terylene ®

terme [tɛʀm] *nm* term; (*fin*) end; **à court/long ~** ♦ *adj* short-/long-term ♦ *adv* in the short/long term; **avant ~** (*MÉD*) prematurely; **mettre un ~ à** to put an end *ou* a stop to; **en bons ~s** on good terms

terminaison [tɛʀminɛzɔ̃] *nf* (*LING*) ending

terminal [tɛʀminal, o] *nm* terminal; **termi-**

nale *nf* (*SCOL*) ≃ sixth form *ou* year (*BRIT*), ≃ twelfth grade (*US*)

terminer [tɛʀmine] *vt* to finish; **se ~** *vi* to end

terne [tɛʀn] *adj* dull

ternir [tɛʀniʀ] *vt* to dull; (*fig*) to sully, tarnish; **se ~** *vi* to become dull

terrain [teʀɛ̃] *nm* (*sol, fig*) ground; (*COMM: étendue de terre*) land *no pl*; (*parcelle*) plot (of land); (*à bâtir*) site; **sur le ~** (*fig*) on the field; **~ d'aviation** airfield; **~ de camping** campsite; **~ de football/rugby** football/rugby pitch (*BRIT*) *ou* field (*US*); **~ de golf** golf course; **~ de jeu** games field; (*pour les petits*) playground; **~ de sport** sports ground; **~ vague** waste ground *no pl*

terrasse [teʀas] *nf* terrace; **à la ~** (*café*) outside; **terrasser** *vt* (*adversaire*) to floor; (*suj: maladie etc*) to strike down

terre [tɛʀ] *nf* (*gén, aussi ÉLEC*) earth; (*substance*) soil, earth; (*opposé à mer*) land *no pl*; (*contrée*) land; **~s** *nfpl* (*terrains*) lands, land *sg*; **en ~** (*pipe, poterie*) clay *cpd*; **à ~ ou par ~** (*mettre, être, s'asseoir*) on the ground (*ou* floor); (*jeter, tomber*) to the ground, down; **~ à ~** *adj inv* down-to-earth; **~ cuite** terracotta; **la ~ ferme** dry land; **~ glaise** clay

terreau [teʀo] *nm* compost

terre-plein [tɛʀplɛ̃] *nm* platform; (*sur chaussée*) central reservation

terrer [teʀe]: **se ~** *vi* to hide away

terrestre [teʀɛstʀ] *adj* (*surface*) earth's, of the earth; (*BOT, ZOOL, MIL*) land *cpd*; (*REL*) earthly

terreur [teʀœʀ] *nf* terror *no pl*

terrible [teʀibl] *adj* terrible, dreadful; (*fam*) terrific; **pas ~** nothing special

terrien, ne [teʀjɛ̃, jɛn] *adj:* **propriétaire ~** landowner ♦ *nm/f* (*non martien etc*) earthling

terrier [teʀje] *nm* burrow, hole; (*chien*) terrier

terrifier [teʀifje] *vt* to terrify

terrine [teʀin] *nf* (*récipient*) terrine; (*CULIN*)

pâté

territoire [teʀitwaʀ] *nm* territory

terroir [teʀwaʀ] *nm*: **accent du ~** country accent

terroriser [teʀɔʀize] *vt* to terrorize

terrorisme [teʀɔʀism] *nm* terrorism; **terroriste** *nm/f* terrorist

tertiaire [teʀsjɛʀ] *adj* tertiary ♦ *nm* (*ÉCON*) service industries *pl*

tertre [teʀtʀ] *nm* hillock, mound

tes [te] *adj voir* **ton**[1]

tesson [tesɔ̃] *nm*: **~ de bouteille** piece of broken bottle

test [test] *nm* test

testament [testamɑ̃] *nm* (*JUR*) will; (*REL*) Testament; (*fig*) legacy

tester [teste] *vt* to test

testicule [testikyl] *nm* testicle

tétanos [tetanɔs] *nm* tetanus

têtard [tetaʀ] *nm* tadpole

tête [tɛt] *nf* head; (*cheveux*) hair *no pl*; (*visage*) face; **de ~** *adj* (*wagon etc*) front *cpd* ♦ *adv* (*calculer*) in one's head, mentally; **tenir ~ à qn** to stand up to sb; **la ~ en bas** with one's head down; **la ~ la première** (*tomber*) headfirst; **faire une ~** (*FOOTBALL*) to head the ball; **faire la ~** (*fig*) to sulk; **en ~** at the front; (*SPORT*) in the lead; **à la ~ de** at the head of; **à ~ reposée** in a more leisurely moment; **n'en faire qu'à sa ~** to do as one pleases; **en avoir par-dessus la ~** to be fed up; **en ~ à ~** in private, alone together; **de la ~ aux pieds** from head to toe; **~ de lecture** (*playback*) head; **~ de liste** (*POL*) chief candidate; **~ de série** (*TENNIS*) seeded player, seed; **tête-à-queue** *nm inv*: **faire un tête-à-queue** to spin round

téter [tete] *vt*: **~ (sa mère)** to suck at one's mother's breast, feed

tétine [tetin] *nf* teat; (*sucette*) dummy (*BRIT*), pacifier (*US*)

têtu, e [tety] *adj* stubborn, pigheaded

texte [tɛkst] *nm* text; (*morceau choisi*) passage

textile [tɛkstil] *adj* textile *cpd* ♦ *nm* textile;

le ~ the textile industry

texto [tɛksto] (*fam*) *adj* word for word

texture [tɛkstyʀ] *nf* texture

thaïlandais, e [tajlɑ̃dɛ, ɛz] *adj* Thai ♦ *nm/f*: **T~, e** Thai

Thaïlande [tajlɑ̃d] *nf* Thailand

TGV *sigle m* (= *train à grande vitesse*) high-speed train

thé [te] *nm* tea; **~ au citron** lemon tea; **~ au lait** tea with milk; **prendre le ~** to have tea; **faire le ~** to make the tea

théâtral, e, -aux [teɑtʀal, o] *adj* theatrical

théâtre [teɑtʀ] *nm* theatre; (*péj: simulation*) playacting; (*fig: lieu*): **le ~ de** the scene of; **faire du ~** to act

théière [tejɛʀ] *nf* teapot

thème [tɛm] *nm* theme; (*SCOL: traduction*) prose (composition)

théologie [teɔlɔʒi] *nf* theology

théorie [teɔʀi] *nf* theory; **théorique** *adj* theoretical

thérapie [teʀapi] *nf* therapy

thermal, e, -aux [tɛʀmal, o] *adj*: **station ~e** spa; **cure ~e** water cure

thermes [tɛʀm] *nmpl* thermal baths

thermomètre [tɛʀmɔmɛtʀ] *nm* thermometer

thermos ® [tɛʀmos] *nm ou nf*: **(bouteille) ~** vacuum *ou* Thermos ® flask

thermostat [tɛʀmɔsta] *nm* thermostat

thèse [tɛz] *nf* thesis

thon [tɔ̃] *nm* tuna (fish)

thym [tɛ̃] *nm* thyme

tibia [tibja] *nm* shinbone, tibia; (*partie antérieure de la jambe*) shin

tic [tik] *nm* tic, (nervous) twitch; (*de langage etc*) mannerism

ticket [tikɛ] *nm* ticket; **~ de caisse** receipt; **~ de quai** platform ticket

tic-tac [tiktak] *nm* ticking; **faire ~-~** to tick

tiède [tjɛd] *adj* lukewarm; (*vent, air*) mild, warm; **tiédir** *vi* to cool; (*se réchauffer*) to grow warmer

tien, ne [tjɛ̃, tjɛn] *pron*: **le(la) ~(ne), les**

~(ne)s yours; **à la ~ne!** cheers!

tiens [tjɛ̃] *vb, excl voir* **tenir**

tierce [tjɛʀs] *adj voir* **tiers**

tiercé [tjɛʀse] *nm* system of forecast betting giving first 3 horses

tiers, tierce [tjɛʀ, tjɛʀs] *adj* third ♦ *nm* (*JUR*) third party; (*fraction*) third; **le ~ monde** the Third World

tifs [tif] (*fam*) *nmpl* hair

tige [tiʒ] *nf* stem; (*baguette*) rod

tignasse [tiɲas] (*péj*) *nf* mop of hair

tigre [tigʀ] *nm* tiger; **tigresse** *nf* tigress; **tigré, e** *adj* (*rayé*) striped; (*tacheté*) spotted; (*chat*) tabby

tilleul [tijœl] *nm* lime (tree), linden (tree); (*boisson*) lime(-blossom) tea

timbale [tɛ̃bal] *nf* (metal) tumbler; **~s** *nfpl* (*MUS*) timpani, kettledrums ·

timbre [tɛ̃bʀ] *nm* (*tampon*) stamp; (*aussi:* **~-poste**) (postage) stamp; (*MUS: de voix, instrument*) timbre, tone

timbré, e [tɛ̃bʀe] (*fam*) *adj* cracked

timide [timid] *adj* shy; (*timoré*) timid; **timidement** *adv* shyly; timidly; **timidité** *nf* shyness; timidity

tins *etc* [tɛ̃] *vb voir* **tenir**

tintamarre [tɛ̃tamaʀ] *nm* din, uproar

tinter [tɛ̃te] *vi* to ring, chime; (*argent, clefs*) to jingle

tique [tik] *nf* (*parasite*) tick

tir [tiʀ] *nm* (*sport*) shooting; (*fait ou manière de ~er*) firing *no pl*; (*rafale*) fire; (*stand*) shooting gallery; **~ à l'arc** archery; **~ au pigeon** clay pigeon shooting

tirage [tiʀaʒ] *nm* (*action*) printing; (*PHOTO*) print; (*de journal*) circulation; (*de livre: nombre d'exemplaires*) (print) run; (*: édition*) edition; (*de loterie*) draw; **par ~ au sort** by drawing lots

tirailler [tiʀaje] *vt:* **être tiraillé entre** to be torn between

tire [tiʀ] *nf:* **vol à la ~** pickpocketing

tiré, e [tiʀe] *adj* (*traits*) drawn; **~ par les cheveux** far-fetched

tire-au-flanc [tiʀɔflɑ̃] (*péj*) *nm inv* skiver

tire-bouchon [tiʀbuʃɔ̃] *nm* corkscrew

tirelire [tiʀliʀ] *nf* moneybox

tirer [tiʀe] *vt* (*gén*) to pull; (*extraire*): **~ qch de** to take *ou* pull sth out of; (*trait, rideau, carte, conclusion, chèque*) to draw; (*langue*) to stick out; (*en faisant feu: balle, coup*) to fire; (*: animal*) to shoot; (*journal, livre, photo*) to print; (*FOOTBALL: corner etc*) to take ♦ *vi* (*faire feu*) to fire; (*faire du tir, FOOTBALL*) to shoot; **s'en ~** *vi* (*fam*) to push off; **s'en ~** (*éviter le pire*) to get off; (*survivre*) to pull through; (*se débrouiller*) to manage; **~ sur** (*corde*) to pull on *ou* at; (*faire feu sur*) to shoot *ou* fire at; (*pipe*) to draw on; (*approcher de: couleur*) to verge *ou* border on; **~ qn de** (*embarras etc*) to help *ou* get sb out of; **~ à l'arc/la carabine** to shoot with a bow and arrow/with a rifle; **~ à sa fin** to be drawing to a close; **~ qch au clair** to clear sth up; **~ au sort** to draw lots; **~ parti de** to take advantage of; **~ profit de** to profit from

tiret [tiʀe] *nm* dash

tireur [tiʀœʀ] *nm* gunman; **~ d'élite** marksman

tiroir [tiʀwaʀ] *nm* drawer; **tiroir-caisse** *nm* till

tisane [tizan] *nf* herb tea

tisonnier [tizɔnje] *nm* poker

tisser [tise] *vt* to weave; **tisserand** *nm* weaver

tissu [tisy] *nm* fabric, material, cloth *no pl*; (*ANAT, BIO*) tissue; **tissu-éponge** *nm* (terry) towelling *no pl*

titre [titʀ] *nm* (*gén*) title; (*de journal*) headline; (*diplôme*) qualification; (*COMM*) security; **en ~** (*champion*) official; **à juste ~** rightly; **à quel ~?** on what grounds?; **à aucun ~** on no account; **au même ~ (que)** in the same way (as); **à ~ d'information** for (your) information; **à ~ gracieux** free of charge; **à ~ d'essai** on a trial basis; **à ~ privé** in a private capacity; **~ de propriété** title deed; **~ de transport** ticket

tituber [titybe] *vi* to stagger (along)

titulaire [titylɛʀ] *adj* (*ADMIN*) with tenure ♦ *nm/f* (*de permis*) holder

toast [tost] *nm* slice *ou* piece of toast; (*de bienvenue*) (welcoming) toast; **porter un ~ à qn** to propose *ou* drink a toast to sb

toboggan [tɔbɔgɑ̃] *nm* slide; (*AUTO*) flyover

toc [tɔk] *excl:* ~, ~ knock knock ♦ *nm:* **en ~** fake

tocsin [tɔksɛ̃] *nm* alarm (bell)

toge [tɔʒ] *nf* toga; (*de juge*) gown

tohu-bohu [tɔybɔy] *nm* hubbub

toi [twa] *pron* you

Toile [twal] *nf* Web

toile *nf* (*tableau*) canvas; **de** *ou* **en ~** (*pantalon*) cotton; (*sac*) canvas; **~ cirée** oilcloth; **~ d'araignée** cobweb; **~ de fond** (*fig*) backdrop

toilette [twalɛt] *nf* (*habits*) outfit; **~s** *nfpl* (*w.-c.*) toilet *sg*; **faire sa ~** to get washed; **articles de ~** toiletries

toi-même [twamɛm] *pron* yourself

toiser [twaze] *vt* to eye up and down

toison [twazɔ̃] *nf* (*de mouton*) fleece

toit [twa] *nm* roof; **~ ouvrant** sunroof

toiture [twatyʀ] *nf* roof

tôle [tol] *nf* (*plaque*) steel *ou* iron sheet; **~ ondulée** corrugated iron

tolérable [tɔleʀabl] *adj* tolerable

tolérant, e [tɔleʀɑ̃, ɑ̃t] *adj* tolerant

tolérer [tɔleʀe] *vt* to tolerate; (*ADMIN: hors taxe etc*) to allow

tollé [tɔ(l)le] *nm* outcry

tomate [tɔmat] *nf* tomato; **~s farcies** stuffed tomatoes

tombe [tɔ̃b] *nf* (*sépulture*) grave; (*avec monument*) tomb

tombeau, x [tɔ̃bo] *nm* tomb

tombée [tɔ̃be] *nf:* **à la ~ de la nuit** at nightfall

tomber [tɔ̃be] *vi* to fall; (*fièvre, vent*) to drop; (*objet*) **laisser ~** to drop; (*personne*) to let down; (*activité*) to give up; **laisse ~!** forget it!; **faire ~** to knock over; **~ sur** (*rencontrer*) to bump into; **~ de fatigue/sommeil** to drop from exhaustion/be falling asleep on one's feet; **ça tombe bien** that's come at the right time; **il est bien tombé** he's been lucky; **~ à l'eau** (*projet*) to fall through; **~ en panne** to break down

tombola [tɔ̃bɔla] *nf* raffle

tome [tɔm] *nm* volume

ton¹, ta [tɔ̃, ta] (*pl* **tes**) *adj* your

ton² [tɔ̃] *nm* (*gén*) tone; (*couleur*) shade, tone; **de bon ~** in good taste

tonalité [tɔnalite] *nf* (*au téléphone*) dialling tone

tondeuse [tɔ̃døz] *nf* (*à gazon*) (lawn)mower; (*du coiffeur*) clippers *pl*; (*pour les moutons*) shears *pl*

tondre [tɔ̃dʀ] *vt* (*pelouse, herbe*) to mow; (*haie*) to cut, clip; (*mouton, toison*) to shear; (*cheveux*) to crop

tongs [tɔ̃g] *nfpl* flip-flops

tonifier [tɔnifje] *vt* (*peau, organisme*) to tone up

tonique [tɔnik] *adj* fortifying ♦ *nm* tonic

tonne [tɔn] *nf* metric ton, tonne

tonneau, x [tɔno] *nm* (*à vin, cidre*) barrel; **faire des ~x** (*voiture, avion*) to roll over

tonnelle [tɔnɛl] *nf* bower, arbour

tonner [tɔne] *vi* to thunder; **il tonne** it is thundering, there's some thunder

tonnerre [tɔnɛʀ] *nm* thunder

tonton [tɔ̃tɔ̃] *nm* uncle

tonus [tɔnys] *nm* energy

top [tɔp] *nm:* **au 3ème ~** at the 3rd stroke

topinambour [tɔpinɑ̃buʀ] *nm* Jerusalem artichoke

topo [tɔpo] (*fam*) *nm* rundown; **c'est le même ~** it's the same old story

toque [tɔk] *nf* (*de fourrure*) fur hat; **~ de cuisinier** chef's hat; **~ de jockey/juge** jockey's/judge's cap

toqué, e [tɔke] (*fam*) *adj* cracked

torche [tɔʀʃ] *nf* torch

torchon [tɔʀʃɔ̃] *nm* cloth; (*à vaisselle*) tea towel *ou* cloth

tordre [tɔʀdʀ] *vt* (*chiffon*) to wring; (*barre, fig: visage*) to twist; **se ~** *vi:* **se ~ le**

poignet/la cheville to twist one's wrist/ankle; **se ~ de douleur/rire** to be doubled up with pain/laughter; **tordu, e** *adj* bent; *(fig)* crazy

tornade [tɔʀnad] *nf* tornado

torpille [tɔʀpij] *nf* torpedo

torréfier [tɔʀefje] *vt* to roast

torrent [tɔʀɑ̃] *nm* mountain stream

torsade [tɔʀsad] *nf*: **un pull à ~s** a cable sweater

torse [tɔʀs] *nm* chest; *(ANAT, SCULPTURE)* torso; **~ nu** stripped to the waist

tort [tɔʀ] *nm (défaut)* fault; **~s** *nmpl (JUR)* fault *sg*; **avoir ~** to be wrong; **être dans son ~** to be in the wrong; **donner ~ à qn** to lay the blame on sb; **causer du ~ à** to harm; **à ~** wrongly; **à ~ et à travers** wildly

torticolis [tɔʀtikɔli] *nm* stiff neck

tortiller [tɔʀtije] *vt* to twist; *(moustache)* to twirl; **se ~** *vi* to wriggle; *(en dansant)* to wiggle

tortionnaire [tɔʀsjɔnɛʀ] *nm* torturer

tortue [tɔʀty] *nf* tortoise; *(d'eau douce)* terrapin; *(d'eau de mer)* turtle

tortueux, -euse [tɔʀtɥø, øz] *adj (rue)* twisting; *(fig)* tortuous

torture [tɔʀtyʀ] *nf* torture; **torturer** *vt* to torture; *(fig)* to torment

tôt [to] *adv* early; **~ ou tard** sooner or later; **si ~** so early; *(déjà)* so soon; **plus ~** earlier; **au plus ~** at the earliest; **il eut ~ fait de faire** he soon did

total, e, -aux [tɔtal, o] *adj, nm* total; **au ~** in total; *(fig)* on the whole; **faire le ~** to work out the total; **totalement** *adv* totally; **totaliser** *vt* to total; **totalitaire** *adj* totalitarian; **totalité** *nf*: **la totalité de** all (of); the whole +*sg*; **en totalité** entirely

toubib [tubib] *(fam) nm* doctor

touchant, e [tuʃɑ̃, ɑ̃t] *adj* touching

touche [tuʃ] *nf (de piano, de machine à écrire)* key; *(de téléphone)* button; *(PEINTURE etc)* stroke, touch; *(fig: de nostalgie)* touch; *(FOOTBALL: aussi:* **remise en ~**) throw-in; *(aussi:* **ligne de ~**) touch-line

toucher [tuʃe] *nm* touch ♦ *vt* to touch; *(palper)* to feel; *(atteindre: d'un coup de feu etc)* to hit; *(concerner)* to concern, affect; *(contacter)* to reach, contact; *(recevoir: récompense)* to receive, get; *(: salaire)* to draw, get; *(: chèque)* to cash; **se ~** *(être en contact)* to touch; **au ~** to the touch; **~ à** to touch; *(concerner)* to have to do with, concern; **je vais lui en ~ un mot** I'll have a word with him about it; **~ à sa fin** to be drawing to a close

touffe [tuf] *nf* tuft

touffu, e [tufy] *adj* thick, dense

toujours [tuʒuʀ] *adv* always; *(encore)* still; *(constamment)* forever; **~ plus** more and more; **pour ~** forever; **~ est-il que** the fact remains that; **essaie ~** (you can) try anyway

toupet [tupɛ] *(fam) nm* cheek

toupie [tupi] *nf* (spinning) top

tour [tuʀ] *nf* tower; *(immeuble)* high-rise block *(BRIT)* ou building *(US)*; *(ÉCHECS)* castle, rook ♦ *nm (excursion)* trip; *(à pied)* stroll, walk; *(en voiture)* run, ride; *(SPORT: aussi:* **~ de piste**) lap; *(d'être servi ou de jouer etc)* turn; *(de roue etc)* revolution; *(POL: aussi:* **~ de scrutin**) ballot; *(ruse, de prestidigitation)* trick; *(de potier)* wheel; *(à bois, métaux)* lathe; *(circonférence):* **de 3 m de ~** 3 m round, with a circumference *ou* girth of 3 m; **faire le ~ de** to go round; *(à pied)* to walk round; **c'est au ~ de Renée** it's Renée's turn; **à ~ de rôle, ~ à ~** in turn; **~ de chant** *nm* song recital; **~ de contrôle** *nf* control tower; **~ de garde** *nm* spell of duty; **~ d'horizon** *nm (fig)* general survey; **~ de taille/tête** *nm* waist/head measurement; **un 33 ~s** an LP; **un 45 ~s** a single

tourbe [tuʀb] *nf* peat

tourbillon [tuʀbijɔ̃] *nm* whirlwind; *(d'eau)* whirlpool; *(fig)* whirl, swirl; **tourbillonner** *vi* to whirl (round)

tourelle [tuʀɛl] *nf* turret

tourisme [tuʀism] *nm* tourism; **agence de ~** tourist agency; **faire du ~** to go touring; (*en ville*) to go sightseeing; **touriste** *nm/f* tourist; **touristique** *adj* tourist *cpd*; (*région*) touristic

tourment [tuʀmɑ̃] *nm* torment; **tourmenter** *vt* to torment; **se tourmenter** *vi* to fret, worry o.s.

tournage [tuʀnaʒ] *nm* (*CINÉMA*) shooting

tournant [tuʀnɑ̃] *nm* (*de route*) bend; (*fig*) turning point

tournebroche [tuʀnəbʀɔʃ] *nm* roasting spit

tourne-disque [tuʀnədisk] *nm* record player

tournée [tuʀne] *nf* (*du facteur etc*) round; (*d'artiste, politicien*) tour; (*au café*) round (of drinks)

tournemain [tuʀnəmɛ̃]: **en un ~** *adv* (as) quick as a flash

tourner [tuʀne] *vt* to turn; (*sauce, mélange*) to stir; (*CINÉMA: faire les prises de vues*) to shoot; (: *produire*) to make ♦ *vi* to turn; (*moteur*) to run; (*taximètre*) to tick away; (*lait etc*) to turn (sour); **se ~** *vi* to turn round; **mal ~** to go wrong; **~ autour de** to go round; (*péj*) to hang round; **~ à/en** to turn into; **~ à gauche/droite** to turn left/right; **~ le dos à** to turn one's back on; to have one's back to; **~ de l'œil** to pass out; **se ~ vers** to turn towards; (*fig*) to turn to

tournesol [tuʀnəsɔl] *nm* sunflower

tournevis [tuʀnəvis] *nm* screwdriver

tourniquet [tuʀnikɛ] *nm* (*pour arroser*) sprinkler; (*portillon*) turnstile; (*présentoir*) revolving stand

tournoi [tuʀnwa] *nm* tournament

tournoyer [tuʀnwaje] *vi* to swirl (round)

tournure [tuʀnyʀ] *nf* (*LING*) turn of phrase; (*évolution*): **la ~ de qch** the way sth is developing; **~ d'esprit** turn *ou* cast of mind; **la ~ des événements** the turn of events

tourte [tuʀt] *nf* pie

tourterelle [tuʀtəʀɛl] *nf* turtledove

tous [tu] *adj, pron voir* **tout**

Toussaint [tusɛ̃] *nf*: **la ~** All Saints' Day

Toussaint

ⓘ **La Toussaint**, *November 1, is a public holiday in France. People traditionally visit the graves of friends and relatives to lay wreaths of heather and chrysanthemums.*

---

tousser [tuse] *vi* to cough

MOT-CLÉ

tout, e [tu, tut] (*mpl* **tous**, *fpl* **toutes**) *adj*
1 (*avec article singulier*) all; **tout le lait** all the milk; **toute la nuit** all night, the whole night; **tout le livre** the whole book; **tout un pain** a whole loaf; **tout le temps** all the time; the whole time; **c'est tout le contraire** it's quite the opposite
2 (*avec article pluriel*) every, all; **tous les livres** all the books; **toutes les nuits** every night; **toutes les fois** every time; **toutes les trois/deux semaines** every third/other *ou* second week, every three/two weeks; **tous les deux** both *ou* each of us (*ou* them *ou* you); **toutes les trois** all three of us (*ou* them *ou* you)
3 (*sans article*): **à tout âge** at any age; **pour toute nourriture, il avait ...** his only food was ...
♦ *pron* everything, all; **il a tout fait** he's done everything; **je les vois tous** I can see them all *ou* all of them; **nous y sommes tous allés** all of us went, we all went; **en tout** in all; **tout ce qu'il sait** all he knows
♦ *nm* whole; **le tout** all of it (*ou* them); **le tout est de ...** the main thing is to ...; **pas du tout** not at all
♦ *adv* **1** (*très, complètement*) very; **tout près** very near; **le tout premier** the very first; **tout seul** all alone; **le livre tout entier** the whole book; **tout en haut** right at the top; **tout droit** straight ahead
2: **tout en** while; **tout en travaillant** while working, as he *etc* works
3: **tout d'abord** first of all; **tout à coup**

suddenly; **tout à fait** absolutely; **tout à l'heure** a short while ago; (*futur*) in a short while, shortly; **à tout à l'heure!** see you later!; **tout de même** all the same; **tout le monde** everybody; **tout de suite** immediately, straight away; **tout terrain** *ou* **tous terrains** all-terrain

toutefois [tutfwa] *adv* however

toutes [tut] *adj, pron voir* **tout**

toux [tu] *nf* cough

toxicomane [tɔksikɔman] *nm/f* drug addict

toxique [tɔksik] *adj* toxic

trac [tʀak] *nm* (*au théâtre, en public*) stage fright; (*aux examens*) nerves *pl*; **avoir le ~** (*au théâtre, en public*) to have stage fright; (*aux examens*) to be feeling nervous

tracasser [tʀakase] *vt* to worry, bother; **se ~** to worry

trace [tʀas] *nf* (*empreintes*) tracks *pl*; (*marques, aussi fig*) mark; (*quantité infime, indice, vestige*) trace; **~s de pas** footprints

tracé [tʀase] *nm* (*parcours*) line; (*plan*) layout

tracer [tʀase] *vt* to draw; (*piste*) to open up

tract [tʀakt] *nm* tract, pamphlet

tractations [tʀaktasjɔ̃] *nfpl* dealings, bargaining *sg*

tracteur [tʀaktœʀ] *nm* tractor

traction [tʀaksjɔ̃] *nf*: **~ avant/arrière** front-wheel/rear-wheel drive

tradition [tʀadisjɔ̃] *nf* tradition; **traditionnel, le** *adj* traditional

traducteur, -trice [tʀadyktœʀ, tʀis] *nm/f* translator

traduction [tʀadyksjɔ̃] *nf* translation

traduire [tʀaduiʀ] *vt* to translate; (*exprimer*) to convey; **~ qn en justice** to bring sb before the courts

trafic [tʀafik] *nm* traffic; **~ d'armes** arms dealing; **trafiquant, e** *nm/f* trafficker; (*d'armes*) dealer; **trafiquer** (*péj*) *vt* (*vin*) to doctor; (*moteur, document*) to tamper with

tragédie [tʀaʒedi] *nf* tragedy; **tragique** *adj* tragic

trahir [tʀaiʀ] *vt* to betray; **trahison** *nf* betrayal; (*JUR*) treason

train [tʀɛ̃] *nm* (*RAIL*) train; (*allure*) pace; **être en ~ de faire qch** to be doing sth; **mettre qn en ~** to put sb in good spirits; **se sentir en ~** to feel in good form; **~ d'atterrissage** undercarriage; **~ de vie** style of living; **~ électrique** (*jouet*) (electric) train set; **~-autos-couchettes** car-sleeper train

traîne [tʀɛn] *nf* (*de robe*) train; **être à la ~** to lag behind

traîneau, x [tʀɛno] *nm* sleigh, sledge

traînée [tʀɛne] *nf* trail; (*sur un mur, dans le ciel*) streak; (*péj*) slut

traîner [tʀɛne] *vt* (*remorque*) to pull; (*enfant, chien*) to drag *ou* trail along ♦ *vi* (*robe, manteau*) to trail; (*être en désordre*) to lie around; (*aller lentement*) to dawdle (along); (*vagabonder, agir lentement*) to hang about; (*durer*) to drag on; **se ~** *vi* to drag o.s. along; **~ les pieds** to drag one's feet

train-train [tʀɛ̃tʀɛ̃] *nm* humdrum routine

traire [tʀɛʀ] *vt* to milk

trait [tʀɛ] *nm* (*ligne*) line; (*de dessin*) stroke; (*caractéristique*) feature, trait; **~s** *nmpl* (*du visage*) features; **d'un ~** (*boire*) in one gulp; **de ~** (*animal*) draught; **avoir ~ à** to concern; **~ d'union** hyphen

traitant, e [tʀɛtɑ̃, ɑ̃t] *adj* (*shampooing*) medicated; **votre médecin ~** your usual *ou* family doctor

traite [tʀɛt] *nf* (*COMM*) draft; (*AGR*) milking; **d'une ~** without stopping; **la ~ des noirs** the slave trade

traité [tʀɛte] *nm* treaty

traitement [tʀɛtmɑ̃] *nm* treatment; (*salaire*) salary; **~ de données** data processing; **~ de texte** word processing; (*logiciel*) word processing package

traiter [tʀɛte] *vt* to treat; (*qualifier*): **~ qn d'idiot** to call sb a fool ♦ *vi* to deal; **~ de** to deal with

traiteur [tʀɛtœʀ] *nm* caterer

traître, -esse [tʀɛtʀ, tʀɛtʀɛs] *adj* (*dangereux*) treacherous ♦ *nm* traitor

trajectoire [tʀaʒɛktwaʀ] *nf* path

trajet [tʀaʒɛ] *nm* (*parcours, voyage*) journey; (*itinéraire*) route; (*distance à parcourir*) distance

trame [tʀam] *nf* (*de tissu*) weft; (*fig*) framework; **usé jusqu'à la ~** threadbare

tramer [tʀame] *vt*: **il se trame quelque chose** there's something brewing

trampoline [tʀɑ̃pɔlin] *nm* trampoline

tramway [tʀamwɛ] *nm* tram(way); (*voiture*) tram(car), (*BRIT*), streetcar (*US*)

tranchant, e [tʀɑ̃ʃɑ̃, ɑ̃t] *adj* sharp; (*fig*) peremptory ♦ *nm* (*d'un couteau*) cutting edge; (*de la main*) edge; **à double ~** double-edged

tranche [tʀɑ̃ʃ] *nf* (*morceau*) slice; (*arête*) edge; **~ d'âge/de salaires** age/wage bracket

tranché, e [tʀɑ̃ʃe] *adj* (*couleurs*) distinct; (*opinions*) clear-cut; **tranchée** *nf* trench

trancher [tʀɑ̃ʃe] *vt* to cut, sever ♦ *vi* to take a decision; **~ avec** to contrast sharply with

tranquille [tʀɑ̃kil] *adj* quiet; (*rassuré*) easy in one's mind, with one's mind at rest; **se tenir ~** (*enfant*) to be quiet; **laisse-moi/laisse-ça ~** leave me/it alone; **avoir la conscience ~** to have a clear conscience; **tranquillisant** *nm* tranquillizer; **tranquillité** *nf* peace (and quiet); (*d'esprit*) peace of mind

transat [tʀɑ̃zat] *nm* deckchair

transborder [tʀɑ̃sbɔʀde] *vt* to tran(s)ship

transcription [tʀɑ̃skʀipsjɔ̃] *nf* transcription; (*copie*) transcript

transférer [tʀɑ̃sfeʀe] *vt* to transfer; **transfert** *nm* transfer

transformation [tʀɑ̃sfɔʀmasjɔ̃] *nf* change; transformation; alteration; (*RUGBY*) conversion

transformer [tʀɑ̃sfɔʀme] *vt* to change; (*radicalement*) to transform; (*vêtement*) to alter; (*matière première, appartement, RUGBY*) to convert; **(se) ~ en** to turn into

transfusion [tʀɑ̃sfyzjɔ̃] *nf*: **~ sanguine** blood transfusion

transgresser [tʀɑ̃sgʀese] *vt* to contravene

transi, e [tʀɑ̃zi] *adj* numb (with cold), chilled to the bone

transiger [tʀɑ̃ziʒe] *vi* to compromise

transit [tʀɑ̃zit] *nm* transit; **transiter** *vi* to pass in transit

transitif, -ive [tʀɑ̃zitif, iv] *adj* transitive

transition [tʀɑ̃zisjɔ̃] *nf* transition; **transitoire** *adj* transitional

translucide [tʀɑ̃slysid] *adj* translucent

transmettre [tʀɑ̃smɛtʀ] *vt* (*passer*): **~ qch à qn** to pass sth on to sb; (*TECH, TÉL, MÉD*) to transmit; (*TV, RADIO: retransmettre*) to broadcast; **transmission** *nf* transmission

transparent, e [tʀɑ̃spaʀɑ̃, ɑ̃t] *adj* transparent

transpercer [tʀɑ̃spɛʀse] *vt* (*froid, pluie*) to go through, pierce; (*balle*) to go through

transpiration [tʀɑ̃spiʀasjɔ̃] *nf* perspiration

transpirer [tʀɑ̃spiʀe] *vi* to perspire

transplanter [tʀɑ̃splɑ̃te] *vt* (*MÉD, BOT*) to transplant; **transplantation** *nf* (*MÉD*) transplant

transport [tʀɑ̃spɔʀ] *nm* transport; **~s en commun** public transport *sg*; **transporter** *vt* to carry, move; (*COMM*) to transport, convey; **transporteur** *nm* haulage contractor (*BRIT*), trucker (*US*)

transvaser [tʀɑ̃svaze] *vt* to decant

transversal, e, -aux [tʀɑ̃svɛʀsal, o] *adj* (*rue*) which runs across; **coupe ~e** cross section

trapèze [tʀapɛz] *nm* (*au cirque*) trapeze

trappe [tʀap] *nf* trap door

trapu, e [tʀapy] *adj* squat, stocky

traquenard [tʀaknaʀ] *nm* trap

traquer [tʀake] *vt* to track down; (*harceler*) to hound

traumatiser [tʀomatize] *vt* to traumatize

travail, -aux [tʀavaj] *nm* (*gén*) work; (*tâche, métier*) work *no pl*, job; (*ÉCON, MÉD*) labour; **être sans ~** (*employé*) to be out of work *ou* unemployed; *voir aussi* **tra-**

vaux; ~ **(au) noir** moonlighting

travailler [tʀavaje] *vi* to work; (*bois*) to warp ♦ *vt* (*bois, métal*) to work; (*objet d'art, discipline*) to work on; **cela le travaille** it is on his mind; **travailleur, -euse** *adj* hard-working ♦ *nm/f* worker; **travailliste** *adj* ≈ Labour *cpd*

travaux [tʀavo] *nmpl* (*de réparation, agricoles etc*) work *sg*; (*sur route*) roadworks *pl*; (*de construction*) building (work); **travaux des champs** farmwork *sg*; **travaux dirigés** (*SCOL*) tutorial; **travaux forcés** hard labour *sg*; **travaux manuels** (*SCOL*) handicrafts; **travaux ménagers** housework *sg*; **travaux pratiques** (*SCOL*) practical work; (*en laboratoire*) lab work

travers [tʀavɛʀ] *nm* fault, failing; **en** ~ **(de)** across; **au** ~ **(de)/à** ~ through; **de** ~ (*nez, bouche*) crooked; (*chapeau*) askew; **comprendre de** ~ to misunderstand; **regarder de** ~ (*fig*) to look askance at

traverse [tʀavɛʀs] *nf* (*de voie ferrée*) sleeper; **chemin de** ~ shortcut

traversée [tʀavɛʀse] *nf* crossing

traverser [tʀavɛʀse] *vt* (*gén*) to cross; (*ville, tunnel, aussi: percer, fig*) to go through; (*suj: ligne, trait*) to run across

traversin [tʀavɛʀsɛ̃] *nm* bolster

travesti [tʀavɛsti] *nm* transvestite

trébucher [tʀebyʃe] *vi*: ~ **(sur)** to stumble (over), trip (against)

trèfle [tʀɛfl] *nm* (*BOT*) clover; (*CARTES: couleur*) clubs *pl*; (*: carte*) club

treille [tʀɛj] *nf* vine arbour

treillis [tʀeji] *nm* (*métallique*) wire-mesh; (*MIL: tenue*) combat uniform; (*pantalon*) combat trousers *pl*

treize [tʀɛz] *num* thirteen; **treizième** *num* thirteenth

---
treizième mois
---

i Le **treizième mois** *is an end-of-year bonus roughly equal to one month's salary. For many employees it is a standard part of their salary package.*

tréma [tʀema] *nm* diaeresis

tremblement [tʀɑ̃bləmɑ̃] *nm*: ~ **de terre** earthquake

trembler [tʀɑ̃ble] *vi* to tremble, shake; ~ **de** (*froid, fièvre*) to shiver *ou* tremble with; (*peur*) to shake *ou* tremble with; ~ **pour qn** to fear for sb

trémousser [tʀemuse]: **se** ~ *vi* to jig about, wriggle about

trempe [tʀɑ̃p] *nf* (*fig*): **de cette/sa** ~ of this/his calibre

trempé, e [tʀɑ̃pe] *adj* soaking (wet), drenched; (*TECH*) tempered

tremper [tʀɑ̃pe] *vt* to soak, drench; (*aussi:* **faire** ~, **mettre à** ~) to soak; (*plonger*): ~ **qch dans** to dip sth in(to) ♦ *vi* to soak; (*fig*): ~ **dans** to be involved *ou* have a hand in; **se** ~ *vi* to have a quick dip; **trempette** *nf*: **faire trempette** to go paddling

tremplin [tʀɑ̃plɛ̃] *nm* springboard; (*SKI*) ski-jump

trentaine [tʀɑ̃tɛn] *nf*: **une** ~ **(de)** thirty or so, about thirty; **avoir la** ~ (*âge*) to be around thirty

trente [tʀɑ̃t] *num* thirty; **être sur son** ~ **et un** to be wearing one's Sunday best; **trentième** *num* thirtieth

trépidant, e [tʀepidɑ̃, ɑ̃t] *adj* (*fig: rythme*) pulsating; (*: vie*) hectic

trépied [tʀepje] *nm* tripod

trépigner [tʀepiɲe] *vi* to stamp (one's feet)

très [tʀɛ] *adv* very; much +*pp*, highly +*pp*

trésor [tʀezɔʀ] *nm* treasure; **T~ (public)** public revenue; **trésorerie** *nf* (*gestion*) accounts *pl*; (*bureaux*) accounts department; **difficultés de trésorerie** cash problems, shortage of cash *ou* funds; **trésorier, -ière** *nm/f* treasurer

tressaillir [tʀesajiʀ] *vi* to shiver, shudder

tressauter [tʀesote] *vi* to start, jump

tresse [tʀɛs] *nf* braid, plait; **tresser** *vt* (*cheveux*) to braid, plait; (*corbeille*) to weave

tréteau, x [tʀeto] *nm* trestle

treuil [tʀœj] *nm* winch

trêve [tʀɛv] *nf* (*MIL, POL*) truce; (*fig*) respite; **~ de ...** enough of this ...

tri [tʀi] *nm*: **faire le ~ (de)** to sort out; **le (bureau de) ~** (*POSTES*) the sorting office

triangle [tʀijɑ̃gl] *nm* triangle; **triangulaire** *adj* triangular

tribord [tʀibɔʀ] *nm*: **à ~** to starboard, on the starboard side

tribu [tʀiby] *nf* tribe

tribunal, -aux [tʀibynal, o] *nm* (*JUR*) court; (*MIL*) tribunal

tribune [tʀibyn] *nf* (*estrade*) platform, rostrum; (*débat*) forum; (*d'église, de tribunal*) gallery; (*de stade*) stand

tribut [tʀiby] *nm* tribute

tributaire [tʀibytɛʀ] *adj*: **être ~ de** to be dependent on

tricher [tʀiʃe] *vi* to cheat; **tricheur, -euse** *nm/f* cheat(er)

tricolore [tʀikɔlɔʀ] *adj* three-coloured; (*français*) red, white and blue

tricot [tʀiko] *nm* (*technique, ouvrage*) knitting *no pl*; (*vêtement*) jersey, sweater; **~ de peau** vest; **tricoter** *vt* to knit

trictrac [tʀiktʀak] *nm* backgammon

tricycle [tʀisikl] *nm* tricycle

triennal, e, -aux [tʀijenal, o] *adj* three-year

trier [tʀije] *vt* to sort out; (*POSTES, fruits*) to sort

trimestre [tʀimɛstʀ] *nm* (*SCOL*) term; (*COMM*) quarter; **trimestriel, le** *adj* quarterly; (*SCOL*) end-of-term

tringle [tʀɛ̃gl] *nf* rod

trinquer [tʀɛ̃ke] *vi* to clink glasses

triomphe [tʀijɔ̃f] *nm* triumph; **triompher** *vi* to triumph, win; **triompher de** to triumph over, overcome

tripes [tʀip] *nfpl* (*CULIN*) tripe *sg*

triple [tʀipl] *adj* triple ♦ *nm*: **le ~ (de)** (*comparaison*) three times as much (as); **en ~ exemplaire** in triplicate; **tripler** *vi, vt* to triple, treble

triplés, -ées [tʀiple] *nm/fpl* triplets

tripoter [tʀipɔte] *vt* to fiddle with

triste [tʀist] *adj* sad; (*couleur, temps, journée*) dreary; (*péj*): **~ personnage/affaire** sorry individual/affair; **tristesse** *nf* sadness

trivial, e, -aux [tʀivjal, jo] *adj* coarse, crude; (*commun*) mundane

troc [tʀɔk] *nm* barter

troène [tʀɔɛn] *nm* privet

trognon [tʀɔɲɔ̃] *nm* (*de fruit*) core; (*de légume*) stalk

trois [tʀwa] *num* three; **troisième** *num* third; **trois quarts** *nmpl*: **les trois quarts de** three-quarters of

trombe [tʀɔ̃b] *nf*: **des ~s d'eau** a downpour; **en ~** like a whirlwind

trombone [tʀɔ̃bɔn] *nm* (*MUS*) trombone; (*de bureau*) paper clip

trompe [tʀɔ̃p] *nf* (*d'éléphant*) trunk; (*MUS*) trumpet, horn

tromper [tʀɔ̃pe] *vt* to deceive; (*vigilance, poursuivants*) to elude; **se ~** *vi* to make a mistake, be mistaken; **se ~ de voiture/ jour** to take the wrong car/get the day wrong; **se ~ de 3 cm/20 euros** to be out by 3 cm/20 euros; **tromperie** *nf* deception, trickery *no pl*

trompette [tʀɔ̃pɛt] *nf* trumpet; **en ~** (*nez*) turned-up

trompeur, -euse [tʀɔ̃pœʀ, øz] *adj* deceptive

tronc [tʀɔ̃] *nm* (*BOT, ANAT*) trunk; (*d'église*) collection box

tronçon [tʀɔ̃sɔ̃] *nm* section; **tronçonner** *vt* to saw up

trône [tʀon] *nm* throne

trop [tʀo] *adv* (*+vb*) too much; (*+adjectif, adverbe*) too; **~ (nombreux)** too many; **~ peu (nombreux)** too few; **~ (souvent)** too often; **~ (longtemps)** (for) too long; **~ de** (*nombre*) too many; (*quantité*) too much; **de ~, en ~**: **des livres en ~** a few books too many; **du lait en ~** too much milk; **3 livres/3 F de ~** 3 books too many/3 F too much

tropical, e, -aux [tʀɔpikal, o] *adj* tropical

tropique [tʀɔpik] *nm* tropic

trop-plein [tʀoplɛ̃] *nm* (*tuyau*) overflow *ou*

outlet (pipe); (*liquide*) overflow

troquer [tʀɔke] *vt*: ~ **qch contre** to barter *ou* trade sth for; (*fig*) to swap sth for

trot [tʀo] *nm* trot; **trotter** *vi* to trot

trotteuse [tʀɔtøz] *nf* (sweep) second hand

trottinette [tʀɔtinɛt] *nf* (child's) scooter

trottoir [tʀɔtwaʀ] *nm* pavement; **faire le** ~ (*péj*) to walk the streets; ~ **roulant** moving walkway, travellator

trou [tʀu] *nm* hole; (*fig*) gap; (*COMM*) deficit; ~ **d'air** air pocket; ~ **d'ozone** ozone hole; **le** ~ **de la serrure** the keyhole; ~ **de mémoire** blank, lapse of memory

troublant, e [tʀublɑ̃, ɑ̃t] *adj* disturbing

trouble [tʀubl] *adj* (*liquide*) cloudy; (*image, photo*) blurred; (*affaire*) shady, murky ♦ *nm* agitation; ~**s** *nmpl* (*POL*) disturbances, troubles, unrest *sg*; (*MÉD*) trouble *sg*, disorders; **trouble-fête** *nm spoilsport*

troubler [tʀuble] *vt* to disturb; (*liquide*) to make cloudy; (*intriguer*) to bother; **se** ~ *vi* (*personne*) to become flustered *ou* confused

trouer [tʀue] *vt* to make a hole (*ou* holes) in

trouille [tʀuj] (*fam*) *nf*: **avoir la** ~ to be scared to death

troupe [tʀup] *nf* troop; ~ **(de théâtre)** (theatrical) company

troupeau, x [tʀupo] *nm* (*de moutons*) flock; (*de vaches*) herd

trousse [tʀus] *nf* case, kit; (*d'écolier*) pencil case; **aux** ~**s de** (*fig*) on the heels *ou* tail of; ~ **à outils** toolkit; ~ **de toilette** toilet bag

trousseau, x [tʀuso] *nm* (*de mariée*) trousseau; ~ **de clefs** bunch of keys

trouvaille [tʀuvaj] *nf* find

trouver [tʀuve] *vt* to find; (*rendre visite*): **aller/venir** ~ **qn** to go/come and see sb; **se** ~ *vi* (*être*) to be; **je trouve que** I find *ou* think that; ~ **à boire/critiquer** to find something to drink/criticize; **se** ~ **bien** to feel well; **se** ~ **mal** to pass out

truand [tʀyɑ̃] *nm* gangster; **truander** *vt*: **se faire truander** to be swindled

truc [tʀyk] *nm* (*astuce*) way, trick; (*de cinéma, prestidigitateur*) trick, effect; (*chose*) thing, thingumajig; **avoir le** ~ to have the knack

truelle [tʀyɛl] *nf* trowel

truffe [tʀyf] *nf* truffle; (*nez*) nose

truffé, e [tʀyfe] *adj*: ~ **de** (*fig*) peppered with; (*fautes*) riddled with; (*pièges*) bristling with

truie [tʀɥi] *nf* sow

truite [tʀɥit] *nf* trout *inv*

truquage [tʀykaʒ] *nm* special effects

truquer [tʀyke] *vt* (*élections, serrure, dés*) to fix

TSVP *sigle* (= *tournez svp*) PTO

TTC *sigle* (= *toutes taxes comprises*) inclusive of tax

tu[1] [ty] *pron* you

tu[2], **e** [ty] *pp de* **taire**

tuba [tyba] *nm* (*MUS*) tuba; (*SPORT*) snorkel

tube [tyb] *nm* tube; (*chanson*) hit

tuberculose [tybɛʀkyloz] *nf* tuberculosis

tuer [tɥe] *vt* to kill; **se** ~ *vi* to be killed; (*suicide*) to kill o.s.; **tuerie** *nf* slaughter *no pl*

tue-tête [tytɛt]: **à** ~-~ *adv* at the top of one's voice

tueur [tɥœʀ] *nm* killer; ~ **à gages** hired killer

tuile [tɥil] *nf* tile; (*fam*) spot of bad luck, blow

tulipe [tylip] *nf* tulip

tuméfié, e [tymefje] *adj* puffed-up, swollen

tumeur [tymœʀ] *nf* growth, tumour

tumulte [tymylt] *nm* commotion; **tumultueux, -euse** *adj* stormy, turbulent

tunique [tynik] *nf* tunic

Tunisie [tynizi] *nf*: **la** ~ Tunisia; **tunisien, ne** *adj* Tunisian ♦ *nm/f*: **Tunisien, ne** Tunisian

tunnel [tynɛl] *nm* tunnel; **le** ~ **sous la Manche** the Channel Tunnel

turbulences [tyʀbylɑ̃s] *nfpl* (*AVIAT*) turbulence *sg*

turbulent, e [tyʀbylɑ̃, ɑ̃t] *adj* boisterous,

unruly

turc, turque [tyʀk] *adj* Turkish ♦ *nm/f*: **T~, -que** Turk/Turkish woman ♦ *nm* (*LING*) Turkish

turf [tyʀf] *nm* racing; **turfiste** *nm/f* race-goer

Turquie [tyʀki] *nf*: **la ~** Turkey

turquoise [tyʀkwaz] *nf* turquoise ♦ *adj inv* turquoise

tus *etc* [ty] *vb voir* **taire**

tutelle [tytɛl] *nf* (*JUR*) guardianship; (*POL*) trusteeship; **sous la ~ de** (*fig*) under the supervision of

tuteur [tytœʀ] *nm* (*JUR*) guardian; (*de plante*) stake, support

tutoyer [tytwaje] *vt*: **~ qn** to address sb as "tu"

tuyau, x [tɥijo] *nm* pipe; (*flexible*) tube; (*fam*) tip; **~ d'arrosage** hosepipe; **~ d'échappement** exhaust pipe; **tuyauterie** *nf* piping *no pl*

TVA *sigle f* (= *taxe à la valeur ajoutée*) VAT

tympan [tɛ̃pɑ̃] *nm* (*ANAT*) eardrum

type [tip] *nm* type; (*fam*) chap, guy ♦ *adj* typical, classic

typé, e [tipe] *adj* ethnic

typique [tipik] *adj* typical

tyran [tiʀɑ̃] *nm* tyrant; **tyrannique** *adj* tyrannical

tzigane [dzigan] *adj* gipsy, tzigane

U, u

UEM *sigle f* (= *union économique et monétaire*) EMU

ulcère [ylsɛʀ] *nm* ulcer; **ulcérer** *vt* (*fig*) to sicken, appal

ultérieur, e [ylteʀjœʀ] *adj* later, subsequent; **remis à une date ~e** postponed to a later date; **ultérieurement** *adv* later, subsequently

ultime [yltim] *adj* final

ultra... [yltʀa] *préfixe*: **~moderne/-rapide** ultra-modern/-fast

---

un, une [œ̃, yn] *art indéf* a; (*devant voyelle*) an; **un garçon/vieillard** a boy/an old man; **une fille** a girl

♦ *pron* one; **l'un des meilleurs** one of the best; **l'un ..., l'autre** (the) one ..., the other; **les uns ..., les autres** some ..., others; **l'un et l'autre** both (of them); **l'un ou l'autre** either (of them); **l'un l'autre, les uns les autres** each other, one another; **pas un seul** not a single one; **un par un** one by one

♦ *num* one; **une pomme seulement** one apple only

---

unanime [ynanim] *adj* unanimous; **unanimité** *nf*: **à l'unanimité** unanimously

uni, e [yni] *adj* (*ton, tissu*) plain; (*surface*) smooth, even; (*famille*) close(-knit); (*pays*) united

unifier [ynifje] *vt* to unite, unify

uniforme [ynifɔʀm] *adj* uniform; (*surface, ton*) even ♦ *nm* uniform; **uniformiser** *vt* (*systèmes*) to standardize

union [ynjɔ̃] *nf* union; **~ de consommateurs** consumers' association; **U~ européenne** European Union; **U~ soviétique** Soviet Union

unique [ynik] *adj* (*seul*) only; (*exceptionnel*) unique; (*le même*): **un prix/système ~** a single price/system; **fils/fille ~** only son/daughter, only child; **sens ~** one-way street; **uniquement** *adv* only, solely; (*juste*) only, merely

unir [yniʀ] *vt* (*nations*) to unite; (*en mariage*) to unite, join together; **s'~** *vi* to unite; (*en mariage*) to be joined together

unitaire [yniteʀ] *adj*: **prix ~** unit price

unité [ynite] *nf* unit; (*harmonie, cohésion*) unity

univers [yniveʀ] *nm* universe; **universel, le** *adj* universal

universitaire [yniveʀsiteʀ] *adj* university *cpd*; (*diplôme, études*) academic, university *cpd* ♦ *nm/f* academic

université [yniveʀsite] *nf* university
urbain, e [yʀbɛ̃, ɛn] *adj* urban, city *cpd*, town *cpd*; **urbanisme** *nm* town planning
urgence [yʀʒɑ̃s] *nf* urgency; (*MÉD etc*) emergency; **d'~** *adj* emergency *cpd* ♦ *adv* as a matter of urgency; (**service des**) **~s** casualty
urgent, e [yʀʒɑ̃, ɑ̃t] *adj* urgent
urine [yʀin] *nf* urine; **urinoir** *nm* (public) urinal
urne [yʀn] *nf* (*électorale*) ballot box; (*vase*) urn
urticaire [yʀtikɛʀ] *nf* nettle rash
us [ys] *nmpl*: **~ et coutumes** (habits and) customs
USA *sigle mpl*: **les USA** the USA
usage [yzaʒ] *nm* (*emploi, utilisation*) use; (*coutume*) custom; **à l'~** with use; **à l'~ de** (*pour*) (for use of); **hors d'~** out of service; **à ~ interne** (*MÉD*) to be taken; **à ~ externe** (*MÉD*) for external use only; **usagé, e** *adj* (*usé*) worn; **usager, -ère** *nm/f* user
usé, e [yze] *adj* worn; (*banal: argument etc*) hackneyed
user [yze] *vt* (*outil*) to wear down; (*vêtement*) to wear out; (*matière*) to wear away; (*consommer: charbon etc*) to use; **s'~** *vi* (*tissu, vêtement*) to wear out; **~ de** (*moyen, procédé*) to use, employ; (*droit*) to exercise
usine [yzin] *nf* factory
usité, e [yzite] *adj* common
ustensile [ystɑ̃sil] *nm* implement; **~ de cuisine** kitchen utensil
usuel, le [yzɥɛl] *adj* everyday, common
usure [yzyʀ] *nf* wear
utérus [yteʀys] *nm* uterus, womb
utile [ytil] *adj* useful
utilisation [ytilizasjɔ̃] *nf* use
utiliser [ytilize] *vt* to use
utilitaire [ytilitɛʀ] *adj* utilitarian
utilité [ytilite] *nf* usefulness *no pl*; **de peu d'~** of little use *ou* help
utopie [ytɔpi] *nf* utopia

V, v

va [va] *vb voir* **aller**
vacance [vakɑ̃s] *nf* (*ADMIN*) vacancy; **~s** *nfpl* holiday(s *pl*), vacation *sg*; **les grandes ~s** the summer holidays; **prendre des/ses ~s** to take a holiday/one's holiday(s); **aller en ~s** to go on holiday; **vacancier, -ière** *nm/f* holiday-maker
vacant, e [vakɑ̃, ɑ̃t] *adj* vacant
vacarme [vakaʀm] *nm* (*bruit*) racket
vaccin [vaksɛ̃] *nm* vaccine; (*opération*) vaccination; **vaccination** *nf* vaccination; **vacciner** *vt* to vaccinate; **être vacciné contre qch** (*fam*) to be cured of sth
vache [vaʃ] *nf* (*ZOOL*) cow; (*cuir*) cowhide ♦ *adj* (*fam*) rotten, mean; **vachement** (*fam*) *adv* (*très*) really; (*pleuvoir, travailler*) a hell of a lot; **vacherie** *nf* (*action*) dirty trick; (*remarque*) nasty remark
vaciller [vasije] *vi* to sway, wobble; (*bougie, lumière*) to flicker; (*fig*) to be failing, falter
va-et-vient [vaevjɛ̃] *nm inv* (*de personnes, véhicules*) comings and goings *pl*, to-ings and fro-ings *pl*
vagabond [vagabɔ̃] *nm* (*rôdeur*) tramp, vagrant; (*voyageur*) wanderer; **vagabonder** *vi* to roam, wander
vagin [vaʒɛ̃] *nm* vagina
vague [vag] *nf* wave ♦ *adj* vague; (*regard*) faraway; (*manteau, robe*) loose(-fitting); (*quelconque*): **un ~ bureau/cousin** some office/cousin or other; **~ de fond** ground swell; **~ de froid** cold spell
vaillant, e [vajɑ̃, ɑ̃t] *adj* (*courageux*) gallant; (*robuste*) hale and hearty
vaille [vaj] *vb voir* **valoir**
vain, e [vɛ̃, vɛn] *adj* vain; **en ~** in vain
vaincre [vɛ̃kʀ] *vt* to defeat; (*fig*) to conquer, overcome; **vaincu, e** *nm/f* defeated party; **vainqueur** *nm* victor; (*SPORT*) winner
vais [vɛ] *vb voir* **aller**

vaisseau, x [veso] *nm* (*ANAT*) vessel; (*NA-VIG*) ship, vessel; **~ spatial** spaceship
vaisselier [vesəlje] *nm* dresser
vaisselle [vesɛl] *nf* (*service*) crockery; (*plats etc à laver*) (dirty) dishes *pl*; **faire la ~** to do the washing-up (*BRIT*) *ou* the dishes
val [val, vo] (*pl* **vaux** *ou* **~s**) *nm* valley
valable [valabl] *adj* valid; (*acceptable*) decent, worthwhile
valent *etc* [val] *vb voir* **valoir**
valet [valɛ] *nm* manservant; (*CARTES*) jack
valeur [valœʀ] *nf* (*gén*) value; (*mérite*) worth, merit; (*COMM: titre*) security; **mettre en ~** (*détail*) to highlight; (*objet décoratif*) to show off to advantage; **avoir de la ~** to be valuable; **sans ~** worthless; **prendre de la ~** to go up *ou* gain in value
valide [valid] *adj* (*en bonne santé*) fit; (*valable*) valid; **valider** *vt* to validate
valions [valjɔ̃] *vb voir* **valoir**
valise [valiz] *nf* (suit)case; **faire ses ~s** to pack one's bags
vallée [vale] *nf* valley
vallon [valɔ̃] *nm* small valley; **vallonné, e** *adj* hilly
valoir [valwaʀ] *vi* (*être valable*) to hold, apply ♦ *vt* (*prix, valeur, effort*) to be worth; (*causer*): **~ qch à qn** to earn sb sth; **se ~** *vi* to be of equal merit; (*péj*) to be two of a kind; **faire ~** (*droits, prérogatives*) to assert; **faire ~ que** to point out that; **à ~ sur** to be deducted from; **vaille que vaille** somehow or other; **cela ne me dit rien qui vaille** I don't like the look of it at all; **ce climat ne me vaut rien** this climate doesn't suit me; **~ le coup** *ou* **la peine** to be worth the trouble *ou* worth it; **~ mieux: il vaut mieux se taire** it's better to say nothing; **ça ne vaut rien** it's worthless; **que vaut ce candidat?** how good is this applicant?
valse [vals] *nf* waltz
valu, e [valy] *pp de* **valoir**
vandalisme [vɑ̃dalism] *nm* vandalism
vanille [vanij] *nf* vanilla

vanité [vanite] *nf* vanity; **vaniteux, -euse** *adj* vain, conceited
vanne [van] *nf* gate; (*fig*) joke
vannerie [vanʀi] *nf* basketwork
vantard, e [vɑ̃taʀ, aʀd] *adj* boastful
vanter [vɑ̃te] *vt* to speak highly of, praise; **se ~** *vi* to boast, brag; **se ~ de** to pride o.s. on; (*péj*) to boast of
vapeur [vapœʀ] *nf* steam; (*émanation*) vapour, fumes *pl*; **~s** *nfpl* (*bouffées*) vapours; **à ~** steam-powered, steam *cpd*; **cuit à la ~** steamed; **vaporeux, -euse** *adj* (*flou*) hazy, misty; (*léger*) filmy; **vaporisateur** *nm* spray; **vaporiser** *vt* (*parfum etc*) to spray
varappe [vaʀap] *nf* rock climbing
vareuse [vaʀøz] *nf* (*blouson*) pea jacket; (*d'uniforme*) tunic
variable [vaʀjabl] *adj* variable; (*temps, humeur*) changeable; (*divers: résultats*) varied, various
varice [vaʀis] *nf* varicose vein
varicelle [vaʀisɛl] *nf* chickenpox
varié, e [vaʀje] *adj* varied; (*divers*) various
varier [vaʀje] *vi* to vary; (*temps, humeur*) to change ♦ *vt* to vary; **variété** *nf* variety; **variétés** *nfpl*: **spectacle/émission de variétés** variety show
variole [vaʀjɔl] *nf* smallpox
vas [va] *vb voir* **aller**
vase [vɑz] *nm* vase ♦ *nf* silt, mud; **vaseux, -euse** *adj* silty, muddy; (*fig: confus*) woolly, hazy; (: *fatigué*) woozy
vasistas [vazistas] *nm* fanlight
vaste [vast] *adj* vast, immense
vaudrai *etc* [vodʀe] *vb voir* **valoir**
vaurien, ne [voʀjɛ̃, jɛn] *nm/f* good-for-nothing
vaut [vo] *vb voir* **valoir**
vautour [votuʀ] *nm* vulture
vautrer [votʀe] *vb*: **se ~ dans/sur** to wallow in/sprawl on
vaux [vo] *nmpl de* **val** ♦ *vb voir* **valoir**
va-vite [vavit]: **à la ~~** *adv* in a rush *ou* hurry

VDQS

i **VDQS** *(vin délimité de qualité supérieure) is the second highest French
wine classification after AOC, indicating
high-quality wine from an approved regional vineyard. It is followed by* **vin de
pays.** **Vin de table** *or* **vin ordinaire** *is
table wine of unspecified origin, often
blended.*

---

veau, x [vo] *nm* (*ZOOL*) calf; (*CULIN*) veal;
(*peau*) calfskin

vécu, e [veky] *pp de* **vivre**

vedette [vədɛt] *nf* (*artiste etc*) star; (*canot*)
motor boat; (*police*) launch

végétal, e, -aux [veʒetal, o] *adj* vegetable ♦ *nm* vegetable, plant; **végétalien,
ne** *adj, nm/f* vegan

végétarien, ne [veʒetaʀjɛ̃, jɛn] *adj, nm/f*
vegetarian

végétation [veʒetasjɔ̃] *nf* vegetation; **~s**
nfpl (*MÉD*) adenoids

véhicule [veikyl] *nm* vehicle; **~ utilitaire**
commercial vehicle

veille [vɛj] *nf* (*état*) wakefulness; (*jour*): **la
~ (de)** the day before; **la ~ au soir** the
previous evening; **à la ~ de** on the eve
of; **la ~ de Noël** Christmas Eve; **la ~ du
jour de l'An** New Year's Eve

veillée [veje] *nf* (*soirée*) evening; (*réunion*)
evening gathering; **~ (funèbre)** wake

veiller [veje] *vi* to stay up ♦ *vt* (*malade,
mort*) to watch over, sit up with; **~ à** to
attend to, see to; **~ à ce que** to make
sure that; **~ sur** to watch over; **veilleur**
nm: **veilleur de nuit** night watchman;
veilleuse *nf* (*lampe*) night light; (*AUTO*)
sidelight; (*flamme*) pilot light

veinard, e [venaʀ, aʀd] *nm/f* lucky devil

veine [vɛn] *nf* (*ANAT, du bois etc*) vein;
(*filon*) vein, seam; (*fam: chance*): **avoir de
la ~** to be lucky

véliplanchiste [veliplɑ̃ʃist] *nm/f* windsurf-
er

vélo [velo] *nm* bike, cycle; **faire du ~** to

go cycling; **~ tout-terrain** mountain bike;
vélomoteur *nm* moped

velours [v(ə)luʀ] *nm* velvet; **~ côtelé** corduroy; **velouté, e** *adj* velvety ♦ *nm*: **velouté de tomates** cream of tomato soup

velu, e [vəly] *adj* hairy

venais *etc* [vənɛ] *vb voir* **venir**

venaison [vənɛzɔ̃] *nf* venison

vendange [vɑ̃dɑ̃ʒ] *nf* (*aussi:* **~s**) grape
harvest; **vendanger** *vi* to harvest the
grapes

vendeur, -euse [vɑ̃dœʀ, øz] *nm/f* shop
assistant ♦ *nm* (*JUR*) vendor, seller; **~ de
journaux** newspaper seller

vendre [vɑ̃dʀ] *vt* to sell; **~ qch à qn** to sell
sb sth; **"à ~"** "for sale"

vendredi [vɑ̃dʀədi] *nm* Friday; **V~ saint**
Good Friday

vénéneux, -euse [venenø, øz] *adj* poi-
sonous

vénérien, ne [veneʀjɛ̃, jɛn] *adj* venereal

vengeance [vɑ̃ʒɑ̃s] *nf* vengeance *no pl*,
revenge *no pl*

venger [vɑ̃ʒe] *vt* to avenge; **se ~** *vi* to
avenge o.s.; **se ~ de qch** to avenge o.s.
for sth, take one's revenge for sth; **se ~
de qn** to take revenge on sb; **se ~ sur** to
take revenge on

venimeux, -euse [vənimø, øz] *adj* poi-
sonous, venomous; (*fig: haineux*) venomous, vicious

venin [vənɛ̃] *nm* venom, poison

venir [v(ə)niʀ] *vi* to come; **~ de** to come
from; **~ de faire: je viens d'y aller/de le
voir** I've just been there/seen him; **s'il
vient à pleuvoir** if it should rain; **j'en
viens à croire que** I have come to believe that; **faire ~** (*docteur, plombier*) to
call (out)

vent [vɑ̃] *nm* wind; **il y a du ~** it's windy;
c'est du ~ it's all hot air; **au ~** to wind-
ward; **sous le ~** to leeward; **avoir le ~
debout/arrière** to head into the wind/
have the wind astern; **dans le ~** (*fam*)
trendy

vente [vɑ̃t] *nf* sale; **la ~** (*activité*) selling;
(*secteur*) sales *pl*; **mettre en ~** (*produit*) to

put on sale; (*maison, objet personnel*) to put up for sale; **~ aux enchères** auction sale; **~ de charité** jumble sale

venteux, -euse [vãtø, øz] *adj* windy

ventilateur [vãtilatœʀ] *nm* fan

ventiler [vãtile] *vt* to ventilate

ventouse [vãtuz] *nf* (*de caoutchouc*) suction pad

ventre [vãtʀ] *nm* (ANAT) stomach; (*légèrement péj*) belly; (*utérus*) womb; **avoir mal au ~** to have stomach ache (BRIT) *ou* a stomach ache (US)

ventriloque [vãtʀilɔk] *nm/f* ventriloquist

venu, e [v(ə)ny] *pp de* **venir** ♦ *adj*: **bien ~** timely; **mal ~** out of place; **être mal ~ à** *ou* **de faire** to have no grounds for doing, be in no position to do

ver [vɛʀ] *nm* worm; (*des fruits etc*) maggot; (*du bois*) woodworm *no pl; voir aussi* **vers**; **~ à soie** silkworm; **~ de terre** earthworm; **~ luisant** glow-worm; **~ solitaire** tapeworm

verbaliser [vɛʀbalize] *vi* (POLICE) to book *ou* report an offender

verbe [vɛʀb] *nm* verb

verdâtre [vɛʀdɑtʀ] *adj* greenish

verdict [vɛʀdik(t)] *nm* verdict

verdir [vɛʀdiʀ] *vi, vt* to turn green; **verdure** *nf* greenery

véreux, -euse [veʀø, øz] *adj* worm-eaten; (*malhonnête*) shady, corrupt

verge [vɛʀʒ] *nf* (ANAT) penis

verger [vɛʀʒe] *nm* orchard

verglacé, e [vɛʀglase] *adj* icy, iced-over

verglas [vɛʀgla] *nm* (black) ice

vergogne [vɛʀgɔɲ]: **sans ~** *adv* shamelessly

véridique [veʀidik] *adj* truthful

vérification [veʀifikasjɔ̃] *nf* (*action*) checking *no pl*; (*contrôle*) check

vérifier [veʀifje] *vt* to check; (*corroborer*) to confirm, bear out

véritable [veʀitabl] *adj* real; (*ami, amour*) true

vérité [veʀite] *nf* truth; **en ~** really, actually

vermeil, le [vɛʀmɛj] *adj* ruby red

vermine [vɛʀmin] *nf* vermin *pl*

vermoulu, e [vɛʀmuly] *adj* worm-eaten

verni, e [vɛʀni] *adj* (*fam*) lucky; **cuir ~** patent leather

vernir [vɛʀniʀ] *vt* (*bois, tableau, ongles*) to varnish; (*poterie*) to glaze

vernis *nm* (*enduit*) varnish; glaze; (*fig*) veneer; **~ à ongles** nail polish *ou* varnish; **vernissage** *nm* (*d'une exposition*) preview

vérole [veʀɔl] *nf* (*variole*) smallpox

verrai *etc* [veʀe] *vb voir* **voir**

verre [vɛʀ] *nm* glass; (*de lunettes*) lens *sg*; **boire** *ou* **prendre un ~** to have a drink; **~ dépoli** frosted glass; **~s de contact** contact lenses; **verrerie** *nf* (*fabrique*) glassworks *sg*; (*activité*) glass-making; (*objets*) glassware; **verrière** *nf* (*paroi vitrée*) glass wall; (*toit vitré*) glass roof

verrons *etc* [veʀɔ̃] *vb voir* **voir**

verrou [veʀu] *nm* (*targette*) bolt; **mettre qn sous les ~s** to put sb behind bars; **verrouillage** *nm* locking; **verrouillage centralisé** central locking; **verrouiller** *vt* (*porte*) to bolt; (*ordinateur*) to lock

verrue [veʀy] *nf* wart

vers [vɛʀ] *nm* line ♦ *nmpl* (*poésie*) verse *sg* ♦ *prép* (*en direction de*) toward(s); (*près de*) around (about); (*temporel*) about, around

versant [vɛʀsã] *nm* slopes *pl*, side

versatile [vɛʀsatil] *adj* fickle, changeable

verse [vɛʀs]: **à ~** *adv*: **il pleut à ~** it's pouring (with rain)

Verseau [vɛʀso] *nm*: **le ~** Aquarius

versement [vɛʀsəmã] *nm* payment; **en 3 ~s** in 3 instalments

verser [vɛʀse] *vt* (*liquide, grains*) to pour; (*larmes, sang*) to shed; (*argent*) to pay ♦ *vi* (*véhicule*) to overturn; (*fig*): **~ dans** to lapse into

verset [vɛʀse] *nm* verse

version [vɛʀsjɔ̃] *nf* version; (SCOL) translation (*into the mother tongue*); **film en ~ originale** film in the original language

verso [vɛʀso] *nm* back; **voir au ~** see over(leaf)

vert, e [vɛʀ, vɛʀt] *adj* green; *(vin)* young; *(vigoureux)* sprightly ♦ *nm* green

vertèbre [vɛʀtɛbʀ] *nf* vertebra

vertement [vɛʀtəmɑ̃] *adv (réprimander)* sharply

vertical, e, -aux [vɛʀtikal, o] *adj* vertical; **verticale** *nf* vertical; **à la verticale** vertically; **verticalement** *adv* vertically

vertige [vɛʀtiʒ] *nm (peur du vide)* vertigo; *(étourdissement)* dizzy spell; *(fig)* fever; **vertigineux, -euse** *adj* breathtaking

vertu [vɛʀty] *nf* virtue; **en ~ de** in accordance with; **vertueux, -euse** *adj* virtuous

verve [vɛʀv] *nf* witty eloquence; **être en ~** to be in brilliant form

verveine [vɛʀvɛn] *nf (BOT)* verbena, vervain; *(infusion)* verbena tea

vésicule [vezikyl] *nf* vesicle; **~ biliaire** gall-bladder

vessie [vesi] *nf* bladder

veste [vɛst] *nf* jacket; **~ droite/croisée** single-/double-breasted jacket

vestiaire [vɛstjɛʀ] *nm (au théâtre etc)* cloakroom; *(de stade etc)* changing-room *(BRIT)*, locker-room *(US)*

vestibule [vɛstibyl] *nm* hall

vestige [vɛstiʒ] *nm* relic; *(fig)* vestige; **~s** *nmpl (de ville)* remains

vestimentaire [vɛstimɑ̃tɛʀ] *adj (détail)* of dress; *(élégance)* sartorial; **dépenses ~s** clothing expenditure

veston [vɛstɔ̃] *nm* jacket

vêtement [vɛtmɑ̃] *nm* garment, item of clothing; **~s** *nmpl* clothes

vétérinaire [veteʀinɛʀ] *nm/f* vet, veterinary surgeon

vêtir [vetiʀ] *vt* to clothe, dress

veto [veto] *nm* veto; **opposer un ~ à** to veto

vêtu, e [vety] *pp de* **vêtir**

vétuste [vetyst] *adj* ancient, timeworn

veuf, veuve [vœf, vœv] *adj* widowed ♦ *nm* widower

veuille [vœj] *vb voir* **vouloir**

veuillez [vœje] *vb voir* **vouloir**

veule [vøl] *adj* spineless

veuve [vœv] *nf* widow

veux [vø] *vb voir* **vouloir**

vexant, e [vɛksɑ̃, ɑ̃t] *adj (contrariant)* annoying; *(blessant)* hurtful

vexation [vɛksasjɔ̃] *nf* humiliation

vexer [vɛkse] *vt*: **~ qn** to hurt sb's feelings; **se ~** *vi* to be offended

viable [vjabl] *adj* viable; *(économie, industrie etc)* sustainable

viaduc [vjadyk] *nm* viaduct

viager, -ère [vjaʒe, ɛʀ] *adj*: **rente viagère** life annuity

viande [vjɑ̃d] *nf* meat

vibrer [vibʀe] *vi* to vibrate; *(son, voix)* to be vibrant; *(fig)* to be stirred; **faire ~** to (cause to) vibrate; *(fig)* to stir, thrill

vice [vis] *nm* vice; *(défaut)* fault ♦ *préfixe*: **~...** vice-; **~ de forme** legal flaw *ou* irregularity

vichy [viʃi] *nm (toile)* gingham

vicié, e [visje] *adj (air)* polluted, tainted; *(JUR)* invalidated

vicieux, -euse [visjø, jøz] *adj (pervers)* lecherous; *(rétif)* unruly ♦ *nm/f* lecher

vicinal, e, -aux [visinal, o] *adj*: **chemin ~** by-road, byway

victime [viktim] *nf* victim; *(d'accident)* casualty

victoire [viktwaʀ] *nf* victory

victuailles [viktɥɑj] *nfpl* provisions

vidange [vidɑ̃ʒ] *nf (d'un fossé, réservoir)* emptying; *(AUTO)* oil change; *(de lavabo: bonde)* waste outlet; **~s** *nfpl (matières)* sewage *sg*; **vidanger** *vt* to empty

vide [vid] *adj* empty ♦ *nm (PHYSIQUE)* vacuum; *(espace)* (empty) space, gap; *(futilité, néant)* void; **avoir peur du ~** to be afraid of heights; **emballé sous ~** vacuum packed; **à ~** *(sans occupants)* empty; *(sans charge)* unladen

vidéo [video] *nf* video ♦ *adj*: **cassette ~** video cassette; **jeu ~** video game; **vidéoclip** *nm* music video; **vidéoclub** *nm* video shop

vide-ordures [vidɔʀdyʀ] *nm inv* (rubbish)

chute

vidéothèque [videɔtɛk] *nf* video library

vide-poches [vidpɔʃ] *nm inv* tidy; (AUTO) glove compartment

vider [vide] *vt* to empty; (CULIN: *volaille, poisson*) to gut, clean out; **se ~** *vi* to empty; **~ les lieux** to quit *ou* vacate the premises; **videur** *nm* (*de boîte de nuit*) bouncer

vie [vi] *nf* life; **être en ~** to be alive; **sans ~** lifeless; **à ~** for life

vieil [vjɛj] *adj m voir* **vieux**; **vieillard** *nm* old man; **les vieillards** old people, the elderly; **vieille** *adj, nf voir* **vieux**; **vieilleries** *nfpl* old things; **vieillesse** *nf* old age; **vieillir** *vi* (*prendre de l'âge*) to grow old; (*population, vin*) to age; (*doctrine, auteur*) to become dated ♦ *vt* to age; **vieillissement** *nm* growing old; ageing

Vienne [vjɛn] *nf* Vienna

viens [vjɛ̃] *vb voir* **venir**

vierge [vjɛrʒ] *adj* virgin; (*page*) clean, blank ♦ *nf* virgin; (*signe*): **la V~** Virgo

Vietnam, Viet-Nam [vjɛtnam] *nm* Vietnam; **vietnamien, ne** *adj* Vietnamese ♦ *nm/f*: **Vietnamien, ne** Vietnamese

vieux (vieil), vieille [vjø, vjɛj] *adj* old ♦ *nm/f* old man (woman) ♦ *nmpl* old people; **mon ~/ma vieille** (*fam*) old man/girl; **prendre un coup de ~** to put years on; **vieille fille** spinster; **~ garçon** bachelor; **~ jeu** *adj inv* old-fashioned

vif, vive [vif, viv] *adj* (*animé*) lively; (*alerte, brusque, aigu*) sharp; (*lumière, couleur*) bright; (*air*) crisp; (*vent, émotion*) keen; (*fort: regret, déception*) great, deep; (*vivant*): **brûlé ~** burnt alive; **de vive voix** personally; **avoir l'esprit ~** to be quick-witted; **piquer au ~** to cut sb to the quick; **à ~** (*plaie*) open; **avoir les nerfs à ~** to be on edge

vigne [viɲ] *nf* (*plante*) vine; (*plantation*) vineyard; **vigneron** *nm* wine grower

vignette [viɲɛt] *nf* (ADMIN) ≃ (road) tax disc (BRIT), ≃ license plate sticker (US); (*de médicament*) price label (*used for reimburse-*

ment)

vignoble [viɲɔbl] *nm* (*plantation*) vineyard; (*vignes d'une région*) vineyards *pl*

vigoureux, -euse [vigurø, øz] *adj* vigorous, robust

vigueur [vigœr] *nf* vigour; **entrer en ~** to come into force; **en ~** current

vil, e [vil] *adj* vile, base

vilain, e [vilɛ̃, ɛn] *adj* (*laid*) ugly; (*affaire, blessure*) nasty; (*pas sage: enfant*) naughty

villa [villa] *nf* (detached) house; **~ en multipropriété** time-share villa

village [vilaʒ] *nm* village; **villageois, e** *adj* village *cpd* ♦ *nm/f* villager

ville [vil] *nf* town; (*importante*) city; (*administration*): **la ~** ≃ the Corporation; ≃ the (town) council; **~ d'eaux** spa

villégiature [vi(l)leʒjatyr] *nf* holiday; (**lieu de**) ~ (holiday) resort

vin [vɛ̃] *nm* wine; **avoir le ~ gai** to get happy after a few drinks; **~ d'honneur** reception (*with wine and snacks*); **~ de pays** local wine; **~ ordinaire** table wine

vinaigre [vinɛgr] *nm* vinegar; **vinaigrette** *nf* vinaigrette, French dressing

vindicatif, -ive [vɛ̃dikatif, iv] *adj* vindictive

vineux, -euse [vinø, øz] *adj* win(e)y

vingt [vɛ̃] *num* twenty; **vingtaine** *nf*: **une vingtaine (de)** about twenty, twenty or so; **vingtième** *num* twentieth

vinicole [vinikɔl] *adj* wine *cpd*, wine-growing

vins *etc* [vɛ̃] *vb voir* **venir**

vinyle [vinil] *nm* vinyl

viol [vjɔl] *nm* (*d'une femme*) rape; (*d'un lieu sacré*) violation

violacé, e [vjɔlase] *adj* purplish, mauvish

violemment [vjɔlamɑ̃] *adv* violently

violence [vjɔlɑ̃s] *nf* violence

violent, e [vjɔlɑ̃, ɑ̃t] *adj* violent; (*remède*) drastic

violer [vjɔle] *vt* (*femme*) to rape; (*sépulture, loi, traité*) to violate

violet, te [vjɔlɛ, ɛt] *adj, nm* purple, mauve; **violette** *nf* (*fleur*) violet

violon [vjɔlɔ̃] *nm* violin; *(fam: prison)* lock-up; **~ d'Ingres** hobby; **violoncelle** *nm* cello; **violoniste** *nm/f* violinist

vipère [vipɛʀ] *nf* viper, adder

virage [viʀaʒ] *nm* *(d'un véhicule)* turn; *(d'une route, piste)* bend

virée [viʀe] *nf* trip; *(à pied)* walk; *(longue)* walking tour; *(dans les cafés)* tour

virement [viʀmɑ̃] *nm* (COMM) transfer

virent [viʀ] *vb voir* **voir**

virer [viʀe] *vt* (COMM): **~ qch (sur)** to transfer sth (into); *(fam: expulser)*: **~ qn** to kick sb out ♦ *vi* to turn; (CHIMIE) to change colour; **~ de bord** to tack

virevolter [viʀvɔlte] *vi* to twirl around

virgule [viʀgyl] *nf* comma; (MATH) point

viril, e [viʀil] *adj* *(propre à l'homme)* masculine; *(énergique, courageux)* manly, virile

virtuel, le [viʀtɥɛl] *adj* potential; *(théorique)* virtual

virtuose [viʀtɥoz] *nm/f* (MUS) virtuoso; *(gén)* master

virus [viʀys] *nm* virus

vis¹ [vi] *vb voir* **voir; vivre**

vis² [vi] *nf* screw

visa [viza] *nm* *(sceau)* stamp; *(validation de passeport)* visa

visage [vizaʒ] *nm* face

vis-à-vis [vizavi] *prép*: **~-~-~ de qn** to(wards) sb; **en ~-~-~** facing each other

viscéral, e, -aux [viseʀal, o] *adj* *(fig)* deep-seated, deep-rooted

visées [vize] *nfpl (intentions)* designs

viser [vize] *vi* to aim ♦ *vt* to aim at; *(concerner)* to be aimed *ou* directed at; *(apposer un visa sur)* to stamp, visa; **~ à qch/faire** to aim at sth/at doing *ou* to do; **viseur** *nm (d'arme)* sights *pl*; (PHOTO) viewfinder

visibilité [vizibilite] *nf* visibility

visible [vizibl] *adj* visible; *(disponible)*: **est-il ~?** can he see me?, will he see visitors?

visière [vizjɛʀ] *nf (de casquette)* peak; *(qui s'attache)* eyeshade

vision [vizjɔ̃] *nf* vision; *(sens)* (eye)sight, vision; *(fait de voir)*: **la ~ de** the sight of; **vi-**sionneuse *nf* viewer

visite [vizit] *nf* visit; **~ médicale** medical examination; **~ accompagnée** *ou* **guidée** guided tour; **faire une ~ à qn** to call on sb, pay sb a visit; **rendre ~ à qn** to visit sb, pay sb a visit; **être en ~ (chez qn)** to be visiting (sb); **avoir de la ~** to have visitors; **heures de ~** *(hôpital, prison)* visiting hours

visiter [vizite] *vt* to visit; **visiteur, -euse** *nm/f* visitor

vison [vizɔ̃] *nm* mink

visser [vise] *vt*: **~ qch** *(fixer, serrer)* to screw sth on

visuel, le [vizɥɛl] *adj* visual

vit [vi] *vb voir* **voir; vivre**

vital, e, -aux [vital, o] *adj* vital

vitamine [vitamin] *nf* vitamin

vite [vit] *adv (rapidement)* quickly, fast; *(sans délai)* quickly; *(sous peu)* soon; **~!** quick!; **faire ~** to be quick; **le temps passe ~** time flies

vitesse [vites] *nf* speed; (AUTO: *dispositif)* gear; **prendre de la ~** to pick up *ou* gather speed; **à toute ~** at full *ou* top speed; **en ~** *(rapidement)* quickly; *(en hâte)* in a hurry

viticole [vitikɔl] *adj* wine *cpd*, wine-growing; **viticulteur** *nm* wine grower

vitrage [vitʀaʒ] *nm*: **double ~** double glazing

vitrail, -aux [vitʀaj, o] *nm* stained-glass window

vitre [vitʀ] *nf* (window) pane; *(de portière, voiture)* window; **vitré, e** *adj* glass *cpd*; **vitrer** *vt* to glaze; **vitreux, -euse** *adj (terne)* glassy

vitrine [vitʀin] *nf* (shop) window; *(petite armoire)* display cabinet; **en ~** in the window; **~ publicitaire** display case, showcase

vivable [vivabl] *adj (personne)* livable-with; *(maison)* fit to live in

vivace [vivas] *adj (arbre, plante)* hardy; *(fig)* indestructible, inveterate

vivacité [vivasite] *nf* liveliness, vivacity

vivant, e [vivɑ̃, ɑ̃t] *adj* (*qui vit*) living, alive; (*animé*) lively; (*preuve, exemple*) living ♦ *nm*: **du ~ de qn** in sb's lifetime; **les ~s** the living

vive [viv] *adj voir* **vif** ♦ *vb voir* **vivre** ♦ *excl*: **~ le roi!** long live the king!; **vivement** *adv* deeply ♦ *excl*: **vivement les vacances!** roll on the holidays!

vivier [vivje] *nm* (*étang*) fish tank; (*réservoir*) fishpond

vivifiant, e [vivifjɑ̃, jɑ̃t] *adj* invigorating

vivions [vivjɔ̃] *vb voir* **vivre**

vivoter [vivɔte] *vi* (*personne*) to scrape a living, get by; (*fig: affaire etc*) to struggle along

vivre [vivʀ] *vi, vt* to live; (*période*) to live through; **~ de** to live on; **il vit encore** he is still alive; **se laisser ~** to take life as it comes; **ne plus ~** (*être anxieux*) to live on one's nerves; **il a vécu** (*eu une vie aventureuse*) he has seen life; **être facile à ~** to be easy to get on with; **faire ~ qn** (*pourvoir à sa subsistance*) to provide a (living) for sb; **vivres** *nmpl* provisions, food supplies

vlan [vlɑ̃] *excl* wham!, bang!

VO [veo] *nf*: **film en ~** film in the original version; **en ~ sous-titrée** in the original version with subtitles

vocable [vɔkabl] *nm* term

vocabulaire [vɔkabylɛʀ] *nm* vocabulary

vocation [vɔkasjɔ̃] *nf* vocation, calling

vociférer [vɔsifeʀe] *vi, vt* to scream

vœu, x [vø] *nm* wish; (*promesse*) vow; **faire ~ de** to take a vow of; **tous nos ~x de bonne année, meilleurs ~x** best wishes for the New Year

vogue [vɔg] *nf* fashion, vogue

voguer [vɔge] *vi* to sail

voici [vwasi] *prép* (*pour introduire, désigner*) here is +*sg*, here are +*pl*; **et ~ que ...** and now it (*ou* he) ...; *voir aussi* **voilà**

voie [vwa] *nf* way; (*RAIL*) track, line; (*AUTO*) lane; **être en bonne ~** to be going well; **mettre qn sur la ~** to put sb on the right track; **pays en ~ de développe-**ment developing country; **être en ~ d'achèvement/de rénovation** to be nearing completion/in the process of renovation; **par ~ buccale** *ou* **orale** orally; **à ~ étroite** narrow-gauge; **~ d'eau** (*NAVIG*) leak; **~ de garage** (*RAIL*) siding; **~ ferrée** track; railway line; **la ~ publique** the public highway

voilà [vwala] *prép* (*en désignant*) there is +*sg*, there are +*pl*; **les ~** *ou* **voici** here *ou* there they are; **en ~** *ou* **voici un** here's one, there's one; **voici mon frère et ~ ma sœur** this is my brother and that's my sister; **~** *ou* **voici deux ans** two years ago; **~** *ou* **voici deux ans que** it's two years since; **et ~!** there we are!; **~ tout** that's all; **~** *ou* **voici** (*en offrant etc*) there *ou* here you are; **tiens! ~ Paul** look! there's Paul

voile [vwal] *nm* veil; (*tissu léger*) net ♦ *nf* sail; (*sport*) sailing; **voiler** *vt* to veil; (*fausser: roue*) to buckle; (: *bois*) to warp; **se voiler** *vi* (*lune, regard*) to mist over; (*voix*) to become husky; (*roue, disque*) to buckle; (*planche*) to warp; **voilier** *nm* sailing ship; (*de plaisance*) sailing boat; **voilure** *nf* (*de voilier*) sails *pl*

voir [vwaʀ] *vi, vt* to see; **se ~** *vt* (*être visible*) to show; (*se fréquenter*) to see each other; (*se produire*) to happen; **se ~ critiquer/transformer** to be criticized/transformed; **cela se voit** (*c'est visible*) that's obvious, it shows; **faire ~ qch à qn** to show sb sth; **en faire ~ à qn** (*fig*) to give sb a hard time; **ne pas pouvoir ~ qn** not to be able to stand sb; **voyons!** let's see now; (*indignation etc*) come on!; **avoir quelque chose à ~ avec** to have something to do with

voire [vwaʀ] *adv* even

voisin, e [vwazɛ̃, in] *adj* (*proche*) neighbouring; (*contigu*) next; (*ressemblant*) connected ♦ *nm/f* neighbour; **voisinage** *nm* (*proximité*) proximity; (*environs*) vicinity; (*quartier, voisins*) neighbourhood

voiture [vwatyʀ] *nf* car; (*wagon*) coach,

carriage; **~ de course** racing car; **~ de sport** sports car

voix [vwa] *nf* voice; (*POL*) vote; **à haute ~** aloud; **à ~ basse** in a low voice; **à 2/4** (*MUS*) in 2/4 parts; **avoir ~ au chapitre** to have a say in the matter

vol [vɔl] *nm* (*d'oiseau, d'avion*) flight; (*larcin*) theft; **~ régulier** scheduled flight; **à d'oiseau** as the crow flies; **au ~: attraper qch au ~** to catch sth as it flies past; **en ~** in flight; **~ à main armée** armed robbery; **~ à voile** gliding; **~ libre** hang-gliding

volage [vɔlaʒ] *adj* fickle

volaille [vɔlaj] *nf* (*oiseaux*) poultry *pl*; (*viande*) poultry *no pl*; (*oiseau*) fowl

volant, e [vɔlɑ̃, ɑ̃t] *adj voir* **feuille** *etc*
♦ *nm* (*d'automobile*) (steering) wheel; (*de commande*) wheel; (*objet lancé*) shuttlecock; (*bande de tissu*) flounce

volcan [vɔlkɑ̃] *nm* volcano

volée [vɔle] *nf* (*TENNIS*) volley; **à la ~: rattraper à la ~** to catch in mid-air; **à toute ~** (*sonner les cloches*) vigorously; (*lancer un projectile*) with full force; **~ de coups/de flèches** volley of blows/arrows

voler [vɔle] *vi* (*avion, oiseau, fig*) to fly; (*voleur*) to steal ♦ *vt* (*objet*) to steal; (*personne*) to rob; **~ qch à qn** to steal sth from sb; **il ne l'a pas volé!** he asked for it!

volet [vɔlε] *nm* (*de fenêtre*) shutter; (*de feuillet, document*) section

voleur, -euse [vɔlœʀ, øz] *nm/f* thief ♦ *adj* thieving; **"au ~!"** "stop thief!"

volière [vɔljεʀ] *nf* aviary

volley [vɔlε] *nm* volleyball

volontaire [vɔlɔ̃tεʀ] *adj* (*acte, enrôlement, prisonnier*) voluntary; (*oubli*) intentional; (*caractère, personne: décidé*) self-willed ♦ *nm/f* volunteer

volonté [vɔlɔ̃te] *nf* (*faculté de vouloir*) will; (*énergie, fermeté*) will(power); (*souhait, désir*) wish; **à ~** as much as one likes; **bonne ~** goodwill, willingness; **mauvaise ~** lack of goodwill, unwillingness

volontiers [vɔlɔ̃tje] *adv* (*avec plaisir*) willingly, gladly; (*habituellement, souvent*) readily, willingly; **voulez-vous boire quelque chose? - ~!** would you like something to drink? - yes, please!

volt [vɔlt] *nm* volt

volte-face [vɔltəfas] *nf inv*: **faire ~-~** to turn round

voltige [vɔltiʒ] *nf* (*ÉQUITATION*) trick riding; (*au cirque*) acrobatics *sg*; **voltiger** *vi* to flutter (about)

volubile [vɔlybil] *adj* voluble

volume [vɔlym] *nm* volume; (*GÉOM: solide*) solid; **volumineux, -euse** *adj* voluminous, bulky

volupté [vɔlypte] *nf* sensual delight *ou* pleasure

vomi [vɔmi] *nm* vomit; **vomir** *vi* to vomit, be sick ♦ *vt* to vomit, bring up; (*fig*) to belch out, spew out; (*exécrer*) to loathe, abhor; **vomissements** *nmpl*: **être pris de vomissements** to (suddenly) start vomiting

vont [vɔ̃] *vb voir* **aller**

vorace [vɔʀas] *adj* voracious

vos [vo] *adj voir* **votre**

vote [vɔt] *nm* vote; **~ par correspondance/procuration** postal/proxy vote; **voter** *vi* to vote ♦ *vt* (*projet de loi*) to vote for; (*loi, réforme*) to pass

votre [vɔtʀ] (*pl* **vos**) *adj* your

vôtre [votʀ] *pron*: **le ~, la ~, les ~s** yours; **les ~s** (*fig*) your family *ou* folks; **à la ~** (*toast*) your (good) health!

voudrai *etc* [vudʀe] *vb voir* **vouloir**

voué, e [vwe] *adj*: **~ à** doomed to

vouer [vwe] *vt*: **~ qch à** (*Dieu, un saint*) to dedicate sth to; **~ sa vie à** (*étude, cause etc*) to devote one's life to; **~ une amitié éternelle à qn** to vow undying friendship to sb

---

MOT-CLÉ

---

vouloir [vulwaʀ] *nm*: **le bon vouloir de qn** sb's goodwill; sb's pleasure
♦ *vt* **1** (*exiger, désirer*) to want; **vouloir**

faire/que qn fasse to want to do/sb to do; **voulez-vous du thé?** would you like *ou* do you want some tea?; **que me veut-il?** what does he want with ·me?; **sans le vouloir** (*involontairement*) without meaning to, unintentionally; **je voudrais ceci/faire** I would *ou* I'd like this/to do

2 (*consentir*): **je veux bien** (*bonne volonté*) I'll be happy to; (*concession*) fair enough, that's fine; **oui, si on veut** (*en quelque sorte*) yes, if you like; **veuillez attendre** please wait; **veuillez agréer ...** (*formule épistolaire*) yours faithfully

3: **en vouloir à qn** to bear sb a grudge; **s'en vouloir (de)** to be annoyed with o.s. (for); **il en veut à mon argent** he's after my money

4: **vouloir de: l'entreprise ne veut plus de lui** the firm doesn't want him any more; **elle ne veut pas de son aide** she doesn't want his help

5: **vouloir dire** to mean

voulu, e [vuly] *adj* (*requis*) required, requisite; (*délibéré*) deliberate, intentional; *voir aussi* **vouloir**

vous [vu] *pron* you; (*objet indirect*) (to) you; (*réfléchi: sg*) yourself; (: *pl*) yourselves; (*réciproque*) each other; **~-même** yourself; **~-mêmes** yourselves

voûte [vut] *nf* vault; **voûter: se voûter** *vi* (*dos, personne*) to become stooped

vouvoyer [vuvwaje] *vt:* **~ qn** to address sb as "vous"

voyage [vwajaʒ] *nm* journey, trip; (*fait de ~r*) **le ~** travel(ling); **partir/être en ~** to go off/be away on a journey *ou* trip; **faire bon ~** to have a good journey; **~ d'agrément/d'affaires** pleasure/business trip; **~ de noces** honeymoon; **~ organisé** package tour

voyager [vwajaʒe] *vi* to travel; **voyageur, -euse** *nm/f* traveller; (*passager*) passenger

voyant, e [vwajɑ̃, ɑ̃t] *adj* (*couleur*) loud, gaudy ♦ *nm* (*signal*) (warning) light; **voyante** *nf* clairvoyant

voyelle [vwajɛl] *nf* vowel

voyons *etc* [vwajɔ̃] *vb voir* **voir**

voyou [vwaju] *nm* hooligan

vrac [vʀak]: **en ~** *adv* (*au détail*) loose; (*en gros*) in bulk; (*en désordre*) in a jumble

vrai, e [vʀɛ] *adj* (*véridique: récit, faits*) true; (*non factice, authentique*) real; **à ~ dire** to tell the truth; **vraiment** *adv* really; **vraisemblable** *adj* likely; (*excuse*) convincing; **vraisemblablement** *adv* probably; **vraisemblance** *nf* likelihood; (*romanesque*) verisimilitude

vrille [vʀij] *nf* (*de plante*) tendril; (*outil*) gimlet; (*spirale*) spiral; (*AVIAT*) spin

vrombir [vʀɔ̃biʀ] *vi* to hum

VRP *sigle m* (= *voyageur, représentant, placier*) sales rep (*fam*)

VTT *sigle m* (= *vélo tout-terrain*) mountain bike

vu, e [vy] *pp de* **voir** ♦ *adj:* **bien/mal ~** (*fig: personne*) popular/unpopular; (: *chose*) approved/disapproved of ♦ *prép* (*en raison de*) in view of; **~ que** in view of the fact that

vue [vy] *nf* (*fait de voir*): **la ~ de** the sight of; (*sens, faculté*) (eye)sight; (*panorama, image, photo*) view; **~s** *nfpl* (*idées*) views; (*dessein*) designs; **hors de ~** out of sight; **avoir en ~** to have in mind; **tirer à ~** to shoot on sight; **à ~ d'œil** visibly; **de ~** by sight; **perdre de ~** to lose sight of; **en ~** (*visible*) in sight; (*célèbre*) in the public eye; **en ~ de faire** with a view to doing

vulgaire [vylgɛʀ] *adj* (*grossier*) vulgar, coarse; (*ordinaire*) commonplace, mundane; (*péj: quelconque*): **de ~s touristes** common tourists; (*BOT, ZOOL: non latin*) common; **vulgariser** *vt* to popularize

vulnérable [vylneʀabl] *adj* vulnerable

W, w

wagon [vagɔ̃] *nm* (*de voyageurs*) carriage; (*de marchandises*) truck, wagon; **wagon-lit** *nm* sleeper, sleeping car; **wagon-restaurant** *nm* restaurant *ou* dining car
wallon, ne [walɔ̃, ɔn] *adj* Walloon
waters [watɛʀ] *nmpl* toilet *sg*
watt [wat] *nm* watt
WC *sigle mpl* (= *water-closet(s)*) toilet
Web [wɛb] *nm inv*: **le ~** the (World Wide) Web
week-end [wikɛnd] *nm* weekend
western [wɛstɛʀn] *nm* western
whisky [wiski] (*pl* **whiskies**) *nm* whisky

X, x

xénophobe [gzenɔfɔb] *adj* xenophobic ♦ *nm/f* xenophobe
xérès [gzeʀɛs] *nm* sherry
xylophone [gzilɔfɔn] *nm* xylophone

Y, y

y [i] *adv* (*à cet endroit*) there; (*dessus*) on it (*ou* them); (*dedans*) in it (*ou* them) ♦ *pron* (*about ou* on *ou* of) it (*d'après le verbe employé*); **j'~ pense** I'm thinking about it; **ça ~ est!** that's it!; *voir aussi* **aller**; **avoir**
yacht [jɔt] *nm* yacht
yaourt [jauʀt] *nm* yoghourt; **~ nature/aux fruits** plain/fruit yogurt
yeux [jø] *nmpl de* **œil**
yoga [jɔga] *nm* yoga

yoghourt [jɔguʀt] *nm* = **yaourt**
yougoslave [jugɔslav] (*HISTOIRE*) *adj* Yugoslav(ian) ♦ *nm/f*: **Y~** Yugoslav
Yougoslavie [jugɔslavi] (*HISTOIRE*) *nf* Yugoslavia

Z, z

zapper [zape] *vi* to zap
zapping [zapiŋ] *nm*: **faire du ~** to flick through the channels
zèbre [zɛbʀ(ə)] *nm* (*ZOOL*) zebra; **zébré, e** *adj* striped, streaked
zèle [zɛl] *nm* zeal; **faire du ~** (*péj*) to be over-zealous; **zélé, e** *adj* zealous
zéro [zeʀo] *nm* zero, nought (*BRIT*); **au-dessous de ~** below zero (Centigrade) *ou* freezing; **partir de ~** to start from scratch; **trois (buts) à ~** 3 (goals to) nil
zeste [zɛst] *nm* peel, zest
zézayer [zezeje] *vi* to have a lisp
zigzag [zigzag] *nm* zigzag; **zigzaguer** *vi* to zigzag
zinc [zɛ̃g] *nm* (*CHIMIE*) zinc
zizanie [zizani] *nf*: **semer la ~** to stir up ill-feeling
zizi [zizi] *nm* (*langage enfantin*) willy
zodiaque [zɔdjak] *nm* zodiac
zona [zona] *nm* shingles *sg*
zone [zon] *nf* zone, area; **~ bleue** ≃ restricted parking area; **~ industrielle** industrial estate
zoo [zo(o)] *nm* zoo
zoologie [zɔɔlɔʒi] *nf* zoology; **zoologique** *adj* zoological
zut [zyt] *excl* dash (it)! (*BRIT*), nuts! (*US*)

VERB TABLES

Introduction

The **Verb Tables** in the following section contain 32 tables of French verbs (some regular and some irregular) in alphabetical order. Each table shows you the following forms: **Present, Perfect, Future, Subjunctive, Imperfect, Conditional, Imperative** and the **Present** and **Past Participles**.

In order to help you use the verbs shown in Verb Tables correctly, there are also a number of example phrases at the bottom of each page to show the verb as it is used in context.

In French there are both **regular** verbs (their forms follow the normal rules) and **irregular** verbs (their forms do not follow the normal rules). The regular verbs in these tables are:

donner (regular -er verb, Verb Table 11)
finir (regular -ir verb, Verb Table 16)
attendre (regular -re verb, Verb Table 3)

The irregular verbs are shown in full.

For a further list of French irregular verb forms see pages 585–588.

▶ aller (to go)

PRESENT

je	vais
tu	vas
il/elle/on	va
nous	allons
vous	allez
ils/elles	vont

PRESENT SUBJUNCTIVE

j'	aille
tu	ailles
il/elle/on	aille
nous	allions
vous	alliez
ils/elles	aillent

PERFECT

je	suis allé(e)
tu	es allé(e)
il/elle/on	est allé(e)
nous	sommes allé(e)s
vous	êtes allé(e)(s)
ils/elles	sont allé(e)s

IMPERFECT

j'	allais
tu	allais
il/elle/on	allait
nous	allions
vous	alliez
ils/elles	allaient

FUTURE

j'	irai
tu	iras
il/elle/on	ira
nous	irons
vous	irez
ils/elles	iront

CONDITIONAL

j'	irais
tu	irais
il/elle/on	irait
nous	irions
vous	iriez
ils/elles	iraient

IMPERATIVE

va / allons / allez

PAST PARTICIPLE

allé

PRESENT PARTICIPLE

allant

EXAMPLE PHRASES

*Vous **allez** au cinéma?* Are you going to the cinema?
*Je **suis allé** à Londres.* I went to London.
*Est-ce que tu **es** déjà **allé** en Allemagne?* Have you ever been to Germany?

---

je/j' = I **tu** = you **il** = he/it **elle** = she/it **on** = we/one **nous** = we **vous** = you **ils/elles** = they

▶ **attendre** (to wait)

PRESENT

j'	attends
tu	attends
il/elle/on	attend
nous	attendons
vous	attendez
ils/elles	attendent

PRESENT SUBJUNCTIVE

j'	attende
tu	attendes
il/elle/on	attende
nous	attendions
vous	attendiez
ils/elles	attendent

PERFECT

j'	ai attendu
tu	as attendu
il/elle/on	a attendu
nous	avons attendu
vous	avez attendu
ils/elles	ont attendu

IMPERFECT

j'	attendais
tu	attendais
il/elle/on	attendait
nous	attendions
vous	attendiez
ils/elles	attendaient

FUTURE

j'	attendrai
tu	attendras
il/elle/on	attendra
nous	attendrons
vous	attendrez
ils/elles	attendront

CONDITIONAL

j'	attendrais
tu	attendrais
il/elle/on	attendrait
nous	attendrions
vous	attendriez
ils/elles	attendraient

IMPERATIVE

attends / attendons / attendez

PAST PARTICIPLE

attendu

PRESENT PARTICIPLE

attendant

EXAMPLE PHRASES

***Attends**-moi!* Wait for me!
*Tu **attends** depuis longtemps?* Have you been waiting long?
*Je l'**ai attendu** à la poste.* I waited for him at the post office.
*Je m'**attends** à ce qu'il soit en retard.* I expect he'll be late.

---

je/j' = I **tu** = you **il** = he/it **elle** = she/it **on** = we/one **nous** = we **vous** = you **ils/elles** = they

▶ **avoir** (to have)

PRESENT

j'	ai
tu	as
il/elle/on	a
nous	avons
vous	avez
ils/elles	ont

PRESENT SUBJUNCTIVE

j'	aie
tu	aies
il/elle/on	ait
nous	ayons
vous	ayez
ils/elles	aient

PERFECT

j'	ai eu
tu	as eu
il/elle/on	a eu
nous	avons eu
vous	avez eu
ils/elles	ont eu

IMPERFECT

j'	avais
tu	avais
il/elle/on	avait
nous	avions
vous	aviez
ils/elles	avaient

FUTURE

j'	aurai
tu	auras
il/elle/on	aura
nous	aurons
vous	aurez
ils/elles	auront

CONDITIONAL

j'	aurais
tu	aurais
il/elle/on	aurait
nous	aurions
vous	auriez
ils/elles	auraient

IMPERATIVE

aie / ayons / ayez

PAST PARTICIPLE

eu

PRESENT PARTICIPLE

ayant

EXAMPLE PHRASES

*Il **a** les yeux bleus.* He's got blue eyes.
*Quel âge **as**-tu?* How old are you?
*Il **a eu** un accident.* He's had an accident.
*J'**avais** faim.* I was hungry.
*Il y **a** beaucoup de monde.* There are lots of people.

---

je/j' = I **tu** = you **il** = he/it **elle** = she/it **on** = we/one **nous** = we **vous** = you **ils/elles** = they

▶ boire (to drink)

PRESENT

je	bois
tu	bois
il/elle/on	boit
nous	buvons
vous	buvez
ils/elles	boivent

PRESENT SUBJUNCTIVE

je	boive
tu	boives
il/elle/on	boive
nous	buvions
vous	buviez
ils/elles	boivent

PERFECT

j'	ai bu
tu	as bu
il/elle/on	a bu
nous	avons bu
vous	avez bu
ils/elles	ont bu

IMPERFECT

je	buvais
tu	buvais
il/elle/on	buvait
nous	buvions
vous	buviez
ils/elles	buvaient

FUTURE

je	boirai
tu	boiras
il/elle/on	boira
nous	boirons
vous	boirez
ils/elles	boiront

CONDITIONAL

je	boirais
tu	boirais
il/elle/on	boirait
nous	boirions
vous	boiriez
ils/elles	boiraient

IMPERATIVE

bois / buvons / buvez

PAST PARTICIPLE

bu

PRESENT PARTICIPLE

buvant

EXAMPLE PHRASES

*Qu'est-ce que tu veux **boire**?* What would you like to drink?
*Il ne **boit** jamais d'alcool.* He never drinks alcohol.
*J'**ai bu** un litre d'eau.* I drank a litre of water.

---

je/j' = I **tu** = you **il** = he/it **elle** = she/it **on** = we/one **nous** = we **vous** = you **ils/elles** = they

▶ connaître (to know)

PRESENT

je	connais
tu	connais
il/elle/on	connaît
nous	connaissons
vous	connaissez
ils/elles	connaissent

PRESENT SUBJUNCTIVE

je	connaisse
tu	connaisses
il/elle/on	connaisse
nous	connaissions
vous	connaissiez
ils/elles	connaissent

PERFECT

j'	ai connu
tu	as connu
il/elle/on	a connu
nous	avons connu
vous	avez connu
ils/elles	ont connu

IMPERFECT

je	connaissais
tu	connaissais
il/elle/on	connaissait
nous	connaissions
vous	connaissiez
ils/elles	connaissaient

FUTURE

je	connaîtrai
tu	connaîtras
il/elle/on	connaîtra
nous	connaîtrons
vous	connaîtrez
ils/elles	connaîtront

CONDITIONAL

je	connaîtrais
tu	connaîtrais
il/elle/on	connaîtrait
nous	connaîtrions
vous	connaîtriez
ils/elles	connaîtraient

IMPERATIVE

connais / connaissons / connaissez

PAST PARTICIPLE

connu

PRESENT PARTICIPLE

connaissant

EXAMPLE PHRASES

*Je ne **connais** pas du tout cette région.* I don't know the area at all.
*Vous **connaissez** M Amiot?* Do you know Mr Amiot?
*Il n'**a** pas **connu** son grand-père.* He never knew his granddad.
*Ils **se sont connus** à Rouen.* They first met in Rouen.

▶ **courir** (to run)

PRESENT

je	cours
tu	cours
il/elle/on	court
nous	courons
vous	courez
ils/elles	courent

PRESENT SUBJUNCTIVE

je	coure
tu	coures
il/elle/on	coure
nous	courions
vous	couriez
ils/elles	courent

PERFECT

j'	ai couru
tu	as couru
il/elle/on	a couru
nous	avons couru
vous	avez couru
ils/elles	ont couru

IMPERFECT

je	courais
tu	courais
il/elle/on	courait
nous	courions
vous	couriez
ils/elles	couraient

FUTURE

je	courrai
tu	courras
il/elle/on	courra
nous	courrons
vous	courrez
ils/elles	courront

CONDITIONAL

je	courrais
tu	courrais
il/elle/on	courrait
nous	courrions
vous	courriez
ils/elles	courraient

IMPERATIVE

cours / courons / courez

PAST PARTICIPLE

couru

PRESENT PARTICIPLE

courant

EXAMPLE PHRASES

*Je ne **cours** pas très vite.* I can't run very fast.
*Elle est sortie en **courant**.* She ran out.
*Ne **courez** pas dans le couloir.* Don't run in the corridor.
*J'**ai couru** jusqu'à l'école.* I ran all the way to school.

---

je/j' = I **tu** = you **il** = he/it **elle** = she/it **on** = we/one **nous** = we **vous** = you **ils/elles** = they

▶ **croire** (to believe)

PRESENT

je	crois
tu	crois
il/elle/on	croit
nous	croyons
vous	croyez
ils/elles	croient

PRESENT SUBJUNCTIVE

je	croie
tu	croies
il/elle/on	croie
nous	croyions
vous	croyiez
ils/elles	croient

PERFECT

j'	ai cru
tu	as cru
il/elle/on	a cru
nous	avons cru
vous	avez cru
ils/elles	ont cru

IMPERFECT

je	croyais
tu	croyais
il/elle/on	croyait
nous	croyions
vous	croyiez
ils/elles	croyaient

FUTURE

je	croirai
tu	croiras
il/elle/on	croira
nous	croirons
vous	croirez
ils/elles	croiront

CONDITIONAL

je	croirais
tu	croirais
il/elle/on	croirait
nous	croirions
vous	croiriez
ils/elles	croiraient

IMPERATIVE

crois / croyons / croyez

PAST PARTICIPLE

cru

PRESENT PARTICIPLE

croyant

EXAMPLE PHRASES

*Je ne te **crois** pas.* I don't believe you.
*J'**ai cru** que tu n'allais pas venir.* I thought you weren't going to come.
*Elle **croyait** encore au père Noël.* She still believed in Santa.

---

je/j' = I **tu** = you **il** = he/it **elle** = she/it **on** = we/one **nous** = we **vous** = you **ils/elles** = they

▶ **devoir** (to have to; to owe)

PRESENT

je	dois
tu	dois
il/elle/on	doit
nous	devons
vous	devez
ils/elles	doivent

PRESENT SUBJUNCTIVE

je	doive
tu	doives
il/elle/on	doive
nous	devions
vous	deviez
ils/elles	doivent

PERFECT

j'	ai dû
tu	as dû
il/elle/on	a dû
nous	avons dû
vous	avez dû
ils/elles	ont dû

IMPERFECT

je	devais
tu	devais
il/elle/on	devait
nous	devions
vous	deviez
ils/elles	devaient

FUTURE

je	devrai
tu	devras
il/elle/on	devra
nous	devrons
vous	devrez
ils/elles	devront

CONDITIONAL

je	devrais
tu	devrais
il/elle/on	devrait
nous	devrions
vous	devriez
ils/elles	devraient

IMPERATIVE

dois / devons / devez

PAST PARTICIPLE

dû (*NB*: due, dus, dues)

PRESENT PARTICIPLE

devant

EXAMPLE PHRASES

*Je **dois** aller faire les courses ce matin.* I have to do the shopping this morning.
*À quelle heure est-ce que tu **dois** partir?* What time do you have to leave?
*Il **a dû** faire ses devoirs hier soir.* He had to do his homework last night.
*Il **devait** prendre le train pour aller travailler.* He had to go to work by train.

---

je/j' = I **tu** = you **il** = he/it **elle** = she/it **on** = we/one **nous** = we **vous** = you **ils/elles** = they

▶ dire (to say)

PRESENT

je	dis
tu	dis
il/elle/on	dit
nous	disons
vous	dites
ils/elles	disent

PRESENT SUBJUNCTIVE

je	dise
tu	dises
il/elle/on	dise
nous	disions
vous	disiez
ils/elles	disent

PERFECT

j'	ai dit
tu	as dit
il/elle/on	a dit
nous	avons dit
vous	avez dit
ils/elles	ont dit

IMPERFECT

je	disais
tu	disais
il/elle/on	disait
nous	disions
vous	disiez
ils/elles	disaient

FUTURE

je	dirai
tu	diras
il/elle/on	dira
nous	dirons
vous	direz
ils/elles	diront

CONDITIONAL

je	dirais
tu	dirais
il/elle/on	dirait
nous	dirions
vous	diriez
ils/elles	diraient

IMPERATIVE

dis / disons / dites

PAST PARTICIPLE

dit

PRESENT PARTICIPLE

disant

EXAMPLE PHRASES

*Qu'est-ce qu'elle **dit**?* What is she saying?
*"Bonjour!", a-t-il **dit**.* "Hello!" he said.
*Ils m'**ont dit** que le film était nul.* They told me that the film was rubbish.
*Comment ça **se dit** en anglais?* How do you say that in English?

je/j' = I **tu** = you **il** = he/it **elle** = she/it **on** = we/one **nous** = we **vous** = you **ils/elles** = they

▶ **donner** (to give)

PRESENT

je	donne
tu	donnes
il/elle/on	donne
nous	donnons
vous	donnez
ils/elles	donnent

PRESENT SUBJUNCTIVE

je	donne
tu	donnes
il/elle/on	donne
nous	donnions
vous	donniez
ils/elles	donnent

PERFECT

j'	ai donné
tu	as donné
il/elle/on	a donné
nous	avons donné
vous	avez donné
ils/elles	ont donné

IMPERFECT

je	donnais
tu	donnais
il/elle/on	donnait
nous	donnions
vous	donniez
ils/elles	donnaient

FUTURE

je	donnerai
tu	donneras
il/elle/on	donnera
nous	donnerons
vous	donnerez
ils/elles	donneront

CONDITIONAL

je	donnerais
tu	donnerais
il/elle/on	donnerait
nous	donnerions
vous	donneriez
ils/elles	donneraient

IMPERATIVE

donne / donnons / donnez

PAST PARTICIPLE

donné

PRESENT PARTICIPLE

donnant

EXAMPLE PHRASES

***Donne**-moi la main.* Give me your hand.
*Est-ce que je t'**ai donné** mon adresse?* Did I give you my address?
*L'appartement **donne** sur la place.* The flat overlooks the square.

---

je/j' = I **tu** = you **il** = he/it **elle** = she/it **on** = we/one **nous** = we **vous** = you **ils/elles** = they

▶ écrire (to write)

PRESENT

j'	écris
tu	écris
il/elle/on	écrit
nous	écrivons
vous	écrivez
ils/elles	écrivent

PRESENT SUBJUNCTIVE

j'	écrive
tu	écrives
il/elle/on	écrive
nous	écrivions
vous	écriviez
ils/elles	écrivent

PERFECT

j'	ai écrit
tu	as écrit
il/elle/on	a écrit
nous	avons écrit
vous	avez écrit
ils/elles	ont écrit

IMPERFECT

j'	écrivais
tu	écrivais
il/elle/on	écrivait
nous	écrivions
vous	écriviez
ils/elles	écrivaient

FUTURE

j'	écrirai
tu	écriras
il/elle/on	écrira
nous	écrirons
vous	écrirez
ils/elles	écriront

CONDITIONAL

j'	écrirais
tu	écrirais
il/elle/on	écrirait
nous	écririons
vous	écririez
ils/elles	écriraient

IMPERATIVE

écris / écrivons / écrivez

PAST PARTICIPLE

écrit

PRESENT PARTICIPLE

écrivant

EXAMPLE PHRASES

*Tu **as écrit** à ta correspondante récemment?* Have you written to your penfriend lately?
*Elle **écrit** des romans.* She writes novels.
*Comment ça s'**écrit**, "brouillard"?* How do you spell "brouillard"?

---

je/j' = I **tu** = you **il** = he/it **elle** = she/it **on** = we/one **nous** = we **vous** = you **ils/elles** = they

▶ être (to be)

PRESENT

je	suis
tu	es
il/elle/on	est
nous	sommes
vous	êtes
ils/elles	sont

PRESENT SUBJUNCTIVE

je	sois
tu	sois
il/elle/on	soit
nous	soyons
vous	soyez
ils/elles	soient

PERFECT

j'	ai été
tu	as été
il/elle/on	a été
nous	avons été
vous	avez été
ils/elles	ont été

IMPERFECT

j'	étais
tu	étais
il/elle/on	était
nous	étions
vous	étiez
ils/elles	étaient

FUTURE

je	serai
tu	seras
il/elle/on	sera
nous	serons
vous	serez
ils/elles	seront

CONDITIONAL

je	serais
tu	serais
il/elle/on	serait
nous	serions
vous	seriez
ils/elles	seraient

IMPERATIVE

sois / soyons / soyez

PAST PARTICIPLE

été

PRESENT PARTICIPLE

étant

EXAMPLE PHRASES

*Mon père **est** professeur.* My father's a teacher.
*Quelle heure est-il? – Il **est** dix heures.* What time is it? – It's 10 o'clock.
*Ils ne **sont** pas encore arrivés.* They haven't arrived yet.

---

je/j' = I **tu** = you **il** = he/it **elle** = she/it **on** = we/one **nous** = we **vous** = you **ils/elles** = they

▶ faire (to do; to make)

PRESENT

je	fais
tu	fais
il/elle/on	fait
nous	faisons
vous	faites
ils/elles	font

PRESENT SUBJUNCTIVE

je	fasse
tu	fasses
il/elle/on	fasse
nous	fassions
vous	fassiez
ils/elles	fassent

PERFECT

j'	ai fait
tu	as fait
il/elle/on	a fait
nous	avons fait
vous	avez fait
ils/elles	ont fait

IMPERFECT

je	faisais
tu	faisais
il/elle/on	faisait
nous	faisions
vous	faisiez
ils/elles	faisaient

FUTURE

je	ferai
tu	feras
il/elle/on	fera
nous	ferons
vous	ferez
ils/elles	feront

CONDITIONAL

je	ferais
tu	ferais
il/elle/on	ferait
nous	ferions
vous	feriez
ils/elles	feraient

IMPERATIVE

fais / faisons / faites

PAST PARTICIPLE

fait

PRESENT PARTICIPLE

faisant

EXAMPLE PHRASES

*Qu'est-ce que tu **fais**?* What are you doing?
*Qu'est-ce qu'il **a fait**?* What has he done? *or* What did he do?
*J'**ai fait** un gâteau.* I've made a cake *or* I made a cake.
*Il s'**est fait** couper les cheveux.* He's had his hair cut.

---

je/j' = I **tu** = you **il** = he/it **elle** = she/it **on** = we/one **nous** = we **vous** = you **ils/elles** = they

▶ falloir (to be necessary)

PRESENT

il faut

PRESENT SUBJUNCTIVE

il faille

PERFECT

il a fallu

IMPERFECT

il fallait

FUTURE

il faudra

CONDITIONAL

il faudrait

IMPERATIVE

not used

PAST PARTICIPLE

fallu

PRESENT PARTICIPLE

not used

EXAMPLE PHRASES

*Il **faut** se dépêcher!* We have to hurry up!
*Il me **fallait** de l'argent.* I needed money.
*Il **faudra** que tu sois là à 8 heures.* You'll have to be there at 8.

---

je/j' = I **tu** = you **il** = he/it **elle** = she/it **on** = we/one **nous** = we **vous** = you **ils/elles** = they

▶ finir (to finish)

PRESENT

je	finis
tu	finis
il/elle/on	finit
nous	finissons
vous	finissez
ils/elles	finissent

PRESENT SUBJUNCTIVE

je	finisse
tu	finisses
il/elle/on	finisse
nous	finissions
vous	finissiez
ils/elles	finissent

PERFECT

j'	ai fini
tu	as fini
il/elle/on	a fini
nous	avons fini
vous	avez fini
ils/elles	ont fini

IMPERFECT

je	finissais
tu	finissais
il/elle/on	finissait
nous	finissions
vous	finissiez
ils/elles	finissaient

FUTURE

je	finirai
tu	finiras
il/elle/on	finira
nous	finirons
vous	finirez
ils/elles	finiront

CONDITIONAL

je	finirais
tu	finirais
il/elle/on	finirait
nous	finirions
vous	finiriez
ils/elles	finiraient

IMPERATIVE

finis / finissons / finissez

PAST PARTICIPLE

fini

PRESENT PARTICIPLE

finissant

EXAMPLE PHRASES

***Finis** ta soupe!* Finish your soup!
*J'ai **fini**!* I've finished!
*Je **finirai** mes devoirs demain.* I'll finish my homework tomorrow.

---

je/j' = I **tu** = you **il** = he/it **elle** = she/it **on** = we/one **nous** = we **vous** = you **ils/elles** = they

▶ se laver (to wash oneself)

PRESENT

je	me lave
tu	te laves
il/elle/on	se lave
nous	nous lavons
vous	vous lavez
ils/elles	se lavent

PRESENT SUBJUNCTIVE

je	me lave
tu	te laves
il/elle/on	se lave
nous	nous lavions
vous	vous laviez
ils/elles	se lavent

PERFECT

je	me suis lavé(e)
tu	t'es lavé(e)
il/elle/on	s'est lavé(e)
nous	nous sommes lavé(e)s
vous	vous êtes lavé(e)(s)
ils/elles	se sont lavé(e)s

IMPERFECT

je	me lavais
tu	te lavais
il/elle/on	se lavait
nous	nous lavions
vous	vous laviez
ils/elles	se lavient

FUTURE

je	me laverai
tu	te laveras
il/elle/on	se lavera
nous	nous laverons
vous	vous laverez
ils/elles	se laveront

CONDITIONAL

je	me laverais
tu	te laverais
il/elle/on	se laverait
nous	nous laverions
vous	vous laveriez
ils/elles	se laveraient

IMPERATIVE

lave-toi / lavons-nous / lavez-vous

PAST PARTICIPLE

lavé(e)

PRESENT PARTICIPLE

se lavant

EXAMPLE PHRASES

Lave-toi vite, tu vas être en retard. Have a quick wash, you're going to be late.

Lavez-vous les mains avant de vous mettre à table. Wash your hands before you sit at the table.

Nous nous sommes **lavé** les dents puis nous sommes allés nous coucher. We cleaned our teeth and went to bed.

---

je/j' = I **tu** = you **il** = he/it **elle** = she/it **on** = we/one **nous** = we **vous** = you **ils/elles** = they

▶ **lire** (to read)

PRESENT

je	lis
tu	lis
il/elle/on	lit
nous	lisons
vous	lisez
ils/elles	lisent

PRESENT SUBJUNCTIVE

je	lise
tu	lises
il/elle/on	lise
nous	lisions
vous	lisiez
ils/elles	lisent

PERFECT

j'	ai lu
tu	as lu
il/elle/on	a lu
nous	avons lu
vous	avez lu
ils/elles	ont lu

IMPERFECT

je	lisais
tu	lisais
il/elle/on	lisait
nous	lisions
vous	lisiez
ils/elles	lisaient

FUTURE

je	lirai
tu	liras
il/elle/on	lira
nous	lirons
vous	lirez
ils/elles	liront

CONDITIONAL

je	lirais
tu	lirais
il/elle/on	lirait
nous	lirions
vous	liriez
ils/elles	liraient

IMPERATIVE

lis / lisons / lisez

PAST PARTICIPLE

lu

PRESENT PARTICIPLE

lisant

EXAMPLE PHRASES

*Vous **avez lu** "Madame Bovary"?* Have you read "Madame Bovary"?
*Je le **lirai** dans l'avion.* I'll read it on the plane.
*Elle lui **lisait** une histoire.* She was reading him a story.

---

je/j' = I **tu** = you **il** = he/it **elle** = she/it **on** = we/one **nous** = we **vous** = you **ils/elles** = they

▶ **mettre** (to put)

PRESENT

je	mets
tu	mets
il/elle/on	met
nous	mettons
vous	mettez
ils/elles	mettent

PRESENT SUBJUNCTIVE

je	mette
tu	mettes
il/elle/on	mette
nous	mettions
vous	mettiez
ils/elles	mettent

PERFECT

j'	ai mis
tu	as mis
il/elle/on	a mis
nous	avons mis
vous	avez mis
ils/elles	ont mis

IMPERFECT

je	mettais
tu	mettais
il/elle/on	mettait
nous	mettions
vous	mettiez
ils/elles	mettaient

FUTURE

je	mettrai
tu	mettras
il/elle/on	mettra
nous	mettrons
vous	mettrez
ils/elles	mettront

CONDITIONAL

je	mettrais
tu	mettrais
il/elle/on	mettrait
nous	mettrions
vous	mettriez
ils/elles	mettraient

IMPERATIVE

mets / mettons / mettez

PAST PARTICIPLE

mis

PRESENT PARTICIPLE

mettant

EXAMPLE PHRASES

***Mets** ton manteau!* Put your coat on!
*Où est-ce que tu **as mis** les clés?* Where have you put the keys?
*J'**ai mis** le livre sur la table.* I put the book on the table.
*Elle s'est **mise** à pleurer.* She started crying.

---

je/j' = I **tu** = you **il** = he/it **elle** = she/it **on** = we/one **nous** = we **vous** = you **ils/elles** = they

▶ mourir (to die)

PRESENT

je	meurs
tu	meurs
il/elle/on	meurt
nous	mourons
vous	mourez
ils/elles	meurent

PERFECT

je	suis mort(e)
tu	es mort(e)
il/elle/on	est mort(e)
nous	sommes mort(e)s
vous	êtes mort(e)(s)
ils/elles	sont mort(e)s

FUTURE

je	mourrai
tu	mourras
il/elle/on	mourra
nous	mourrons
vous	mourrez
ils/elles	mourront

IMPERATIVE

meurs / mourons / mourez

PRESENT PARTICIPLE

mourant

PRESENT SUBJUNCTIVE

je	meure
tu	meures
il/elle/on	meure
nous	mourions
vous	mouriez
ils/elles	meurent

IMPERFECT

je	mourais
tu	mourais
il/elle/on	mourait
nous	mourions
vous	mouriez
ils/elles	mouraient

CONDITIONAL

je	mourrais
tu	mourrais
il/elle/on	mourrait
nous	mourrions
vous	mourriez
ils/elles	mourraient

PAST PARTICIPLE

mort

EXAMPLE PHRASES

*Elle **est morte** en 1998.* She died in 1998.
*Ils **sont morts**.* They're dead.
*On **meurt** de froid ici!* We're freezing to death in here!

---

je/j' = I **tu** = you **il** = he/it **elle** = she/it **on** = we/one **nous** = we **vous** = you **ils/elles** = they

▶ naître (to be born)

PRESENT

je	nais
tu	nais
il/elle/on	naît
nous	naissons
vous	naissez
ils/elles	naissent

PERFECT

je	suis né(e)
tu	es né(e)
il/elle/on	est né(e)
nous	sommes né(e)s
vous	êtes né(e)(s)
ils/elles	sont né(e)s

FUTURE

je	naîtrai
tu	naîtras
il/elle/on	naîtra
nous	naîtrons
vous	naîtrez
ils/elles	naîtront

IMPERATIVE

nais / naissons / naissez

PRESENT PARTICIPLE

naissant

PRESENT SUBJUNCTIVE

je	naisse
tu	naisses
il/elle/on	naisse
nous	naissions
vous	naissiez
ils/elles	naissent

IMPERFECT

je	naissais
tu	naissais
il/elle/on	naissait
nous	naissions
vous	naissiez
ils/elles	naissaient

CONDITIONAL

je	naîtrais
tu	naîtrais
il/elle/on	naîtrait
nous	naîtrions
vous	naîtriez
ils/elles	naîtraient

PAST PARTICIPLE

né

EXAMPLE PHRASES

*Je **suis née** le 12 février.* I was born on 12 February.
*Le bébé de Delphine **naîtra** en mars.* Delphine is going to have a baby in March.
*Quand est-ce que tu **es né**?* When were you born?

---

je/j' = I **tu** = you **il** = he/it **elle** = she/it **on** = we/one **nous** = we **vous** = you **ils/elles** = they

▶ ouvrir (to open)

PRESENT

j'	ouvre
tu	ouvres
il/elle/on	ouvre
nous	ouvrons
vous	ouvrez
ils/elles	ouvrent

PRESENT SUBJUNCTIVE

j'	ouvre
tu	ouvres
il/elle/on	ouvre
nous	ouvrions
vous	ouvriez
ils/elles	ouvrent

PERFECT

j'	ai ouvert
tu	as ouvert
il/elle/on	a ouvert
nous	avons ouvert
vous	avez ouvert
ils/elles	ont ouvert

IMPERFECT

j'	ouvrais
tu	ouvrais
il/elle/on	ouvrait
nous	ouvrions
vous	ouvriez
ils/elles	ouvraient

FUTURE

j'	ouvrirai
tu	ouvriras
il/elle/on	ouvrira
nous	ouvrirons
vous	ouvrirez
ils/elles	ouvriront

CONDITIONAL

j'	ouvrirais
tu	ouvrirais
il/elle/on	ouvrirait
nous	ouvririons
vous	ouvririez
ils/elles	ouvriraient

IMPERATIVE

ouvre / ouvrons / ouvrez

PAST PARTICIPLE

ouvert

PRESENT PARTICIPLE

ouvrant

EXAMPLE PHRASES

*Elle **a ouvert** la porte.* She opened the door.
*Est-ce que tu pourrais **ouvrir** la fenêtre?* Could you open the window?
*Je me suis coupé en **ouvrant** une boîte de conserve.* I cut myself opening a tin.
*La porte s'est **ouverte**.* The door opened.

▶ pouvoir (to be able)

PRESENT

je	peux
tu	peux
il/elle/on	peut
nous	pouvons
vous	pouvez
ils/elles	peuvent

PRESENT SUBJUNCTIVE

je	puisse
tu	puisses
il/elle/on	puisse
nous	puissions
vous	puissiez
ils/elles	puissent

PERFECT

j'	ai pu
tu	as pu
il/elle/on	a pu
nous	avons pu
vous	avez pu
ils/elles	ont pu

IMPERFECT

je	pouvais
tu	pouvais
il/elle/on	pouvait
nous	pouvions
vous	pouviez
ils/elles	pouvaient

FUTURE

je	pourrai
tu	pourras
il/elle/on	pourra
nous	pourrons
vous	pourrez
ils/elles	pourront

CONDITIONAL

je	pourrais
tu	pourrais
il/elle/on	pourrait
nous	pourrions
vous	pourriez
ils/elles	pourraient

IMPERATIVE

not used

PAST PARTICIPLE

pu

PRESENT PARTICIPLE

pouvant

EXAMPLE PHRASES

*Je **peux** t'aider, si tu veux.* I can help you if you like.
*J'ai fait tout ce que j'**ai pu**.* I did all I could.
*Je ne **pourrai** pas venir samedi.* I won't be able to come on Saturday.

▶ **prendre** (to take)

PRESENT

je	prends
tu	prends
il/elle/on	prend
nous	prenons
vous	prenez
ils/elles	prennent

PRESENT SUBJUNCTIVE

je	prenne
tu	prennes
il/elle/on	prenne
nous	prenions
vous	preniez
ils/elles	prennent

PERFECT

j'	ai pris
tu	as pris
il/elle/on	a pris
nous	avons pris
vous	avez pris
ils/elles	ont pris

IMPERFECT

je	prenais
tu	prenais
il/elle/on	prenait
nous	prenions
vous	preniez
ils/elles	prenaient

FUTURE

je	prendrai
tu	prendras
il/elle/on	prendra
nous	prendrons
vous	prendrez
ils/elles	prendront

CONDITIONAL

je	prendrais
tu	prendrais
il/elle/on	prendrait
nous	prendrions
vous	prendriez
ils/elles	prendraient

IMPERATIVE

prends / prenons / prenez

PAST PARTICIPLE

pris

PRESENT PARTICIPLE

prenant

EXAMPLE PHRASES

J'**ai pris** plein de photos. I took lots of pictures.
N'oublie pas de **prendre** ton passeport. Don't forget to take your passport.
Il **prendra** le train de 8h20. He'll take the 8.20 train.
Pour qui est-ce qu'il **se prend**? Who does he think he is?

---

je/j' = I **tu** = you **il** = he/it **elle** = she/it **on** = we/one **nous** = we **vous** = you **ils/elles** = they

▶ rire (to laugh)

PRESENT

je	ris
tu	ris
il/elle/on	rit
nous	rions
vous	riez
ils/elles	rient

PRESENT SUBJUNCTIVE

je	rie
tu	ries
il/elle/on	rie
nous	riions
vous	riiez
ils/elles	rient

PERFECT

j'	ai ri
tu	as ri
il/elle/on	a ri
nous	avons ri
vous	avez ri
ils/elles	ont ri

IMPERFECT

je	riais
tu	riais
il/elle/on	riait
nous	riions
vous	riiez
ils/elles	riaient

FUTURE

je	rirai
tu	riras
il/elle/on	rira
nous	rirons
vous	rirez
ils/elles	riront

CONDITIONAL

je	rirais
tu	rirais
il/elle/on	rirait
nous	ririons
vous	ririez
ils/elles	riraient

IMPERATIVE

ris / rions / riez

PAST PARTICIPLE

ri

PRESENT PARTICIPLE

riant

EXAMPLE PHRASES

On *a* bien **ri**. We had a good laugh.
Ne **ris** pas, ce n'est pas drôle! Don't laugh, it's not funny!
C'était juste pour **rire**. It was only for a laugh.

▶ savoir (to know)

PRESENT

je	sais
tu	sais
il/elle/on	sait
nous	savons
vous	savez
ils/elles	savent

PRESENT SUBJUNCTIVE

je	sache
tu	saches
il/elle/on	sache
nous	sachions
vous	sachiez
ils/elles	sachent

PERFECT

j'	ai su
tu	as su
il/elle/on	a su
nous	avons su
vous	avez su
ils/elles	ont su

IMPERFECT

je	savais
tu	savais
il/elle/on	savait
nous	savions
vous	saviez
ils/elles	savaient

FUTURE

je	saurai
tu	sauras
il/elle/on	saura
nous	saurons
vous	saurez
ils/elles	sauront

CONDITIONAL

je	saurais
tu	saurais
il/elle/on	saurait
nous	saurions
vous	sauriez
ils/elles	sauraient

IMPERATIVE

sache / sachons / sachez

PAST PARTICIPLE

su

PRESENT PARTICIPLE

sachant

EXAMPLE PHRASES

*Tu **sais** ce que tu vas faire l'année prochaine?* Do you know what you're doing next year?
*Je ne **sais** pas.* I don't know.
*Elle ne **sait** pas nager.* She can't swim.
*Tu **savais** que son père était pakistanais?* Did you know her father was Pakistani?

---

je/j' = I **tu** = you **il** = he/it **elle** = she/it **on** = we/one **nous** = we **vous** = you **ils/elles** = they

▶ **sortir** (to go out)

PRESENT

je	sors
tu	sors
il/elle/on	sort
nous	sortons
vous	sortez
ils/elles	sortent

PRESENT SUBJUNCTIVE

je	sorte
tu	sortes
il/elle/on	sorte
nous	sortions
vous	sortiez
ils/elles	sortent

PERFECT

je	suis sorti(e)
tu	es sorti(e)
il/elle/on	est sorti(e)
nous	sommes sorti(e)s
vous	êtes sorti(e)(s)
ils/elles	sont sorti(e)s

IMPERFECT

je	sortais
tu	sortais
il/elle/on	sortait
nous	sortions
vous	sortiez
ils/elles	sortaient

FUTURE

je	sortirai
tu	sortiras
il/elle/on	sortira
nous	sortirons
vous	sortirez
ils/elles	sortiront

CONDITIONAL

je	sortirais
tu	sortirais
il/elle/on	sortirait
nous	sortirions
vous	sortiriez
ils/elles	sortiraient

IMPERATIVE

sors / sortons / sortez

PAST PARTICIPLE

sorti

PRESENT PARTICIPLE

sortant

EXAMPLE PHRASES

*Je ne **suis pas sortie** ce week-end.* I didn't go out this weekend.
*Aurélie **sort** avec Bruno.* Aurélie is going out with Bruno.
*Elle **est sortie** de l'hôpital hier.* She came out of hospital yesterday.
*Je n'**ai pas sorti** le chien parce qu'il pleuvait.* I didn't take the dog out for a walk
because it was raining.

📝 Note that **sortir** takes **avoir** in the perfect tense when it is used with a direct object.

je/j' = I **tu** = you **il** = he/it **elle** = she/it **on** = we/one **nous** = we **vous** = you **ils/elles** = they

▶ **tenir** (to hold)

PRESENT

je	tiens
tu	tiens
il/elle/on	tient
nous	tenons
vous	tenez
ils/elles	tiennent

PRESENT SUBJUNCTIVE

je	tienne
tu	tiennes
il/elle/on	tienne
nous	tenions
vous	teniez
ils/elles	tiennent

PERFECT

j'	ai tenu
tu	as tenu
il/elle/on	a tenu
nous	avons tenu
vous	avez tenu
ils/elles	ont tenu

IMPERFECT

je	tenais
tu	tenais
il/elle/on	tenait
nous	tenions
vous	teniez
ils/elles	tenaient

FUTURE

je	tiendrai
tu	tiendras
il/elle/on	tiendra
nous	tiendrons
vous	tiendrez
ils/elles	tiendront

CONDITIONAL

je	tiendrais
tu	tiendrais
il/elle/on	tiendrait
nous	tiendrions
vous	tiendriez
ils/elles	tiendraient

IMPERATIVE

tiens / tenons / tenez

PAST PARTICIPLE

tenu

PRESENT PARTICIPLE

tenant

EXAMPLE PHRASES

Tiens-moi la main. Hold my hand.
*Elle **tenait** beaucoup à son chat.* She was really attached to her cat.
Tiens, prends mon stylo. Here, have my pen.
Tiens-toi droit! Sit up straight!

---

je/j' = I **tu** = you **il** = he/it **elle** = she/it **on** = we/one **nous** = we **vous** = you **ils/elles** = they

▶ **venir** (to come)

PRESENT

je	viens
tu	viens
il/elle/on	vient
nous	venons
vous	venez
ils/elles	viennent

PRESENT SUBJUNCTIVE

je	vienne
tu	viennes
il/elle/on	vienne
nous	venions
vous	veniez
ils/elles	viennent

PERFECT

je	suis venu(e)
tu	es venu(e)
il/elle/on	est venu(e)
nous	sommes venu(e)s
vous	êtes venu(e)(s)
ils/elles	sont venu(e)s

IMPERFECT

je	venais
tu	venais
il/elle/on	venait
nous	venions
vous	veniez
ils/elles	venaient

FUTURE

je	viendrai
tu	viendras
il/elle/on	viendra
nous	viendrons
vous	viendrez
ils/elles	viendront

CONDITIONAL

je	viendrais
tu	viendrais
il/elle/on	viendrait
nous	viendrions
vous	viendriez
ils/elles	viendraient

IMPERATIVE

viens / venons / venez

PAST PARTICIPLE

venu

PRESENT PARTICIPLE

venant

EXAMPLE PHRASES

*Elle ne **viendra** pas cette année.* She won't be coming this year.
*Fatou et Malik **viennent** du Sénégal.* Fatou and Malik come from Senegal.
*Je **viens** de manger.* I've just eaten.

---

je/j' = I **tu** = you **il** = he/it **elle** = she/it **on** = we/one **nous** = we **vous** = you **ils/elles** = they

▶ **vivre** (to live)

PRESENT

je	vis
tu	vis
il/elle/on	vit
nous	vivons
vous	vivez
ils/elles	vivent

PRESENT SUBJUNCTIVE

je	vive
tu	vives
il/elle/on	vive
nous	vivions
vous	viviez
ils/elles	vivent

PERFECT

j'	ai vécu
tu	as vécu
il/elle/on	a vécu
nous	avons vécu
vous	avez vécu
ils/elles	ont vécu

IMPERFECT

je	vivais
tu	vivais
il/elle/on	vivait
nous	vivions
vous	viviez
ils/elles	vivaient

FUTURE

je	vivrai
tu	vivras
il/elle/on	vivra
nous	vivrons
vous	vivrez
ils/elles	vivront

CONDITIONAL

je	vivrais
tu	vivrais
il/elle/on	vivrait
nous	vivrions
vous	vivriez
ils/elles	vivraient

IMPERATIVE

vis / vivons / vivez

PAST PARTICIPLE

vécu

PRESENT PARTICIPLE

vivant

EXAMPLE PHRASES

*Ma sœur **vit** en Espagne.* My sister lives in Spain.
*Il **a vécu** dix ans à Lyon.* He lived in Lyons for 10 years.
*Les gorilles **vivent** surtout dans la forêt.* Gorillas mostly live in the forest.

---

je/j' = I **tu** = you **il** = he/it **elle** = she/it **on** = we/one **nous** = we **vous** = you **ils/elles** = they

▶ **voir** (to see)

PRESENT

je	vois
tu	vois
il/elle/on	voit
nous	voyons
vous	voyez
ils/elles	voient

PRESENT SUBJUNCTIVE

je	voie
tu	voies
il/elle/on	voie
nous	voyions
vous	voyiez
ils/elles	voient

PERFECT

j'	ai vu
tu	as vu
il/elle/on	a vu
nous	avons vu
vous	avez vu
ils/elles	ont vu

IMPERFECT

je	voyais
tu	voyais
il/elle/on	voyait
nous	voyions
vous	voyiez
ils/elles	voyaient

FUTURE

je	verrai
tu	verras
il/elle/on	verra
nous	verrons
vous	verrez
ils/elles	verront

CONDITIONAL

je	verrais
tu	verrais
il/elle/on	verrait
nous	verrions
vous	verriez
ils/elles	verraient

IMPERATIVE

vois / voyons / voyez

PAST PARTICIPLE

vu

PRESENT PARTICIPLE

voyant

EXAMPLE PHRASES

*Venez me **voir** quand vous serez à Paris.* Come and see me when you're in Paris.
*Je ne **vois** rien sans mes lunettes.* I can't see anything without my glasses.
*Est-ce que tu l'**as vu**?* Did you see him? or Have you seen him?
*Est-ce que cette tache **se voit**?* Does that stain show?

---

je/j' = I **tu** = you **il** = he/it **elle** = she/it **on** = we/one **nous** = we **vous** = you **ils/elles** = they

▶ **vouloir** (to want)

<table>
<tr><td>

PRESENT

je	veux
tu	veux
il/elle/on	veut
nous	voulons
vous	voulez
ils/elles	veulent

</td><td>

PRESENT SUBJUNCTIVE

je	veuille
tu	veuilles
il/elle/on	veuille
nous	voulions
vous	vouliez
ils/elles	veuillent

</td></tr>
<tr><td>

PERFECT

j'	ai voulu
tu	as voulu
il/elle/on	a voulu
nous	avons voulu
vous	avez voulu
ils/elles	ont voulu

</td><td>

IMPERFECT

je	voulais
tu	voulais
il/elle/on	voulait
nous	voulions
vous	vouliez
ils/elles	voulaient

</td></tr>
<tr><td>

FUTURE

je	voudrai
tu	voudras
il/elle/on	voudra
nous	voudrons
vous	voudrez
ils/elles	voudront

</td><td>

CONDITIONAL

je	voudrais
tu	voudrais
il/elle/on	voudrait
nous	voudrions
vous	voudriez
ils/elles	voudraient

</td></tr>
<tr><td>

IMPERATIVE

veuille / veuillons / veuillez

</td><td>

PAST PARTICIPLE

voulu

</td></tr>
</table>

PRESENT PARTICIPLE

voulant

EXAMPLE PHRASES

*Elle **veut** un vélo pour Noël.* She wants a bike for Christmas.
*Ils **voulaient** aller au cinéma.* They wanted to go to the cinema.
*Tu **voudrais** une tasse de thé?* Would you like a cup of tea?

A, a

A [eɪ] *n* (MUS) la *m*

KEYWORD

a [eɪ, ə] *indef art* (*before vowel or silent h: an*)
1 un(e); **a book** un livre; **an apple** une
pomme; **she's a doctor** elle est médecin
2 (*instead of the number "one"*) un(e); **a
year ago** il y a un an; **a hundred/
thousand** *etc* **pounds** cent/mille *etc* livres
3 (*in expressing ratios, prices etc*): **3 a day/
week** 3 par jour/semaine; **10 km an hour**
10 km à l'heure; **30p a kilo** 30p le kilo

A.A. *n abbr* = **Alcoholics Anonymous**;
(*BRIT: Automobile Association*) ≃ TCF *m*
A.A.A. (*US*) *n abbr* (= **American Automobile
Association**) ≃ TCF *m*
aback [ə'bæk] *adv*: **to be taken ~** être
stupéfait(e), être décontenancé(e)
abandon [ə'bændən] *vt* abandonner
abate [ə'beɪt] *vi* s'apaiser, se calmer
abbey ['æbɪ] *n* abbaye *f*
abbot ['æbət] *n* père supérieur
abbreviation [əbriːvɪ'eɪʃən] *n* abréviation *f*
abdicate ['æbdɪkeɪt] *vt, vi* abdiquer
abdomen ['æbdəmen] *n* abdomen *m*
abduct [æb'dʌkt] *vt* enlever
aberration [æbə'reɪʃən] *n* anomalie *f*
abide [ə'baɪd] *vt*: **I can't ~ it/him** je ne
peux pas le souffrir *or* supporter; **~ by** *vt
fus* observer, respecter
ability [ə'bɪlɪtɪ] *n* compétence *f*; capacité *f*;
(*skill*) talent *m*
abject ['æbdʒekt] *adj* (*poverty*) sordide;
(*apology*) plat(e)
ablaze [ə'bleɪz] *adj* en feu, en flammes
able ['eɪbl] *adj* capable, compétent(e); **to
be ~ to do sth** être capable de faire qch,
pouvoir faire qch; **~-bodied** *adj* robuste;
ably *adv* avec compétence *or* talent, habilement
abnormal [æb'nɔːməl] *adj* anormal(e)
aboard [ə'bɔːd] *adv* à bord ♦ *prep* à bord
de
abode [ə'bəud] *n* (LAW): **of no fixed ~** sans
domicile fixe
abolish [ə'bɔlɪʃ] *vt* abolir
aborigine [æbə'rɪdʒɪnɪ] *n* aborigène *m/f*
abort [ə'bɔːt] *vt* faire avorter; **~ion** *n* avortement *m*; **to have an ~ion** se faire avorter; **~ive** [ə'bɔːtɪv] *adj* manqué(e)

KEYWORD

about [ə'baut] *adv* 1 (*approximately*) environ, à peu près; **about a hundred/
thousand** *etc* environ cent/mille *etc*, une
centaine/un millier *etc*; **it takes about 10
hours** ça prend environ *or* à peu près 10
heures; **at about 2 o'clock** vers 2 heures;
I've just about finished j'ai presque fini
2 (*referring to place*) çà et là, de côté et
d'autre; **to run about** courir çà et là; **to
walk about** se promener, aller et venir
3: **to be about to do sth** être sur le point
de faire qch
♦ *prep* 1 (*relating to*) au sujet de, à propos
de; **a book about London** un livre sur
Londres; **what is it about?** de quoi
s'agit-il?; **we talked about it** nous en
avons parlé; **what** *or* **how about doing
this?** et si nous faisions ceci?
2 (*referring to place*) dans; **to walk about
the town** se promener dans la ville

about-face [ə'baut'feɪs] *n* demi-tour *m*
about-turn [ə'baut'tɜːn] *n* (MIL) demi-tour
m; (*fig*) volte-face *f*
above [ə'bʌv] *adv* au-dessus ♦ *prep* au-
dessus de; (*more*) plus de; **mentioned ~**
mentionné ci-dessus; **~ all** par-dessus

tout, surtout; **~board** *adj* franc (franche); honnête

abrasive [ə'breɪzɪv] *adj* abrasif(-ive); (*fig*) caustique, agressif(-ive)

abreast [ə'brest] *adv* de front; **to keep ~ of** se tenir au courant de

abroad [ə'brɔːd] *adv* à l'étranger

abrupt [ə'brʌpt] *adj* (*steep, blunt*) abrupt(e); (*sudden, gruff*) brusque; **~ly** *adv* (*speak, end*) brusquement

abscess ['æbsɪs] *n* abcès *m*

absence ['æbsəns] *n* absence *f*

absent ['æbsənt] *adj* absent(e); **~ee** [æbsən'tiː] *n* absent(e); (*habitual*) absentéiste *m/f*; **~-minded** *adj* distrait(e)

absolute ['æbsəluːt] *adj* absolu(e); **~ly** [æbsə'luːtlɪ] *adv* absolument

absolve [ab'zɔlv] *vt*: **to ~ sb (from)** (*blame, responsibility, sin*) absoudre qn (de)

absorb [ab'zɔːb] *vt* absorber; **to be ~ed in a book** être plongé(e) dans un livre; **~ent cotton** (*US*) *n* coton *m* hydrophile

abstain [ab'steɪn] *vi*: **to ~ (from)** s'abstenir (de)

abstract ['æbstrækt] *adj* abstrait(e)

absurd [ab'səːd] *adj* absurde

abundant [ə'bandənt] *adj* abondant(e)

abuse [*n* ə'bjuːs, *vb* ə'bjuːz] *n* abus *m*; (*insults*) insultes *fpl*, injures *fpl* ♦ *vt* abuser de; (*insult*) insulter; **abusive** [ə'bjuːsɪv] *adj* grossier(-ère), injurieux(-euse)

abysmal [ə'bɪzməl] *adj* exécrable; (*ignorance etc*) sans bornes

abyss [ə'bɪs] *n* abîme *m*, gouffre *m*

AC *abbr* (= *alternating current*) courant alternatif

academic [ækə'demɪk] *adj* universitaire; (*person: scholarly*) intellectuel(le); (*pej: issue*) oiseux(-euse), purement théorique ♦ *n* universitaire *m/f*; **~ year** *n* année *f* universitaire

academy [ə'kædəmɪ] *n* (*learned body*) académie *f*; (*school*) collège *m*; **~ of music** conservatoire *m*

accelerate [æk'seləreɪt] *vt, vi* accélérer; **accelerator** *n* accélérateur *m*

accent ['æksənt] *n* accent *m*

accept [ak'sept] *vt* accepter; **~able** *adj* acceptable; **~ance** *n* acceptation *f*

access ['ækses] *n* accès *m*; (*LAW: in divorce*) droit *m* de visite; **~ible** [æk'sesəbl] *adj* accessible

accessory [æk'sesərɪ] *n* accessoire *m*

accident ['æksɪdənt] *n* accident *m*; (*chance*) hasard *m*; **by ~** accidentellement; par hasard; **~al** [æksɪ'dentl] *adj* accidentel(le); **~ally** [æksɪ'dentəlɪ] *adv* accidentellement; **~ insurance** *n* assurance *f* accident; **~-prone** *adj* sujet(te) aux accidents

acclaim [ə'kleɪm] *n* acclamations *fpl* ♦ *vt* acclamer

accommodate [ə'kɔmədeɪt] *vt* loger, recevoir; (*oblige, help*) obliger; (*car etc*) contenir; **accommodating** *adj* obligeant(e), arrangeant(e); **accommodation** [əkɔmə'deɪʃən] (*US* **accommodations**) *n* logement *m*

accompany [ə'kʌmpənɪ] *vt* accompagner

accomplice [ə'kʌmplɪs] *n* complice *m/f*

accomplish [ə'kʌmplɪʃ] *vt* accomplir; **~ment** *n* accomplissement *m*; réussite *f*; (*skill: gen pl*) talent *m*

accord [ə'kɔːd] *n* accord *m* ♦ *vt* accorder; **of his own ~** de son plein gré; **~ance** [ə'kɔːdəns] *n*: **in ~ance with** conformément à; **~ing: ~ing to** *prep* selon; **~ingly** *adv* en conséquence

accordion [ə'kɔːdɪən] *n* accordéon *m*

account [ə'kaunt] *n* (*COMM*) compte *m*; (*report*) compte rendu; récit *m*; **~s** *npl* (*COMM*) comptabilité *f*, comptes; **of no ~** sans importance; **on ~** en acompte; **on no ~** en aucun cas; **on ~ of** à cause de; **to take into ~, take ~ of** tenir compte de; **~ for** *vt fus* expliquer, rendre compte de; **~able (to)** *adj*: **~able (to)** responsable (devant); **~ancy** *n* comptabilité *f*; **~ant** *n* comptable *m/f*; **~ number** *n* (*at bank etc*) numéro *m* de compte

accrued interest [ə'kruːd-] *n* intérêt *m* cumulé

accumulate [ə'kjuːmjuleɪt] *vt* accumuler, amasser ♦ *vi* s'accumuler, s'amasser

accuracy ['ækjurəsɪ] *n* exactitude *f*, précision f

accurate ['ækjurɪt] *adj* exact(e), précis(e); **~ly** *adv* avec précision

accusation [ækju'zeɪʃən] *n* accusation f

accuse [ə'kju:z] *vt*: **to ~ sb (of sth)** accuser qn (de qch); **the ~d** l'accusé(e)

accustom [ə'kʌstəm] *vt* accoutumer, habituer; **~ed** *adj* (*usual*) habituel(le); (*in the habit*): **~ed to** habitué(e) *or* accoutumé(e) à

ace [eɪs] *n* as m

ache [eɪk] *n* mal m, douleur f ♦ *vi* (*yearn*): **to ~ to do sth** mourir d'envie de faire qch; **my head ~s** j'ai mal à la tête

achieve [ə'tʃi:v] *vt* (*aim*) atteindre; (*victory, success*) remporter, obtenir; **~ment** *n* exploit m, réussite f

acid ['æsɪd] *adj* acide ♦ *n* acide m; **~ rain** *n* pluies fpl acides

acknowledge [ək'nɔlɪdʒ] *vt* (*letter: also:* **~ receipt of**) accuser réception de; (*fact*) reconnaître; **~ment** *n* (*of letter*) accusé m de réception

acne ['æknɪ] *n* acné m

acorn ['eɪkɔ:n] *n* gland m

acoustic [ə'ku:stɪk] *adj* acoustique; **~s** *n*, *npl* acoustique f

acquaint [ə'kweɪnt] *vt*: **to ~ sb with sth** mettre qn au courant de qch; **to be ~ed with** connaître; **~ance** *n* connaissance f

acquire [ə'kwaɪər] *vt* acquérir

acquit [ə'kwɪt] *vt* acquitter; **to ~ o.s. well** bien se comporter, s'en tirer très honorablement

acre ['eɪkər] *n* acre f (= 4047 m²)

acrid ['ækrɪd] *adj* âcre

acrobat ['ækrəbæt] *n* acrobate m/f

across [ə'krɔs] *prep* (*on the other side*) de l'autre côté de; (*crosswise*) en travers de ♦ *adv* de l'autre côté; en travers; **to run/ swim ~** traverser en courant/à la nage; **~ from** en face de

acrylic [ə'krɪlɪk] *adj* acrylique

act [ækt] *n* acte m, action f; (*of play*) acte m; (*in music-hall etc*) numéro m; (*LAW*) loi f ♦ *vi* agir; (*THEATRE*) jouer; (*pretend*) jouer la comédie ♦ *vt* (*part*) jouer, tenir; **in the ~ of** en train de; **to ~ as** servir de; **~ing** *adj* suppléant(e), par intérim ♦ *n* (*activity*): **to do some ~ing** faire du théâtre (*or* du cinéma)

action ['ækʃən] *n* action f; (*MIL*) combat(s) m(pl); **out of ~** hors de combat; (*machine*) hors d'usage; **to take ~** agir, prendre des mesures; **~ replay** *n* (*TV*) ralenti m

activate ['æktɪveɪt] *vt* (*mechanism*) actionner, faire fonctionner

active ['æktɪv] *adj* actif(-ive); (*volcano*) en activité; **~ly** *adv* activement; **activity** [æk'tɪvɪtɪ] *n* activité f; **activity holiday** *n* vacances actives

actor ['æktər] *n* acteur m

actress ['æktrɪs] *n* actrice f

actual ['æktjuəl] *adj* réel(le), véritable; **~ly** *adv* (*really*) réellement, véritablement; (*in fact*) en fait

acute [ə'kju:t] *adj* aigu(ë); (*mind, observer*) pénétrant(e), perspicace

ad [æd] *n abbr* = **advertisement**

A.D. *adv abbr* (= *anno Domini*) ap. J.-C.

adamant ['ædəmənt] *adj* inflexible

adapt [ə'dæpt] *vt* adapter ♦ *vi*: **to ~ (to)** s'adapter (à); **~able** *adj* (*device*) adaptable; (*person*) qui s'adapte facilement; **~er**, **~or** *n* (*ELEC*) adaptateur m

add [æd] *vt* ajouter; (*figures: also:* **to ~ up**) additionner ♦ *vi*: **to ~ to** (*increase*) ajouter à, accroître

adder ['ædər] *n* vipère f

addict ['ædɪkt] *n* intoxiqué(e); (*fig*) fanatique m/f; **~ed** [ə'dɪktɪd] *adj*: **to be ~ed to** (*drugs, drink etc*) être adonné(e) à; (*fig: football etc*) être un(e) fanatique de; **~ion** *n* (*MED*) dépendance f; **~ive** *adj* qui crée une dépendance

addition [ə'dɪʃən] *n* addition f; (*thing added*) ajout m; **in ~** de plus; de surcroît; **in ~ to** en plus de; **~al** *adj* supplémentaire

additive ['ædɪtɪv] *n* additif m

address [ə'drɛs] *n* adresse f; (*talk*) discours m, allocution f ♦ *vt* adresser; (*speak to*) s'adresser à; **to ~ (o.s. to) a problem** s'attaquer à un problème

adept ['ædɛpt] *adj*: **~ at** expert(e) à *or* en

adequate ['ædɪkwɪt] *adj* adéquat(e); suffisant(e)

adhere [əd'hɪəʳ] *vi*: **to ~ to** adhérer à; (*fig: rule, decision*) se tenir à

adhesive [əd'hi:zɪv] *n* adhésif *m*; **~ tape** *n* (*BRIT*) ruban adhésif; (*US: MED*) sparadrap *m*

ad hoc [æd'hɔk] *adj* improvisé(e), ad hoc

adjacent [ə'dʒeɪsənt] *adj*: **~ (to)** adjacent (à)

adjective ['ædʒɛktɪv] *n* adjectif *m*

adjoining [ə'dʒɔɪnɪŋ] *adj* voisin(e), adjacent(e), attenant(e)

adjourn [ə'dʒə:n] *vt* ajourner ♦ *vi* suspendre la séance; clore la session

adjust [ə'dʒʌst] *vt* (*machine*) ajuster, régler; (*prices, wages*) rajuster ♦ *vi*: **to ~ (to)** s'adapter (à); **~able** *adj* réglable; **~ment** *n* (*PSYCH*) adaptation *f*; (*to machine*) ajustage *m*, réglage *m*; (*of prices, wages*) rajustement *m*

ad-lib [æd'lɪb] *vt, vi* improviser; **ad lib** *adv* à volonté, à loisir

administer [əd'mɪnɪstəʳ] *vt* administrer; (*justice*) rendre; **administration** [ədmɪnɪs'treɪʃən] *n* administration *f*; **administrative** [əd'mɪnɪstrətɪv] *adj* administratif(-ive)

admiral ['ædmərəl] *n* amiral *m*; **A~ty** ['ædmərəltɪ] (*BRIT*) *n*: **the A~ty** ministère *m* de la Marine

admire [əd'maɪəʳ] *vt* admirer

admission [əd'mɪʃən] *n* admission *f*; (*to exhibition, night club etc*) entrée *f*; (*confession*) aveu *m*; **~ charge** *n* droits *mpl* d'admission

admit [əd'mɪt] *vt* laisser entrer; admettre; (*agree*) reconnaître, admettre; **~ to** *vt fus* reconnaître, avouer; **~tance** *n* admission *f*, (droit *m* d')entrée *f*; **~tedly** *adv* il faut en convenir

ado [ə'du:] *n*: **without (any) more ~** sans plus de cérémonies

adolescence [ædəu'lɛsns] *n* adolescence *f*; **adolescent** *adj, n* adolescent(e)

adopt [ə'dɔpt] *vt* adopter; **~ed** *adj* adoptif(-ive), adopté(e); **~ion** *n* adoption *f*

adore [ə'dɔːʳ] *vt* adorer

adorn [ə'dɔːn] *vt* orner

Adriatic (Sea) [eɪdrɪ'ætɪk-] *n* Adriatique *f*

adrift [ə'drɪft] *adv* à la dérive

adult ['ædʌlt] *n* adulte *m/f* ♦ *adj* adulte; (*literature, education*) pour adultes

adultery [ə'dʌltərɪ] *n* adultère *m*

advance [əd'vɑːns] *n* avance *f* ♦ *adj*: **~ booking** réservation *f* ♦ *vt* avancer ♦ *vi* avancer, s'avancer; **~ notice** avertissement *m*; **to make ~s (to sb)** faire des propositions (à qn); (*amorously*) faire des avances (à qn); **in ~** à l'avance, d'avance; **~d** *adj* avancé(e); (*SCOL: studies*) supérieur(e)

advantage [əd'vɑːntɪdʒ] *n* (*also TENNIS*) avantage *m*; **to take ~ of** (*person*) exploiter

advent ['ædvənt] *n* avènement *m*, venue *f*; **A~** Avent *m*

adventure [əd'vɛntʃəʳ] *n* aventure *f*

adverb ['ædvə:b] *n* adverbe *m*

adverse ['ædvə:s] *adj* défavorable, contraire

advert ['ædvə:t] (*BRIT*) *n abbr* = **advertisement**

advertise ['ædvətaɪz] *vi, vt* faire de la publicité (pour); (*in classified ads etc*) mettre une annonce (pour vendre); **to ~ for** (*staff, accommodation*) faire paraître une annonce pour trouver; **~ment** [əd'və:tɪsmənt] *n* (*COMM*) réclame *f*, publicité *f*; (*in classified ads*) annonce *f*; **advertising** *n* publicité *f*

advice [əd'vaɪs] *n* conseils *mpl*; (*notification*) avis *m*; **piece of ~** conseil; **to take legal ~** consulter un avocat

advisable [əd'vaɪzəbl] *adj* conseillé(e), indiqué(e)

advise [əd'vaɪz] *vt* conseiller; **to ~ sb of sth** aviser *or* informer qn de qch; **to ~ against sth/doing sth** déconseiller qch/ conseiller de ne pas faire qch; **~r, advisor** *n* conseiller(-ère); **advisory** *adj* consultatif(-ive)

advocate [*n* 'ædvəkɪt, *vb* 'ædvəkeɪt] *n* (*upholder*) défenseur *m*, avocat(e); (*LAW*) avocat(e) ♦ vt recommander, prôner

Aegean (Sea) [iː'dʒiːən-] n (mer f) Égée f

aerial ['ɛərɪəl] n antenne f ♦ adj aérien(ne)

aerobics [ɛə'rəubɪks] n aérobic f

aeroplane ['ɛərəpleɪn] (BRIT) n avion m

aerosol ['ɛərəsɔl] n aérosol m

aesthetic [iːs'θetɪk] adj esthétique

afar [ə'fɑːr] adv: **from ~** de loin

affair [ə'fɛər] n affaire f; (also: **love ~**) liaison f; aventure f

affect [ə'fekt] vt affecter; (disease) atteindre; **~ed** adj affecté(e); **~ion** n affection f; **~ionate** adj affectueux(-euse)

affinity [ə'fɪnɪtɪ] n (bond, rapport): **to have an ~ with/for** avoir une affinité avec/pour

afflict [ə'flɪkt] vt affliger

affluence ['æfluəns] n abondance f, opulence f

affluent ['æfluənt] adj (person, family, surroundings) aisé(e), riche; **the ~ society** la société d'abondance

afford [ə'fɔːd] vt se permettre; (provide) fournir, procurer

afloat [ə'fləut] adj, adv à flot; **to stay ~** surnager

afoot [ə'fut] adv: **there is something ~** il se prépare quelque chose

afraid [ə'freɪd] adj effrayé(e); **to be ~ of** or **to** avoir peur de; **I am ~ that ...** je suis désolé(e), mais ...; **I am ~ so/not** hélas oui/non

Africa ['æfrɪkə] n Afrique f; **~n** adj africain(e) ♦ n Africain(e)

after ['ɑːftər] prep, adv après ♦ conj après que, après avoir or être +pp; **what/who are you ~?** que/qui cherchez-vous?; **~ he left/having done** après qu'il fut parti/après avoir fait; **ask ~ him** demandez de ses nouvelles; **to name sb ~ sb** donner à qn le nom de qn; **twenty ~ eight** (US) huit heures vingt; **~ all** après tout; **~ you!** après vous, Monsieur (or Madame etc); **~effects** npl (of disaster, radiation, drink etc) répercussions fpl; (of illness) séquelles fpl, suites fpl; **~math** n conséquences fpl, suites fpl; **~noon** n après-midi m or f; **~s**

(inf) n (dessert) dessert m; **~-sales service** (BRIT) n (for car, washing machine etc) service m après-vente; **~-shave (lotion)** n after-shave m; **~sun** n après-soleil m inv; **~thought** n: **I had an ~thought** il m'est venu une idée après coup; **~wards** (US **afterward**) adv après

again [ə'gen] adv de nouveau; encore (une fois); **to do sth ~** refaire qch; **not ... ~** ne ... plus; **~ and ~** à plusieurs reprises

against [ə'genst] prep contre; (compared to) par rapport à

age [eɪdʒ] n âge m ♦ vt, vi vieillir; **it's been ~s since** ça fait une éternité que ...; **he is 20 years of ~** il a 20 ans; **to come of ~** atteindre sa majorité; **~d** [adj eɪdʒd, npl 'eɪdʒɪd] adj: **~d 10** âgé(e) de 10 ans ♦ npl: **the ~d** les personnes âgées; **~ group** n tranche f d'âge; **~ limit** n limite f d'âge

agency ['eɪdʒənsɪ] n agence f; (government body) organisme m, office m

agenda [ə'dʒendə] n ordre m du jour

agent ['eɪdʒənt] n agent m, représentant m; (firm) concessionnaire m

aggravate ['ægrəveɪt] vt aggraver; (annoy) exaspérer

aggressive [ə'gresɪv] adj agressif(-ive)

agitate ['ædʒɪteɪt] vt (person) agiter, émouvoir, troubler ♦ vi: **to ~ for/against** faire campagne pour/contre

AGM n abbr (= annual general meeting) AG f

ago [ə'gəu] adv: **2 days ~** il y a deux jours; **not long ~** il n'y a pas longtemps; **how long ~?** il y a combien de temps (de cela)?

agony ['ægənɪ] n (pain) douleur f atroce; **to be in ~** souffrir le martyre

agree [ə'griː] vt (price) convenir de ♦ vi: **to ~ with** (person) être d'accord avec; (statements etc) concorder avec; (LING) s'accorder avec; **to ~ to do** accepter de or consentir à faire; **to ~ to sth** consentir à qch; **to ~ that** (admit) convenir or reconnaître que; **garlic doesn't ~ with me** je ne supporte pas l'ail; **~able** adj agréable; (*willing*) consentant(e), d'accord; ~d *adj* (*time, place*) convenu(e); ~ment *n* accord *m*; **in ~ment** d'accord

agricultural [ægrɪˈkʌltʃərəl] *adj* agricole

agriculture [ˈægrɪkʌltʃəʳ] *n* agriculture *f*

aground [əˈɡraʊnd] *adv*: **to run ~** échouer, s'échouer

ahead [əˈhɛd] *adv* (*in front: of position, place*) devant; (: *at the head*) en avant; (*look, plan, think*) en avant; ~ **of** devant; (*fig: schedule etc*) en avance sur; ~ **of time** en avance; **go right** *or* **straight ~** allez tout droit; **go ~!** (*fig: permission*) allez-y!

aid [eɪd] *n* aide *f*; (*device*) appareil *m* ♦ *vt* aider; **in ~ of** en faveur de; *see also* **hearing**

aide [eɪd] *n* (*person*) aide *mf*, assistant(e)

AIDS [eɪdz] *n abbr* (= *acquired immune deficiency syndrome*) SIDA *m*; **AIDS-related** *adj* associé(e) au sida

aim [eɪm] *vt*: **to ~ sth (at)** (*gun, camera*) braquer *or* pointer qch (sur); (*missile*) lancer qch (à *or* contre *or* en direction de); (*blow*) allonger qch (à); (*remark*) destiner *or* adresser qch (à) ♦ *vi* (*also*: **to take ~**) viser ♦ *n* but *m*; (*skill*): **his ~ is bad** il vise mal; **to ~ at** viser; (*fig*) viser (à); **to ~ to do** avoir l'intention de faire; ~**less** *adj* sans but

ain't [eɪnt] (*inf*) = **am not; aren't; isn't**

air [ɛəʳ] *n* air *m* ♦ *vt* (*room, bed, clothes*) aérer; (*grievances, views, ideas*) exposer, faire connaître ♦ *cpd* (*currents, attack etc*) aérien(ne); **to throw sth into the ~** jeter qch en l'air; **by ~** (*travel*) par avion; **to be on the ~** (*RADIO, TV: programme*) être diffusé(e); (: *station*) diffuser; ~**bed** *n* matelas *m* pneumatique; ~-**conditioned** *adj* climatisé(e); ~ **conditioning** *n* climatisation *f*; ~**craft** *n inv* avion *m*; ~**craft carrier** *n* porte-avions *m inv*; ~**field** *n* terrain *m* d'aviation; **A~ Force** *n* armée *f* de l'air; ~ **freshener** *n* désodorisant *m*; ~**gun** *n* fusil *m* à air comprimé; ~ **hostess** *n* (*BRIT*) hôtesse *f* de l'air; ~ **letter** *n* (*BRIT*) aérogramme *m*; ~**lift** *n* pont aérien; ~**line** *n* ligne aérienne, compagnie *f*

d'aviation; ~**liner** *n* avion *m* de ligne; ~**mail** *n*: **by ~mail** par avion; ~ **mile** *n* air mile *m*; ~**plane** *n* (*US*) avion *m*; ~**port** *n* aéroport *m*; ~ **raid** *n* attaque *or* raid aérien(ne); ~**sick** *adj*: **to be ~sick** avoir le mal de l'air; ~**tight** *adj* hermétique; ~-**traffic controller** *n* aiguilleur *m* du ciel; ~**y** *adj* bien aéré(e); (*manners*) dégagé(e)

aisle [aɪl] *n* (*of church*) allée centrale; nef latérale; (*of theatre etc*) couloir *m*, passage *m*, allée; ~ **seat** *n* place *m* côté couloir

ajar [əˈdʒɑːʳ] *adj* entrouvert(e)

akin [əˈkɪn] *adj*: ~ **to** (*similar*) qui tient de *or* ressemble à

alarm [əˈlɑːm] *n* alarme *f* ♦ *vt* alarmer; ~ **call** *n* coup de fil *m* pour réveiller; ~ **clock** *n* réveille-matin *m inv*, réveil *m*

alas [əˈlæs] *excl* hélas!

album [ˈælbəm] *n* album *m*

alcohol [ˈælkəhɔl] *n* alcool *m*; ~-**free** *adj* sans alcool; ~**ic** [ælkəˈhɔlɪk] *adj* alcoolique ♦ *n* alcoolique *m/f*; **A~ics Anonymous** Alcooliques anonymes

ale [eɪl] *n* bière *f*

alert [əˈlɜːt] *adj* alerte, vif (vive); vigilant(e) ♦ *n* alerte *f* ♦ *vt* alerter; **on the ~** sur le qui-vive; (*MIL*) en état d'alerte

algebra [ˈældʒɪbrə] *n* algèbre *m*

Algeria [ælˈdʒɪərɪə] *n* Algérie *f*

alias [ˈeɪlɪəs] *adv* alias ♦ *n* faux nom, nom d'emprunt; (*writer*) pseudonyme *m*

alibi [ˈælɪbaɪ] *n* alibi *m*

alien [ˈeɪlɪən] *n* étranger(-ère); (*from outer space*) extraterrestre *mf* ♦ *adj*: ~ **(to)** étranger(-ère) (à)

alight [əˈlaɪt] *adj, adv* en feu ♦ *vi* mettre pied à terre; (*passenger*) descendre

alike [əˈlaɪk] *adj* semblable, pareil(le) ♦ *adv* de même; **to look ~** se ressembler

alimony [ˈælɪmənɪ] *n* (*payment*) pension *f* alimentaire

alive [əˈlaɪv] *adj* vivant(e); (*lively*) plein(e) de vie

KEYWORD

---

all [ɔːl] *adj* (*singular*) tout(e); (*plural*) tous (toutes); **all day** toute la journée; **all**

night toute la nuit; **all men** tous les hommes; **all five** tous les cinq; **all the food** toute la nourriture; **all the books** tous les livres; **all the time** tout le temps; **all his life** toute sa vie

♦ *pron* 1 tout; **I ate it all, I ate all of it** j'ai tout mangé; **all of us went** nous y sommes tous allés; **all of the boys went** tous les garçons y sont allés

2 (*in phrases*): **above all** surtout, par-dessus tout; **after all** après tout; **not at all** (*in answer to question*) pas du tout; (*in answer to thanks*) je vous en prie!; **I'm not at all** tired je ne suis pas du tout fatigué(e); **anything at all will do** n'importe quoi fera l'affaire; **all in all** tout bien considéré, en fin de compte

♦ *adv*: **all alone** tout(e) seul(e); **it's not as hard as all that** ce n'est pas si difficile que ça; **all the more/the better** d'autant plus/mieux; **all but** presque, pratiquement; **the score is 2 all** le score est de 2 partout

allege [ə'lɛdʒ] *vt* alléguer, prétendre; **~dly** [ə'lɛdʒɪdlɪ] *adv* à ce que l'on prétend, paraît-il

allegiance [ə'liːdʒəns] *n* allégeance *f*, fidélité *f*, obéissance *f*

allergic [ə'lɔːdʒɪk] *adj*: **~ to** allergique à

allergy ['ælədʒɪ] *n* allergie *f*

alleviate [ə'liːvɪeɪt] *vt* soulager, adoucir

alley ['ælɪ] *n* ruelle *f*

alliance [ə'laɪəns] *n* alliance *f*

allied ['ælaɪd] *adj* allié(e)

all-in ['ɔːlɪn] (*BRIT*) *adj* (*also adv*: *charge*) tout compris

all-night ['ɔːl'naɪt] *adj* ouvert(e) *or* qui dure toute la nuit

allocate ['æləkeɪt] *vt* (*share out*) répartir, distribuer; **to ~ sth to** (*duties*) assigner *or* attribuer qch à; (*sum, time*) allouer qch à

allot [ə'lɔt] *vt*: **to ~ (to)** (*money*) répartir (entre), distribuer (à); (*time*) allouer (à); **~ment** *n* (*share*) part *f*; (*garden*) lopin *m* de terre (*loué à la municipalité*)

all-out ['ɔːlaut] *adj* (*effort etc*) total(e)

♦ *adv*: **all out** à fond

allow [ə'lau] *vt* (*practice, behaviour*) permettre, autoriser; (*sum to spend etc*) accorder, allouer; (*sum, time estimated*) compter, prévoir; (*claim, goal*) admettre; (*concede*): **to ~ that** convenir que; **to ~ sb to do** permettre à qn de faire, autoriser qn à faire; **he is ~ed to ...** on lui permet de ...; **~ for** *vt fus* tenir compte de; **~ance** [ə'lauəns] *n* (*money received*) allocation *f*; subside *m*; indemnité *f*; (*TAX*) somme *f* déductible du revenu imposable, abattement *m*; **to make ~ances for** tenir compte de

alloy ['ælɔɪ] *n* alliage *m*

all: **~ right** *adv* (*feel, work*) bien; (*as answer*) d'accord; **~-rounder** *n*: **to be a good ~-rounder** être doué(e) en tout; **~-time** *adj* (*record*) sans précédent, absolu(e)

ally [*n* 'ælaɪ, *vb* ə'laɪ] *n* allié *m* ♦ *vt*: **to ~ o.s. with** s'allier avec

almighty [ɔːl'maɪtɪ] *adj* tout-puissant; (*tremendous*) énorme

almond ['ɑːmənd] *n* amande *f*

almost ['ɔːlməust] *adv* presque

alone [ə'ləun] *adj, adv* seul(e); **to leave sb ~** laisser qn tranquille; **to leave sth ~** ne pas toucher à qch; **let ~ ...** sans parler de ...; encore moins ...

along [ə'lɔŋ] *prep* le long de ♦ *adv*: **is he coming ~ with us?** vient-il avec nous?; **he was hopping/limping ~** il avançait en sautillant/boitant; **~ with** (*together with*: *person*) en compagnie de; (: *thing*) avec, en plus de; **all ~** (*all the time*) depuis le début; **~side** *prep* le long de; à côté de ♦ *adv* bord à bord

aloof [ə'luːf] *adj* distant(e) ♦ *adv*: **to stand ~** se tenir à distance *or* à l'écart

aloud [ə'laud] *adv* à haute voix

alphabet ['ælfəbɛt] *n* alphabet *m*; **~ical** [ælfə'bɛtɪkl] *adj* alphabétique

alpine ['ælpaɪn] *adj* alpin(e), alpestre

Alps [ælps] *npl*: **the ~** les Alpes *fpl*

already [ɔːl'rɛdɪ] *adv* déjà

alright ['ɔːl'raɪt] (*BRIT*) *adv* = **all right**

Alsatian [æl'seɪʃən] (*BRIT*) *n* (*dog*) berger allemand

also ['ɔːlsəʊ] *adv* aussi

altar ['ɔːltər] *n* autel *m*

alter ['ɔːltər] *vt, vi* changer

alternate [*adj* ɔl'tɜːnɪt, *vb* 'ɔːltəneɪt] *adj* alterné(e), alternant(e), alternatif(-ive) ♦ *vi* alterner; **on ~ days** un jour sur deux, tous les deux jours; **alternating current** *n* courant alternatif

alternative [ɔl'tɜːnətɪv] *adj* (*solutions*) possible, au choix; (*plan*) autre, de rechange; (*lifestyle etc*) parallèle ♦ *n* (*choice*) alternative *f*; (*other possibility*) autre possibilité *f*; **an ~ comedian** un nouveau comique; **~ medicine** médicines *fpl* parallèles *or* douces; **~ly** *adv*: **~ly one could** une autre *or* l'autre solution serait de, on pourrait aussi

alternator ['ɔːltəneɪtər] *n* (*AUT*) alternateur *m*

although [ɔːl'ðəʊ] *conj* bien que +*sub*

altitude ['æltɪtjuːd] *n* altitude *f*

alto ['æltəʊ] *n* (*female*) contralto *m*; (*male*) haute-contre *f*

altogether [ɔːltə'gɛðər] *adv* entièrement, tout à fait; (*on the whole*) tout compte fait; (*in all*) en tout

aluminium [æljuˈmɪnɪəm] (*BRIT*), **aluminum** [ə'luːmɪnəm] (*US*) *n* aluminium *m*

always ['ɔːlweɪz] *adv* toujours

Alzheimer's (disease) ['æltshaɪməz-] *n* maladie *f* d'Alzheimer

AM *n abbr* (= *Assembly Member*) député *m* au Parlement gallois

am [æm] *vb see* **be**

a.m. *adv abbr* (= *ante meridiem*) du matin

amalgamate [ə'mælgəmeɪt] *vt, vi* fusionner

amateur ['æmətər] *n* amateur *m*; **~ish** (*pej*) *adj* d'amateur

amaze [ə'meɪz] *vt* stupéfier; **to be ~d (at)** être stupéfait(e) (de); **~ment** *n* stupéfaction *f*, stupeur *f*; **amazing** *adj* étonnant(e); exceptionnel(le)

ambassador [æm'bæsədər] *n* ambassadeur *m*

amber ['æmbər] *n* ambre *m*; **at ~** (*BRIT*: *AUT*) à l'orange

ambiguous [æm'bɪgjuəs] *adj* ambigu(ë)

ambition [æm'bɪʃən] *n* ambition *f*; **ambitious** *adj* ambitieux(-euse)

ambulance ['æmbjuləns] *n* ambulance *f*

ambush ['æmbuʃ] *n* embuscade *f* ♦ *vt* tendre une embuscade à

amenable [ə'miːnəbl] *adj*: **~ to** (*advice etc*) disposé(e) à écouter

amend [ə'mɛnd] *vt* (*law*) amender; (*text*) corriger; **to make ~s** réparer ses torts, faire amende honorable

amenities [ə'miːnɪtɪz] *npl* aménagements *mpl*, équipements *mpl*

America [ə'mɛrɪkə] *n* Amérique *f*; **~n** *adj* américain(e) ♦ *n* Américain(e)

amiable ['eɪmɪəbl] *adj* aimable, affable

amicable ['æmɪkəbl] *adj* amical(e); (*LAW*) à l'amiable

amid(st) [ə'mɪd(st)] *prep* parmi, au milieu de

amiss [ə'mɪs] *adj, adv*: **there's something ~** il y a quelque chose qui ne va pas *or* qui cloche; **to take sth ~** prendre qch mal *or* de travers

ammonia [ə'məʊnɪə] *n* (*gas*) ammoniac *m*; (*liquid*) ammoniaque *f*

ammunition [æmju'nɪʃən] *n* munitions *fpl*

amok [ə'mɔk] *adv*: **to run ~** être pris(e) d'un accès de folie furieuse

among(st) [ə'mʌŋ(st)] *prep* parmi, entre

amorous ['æmərəs] *adj* amoureux(-euse)

amount [ə'maʊnt] *n* (*sum*) somme *f*, montant *m*; (*quantity*) quantité *f*, nombre *m* ♦ *vi*: **to ~ to** (*total*) s'élever à; (*be same as*) équivaloir à, revenir à

amp(ere) ['æmp(ɛər)] *n* ampère *m*

ample ['æmpl] *adj* ample; spacieux(-euse); (*enough*): **this is ~** c'est largement suffisant; **to have ~ time/room** avoir bien assez de temps/place

amplifier ['æmplɪfaɪər] *n* amplificateur *m*

amuse [ə'mjuːz] *vt* amuser, divertir; **~ment** *n* amusement *m*; **~ment arcade** *n* salle *f* de jeu; **~ment park** *n* parc *m* d'attractions

an [æn, ən] *indef art see* **a**

anaemic [ə'ni:mɪk] (*US* **anemic**) *adj* anémique

anaesthetic [ænɪs'θetɪk] (*US* **anesthetic**) *n* anesthésique *m*

analog(ue) ['ænələg] *adj* (*watch, computer*) analogique

analyse ['ænəlaɪz] (*US* **analyze**) *vt* analyser; **analysis** [ə'næləsɪs] (*pl* **analyses**) *n* analyse *f*; **analyst** ['ænəlɪst] *n* (*POL etc*) spécialiste *m/f*; (*US*) psychanalyste *m/f*

analyze ['ænəlaɪz] (*US*) *vt* = **analyse**

anarchist ['ænəkɪst] *n* anarchiste *m/f*

anarchy ['ænəkɪ] *n* anarchie *f*

anatomy [ə'nætəmɪ] *n* anatomie *f*

ancestor ['ænsɪstə*] *n* ancêtre *m*, aïeul *m*

anchor ['ænkə*] *n* ancre *f* ♦ *vi* (*also:* **to drop** ~) jeter l'ancre, mouiller ♦ *vt* mettre à l'ancre; (*fig*): **to** ~ **sth to** fixer qch à

anchovy ['æntʃəvɪ] *n* anchois *m*

ancient ['eɪnʃənt] *adj* ancien(ne), antique; (*person*) d'un âge vénérable; (*car*) antédiluvien(ne)

ancillary [æn'sɪlərɪ] *adj* auxiliaire

and [ænd] *conj* et; ~ **so on** et ainsi de suite; **try** ~ **come** tâchez de venir; **he talked** ~ **talked** il n'a pas arrêté de parler; **better** ~ **better** de mieux en mieux

anew [ə'nju:] *adv* à nouveau

angel ['eɪndʒəl] *n* ange *m*

anger ['æŋɡə*] *n* colère *f*

angina [æn'dʒaɪnə] *n* angine *f* de poitrine

angle ['æŋɡl] *n* angle *m*; **from their** ~ de leur point de vue

angler ['æŋɡlə*] *n* pêcheur(-euse) à la ligne

Anglican ['æŋɡlɪkən] *adj, n* anglican(e)

angling ['æŋɡlɪŋ] *n* pêche *f* à la ligne

Anglo- ['æŋɡləʊ] *prefix* anglo(-)

angrily ['æŋɡrɪlɪ] *adv* avec colère

angry ['æŋɡrɪ] *adj* en colère, furieux(-euse); (*wound*) enflammé(e); **to be** ~ **with sb/at sth** être furieux contre qn/de qch; **to get** ~ se fâcher, se mettre en colère

anguish ['æŋɡwɪʃ] *n* (*mental*) angoisse *f*

animal ['ænɪməl] *n* animal *m* ♦ *adj* animal(e)

animate [*vb* 'ænɪmeɪt, *adj* 'ænɪmɪt] *vt* animer ♦ *adj* animé(e), vivant(e); ~**d** *adj* ani-

mé(e)

aniseed ['ænɪsi:d] *n* anis *m*

ankle ['æŋkl] *n* cheville *f*; ~ **sock** *n* socquette *f*

annex [*n* 'æneks, *vb* ə'neks] *n* (*BRIT:* ~**e**) annexe *f* ♦ *vt* annexer

anniversary [ænɪ'vɜ:sərɪ] *n* anniversaire *m*

announce [ə'naʊns] *vt* annoncer; (*birth, death*) faire part de; ~**ment** *n* annonce *f*; (*for births etc: in newspaper*) avis *m* de faire-part; (*: letter, card*) faire-part *m*; ~**r** *n* (*RADIO, TV: between programmes*) speaker(ine)

annoy [ə'nɔɪ] *vt* agacer, ennuyer, contrarier; **don't get** ~**ed!** ne vous fâchez pas!; ~**ance** *n* mécontentement *m*, contrariété *f*; ~**ing** *adj* agaçant(e), contrariant(e)

annual ['ænjuəl] *adj* annuel(le) ♦ *n* (*BOT*) plante annuelle; (*children's book*) album *m*

annul [ə'nʌl] *vt* annuler

annum ['ænəm] *n see* **per**

anonymous [ə'nɒnɪməs] *adj* anonyme

anorak ['ænəræk] *n* anorak *m*

anorexia [ænə'reksɪə] *n* (*also:* ~ **nervosa**) anorexie *f*

another [ə'nʌðə*] *adj:* ~ **book** (*one more*) un autre livre, encore un livre, un livre de plus; (*a different one*) un autre livre ♦ *pron* un(e) autre, encore un(e), un(e) de plus; *see also* **one**

answer ['ɑ:nsə*] *n* réponse *f*; (*to problem*) solution *f* ♦ *vi* répondre ♦ *vt* (*reply to*) répondre à; (*problem*) résoudre; (*prayer*) exaucer; **in** ~ **to your letter** en réponse à votre lettre; **to** ~ **the phone** répondre (au téléphone); **to** ~ **the bell** *or* **the door** aller *or* venir ouvrir (la porte); ~ **back** *vi* répondre, répliquer; ~ **for** *vt fus* (*person*) répondre de, se porter garant de; (*crime, one's actions*) être responsable de; ~ **to** *vt fus* (*description*) répondre *or* correspondre à; ~**able** *adj:* ~**able** (**to sb/for sth**) responsable (devant qn/de qch); ~**ing machine** *n* répondeur *m* automatique

ant [ænt] *n* fourmi *f*

antagonism [æn'tæɡənɪzəm] *n* antagonisme *m*

antagonize [æn'tægənaɪz] *vt* éveiller l'hostilité de, contrarier

Antarctic [ænt'ɑːktɪk] *n*: **the ~** l'Antarctique *m*

antenatal ['æntɪ'neɪtl] *adj* prénatal(e); ~ **clinic** *n* service *m* de consultation prénatale

anthem ['ænθəm] *n*: **national ~** hymne national

anti: ~**-aircraft** *adj* (*missile*) antiaérien(ne); ~**biotic** ['æntɪbaɪ'ɔtɪk] *n* antibiotique *m*; ~**body** *n* anticorps *m*

anticipate [æn'tɪsɪpeɪt] *vt* s'attendre à; prévoir; (*wishes, request*) aller au devant de, devancer

anticipation [æntɪsɪ'peɪʃən] *n* attente *f*; **in ~** par anticipation, à l'avance

anticlimax ['æntɪ'klaɪmæks] *n* déception *f*, douche froide (*fam*)

anticlockwise ['æntɪ'klɔkwaɪz] *adj, adv* dans le sens inverse des aiguilles d'une montre

antics ['æntɪks] *npl* singeries *fpl*

antidepressant ['æntɪdɪ'presənt] *n* antidépresseur *m*

antifreeze ['æntɪfriːz] *n* antigel *m*

antihistamine ['æntɪ'hɪstəmɪn] *n* antihistaminique *m*

antiquated ['æntɪkweɪtɪd] *adj* vieilli(e), suranné(e), vieillot(te)

antique [æn'tiːk] *n* objet *m* d'art ancien, meuble ancien *or* d'époque, antiquité *f* ♦ *adj* ancien(ne); ~ **dealer** *n* antiquaire *m*; ~ **shop** *n* magasin *m* d'antiquités

anti: ~**-Semitism** ['æntɪ'semɪtɪzəm] *n* antisémitisme *m*; ~**septic** [æntɪ'septɪk] *n* antiseptique *m*; ~**social** ['æntɪ'səʊʃəl] *adj* peu liant(e), sauvage, insociable; (*against society*) antisocial(e)

antlers ['æntləz] *npl* bois *mpl*, ramure *f*

anvil ['ænvɪl] *n* enclume *f*

anxiety [æŋ'zaɪətɪ] *n* anxiété *f*; (*keenness*): ~ **to do** grand désir *or* impatience *f* de faire

anxious ['æŋkʃəs] *adj* anxieux(-euse); (*worrying: time, situation*) inquiétant(e); (*keen*): ~ **to do/that** qui tient beaucoup à faire/à

ce que; impatient(e) de faire/que

KEYWORD

---

any ['enɪ] *adj* **1** (*in questions etc: singular*) du, de l', de la; (: *plural*) des; **have you any butter/children/ink?** avez-vous du beurre/des enfants/de l'encre?

2 (*with negative*) de, d'; **I haven't any books** je n'ai pas de livres

3 (*no matter which*) n'importe quel(le); **choose any book you like** vous pouvez choisir n'importe quel livre

4 (*in phrases*): **in any case** de toute façon; **any day now** d'un jour à l'autre; **at any moment** à tout moment, d'un instant à l'autre; **at any rate** en tout cas

♦ *pron* **1** (*in questions etc*) en; **have you got any?** est-ce que vous en avez?; **can any of you sing?** est-ce que parmi vous il y en a qui savent chanter?

2 (*with negative*) en; **I haven't any (of them)** je n'en ai pas, je n'en ai aucun

3 (*no matter which one(s)*) n'importe lequel (*or* laquelle); **take any of those books (you like)** vous pouvez prendre n'importe lequel de ces livres

♦ *adv* **1** (*in questions etc*): **do you want any more soup/sandwiches?** voulez-vous encore de la soupe/des sandwichs?; **are you feeling any better?** est-ce que vous vous sentez mieux?

2 (*with negative*): **I can't hear him any more** je ne l'entends plus; **don't wait any longer** n'attendez pas plus longtemps

---

any: ~**body** *pron* n'importe qui; (*in interrogative sentences*) quelqu'un; (*in negative sentences*): **I don't see ~body** je ne vois personne; ~**how** *adv* (*at any rate*) de toute façon, quand même; (*haphazard*) n'importe comment; ~**one** *pron* = **anybody**; ~**thing** *pron* n'importe quoi, quelque chose, ne ... rien; ~**way** *adv* de toute façon; ~**where** *adv* n'importe où, quelque part; **I don't see him ~where** je ne le vois nulle part

apart [ə'pɑːt] *adv* (*to one side*) à part; de

côté; à l'écart; (*separately*) séparément; **10 miles ~** à 10 miles l'un de l'autre; **to take ~** démonter; **~ from** à part, excepté

apartheid [ə'pɑːteɪt] *n* apartheid *m*

apartment [ə'pɑːtmənt] *n* (*US*) appartement *m*, logement *m*; (*room*) chambre *f*; **~ building** (*US*) *n* immeuble *m*; (*divided house*) maison divisée en appartements

ape [eɪp] *n* (grand) singe ♦ *vt* singer

apéritif [ə'perɪtiːf] *n* apéritif *m*

aperture ['æpətjuəʳ] *n* orifice *m*, ouverture *f*; (*PHOT*) ouverture (du diaphragme)

APEX ['eɪpeks] *n abbr* (*AVIAT*) (= *advance purchase excursion*) APEX *m*

apologetic [əpɔlə'dʒetɪk] *adj* (*tone, letter*) d'excuse; (*person*): **to be ~** s'excuser

apologize [ə'pɔlədʒaɪz] *vi*: **to ~ (for sth to sb)** s'excuser (de qch auprès de qn), présenter des excuses (à qn pour qch)

apology [ə'pɔlədʒɪ] *n* excuses *fpl*

apostle [ə'pɔsl] *n* apôtre *m*

apostrophe [ə'pɔstrəfɪ] *n* apostrophe *f*

appalling [ə'pɔːlɪŋ] *adj* épouvantable; (*stupidity*) consternant(e)

apparatus [æpə'reɪtəs] *n* appareil *m*, dispositif *m*; (*in gymnasium*) agrès *mpl*; (*of government*) dispositif *m*

apparel [ə'pærəl] (*US*) *n* habillement *m*

apparent [ə'pærənt] *adj* apparent(e); **~ly** *adv* apparemment

appeal [ə'piːl] *vi* (*LAW*) faire *or* interjeter appel ♦ *n* appel *m*; (*request*) prière *f*; appel *m*; (*charm*) attrait *m*, charme *m*; **to ~ for** lancer un appel pour; **to ~ to** (*beg*) faire appel à; (*be attractive*) plaire à; **it doesn't ~ to me** cela ne m'attire pas; **~ing** *adj* (*attractive*) attrayant(e)

appear [ə'pɪəʳ] *vi* apparaître, se montrer; (*LAW*) comparaître; (*publication*) paraître, sortir, être publié(e); (*seem*) paraître, sembler; **it would ~ that** il semble que; **to ~ in Hamlet** jouer dans Hamlet; **to ~ on TV** passer à la télé; **~ance** *n* apparition *f*; parution *f*; (*look, aspect*) apparence *f*, aspect *m*

appease [ə'piːz] *vt* apaiser, calmer

appendicitis [əpendɪ'saɪtɪs] *n* appendicite *f*

appendix [ə'pendɪks] (*pl* **appendices**) *n* appendice *m*

appetite ['æpɪtaɪt] *n* appétit *m*; **appetizer** *n* amuse-gueule *m*; (*drink*) apéritif *m*

applaud [ə'plɔːd] *vt, vi* applaudir

applause [ə'plɔːz] *n* applaudissements *mpl*

apple ['æpl] *n* pomme *f*; **~ tree** *n* pommier *m*

appliance [ə'plaɪəns] *n* appareil *m*

applicable [ə'plɪkəbl] *adj* (*relevant*): **to be ~ to** valoir pour

applicant ['æplɪkənt] *n*: **~ (for)** candidat(e) (à)

application [æplɪ'keɪʃən] *n* application *f*; (*for a job, a grant etc*) demande *f*; candidature *f*; **~ form** *n* formulaire *m* de demande

applied [ə'plaɪd] *adj* appliqué(e)

apply [ə'plaɪ] *vt*: **to ~ (to)** (*paint, ointment*) appliquer (sur); (*law etc*) appliquer (à) ♦ *vi*: **to ~ to** (*be suitable for, relevant to*) s'appliquer à; (*ask*) s'adresser à; **to ~ (for)** (*permit, grant*) faire une demande (en vue d'obtenir); (*job*) poser sa candidature (pour), faire une demande d'emploi (concernant); **to ~ o.s. to** s'appliquer à

appoint [ə'pɔɪnt] *vt* nommer, engager; **~ed** *adj*: **at the ~ed time** à l'heure dite; **~ment** *n* nomination *f*; (*meeting*) rendez-vous *m*; **to make an ~ment (with)** prendre rendez-vous (avec)

appraisal [ə'preɪzl] *n* évaluation *f*

appreciate [ə'priːʃieɪt] *vt* (*like*) apprécier; (*be grateful for*) être reconnaissant(e) de; (*understand*) comprendre; se rendre compte de ♦ *vi* (*FINANCE*) prendre de la valeur

appreciation [əpriːʃi'eɪʃən] *n* appréciation *f*; (*gratitude*) reconnaissance *f*; (*COMM*) hausse *f*, valorisation *f*

appreciative [ə'priːʃiətɪv] *adj* (*person*) sensible; (*comment*) élogieux(-euse)

apprehensive [æprɪ'hensɪv] *adj* inquiet(-ète), appréhensif(-ive)

apprentice [ə'prentɪs] *n* apprenti *m*; **~ship** *n* apprentissage *m*

approach [ə'prəʊtʃ] *vi* approcher ♦ *vt*
(*come near*) approcher de; (*ask, apply to*)
s'adresser à; (*situation, problem*) aborder
♦ *n* approche *f*; (*access*) accès *m*; **~able**
adj accessible

appropriate [*adj* ə'prəʊprɪɪt, *vb*
ə'prəʊprɪeɪt] *adj* (*moment, remark*) oppor-
tun(e); (*tool etc*) approprié(e) ♦ *vt* (*take*)
s'approprier

approval [ə'pru:vəl] *n* approbation *f*; **on ~**
(*COMM*) à l'examen

approve [ə'pru:v] *vt* approuver; **~ of** *vt*
fus approuver

approximate [*adj* ə'prɒksɪmɪt, *vb*
ə'prɒksɪmeɪt] *adj* approximatif(-ive) ♦ *vt* se
rapprocher de, être proche de; **~ly** *adv*
approximativement

apricot ['eɪprɪkɒt] *n* abricot *m*

April ['eɪprəl] *n* avril *m*; **~ Fool's Day** le
premier avril

April Fool's Day

ⓘ April Fool's Day *est le 1er avril, à*
l'occasion duquel on fait des farces de
toutes sortes. Les victimes de ces farces
sont les "April fools". Les médias britanni-
ques se prennent aussi au jeu, diffusant de
fausses nouvelles, comme la découverte
d'îles de la taille de l'Irlande, ou faisant
des reportages bidon, montrant par exem-
ple la culture d'arbres à spaghettis en Ita-
lie.

---

apron ['eɪprən] *n* tablier *m*

apt [æpt] *adj* (*suitable*) approprié(e); (*likely*):
~ to do susceptible de faire; qui a une tendance à faire

Aquarius [ə'kwɛərɪəs] *n* le Verseau

Arab ['ærəb] *adj* arabe ♦ *n* Arabe *m/f*; **~ian**
[ə'reɪbɪən] *adj* arabe; **~ic** *adj* arabe ♦ *n*
arabe *m*

arbitrary ['ɑ:bɪtrərɪ] *adj* arbitraire

arbitration [ɑ:bɪ'treɪʃən] *n* arbitrage *m*

arcade [ɑ:'keɪd] *n* arcade *f*; (*passage with
shops*) passage *m*, galerie marchande;
(*with video games*) salle *f* de jeu

arch [ɑ:tʃ] *n* arc *m*; (*of foot*) cambrure *f*,

voûte *f* plantaire ♦ *vt* arquer, cambrer

archaeologist [ɑ:kɪ'ɒlədʒɪst] *n* archéologue *m/f*

archaeology [ɑ:kɪ'ɒlədʒɪ] *n* archéologie *f*

archbishop [ɑ:tʃ'bɪʃəp] *n* archevêque *m*

archeology *etc* (*US*) [ɑ:kɪ'ɒlədʒɪ] = **archaeology** *etc*

archery ['ɑ:tʃərɪ] *n* tir *m* à l'arc

architect ['ɑ:kɪtekt] *n* architecte *m*; **~ure**
n architecture *f*

archives ['ɑ:kaɪvz] *npl* archives *fpl*

Arctic ['ɑ:ktɪk] *adj* arctique ♦ *n* Arctique *m*

ardent ['ɑ:dənt] *adj* fervent(e)

are [ɑ:ʳ] *vb see* **be**

area ['ɛərɪə] *n* (*GEOM*) superficie *f*; (*zone*)
région *f*; (: *smaller*) secteur *m*, partie *f*; (*in
room*) coin *m*; (*knowledge, research*) domaine *m*; **~ code** (*US*) *n* (*TEL*) indicatif *m* téléphonique

aren't [ɑ:nt] = **are not**

Argentina [ɑ:dʒən'ti:nə] *n* Argentine *f*;
Argentinian [ɑ:dʒən'tɪnɪən] *adj* argen-
tin(e) ♦ *n* Argentin(e)

arguably ['ɑ:gjuəblɪ] *adv*: **it is ~ ...** on
peut soutenir que ...

argue ['ɑ:gju:] *vi* (*quarrel*) se disputer; (*reason*) argumenter; **to ~ that** objecter *or* alléguer que

argument ['ɑ:gjumənt] *n* (*reasons*) argument *m*; (*quarrel*) dispute *f*; **~ative**
[ɑ:gju'mentətɪv] *adj* ergoteur(-euse),
raisonneur(-euse)

Aries ['ɛərɪz] *n* le Bélier

arise [ə'raɪz] (*pt* **arose**, *pp* **arisen**) *vi* survenir, se présenter

aristocrat ['ærɪstəkræt] *n* aristocrate *m/f*

arithmetic [ə'rɪθmətɪk] *n* arithmétique *f*

ark [ɑ:k] *n*: **Noah's A~** l'Arche *f* de Noé

arm [ɑ:m] *n* bras *m* ♦ *vt* armer; **~s** *npl*
(*weapons, HERALDRY*) armes *fpl*; **~ in ~** bras
dessus bras dessous

armaments ['ɑ:məmənts] *npl* armement
m

armchair ['ɑ:mtʃɛəʳ] *n* fauteuil *m*

armed [ɑ:md] *adj* armé(e); **~ robbery** *n*
vol *m* à main armée

armour ['ɑ:məʳ] (*US* **armor**) *n* armure *f*;

(MIL: *tanks*) blindés *mpl*; **~ed car** *n* véhicule blindé

armpit ['ɑ:mpɪt] *n* aisselle *f*

armrest ['ɑ:mrɛst] *n* accoudoir *m*

army ['ɑ:mɪ] *n* armée *f*

A road (BRIT) *n* (AUT) route nationale

aroma [ə'rəumə] *n* arôme *m*; **~therapy** *n* aromathérapie *f*

arose [ə'rəuz] *pt of* **arise**

around [ə'raund] *adv* autour (de); (*nearby*) dans les parages ♦ *prep* autour de; (*near*) près de; (*fig: about*) environ; (: *date, time*) vers

arouse [ə'rauz] *vt* (*sleeper*) éveiller; (*curiosity, passions*) éveiller, susciter; (*anger*) exciter

arrange [ə'reɪndʒ] *vt* arranger; **to ~ to do sth** prévoir de faire qch; **~ment** *n* arrangement *m*; **~ments** *npl* (*plans etc*) arrangements *mpl*, dispositions *fpl*

array [ə'reɪ] *n*: **~ of** déploiement *m or* étalage *m* de

arrears [ə'rɪəz] *npl* arriéré *m*; **to be in ~ with one's rent** devoir un arriéré de loyer

arrest [ə'rɛst] *vt* arrêter; (*sb's attention*) retenir, attirer ♦ *n* arrestation *f*; **under ~** en état d'arrestation

arrival [ə'raɪvl] *n* arrivée *f*; **new ~** nouveau venu, nouvelle venue; (*baby*) nouveau-né(e)

arrive [ə'raɪv] *vi* arriver

arrogant ['ærəgənt] *adj* arrogant(e)

arrow ['ærəu] *n* flèche *f*

arse [ɑ:s] (BRIT: *inf!*) *n* cul *m* (!)

arson ['ɑ:sn] *n* incendie criminel

art [ɑ:t] *n* art *m*; **A~s** *npl* (SCOL) les lettres *fpl*

artery ['ɑ:tərɪ] *n* artère *f*

art gallery *n* musée *m* d'art; (*small and private*) galerie *f* de peinture

arthritis [ɑ:'θraɪtɪs] *n* arthrite *f*

artichoke ['ɑ:tɪtʃəuk] *n* (*also*: **globe ~**) artichaut *m*; (*also*: **Jerusalem ~**) topinambour *m*

article ['ɑ:tɪkl] *n* article *m*; **~s** *npl* (BRIT: LAW: *training*) ≃ stage *m*; **~ of clothing** vêtement *m*

articulate [*adj* ɑ:'tɪkjulɪt, *vb* ɑ:'tɪkjuleɪt] *adj*

(*person*) qui s'exprime bien; (*speech*) bien articulé(e), prononcé(e) clairement ♦ *vt* exprimer; **~d lorry** (BRIT) *n* (camion *m*) semi-remorque *m*

artificial [ɑ:tɪ'fɪʃəl] *adj* artificiel(le); **~ respiration** *n* respiration artificielle

artist ['ɑ:tɪst] *n* artiste *m/f*; **~ic** [ɑ:'tɪstɪk] *adj* artistique; **~ry** *n* art *m*, talent *m*

art school *n* ≃ école *f* des beaux-arts

KEYWORD

as [æz, əz] *conj* **1** (*referring to time*) comme, alors que; à mesure que; **he came in as I was leaving** il est arrivé comme je partais; **as the years went by** à mesure que les années passaient; **as from tomorrow** à partir de demain

2 (*in comparisons*): **as big as** aussi grand que; **twice as big as** deux fois plus grand que; **as much or many as** autant que; **as much money/many books** autant d'argent/de livres que; **as soon as** dès que

3 (*since, because*) comme, puisque; **as he had to be home by 10 ...** comme il *or* puisqu'il devait être de retour avant 10 h ...

4 (*referring to manner, way*) comme; **do as you wish** faites comme vous voudrez

5 (*concerning*): **as for or to that** quant à cela, pour ce qui est de cela

6: as if or though comme si; **he looked as if he was ill** il avait l'air d'être malade; *see also* **long**; **such**; **well**

♦ *prep*: **he works as a driver** il travaille comme chauffeur; **as chairman of the company, he ...** en tant que président de la société, il ...; **dressed up as a cowboy** déguisé en cowboy; **he gave me it as a present** il me l'a offert, il m'en a fait cadeau

---

a.s.a.p. *abbr* (= *as soon as possible*) dès que possible

asbestos [æz'bɛstəs] *n* amiante *f*

ascend [ə'sɛnd] *vt* gravir; (*throne*) monter sur

ascertain [æsə'teɪn] *vt* vérifier
ash [æʃ] *n* (*dust*) cendre *f*; (*also:* ~ **tree**) frêne *m*
ashamed [ə'ʃeɪmd] *adj* honteux(-euse), confus(e); **to be ~ of** avoir honte de
ashore [ə'ʃɔ:ʳ] *adv* à terre
ashtray ['æʃtreɪ] *n* cendrier *m*
Ash Wednesday *n* mercredi *m* des cendres
Asia ['eɪʃə] *n* Asie *f*; ~**n** *n* Asiatique *m/f* ♦ *adj* asiatique
aside [ə'saɪd] *adv* de côté; à l'écart ♦ *n* aparté *m*
ask [ɑ:sk] *vt* demander; (*invite*) inviter; **to ~ sb sth/to do sth** demander qch à qn/à qn de faire qch; **to ~ sb about sth** questionner qn sur qch; se renseigner auprès de qn sur qch; **to ~ (sb) a question** poser une question (à qn); **to ~ sb out to dinner** inviter qn au restaurant; ~ **after** *vt fus* demander des nouvelles de; ~ **for** *vt fus* demander; (*trouble*) chercher
asking price ['ɑ:skɪŋ-] *n*: **the ~** le prix de départ
asleep [ə'sli:p] *adj* endormi(e); **to fall ~** s'endormir
asparagus [əs'pærəgəs] *n* asperges *fpl*
aspect ['æspɛkt] *n* aspect *m*; (*direction in which a building etc faces*) orientation *f*, exposition *f*
aspire [əs'paɪəʳ] *vi*: **to ~ to** aspirer à
aspirin ['æsprɪn] *n* aspirine *f*
ass [æs] *n* âne *m*; (*inf*) imbécile *m/f*; (*US: inf!*) cul *m* (!)
assailant [ə'seɪlənt] *n* agresseur *m*; assaillant *m*
assassinate [ə'sæsɪneɪt] *vt* assassiner; **assassination** [əsæsɪ'neɪʃən] *n* assassinat *m*
assault [ə'sɔ:lt] *n* (*MIL*) assaut *m*; (*gen: attack*) agression *f* ♦ *vt* attaquer; (*sexually*) violenter
assemble [ə'sɛmbl] *vt* assembler ♦ *vi* s'assembler, se rassembler; **assembly** *n* assemblée *f*, réunion *f*; (*institution*) assemblée; (*construction*) assemblage *m*; **assembly line** *n* chaîne *f* de montage

assent [ə'sɛnt] *n* assentiment *m*, consentement *m*
assert [ə'sɜ:t] *vt* affirmer, déclarer; (*one's authority*) faire valoir; (*one's innocence*) protester de
assess [ə'sɛs] *vt* évaluer; (*tax, payment*) établir *or* fixer le montant de; (*property etc: for tax*) calculer la valeur imposable de; (*person*) juger la valeur de; ~**ment** *n* évaluation *f*, fixation *f*, calcul *m* de la valeur imposable de, jugement *m*; ~**or** *n* expert *m* (*impôt et assurance*)
asset ['æsɛt] *n* avantage *m*, atout *m*; ~**s** *npl* (*FINANCE*) capital *m*; avoir(s) *m(pl)*; actif *m*
assign [ə'saɪn] *vt* (*date*) fixer; (*task*) assigner à; (*resources*) affecter à; ~**ment** *n* tâche *f*, mission *f*
assist [ə'sɪst] *vt* aider, assister; ~**ance** *n* aide *f*, assistance *f*; ~**ant** *n* assistant(e), adjoint(e); (*BRIT: also:* **shop ~ant**) vendeur(-euse)
associate [*n, adj* ə'səʊʃɪɪt, *vb* ə'səʊʃɪeɪt] *adj, n* associé(e) ♦ *vt* associer ♦ *vi*: **to ~ with** fréquenter qn; **association** [əsəʊsɪ'eɪʃən] *n* association *f*
assorted [ə'sɔ:tɪd] *adj* assorti(e)
assortment [ə'sɔ:tmənt] *n* assortiment *m*
assume [ə'sju:m] *vt* supposer; (*responsibilities etc*) assumer; (*attitude, name*) prendre, adopter; **assumption** [ə'sʌmpʃən] *n* supposition *f*, hypothèse *f*; (*of power*) assomption *f*, prise *f*
assurance [ə'ʃʊərəns] *n* assurance *f*
assure [ə'ʃʊəʳ] *vt* assurer
asthma ['æsmə] *n* asthme *m*
astonish [ə'stɒnɪʃ] *vt* étonner, stupéfier; ~**ment** *n* étonnement *m*
astound [ə'staʊnd] *vt* stupéfier, sidérer
astray [ə'streɪ] *adv*: **to go ~** s'égarer; (*fig*) quitter le droit chemin; **to lead ~** détourner du droit chemin
astride [ə'straɪd] *prep* à cheval sur
astrology [əs'trɒlədʒɪ] *n* astrologie *f*
astronaut ['æstrənɔ:t] *n* astronaute *m/f*
astronomy [əs'trɒnəmɪ] *n* astronomie *f*
asylum [ə'saɪləm] *n* asile *m*

KEYWORD

at [æt] *prep* **1** (*referring to position, direction*) à; **at the top** au sommet; **at home/school** à la maison *or* chez soi/à l'école; **at the baker's** à la boulangerie, chez le boulanger; **to look at sth** regarder qch
2 (*referring to time*): **at 4 o'clock** à 4 heures; **at Christmas** à Noël; **at night** la nuit; **at times** par moments, parfois
3 (*referring to rates, speed etc*) à; **at £1 a kilo** une livre le kilo; **two at a time** deux à la fois; **at 50 km/h** à 50 km/h
4 (*referring to manner*): **at a stroke** d'un seul coup; **at peace** en paix
5 (*referring to activity*): **to be at work** être au travail, travailler; **to play at cowboys** jouer aux cowboys; **to be good at sth** être bon en qch
6 (*referring to cause*): **shocked/surprised/annoyed at sth** choqué par/étonné de/agacé par qch; **I went at his suggestion** j'y suis allé sur son conseil

ate [eɪt] *pt of* **eat**
atheist [ˈeɪθɪɪst] *n* athée *m/f*
Athens [ˈæθɪnz] *n* Athènes
athlete [ˈæθliːt] *n* athlète *m/f*; **athletic** [æθˈletɪk] *adj* athlétique; **athletics** *n* athlétisme *m*
Atlantic [ətˈlæntɪk] *adj* atlantique ♦ *n*: **the ~ (Ocean)** l'(océan *m*) Atlantique *m*
atlas [ˈætləs] *n* atlas *m*
ATM *n abbr* (= *automated telling machine*) guichet *m* automatique
atmosphere [ˈætməsfɪər] *n* atmosphère *f*
atom [ˈætəm] *n* atome *m*; **~ic** [əˈtɒmɪk] *adj* atomique; **~(ic) bomb** *n* bombe *f* atomique; **~izer** *n* atomiseur *m*
atone [əˈtəun] *vi*: **to ~ for** expier, racheter
atrocious [əˈtrəuʃəs] *adj* (*very bad*) atroce, exécrable
attach [əˈtætʃ] *vt* attacher; (*document, letter*) joindre; **to be ~ed to sb/sth** être attaché à qn/qch
attaché case [əˈtæʃeɪ] *n* mallette *f*, attaché-case *m*

attachment [əˈtætʃmənt] *n* (*tool*) accessoire *m*; (*love*): **~ (to)** affection *f* (pour), attachement *m* (à)
attack [əˈtæk] *vt* attaquer; (*task etc*) s'attaquer à ♦ *n* attaque *f*; (*also*: **heart ~**) crise *f* cardiaque
attain [əˈteɪn] *vt* (*also*: **to ~ to**) parvenir à, atteindre; (: *knowledge*) acquérir
attempt [əˈtempt] *n* tentative *f* ♦ *vt* essayer, tenter; **to make an ~ on sb's life** attenter à la vie de qn; **~ed** *adj*: **~ed murder/suicide** tentative *f* de meurtre/suicide
attend [əˈtend] *vt* (*course*) suivre; (*meeting, talk*) assister à; (*school, church*) aller à, fréquenter; (*patient*) soigner, s'occuper de; **~ to** *vt fus* (*needs, affairs etc*) s'occuper de; (*customer, patient*) s'occuper de; **~ance** *n* (*being present*) présence *f*; (*people present*) assistance *f*; **~ant** *n* employé(e) ♦ *adj* (*dangers*) inhérent(e), concomitant(e)
attention [əˈtenʃən] *n* attention *f*; **~!** (*MIL*) garde-à-vous!; **for the ~ of** (*ADMIN*) à l'attention de
attentive [əˈtentɪv] *adj* attentif(-ive); (*kind*) prévenant(e)
attest [əˈtest] *vi*: **to ~ to** (*demonstrate*) démontrer; (*confirm*) témoigner
attic [ˈætɪk] *n* grenier *m*
attitude [ˈætɪtjuːd] *n* attitude *f*; pose *f*, maintien *m*
attorney [əˈtəːnɪ] *n* (*US: lawyer*) avoué *m*; **A~ General** *n* (*BRIT*) ≈ procureur général; (*US*) ≈ garde *m* des Sceaux, ministre *m* de la Justice
attract [əˈtrækt] *vt* attirer; **~ion** *n* (*gen pl: pleasant things*) attraction *f*, attrait *m*; (*PHYSICS*) attraction *f*; (*fig: towards sb or sth*) attirance *f*; **~ive** *adj* attrayant(e); (*person*) séduisant(e)
attribute [*n* ˈætrɪbjuːt, *vb* əˈtrɪbjuːt] *n* attribut *m* ♦ *vt*: **to ~ sth to** attribuer qch à
attrition [əˈtrɪʃən] *n*: **war of ~** guerre *f* d'usure
aubergine [ˈəubəʒiːn] *n* aubergine *f*
auction [ˈɔːkʃən] *n* (*also*: **sale by ~**) vente *f* aux enchères ♦ *vt* (*also*: **sell by ~**) ven-

dre aux enchères; (*also:* **put up for** ~) mettre aux enchères; ~**eer** [ɔ:kʃə'nɪər] *n* commissaire-priseur *m*

audience ['ɔ:dɪəns] *n* (*people*) assistance *f*; public *m*; spectateurs *mpl*; (*interview*) audience *f*

audiovisual ['ɔ:dɪəu'vɪzjuəl] *adj* audiovisuel(le); ~ **aids** *npl* supports *or* moyens audiovisuels

audit ['ɔ:dɪt] *vt* vérifier

audition [ɔ:'dɪʃən] *n* audition *f*

auditor ['ɔ:dɪtər] *n* vérificateur *m* des comptes

augur ['ɔ:gər] *vi*: **it ~s well** c'est bon signe *or* de bon augure

August ['ɔ:gəst] *n* août *m*

aunt [ɑ:nt] *n* tante *f*; ~**ie**, ~**y** ['ɑ:ntɪ] *n dimin of* **aunt**

au pair ['əu'pɛər] *n* (*also:* ~ **girl**) jeune fille *f* au pair

auspicious [ɔ:s'pɪʃəs] *adj* de bon augure, propice

Australia [ɔs'treɪlɪə] *n* Australie *f*; ~**n** *adj* australien(ne) ♦ *n* Australien(ne)

Austria ['ɔstrɪə] *n* Autriche *f*; ~**n** *adj* autrichien(ne) ♦ *n* Autrichien(ne)

authentic [ɔ:'θɛntɪk] *adj* authentique

author ['ɔ:θər] *n* auteur *m*

authoritarian [ɔ:θɔrɪ'tɛərɪən] *adj* autoritaire

authoritative [ɔ:'θɔrɪtətɪv] *adj* (*account*) digne de foi; (*study, treatise*) qui fait autorité; (*person, manner*) autoritaire

authority [ɔ:'θɔrɪtɪ] *n* autorité *f*; (*permission*) autorisation (formelle); **the authorities** *npl* (*ruling body*) les autorités *fpl*, l'administration *f*

authorize ['ɔ:θəraɪz] *vt* autoriser

auto ['ɔ:təu] (*US*) *n* auto *f*, voiture *f*

auto: ~**biography** [ɔ:təbaɪ'ɔgrəfɪ] *n* autobiographie *f*; ~**graph** ['ɔ:təgrɑ:f] *n* autographe *m* ♦ *vt* signer, dédicacer; ~**mated** ['ɔ:təmeɪtɪd] *adj* automatisé(e), automatique; ~**matic** [ɔ:tə'mætɪk] *adj* automatique ♦ *n* (*gun*) automatique *m*; (*washing machine*) machine *f* à laver automatique; (*BRIT: AUT*) voiture *f* à transmission auto-

matique; ~**matically** *adv* automatiquement; ~**mation** [ɔ:tə'meɪʃən] *n* automatisation *f* (électronique); ~**mobile** ['ɔ:təməbi:l] (*US*) *n* automobile *f*; ~**nomy** [ɔ:'tɔnəmɪ] *n* autonomie *f*

autumn ['ɔ:təm] *n* automne *m*; **in** ~ en automne

auxiliary [ɔ:g'zɪlɪərɪ] *adj* auxiliaire ♦ *n* auxiliaire *m/f*

avail [ə'veɪl] *vt*: **to ~ o.s. of** profiter de ♦ *n*: **to no** ~ sans résultat, en vain, en pure perte

availability [əveɪlə'bɪlɪtɪ] *n* disponibilité *f*

available [ə'veɪləbl] *adj* disponible

avalanche ['ævəlɑ:nʃ] *n* avalanche *f*

Ave *abbr* = **avenue**

avenge [ə'vɛndʒ] *vt* venger

avenue ['ævənju:] *n* avenue *f*; (*fig*) moyen *m*

average ['ævərɪdʒ] *n* moyenne *f*; (*fig*) moyen *m* ♦ *adj* moyen(ne) ♦ *vt* (*a certain figure*) atteindre *or* faire *etc* en moyenne; **on** ~ en moyenne; ~ **out** *vi*: **to ~ out at** représenter en moyenne, donner une moyenne de

averse [ə'vɜ:s] *adj*: **to be ~ to sth/doing sth** éprouver une forte répugnance envers qch/à faire qch

avert [ə'vɜ:t] *vt* (*danger*) prévenir, écarter; (*one's eyes*) détourner

aviary ['eɪvɪərɪ] *n* volière *f*

avocado [ævə'kɑ:dəu] *n* (*BRIT:* ~ *pear*) avocat *m*

avoid [ə'vɔɪd] *vt* éviter

await [ə'weɪt] *vt* attendre

awake [ə'weɪk] (*pt* **awoke**, *pp* **awoken**) *adj* éveillé(e) ♦ *vt* éveiller ♦ *vi* s'éveiller; ~ **to** (*dangers, possibilities*) conscient(e) de; **to be** ~ être réveillé(e); **he was still** ~ il ne dormait pas encore; ~**ning** *n* réveil *m*

award [ə'wɔ:d] *n* récompense *f*, prix *m*; (*LAW: damages*) dommages-intérêts *mpl* ♦ *vt* (*prize*) décerner; (*LAW: damages*) accorder

aware [ə'wɛər] *adj*: ~ (**of**) (*conscious*) conscient(e) (de); (*informed*) au courant (de); **to become** ~ **of/that** prendre conscience de/que; se rendre compte de/que; **~ness** *n* conscience *f*, connaissance *f*

away [ə'weɪ] *adj, adv* (au) loin; absent(e); **two kilometres ~** à (une distance de) deux kilomètres, à deux kilomètres de distance; **two hours ~ by car** à deux heures de voiture *or* de route; **the holiday was two weeks ~** il restait deux semaines jusqu'aux vacances; **~ from** loin de; **he's ~ for a week** il est parti (pour) une semaine; **to pedal/work/laugh ~** être en train de pédaler/travailler/rire; **to fade ~** (*sound*) s'affaiblir; (*colour*) s'estomper; **to wither ~** (*plant*) se dessécher; **to take ~** emporter; (*subtract*) enlever; **~ game** *n* (*SPORT*) match *m* à l'extérieur

awe [ɔ:] *n* respect mêlé de crainte; **~-inspiring** ['ɔ:ɪnspaɪərɪŋ] *adj* impressionnant(e)

awful ['ɔ:fəl] *adj* affreux(-euse); **an ~ lot (of)** un nombre incroyable (de); **~ly** *adv* (*very*) terriblement, vraiment

awkward ['ɔ:kwəd] *adj* (*clumsy*) gauche, maladroit(e); (*inconvenient*) peu pratique; (*embarrassing*) gênant(e), délicat(e)

awning ['ɔ:nɪŋ] *n* (*of tent*) auvent *m*; (*of shop*) store *m*; (*of hotel etc*) marquise *f*

awoke [ə'wəuk] *pt of* **awake**; **~n** [ə'wəukən] *pp of* **awake**

axe [æks] (*US* **ax**) *n* hache *f* ♦ *vt* (*project etc*) abandonner; (*jobs*) supprimer

axes[1] ['æksɪz] *npl of* **axe**

axes[2] ['æksi:z] *npl of* **axis**

axis ['æksɪs] (*pl* **axes**) *n* axe *m*

axle ['æksl] *n* (*also:* **~-tree**: *AUT*) essieu *m*

ay(e) [aɪ] *excl* (yes) oui

B, b

B [bi:] *n* (*MUS*) si *m*; **~ road** (*BRIT*) route départmentale

B.A. *abbr* = **Bachelor of Arts**

babble ['bæbl] *vi* bredouiller; (*baby, stream*) gazouiller

baby ['beɪbɪ] *n* bébé *m*; (*US: inf: darling*):

come on, ~! viens ma belle/mon gars!; **~ carriage** (*US*) *n* voiture *f* d'enfant; **~ food** *n* aliments *mpl* pour bébé(s); **~-sit** *vi* garder les enfants; **~-sitter** *n* babysitter *m/f*; **~ wipe** *n* lingette *f* (*pour bébé*)

bachelor ['bætʃələ*] *n* célibataire *m*; **B~ of Arts/Science** ≃ licencié(e) ès *or* en lettres/sciences

back [bæk] *n* (*of person, horse, book*) dos *m*; (*of hand*) dos, revers *m*; (*of house*) derrière *m*; (*of car, train*) arrière *m*; (*of chair*) dossier *m*; (*of page*) verso *m*; (*of room, audience*) fond *m*; (*SPORT*) arrière *m* ♦ *vt* (*candidate: also:* **~ up**) soutenir, appuyer; (*horse: at races*) parier *or* miser sur; (*car*) (faire) reculer ♦ *vi* (*also:* **~ up**) reculer; (*also:* **~ up**: *car etc*) faire marche arrière ♦ *adj* (*in compounds*) de derrière, à l'arrière ♦ *adv* (*not forward*) en arrière; (*returned*): **he's ~** il est rentré, il est de retour; (*restitution*): **throw the ball ~** renvoie la balle; (*again*): **he called ~** il a rappelé; **~ seat/wheels** (*AUT*) sièges *mpl*/roues *fpl* arrières; **~ payments/rent** arriéré *m* de paiements/ loyer; **he ran ~** il est revenu en courant; **~ down** *vi* rabattre de ses prétentions; **~ out** *vi* (*of promise*) se dédire; **~ up** *vt* (*candidate etc*) soutenir, appuyer; (*COMPUT*) sauvegarder; **~ache** *n* mal *m* de dos; **~bencher** (*BRIT*) *n* membre du parlement sans portefeuille; **~bone** *n* colonne vertébrale, épine dorsale; **~date** *vt* (*letter*) antidater; **~dated pay rise** augmentation *f* avec effet rétroactif; **~fire** *vi* (*AUT*) pétarader; (*plans*) mal tourner; **~ground** *n* arrière-plan *m*; (*of events*) situation *f*, conjoncture *f*; (*basic knowledge*) éléments *mpl* de base; (*experience*) formation *f*; **family ~ground** milieu familial; **~hand** *n* (*TENNIS: also:* **~hand stroke**) revers *m*; **~hander** (*BRIT*) *n* (*bribe*) pot-de-vin *m*; **~ing** *n* (*fig*) soutien *m*, appui *m*; **~lash** *n* contre-coup *m*, répercussion *f*; **~log** *n*: **~log of work** travail *m* en retard; **~ number** *n* (*of magazine etc*) vieux numéro; **~pack** *n* sac *m* à dos; **~packer** *n* randonneur(-euse); **~ pain** *n* mal *m* de dos; **~ pay** *n* rappel *m* de salaire; **~side** (*inf*) *n* derrière *m*, postérieur *m*; **~stage** *adv* ♦ *n* derrière la scène, dans la coulisse; **~stroke** *n* dos crawlé; **~up** *adj* (*train, plane*) supplémentaire, de réserve; (COM-PUT) de sauvegarde ♦ *n* (*support*) appui *m*, soutien *m*; (*also*: **~up disk/file**) sauvegar-de *f*; **~ward** *adj* (*movement*) en arrière; (*person, country*) arriéré(e); attardé(e); **~wards** *adv* (*move, go*) en arrière; (*read a list*) à l'envers, à rebours; (*fall*) à la renver-se; (*walk*) à reculons; **~water** *n* (*fig*) coin reculé; bled perdu (*péj*); **~yard** *n* arrière-cour *f*

bacon ['beɪkən] *n* bacon *m*, lard *m*

bacteria [bæk'tɪərɪə] *npl* bactéries *fpl*

bad [bæd] *adj* mauvais(e); (*child*) vilain(e); (*mistake, accident etc*) grave; (*meat, food*) gâté(e), avarié(e); **his ~ leg** sa jambe ma-lade; **to go ~** (*meat, food*) se gâter

badge [bædʒ] *n* insigne *m*; (*of policeman*) plaque *f*

badger ['bædʒər] *n* blaireau *m*

badly ['bædlɪ] *adv* (*work, dress etc*) mal; **~ wounded** grièvement blessé; **he needs it ~** il en a absolument besoin; **~ off** *adj, adv* dans la gêne

badminton ['bædmɪntən] *n* badminton *m*

bad-tempered ['bæd'tempəd] *adj* (*person: by nature*) ayant mauvais caractère; (: *on one occasion*) de mauvaise humeur

baffle ['bæfl] *vt* (*puzzle*) déconcerter

bag [bæg] *n* sac *m* ♦ *vt* (*inf: take*) empo-cher; s'approprier; **~s of** (*inf: lots of*) des masses de; **~gage** *n* bagages *mpl*; **~gage allowance** *n* franchise *f* de baga-ges; **~gage reclaim** *n* livraison *f* de ba-gages; **~gy** *adj* avachi(e), qui fait des po-ches; **~pipes** *npl* cornemuse *f*

bail [beɪl] *n* (*payment*) caution *f*; (*release*) mise *f* en liberté sous caution ♦ *vt* (*pris-oner: also:* **grant ~ to**) mettre en liberté sous caution; (*boat: also:* **~ out**) écoper; **on ~** (*prisoner*) sous caution; *see also* **bale**; **~ out** *vt* (*prisoner*) payer la caution de

bailiff ['beɪlɪf] *n* (BRIT) ≃ huissier *m*; (US) ≃ huissier-audiencier *m*

bait [beɪt] *n* appât *m* ♦ *vt* appâter; (*fig: tease*) tourmenter

bake [beɪk] *vt* (faire) cuire au four ♦ *vi* (*bread etc*) cuire (au four); (*make cakes etc*) faire de la pâtisserie; **~d beans** *npl* hari-cots blancs à la sauce tomate; **~d potato** *n* pomme *f* de terre en robe des champs; **~r** *n* boulanger *m*; **~ry** *n* boulangerie *f*; boulangerie industrielle; **baking** *n* cuisson *f*; **baking powder** *n* levure *f* (chimique)

balance ['bæləns] *n* équilibre *m*; (COMM: *sum*) solde *m*; (*remainder*) reste *m*; (*scales*) balance *f* ♦ *vt* mettre ou faire tenir en équilibre; (*pros and cons*) peser; (*budget*) équilibrer; (*account*) balancer; **~ of trade/ payments** balance commerciale/des comptes *or* paiements; **~d** *adj* (*personality, diet*) équilibré(e); (*report*) objectif(-ive); **~ sheet** *n* bilan *m*

balcony ['bælkənɪ] *n* balcon *m*; (*in theatre*) deuxième balcon

bald [bɔːld] *adj* chauve; (*tyre*) lisse

bale [beɪl] *n* balle *f*, ballot *m*; **~ out** *vi* (*of a plane*) sauter en parachute

ball [bɔːl] *n* boule *f*; (*football*) ballon *m*; (*for tennis, golf*) balle *f*; (*of wool*) pelote *f*; (*of string*) bobine *f*; (*dance*) bal *m*; **to play ~ (with sb)** (*fig*) coopérer (avec qn)

ballast ['bæləst] *n* lest *m*

ball bearings *npl* roulement *m* à billes

ballerina [bælə'riːnə] *n* ballerine *f*

ballet ['bæleɪ] *n* ballet *m*; (*art*) danse *f* (classique); **~ dancer** *n* danseur(-euse) *m/f* de ballet; **~ shoe** *n* chausson *m* de danse

balloon [bə'luːn] *n* ballon *m*; (*in comic strip*) bulle *f*

ballot ['bælət] *n* scrutin *m*; **~ paper** *n* bul-letin *m* de vote

ballpoint (pen) ['bɔːlpɔɪnt(-)] *n* stylo *m* à bille

ballroom ['bɔːlrum] *n* salle *f* de bal

ban [bæn] *n* interdiction *f* ♦ *vt* interdire

banana [bə'nɑːnə] *n* banane *f*

band [bænd] *n* bande *f*; (*at a dance*) or-chestre *m*; (MIL) musique *f*, fanfare *f*; **~**

together *vi* se liguer

bandage ['bændɪdʒ] *n* bandage *m*, pansement *m* ♦ *vt* bander

Bandaid ® ['bændeɪd] (*US*) *n* pansement adhésif

bandit *n* bandit *m*

bandy-legged ['bændɪˈlɛgɪd] *adj* aux jambes arquées

bang [bæŋ] *n* détonation *f*; (*of door*) claquement *m*; (*blow*) coup (violent) ♦ *vt* frapper (violemment); (*door*) claquer ♦ *vi* détoner; claquer ♦ *excl* pan!; ~s (*US*) *npl* (*fringe*) frange *f*

banish ['bænɪʃ] *vt* bannir

banister(s) ['bænɪstə(z)] *n(pl)* rampe *f* (d'escalier)

bank [bæŋk] *n* banque *f*; (*of river, lake*) bord *m*, rive *f*; (*of earth*) talus *m*, remblai *m* ♦ *vi* (*AVIAT*) virer sur l'aile; ~ **on** *vt fus* miser *or* tabler sur; ~ **account** *n* compte *m* en banque; ~ **card** *n* carte *f* d'identité bancaire; ~**er** *n* banquier *m*; ~**er's card** (*BRIT*) *n* = **bank card**; ~ **holiday** (*BRIT*) *n* jour férié (*les banques sont fermées*); ~**ing** *n* opérations *fpl* bancaires; profession *f* de banquier; ~**note** *n* billet *m* de banque; ~ **rate** *n* taux *m* de l'escompte

---

bank holiday

i Un **bank holiday** en Grande-Bretagne est un lundi férié et donc l'occasion d'un week-end prolongé. La circulation sur les routes et le trafic dans les gares et les aéroports augmentent considérablement à ces périodes. Les principaux bank holidays, à part Pâques et Noël, ont lieu au mois de mai et fin août.

---

bankrupt ['bæŋkrʌpt] *adj* en faillite; **to go** ~ faire faillite; ~**cy** *n* faillite *f*

bank statement *n* relevé *m* de compte

banner ['bænə'] *n* bannière *f*

bannister(s) ['bænɪstə(z)] *n(pl)* = **banister(s)**

baptism ['bæptɪzəm] *n* baptême *m*

bar [bɑː'] *n* (*pub*) bar *m*; (*counter: in pub*) comptoir *m*, bar; (*rod: of metal etc*) barre *f*; (*on window etc*) barreau *m*; (*of chocolate*) tablette *f*, plaque *f*; (*fig*) obstacle *m*; (*prohibition*) mesure *f* d'exclusion; (*MUS*) mesure *f* ♦ *vt* (*road*) barrer; (*window*) munir de barreaux; (*person*) exclure; (*activity*) interdire; ~ **of soap** savonnette *f*; **the B~** (*LAW*) le barreau; **behind ~s** (*prisoner*) sous les verrous; ~ **none** sans exception

barbaric [bɑːˈbærɪk] *adj* barbare

barbecue ['bɑːbɪkjuː] *n* barbecue *m*

barbed wire ['bɑːbd-] *n* fil *m* de fer barbelé

barber ['bɑːbə'] *n* coiffeur *m* (pour hommes)

bar code *n* (*on goods*) code *m* à barres

bare [bɛə'] *adj* nu(e) ♦ *vt* mettre à nu, dénuder; (*teeth*) montrer; **the ~ necessities** le strict nécessaire; ~**back** *adv* à cru, sans selle; ~**faced** *adj* impudent(e), effronté(e); ~**foot** *adj, adv* nu-pieds, (les) pieds nus; ~**ly** *adv* à peine

bargain ['bɑːgɪn] *n* (*transaction*) marché *m*; (*good buy*) affaire *f*, occasion *f* ♦ *vi* (*haggle*) marchander; (*negotiate*): **to ~ (with sb)** négocier (avec qn), traiter (avec qn); **into the ~** par-dessus le marché; ~ **for** *vt fus*: **he got more than he ~ed for** il ne s'attendait pas à un coup pareil

barge [bɑːdʒ] *n* péniche *f*; ~ **in** *vi* (*walk in*) faire irruption; (*interrupt talk*) intervenir mal à propos

bark [bɑːk] *n* (*of tree*) écorce *f*; (*of dog*) aboiement *m* ♦ *vi* aboyer

barley ['bɑːlɪ] *n* orge *f*; ~ **sugar** *n* sucre *m* d'orge

bar: ~**maid** *n* serveuse *f* de bar, barmaid *f*; ~**man** (*irreg*) *n* barman *m*; ~ **meal** *n* repas *m* de bistrot; **to go for a ~ meal** aller manger au bistrot

barn [bɑːn] *n* grange *f*

barometer [bəˈrɒmɪtə'] *n* baromètre *m*

baron ['bærən] *n* baron *m*; ~**ess** ['bærənɪs] *n* baronne *f*

barracks ['bærəks] *npl* caserne *f*

barrage ['bærɑːʒ] *n* (*MIL*) tir *m* de barrage; (*dam*) barrage *m*; (*fig*) pluie *f*

barrel ['bærəl] *n* tonneau *m*; (*of oil*) baril

m; (*of gun*) canon *m*

barren ['bærən] *adj* stérile

barricade [,bærɪ'keɪd] *n* barricade *f*

barrier ['bærɪəʳ] *n* barrière *f*; (*fig: to progress etc*) obstacle *m*

barring ['bɑːrɪŋ] *prep* sauf

barrister ['bærɪstəʳ] (*BRIT*) *n* avocat (plaidant)

barrow ['bærəu] *n* (*wheelbarrow*) charrette *f* à bras

bartender ['bɑːtendəʳ] (*US*) *n* barman *m*

barter ['bɑːtəʳ] *vt*: **to ~ sth for** échanger qch contre

base [beɪs] *n* base *f*; (*of tree, post*) pied *m* ♦ *vt*: **to ~ sth on** baser *or* fonder qch sur ♦ *adj* vil(e), bas(se)

baseball ['beɪsbɔːl] *n* base-ball *m*

basement ['beɪsmənt] *n* sous-sol *m*

bases[1] ['beɪsɪz] *npl of* **base**

bases[2] ['beɪsiːz] *npl of* **basis**

bash [bæʃ] (*inf*) *vt* frapper, cogner

bashful ['bæʃful] *adj* timide; modeste

basic ['beɪsɪk] *adj* fondamental(e), de base; (*minimal*) rudimentaire; **~ally** *adv* fondamentalement, à la base; (*in fact*) en fait, au fond; **~s** *npl*: **the ~s** l'essentiel *m*

basil ['bæzl] *n* basilic *m*

basin ['beɪsn] *n* (*vessel, also GEO*) cuvette *f*, bassin *m*; (*also*: **washbasin**) lavabo *m*

basis ['beɪsɪs] (*pl* **bases**) *n* base *f*; **on a trial ~** à titre d'essai; **on a part-time ~** à temps partiel

bask [bɑːsk] *vi*: **to ~ in the sun** se chauffer au soleil

basket ['bɑːskɪt] *n* corbeille *f*; (*with handle*) panier *m*; **~ball** *n* basket-ball *m*

bass [beɪs] *n* (*MUS*) basse *f*; **~ drum** *n* grosse caisse *f*

bassoon [bə'suːn] *n* (*MUS*) basson *m*

bastard ['bɑːstəd] *n* enfant naturel(le), bâtard(e); (*inf!*) salaud *m* (!)

bat [bæt] *n* chauve-souris *f*; (*for baseball etc*) batte *f*; (*BRIT: for table tennis*) raquette *f* ♦ *vt*: **he didn't ~ an eyelid** il n'a pas sourcillé *or* bronché

batch [bætʃ] *n* (*of bread*) fournée *f*; (*of papers*) liasse *f*

bated ['beɪtɪd] *adj*: **with ~ breath** en retenant son souffle

bath [bɑːθ] *n* bain *m*; (*~tub*) baignoire *f* ♦ *vt* baigner, donner un bain à; **to have a ~** prendre un bain; *see also* **baths**

bathe [beɪð] *vi* se baigner ♦ *vt* (*wound*) laver; **bathing** *n* baignade *f*; **bathing costume**, **bathing suit** (*US*) *n* maillot *m* (de bain)

bath: **~robe** *n* peignoir *m* de bain; **~room** *n* salle *f* de bains; **~s** *npl* (*also*: **swimming ~s**) piscine *f*; **~ towel** *n* serviette *f* de bain

baton ['bætən] *n* bâton *m*; (*MUS*) baguette *f*; (*club*) matraque *f*

batter ['bætəʳ] *vt* battre ♦ *n* pâte *f* à frire; **~ed** ['bætəd] *adj* (*hat, pan*) cabossé(e)

battery ['bætərɪ] *n* batterie *f*; (*of torch*) pile *f*; **~ farming** *n* élevage *m* en batterie

battle ['bætl] *n* bataille *f*, combat *m* ♦ *vi* se battre, lutter; **~field** *n* champ *m* de bataille; **~ship** *n* cuirassé *m*

Bavaria [bə'vɛərɪə] *n* Bavière *f*

bawl [bɔːl] *vi* hurler; (*child*) brailler

bay [beɪ] *n* (*of sea*) baie *f*; **to hold sb at ~** tenir qn à distance *or* en échec; **~ leaf** *n* laurier *m*; **~ window** *n* baie vitrée

bazaar [bə'zɑːʳ] *n* bazar *m*; vente *f* de charité

B & B *n abbr* = **bed and breakfast**

BBC *n abbr* (= *British Broadcasting Corporation*) *office de la radiodiffusion et télévision britannique*

B.C. *adv abbr* (= *before Christ*) av. J.-C.

KEYWORD
---

be [biː] (*pt* **was**, **were**, *pp* **been**) *aux vb* **1** (*with present participle: forming continuous tenses*): **what are you doing?** que faites-vous?; **they're coming tomorrow** ils viennent demain; **I've been waiting for you for 2 hours** je t'attends depuis 2 heures

2 (*with pp: forming passives*) être; **to be killed** être tué(e); **he was nowhere to be seen** on ne le voyait nulle part

3 (*in tag questions*): **it was fun, wasn't it?** c'était drôle, n'est-ce pas?; **she's back, is**

she? elle est rentrée, n'est-ce pas *or* alors?

4 (*+to +infinitive*): **the house is to be sold** la maison doit être vendue; **he's not to open it** il ne doit pas l'ouvrir

♦ *vb + complement* **1** (*gen*) être; **I'm English** je suis anglais(e); **I'm tired** je suis fatigué(e); **I'm hot/cold** j'ai chaud/froid; **he's a doctor** il est médecin; **2 and 2 are 4** 2 et 2 font 4

2 (*of health*) aller; **how are you?** comment allez-vous?; **he's fine now** il va bien maintenant; **he's very ill** il est très malade

3 (*of age*) avoir; **how old are you?** quel âge avez-vous?; **I'm sixteen (years old)** j'ai seize ans

4 (*cost*) coûter; **how much was the meal?** combien a coûté le repas?; **that'll be £5, please** ça fera 5 livres, s'il vous plaît

♦ *vi* **1** (*exist, occur etc*) être, exister; **the prettiest girl that ever was** la fille la plus jolie qui ait jamais existé; **be that as it may** quoi qu'il en soit; **so be it** soit

2 (*referring to place*) être, se trouver; **I won't be here tomorrow** je ne serai pas là demain; **Edinburgh is in Scotland** Édimbourg est *or* se trouve en Écosse

3 (*referring to movement*) aller; **where have you been?** où êtes-vous allé(s)?

♦ *impers vb* **1** (*referring to time, distance*) être; **it's 5 o'clock** il est 5 heures; **it's the 28th of April** c'est le 28 avril; **it's 10 km to the village** le village est à 10 km

2 (*referring to the weather*) faire; **it's too hot/cold** il fait trop chaud/froid; **it's windy** il y a du vent

3 (*emphatic*): **it's me/the postman** c'est moi/le facteur

beach [biːtʃ] *n* plage *f* ♦ *vt* échouer
beacon ['biːkən] *n* (*lighthouse*) fanal *m*; (*marker*) balise *f*
bead [biːd] *n* perle *f*
beak [biːk] *n* bec *m*
beaker ['biːkər] *n* gobelet *m*

beam [biːm] *n* poutre *f*; (*of light*) rayon *m* ♦ *vi* rayonner
bean [biːn] *n* haricot *m*; (*of coffee*) grain *m*; **runner ~** haricot *m* (à rames); **broad ~** fève *f*; **~sprouts** *npl* germes *mpl* de soja
bear [bɛər] (*pt bore, pp borne*) *n* ours *m* ♦ *vt* porter; (*endure*) supporter ♦ *vi*: **to ~ right/left** obliquer à droite/gauche, se diriger vers la droite/gauche; **~ out** *vt* corroborer, confirmer; **~ up** *vi* (*person*) tenir le coup
beard [biəd] *n* barbe *f*; **~ed** *adj* barbu(e)
bearer ['bɛərər] *n* porteur *m*; (*of passport*) titulaire *m/f*
bearing ['bɛərɪŋ] *n* maintien *m*, allure *f*; (*connection*) rapport *m*; **~s** *npl* (*also:* **ball ~s**) roulement *m* (à billes); **to take a ~** faire le point
beast [biːst] *n* bête *f*; (*inf: person*) brute *f*; **~ly** *adj* infect(e)
beat [biːt] (*pt beat, pp beaten*) *n* battement *m*; (*MUS*) temps *m*, mesure *f*; (*of policeman*) ronde *f* ♦ *vt, vi* battre; **off the ~en track** hors des chemins *or* sentiers battus; **~ it!** (*inf*) fiche(-moi) le camp!; **~ off** *vt* repousser; **~ up** *vt* (*inf: person*) tabasser; (*eggs*) battre; **~ing** *n* raclée *f*
beautiful ['bjuːtɪful] *adj* beau (belle); **~ly** *adv* admirablement
beauty ['bjuːtɪ] *n* beauté *f*; **~ salon** *n* institut *m* de beauté; **~ spot** (*BRIT*) *n* (*TOURISM*) site naturel (d'une grande beauté)
beaver ['biːvər] *n* castor *m*
because [bɪˈkɔz] *conj* parce que; **~ of** *prep* à cause de
beck [bɛk] *n*: **to be at sb's ~ and call** être à l'entière disposition de qn
beckon ['bɛkən] *vt* (*also:* **~ to**) faire signe (de venir) à
become [bɪˈkʌm] (*irreg: like come*) *vi* devenir; **to ~ fat/thin** grossir/maigrir; **becoming** *adj* (*behaviour*) convenable, bienséant(e); (*clothes*) seyant(e)
bed [bɛd] *n* lit *m*; (*of flowers*) parterre *m*; (*of coal, clay*) couche *f*; (*of sea*) fond *m*; **to go to ~** aller se coucher; **~ and breakfast** *n* (*terms*) chambre et petit déjeuner;

(*place*) ≈ chambre f d'hôte; ~**clothes** npl couvertures fpl et draps mpl; ~**ding** n literie f; ~ **linen** n draps mpl de lit (et taies fpl d'oreillers), literie f

---
bed and breakfast
---

i *Un* **bed and breakfast** *est une petite pension dans une maison particulière ou une ferme où l'on peut louer une chambre avec petit déjeuner compris pour un prix modique par rapport à ce que l'on paierait dans un hôtel. Ces établissements sont communément appelés B & B, et sont signalés par une pancarte dans le jardin ou au-dessus de la porte.*

bedraggled [bɪˈdrægld] adj (*person, clothes*) débraillé(e); (*hair: wet*) trempé(e)
bed: ~**ridden** adj cloué(e) au lit; ~**room** n chambre f (à coucher); ~**side** n: **at sb's** ~**side** au chevet de qn; ~**sit(ter)** n (*BRIT*) chambre meublée, studio m; ~**spread** n couvre-lit m, dessus-de-lit m inv; ~**time** n heure f du coucher
bee [biː] n abeille f
beech [biːtʃ] n hêtre m
beef [biːf] n bœuf m; **roast** ~ rosbif m; ~**burger** n hamburger m; ~**eater** n hallebardier de la Tour de Londres
bee: ~**hive** n ruche f; ~**line** n: **to make a** ~**line for** se diriger tout droit vers
been [biːn] pp of **be**
beer [bɪəʳ] n bière f
beet [biːt] n (*vegetable*) betterave f; (*US: also:* **red** ~) betterave (potagère)
beetle [ˈbiːtl] n scarabée m
beetroot [ˈbiːtruːt] n (*BRIT*) n betterave f
before [bɪˈfɔːʳ] prep (*in time*) avant; (*in space*) devant ♦ conj avant que +sub; avant de ♦ adv avant; devant; ~ **going** avant de partir; ~ **she goes** avant qu'elle ne parte; **the week** ~ la semaine précédente or d'avant; **I've seen it** ~ je l'ai déjà vu; ~**hand** adv au préalable, à l'avance
beg [bɛg] vi mendier ♦ vt mendier; (*forgiveness, mercy etc*) demander; (*entreat*) supplier; *see also* **pardon**

began [bɪˈgæn] pt of **begin**
beggar [ˈbɛgəʳ] n mendiant(e)
begin [bɪˈgɪn] (pt **began**, pp **begun**) vt, vi commencer; **to** ~ **doing** or **to do sth** commencer à or de faire qch; ~**ner** n débutant(e); ~**ning** n commencement m, début m
behalf [bɪˈhɑːf] n: **on** ~ **of**, (*US*) **in** ~ **of** (*representing*) de la part de; (*for benefit of*) pour le compte de; **on my/his** ~ pour moi/lui
behave [bɪˈheɪv] vi se conduire, se comporter; (*well: also:* ~ **o.s.**) se conduire bien or comme il faut; **behaviour** (*US* **behavior**) [bɪˈheɪvjəʳ] n comportement m, conduite f
behead [bɪˈhɛd] vt décapiter
behind [bɪˈhaɪnd] prep derrière; (*time, progress*) en retard sur; (*work, studies*) en retard dans ♦ adv derrière ♦ n derrière m; **to be** ~ (**schedule**) avoir du retard; ~ **the scenes** dans les coulisses
behold [bɪˈhəʊld] (*irreg: like* **hold**) vt apercevoir, voir
beige [beɪʒ] adj beige
Beijing [ˈbeɪˈdʒɪŋ] n Bei-jing, Pékin
being [ˈbiːɪŋ] n être m
Beirut [beɪˈruːt] n Beyrouth
Belarus [bɛləˈrus] n Bélarus f
belated [bɪˈleɪtɪd] adj tardif(-ive)
belch [bɛltʃ] vi avoir un renvoi, roter ♦ vt (*also:* ~ **out**: *smoke etc*) vomir, cracher
Belgian [ˈbɛldʒən] adj belge, de Belgique ♦ n Belge m/f
Belgium [ˈbɛldʒəm] n Belgique f
belie [bɪˈlaɪ] vt démentir
belief [bɪˈliːf] n (*opinion*) conviction f; (*trust, faith*) foi f
believe [bɪˈliːv] vt, vi croire; **to** ~ **in** (*God*) croire en; (*method, ghosts*) croire à; ~**r** n (*in idea, activity*): ~**r in** partisan(e) de; (*REL*) croyant(e)
belittle [bɪˈlɪtl] vt déprécier, rabaisser
bell [bɛl] n cloche f; (*small*) clochette f, grelot m; (*on door*) sonnette f; (*electric*) sonnerie f
belligerent [bɪˈlɪdʒərənt] adj (*person, atti-*

tude) agressif(-ive)

bellow ['bɛləʊ] *vi* (*bull*) meugler; (*person*) brailler

belly ['bɛlɪ] *n* ventre *m*

belong [bɪ'lɒŋ] *vi*: **to ~ to** appartenir à; (*club etc*) faire partie de; **this book ~s here** ce livre va ici; **~ings** *npl* affaires *fpl*, possessions *fpl*

beloved [bɪ'lʌvɪd] *adj* (bien-)aimé(e)

below [bɪ'ləʊ] *prep* sous, au-dessous de ♦ *adv* en dessous; **see ~** voir plus bas *or* plus loin *or* ci-dessous

belt [bɛlt] *n* ceinture *f*; (*of land*) région *f*; (*TECH*) courroie *f* ♦ *vt* (*thrash*) donner une raclée à; **~way** (*US*) *n* (*AUT*) route *f* de ceinture; (: *motorway*) périphérique *m*

bemused [bɪ'mjuːzd] *adj* stupéfié(e)

bench [bɛntʃ] *n* (*gen, also BRIT: POL*) banc *m*; (*in workshop*) établi *m*; **the B~** (*LAW: judge*) le juge; (: *judges collectively*) la magistrature, la Cour

bend [bɛnd] (*pt, pp* **bent**) *vt* courber; (*leg, arm*) plier ♦ *vi* se courber ♦ *n* (*BRIT: in road*) virage *m*, tournant *m*; (*in pipe, river*) coude *m*; **~ down** *vi* se baisser; **~ over** *vi* se pencher

beneath [bɪ'niːθ] *prep* sous, au-dessous de; (*unworthy of*) indigne de ♦ *adv* dessous, au-dessous, en bas

benefactor ['bɛnɪfæktə'] *n* bienfaiteur *m*

beneficial [bɛnɪ'fɪʃəl] *adj* salutaire; avantageux(-euse); **~ to the health** bon(ne) pour la santé

benefit ['bɛnɪfɪt] *n* avantage *m*, profit *m*; (*allowance of money*) allocation *f* ♦ *vt* faire du bien à, profiter à ♦ *vi*: **he'll ~ from it** cela lui fera du bien, il y gagnera *or* s'en trouvera bien

Benelux ['bɛnɪlʌks] *n* Bénélux *m*

benevolent [bɪ'nɛvələnt] *adj* bienveillant(e); (*organization*) bénévole

benign [bɪ'naɪn] *adj* (*person, smile*) bienveillant(e), affable; (*MED*) bénin(-igne)

bent [bɛnt] *pt, pp of* **bend** ♦ *n* inclination *f*, penchant *m*; **to be ~ on** être résolu(e) à

bequest [bɪ'kwɛst] *n* legs *m*

bereaved [bɪ'riːvd] *n*: **the ~** la famille du disparu

beret ['bɛreɪ] *n* béret *m*

Berlin [bəː'lɪn] *n* Berlin

berm [bəːm] (*US*) *n* (*AUT*) accotement *m*

Bermuda [bəː'mjuːdə] *n* Bermudes *fpl*

berry ['bɛrɪ] *n* baie *f*

berserk [bə'səːk] *adj*: **to go ~** (*madman, crowd*) se déchaîner

berth [bəːθ] *n* (*bed*) couchette *f*; (*for ship*) poste *m* d'amarrage, mouillage *m* ♦ *vi* (*in harbour*) venir à quai; (*at anchor*) mouiller

beseech [bɪ'siːtʃ] (*pt, pp* **besought**) *vt* implorer, supplier

beset [bɪ'sɛt] (*pt, pp* **beset**) *vt* assaillir

beside [bɪ'saɪd] *prep* à côté de; **to be ~ o.s. (with anger)** être hors de soi; **that's ~ the point** cela n'a rien à voir; **~s** *adv* en outre, de plus; (*in any case*) d'ailleurs ♦ *prep* (*as well as*) en plus de

besiege [bɪ'siːdʒ] *vt* (*town*) assiéger; (*fig*) assaillir

best [bɛst] *adj* meilleur(e) ♦ *adv* le mieux; **the ~ part of** (*quantity*) le plus clair de, la plus grande partie de; **at ~** au mieux; **to make the ~ of sth** s'accommoder de qch (du mieux que l'on peut); **to do one's ~** faire de son mieux; **to the ~ of my knowledge** pour autant que je sache; **to the ~ of my ability** du mieux que je pourrai; **~ before date** *n* date *f* de limite d'utilisation *or* de consommation; **~ man** *n* garçon *m* d'honneur

bestow [bɪ'stəʊ] *vt*: **to ~ sth on sb** accorder qch à qn; (*title*) conférer qch à qn

bet [bɛt] (*pt, pp* **bet** *or* **betted**) *n* pari *m* ♦ *vt, vi* parier

betray [bɪ'treɪ] *vt* trahir

better ['bɛtə'] *adj* meilleur(e) ♦ *adv* mieux ♦ *vt* améliorer ♦ *n*: **to get the ~ of** triompher de, l'emporter sur; **you had ~ do it** vous feriez mieux de le faire; **he thought ~ of it** il s'est ravisé; **to get ~** aller mieux; s'améliorer; **~ off** *adj* plus à l'aise financièrement; (*fig*): **you'd be ~ off this way** vous vous en trouveriez mieux ainsi

betting ['bɛtɪŋ] *n* paris *mpl*; **~ shop** (*BRIT*) *n* bureau *m* de paris

between [bɪ'twiːn] *prep* entre ♦ *adv*: **(in)** ~ au milieu; dans l'intervalle; (*in time*) dans l'intervalle

beverage ['bεvərɪdʒ] *n* boisson *f* (*gén sans alcool*)

beware [bɪ'wεəʳ] *vi*: **to ~ (of)** prendre garde (à); **"~ of the dog"** "(attention) chien méchant"

bewildered [bɪ'wɪldəd] *adj* dérouté(e), ahuri(e)

beyond [bɪ'jɔnd] *prep* (*in space, time*) audelà de; (*exceeding*) au-dessus de ♦ *adv* au-delà; ~ **doubt** hors de doute; ~ **repair** irréparable

bias ['baɪəs] *n* (*prejudice*) préjugé *m*, parti pris; ~**(s)ed** *adj* partial(e), montrant un parti pris

bib [bɪb] *n* bavoir *m*, bavette *f*

Bible ['baɪbl] *n* Bible *f*

bicarbonate of soda [baɪ'kɑːbənɪt-] *n* bicarbonate *m* de soude

bicker ['bɪkəʳ] *vi* se chamailler

bicycle ['baɪsɪkl] *n* bicyclette *f*

bid [bɪd] (*pt* **bid** *or* **bade**, *pp* **bid(den)**) *n* offre *f*; (*at auction*) enchère *f*; (*attempt*) tentative *f* ♦ *vi* faire une enchère *or* offre ♦ *vt* faire une enchère *or* offre de; **to ~ sb good day** souhaiter le bonjour à qn; ~**der** *n*: **the highest ~der** le plus offrant; ~**ding** *n* enchères *fpl*

bide [baɪd] *vt*: **to ~ one's time** attendre son heure

bifocals [baɪ'fəʊklz] *npl* verres *mpl* à double foyer, lunettes bifocales

big [bɪg] *adj* grand(e); gros(se); ~**headed** *adj* prétentieux(-euse)

bigot ['bɪgət] *n* fanatique *m/f*, sectaire *m/f*; ~**ed** *adj* fanatique, sectaire; ~**ry** *n* fanatisme *m*, sectarisme *m*

big top *n* grand chapiteau

bike [baɪk] *n* vélo *m*, bécane *f*

bikini [bɪ'kiːnɪ] *n* bikini *m*

bilingual [baɪ'lɪŋgwəl] *adj* bilingue

bill [bɪl] *n* note *f*, facture *f*; (*POL*) projet *m* de loi; (*US: banknote*) billet *m* (de banque); (*of bird*) bec *m*; (*THEATRE*): **on the ~** à l'affiche; **"post no ~s"** "défense d'affi-cher"; **to fit** *or* **fill the ~** (*fig*) faire l'affai-re; ~**board** *n* panneau *m* d'affichage

billet ['bɪlɪt] *n* cantonnement *m* (chez l'ha-bitant)

billfold ['bɪlfəʊld] (*US*) *n* portefeuille *m*

billiards ['bɪljədz] *n* (jeu *m* de) billard *m*

billion ['bɪljən] *n* (*BRIT*) billion *m* (*million de millions*); (*US*) milliard *m*

bimbo ['bɪmbəʊ] (*inf*) *n* ravissante idiote *f*, potiche *f*

bin [bɪn] *n* boîte *f*; (*also*: **dustbin**) poubelle *f*; (*for coal*) coffre *m*

bind [baɪnd] (*pt, pp* **bound**) *vt* attacher; (*book*) relier; (*oblige*) obliger, contraindre ♦ *n* (*inf: nuisance*) scie *f*; ~**ing** *adj* (*contract*) constituant une obligation

binge [bɪndʒ] (*inf*) *n*: **to go on a/the ~** al-ler faire la bringue

bingo ['bɪŋgəʊ] *n* jeu de loto pratiqué dans des établissements publics

binoculars [bɪ'nɔkjuləz] *npl* jumelles *fpl*

bio *prefix*: ~**chemistry** *n* biochimie *f*; ~**degradable** *adj* biodégradable; ~**gra-phy** *n* biographie *f*; ~**logical** *adj* biologi-que; ~**logy** *n* biologie *f*

birch [bəːtʃ] *n* bouleau *m*

bird [bəːd] *n* oiseau *m*; (*BRIT: inf: girl*) nana *f*; ~**'s-eye view** *n* vue *f* à vol d'oiseau; (*fig*) vue d'ensemble *or* générale; ~**watcher** *n* ornithologue *m/f* amateur

Biro ['baɪərəʊ] ® *n* stylo *m* à bille

birth [bəːθ] *n* naissance *f*; **to give ~ to** (*subj: woman*) donner naissance à; (*: ani-mal*) mettre bas; ~ **certificate** *n* acte *m* de naissance; ~ **control** *n* (*policy*) limita-tion *f* des naissances; (*method*) métho-de(s) contraceptive(s); ~**day** *n* anniversai-re *m* ♦ *cpd* d'anniversaire; ~**place** *n* lieu *m* de naissance; (*fig*) berceau *m*; ~ **rate** *n* (taux *m* de) natalité *f*

biscuit ['bɪskɪt] *n* (*BRIT*) biscuit *m*; (*US*) petit pain au lait

bisect [baɪ'sεkt] *vt* couper *or* diviser en deux

bishop ['bɪʃəp] *n* évêque *m*; (*CHESS*) fou *m*

bit [bɪt] *pt* *of* **bite** ♦ *n* morceau *m*; (*of tool*) mèche *f*; (*of horse*) mors *m*; (*COMPUT*) élément *m* binaire; **a ~ of** un peu de; **a ~ mad** un peu fou; **~ by ~** petit à petit

bitch [bɪtʃ] *n* (*dog*) chienne *f*; (*inf!*) salope *f* (*!*), garce *f*

bite [baɪt] (*pt* **bit**, *pp* **bitten**) *vt, vi* mordre; (*insect*) piquer ♦ *n* (*insect* ~) piqûre *f*; (*mouthful*) bouchée *f*; **let's have a ~ (to eat)** (*inf*) mangeons un morceau; **to ~ one's nails** se ronger les ongles

bitter ['bɪtəʳ] *adj* amer(-ère); (*weather, wind*) glacial(e); (*criticism*) cinglant(e); (*struggle*) acharné(e) ♦ *n* (BRIT: *beer*) bière *f* (forte); **~ness** *n* amertume *f*; (*taste*) goût amer

black [blæk] *adj* noir(e) ♦ *n* (*colour*) noir *m*; (*person*): **B~** noir(e) ♦ *vt* (BRIT: INDUSTRY) boycotter; **to give sb a ~ eye** pocher l'œil à qn, faire un œil au beurre noir à qn; **~ and blue** couvert(e) de bleus; **to be in the ~** (*in credit*) être créditeur(-trice); **~berry** *n* mûre *f*; **~bird** *n* merle *m*; **~board** *n* tableau noir; **~ coffee** *n* café noir; **~currant** *n* cassis *m*; **~en** *vt* noircir; **~ ice** *n* verglas *m*; **~leg** *n* (BRIT) briseur *m* de grève, jaune *m*; **~list** *n* liste noire; **~mail** *n* chantage *m* ♦ *vt* faire chanter, soumettre au chantage; **~ market** *n* marché noir; **~out** *n* panne *f* d'électricité; (TV *etc*) interruption *f* d'émission; (*fainting*) syncope *f*; **~ pudding** *n* boudin (noir); **B~ Sea** *n*: **the B~ Sea** la mer Noire; **~ sheep** *n* brebis galeuse; **~smith** *n* forgeron *m*; **~ spot** *n* (AUT) point noir

bladder ['blædəʳ] *n* vessie *f*

blade [bleɪd] *n* lame *f*; (*of propeller*) pale *f*; **~ of grass** brin *m* d'herbe

blame [bleɪm] *n* faute *f*, blâme *m* ♦ *vt*: **to ~ sb/sth for sth** attribuer à qn/qch la responsabilité de qch; reprocher qch à qn/qch; **who's to ~?** qui est le fautif *or* coupable *or* responsable?

bland [blænd] *adj* (*taste, food*) doux (douce), fade

blank [blæŋk] *adj* blanc (blanche); (*look*) sans expression, dénué(e) d'expression ♦ *n* espace *m* vide, blanc *m*; (*cartridge*) cartouche *f* à blanc; **his mind was a ~** il avait la tête vide; **~ cheque** chèque *m* en blanc

blanket ['blæŋkɪt] *n* couverture *f*; (*of snow, cloud*) couche *f*

blare [blɛəʳ] *vi* beugler

blast [blɑːst] *n* souffle *m*; (*of explosive*) explosion *f* ♦ *vt* faire sauter *or* exploser; **~-off** *n* (SPACE) lancement *m*

blatant ['bleɪtənt] *adj* flagrant(e), criant(e)

blaze [bleɪz] *n* (*fire*) incendie *m*; (*fig*) flamboiement *m* ♦ *vi* (*fire*) flamber; (*fig: eyes*) flamboyer; (: *guns*) crépiter ♦ *vt*: **to ~ a trail** (*fig*) montrer la voie

blazer ['bleɪzəʳ] *n* blazer *m*

bleach [bliːtʃ] *n* (*also:* **household ~**) eau *f* de Javel ♦ *vt* (*linen etc*) blanchir; **~ed** *adj* (*hair*) oxygéné(e), décoloré(e)

bleak [bliːk] *adj* morne, triste; (*countryside*) désolé(e)

bleat [bliːt] *vi* bêler

bleed [bliːd] (*pt, pp* **bled**) *vt, vi* saigner; **my nose is ~ing** je saigne du nez

bleeper ['bliːpəʳ] *n* (*device*) bip *m*

blemish ['blɛmɪʃ] *n* défaut *m*; (*on fruit, reputation*) tache *f*

blend [blɛnd] *n* mélange *m* ♦ *vt* mélanger ♦ *vi* (*colours etc: also:* **~ in**) se mélanger, se fondre; **~er** *n* mixeur *m*

bless [blɛs] (*pt, pp* **blessed** *or* **blest**) *vt* bénir; **~ you!** (*after sneeze*) à vos souhaits!; **~ing** *n* bénédiction *f*; (*godsend*) bienfait *m*

blew [bluː] *pt of* **blow**

blight [blaɪt] *vt* (*hopes etc*) anéantir; (*life*) briser

blimey ['blaɪmɪ] (BRIT: *inf*) *excl* mince alors!

blind [blaɪnd] *adj* aveugle ♦ *n* (*for window*) store *m* ♦ *vt* aveugler; **~ alley** *n* impasse *f*; **~ corner** (BRIT) *n* virage *m* sans visibilité; **~fold** *n* bandeau *m* ♦ *adj, adv* les yeux bandés ♦ *vt* bander les yeux à; **~ly** *adv* aveuglément; **~ness** *n* cécité *f*; **~ spot** *n* (AUT *etc*) angle mort; **that is her ~ spot** (*fig*) elle refuse d'y voir clair sur ce point

blink [blɪŋk] *vi* cligner des yeux; (*light*) clignoter; **~ers** *npl* œillères *fpl*

bliss [blɪs] *n* félicité *f*, bonheur *m* sans mélange

blister ['blɪstəʳ] n (*on skin*) ampoule f, cloque f; (*on paintwork, rubber*) boursouflure f ♦ vi (*paint*) se boursoufler, se cloquer

blizzard ['blɪzəd] n blizzard m, tempête f de neige

bloated ['bləʊtɪd] adj (*face*) bouffi(e); (*stomach, person*) gonflé(e)

blob [blɔb] n (*drop*) goutte f; (*stain, spot*) tache f

block [blɔk] n bloc m; (*in pipes*) obstruction f; (*toy*) cube m; (*of buildings*) pâté m (de maisons) ♦ vt bloquer; (*fig*) faire obstacle à; **~ of flats** (*BRIT*) immeuble (locatif); **mental ~** trou m de mémoire; **~ade** [blɔ'keɪd] n blocus m; **~age** n obstruction f; **~buster** n (*film, book*) grand succès; **~ letters** npl majuscules fpl

bloke [bləʊk] (*BRIT: inf*) n type m

blond(e) [blɔnd] adj, n blond(e)

blood [blʌd] n sang m; **~ donor** n donneur(-euse) de sang; **~ group** n groupe sanguin; **~hound** n limier m; **~ poisoning** n empoisonnement m du sang; **~ pressure** n tension f (artérielle); **~shed** n effusion f de sang, carnage m; **~ sports** npl sports mpl sanguinaires; **~shot** adj: **~shot eyes** yeux injectés de sang; **~stream** n sang m, système sanguin; **~ test** n prise f de sang; **~thirsty** adj sanguinaire; **~ vessel** n vaisseau sanguin; **~y** adj sanglant(e); (*nose*) en sang; (*BRIT: inf!*): **this ~y ...** ce foutu ... (!), ce putain de ... (!); **~y strong/good** vachement or sacrément fort/bon; **~y-minded** (*BRIT: inf*) adj contrariant(e), obstiné(e)

bloom [bluːm] n fleur f ♦ vi être en fleur

blossom ['blɔsəm] n fleur(s) f(pl) ♦ vi être en fleurs; (*fig*) s'épanouir; **to ~ into** devenir

blot [blɔt] n tache f ♦ vt tacher; **~ out** vt (*memories*) effacer; (*view*) cacher, masquer

blotchy ['blɔtʃi] adj (*complexion*) couvert(e) de marbrures

blotting paper ['blɔtɪŋ-] n buvard m

blouse [blauz] n chemisier m, corsage m

blow [bləʊ] (*pt* **blew**, *pp* **blown**) n coup m ♦ vi souffler ♦ vt souffler; (*fuse*) faire sauter; (*instrument*) jouer de; **to ~ one's nose** se moucher; **to ~ a whistle** siffler; **~ away** vt chasser, faire s'envoler; **~ down** vt faire tomber, renverser; **~ off** vt emporter; **~ out** vi (*fire, flame*) s'éteindre; **~ over** vi s'apaiser; **~ up** vi faire sauter; (*tyre*) gonfler; (*PHOT*) agrandir ♦ vi exploser, sauter; **~-dry** n brushing m; **~lamp** (*BRIT*) n chalumeau m; **~-out** n (*of tyre*) éclatement m; **~-torch** ♦ n = **blowlamp**

blue [bluː] adj bleu(e); (*fig*) triste; **~s** n (*MUS*): **the ~s** le blues; **~ film/joke** film m/histoire f pornographique; **to come out of the ~** (*fig*) être complètement inattendu; **~bell** n jacinthe f des bois; **~bottle** n mouche f à viande; **~print** n (*fig*) projet m, plan directeur

bluff [blʌf] vi bluffer ♦ n bluff m; **to call sb's ~** mettre qn au défi d'exécuter ses menaces

blunder ['blʌndəʳ] n gaffe f, bévue f ♦ vi faire une gaffe or une bévue

blunt [blʌnt] adj (*person*) brusque, ne mâchant pas ses mots; (*knife*) émoussé(e), peu tranchant(e); (*pencil*) mal taillé

blur [bləːʳ] n tache or masse floue or confuse ♦ vt brouiller

blush [blʌʃ] vi rougir ♦ n rougeur f

blustery ['blʌstəri] adj (*weather*) à bourrasques

boar [bɔːʳ] n sanglier m

board [bɔːd] n planche f; (*on wall*) panneau m; (*for chess*) échiquier m; (*cardboard*) carton m; (*committee*) conseil m, comité m; (*in firm*) conseil d'administration; (*NAUT, AVIAT*): **on ~** à bord ♦ vt (*ship*) monter à bord de; (*train*) monter dans; **full ~** (*BRIT*) pension complète; **half ~** demi-pension f; **~ and lodging** chambre f avec pension; **which goes by the ~** (*fig*) qu'on laisse tomber, qu'on abandonne; **~ up** vt (*door, window*) boucher; **~er** n (*SCOL*) interne m/f, pensionnaire; **~ game** n jeu m de société; **~ing card** n = **boarding pass**; **~ing house** n pension f; **~ing pass** n (*AVIAT, NAUT*) carte f d'embarquement; **~ing school** n internat m, pensionnat *m*; ~ **room** *n* salle *f* du conseil d'administration

boast [bəʊst] *vi*: **to ~ (about** *or* **of)** se vanter (de)

boat [bəʊt] *n* bateau *m*; (*small*) canot *m*; barque *f*; ~ **train** *n* train *m* (qui assue correspondance avec le ferry)

bob [bɔb] *vi* (*boat, cork on water: also:* ~ **up and down**) danser, se balancer

bobby ['bɔbɪ] (*BRIT: inf*) *n* ≈ agent *m* (de police)

bobsleigh ['bɔbsleɪ] *n* bob *m*

bode [bəʊd] *vi*: **to ~ well/ill (for)** être de bon/mauvais augure (pour)

bodily ['bɔdɪlɪ] *adj* corporel(le) ♦ *adv* dans ses bras

body ['bɔdɪ] *n* corps *m*; (*of car*) carrosserie *f*; (*of plane*) fuselage *m*; (*fig: society*) organe *m*, organisme *m*; (*: quantity*) ensemble *m*, masse *f*; (*of wine*) corps *m*; ~-**building** *n* culturisme *m*; ~**guard** *n* garde *m* du corps; ~**work** *n* carrosserie *f*

bog [bɔg] *n* tourbière *f* ♦ *vt*: **to get ~ged down** (*fig*) s'enliser

bog-standard (*inf*) *adj* tout à fait ordinaire

bogus ['bəʊgəs] *adj* bidon *inv*; fantôme

boil [bɔɪl] *vt* (*faire*) bouillir ♦ *vi* bouillir ♦ *n* (*MED*) furoncle *m*; **to come to the** (*BRIT*) ~ *or* **a** (*US*) ~ bouillir; ~ **down to** *vt fus* (*fig*) se réduire *or* ramener à; ~ **over** *vi* déborder; ~**ed egg** *n* œuf *m* à la coque; ~**ed potatoes** *npl* pommes *fpl* à l'anglaise *or* à l'eau; ~**er** *n* chaudière *f*; ~**ing point** *n* point *m* d'ébullition

boisterous ['bɔɪstərəs] *adj* bruyant(e), tapageur(-euse)

bold [bəʊld] *adj* hardi(e), audacieux(-euse); (*pej*) effronté(e); (*outline, colour*) franc (franche), tranché(e), marqué(e); (*pattern*) grand(e)

bollard ['bɔləd] (*BRIT*) *n* (*AUT*) borne lumineuse *or* de signalisation

bolt [bəʊlt] *n* (*lock*) verrou *m*; (*with nut*) boulon *m* ♦ *adv*: ~ **upright** droit(e) comme un piquet ♦ *vt* verrouiller; (*TECH: also:* ~ **on**, ~ **together**) boulonner; (*food*)

engloutir ♦ *vi* (*horse*) s'emballer

bomb [bɔm] *n* bombe *f* ♦ *vt* bombarder; ~**ing** *n* (*by terrorist*) attentat *m* à la bombe; ~ **disposal unit** *n* section *f* de déminage; ~**er** *n* (*AVIAT*) bombardier *m*; ~**shell** *n* (*fig*) bombe *f*

bond [bɔnd] *n* lien *m*; (*binding promise*) engagement *m*, obligation *f*; (*COMM*) obligation; **in ~** (*of goods*) en douane

bondage ['bɔndɪdʒ] *n* esclavage *m*

bone [bəʊn] *n* os *m*; (*of fish*) arête *f* ♦ *vt* désosser; ôter les arêtes de; ~ **dry** *adj* complètement sec (sèche); ~ **idle** *adj* fainéant(e); ~ **marrow** *n* moelle *f* osseuse

bonfire ['bɔnfaɪər] *n* feu *m* (de joie); (*for rubbish*) feu

bonnet ['bɔnɪt] *n* bonnet *m*; (*BRIT: of car*) capot *m*

bonus ['bəʊnəs] *n* prime *f*, gratification *f*

bony ['bəʊnɪ] *adj* (*arm, face, MED: tissue*) osseux(-euse); (*meat*) plein(e) d'os; (*fish*) plein d'arêtes

boo [buː] *excl* hou!, peuh! ♦ *vt* huer

booby trap ['buːbɪ-] *n* engin piégé

book [bʊk] *n* livre *m*; (*of stamps, tickets*) carnet *m* ♦ *vt* (*ticket*) prendre; (*seat, room*) réserver; (*driver*) dresser un procès-verbal à; (*football player*) prendre le nom de; ~**s** *npl* (*accounts*) comptes *mpl*, comptabilité *f*; ~**case** *n* bibliothèque *f* (*meuble*); ~**ing office** (*BRIT*) *n* bureau *m* de location; ~-**keeping** *n* comptabilité *f*; ~**let** *n* brochure *f*; ~**maker** *n* bookmaker *m*; ~**seller** *n* libraire *m/f*; ~**shelf** *n* (*single*) étagère *f* (à livres); ~**shop** *n* librairie *f*; ~**store** *n* librairie *f*

boom [buːm] *n* (*noise*) grondement *m*; (*in prices, population*) forte augmentation ♦ *vi* gronder; prospérer

boon [buːn] *n* bénédiction *f*, grand avantage

boost [buːst] *n* stimulant *m*, remontant *m* ♦ *vt* stimuler; ~**er** *n* (*MED*) rappel *m*

boot [buːt] *n* botte *f*; (*for hiking*) chaussure *f* (de marche); (*for football etc*) soulier *m*; (*BRIT: of car*) coffre *m* ♦ *vt* (*COMPUT*) amorcer, initialiser; **to ~** (*in addition*) par-dessus le marché

booth [buːð] *n* (*at fair*) baraque (foraine); (*telephone etc*) cabine *f*; (*also:* **voting ~**) isoloir *m*

booze [buːz] (*inf*) *n* boissons *fpl* alcooliques, alcool *m*

border ['bɔːdəʳ] *n* bordure *f*; bord *m*; (*of a country*) frontière *f* ♦ *vt* border; (*also:* **~ on:** *country*) être limitrophe de; **B~s** *n* (GEO): **the B~s** *la région frontière entre l'Écosse et l'Angleterre*; **~ on** *vt fus* être voisin(e) de, toucher à; **~line** *n* (*fig*) ligne *f* de démarcation; **~line case** cas *m* limite

bore [bɔːʳ] *pt of* **bear** ♦ *vt* (*hole*) percer; (*oil well, tunnel*) creuser; (*person*) ennuyer, raser ♦ *n* raseur(-euse); (*of gun*) calibre *m*; **to be ~d** s'ennuyer; **~dom** *n* ennui *m*; **boring** *adj* ennuyeux(-euse)

born [bɔːn] *adj*: **to be ~** naître; **I was ~ in 1960** je suis né en 1960

borne [bɔːn] *pp of* **bear**

borough ['bʌrə] *n* municipalité *f*

borrow ['bɔrəu] *vt*: **to ~ sth (from sb)** emprunter qch (à qn)

Bosnia (and) Herzegovina ['bɔznɪə-(ənd)hɜːtsəgəu'viːnə] *n* Bosnie-Herzégovine *f*; **Bosnian** *adj* bosniaque, bosnien(ne) ♦ *n* Bosniaque *m/f*

bosom ['buzəm] *n* poitrine *f*; (*fig*) sein *m*

boss [bɔs] *n* patron(ne) ♦ *vt* (*also:* **~ around/about**) mener à la baguette; **~y** *adj* autoritaire

bosun ['bəusn] *n* maître *m* d'équipage

botany ['bɔtənɪ] *n* botanique *f*

botch [bɔtʃ] *vt* (*also:* **~ up**) saboter, bâcler

both [bəuθ] *adj* les deux, l'un(e) et l'autre ♦ *pron*: **~ (of them)** les deux, tous (toutes) (les) deux, l'un(e) et l'autre; **they sell ~ the fabric and the finished curtains** ils vendent (et) le tissu et les rideaux (finis), ils vendent à la fois le tissu et les rideaux (finis); **~ of us went, we ~ went** nous y sommes allés (tous) les deux

bother ['bɔðəʳ] *vt* (*worry*) tracasser; (*disturb*) déranger ♦ *vi* (*also:* **~ o.s.**) se tracasser, se faire du souci ♦ *n*: **it is a ~ to have to do** c'est vraiment ennuyeux d'avoir à fai-

re; **it's no ~** aucun problème; **to ~ doing** prendre la peine de faire

bottle ['bɔtl] *n* bouteille *f*; (*baby's*) biberon *m* ♦ *vt* mettre en bouteille(s); **~d beer** bière *f* en canette; **~d water** eau minérale; **~ up** *vt* refouler, contenir; **~ bank** *n* conteneur *m* à verre; **~neck** *n* étranglement *m*; **~-opener** *n* ouvre-bouteille *m*

bottom ['bɔtəm] *n* (*of container, sea etc*) fond *m*; (*buttocks*) derrière *m*; (*of page, list*) bas *m* ♦ *adj* du fond; du bas; **the ~ of the class** le dernier de la classe

bough [bau] *n* branche *f*, rameau *m*

bought [bɔːt] *pt, pp of* **buy**

boulder ['bəuldəʳ] *n* gros rocher

bounce [bauns] *vi* (*ball*) rebondir; (*cheque*) être refusé(e) (*étant sans provision*) ♦ *vt* faire rebondir ♦ *n* (*rebound*) rebond *m*; **~r** (*inf*) *n* (*at dance, club*) videur *m*

bound [baund] *pt, pp of* **bind** ♦ *n* (*gen pl*) limite *f*; (*leap*) bond *m* ♦ *vi* (*leap*) bondir ♦ *vt* (*limit*) borner ♦ *adj*: **to be ~ to do sth** (*obliged*) être obligé(e) *or* avoir obligation de faire qch; **he's ~ to fail** (*likely*) il est sûr d'échouer, son échec est inévitable *or* assuré; **~ by** (*law, regulation*) engagé(e) par; **~ for** à destination de; **out of ~s** dont l'accès est interdit

boundary ['baundrɪ] *n* frontière *f*

bout [baut] *n* période *f*; (*of malaria etc*) accès *m*, crise *f*, attaque *f*; (BOXING *etc*) combat *m*, match *m*

bow¹ [bəu] *n* nœud *m*; (*weapon*) arc *m*; (MUS) archet *m*

bow² [bau] *n* (*with body*) révérence *f*, inclination *f* (*du buste or corps*); (NAUT: *also:* **~s**) proue *f* ♦ *vi* faire une révérence, s'incliner; (*yield*): **to ~ to** *or* **before** s'incliner devant, se soumettre à

bowels ['bauəlz] *npl* intestins *mpl*; (*fig*) entrailles *fpl*

bowl [bəul] *n* (*for eating*) bol *m*; (*ball*) boule *f* ♦ *vi* (CRICKET, BASEBALL) lancer (la balle)

bow-legged ['bəu'legɪd] *adj* aux jambes arquées

bowler ['bəuləʳ] *n* (CRICKET, BASEBALL) lanceur *m* (de la balle); (BRIT: *also:* **~ hat**) (chapeau *m*) melon *m*

bowling ['bəʊlɪŋ] *n* (*game*) jeu *m* de boules; jeu *m* de quilles; ~ **alley** *n* bowling *m*; ~ **green** *n* terrain *m* de boules (*gazonné et carré*)

bowls [bəʊlz] *n* (*game*) (jeu *m* de) boules *fpl*

bow tie [bəʊ-] *n* nœud *m* papillon

box [bɒks] *n* boîte *f*; (*also:* **cardboard ~**) carton *m*; (*THEATRE*) loge *f* ♦ *vt* mettre en boîte; (*SPORT*) boxer avec ♦ *vi* boxer, faire de la boxe; ~**er** *n* (*person*) boxeur *m*; ~**er shorts** *npl* caleçon *msg*; ~**ing** *n* (*SPORT*) boxe *f*; B~**ing Day** (*BRIT*) *n* le lendemain de Noël; ~**ing gloves** *npl* gants *mpl* de boxe; ~**ing ring** *n* ring *m*; ~ **office** *n* bureau *m* de location; ~**room** *n* débarras *m*; chambrette *f*

Boxing Day

i Boxing Day *est le lendemain de Noël, férié en Grande-Bretagne. Si Noël tombe un samedi, le jour férié est reculé jusqu'au lundi suivant. Ce nom vient d'une coutume du XIXe siècle qui consistait à donner des cadeaux de Noël (dans des boîtes) à ses employés etc le 26 décembre.*

boy [bɔɪ] *n* garçon *m*

boycott ['bɔɪkɒt] *n* boycottage *m* ♦ *vt* boycotter

boyfriend ['bɔɪfrɛnd] *n* (petit) ami

boyish ['bɔɪɪʃ] *adj* (*behaviour*) de garçon; (*girl*) garçonnier(-ière)

BR *n abbr* = **British Rail**

bra [brɑː] *n* soutien-gorge *m*

brace [breɪs] *n* (*on teeth*) appareil *m* (dentaire); (*tool*) vilbrequin *m* ♦ *vt* (*knees, shoulders*) appuyer; ~**s** *npl* (*BRIT: for trousers*) bretelles *fpl*; ~ **o.s.** (*lit*) s'arcbouter; (*fig*) se préparer mentalement

bracelet ['breɪslɪt] *n* bracelet *m*

bracing ['breɪsɪŋ] *adj* tonifiant(e), tonique

bracket ['brækɪt] *n* (*TECH*) tasseau *m*, support *m*; (*group*) classe *f*, tranche *f*; (*also:* **brace ~**) accolade *f*; (*also:* **round ~**) pa-

renthèse *f*; (*also:* **square ~**) crochet *m* ♦ *vt* mettre entre parenthèse(s); (*fig: also:* ~ **together**) regrouper

brag [bræg] *vi* se vanter

braid [breɪd] *n* (*trimming*) galon *m*; (*of hair*) tresse *f*

brain [breɪn] *n* cerveau *m*; ~**s** *npl* (*intellect, CULIN*) cervelle *f*; **he's got ~s** il est intelligent; ~**wash** *vt* faire subir un lavage de cerveau à; ~**wave** *n* idée géniale; ~**y** *adj* intelligent(e), doué(e)

braise [breɪz] *vt* braiser

brake [breɪk] *n* (*on vehicle, also fig*) frein *m* ♦ *vi* freiner; ~ **light** *n* feu *m* de stop

bran [bræn] *n* son *m*

branch [brɑːntʃ] *n* branche *f*; (*COMM*) succursale *f* ♦ *vi* bifurquer; ~ **out** *vi* (*fig*): **to** ~ **out into** étendre ses activités à

brand [brænd] *n* marque (commerciale) ♦ *vt* (*cattle*) marquer (au fer rouge); ~**new** *adj* tout(e) neuf (neuve), flambant neuf (neuve)

brandy ['brændɪ] *n* cognac *m*, fine *f*

brash [bræʃ] *adj* effronté(e)

brass [brɑːs] *n* cuivre *m* (jaune), laiton *m*; **the** ~ (*MUS*) les cuivres; ~ **band** *n* fanfare *f*

brat [bræt] (*pej*) *n* mioche *m/f*, môme *m/f*

brave [breɪv] *adj* courageux(-euse), brave ♦ *n* guerrier indien ♦ *vt* braver, affronter; ~**ry** *n* bravoure *f*, courage *m*

brawl [brɔːl] *n* rixe *f*, bagarre *f*

brazen ['breɪzn] *adj* impudent(e), effronté(e) ♦ *vt*: **to** ~ **it out** payer d'effronterie, crâner

brazier ['breɪzɪər] *n* brasero *m*

Brazil [brə'zɪl] *n* Brésil *m*

breach [briːtʃ] *vt* ouvrir une brèche dans ♦ *n* (*gap*) brèche *f*; (*breaking*): ~ **of contract** rupture *f* de contrat; ~ **of the peace** attentat *m* à l'ordre public

bread [brɛd] *n* pain *m*; ~ **and butter** *n* tartines (beurrées); (*fig*) subsistance *f*; ~**bin** (*BRIT*) *n* boîte *f* à pain; (*bigger*) huche *f* à pain; ~**crumbs** *npl* miettes *fpl* de pain; (*CULIN*) chapelure *f*, panure *f*; ~**line** *n*: **to be on the ~line** être sans le sou or dans l'indigence

breadth [brɛtθ] *n* largeur *f*; (*fig*) ampleur *f*

breadwinner ['brɛdwɪnər] *n* soutien *m* de famille

break [breɪk] (*pt* **broke**, *pp* **broken**) *vt* casser, briser; (*promise*) rompre; (*law*) violer ♦ *vi* (se) casser, se briser; (*weather*) tourner; (*story*, *news*) se répandre; (*day*) se lever ♦ *n* (*gap*) brèche *f*; (*fracture*) cassure *f*; (*pause*, *interval*) interruption *f*, arrêt *m*; (: *short*) pause *f*; (: *at school*) récréation *f*; (*chance*) chance *f*, occasion *f* favorable; **to ~ one's leg** *etc* se casser la jambe *etc*; **to ~ a record** battre un record; **to ~ the news to sb** annoncer la nouvelle à qn; **~ even** rentrer dans ses frais; **~ free** *or* **loose** se dégager, s'échapper; **~ open** (*door etc*) forcer, fracturer; **~ down** *vt* (*figures*, *data*) décomposer, analyser ♦ *vi* s'effondrer; (*MED*) faire une dépression (nerveuse); (*AUT*) tomber en panne; **~ in** *vt* (*horse etc*) dresser ♦ *vi* (*burglar*) entrer par effraction; (*interrupt*) interrompre; **~ into** *vt fus* (*house*) s'introduire *or* pénétrer par effraction dans; **~ off** *vi* (*speaker*) s'interrompre; (*branch*) se rompre; **~ out** *vi* éclater, se déclarer; (*prisoner*) s'évader; **to ~ out in spots** *or* **a rash** avoir une éruption de boutons; **~ up** *vi* (*ship*) se disloquer; (*crowd*, *meeting*) se disperser, se séparer; (*marriage*) se briser; (*SCOL*) entrer en vacances ♦ *vt* casser; (*fight etc*) interrompre, faire cesser; **~age** *n* casse *f*; **~down** *n* (*AUT*) panne *f*; (*in communications*, *marriage*) rupture *f*; (*MED*: *also*: **nervous ~down**) dépression (nerveuse); (*of statistics*) ventilation *f*; **~down van** (*BRIT*) *n* dépanneuse *f*; **~er** *n* brisant *m*

breakfast ['brɛkfəst] *n* petit déjeuner

break: **~-in** *n* cambriolage *m*; **~ing and entering** *n* (*LAW*) effraction *f*; **~through** *n* percée *f*; **~water** *n* brise-lames *m inv*, digue *f*

breast [brɛst] *n* (*of woman*) sein *m*; (*chest*, *of meat*) poitrine *f*; **~-feed** (*irreg*: *like* **feed**) *vt*, *vi* allaiter; **~stroke** *n* brasse *f*

breath [brɛθ] *n* haleine *f*; **out of ~** à bout de souffle, essoufflé(e); **B~alyser** ® ['brɛθəlaɪzər] *n* Alcootest ® *m*

breathe [briːð] *vt*, *vi* respirer; **~ in** *vt*, *vi* aspirer, inspirer; **~ out** *vt*, *vi* expirer; **~r** *n* moment *m* de repos *or* de répit; **breathing** *n* respiration *f*

breathless ['brɛθlɪs] *adj* essoufflé(e), haletant(e)

breathtaking ['brɛθteɪkɪŋ] *adj* stupéfiant(e)

breed [briːd] (*pt,pp* **bred**) *vt* élever, faire l'élevage de ♦ *vi* se reproduire ♦ *n* race *f*, variété *f*; **~ing** *n* (*upbringing*) éducation *f*

breeze [briːz] *n* brise *f*; **breezy** *adj* frais (fraîche); aéré(e); (*manner etc*) désinvolte, jovial(e)

brevity ['brɛvɪtɪ] *n* brièveté *f*

brew [bruː] *vt* (*tea*) faire infuser; (*beer*) brasser ♦ *vi* (*fig*) se préparer, couver; **~ery** *n* brasserie *f* (*fabrique*)

bribe [braɪb] *n* pot-de-vin *m* ♦ *vt* acheter, soudoyer; **~ry** *n* corruption *f*

brick [brɪk] *n* brique *f*; **~layer** *n* maçon *m*

bridal ['braɪdl] *adj* nuptial(e)

bride [braɪd] *n* mariée *f*, épouse *f*; **~groom** *n* marié *m*, époux *m*; **~smaid** *n* demoiselle *f* d'honneur

bridge [brɪdʒ] *n* pont *m*; (*NAUT*) passerelle *f* (de commandement); (*of nose*) arête *f*; (*CARDS*, *DENTISTRY*) bridge *m* ♦ *vt* (*fig: gap, gulf*) combler

bridle ['braɪdl] *n* bride *f*; **~ path** *n* piste *or* allée cavalière

brief [briːf] *adj* bref (brève) ♦ *n* (*LAW*) dossier *m*, cause *f*; (*gen*) tâche *f* ♦ *vt* mettre au courant; **~s** *npl* (*undergarment*) slip *m*; **~case** *n* serviette *f*; porte-documents *m inv*; **~ly** *adv* brièvement

bright [braɪt] *adj* brillant(e); (*room*, *weather*) clair(e); (*clever: person, idea*) intelligent(e); (*cheerful: colour, person*) vif (vive)

brighten ['braɪtn] (*also*: **~ up**) *vt* (*room*) éclaircir, égayer; (*event*) égayer ♦ *vi* s'éclaircir; (*person*) retrouver un peu de sa gaieté; (*face*) s'éclairer; (*prospects*) s'améliorer

brilliance ['brɪljəns] *n* éclat *m*

brilliant ['brɪljənt] *adj* brillant(e); (*sunshine, light*) éclatant(e); (*inf: holiday etc*) super

brim [brɪm] *n* bord *m*

brine [braɪn] *n* (CULIN) saumure *f*

bring [brɪŋ] (*pt, pp* **brought**) *vt* apporter; (*person*) amener; ~ **about** *vt* provoquer, entraîner; ~ **back** *vt* rapporter; ramener; (*restore: hanging*) réinstaurer; ~ **down** *vt* (*price*) faire baisser; (*enemy plane*) descendre; (*government*) faire tomber; ~ **forward** *vt* avancer; ~ **off** *vt* (*task, plan*) réussir, mener à bien; ~ **out** *vt* (*meaning*) faire ressortir; (*book*) publier; (*object*) sortir; ~ **round** *vt* (*unconscious person*) ranimer; ~ **up** *vt* (*child*) élever; (*carry up*) monter; (*question*) soulever; (*food: vomit*) vomir, rendre

brink [brɪŋk] *n* bord *m*

brisk [brɪsk] *adj* vif (vive)

bristle ['brɪsl] *n* poil *m* ♦ *vi* se hérisser

Britain ['brɪtən] *n* (*also:* **Great ~**) Grande-Bretagne *f*

British ['brɪtɪʃ] *adj* britannique ♦ *npl*: **the ~** les Britanniques *mpl*; ~ **Isles** *npl*: **the ~ Isles** les Îles *fpl* Britanniques; ~ **Rail** *n* compagnie ferroviaire britannique

Briton ['brɪtən] *n* Britannique *m/f*

Brittany ['brɪtənɪ] *n* Bretagne *f*

brittle ['brɪtl] *adj* cassant(e), fragile

broach [brəutʃ] *vt* (*subject*) aborder

broad [brɔːd] *adj* large; (*general: outlines*) grand(e); (: *distinction*) général(e); (*accent*) prononcé(e); **in ~ daylight** en plein jour; ~**band** *n* haut débit *m*; ~**cast** (*pt, pp* **broadcast**) *n* émission *f* ♦ *vt* radiodiffuser; téléviser ♦ *vi* émettre; ~**en** *vt* élargir ♦ *vi* s'élargir; **to ~en one's mind** élargir ses horizons; ~**ly** *adv* en gros, généralement; ~**-minded** *adj* large d'esprit

broccoli ['brɔkəlɪ] *n* brocoli *m*

brochure ['brəʊʃjʊər] *n* prospectus *m*, dépliant *m*

broil [brɔɪl] *vt* griller

broke [brəuk] *pt of* **break** ♦ *adj* (*inf*) fauché(e)

broken ['brəʊkn] *pp of* **break** ♦ *adj* cassé(e); (*machine: also:* ~ **down**) fichu(e); **in ~ English/French** dans un anglais/français approximatif *or* hésitant; ~ **leg** *etc* jambe *etc* cassée; ~**-hearted** *adj* (ayant) le cœur brisé

broker ['brəʊkər] *n* courtier *m*

brolly ['brɔlɪ] *n* (BRIT: *inf*) pépin *m*, parapluie *m*

bronchitis [brɔŋ'kaɪtɪs] *n* bronchite *f*

brooch [brəutʃ] *n* broche *f*

brood [bruːd] *n* couvée *f* ♦ *vi* (*person*) méditer (sombrement), ruminer

broom [brum] *n* balai *m*; (BOT) genêt *m*; ~**stick** *n* manche *m* à balai

Bros. *abbr* = **Brothers**

broth [brɔθ] *n* bouillon *m* de viande et de légumes

brothel ['brɔθl] *n* maison close, bordel *m*

brother ['brʌðər] *n* frère *m*; ~**-in-law** *n* beau-frère *m*

brought [brɔːt] *pt, pp of* **bring**

brow [brau] *n* front *m*; (*eyebrow*) sourcil *m*; (*of hill*) sommet *m*

brown [braun] *adj* brun(e), marron *inv*; (*hair*) châtain *inv*, brun; (*eyes*) marron *inv*; (*tanned*) bronzé(e) ♦ *n* (*colour*) brun *m* ♦ *vt* (CULIN) faire dorer; ~ **bread** *n* pain *m* bis; B~**ie** *n* (*also:* **B~ie Guide**) jeannette *f*, éclaireuse (cadette); ~**ie** (US) *n* (*cake*) gâteau *m* au chocolat et aux noix; ~ **paper** *n* papier *m* d'emballage; ~ **sugar** *n* cassonade *f*

browse [brauz] *vi* (*among books*) bouquiner, feuilleter les livres; **to ~ through a book** feuilleter un livre; ~**r** *n* navigateur *m*

bruise [bruːz] *n* bleu *m*, contusion *f* ♦ *vt* contusionner, meurtrir

brunette [bruː'net] *n* (femme) brune

brunt [brʌnt] *n*: **the ~ of** (*attack, criticism etc*) le plus gros de

brush [brʌʃ] *n* brosse *f*; (*painting*) pinceau *m*; (*shaving*) blaireau *m*; (*quarrel*) accrochage *m*, prise *f* de bec ♦ *vt* brosser; (*also:* ~ **against**) effleurer, frôler; ~ **aside** *vt* écarter, balayer; ~ **up** *vt* (*knowledge*) rafraîchir, réviser; ~**wood** *n* broussailles *fpl*, taillis *m*

Brussels ['brʌslz] n Bruxelles; ~ **sprout** n chou m de Bruxelles

brutal ['bruːtl] adj brutal(e)

brute [bruːt] n brute f ♦ adj: **by ~ force** par la force

BSc abbr = **Bachelor of Science**

BSE n abbr (= bovine spongiform encephalopathy) ESB f, BSE f

bubble ['bʌbl] n bulle f ♦ vi bouillonner, faire des bulles; (sparkle) pétiller; ~ **bath** n bain moussant; ~ **gum** n bubblegum m

buck [bʌk] n mâle m (d'un lapin, daim etc); (US: inf) dollar m ♦ vi ruer, lancer une ruade; **to pass the ~ (to sb)** se décharger de la responsabilité (sur qn); ~ **up** vi (cheer up) reprendre du poil de la bête, se remonter

bucket ['bʌkɪt] n seau m

Buckingham Palace

buckle ['bʌkl] n boucle f ♦ vt (belt etc) boucler, attacher ♦ vi (warp) tordre, gauchir; (: wheel) se voiler; se déformer

bud [bʌd] n bourgeon m; (of flower) bouton m ♦ vi bourgeonner; (flower) éclore

Buddhism ['budɪzəm] n bouddhisme m

Buddhist ['budɪst] adj bouddhiste ♦ n Bouddhiste m/f

budding ['bʌdɪŋ] adj (poet etc) en herbe; (passion etc) naissant(e)

buddy ['bʌdɪ] (US) n copain m

budge [bʌdʒ] vt faire bouger; (fig: person) faire changer d'avis ♦ vi bouger; changer d'avis

budgerigar ['bʌdʒərɪɡɑːʳ] (BRIT) n perruche f

budget ['bʌdʒɪt] n budget m ♦ vi: **to ~ for sth** inscrire qch au budget

budgie ['bʌdʒɪ] (BRIT) n = **budgerigar**

buff [bʌf] adj (couleur f) chamois m ♦ n (inf: enthusiast) mordu(e); **he's a ... ~** c'est un mordu de ...

buffalo ['bʌfələu] (pl ~ or ~**es**) n buffle m; (US) bison m

buffer ['bʌfəʳ] n tampon m; (COMPUT) mémoire f tampon

buffet¹ ['bʌfɪt] vt secouer, ébranler

buffet² ['bufeɪ] n (food, BRIT: bar) buffet m; ~ **car** (BRIT) n (RAIL) voiture-buffet f

bug [bʌg] n (insect) punaise f; (: gen) insecte m, bestiole f; (fig: germ) virus m, microbe m; (COMPUT) erreur f; (fig: spy device) dispositif m d'écoute (électronique) ♦ vt garnir de dispositifs d'écoute; (inf: annoy) embêter; ~**ged** adj sur écoute

bugle ['bjuːɡl] n clairon m

build [bɪld] (pt, pp **built**) n (of person) carrure f, charpente f ♦ vt construire, bâtir; ~ **up** vt accumuler, amasser; accroître; ~**er** n entrepreneur m; ~**ing** n (trade) construction f; (house, structure) bâtiment m, construction; (offices, flats) immeuble m; ~**ing society** (BRIT) n société f de crédit immobilier

building society

built [bɪlt] pt, pp of **build**; ~-**in** ['bɪltɪn] adj (cupboard, oven) encastré(e); (device) incorporé(e); intégré(e); ~-**up area** ['bɪltʌp-] n zone urbanisée

bulb [bʌlb] n (BOT) bulbe m, oignon m; (ELEC) ampoule f

Bulgaria [bʌlˈɡeərɪə] n Bulgarie f

bulge [bʌldʒ] n renflement m, gonflement m ♦ vi (pocket, file etc) être plein(e) à craquer; (cheeks) être gonflé(e)

bulk [bʌlk] n masse f, volume m; (of person) corpulence f; **in ~** (COMM) en vrac; **the ~ of** la plus grande or grosse partie de; **~y** adj volumineux(-euse), encombrant(e)

bull [bul] n taureau m; (male elephant/whale) mâle m; **~dog** n bouledogue m

bulldozer ['buldəuzəʳ] n bulldozer m

bullet ['bulɪt] n balle f (de fusil etc)

bulletin ['bulɪtɪn] n bulletin m, communiqué m; (news ~) (bulletin d')informations fpl; **~ board** n (Internet) messagerie f électronique

bulletproof ['bulɪtpruːf] adj (car) blindé(e); (vest etc) pare-balles inv

bullfight ['bulfaɪt] n corrida f, course f de taureaux; **~er** n torero m; **~ing** n tauromachie f

bullion ['buljən] n or m ou argent m en lingots

bullock ['bulək] n bœuf m

bullring ['bulrɪŋ] n arènes fpl

bull's-eye ['bulzaɪ] n centre m (de la cible)

bully ['bulɪ] n brute f, tyran m ♦ vt tyranniser, rudoyer

bum [bʌm] n (inf: backside) derrière m; (esp US: tramp) vagabond(e), traîne-savates m/f inv

bumblebee ['bʌmblbiː] n bourdon m

bump [bʌmp] n (in car: minor accident) accrochage m; (jolt) cahot m; (on road etc, on head) bosse f ♦ vt heurter, cogner; **~ into** vt fus rentrer dans, tamponner; (meet) tomber sur; **~er** n pare-chocs m inv ♦ adj: **~er crop/harvest** récolte/moisson exceptionnelle; **~er cars** (US) npl autos tamponneuses; **~y** adj cahoteux(-euse)

bun [bʌn] n petit pain au lait; (of hair) chignon m

bunch [bʌntʃ] n (of flowers) bouquet m; (of keys) trousseau m; (of bananas) régime m; (of people) groupe m; **~es** npl (in hair) couettes fpl; **~ of grapes** grappe f de raisin

bundle ['bʌndl] n paquet m ♦ vt (also: **~ up**) faire un paquet de; (put): **to ~ sth/sb into** fourrer ou enfourner qch/qn dans

bungalow ['bʌŋgələu] n bungalow m

bungle ['bʌŋgl] vt bâcler, gâcher

bunion ['bʌnjən] n oignon m (au pied)

bunk [bʌŋk] n couchette f; **~ beds** npl lits superposés

bunker ['bʌŋkəʳ] n (coal store) soute f à charbon; (MIL, GOLF) bunker m

bunting ['bʌntɪŋ] n pavoisement m, drapeaux mpl

buoy [bɔɪ] n bouée f; **~ up** vt faire flotter; (fig) soutenir, épauler; **~ant** adj capable de flotter; (carefree) gai(e), plein(e) d'entrain; (economy) ferme, actif

burden ['bəːdn] n fardeau m ♦ vt (trouble) accabler, surcharger

bureau ['bjuərəu] (pl **~x**) n (BRIT: writing desk) bureau m, secrétaire m; (US: chest of drawers) commode f; (office) bureau, office m; **~cracy** [bjuə'rɔkrəsɪ] n bureaucratie f

burglar ['bəːgləʳ] n cambrioleur m; **~ alarm** n sonnerie f d'alarme

Burgundy ['bəːgəndɪ] n Bourgogne f

burial ['berɪəl] n enterrement m

burly ['bəːlɪ] adj de forte carrure, costaud(e)

Burma ['bəːmə] n Birmanie f

burn [bəːn] (pt, pp **burned** or **burnt**) vt, vi brûler ♦ n brûlure f; **~ down** vt incendier, détruire par le feu; **~er** n brûleur m; **~ing** adj brûlant(e); (house) en flammes; (ambition) dévorant(e)

burrow ['bʌrəu] n terrier m ♦ vt creuser

bursary ['bəːsərɪ] (BRIT) n bourse f (d'études)

burst [bəːst] (pt,pp **burst**) vt crever; faire éclater; (subj: river: banks etc) rompre ♦ vi éclater; (tyre) crever ♦ n (of gunfire) rafale f (de tir); (also: **~ pipe**) rupture f; fuite f; **a ~ of enthusiasm/energy** un accès d'enthousiasme/d'énergie; **to ~ into flames** s'enflammer soudainement; **to ~ out laughing** éclater de rire; **to ~ into tears** fondre en larmes; **to be ~ing with** être plein (à craquer) de; (fig) être débordant(e) de; **~ into** vt fus (room etc) faire irruption dans

bury ['berɪ] vt enterrer

bus [bʌs] (pl ~es) n autobus m

bush [buʃ] n buisson m; (scrubland) brousse f; **to beat about the ~** tourner autour du pot; ~y adj broussailleux(-euse), touffu(e)

busily ['bɪzɪlɪ] adv activement

business ['bɪznɪs] n (matter, firm) affaire f; (trading) affaires fpl; (job, duty) travail m; **to be away on ~** être en déplacement d'affaires; **it's none of my ~** cela ne me regarde pas, ce ne sont pas mes affaires; **he means ~** il ne plaisante pas, il est sérieux; ~**like** adj (firm) sérieux(-euse); (method) efficace; ~**man** (irreg) n homme m d'affaires; ~ **trip** n voyage m d'affaires; ~**woman** (irreg) n femme f d'affaires

busker ['bʌskər] (BRIT) n musicien ambulant

bus: ~ **shelter** n abribus m; ~ **station** n gare routière; ~ **stop** n arrêt m d'autobus

bust [bʌst] n buste m; (measurement) tour m de poitrine ♦ adj (inf: broken) fichu(e), fini(e); **to go ~** faire faillite

bustle ['bʌsl] n remue-ménage m, affairement m ♦ vi s'affairer, se démener; **bustling** adj (town) bruyant(e), affairé(e)

busy ['bɪzɪ] adj occupé(e); (shop, street) très fréquenté(e) ♦ vt: **to ~ o.s.** s'occuper; ~**body** n mouche f du coche, âme f charitable; ~ **signal** (US) n (TEL) tonalité f occupé inv

but [bʌt] conj mais; **I'd love to come, but I'm busy** j'aimerais venir mais je suis occupé

♦ prep (apart from, except) sauf, excepté; **we've had nothing but trouble** nous n'avons eu que des ennuis; **no-one but him can do it** lui seul peut le faire; **but for you/your help** sans toi/ton aide; **anything but that** tout sauf or excepté ça, tout mais pas ça

♦ adv (just, only) ne ... que; **she's but a child** elle n'est qu'une enfant; **had I but known** si seulement j'avais su; **all but finished** pratiquement terminé

butcher ['butʃər] n boucher m ♦ vt massacrer; (cattle etc for meat) tuer; ~'s **(shop)** n boucherie f

butler ['bʌtlər] n maître m d'hôtel

butt [bʌt] n (large barrel) gros tonneau; (of gun) crosse f; (of cigarette) mégot m; (BRIT: fig: target) cible f ♦ vt donner un coup de tête à; ~ **in** vi (interrupt) s'immiscer dans la conversation

butter ['bʌtər] n beurre m ♦ vt beurrer; ~**cup** n bouton m d'or

butterfly ['bʌtəflaɪ] n papillon m; (SWIMMING: also: ~ **stroke**) brasse f papillon

buttocks ['bʌtəks] npl fesses fpl

button ['bʌtn] n bouton m; (US: badge) pin m ♦ vt (also: ~ **up**) boutonner ♦ vi se boutonner

buttress ['bʌtrɪs] n contrefort m

buy [baɪ] (pt, pp **bought**) vt acheter ♦ n achat m; **to give sb a ~** achat m; **to ~ sb sth/sth from sb** acheter qch à qn; **to ~ sb a drink** offrir un verre or à boire à qn; ~**er** n acheteur(-euse)

buzz [bʌz] n bourdonnement m; (inf: phone call): **to give sb a ~** passer un coup m de fil à qn ♦ vi bourdonner; ~**er** n timbre m électrique; ~ **word** n (inf) mot m à la mode

by [baɪ] prep 1 (referring to cause, agent) par, de; **killed by lightning** tué par la foudre; **surrounded by a fence** entouré d'une barrière; **a painting by Picasso** un tableau de Picasso

2 (referring to method, manner, means): **by bus/car** en autobus/voiture; **by train** par le or en train; **to pay by cheque** payer par chèque; **by saving hard, he ...** à force d'économiser, il ...

3 (via, through) par; **we came by Dover** nous sommes venus par Douvres

4 (close to, past) à côté de; **the house by the school** la maison à côté de l'école; **a holiday by the sea** des vacances au bord de la mer; **she sat by his bed** elle était assise à son chevet; **she went by me** elle

est passée à côté de moi; **I go by the post office every day** je passe devant la poste tous les jours
5 (*with time: not later than*) avant; (: *during*): **by daylight** à la lumière du jour; **by night** la nuit, de nuit; **by 4 o'clock** avant 4 heures; **by this time tomorrow** d'ici demain à la même heure; **by the time I got here it was too late** lorsque je suis arrivé il était déjà trop tard
6 (*amount*) à; **by the kilo/metre** au kilo/au mètre; **paid by the hour** payé à l'heure
7 (*MATH, measure*): **to divide/multiply by 3** diviser/multiplier par 3; **a room 3 metres by 4** une pièce de 3 mètres sur 4; **it's broader by a metre** c'est plus large d'un mètre; **one by one** un à un; **little by little** petit à petit, peu à peu
8 (*according to*) d'après, selon; **it's 3 o'clock by my watch** il est 3 heures à ma montre; **it's all right by me** je n'ai rien contre
9: (all) by oneself *etc* tout(e) seul(e)
10: by the way au fait, à propos
♦ *adv* **1** *see* **go**; **pass** *etc*
2: by and by un peu plus tard, bientôt; **by and large** dans l'ensemble

bye(-bye) ['baɪ('baɪ)] *excl* au revoir!, salut!
by(e)-law ['baɪlɔ:] *n* arrêté municipal
by: ~**-election** (*BRIT*) *n* élection (législative) partielle; ~**gone** *adj* passé(e) ♦ *n*: **let** ~**gones be** ~**gones** passons l'éponge, oublions le passé; ~**pass** *n* (route *f* de) contournement *m*; (*MED*) pontage *m* ♦ *vt* éviter; ~**-product** *n* sous-produit *m*, dérivé *m*; (*fig*) conséquence *f* secondaire, retombée *f*; ~**stander** *n* spectateur(-trice), badaud(e)
byte [baɪt] *n* (*COMPUT*) octet *m*
byword ['baɪwə:d] *n*: **to be a** ~ **for** être synonyme de (*fig*)

C, c

C [si:] *n* (*MUS*) do *m*
CA *abbr* = **chartered accountant**
cab [kæb] *n* taxi *m*; (*of train, truck*) cabine *f*
cabaret ['kæbəreɪ] *n* (*show*) spectacle *m* de cabaret
cabbage ['kæbɪdʒ] *n* chou *m*
cabin ['kæbɪn] *n* (*house*) cabane *f*, hutte *f*; (*on ship*) cabine *f*; (*on plane*) compartiment *m*; ~ **crew** *n* (*AVIAT*) équipage *m*; ~ **cruiser** *n* cruiser *m*
cabinet ['kæbɪnɪt] *n* (*POL*) cabinet *m*; (*furniture*) petit meuble à tiroirs et rayons; (*also*: **display** ~) vitrine *f*, petite armoire vitrée
cable ['keɪbl] *n* câble *m* ♦ *vt* câbler, télégraphier; ~**-car** *n* téléphérique *m*; ~ **television** *n* télévision *f* par câble
cache [kæʃ] *n* stock *m*
cackle ['kækl] *vi* caqueter
cactus ['kæktəs] (*pl* **cacti**) *n* cactus *m*
cadet [kə'dɛt] *n* (*MIL*) élève *m* officier
cadge [kædʒ] (*inf*) *vt*: **to** ~ **(from** *or* **off)** se faire donner (par)
Caesarian [sɪ'zɛərɪən] *n* (*also*: ~ **section**) césarienne *f*
café ['kæfeɪ] *n* ≃ café(-restaurant) *m* (*sans alcool*)
cage [keɪdʒ] *n* cage *f*
cagey ['keɪdʒɪ] (*inf*) *adj* réticent(e); méfiant(e)
cagoule [kə'gu:l] *n* K-way ® *m*
Cairo ['kaɪərəu] *n* le Caire
cajole [kə'dʒəul] *vt* couvrir de flatteries *or* de gentillesses
cake [keɪk] *n* gâteau *m*; ~**d** *adj*: ~**d with** raidi(e) par, couvert(e) d'une croûte de
calculate ['kælkjuleɪt] *vt* calculer; (*estimate: chances, effect*) évaluer; **calculation** *n* calcul *m*; **calculator** *n* machine *f* à calculer, calculatrice *f*; (*pocket*) calculette *f*
calendar ['kæləndə'] *n* calendrier *m*; ~ **year** *n* année civile
calf [kɑ:f] (*pl* **calves**) *n* (*of cow*) veau *m*; (*of*

other animals) petit *m*; *(also:* **~skin)** veau *m*, vachette *f*; *(ANAT)* mollet *m*

calibre ['kælɪbəʳ] *(US* **caliber)** *n* calibre *m*

call [kɔːl] *vt* appeler; *(meeting)* convoquer ♦ *vi* appeler; *(visit: also:* **~ in, ~ round)** passer ♦ *n* (*shout*) appel *m*, cri *m*; *(also:* **telephone ~)** coup *m* de téléphone; *(visit)* visite *f*; **she's ~ed Suzanne** elle s'appelle Suzanne; **to be on ~** être de permanence; **~ back** *vi* (*return*) repasser; *(TEL)* rappeler; **~ for** *vt fus* (*demand*) demander; (*fetch*) passer prendre; **~ off** *vt* annuler; **~ on** *vt fus* (*visit*) rendre visite à, passer voir; (*request*): **to ~ on sb to do** inviter qn à faire ♦ **~ out** *vi* pousser un cri ou des cris; **~ up** *vt* (*MIL*) appeler, mobiliser; *(TEL)* appeler; **~box** *n* (*BRIT*) *(TEL)* cabine *f* téléphonique; **~ centre** *n* centre *m* d'appels; **~er** *n* (*TEL*) personne *f* qui appelle; *(visitor)* visiteur *m*; **~ girl** *n* call-girl *f*; **~-in** (*US*) *n* (*RADIO, TV: phone-in*) programme *m* à ligne ouverte; **~ing** *n* vocation *f*; (*trade, occupation*) état *m*; **~ing card** (*US*) *n* carte *f* de visite

callous ['kæləs] *adj* dur(e), insensible

calm [kɑːm] *adj* calme ♦ *n* calme *m* ♦ *vt* calmer, apaiser; **~ down** *vi* se calmer ♦ *vt* calmer, apaiser

Calor gas ® ['kæləʳ-] *n* butane *m*, butagaz *m* ®

calorie ['kælərɪ] *n* calorie *f*

calves [kɑːvz] *npl of* **calf**

camber ['kæmbəʳ] *(of road)* bombement *m*

Cambodia [kæm'bəʊdɪə] *n* Cambodge *m*

camcorder ['kæmkɔːdəʳ] *n* caméscope *m*

came [keɪm] *pt of* **come**

camel ['kæməl] *n* chameau *m*

camera ['kæmərə] *n* (*PHOT*) appareil-photo *m*; *(also:* **cine-~, movie ~)** caméra *f*; **in ~** à huis clos; **~man** (*irreg*) *n* caméraman *m*; **~phone** *n* téléphone *m* avec appareil-photo numérique intégré

camouflage ['kæməflɑːʒ] *n* camouflage *m* ♦ *vt* camoufler

camp [kæmp] *n* camp *m* ♦ *vi* camper ♦ *adj* (*man*) efféminé(e)

campaign [kæm'peɪn] *n* (*MIL, POL etc*) campagne *f* ♦ *vi* faire campagne

camp: **~bed** (*BRIT*) *n* lit *m* de camp; **~er** *n* campeur(-euse); *(vehicle)* camping-car *m*; **~ing** *n* camping *m*; **to go ~ing** faire du camping; **~ing gas** ® *n* butane *m*; **~site** *n* (terrain *m* de) camping *m*

can¹ [kæn] *n* (*of milk, oil, water*) bidon *m*; (*tin*) boîte *f* de conserve ♦ *vt* mettre en conserve

---
KEYWORD
---

can² [kæn] (*negative* **cannot, can't,** *conditional and pt* **could**) *aux vb* **1** (*be able to*) pouvoir; **you can do it if you try** vous pouvez le faire si vous essayez; **I can't hear you** je ne t'entends pas

2 (*know how to*) savoir; **I can swim/play tennis/drive** je sais nager/jouer au tennis/conduire; **can you speak French?** parlez-vous français?

3 (*may*) pouvoir; **can I use your phone?** puis-je me servir de votre téléphone?

4 (*expressing disbelief, puzzlement etc*): **it can't be true!** ce n'est pas possible!; **what CAN he want?** qu'est-ce qu'il peut bien vouloir?

5 (*expressing possibility, suggestion etc*): **he could be in the library** il est peut-être dans la bibliothèque; **she could have been delayed** il se peut qu'elle ait été retardée

---

Canada ['kænədə] *n* Canada *m*; **Canadian** [kə'neɪdɪən] *adj* canadien(ne) ♦ *n* Canadien(ne)

canal [kə'næl] *n* canal *m*

canapé ['kænəpeɪ] *n* canapé *m*

canary [kə'nɛərɪ] *n* canari *m*, serin *m*

cancel ['kænsəl] *vt* annuler; (*train*) supprimer; (*party, appointment*) décommander; (*cross out*) barrer, rayer; **~lation** [kænsə'leɪʃən] *n* annulation *f*; suppression *f*

cancer ['kænsəʳ] *n* (*MED*) cancer *m*; **C~** (*ASTROLOGY*) le Cancer

candid ['kændɪd] *adj* (très) franc (franche), sincère

candidate ['kændɪdeɪt] *n* candidat(e)

candle ['kændl] n bougie f; (of tallow) chandelle f; (in church) cierge m; **~light** n: **by ~light** à la lumière d'une bougie; (dinner) aux chandelles; **~stick** n (also: **~ holder**) bougeoir m; (bigger, ornate) chandelier m

candour ['kændər] (US **candor**) n (grande) franchise or sincérité

candy ['kændɪ] n sucre candi; (US) bonbon m; (BRIT) capsule f

cane [keɪn] n canne f; (for furniture, baskets etc) rotin m ♦ vt (BRIT: SCOL) administrer des coups de bâton à

canister ['kænɪstər] n boîte f; (of gas, pressurized substance) bombe f

cannabis ['kænəbɪs] n (drug) cannabis m

canned [kænd] adj (food) en boîte, en conserve

cannon ['kænən] (pl **~** or **~s**) n (gun) canon m

cannot ['kænɔt] = **can not**

canoe [kə'nuː] n pirogue f; (SPORT) canoë m; **~ing** n: **to go ~ing** faire du canoë

canon ['kænən] n (clergyman) chanoine m; (standard) canon m

can-opener ['kænəupnər] n ouvre-boîte m

canopy ['kænəpɪ] n baldaquin m; dais m

can't [kænt] = **cannot**

canteen [kæn'tiːn] n cantine f; (BRIT: of cutlery) ménagère f

canter ['kæntər] vi (horse) aller au petit galop

canvas ['kænvəs] n toile f

canvass ['kænvəs] vi (POL): **to ~ for** faire campagne pour ♦ vt (investigate: opinions etc) sonder

canyon ['kænjən] n cañon m, gorge (profonde)

cap [kæp] n casquette f; (of pen) capuchon m; (of bottle) capsule f; (contraceptive: also: **Dutch ~**) diaphragme m; (for toy gun) amorce f ♦ vt (outdo) surpasser; (put limit on) plafonner

capability [keɪpə'bɪlɪtɪ] n aptitude f, capacité f

capable ['keɪpəbl] adj capable

capacity [kə'pæsɪtɪ] n capacité f; (capabili-

ty) aptitude f; (of factory) rendement m

cape [keɪp] n (garment) cape f; (GEO) cap m

caper ['keɪpər] n (CULIN: gen pl) câpre f; (prank) farce f

capital ['kæpɪtl] n (also: **~ city**) capitale f; (money) capital m; (also: **~ letter**) majuscule f; **~ gains tax** n (COMM) impôt m sur les plus-values; **~ism** n capitalisme m; **~ist** adj capitaliste ♦ n capitaliste m/f; **~ize** ['kæpɪtəlaɪz] vi: **to ~ize on** tirer parti de; **~ punishment** n peine capitale

---
Capitol

ⓘ Le **Capitol** est le siège du **Congress**, à Washington. Il est situé sur Capitol Hill.

Capricorn ['kæprɪkɔːn] n le Capricorne

capsize [kæp'saɪz] vt faire chavirer ♦ vi chavirer

capsule ['kæpsjuːl] n capsule f

captain ['kæptɪn] n capitaine m

caption ['kæpʃən] n légende f

captive ['kæptɪv] adj, n captif(-ive)

capture ['kæptʃər] vt capturer, prendre; (attention) capter; (COMPUT) saisir ♦ n capture f; (data ~) saisie f de données

car [kɑːr] n voiture f, auto f; (RAIL) wagon m, voiture

caramel ['kærəməl] n caramel m

caravan ['kærəvæn] n caravane f; **~ning** n: **to go ~ning** faire du caravaning; **~ site** (BRIT) n camping m pour caravanes

carbohydrate [kɑːbəu'haɪdreɪt] n hydrate m de carbone; (food) féculent m

carbon ['kɑːbən] n carbone m; **~ dioxide** n gaz m carbonique; **~ monoxide** n oxyde m de carbone; **~ paper** n papier m carbone

car boot sale n marché aux puces où les particuliers vendent des objets entreposés dans le coffre de leur voiture

carburettor [kɑːbju'retər] (US **carburetor**) n carburateur m

card [kɑːd] n carte f; (material) carton m; **~board** n carton m; **~ game** n jeu m de cartes

cardiac ['kɑːdɪæk] *adj* cardiaque

cardigan ['kɑːdɪɡən] *n* cardigan *m*

cardinal ['kɑːdɪnl] *adj* cardinal(e) ♦ *n* cardinal *m*

card index *n* fichier *m*

cardphone *n* téléphone *m* à carte

care [kɛəʳ] *n* soin *m*, attention *f*; (*worry*) souci *m*; (*charge*) charge *f*, garde *f* ♦ *vi*: **to ~ about** se soucier de, s'intéresser à; (*person*) être attaché(e) à; **~ of** chez, aux bons soins de; **in sb's ~** à la garde de qn, confié(e) à qn; **to take ~ (to do)** faire attention (à faire); **to take ~ of** s'occuper de; **I don't ~** ça m'est bien égal; **I couldn't ~ less** je m'en fiche complètement (*inf*); **~ for** *vt fus* s'occuper de; (*like*) aimer

career [kə'rɪəʳ] *n* carrière *f* ♦ *vi* (*also:* **~ along**) aller à toute allure; **~ woman** (*irreg*) *n* femme ambitieuse

care: **~free** *adj* sans souci, insouciant(e); **~ful** (*thorough*) soigneux(-euse); (*cautious*) prudent(e); **(be) ~ful!** (fais) attention!; **~fully** *adv* avec soin, soigneusement; prudemment; **~less** *adj* négligent(e); (*heedless*) insouciant(e); **~r** *n* (*MED*) aide *f*

caress [kə'rɛs] *n* caresse *f* ♦ *vt* caresser

caretaker ['kɛəteɪkəʳ] *n* gardien(ne), concierge *m/f*

car-ferry ['kɑːfɛrɪ] *n* (*on sea*) ferry(-boat) *m*

cargo ['kɑːɡəʊ] (*pl* **~es**) *n* cargaison *f*, chargement *m*

car hire *n* location *f* de voitures

Caribbean [kærɪ'biːən] *adj*: **the ~ (Sea)** la mer des Antilles *or* Caraïbes

caring ['kɛərɪŋ] *adj* (*person*) bienveillant(e); (*society, organization*) humanitaire

carnation [kɑː'neɪʃən] *n* œillet *m*

carnival ['kɑːnɪvl] *n* (*public celebration*) carnaval *m*; (*US: funfair*) fête foraine

carol ['kærəl] *n*: **(Christmas) ~** chant *m* de Noël

carp [kɑːp] *n* (*fish*) carpe *f*

car park (*BRIT*) *n* parking *m*, parc *m* de stationnement

carpenter ['kɑːpɪntəʳ] *n* charpentier *m*; **carpentry** *n* menuiserie *f*

carpet ['kɑːpɪt] *n* tapis *m* ♦ *vt* recouvrir d'un tapis; **~ sweeper** *n* balai *m* mécanique

car phone *n* (*TEL*) téléphone *m* de voiture

car rental *n* location *f* de voitures

carriage ['kærɪdʒ] *n* voiture *f*; (*of goods*) transport *m*; (*: cost*) port *m*; **~way** (*BRIT*) *n* (*part of road*) chaussée *f*

carrier ['kærɪəʳ] *n* transporteur *m*, camionneur *m*; (*company*) entreprise *f* de transport; (*MED*) porteur(-euse); **~ bag** (*BRIT*) *n* sac *m* (en papier *or* en plastique)

carrot ['kærət] *n* carotte *f*

carry ['kærɪ] *vt* (*subj: person*) porter; (*: vehicle*) transporter; (*involve: responsibilities etc*) comporter, impliquer ♦ *vi* (*sound*) porter; **to get carried away** (fig) s'emballer, s'enthousiasmer; **~ on** *vi*: **to ~ on with sth/doing** continuer qch/de faire ♦ *vt* poursuivre; **~ out** *vt* (*orders*) exécuter; (*investigation*) mener; **~cot** (*BRIT*) *n* porte-bébé *m*; **~-on** (*inf*) *n* (*fuss*) histoires *fpl*

cart [kɑːt] *n* charrette *f* ♦ *vt* (*inf*) transporter, trimballer (*inf*)

carton ['kɑːtən] *n* (*box*) carton *m*; (*of yogurt*) pot *m*; (*of cigarettes*) cartouche *f*

cartoon [kɑː'tuːn] *n* (*PRESS*) dessin *m* (humoristique), caricature *f*; (*BRIT: comic strip*) bande dessinée; (*CINEMA*) dessin animé

cartridge ['kɑːtrɪdʒ] *n* cartouche *f*

carve [kɑːv] *vt* (*meat*) découper; (*wood, stone*) tailler, sculpter; **~ up** *vt* découper; (fig: *country*) morceler; **carving** *n* sculpture *f*; **carving knife** *n* couteau *m* à découper

car wash *n* station *f* de lavage (de voitures)

case [keɪs] *n* cas *m*; (*LAW*) affaire *f*, procès *m*; (*box*) caisse *f*, boîte *f*, étui *m*; (*BRIT: also:* **suitcase**) valise *f*; **in ~ of** en cas de; **in ~ he ...** au cas où il ...; **just in ~** à tout hasard; **in any ~** en tout cas, de toute façon

cash [kæʃ] *n* argent *m*; (*COMM*) argent liquide, espèces *fpl* ♦ *vt* encaisser; **to pay (in)** ~ payer comptant; ~ **on delivery** payable *or* paiement à la livraison; ~**book** *n* livre *m* de caisse; ~ **card** (*BRIT*) *n* carte *f* de retrait; ~ **desk** (*BRIT*) *n* caisse *f*; ~ **dispenser** (*BRIT*) *n* distributeur *m* automatique de billets, billeterie *f*

cashew [kæ'ʃuː] *n* (*also*: ~ **nut**) noix *f* de cajou

cashier [kæ'ʃɪəʳ] *n* caissier(-ère)

cashmere ['kæʃmɪəʳ] *n* cachemire *m*

cash register *n* caisse (enregistreuse)

casing ['keɪsɪŋ] *n* revêtement (protecteur), enveloppe (protectrice)

casino [kə'siːnəu] *n* casino *m*

casket ['kɑːskɪt] *n* coffret *m*; (*US*: *coffin*) cercueil *m*

casserole ['kæsərəul] *n* (*container*) cocotte *f*; (*food*) ragoût *m* (en cocotte)

cassette [kæ'set] *n* cassette *f*, musicassette *f*; ~ **player** *n* lecteur *m* de cassettes; ~ **recorder** *n* magnétophone *m* à cassettes

cast [kɑːst] (*pt*, *pp* **cast**) *vt* (*throw*) jeter; (*shed*) perdre; se dépouiller de; (*statue*) mouler; (*THEATRE*): **to ~ sb as Hamlet** attribuer à qn le rôle de Hamlet ♦ *n* (*THEATRE*) distribution *f*; (*also*: **plaster ~**) plâtre *m*; **to ~ one's vote** voter; ~ **off** *vi* (*NAUT*) larguer les amarres; (*KNITTING*) arrêter les mailles; ~ **on** *vi* (*KNITTING*) monter les mailles

castaway ['kɑːstəweɪ] *n* naufragé(e)

caster sugar ['kɑːstə-] (*BRIT*) *n* sucre *m* semoule

casting vote (*BRIT*) *n* voix prépondérante (*pour départager*)

cast iron *n* fonte *f*

castle ['kɑːsl] *n* château (fort); (*CHESS*) tour *f*

castor ['kɑːstəʳ] *n* (*wheel*) roulette *f*; ~ **oil** *n* huile *f* de ricin

castrate [kæs'treɪt] *vt* châtrer

casual ['kæʒjul] *adj* (*by chance*) de hasard, fait(e) au hasard, fortuit(e); (*irregular*: *work etc*) temporaire; (*unconcerned*) désinvolte; ~**ly** *adv* avec désinvolture, négligemment; (*dress*) de façon décontractée

casualty ['kæʒjultɪ] *n* accidenté(e), blessé(e); (*dead*) victime *f*, mort(e); (*MED*: *department*) urgences *fpl*

casual wear *n* vêtements *mpl* décontractés

cat [kæt] *n* chat *m*

catalogue ['kætəlɔg] (*US* **catalog**) *n* catalogue *m* ♦ *vt* cataloguer

catalyst ['kætəlɪst] *n* catalyseur *m*

catalytic converter [kætə'lɪtɪk kən'vəːtəʳ] *n* pot *m* catalytique

catapult ['kætəpʌlt] (*BRIT*) *n* (*sling*) lance-pierres *m inv*, fronde *m*

catarrh [kə'tɑːʳ] *n* rhume *m* chronique, catarrhe *m*

catastrophe [kə'tæstrəfɪ] *n* catastrophe *f*

catch [kætʃ] (*pt*, *pp* **caught**) *vt* attraper; (*person*: *by surprise*) prendre, surprendre; (*understand*, *hear*) saisir ♦ *vi* (*fire*) prendre; (*become trapped*) se prendre, s'accrocher ♦ *n* prise *f*; (*trick*) attrape *f*; (*of lock*) loquet *m*; **to ~ sb's attention** *or* **eye** attirer l'attention de qn; **to ~ one's breath** retenir son souffle; **to ~ fire** prendre feu; **to ~ sight of** apercevoir; ~ **on** *vi* saisir; (*grow popular*) prendre; ~ **up** *vi* se rattraper, combler son retard ♦ *vt* (*also*: ~ **up with**) rattraper; ~**ing** *adj* (*MED*) contagieux(-euse); ~**ment area** ['kætʃmənt-] (*BRIT*) *n* (*SCOL*) secteur *m* de recrutement; (*of hospital*) circonscription hospitalière; ~ **phrase** *n* slogan *m*; expression *f* (à la mode); ~**y** *adj* (*tune*) facile à retenir

category ['kætɪgərɪ] *n* catégorie *f*

cater ['keɪtəʳ] *vi* (*provide food*): **to ~ (for)** préparer des repas (pour), se charger de la restauration (pour); ~ **for** (*BRIT*) *vt fus* (*needs*) satisfaire, pourvoir à; (*readers*, *consumers*) s'adresser à, pourvoir aux besoins de; ~**er** *n* traiteur *m*; fournisseur *m*; ~**ing** *n* restauration *f*; approvisionnement *m*, ravitaillement *m*

caterpillar ['kætəpɪləʳ] *n* chenille *f*

cathedral [kə'θiːdrəl] *n* cathédrale *f*

catholic ['kæθəlɪk] *adj* (*tastes*) éclectique, varié(e); **C~** *adj* catholique ♦ *n* catholique *m/f*

Catseye ® ['kæts'aɪ] (*BRIT*) *n* (*AUT*) cata-dioptre *m*

cattle ['kætl] *npl* bétail *m*

catty ['kætɪ] *adj* méchant(e)

caucus ['kɔːkəs] *n* (*POL: group*) comité local d'un parti politique; (*US: POL*) comité électoral (pour désigner des candidats)

caught [kɔːt] *pt, pp of* **catch**

cauliflower ['kɒlɪflauə'] *n* chou-fleur *m*

cause [kɔːz] *n* cause *f ♦ vt* causer

caution ['kɔːʃən] *n* prudence *f*; (*warning*) avertissement *m ♦ vt* avertir, donner un avertissement à; **cautious** *adj* prudent(e)

cavalry ['kævəlrɪ] *n* cavalerie *f*

cave [keɪv] *n* caverne *f*, grotte *f*; ~ **in** *vi* (*roof etc*) s'effondrer; ~**man** ['keɪvmæn] (*irreg*) *n* homme *m* des cavernes

caviar(e) ['kævɪɑː'] *n* caviar *m*

CB *n abbr* (= *Citizens' Band (Radio)*) CB *f*

CBI *n abbr* (= *Confederation of British Industries*) groupement du patronat

cc *abbr* = **carbon copy**; **cubic centimetres**

CCTV *n abbr* (= *closed-circuit television*) télévision *f* en circuit fermé

CD *n abbr* (= *compact disc (player)*) CD *m*; **CDI** *n abbr* (= *Compact Disk Interactive*) CD-I *m*; **CD player** *n* platine *f* laser; **CD-ROM** [siːdiːˈrɔm] *n abbr* (= *compact disc read-only memory*) CD-Rom *m*

cease [siːs] *vt, vi* cesser; ~**fire** *n* cessez-le-feu *m*; ~**less** *adj* incessant(e), continuel(le)

cedar ['siːdə'] *n* cèdre *m*

ceiling ['siːlɪŋ] *n* plafond *m*

celebrate ['sɛlɪbreɪt] *vt, vi* célébrer; ~**d** *adj* célèbre; **celebration** [sɛlɪˈbreɪʃən] *n* célébration *f*; **celebrity** [sɪˈlɛbrɪtɪ] *n* célébrité *f*

celery ['sɛlərɪ] *n* céleri *m* (à côtes)

cell [sɛl] *n* cellule *f*; (*ELEC*) élément *m* (de pile)

cellar ['sɛlə'] *n* cave *f*

cello ['tʃɛləu] *n* violoncelle *m*

cellphone ['sɛlfəun] *n* téléphone *m* cellulaire

Celt [kɛlt, sɛlt] *n* Celte *m/f*; ~**ic** *adj* celte

cement [sə'mɛnt] *n* ciment *m*

cemetery ['sɛmɪtrɪ] *n* cimetière *m*

censor ['sɛnsə'] *n* censeur *m ♦ vt* censurer; ~**ship** *n* censure *f*

censure ['sɛnʃə'] *vt* blâmer, critiquer

census ['sɛnsəs] *n* recensement *m*

cent [sɛnt] *n* (*US etc: coin*) cent *m* (= *un centième du dollar, de l'euro*); *see also* **per**

centenary [sɛn'tiːnərɪ] *n* centenaire *m*

center ['sɛntə'] (*US*) *n* = **centre**

centigrade ['sɛntɪɡreɪd] *adj* centigrade

centimetre ['sɛntɪmiːtə'] (*US* **centimeter**) *n* centimètre *m*

centipede ['sɛntɪpiːd] *n* mille-pattes *m inv*

central ['sɛntrəl] *adj* central(e); **C~ America** *n* Amérique centrale; ~ **heating** *n* chauffage central; ~ **reservation** (*BRIT*) *n* (*AUT*) terre-plein central

centre ['sɛntə'] (*US* **center**) *n* centre *m ♦ vt* centrer; ~**-forward** *n* (*SPORT*) avant-centre *m*; ~**-half** *n* (*SPORT*) demi-centre *m*

century ['sɛntjurɪ] *n* siècle *m*; **20th** ~ XXe siècle

ceramic [sɪ'ræmɪk] *adj* céramique

cereal ['siːrɪəl] *n* céréale *f*

ceremony ['sɛrɪmənɪ] *n* cérémonie *f*; **to stand on** ~ faire des façons

certain ['səːtən] *adj* certain(e); **for** ~ certainement, sûrement; ~**ly** *adv* certainement; ~**ty** *n* certitude *f*

certificate [sə'tɪfɪkɪt] *n* certificat *m*

certified ['səːtɪfaɪd] *adj*: **by** ~ **mail** (*US*) en recommandé, avec avis de réception; ~ **public accountant** (*US*) expert-comptable *m*

certify ['səːtɪfaɪ] *vt* certifier; (*award diploma to*) conférer un diplôme *etc* à; (*declare insane*) déclarer malade mental(e)

cervical ['səːvɪkl] *adj*: ~ **cancer** cancer *m* du col de l'utérus; ~ **smear** frottis vaginal

cervix ['səːvɪks] *n* col *m* de l'utérus

cf. *abbr* (= *compare*) cf., voir

CFC *n abbr* (= *chlorofluorocarbon*) CFC *m*

ch. *abbr* (= *chapter*) chap

chafe [tʃeɪf] *vt* irriter, frotter contre

chain [tʃeɪn] *n* chaîne *f ♦ vt* (*also:* ~ **up**) enchaîner, attacher (avec une chaîne); ~ **reaction** *n* réaction *f* en chaîne; ~-

smoke vi fumer cigarette sur cigarette; ~ **store** n magasin m à succursales multiples

chair [tʃɛəʳ] n chaise f; (armchair) fauteuil m; (of university) chaire f; (of meeting, committee) présidence f ♦ vt (meeting) présider; ~**lift** n télésiège m; ~**man** (irreg) n président m

chalet [ˈʃæleɪ] n chalet m

chalk [tʃɔːk] n craie f

challenge [ˈtʃælɪndʒ] n défi m ♦ vt défier; (statement, right) mettre en question, contester; **to ~ sb to do** mettre qn au défi de faire; **challenging** adj (tone, look) de défi, provocateur(-trice); (task, career) qui représente un défi or une gageure

chamber [ˈtʃeɪmbəʳ] n chambre f; ~ **of commerce** chambre de commerce; ~**maid** n femme f de chambre; ~ **music** n musique f de chambre

champagne [ʃæmˈpeɪn] n champagne m

champion [ˈtʃæmpɪən] n champion(ne); ~**ship** n championnat m

chance [tʃɑːns] n (opportunity) occasion f, possibilité f; (hope, likelihood) chance f; (risk) risque m ♦ vt: **to ~ it** risquer (le coup), essayer ♦ adj fortuit(e), de hasard; **to take a ~** prendre un risque; **by ~** par hasard

chancellor [ˈtʃɑːnsələʳ] n chancelier m; **C~ of the Exchequer** (BRIT) n chancelier m de l'Échiquier; ≈ ministre m des Finances

chandelier [ʃændəˈlɪəʳ] n lustre m

change [tʃeɪndʒ] vt (alter, replace, COMM: money) changer; (hands, trains, clothes, one's name) changer de; (transform): **to ~ sb into** changer or transformer qn en ♦ vi (gen) changer; (one's clothes) se changer; (be transformed): **to ~ into** se changer or transformer en ♦ n changement m; (money) monnaie f; **to ~ gear** (AUT) changer de vitesse; **to ~ one's mind** changer d'avis; **a ~ of clothes** des vêtements de rechange; **for a ~** pour changer; ~**able** adj (weather) variable; ~ **machine** n distributeur m de monnaie; ~**over** n (to new

system) changement m, passage m; **changing** adj changeant(e); **changing room** (BRIT) n (in shop) salon m d'essayage; (SPORT) vestiaire m

channel [ˈtʃænl] n (TV) chaîne f; (navigable passage) chenal m; (irrigation) canal m ♦ vt canaliser; **the (English) C~** la Manche; **the C~ Islands** les îles de la Manche, les îles Anglo-Normandes; **the C~ Tunnel** le tunnel sous la Manche; ~-**hopping** n (TV) zapping m

chant [tʃɑːnt] n chant m; (REL) psalmodie f ♦ vt chanter, scander

chaos [ˈkeɪɒs] n chaos m

chap [tʃæp] (BRIT: inf) n (man) type m

chapel [ˈtʃæpl] n chapelle f; (BRIT: non-conformist ~) église f

chaplain [ˈtʃæplɪn] n aumônier m

chapped [tʃæpt] adj (skin, lips) gercé(e)

chapter [ˈtʃæptəʳ] n chapitre m

char [tʃɑːʳ] vt (burn) carboniser

character [ˈkærɪktəʳ] n caractère m; (in novel, film) personnage m; (eccentric) numéro m, phénomène m; ~**istic** [kærɪktəˈrɪstɪk] adj caractéristique ♦ n caractéristique f

charcoal [ˈtʃɑːkəʊl] n charbon m de bois; (for drawing) charbon m

charge [tʃɑːdʒ] n (cost) prix (demandé); (accusation) accusation f; (LAW) inculpation f ♦ vt: **to ~ sb (with)** inculper qn (de); (battery, enemy) charger; (customer, sum) faire payer ♦ vi foncer; ~**s** npl (costs) frais mpl; **to reverse the ~s** (TEL) téléphoner en P.C.V.; **to take ~ of** se charger de; **to be in ~ of** être responsable de, s'occuper de; **how much do you ~?** combien prenez-vous?; **to ~ an expense (up) to sb** mettre une dépense sur le compte de qn; ~ **card** n carte f de client

charity [ˈtʃærɪtɪ] n charité f; (organization) institution f charitable or de bienfaisance, œuvre f (de charité)

charm [tʃɑːm] n charme m; (on bracelet) breloque f ♦ vt charmer, enchanter; ~**ing** adj charmant(e)

chart [tʃɑːt] n tableau m, diagramme m; graphique m; (map) carte marine ♦ vt dresser *or* établir la carte de; **~s** *npl* (*hit parade*) hit-parade *m*

charter ['tʃɑːtəʳ] *vt* (*plane*) affréter ♦ *n* (*document*) charte *f*; **~ed accountant** (*BRIT*) *n* expert-comptable *m*; **~ flight** *n* charter *m*

chase [tʃeɪs] *vt* poursuivre, pourchasser; (*also:* **~ away**) chasser ♦ *n* poursuite *f*, chasse *f*

chasm ['kæzəm] *n* gouffre *m*, abîme *m*

chat [tʃæt] *vi* (*also:* **have a ~**) bavarder, causer ♦ *n* conversation *f*; **~ show** (*BRIT*) *n* causerie télévisée

chatter ['tʃætəʳ] *vi* (*person*) bavarder; (*animal*) jacasser ♦ *n* bavardage *m*; jacassement *m*; **my teeth are ~ing** je claque des dents; **~box** (*inf*) *n* moulin *m* à paroles

chatty ['tʃætɪ] *adj* (*style*) familier(-ère); (*person*) bavard(e)

chauffeur ['ʃəʊfəʳ] *n* chauffeur *m* (de maître)

chauvinist ['ʃəʊvɪnɪst] *n* (*male ~*) phallocrate *m*; (*nationalist*) chauvin(e)

cheap [tʃiːp] *adj* bon marché *inv*, pas cher (chère), (*joke*) facile, d'un goût douteux; (*poor quality*) à bon marché, de qualité médiocre ♦ *adv* à bon marché, pour pas cher; **~ day return** billet *m* d'aller et retour réduit (*valable pour la journée*); **~er** *adj* moins cher (chère); **~ly** *adv* à bon marché, à bon compte

cheat [tʃiːt] *vi* tricher ♦ *vt* tromper, duper; (*rob*): **to ~ sb out of sth** escroquer qch à qn ♦ *n* tricheur(-euse); escroc *m*

check [tʃɛk] *vt* vérifier; (*passport, ticket*) contrôler; (*halt*) arrêter; (*restrain*) maîtriser ♦ *n* vérification *f*; contrôle *m*; (*curb*) frein *m*; (*US: bill*) addition *f*; (*pattern: gen pl*) carreaux *mpl*; (*US*) = **cheque** ♦ *adj* (*pattern, cloth*) à carreaux; **~ in** *vi* (*in hotel*) remplir sa fiche (d'hôtel); (*at airport*) se présenter à l'enregistrement ♦ *vt* (*luggage*) (faire) enregistrer; **~ out** *vi* (*in hotel*) régler sa note; **~ up** *vi*: **to ~ up (on sth)** vérifier (qch); **to ~ up on sb** se renseigner sur le compte de qn; **~ered** (*US*) *adj* = **chequered**; **~ers** (*US*) *npl* jeu *m* de dames; **~-in** (*desk*) *n* enregistrement *m*; **~ing account** (*US*) *n* (*current account*) compte courant; **~mate** *n* échec et mat *m*; **~out** *n* (*in shop*) caisse *f*; **~point** *n* contrôle *m*; **~room** (*US*) *n* (*left-luggage office*) consigne *f*; **~up** *n* (*MED*) examen médical, check-up *m*

cheek [tʃiːk] *n* joue *f*; (*impudence*) toupet *m*, culot *m*; **~bone** *n* pommette *f*; **~y** *adj* effronté(e), culotté(e)

cheep [tʃiːp] *vi* piauler

cheer [tʃɪəʳ] *vt* acclamer, applaudir; (*gladden*) réjouir, réconforter ♦ *vi* applaudir ♦ *n* (*gen pl*) acclamations *fpl*, applaudissements *mpl*; bravos *mpl*, hourras *mpl*; **~s!** à la vôtre!; **~ up** *vi* se dérider, reprendre courage ♦ *vt* remonter le moral à *or* de, dérider; **~ful** *adj* gai(e), joyeux(-euse)

cheerio [tʃɪərɪˈəʊ] (*BRIT*) *excl* salut!, au revoir!

cheese [tʃiːz] *n* fromage *m*; **~board** *n* plateau *m* de fromages

cheetah ['tʃiːtə] *n* guépard *m*

chef [ʃɛf] *n* chef (cuisinier)

chemical ['kɛmɪkl] *adj* chimique ♦ *n* produit *m* chimique

chemist ['kɛmɪst] *n* (*BRIT: pharmacist*) pharmacien(ne); (*scientist*) chimiste *m/f*; **~ry** *n* chimie *f*; **~'s (shop)** (*BRIT*) *n* pharmacie *f*

cheque [tʃɛk] (*BRIT*) *n* chèque *m*; **~book** *n* chéquier *m*, carnet *m* de chèques; **~ card** *n* carte *f* (d'identité) bancaire

chequered ['tʃɛkəd] (*US* **checkered**) *adj* (*fig*) varié(e)

cherish ['tʃɛrɪʃ] *vt* chérir

cherry ['tʃɛrɪ] *n* cerise *f*; (*also:* **~ tree**) cerisier *m*

chess [tʃɛs] *n* échecs *mpl*; **~board** *n* échiquier *m*

chest [tʃɛst] *n* poitrine *f*; (*box*) coffre *m*, caisse *f*; **~ of drawers** *n* commode *f*

chestnut ['tʃɛsnʌt] *n* châtaigne *f*; (*also:* **~ tree**) châtaignier *m*

chew [tʃuː] *vt* mâcher; **~ing gum** *n* chewing-gum *m*

chic [ʃiːk] adj chic inv, élégant(e)

chick [tʃɪk] n poussin m; (inf) nana f

chicken ['tʃɪkɪn] n poulet m; (inf: coward) poule mouillée; ~ out (inf) vi se dégonfler; ~pox n varicelle f.

chicory ['tʃɪkərɪ] n (for coffee) chicorée f; (salad) endive f

chief [tʃiːf] n chef ♦ adj principal(e); ~ executive (US chief executive officer) n directeur(-trice) général(e); ~ly adv principalement, surtout

chiffon ['ʃɪfɔn] n mousseline f de soie

chilblain ['tʃɪlbleɪn] n engelure f

child [tʃaɪld] (pl ~ren) n enfant m/f; ~birth n accouchement m; ~hood n enfance f; ~ish adj puéril(e), enfantin(e); ~like adj d'enfant, innocent(e); ~ minder (BRIT) n garde f d'enfants; ~ren ['tʃɪldrən] npl of child

Chile ['tʃɪlɪ] n Chili m

chill [tʃɪl] n (of water) froid m; (of air) fraîcheur f; (MED) refroidissement m, coup m de froid ♦ vt (person) faire frissonner; (CULIN) mettre au frais, rafraîchir

chil(l)i ['tʃɪlɪ] n piment m (rouge)

chilly ['tʃɪlɪ] adj froid(e), glacé(e); (sensitive to cold) frileux(-euse); to feel ~ avoir froid

chime [tʃaɪm] n carillon m ♦ vi carillonner, sonner

chimney ['tʃɪmnɪ] n cheminée f; ~ sweep n ramoneur m

chimpanzee [tʃɪmpæn'ziː] n chimpanzé m

chin [tʃɪn] n menton m

China ['tʃaɪnə] n Chine f

china ['tʃaɪnə] n porcelaine f; (crockery) (vaisselle f en) porcelaine

Chinese [tʃaɪ'niːz] adj chinois(e) ♦ n inv (person) Chinois(e); (LING) chinois m

chink [tʃɪŋk] n (opening) fente f, fissure f; (noise) tintement m

chip [tʃɪp] n (gen pl: CULIN: BRIT) frite f; (: US: potato ~) chip m; (of wood) copeau m; (of glass, stone) éclat m; (also: microchip) puce f ♦ vt (cup, plate) ébrécher

---

| chip shop |

🛈 Un **chip shop**, que l'on appelle également un "fish-and-chip shop", est un magasin où l'on vend des plats à emporter. Les chip shops sont d'ailleurs à l'origine des *takeaways*. On y achète en particulier du poisson frit et des frites, mais on y trouve également des plats traditionnels britanniques (steak pies, saucisses, etc). Tous les plats étaient à l'origine emballés dans du papier journal. Dans certains de ces magasins, on peut s'asseoir pour consommer sur place.

---

chiropodist [kɪ'rɔpədɪst] (BRIT) n pédicure m/f

chirp [tʃəːp] vi pépier, gazouiller

chisel ['tʃɪzl] n ciseau m

chit [tʃɪt] n mot m, note f

chitchat ['tʃɪttʃæt] n bavardage m

chivalry ['ʃɪvəlrɪ] n esprit m chevaleresque, galanterie f

chives [tʃaɪvz] npl ciboulette f, civette f

chock-a-block ['tʃɔkə'blɔk], chock-full ['tʃɔk'ful] adj plein(e) à craquer

chocolate ['tʃɔklɪt] n chocolat m

choice [tʃɔɪs] n choix m ♦ adj de choix

choir ['kwaɪər] n chœur m, chorale f; ~boy n jeune choriste m

choke [tʃəuk] vi étouffer ♦ vt étrangler; étouffer ♦ n (AUT) starter m; street ~d with traffic rue engorgée ou embouteillée

cholesterol [kə'lɛstərɔl] n cholestérol m

choose [tʃuːz] (pt chose, pp chosen) vt choisir; to ~ to do décider de faire, juger bon de faire; choosy adj: (to be) choosy (faire le/la) difficile

chop [tʃɔp] vt (wood) couper (à la hache); (CULIN: also: ~ up) couper (fin), émincer, hacher (en morceaux) ♦ n (CULIN) côtelette f; ~s npl (jaws) mâchoires fpl

chopper ['tʃɔpər] n (helicopter) hélicoptère m, hélico m

choppy ['tʃɔpɪ] adj (sea) un peu agité(e)

chopsticks ['tʃɔpstɪks] npl baguettes fpl

chord [kɔːd] n (MUS) accord m

chore [tʃɔːʳ] n travail m de routine; **household ~s** travaux mpl du ménage

chortle ['tʃɔːtl] vi glousser

chorus ['kɔːrəs] n chœur m; (*repeated part of song: also fig*) refrain m

chose [tʃəuz] pt of **choose**; **~n** pp of **choose**

chowder ['tʃaudəʳ] n soupe f de poisson

Christ [kraɪst] n Christ m

christen ['krɪsn] vt baptiser

christening ['krɪsnɪŋ] n baptême m

Christian ['krɪstɪən] adj, n chrétien(ne); **~ity** [krɪstɪ'ænɪtɪ] n christianisme m; **~ name** n prénom m

Christmas ['krɪsməs] n Noël m or f; **Happy** or **Merry ~!** joyeux Noël!; **~ card** n carte f de Noël; **~ Day** n le jour de Noël; **~ Eve** n la veille de Noël; la nuit de Noël; **~ tree** n arbre m de Noël

chrome [krəum] n chrome m

chromium ['krəumɪəm] n chrome m

chronic ['krɔnɪk] adj chronique

chronicle ['krɔnɪkl] n chronique f

chronological [krɔnə'lɔdʒɪkl] adj chronologique

chrysanthemum [krɪ'sænθəməm] n chrysanthème m

chubby ['tʃʌbɪ] adj potelé(e), rondelet(te)

chuck [tʃʌk] (inf) vt (throw) lancer, jeter; (BRIT: person) (: also: **~ up**: job) lâcher; **~ out** vt flanquer dehors or à la porte; (rubbish) jeter

chuckle ['tʃʌkl] vi glousser

chug [tʃʌg] vi faire teuf-teuf; (: also: **~ along**) avancer en faisant teuf-teuf

chum [tʃʌm] n copain (copine)

chunk [tʃʌŋk] n gros morceau

church [tʃəːtʃ] n église f; **~yard** n cimetière m

churn [tʃəːn] n (for butter) baratte f; (: also: **milk ~**) (grand) bidon à lait; **~ out** vt débiter

chute [ʃuːt] n glissoire f; (: also: **rubbish ~**) vide-ordures m inv

chutney ['tʃʌtnɪ] n condiment m à base de fruits au vinaigre

CIA n abbr (= Central Intelligence Agency)

CIA f

CID (BRIT) n abbr (= Criminal Investigation Department) P.J. f

cider ['saɪdəʳ] n cidre m

cigar [sɪ'gɑːʳ] n cigare m

cigarette [sɪgə'rɛt] n cigarette f; **~ case** n étui m à cigarettes; **~ end** n mégot m

Cinderella [sɪndə'rɛlə] n Cendrillon

cinders ['sɪndəz] npl cendres fpl

cine-camera ['sɪnɪ'kæmərə] (BRIT) n caméra f

cinema ['sɪnəmə] n cinéma m

cinnamon ['sɪnəmən] n cannelle f

circle ['səːkl] n cercle m; (in cinema, theatre) balcon m ♦ vi faire or décrire des cercles ♦ vt (move round) faire le tour de, tourner autour de; (surround) entourer, encercler

circuit ['səːkɪt] n circuit m; **~ous** [səː'kjuɪtəs] adj indirect(e), qui fait un détour

circular ['səːkjuləʳ] adj circulaire ♦ n circulaire f

circulate ['səːkjuleɪt] vi circuler ♦ vt faire circuler; **circulation** [səːkju'leɪʃən] n circulation f; (of newspaper) tirage m

circumflex ['səːkəmflɛks] n (also: **~ accent**) accent m circonflexe

circumstances ['səːkəmstənsɪz] npl circonstances fpl; (financial condition) moyens mpl, situation financière

circus ['səːkəs] n cirque m

CIS n abbr (= Commonwealth of Independent States) CEI f

cistern ['sɪstən] n réservoir m (d'eau); (in toilet) réservoir de la chasse d'eau

citizen ['sɪtɪzn] n (resident): **the ~s of this town** les habitants de cette ville; **~ship** n citoyenneté f

citrus fruit ['sɪtrəs-] n agrume m

city ['sɪtɪ] n ville f, cité f; **the C~** la Cité de Londres (centre des affaires); **~ technology college** n établissement m d'enseignement technologique

civic ['sɪvɪk] adj civique; (authorities) municipal(e); **~ centre** (BRIT) n centre administratif (municipal)

civil ['sɪvɪl] *adj* civil(e); (*polite*) poli(e), courtois(e); (*disobedience, defence*) passif(-ive); ~ **engineer** *n* ingénieur *m* des travaux publics; **~ian** [sɪ'vɪlɪən] *adj, n* civil(e)

civilization [sɪvɪlaɪ'zeɪʃən] *n* civilisation *f*

civilized ['sɪvɪlaɪzd] *adj* civilisé(e); (*fig*) où règnent les bonnes manières

civil: ~ **law** *n* code civil; (*study*) droit civil; ~ **servant** *n* fonctionnaire *m/f*; **C~ Service** *n* fonction publique, administration *f*; ~ **war** *n* guerre civile

clad [klæd] *adj:* ~ **(in)** habillé(e) (de)

claim [kleɪm] *vt* revendiquer; (*rights, inheritance*) demander, prétendre à; (*assert*) déclarer, prétendre ♦ *vi* (*for insurance*) faire une déclaration de sinistre ♦ *n* revendication *f*; demande *f*; prétention *f*, déclaration *f*; (*right*) droit *m*, titre *m*; **~ant** *n* (*ADMIN, LAW*) requérant(e)

clairvoyant [kleə'vɔɪənt] *n* voyant(e), extra-lucide *m/f*

clam [klæm] *n* palourde *f*

clamber ['klæmbə'] *vi* grimper, se hisser

clammy ['klæmɪ] *adj* humide (et froid(e)), moite

clamour ['klæmə'] (*US* **clamor**) *vi:* **to ~ for** réclamer à grands cris

clamp [klæmp] *n* agrafe *f*, crampon *m* ♦ *vt* serrer; (*sth to sth*) fixer; (*wheel*) mettre un sabot à; ~ **down on** *vt fus* sévir or prendre des mesures draconiennes contre

clan [klæn] *n* clan *m*

clang [klæŋ] *vi* émettre un bruit or fracas métallique

clap [klæp] *vi* applaudir; **~ping** *n* applaudissements *mpl*

claret ['klærət] *n* (vin *m* de) bordeaux *m* (rouge)

clarinet [klærɪ'net] *n* clarinette *f*

clarity ['klærɪtɪ] *n* clarté *f*

clash [klæʃ] *n* choc *m*; (*fig*) conflit *m* ♦ *vi* se heurter; être or entrer en conflit; (*colours*) jurer; (*two events*) tomber en même temps

clasp [klɑːsp] *n* (*of necklace, bag*) fermoir *m*; (*hold, embrace*) étreinte *f* ♦ *vt* serrer, étreindre

class [klɑːs] *n* classe *f* ♦ *vt* classer, classifier

classic ['klæsɪk] *adj* classique ♦ *n* (*author, work*) classique *m*; **~al** *adj* classique

classified ['klæsɪfaɪd] *adj* (*information*) secret(-ète); ~ **advertisement** *n* petite annonce

classmate ['klɑːsmeɪt] *n* camarade *m/f* de classe

classroom ['klɑːsrum] *n* (salle *f* de) classe *f*

clatter ['klætə'] *n* cliquetis *m* ♦ *vi* cliqueter

clause [klɔːz] *n* clause *f*; (*LING*) proposition *f*

claw [klɔː] *n* griffe *f*; (*of bird of prey*) serre *f*; (*of lobster*) pince *f*

clay [kleɪ] *n* argile *f*

clean [kliːn] *adj* propre; (*clear, smooth*) net(te); (*record, reputation*) sans tache; (*joke, story*) correct(e) ♦ *vt* nettoyer; ~ **out** *vt* nettoyer (à fond); ~ **up** *vt* nettoyer; (*fig*) remettre de l'ordre dans; **~-cut** *adj* (*person*) net(te), soigné(e); **~er** *n* (*person*) nettoyeur(-euse), femme *f* de ménage; (*product*) détachant *m*; **~er's** *n* (*also:* **dry ~er's**) teinturier *m*; **~ing** *n* nettoyage *m*; **~liness** ['klɛnlɪnɪs] *n* propreté *f*

cleanse [klɛnz] *vt* nettoyer; (*purify*) purifier; **~r** *n* (*for face*) démaquillant *m*

clean-shaven ['kliːn'ʃeɪvn] *adj* rasé(e) de près

cleansing department ['klɛnzɪŋ-] (*BRIT*) *n* service *m* de voirie

clear [klɪə'] *adj* clair(e); (*glass, plastic*) transparent(e); (*road, way*) libre, dégagé(e); (*conscience*) net(te) ♦ *vt* (*room*) débarrasser; (*of people*) faire évacuer; (*cheque*) compenser; (*LAW: suspect*) innocenter; (*obstacle*) franchir or sauter sans heurter ♦ *vi* (*weather*) s'éclaircir; (*fog*) se dissiper ♦ *adv:* ~ **of** à distance de, à l'écart de; **to ~ the table** débarrasser la table, desservir; ~ **up** *vt* ranger, mettre en ordre; (*mystery*) éclaircir, résoudre; **~ance** *n* (*removal*) déblaiement *m*; (*permission*) autorisation *f*; **~-cut** *adj* clair(e), nettement défini(e); **~ing** *n* (*in forest*) clairière *f*; **~ing bank** (*BRIT*) *n* banque qui appartient à une

chambre de compensation; **~ly** *adv* clairement; *(evidently)* de toute évidence; **~way**
(BRIT) *n* route *f* à stationnement interdit

clef [klɛf] *n* *(MUS)* clé *f*

cleft [klɛft] *n* *(in rock)* crevasse *f*, fissure *f*

clementine ['klɛməntaɪn] *n* clémentine *f*

clench [klɛntʃ] *vt* serrer

clergy ['kləːdʒɪ] *n* clergé *m*; **~man** *(irreg)*
n ecclésiastique *m*

clerical ['klɛrɪkl] *adj* de bureau, d'employé
de bureau; *(REL)* clérical(e), du clergé

clerk [klɑːk, *(US)* kləːrk] *n* employé(e) de
bureau; *(US: salesperson)* vendeur(-euse)

clever ['klɛvər] *adj* *(mentally)* intelligent(e);
(crafty) habile, adroit(e); *(device, arrangement)* ingénieux(-euse), astucieux(-euse)

click [klɪk] *vi* faire un bruit sec *or* un déclic; **~ on** *vt* *(COMPUT)* cliquer sur

client ['klaɪənt] *n* client(e)

cliff [klɪf] *n* falaise *f*

climate ['klaɪmɪt] *n* climat *m*

climax ['klaɪmæks] *n* apogée *m*, point culminant; *(sexual)* orgasme *m*

climb [klaɪm] *vi* grimper, monter ♦ *vt* gravir,
escalader, monter sur ♦ *n* montée *f*, escalade
f; **~-down** *n* reculade *f*; **~er** *n* *(mountaineer)*
grimpeur(-euse), varappeur(-euse); *(plant)*
plante grimpante; **~ing** *n* *(mountaineering)*
escalade *f*, varappe *f*

clinch [klɪntʃ] *vt* *(deal)* conclure, sceller

cling [klɪŋ] *(pt, pp* **clung)** *vi*: **to ~ (to)** se
cramponner (à), s'accrocher (à); *(of
clothes)* coller (à)

clinic ['klɪnɪk] *n* centre médical; **~al** *adj*
clinique; *(attitude)* froid(e), détaché(e)

clink [klɪŋk] *vi* tinter, cliqueter

clip [klɪp] *n* *(for hair)* barrette *f*; *(also:* **paper ~)** trombone *m* ♦ *vt* *(fasten)* attacher;
(hair, nails) couper; *(hedge)* tailler; **~pers**
npl *(for hedge)* sécateur *m*; *(also:* **nail
~pers)** coupe-ongles *m inv*; **~ping** *n*
(from newspaper) coupure *f* de journal

cloak [kləuk] *n* grande cape ♦ *vt* *(fig)* masquer, cacher; **~room** *n* *(for coats etc)* vestiaire *m*; *(BRIT: WC)* toilettes *fpl*

clock [klɔk] *n* *(large)* horloge *f*; *(small)* pendule *f*; **~ in** *(BRIT)* *vi* pointer (en arrivant);

~ off *(BRIT)* *vi* pointer (en partant); **~ on**
(BRIT) *vi* = **clock in**; **~ out** *(BRIT)* *vi* =
clock off; **~wise** *adv* dans le sens des
aiguilles d'une montre; **~work** *n* rouages
mpl, mécanisme *m*; *(of clock)* mouvement
m (d'horlogerie) ♦ *adj* mécanique

clog [klɔg] *n* sabot *m* ♦ *vt* boucher ♦ *vi*
(also: **~ up)** se boucher

cloister ['klɔɪstər] *n* cloître *m*

clone [kləun] *n* clone *m* ♦ *vt* cloner

close¹ [kləus] *adj* *(near)* près, proche;
(contact, link) étroit(e); *(contest)* très ser-
ré(e); *(watch)* étroit(e), strict(e); *(examination)* attentif(-ive), minutieux(-euse);
(weather) lourd(e), étouffant(e) ♦ *adv* près,
à proximité; **~ to** près de, proche de; **~ by**
adj proche ♦ *adv* tout(e) près; **~ at hand**
= **close by**; **a ~ friend** un ami intime; **to
have a ~ shave** *(fig)* l'échapper belle

close² [kləuz] *vt* fermer ♦ *vi* *(shop etc)*
fermer; *(lid, door etc)* se fermer; *(end)* se
terminer, se conclure ♦ *n* *(end)* conclusion
f, fin *f*; **~ down** *vt, vi* fermer *(définitivement)*; **~d** *adj* fermé(e); **~d shop** *n* organisation *f* qui n'admet que des travailleurs
syndiqués

close-knit ['kləus'nɪt] *adj* *(family, community)* très uni(e)

closely ['kləuslɪ] *adv* *(examine, watch)* de
près

closet ['klɔzɪt] *n* *(cupboard)* placard *m*, réduit *m*

close-up ['kləusʌp] *n* gros plan

closure ['kləuʒər] *n* fermeture *f*

clot [klɔt] *n* *(gen: blood ~)* caillot *m*; *(inf:
person)* ballot *m* ♦ *vi* *(blood)* se coaguler;
~ted cream crème fraîche très épaisse

cloth [klɔθ] *n* *(material)* tissu *m*, étoffe *f*;
(also: **teacloth)** torchon *m*; lavette *f*

clothe [kləuð] *vt* habiller, vêtir; **~s** *npl*
vêtements *mpl*, habits *mpl*; **~s brush** *n*
brosse *f* à habits; **~s line** *n* corde *f* (à linge); **~s peg** *(US* **clothes pin)** *n* pince *f* à
linge; **clothing** *n* = **clothes**

cloud [klaud] *n* nuage *m*; **~burst** *n* grosse
averse; **~y** *adj* nuageux(-euse), couvert(e);
(liquid) trouble

clout [klaut] *vt* flanquer une taloche à

clove [kləuv] *n* (CULIN: *spice*) clou *m* de girofle; **~ of garlic** gousse *f* d'ail

clover ['kləuvə^r] *n* trèfle *m*

clown [klaun] *n* clown *m* ♦ *vi* (*also:* **~ about, ~ around**) faire le clown

cloying ['klɔɪɪŋ] *adj* (*taste, smell*) écœurant(e)

club [klʌb] *n* (*society, place: also:* **golf ~**) club *m*; (*weapon*) massue *f*, matraque *f* ♦ *vt* matraquer ♦ *vi:* **to ~ together** s'associer; **~s** *npl* (CARDS) trèfle *m*; **~ class** *n* (AVIAT) classe *f* club; **~house** *n* club *m*

cluck [klʌk] *vi* glousser

clue [kluː] *n* indice *m*; (*in crosswords*) définition *f*; **I haven't a ~** je n'en ai pas la moindre idée

clump [klʌmp] *n:* **~ of trees** bouquet *m* d'arbres

clumsy ['klʌmzɪ] *adj* gauche, maladroit(e)

clung [klʌŋ] *pt, pp of* **cling**

cluster ['klʌstə^r] *n* (*of people*) (petit) groupe; (*of flowers*) grappe *f*; (*of stars*) amas *m* ♦ *vi* se rassembler

clutch [klʌtʃ] *n* (*grip, grasp*) étreinte *f*, prise *f*; (AUT) embrayage *m* ♦ *vt* (*grasp*) agripper; (*hold tightly*) serrer fort; (*hold on to*) se cramponner à

clutter ['klʌtə^r] *vt* (*also:* **~ up**) encombrer

CND *n abbr* (= *Campaign for Nuclear Disarmament*) mouvement pour le désarmement nucléaire

Co. *abbr* = **county**; **company**

c/o *abbr* (= *care of*) c/o, aux bons soins de

coach [kəutʃ] *n* (*bus*) autocar *m*; (*horse-drawn*) diligence *f*; (*of train*) voiture *f*, wagon *m*; (SPORT: *trainer*) entraîneur(-euse); (SCOL: *tutor*) répétiteur(-trice) ♦ *vt* entraîner; (*student*) faire travailler; **~ trip** *n* excursion *f* en car

coal [kəul] *n* charbon *m*; **~ face** *n* front *m* de taille; **~field** *n* bassin houiller

coalition [kəuə'lɪʃən] *n* coalition *f*

coalman (*irreg*) *n* charbonnier *m*, marchand *m* de charbon

coalmine *n* mine *f* de charbon

coarse [kɔːs] *adj* grossier(-ère), rude

coast [kəust] *n* côte *f* ♦ *vi* (*car, cycle etc*) descendre en roue libre; **~al** *adj* côtier(-ère); **~guard** *n* garde-côte *m*; (*service*) gendarmerie *f* maritime; **~line** *n* côte *f*, littoral *m*

coat [kəut] *n* manteau *m*; (*of animal*) pelage *m*, poil *m*; (*of paint*) couche *f* ♦ *vt* couvrir; **~ hanger** *n* cintre *m*; **~ing** *n* couche *f*, revêtement *m*; **~ of arms** *n* blason *m*, armoiries *fpl*

coax [kəuks] *vt* persuader par des cajoleries

cobbler ['kɔblə^r] *n* cordonnier *m*

cobbles ['kɔblz] (*also:* **~tones**) *npl* pavés (ronds)

cobweb ['kɔbwɛb] *n* toile *f* d'araignée

cocaine [kə'keɪn] *n* cocaïne *f*

cock [kɔk] *n* (*rooster*) coq *m*; (*male bird*) mâle *m* ♦ *vt* (*gun*) armer; **~erel** *n* jeune coq *m*

cockle ['kɔkl] *n* coque *f*

cockney ['kɔknɪ] *n* cockney *m*, *habitant des quartiers populaires de l'East End de Londres*, ≈ faubourien(ne)

cockpit ['kɔkpɪt] *n* (*in aircraft*) poste *m* de pilotage, cockpit *m*

cockroach ['kɔkrəutʃ] *n* cafard *m*

cocktail ['kɔkteɪl] *n* cocktail *m*; (*fruit ~ etc*) salade *f*; **~ cabinet** *n* (meuble-)bar *m*; **~ party** *n* cocktail *m*

cocoa ['kəukəu] *n* cacao *m*

coconut ['kəukənʌt] *n* noix *f* de coco

COD *abbr* = **cash on delivery**

cod [kɔd] *n* morue fraîche, cabillaud *m*

code [kəud] *n* code *m*

cod-liver oil *n* huile *f* de foie de morue

coercion [kəu'əːʃən] *n* contrainte *f*

coffee ['kɔfɪ] *n* café *m*; **~ bar** (BRIT) *n* café *m*; **~ bean** *n* grain *m* de café; **~ break** *n* pause-café *f*; **~pot** *n* cafetière *f*; **~ table** *n* (petite) table basse

coffin ['kɔfɪn] *n* cercueil *m*

cog [kɔg] *n* dent *f* (d'engrenage); (*wheel*) roue dentée

cogent ['kəudʒənt] *adj* puissant(e), convaincant(e)

coil [kɔɪl] *n* rouleau *m*, bobine *f*; (*contraceptive*) stérilet *m* ♦ *vt* enrouler

coin [kɔɪn] n pièce f de monnaie ♦ vt (word) inventer; ~age n monnaie f, système m monétaire; ~ box (BRIT) n cabine f téléphonique

coincide [kəʊɪn'saɪd] vi coïncider; ~nce [kəʊ'ɪnsɪdəns] n coïncidence f

Coke [kəʊk] ® n coca m

coke [kəʊk] n coke m

colander ['kɔləndəʳ] n passoire f

cold [kəʊld] adj froid(e) ♦ n froid m; (MED) rhume m; **it's ~** il fait froid; **to be** or **feel ~** (person) avoir froid; **to catch ~** prendre or attraper froid; **to catch a ~** attraper un rhume; **in ~ blood** de sang-froid; **~-shoulder** vt se montrer froid(e) envers, snober; **~ sore** n bouton m de fièvre

coleslaw ['kəʊlslɔː] n sorte de salade de chou cru

colic ['kɔlɪk] n colique(s) f(pl)

collapse [kə'læps] vi s'effondrer, s'écrouler ♦ n effondrement m, écroulement m; **collapsible** adj pliant(e); télescopique

collar ['kɔləʳ] n (of coat, shirt) col m; (for animal) collier m; ~bone n clavicule f

collateral [kə'lætərl] n nantissement m

colleague ['kɔliːg] n collègue m/f

collect [kə'lekt] vt rassembler; ramasser; (as a hobby) collectionner; (BRIT: call and pick up) (passer) prendre; (mail) faire la levée de, ramasser; (money owed) encaisser; (donations, subscriptions) recueillir ♦ vi (people) se rassembler; (things) s'amasser; **to call ~** (US: TEL) téléphoner en P.C.V.; ~ion n collection f; (of mail) levée f; (for money) collecte f, quête f; ~or n collectionneur m

college ['kɔlɪdʒ] n collège m

collide [kə'laɪd] vi entrer en collision

colliery ['kɔlɪərɪ] (BRIT) n mine f de charbon, houillère f

collision [kə'lɪʒən] n collision f

colloquial [kə'ləʊkwɪəl] adj familier(-ère)

colon ['kəʊlən] n (sign) deux-points m inv; (MED) côlon m

colonel ['kɔːnl] n colonel m

colony ['kɔlənɪ] n colonie f

colour ['kʌləʳ] (US color) n couleur f ♦ vt (paint) peindre; (dye) teindre; (news) fausser, exagérer ♦ vi (blush) rougir; ~s npl (of party, club) couleurs fpl; ~ in vt colorier; ~ bar n discrimination raciale (dans un établissement); ~-blind adj daltonien(ne); ~ed adj (person) de couleur; (illustration) en couleur; ~ film n (for camera) pellicule f (en) couleur; ~ful adj coloré(e), vif (vive); (personality) pittoresque, haut(e) en couleurs; ~ing ['kʌlərɪŋ] n colorant m; (complexion) teint m; ~ scheme n combinaison f de(s) couleurs; ~ television n télévision f (en) couleur

colt [kəʊlt] n poulain m

column ['kɔləm] n colonne f; ~ist ['kɔləmnɪst] n chroniqueur(-euse)

coma ['kəʊmə] n coma m

comb [kəʊm] n peigne m ♦ vt (hair) peigner; (area) ratisser, passer au peigne fin

combat ['kɔmbæt] n combat m ♦ vt combattre, lutter contre

combination [kɔmbɪ'neɪʃən] n combinaison f

combine [vb kəm'baɪn, n 'kɔmbaɪn] vt: **to ~ sth with sth** combiner qch avec qch; (one quality with another) joindre or allier qch à qch ♦ vi s'associer; (CHEM) se combiner ♦ n (ECON) trust m; ~ (harvester) n moissonneuse-batteuse(-lieuse) f

come [kʌm] (pt **came**, pp **come**) vi venir, arriver; **to ~ to** (decision etc) parvenir or arriver à; **to ~ undone/loose** se défaire/ desserrer; ~ **about** vi se produire, arriver; ~ **across** vt fus rencontrer par hasard, tomber sur; ~ **along** vi = **come on**; ~ **away** vi partir, s'en aller, se détacher; ~ **back** vi revenir; ~ **by** vt fus (acquire) obtenir, se procurer; ~ **down** vi descendre; (prices) baisser; (buildings) s'écrouler, être démoli(e); ~ **forward** vi s'avancer, se présenter, s'annoncer; ~ **from** vt fus être originaire de, venir de; ~ **in** vi entrer; ~ **in for** vt fus (criticism etc) être l'objet de; ~ **into** vt fus (money) hériter de; ~ **off** vi (button) se détacher; (stain) s'enlever; (attempt) réussir; ~ **on** vi (pupil, work, project) faire des progrès, s'avancer; (lights, electri-

city) s'allumer; *(central heating)* se mettre en marche; ~ **on!** viens!, allons!, allez!; ~ **out** *vi* sortir; *(book)* paraître; *(strike)* cesser le travail, se mettre en grève; ~ **round** *vi (after faint, operation)* revenir à soi, reprendre connaissance; ~ **to** *vi* revenir à soi; ~ **up** *vi* monter; ~ **up against** *vt fus (resistance, difficulties)* rencontrer; ~ **up with** *vt fus:* **he came up with an idea** il a eu une idée, il a proposé quelque chose; ~ **upon** *vt fus* tomber sur; ~**back** *n (THEATRE etc)* rentrée *f*

comedian [kə'miːdɪən] *n (in music hall etc)* comique *m; (THEATRE)* comédien *m*

comedy ['kɒmɪdɪ] *n* comédie *f*

comeuppance [kʌm'ʌpəns] *n:* **to get one's ~** recevoir ce qu'on mérite

comfort ['kʌmfət] *n* confort *m*, bien-être *m; (relief)* soulagement *m*, réconfort *m* ♦ *vt* consoler, réconforter; **the ~s of home** les commodités *fpl* de la maison; ~**able** *adj* confortable; *(person)* à l'aise; *(patient)* dont l'état est stationnaire; *(walk etc)* facile; ~**ably** *adv (sit)* confortablement; *(live)* à l'aise; ~ **station** *n (US)* toilettes *fpl*

comic ['kɒmɪk] *adj (also:* ~**al)** comique ♦ *n* comique *m; (BRIT: magazine)* illustré *m*; ~ **strip** *n* bande dessinée

coming ['kʌmɪŋ] *n* arrivée *f* ♦ *adj* prochain(e), à venir; ~**(s) and going(s)** *n(pl)* va-et-vient *m inv*

comma ['kɒmə] *n* virgule *f*

command [kə'mɑːnd] *n* ordre *m*, commandement *m; (MIL: authority)* commandement *m; (mastery)* maîtrise *f* ♦ *vt (troops)* commander; **to ~ sb to do** ordonner à qn de faire; ~**eer** [kɒmən'dɪər] *vt* réquisitionner; ~**er** *n (MIL)* commandant *m*

commando [kə'mɑːndəu] *n* commando *m*; membre *m* d'un commando

commemorate [kə'meməreit] *vt* commémorer

commence [kə'mens] *vt, vi* commencer

commend [kə'mend] *vt* louer; *(recommend)* recommander

commensurate [kə'menʃərɪt] *adj:* ~ **with** *or* **to** en proportion de, proportionné(e) à

comment ['kɒment] *n* commentaire *m* ♦ *vi:* **to ~ (on)** faire des remarques (sur); **"no ~"** "je n'ai rien à dire"; ~**ary** ['kɒməntərɪ] *n* commentaire *m; (SPORT)* reportage *m* (en direct); ~**ator** ['kɒmənteitər] *n* commentateur *m*; reporter *m*

commerce ['kɒməːs] *n* commerce *m*

commercial [kə'məːʃəl] *adj* commercial(e) ♦ *n (TV, RADIO)* annonce *f* publicitaire, spot *m* (publicitaire)

commiserate [kə'mɪzəreit] *vi:* **to ~ with sb** témoigner de la sympathie pour qn

commission [kə'mɪʃən] *n (order for work)* commande *f; (committee, fee)* commission *f* ♦ *vt (work of art etc)* commander, charger un artiste de l'exécution de; **out of ~** *(not working)* hors service; ~**aire** [kəmɪʃə'neər] *(BRIT) n (at shop, cinema etc)* portier *m* (en uniforme); ~**er** *n (POLICE)* préfet *m* (de police)

commit [kə'mɪt] *vt (act)* commettre; *(resources)* consacrer; *(to sb's care)* confier (à); **to ~ o.s. (to do)** s'engager (à faire); **to ~ suicide** se suicider; ~**ment** *n* engagement *m; (obligation)* responsabilité(s) *f(pl)*

committee [kə'mɪtɪ] *n* comité *m*

commodity [kə'mɒdɪtɪ] *n* produit *m*, marchandise *f*, article *m*

common ['kɒmən] *adj* commun(e); *(usual)* courant(e) ♦ *n* terrain communal; **the C~s** *(BRIT) npl* la chambre des Communes; **in ~** en commun; ~**er** *n* roturier(-ière); ~ **law** *n* droit coutumier; ~**ly** *adv* communément, généralement; couramment; **C~ Market** *n* Marché commun; ~**place** *adj* banal(e), ordinaire; ~ **room** *n* salle commune; ~ **sense** *n* bon sens; **C~wealth** *(BRIT) n* Commonwealth *m*

commotion [kə'məuʃən] *n* désordre *m*, tumulte *m*

communal ['kɒmjuːnl] *adj (life)* communautaire; *(for common use)* commun(e)

commune [*n* 'kɒmjuːn, *vb* kə'mjuːn] *n (group)* communauté *f* ♦ *vi:* **to ~ with** communier avec

communicate [kə'mjuːnɪkeɪt] *vt, vi* communiquer; **communication** [kəmjuːnɪ'keɪʃən] *n* communication *f*; **communication cord** (*BRIT*) *n* sonnette *f* d'alarme

communion [kə'mjuːnɪən] *n* (*also:* **Holy C~**) communion *f*

communism ['kɔmjunɪzəm] *n* communisme *m*; **communist** *adj* communiste ♦ *n* communiste *m/f*

community [kə'mjuːnɪtɪ] *n* communauté *f*; **~ centre** *n* centre *m* de loisirs; **~ chest** (*US*) *n* fonds commun

commutation ticket [kɔmjuː'teɪʃən-] (*US*) *n* carte *f* d'abonnement

commute [kə'mjuːt] *vi* faire un trajet journalier pour se rendre à son travail ♦ *vt* (*LAW*) commuer; **~r** *n* banlieusard(e) (*qui fait un trajet journalier pour se rendre à son travail*)

compact [*adj* kəm'pækt, *n* 'kɔmpækt] *adj* compact(e) ♦ *n* (*also:* **powder ~**) poudrier *m*; **~ disc** *n* disque compact; **~ disc player** *n* lecteur *m* de disque compact

companion [kəm'pænjən] *n* compagnon (compagne); **~ship** *n* camaraderie *f*

company ['kʌmpənɪ] *n* compagnie *f*; **to keep sb ~** tenir compagnie à qn; **~ secretary** (*BRIT*) *n* (*COMM*) secrétaire général (*d'une société*)

comparative [kəm'pærətɪv] *adj* (*study*) comparatif(-ive); (*relative*) relatif(-ive); **~ly** *adv* (*relatively*) relativement

compare [kəm'pɛəʳ] *vt*: **to ~ sth/sb with/to** comparer qch/qn avec *or* et/à ♦ *vi*: **to ~ (with)** se comparer (à); être comparable (à); **comparison** [kəm'pærɪsn] *n* comparaison *f*

compartment [kəm'pɑːtmənt] *n* compartiment *m*

compass ['kʌmpəs] *n* boussole *f*; **~es** *npl* (*GEOM: also:* **pair of ~es**) compas *m*

compassion [kəm'pæʃən] *n* compassion *f*; **~ate** *adj* compatissant(e)

compatible [kəm'pætɪbl] *adj* compatible

compel [kəm'pɛl] *vt* contraindre, obliger

compensate ['kɔmpənseɪt] *vt* indemniser, dédommager ♦ *vi*: **to ~ for** compenser; **compensation** [kɔmpən'seɪʃən] *n* compensation *f*; (*money*) dédommagement *m*, indemnité *f*

compère ['kɔmpɛəʳ] *n* (*TV*) animateur(-trice)

compete [kəm'piːt] *vi*: **to ~ (with)** rivaliser (avec), faire concurrence (à)

competent ['kɔmpɪtənt] *adj* compétent(e), capable

competition [kɔmpɪ'tɪʃən] *n* (*contest*) compétition *f*, concours *m*; (*ECON*) concurrence *f*

competitive [kəm'petɪtɪv] *adj* (*ECON*) concurrentiel(le); (*sport*) de compétition; (*person*) qui a l'esprit de compétition; **competitor** *n* concurrent(e)

complacency [kəm'pleɪsnsɪ] *n* suffisance *f*, vaine complaisance

complain [kəm'pleɪn] *vi*: **to ~ (about)** se plaindre (de); (*in shop etc*) réclamer (au sujet de); **to ~ of** (*pain*) se plaindre de; **~t** *n* plainte *f*; réclamation *f*; (*MED*) affection *f*

complement [*n* 'kɔmplɪmənt, *vb* 'kɔmplɪment] *n* complément *m*; (*especially of ship's crew etc*) effectif complet ♦ *vt* (*enhance*) compléter; **~ary** [kɔmplɪ'mentərɪ] *adj* complémentaire

complete [kəm'pliːt] *adj* complet(-ète) ♦ *vt* achever, parachever; (*set, group*) compléter; (*a form*) remplir; **~ly** *adv* complètement; **completion** *n* achèvement *m*; (*of contract*) exécution *f*

complex ['kɔmpleks] *adj* complexe ♦ *n* complexe *m*

complexion [kəm'plekʃən] *n* (*of face*) teint *m*

compliance [kəm'plaɪəns] *n* (*submission*) docilité *f*; (*agreement*): **~ with** le fait de se conformer à; **in ~ with** en accord avec

complicate ['kɔmplɪkeɪt] *vt* compliquer; **~d** *adj* compliqué(e); **complication** [kɔmplɪ'keɪʃən] *n* complication *f*

compliment [*n* 'kɔmplɪmənt, *vb* 'kɔmplɪment] *n* compliment *m* ♦ *vt* complimenter; **~s** *npl* (*respects*) compliments *mpl*, hommages *mpl*; **to pay sb a** ~ faire *or* adresser un compliment à qn; ~**ary** [kɔmplɪ'mɛntərɪ] *adj* flatteur(-euse); *(free)* (offert(e)) à titre gracieux; ~**ary ticket** *n* billet *m* de faveur

comply [kəm'plaɪ] *vi:* **to ~ with** se soumettre à, se conformer à

component [kəm'pəunənt] *n* composant *m*, élément *m*

compose [kəm'pəuz] *vt* composer; *(form):* **to be ~d of** se composer de; **to ~ o.s.** se calmer, se maîtriser; prendre une contenance; ~**d** *adj* calme, posé(e); ~**r** *n* (MUS) compositeur *m*; **composition** [kɔmpə'zɪʃən] *n* composition *f*; **composure** [kəm'pəuʒər] *n* calme *m*, maîtrise *f* de soi

compound ['kɔmpaund] *n* composé *m*; *(enclosure)* enclos *m*, enceinte *f*; ~ **fracture** *n* fracture compliquée; ~ **interest** *n* intérêt composé

comprehend [kɔmprɪ'hɛnd] *vt* comprendre; **comprehension** *n* compréhension *f*

comprehensive [kɔmprɪ'hɛnsɪv] *adj* (très) complet(-ète); ~ **policy** *n* (INSURANCE) assurance *f* tous risques; ~ **(school)** (BRIT) *n* école secondaire polyvalente; ≈ C.E.S. *m*

compress [*vb* kəm'prɛs, *n* 'kɔmprɛs] *vt* comprimer; *(text, information)* condenser ♦ *n* (MED) compresse *f*

comprise [kəm'praɪz] *vt (also:* **be ~d of)** comprendre; *(constitute)* constituer, représenter

compromise ['kɔmprəmaɪz] *n* compromis *m* ♦ *vt* compromettre ♦ *vi* transiger, accepter un compromis

compulsion [kəm'pʌlʃən] *n* contrainte *f*, force *f*

compulsive [kəm'pʌlsɪv] *adj* (PSYCH) compulsif(-ive); *(book, film etc)* captivant(e)

compulsory [kəm'pʌlsərɪ] *adj* obligatoire

computer [kəm'pju:tər] *n* ordinateur *m*; ~ **game** *n* jeu *m* vidéo; ~-**generated** *adj* de synthèse; ~**ize** *vt* informatiser; ~ **programmer** *n* programmeur(-euse); ~ **programming** *n* programmation *f*; ~ **sci-**

ence *n* informatique *f*; **computing** *n* = **computer science**

comrade ['kɔmrɪd] *n* camarade *m/f*

con [kɔn] *vt* duper; *(cheat)* escroquer ♦ *n* escroquerie *f*

conceal [kən'si:l] *vt* cacher, dissimuler

conceit [kən'si:t] *n* vanité *f*, suffisance *f*, prétention *f*; ~**ed** *adj* vaniteux(-euse), suffisant(e)

conceive [kən'si:v] *vt, vi* concevoir

concentrate ['kɔnsəntreɪt] *vi* se concentrer ♦ *vt* concentrer; **concentration** *n* concentration *f*; **concentration camp** *n* camp *m* de concentration

concept ['kɔnsɛpt] *n* concept *m*

concern [kən'sə:n] *n* affaire *f*; (COMM) entreprise *f*, firme *f*; *(anxiety)* inquiétude *f*, souci *m* ♦ *vt* concerner; **to be ~ed (about)** s'inquiéter (de), être inquiet(-ète) (au sujet de); ~**ing** *prep* en ce qui concerne, à propos de

concert ['kɔnsət] *n* concert *m*; ~**ed** [kən'sə:tɪd] *adj* concerté(e); ~ **hall** *n* salle *f* de concert

concerto [kən'tʃə:təu] *n* concerto *m*

concession [kən'sɛʃən] *n* concession *f*; **tax ~** dégrèvement fiscal

conclude [kən'klu:d] *vt* conclure; **conclusion** [kən'klu:ʒən] *n* conclusion *f*; **conclusive** [kən'klu:sɪv] *adj* concluant(e), définitif(-ive)

concoct [kən'kɔkt] *vt* confectionner, composer; *(fig)* inventer; ~**ion** *n* mélange *m*

concourse ['kɔnkɔ:s] *n (hall)* hall *m*, salle *f* des pas perdus

concrete ['kɔnkri:t] *n* béton *m* ♦ *adj* concret(-ète); *(floor etc)* en béton

concur [kən'kə:r] *vi (agree)* être d'accord

concurrently [kən'kʌrntlɪ] *adv* simultanément

concussion [kən'kʌʃən] *n* (MED) commotion (cérébrale)

condemn [kən'dɛm] *vt* condamner

condensation [kɔndɛn'seɪʃən] *n* condensation *f*

condense [kən'dɛns] *vi* se condenser ♦ *vt*

condenser; ~**d milk** *n* lait concentré (sucré)

condition [kən'dɪʃən] *n* condition *f*; (*MED*) état *m* ♦ *vt* déterminer, conditionner; **on ~ that** à condition que +*sub*, à condition de; ~**al** *adj* conditionnel(le); ~**er** *n* (*for hair*) baume après-shampooing *m*; (*for fabrics*) assouplissant *m*

condolences [kən'dəʊlənsɪz] *npl* condoléances *fpl*

condom ['kɔndəm] *n* préservatif *m*

condominium [kɔndə'mɪnɪəm] (*US*) *n* (*building*) immeuble *m* (en copropriété)

condone [kən'dəʊn] *vt* fermer les yeux sur, approuver (tacitement)

conducive [kən'djuːsɪv] *adj*: ~ **to** favorable à, qui contribue à

conduct [*n* 'kɔndʌkt, *vb* kən'dʌkt] *n* conduite *f* ♦ *vt* conduire; (*MUS*) diriger; **to ~ o.s.** se conduire, se comporter; ~**ed tour** *n* voyage organisé; (*of building*) visite guidée; ~**or** *n* (*of orchestra*) chef *m* d'orchestre; (*on bus*) receveur *m*; (*US*: *on train*) chef *m* de train; (*ELEC*) conducteur *m*; ~**ress** *n* (*on bus*) receveuse *f*

cone [kəʊn] *n* cône *m*; (*for ice-cream*) cornet *m*; (*BOT*) pomme *f* de pin, cône

confectioner [kən'fekʃənər] *n* confiseur(euse); ~'**s (shop)** *n* confiserie *f*; ~**y** *n* confiserie *f*

confer [kən'fəːr] *vt*: **to ~ sth on** conférer qch à ♦ *vi* conférer, s'entretenir

conference ['kɔnfərəns] *n* conférence *f*

confess [kən'fes] *vt* confesser, avouer ♦ *vi* se confesser; ~**ion** *n* confession *f*

confetti [kən'fetɪ] *n* confettis *mpl*

confide [kən'faɪd] *vi*: **to ~ in** se confier à

confidence ['kɔnfɪdns] *n* confiance *f*; (*also*: **self-~**) assurance *f*, confiance en soi; (*secret*) confidence *f*; **in ~** (*speak, write*) en confidence, confidentiellement; ~ **trick** *n* escroquerie *f*; **confident** *adj* sûr(e), assuré(e); **confidential** [kɔnfɪ'denʃəl] *adj* confidentiel(le)

confine [kən'faɪn] *vt* limiter, borner; (*shut up*) confiner, enfermer; ~**d** *adj* (*space*) restreint(e), réduit(e); ~**ment** *n* emprisonne-

ment *m*, détention *f*; ~**s** ['kɔnfaɪnz] *npl* confins *mpl*, bornes *fpl*

confirm [kən'fəːm] *vt* confirmer; (*appointment*) ratifier; ~**ation** [kɔnfə'meɪʃən] *n* confirmation *f*; ~**ed** *adj* invétéré(e), incorrigible

confiscate ['kɔnfɪskeɪt] *vt* confisquer

conflict [*n* 'kɔnflɪkt, *vb* kən'flɪkt] *n* conflit *m*, lutte *f* ♦ *vi* être *or* entrer en conflit; (*opinions*) s'opposer, se heurter; ~**ing** [kən'flɪktɪŋ] *adj* contradictoire

conform [kən'fɔːm] *vi*: **to ~ (to)** se conformer (à)

confound [kən'faʊnd] *vt* confondre

confront [kən'frʌnt] *vt* confronter, mettre en présence; (*enemy, danger*) affronter, faire face à; ~**ation** [kɔnfrən'teɪʃən] *n* confrontation *f*

confuse [kən'fjuːz] *vt* (*person*) troubler; (*situation*) embrouiller; (*one thing with another*) confondre; ~**d** *adj* (*person*) dérouté(e), désorienté(e); **confusing** *adj* peu clair(e), déroutant(e); **confusion** [kən'fjuːʒən] *n* confusion *f*

congeal [kən'dʒiːl] *vi* (*blood*) se coaguler; (*oil etc*) se figer

congenial [kən'dʒiːnɪəl] *adj* sympathique, agréable

congested [kən'dʒestɪd] *adj* (*MED*) congestionné(e); (*area*) surpeuplé(e); (*road*) bloqué(e); **congestion** *n* congestion *f*; (*fig*) encombrement *m*

congratulate [kən'grætjuleɪt] *vt*: **to ~ sb (on)** féliciter qn (de); **congratulations** [kəngrætju'leɪʃənz] *npl* félicitations *fpl*

congregate ['kɔngrɪgeɪt] *vi* se rassembler, se réunir; **congregation** [kɔngrɪ'geɪʃən] *n* assemblée *f* (des fidèles)

congress ['kɔngres] *n* congrès *m*; ~**man** (*irreg*) (*US*) *n* membre *m* du Congrès

conjunction [kən'dʒʌŋkʃən] *n* (*LING*) conjonction *f*

conjunctivitis [kəndʒʌŋktɪ'vaɪtɪs] *n* conjonctivite *f*

conjure ['kʌndʒər] *vi* faire des tours de passe-passe; ~ **up** *vt* (*ghost, spirit*) faire apparaître; (*memories*) évoquer; ~**r** *n* pres-

tidigitateur *m*, illusionniste *m/f*
con man (*irreg*) *n* escroc *m*
connect [kə'nɛkt] *vt* joindre, relier; (*ELEC*)
connecter; (*TEL: caller*) mettre en connection (*with* avec); (: *new subscriber*) brancher; (*fig*) établir un rapport entre, faire un rapprochement entre ♦ *vi* (*train*): **to ~ with** assurer la correspondance avec; **to be ~ed with** (*fig*) avoir un rapport avec, avoir des rapports avec, être en relation avec; **~ion** *n* relation *f*, lien *m*; (*ELEC*) connexion *f*; (*train, plane etc*) correspondance *f*; (*TEL*) branchement *m*, communication *f*
connive [kə'naɪv] *vi*: **to ~ at** se faire le complice de
conquer ['kɔŋkəʳ] *vt* conquérir; (*feelings*) vaincre, surmonter; **conquest** ['kɔŋkwɛst] *n* conquête *f*
cons [kɔnz] *npl see* **convenience; pro**
conscience ['kɔnʃəns] *n* conscience *f*; **conscientious** [kɔnʃɪ'ɛnʃəs] *adj* consciencieux(-euse)
conscious ['kɔnʃəs] *adj* conscient(e); **~ness** *n* conscience *f*; (*MED*) connaissance *f*
conscript ['kɔnskrɪpt] *n* conscrit *m*
consent [kən'sɛnt] *n* consentement *m* ♦ *vi*: **to ~ (to)** consentir (à)
consequence ['kɔnsɪkwəns] *n* conséquence *f*, suites *fpl*; (*significance*) importance *f*; **consequently** *adv* par conséquent, donc
conservation [kɔnsə'veɪʃən] *n* préservation *f*, protection *f*
conservative [kən'sɜːvətɪv] *adj* conservateur(-trice); **at a ~ estimate** au bas mot; **C~** (*BRIT*) *adj, n* (*POL*) conservateur(-trice)
conservatory [kən'sɜːvətrɪ] *n* (*greenhouse*) serre *f*
conserve [kən'sɜːv] *vt* conserver, préserver; (*supplies, energy*) économiser ♦ *n* confiture *f*
consider [kən'sɪdəʳ] *vt* (*study*) considérer, réfléchir à; (*take into account*) penser à, prendre en considération; (*regard, judge*)

considérer, estimer; **to ~ doing sth** envisager de faire qch; **~able** *adj* considérable; **~ably** *adv* nettement; **~ate** *adj* prévenant(e), plein(e) d'égards; **~ation** [kənsɪdə'reɪʃən] *n* considération *f*; **~ing** *prep* étant donné
consign [kən'saɪn] *vt* expédier; (*to sb's care*) confier; (*fig*) livrer; **~ment** *n* arrivage *m*, envoi *m*
consist [kən'sɪst] *vi*: **to ~ of** consister en, se composer de
consistency [kən'sɪstənsɪ] *n* consistance *f*; (*fig*) cohérence *f*
consistent [kən'sɪstənt] *adj* logique, cohérent(e)
consolation [kɔnsə'leɪʃən] *n* consolation *f*
console[1] [kən'səul] *vt* consoler
console[2] ['kɔnsəul] *n* (*COMPUT*) console *f*
consonant ['kɔnsənənt] *n* consonne *f*
conspicuous [kən'spɪkjuəs] *adj* voyant(e), qui attire l'attention
conspiracy [kən'spɪrəsɪ] *n* conspiration *f*, complot *m*
constable ['kʌnstəbl] (*BRIT*) *n* ≃ agent *m* de police, gendarme *m*; **chief ~** ≃ préfet *m* de police; **constabulary** [kən'stæbjulərɪ] (*BRIT*) *n* ≃ police *f*, gendarmerie *f* .
constant ['kɔnstənt] *adj* constant(e); incessant(e); **~ly** *adv* constamment, sans cesse
constipated ['kɔnstɪpeɪtɪd] *adj* constipé(e); **constipation** [kɔnstɪ'peɪʃən] *n* constipation *f*
constituency [kən'stɪtjuənsɪ] *n* circonscription électorale
constituent [kən'stɪtjuənt] *n* (*POL*) électeur(-trice); (*part*) élément constitutif, composant *m*
constitution [kɔnstɪ'tjuːʃən] *n* constitution *f*; **~al** *adj* constitutionnel(le)
constraint [kən'streɪnt] *n* contrainte *f*
construct [kən'strʌkt] *vt* construire; **~ion** *n* construction *f*; **~ive** *adj* constructif(-ive); **~ive dismissal** démission forcée
consul ['kɔnsl] *n* consul *m*; **~ate** ['kɔnsjulɪt] *n* consulat *m*
consult [kən'sʌlt] *vt* consulter; **~ant** *n*

(*MED*) médecin consultant; (*other specialist*) consultant *m*, (expert-)conseil *m*; ~**ing room** (*BRIT*) *n* cabinet *m* de consultation

consume [kən'sju:m] *vt* consommer; ~**r** *n* consommateur(-trice); ~**r goods** *npl* biens *mpl* de consommation; ~**r society** *n* société *f* de consommation

consummate ['kɔnsʌmeɪt] *vt* consommer

consumption [kən'sʌmpʃən] *n* consommation *f*

cont. *abbr* (= *continued*) suite

contact ['kɔntækt] *n* contact *m*; (*person*) connaissance *f*, relation *f* ♦ *vt* contacter, se mettre en contact *or* en rapport avec; ~ **lenses** *npl* verres *mpl* de contact, lentilles *fpl*

contagious [kən'teɪdʒəs] *adj* contagieux(-euse)

contain [kən'teɪn] *vt* contenir; **to ~ o.s.** se contenir, se maîtriser; ~**er** *n* récipient *m*; (*for shipping etc*) container *m*

contaminate [kən'tæmɪneɪt] *vt* contaminer

cont'd *abbr* (= *continued*) suite

contemplate ['kɔntəmpleɪt] *vt* contempler; (*consider*) envisager

contemporary [kən'tempərərɪ] *adj* contemporain(e); (*design, wallpaper*) moderne ♦ *n* contemporain(e)

contempt [kən'tempt] *n* mépris *m*, dédain *m*; ~ **of court** (*LAW*) outrage *m* à l'autorité de la justice; ~**uous** [kən'temptjuəs] *adj* dédaigneux(-euse), méprisant(e)

contend [kən'tend] *vt*: **to ~ that** soutenir *or* prétendre que ♦ *vi*: **to ~ with** (*compete*) rivaliser avec; (*struggle*) lutter avec; ~**er** *n* concurrent(e); (*POL*) candidat(e)

content [*adj, vb* kən'tent, *n* 'kɔntent] *adj* content(e), satisfait(e) ♦ *vt* contenter, satisfaire ♦ *n* contenu *m*; (*of fat, moisture*) teneur *f*; ~**s** *npl* (*of container etc*) contenu *m*; (**table of**) ~**s** table *f* des matières; ~**ed** *adj* content(e), satisfait(e)

contention [kən'tenʃən] *n* dispute *f*, contestation *f*; (*argument*) assertion *f*, affirmation *f*

contest [*n* 'kɔntest, *vb* kən'test] *n* combat *m*, lutte *f*; (*competition*) concours *m* ♦ *vt* (*decision, statement*) contester, discuter; (*compete for*) disputer; ~**ant** [kən'testənt] *n* concurrent(e); (*in fight*) adversaire *m/f*

context ['kɔntekst] *n* contexte *m*

continent ['kɔntɪnənt] *n* continent *m*; **the C~** (*BRIT*) l'Europe continentale; ~**al** [kɔntɪ'nentl] *adj* continental(e); ~**al breakfast** *n* petit déjeuner *m* à la française; ~**al quilt** (*BRIT*) *n* couette *f*

contingency [kən'tɪndʒənsɪ] *n* éventualité *f*, événement imprévu

continual [kən'tɪnjuəl] *adj* continuel(le)

continuation [kəntɪnju'eɪʃən] *n* continuation *f*; (*after interruption*) reprise *f*; (*of story*) suite *f*

continue [kən'tɪnju:] *vi, vt* continuer; (*after interruption*) reprendre, poursuivre; **continuity** [kɔntɪ'nju:ɪtɪ] *n* continuité *f*; (*TV etc*) enchaînement *m*; **continuous** [kən'tɪnjuəs] *adj* continu(e); (*LING*) progressif(-ive)

contort [kən'tɔ:t] *vt* tordre, crisper

contour ['kɔntuər] *n* contour *m*, profil *m*; (*on map: also:* ~ **line**) courbe *f* de niveau

contraband ['kɔntrəbænd] *n* contrebande *f*

contraceptive [kɔntrə'septɪv] *adj* contraceptif(-ive), anticonceptionnel(le) ♦ *n* contraceptif *m*

contract [*n* 'kɔntrækt, *vb* kən'trækt] *n* contrat *m* ♦ *vi* (*become smaller*) se contracter, se resserrer; (*COMM*): **to ~ to do sth** s'engager (par contrat) à faire qch; ~**ion** [kən'trækʃən] *n* contraction *f*; ~**or** [kən'træktər] *n* entrepreneur *m*

contradict [kɔntrə'dɪkt] *vt* contredire

contraflow ['kɔntrəfləu] *n* (*AUT*): ~ **lane** voie *f* à contresens; **there's a ~ system in operation on ...** une voie a été mise en sens inverse sur ...

contraption [kən'træpʃən] (*pej*) *n* machin *m*, truc *m*

contrary[1] ['kɔntrərɪ] *adj* contraire, opposé(e) ♦ *n* contraire *m*; **on the ~** au contraire; **unless you hear to the ~** sauf avis contraire

contrary² [kən'treəri] *adj* (*perverse*) contrariant(e), entêté(e)

contrast [*n* 'kɔntrɑːst, *vb* kən'trɑːst] *n* contraste *m* ♦ *vt* mettre en contraste, contraster; **in ~ to** *or* **with** contrairement à

contravene [kɔntrə'viːn] *vt* enfreindre, violer, contrevenir à

contribute [kən'trɪbjuːt] *vi* contribuer ♦ *vt*: **to ~ £10/an article to** donner 10 livres/un article à; **to ~ to** contribuer à; (*newspaper*) collaborer à; **contribution** [kɔntrɪ'bjuːʃən] *n* contribution *f*; **contributor** [kən'trɪbjutə'] *n* (*to newspaper*) collaborateur(-trice)

contrive [kən'traɪv] *vi*: **to ~ to do** s'arranger pour faire, trouver le moyen de faire

control [kən'trəul] *vt* maîtriser, commander; (*check*) contrôler ♦ *n* contrôle *m*, autorité *f*; maîtrise *f*; **~s** *npl* (*of machine etc*) commandes *fpl*; (*on radio, TV*) boutons *mpl* de réglage; **~led substance** narcotique *m*; **everything is under ~** tout va bien, j'ai (*or* il a *etc*) la situation en main; **to be in ~ of** être maître de, maîtriser; **the car went out of ~** j'ai (*or* il a *etc*) perdu le contrôle du véhicule; **~ panel** *n* tableau *m* de commande; **~ room** *n* salle *f* des commandes; **~ tower** *n* (*AVIAT*) tour *f* de contrôle

controversial [kɔntrə'vəːʃl] *adj* (*topic*) discutable, controversé(e); (*person*) qui fait beaucoup parler de lui; **controversy** ['kɔntrəvəːsɪ] *n* controverse *f*, polémique *f*

convalesce [kɔnvə'lɛs] *vi* relever de maladie, se remettre (d'une maladie)

convector [kən'vɛktə'] *n* (*heater*) radiateur *m* (à convexion)

convene [kən'viːn] *vt* convoquer, assembler ♦ *vi* se réunir, s'assembler

convenience [kən'viːnɪəns] *n* commodité *f*; **at your ~** quand *or* comme cela vous convient; **all modern ~s**, (*BRIT*) **all mod cons** avec tout le confort moderne, tout confort

convenient [kən'viːnɪənt] *adj* commode

convent ['kɔnvənt] *n* couvent *m*; ~

school *n* couvent *m*

convention [kən'vɛnʃən] *n* convention *f*; **~al** *adj* conventionnel(le)

conversant [kən'vəːsnt] *adj*: **to be ~ with** s'y connaître en; être au courant de

conversation [kɔnvə'seɪʃən] *n* conversation *f*

converse [*n* 'kɔnvəːs, *vb* kən'vəːs] *n* contraire *m*, inverse *m* ♦ *vi* s'entretenir; **~ly** [kɔn'vəːslɪ] *adv* inversement, réciproquement

convert [*vb* kən'vəːt, *n* 'kɔnvəːt] *vt* (*REL, COMM*) convertir; (*alter*) transformer; (*house*) aménager ♦ *n* converti(e); **~ible** [kən'vəːtəbl] *n* (*voiture f*) décapotable *f*

convey [kən'veɪ] *vt* transporter; (*thanks*) transmettre; (*idea*) communiquer; **~or belt** *n* convoyeur *m*, tapis roulant

convict [*vb* kən'vɪkt, *n* 'kɔnvɪkt] *vt* déclarer (*or* reconnaître) coupable ♦ *n* forçat *m*, détenu *m*; (*on radio, TV*) ~ion (*LAW*) condamnation *f*; (*belief*) conviction *f*

convince [kən'vɪns] *vt* convaincre, persuader; **convincing** *adj* persuasif(-ive), convaincant(e)

convoluted ['kɔnvəluːtɪd] *adj* (*argument*) compliqué(e)

convulse [kən'vʌls] *vt*: **to be ~d with laughter/pain** se tordre de rire/douleur

cook [kuk] *vt* (faire) cuire ♦ *vi* cuire; (*person*) faire la cuisine ♦ *n* cuisinier(-ière); **~book** *n* livre *m* de cuisine; **~er** *n* cuisinière *f*; **~ery** *n* cuisine *f*; **~ery book** (*BRIT*) *n* = **cookbook**; **~ie** (*US*) *n* biscuit *m*, petit gâteau sec; **~ing** *n* cuisine *f*

cool [kuːl] *adj* frais (fraîche), (*calm, unemotional*) calme; (*unfriendly*) froid(e) ♦ *vt, vi* rafraîchir, refroidir

coop [kuːp] *n* poulailler *m*; (*for rabbits*) clapier *m* ♦ *vt*: **to ~ up** (*fig*) cloîtrer, enfermer

cooperate [kəu'ɔpəreɪt] *vi* coopérer, collaborer; **cooperation** [kəuɔpə'reɪʃən] *n* coopération *f*, collaboration *f*; **cooperative** [kəu'ɔpərətɪv] *adj* coopératif(-ive) ♦ *n* coopérative *f*

coordinate [*vb* kəu'ɔːdɪneɪt, *n* kəu'ɔːdɪnət]

vt· coordonner ♦ *n (MATH)* coordonnée *f*; **~s** *npl (clothes)* ensemble *m*, coordonnés *mpl*

co-ownership [kəu'əunəʃip] *n* co-propriété *f*

cop [kɔp] *(inf) n* flic *m*

cope [kəup] *vi*: **to ~ with** faire face à; *(solve)* venir à bout de

copper ['kɔpəʳ] *n* cuivre *m*; *(BRIT: inf: policeman)* flic *m*; **~s** *npl (coins)* petite monnaie

copy ['kɔpi] *n* copie *f*; *(of book etc)* exemplaire *m* ♦ *vt* copier; **~right** *n* droit *m* d'auteur, copyright *m*

coral ['kɔrəl] *n* corail *m*

cord [kɔ:d] *n* corde *f*; *(fabric)* velours côtelé; *(ELEC)* cordon *m*, fil *m*

cordial ['kɔ:diəl] *adj* cordial(e), chaleureux(-euse) ♦ *n* cordial *m*

cordon ['kɔ:dn] *n* cordon *m*; **~ off** *vt* boucler *(par cordon de police)*

corduroy ['kɔ:dərɔi] *n* velours côtelé

core [kɔ:ʳ] *n* noyau *m*; *(of fruit)* trognon *m*, cœur *m*; *(of building, problem)* cœur ♦ *vt* enlever le trognon *or* le cœur de

cork [kɔ:k] *n* liège *m*; *(of bottle)* bouchon *m*; **~screw** *n* tire-bouchon *m*

corn [kɔ:n] *n (BRIT: wheat)* blé *m*; *(US: maize)* maïs *m*; *(on foot)* cor *m*; **~ on the cob** *(CULIN)* épi *m* de maïs; **~ed beef** *n* corned-beef *m*

corner ['kɔ:nəʳ] *n* coin *m*; *(AUT)* tournant *m*, virage *m*; *(FOOTBALL: also:* **~ kick**) corner *m* ♦ *vt* acculer, mettre au pied du mur; coincer; *(COMM: market)* accaparer ♦ *vi* prendre un virage; **~stone** *n* pierre *f* angulaire

cornet ['kɔ:nit] *n (MUS)* cornet *m* à pistons; *(BRIT: of ice-cream)* cornet (de glace)

cornflakes ['kɔ:nfleiks] *npl* corn-flakes *mpl*

cornflour ['kɔ:nflauəʳ] *(BRIT)*, **cornstarch** ['kɔ:nsta:tʃ] *(US)* *n* farine *f* de maïs, maïzena *f* ®

Cornwall ['kɔ:nwəl] *n* Cornouailles *f*

corny ['kɔ:ni] *(inf) adj* rebattu(e)

coronary ['kɔrənəri] *n (also:* **~ thrombosis**) infarctus *m* (du myocarde), thrombo-se *f* coronarienne

coronation [kɔrə'neiʃən] *n* couronnement *m*

coroner ['kɔrənəʳ] *n* officiel chargé de déterminer les causes d'un décès

corporal ['kɔ:pərl] *n* caporal *m*, brigadier *m* ♦ *adj*: **~ punishment** châtiment corporel

corporate ['kɔ:pərit] *adj* en commun, collectif(-ive); *(COMM)* de l'entreprise

corporation [kɔ:pə'reiʃən] *n (of town)* municipalité *f*, conseil municipal; *(COMM)* société *f*

corps [kɔ:ʳ] *(pl* **~**) *n* corps *m*

corpse [kɔ:ps] *n* cadavre *m*

correct [kə'rekt] *adj (accurate)* correct(e), exact(e); *(proper)* correct, convenable ♦ *vt* corriger; **~ion** *n* correction *f*

correspond [kɔris'pɔnd] *vi* correspondre; **~ence** *n* correspondance *f*; **~ence course** *n* cours *m* par correspondance; **~ent** *n* correspondant(e)

corridor ['kɔridɔ:ʳ] *n* couloir *m*, corridor *m*

corrode [kə'rəud] *vt* corroder, ronger ♦ *vi* se corroder

corrugated ['kɔrəgeitid] *adj* plissé(e); ondulé(e); **~ iron** *n* tôle ondulée

corrupt [kə'rʌpt] *adj* corrompu(e) ♦ *vt* corrompre; **~ion** *n* corruption *f*

Corsica ['kɔ:sikə] *n* Corse *f*

cosmetic [kɔz'metik] *n* produit *m* de beauté, cosmétique *m*

cost [kɔst] *(pt, pp* **cost**) *n* coût *m* ♦ *vi* coûter ♦ *vt* établir *or* calculer le prix de revient de; **~s** *npl (COMM)* frais *mpl*; *(LAW)* dépens *mpl*; **it ~s £5/too much** cela coûte cinq livres/c'est trop cher; **at all ~s** coûte que coûte, à tout prix

co-star ['kəusta:ʳ] *n* partenaire *m/f*

cost: **~-effective** *adj* rentable; **~ly** *adj* coûteux(-euse); **~-of-living** *adj*: **~-of-living allowance** indemnité *f* de vie chère; **~-of-living index** index *m* du coût de la vie; **~ price** *(BRIT)* *n* prix coûtant *or* de revient

costume ['kɔstju:m] *n* costume *m*; *(lady's suit)* tailleur *m*; *(BRIT: also:* **swimming ~**)

maillot *m* (de bain); ~ **jewellery** *n* bijoux *mpl* fantaisie

cosy ['kəuzɪ] (*US* **cozy**) *adj* douillet(te); (*person*) à l'aise, au chaud

cot [kɒt] *n* (*BRIT: child's*) lit *m* d'enfant, petit lit; (*US: campbed*) lit de camp

cottage ['kɒtɪdʒ] *n* petite maison (à la campagne), cottage *m*; ~ **cheese** *n* fromage blanc (*maigre*)

cotton ['kɒtn] *n* coton *m*; ~ **on** (*inf*) *vi*: **to ~ on to** piger; ~ **candy** (*US*) *n* barbe *f* à papa; ~ **wool** (*BRIT*) *n* ouate *f*, coton *m* hydrophile

couch [kautʃ] *n* canapé *m*; divan *m*

couchette [kuːˈʃet] *n* couchette *f*

cough [kɒf] *vi* tousser ♦ *n* toux *f*; ~ **sweet** *n* pastille *f* pour or contre la toux

could [kud] *pt of* **can²**; ~**n't** = **could not**

council ['kaunsl] *n* conseil *m*; **city** or **town ~** conseil municipal; ~ **estate** (*BRIT*) *n* (zone *f* de) logements loués à/par la municipalité; ~ **house** (*BRIT*) *n* maison *f* (à loyer modéré) louée par la municipalité; ~**lor** *n* conseiller(-ère)

counsel ['kaunsl] *n* (*lawyer*) avocat(e); (*advice*) conseil *m*, consultation *f*; ~**lor** *n* conseiller(-ère); (*US: lawyer*) avocat(e)

count [kaunt] *vt, vi* compter ♦ *n* compte *m*; (*nobleman*) comte *m*; ~ **on** *vt fus* compter sur; ~**down** *n* compte *m* à rebours

countenance ['kauntɪnəns] *n* expression *f* ♦ *vt* approuver

counter ['kauntəʳ] *n* comptoir *m*; (*in post office, bank*) guichet *m*; (*in game*) jeton *m* ♦ *vt* aller à l'encontre de, opposer ♦ *adv*: ~ **to** contrairement à; ~**act** *vt* neutraliser, contrebalancer; ~**feit** *n* faux *m*, contrefaçon *f* ♦ *vt* contrefaire ♦ *adj* faux (fausse); ~**foil** *n* talon *m*, souche *f*; ~**part** *n* (*of person etc*) homologue *m/f*

countess ['kauntɪs] *n* comtesse *f*

countless ['kauntlɪs] *adj* innombrable

country ['kʌntrɪ] *n* pays *m*; (*native land*) patrie *f*; (*as opposed to town*) campagne *f*; (*region*) région *f*, pays; ~ **dancing** (*BRIT*) *n* danse *f* folklorique; ~ **house** *n* manoir *m*,

(petit) château; ~**man** (*irreg*) *n* (*compatriot*) compatriote *m*; (*country dweller*) habitant *m* de la campagne, campagnard *m*; ~**side** *n* campagne *f*

county ['kauntɪ] *n* comté *m*

coup [kuː] *n* beau coup *m*; (*also*: ~ **d'état**) coup d'État

couple ['kʌpl] *n* couple *m*; **a ~ of** deux; (*a few*) quelques

coupon ['kuːpɒn] *n* coupon *m*, bon-prime *m*, bon-réclame *m*; (*COMM*) coupon

courage ['kʌrɪdʒ] *n* courage *m*

courier ['kurɪəʳ] *n* messager *m*, courrier *m*; (*for tourists*) accompagnateur(-trice), guide *m/f*

course [kɔːs] *n* cours *m*; (*of ship*) route *f*; (*for golf*) terrain *m*; (*part of meal*) plat *m*; **first ~** entrée *f*; **of ~** bien sûr; ~ **of action** parti *m*, ligne *f* de conduite; ~ **of treatment** (*MED*) traitement *m*

court [kɔːt] *n* cour *f*; (*LAW*) cour, tribunal *m*; (*TENNIS*) court *m* ♦ *vt* (*woman*) courtiser, faire la cour à; **to take to ~** actionner or poursuivre en justice

courteous ['kɜːtɪəs] *adj* courtois(e), poli(e); **courtesy** ['kɜːtəsɪ] *n* courtoisie *f*, politesse *f*; **(by) courtesy of** avec l'aimable autorisation de; **courtesy bus** or **coach** *n* navette gratuite

court: ~-**house** (*US*) *n* palais *m* de justice; ~**ier** *n* courtisan *m*, dame *f* de la cour; ~ **martial** (*pl* **courts martial**) *n* cour martiale, conseil *m* de guerre; ~**room** *n* salle *f* de tribunal; ~**yard** *n* cour *f*

cousin ['kʌzn] *n* cousin(e); **first ~** cousin(e) germain(e)

cove [kəuv] *n* petite baie, anse *f*

covenant ['kʌvənənt] *n* engagement *m*

cover ['kʌvəʳ] *vt* couvrir ♦ *n* couverture *f*; (*of pan*) couvercle *m*; (*over furniture*) housse *f*; (*shelter*) abri *m*; **to take ~** se mettre à l'abri; **under ~** à l'abri; **under ~ of darkness** à la faveur de la nuit; **under separate ~** (*COMM*) sous pli séparé; **to ~ up for sb** couvrir qn; ~**age** *n* (*TV, PRESS*) reportage *m*; ~ **charge** *n* couvert *m* (*supplément à payer*); ~**ing** *n* couche *f*; ~**ing**

letter (*US* **cover letter**) *n* lettre explicative; ~ **note** *n* (*INSURANCE*) police *f* provisoire

covert ['kʌvət] *adj* (*threat*) voilé(e), caché(e); (*glance*) furtif(-ive)

cover-up ['kʌvərʌp] *n* tentative *f* pour étouffer une affaire

covet ['kʌvɪt] *vt* convoiter

cow [kau] *n* vache *f* ♦ *vt* effrayer, intimider

coward ['kauəd] *n* lâche *m/f*; ~**ice** *n* lâcheté *f*; ~**ly** *adj* lâche

cowboy ['kaubɔɪ] *n* cow-boy *m*

cower ['kauər] *vi* se recroqueviller

coy [kɔɪ] *adj* faussement effarouché(e) *or* timide

cozy ['kəuzɪ] (*US*) *adj* = **cosy**

CPA (*US*) *n abbr* = **certified public accountant**

crab [kræb] *n* crabe *m*; ~ **apple** *n* pomme *f* sauvage

crack [kræk] *n* (*split*) fente *f*, fissure *f*; (*in cup, bone etc*) fêlure *f*; (*in wall*) lézarde *f*; (*noise*) craquement *m*, coup (sec); (*drug*) crack *m* ♦ *vt* fendre, fissurer; fêler; lézarder; (*whip*) faire claquer; (*nut*) casser; (*code*) déchiffrer; (*problem*) résoudre ♦ *adj* (*athlete*) de première classe, d'élite; ~ **down on** *vt fus* mettre un frein à; ~ **up** *vi* être au bout du rouleau, s'effondrer; ~**ed** *adj* (*cup, bone*) fêlé(e); (*broken*) cassé(e); (*wall*) lézardé(e); (*surface*) craquelé(e); (*inf: mad*) cinglé(e); ~**er** *n* (*Christmas cracker*) pétard *m*; (*biscuit*) biscuit (salé)

crackle ['krækl] *vi* crépiter, grésiller

cradle ['kreɪdl] *n* berceau *m*

craft [krɑ:ft] *n* métier (artisanal); (*pl inv: boat*) embarcation *f*, barque *f*; (: *plane*) appareil *m*; ~**sman** (*irreg*) *n* artisan *m*, ouvrier (qualifié); ~**smanship** *n* travail *m*; ~**y** *adj* rusé(e), malin(-igne)

crag [kræg] *n* rocher escarpé

cram [kræm] *vt* (*fill*): **to ~ sth with** bourrer qch de; (*put*): **to ~ sth into** fourrer qch dans ♦ *vi* (*for exams*) bachoter

cramp [kræmp] *n* crampe *f* ♦ *vt* gêner, entraver; ~**ed** *adj* à l'étroit, très serré(e)

cranberry ['krænbərɪ] *n* canneberge *f*

crane [kreɪn] *n* grue *f*

crank [kræŋk] *n* manivelle *f*; (*person*) excentrique *m/f*

cranny ['krænɪ] *n see* **nook**

crash [kræʃ] *n* fracas *m*; (*of car*) collision *f*; (*of plane*) accident *m* ♦ *vt* avoir un accident avec ♦ *vi* (*plane*) s'écraser; (*two cars*) se percuter, s'emboutir; (*COMM*) s'effondrer; **to ~ into** se jeter *or* se fracasser contre; ~ **course** *n* cours intensif; ~ **helmet** *n* casque (protecteur); ~ **landing** *n* atterrissage forcé *or* en catastrophe

crate [kreɪt] *n* cageot *m*; (*for bottles*) caisse *f*

cravat(e) [krə'væt] *n* foulard (noué autour du cou)

crave [kreɪv] *vt, vi*: **to ~ (for)** avoir une envie irrésistible de

crawl [krɔ:l] *vi* ramper; (*vehicle*) avancer au pas ♦ *n* (*SWIMMING*) crawl *m*

crayfish ['kreɪfɪʃ] *n inv* (*freshwater*) écrevisse *f*; (*saltwater*) langoustine *f*

crayon ['kreɪən] *n* crayon *m* (de couleur)

craze [kreɪz] *n* engouement *m*

crazy ['kreɪzɪ] *adj* fou (folle)

creak [kri:k] *vi* grincer; craquer

cream [kri:m] *n* crème *f* ♦ *adj* (*colour*) crème *inv*; ~ **cake** *n* (petit) gâteau à la crème; ~ **cheese** *n* fromage *m* à la crème, fromage blanc; ~**y** *adj* crémeux(-euse)

crease [kri:s] *n* pli *m* ♦ *vt* froisser, chiffonner ♦ *vi* se froisser, se chiffonner

create [kri:'eɪt] *vt* créer; **creation** *n* création *f*; **creative** *adj* (*artistic*) créatif(-ive); (*ingenious*) ingénieux(-euse)

creature ['kri:tʃər] *n* créature *f*

crèche [kreʃ] *n* garderie *f*, crèche *f*

credence ['kri:dns] *n*: **to lend** *or* **give ~ to** ajouter foi à

credentials [krɪ'dɛnʃlz] *npl* (*references*) références *fpl*; (*papers of identity*) pièce *f* d'identité

credit ['krɛdɪt] *n* crédit *m*; (*recognition*) honneur *m* ♦ *vt* (*COMM*) créditer; (*believe: also:* **give ~ to**) ajouter foi à, croire; ~**s** *npl* (*CINEMA, TV*) générique *m*; **to be in ~**

(*person, bank account*) être créditeur(-trice); **to ~ sb with** (*fig*) prêter *or* attribuer à qn; **~ card** *n* carte *f* de crédit; **~or** *n* créancier(-ière)

creed [kriːd] *n* croyance *f*; credo *m*

creek [kriːk] *n* crique *f*, anse *f*; (*US: stream*) ruisseau *m*, petit cours d'eau

creep [kriːp] (*pt, pp* **crept**) *vi* ramper; **~er** *n* plante grimpante; **~y** *adj* (*frightening*) qui fait frissonner, qui donne la chair de poule

cremate [krɪˈmeɪt] *vt* incinérer; **crematorium** [kremə'tɔːrɪəm] (*pl* **crematoria**) *n* four *m* crématoire

crêpe [kreɪp] *n* crêpe *m*; **~ bandage** (*BRIT*) *n* bande *f* Velpeau ®

crept [krept] *pt, pp of* **creep**

crescent ['krɛsnt] *n* croissant *m*; (*street*) rue *f* (*en arc de cercle*)

cress [krɛs] *n* cresson *m*

crest [krɛst] *n* crête *f*; **~fallen** *adj* déconfit(e), découragé(e)

Crete [kriːt] *n* Crète *f*

crevice ['krɛvɪs] *n* fissure *f*, lézarde *f*, fente *f*

crew [kruː] *n* équipage *m*; (*CINEMA*) équipe *f*; **~-cut** *n*: **to have a ~-cut** avoir les cheveux en brosse; **~-neck** *n* col ras du cou

crib [krɪb] *n* lit *m* d'enfant; (*for baby*) berceau *m* ♦ *vt* (*inf*) copier

crick [krɪk] *n*: **~ in the neck** torticolis *m*; **~ in the back** tour *m* de reins

cricket ['krɪkɪt] *n* (*insect*) grillon *m*, cri-cri *m inv*; (*game*) cricket *m*

crime [kraɪm] *n* crime *m*; **criminal** ['krɪmɪnl] *adj, n* criminel(le)

crimson ['krɪmzn] *adj* cramoisi(e)

cringe [krɪndʒ] *vi* avoir un mouvement de recul

crinkle ['krɪŋkl] *vt* froisser, chiffonner

cripple ['krɪpl] *n* boiteux(-euse), infirme *m/f* ♦ *vt* estropier

crisis ['kraɪsɪs] (*pl* **crises**) *n* crise *f*

crisp [krɪsp] *adj* croquant(e); (*weather*) vif (vive); (*manner etc*) brusque; **~s** (*BRIT*) *npl* (pommes) chips *fpl*

crisscross ['krɪskrɔs] *adj* entrecroisé(e)

criterion [kraɪˈtɪərɪən] (*pl* **criteria**) *n* critère *m*

critic ['krɪtɪk] *n* critique *m*; **~al** *adj* critique; **~ally** *adv* (*examine*) d'un œil critique; (*speak etc*) sévèrement; **~ally ill** gravement malade; **~ism** ['krɪtɪsɪzəm] *n* critique *f*; **~ize** ['krɪtɪsaɪz] *vt* critiquer

croak [krəuk] *vi* (*frog*) coasser; (*raven*) croasser; (*person*) parler d'une voix rauque

Croatia [krəu'eɪʃə] *n* Croatie *f*

crochet ['krəuʃeɪ] *n* travail *m* au crochet

crockery ['krɔkərɪ] *n* vaisselle *f*

crocodile ['krɔkədaɪl] *n* crocodile *m*

crocus ['krəukəs] *n* crocus *m*

croft [krɔft] (*BRIT*) *n* petite ferme *f*

crony ['krəunɪ] (*inf: pej*) *n* copain (copine)

crook [kruk] *n* escroc *m*; (*of shepherd*) houlette *f*; **~ed** ['krukɪd] *adj* courbé(e), tordu(e); (*action*) malhonnête

crop [krɔp] *n* (*produce*) culture *f*; (*amount produced*) récolte *f*; (*riding ~*) cravache *f* ♦ *vt* (*hair*) tondre; **~ up** *vi* surgir, se présenter, survenir

cross [krɔs] *n* croix *f*; (*BIO etc*) croisement *m* ♦ *vt* (*street etc*) traverser; (*arms, legs, BIO*) croiser; (*cheque*) barrer ♦ *adj* en colère, fâché(e); **~ out** *vt* barrer, biffer; **~ over** *vi* traverser; **~bar** *n* barre (transversale); **~-country (race)** *n* cross-(country) *m*; **~-examine** *vt* (*LAW*) faire subir un examen contradictoire à; **~-eyed** *adj* qui louche; **~fire** *n* feux croisés; **~ing** *n* (*sea passage*) traversée *f*; (*also:* **pedestrian ~ing**) passage clouté; **~ing guard** (*US*) *n contractuel qui fait traverser la rue aux enfants*; **~ purposes** *npl*: **to be at ~ purposes with sb** comprendre qn de travers; **~-reference** *n* renvoi *m*, référence *f*; **~roads** *n* carrefour *m*; **~ section** *n* (*of object*) coupe transversale; (*in population*) échantillon *m*; **~walk** (*US*) *n* passage clouté; **~wind** *n* vent *m* de travers; **~word** *n* mots *mpl* croisés

crotch [krɔtʃ] *n* (*ANAT, of garment*) entrejambes *m inv*

crouch [krautʃ] *vi* s'accroupir; se tapir

crow [krəu] *n* (*bird*) corneille *f*; (*of cock*)

chant *m* du coq, cocorico *m* ♦ *vi* (*cock*) chanter

crowbar [ˈkrəʊbɑːʳ] *n* levier *m*

crowd [kraʊd] *n* foule *f* ♦ *vt* remplir ♦ *vi* affluer, s'attrouper, s'entasser; **to ~ in** entrer en foule; **~ed** *adj* bondé(e), plein(e)

crown [kraʊn] *n* couronne *f*; (*of head*) sommet *m* de la tête; (*of hill*) sommet *m* ♦ *vt* couronner; **~ jewels** *npl* joyaux *mpl* de la Couronne

crow's-feet [ˈkrəʊzfiːt] *npl* pattes *fpl* d'oie

crucial [ˈkruːʃl] *adj* crucial(e), décisif(-ive)

crucifix [ˈkruːsɪfɪks] *n* (*REL*) crucifix *m*; **~ion** [kruːsɪˈfɪkʃən] *n* (*REL*) crucifixion *f*

crude [kruːd] *adj* (*materials*) brut(e); non raffiné(e); (*fig: basic*) rudimentaire, sommaire; (: *vulgar*) cru(e), grossier(-ère); **~** (**oil**) *n* (*pétrole*) brut *m*

cruel [ˈkruəl] *adj* cruel(le); **~ty** *n* cruauté *f*

cruise [kruːz] *n* croisière *f* ♦ *vi* (*ship*) croiser; (*car*) rouler; **~r** *n* croiseur *m*; (*motorboat*) yacht *m* de croisière

crumb [krʌm] *n* miette *f*

crumble [ˈkrʌmbl] *vt* émietter ♦ *vi* (*plaster etc*) s'effriter; (*land, earth*) s'ébouler; (*building*) s'écrouler, crouler; (*fig*) s'effondrer; **crumbly** *adj* friable

crumpet [ˈkrʌmpɪt] *n* petite crêpe (épaisse)

crumple [ˈkrʌmpl] *vt* froisser, friper

crunch [krʌntʃ] *vt* croquer; (*underfoot*) faire craquer *or* crisser, écraser ♦ *n* (*fig*) instant *m* *or* moment *m* critique, moment de vérité; **~y** *adj* croquant(e), croustillant(e)

crusade [kruːˈseɪd] *n* croisade *f*

crush [krʌʃ] *n* foule *f*, cohue *f*; (*love*): **to have a ~ on sb** avoir le béguin pour qn (*inf*); (*drink*): **lemon ~** citron pressé ♦ *vt* écraser; (*crumple*) froisser; (*fig: hopes*) anéantir

crust [krʌst] *n* croûte *f*

crutch [krʌtʃ] *n* béquille *f*

crux [krʌks] *n* point crucial

cry [kraɪ] *vi* pleurer; (*shout: also: ~ out*) crier ♦ *n* cri *m*; **~ off** (*inf*) *vi* se dédire; se décommander

cryptic [ˈkrɪptɪk] *adj* énigmatique

crystal [ˈkrɪstl] *n* cristal *m*; **~-clear** *adj* clair(e) comme de l'eau de roche

CSA *n abbr* (= *Child Support Agency*) organisme pour la protection des enfants de parents séparés, qui contrôle le versement des pensions alimentaires

CTC *n abbr* = **city technology college**

cub [kʌb] *n* petit *m* (*d'un animal*); (*also:* **C~ scout**) louveteau *m*

Cuba [ˈkjuːbə] *n* Cuba *m*

cube [kjuːb] *n* cube *m* ♦ *vt* (*MATH*) élever au cube; **cubic** *adj* cubique; **cubic metre** *etc* mètre *m* *etc* cube; **cubic capacity** *n* cylindrée *f*

cubicle [ˈkjuːbɪkl] *n* (*in hospital*) box *m*; (*at pool*) cabine *f*

cuckoo [ˈkuːkuː] *n* coucou *m*; **~ clock** *n* (*pendule f à*) coucou *m*

cucumber [ˈkjuːkʌmbəʳ] *n* concombre *m*

cuddle [ˈkʌdl] *vt* câliner, caresser ♦ *vi* se blottir l'un contre l'autre

cue [kjuː] *n* (*snooker ~*) queue *f* de billard; (*THEATRE etc*) signal *m*

cuff [kʌf] *n* (*BRIT: of shirt, coat etc*) poignet *m*, manchette *f*; (*US: of trousers*) revers *m*; (*blow*) tape *f*; **off the ~** à l'improviste; **~ links** *npl* boutons *mpl* de manchette

cul-de-sac [ˈkʌldəsæk] *n* cul-de-sac *m*, impasse *f*

cull [kʌl] *vt* sélectionner ♦ *n* (*of animals*) massacre *m*

culminate [ˈkʌlmɪneɪt] *vi*: **to ~ in** finir *or* se terminer par; (*end in*) mener à; **culmination** [kʌlmɪˈneɪʃən] *n* point culminant

culottes [kjuːˈlɒts] *npl* jupe-culotte *f*

culprit [ˈkʌlprɪt] *n* coupable *m/f*

cult [kʌlt] *n* culte *m*

cultivate [ˈkʌltɪveɪt] *vt* cultiver; **cultivation** [kʌltɪˈveɪʃən] *n* culture *f*

cultural [ˈkʌltʃərəl] *adj* culturel(le)

culture [ˈkʌltʃəʳ] *n* culture *f*; **~d** *adj* (*person*) cultivé(e)

cumbersome [ˈkʌmbəsəm] *adj* encombrant(e), embarrassant(e)

cunning [ˈkʌnɪŋ] *n* ruse *f*, astuce *f* ♦ *adj* rusé(e), malin(-igne); (*device, idea*) astucieux(-euse)

cup [kʌp] *n* tasse *f*; (*as prize*) coupe *f*; (*of bra*) bonnet *m*

cupboard ['kʌbəd] *n* armoire *f*; (*built-in*) placard *m*

cup tie (*BRIT*) *n* match *m* de coupe

curate ['kjuərɪt] *n* vicaire *m*

curator [kjuə'reɪtər] *n* conservateur *m* (*d'un musée etc*)

curb [kəːb] *vt* refréner, mettre un frein à ♦ *n* (*fig*) frein *m*, restriction *f*; (*US: kerb*) bord *m* du trottoir

curdle ['kəːdl] *vi* se cailler

cure [kjuər] *vt* guérir; (*CULIN: salt*) saler; (*: smoke*) fumer; (*: dry*) sécher ♦ *n* remède *m*

curfew ['kəːfjuː] *n* couvre-feu *m*

curiosity [kjuərɪ'ɔsɪtɪ] *n* curiosité *f*

curious ['kjuərɪəs] *adj* curieux(-euse)

curl [kəːl] *n* boucle *f* (*de cheveux*) ♦ *vt, vi* boucler; (*tightly*) friser; ~ **up** *vi* s'enrouler; se pelotonner; ~**er** *n* bigoudi *m*, rouleau *m*; ~**y** *adj* bouclé(e); frisé(e)

currant ['kʌrnt] *n* (*dried*) raisin *m* de Corinthe, raisin sec; (*bush*) groseiller *m*; (*fruit*) groseille *f*

currency ['kʌrnsɪ] *n* monnaie *f*; **to gain ~** (*fig*) s'accréditer

current ['kʌrnt] *n* courant *m* ♦ *adj* courant(e); ~ **account** (*BRIT*) *n* compte courant; ~ **affairs** *npl* (questions *fpl* d')actualité *f*; ~**ly** *adv* actuellement

curriculum [kə'rɪkjuləm] (*pl* ~**s** *or* **curricula**) *n* programme *m* d'études; ~ **vitae** *n* curriculum vitae *m*

curry ['kʌrɪ] *n* curry *m* ♦ *vt*: **to ~ favour with** chercher à s'attirer les bonnes grâces de

curse [kəːs] *vi* jurer, blasphémer ♦ *vt* maudire ♦ *n* (*spell*) malédiction *f*; (*problem, scourge*) fléau *m*; (*swearword*) juron *m*

cursor ['kəːsər] *n* (*COMPUT*) curseur *m*

cursory ['kəːsərɪ] *adj* superficiel(le), hâtif(-ive)

curt [kəːt] *adj* brusque, sec (sèche)

curtail [kəː'teɪl] *vt* (*visit etc*) écourter; (*expenses, freedom etc*) réduire

curtain ['kəːtn] *n* rideau *m*

curts(e)y ['kəːtsɪ] *vi* faire une révérence

curve [kəːv] *n* courbe *f*; (*in the road*) tournant *m*, virage *m* ♦ *vi* se courber; (*road*) faire une courbe

cushion ['kuʃən] *n* coussin *m* ♦ *vt* (*fall, shock*) amortir

custard ['kʌstəd] *n* (*for pouring*) crème anglaise

custody ['kʌstədɪ] *n* (*of child*) garde *f*; **to take sb into ~** (*suspect*) placer qn en détention préventive

custom ['kʌstəm] *n* coutume *f*, usage *m*; (*COMM*) clientèle *f*; ~**ary** *adj* habituel(le)

customer ['kʌstəmər] *n* client(e)

customized ['kʌstəmaɪzd] *adj* (*car etc*) construit(e) sur commande

custom-made ['kʌstəm'meɪd] *adj* (*clothes*) fait(e) sur mesure; (*other goods*) hors série, fait(e) sur commande

customs ['kʌstəmz] *npl* douane *f*; ~ **officer** *n* douanier(-ière)

cut [kʌt] (*pt, pp* **cut**) *vt* couper; (*meat*) découper; (*reduce*) réduire ♦ *vi* couper ♦ *n* coupure *f*; (*of clothes*) coupe *f*; (*in salary etc*) réduction *f*; (*of meat*) morceau *m*; **to ~ one's hand** se couper la main; **to ~ a tooth** percer une dent; ~ **down** *vt fus* (*tree etc*) abattre; (*consumption*) réduire; ~ **off** *vt* couper; (*fig*) isoler; ~ **out** *vt* découper; (*stop*) arrêter; (*remove*) ôter; ~ **up** *vt* (*meat*) découper; ~**back** *n* réduction *f*

cute [kjuːt] *adj* mignon(ne), adorable

cutlery ['kʌtlərɪ] *n* couverts *mpl*

cutlet ['kʌtlɪt] *n* côtelette *f*

cut: ~**out** *n* (*switch*) coupe-circuit *m inv*; (*cardboard cutout*) découpage *m*; ~**-price** (*US* **cut-rate**) *adj* au rabais, à prix réduit; ~**-throat** *n* assassin *m* ♦ *adj* acharné(e); ~**ting** *adj* tranchant(e), coupant(e); (*fig*) cinglant(e), mordant(e) ♦ *n* (*BRIT: from newspaper*) coupure *f* (*de journal*); (*from plant*) bouture *f*

CV *n abbr* = **curriculum vitae**

cwt *abbr* = **hundredweight(s)**

cyanide ['saɪənaɪd] *n* cyanure *m*

cybercafé ['saɪbəkæfeɪ] *n* cybercafé *m*

cyberspace ['saɪbəspeɪs] *n* cyberspace *m*

cycle ['saɪkl] *n* cycle *m*; (*bicycle*) bicyclette *f*, vélo *m* ♦ *vi* faire de la bicyclette; ~ **hire** *n* location *f* de vélos; ~ **lane** *or* **path** *n* piste *f* cyclable; **cycling** *n* cyclisme *m*; **cyclist** ['saɪklɪst] *n* cycliste *m/f*

cygnet ['sɪgnɪt] *n* jeune cygne *m*

cylinder ['sɪlɪndə'] *n* cylindre *m*; ~-**head gasket** *n* joint *m* de culasse

cymbals ['sɪmblz] *npl* cymbales *fpl*

cynic ['sɪnɪk] *n* cynique *m/f*; ~**al** *adj* cynique; ~**ism** ['sɪnɪsɪzəm] *n* cynisme *m*

Cypriot ['sɪprɪət] *adj* cypriote, chypriote ♦ *n* Cypriote *m/f*, Chypriote *m/f*

Cyprus ['saɪprəs] *n* Chypre *f*

cyst [sɪst] *n* kyste *m*

cystitis [sɪs'taɪtɪs] *n* cystite *f*

czar [zɑ:'] *n* tsar *m*

Czech [tʃɛk] *adj* tchèque ♦ *n* Tchèque *m/f*; (*LING*) tchèque *m*

Czechoslovak [tʃɛkə'sləʊvæk] *adj* tchécoslovaque ♦ *n* Tchécoslovaque *m/f*

Czechoslovakia [tʃɛkəslə'vækɪə] *n* Tchécoslovaquie *f*

D, d

D [di:] *n* (*MUS*) ré *m*

dab [dæb] *vt* (*eyes, wound*) tamponner; (*paint, cream*) appliquer (par petites touches *or* rapidement)

dabble ['dæbl] *vi*: **to ~ in** faire *or* se mêler *or* s'occuper un peu de

dad [dæd] *n*, **daddy** ['dædɪ] *n* papa *m*

daffodil ['dæfədɪl] *n* jonquille *f*

daft [dɑ:ft] *adj* idiot(e), stupide

dagger ['dægə'] *n* poignard *m*

daily ['deɪlɪ] *adj* quotidien(ne), journalier(ère) ♦ *n* quotidien *m* ♦ *adv* tous les jours

dainty ['deɪntɪ] *adj* délicat(e), mignon(ne)

dairy ['dɛərɪ] *n* (*BRIT: shop*) crémerie, laiterie *f*; (*on farm*) laiterie; ~ **products** *npl* produits laitiers; ~ **store** (*US*) *n* crémerie *f*, laiterie *f*

daisy ['deɪzɪ] *n* pâquerette *f*

dale [deɪl] *n* vallon *m*

dam [dæm] *n* barrage *m* ♦ *vt* endiguer

damage ['dæmɪdʒ] *n* dégâts *mpl*, dommages *mpl*; (*fig*) tort *m* ♦ *vt* endommager, abîmer; (*fig*) faire du tort à; ~**s** *npl* (*LAW*) dommages-intérêts *mpl*

damn [dæm] *vt* condamner; (*curse*) maudire ♦ *n* (*inf*): **I don't give a ~** je m'en fous ♦ *adj* (*inf: also:* ~**ed**): **this ~ ...** ce sacré *or* foutu ...; ~ **(it)!** zut!; ~**ing** *adj* accablant(e)

damp [dæmp] *adj* humide ♦ *n* humidité *f* ♦ *vt* (*also:* ~**en**: *cloth, rag*) humecter; (: *enthusiasm*) refroidir

damson ['dæmzən] *n* prune *f* de Damas

dance [dɑ:ns] *n* danse *f*; (*social event*) bal *m* ♦ *vi* danser; ~ **hall** *n* salle *f* de bal, dancing *m*; ~**r** *n* danseur(-euse); **dancing** *n* danse *f*

dandelion ['dændɪlaɪən] *n* pissenlit *m*

dandruff ['dændrəf] *n* pellicules *fpl*

Dane [deɪn] *n* Danois(e)

danger ['deɪndʒə'] *n* danger *m*; **there is a ~ of fire** il y a (un) risque d'incendie; **in ~** en danger; **he was in ~ of falling** il risquait de tomber; ~**ous** *adj* dangereux(-euse)

dangle ['dæŋgl] *vt* balancer ♦ *vi* pendre

Danish ['deɪnɪʃ] *adj* danois(e) ♦ *n* (*LING*) danois *m*

dare [dɛə'] *vt*: **to ~ sb to do** défier qn de faire ♦ *vi*: **to ~ (to) do sth** oser faire qch; **I ~ say** (*I suppose*) il est probable (que); **daring** *adj* hardi(e), audacieux(-euse); (*dress*) osé(e) ♦ *n* audace *f*, hardiesse *f*

dark [dɑ:k] *adj* (*night, room*) obscur(e), sombre; (*colour, complexion*) foncé(e), sombre ♦ *n*: **in the ~** dans le noir; **in the ~ about** tout ignorant tout de; **after ~** après la tombée de la nuit; ~**en** *vt* obscurcir, assombrir ♦ *vi* s'obscurcir, s'assombrir; ~ **glasses** *npl* lunettes noires; ~**ness** *n* obscurité *f*; ~**room** *n* chambre noire

darling ['dɑ:lɪŋ] *adj* chéri(e) ♦ *n* chéri(e); (*favourite*): **to be the ~ of** être la coqueluche de

darn [dɑ:n] *vt* repriser, raccommoder

dart [dɑ:t] *n* fléchette *f*; (*sewing*) pince *f*

♦ *vi*: **to ~ towards** (*also:* **make a ~ to-wards**) se précipiter *or* s'élancer vers; **to ~ away/along** partir/passer comme une flèche; **~board** *n* cible *f* (de jeu de fléchettes); **~s** *n* (*jeu de*) fléchettes *fpl*

dash [dæʃ] *n* (*sign*) tiret *m*; (*small quantity*) goutte *f*, larme *f* ♦ *vt* (*missile*) jeter *or* lancer violemment; (*hopes*) anéantir ♦ *vi*: **to ~ towards** (*also:* **make a ~ towards**) se précipiter *or* se ruer vers; **~ away** *vi* partir à toute allure, filer; **~ off** *vi* = **dash away**

dashboard ['dæʃbɔ:d] *n* (*AUT*) tableau *m* de bord

dashing ['dæʃɪŋ] *adj* fringant(e)

data ['deɪtə] *npl* données *fpl*; **~base** *n* (*COMPUT*) base *f* de données; **~ process-ing** *n* traitement *m* de données

date [deɪt] *n* date *f*; (*with sb*) rendez-vous *m*; (*fruit*) datte *f* ♦ *vt* dater; (*person*) sortir avec; **~ of birth** date de naissance; **to ~** (*until now*) à ce jour; **out of ~** (*passport*) périmé(e); (*theory etc*) dépassé(e); (*clothes etc*) démodé(e); **up to ~** moderne; (*news*) très récent; **~d** ['deɪtɪd] *adj* démodé(e); **~ rape** *n* viol *m* (*à l'issue d'un rendez-vous galant*)

daub [dɔ:b] *vt* barbouiller

daughter ['dɔ:tə'] *n* fille *f*; **~-in-law** *n* belle-fille *f*, bru *f*

daunting ['dɔ:ntɪŋ] *adj* décourageant(e)

dawdle ['dɔ:dl] *vi* traîner, lambiner

dawn [dɔ:n] *n* aube *f*, aurore *f* ♦ *vi* (*day*) se lever, poindre; (*fig*): **it ~ed on him that ...** il lui vint à l'esprit que ...

day [deɪ] *n* jour *m*; (*as duration*) journée *f*; (*period of time, age*) époque *f*, temps *m*; **the ~ before** la veille, le jour précédent; **the ~ after, the following ~** le lende-main, le jour suivant; **the ~ after tomor-row** après-demain; **the ~ before yester-day** avant-hier; **by ~** de jour; **~break** *n* point *m* du jour; **~dream** *vi* rêver (tout éveillé), **~light** *n* (lumière *f* du) jour *m*; **~ return** (*BRIT*) *n* billet *m* d'aller-retour (va-lable pour la journée); **~time** *n* jour *m*, journée *f*; **~-to-~** *adj* quotidien(ne);

(*event*) journalier(-ère)

daze [deɪz] *vt* (*stun*) étourdir ♦ *n*: **in a ~** étourdi(e), hébété(e)

dazzle ['dæzl] *vt* éblouir, aveugler

DC *abbr* (= *direct current*) courant continu

D-day ['di:deɪ] *n* le jour J

dead [dɛd] *adj* mort(e); (*numb*) engour-di(e), insensible; (*battery*) à plat; (*tele-phone*): **the line is ~** la ligne est coupée ♦ *adv* absolument, complètement ♦ *npl*: **the ~** les morts; **he was shot ~** il a été tué d'un coup de revolver; **~ on time** à l'heure pile; **~ tired** éreinté(e), complètement fourbu(e); **to stop ~** s'ar-rêter pile *or* net; **~en** *vt* (*blow, sound*) amortir; (*pain*) calmer; **~ end** *n* impasse *f*; **~ heat** *n* (*SPORT*): **to finish in a ~ heat** terminer ex-æquo; **~line** *n* date *f* *or* heu-re *f* limite; **~lock** (*fig*) *n* impasse *f*; **~ loss** *n*: **to be a ~ loss** (*inf: person*) n'être bon(ne) à rien; **~ly** *adj* mortel(le); (*weap-on*) meurtrier(-ère); (*accuracy*) extrême; **~pan** *adj* impassible; **D~ Sea** *n*: **the D~ Sea** la mer Morte

deaf [dɛf] *adj* sourd(e); **~en** *vt* rendre sourd; **~ening** *adj* assourdissant(e); **~-mute** *n* sourd(e)-muet(te); **~ness** *n* sur-dité *f*

deal [di:l] (*pt, pp* **dealt**) *n* affaire *f*, marché *m* ♦ *vt* (*blow*) porter; (*cards*) donner, dis-tribuer; **a great ~ (of)** beaucoup (de); **~ in** *vt fus* faire le commerce de; **~ with** *vt fus* (*person, problem*) s'occuper *or* se char-ger de; (*be about: book etc*) traiter de; **~er** *n* marchand *m*; **~ings** *npl* (*COMM*) trans-actions *fpl*; (*relations*) relations *fpl*, rap-ports *mpl*

dean [di:n] *n* (*REL, BRIT: SCOL*) doyen *m*; (*US: SCOL*) conseiller(-ère) (principal(e)) d'édu-cation

dear [dɪə'] *adj* cher (chère); (*expensive*) cher, coûteux(-euse) ♦ *n*: **my ~** mon cher/ma chère; **~ me!** mon Dieu!; **D~ Sir/Madam** (*in letter*) Monsieur/Madame; **D~ Mr/Mrs X** Cher Monsieur/Chère Ma-dame; **~ly** *adv* (*love*) tendrement; (*pay*) cher

death [deθ] *n* mort *f*; (*fatality*) mort *m*; (*ADMIN*) décès *m*; ~ **certificate** *n* acte *m* de décès; ~**ly** *adj* de mort; ~ **penalty** *n* peine *f* de mort; ~ **rate** *n* (taux *m* de) mortalité *f*; ~ **toll** *n* nombre *m* de morts

debase [dɪ'beɪs] *vt* (*value*) déprécier, dévaloriser

debatable [dɪ'beɪtəbl] *adj* discutable

debate [dɪ'beɪt] *n* discussion *f*, débat *m* ♦ *vt* discuter, débattre

debit ['debɪt] *n* débit *m* ♦ *vt*: **to ~ a sum to sb** *or* **to sb's account** porter une somme au débit de qn, débiter qn d'une somme; *see also* **direct**

debt [det] *n* dette *f*; **to be in ~** avoir des dettes, être endetté(e); ~**or** *n* débiteur(-trice)

decade ['dekeɪd] *n* décennie *f*, décade *f*

decadence ['dekədəns] *n* décadence *f*

decaff ['di:kæf] (*inf*) *n* déca *m*

decaffeinated [dɪ'kæfɪneɪtɪd] *adj* décaféiné(e)

decanter [dɪ'kæntər] *n* carafe *f*

decay [dɪ'keɪ] *n* (*of building*) délabrement *m*; (*also*: **tooth ~**) carie *f* (dentaire) ♦ *vi* (*rot*) se décomposer, pourrir; (*: teeth*) se carier

deceased [dɪ'si:st] *n* défunt *m*

deceit [dɪ'si:t] *n* tromperie *f*, supercherie *f*; ~**ful** *adj* trompeur(-euse); **deceive** *vt* tromper

December [dɪ'sembər] *n* décembre *m*

decent ['di:sənt] *adj* décent(e), convenable

deception [dɪ'sepʃən] *n* tromperie *f*

deceptive [dɪ'septɪv] *adj* trompeur(-euse)

decide [dɪ'saɪd] *vt* (*person*) décider; (*question, argument*) trancher, régler ♦ *vi* se décider, décider; **to ~ to do/that** décider de faire/que; **to ~ on** décider, se décider pour; ~**d** *adj* (*resolute*) résolu(e), décidé(e); (*clear, definite*) net(te), marqué(e); ~**dly** *adv* résolument; (*distinctly*) incontestablement, nettement

deciduous [dɪ'sɪdjuəs] *adj* à feuilles caduques

decimal ['desɪməl] *adj* décimal(e) ♦ *n* décimale *f*; ~ **point** *n* ≃ virgule *f*

decipher [dɪ'saɪfər] *vt* déchiffrer

decision [dɪ'sɪʒən] *n* décision *f*

decisive [dɪ'saɪsɪv] *adj* décisif(-ive); (*person*) décidé(e)

deck [dek] *n* (*NAUT*) pont *m*; (*of bus*): **top ~** impériale *f*; (*of cards*) jeu *m*; (*record ~*) platine *f*; ~**chair** *n* chaise longue

declare [dɪ'kleər] *vt* déclarer

decline [dɪ'klaɪn] *n* (*decay*) déclin *m*; (*lessening*) baisse *f* ♦ *vt* refuser, décliner ♦ *vi* décliner; (*business*) baisser

decoder [di:'kəudər] *n* (*TV*) décodeur *m*

decorate ['dekəreɪt] *vt* (*adorn, give a medal to*) décorer; (*paint and paper*) peindre et tapisser; **decoration** [dekə'reɪʃən] *n* (*medal etc, adornment*) décoration *f*; **decorator** *n* peintre-décorateur *m*

decoy ['di:kɔɪ] *n* piège *m*; (*person*) compère *m*

decrease [*n* 'di:kri:s, *vb* di:'kri:s] *n*: ~ **(in)** diminution *f* (de) ♦ *vt*, *vi* diminuer

decree [dɪ'kri:] *n* (*POL, REL*) décret *m*; (*LAW*) arrêt *m*, jugement *m*; ~ **nisi** [-'naɪsaɪ] *n* jugement *m* provisoire de divorce

dedicate ['dedɪkeɪt] *vt* consacrer; (*book etc*) dédier; ~**d** *adj* (*person*) dévoué(e); (*COMPUT*) spécialisé(e), dédié(e); **dedication** [dedɪ'keɪʃən] *n* (*devotion*) dévouement *m*; (*in book*) dédicace *f*

deduce [dɪ'dju:s] *vt* déduire, conclure

deduct [dɪ'dʌkt] *vt*: **to ~ sth (from)** déduire qch (de), retrancher qch (de); ~**ion** *n* (*deducting, deducing*) déduction *f*; (*from wage etc*) prélèvement *m*, retenue *f*

deed [di:d] *n* action *f*, acte *m*; (*LAW*) acte notarié, contrat *m*

deep [di:p] *adj* profond(e); (*voice*) grave ♦ *adv*: **spectators stood 20 ~** il y avait 20 rangs de spectateurs; **4 metres ~** de 4 mètres de profondeur; ~ **end** (*of swimming pool*) grand bain; ~**en** *vt* approfondir ♦ *vi* (*fig*) s'épaissir; ~**freeze** *n* congélateur *m*; ~**fry** *vt* faire frire (en friteuse); ~**ly** *adv* profondément; (*interested*) vivement; ~**-sea diver** *n* sous-marin(e); ~**-sea diving** *n* plongée sous-marine; ~**-sea fishing** *n* grande pêche; ~**-seated** *adj* profond(e), profondément enraciné(e)

deer [dɪəʳ] *n inv*: **(red) ~** cerf *m*, biche *f*; **(fallow) ~** daim *m*; **(roe) ~** chevreuil *m*; **~skin** *n* daim

deface [dɪˈfeɪs] *vt* dégrader; (*notice, poster*) barbouiller

default [dɪˈfɔːlt] *n* (*COMPUT: also:* **~ value**) valeur *f* par défaut; **by ~** (*LAW*) par défaut, par contumace; (*SPORT*) par forfait

defeat [dɪˈfiːt] *n* défaite *f* ♦ *vt* (*team, opponents*) battre

defect [*n* ˈdiːfekt, *vb* dɪˈfekt] *n* défaut *m* ♦ *vi*: **to ~ to the enemy** passer à l'ennemi; **~ive** [dɪˈfektɪv] *adj* défectueux(-euse)

defence [dɪˈfens] (*US* **defense**) *n* défense *f*; **~less** *adj* sans défense

defend [dɪˈfend] *vt* défendre; **~ant** *n* défendeur(-deresse); (*in criminal case*) accusé(e), prévenu(e); **~er** *n* défenseur *m*

defer [dɪˈfɜːʳ] *vt* (*postpone*) différer, ajourner

defiance [dɪˈfaɪəns] *n* défi *m*; **in ~ of** au mépris de; **defiant** *adj* provocant(e), de défi; (*person*) rebelle, intraitable

deficiency [dɪˈfɪʃənsɪ] *n* insuffisance *f*, déficience *f*; **deficient** *adj* (*inadequate*) insuffisant(e); **to be deficient in** manquer de

deficit [ˈdefɪsɪt] *n* déficit *m*

define [dɪˈfaɪn] *vt* définir

definite [ˈdefɪnɪt] *adj* (*fixed*) défini(e), (bien) déterminé(e); (*clear, obvious*) net(te), manifeste; (*certain*) sûr(e); **he was ~ about it** il a été catégorique; **~ly** *adv* sans aucun doute

definition [defɪˈnɪʃən] *n* définition *f*; (*clearness*) netteté *f*

deflate [diːˈfleɪt] *vt* dégonfler

deflect [dɪˈflekt] *vt* détourner, faire dévier

deformed [dɪˈfɔːmd] *adj* difforme

defraud [dɪˈfrɔːd] *vt* frauder; **to ~ sb of sth** escroquer qch à qn

defrost [diːˈfrɒst] *vt* dégivrer; (*food*) décongeler; **~er** (*US*) *n* (*demister*) dispositif *m* anti-buée *inv*

deft [deft] *adj* adroit(e), preste

defunct [dɪˈfʌŋkt] *adj* défunt(e)

defuse [diːˈfjuːz] *vt* désamorcer

defy [dɪˈfaɪ] *vt* défier; (*efforts etc*) résister à

degenerate [*vb* dɪˈdʒenəreɪt, *adj* dɪˈdʒenərɪt] *vi* dégénérer ♦ *adj* dégénéré(e)

degree [dɪˈgriː] *n* degré *m*; (*SCOL*) diplôme *m* (universitaire); **a (first) ~ in maths** une licence en maths; **by ~s** (*gradually*) par degrés; **to some ~, to a certain ~** jusqu'à un certain point, dans une certaine mesure

dehydrated [diːhaɪˈdreɪtɪd] *adj* déshydraté(e); (*milk, eggs*) en poudre

de-ice [diːˈaɪs] *vt* (*windscreen*) dégivrer

deign [deɪn] *vi*: **to ~ to do** daigner faire

dejected [dɪˈdʒektɪd] *adj* abattu(e), déprimé(e)

delay [dɪˈleɪ] *vt* retarder ♦ *vi* s'attarder ♦ *n* délai *m*, retard *m*; **to be ~ed** être en retard

delectable [dɪˈlektəbl] *adj* délicieux(-euse)

delegate [*n* ˈdelɪgɪt, *vb* ˈdelɪgeɪt] *n* délégué(e) ♦ *vt* déléguer

delete [dɪˈliːt] *vt* rayer, supprimer

deliberate [*adj* dɪˈlɪbərɪt, *vb* dɪˈlɪbəreɪt] *adj* (*intentional*) délibéré(e); (*slow*) mesuré(e) ♦ *vi* délibérer, réfléchir; **~ly** [dɪˈlɪbərɪtlɪ] *adv* (*on purpose*) exprès, délibérément

delicacy [ˈdelɪkəsɪ] *n* délicatesse *f*; (*food*) mets fin *or* délicat, friandise *f*

delicate [ˈdelɪkɪt] *adj* délicat(e)

delicatessen [delɪkəˈtesn] *n* épicerie fine

delicious [dɪˈlɪʃəs] *adj* délicieux(-euse)

delight [dɪˈlaɪt] *n* (grande) joie, grand plaisir ♦ *vt* enchanter; **to take (a) ~ in** prendre grand plaisir à; **~ed** *adj*: **~ed (at *or* with/to do)** ravi(e) (de/de faire); **~ful** *adj* (*person*) adorable; (*meal, evening*) merveilleux(-euse)

delinquent [dɪˈlɪŋkwənt] *adj, n* délinquant(e)

delirious [dɪˈlɪrɪəs] *adj*: **to be ~** délirer

deliver [dɪˈlɪvəʳ] *vt* (*mail*) distribuer; (*goods*) livrer; (*message*) remettre; (*speech*) prononcer; (*MED: baby*) mettre au monde; **~y** *n* distribution *f*; livraison *f*; (*of speaker*) élocution *f*; (*MED*) accouchement *m*; **to take ~y of** prendre livraison de

delude [dɪ'luːd] *vt* tromper, leurrer; **delusion** *n* illusion *f*

demand [dɪ'maːnd] *vt* réclamer, exiger ♦ *n* exigence *f*; (*claim*) revendication *f*; (*ECON*) demande *f*; **in ~** demandé(e), recherché(e); **on ~** sur demande; **~ing** *adj* (*person*) exigeant(e); (*work*) astreignant(e)

demean [dɪ'miːn] *vt*: **to ~ o.s.** s'abaisser

demeanour [dɪ'miːnər] (*US* **demeanor**) *n* comportement *m*; maintien *m*

demented [dɪ'mɛntɪd] *adj* dément(e), fou (folle)

demise [dɪ'maɪz] *n* mort *f*

demister [diː'mɪstər] (*BRIT*) *n* (*AUT*) dispositif *m* anti-buée *inv*

demo ['dɛməʊ] (*inf*) *n abbr* (= *demonstration*) manif *f*

democracy [dɪ'mɔkrəsɪ] *n* démocratie *f*; **democrat** ['dɛməkræt] *n* démocrate *m/f*; **democratic** [dɛmə'krætɪk] *adj* démocratique

demolish [dɪ'mɔlɪʃ] *vt* démolir

demonstrate ['dɛmənstreɪt] *vt* démontrer, prouver; (*show*) faire une démonstration de ♦ *vi*: **to ~ (for/against)** manifester (en faveur de/contre); **demonstration** [dɛmən'streɪʃən] *n* démonstration *f*, manifestation *f*; **demonstrator** *n* (*POL*) manifestant(e)

demote [dɪ'məʊt] *vt* rétrograder

demure [dɪ'mjʊər] *adj* sage, réservé(e)

den [dɛn] *n* tanière *f*, antre *m*

denial [dɪ'naɪəl] *n* démenti *m*; (*refusal*) dénégation *f*

denim ['dɛnɪm] *n* jean *m*; **~s** *npl* (*jeans*) (blue-)jean(s) *m(pl)*

Denmark ['dɛnmaːk] *n* Danemark *m*

denomination [dɪnɔmɪ'neɪʃən] *n* (*of money*) valeur *f*; (*REL*) confession *f*

denounce [dɪ'naʊns] *vt* dénoncer

dense [dɛns] *adj* dense; (*stupid*) obtus(e), bouché(e); **~ly** *adv*: **~ly populated** à forte densité de population; **density** ['dɛnsɪtɪ] *n* densité *f*; **double/high-density diskette** disquette *f* double densité/haute densité

dent [dɛnt] *n* bosse *f* ♦ *vt* (*also:* **make a ~ in**) cabosser

dental ['dɛntl] *adj* dentaire; **~ surgeon** *n* (chirurgien(ne)) dentiste

dentist ['dɛntɪst] *n* dentiste *m/f*

dentures ['dɛntʃəz] *npl* dentier *m sg*

deny [dɪ'naɪ] *vt* nier; (*refuse*) refuser

deodorant [diː'əʊdərənt] *n* déodorant *m*, désodorisant *m*

depart [dɪ'paːt] *vi* partir; **to ~ from** (*fig: differ from*) s'écarter de

department [dɪ'paːtmənt] *n* (*COMM*) rayon *m*; (*SCOL*) section *f*; (*POL*) ministère *m*, département *m*; **~ store** *n* grand magasin

departure [dɪ'paːtʃər] *n* départ *m*; **a new ~** une nouvelle voie; **~ lounge** *n* (*at airport*) salle *f* d'embarquement

depend [dɪ'pɛnd] *vi*: **to ~ on** dépendre de; (*rely on*) compter sur; **it ~s** cela dépend; **~ing on the result** selon le résultat; **~able** *adj* (*person*) sérieux(-euse), sûr(e); (*car, watch*) solide, fiable; **~ant** *n* personne *f* à charge; **~ent** *adj*: **to be ~ent (on)** dépendre (de) ♦ *n* = **dependant**

depict [dɪ'pɪkt] *vt* (*in picture*) représenter; (*in words*) (dé)peindre, décrire

depleted [dɪ'pliːtɪd] *adj* (considérablement) réduit(e) *or* diminué(e)

deport [dɪ'pɔːt] *vt* expulser

deposit [dɪ'pɔzɪt] *n* (*CHEM, COMM, GEO*) dépôt *m*; (*of ore, oil*) gisement *m*; (*part payment*) arrhes *fpl*, acompte *m*; (*on bottle etc*) consigne *f*; (*for hired goods etc*) cautionnement *m*, garantie *f* ♦ *vt* déposer; **~ account** *n* compte *m* sur livret

depot ['dɛpəʊ] *n* dépôt *m*; (*US: RAIL*) gare *f*

depress [dɪ'prɛs] *vt* déprimer; (*press down*) appuyer sur, abaisser; (*prices, wages*) faire baisser; **~ed** *adj* (*person*) déprimé(e); (*area*) en déclin, touché(e) par le sous-emploi; **~ing** *adj* déprimant(e); **~ion** *n* dépression *f*; (*hollow*) creux *m*

deprivation [dɛprɪ'veɪʃən] *n* privation *f*; (*loss*) perte *f*

deprive [dɪ'praɪv] *vt*: **to ~ sb of** priver qn de; **~d** *adj* déshérité(e)

depth [dɛpθ] *n* profondeur *f*; **in the ~s of despair** au plus profond du désespoir; **to be out of one's ~** avoir perdu pied, nager

deputize ['depjutaɪz] *vi*: **to ~ for** assurer l'intérim de

deputy ['depjutɪ] *adj* adjoint(e) ♦ *n* (*second in command*) adjoint(e); (*US: also:* **~ sheriff**) shérif adjoint; **~ head** directeur adjoint, sous-directeur *m*

derail [dɪ'reɪl] *vt*: **to be ~ed** dérailler

deranged [dɪ'reɪndʒd] *adj*: **to be (mentally) ~** avoir le cerveau dérangé

derby ['dɑːrbɪ] (*US*) *n* (*bowler hat*) (chapeau *m*) melon *m*

derelict ['derɪlɪkt] *adj* abandonné(e), à l'abandon

derisory [dɪ'raɪsərɪ] *adj* (*sum*) dérisoire; (*smile, person*) moqueur(-euse)

derive [dɪ'raɪv] *vt*: **to ~ sth from** tirer qch de; trouver qch dans ♦ *vi*: **to ~ from** provenir de, dériver de

derogatory [dɪ'rɔgətərɪ] *adj* désobligeant(e); péjoratif(-ive)

descend [dɪ'send] *vt, vi* descendre; **to ~ from** descendre de, être issu(e) de; **to ~ to (doing) sth** s'abaisser à (faire) qch; **descent** *n* descente *f*; (*origin*) origine *f*

describe [dɪs'kraɪb] *vt* décrire; **description** [dɪs'krɪpʃən] *n* description *f*; (*sort*) sorte *f*, espèce *f*

desecrate ['desɪkreɪt] *vt* profaner

desert [*n* 'dezət, *vb* dɪ'zəːt] *n* désert *m* ♦ *vt* déserter, abandonner ♦ *vi* (*MIL*) déserter; **~s** *npl*: **to get one's just ~s** n'avoir que ce qu'on mérite; **~er** [dɪ'zəːtər] *n* déserteur *m*; **~ion** [dɪ'zəːʃən] *n* (*MIL*) désertion *f*; (*LAW: of spouse*) abandon *m* du domicile conjugal; **~ island** *n* île déserte

deserve [dɪ'zəːv] *vt* mériter; **deserving** *adj* (*person*) méritant(e); (*action, cause*) méritoire

design [dɪ'zaɪn] *n* (*sketch*) plan *m*, dessin *m*; (*layout, shape*) conception *f*, ligne *f*; (*pattern*) dessin *m*, motif(s) *m(pl)*; (*COMM, art*) design *m*, stylisme *m*; (*intention*) dessein *m* ♦ *vt* dessiner; élaborer; **~er** *n* (*TECH*) concepteur-projeteur *m*; (*ART*) dessinateur(-trice), designer *m*; (*fashion*) styliste *m/f*

desire [dɪ'zaɪər] *n* désir *m* ♦ *vt* désirer

desk [desk] *n* (*in office*) bureau *m*; (*for pupil*) pupitre *m*; (*BRIT: in shop, restaurant*) caisse *f*; (*in hotel, at airport*) réception *f*; **~-top publishing** *n* publication assistée par ordinateur, PAO *f*

desolate ['desəlɪt] *adj* désolé(e); (*person*) affligé(e)

despair [dɪs'peər] *n* désespoir *m* ♦ *vi*: **to ~ of** désespérer de

despatch [dɪs'pætʃ] *n, vt* = **dispatch**

desperate ['despərɪt] *adj* désespéré(e); (*criminal*) prêt(e) à tout; **to be ~ for sth/ to do sth** avoir désespérément besoin de qch/de faire qch; **~ly** *adv* désespérément; (*very*) terriblement, extrêmement; **desperation** [despə'reɪʃən] *n* désespoir *m*; **in (sheer) desperation** en désespoir de cause

despicable [dɪs'pɪkəbl] *adj* méprisable

despise [dɪs'paɪz] *vt* mépriser

despite [dɪs'paɪt] *prep* malgré, en dépit de

despondent [dɪs'pɔndənt] *adj* découragé(e), abattu(e)

dessert [dɪ'zəːt] *n* dessert *m*; **~spoon** *n* cuiller *f* à dessert

destination [destɪ'neɪʃən] *n* destination *f*

destined ['destɪnd] *adj*: **to be ~ to do/for sth** être destiné(e) à faire/à qch

destiny ['destɪnɪ] *n* destinée *f*, destin *m*

destitute ['destɪtjuːt] *adj* indigent(e)

destroy [dɪs'trɔɪ] *vt* détruire; (*injured horse*) abattre; (*dog*) faire piquer; **~er** *n* (*NAUT*) contre-torpilleur *m*

destruction [dɪs'trʌkʃən] *n* destruction *f*

detach [dɪ'tætʃ] *vt* détacher; **~ed** *adj* (*attitude, person*) détaché(e); **~ed house** *n* pavillon *m*, maison(nette) (individuelle); **~ment** *n* (*MIL*) détachement *m*; (*fig*) détachement, indifférence *f*

detail ['diːteɪl] *n* détail *m* ♦ *vt* raconter en détail, énumérer; **in ~** en détail; **~ed** *adj* détaillé(e)

detain [dɪ'teɪn] *vt* retenir; (*in captivity*) détenir; (*in hospital*) hospitaliser

detect [dɪ'tekt] *vt* déceler, percevoir; (*MED, POLICE*) dépister; (*MIL, RADAR, TECH*) détecter; **~ion** n découverte f; **~ive** n agent m de la sûreté, policier m; **private ~ive** détective privé; **~ive story** n roman policier

detention [dɪ'tɛnʃən] n détention f; (SCOL) retenue f, consigne f

deter [dɪ'tə:ʳ] vt dissuader

detergent [dɪ'tə:dʒənt] n détergent m, détersif m

deteriorate [dɪ'tɪərɪəreɪt] vi se détériorer, se dégrader

determine [dɪ'tə:mɪn] vt déterminer; **to ~ to do** résoudre de faire, se déterminer à faire; **~d** adj (person) déterminé(e), décidé(e)

deterrent [dɪ'tɛrənt] n effet m de dissuasion; force f de dissuasion

detest [dɪ'tɛst] vt détester, avoir horreur de

detonate ['dɛtəneɪt] vt faire détoner or exploser

detour ['di:tuəʳ] n détour m; (US: AUT: diversion) déviation f

detract [dɪ'trækt] vt: **to ~ from** (quality, pleasure) diminuer; (reputation) porter atteinte à

detriment ['dɛtrɪmənt] n: **to the ~ of** au détriment de, au préjudice de; **~al** [dɛtrɪ'mɛntl] adj: **~al to** préjudiciable or nuisible à

devaluation [dɪvælju'eɪʃən] n dévaluation f

devastate ['dɛvəsteɪt] vt dévaster; **~d** adj (fig) anéanti(e); **devastating** adj dévastateur(-trice); (news) accablant(e)

develop [dɪ'vɛləp] vt (gen) développer; (disease) commencer à souffrir de; (resources) mettre en valeur, exploiter ♦ vi se développer; (situation, disease: evolve) évoluer; (facts, symptoms: appear) se manifester, se produire; **~ing country** pays m en voie de développement; **the machine has ~ed a fault** un problème s'est manifesté dans cette machine; **~er** n (also: **property ~er**) promoteur m; **~ment** [dɪ'vɛləpmənt] n développement m; (of affair, case) rebondissement m, fait(s) nouveau(x)

device [dɪ'vaɪs] n (apparatus) engin m, dispositif m

devil ['dɛvl] n diable m; démon m

devious ['di:vɪəs] adj (person) sournois(e), dissimulé(e)

devise [dɪ'vaɪz] vt imaginer, concevoir

devoid [dɪ'vɔɪd] adj: **~ of** dépourvu(e) de, dénué(e) de

devolution [di:və'lu:ʃən] n (POL) décentralisation f

devote [dɪ'vəut] vt: **to ~ sth to** consacrer qch à; **~d** [dɪ'vəutɪd] adj dévoué(e); **to be ~d to** (book etc) être consacré(e) à; (person) être très attaché(e) à; **~e** [dɛvəu'ti:] n (REL) adepte m/f; (MUS, SPORT) fervent(e); **devotion** n dévouement m, attachement m; (REL) dévotion f, piété f

devour [dɪ'vauəʳ] vt dévorer

devout [dɪ'vaut] adj pieux(-euse), dévot(e)

dew [dju:] n rosée f

diabetes [daɪə'bi:ti:z] n diabète m; **diabetic** [daɪə'bɛtɪk] adj diabétique ♦ n diabétique m/f

diabolical [daɪə'bɔlɪkl] (inf) adj (weather) atroce; (behaviour) infernal(e)

diagnosis [daɪəg'nəusɪs] (pl **diagnoses**) n diagnostic m

diagonal [daɪ'ægənl] adj diagonal(e) ♦ n diagonale f

diagram ['daɪəgræm] n diagramme m, schéma m

dial ['daɪəl] n cadran m ♦ vt (number) faire, composer

dialect ['daɪəlɛkt] n dialecte m

dialling code (BRIT) n indicatif m (téléphonique)

dialling tone (BRIT) n tonalité f

dialogue ['daɪəlɔg] n dialogue m

dial tone (US) n = **dialling tone**

diameter [daɪ'æmɪtəʳ] n diamètre m

diamond ['daɪəmənd] n diamant m; (shape) losange m; **~s** npl (CARDS) carreau m

diaper ['daɪəpəʳ] (US) n couche f

diaphragm ['daɪəfræm] n diaphragme m

diarrhoea [daɪə'ri:ə] (US **diarrhea**) n diarrhée f

diary ['daɪərɪ] n (daily account) journal m;

(book) agenda m

dice [daɪs] n inv dé m ♦ vt (CULIN) couper en dés or en cubes

dictate [dɪk'teɪt] vt dicter; **dictation** n dictée f

dictator [dɪk'teɪtər] n dictateur m; **~ship** n dictature f

dictionary ['dɪkʃənrɪ] n dictionnaire m

did [dɪd] pt of **do**; **~n't = did not**

die [daɪ] vi mourir; **to be dying for sth** avoir une envie folle de qch; **to be dying to do sth** mourir d'envie de faire qch; **~ away** vi s'éteindre; **~ down** vi se calmer, s'apaiser; **~ out** vi disparaître

diesel ['diːzl] n (vehicle) diesel m; (also: **~ oil**) carburant m diesel, gas-oil m; **~ engine** n moteur m diesel

diet ['daɪət] n alimentation f; (restricted food) régime m ♦ vi (also: **be on a ~**) suivre un régime

differ ['dɪfər] vi (be different): **to ~ (from)** être différent (de); différer (de); (disagree): **to ~ (from sb over sth)** ne pas être d'accord (avec qn au sujet de qch); **~ence** n différence f; (quarrel) différend m, désaccord m; **~ent** adj différent(e); **~entiate** [dɪfə'renʃɪeɪt] vi: **to ~entiate (between)** faire une différence (entre)

difficult ['dɪfɪkəlt] adj difficile; **~y** n difficulté f

diffident ['dɪfɪdənt] adj qui manque de confiance or d'assurance

dig [dɪg] (pt, pp **dug**) vt (hole) creuser; (garden) bêcher ♦ n (prod) coup m de coude; (fig) coup de griffe or de patte; (archeological) fouilles fpl; **~ in** vi (MIL: also: **~ o.s. in**) se retrancher; **~ into** vt fus (savings) puiser dans; **to ~ one's nails into sth** enfoncer ses ongles dans qch; **~ up** vt déterrer

digest [vb daɪ'dʒest, n 'daɪdʒest] vt digérer ♦ n sommaire m, résumé m; **~ion** [dɪ'dʒestʃən] n digestion f

digit ['dɪdʒɪt] n (number) chiffre m; (finger) doigt m; **~al** adj digital(e), à affichage numérique or digital; **~al camera** appareil m photo numérique; **~al computer** cal-

culateur m numérique; **~al TV** télévision f numérique; **~al watch** montre f à affichage numérique

dignified ['dɪgnɪfaɪd] adj digne

dignity ['dɪgnɪtɪ] n dignité f

digress [daɪ'gres] vi: **to ~ from** s'écarter de, s'éloigner de

digs [dɪgz] (BRIT: inf) npl piaule f, chambre meublée

dilapidated [dɪ'læpɪdeɪtɪd] adj délabré(e)

dilemma [daɪ'lemə] n dilemme m

diligent ['dɪlɪdʒənt] adj appliqué(e)

dilute [daɪ'luːt] vt diluer

dim [dɪm] adj (light) faible; (memory, outline) vague, indécis(e); (room) sombre; (stupid) borné(e), obtus(e) ♦ vt (light) réduire, baisser; (US: AUT) mettre en code

dime [daɪm] (US) n **= 10 cents**

dimension [daɪ'menʃən] n dimension f

diminish [dɪ'mɪnɪʃ] vt, vi diminuer

diminutive [dɪ'mɪnjutɪv] adj minuscule, tout(e) petit(e)

dimmers ['dɪməz] (US) npl (AUT) phares mpl code inv; feux mpl de position

dimple ['dɪmpl] n fossette f

din [dɪn] n vacarme m

dine [daɪn] vi dîner; **~r** n (person) dîneur(-euse); (US: restaurant) petit restaurant

dinghy ['dɪŋgɪ] n youyou m; (also: **rubber ~**) canot m pneumatique; (also: **sailing ~**) voilier m, dériveur m

dingy ['dɪndʒɪ] adj miteux(-euse), minable

dining car (BRIT) n wagon-restaurant m

dining room n salle f à manger

dinner ['dɪnər] n dîner m; (lunch) déjeuner m; (public) banquet m; **~ jacket** n smoking m; **~ party** n dîner m; **~ time** n heure f du dîner; (midday) heure du déjeuner

dinosaur ['daɪnəsɔːr] n dinosaure m

dip [dɪp] n déclivité f; (in sea) baignade f, bain m; (CULIN) ≈ sauce f ♦ vt tremper, plonger; (BRIT: AUT: lights) mettre en code, baisser ♦ vi plonger

diploma [dɪ'pləumə] n diplôme m

diplomacy [dɪ'pləuməsɪ] n diplomatie f

diplomat ['dɪpləmæt] n diplomate m; **~ic**

[dɪplə'mætɪk] *adj* diplomatique

dipstick ['dɪpstɪk] *n* (AUT) jauge *f* de niveau d'huile

dipswitch ['dɪpswɪtʃ] (BRIT) *n* (AUT) interrupteur *m* de lumière réduite

dire [daɪər] *adj* terrible, extrême, affreux(-euse)

direct [daɪ'rɛkt] *adj* direct(e) ♦ *vt* diriger, orienter; (letter, remark) adresser; (film, programme) réaliser; (play) mettre en scène; (order): **to ~ sb to do sth** ordonner à qn de faire qch ♦ *adv* directement; **can you ~ me to ...?** pouvez-vous m'indiquer le chemin de ...?; ~ **debit** (BRIT) *n* prélèvement *m* automatique

direction [dɪ'rɛkʃən] *n* direction *f*; ~**s** *npl* (advice) indications *fpl*; **sense of ~** sens *m* de l'orientation; ~**s for use** mode *m* d'emploi

directly [dɪ'rɛktlɪ] *adv* (in a straight line) directement, tout droit; (at once) tout de suite, immédiatement

director [dɪ'rɛktər] *n* directeur *m*; (THEATRE) metteur *m* en scène; (CINEMA, TV) réalisateur(-trice)

directory [dɪ'rɛktərɪ] *n* annuaire *m*; (COMPUT) répertoire *m*; ~ **enquiries** (US **directory assistance**) *n* renseignements *mpl*

dirt [dɜːt] *n* saleté *f*; crasse *f*; (earth) terre *f*, boue *f*; ~-**cheap** *adj* très bon marché *inv*; ~**y** *adj* sale ♦ *vt* salir; ~**y trick** coup tordu

disability [dɪsə'bɪlɪtɪ] *n* invalidité *f*, infirmité *f*

disabled [dɪs'eɪbld] *adj* infirme, invalide ♦ *npl*: **the ~** les handicapés

disadvantage [dɪsəd'vɑːntɪdʒ] *n* désavantage *m*, inconvénient *m*

disagree [dɪsə'griː] *vi* (be different) ne pas concorder; (be against, think otherwise): **to ~ (with)** ne pas être d'accord (avec); ~**able** *adj* désagréable; ~**ment** *n* désaccord *m*, différend *m*

disallow ['dɪsə'laʊ] *vt* rejeter

disappear [dɪsə'pɪər] *vi* disparaître; ~**ance** *n* disparition *f*

disappoint [dɪsə'pɔɪnt] *vt* décevoir; ~**ed** *adj* déçu(e); ~**ing** *adj* décevant(e); ~**ment** *n* déception *f*

disapproval [dɪsə'pruːvəl] *n* désapprobation *f*

disapprove [dɪsə'pruːv] *vi*: **to ~ (of)** désapprouver

disarmament [dɪs'ɑːməmənt] *n* désarmement *m*

disarray [dɪsə'reɪ] *n*: **in ~** (army) en déroute; (organization) en désarroi; (hair, clothes) en désordre

disaster [dɪ'zɑːstər] *n* catastrophe *f*, désastre *m*; **disastrous** *adj* désastreux(-euse)

disband [dɪs'bænd] *vt* démobiliser; disperser ♦ *vi* se séparer; se disperser

disbelief ['dɪsbə'liːf] *n* incrédulité *f*

disc [dɪsk] *n* disque *m*; (COMPUT) = **disk**

discard [dɪs'kɑːd] *vt* (old things) se débarrasser de; (fig) écarter, renoncer à

discern [dɪ'sɜːn] *vt* discerner, distinguer; ~**ing** *adj* perspicace

discharge [*vb* dɪs'tʃɑːdʒ, *n* 'dɪstʃɑːdʒ] *vt* décharger; (duties) s'acquitter de; (patient) renvoyer (chez lui); (employee) congédier, licencier; (soldier) rendre à la vie civile, réformer; (defendant) relaxer, élargir ♦ *n* décharge *f*; (dismissal) renvoi *m*; licenciement *m*; élargissement *m*; (MED) écoulement *m*

discipline ['dɪsɪplɪn] *n* discipline *f*

disc jockey *n* disc-jockey *m*

disclaim [dɪs'kleɪm] *vt* nier

disclose [dɪs'kləʊz] *vt* révéler, divulguer; **disclosure** *n* révélation *f*

disco ['dɪskəʊ] *n abbr* = **discothèque**

discomfort [dɪs'kʌmfət] *n* malaise *m*, gêne *f*; (lack of comfort) manque *m* de confort

disconcert [dɪskən'sɜːt] *vt* déconcerter

disconnect [dɪskə'nɛkt] *vt* (ELEC, RADIO, pipe) débrancher; (TEL, water) couper

discontent [dɪskən'tɛnt] *n* mécontentement *m*; ~**ed** *adj* mécontent(e)

discontinue [dɪskən'tɪnjuː] *vt* cesser, interrompre; "~**d**" (COMM) "fin de série"

discord ['dɪskɔːd] *n* discorde *f*, dissension

f; (MUS) dissonance f

discotheque ['dɪskəutek] n discothèque f

discount [n 'dɪskaunt, vb dɪs'kaunt] n remise f, rabais m ♦ vt (sum) faire une remise de; (fig) ne pas tenir compte de

discourage [dɪs'kʌrɪdʒ] vt décourager

discover [dɪs'kʌvəʳ] vt découvrir; ~y n découverte f

discredit [dɪs'krɛdɪt] vt (idea) mettre en doute; discréditer

discreet [dɪs'kriːt] adj discret(-ète)

discrepancy [dɪs'krɛpənsɪ] n divergence f, contradiction f

discretion [dɪs'krɛʃən] n discrétion f; **use your own ~** à vous de juger

discriminate [dɪs'krɪmɪneɪt] vi: **to ~ between** établir une distinction entre, faire la différence entre; **to ~ against** pratiquer une discrimination contre; **discriminating** adj qui a du discernement; **discrimination** [dɪskrɪmɪ'neɪʃən] n discrimination f; (judgment) discernement m

discuss [dɪs'kʌs] vt discuter de; (debate) discuter; ~ion n discussion f

disdain [dɪs'deɪn] n dédain m

disease [dɪ'ziːz] n maladie f

disembark [dɪsɪm'bɑːk] vi débarquer

disentangle [dɪsɪn'tæŋgl] vt (wool, wire) démêler, débrouiller; (from wreckage) dégager

disfigure [dɪs'fɪgəʳ] vt défigurer

disgrace [dɪs'greɪs] n honte f; (disfavour) disgrâce f ♦ vt déshonorer, couvrir de honte; ~ful adj scandaleux(-euse), honteux(-euse)

disgruntled [dɪs'grʌntld] adj mécontent(e)

disguise [dɪs'gaɪz] n déguisement m ♦ vt déguiser; **in ~** déguisé(e)

disgust [dɪs'gʌst] n dégoût m, aversion f ♦ vt dégoûter, écœurer; ~ing adj dégoûtant(e); révoltant(e)

dish [dɪʃ] n plat m; **to do** or **wash the ~es** faire la vaisselle; ~ **out** vt servir, distribuer; ~ **up** vt servir; ~**cloth** n (for washing) lavette f

dishearten [dɪs'hɑːtn] vt décourager

dishevelled [dɪ'ʃɛvəld] (US **disheveled**) adj ébouriffé(e); décoiffé(e); débraillé(e)

dishonest [dɪs'ɔnɪst] adj malhonnête

dishonour [dɪs'ɔnəʳ] (US **dishonor**) n déshonneur m; ~**able** adj (behaviour) déshonorant(e); (person) peu honorable

dishtowel ['dɪʃtauəl] (US) n torchon m

dishwasher ['dɪʃwɔʃəʳ] n lave-vaisselle m

disillusion [dɪsɪ'luːʒən] vt désabuser, désillusionner

disinfect [dɪsɪn'fɛkt] vt désinfecter; ~**ant** n désinfectant m

disintegrate [dɪs'ɪntɪgreɪt] vi se désintégrer

disinterested [dɪs'ɪntrəstɪd] adj désintéressé(e)

disjointed [dɪs'dʒɔɪntɪd] adj décousu(e), incohérent(e)

disk [dɪsk] n (COMPUT) disque m; (: floppy ~) disquette f; **single-/double-sided ~** disquette simple/double face; ~ **drive** n lecteur m de disquettes; ~**ette** [dɪs'kɛt] n disquette f, disque m souple

dislike [dɪs'laɪk] n aversion f, antipathie f ♦ vt ne pas aimer

dislocate ['dɪsləkeɪt] vt disloquer; déboiter

dislodge [dɪs'lɔdʒ] vt déplacer, faire bouger

disloyal [dɪs'lɔɪəl] adj déloyal(e)

dismal ['dɪzml] adj lugubre, maussade

dismantle [dɪs'mæntl] vt démonter

dismay [dɪs'meɪ] n consternation f

dismiss [dɪs'mɪs] vt congédier, renvoyer; (soldiers) faire rompre les rangs à; (idea) écarter; (LAW): **to ~ a case** rendre une fin de non-recevoir; ~**al** n renvoi m

dismount [dɪs'maunt] vi mettre pied à terre, descendre

disobedient [dɪsə'biːdɪənt] adj désobéissant(e)

disobey [dɪsə'beɪ] vt désobéir à

disorder [dɪs'ɔːdəʳ] n désordre m; (rioting) désordres mpl; (MED) troubles mpl; ~**ly** adj en désordre; désordonné(e)

disorientated [dɪs'ɔːrɪenteɪtɪd] adj désorienté(e)

disown [dɪs'əun] vt renier

disparaging [dɪs'pærɪdʒɪŋ] *adj* désobligeant(e)

dispassionate [dɪs'pæʃənət] *adj* calme, froid(e); impartial(e), objectif(-ive)

dispatch [dɪs'pætʃ] *vt* expédier, envoyer ♦ *n* envoi *m*, expédition *f*; (*MIL, PRESS*) dépêche *f*

dispel [dɪs'pɛl] *vt* dissiper, chasser

dispense [dɪs'pɛns] *vt* distribuer, administrer; ~ **with** *vt fus* se passer de; ~**r** *n* (*machine*) distributeur *m*; **dispensing chemist** (*BRIT*) *n* pharmacie *f*

disperse [dɪs'pə:s] *vt* disperser ♦ *vi* se disperser

dispirited [dɪs'pɪrɪtɪd] *adj* découragé(e), déprimé(e)

displace [dɪs'pleɪs] *vt* déplacer

display [dɪs'pleɪ] *n* étalage *m*; déploiement *m*; affichage *m*; (*screen*) écran *m*, visuel *m*; (*of feeling*) manifestation *f* ♦ *vt* montrer; (*goods*) mettre à l'étalage, exposer; (*results, departure times*) afficher; (*pej*) faire étalage de

displease [dɪs'pli:z] *vt* mécontenter, contrarier; ~**d** *adj*: ~**d with** mécontent(e) de; **displeasure** [dɪs'plɛʒəʳ] *n* mécontentement *m*

disposable [dɪs'pəuzəbl] *adj* (*pack etc*) jetable, à jeter; (*income*) disponible; ~ **nappy** (*BRIT*) *n* couche *f* à jeter, couche-culotte *f*

disposal [dɪs'pəuzl] *n* (*of goods for sale*) vente *f*; (*of property*) disposition *f*, cession *f*; (*of rubbish*) enlèvement *m*; destruction *f*; **at one's** ~ à sa disposition

dispose [dɪs'pəuz] *vt* disposer; ~ **of** *vt fus* (*unwanted goods etc*) se débarrasser de, se défaire de; (*problem*) expédier; ~**d** *adj*: **to be** ~**d to do sth** être disposé(e) à faire qch; **disposition** [dɪspə'zɪʃən] *n* disposition *f*; (*temperament*) naturel *m*

disprove [dɪs'pru:v] *vt* réfuter

dispute [dɪs'pju:t] *n* discussion *f*; (*also:* **industrial** ~) conflit *m* ♦ *vt* contester; (*matter*) discuter; (*victory*) disputer

disqualify [dɪs'kwɔlɪfaɪ] *vt* (*SPORT*) disqualifier; **to** ~ **sb for sth/from doing** rendre qn inapte à qch/à faire

disquiet [dɪs'kwaɪət] *n* inquiétude *f*, trouble *m*

disregard [dɪsrɪ'ga:d] *vt* ne pas tenir compte de

disrepair ['dɪsrɪ'pɛəʳ] *n*: **to fall into** ~ (*building*) tomber en ruine

disreputable [dɪs'rɛpjutəbl] *adj* (*person*) de mauvaise réputation; (*behaviour*) déshonorant(e)

disrespectful [dɪsrɪ'spɛktful] *adj* irrespectueux(-euse)

disrupt [dɪs'rʌpt] *vt* (*plans*) déranger; (*conversation*) interrompre

dissatisfied [dɪs'sætɪsfaɪd] *adj*: ~ **(with)** insatisfait(e) (de)

dissect [dɪ'sɛkt] *vt* disséquer

dissent [dɪ'sɛnt] *n* dissentiment *m*, différence *f* d'opinion

dissertation [dɪsə'teɪʃən] *n* mémoire *m*

disservice [dɪs'sə:vɪs] *n*: **to do sb a** ~ rendre un mauvais service à qn

dissimilar [dɪ'sɪmɪləʳ] *adj*: ~ **(to)** dissemblable (à), différent(e) (de)

dissipate ['dɪsɪpeɪt] *vt* dissiper; (*money, efforts*) disperser

dissolute ['dɪsəlu:t] *adj* débauché(e), dissolu(e)

dissolve [dɪ'zɔlv] *vt* dissoudre ♦ *vi* se dissoudre, fondre; **to** ~ **in(to) tears** fondre en larmes

distance ['dɪstns] *n* distance *f*; **in the** ~ au loin

distant ['dɪstnt] *adj* lointain(e), éloigné(e); (*manner*) distant(e), froid(e)

distaste [dɪs'teɪst] *n* dégoût *m*; ~**ful** *adj* déplaisant(e), désagréable

distended [dɪs'tɛndɪd] *adj* (*stomach*) dilaté(e)

distil [dɪs'tɪl] (*US* **distill**) *vt* distiller; ~**lery** *n* distillerie *f*

distinct [dɪs'tɪŋkt] *adj* distinct(e); (*clear*) marqué(e); **as** ~ **from** par opposition à; ~**ion** *n* distinction *f*; (*in exam*) mention *f* très bien; ~**ive** *adj* distinctif(-ive)

distinguish [dɪs'tɪŋgwɪʃ] *vt* distinguer; ~**ed** *adj* (*eminent*) distingué(e); ~**ing** *adj*

(feature) distinctif(-ive), caractéristique
distort [dɪs'tɔːt] *vt* déformer
distract [dɪs'trækt] *vt* distraire, déranger;
~**ed** *adj* distrait(e); *(anxious)* éperdu(e),
égaré(e); ~**ion** *n* distraction *f*; égarement
m
distraught [dɪs'trɔːt] *adj* éperdu(e)
distress [dɪs'trɛs] *n* détresse *f* ♦ *vt* affliger;
~**ing** *adj* douloureux(-euse), pénible
distribute [dɪs'trɪbjuːt] *vt* distribuer; **distribution** [dɪstrɪ'bjuːʃən] *n* distribution *f*;
distributor *n* distributeur *m*
district ['dɪstrɪkt] *n* *(of country)* région *f*; *(of
town)* quartier *m*; *(ADMIN)* district *m*; ~ **attorney** *(US)* *n* ≃ procureur *m* de la République; ~ **nurse** *(BRIT)* *n* infirmière visiteuse
distrust [dɪs'trʌst] *n* méfiance *f* ♦ *vt* se
méfier de
disturb [dɪs'təːb] *vt* troubler; *(inconvenience)*
déranger; ~**ance** *n* dérangement *m*; *(violent event, political etc)* troubles *mpl*; ~**ed**
adj *(worried, upset)* agité(e), troublé(e); **to
be emotionally** ~**ed** avoir des problèmes
affectifs; ~**ing** *adj* troublant(e), inquiétant(e)
disuse [dɪs'juːs] *n*: **to fall into** ~ tomber
en désuétude; ~**d** [dɪs'juːzd] *adj* désaffecté(e)
ditch [dɪtʃ] *n* fossé *m*; *(irrigation)* rigole *f*
♦ *vt* *(inf)* abandonner; *(person)* plaquer
dither ['dɪðəʳ] *vi* hésiter
ditto ['dɪtəu] *adv* idem
dive [daɪv] *n* plongeon *m*; *(of submarine)*
plongée *f* ♦ *vi* plonger; **to** ~ **into** *(bag,
drawer etc)* plonger la main dans; *(shop,
car etc)* se précipiter dans; ~**r** *n* plongeur *m*
diversion [daɪ'vəːʃən] *n* *(BRIT: AUT)* déviation *f*; *(distraction, MIL)* diversion *f*
divert [daɪ'vəːt] *vt* *(funds, BRIT: traffic)* dévier; *(river, attention)* détourner
divide [dɪ'vaɪd] *vt* diviser; *(separate)* séparer
♦ *vi* se diviser; ~**d highway** *(US)* *n* route
f à quatre voies
dividend ['dɪvɪdɛnd] *n* dividende *m*
divine [dɪ'vaɪn] *adj* divin(e)

diving ['daɪvɪŋ] *n* plongée (sous-marine); ~
board *n* plongeoir *m*
divinity [dɪ'vɪnɪtɪ] *n* divinité *f*; *(SCOL)* théologie *f*
division [dɪ'vɪʒən] *n* division *f*
divorce [dɪ'vɔːs] *n* divorce *m* ♦ *vt* divorcer
d'avec; *(dissociate)* séparer; ~**d** *adj* divorcé(e); ~**e** *n* divorcé(e)
D.I.Y. *(BRIT)* *n abbr* = **do-it-yourself**
dizzy ['dɪzɪ] *adj*: **to make sb** ~ donner le
vertige à qn; **to feel** ~ avoir la tête qui
tourne
DJ *n abbr* = **disc jockey**
DNA fingerprinting *n* technique *f* des
empreintes génétiques

KEYWORD

do [duː] *(pt* **did**, *pp* **done**) *n (inf: party etc)*
soirée *f*, fête *f*
♦ *vb* **1** *(in negative constructions)* non traduit; **I don't understand** je ne
comprends pas
2 *(to form questions)* non traduit; **didn't
you know?** vous ne le saviez pas?; **why
didn't you come?** pourquoi n'êtes-vous
pas venu?
3 *(for emphasis, in polite expressions)*: **she
does seem rather late** je trouve qu'elle
est bien en retard; **do sit down/help
yourself** asseyez-vous/servez-vous je vous
en prie
4 *(used to avoid repeating vb)*: **she swims
better than I do** elle nage mieux que
moi; **do you agree? - yes, I do/no, I
don't** vous êtes d'accord? - oui/non; **she
lives in Glasgow - so do I** elle habite
Glasgow - moi aussi; **who broke it? - I
did** qui l'a cassé? - c'est moi
5 *(in question tags)*: **he laughed, didn't
he?** il a ri, n'est-ce pas?; **I don't know
him, do I?** je ne crois pas le connaître
♦ *vt (gen: carry out, perform etc)* faire; **what
are you doing tonight?** qu'est-ce que
vous faites ce soir?; **to do the cooking/
washing-up** faire la cuisine/la vaisselle; **to
do one's teeth/hair/nails** se brosser les
dents/se coiffer/se faire les ongles; **the**

car was doing 100 ≃ la voiture faisait du 160 (à l'heure)
♦ *vi* 1 (*act, behave*) faire; **do as I do** faites comme moi
2 (*get on, fare*) marcher; **the firm is doing well** l'entreprise marche bien; **how do you do?** comment allez-vous?; (*on being introduced*) enchanté(e)!
3 (*suit*) aller; **will it do?** est-ce que ça ira?
4 (*be sufficient*) suffire, aller; **will £10 do?** est-ce que 10 livres suffiront?; **that'll do** ça suffit, ça ira; **that'll do!** (*in annoyance*) ça va *or* suffit comme ça!; **to make do (with)** se contenter (de)

do away with *vt fus* supprimer

do up *vt* (*laces, dress*) attacher; (*buttons*) boutonner; (*zip*) fermer; (*renovate: room*) refaire; (: *house*) remettre à neuf

do with *vt fus* (*need*): **I could do with a drink/some help** quelque chose à boire/un peu d'aide ne serait pas de refus; (*be connected*): **that has nothing to do with you** cela ne vous concerne pas; **I won't have anything to do with it** je ne veux pas m'en mêler

do without *vi* s'en passer ♦ *vt fus* se passer de

dock [dɔk] *n* dock *m*; (*LAW*) banc *m* des accusés ♦ *vi* se mettre à quai; (*SPACE*) s'arrimer; ~**er** *n* docker *m*; ~**yard** *n* chantier *m* de construction navale

doctor ['dɔktə'] *n* médecin *m*, docteur *m*; (*PhD etc*) docteur ♦ *vt* (*drink*) frelater; **D~ of Philosophy** *n* (*degree*) doctorat *m*; (*person*) Docteur *m* en Droit *or* Lettres *etc*, titulaire *m/f* d'un doctorat

document ['dɔkjumənt] *n* document *m*; ~**ary** [dɔkju'mentəri] *adj* documentaire ♦ *n* documentaire *m*

dodge [dɔdʒ] *n* truc *m*; combine *f* ♦ *vt* esquiver, éviter

dodgems ['dɔdʒəmz] (*BRIT*) *npl* autos tamponneuses

doe [dəu] *n* (*deer*) biche *f*; (*rabbit*) lapine *f*

does [dʌz] *vb see* **do**; ~**n't** = **does not**

dog [dɔg] *n* chien(ne) ♦ *vt* suivre de près;

poursuivre, harceler; ~ **collar** *n* collier *m* de chien; (*fig*) faux-col *m* d'ecclésiastique; ~**-eared** *adj* corné(e); ~**ged** ['dɔgid] *adj* obstiné(e), opiniâtre; ~**sbody** *n* bonne *f* à tout faire, tâcheron *m*

doings ['duːɪŋz] *npl* activités *fpl*

do-it-yourself ['duːɪtjɔː'self] *n* bricolage *m*

doldrums ['dɔldrəmz] *npl*: **to be in the ~** avoir le cafard; (*business*) être dans le marasme

dole [dəul] *n* (*BRIT: payment*) allocation *f* de chômage; **on the ~** au chômage; ~ **out** *vt* donner au compte-goutte

doll [dɔl] *n* poupée *f*

dollar ['dɔlə'] *n* dollar *m*

dolled up (*inf*) *adj*: **(all) ~** sur son trente et un

dolphin ['dɔlfɪn] *n* dauphin *m*

dome [dəum] *n* dôme *m*

domestic [də'mestɪk] *adj* (*task, appliances*) ménager(-ère); (*of country: trade, situation etc*) intérieur(e); (*animal*) domestique; ~**ated** *adj* (*animal*) domestiqué(e); (*husband*) pantouflard(e)

dominate ['dɔmɪneɪt] *vt* dominer

domineering [dɔmɪ'nɪərɪŋ] *adj* dominateur(-trice), autoritaire

dominion [də'mɪnɪən] *n* (*territory*) territoire *m*; **to have ~ over** contrôler

domino ['dɔmɪnəu] (*pl* ~**es**) *n* domino *m*; ~**es** *n* (*game*) dominos *mpl*

don [dɔn] (*BRIT*) *n* professeur *m* d'université

donate [də'neɪt] *vt* faire don de, donner

done [dʌn] *pp of* **do**

donkey ['dɔŋkɪ] *n* âne *m*

donor ['dəunə'] *n* (*of blood etc*) donneur(-euse); (*to charity*) donateur(-trice); ~ **card** *n* carte *f* de don d'organes

don't [dəunt] *vb* = **do not**

donut ['dəunʌt] (*US*) *n* = **doughnut**

doodle ['duːdl] *vi* griffonner, gribouiller

doom [duːm] *n* destin *m* ♦ *vt*: **to be ~ed (to failure)** être voué(e) à l'échec

door [dɔː'] *n* porte *f*; (*RAIL, car*) portière *f*; ~**bell** *n* sonnette *f*; ~**handle** *n* poignée *f* de la porte; (*car*) poignée de portière; ~**man** (*irreg*) *n* (*in hotel*) portier *m*; ~**mat**

n paillasson *m*; ~step *n* pas *m* de (la) porte, seuil *m*; ~way *n* (embrasure *f* de la) porte *f*

dope [dəup] *n* (*inf: drug*) drogue *f*; (: *person*) andouille *f* ♦ *vt* (*horse etc*) doper

dormant ['dɔ:mənt] *adj* assoupi(e), en veilleuse

dormitory ['dɔ:mɪtrɪ] *n* dortoir *m*; (*US: building*) résidence *f* universitaire

dormouse ['dɔ:maus] (*pl* **dormice**) *n* loir *m*

DOS [dɔs] *n abbr* (= *disk operating system*) DOS

dose [dəus] *n* dose *f*

dosh [dɔʃ] (*inf*) *n* fric *m*

doss house ['dɔs-] (*BRIT*) *n* asile *m* de nuit

dot [dɔt] *n* point *m*; (*on material*) pois *m* ♦ *vt*: ~ted with parsemé(e) de; on the ~ à l'heure tapante *or* pile; ~ted line *n* pointillé(s) *m(pl)*

double ['dʌbl] *adj* double ♦ *adv* (*twice*): to cost ~ (sth) coûter le double (de qch) *or* deux fois plus (que qch) ♦ *n* double *m* ♦ *vt* doubler; (*fold*) plier en deux ♦ *vi* doubler; ~s *n* (*TENNIS*) double *m*; on the ~ (*BRIT*) at the ~ au pas de course; ~ bass (*BRIT*) *n* contrebasse *f*; ~ bed *n* grand lit; ~ bend (*BRIT*) *n* virage *m* en S; ~-breasted *adj* croisé(e); ~-click (*COMPUT*) *n* double-cliquer; ~-cross *vt* doubler, trahir; ~-decker *n* autobus *m* à impériale; ~ glazing (*BRIT*) *n* double vitrage *m*; ~ room *n* chambre *f* pour deux personnes; doubly *adv* doublement, deux fois plus

doubt [daut] *n* doute *m* ♦ *vt* douter de; to ~ that douter que; ~ful *adj* douteux(-euse); (*person*) incertain(e); ~less *adv* sans doute, sûrement

dough [dəu] *n* pâte *f*; ~nut (*US* **donut**) *n* beignet *m*

dove [dʌv] *n* colombe *f*

Dover ['dəuvəʳ] *n* Douvres

dovetail ['dʌvteɪl] *vi* (*fig*) concorder

dowdy ['daudɪ] *adj* démodé(e); mal fagoté(e) (*inf*)

down [daun] *n* (*soft feathers*) duvet *m*

♦ *adv* en bas, vers le bas; (*on the ground*) par terre ♦ *prep* en bas de ♦ *vt* (*inf: drink, food*) s'envoyer; ~ with X! à bas X!; ~-and-out *n* clochard(e); ~-at-heel *adj* (*fig*) miteux(-euse); ~cast *adj* démoralisé(e); ~fall *n* chute *f*; ruine *f*; ~hearted *adj* découragé(e); ~hill *adv*: to go ~hill descendre; (*fig*) péricliter; ~load *vt* (*COMPUT*) télécharger; ~ payment *n* acompte *m*; ~pour *n* pluie torrentielle, déluge *m*; ~right *adj* (*lie etc*) effronté(e); (*refusal*) catégorique; ~size *vt* (*ECON*) réduire ses effectifs

---

Downing Street

i **Downing Street** *est une rue de Westminster (à Londres) où se trouve la résidence officielle du Premier minister (numéro 10) et celle du ministre des Finances (numéro 11). Le nom "***Downing Street***" est souvent utilisé pour désigner le gouvernement britannique.*

Down's syndrome [daunz-] *n* (*MED*) trisomie *f*

down: ~stairs *adv* au rez-de-chaussée; à l'étage inférieur; ~stream *adv* en aval; ~-to-earth *adj* terre à terre *inv*; ~town *adv* en ville; ~ under *adv* en Australie/Nouvelle-Zélande; ~ward *adj*, *adv* vers le bas; ~wards *adv* vers le bas

dowry ['daurɪ] *n* dot *f*

doz. *abbr* = **dozen**

doze [dəuz] *vi* sommeiller; ~ off *vi* s'assoupir

dozen ['dʌzn] *n* douzaine *f*; a ~ books une douzaine de livres; ~s of des centaines de

Dr. *abbr* = **doctor**; **drive**

drab [dræb] *adj* terne, morne

draft [drɑ:ft] *n* ébauche *f*; (*of letter, essay etc*) brouillon *m*; (*COMM*) traite *f*; (*US: call-up*) conscription *f* ♦ *vt* faire le brouillon *or* un projet de; (*MIL: send*) détacher; *see also* **draught**

draftsman ['drɑ:ftsmən] (*irreg*) (*US*) *n* = **draughtsman**

drag [dræg] *vt* traîner; (*river*) draguer ♦ *vi*

traîner ♦ n (inf) casse-pieds m/f; (women's clothing): **in ~** (en) travesti; **~ on** vi s'éterniser

dragon ['drægn] n dragon m

dragonfly ['drægənflaɪ] n libellule f

drain [dreɪn] n égout m, canalisation f; (on resources) saignée f ♦ vt (land, marshes etc) drainer, assécher; (vegetables) égoutter; (glass) vider ♦ vi (water) s'écouler; **~age** n drainage m; système m d'égouts ou de canalisations; **~ing board** (US **drain board**) n égouttoir m; **~pipe** n tuyau m d'écoulement

drama ['drɑːmə] n (art) théâtre m, art m dramatique; (play) pièce f (de théâtre); (event) drame m; **~tic** [drə'mætɪk] adj dramatique; spectaculaire; **~tist** ['dræmətɪst] n auteur m dramatique; **~tize** ['dræmətaɪz] vt (events) dramatiser; (adapt: for TV/cinema) adapter pour la télévision/pour l'écran

drank [dræŋk] pt of **drink**

drape [dreɪp] vt draper; **~s** (US) npl rideaux mpl

drastic ['dræstɪk] adj sévère; énergique; (change) radical(e)

draught [drɑːft] (US **draft**) n courant m d'air; (NAUT) tirant m d'eau; **on ~** (beer) à la pression; **~board** (BRIT) n damier m; **~s** (BRIT) n (jeu m de) dames fpl

draughtsman ['drɑːftsmən] (irreg) n dessinateur(-trice) (industriel(le))

draw [drɔː] (pt **drew**, pp **drawn**) vt tirer; (tooth) arracher, extraire; (attract) attirer; (picture) dessiner; (line, circle) tracer; (money) retirer; (wages) toucher ♦ vi (SPORT) faire match nul ♦ n match nul; (lottery) tirage m au sort; loterie f; **to ~ near** s'approcher; approcher; **~ out** vi (lengthen) s'allonger ♦ vt (money) retirer; **~ up** vi (stop) s'arrêter ♦ vt (chair) approcher; (document) établir, dresser; **~back** n inconvénient m, désavantage m; **~bridge** n pont-levis m

drawer [drɔːr] n tiroir m

drawing ['drɔːɪŋ] n dessin m; **~ board** n planche f à dessin; **~ pin** (BRIT) n punaise

f; **~ room** n salon m

drawl [drɔːl] n accent traînant

drawn [drɔːn] pp of **draw**

dread [drɛd] n terreur f, effroi m ♦ vt redouter, appréhender; **~ful** adj affreux(-euse)

dream [driːm] (pt, pp **dreamed** or **dreamt**) n rêve m ♦ vt, vi rêver; **~y** adj rêveur(-euse); (music) langoureux(-euse)

dreary ['drɪərɪ] adj morne; monotone

dredge [drɛdʒ] vt draguer

dregs [drɛgz] npl lie f

drench [drɛntʃ] vt tremper

dress [drɛs] n robe f; (no pl: clothing) habillement m, tenue f ♦ vi s'habiller ♦ vt habiller; (wound) panser; **to get ~ed** s'habiller; **~ up** vi s'habiller; (in fancy ~) se déguiser; **~ circle** (BRIT) n (THEATRE) premier balcon; **~er** n (furniture) vaisselier m; (: US) coiffeuse f, commode f; **~ing** n (MED) pansement m; (CULIN) sauce f, assaisonnement m; **~ing gown** (BRIT) n robe f de chambre; **~ing room** n (THEATRE) loge f; (SPORT) vestiaire m; **~ing table** n coiffeuse f; **~maker** n couturière f; **~ rehearsal** n (répétition) générale f

drew [druː] pt of **draw**

dribble ['drɪbl] vi (baby) baver ♦ vt (ball) dribbler

dried [draɪd] adj (fruit, beans) sec (sèche); (eggs, milk) en poudre

drier ['draɪər] n = **dryer**

drift [drɪft] n (of current etc) force f; direction f, mouvement m; (of snow) rafale f; (: on ground) congère f; (general meaning) sens (général) ♦ vi (boat) aller à la dérive, dériver; (sand, snow) s'amonceler, s'entasser; **~wood** n bois flotté

drill [drɪl] n perceuse f; (~ bit) foret m, mèche f; (of dentist) roulette f, fraise f; (MIL) exercice m ♦ vt percer; (troops) entraîner ♦ vi (for oil) faire un or des forage(s)

drink [drɪŋk] (pt **drank**, pp **drunk**) n boisson f; (alcoholic) verre m ♦ vt, vi boire; **to have a ~** boire quelque chose, boire un verre; prendre l'apéritif; **a ~ of water** un verre d'eau; ~**er** *n* buveur(-euse); ~**ing water** *n* eau *f* potable

drip [drɪp] *n* goutte *f*; (MED) goutte-à-goutte *m inv*, perfusion *f* ♦ *vi* tomber goutte à goutte; (*tap*) goutter; ~-**dry** *adj* (*shirt*) sans repassage; ~**ping** *n* graisse *f* (de rôti)

drive [draɪv] (*pt* **drove**, *pp* **driven**) *n* promenade *f or* trajet *m* en voiture; (*also:* ~**way**) allée *f*; (*energy*) dynamisme *m*, énergie *f*; (*push*) effort (concerté), campagne *f*; (*also: disk* ~) lecteur *m* de disquettes ♦ *vt* conduire; (*push*) chasser, pousser; (TECH: *motor, wheel*) faire fonctionner; entraîner; (*nail, stake etc*): **to ~ sth into sth** enfoncer qch dans qch ♦ *vi* (AUT: *at controls*) conduire; (: *travel*) aller en voiture; **left-/right-hand** ~ conduite *f* à gauche/droite; **to ~ sb mad** rendre qn fou (folle); **to ~ sb home/to the airport** reconduire qn chez lui/conduire qn à l'aéroport; ~-**by shooting** *n* (*tentative d'*)assassinat par coups de feu tirés d'un voiture

drivel ['drɪvl] (*inf*) *n* idioties *fpl*

driver ['draɪvə*r*] *n* conducteur(-trice); (*of taxi, bus*) chauffeur *m*; ~**'s license** (US) *n* permis *m* de conduire

driveway ['draɪvweɪ] *n* allée *f*

driving ['draɪvɪŋ] *n* conduite *f*; ~ **instructor** *n* moniteur *m* d'auto-école; ~ **lesson** *n* leçon *f* de conduite; ~ **licence** (BRIT) *n* permis *m* de conduire; ~ **school** *n* auto-école *f*; ~ **test** *n* examen *m* du permis de conduire

drizzle ['drɪzl] *n* bruine *f*, crachin *m*

drool [druːl] *vi* baver

droop [druːp] *vi* (*shoulders*) tomber; (*head*) pencher; (*flower*) pencher la tête

drop [drɔp] *n* goutte *f*; (*fall*) baisse *f*; (*also:* **parachute** ~) saut *m* ♦ *vt* laisser tomber; (*voice, eyes, price*) baisser; (*set down from car*) déposer ♦ *vi* tomber; ~**s** *npl* (MED) gouttes; ~ **off** *vi* (*sleep*) s'assoupir ♦ *vt* (*passenger*) déposer; ~ **out** *vi* (*withdraw*) se retirer; (*student etc*) abandonner, décrocher; ~**out** *n* marginal(e); ~**per** *n* compte-gouttes *m inv*; ~**pings** *npl* crottes *fpl*

drought [draut] *n* sécheresse *f*

drove [drəuv] *pt of* **drive**

drown [draun] *vt* noyer ♦ *vi* se noyer

drowsy ['drauzɪ] *adj* somnolent(e)

drug [drʌg] *n* médicament *m*; (*narcotic*) drogue *f* ♦ *vt* droguer; **to be on ~s** se droguer; ~ **addict** *n* toxicomane *m/f*; ~**gist** (US) *n* pharmacien(ne)-droguiste; ~**store** (US) *n* pharmacie-droguerie *f*, drugstore *m*

drum [drʌm] *n* tambour *m*; (*for oil, petrol*) bidon *m*; ~**s** *npl* (*kit*) batterie *f*; ~**mer** *n* (joueur *m* de) tambour *m*

drunk [drʌŋk] *pp of* **drink** ♦ *adj* ivre, soûl(e) ♦ *n* (*also:* ~**ard**) ivrogne *m/f*; ~**en** *adj* (*person*) ivre, soûl(e); (*rage, stupor*) ivrogne, d'ivrogne

dry [draɪ] *adj* sec (sèche); (*day*) sans pluie; (*humour*) pince-sans-rire *inv*; (*lake, riverbed, well*) à sec ♦ *vt* sécher; (*clothes*) faire sécher ♦ *vi* sécher; ~ **up** *vi* tarir; ~-**cleaner's** *n* teinturerie *f*; ~**er** *n* séchoir *m*; (*spin-dryer*) essoreuse *f*; ~**ness** *n* sécheresse *f*; ~ **rot** *n* pourriture sèche (*du bois*)

DSS *n abbr* (= Department of Social Security) ≃ Sécurité sociale

DTP *n abbr* (= desk-top publishing) PAO *f*

dual ['djuəl] *adj* double; ~ **carriageway** (BRIT) *n* route *f* à quatre voies *or* à chaussées séparées; ~-**purpose** *adj* à double usage

dubbed [dʌbd] *adj* (CINEMA) doublé(e)

dubious ['djuːbɪəs] *adj* hésitant(e), incertain(e); (*reputation, company*) douteux(-euse)

duchess ['dʌtʃɪs] *n* duchesse *f*

duck [dʌk] *n* canard *m* ♦ *vi* se baisser vivement, baisser subitement la tête; ~**ling** ['dʌklɪŋ] *n* caneton *m*

duct [dʌkt] *n* conduite *f*, canalisation *f*; (ANAT) conduit *m*

dud [dʌd] *n* (*object, tool*): **it's a** ~ c'est de la camelote, ça ne marche pas ♦ *adj*: ~ **cheque** (BRIT) chèque sans provision

due [dju:] *adj* dû (due); (*expected*) attendu(e); (*fitting*) qui convient ♦ *n*: **to give sb his** (*or* **her**) **~** être juste envers qn ♦ *adv*: **~ north** droit vers le nord; **~s** *npl* (*for club, union*) cotisation *f*; **in ~ course** en temps utile *or* voulu; finalement; **~ to** dû (due) à; causé(e) par; **he's ~ to finish tomorrow** normalement il doit finir demain

duet [dju:'et] *n* duo *m*

duffel bag ['dʌfl-] *n* sac duffel *m* marin

duffel coat *n* duffel-coat *m*

dug [dʌg] *pt, pp of* **dig**

duke [dju:k] *n* duc *m*

dull [dʌl] *adj* terne, morne; (*boring*) ennuyeux(-euse); (*sound, pain*) sourd(e); (*weather, day*) gris(e), maussade ♦ *vt* (*pain, grief*) atténuer; (*mind, senses*) engourdir

duly ['dju:lɪ] *adv* (*on time*) en temps voulu; (*as expected*) comme il se doit

dumb [dʌm] *adj* muet(te); (*stupid*) bête; **~founded** *adj* sidéré(e)

dummy ['dʌmɪ] *n* (*tailor's model*) mannequin *m*; (*mock-up*) factice *m*, maquette *f*; (*BRIT: for baby*) tétine *f* ♦ *adj* faux (fausse), factice

dump [dʌmp] *n* (*also:* **rubbish ~**) décharge (publique); (*pej*) trou *m* ♦ *vt* (*put down*) déposer; déverser; (*get rid of*) se débarrasser de; (*COMPUT: data*) vider

dumpling ['dʌmplɪŋ] *n* boulette *f* (de pâte)

dumpy ['dʌmpɪ] *adj* boulot(te)

dunce [dʌns] *n* âne *m*, cancre *m*

dune [dju:n] *n* dune *f*

dung [dʌŋ] *n* fumier *m*

dungarees [dʌŋɡə'ri:z] *npl* salopette *f*; bleu(s) *m(pl)*

dungeon ['dʌndʒən] *n* cachot *m*

duplex ['dju:pleks] (*US*) *n* maison jumelée; (*apartment*) duplex *m*

duplicate [*n* 'dju:plɪkət, *vb* 'dju:plɪkeɪt] *n* double *m* ♦ *vt* faire un double de; (*on machine*) polycopier; photocopier; **in ~** en deux exemplaires

durable ['djuərəbl] *adj* durable, (*clothes, metal*) résistant(e), solide

duration [djuə'reɪʃən] *n* durée *f*

during ['djuərɪŋ] *prep* pendant, au cours de

dusk [dʌsk] *n* crépuscule *m*

dust [dʌst] *n* poussière *f* ♦ *vt* (*furniture*) épousseter, essuyer; (*cake etc*): **to ~ with** saupoudrer de; **~bin** (*BRIT*) *n* poubelle *f*; **~er** *n* chiffon *m*; **~man** (*BRIT*) (*irreg*) *n* boueux *m*, éboueur *m*; **~y** *adj* poussiéreux(-euse)

Dutch [dʌtʃ] *adj* hollandais(e), néerlandais(e) ♦ *n* (*LING*) hollandais *m* ♦ *adv* (*inf*): **to go ~** partager les frais; **the ~** *npl* (*people*) les Hollandais; **~man** (*irreg*) *n* Hollandais; **~woman** (*irreg*) *n* Hollandaise *f*

duty ['dju:tɪ] *n* devoir *m*; (*tax*) droit *m*, taxe *f*; **on ~** de service; (*at night etc*) de garde; **off ~** libre, pas de service *or* de garde; **~-free** *adj* exempté(e) de douane, hors taxe *inv*

duvet ['du:veɪ] (*BRIT*) *n* couette *f*

DVD *n abbr* (= *digital versatile disc*) DVD *m*

dwarf [dwɔ:f] (*pl* **dwarves**) *n* nain(e) *f* ♦ *vt* écraser

dwell [dwel] (*pt, pp* **dwelt**) *vi* demeurer; **~ on** *vt fus* s'appesantir sur

dwindle ['dwɪndl] *vi* diminuer, décroître

dye [daɪ] *n* teinture *f* ♦ *vt* teindre

dying ['daɪɪŋ] *adj* mourant(e), agonisant(e)

dyke [daɪk] (*BRIT*) *n* digue *f*

dynamic [daɪ'næmɪk] *adj* dynamique

dynamite ['daɪnəmaɪt] *n* dynamite *f*

dynamo ['daɪnəməu] *n* dynamo *f*

dyslexia [dɪs'leksɪə] *n* dyslexie *f*

E, e

E [i:] *n* (*MUS*) mi *m*

each [i:tʃ] *adj* chaque ♦ *pron* chacun(e); **~ other** l'un(e) l'autre; **they hate ~ other** ils se détestent (mutuellement); **you are jealous of ~ other** vous êtes jaloux l'un de l'autre; **they have 2 books ~** ils ont 2 livres chacun

eager ['i:ɡə'] *adj* (*keen*) avide; **to be ~ to do sth** avoir très envie de faire qch; **to be**

~ **for** désirer vivement, être avide de

eagle ['i:gl] n aigle m

ear [ɪəʳ] n oreille f; (of corn) épi m; ~**ache** n mal m aux oreilles; ~**drum** n tympan m

earl [ə:l] (BRIT) n comte m

earlier ['ə:lɪəʳ] adj (date etc) plus rapproché(e); (edition, fashion etc) plus ancien(ne), antérieur(e) ♦ adv plus tôt

early ['ə:lɪ] adv tôt, de bonne heure; (ahead of time) en avance; (near the beginning) au début ♦ adj qui se manifeste (or se fait) tôt or de bonne heure; (work) de jeunesse; (settler, Christian) premier(-ère); (reply) rapide; (death) prématuré(e); **to have an ~ night** se coucher tôt or de bonne heure; **in the ~** or **~ in the spring/19th century** au début du printemps/19ème siècle; ~ **retirement** n: **to take ~ retirement** prendre sa retraite anticipée

earmark ['ɪəmɑ:k] vt: **to ~ sth for** réserver or destiner qch à

earn [ə:n] vt gagner; (COMM: yield) rapporter

earnest ['ə:nɪst] adj sérieux(-euse); **in ~** ♦ adv sérieusement

earnings ['ə:nɪŋz] npl salaire m; (of company) bénéfices mpl

ear: ~**phones** npl écouteurs mpl; ~**ring** n boucle f d'oreille; ~**shot** n: **within ~shot** à portée de voix

earth [ə:θ] n (gen, also BRIT: ELEC) terre f ♦ vt relier à la terre; ~**enware** n poterie f; faïence f; ~**quake** n tremblement m de terre, séisme m; ~**y** adj (vulgar: humour) truculent(e)

ease [i:z] n facilité f, aisance f; (comfort) bien-être m ♦ vt (soothe) calmer; (loosen) relâcher, détendre; **to ~ sth in/out** faire pénétrer/sortir qch délicatement or avec douceur; faciliter la pénétration/la sortie de qch; **at ~!** (MIL) repos!; ~ **off** or **up** vi diminuer; (slow down) ralentir

easel ['i:zl] n chevalet m

easily ['i:zɪlɪ] adv facilement

east [i:st] n est m ♦ adj (wind) d'est; (side) est inv ♦ adv à l'est, vers l'est; **the E~**

l'Orient m; (POL) les pays mpl de l'Est

Easter ['i:stəʳ] n Pâques fpl; ~ **egg** n œuf m de Pâques

east: ~**erly** ['i:stəlɪ] adj (wind) d'est; (direction) est inv; (point) à l'est; ~**ern** ['i:stən] adj de l'est, oriental(e); ~**ward(s)** ['i:stwəd(z)] adv vers l'est, à l'est

easy ['i:zɪ] adj facile; (manner) aisé(e) ♦ adv: **to take it** or **things ~** ne pas se fatiguer; (not worry) ne pas (trop) s'en faire; ~ **chair** n fauteuil m; ~-**going** adj accommodant(e), facile à vivre

eat [i:t] (pt **ate**, pp **eaten**) vt, vi manger; ~ **away at**, ~ **into** vt fus ronger, attaquer; (savings) entamer

eaves [i:vz] npl avant-toit m

eavesdrop ['i:vzdrɔp] vi: **to ~ (on a conversation)** écouter (une conversation) de façon indiscrète

ebb [eb] n reflux m ♦ vi refluer; (fig: also: ~ **away**) décliner

ebony ['ebənɪ] n ébène f

EC n abbr (= European Community) C.E. f

ECB n abbr (= European Central Bank) BCE f

eccentric [ɪk'sentrɪk] adj excentrique

echo ['ekəu] (pl ~**es**) n écho m ♦ vt répéter ♦ vi résonner, faire écho

eclipse [ɪ'klɪps] n éclipse f

ecology [ɪ'kɔlədʒɪ] n écologie f

e-commerce ['i:kɔmə:s] n commerce m électronique

economic [i:kə'nɔmɪk] adj économique; (business etc) rentable; **economical** adj économique; (person) économe

economics [i:kə'nɔmɪks] n économie f politique ♦ npl (of project, situation) aspect m financier

economize [ɪ'kɔnəmaɪz] vi économiser, faire des économies

economy [ɪ'kɔnəmɪ] n économie f; ~ **class** n classe f touriste; ~ **size** n format m économique

ecstasy ['ekstəsɪ] n extase f (drogue aussi); **ecstatic** [eks'tætɪk] adj extatique

ECU ['eɪkju:] n abbr (= European Currency Unit) ECU m

eczema ['ɛksɪmə] *n* eczéma *m*

edge [ɛdʒ] *n* bord *m*; (*of knife etc*) tranchant *m*, fil *m* ♦ *vt* border; **on ~** (*fig*) crispé(e), tendu(e); **to ~ away from** s'éloigner furtivement de; **~ways** *adv*: **he couldn't get a word in ~ways** il ne pouvait pas placer un mot

edgy ['ɛdʒɪ] *adj* crispé(e), tendu(e)

edible ['ɛdɪbl] *adj* comestible

Edinburgh ['ɛdɪnbərə] *n* Édimbourg

edit ['ɛdɪt] *vt* (*text, book*) éditer; (*report*) préparer; (*film*) monter; (*broadcast*) réaliser; **~ion** [ɪ'dɪʃən] *n* édition *f*; **~or** *n* (*of column*) rédacteur(-trice); (*of newspaper*) rédacteur(-trice) en chef; (*of sb's work*) éditeur(-trice); **~orial** [ɛdɪ'tɔːrɪəl] *adj* de la rédaction, éditorial(e) ♦ *n* éditorial *m*

educate ['ɛdjukeɪt] *vt* (*teach*) instruire; (*instruct*) éduquer; **~d** *adj* (*person*) cultivé(e); **education** [ɛdju'keɪʃən] *n* éducation *f*; (*studies*) études *fpl*; (*teaching*) enseignement *m*, instruction *f*; **educational** *adj* (*experience, toy*) pédagogique; (*institution*) scolaire; (*policy*) d'éducation

eel [iːl] *n* anguille *f*

eerie ['ɪərɪ] *adj* inquiétant(e)

effect [ɪ'fɛkt] *n* effet *m* ♦ *vt* effectuer; **to take ~** (*law*) entrer en vigueur, prendre effet; (*drug*) agir, faire son effet; **in ~** en fait; **~ive** [ɪ'fɛktɪv] *adj* efficace; (*actual*) véritable; **~ively** *adv* effectivement; (*in reality*) effectivement; **~iveness** *n* efficacité *f*

effeminate [ɪ'fɛmɪnɪt] *adj* efféminé(e)

effervescent [ɛfə'vɛsnt] *adj* (*drink*) gazeux(-euse)

efficiency [ɪ'fɪʃənsɪ] *n* efficacité *f*; (*of machine*) rendement *m*

efficient [ɪ'fɪʃənt] *adj* efficace; (*machine*) qui a un bon rendement

effort ['ɛfət] *n* effort *m*; **~less** *adj* (*style*) aisé(e); (*achievement*) facile

effusive [ɪ'fjuːsɪv] *adj* chaleureux(-euse)

e.g. *adv abbr* (= *exempli gratia*) par exemple, p. ex.

egg [ɛg] *n* œuf *m*; **hard-boiled/soft-boiled ~** œuf dur/à la coque; **~ on** *vt* pousser; **~cup** *n* coquetier *m*; **~plant** *n*

(*esp US*) aubergine *f*; **~shell** *n* coquille *f* d'œuf

ego ['iːgəu] *n* (*self-esteem*) amour-propre *m*

egotism ['ɛgəutɪzəm] *n* égotisme *m*

egotist ['ɛgəutɪst] *n* égocentrique *m/f*

Egypt ['iːdʒɪpt] *n* Égypte *f*; **~ian** [ɪ'dʒɪpʃən] *adj* égyptien(ne) ♦ *n* Égyptien(ne)

eiderdown ['aɪdədaun] *n* édredon *m*

Eiffel Tower ['aɪfəl-] *n* tour *f* Eiffel

eight [eɪt] *num* huit; **~een** [eɪ'tiːn] *num* dix-huit; **~h** [eɪtθ] *num* huitième; **~y** ['eɪtɪ] *num* quatre-vingt(s)

Eire ['ɛərə] *n* République *f* d'Irlande

either ['aɪðər] *adj* l'un ou l'autre; (*both, each*) chaque ♦ *pron*: **~ (of them)** l'un ou l'autre ♦ *adv* non plus ♦ *conj*: **~ good or bad** ou bon ou mauvais, soit bon soit mauvais; **on ~ side** de chaque côté; **I don't like ~** je n'aime ni l'un ni l'autre; **no, I don't ~** moi non plus

eject [ɪ'dʒɛkt] *vt* (*tenant etc*) expulser; (*object*) éjecter

elaborate [*adj* ɪ'læbərɪt, *vb* ɪ'læbəreɪt] *adj* compliqué(e), recherché(e) ♦ *vt* élaborer ♦ *vi*: **to ~ (on)** entrer dans les détails (de)

elastic [ɪ'læstɪk] *adj* élastique ♦ *n* élastique *m*; **~ band** *n* élastique *m*

elated [ɪ'leɪtɪd] *adj* transporté(e) de joie

elation [ɪ'leɪʃən] *n* allégresse *f*

elbow ['ɛlbəu] *n* coude *m*

elder ['ɛldər] *adj* aîné(e) ♦ *n* (*tree*) sureau *m*; **one's ~s** ses aînés; **~ly** *adj* âgé(e) ♦ *npl*: **the ~ly** les personnes âgées

eldest ['ɛldɪst] *adj*, *n*: **the ~ (child)** l'aîné(e) (des enfants)

elect [ɪ'lɛkt] *vt* élire ♦ *adj*: **the president ~** le président désigné; **to ~ to do** choisir de faire; **~ion** *n* élection *f*; **~ioneering** [ɪlɛkʃə'nɪərɪŋ] *n* propagande électorale, manœuvres électorales; **~or** *n* électeur(-trice); **~orate** *n* électorat *m*

electric [ɪ'lɛktrɪk] *adj* électrique; **~al** *adj* électrique; **~ blanket** *n* couverture chauffante; **~ fire** (*BRIT*) *n* radiateur *m* électrique; **~ian** [ɪlɛk'trɪʃən] *n* électricien *m*; **~ity** [ɪlɛk'trɪsɪtɪ] *n* électricité *f*; **electrify** [ɪ'lɛktrɪfaɪ] *vt* (*RAIL, fence*) électrifier; (*audi-*

ence) électriser

electronic [ɪlɛk'trɒnɪk] *adj* électronique; ~ **mail** *n* courrier *m* électronique; **~s** *n* électronique *f*

elegant ['ɛlɪgənt] *adj* élégant(e)

element ['ɛlɪmənt] *n* (*gen*) élément *m*; (*of heater, kettle etc*) résistance *f*; **~ary** [ɛlɪ'mɛntərɪ] *adj* élémentaire; (*school, education*) primaire

elephant ['ɛlɪfənt] *n* éléphant *m*

elevation [ɛlɪ'veɪʃən] *n* (*raising, promotion*) avancement *m*, promotion *f*; (*height*) hauteur *f*

elevator ['ɛlɪveɪtə*r*] *n* (*in warehouse etc*) élévateur *m*, monte-charge *m inv*; (*US: lift*) ascenseur *m*

eleven [ɪ'lɛvn] *num* onze; **~ses** [ɪ'lɛvnzɪz] *npl* ≃ pause-café *f*; **~th** *num* onzième

elicit [ɪ'lɪsɪt] *vt*: **to ~ (from)** obtenir (de), arracher (à)

eligible ['ɛlɪdʒəbl] *adj*: **to be ~ for** remplir les conditions requises pour; **an ~ young man/woman** un beau parti

elm [ɛlm] *n* orme *m*

elongated ['iːlɒŋgeɪtɪd] *adj* allongé(e)

elope [ɪ'ləup] *vi* (*lovers*) s'enfuir (ensemble)

eloquent ['ɛləkwənt] *adj* éloquent(e)

else [ɛls] *adv* d'autre; **something ~** quelque chose d'autre, autre chose; **somewhere ~** ailleurs, autre part; **everywhere ~** partout ailleurs; **nobody ~** personne d'autre; **where ~?** à quel autre endroit?; **little ~** pas grand-chose d'autre; **~where** *adv* ailleurs, autre part

elude [ɪ'luːd] *vt* échapper à

elusive [ɪ'luːsɪv] *adj* insaisissable

emaciated [ɪ'meɪsɪeɪtɪd] *adj* émacié(e), décharné(e)

e-mail [iː'meɪl] *n* courrier *m* électronique ♦ *vt* (*person*) envoyer un message électronique à

emancipate [ɪ'mænsɪpeɪt] *vt* émanciper

embankment [ɪm'bæŋkmənt] *n* (*of road, railway*) remblai *m*, talus *m*; (*of river*) berge *f*, quai *m*

embark [ɪm'bɑːk] *vi* embarquer; **to ~ on** (*journey*) entreprendre; (*fig*) se lancer or

s'embarquer dans; **~ation** [ɛmbɑː'keɪʃən] *n* embarquement *m*

embarrass [ɪm'bærəs] *vt* embarrasser, gêner; **~ed** *adj* gêné(e); **~ing** *adj* gênant(e), embarrassant(e); **~ment** *n* embarras *m*, gêne *f*

embassy ['ɛmbəsɪ] *n* ambassade *f*

embedded [ɪm'bɛdɪd] *adj* enfoncé(e)

embellish [ɪm'bɛlɪʃ] *vt* orner, décorer; (*fig: account*) enjoliver

embers ['ɛmbəz] *npl* braise *f*

embezzle [ɪm'bɛzl] *vt* détourner; **~ment** *n* détournement *m* de fonds

embitter [ɪm'bɪtə*r*] *vt* (*person*) aigrir; (*relations*) envenimer

embody [ɪm'bɒdɪ] *vt* (*features*) réunir, comprendre; (*ideas*) formuler, exprimer

embossed [ɪm'bɒst] *adj* (*metal*) estampé(e); (*leather*) frappé(e); **~ wallpaper** papier gaufré

embrace [ɪm'breɪs] *vt* embrasser, étreindre; (*include*) embrasser ♦ *vi* s'étreindre, s'embrasser ♦ *n* étreinte *f*

embroider [ɪm'brɔɪdə*r*] *vt* broder; **~y** *n* broderie *f*

emerald ['ɛmərəld] *n* émeraude *f*

emerge [ɪ'mɜːdʒ] *vi* apparaître; (*from room, car*) surgir; (*from sleep, imprisonment*) sortir

emergency [ɪ'mɜːdʒənsɪ] *n* urgence *f*; **in an ~** en cas d'urgence; **~ cord** *n* sonnette *f* d'alarme; **~ exit** *n* sortie *f* de secours; **~ landing** *n* atterrissage forcé; **~ services** *npl*: **the ~ services** (*fire, police, ambulance*) les services *mpl* d'urgence

emery board ['ɛmərɪ-] *n* lime *f* à ongles (*en carton émerisé*)

emigrate ['ɛmɪgreɪt] *vi* émigrer

eminent ['ɛmɪnənt] *adj* éminent(e)

emissions [ɪ'mɪʃənz] *npl* émissions *fpl*

emit [ɪ'mɪt] *vt* émettre

emotion [ɪ'məuʃən] *n* émotion *f*; **~al** *adj* (*person*) émotif(-ive), très sensible; (*needs, exhaustion*) affectif(-ive); (*scene*) émouvant(e); (*tone, speech*) qui fait appel aux sentiments; **emotive** *adj* chargé(e) d'émotion; (*subject*) sensible

emperor ['ɛmpərə*r*] *n* empereur *m*

emphasis ['ɛmfəsɪs] (*pl* **-ases**) *n* (*stress*) accent *m*; (*importance*) insistance *f*

emphasize ['ɛmfəsaɪz] *vt* (*syllable, word, point*) appuyer *or* insister sur; (*feature*) souligner, accentuer

emphatic [ɛm'fætɪk] *adj* (*strong*) énergique, vigoureux(-euse); (*unambiguous, clear*) catégorique

empire ['ɛmpaɪə'] *n* empire *m*

employ [ɪm'plɔɪ] *vt* employer; **~ee** *n* employé(e); **~er** *n* employeur(-euse); **~ment** *n* emploi *m*; **~ment agency** *n* agence *f* *or* bureau *m* de placement

empower [ɪm'pauə'] *vt*: **to ~ sb to do** autoriser *or* habiliter qn à faire

empress ['ɛmprɪs] *n* impératrice *f*

emptiness ['ɛmptɪnɪs] *n* (*of area, region*) aspect *m* désertique; (*of life*) vide *m*, vacuité *f*

empty ['ɛmptɪ] *adj* vide; (*threat, promise*) en l'air, vain(e) ♦ *vt* vider ♦ *vi* se vider; (*liquid*) s'écouler; **~-handed** *adj* les mains vides

EMU *n abbr* (= *economic and monetary union*) UME *f*

emulate ['ɛmjuleɪt] *vt* rivaliser avec, imiter

emulsion [ɪ'mʌlʃən] *n* émulsion *f*; (*also: ~ paint*) peinture mate

enable [ɪ'neɪbl] *vt*: **to ~ sb to do** permettre à qn de faire

enamel [ɪ'næməl] *n* émail *m*; (*also: ~ paint*) peinture laquée

enchant [ɪn'tʃɑːnt] *vt* enchanter; **~ing** *adj* ravissant(e), enchanteur(-teresse)

encl. *abbr* = **enclosed**

enclose [ɪn'kləuz] *vt* (*land*) clôturer; (*space, object*) entourer; (*letter etc*) **to ~ (with)** joindre (à); **please find ~d** veuillez trouver ci-joint; **enclosure** *n* enceinte *f*

encompass [ɪn'kʌmpəs] *vt* (*include*) contenir, inclure

encore [ɔŋ'kɔːr] *excl* bis ♦ *n* bis *m*

encounter [ɪn'kauntə'] *n* rencontre *f* ♦ *vt* rencontrer

encourage [ɪn'kʌrɪdʒ] *vt* encourager; **~ment** *n* encouragement *m*

encroach [ɪn'krəutʃ] *vi*: **to ~ (up)on** empiéter sur

encyclop(a)edia [ɛnsaɪkləu'piːdɪə] *n* encyclopédie *f*

end [ɛnd] *n* (*gen, also: aim*) fin *f*; (*of table, street, rope etc*) bout *m*, extrémité *f* ♦ *vt* terminer; (*also:* **bring to an ~, put an ~ to**) mettre fin à ♦ *vi* se terminer, finir; **in the ~** finalement; **on ~** (*object*) debout, dressé(e); **to stand on ~** (*hair*) se dresser sur la tête; **for hours on ~** pendant des heures et des heures; **~ up** *vi*: **to ~ up in** (*condition*) finir *or* se terminer par; (*place*) finir *or* aboutir à

endanger [ɪn'deɪndʒə'] *vt* mettre en danger; **an ~ed species** une espèce en voie de disparition

endearing [ɪn'dɪərɪŋ] *adj* attachant(e)

endeavour [ɪn'dɛvə'] (*US* **endeavor**) *n* tentative *f*, effort *m* ♦ *vi*: **to ~ to do** tenter *or* s'efforcer de faire

ending ['ɛndɪŋ] *n* dénouement *m*, fin *f*; (*LING*) terminaison *f*

endive ['ɛndaɪv] *n* chicorée *f*; (*smooth*) endive *f*

endless ['ɛndlɪs] *adj* sans fin, interminable

endorse [ɪn'dɔːs] *vt* (*cheque*) endosser; (*approve*) appuyer, approuver, sanctionner; **~ment** *n* (*approval*) appui *m*, aval *m*; (*BRIT: on driving licence*) contravention portée au permis de conduire

endure [ɪn'djuə'] *vt* supporter, endurer ♦ *vi* durer

enemy ['ɛnəmɪ] *adj, n* ennemi(e)

energetic [ɛnə'dʒɛtɪk] *adj* énergique; (*activity*) qui fait se dépenser (physiquement)

energy ['ɛnədʒɪ] *n* énergie *f*

enforce [ɪn'fɔːs] *vt* (*law*) appliquer, faire respecter

engage [ɪn'geɪdʒ] *vt* engager; (*attention etc*) retenir ♦ *vi* (*TECH*) s'enclencher, s'engrener; **to ~ in** se lancer dans; **~d** *adj* (*BRIT: busy, in use*) occupé(e); (*betrothed*) fiancé(e); **to get ~d** se fiancer; **~d tone** *n* (*TEL*) tonalité *f* occupé *inv* *or* pas libre; **~ment** *n* obligation *f*, engagement *m*; rendez-vous *m inv*; (*to marry*) fiançailles *fpl*; **~ment ring** *n* bague *f* de fiançailles;

engaging adj engageant(e), attirant(e)

engine ['endʒɪn] n (AUT) moteur m; (RAIL) locomotive f; ~ **driver** n mécanicien m

engineer [endʒɪ'nɪəʳ] n ingénieur m; (BRIT: repairer) dépanneur m; (NAVY, US RAIL) mécanicien m; ~**ing** n engineering m, ingénierie f; (of bridges, ships) génie m; (of machine) mécanique f

England ['ɪŋɡlənd] n Angleterre f; **English** adj anglais(e) ♦ n (LING) anglais m; **the English** npl (people) les Anglais; **the English Channel** la Manche; **Englishman** (irreg) n Anglais; **Englishwoman** (irreg) n Anglaise f

engraving [ɪn'ɡreɪvɪŋ] n gravure f

engrossed [ɪn'ɡrəʊst] adj: ~ **in** absorbé(e) par, plongé(e) dans

engulf [ɪn'ɡʌlf] vt engloutir

enhance [ɪn'hɑ:ns] vt rehausser, mettre en valeur

enjoy [ɪn'dʒɔɪ] vt aimer, prendre plaisir à; (have: health, fortune) jouir de; (: success) connaître; **to ~ o.s.** s'amuser; ~**able** adj agréable; ~**ment** n plaisir m

enlarge [ɪn'lɑ:dʒ] vt accroître, (PHOT) agrandir ♦ vi: **to ~ on** (subject) s'étendre sur; ~**ment** [ɪn'lɑ:dʒmənt] n (PHOT) agrandissement m

enlighten [ɪn'laɪtn] vt éclairer; ~**ed** adj éclairé(e); ~**ment** n: **the E~ment** (HISTORY) ≃ le Siècle des lumières

enlist [ɪn'lɪst] vt recruter; (support) s'assurer ♦ vi s'engager

enmity ['enmɪtɪ] n inimitié f

enormous [ɪ'nɔ:məs] adj énorme

enough [ɪ'nʌf] adj, pron: ~ **time/books** assez or suffisamment de temps/livres ♦ adv: **big** ~ assez or suffisamment grand; **have you got ~?** en avez-vous assez?; **he has not worked** ~ il n'a pas assez or suffisamment travaillé; ~ **to eat** assez à manger; ~**! assez!**, ça suffit!; **that's** ~, **thanks** cela suffit or c'est assez, merci; **I've had** ~ **of him** j'en ai assez de lui; ... **which, funnily** or **oddly** ~ ... qui, chose curieuse

enquire [ɪn'kwaɪəʳ] vt, vi = **inquire**

enrage [ɪn'reɪdʒ] vt mettre en fureur or en rage, rendre furieux(-euse)

enrol [ɪn'rəʊl] (US **enroll**) vt inscrire ♦ vi s'inscrire; ~**ment** (US **enrollment**) n inscription f

en suite ['ɒnswi:t] adj: **with** ~ **bathroom** avec salle de bains en attenante

ensure [ɪn'ʃʊəʳ] vt assurer; garantir; **to ~ that** s'assurer que

entail [ɪn'teɪl] vt entraîner, occasionner

entangled [ɪn'tæŋɡld] adj: **to become** ~ **(in)** s'empêtrer (dans)

enter ['entəʳ] vt (room) entrer dans, pénétrer dans; (club, army) entrer à; (competition) s'inscrire à or pour; (sb for a competition) (faire) inscrire; (write down) inscrire, noter; (COMPUT) entrer, introduire ♦ vi entrer; ~ **for** vt fus s'inscrire à, se présenter pour or à; ~ **into** vt fus (explanation) se lancer dans; (discussion, negotiations) entamer; (agreement) conclure

enterprise ['entəpraɪz] n entreprise f; (initiative) (esprit m d')initiative f; **free** ~ libre entreprise; **private** ~ entreprise privée; **enterprising** adj entreprenant(e), dynamique; (scheme) audacieux(-euse)

entertain [entə'teɪn] vt amuser, distraire; (invite) recevoir (à dîner); (idea, plan) envisager; ~**er** n artiste m/f de variétés; ~**ing** adj amusant(e), distrayant(e); ~**ment** n (amusement) divertissement m, amusement m; (show) spectacle m

enthralled [ɪn'θrɔ:ld] adj captivé(e)

enthusiasm [ɪn'θu:zɪæzəm] n enthousiasme m

enthusiast [ɪn'θu:zɪæst] n enthousiaste m/f; ~**ic** [ɪnθu:zɪ'æstɪk] adj enthousiaste; **to be** ~**ic about** être enthousiasmé(e) par

entire [ɪn'taɪəʳ] adj (tout) entier(-ère); ~**ly** adv entièrement, complètement; ~**ty** [ɪn'taɪərətɪ] n: **in its** ~**ty** dans sa totalité

entitle [ɪn'taɪtl] vt: **to** ~ **sb to sth** donner droit à qch à qn; ~**d** [ɪn'taɪtld] adj (book) intitulé(e); **to be** ~**d to do** avoir le droit de or être habilité à faire

entrance [n 'entrns, vb ɪn'trɑ:ns] n entrée f ♦ vt enchanter, ravir; **to gain** ~ **to** (university etc) être admis à; ~ **examination**

n examen *m* d'entrée; ~ **fee** *n* (*to museum etc*) prix *m* d'entrée; (*to join club etc*) droit *m* d'inscription; ~ **ramp** (*US*) *n* (*AUT*) bretelle *f* d'accès; **entrant** *n* participant(e); concurrent(e); (*BRIT: in exam*) candidat(e)

entrenched [ɛn'trɛntʃt] *adj* retranché(e); (*ideas*) arrêté(e)

entrepreneur ['ɔntrəprə'nɜːʳ] *n* entrepreneur *m*

entrust [ɪn'trʌst] *vt*: **to ~ sth to** confier qch à

entry ['ɛntrɪ] *n* entrée *f*; (*in register*) inscription *f*; **no ~** défense d'entrer, entrée interdite; (*AUT*) sens interdit; ~ **form** feuille *f* d'inscription; ~ **phone** (*BRIT*) *n* interphone *m*

envelop [ɪn'vɛləp] *vt* envelopper

envelope ['ɛnvələup] *n* enveloppe *f*

envious ['ɛnvɪəs] *adj* envieux(-euse)

environment [ɪn'vaɪərnmənt] *n* environnement *m*; (*social, moral*) milieu *m*; **~al** [ɪnvaɪərn'mɛntl] *adj* écologique; du milieu; **~-friendly** *adj* écologique

envisage [ɪn'vɪzɪdʒ] *vt* (*foresee*) prévoir

envoy ['ɛnvɔɪ] *n* (*diplomat*) ministre *m* plénipotentiaire

envy ['ɛnvɪ] *n* envie *f* ♦ *vt* envier; **to ~ sb sth** envier qch à qn

epic ['ɛpɪk] *n* épopée *f* ♦ *adj* épique

epidemic [ɛpɪ'dɛmɪk] *n* épidémie *f*

epilepsy ['ɛpɪlɛpsɪ] *n* épilepsie *f*; **epileptic** *n* épileptique *m/f*

episode ['ɛpɪsəud] *n* épisode *m*

epitome [ɪ'pɪtəmɪ] *n* modèle *m*; **epitomize** *vt* incarner

equal ['iːkwl] *adj* égal(e) ♦ *n* égal(e) ♦ *vt* égaler; ~ **to** (*task*) à la hauteur de; **~ity** [iː'kwɔlɪtɪ] *n* égalité *f*; **~ize** *vi* (*SPORT*) égaliser; **~ly** *adv* également; (*just as*) tout aussi

equanimity [ɛkwə'nɪmɪtɪ] *n* égalité *f* d'humeur

equate [ɪ'kweɪt] *vt*: **to ~ sth with** comparer qch à; assimiler qch à; **equation** *n* (*MATH*) équation *f*

equator [ɪ'kweɪtəʳ] *n* équateur *m*

equilibrium [iːkwɪ'lɪbrɪəm] *n* équilibre *m*

equip [ɪ'kwɪp] *vt*: **to ~ (with)** équiper (de); **to be well ~ped** être bien équipé(e); **~ment** *n* équipement *m*; (*electrical etc*) appareillage *m*, installation *f*

equities ['ɛkwɪtɪz] (*BRIT*) *npl* (*COMM*) actions cotées en Bourse

equivalent [ɪ'kwɪvələnt] *adj*: ~ **(to)** équivalent(e) (à) ♦ *n* équivalent *m*

era ['ɪərə] *n* ère *f*, époque *f*

eradicate [ɪ'rædɪkeɪt] *vt* éliminer

erase [ɪ'reɪz] *vt* effacer; ~**r** *n* gomme *f*

erect [ɪ'rɛkt] *adj* droit(e) ♦ *vt* construire; (*monument*) ériger, élever; (*tent etc*) dresser; ~**ion** *n* érection *f*

ERM *n abbr* (= *Exchange Rate Mechanism*) MTC *m*

erode [ɪ'rəud] *vt* éroder; (*metal*) ronger

erotic [ɪ'rɔtɪk] *adj* érotique

errand ['ɛrənd] *n* course *f*, commission *f*

erratic [ɪ'rætɪk] *adj* irrégulier(-ère); inconstant(e)

error ['ɛrəʳ] *n* erreur *f*

erupt [ɪ'rʌpt] *vi* entrer en éruption; (*fig*) éclater; ~**ion** *n* éruption *f*

escalate ['ɛskəleɪt] *vi* s'intensifier

escalator ['ɛskəleɪtəʳ] *n* escalier roulant

escapade [ɛskə'peɪd] *n* (*misdeed*) fredaine *f*; (*adventure*) équipée *f*

escape [ɪs'keɪp] *n* fuite *f*; (*from prison*) évasion *f* ♦ *vi* s'échapper, fuir; (*from jail*) s'évader; (*fig*) s'en tirer; (*leak*) s'échapper ♦ *vt* échapper à; **to ~ from** (*person*) échapper à; (*place*) s'échapper de; (*fig*) fuir; **escapism** *n* (*fig*) évasion *f*

escort [*n* 'ɛskɔːt, *vb* ɪs'kɔːt] *n* escorte *f* ♦ *vt* escorter

Eskimo ['ɛskɪməu] *n* Esquimau(de)

especially [ɪs'pɛʃlɪ] *adv* (*particularly*) particulièrement; (*above all*) surtout

espionage ['ɛspɪənɑːʒ] *n* espionnage *m*

Esquire [ɪs'kwaɪəʳ] *n*: **J Brown, ~** Monsieur J. Brown

essay ['ɛseɪ] *n* (*SCOL*) dissertation *f*; (*LITERATURE*) essai *m*

essence ['ɛsns] *n* essence *f*

essential [ɪ'sɛnʃl] *adj* essentiel(le); (*basic*) fondamental(e) ♦ *n*: ~**s** éléments essentiels; **~ly** *adv* essentiellement

establish [ɪsˈtæblɪʃ] *vt* établir; (*business*) fonder, créer; (*one's power etc*) asseoir, affermir; **~ed** *adj* bien établi(e); **~ment** *n* établissement *m*; (*founding*) création *f*

estate [ɪsˈteɪt] *n* (*land*) domaine *m*, propriété *f*; (*LAW*) biens *mpl*, succession *f*; (*BRIT: also: housing ~*) lotissement *m*, cité *f*; **~ agent** *n* agent immobilier; **~ car** (*BRIT*) *n* break *m*

esteem [ɪsˈtiːm] *n* estime *f*

esthetic [ɪsˈθetɪk] (*US*) *adj* = **aesthetic**

estimate [*n* ˈestɪmət, *vb* ˈestɪmeɪt] *n* estimation *f*; (*COMM*) devis *m* ♦ *vt* estimer; **estimation** [estɪˈmeɪʃən] *n* opinion *f*; (*calculation*) estimation *f*

estranged [ɪsˈtreɪndʒd] *adj* séparé(e); dont on s'est séparé(e)

eternal [ɪˈtəːnl] *adj* éternel(le)

eternity [ɪˈtəːnɪtɪ] *n* éternité *f*

ethical [ˈeθɪkl] *adj* moral(e); **ethics** *n* éthique *f* ♦ *npl* moralité *f*

Ethiopia [iːθɪˈəupɪə] *n* Éthiopie *f*

ethnic [ˈeθnɪk] *adj* ethnique; (*music etc*) folklorique; **~ minority** minorité *f* ethnique

ethos [ˈiːθɔs] *n* génie *m*

e-ticket *n* billet *m* électronique

etiquette [ˈetɪket] *n* convenances *fpl*, étiquette *f*

EU *n abbr* (= *European Union*) UE *f*

euro [ˈjuərəu] *n* (*currency*) euro *m*

Eurocheque [ˈjuərəutʃek] *n* eurochèque *m*

Euroland [ˈjuərəulænd] *n* Euroland *m*

Europe [ˈjuərəp] *n* Europe *f*; **~an** [juərəˈpiːən] *adj* européen(ne) ♦ *n* Européen(ne); **~an Community** Communauté européenne

evacuate [ɪˈvækjueɪt] *vt* évacuer

evade [ɪˈveɪd] *vt* échapper à; (*question etc*) éluder; (*duties*) se dérober à; **to ~ tax** frauder le fisc

evaporate [ɪˈvæpəreɪt] *vi* s'évaporer; **~d milk** *n* lait condensé non sucré

evasion [ɪˈveɪʒən] *n* dérobade *f*; **tax ~** fraude fiscale

eve [iːv] *n*: **on the ~ of** à la veille de

even [ˈiːvn] *adj* (*level, smooth*) régulier(-ère); (*equal*) égal(e); (*number*) pair(e) ♦ *adv* même; **~ if** même si +*indic*; **~ though** alors même que +*cond*; **~ more** encore plus; **~ so** quand même; **not ~** pas même; **to get ~ with sb** prendre sa revanche sur qn

evening [ˈiːvnɪŋ] *n* soir *m*; (*as duration, event*) soirée *f*; **in the ~** le soir; **~ class** *n* cours *m* du soir; **~ dress** *n* tenue *f* de soirée

event [ɪˈvent] *n* événement *m*; (*SPORT*) épreuve *f*; **in the ~ of** en cas de; **~ful** *adj* mouvementé(e)

eventual [ɪˈventʃuəl] *adj* final(e); **~ity** [ɪventʃuˈælɪtɪ] *n* possibilité *f*, éventualité *f*; **~ly** *adv* finalement

ever [ˈevə*] *adv* jamais; (*at all times*) toujours; **the best ~** le meilleur qu'on ait jamais vu; **have you ~ seen it?** l'as-tu déjà vu?, as-tu eu l'occasion *or* t'est-il arrivé de le voir?; **why ~ not?** mais enfin, pourquoi pas?; **~ since** *adv* depuis ♦ *conj* depuis que; **~green** *n* arbre *m* à feuilles persistantes; **~lasting** *adj* éternel(le)

every [ˈevrɪ] *adj* chaque; **~ day** tous les jours, chaque jour; **~ other/third day** tous les deux/trois jours; **~ other car** une voiture sur deux; **~ now and then** de temps en temps; **~body** *pron* tout le monde, tous *pl*; **~day** *adj* quotidien(ne), de tous les jours; **~one** *pron* = **everybody**; **~thing** *pron* tout; **~where** *adv* partout

evict [ɪˈvɪkt] *vt* expulser; **~ion** *n* expulsion *f*

evidence [ˈevɪdns] *n* (*proof*) preuve(s) *f(pl)*; (*of witness*) témoignage *m*; (*sign*): **to show ~ of** présenter des signes de; **to give ~** témoigner, déposer

evident [ˈevɪdnt] *adj* évident(e); **~ly** *adv* de toute évidence; (*apparently*) apparemment

evil [ˈiːvl] *adj* mauvais(e) ♦ *n* mal *m*

evoke [ɪˈvəuk] *vt* évoquer

evolution [iːvəˈluːʃən] *n* évolution *f*

evolve [ɪˈvɔlv] *vt* élaborer ♦ *vi* évoluer

ewe [juː] n brebis f

ex- [eks] prefix ex-

exact [ɪgˈzækt] adj exact(e) ♦ vt: **to ~ sth (from)** extorquer qch (à); exiger qch (de); **~ing** adj exigeant(e); (work) astreignant(e); **~ly** adv exactement

exaggerate [ɪgˈzædʒəreɪt] vt, vi exagérer; **exaggeration** [ɪgzædʒəˈreɪʃən] n exagération f

exalted [ɪgˈzɔːltɪd] adj (prominent) élevé(e); (: person) haut placé(e)

exam [ɪgˈzæm] n abbr (SCOL) = **examination**

examination [ɪgzæmɪˈneɪʃən] n (SCOL, MED) examen m

examine [ɪgˈzæmɪn] vt (gen) examiner; (SCOL: person) interroger; **~r** n examinateur(-trice)

example [ɪgˈzɑːmpl] n exemple m; **for ~** par exemple

exasperate [ɪgˈzɑːspəreɪt] vt exaspérer; **exasperation** [ɪgzɑːspəˈreɪʃən] n exaspération f, irritation f

excavate [ˈekskəveɪt] vt excaver; **excavation** [ekskəˈveɪʃən] n fouilles fpl

exceed [ɪkˈsiːd] vt dépasser; (one's powers) outrepasser; **~ingly** adv extrêmement

excellent [ˈeksələnt] adj excellent(e)

except [ɪkˈsept] prep (also: **~ for, ~ing**) sauf, excepté ♦ vt excepter; **~ if/when** sauf si/quand; **~ that** sauf que, si ce n'est que; **~ion** n exception f; **to take ~ion to** s'offusquer de; **~ional** adj exceptionnel(le)

excerpt [ˈeksɜːpt] n extrait m

excess [ɪkˈses] n excès m; **~ baggage** n excédent m de bagages; **~ fare** (BRIT) n supplément m; **~ive** adj excessif(-ive)

exchange [ɪksˈtʃeɪndʒ] n échange m; (also: **telephone ~**) central m ♦ vt: **to ~ (for)** échanger (contre); **~ rate** n taux m de change

Exchequer [ɪksˈtʃekər] (BRIT) n: **the ~** l'Échiquier m, ≈ le ministère des Finances

excise [n ˈeksaɪz, vb ekˈsaɪz] n taxe f ♦ vt exciser

excite [ɪkˈsaɪt] vt exciter; **to get ~d** s'exci-

ter; **~ment** n excitation f; **exciting** adj passionnant(e)

exclaim [ɪksˈkleɪm] vi s'exclamer; **exclamation** [ekskləˈmeɪʃən] n exclamation f; **exclamation mark** n point m d'exclamation

exclude [ɪksˈkluːd] vt exclure; **exclusion zone** n zone interdite; **exclusive** adj exclusif(-ive); (club, district) sélect(e); (item of news) en exclusivité; **exclusive of VAT** TVA non comprise; **mutually exclusive** qui s'excluent l'un(e) l'autre

excruciating [ɪksˈkruːʃɪeɪtɪŋ] adj atroce

excursion [ɪksˈkɜːʃən] n excursion f

excuse [n ɪksˈkjuːs, vb ɪksˈkjuːz] n excuse f ♦ vt excuser; **to ~ sb from** (activity) dispenser qn de; **~ me!** excusez-moi!, pardon!; **now if you will ~ me, ...** maintenant, si vous (le) permettez ...

ex-directory [ˈeksdɪˈrektərɪ] (BRIT) adj sur la liste rouge

execute [ˈeksɪkjuːt] vt exécuter; **execution** n exécution f

executive [ɪgˈzekjʊtɪv] n (COMM) cadre m; (of organization, political party) bureau m ♦ adj exécutif(-ive)

exemplify [ɪgˈzemplɪfaɪ] vt illustrer; (typify) incarner

exempt [ɪgˈzempt] adj: **~ from** exempté(e) or dispensé(e) de ♦ vt: **to ~ sb from** exempter or dispenser qn de

exercise [ˈeksəsaɪz] n exercice m ♦ vt exercer; (patience etc) faire preuve de; (dog) promener ♦ vi prendre de l'exercice; **~ book** n cahier m

exert [ɪgˈzɜːt] vt exercer, employer; **to ~ o.s.** se dépenser; **~ion** n effort m

exhale [eksˈheɪl] vt exhaler ♦ vi expirer

exhaust [ɪgˈzɔːst] n (also: **~ fumes**) gaz mpl d'échappement; (also: **~ pipe**) tuyau m d'échappement ♦ vt épuiser; **~ed** adj épuisé(e); **~ion** n épuisement m; **nervous ~ion** fatigue nerveuse; surmenage mental; **~ive** adj très complet(-ète)

exhibit [ɪgˈzɪbɪt] n (ART) pièce exposée, objet exposé; (LAW) pièce à conviction ♦ vt exposer; (courage, skill) faire preuve de;

~ion [ɛksɪ'bɪʃən] n exposition f; (of ill-temper, talent etc) démonstration f

exhilarating [ɪg'zɪləreɪtɪŋ] adj grisant(e); stimulant(e)

ex-husband n ex-mari m

exile ['ɛksaɪl] n exil m; (person) exilé(e) ♦ vt exiler

exist [ɪg'zɪst] vi exister; ~ence n existence f; ~ing adj actuel(le)

exit ['ɛksɪt] n sortie f ♦ vi (COMPUT, THEATRE) sortir; ~ poll n sondage m (fait à la sortie de l'isoloir); ~ ramp n (AUT) bretelle f d'accès

exodus ['ɛksədəs] n exode m

exonerate [ɪg'zɔnəreɪt] vt: **to ~ from** disculper de

exotic [ɪg'zɔtɪk] adj exotique

expand [ɪks'pænd] vt agrandir; accroître ♦ vi (trade etc) se développer, s'accroître; (gas, metal) se dilater

expanse [ɪks'pæns] n étendue f

expansion [ɪks'pænʃən] n développement m, accroissement m

expect [ɪks'pɛkt] vt (anticipate) s'attendre à, s'attendre à ce que +sub; (count on) compter sur, escompter; (require) demander, exiger; (suppose) supposer; (await, also baby) attendre ♦ vi: **to be ~ing** être enceinte; ~ancy n (anticipation) attente f; **life ~ancy** espérance f de vie; ~ant mother n future maman; ~ation [ɛkspɛk'teɪʃən] n attente f; espérance(s) f(pl)

expedient [ɪks'piːdɪənt] adj indiqué(e), opportun(e) ♦ n expédient m

expedition [ɛkspə'dɪʃən] n expédition f

expel [ɪks'pɛl] vt chasser, expulser; (SCOL) renvoyer

expend [ɪks'pɛnd] vt consacrer; (money) dépenser; ~iture [ɪks'pɛndɪtʃər] n dépense f; dépenses fpl

expense [ɪks'pɛns] n dépense f, frais mpl; (high cost) coût m; ~s npl (COMM) frais mpl; **at the ~ of** aux dépens de; ~ account n (note f de) frais mpl; **expensive** adj cher (chère), coûteux(-euse); **to be expensive** coûter cher

experience [ɪks'pɪərɪəns] n expérience f ♦ vt connaître, faire l'expérience de; (feeling) éprouver; ~d adj expérimenté(e)

experiment [ɪks'pɛrɪmənt] n expérience f ♦ vi faire une expérience; **to ~ with** expérimenter

expert ['ɛkspəːt] adj expert(e) ♦ n expert m; ~ise [ɛkspəː'tiːz] n (grande) compétence

expire [ɪks'paɪər] vi expirer; **expiry** n expiration f

explain [ɪks'pleɪn] vt expliquer; **explanation** [ɛksplə'neɪʃən] n explication f; **explanatory** [ɪks'plænətrɪ] adj explicatif(-ive)

explicit [ɪks'plɪsɪt] adj explicite; (definite) formel(le)

explode [ɪks'pləud] vi exploser

exploit [n 'ɛksplɔɪt, vb ɪks'plɔɪt] n exploit m ♦ vt exploiter; ~ation [ɛksplɔɪ'teɪʃən] n exploitation f

exploratory [ɪks'plɔrətrɪ] adj (expedition) d'exploration; (fig: talks) préliminaire

explore [ɪks'plɔːr] vt explorer; (possibilities) étudier, examiner; ~r n explorateur(-trice)

explosion [ɪks'pləuʒən] n explosion f; **explosive** adj explosif(-ive) ♦ n explosif m

exponent [ɪks'pəunənt] n (of school of thought etc) interprète m, représentant m

export [vb ɛks'pɔːt, n 'ɛkspɔːt] vt exporter ♦ n exportation f ♦ cpd d'exportation; ~er n exportateur m

expose [ɪks'pəuz] vt exposer; (unmask) démasquer, dévoiler; ~d adj (position, house) exposé(e); **exposure** n exposition f; (publicity) couverture f; (PHOT) (temps m de) pose f; (: shot) pose; **to die from exposure** (MED) mourir de froid; **exposure meter** n posemètre m

express [ɪks'prɛs] adj (definite) formel(le), exprès(-esse); (BRIT: letter etc) exprès inv ♦ n (train) rapide m; (bus) car m express ♦ vt exprimer; ~ion n expression f; ~ly adv expressément, formellement; ~way n (US) n (urban motorway) voie f express (à plusieurs files)

exquisite ['ɛks'kwɪzɪt] adj exquis(e)

extend [ɪks'tɛnd] vt (visit, street) prolonger;

(*building*) agrandir; (*offer*) présenter, offrir; (*hand, arm*) tendre ♦ *vi* s'étendre; **extension** *n* prolongation *f*; agrandissement *m*; (*building*) annexe *f*; (*to wire, table*) rallonge *f*; (*telephone: in offices*) poste *m*; (: *in private house*) téléphone *m* supplémentaire; **extensive** *adj* étendu(e), vaste; (*damage, alterations*) considérable; (*inquiries*) approfondi(e); **extensively** *adv*: **he's travelled extensively** il a beaucoup voyagé

extent [ɪks'tɛnt] *n* étendue *f*; **to some ~** dans une certaine mesure; **to what ~?** dans quelle mesure?, jusqu'à quel point?; **to the ~ of ...** au point de ...; **to such an ~ that ...** à tel point que ...

extenuating [ɪks'tɛnjueɪtɪŋ] *adj*: **~ circumstances** circonstances atténuantes

exterior [ɛks'tɪərɪəʳ] *adj* extérieur(e) ♦ *n* extérieur *m*; dehors *m*

external [ɛks'tɔːnl] *adj* externe

extinct [ɪks'tɪŋkt] *adj* éteint(e)

extinguish [ɪks'tɪŋgwɪʃ] *vt* éteindre

extort [ɪks'tɔːt] *vt*: **to ~ sth (from)** extorquer qch (à); **~ionate** *adj* exorbitant(e)

extra ['ɛkstrə] *adj* supplémentaire, de plus ♦ *adv* (*in addition*) en plus ♦ *n* supplément *m*; (*perk*) à-côté *m*; (*THEATRE*) figurant(e) ♦ *prefix* extra...

extract [*vb* ɪks'trækt, *n* 'ɛkstrækt] *vt* extraire; (*tooth*) arracher; (*money, promise*) soutirer ♦ *n* extrait *m*

extracurricular ['ɛkstrəkə'rɪkjuləʳ] *adj* parascolaire

extradite ['ɛkstrədaɪt] *vt* extrader

extra...: **~marital** ['ɛkstrə'mærɪtl] *adj* extra-conjugal(e); **~mural** ['ɛkstrə'mjuərl] *adj* hors faculté *inv*; (*lecture*) public(-que); **~ordinary** [ɪks'trɔːdnrɪ] *adj* extraordinaire

extravagance [ɪks'trævəgəns] *n* prodigalités *fpl*; (*thing bought*) folie *f*, dépense excessive; **extravagant** *adj* extravagant(e); (*in spending: person*) prodigue, dépensier(-ère); (: *tastes*) dispendieux(-euse)

extreme [ɪks'triːm] *adj* extrême ♦ *n* extrême *m*; **~ly** *adv* extrêmement; **extremist** *adj, n* extrémiste *m/f*

extricate ['ɛkstrɪkeɪt] *vt*: **to ~ sth (from)** dégager qch (de)

extrovert ['ɛkstrəvɔːt] *n* extraverti(e)

ex-wife *n* ex-femme *f*

eye [aɪ] *n* œil *m* (*pl* yeux); (*of needle*) trou *m*, chas *m* ♦ *vt* examiner; **to keep an ~ on** surveiller; **~brow** *n* sourcil *m*; **~drops** *npl* gouttes *fpl* pour les yeux; **~lash** *n* cil *m*; **~lid** *n* paupière *f*; **~liner** *n* eye-liner *m*; **~-opener** *n* révélation *f*; **~shadow** *n* ombre *f* à paupières; **~sight** *n* vue *f*; **~sore** *n* horreur *f*; **~ witness** *n* témoin *m* oculaire

F, f

F [ɛf] *n* (*MUS*) fa *m*

fable ['feɪbl] *n* fable *f*

fabric ['fæbrɪk] *n* tissu *m*

fabulous ['fæbjuləs] *adj* fabuleux(-euse); (*inf: super*) formidable

face [feɪs] *n* visage *m*, figure *f*; (*expression*) expression *f*; (*of clock*) cadran *m*; (*of cliff*) paroi *f*; (*of mountain*) face *f*; (*of building*) façade *f* ♦ *vt* faire face à; **~ down** (*person*) à plat ventre; (*card*) face en dessous; **to lose/save ~** perdre/sauver la face; **to make** *or* **pull a ~** faire une grimace; **in the ~ of** (*difficulties etc*) face à, devant; **on the ~ of it** à première vue; **~ to ~** face à face; **~ up to** *vt fus* faire face à, affronter; **~ cloth** (*BRIT*) *n* gant *m* de toilette; **~ cream** *n* crème *f* pour le visage; **~ lift** *n* lifting *m*; (*of building etc*) ravalement *m*, retapage *m*; **~ powder** *n* poudre *f* de riz; **~ value** *n* (*of coin*) valeur nominale; **to take sth at ~ value** (*fig*) prendre qch pour argent comptant

facilities [fə'sɪlɪtɪz] *npl* installations *fpl*, équipement *m*; **credit ~** facilités *fpl* de paiement

facing ['feɪsɪŋ] *prep* face à, en face de

facsimile [fæk'sɪmɪlɪ] *n* (*exact replica*) facsimilé *m*; (*fax*) télécopie *f*

fact [fækt] *n* fait *m*; **in ~** en fait

factor ['fæktəʳ] *n* facteur *m*

factory ['fæktərɪ] *n* usine *f*, fabrique *f*

factual ['fæktjuəl] *adj* basé(e) sur les faits

faculty ['fækəltɪ] *n* faculté *f*; (*US: teaching staff*) corps enseignant

fad [fæd] *n* (*craze*) engouement *m*

fade [feɪd] *vi* se décolorer, passer; (*light, sound*) s'affaiblir; (*flower*) se faner

fag [fæg] (*BRIT: inf*) *n* (*cigarette*) sèche *f*

fail [feɪl] *vt* (*exam*) échouer à; (*candidate*) recaler; (*subj: courage, memory*) faire défaut à ♦ *vi* échouer; (*brakes*) lâcher; (*eyesight, health, light*) baisser, s'affaiblir; **to ~ to do sth** (*neglect*) négliger de faire qch; (*be unable*) ne pas arriver *or* parvenir à faire qch; **without ~** à coup sûr; sans faute; **~ing** *n* défaut *m* ♦ *prep* faute de; **~ure** *n* échec *m*; (*person*) raté(e); (*mechanical etc*) défaillance *f*

faint [feɪnt] *adj* faible; (*recollection*) vague; (*mark*) à peine visible ♦ *n* évanouissement *m* ♦ *vi* s'évanouir; **to feel ~** défaillir

fair [fɛər] *adj* équitable, juste, impartial(e); (*hair*) blond(e); (*skin, complexion*) pâle, blanc (blanche); (*weather*) beau (belle); (*good enough*) assez bon(ne); (*sizeable*) considérable ♦ *adv*: **to play ~** jouer franc-jeu ♦ *n* foire *f*; (*BRIT: funfair*) fête (foraine); **~ly** *adv* équitablement; (*quite*) assez; **~ness** *n* justice *f*, équité *f*, impartialité *f*

fairy ['fɛərɪ] *n* fée *f*; **~ tale** *n* conte *m* de fées

faith [feɪθ] *n* foi *f*; (*trust*) confiance *f*; (*specific religion*) religion *f*; **~ful** *adj* fidèle; **~fully** *adv see* **yours**

fake [feɪk] *n* (*painting etc*) faux *m*; (*person*) imposteur *m* ♦ *adj* faux (fausse) ♦ *vt* simuler; (*painting*) faire un faux de

falcon ['fɔːlkən] *n* faucon *m*

fall [fɔːl] (*pt* **fell**, *pp* **fallen**) *n* chute *f*; (*US: autumn*) automne *m* ♦ *vi* tomber; (*price, temperature, dollar*) baisser; **~s** *npl* (*waterfall*) chute *f* d'eau, cascade *f*; **to ~ flat** (*on one's face*) tomber de tout son long, s'étaler; (*joke*) tomber à plat; (*plan*) échouer; **~ back** *vi* reculer, se retirer; **~ back on** *vt fus* se rabattre sur; **~ behind** *vi* prendre du retard; **~ down** *vi* (*person*) tomber;

(*building*) s'effondrer, s'écrouler; **~ for** *vt fus* (*trick, story etc*) se laisser prendre à; (*person*) tomber amoureux de; **~ in** *vi* s'effondrer; (*MIL*) se mettre en rangs; **~ off** *vi* tomber; (*diminish*) baisser, diminuer; **~ out** *vi* (*hair, teeth*) tomber; (*MIL*) rompre les rangs; (*friends etc*) se brouiller; **~ through** *vi* (*plan, project*) tomber à l'eau

fallacy ['fæləsɪ] *n* erreur *f*, illusion *f*

fallout ['fɔːlaʊt] *n* retombées (radioactives)

fallow ['fæləʊ] *adj* en jachère; en friche

false [fɔːls] *adj* faux (fausse); **~ alarm** *n* fausse alerte; **~ pretences** *npl*: **under ~ pretences** sous un faux prétexte; **~ teeth** (*BRIT*) *npl* fausses dents

falter ['fɔːltər] *vi* chanceler, vaciller

fame [feɪm] *n* renommée *f*, renom *m*

familiar [fə'mɪlɪər] *adj* familier(-ère); **to be ~ with** (*subject*) connaître

family ['fæmɪlɪ] *n* famille *f* ♦ *cpd* (*business, doctor etc*) de famille; **has he any ~?** (*children*) a-t-il des enfants?

famine ['fæmɪn] *n* famine *f*

famished ['fæmɪʃt] (*inf*) *adj* affamé(e)

famous ['feɪməs] *adj* célèbre; **~ly** *adv* (*get on*) fameusement, à merveille

fan [fæn] *n* (*folding*) éventail *m*; (*ELEC*) ventilateur *m*; (*of person*) fan *m*, admirateur(-trice); (*of team, sport etc*) supporter *m/f* ♦ *vt* éventer; (*fire, quarrel*) attiser

fanatic [fə'nætɪk] *n* fanatique *m/f*

fan belt *n* courroie *f* de ventilateur

fancy ['fænsɪ] *n* fantaisie *f*, envie *f*; imagination *f* ♦ *adj* (de) fantaisie *inv* ♦ *vt* (*feel like, want*) avoir envie de; (*imagine, think*) imaginer; **to take a ~ to** se prendre d'affection pour; s'enticher de; **he fancies her** (*inf*) elle lui plaît; **~ dress** *n* déguisement *m*, travesti *m*; **~-dress ball** *n* bal masqué *or* costumé

fang [fæŋ] *n* croc *m*; (*of snake*) crochet *m*

fantastic [fæn'tæstɪk] *adj* fantastique

fantasy ['fæntəsɪ] *n* imagination *f*, fantaisie *f*; (*dream*) chimère *f*

far [fɑːr] *adj* lointain(e), éloigné(e) ♦ *adv* loin; **~ away** *or* **off** au loin, dans le lointain; **at the ~ side/end** à l'autre côté/

bout; **~ better** beaucoup mieux; **~ from** loin de; **by ~** de loin, de beaucoup; **go as ~ as the farm** allez jusqu'à la ferme; **as ~ as I know** pour autant que je sache; **how ~ is it to ...?** combien y a-t-il jusqu'à ...?; **how ~ have you got?** où en êtes-vous?; **~away** ['fɑːrəweɪ] *adj* lointain(e); *(look)* distrait(e)

farce [fɑːs] *n* farce *f*

fare [fɛəʳ] *n (on trains, buses)* prix *m* du billet; *(in taxi)* prix de la course; *(food)* table *f*, chère *f*; **half ~** demi-tarif; **full ~** plein tarif

Far East *n* Extrême-Orient *m*

farewell [fɛəˈwel] *excl* adieu ♦ *n* adieu *m*

farm [fɑːm] *n* ferme *f* ♦ *vt* cultiver; **~er** *n* fermier(-ère); cultivateur(-trice); **~hand** *n* ouvrier(-ère) agricole; **~house** *n* (maison *f* de) ferme *f*; **~ing** *n* agriculture *f*; *(of animals)* élevage *m*; **~land** *n* terres cultivées; **~ worker** *n* = **farmhand**; **~yard** *n* cour *f* de ferme

far-reaching ['fɑːˈriːtʃɪŋ] *adj* d'une grande portée

fart [fɑːt] *(inf!)* *vi* péter

farther ['fɑːðəʳ] *adv* plus loin ♦ *adj* plus éloigné(e), plus lointain(e)

farthest ['fɑːðɪst] *superl* of **far**

fascinate ['fæsɪneɪt] *vt* fasciner; **fascinating** *adj* fascinant(e)

fascism ['fæʃɪzəm] *n* fascisme *m*

fashion ['fæʃən] *n* mode *f*; *(manner)* façon *f*, manière *f* ♦ *vt* façonner; **in ~** à la mode; **out of ~** démodé(e); **~able** *adj* à la mode; **~ show** *n* défilé *m* de mannequins *or* de mode

fast [fɑːst] *adj* rapide; *(clock):* **to be ~** avancer; *(dye, colour)* grand *or* bon teint *inv* ♦ *adv* vite, rapidement; *(stuck, held)* solidement ♦ *n* jeûne *m* ♦ *vi* jeûner; **~ asleep** profondément endormi

fasten ['fɑːsn] *vt* attacher, fixer; *(coat)* attacher, fermer ♦ *vi* se fermer, s'attacher; **~er**, **~ing** *n* attache *f*

fast food *n* fast food *m*, restauration *f* rapide

fastidious [fæsˈtɪdɪəs] *adj* exigeant(e), difficile

fat [fæt] *adj* gros(se) ♦ *n* graisse *f*; *(on meat)* gras *m*; *(for cooking)* matière grasse

fatal ['feɪtl] *adj (injury etc)* mortel(le); *(mistake)* fatal(e); **~ity** [fəˈtælɪtɪ] *n (road death etc)* victime *f*, décès *m*

fate [feɪt] *n* destin *m*; *(of person)* sort *m*; **~ful** *adj* fatidique

father ['fɑːðəʳ] *n* père *m*; **~-in-law** *n* beau-père *m*; **~ly** *adj* paternel(le)

fathom ['fæðəm] *n* brasse *f* (= 1828 mm) ♦ *vt (mystery)* sonder, pénétrer

fatigue [fəˈtiːg] *n* fatigue *f*

fatten ['fætn] *vt, vi* engraisser

fatty ['fætɪ] *adj (food)* gras(se) ♦ *n (inf)* gros(se)

fatuous ['fætjuəs] *adj* stupide

faucet ['fɔːsɪt] *(US)* *n* robinet *m*

fault [fɔːlt] *n* faute *f*; *(defect)* défaut *m*; *(GEO)* faille *f* ♦ *vt* trouver des défauts à; **it's my ~** c'est de ma faute; **to find ~ with** trouver à redire *or* à critiquer à; **at ~** fautif(-ive), coupable; **~y** *adj* défectueux(-euse)

fauna ['fɔːnə] *n* faune *f*

favour ['feɪvəʳ] *(US* **favor**) *n* faveur *f*; *(help)* service *m* ♦ *vt (proposition)* être en faveur de; *(pupil etc)* favoriser; *(team, horse)* donner gagnant; **to do sb a ~** rendre un service à qn; **to find ~ with** trouver grâce aux yeux de; **in ~ of** en faveur de; **~able** *adj* favorable; **~ite** ['feɪvrɪt] *adj, n* favori(te)

fawn [fɔːn] *n* faon *m* ♦ *adj (colour)* fauve ♦ *vi:* **to ~ (up)on** flatter servilement

fax [fæks] *n (document)* télécopie *f*; *(machine)* télécopieur *m* ♦ *vt* envoyer par télécopie

FBI *n abbr (US: Federal Bureau of Investigation)* F.B.I. *f*

fear [fɪəʳ] *n* crainte *f*, peur *f* ♦ *vt* craindre; **for ~ of** de peur que +*sub*, de peur de +*infin*; **~ful** *adj* craintif(-ive); *(sight, noise)* affreux(-euse), épouvantable; **~less** *adj* intrépide

feasible ['fiːzəbl] *adj* faisable, réalisable

feast [fiːst] *n* festin *m*, banquet *m*; *(REL:*

also: ~ **day**) fête *f* ♦ *vi* festoyer

feat [fiːt] *n* exploit *m*, prouesse *f*

feather ['feðə*r*] *n* plume *f*

feature ['fiːtʃə*r*] *n* caractéristique *f*; (*article*) chronique *f*, rubrique *f* ♦ *vt* (*subj: film*) avoir pour vedette(s) ♦ *vi:* **to ~ in** figurer (en bonne place) dans; (*in film*) jouer dans; **~s** *npl* (*of face*) traits *mpl*; ~ **film** *n* long métrage

February ['februərɪ] *n* février *m*

fed [fed] *pt, pp of* **feed**

federal ['fedərəl] *adj* fédéral(e)

fed up *adj:* **to be ~** en avoir marre, en avoir plein le dos

fee [fiː] *n* rémunération *f*; (*of doctor, lawyer*) honoraires *mpl*; (*for examination*) droits *mpl*; **school ~s** frais *mpl* de scolarité

feeble ['fiːbl] *adj* faible; (*pathetic: attempt, excuse*) pauvre; (: *joke*) piteux(-euse)

feed [fiːd] (*pt, pp* **fed**) *n* (*of animal*) fourrage *m*; pâture *f*; (*on printer*) mécanisme *m* d'alimentation ♦ *vt* (*person*) nourrir; (*BRIT: baby*) allaiter; (: *with bottle*) donner le biberon à; (*horse etc*) donner à manger à; (*machine*) alimenter; (*data, information*): **to ~ sth into** fournir qch à; ~ **on** *vt fus* se nourrir de; **~back** *n* feed-back *m inv*

feel [fiːl] (*pt, pp* **felt**) *n* sensation *f*; (*impression*) impression *f* ♦ *vt* toucher; (*explore*) tâter, palper; (*cold, pain*) sentir; (*grief, anger*) ressentir, éprouver; (*think, believe*) trouver; **to ~ hungry/cold** avoir faim/froid; **to ~ lonely/better** se sentir seul/mieux; **I don't ~ well** je ne me sens pas bien; **it ~s soft** c'est doux (douce) au toucher; **to ~ like** (*want*) avoir envie de; ~ **about** *vi* fouiller, tâtonner; **~er** *n* (*of insect*) antenne *f*; **~ing** *n* (*physical*) sensation *f*; (*emotional*) sentiment *m*

feet [fiːt] *npl of* **foot**

feign [feɪn] *vt* feindre, simuler

fell [fel] *pt of* **fall** ♦ *vt* (*tree, person*) abattre

fellow ['feləu] *n* type *m*; (*comrade*) compagnon *m*; (*of learned society*) membre *m* ♦ *cpd:* **their ~ prisoners/students** leurs camarades prisonniers/d'étude; ~ **citizen** *n* concitoyen(ne) *m/f*; ~ **countryman** (*ir-*

reg) *n* compatriote *m*; ~ **men** *npl* semblables *mpl*; **~ship** *n* (*society*) association *f*; (*comradeship*) amitié *f*, camaraderie *f*; (*grant*) sorte de bourse universitaire

felony ['felənɪ] *n* crime *m*, forfait *m*

felt [felt] *pt, pp of* **feel** ♦ *n* feutre *m*; **~-tip pen** *n* stylo-feutre *m*

female ['fiːmeɪl] *n* (*ZOOL*) femelle *f*; (*pej: woman*) bonne femme ♦ *adj* (*BIO*) femelle; (*sex, character*) féminin(e); (*vote etc*) des femmes

feminine ['femɪnɪn] *adj* féminin(e)

feminist ['femɪnɪst] *n* féministe *m/f*

fence [fens] *n* barrière *f* ♦ *vt* (*also:* ~ **in**) clôturer ♦ *vi* faire de l'escrime; **fencing** *n* escrime *m*

fend [fend] *vi:* **to ~ for o.s.** se débrouiller (tout seul); ~ **off** *vt* (*attack etc*) parer

fender ['fendə*r*] *n* garde-feu *m inv*; (*on boat*) défense *f*; (*US: of car*) aile *f*

ferment [*vb* fə'ment, *n* 'fɜːment] *vi* fermenter ♦ *n* agitation *f*, effervescence *f*

fern [fɜːn] *n* fougère *f*

ferocious [fə'rəuʃəs] *adj* féroce

ferret ['ferɪt] *n* furet *m*

ferry ['ferɪ] *n* (*small*) bac *m*; (*large: also:* **~boat**) ferry(-boat) *m* ♦ *vt* transporter

fertile ['fɜːtaɪl] *adj* fertile; (*BIO*) fécond(e); **fertilizer** ['fɜːtɪlaɪzə*r*] *n* engrais *m*

fester ['festə*r*] *vi* suppurer

festival ['festɪvəl] *n* (*REL*) fête *f*; (*ART, MUS*) festival *m*

festive ['festɪv] *adj* de fête; **the ~ season** (*BRIT: Christmas*) la période des fêtes; **festivities** *npl* réjouissances *fpl*

festoon [fes'tuːn] *vt:* **to ~ with** orner de

fetch [fetʃ] *vt* aller chercher; (*sell for*) se vendre

fête [feɪt] *n* fête *f*, kermesse *f*

feud [fjuːd] *n* dispute *f*, dissension *f*

fever ['fiːvə*r*] *n* fièvre *f*; **~ish** *adj* fiévreux(-euse), fébrile

few [fjuː] *adj* (*not many*) peu de; **a ~** *adj* quelques ♦ *pron* quelques-uns(-unes); **~er** ['fjuːə*r*] *adj* moins de; moins (nombreux); **~est** ['fjuːɪst] *adj* le moins (de)

fiancé, e [fɪ'ɑ̃ːnseɪ] *n* fiancé(e) *m/f*

fib [fɪb] *n* bobard *m*

fibre ['faɪbə^r] (*US* **fiber**) *n* fibre *f*; **~glass** ['faɪbəglɑːs] (*US* **Fiberglass** ®) *n* fibre de verre

fickle ['fɪkl] *adj* inconstant(e), volage, capricieux(-euse)

fiction ['fɪkʃən] *n* romans *mpl*, littérature *f* romanesque; (*invention*) fiction *f*; **~al** *adj* fictif(-ive)

fictitious *adj* fictif(-ive), imaginaire

fiddle ['fɪdl] *n* (*MUS*) violon *m*; (*cheating*) combine *f*; escroquerie *f* ♦ *vt* (*BRIT: accounts*) falsifier, maquiller; **~ with** *vt fus* tripoter

fidget ['fɪdʒɪt] *vi* se trémousser, remuer

field [fiːld] *n* champ *m*; (*fig*) domaine *m*, champ; (*SPORT: ground*) terrain *m*; **~work** *n* travaux *mpl* pratiques (sur le terrain)

fiend [fiːnd] *n* démon *m*

fierce [fɪəs] *adj* (*look, animal*) féroce, sauvage; (*wind, attack, person*) (très) violent(e); (*fighting, enemy*) acharné(e)

fiery ['faɪərɪ] *adj* ardent(e), brûlant(e); (*temperament*) fougueux(-euse)

fifteen [fɪf'tiːn] *num* quinze

fifth [fɪfθ] *num* cinquième

fifty ['fɪftɪ] *num* cinquante; **~-fifty** *adj*: **a ~-fifty chance** *etc* une chance *etc* sur deux ♦ *adv* moitié-moitié

fig [fɪg] *n* figue *f*

fight [faɪt] (*pt, pp* **fought**) *n* (*MIL*) combat *m*; (*between persons*) bagarre *f*; (*against cancer etc*) lutte *f* ♦ *vt* se battre contre; (*cancer, alcoholism, emotion*) combattre, lutter contre; (*election*) se présenter à ♦ *vi* se battre; **~er** *n* (*fig*) lutteur *m*; (*plane*) chasseur *m*; **~ing** *n* combats *mpl*; (*brawl*) bagarres *fpl*

figment ['fɪgmənt] *n*: **a ~ of the imagination** une invention

figurative ['fɪgjurətɪv] *adj* figuré(e)

figure ['fɪgə^r] *n* figure *f*; (*number, cipher*) chiffre *m*; (*body, outline*) silhouette *f*; (*shape*) ligne *f*, formes *fpl* ♦ *vt* (*think: esp US*) supposer ♦ *vi* (*appear*) figurer; **~ out** *vt* (*work out*) calculer; **~head** *n* (*NAUT*) figure *f* de proue; (*pej*) prête-nom *m*; **~**

of speech *n* figure *f* de rhétorique

file [faɪl] *n* (*dossier*) dossier *m*; (*folder*) dossier, chemise *f*; (*COMPUT*) fichier *m*; (*row*) file *f*; (*tool*) lime *f* ♦ *vt* (*nails, wood*) limer; (*papers*) classer; (*LAW: claim*) faire enregistrer; déposer ♦ *vi*: **to ~ in/out** entrer/sortir l'un derrière l'autre; **to ~ for divorce** faire une demande en divorce; **filing cabinet** *n* classeur *m* (*meuble*)

fill [fɪl] *vt* remplir; (*need*) répondre à ♦ *n*: **to eat one's ~** manger à sa faim; **to ~ with** remplir de; **~ in** *vt* (*hole*) boucher; (*form*) remplir; **~ up** *vt* remplir; **~ it up, please** (*AUT*) le plein, s'il vous plaît

fillet ['fɪlɪt] *n* filet *m*; **~ steak** *n* filet *m* de bœuf, tournedos *m*

filling ['fɪlɪŋ] *n* (*CULIN*) garniture *f*, farce *f*; (*for tooth*) plombage *m*; **~ station** *n* station-service *f*

film [fɪlm] *n* film *m*; (*PHOT*) pellicule *f*, film; (*of powder, liquid*) couche *f*, pellicule ♦ *vt* (*scene*) filmer ♦ *vi* tourner; **~ star** *n* vedette *f* de cinéma

filter ['fɪltə^r] *n* filtre *m* ♦ *vt* filtrer; **~ lane** *n* (*AUT*) voie *f* de sortie; **~-tipped** *adj* à bout filtre

filth [fɪlθ] *n* saleté *f*; **~y** *adj* sale, dégoûtant(e); (*language*) ordurier(-ère)

final ['faɪnl] *adj* final(e); (*definitive*) définitif(-ive) ♦ *n* (*SPORT*) finale *f*; **~s** *npl* (*SCOL*) examens *mpl* de dernière année; **~e** [fɪ'nɑːlɪ] *n* finale *m*; **~ist** *n* finaliste *m/f*; **~ize** *vt* mettre au point; **~ly** *adv* (*eventually*) enfin, finalement; (*lastly*) en dernier lieu

finance [faɪ'næns] *n* finance *f* ♦ *vt* financer; **~s** *npl* (*financial position*) finances *fpl*; **financial** [faɪ'nænʃəl] *adj* financier(-ère)

find [faɪnd] (*pt, pp* **found**) *vt* trouver; (*lost object*) retrouver ♦ *n* trouvaille *f*, découverte *f*; **to ~ sb guilty** (*LAW*) déclarer qn coupable; **~ out** *vt* (*truth, secret*) découvrir; (*person*) démasquer ♦ *vi*: **to ~ out about** (*make enquiries*) se renseigner; (*by chance*) apprendre; **~ings** *npl* (*LAW*) conclusions *fpl*, verdict *m*; (*of report*) conclusions

fine [faɪn] *adj* (*excellent*) excellent(e); (*thin, not coarse, subtle*) fin(e); (*weather*) beau (belle) ♦ *adv* (*well*) très bien ♦ *n* (*LAW*) amende *f*; contravention *f* ♦ *vt* (*LAW*) condamner à une amende; donner une contravention à; **to be ~** (*person*) aller bien; (*weather*) être beau; **~ arts** *npl* beaux-arts *mpl*; **~ry** *n* parure *f*

finger ['fɪŋgəʳ] *n* doigt *m* ♦ *vt* palper, toucher; **little ~** auriculaire *m*, petit doigt; **index ~** index *m*; **~nail** *n* ongle *m* (de la main); **~print** *n* empreinte digitale; **~tip** *n* bout *m* du doigt

finish ['fɪnɪʃ] *n* fin *f*; (*SPORT*) arrivée *f*; (*polish etc*) finition *f* ♦ *vt* finir, terminer ♦ *vi* finir, se terminer; **to ~ doing sth** finir de faire qch; **to ~ third** arriver *or* terminer troisième; **~ off** *vt* finir, terminer; (*kill*) achever; **~ up** *vi, vt* finir, terminer; **~ing line** *n* ligne *f* d'arrivée

finite ['faɪnaɪt] *adj* fini(e); (*verb*) conjugué(e)

Finland ['fɪnlənd] *n* Finlande *f*; **Finn** [fɪn] *n* Finlandais(e); **Finnish** *adj* finlandais(e) ♦ *n* (*LING*) finnois *m*

fir [fɜːʳ] *n* sapin *m*

fire ['faɪəʳ] *n* feu *m*; (*accidental*) incendie *m*; (*heater*) radiateur *m* ♦ *vt* (*fig*) enflammer, animer; (*inf: dismiss*) mettre à la porte, renvoyer; (*discharge*): **to ~ a gun** tirer un coup de feu ♦ *vi* (*shoot*) tirer, faire feu; **on ~** en feu; **~ alarm** *n* avertisseur *m* d'incendie; **~arm** *n* arme *f* à feu; **~ brigade** *n* (sapeurs-)pompiers *mpl*; **~ department** (*US*) *n* = **fire brigade**; **~ engine** *n* (*vehicle*) voiture *f* des pompiers; **~ escape** *n* escalier *m* de secours; **~ extinguisher** *n* extincteur *m*; **~man** *n* pompier *m*; **~place** *n* cheminée *f*; **~side** *n* foyer *m*, coin *m* du feu; **~ station** *n* caserne *f* de pompiers; **~wood** *n* bois *m* de chauffage; **~works** *npl* feux *mpl* d'artifice; (*display*) feu(x) d'artifice

firing squad ['faɪərɪŋ-] *n* peloton *m* d'exécution

firm [fɜːm] *adj* ferme ♦ *n* compagnie *f*, firme *f*

first [fɜːst] *adj* premier(-ère) ♦ *adv* (*before all others*) le premier, la première; (*before all other things*) en premier, d'abord; (*when listing reasons etc*) en premier lieu, premièrement ♦ *n* (*person: in race*) premier(-ère); (*BRIT: SCOL*) mention *f* très bien; (*AUT*) première *f*; **at ~** au commencement, au début; **~ of all** tout d'abord, pour commencer; **~ aid** *n* premiers secours *or* soins; **~-aid kit** *n* trousse *f* à pharmacie; **~-class** *adj* de première classe; (*excellent*) excellent(e), exceptionnel(le); **~-hand** *adj* de première main; **~ lady** (*US*) *n* femme *f* du président; **~ly** *adv* premièrement, en premier lieu; **~ name** *n* prénom *m*; **~-rate** *adj* excellent(e)

fish [fɪʃ] *n inv* poisson *m* ♦ *vt, vi* pêcher; **to go ~ing** aller à la pêche; **~erman** *n* pêcheur *m*; **~ farm** *n* établissement *m* piscicole; **~ fingers** (*BRIT*) *npl* bâtonnets de poisson (congelés); **~ing boat** *n* barque *f or* bateau *m* de pêche; **~ing line** *n* ligne *f* (de pêche); **~ing rod** *n* canne *f* à pêche; **~ing tackle** *n* attirail *m* de pêche; **~monger's (shop)** *n* poissonnerie *f*; **~ slice** *n* pelle *f* à poisson; **~ sticks** (*US*) *npl* = **fish fingers**; **~y** (*inf*) *adj* suspect(e), louche

fist [fɪst] *n* poing *m*

fit [fɪt] *adj* (*healthy*) en (bonne) forme; (*proper*) convenable; approprié(e) ♦ *vt* (*subj: clothes*) aller à; (*put in, attach*) installer, poser; adapter; (*equip*) équiper, garnir, munir; (*suit*) convenir à ♦ *vi* (*clothes*) aller; (*parts*) s'adapter; (*in space, gap*) entrer, s'adapter ♦ *n* (*MED*) accès *m*, crise *f* (*of anger*) accès; (*of hysterics, jealousy*) crise; **~ to** en état de; **~ for** digne de; apte à; **~ of coughing** quinte *f* de toux; **a ~ of giggles** le fou rire; **this dress is a good ~** cette robe (me) va très bien; **by ~s and starts** par à-coups; **~ in** *vi* s'accorder; s'adapter; **~ful** *adj* (*sleep*) agité(e); **~ment** *n* meuble encastré, élément *m*; **~ness** *n*

(MED) forme *f* physique; ~**ted carpet** *n* moquette *f*; ~**ted kitchen** *(BRIT)* *n* cuisine équipée; ~**ter** *n* monteur *m*; ~**ting** *adj* approprié(e) ♦ *n (of dress)* essayage *m*; *(of piece of equipment)* pose *f*, installation *f*; ~**tings** *npl (in building)* installations *fpl*; ~**ting room** *n* cabine *f* d'essayage

five [faɪv] *num* cinq; ~**r** *(inf)* *n (BRIT)* billet *m* de cinq livres; *(US)* billet de cinq dollars

fix [fɪks] *vt (date, amount etc)* fixer; *(organize)* arranger; *(mend)* réparer; *(meal, drink)* préparer ♦ *n*: **to be in a** ~ être dans le pétrin; ~ **up** *vt (meeting)* arranger; **to** ~ **sb up with sth** faire avoir qch à qn; ~**ation** [fɪk'seɪʃən] *n (PSYCH)* fixation *f*; *(fig)* obsession *f*; ~**ed** *adj (prices etc)* fixe; *(smile)* figé(e); ~**ture** *n* installation *f* (fixe); *(SPORT)* rencontre *f* (au programme)

fizzy ['fɪzɪ] *adj* pétillant(e); gazeux(-euse)

flabbergasted ['flæbəgɑːstɪd] *adj* sidéré(e), ahuri(e)

flabby ['flæbɪ] *adj* mou (molle)

flag [flæg] *n* drapeau *m*; *(also:* ~**stone)** dalle *f* ♦ *vi* faiblir; fléchir; ~ **down** *vt* héler, faire signe (de s'arrêter) à; ~**pole** *n* mât *m*; ~**ship** *n* vaisseau *m* amiral; *(fig)* produit *m* vedette

flair [flɛəʳ] *n* flair *m*

flak [flæk] *n (MIL)* tir antiaérien; *(inf: criticism)* critiques *fpl*

flake [fleɪk] *n (of rust, paint)* écaille *f*; *(of snow, soap powder)* flocon *m* ♦ *vi (also:* ~ **off)** s'écailler

flamboyant [flæm'bɔɪənt] *adj* flamboyant(e), éclatant(e); *(person)* haut(e) en couleur

flame [fleɪm] *n* flamme *f*

flamingo [flə'mɪŋgəu] *n* flamant *m* (rose)

flammable ['flæməbl] *adj* inflammable

flan [flæn] *(BRIT)* *n* tarte *f*

flank [flæŋk] *n* flanc *m* ♦ *vt* flanquer

flannel ['flænl] *n (fabric)* flanelle *f*; *(BRIT: also:* **face** ~**)** gant *m* de toilette

flap [flæp] *n (of pocket, envelope)* rabat *m* ♦ *vt (wings)* battre (de) ♦ *vi (sail, flag)* claquer; *(inf: also:* **be in a** ~**)** paniquer

flare [flɛəʳ] *n (signal)* signal lumineux; *(in*

skirt etc) évasement *m*; ~ **up** *vi* s'embraser; *(fig: person)* se mettre en colère, s'emporter; *(: revolt etc)* éclater

flash [flæʃ] *n* éclair *m*; *(also:* **news** ~**)** flash *m* (d'information); *(PHOT)* flash ♦ *vt (light)* projeter; *(send: message)* câbler; *(look)* jeter; *(smile)* lancer ♦ *vi (light)* clignoter; **a** ~ **of lightning** un éclair; **in a** ~ en un clin d'œil; **to** ~ **one's headlights** faire un appel de phares; **to** ~ **by** *or* **past** *(person)* passer (devant) comme un éclair; ~**bulb** *n* ampoule *f* de flash; ~**cube** *n* cube-flash *m*; ~**light** *n* lampe *f* de poche; ~**y** *(pej)* *adj* tape-à-l'œil *inv*, tapageur(-euse)

flask [flɑːsk] *n* flacon *m*, bouteille *f*; *(also:* **vacuum** ~**)** thermos ® *m or f*

flat [flæt] *adj* plat(e); *(tyre)* dégonflé(e), à plat; *(beer)* éventé(e); *(denial)* catégorique; *(MUS)* bémol *inv*; *(: voice)* faux (fausse); *(fee, rate)* fixe ♦ *n (BRIT: apartment)* appartement *m*; *(AUT)* crevaison *f*; *(MUS)* bémol *m*; **to work** ~ **out** travailler d'arrache-pied; ~**ly** *adv* catégoriquement; ~**ten** *vt (also:* ~**ten out)** aplatir; *(crop)* coucher; *(building(s))* raser

flatter ['flætəʳ] *vt* flatter; ~**ing** *adj* flatteur(-euse); ~**y** *n* flatterie *f*

flaunt [flɔːnt] *vt* faire étalage de

flavour ['fleɪvəʳ] *(US* **flavor)** *n* goût *m*, saveur *f*; *(of ice cream etc)* parfum *m* ♦ *vt* parfumer; **vanilla-**~**ed** à l'arôme de vanille, à la vanille; ~**ing** *n* arôme *m*

flaw [flɔː] *n* défaut *m*; ~**less** *adj* sans défaut

flax [flæks] *n* lin *m*

flea [fliː] *n* puce *f*

fleck [flɛk] *n* tacheture *f*, moucheture *f*

flee [fliː] *(pt, pp* **fled)** *vt* fuir ♦ *vi* fuir, s'enfuir

fleece [fliːs] *n* toison *f* ♦ *vt (inf)* voler, filouter

fleet [fliːt] *n* flotte *f*; *(of lorries etc)* parc *m*, convoi *m*

fleeting ['fliːtɪŋ] *adj* fugace, fugitif(-ive); *(visit)* très bref (brève)

Flemish ['flemɪʃ] *adj* flamand(e)

flesh [fleʃ] *n* chair *f*; ~ **wound** *n* blessure

superficielle

flew [fluː] *pt of* **fly**

flex [fleks] *n* fil *m or* câble *m* électrique ♦ *vt* (*knee*) fléchir; (*muscles*) tendre; ~**ible** *adj* flexible

flick [flɪk] *n* petite tape; chiquenaude *f*; (*of duster*) petit coup ♦ *vt* donner un petit coup à; (*switch*) appuyer sur; ~ **through** *vt fus* feuilleter

flicker ['flɪkəʳ] *vi* (*light*) vaciller; **his eyelids ~ed** il a cillé

flier ['flaɪəʳ] *n* aviateur *m*

flight [flaɪt] *n* vol *m*; (*escape*) fuite *f*; (*also:* ~ **of steps**) escalier *m*; ~ **attendant** (*US*) *n* steward *m*, hôtesse *f* de l'air; ~ **deck** *n* (*AVIAT*) poste *m* de pilotage; (*NAUT*) pont *m* d'envol

flimsy ['flɪmzɪ] *adj* peu solide; (*clothes*) trop léger(-ère); (*excuse*) pauvre, mince

flinch [flɪntʃ] *vi* tressaillir; **to ~ from** se dérober à, reculer devant

fling [flɪŋ] (*pt, pp* **flung**) *vt* jeter, lancer

flint [flɪnt] *n* silex *m*; (*in lighter*) pierre *f* (à briquet)

flip [flɪp] *vt* (*throw*) lancer (d'une chiquenaude); **to ~ sth over** retourner qch

flippant ['flɪpənt] *adj* désinvolte, irrévérencieux(-euse)

flipper ['flɪpəʳ] *n* (*of seal etc*) nageoire *f*; (*for swimming*) palme *f*

flirt [fləːt] *vi* flirter ♦ *n* flirteur(-euse) *m/f*

float [fləut] *n* flotteur *m*; (*in procession*) char *m*; (*money*) réserve *f* ♦ *vi* flotter

flock [flɔk] *n* troupeau *m*; (*of birds*) vol *m*; (*REL*) ouailles *fpl* ♦ *vi*: **to ~ to** se rendre en masse à

flog [flɔg] *vt* fouetter

flood [flʌd] *n* inondation *f*; (*of letters, refugees etc*) flot *m* ♦ *vt* inonder ♦ *vi* (*people*): **to ~ into** envahir; ~**ing** *n* inondation *f*; ~**light** *n* projecteur *m*

floor [flɔːʳ] *n* sol *m*; (*storey*) étage *m*; (*of sea, valley*) fond *m* ♦ *vt* (*subj: question*) décontenancer; (: *blow*) terrasser; **on the ~** par terre; **ground ~**, (*US*) **first ~** rez-de-chaussée *m inv*; **first ~**, (*US*) **second ~** premier étage; ~**board** *n* planche *f* (du

plancher); ~ **show** *n* spectacle *m* de variétés

flop [flɔp] *n* fiasco *m* ♦ *vi* être un fiasco; (*fall: into chair*) s'affaler, s'effondrer; ~**py** *adj* lâche, flottant(e) ♦ *n* (*COMPUT: also:* ~**py disk**) disquette *f*

flora ['flɔːrə] *n* flore *f*

floral ['flɔːrl] *adj* (*dress*) à fleurs

florid ['flɔrɪd] *adj* (*complexion*) coloré(e); (*style*) plein(e) de fioritures

florist ['flɔrɪst] *n* fleuriste *m/f*; ~**'s (shop)** *n* magasin *m or* boutique *f* de fleuriste

flounder ['flaundəʳ] *vi* patauger ♦ *n* (*ZOOL*) flet *m*

flour ['flauəʳ] *n* farine *f*

flourish ['flʌrɪʃ] *vi* prospérer ♦ *n* (*gesture*) moulinet *m*

flout [flaut] *vt* se moquer de, faire fi de

flow [fləu] *n* (*ELEC, of river*) courant *m*; (*of blood in veins*) circulation *f*; (*of tide*) flux *m*; (*of orders, data*) flot *m* ♦ *vi* couler; (*traffic*) s'écouler; (*robes, hair*) flotter; **the ~ of traffic** l'écoulement *m* de la circulation; ~ **chart** *n* organigramme *m*

flower ['flauəʳ] *n* fleur *f* ♦ *vi* fleurir; ~ **bed** *n* plate-bande *f*; ~**pot** *n* pot *m* (de fleurs); ~**y** *adj* fleuri(e)

flown [fləun] *pp of* **fly**

flu [fluː] *n* grippe *f*

fluctuate ['flʌktjueɪt] *vi* varier, fluctuer

fluent ['fluːənt] *adj* (*speech*) coulant(e), aisé(e); **he speaks ~ French, he's ~ in French** il parle couramment le français

fluff [flʌf] *n* duvet *m*; (*on jacket, carpet*) peluche *f* ♦ ~**y** *adj* duveteux(-euse); (*toy*) en peluche

fluid ['fluːɪd] *adj* fluide ♦ *n* fluide *m*

fluke [fluːk] (*inf*) *n* (*luck*) coup *m* de veine

flung [flʌŋ] *pt, pp of* **fling**

fluoride ['fluəraɪd] *n* fluorure *f*; ~ **toothpaste** dentifrice *m* au fluor

flurry ['flʌrɪ] *n* (*of snow*) rafale *f*, bourrasque *f*; ~ **of activity/excitement** affairement *m*/excitation *f* soudain(e)

flush [flʌʃ] *n* (*on face*) rougeur *f*; (*fig: of youth, beauty etc*) éclat *m* ♦ *vt* nettoyer à grande eau ♦ *vi* rougir ♦ *adj:* ~ **with** au ras de, de niveau avec; **to ~ the toilet** tirer la chasse (d'eau); **~ed** *adj* (tout(e)) rouge

flustered ['flʌstəd] *adj* énervé(e)

flute [fluːt] *n* flûte *f*

flutter ['flʌtə'] *n* (*of panic, excitement*) agitation *f*; (*of wings*) battement *m* ♦ *vi* (*bird*) battre des ailes, voleter

flux [flʌks] *n*: **in a state of ~** fluctuant sans cesse

fly [flaɪ] (*pt* **flew**, *pp* **flown**) *n* (*insect*) mouche *f*; (*on trousers: also:* **flies**) braguette *f* ♦ *vt* piloter; (*passengers, cargo*) transporter (par avion); (*distances*) parcourir ♦ *vi* voler; (*passengers*) aller en avion; (*escape*) s'enfuir, fuir; (*flag*) se déployer; **~ away** *vi* (*bird, insect*) s'envoler; **~ off** *vi* = **fly away**; **~-drive** *n* formule *f* avion plus voiture; **~ing** *n* (*activity*) aviation *f*; (*action*) vol *m* ♦ *adj*: **a ~ing visit** une visite éclair; **with ~ing colours** haut la main; **~ing saucer** *n* soucoupe volante; **~ing start** *n*: **to get off to a ~ing start** prendre un excellent départ; **~over** (*BRIT*) *n* (*bridge*) saut-de-mouton *m*; **~sheet** *n* (*for tent*) double toit *m*

foal [fəʊl] *n* poulain *m*

foam [fəʊm] *n* écume *f*; (*on beer*) mousse *f*; (*also:* **~ rubber**) caoutchouc mousse *m* ♦ *vi* (*liquid*) écumer; (*soapy water*) mousser

fob [fɒb] *vt*: **to ~ sb off** se débarrasser de qn

focal point ['fəʊkl-] *n* (*fig*) point central

focus ['fəʊkəs] (*pl* **~es**) *n* foyer *m*; (*of interest*) centre *m* ♦ *vt* (*camera etc*) mettre au point ♦ *vi*: **to ~ (on)** (*with camera*) régler la mise au point (sur); (*person*) fixer son regard (sur); **out of/in ~** (*picture*) flou(e)/net(te); (*camera*) pas au point/au point

fodder ['fɒdə'] *n* fourrage *m*

foe [fəʊ] *n* ennemi *m*

fog [fɒg] *n* brouillard *m*; **~gy** *adj*: **it's ~gy** il y a du brouillard; **~ lamp** (*US* **fog light**) *n* (*AUT*) phare *m* antibrouillard

foil [fɔɪl] *vt* déjouer, contrecarrer ♦ *n* feuille *f* de métal; (*kitchen ~*) papier *m* alu(minium); (*complement*) repoussoir *f*

fold [fəʊld] *n* (*bend, crease*) pli *m*; (*AGR*) parc *m* à moutons; (*fig*) bercail *m* ♦ *vt* plier; (*arms*) croiser; **~ up** *vi* (*map, table etc*) se plier; (*business*) fermer boutique ♦ *vt* (*map, clothes*) plier; **~er** *n* (*for papers*) chemise *f*; (*: with hinges*) classeur *m*; (*COMPUT*) répertoire *m*; **~ing** *adj* (*chair, bed*) pliant(e)

foliage ['fəʊlɪdʒ] *n* feuillage *m*

folk [fəʊk] *npl* gens *mpl* ♦ *cpd* folklorique; **~s** (*inf*) *npl* (*parents*) parents *mpl*; **~lore** ['fəʊklɔː'] *n* folklore *m*; **~ song** *n* chanson *f* folklorique

follow ['fɒləʊ] *vt* suivre ♦ *vi* suivre; (*result*) s'ensuivre; **to ~ suit** (*fig*) faire de même; **~ up** *vt* (*letter, offer*) donner suite à; (*case*) suivre; **~er** *n* disciple *m/f*, partisan(e); **~ing** *adj* suivant(e) ♦ *n* partisans *mpl*, disciples *mpl*

folly ['fɒlɪ] *n* inconscience *f*; folie *f*

fond [fɒnd] *adj* (*memory, look*) tendre; (*hopes, dreams*) un peu fou (folle); **to be ~ of** aimer beaucoup

fondle ['fɒndl] *vt* caresser

font [fɒnt] *n* (*in church: for baptism*) fonts baptismaux; (*TYP*) fonte *f*

food [fuːd] *n* nourriture *f*; **~ mixer** *n* mixer *m*; **~ poisoning** *n* intoxication *f* alimentaire; **~ processor** *n* robot *m* de cuisine; **~stuffs** *npl* denrées *fpl* alimentaires

fool [fuːl] *n* idiot(e); (*CULIN*) mousse *f* de fruits ♦ *vt* berner, duper ♦ *vi* faire l'idiot *or* l'imbécile; **~hardy** *adj* téméraire, imprudent(e); **~ish** *adj* idiot(e), stupide; (*rash*) imprudent(e), insensé(e); **~proof** *adj* (*plan etc*) infaillible

foot [fʊt] (*pl* **feet**) *n* pied *m*; (*of animal*) patte *f*; (*measure*) pied (= 30,48 *cm*; *12 inches*) ♦ *vt* (*bill*) payer; **on ~** à pied; **~age** *n* (*CINEMA: length*) ≈ métrage *m*; (*: material*) séquences *fpl*; **~ball** *n* ballon *m* (de football); (*sport: BRIT*) football *m*, foot *m*; (*: US*) football américain; **~ball player** (*BRIT*) *n* (*also:* **~baller**) joueur *m* de football; **~brake** *n* frein *m* à pédale; **~bridge** *n* passerelle *f*; **~hills** *npl* contreforts *mpl*; **~hold** *n* prise *f* (de pied); **~ing**

n (*fig*) position *f*; **to lose one's ~ing** perdre pied; **~lights** *npl* rampe *f*; **~note** *n* note *f* (en bas de page); **~path** *n* sentier *m*; (*in street*) trottoir *m*; **~print** *n* trace *f* (de pas); **~step** *n* pas *m*; **~wear** *n* chaussure(s) *f(pl)*

---

football pools

i *Les* **football pools** - *ou plus familièrement les "pools" - consistent à parier sur les résultats des matches de football qui se jouent tous les samedis. L'expression consacrée en anglais est "to do the pools". Les parieurs envoient à l'avance les fiches qu'ils ont complétées à l'organisme qui gère les paris et ils attendent 17 h le samedi que les résultats soient annoncés. Les sommes gagnées se comptent parfois en milliers (ou même en millions) de livres sterling.*

KEYWORD

for [fɔːʳ] *prep* **1** (*indicating destination, intention, purpose*) pour; **the train for London** le train pour *or* (à destination) de Londres; **he went for the paper** il est allé chercher le journal; **it's time for lunch** c'est l'heure du déjeuner; **what's it for?** ça sert à quoi?; **what for?** (*why*) pourquoi?
2 (*on behalf of, representing*) pour; **the MP for Hove** le député de Hove; **to work for sb/sth** travailler pour qn/qch; **G for George** G comme Georges
3 (*because of*) pour; **for this reason** pour cette raison; **for fear of being criticized** de peur d'être critiqué
4 (*with regard to*) pour; **it's cold for July** il fait froid pour juillet; **a gift for languages** un don pour les langues
5 (*in exchange for*): **I sold it for £5** je l'ai vendu 5 livres; **to pay 50 pence for a ticket** payer un billet 50 pence
6 (*in favour of*) pour; **are you for or against us?** êtes-vous pour ou contre nous?

7 (*referring to distance*) pendant; sur; **there are roadworks for 5 km** il y a des travaux sur 5 km; **we walked for miles** nous avons marché pendant des kilomètres
8 (*referring to time*) pendant; depuis; pour; **he was away for 2 years** il a été absent pendant 2 ans; **she will be away for a month** elle sera absente (pendant) un mois; **I have known her for years** je la connais depuis des années; **can you do it for tomorrow?** est-ce que tu peux le faire pour demain?
9 (*with infinitive clauses*): **it is not for me to decide** ce n'est pas à moi de décider; **it would be best for you to leave** le mieux serait que vous partiez; **there is still time for you to do it** vous avez encore le temps de le faire; **for this to be possible …** pour que cela soit possible …
10 (*in spite of*): **for all his work/efforts** malgré tout son travail/tous ses efforts; **for all his complaints, he's very fond of her** il a beau se plaindre, il l'aime beaucoup
♦ *conj* (*since, as: rather formal*) car

forage ['fɔrɪdʒ] *vi* fourrager
foray ['fɔreɪ] *n* incursion *f*
forbid [fəˈbɪd] (*pt* **forbad(e)**, *pp* **forbidden**) *vt* défendre, interdire; **to ~ sb to do** défendre *or* interdire à qn de faire; **~ding** *adj* sévère, sombre
force [fɔːs] *n* force *f* ♦ *vt* forcer; (*push*) pousser (de force); **the F~s** *npl* (*MIL*) l'armée *f*; **in ~** en vigueur; **~-feed** *vt* nourrir de force; **~ful** *adj* énergique, volontaire; **forcibly** *adv* par la force, de force; (*express*) énergiquement
ford [fɔːd] *n* gué *m*
fore [fɔːʳ] *n*: **to come to the ~** se faire remarquer; **~arm** *n* avant-bras *m inv*; **~boding** *n* pressentiment *m* (néfaste); **~cast** (*irreg: like* **cast**) *n* prévision *f* ♦ *vt* prévoir; **~court** *n* (*of garage*) devant *m*; **~finger** *n* index *m*; **~front** *n*: **in the ~front of** au premier rang *or* plan de

foregone ['fɔːgɒn] *adj*: **it's a ~ conclusion** c'est couru d'avance

foreground ['fɔːgraund] *n* premier plan

forehead ['fɒrɪd] *n* front *m*

foreign ['fɒrɪn] *adj* étranger(-ère); (*trade*) extérieur(-e); **~er** n étranger(-ère); **~ exchange** *n* change *m*; F**~ Office** (*BRIT*) *n* ministère *m* des affaires étrangères; F**~ Secretary** (*BRIT*) *n* ministre *m* des affaires étrangères

fore: **~leg** *n* (*of cat, dog*) patte *f* de devant; (*of horse*) jambe antérieure; **~man** (*irreg*) *n* (*of factory, building site*) contremaître *m*, chef *m* d'équipe; **~most** *adj* le (la) plus en vue; premier(-ère) ♦ *adv*: **first and ~most** avant tout, tout d'abord

forensic [fə'rɛnsɪk] *adj*: **~ medicine** médecine légale; **~ scientist** médecin *m* légiste

fore: **~runner** *n* précurseur *m*; **~see** (*irreg: like* **see**) *vt* prévoir; **~seeable** *adj* prévisible; **~shadow** *vt* présager, annoncer, laisser prévoir; **~sight** *n* prévoyance *f*

forest ['fɒrɪst] *n* forêt *f*; **~ry** *n* sylviculture *f*

foretaste ['fɔːteɪst] *n* avant-goût *m*

foretell [fɔː'tɛl] (*irreg: like* **tell**) *vt* prédire

forever [fə'rɛvər] *adv* pour toujours; (*fig*) continuellement

foreword ['fɔːwəːd] *n* avant-propos *m inv*

forfeit ['fɔːfɪt] *vt* (*lose*) perdre

forgave [fə'geɪv] *pt of* **forgive**

forge [fɔːdʒ] *n* forge *f* ♦ *vt* (*signature*) contrefaire; (*wrought iron*) forger; **to ~ money** (*BRIT*) fabriquer de la fausse monnaie; **~ ahead** *vi* pousser de l'avant, prendre de l'avance; **~d** *adj* faux (fausse); **~r** *n* faussaire *m*; **~ry** *n* faux *m*, contrefaçon *f*

forget [fə'gɛt] (*pt* **forgot**, *pp* **forgotten**) *vt*, *vi* oublier; **~ful** *adj* distrait(e), étourdi(e); **~-me-not** *n* myosotis *m*

forgive [fə'gɪv] (*pt* **forgave**, *pp* **forgiven**) *vt* pardonner; **to ~ sb for sth/for doing sth** pardonner qch à qn/à qn de faire qch; **~ness** *n* pardon *m*

forgo [fɔː'gəʊ] (*pt* **forwent**, *pp* **forgone**) *vt* renoncer à

fork [fɔːk] *n* (*for eating*) fourchette *f*; (*for gardening*) fourche *f*; (*of roads*) bifurcation *f*; (*of railways*) embranchement *m* ♦ *vi* (*road*) bifurquer; **~ out** *vt* (*inf*) allonger; **~-lift truck** *n* chariot élévateur

forlorn [fə'lɔːn] *adj* (*deserted*) abandonné(e); (*attempt, hope*) désespéré(e)

form [fɔːm] *n* forme *f*; (*SCOL*) classe *f*; (*questionnaire*) formulaire *m* ♦ *vt* former; (*habit*) contracter; **in top ~** en pleine forme

formal ['fɔːməl] *adj* (*offer, receipt*) en bonne et due forme; (*person*) cérémonieux(-euse); (*dinner*) officiel(le); (*clothes*) de soirée; (*garden*) à la française; (*education*) à proprement parler; **~ly** *adv* officiellement; cérémonieusement

format ['fɔːmæt] *n* format *m* ♦ *vt* (*COMPUT*) formater

formation [fɔː'meɪʃən] *n* formation *f*

formative ['fɔːmətɪv] *adj*: **~ years** années *fpl* d'apprentissage or de formation

former ['fɔːmər] *adj* ancien(ne) (*before n*), précédent(e); **the ~ ... the latter** le premier ... le second, celui-là ... celui-ci; **~ly** *adv* autrefois

formidable ['fɔːmɪdəbl] *adj* redoutable

formula ['fɔːmjʊlə] (*pl* **~s** *or* **~e**) *n* formule *f*

forsake [fə'seɪk] (*pt* **forsook**, *pp* **forsaken**) *vt* abandonner

fort [fɔːt] *n* fort *m*

forte ['fɔːtɪ] *n* (point) fort *m*

forth [fɔːθ] *adv* en avant; **to go back and ~** aller et venir; **and so ~** et ainsi de suite; **~coming** *adj* (*event*) qui va avoir lieu prochainement; (*character*) ouvert(e), communicatif(-ive); (*available*) disponible; **~right** *adj* franc (franche), direct(e); **~with** *adv* sur-le-champ

fortify ['fɔːtɪfaɪ] *vt* fortifier

fortitude ['fɔːtɪtjuːd] *n* courage *m*

fortnight ['fɔːtnaɪt] (*BRIT*) *n* quinzaine *f*, quinze jours *mpl*; **~ly** (*BRIT*) *adj* bimensuel(le) ♦ *adv* tous les quinze jours

fortunate ['fɔːtʃənɪt] *adj* heureux(-euse); (*person*) chanceux(-euse); **it is ~ that** c'est une chance que; **~ly** *adv* heureusement

fortune ['fɔːtʃən] n chance f; (wealth) fortune f; ~-**teller** n diseuse f de bonne aventure

forty ['fɔːtɪ] num quarante

forward ['fɔːwəd] adj (ahead of schedule) en avance; (movement, position) en avant, vers l'avant; (not shy) direct(e); effronté(e) ♦ n (SPORT) avant m ♦ vt (letter) faire suivre; (parcel, goods) expédier; (fig) promouvoir, favoriser; ~(s) adv en avant; **to move ~** avancer

fossil ['fɔsl] n fossile m

foster ['fɔstər] vt encourager, favoriser; (child) élever (sans obligation d'adopter); ~ **child** n enfant adoptif(-ive)

fought [fɔːt] pt, pp of **fight**

foul [faul] adj (weather, smell, food) infect(e); (language) ordurier(-ère) ♦ n (SPORT) faute f ♦ vt (dirty) salir, encrasser; **he's got a ~ temper** il a un caractère de chien; ~ **play** n (LAW) acte criminel

found [faund] pt, pp of **find** ♦ vt (establish) fonder; ~**ation** [faun'deɪʃən] n (act) fondation f; (base) fondement m; (also: ~**ation cream**) fond m de teint; ~**ations** npl (of building) fondations fpl

founder ['faundər] n fondateur m ♦ vi couler, sombrer

foundry ['faundrɪ] n fonderie f

fountain ['fauntɪn] n fontaine f; ~ **pen** n stylo m (à encre)

four [fɔːr] num quatre; **on all ~s** à quatre pattes; ~-**poster** n (also: ~-**poster bed**) lit m à baldaquin; ~**teen** num quatorze; ~**th** num quatrième

fowl [faul] n volaille f

fox [fɔks] n renard m ♦ vt mystifier

foyer ['fɔɪeɪ] n (hotel) hall m; (THEATRE) foyer m

fraction ['frækʃən] n fraction f

fracture ['fræktʃər] n fracture f

fragile ['frædʒaɪl] adj fragile

fragment ['frægmənt] n fragment m

fragrant ['freɪgrənt] adj parfumé(e), odorant(e)

frail [freɪl] adj fragile, délicat(e)

frame [freɪm] n charpente f; (of picture, bi-

cycle) cadre m; (of door, window) encadrement m, chambranle m; (of spectacles: also: ~s) monture f ♦ vt encadrer; ~ **of mind** disposition f d'esprit; ~**work** n structure f

France [frɑːns] n France f

franchise ['fræntʃaɪz] n (POL) droit m de vote; (COMM) franchise f

frank [fræŋk] adj franc (franche) ♦ vt (letter) affranchir; ~**ly** adv franchement

frantic ['fræntɪk] adj (hectic) frénétique; (distraught) hors de soi

fraternity [frə'tɜːnɪtɪ] n (spirit) fraternité f; (club) communauté f, confrérie f

fraud [frɔːd] n supercherie f, fraude f, tromperie f; (person) imposteur m

fraught [frɔːt] adj: ~ **with** chargé(e) de, plein(e) de

fray [freɪ] vi s'effilocher

freak [friːk] n (also cpd) phénomène m, créature ou événement exceptionnel par sa rareté

freckle ['frɛkl] n tache f de rousseur

free [friː] adj libre; (gratis) gratuit(e) ♦ vt (prisoner etc) libérer; (jammed object or person) dégager; ~ **(of charge), for ~** gratuitement; ~**dom** n liberté f; F~**fone** ® n numéro vert; ~-**for-all** n mêlée générale; ~ **gift** n prime f; ~**hold** n propriété foncière libre; ~ **kick** n coup franc; ~**lance** adj indépendant(e); ~**ly** adv librement; (liberally) libéralement; F~**mason** n franc-maçon m; F~**post** ® n port payé; ~-**range** adj (hen, eggs) de ferme; ~ **trade** n libre-échange m; ~**way** (US) n autoroute f; ~ **will** n libre arbitre m; **of one's own ~ will** de son plein gré

freeze [friːz] (pt **froze**, pp **frozen**) vi geler ♦ vt geler; (food) congeler; (prices, salaries) bloquer, geler ♦ n gel m; (fig) blocage m; ~-**dried** adj lyophilisé(e); ~**r** n congélateur m; **freezing** adj: **freezing (cold)** (weather, water) glacial(e) ♦ n: **3 degrees below freezing** 3 degrés au-dessous de zéro; **freezing point** n point m de congélation

freight [freɪt] n (goods) fret m, cargaison f;

(*money charged*) fret, prix *m* du transport; ~ **train** *n* train *m* de marchandises

French [frentʃ] *adj* français(e) ♦ *n* (*LING*) français *m*; **the** ~ *npl* (*people*) les Français; ~ **bean** *n* haricot vert; ~ **fried potatoes** (*US* ~ **fries**) *npl* (pommes de terre *fpl*) frites *fpl*; ~ **horn** *n* (*MUS*) cor *m* (d'harmonie); ~ **kiss** *n* baiser profond; ~ **loaf** *n* baguette *f*; ~**man** (*irreg*) *n* Français *m*; ~ **window** *n* porte-fenêtre *f*; ~**woman** (*irreg*) *n* Française *f*

frenzy ['frenzɪ] *n* frénésie *f*

frequency ['friːkwənsɪ] *n* fréquence *f*

frequent [*adj* 'friːkwənt, *vb* frɪ'kwent] *adj* fréquent(e) ♦ *vt* fréquenter; ~**ly** *adv* fréquemment

fresh [freʃ] *adj* frais (fraîche); (*new*) nouveau (nouvelle); (*cheeky*) familier(-ère), culotté(e); ~**en** *vi* (*wind, air*) fraîchir; ~**en up** *vi* faire un brin de toilette; ~**er** (*BRIT*: *inf*) *n* (*SCOL*) bizuth *m*, étudiant(e) de 1ère année; ~**ly** *adv* nouvellement, récemment; ~**man** (*US*) (*irreg*) *n* = **fresher**; ~**ness** *n* fraîcheur *f*; ~**water** *adj* (*fish*) d'eau douce

fret [fret] *vi* s'agiter, se tracasser

friar ['fraɪər] *n* moine *m*, frère *m*

friction ['frɪkʃən] *n* friction *f*

Friday ['fraɪdɪ] *n* vendredi *m*

fridge [frɪdʒ] (*BRIT*) *n* frigo *m*, frigidaire ® *m*

fried [fraɪd] *adj* frit(e); ~ **egg** œuf *m* sur le plat

friend [frend] *n* ami(e); ~**ly** *adj* amical(e); gentil(le); (*place*) accueillant(e); **they were killed by** ~**ly fire** ils sont morts sous les tirs de leur propre camp; ~**ship** *n* amitié *f*

frieze [friːz] *n* frise *f*

fright [fraɪt] *n* peur *f*, effroi *m*; **to take** ~ prendre peur, s'effrayer; ~**en** *vt* effrayer, faire peur à; ~**ened** *adj*: **to be** ~**ened (of)** avoir peur (de); ~**ening** *adj* effrayant(e); ~**ful** *adj* affreux(-euse)

frigid ['frɪdʒɪd] *adj* frigide

frill [frɪl] *n* (*on dress*) volant *m*; (*on shirt*) jabot *m*

fringe [frɪndʒ] *n* (*BRIT*: *of hair*) frange *f*; (*edge*: *of forest etc*) bordure *f*; ~ **benefits** *npl* avantages sociaux *or* en nature

Frisbee ® ['frɪzbɪ] *n* Frisbee ® *m*

frisk [frɪsk] *vt* fouiller

fritter ['frɪtər] *n* beignet *m*; ~ **away** *vt* gaspiller

frivolous ['frɪvələs] *adj* frivole

frizzy ['frɪzɪ] *adj* crépu(e)

fro [frəu] *adv*: **to go to and** ~ aller et venir

frock [frɔk] *n* robe *f*

frog [frɔg] *n* grenouille *f*; ~**man** *n* homme-grenouille *m*

frolic ['frɔlɪk] *vi* folâtrer, batifoler

KEYWORD

from [frɔm] *prep* **1** (*indicating starting place, origin etc*) de; **where do you come from?**, **where are you from?** d'où venez-vous?; **from London to Paris** de Londres à Paris; **a letter from my sister** une lettre de ma sœur; **to drink from the bottle** boire à (même) la bouteille

2 (*indicating time*) (à partir) de; **from one o'clock to** *or* **until** *or* **till two** d'une heure à deux heures; **from January (on)** à partir de janvier

3 (*indicating distance*) de; **the hotel is one kilometre from the beach** l'hôtel est à un kilomètre de la plage

4 (*indicating price, number etc*) de; **the interest rate was increased from 9% to 10%** le taux d'intérêt est passé de 9 à 10%

5 (*indicating difference*) de; **he can't tell red from green** il ne peut pas distinguer le rouge du vert

6 (*because of, on the basis of*): **from what he says** d'après ce qu'il dit; **weak from hunger** affaibli par la faim

front [frʌnt] *n* (*of house, dress*) devant *m*; (*of coach, train*) avant *m*; (*promenade*: *also*: **sea** ~) bord *m* de mer; (*MIL, METEOROLOGY*) front *m*; (*fig*: *appearances*) contenance *f*, façade *f* ♦ *adj* de devant; (*seat*) avant *inv*; **in** ~ **(of)** devant; ~**age** *n* (*of building*) façade f; ~ **door** n porte f d'entrée; (of car) portière f avant; **~ier** ['frʌntɪə'] n frontière f; ~ **page** n première page; ~ **room** (BRIT) n pièce f de devant, salon m; ~**-wheel drive** n traction f avant

frost [frɒst] n gel m, gelée f; (also: **hoarfrost**) givre m; **~bite** n gelures fpl; **~ed** adj (glass) dépoli(e); **~y** adj (weather, welcome) glacial(e)

froth [frɒθ] n mousse f; écume f

frown [fraun] vi froncer les sourcils

froze [frəuz] pt of **freeze**

frozen ['frəuzn] pp of **freeze**

fruit [fru:t] n inv fruit m; **~erer** n fruitier m, marchand(e) de fruits; **~ful** adj (fig) fructueux(-euse); **~ion** [fru:'ɪʃən] n: **to come to ~ion** se réaliser; ~ **juice** n jus m de fruit; ~ **machine** (BRIT) n machine f à sous; ~ **salad** n salade f de fruits

frustrate [frʌs'treɪt] vt frustrer

fry [fraɪ] (pt, pp **fried**) vt (faire) frire; see also **small**; **~ing pan** n poêle f (à frire)

ft. abbr = **foot**; **feet**

fudge [fʌdʒ] n (CULIN) caramel m

fuel ['fjuəl] n (for heating) combustible m; (for propelling) carburant m; ~ **oil** n mazout m; ~ **tank** n (in vehicle) réservoir m

fugitive ['fju:dʒɪtɪv] n fugitif(-ive)

fulfil [ful'fɪl] (US **fulfill**) vt (function, condition) remplir; (order) exécuter; (wish, desire) satisfaire, réaliser; **~ment** (US **fulfillment**) n (of wishes etc) réalisation f; (feeling) contentement m

full [ful] adj plein(e); (details, information) complet(-ète); (skirt) ample, large ♦ adv: **to know ~ well that** savoir fort bien que; **I'm ~ (up)** j'ai bien mangé; **a ~ two hours** deux bonnes heures; **at ~ speed** à toute vitesse; **in ~** (reproduce, quote) intégralement; (write) en toutes lettres; ~ **employment** n plein emploi; **to pay in ~** tout payer; **~-length** adj (film) long métrage; (portrait, mirror) en pied; (coat) long(ue); ~ **moon** n pleine lune; **~-scale** adj (attack, war) complet(-ète), total(e); (model) grandeur nature inv; ~ **stop** n point m; **~-time** adj, adv (work) à plein temps; **~y**

adv entièrement, complètement; (at least) au moins; **~y licensed** (hotel, restaurant) autorisé(e) à vendre des boissons alcoolisées; **~y-fledged** adj (barrister etc) diplômé(e); (citizen, member) à part entière

fumble ['fʌmbl] vi: ~ **with** tripoter

fume [fju:m] vi rager; **~s** npl vapeurs fpl, émanations fpl, gaz mpl

fun [fʌn] n amusement m, divertissement m; **to have ~** s'amuser; **for ~** pour rire; **to make ~ of** se moquer de

function ['fʌŋkʃən] n fonction f; (social occasion) cérémonie f, soirée officielle ♦ vi fonctionner; **~al** adj fonctionnel(le)

fund [fʌnd] n caisse f, fonds m; (source, store) source f, mine f; **~s** npl (money) fonds mpl

fundamental [fʌndə'mentl] adj fondamental(e)

funeral ['fju:nərəl] n enterrement m, obsèques fpl; ~ **parlour** n entreprise f de pompes funèbres; ~ **service** n service m funèbre

funfair ['fʌnfeə'] (BRIT) n fête (foraine)

fungi ['fʌŋgaɪ] npl of **fungus**

fungus ['fʌŋgəs] (pl **fungi**) n champignon m; (mould) moisissure f

funnel ['fʌnl] n entonnoir m; (of ship) cheminée f

funny ['fʌnɪ] adj amusant(e), drôle; (strange) curieux(-euse), bizarre

fur [fə:'] n fourrure f; (BRIT: in kettle etc) (dépôt m de) tartre m

furious ['fjuərəs] adj furieux(-euse); (effort) acharné(e)

furlong ['fə:lɒŋ] n = 201,17 m

furnace ['fə:nɪs] n fourneau m

furnish ['fə:nɪʃ] vt meubler; (supply): **to ~ sb with sth** fournir qch à qn; **~ings** npl mobilier m, ameublement m

furniture ['fə:nɪtʃə'] n meubles mpl, mobilier m; **piece of ~** meuble m

furrow ['fʌrəu] n sillon m

furry ['fə:rɪ] adj (animal) à fourrure; (toy) en peluche

further ['fə:ðə'] adj (additional) supplémentaire, autre; nouveau (nouvelle) ♦ adv plus loin; (more) davantage; (moreover) de plus ♦ vt faire avancer or progresser, promouvoir; ~ education n enseignement m postscolaire; ~more adv de plus, en outre

furthest ['fɜːðɪst] superl of **far**

fury ['fjuərɪ] n fureur f

fuse [fjuːz] (US **fuze**) n fusible m; (for bomb etc) amorce f, détonateur m ♦ vt, vi (metal) fondre; **to ~ the lights** (BRIT) faire sauter les plombs; ~ **box** n boîte f à fusibles

fuss [fʌs] n (excitement) agitation f; (complaining) histoire(s) f(pl); **to make a ~** faire des histoires; **to make a ~ of sb** être aux petits soins pour qn; ~**y** adj (person) tatillon(ne), difficile; (dress, style) tarabiscoté(e)

future ['fjuːtʃər] adj futur(e) ♦ n avenir m; (LING) futur m; **in ~** à l'avenir

fuze [fjuːz] (US) n, vt, vi = **fuse**

fuzzy ['fʌzɪ] adj (PHOT) flou(e); (hair) crépu(e)

G, g

G [dʒiː] n (MUS) sol m

G7 n abbr (= Group of 7) le groupe des 7

gabble ['gæbl] vi bredouiller

gable ['geɪbl] n pignon m

gadget ['gædʒɪt] n gadget m

Gaelic ['geɪlɪk] adj gaélique ♦ n (LING) gaélique m

gag [gæg] n (on mouth) bâillon m; (joke) gag m ♦ vt bâillonner

gaiety ['geɪtɪ] n gaieté f

gain [geɪn] n (improvement) gain m; (profit) gain, profit m; (increase): ~ **(in)** augmentation f (de) ♦ vt gagner ♦ vi (watch) avancer; **to ~ 3 lbs (in weight)** prendre 3 livres; **to ~ on sb** (catch up) rattraper qn; **to ~ from/by** gagner de/à

gal. abbr = **gallon**

gale [geɪl] n coup m de vent

gallant ['gælənt] adj vaillant(e), brave; (towards ladies) galant

gall bladder ['gɔːl-] n vésicule f biliaire

gallery ['gælərɪ] n galerie f; (also: **art ~**) musée m; (: private) galerie

gallon ['gæln] n gallon m (BRIT = 4,5 l; US = 3,8 l)

gallop ['gæləp] n galop m ♦ vi galoper

gallows ['gæləuz] n potence f

gallstone ['gɔːlstəun] n calcul m biliaire

galore [gə'lɔːr] adv en abondance, à gogo

Gambia ['gæmbɪə] n: **(The) ~** la Gambie

gambit ['gæmbɪt] n (fig): **(opening) ~** manœuvre f stratégique

gamble ['gæmbl] n pari m, risque calculé ♦ vt, vi jouer; **to ~ on** (fig) miser sur; ~**r** n joueur m; **gambling** n jeu m

game [geɪm] n jeu m; (match) match m; (strategy, scheme) plan m; projet m; (HUNTING) gibier m ♦ adj (willing): **to be ~ (for)** être prêt(e) (à or pour); **big ~** gros gibier; ~**keeper** n garde-chasse m

gammon ['gæmən] n (bacon) quartier m de lard fumé; (ham) jambon fumé

gamut ['gæmət] n gamme f

gang [gæŋ] n bande f; (of workmen) équipe f; ~ **up** vi: **to ~ up on sb** se liguer contre qn; ~**ster** n gangster m; ~**way** ['gæŋweɪ] n passerelle f; (BRIT: of bus, plane) couloir central; (: in cinema) allée centrale

gaol [dʒeɪl] (BRIT) n = **jail**

gap [gæp] n trou m; (in time) intervalle m; (difference): ~ **between** écart m entre

gape [geɪp] vi (person) être or rester bouche bée; (hole, shirt) être ouvert(e); **gaping** adj (hole) béant(e)

garage ['gærɑːʒ] n garage m

garbage ['gɑːbɪdʒ] n (US: rubbish) ordures fpl, détritus mpl; (inf: nonsense) foutaises fpl; ~ **can** (US) n poubelle f, boîte f à ordures

garbled ['gɑːbld] adj (account, message) embrouillé(e)

garden ['gɑːdn] n jardin m; ~**s** npl jardin public; ~**er** n jardinier m; ~**ing** n jardinage m

gargle ['gɑːgl] vi se gargariser

garish ['gɛərɪʃ] adj criard(e), voyant(e); (light) cru(e)

garland ['gɑːlənd] n guirlande f; couronne

f

garlic ['gɑːlɪk] *n* ail *m*

garment ['gɑːmənt] *n* vêtement *m*

garrison ['gærɪsn] *n* garnison *f*

garter ['gɑːtər] *n* jarretière *f*; (*US*) jarretelle *f*

gas [gæs] *n* gaz *m*; (*US: gasoline*) essence *f* ♦ *vt* asphyxier; ~ **cooker** (*BRIT*) *n* cuisinière *f* à gaz; ~ **cylinder** *n* bouteille *f* de gaz; ~ **fire** (*BRIT*) *n* radiateur *m* à gaz

gash [gæʃ] *n* entaille *f*; (*on face*) balafre *f*

gasket ['gæskɪt] *n* (*AUT*) joint *m* de culasse

gas mask *n* masque *m* à gaz

gas meter *n* compteur *m* à gaz

gasoline ['gæsəliːn] (*US*) *n* essence *f*

gasp [gɑːsp] *vi* haleter

gas: ~ **ring** *n* brûleur *m*; ~ **station** (*US*) *n* station-service *f*; ~ **tap** *n* bouton *m* (de cuisinière à gaz); (*on pipe*) robinet *m* à gaz

gastric ['gæstrɪk] *adj* gastrique; ~ **flu** grippe *f* intestinale

gate [geɪt] *n* (*of garden*) portail *m*; (*of field*) barrière *f*; (*of building, at airport*) porte *f*

gateau ['gætəu] *n* (*pl* **~x**) (gros) gâteau *m* à la crème

gatecrash *vt* s'introduire sans invitation dans

gateway *n* porte *f*

gather ['gæðər] *vt* (*flowers, fruit*) cueillir; (*pick up*) ramasser; (*assemble*) rassembler, réunir; recueillir; (*understand*) comprendre; (*SEWING*) froncer ♦ *vi* (*assemble*) se rassembler; **to ~ speed** prendre de la vitesse; ~**ing** *n* rassemblement *m*

gaudy ['gɔːdɪ] *adj* voyant(e)

gauge [geɪdʒ] *n* (*instrument*) jauge *f* ♦ *vt* jauger

gaunt [gɔːnt] *adj* (*thin*) décharné(e); (*grim, desolate*) désolé(e)

gauntlet ['gɔːntlɪt] *n* (*glove*) gant *m*

gauze [gɔːz] *n* gaze *f*

gave [geɪv] *pt* of **give**

gay [geɪ] *adj* (*homosexual*) homosexuel(le); (*cheerful*) gai(e), réjoui(e); (*colour etc*) gai, vif (vive)

gaze [geɪz] *n* regard *m* fixe ♦ *vi*: **to ~ at** fixer du regard

gazump [gə'zʌmp] (*BRIT*) *vi* revenir sur une promesse de vente (*pour accepter une offre plus intéressante*)

GB *abbr* = **Great Britain**

GCE *n abbr* (*BRIT*) = **General Certificate of Education**

GCSE *n abbr* (*BRIT*) = **General Certificate of Secondary Education**

gear [gɪər] *n* matériel *m*, équipement *m*; attirail *m*; (*TECH*) engrenage *m*; (*AUT*) vitesse *f* ♦ *vt* (*fig: adapt*): **to ~ sth to** adapter qch à; **top** *or* (*US*) **high ~** quatrième (*or* cinquième) vitesse; **low ~** première vitesse; **in ~** en prise; ~ **box** *n* boîte *f* de vitesses; ~ **lever** (*US* **gear shift**) *n* levier *m* de vitesse

geese [giːs] *npl of* **goose**

gel [dʒel] *n* gel *m*

gem [dʒem] *n* pierre précieuse

Gemini ['dʒemɪnaɪ] *n* les Gémeaux *mpl*

gender ['dʒendər] *n* genre *m*

gene [dʒiːn] *n* gène *m*

general ['dʒenərl] *n* général *m* ♦ *adj* général(e); **in ~** en général; ~ **delivery** *n* poste restante; ~ **election** *n* élection(s) législative(s); ~ **knowledge** *n* connaissances générales; ~**ly** *adv* généralement; ~ **practitioner** *n* généraliste *m/f*

generate ['dʒenəreɪt] *vt* engendrer; (*electricity etc*) produire; **generation** *n* génération *f*; (*of electricity etc*) production *f*; **generator** *n* générateur *m*

generosity [dʒenə'rɔsɪtɪ] *n* générosité *f*

generous ['dʒenərəs] *adj* généreux(-euse); (*copious*) copieux(-euse)

genetic [dʒɪ'netɪk] *adj*: ~ **engineering** ingénierie *f* génétique; ~ **fingerprinting** système *m* d'empreinte génétique

genetics [dʒɪ'netɪks] *n* génétique *f*

Geneva [dʒɪ'niːvə] *n* Genève

genial ['dʒiːnɪəl] *adj* cordial(e), chaleureux(-euse)

genitals ['dʒenɪtlz] *npl* organes génitaux

genius ['dʒiːnɪəs] *n* génie *m*

genteel [dʒen'tiːl] *adj* de bon ton, distingué(e)

gentle ['dʒɛntl] *adj* doux (douce)
gentleman ['dʒɛntlmən] *n* monsieur *m*; (*well-bred man*) gentleman *m*
gently ['dʒɛntlɪ] *adv* doucement
gentry ['dʒɛntrɪ] *n inv*: **the ~** la petite noblesse
gents [dʒɛnts] *n* W.-C. *mpl* (pour hommes)
genuine ['dʒɛnjuɪn] *adj* véritable, authentique; (*person*) sincère
geographical [dʒɪə'græfɪkl] *adj* géographique
geography [dʒɪ'ɔgrəfɪ] *n* géographie *f*
geology [dʒɪ'ɔlədʒɪ] *n* géologie *f*
geometric(al) [dʒɪə'mɛtrɪk(l)] *adj* géométrique
geometry [dʒɪ'ɔmətrɪ] *n* géométrie *f*
geranium [dʒɪ'reɪnɪəm] *n* géranium *m*
geriatric [dʒɛrɪ'ætrɪk] *adj* gériatrique
germ [dʒə:m] *n* (*MED*) microbe *m*
German ['dʒə:mən] *adj* allemand(e) ♦ *n* Allemand(e); (*LING*) allemand *m*; ~ **measles** (*BRIT*) *n* rubéole *f*
Germany ['dʒə:mənɪ] *n* Allemagne *f*
gesture ['dʒɛstʃə'] *n* geste *m*

KEYWORD
---

get [gɛt] (*pt, pp* **got**, *pp* **gotten** (*US*)) *vi* 1 (*become, be*) devenir; **to get old/tired** devenir vieux/fatigué, vieillir/se fatiguer; **to get drunk** s'enivrer; **to get killed** se faire tuer; **when do I get paid?** quand est-ce que je serai payé?; **it's getting late** il se fait tard
2 (*go*): **to get to/from** aller à/de; **to get home** rentrer chez soi; **how did you get here?** comment es-tu arrivé ici?
3 (*begin*) commencer *or* se mettre à; **I'm getting to like him** je commence à l'apprécier; **let's get going** *or* **started** allons-y
4 (*modal aux vb*): **you've got to do it** il faut que vous le fassiez; **I've got to tell the police** je dois le dire à la police
♦ *vt* 1: **to get sth done** (*do*) faire qch; (*have done*) faire faire qch; **to get one's hair cut** se faire couper les cheveux; **to**

get sb to do sth faire faire qch à qn; **to get sb drunk** enivrer qn
2 (*obtain*: *money, permission, results*) obtenir, avoir; (*find*: *job, flat*) trouver; (*fetch*: *person, doctor, object*) aller chercher; **to get sth for sb** procurer qch à qn; **get me Mr Jones, please** (*on phone*) passez-moi Mr Jones, s'il vous plaît; **can I get you a drink?** est-ce que je peux vous servir à boire?
3 (*receive*: *present, letter*) recevoir, avoir; (*acquire*: *reputation*) avoir; (: *prize*) obtenir; **what did you get for your birthday?** qu'est-ce que tu as eu pour ton anniversaire?
4 (*catch*) prendre, saisir, attraper; (*hit*: *target etc*) atteindre; **to get sb by the arm/throat** prendre *or* saisir *or* attraper qn par le bras/à la gorge; **get him!** arrête-le!
5 (*take, move*) faire parvenir; **do you think we'll get it through the door?** on arrivera à le faire passer par la porte?; **I'll get you there somehow** je me débrouillerai pour t'y emmener
6 (*catch, take*: *plane, bus etc*) prendre
7 (*understand*) comprendre, saisir; (*hear*) entendre; **I've got it!** j'ai compris!, je saisis!; **I didn't get your name** je n'ai pas entendu votre nom
8 (*have, possess*): **to have got** avoir; **how many have you got?** vous en avez combien?
get about *vi* se déplacer; (*news*) se répandre
get along *vi* (*agree*) s'entendre; (*depart*) s'en aller; (*manage*) = **get by**
get at *vt fus* (*attack*) s'en prendre à; (*reach*) attraper, atteindre
get away *vi* partir, s'en aller; (*escape*) s'échapper
get away with *vt fus* en être quitte pour; se faire passer *or* pardonner
get back *vi* (*return*) rentrer ♦ *vt* récupérer, recouvrer
get by *vi* (*pass*) passer; (*manage*) se débrouiller
get down *vi, vt fus* descendre ♦ *vt* des-

cendre; (*depress*) déprimer
get down to *vt fus* (*work*) se mettre à
(faire)
get in *vi* rentrer; (*train*) arriver
get into *vt fus* entrer dans; (*car, train etc*)
monter dans; (*clothes*) mettre, enfiler, endosser; **to get into bed/a rage** se mettre
au lit/en colère
get off *vi* (*from train etc*) descendre; (*depart: person, car*) s'en aller; (*escape*) s'en tirer ♦ *vt* (*remove: clothes, stain*) enlever ♦ *vt
fus* (*train, bus*) descendre de
get on *vi* (*at exam etc*) se débrouiller;
(*agree*): **to get on (with)** s'entendre (avec)
♦ *vt fus* monter dans; (*horse*) monter sur
get out *vi* sortir; (*of vehicle*) descendre
♦ *vt* sortir
get out of *vt fus* sortir de; (*duty etc*)
échapper à, se soustraire à
get over *vt fus* (*illness*) se remettre de
get round *vt fus* contourner; (*fig: person*)
entortiller
get through *vi* (*TEL*) avoir la communication; **to get through to sb** atteindre qn
get together *vi* se réunir ♦ *vt* assembler
get up *vi* (*rise*) se lever ♦ *vt fus* monter
get up to *vt fus* (*reach*) arriver à; (*prank
etc*) faire

---

getaway ['gɛtəweɪ] *n*: **to make one's ~**
filer
geyser ['giːzəʳ] *n* (*GEO*) geyser *m*; (*BRIT:
water heater*) chauffe-eau *m inv*
Ghana ['gɑːnə] *n* Ghana *m*
ghastly ['gɑːstlɪ] *adj* atroce, horrible; (*pale*)
livide, blême
gherkin ['gəːkɪn] *n* cornichon *m*
ghetto blaster ['gɛtəu'blɑːstəʳ] *n* stéréo *f*
portable
ghost [gəust] *n* fantôme *m*, revenant *m*
giant ['dʒaɪənt] *n* géant(e) ♦ *adj* géant(e),
énorme
gibberish ['dʒɪbərɪʃ] *n* charabia *m*
giblets ['dʒɪblɪts] *npl* abats *mpl*
Gibraltar [dʒɪ'brɔːltəʳ] *n* Gibraltar *m*
giddy ['gɪdɪ] *adj* (*dizzy*): **to be** *or* **feel ~**
avoir le vertige

gift [gɪft] *n* cadeau *m*; (*donation, ability*) don
m; **~ed** *adj* doué(e); **~ shop** *n* boutique
f de cadeaux; **~ token** *n* chèque-cadeau
m
gigantic [dʒaɪ'gæntɪk] *adj* gigantesque
giggle ['gɪgl] *vi* pouffer (de rire), rire sotte-
ment
gill [dʒɪl] *n* (*measure*) = 0.25 pints (*BRIT* =
0.15 l, *US* = 0.12 l)
gills [gɪlz] *npl* (*of fish*) ouïes *fpl*, branchies
fpl
gilt [gɪlt] *adj* doré(e) ♦ *n* dorure *f*; **~-
edged** *adj* (*COMM*) de premier ordre
gimmick ['gɪmɪk] *n* truc *m*
gin [dʒɪn] *n* (*liquor*) gin *m*
ginger ['dʒɪndʒəʳ] *n* gingembre *m*; **~ ale**,
~ beer *n* boisson gazeuse au gingembre;
~bread *n* pain *m* d'épices
gingerly ['dʒɪndʒəlɪ] *adv* avec précaution
gipsy ['dʒɪpsɪ] *n* = **gypsy**
giraffe [dʒɪ'rɑːf] *n* girafe *f*
girder ['gəːdəʳ] *n* poutrelle *f*
girl [gəːl] *n* fille *f*, fillette *f*; (*young unmarried
woman*) jeune fille; (*daughter*) fille; **an
English ~** une jeune Anglaise; **~friend** *n*
(*of girl*) amie *f*; (*of boy*) petite amie; **~ish**
adj de petite *or* de jeune fille; (*for a boy*)
efféminé(e)
giro ['dʒaɪrəu] *n* (*bank ~*) virement *m* bancaire; (*post office ~*) mandat *m*; (*BRIT: welfare cheque*) mandat *m* d'allocation
chômage
gist [dʒɪst] *n* essentiel *m*
give [gɪv] (*pt* **gave**, *pp* **given**) *vt* donner
♦ *vi* (*break*) céder; (*stretch: fabric*) se
prêter; **to ~ sb sth**, **~ sth to sb** donner
qch à qn; **to ~ a cry/sigh** pousser un
cri/un soupir; **~ away** *vt* donner; (*~ free*)
faire cadeau de; (*betray*) donner, trahir;
(*disclose*) révéler; (*bride*) conduire à l'autel;
~ back *vt* rendre; **~ in** *vi* céder ♦ *vt* donner; **~ off** *vt* dégager; **~ out** *vt* distribuer;
annoncer; **~ up** *vi* renoncer ♦ *vt* renoncer
à; **to ~ up smoking** arrêter de fumer; **to
~ o.s. up** se rendre; **~ way** (*BRIT*) *vi* céder; (*AUT*) céder la priorité
glacier ['glæsɪəʳ] *n* glacier *m*

glad [glæd] *adj* content(e); ~**ly** *adv* volontiers

glamorous ['glæmərəs] *adj* (*person*) séduisant(e); (*job*) prestigieux(-euse)

glamour ['glæmər] *n* éclat *m*, prestige *m*

glance [glɑːns] *n* coup *m* d'œil ♦ *vi*: **to ~ at** jeter un coup d'œil à; **glancing** *adj* (*blow*) oblique

gland *n* glande *f*

glare [glɛər] *n* (*of anger*) regard furieux; (*of light*) lumière éblouissante; (*of publicity*) feux *mpl* ♦ *vi* briller d'un éclat aveuglant; **to ~ at** lancer un regard furieux à; **glaring** *adj* (*mistake*) criant(e), qui saute aux yeux

glass [glɑːs] *n* verre *m*; ~**es** *npl* (*spectacles*) lunettes *fpl*; ~**house** (BRIT) *n* (*for plants*) serre *f*; ~**ware** *n* verrerie *f*

glaze [gleɪz] *vt* (*door, window*) vitrer; (*pottery*) vernir ♦ *n* (*on pottery*) vernis *m*; ~**d** *adj* (*pottery*) verni(e); (*eyes*) vitreux(-euse)

glazier ['gleɪzɪər] *n* vitrier *m*

gleam [gliːm] *vi* luire, briller

glean [gliːn] *vt* (*information*) glaner

glee [gliː] *n* joie *f*

glib [glɪb] *adj* (*person*) qui a du bagou; (*response*) désinvolte, facile

glide [glaɪd] *vi* glisser; (AVIAT, birds) planer; ~**r** *n* (AVIAT) planeur *m*; **gliding** *n* (SPORT) vol *m* à voile

glimmer ['glɪmər] *n* lueur *f*

glimpse [glɪmps] *n* vision passagère, aperçu *m* ♦ *vt* entrevoir, apercevoir

glint [glɪnt] *vi* étinceler

glisten ['glɪsn] *vi* briller, luire

glitter ['glɪtər] *vi* scintiller, briller

gloat [gləut] *vi*: **to ~ (over)** jubiler (à propos de)

global ['gləubl] *adj* mondial(e); ~ **warming** réchauffement *m* de la planète

globe [gləub] *n* globe *m*

gloom [gluːm] *n* obscurité *f*; (*sadness*) tristesse *f*, mélancolie *f*; ~**y** *adj* sombre, triste, lugubre

glorious ['glɔːrɪəs] *adj* glorieux(-euse); splendide

glory ['glɔːrɪ] *n* gloire *f*; splendeur *f*

gloss [glɒs] *n* (*shine*) brillant *m*, vernis *m*; ~ **over** *vt fus* glisser sur

glossary ['glɒsərɪ] *n* glossaire *m*

glossy ['glɒsɪ] *adj* brillant(e); ~ **magazine** magazine *m* de luxe

glove [glʌv] *n* gant *m*; ~ **compartment** *n* (AUT) boîte *f* à gants, vide-poches *m inv*

glow [gləu] *vi* rougeoyer; (*face*) rayonner; (*eyes*) briller

glower ['glauər] *vi*: **to ~ (at)** lancer des regards mauvais (à)

glucose ['gluːkəus] *n* glucose *m*

glue [gluː] *n* colle *f* ♦ *vt* coller

glum [glʌm] *adj* sombre, morne

glut [glʌt] *n* surabondance *f*

glutton ['glʌtn] *n* glouton(ne); **a ~ for work** un bourreau de travail; **a ~ for punishment** un masochiste (*fig*)

GM *abbr* (= *genetically modified*) génétiquement modifié(e)

gnat [næt] *n* moucheron *m*

gnaw [nɔː] *vt* ronger

go [gəu] (*pt* **went**, *pp* **gone**, *pl* ~**es**) *vi* aller; (*depart*) partir, s'en aller; (*work*) marcher; (*break etc*) céder; (*be sold*): **to ~ for £10** se vendre 10 livres; (*fit, suit*): **to ~ with** aller avec; (*become*): **to ~ pale/mouldy** pâlir/moisir ♦ *n*: **to have a ~ (at)** essayer (de faire); **to be on the ~** être en mouvement; **whose ~ is it?** à qui est-ce de jouer?; **he's ~ing to do** il va faire, il est sur le point de faire; **to ~ for a walk** aller se promener; **to ~ dancing** aller danser; **how did it ~?** comment est-ce que ça s'est passé?; **to ~ round the back/by the shop** passer par derrière/devant le magasin; ~ **about** *vi* (*rumour*) se répandre ♦ *vt fus*: **how do I ~ about this?** comment dois-je m'y prendre (pour faire ceci)?; ~ **after** *vt fus* (*pursue*) poursuivre, courir après; (*job, record etc*) essayer d'obtenir; ~ **ahead** *vi* (*make progress*) avancer; (*get ~ing*) y aller; ~ **along** *vi* aller, avancer ♦ *vt fus* longer, parcourir; ~ **away** *vi* partir, s'en aller; ~ **back** *vi* rentrer; revenir; (~ *again*) retourner; ~ **back on** *vt fus* (*promise*) revenir sur; ~ **by** *vi* (*years, time*) passer, s'écouler ♦ vt fus s'en tenir à; en croire; ~ **down** vi descendre; (ship) couler; (sun) se coucher ♦ vt fus descendre; ~ **for** vt fus (fetch) aller chercher; (like) aimer; (attack) s'en prendre à, attaquer; ~ **in** vi entrer; ~ **in for** vt fus (competition) se présenter à; (like) aimer; ~ **into** vt fus entrer dans; (investigate) étudier, examiner; (embark on) se lancer dans; ~ **off** vi partir, s'en aller; (food) se gâter; (explode) sauter; (event) se dérouler ♦ vt fus ne plus aimer; **the gun went off** le coup est parti; ~ **on** vi continuer; (happen) se passer; **to ~ on doing** continuer à faire; ~ **out** vi sortir; (fire, light) s'éteindre; ~ **over** vt fus (check) revoir, vérifier; ~ **past** vt fus: **to ~ past sth** passer devant qch; ~ **round** vi (circulate: news, rumour) circuler; (revolve) tourner; (suffice) suffire (pour tout le monde); **to ~ round to sb's** (visit) passer chez qn; **to ~ round (by)** (make a detour) faire un détour (par); ~ **through** vt fus (town etc) traverser; ~ **up** vi monter; (price) augmenter ♦ vt fus gravir; ~ **with** vt fus (suit) aller avec; ~ **without** vt fus se passer de

goad [gəʊd] vt aiguillonner

go-ahead adj dynamique, entreprenant(e) ♦ n feu vert

goal [gəʊl] n but m; ~**keeper** n gardien m de but; ~**post** n poteau m de but

goat [gəʊt] n chèvre f

gobble [ˈgɔbl] vt (also: ~ **down**, ~ **up**) engloutir

go-between [ˈgəʊbɪtwiːn] n intermédiaire m/f

god [gɔd] n dieu m; G~ n Dieu m; ~**child** n filleul(e); ~**daughter** n filleule f; ~**dess** n déesse f; ~**father** n parrain m; ~**forsaken** adj maudit(e); ~**mother** n marraine f; ~**send** n aubaine f; ~**son** n filleul m

goggles [ˈgɔglz] npl (for skiing etc) lunettes protectrices

going [ˈgəʊɪŋ] n (conditions) état m du terrain ♦ adj: **the ~ rate** le tarif (en vigueur)

gold [gəʊld] n or m ♦ adj en or; (reserves) d'or; ~**en** adj (made of gold) en or; (gold in colour) doré(e); ~**fish** n poisson m rouge; ~-**plated** adj plaqué(e) or inv; ~**smith** n orfèvre m

golf [gɔlf] n golf m; ~ **ball** n balle f de golf; (on typewriter) boule m; ~ **club** n club m de golf; (stick) club m, crosse f de golf; ~ **course** n (terrain m de) golf m; ~**er** n joueur(-euse) de golf

gone [gɔn] pp of **go**

gong [gɔŋ] n gong m

good [gʊd] adj bon(ne); (kind) gentil(le); (child) sage ♦ n bien m; ~**s** npl (COMM) marchandises fpl, articles mpl; ~! bon!, très bien!; **to be ~ at** être bon en; **to be ~ for** être bon pour; **would you be ~ enough to ...?** auriez-vous la bonté or l'amabilité de ...?; **a ~ deal (of)** beaucoup (de); **a ~ many** beaucoup (de); **to make ~** vi (succeed) faire son chemin, réussir ♦ vt (deficit) combler; (losses) compenser; **it's no ~ complaining** cela ne sert à rien de se plaindre; **for ~** pour de bon, une fois pour toutes; ~ **morning/afternoon!** bonjour!; ~ **evening!** bonsoir!; ~ **night!** bonsoir!; (on going to bed) bonne nuit!; ~**bye** excl au revoir!; G~ **Friday** n Vendredi saint; ~-**looking** adj beau (belle), bien inv; ~-**natured** adj (person) qui a un bon naturel; ~**ness** n (of person) bonté f; **for ~ness sake!** je vous en prie!; ~**ness gracious!** mon Dieu!; ~**s train** (BRIT) n train m de marchandises; ~**will** n bonne volonté

goose [guːs] n (pl **geese**) oie f

gooseberry [ˈgʊzbərɪ] n groseille f à maquereau; **to play ~** (BRIT) tenir la chandelle

gooseflesh [ˈguːsfleʃ] n, **goose pimples** npl chair f de poule

gore [gɔːr] vt encorner ♦ n sang m

gorge [gɔːdʒ] n gorge f ♦ vt: **to ~ o.s. (on)** se gorger (de)

gorgeous [ˈgɔːdʒəs] adj splendide, superbe

gorilla [gəˈrɪlə] n gorille m

gorse [gɔːs] n ajoncs mpl

gory [ˈgɔːrɪ] adj sanglant(e); (details) horri-

ble
go-slow ['gəʊ'sləʊ] (BRIT) n grève perlée
gospel ['gɔspl] n évangile m
gossip ['gɔsɪp] n (chat) bavardages mpl; commérage m, cancans mpl; (person) commère f ♦ vi bavarder; (maliciously) cancaner, faire des commérages
got [gɔt] pt, pp of **get**; **~ten** (US) pp of **get**
gout [gaʊt] n goutte f
govern ['gʌvən] vt gouverner; **~ess** n gouvernante f; **~ment** n gouvernement m; (BRIT: ministers) ministère m; **~or** n (of state, bank) gouverneur m; (of school, hospital) ≈ membre m/f du conseil d'établissement; (BRIT: of prison) directeur(-trice)
gown [gaʊn] n robe f; (of teacher, BRIT: of judge) toge f
GP n abbr = **general practitioner**
grab [græb] vt saisir, empoigner ♦ vi: **to ~ at** essayer de saisir
grace [greɪs] n grâce f ♦ vt honorer; (adorn) orner; **5 days' ~** cinq jours de répit; **~ful** adj gracieux(-euse), élégant(e); **gracious** ['greɪʃəs] adj bienveillant(e)
grade [greɪd] n (COMM) qualité f; (in hierarchy) catégorie f, grade m, échelon m; (SCOL) note f; (US: school class) classe f ♦ vt classer; **~ crossing** (US) n passage m à niveau; **~ school** (US) n école f primaire
gradient ['greɪdɪənt] n inclinaison f, pente f
gradual ['grædjʊəl] adj graduel(le), progressif(-ive); **~ly** adv peu à peu, graduellement
graduate [n 'grædjuɪt, vb 'grædjueɪt] n diplômé(e), licencié(e); (US: of high school) bachelier(-ère) ♦ vi obtenir son diplôme; (US) obtenir son baccalauréat; **graduation** [grædju'eɪʃən] n (cérémonie f de) remise f des diplômes
graffiti [grə'fi:tɪ] npl graffiti mpl
graft [grɑ:ft] n (AGR, MED) greffe f; (bribery) corruption f ♦ vt greffer; **hard ~** (BRIT: inf) boulot acharné
grain [greɪn] n grain m
gram [græm] n gramme m
grammar ['græmər] n grammaire f; **~**

school (BRIT) n ≈ lycée m; **grammatical** [grə'mætɪkl] adj grammatical(e)
gramme [græm] n = **gram**
grand [grænd] adj magnifique, splendide; (gesture etc) noble; **~children** npl petits-enfants mpl; **~dad** (inf) n grand-papa m; **~daughter** n petite-fille f; **~father** n grand-père m; **~ma** (inf) n grand-maman f; **~mother** n grand-mère f; **~pa** (inf) n = **granddad**; **~parents** npl grands-parents mpl; **~ piano** n piano m à queue; **~son** n petit-fils m; **~stand** n (SPORT) tribune f
granite ['grænɪt] n granit m
granny ['grænɪ] (inf) n grand-maman f
grant [grɑ:nt] vt accorder; (admit) concéder ♦ n (SCOL) bourse f; (ADMIN) subside m, subvention f; **to take it for ~ed that** trouver tout naturel que +sub; **to take sb for ~ed** considérer qn comme faisant partie du décor
granulated sugar ['grænjuleɪtɪd-] n sucre m en poudre
grape [greɪp] n raisin m
grapefruit ['greɪpfru:t] n pamplemousse m
graph [grɑ:f] n graphique m; **~ic** ['græfɪk] adj graphique; (account, description) vivant(e); **~ics** n arts mpl graphiques; graphisme m ♦ npl représentations fpl graphiques
grapple ['græpl] vi: **to ~ with** être aux prises avec
grasp [grɑ:sp] vt saisir ♦ n (grip) prise f; (understanding) compréhension f, connaissance f; **~ing** adj cupide
grass [grɑ:s] n herbe f; (lawn) gazon m; **~hopper** n sauterelle f; **~-roots** adj de la base, du peuple
grate [greɪt] n grille f de cheminée ♦ vi grincer ♦ vt (CULIN) râper
grateful ['greɪtful] adj reconnaissant(e)
grater ['greɪtər] n râpe f
gratifying ['grætɪfaɪɪŋ] adj agréable
grating ['greɪtɪŋ] n (iron bars) grille f ♦ adj (noise) grinçant(e)
gratitude ['grætɪtju:d] n gratitude f
gratuity [grə'tju:ɪtɪ] n pourboire m
grave [greɪv] n tombe f ♦ adj grave,

sérieux(-euse)

gravel ['grævl] *n* gravier *m*

gravestone ['greɪvstəʊn] *n* pierre tombale

graveyard ['greɪvjɑːd] *n* cimetière *m*

gravity ['grævɪtɪ] *n* (*PHYSICS*) gravité *f*; pesanteur *f*; (*seriousness*) gravité

gravy ['greɪvɪ] *n* jus *m* (de viande); sauce *f*

gray [greɪ] (*US*) *adj* = **grey**

graze [greɪz] *vi* paître, brouter ♦ *vt* (*touch lightly*) frôler, effleurer; (*scrape*) écorcher ♦ *n* écorchure *f*

grease [griːs] *n* (*fat*) graisse *f*; (*lubricant*) lubrifiant *m* ♦ *vt* graisser; lubrifier; **~proof paper** (*BRIT*) *n* papier sulfurisé; **greasy** *adj* gras(se), graisseux(-euse)

great [greɪt] *adj* grand(e); (*inf*) formidable; **G~ Britain** *n* Grande-Bretagne *f*; **~-grandfather** *n* arrière-grand-père *m*; **~-grandmother** *n* arrière-grand-mère *f*; **~ly** *adv* très, grandement; (*with verbs*) beaucoup; **~ness** *n* grandeur *f*

Greece [griːs] *n* Grèce *f*

greed [griːd] *n* (*also*: **~iness**) avidité *f*; (*for food*) gourmandise *f*, gloutonnerie *f*; **~y** *adj* avide; gourmand(e), glouton(ne)

Greek [griːk] *adj* grec (grecque) ♦ *n* Grec (Grecque); (*LING*) grec *m*

green [griːn] *adj* vert(e); (*inexperienced*) (bien) jeune, naïf (naïve); (*POL*) vert(e), écologiste; (*ecological*) écologique ♦ *n* vert *m*; (*stretch of grass*) pelouse *f*; **~s** *npl* (*vegetables*) légumes verts; (*POL*): **the G~s** les Verts *mpl*; **the G~ Party** (*BRIT*: *POL*): le parti écologiste; **~ belt** *n* (*round town*) ceinture verte; **~ card** *n* (*AUT*) carte verte; (*US*) permis *m* de travail; **~ery** *n* verdure *f*; **~grocer's** (*BRIT*) *n* marchand *m* de fruits et légumes; **~house** *n* serre *f*; **~house effect** *n* effet *m* de serre; **~house gas** *n* gas *m* à effet de serre; **~ish** *adj* verdâtre

Greenland ['griːnlənd] *n* Groenland *m*

greet [griːt] *vt* accueillir; **~ing** *n* salutation *f*; **~ing(s) card** *n* carte *f* de vœux

gregarious [grə'gɛərɪəs] *adj* (*person*) sociable

grenade [grə'neɪd] *n* grenade *f*

grew [gruː] *pt of* **grow**

grey [greɪ] (*US* **gray**) *adj* gris(e); (*dismal*) sombre; **~-haired** *adj* grisonnant(e); **~hound** *n* lévrier *m*

grid [grɪd] *n* grille *f*, (*ELEC*) réseau *m*; **~lock** *n* (*traffic jam*) embouteillage *m*; **~locked** *adj*: **to be ~locked** (*roads*) être bloqué par un embouteillage; (*talks etc*) être suspendu

grief [griːf] *n* chagrin *m*, douleur *f*

grievance ['griːvəns] *n* doléance *f*, grief *m*

grieve [griːv] *vi* avoir du chagrin; se désoler ♦ *vt* faire de la peine à, affliger; **to ~ for sb** (*dead person*) pleurer qn; **grievous** *adj* (*LAW*): **grievous bodily harm** coups *mpl* et blessures *fpl*

grill [grɪl] *n* (*on cooker*) gril *m*; (*food*: *also* **mixed ~**) grillade(s) *f(pl)* ♦ *vt* (*BRIT*) griller; (*inf*: *question*) cuisiner

grille [grɪl] *n* grille *f*, grillage *m*; (*AUT*) calandre *f*

grim [grɪm] *adj* sinistre, lugubre; (*serious*, *stern*) sévère

grimace [grɪ'meɪs] *n* grimace *f* ♦ *vi* grimacer, faire une grimace

grime [graɪm] *n* crasse *f*, saleté *f*

grin [grɪn] *n* large sourire *m* ♦ *vi* sourire

grind [graɪnd] (*pt*, *pp* **ground**) *vt* écraser; (*coffee*, *pepper etc*) moudre; (*US*: *meat*) hacher; (*make sharp*) aiguiser ♦ *n* (*work*) corvée *f*

grip [grɪp] *n* (*hold*) prise *f*, étreinte *f*; (*control*) emprise *f*; (*grasp*) connaissance *f*; (*handle*) poignée *f*; (*holdall*) sac *m* de voyage ♦ *vt* saisir, empoigner; **to come to ~s with** en venir aux prises avec; **~ping** *adj* prenant(e), palpitant(e)

grisly ['grɪzlɪ] *adj* sinistre, macabre

gristle ['grɪsl] *n* cartilage *m*

grit [grɪt] *n* gravillon *m*; (*courage*) cran *m* ♦ *vt* (*road*) sabler; **to ~ one's teeth** serrer les dents

groan [grəʊn] *n* (*of pain*) gémissement *m* ♦ *vi* gémir

grocer ['grəʊsər] *n* épicier *m*; **~ies** *npl* provisions *fpl*; **~'s (shop)** *n* épicerie *f*

groin [grɔɪn] *n* aine *f*

groom [gruːm] *n* palefrenier *m*; (*also*:

bridegroom) marié *m* ♦ *vt* (*horse*) panser; (*fig*): **to ~ sb for** former qn pour; **well-~ed** très soigné(e)

groove [gru:v] *n* rainure *f*

grope [grəup] *vi*: **to ~ for** chercher à tâtons

gross [grəus] *adj* grossier(-ère); (*COMM*) brut(e); **~ly** *adv* (*greatly*) très, grandement

grotto ['grɔtəu] *n* grotte *f*

grotty ['grɔti] (*inf*) *adj* minable, affreux(-euse)

ground [graund] *pt*, *pp of* **grind** ♦ *n* sol *m*, terre *f*; (*land*) terrain *m*, terres *fpl*; (*SPORT*) terrain; (*US: also:* **~ wire**) terre; (*reason: gen pl*) raison *f* ♦ *vt* (*plane*) empêcher de décoller, retenir au sol; (*US: ELEC*) équiper d'une prise de terre; **~s** *npl* (*of coffee etc*) marc *m*; (*gardens etc*) parc *m*, domaine *m*; **on the ~, to the ~** par terre; **to gain/lose ~** gagner/perdre du terrain; **~ cloth** (*US*) *n* = **groundsheet**; **~ing** *n* (*in education*) connaissances *fpl* de base; **~less** *adj* sans fondement; **~sheet** (*BRIT*) *n* tapis *m* de sol; **~ staff** *n* personnel *m* au sol; **~work** *n* préparation *f*

group [gru:p] *n* groupe *m* ♦ *vt* (*also:* **~ together**) grouper ♦ *vi* se grouper

grouse [graus] *n inv* (*bird*) grouse *f* ♦ *vi* (*complain*) rouspéter, râler

grove [grəuv] *n* bosquet *m*

grovel ['grɔvl] *vi* (*fig*) ramper

grow [grəu] (*pt* **grew**, *pp* **grown**) *vi* pousser, croître; (*person*) grandir; (*increase*) augmenter, se développer; (*become*): **to ~ rich/weak** s'enrichir/s'affaiblir; (*develop*): **he's ~n out of his jacket** sa veste est (devenue) trop petite pour lui ♦ *vt* cultiver, faire pousser; (*beard*) laisser pousser; **he'll ~ out of it!** ça va lui passer!; **~ up** *vi* grandir; **~er** *n* producteur *m*; **~ing** *adj* (*fear, amount*) croissant(e), grandissant(e)

growl [graul] *vi* grogner

grown [grəun] *pp of* **grow**; **~-up** *n* adulte *m/f*, grande personne

growth [grəuθ] *n* croissance *f*, développement *m*; (*what has grown*) pousse *f*; pous-

sée *f*; (*MED*) grosseur *f*, tumeur *f*

grub [grʌb] *n* larve *f*; (*inf: food*) bouffe *f*

grubby ['grʌbi] *adj* crasseux(-euse)

grudge [grʌdʒ] *n* rancune *f* ♦ *vt*: **to ~ sb sth** (*in giving*) donner qch à qn à contre-cœur; (*resent*) reprocher qch à qn; **to bear sb a ~ (for)** garder rancune *or* en vouloir à qn (de)

gruelling ['gruəlɪŋ] (*US* **grueling**) *adj* exténuant(e)

gruesome ['gru:səm] *adj* horrible

gruff [grʌf] *adj* bourru(e)

grumble ['grʌmbl] *vi* rouspéter, ronchonner

grumpy ['grʌmpi] *adj* grincheux(-euse)

grunt [grʌnt] *vi* grogner

G-string ['dʒi:strɪŋ] *n* (*garment*) cache-sexe *m inv*

guarantee [gærən'ti:] *n* garantie *f* ♦ *vt* garantir

guard [gɑ:d] *n* garde *f*; (*one man*) garde *m*; (*BRIT: RAIL*) chef *m* de train; (*on machine*) dispositif *m* de sûreté; (*also:* **fireguard**) garde-feu *m* ♦ *vt* garder, surveiller; (*protect*): **to ~ (against** *or* **from)** protéger (contre); **~ against** *vt* (*prevent*) empêcher, se protéger de; **~ed** *adj* (*fig*) prudent(e); **~ian** *n* gardien(ne); (*of minor*) tuteur(-trice); **~'s van** (*BRIT*) *n* (*RAIL*) fourgon *m*

guerrilla [gə'rɪlə] *n* guérillero *m*

guess [gɛs] *vt* deviner; (*estimate*) évaluer; (*US*) croire, penser ♦ *vi* deviner ♦ *n* supposition *f*, hypothèse *f*; **to take** *or* **have a ~** essayer de deviner; **~work** *n* hypothèse *f*

guest [gɛst] *n* invité(e); (*in hotel*) client(e); **~-house** *n* pension *f*; **~ room** *n* chambre *f* d'amis

guffaw [gʌ'fɔ:] *vi* pouffer de rire

guidance ['gaɪdəns] *n* conseils *mpl*

guide [gaɪd] *n* (*person, book etc*) guide *m*; (*BRIT: also:* **girl ~**) guide *f* ♦ *vt* guider; **~book** *n* guide *m*; **~ dog** *n* chien *m* d'aveugle; **~lines** *npl* (*fig*) instructions (générales), conseils *mpl*

guild [gɪld] *n* corporation *f*; cercle *m*, association f

guillotine ['gɪləti:n] n guillotine f

guilt [gɪlt] n culpabilité f; ~y adj coupable

guinea pig ['gɪnɪ-] n cobaye m

guise [gaɪz] n aspect m, apparence f

guitar [gɪ'tɑ:r] n guitare f

gulf [gʌlf] n golfe m; (abyss) gouffre m

gull [gʌl] n mouette f; (larger) goéland m

gullible ['gʌlɪbl] adj crédule

gully ['gʌlɪ] n ravin m; ravine f; couloir m

gulp [gʌlp] vi avaler sa salive ♦ vt (also: ~ down) avaler

gum [gʌm] n (ANAT) gencive f; (glue) colle f; (sweet: also ~drop) boule f de gomme; (also: **chewing ~**) chewing-gum m ♦ vt coller; ~**boots** (BRIT) npl bottes fpl en caoutchouc

gun [gʌn] n (small) revolver m, pistolet m; (rifle) fusil m, carabine f; (cannon) canon m; ~**boat** n canonnière f; ~**fire** n fusillade f; ~**man** n bandit armé; ~**point** n: **at ~point** sous la menace du pistolet (or fusil); ~**powder** n poudre f à canon; ~**shot** n coup m de feu

gurgle ['gə:gl] vi gargouiller; (baby) gazouiller

gush [gʌʃ] vi jaillir; (fig) se répandre en effusions

gust [gʌst] n (of wind) rafale f; (of smoke) bouffée f

gusto ['gʌstəu] n enthousiasme m

gut [gʌt] n intestin m, boyau m; ~**s** npl (inf: courage) cran m

gutter ['gʌtər] n (in street) caniveau m; (of roof) gouttière f

guy [gaɪ] n (inf: man) type m; (also: ~**rope**) corde f; (BRIT: figure) effigie de Guy Fawkes (brûlée en plein air le 5 novembre)

Guy Fawkes' Night

i **Guy Fawkes' Night**, que l'on appelle également "bonfire night", commémore l'échec du complot (le "Gunpowder Plot") contre James Ist et son parlement le 5 novembre 1605. L'un des conspirateurs, Guy Fawkes, avait été surpris dans les caves du parlement alors qu'il s'apprêtait à y mettre le feu. Chaque année pour le 5 novembre, les enfants préparent à l'avance une effigie de Guy Fawkes et ils demandent aux passants "un penny pour le guy" avec lequel ils pourront s'acheter des fusées de feu d'artifice. Beaucoup de gens font encore un feu dans leur jardin sur lequel ils brûlent le "guy".

guzzle ['gʌzl] vt avaler gloutonnement

gym [dʒɪm] n (also: ~**nasium**) gymnase m; (also: ~**nastics**) gym f; ~**nast** n gymnaste m/f; ~**nastics** [dʒɪm'næstɪks] n, npl gymnastique f; ~ **shoes** npl chaussures fpl de gym; ~**slip** (BRIT) n tunique f (d'écolière)

gynaecologist [gaɪnɪ'kɒlədʒɪst] (US **gynecologist**) n gynécologue m/f

gypsy ['dʒɪpsɪ] n gitan(e), bohémien(ne)

H, h

haberdashery [hæbə'dæʃərɪ] (BRIT) n mercerie f

habit ['hæbɪt] n habitude f; (REL: costume) habit m; ~**ual** adj habituel(le); (drinker, liar) invétéré(e)

hack [hæk] vt hacher, tailler ♦ n (pej: writer) nègre m; ~**er** n (COMPUT) pirate m (informatique); (: enthusiast) passionné(e) m/f des ordinateurs

hackneyed ['hæknɪd] adj usé(e), rebattu(e)

had [hæd] pt, pp of **have**

haddock ['hædək] (pl ~ or ~**s**) n églefin m; **smoked ~** haddock m

hadn't ['hædnt] = **had not**

haemorrhage ['hemərɪdʒ] (US **hemorrhage**) n hémorragie f

haemorrhoids ['hemərɔɪdz] (US **hemorrhoids**) npl hémorroïdes fpl

haggle ['hægl] vi marchander

Hague [heɪg] n: **The ~** La Haye

hail [heɪl] *n* grêle *f* ♦ *vt* (*call*) héler; (*acclaim*) acclamer ♦ *vi* grêler; **~stone** *n* grêlon *m*

hair [hɛəʳ] *n* cheveux *mpl*; (*of animal*) pelage *m*; (*single ~: on head*) cheveu *m*; (: *on body; of animal*) poil *m*; **to do one's ~** se coiffer; **~brush** *n* brosse *f* à cheveux; **~cut** *n* coupe *f* (de cheveux); **~do** *n* coiffure *f*; **~dresser** *n* coiffeur(-euse); **~dresser's** *n* salon *m* de coiffure, coiffeur *m*; **~ dryer** *n* sèche-cheveux *m*; **~ gel** *n* gel *m* pour cheveux; **~grip** *n* pince *f* à cheveux; **~net** *n* filet *m* à cheveux; **~piece** *n* perruque *f*; **~pin** *n* épingle *f* à cheveux; **~pin bend** (*US* **hairpin curve**) *n* virage *m* en épingle à cheveux; **~-raising** *adj* à (vous) faire dresser les cheveux sur la tête; **~ removing cream** *n* crème *f* dépilatoire; **~ spray** *n* laque *f* (pour les cheveux); **~style** *n* coiffure *f*; **~y** *adj* poilu(e); (*inf: fig*) effrayant(e)

hake [heɪk] (*pl* **~** *or* **~s**) *n* colin *m*, merlu *m*

half [hɑːf] (*pl* **halves**) *n* moitié *f*; (*of beer: also: ~ pint*) ≃ demi *m*; (*RAIL, bus: also: ~ fare*) demi-tarif *m* ♦ *adj* demi(e) ♦ *adv* (à) moitié, à demi; **~ a dozen** une demi-douzaine; **~ a pound** une demi-livre, ≃ 250 g; **two and a ~** deux et demi; **to cut sth in ~** couper qch en deux; **~-caste** [ˈhɑːfkɑːst] *n* métis(se); **~-hearted** *adj* tiède, sans enthousiasme; **~-hour** *n* demi-heure *f*; **~-mast: at ~-mast** *adv* (*flag*) en berne; **~penny** (*BRIT*) *n* demi-penny *m*; **~-price** *adj, adv*: (**at**) **~-price** à moitié prix; **~ term** (*BRIT*) *n* (*SCOL*) congé *m* de demi-trimestre; **~-time** *n* mi-temps *f*; **~way** *adv* à mi-chemin

hall [hɔːl] *n* salle *f*; (*entrance way*) hall *m*, entrée *f*

hallmark [ˈhɔːlmɑːk] *n* poinçon *m*; (*fig*) marque *f*

hallo [həˈləu] *excl* = **hello**

hall of residence (*BRIT*) (*pl* **halls of residence**) *n* résidence *f* universitaire

Hallowe'en [ˈhæləuˈiːn] *n* veille *f* de la Toussaint

Hallowe'en

i Selon la tradition, **Hallowe'en** est la nuit des fantômes et des sorcières. En Écosse et aux États-Unis surtout (beaucoup moins en Angleterre) les enfants, pour fêter *Hallowe'en*, se déguisent ce soir-là et ils vont ainsi de porte en porte en demandant de petits cadeaux (du chocolat, une pomme etc).

---

hallucination [həluːsɪˈneɪʃən] *n* hallucination *f*

hallway [ˈhɔːlweɪ] *n* vestibule *m*

halo [ˈheɪləu] *n* (*of saint etc*) auréole *f*

halt [hɔːlt] *n* halte *f*, arrêt *m* ♦ *vt* (*progress etc*) interrompre ♦ *vi* faire halte, s'arrêter

halve [hɑːv] *vt* (*apple etc*) partager *or* diviser en deux; (*expense*) réduire de moitié; **~s** *npl of* **half**

ham [hæm] *n* jambon *m*

hamburger [ˈhæmbəːgəʳ] *n* hamburger *m*

hamlet [ˈhæmlɪt] *n* hameau *m*

hammer [ˈhæməʳ] *n* marteau *m* ♦ *vt* (*nail*) enfoncer; (*fig*) démolir ♦ *vi* (*on door*) frapper à coups redoublés; **to ~ an idea into sb** faire entrer de force une idée dans la tête de qn

hammock [ˈhæmək] *n* hamac *m*

hamper [ˈhæmpəʳ] *vt* gêner ♦ *n* panier *m* (d'osier)

hamster [ˈhæmstəʳ] *n* hamster *m*

hand [hænd] *n* main *f*; (*of clock*) aiguille *f*; (*~writing*) écriture *f*; (*worker*) ouvrier(-ère); (*at cards*) jeu *m* ♦ *vt* passer, donner; **to give *or* lend sb a ~** donner un coup de main à qn; **at ~** à portée de la main; **in ~** (*time*) à disposition; (*job, situation*) en main; **to be on ~** (*person*) être disponible; (*emergency services*) se tenir prêt(e) (à intervenir); **to ~** (*information etc*) sous la main, à portée de la main; **on the one ~ ..., on the other ~** d'une part ..., d'autre part; **~ in** *vt* remettre; **~ out** *vt* distribuer; **~ over** *vt* transmettre; céder; **~bag** *n* sac *m* à main; **~book** *n* manuel *m*; **~brake** *n* frein *m* à main; **~cuffs** *npl* menottes *fpl*;

~ful *n* poignée *f*

handicap ['hændɪkæp] *n* handicap *m* ♦ *vt* handicaper; **mentally/physically ~ped** handicapé(e) mentalement/physiquement

handicraft ['hændɪkrɑːft] *n* (*travail m* d')artisanat *m*, technique artisanale; (*object*) objet artisanal

handiwork ['hændɪwəːk] *n* ouvrage *m*

handkerchief ['hæŋkətʃɪf] *n* mouchoir *m*

handle ['hændl] *n* (*of door etc*) poignée *f*; (*of cup etc*) anse *f*; (*of knife etc*) manche *m*; (*of saucepan*) queue *f*; (*for winding*) manivelle *f* ♦ *vt* toucher, manier; (*deal with*) s'occuper de; (*treat: people*) prendre; **"~ with care"** "fragile"; **to fly off the ~** s'énerver; ~**bar(s)** *n(pl)* guidon *m*

hand: ~**-luggage** *n* bagages *mpl* à main; ~**made** *adj* fait(e) à la main; ~**out** *n* (*from government, parents*) aide *f*, don *m*; (*leaflet*) documentation *f*, prospectus *m*; (*summary of lecture*) polycopié *m*; ~**rail** *n* rampe *f*, main courante; ~**set** *n* (TEL) combiné *m*; **please replace the ~set** raccrochez s'il vous plaît; ~**shake** *n* poignée *f* de main

handsome ['hænsəm] *adj* beau (belle); (*profit, return*) considérable

handwriting ['hændraɪtɪŋ] *n* écriture *f*

handy ['hændɪ] *adj* (*person*) adroit(e); (*close at hand*) sous la main; (*convenient*) pratique

hang [hæŋ] (*pt, pp* **hung**) *vt* accrocher; (*criminal: pt, pp:* ~*ed*) pendre ♦ *vi* pendre; (*hair, drapery*) tomber; **to get the ~ of (doing) sth** (*inf*) attraper le coup pour faire qch; ~ **about** *vi* traîner; ~ **around** *vi* = **hang about**; ~ **on** *vi* (*wait*) attendre; ~ **up** *vi* (TEL): **to ~ up (on sb)** raccrocher (au nez de qn) ♦ *vt* (*coat, painting etc*) accrocher, suspendre

hangar ['hæŋər] *n* hangar *m*

hanger ['hæŋər] *n* cintre *m*, portemanteau *m*; ~**-on** *n* parasite *m*

hang: ~**-gliding** *n* deltaplane *m*, vol *m* libre; ~**over** *n* (*after drinking*) gueule *f* de bois; ~**-up** *n* complexe *m*

hanker ['hæŋkər] *vi*: **to ~ after** avoir envie de

hankie, hanky ['hæŋkɪ] *n abbr* = **handkerchief**

haphazard [hæpˈhæzəd] *adj* fait(e) au hasard, fait(e) au petit bonheur

happen ['hæpən] *vi* arriver; se passer, se produire; **it so ~s that** il se trouve que; **as it ~s** justement; ~**ing** *n* événement *m*

happily ['hæpɪlɪ] *adv* heureusement; (*cheerfully*) joyeusement

happiness ['hæpɪnɪs] *n* bonheur *m*

happy ['hæpɪ] *adj* heureux(-euse); ~ **with** (*arrangements etc*) satisfait(e) de; **to be ~ to do** faire volontiers; ~ **birthday!** bon anniversaire!; ~**-go-lucky** *adj* insouciant(e); ~ **hour** *n* heure pendant laquelle les consommations sont à prix réduit

harass ['hærəs] *vt* accabler, tourmenter; ~**ment** *n* tracasseries *fpl*

harbour ['hɑːbər] (US **harbor**) *n* port *m* ♦ *vt* héberger, abriter; (*hope, fear etc*) entretenir

hard [hɑːd] *adj* dur(e); (*question, problem*) difficile, dur(e); (*facts, evidence*) concret(-ète) ♦ *adv* (*work*) dur; (*think, try*) sérieusement; **to look ~ at** regarder fixement; (*thing*) regarder de près; **no ~ feelings!** sans rancune!; **to be ~ of hearing** être dur(e) d'oreille; **to be ~ done by** être traité(e) injustement; ~**back** *n* livre relié; ~ **cash** *n* espèces *fpl*; ~ **disk** *n* (COMPUT) disque dur; ~**en** *vt* durcir; (*fig*) endurcir ♦ *vi* durcir; ~**-headed** *adj* réaliste, décidé(e); ~ **labour** *n* travaux forcés

hardly ['hɑːdlɪ] *adv* (*scarcely, no sooner*) à peine; ~ **anywhere/ever** presque nulle part/jamais

hard: ~**ship** *n* épreuves *fpl*; ~ **shoulder** (BRIT) *n* (AUT) accotement stabilisé; ~ **up** (*inf*) *adj* fauché(e); ~**ware** *n* quincaillerie *f*; (COMPUT, MIL) matériel *m*; ~**ware shop** *n* quincaillerie *f*; ~**-wearing** *adj* solide; ~**-working** *adj* travailleur(-euse)

hardy ['hɑːdɪ] *adj* robuste; (*plant*) résistant(e) au gel

hare [hɛər] *n* lièvre *m*; ~**-brained** *adj* farfelu(e)

harm [hɑːm] *n* mal *m*; (*wrong*) tort *m* ♦ *vt* (*person*) faire du mal *or* du tort à; (*thing*) endommager; **out of ~'s way** à l'abri du danger, en lieu sûr; **~ful** *adj* nuisible; **~less** *adj* inoffensif(-ive); sans méchanceté

harmony ['hɑːmənɪ] *n* harmonie *f*

harness ['hɑːnɪs] *n* harnais *m*; (*safety ~*) harnais de sécurité ♦ *vt* (*horse*) harnacher; (*resources*) exploiter

harp [hɑːp] *n* harpe *f* ♦ *vi*: **to ~ on about** rabâcher

harrowing ['hærəʊɪŋ] *adj* déchirant(e), très pénible

harsh [hɑːʃ] *adj* (*hard*) dur(e); (*severe*) sévère; (*unpleasant: sound*) discordant(e); (: *light*) cru(e)

harvest ['hɑːvɪst] *n* (*of corn*) moisson *f*; (*of fruit*) récolte *f*; (*of grapes*) vendange *f* ♦ *vt* moissonner; récolter; vendanger

has [hæz] *vb see* **have**

hash [hæʃ] *n* (CULIN) hachis *m*; (*fig: mess*) gâchis *m*

hasn't ['hæznt] = **has not**

hassle ['hæsl] *n* (*inf: bother*) histoires *fpl*, tracas *mpl*

haste [heɪst] *n* hâte *f*; précipitation *f*; **~n** ['heɪsn] *vt* hâter, accélérer ♦ *vi* se hâter, s'empresser; **hastily** *adv* à la hâte; précipitamment; **hasty** *adj* hâtif(-ive); précipité(e)

hat [hæt] *n* chapeau *m*

hatch [hætʃ] *n* (NAUT: *also*: **~way**) écoutille *f*; (*also*: **service ~**) passe-plats *m inv* ♦ *vi* éclore; **~back** *n* (AUT) modèle *m* avec hayon arrière

hatchet ['hætʃɪt] *n* hachette *f*

hate [heɪt] *vt* haïr, détester ♦ *n* haine *f*; **~ful** *adj* odieux(-euse), détestable; **hatred** ['heɪtrɪd] *n* haine *f*

haughty ['hɔːtɪ] *adj* hautain(e), arrogant(e)

haul [hɔːl] *vt* traîner, tirer ♦ *n* (*of fish*) prise *f*; (*of stolen goods etc*) butin *m*; **~age** *n* transport routier; (*costs*) frais *mpl* de transport

haulier ['hɔːlɪə*] (US **hauler**) *n* (*company*) transporteur (routier); (*driver*) camionneur *m*

haunch [hɔːntʃ] *n* hanche *f*; (*of meat*) cuissot *m*

haunt [hɔːnt] *vt* (*subj: ghost, fear*) hanter; (: *person*) fréquenter ♦ *n* repaire *m*

KEYWORD

have [hæv] (*pt, pp* **had**) *aux vb* **1** (*gen*) avoir; être; **to have arrived/gone** être arrivé(e)/allé(e); **to have eaten/slept** avoir mangé/dormi; **he has been promoted** il a eu une promotion

2 (*in tag questions*): **you've done it, haven't you?** vous l'avez fait, n'est-ce pas?

3 (*in short answers and questions*): **no I haven't/yes we have!** mais non!/mais si!; **so I have!** ah oui!, oui c'est vrai!; **I've been there before, have you?** j'y suis déjà allé, et vous?

♦ *modal aux vb* (*be obliged*): **to have (got) to do sth** devoir faire qch; être obligé(e) de faire qch; **she has (got) to do it** elle doit le faire, il faut qu'elle le fasse; **you haven't to tell her** vous ne devez pas le lui dire

♦ *vt* **1** (*possess, obtain*) avoir; **he has (got) blue eyes/dark hair** il a les yeux bleus/ les cheveux bruns; **may I have your address?** puis-je avoir votre adresse?

2 (+*noun: take, hold etc*): **to have breakfast/a bath/a shower** prendre le petit déjeuner/un bain/une douche; **to have dinner/lunch** dîner/déjeuner; **to have a swim** nager; **to have a meeting** se réunir; **to have a party** organiser une fête

3: **to have sth done** faire faire qch; **to have one's hair cut** se faire couper les cheveux; **to have sb do sth** faire faire qch à qn

4 (*experience, suffer*) avoir; **to have a cold/flu** avoir un rhume/la grippe; **to have an operation** se faire opérer

5 (*inf: dupe*) avoir; **he's been had** il s'est fait avoir *or* rouler

have out *vt*: **to have it out with sb** (*set-*

tle a problem etc) s'expliquer (franchement) avec qn

haven ['heɪvn] *n* port *m*; (*fig*) havre *m*

haven't ['hævnt] = **have not**

havoc ['hævək] *n* ravages *mpl*

hawk [hɔːk] *n* faucon *m*

hay [heɪ] *n* foin *m*; ~ **fever** *n* rhume *m* des foins; **~stack** *n* meule *f* de foin

haywire (*inf*) *adj*: **to go ~** (*machine*) se détraquer; (*plans*) mal tourner

hazard ['hæzəd] *n* danger *m*, risque *m* ♦ *vt* risquer, hasarder; ~ (**warning**) **lights** *npl* (*AUT*) feux *mpl* de détresse

haze [heɪz] *n* brume *f*

hazelnut ['heɪzlnʌt] *n* noisette *f*

hazy ['heɪzɪ] *adj* brumeux(-euse); (*idea*) vague

he [hiː] *pron* il; **it is ~ who ...** c'est lui qui ...

head [hɛd] *n* tête *f*; (*leader*) chef *m*; (*of school*) directeur(-trice) ♦ *vt* (*list*) être en tête de; (*group*) être à la tête de; **~s** (**or tails**) pile (ou face); ~ **first** la tête la première; ~ **over heels in love** follement *or* éperdument amoureux(-euse); **to ~ a ball** faire une tête; **to ~ for** *vt fus* se diriger vers; **~ache** *n* mal *m* de tête; **~dress** (*BRIT*) *n* (*of Red Indian etc*) coiffure *f*; **~ing** *n* titre *m*; **~lamp** (*BRIT*) *n* = **headlight**; **~land** *n* promontoire *m*, cap *m*; **~light** *n* phare *m*; **~line** *n* titre *m*; **~long** *adv* (*fall*) la tête la première; (*rush*) tête baissée; **~master** *n* directeur *m*; **~mistress** *n* directrice *f*; ~ **office** *n* bureau central, siège *m*; **~-on** *adj* (*collision*) de plein fouet; (*confrontation*) en face à face; **~phones** *npl* casque *m* (à écouteurs); **~quarters** *npl* bureau *or* siège central; (*MIL*) quartier général; **~rest** *n* appui-tête *m*; **~room** *n* (*in car*) hauteur *f* de plafond; (*under bridge*) hauteur limite; **~scarf** *n* foulard *m*; **~strong** *adj* têtu(e), entêté(e); ~ **teacher** *n* directeur(-trice) *m* (*of secondary school*) proviseur *m*; ~ **waiter** *n* maître *m* d'hôtel; **~way** *n*: **to make ~way** avancer, faire des progrès; **~wind** *n* vent *m* contraire; (*NAUT*) vent debout; **~y**

adj capiteux(-euse); enivrant(e); (*experience*) grisant(e)

heal [hiːl] *vt, vi* guérir

health [hɛlθ] *n* santé *f*; ~ **food** *n* aliment(s) naturel(s); ~ **food shop** *n* magasin *m* diététique; **H~ Service** (*BRIT*) *n*: **the H~ Service** ≃ la Sécurité sociale; **~y** *adj* (*person*) en bonne santé; (*climate, food, attitude etc*) sain(e), bon(ne) pour la santé

heap [hiːp] *n* tas *m* ♦ *vt*: **to ~ (up)** entasser, amonceler; **she ~ed her plate with cakes** elle a chargé son assiette de gâteaux

hear [hɪəʳ] (*pt, pp* **heard**) *vt* entendre; (*news*) apprendre ♦ *vi* entendre; **to ~ about** entendre parler de; avoir des nouvelles de; **to ~ from sb** recevoir *or* avoir des nouvelles de qn; **~ing** *n* (*sense*) ouïe *f*; (*of witnesses*) audition *f*; (*of a case*) audience *f*; **~ing aid** *n* appareil *m* acoustique; **~say: by ~say** *adv* par ouï-dire *m*

hearse [həːs] *n* corbillard *m*

heart [hɑːt] *n* cœur *m*; **~s** *npl* (*CARDS*) cœur; **to lose/take ~** perdre/prendre courage; **at ~** au fond; **by ~** (*learn, know*) par cœur; ~ **attack** *n* crise *f* cardiaque; **~beat** *n* battement *m* du cœur; **~breaking** *adj* déchirant(e), qui fend le cœur; **~broken** *adj*: **to be ~broken** avoir beaucoup de chagrin *or* le cœur brisé; **~burn** *n* brûlures *fpl* d'estomac; ~ **failure** *n* arrêt *m* du cœur; **~felt** *adj* sincère

hearth [hɑːθ] *n* foyer *m*, cheminée *f*

heartily ['hɑːtɪlɪ] *adv* chaleureusement; (*laugh*) de bon cœur; (*eat*) de bon appétit; **to agree ~** être entièrement d'accord

hearty ['hɑːtɪ] *adj* chaleureux(-euse) (*appetite*) robuste; (*dislike*) cordial(e)

heat [hiːt] *n* chaleur *f*; (*fig*) feu *m*, agitation *f*; (*SPORT: also:* **qualifying ~**) éliminatoire *f* ♦ *vt* chauffer; ~ **up** *vi* (*water*) chauffer; (*room*) se réchauffer ♦ *vt* réchauffer; **~ed** *adj* chauffé(e); (*fig*) passionné(e), échauffé(e); **~er** *n* appareil *m* de chauffage; radiateur *m*; (*in car*) chauffage *m*; (*water heater*) chauffe-eau *m*

heath [hiːθ] (*BRIT*) *n* lande *f*

heather ['hɛðər] *n* bruyère *f*

heating ['hi:tɪŋ] *n* chauffage *m*

heatstroke ['hi:tstrəuk] *n* (*MED*) coup *m* de chaleur

heat wave *n* vague *f* de chaleur

heave [hi:v] *vt* soulever (avec effort); (*drag*) traîner ♦ *vi* se soulever; (*retch*) avoir un haut-le-cœur; **to ~ a sigh** pousser un soupir

heaven ['hɛvn] *n* ciel *m*, paradis *m*; (*fig*) paradis *m*; **~ly** *adj* céleste, divin(e)

heavily ['hɛvɪlɪ] *adv* lourdement; (*drink, smoke*) beaucoup; (*sleep, sigh*) profondément

heavy ['hɛvɪ] *adj* lourd(e); (*work, sea, rain, eater*) gros(se); (*snow*) beaucoup de; (*drinker, smoker*) grand(e); (*breathing*) bruyant(e); (*schedule, week*) chargé(e); **~ goods vehicle** *n* poids lourd; **~weight** *n* (*SPORT*) poids lourd

Hebrew ['hi:bru:] *adj* hébraïque ♦ *n* (*LING*) hébreu *m*

Hebrides ['hɛbrɪdi:z] *npl*: **the ~** les Hébrides *fpl*

heckle ['hɛkl] *vt* interpeller (*un orateur*)

hectic ['hɛktɪk] *adj* agité(e), trépidant(e)

he'd [hi:d] = **he would**; **he had**

hedge [hɛdʒ] *n* haie *f* ♦ *vi* se dérober; **to ~ one's bets** (*fig*) se couvrir

hedgehog ['hɛdʒhɔg] *n* hérisson *m*

heed [hi:d] *vt* (*also:* **take ~ of**) tenir compte de; **~less** *adj* insouciant(e)

heel [hi:l] *n* talon *m* ♦ *vt* retalonner

hefty ['hɛftɪ] *adj* (*person*) costaud(e); (*parcel*) lourd(e); (*profit*) gros(se)

heifer ['hɛfər] *n* génisse *f*

height [haɪt] *n* (*of person*) taille *f*, grandeur *f*; (*of object*) hauteur *f*; (*of plane, mountain*) altitude *f*; (*high ground*) hauteur *f*, éminence *f*; (*fig: of glory*) sommet *m*; (*: of luxury, stupidity*) comble *m*; **~en** *vt* (*fig*) augmenter

heir [ɛər] *n* héritier *m*; **~ess** *n* héritière *f*; **~loom** *n* héritage *m*, meuble *m* (*or* bijou *m or* tableau *m*) de famille

held [hɛld] *pt, pp of* **hold**

helicopter ['hɛlɪkɔptər] *n* hélicoptère *m*

hell [hɛl] *n* enfer *m*; **~!** (*inf!*) merde!

he'll [hi:l] = **he will**; **he shall**

hellish ['hɛlɪʃ] (*inf*) *adj* infernal(e)

hello [hə'ləu] *excl* bonjour!; (*to attract attention*) hé!; (*surprise*) tiens!

helm [hɛlm] *n* (*NAUT*) barre *f*

helmet ['hɛlmɪt] *n* casque *m*

help [hɛlp] *n* aide *f*; (*charwoman*) femme *f* de ménage ♦ *vt* aider; **~!** au secours!; **~ yourself** servez-vous; **he can't ~ it** il ne peut pas s'en empêcher; **~er** *n* aide *m/f*, assistant(e); **~ful** *adj* serviable, obligeant(e); (*useful*) utile; **~ing** *n* portion *f*; **~less** *adj* impuissant(e); (*defenceless*) faible

hem [hɛm] *n* ourlet *m* ♦ *vt* ourler; **~ in** *vt* cerner

hemorrhage ['hɛmərɪdʒ] (*US*) *n* = **haemorrhage**

hemorrhoids ['hɛmərɔɪdz] (*US*) *npl* = **haemorrhoids**

hen [hɛn] *n* poule *f*

hence [hɛns] *adv* (*therefore*) d'où, de là; **2 years ~** d'ici 2 ans, dans 2 ans; **~forth** *adv* dorénavant

her [hə:r] *pron* (*direct*) la, l'; (*indirect*) lui; (*stressed, after prep*) elle ♦ *adj* son (sa), ses *pl*; *see also* **me**; **my**

herald ['hɛrəld] *n* héraut *m* ♦ *vt* annoncer; **~ry** *n* (*study*) héraldique *f*; (*coat of arms*) blason *m*

herb [hə:b] *n* herbe *f*

herd [hə:d] *n* troupeau *m*

here [hɪər] *adv* ici; (*time*) alors ♦ *excl* tiens!, tenez!; **~!** présent!; **~ is, ~ are** voici; **~ he/she is!** le/la voici!; **~after** *adv* après, plus tard; **~by** *adv* (*formal: in letter*) par la présente

hereditary [hɪ'rɛdɪtrɪ] *adj* héréditaire

heresy ['hɛrəsɪ] *n* hérésie *f*

heritage ['hɛrɪtɪdʒ] *n* (*of country*) patrimoine *m*

hermit ['hə:mɪt] *n* ermite *m*

hernia ['hə:nɪə] *n* hernie *f*

hero ['hɪərəu] (*pl* **~es**) *n* héros *m*

heroin ['hɛrəuɪn] *n* héroïne *f*

heroine ['hɛrəuɪn] *n* héroïne *f*

heron ['hɛrən] n héron m

herring ['hɛrɪŋ] n hareng m

hers [hɜːz] pron le (la) sien(ne), les siens (siennes); see also **mine¹**

herself [hɜː'sɛlf] pron (reflexive) se; (emphatic) elle-même; (after prep) elle; see also **oneself**

he's [hiːz] = **he is; he has**

hesitant ['hɛzɪtənt] adj hésitant(e), indécis(e)

hesitate ['hɛzɪteɪt] vi hésiter; **hesitation** [hɛzɪ'teɪʃən] n hésitation f

heterosexual ['hɛtərəʊ'sɛksjʊəl] adj, n hétérosexuel(le)

heyday ['heɪdeɪ] n: **the ~ of** l'âge m d'or de, les beaux jours de

HGV n abbr = **heavy goods vehicle**

hi [haɪ] excl salut!; (to attract attention) hé!

hiatus [haɪ'eɪtəs] n (gap) lacune f; (interruption) pause f

hibernate ['haɪbəneɪt] vi hiberner

hiccough, hiccup ['hɪkʌp] vi hoqueter; **~s** npl hoquet m

hide [haɪd] (pt **hid**, pp **hidden**) n (skin) peau f ♦ vt cacher ♦ vi: **to ~ (from sb)** se cacher (de qn); **~-and-seek** n cachecache m

hideous ['hɪdɪəs] adj hideux(-euse)

hiding ['haɪdɪŋ] n (beating) correction f, volée f de coups; **to be in ~** (concealed) se tenir caché(e)

hierarchy ['haɪərɑːkɪ] n hiérarchie f

hi-fi ['haɪfaɪ] n hi-fi f inv ♦ adj hi-fi inv

high [haɪ] adj haut(e); (speed, respect, number) grand(e); (price) élevé(e); (wind) fort(e), violent(e); (voice) aigu (aiguë) ♦ adv haut; **20 m ~** haut(e) de 20 m; **~brow** adj, n intellectuel(le); **~chair** n (child's) chaise haute; **~er education** n études supérieures; **~-handed** adj très autoritaire; très cavalier(-ère); **~-heeled** adj à hauts talons; **~ jump** n (SPORT) saut m en hauteur; **~lands** npl Highlands mpl; **~light** n (fig: of event) point culminant ♦ vt faire ressortir, souligner; **~lights** npl (in hair) reflets mpl; **~ly** adv très, fort, hautement; **to speak/think ~ly of sb**

dire/penser beaucoup de bien de qn; **~ly paid** adj très bien payé(e); **~ly strung** adj nerveux(-euse), toujours tendu(e); **~ness** n: **Her** (or **His**) **H~ness** Son Altesse f; **~-pitched** adj aigu (aiguë); **~-rise** adj: **~-rise block, ~-rise flats** tour f (d'habitation); **~ school** n lycée m; (US) établissement m d'enseignement supérieur; **~ season** (BRIT) n haute saison; **~ street** (BRIT) n grand-rue f; **~way** n route nationale; **H~way Code** (BRIT) n code m de la route

hijack ['haɪdʒæk] vt (plane) détourner; **~er** n pirate m de l'air

hike [haɪk] vi aller or faire des excursions à pied ♦ n excursion f à pied, randonnée f; **~r** n promeneur(-euse), excursionniste m/f; **hiking** n excursions fpl à pied

hilarious [hɪ'lɛərɪəs] adj (account, event) désopilant(e)

hill [hɪl] n colline f; (fairly high) montagne f; (on road) côte f; **~side** n (flanc m de) coteau m; **~-walking** n randonnée f de basse montagne; **~y** adj vallonné(e); montagneux(-euse)

hilt [hɪlt] n (of sword) garde f; **to the ~** (fig: support) à fond

him [hɪm] pron (direct) le, l'; (stressed, indirect, after prep) lui; see also **me**; **~self** pron (reflexive) se; (emphatic) lui-même; (after prep) lui; see also **oneself**

hinder ['hɪndər] vt gêner; (delay) retarder; **hindrance** n gêne f, obstacle m

hindsight ['haɪndsaɪt] n: **with ~** avec du recul, rétrospectivement

Hindu ['hɪnduː] adj hindou(e)

hinge [hɪndʒ] n charnière f ♦ vi (fig): **to ~ on** dépendre de

hint [hɪnt] n allusion f; (advice) conseil m ♦ vt: **to ~ that** insinuer que ♦ vi: **to ~ at** faire une allusion à

hip [hɪp] n hanche f

hippie ['hɪpɪ] n hippie m/f

hippo ['hɪpəʊ] (pl **~s**), **hippopotamus** [hɪpə'pɒtəməs] (pl **~potamuses** or **~potami**) n hippopotame m

hire ['haɪər] vt (BRIT: car, equipment) louer;

(*worker*) embaucher, engager ♦ *n* location *f*; **for ~** à louer; (*taxi*) libre; **~(d) car** *n* voiture *f* de location; **~ purchase** (*BRIT*) *n* achat *m* (*or* vente *f*) à tempérament *or* crédit

his [hɪz] *pron* le (la) sien(ne), les siens (siennes) ♦ *adj* son (sa), ses *pl*; *see also* **my; mine**[1]

hiss [hɪs] *vi* siffler

historic [hɪ'stɔrɪk] *adj* historique; **~al** *adj* historique

history ['hɪstərɪ] *n* histoire *f*

hit [hɪt] (*pt*, *pp* **hit**) *vt* frapper; (*reach: target*) atteindre, toucher; (*collide with: car*) entrer en collision avec, heurter; (*fig: affect*) toucher ♦ *n* coup *m*; (*success*) succès *m*; (*: song*) tube *m*; **to ~ it off with sb** bien s'entendre avec qn; **~-and-run driver** *n* chauffard *m* (coupable du délit de fuite)

hitch [hɪtʃ] *vt* (*fasten*) accrocher, attacher; (*also*: **~ up**) remonter d'une saccade ♦ *n* (*difficulty*) anicroche *f*, contretemps *m*; **to ~ a lift** faire du stop; **~hike** *vi* faire de l'auto-stop; **~hiker** *n* auto-stoppeur(-euse)

hi-tech ['haɪ'tɛk] *adj* de pointe

hitherto [hɪðə'tuː] *adv* jusqu'ici

hit man *n* tueur *m* à gages

HIV *n*: **~-negative/-positive** *adj* séronégatif(-ive)/-positif(-ive)

hive [haɪv] *n* ruche *f*

HMS *abbr* = **Her/His Majesty's Ship**

hoard [hɔːd] *n* (*of food*) provisions *fpl*, réserves *fpl*; (*of money*) trésor *m* ♦ *vt* amasser; **~ing** (*BRIT*) *n* (*for posters*) panneau *m* d'affichage *or* publicitaire

hoarse [hɔːs] *adj* enroué(e)

hoax [həuks] *n* canular *m*

hob [hɔb] *n* plaque (chauffante)

hobble ['hɔbl] *vi* boitiller

hobby ['hɔbɪ] *n* passe-temps favori

hobo ['həubəu] (*US*) *n* vagabond *m*

hockey ['hɔkɪ] *n* hockey *m*

hog [hɔg] *n* porc (châtré) ♦ *vt* (*fig*) accaparer; **to go the whole ~** aller jusqu'au bout

hoist [hɔɪst] *n* (*apparatus*) palan *m* ♦ *vt* hisser

hold [həuld] (*pt*, *pp* **held**) *vt* tenir; (*contain*) contenir; (*believe*) considérer; (*possess*) avoir; (*detain*) détenir ♦ *vi* (*withstand pressure*) tenir (bon); (*be valid*) valoir ♦ *n* (*also fig*) prise *f*; (*NAUT*) cale *f*; **~ the line!** (*TEL*) ne quittez pas!; **to ~ one's own** (*fig*) (bien) se défendre; **to catch** *or* **get (a) ~ of** saisir; **to get ~ of** (*fig*) trouver; **~ back** *vt* retenir; (*secret*) taire; **~ down** *vt* (*person*) maintenir à terre; (*job*) occuper; **~ off** *vt* tenir à distance; **~ on** *vi* tenir bon; (*wait*) attendre; **~ on!** (*TEL*) ne quittez pas!; **~ on to** *vt fus* se cramponner à; (*keep*) conserver; **~ out** *vt* offrir ♦ *vi* (*resist*) tenir bon; **~ up** *vt* (*raise*) lever; (*support*) soutenir; (*delay*) retarder; (*rob*) braquer; **~all** (*BRIT*) *n* fourre-tout *m inv*; **~er** *n* (*of ticket, record*) détenteur(-trice); (*of office, title etc*) titulaire *m/f*; (*container*) support *m*; **~ing** *n* (*share*) intérêts *mpl*; (*farm*) ferme *f*; **~-up** *n* (*robbery*) hold-up *m*; (*delay*) retard *m*; (*BRIT: in traffic*) bouchon *m*

hole [həul] *n* trou *m*; **~-in-the-wall** *n* (*cash dispenser*) distributeur *m* de billets

holiday ['hɔlɪdeɪ] *n* vacances *fpl*; (*day off*) jour *m* de congé; (*public*) jour férié; **on ~** en congé; **~ camp** *n* (*also*: **~ centre**) camp *m* de vacances; **~-maker** (*BRIT*) *n* vacancier(-ère); **~ resort** *n* centre *m* de villégiature *or* de vacances

Holland ['hɔlənd] *n* Hollande *f*

hollow ['hɔləu] *adj* creux(-euse) ♦ *n* creux *m* ♦ *vt*: **to ~ out** creuser, évider

holly ['hɔlɪ] *n* houx *m*

holocaust ['hɔləkɔːst] *n* holocauste *m*

holster ['həulstə*] *n* étui *m* de revolver

holy ['həulɪ] *adj* saint(e); (*bread, water*) bénit(e); (*ground*) sacré(e); **H~ Ghost** *n* Saint-Esprit *m*

homage ['hɔmɪdʒ] *n* hommage *m*; **to pay ~ to** rendre hommage à

home [həum] *n* foyer *m*, maison *f*; (*country*) pays natal, patrie *f*; (*institution*) maison ♦ *adj* de famille; (*ECON, POL*) national(e), intérieur(e); (SPORT: game) sur leur (or notre) terrain; (team) qui reçoit ♦ adv chez soi, à la maison; au pays natal; (right in: nail etc) à fond; **at ~** chez soi, à la maison; **make yourself at ~** faites comme chez vous; **~ address** n domicile permanent; **~land** n patrie f; **~less** adj sans foyer; sans abri; **~ly** adj (plain) simple, sans prétention; **~-made** adj fait(e) à la maison; **~ match** n match m à domicile; **H~ Office** (BRIT) n ministère m de l'Intérieur; **~ page** n (COMPUT) page f d'accueil; **~ rule** n autonomie f; **H~ Secretary** (BRIT) n ministre m de l'Intérieur; **~sick** adj: **to be ~sick** avoir le mal du pays; s'ennuyer de sa famille; **~ town** n ville natale; **~ward** adj (journey) du retour; **~work** n devoirs mpl

homoeopathic [həumiəu'pæθik] (US **homeopathic**) adj (medicine, methods) homéopathique; (doctor) homéopathe

homogeneous [hɔməu'dʒiːniəs] adj homogène

homosexual [hɔməu'seksjuəl] adj, n homosexuel(le)

honest ['ɔnist] adj honnête; (sincere) franc (franche); **~ly** adv honnêtement; franchement; **~y** n honnêteté f

honey ['hʌni] n miel m; **~comb** n rayon m de miel; **~moon** n lune f de miel, voyage m de noces; **~suckle** (BOT) n chèvrefeuille m

honk [hɔŋk] vi (AUT) klaxonner

honorary ['ɔnərəri] adj honoraire; (duty, title) honorifique

honour ['ɔnər] (US **honor**) vt honorer ♦ n honneur m; **hono(u)rable** adj honorable; **hono(u)rs degree** n (SCOL) licence avec mention

hood [hud] n capuchon m; (of cooker) hotte f; (AUT: BRIT) capote f; (: US) capot m

hoof [huːf] (pl **hooves**) n sabot m

hook [huk] n crochet m; (on dress) agrafe f; (for fishing) hameçon m ♦ vt accrocher; (fish) prendre

hooligan ['huːligən] n voyou m

hoop [huːp] n cerceau m

hooray [huː'rei] excl hourra

hoot [huːt] vi (AUT) klaxonner; (siren) mugir; (owl) hululer; **~er** n (BRIT: AUT) klaxon m; (NAUT, factory) sirène f

Hoover ® ['huːvər] (BRIT) n aspirateur m ♦ vt: **h~** passer l'aspirateur dans or sur

hooves [huːvz] npl of **hoof**

hop [hɔp] vi (on one foot) sauter à cloche-pied; (bird) sautiller

hope [həup] vt, vi espérer ♦ n espoir m; **I ~ so** je l'espère; **I ~ not** j'espère que non; **~ful** adj (person) plein(e) d'espoir; (situation) prometteur(-euse), encourageant(e); **~fully** adv (expectantly) avec espoir, avec optimisme; **~less** adj désespéré(e); (useless) nul(le)

hops [hɔps] npl houblon m

horizon [hə'raizn] n horizon m; **~tal** [hɔri'zɔntl] adj horizontal(e)

horn [hɔːn] n corne f; (MUS: also: **French ~**) cor m; (AUT) klaxon m

hornet ['hɔːnit] n frelon m

horoscope ['hɔrəskəup] n horoscope m

horrendous [hə'rendəs] adj horrible, affreux(-euse)

horrible ['hɔribl] adj horrible, affreux(-euse)

horrid ['hɔrid] adj épouvantable

horrify ['hɔrifai] vt horrifier

horror ['hɔrər] n horreur f; **~ film** n film m d'épouvante

hors d'oeuvre [ɔː'dəːvrə] n (CULIN) hors-d'œuvre m inv

horse [hɔːs] n cheval m; **~back** n: **on ~back** à cheval; **~ chestnut** n marron m (d'Inde); **~man** (irreg) n cavalier m; **~power** n puissance f (en chevaux); **~-racing** n courses fpl de chevaux; **~radish** n raifort m; **~shoe** n fer m à cheval

hose [həuz] n (also: **~pipe**) tuyau m; (also: **garden ~**) tuyau d'arrosage

hospitable ['hɔspitəbl] adj hospitalier(-ère)

hospital ['hɔspitl] n hôpital m; **in ~** à l'hôpital

hospitality [hɔspi'tæliti] n hospitalité f

host [həust] n hôte m; (TV, RADIO)

animateur(-trice); *(REL)* hostie *f*; *(large number)*: **a ~ of** une foule de

hostage ['hɔstɪdʒ] *n* otage *m*

hostel ['hɔstl] *n* foyer *m*; *(also:* **youth ~)** auberge *f* de jeunesse

hostess ['həustɪs] *n* hôtesse *f*; *(TV, RADIO)* animatrice *f*

hostile ['hɔstaɪl] *adj* hostile; **hostility** [hɔ'stɪlɪtɪ] *n* hostilité *f*

hot [hɔt] *adj* chaud(e); *(as opposed to only warm)* très chaud(e); *(spicy)* fort(e); *(fig)* acharné(e); *(temper)* passionné(e); **to be ~** *(person)* avoir chaud; *(object)* être (très) chaud; *(weather)* faire chaud; **~bed** *n (fig)* foyer *m*, pépinière *f*; **~ dog** *n* hot-dog *m*

hotel [həu'tɛl] *n* hôtel *m*

hot: **~house** *n* serre (chaude); **~line** *n* *(POL)* téléphone *m* rouge, ligne directe; **~ly** *adv* passionnément, violemment; **~plate** *n (on cooker)* plaque chauffante; **~pot** *(BRIT) n* ragoût *m*; **~-water bottle** *n* bouillotte *f*

hound [haund] *vt* poursuivre avec acharnement ♦ *n* chien courant

hour ['auə'] *n* heure *f*; **~ly** *adj, adv* toutes les heures; *(rate)* horaire

house [*n* haus, *vb* hauz] *n* maison *f*; *(POL)* chambre *f*; *(THEATRE)* salle *f*; auditoire *m* ♦ *vt (person)* loger, héberger; *(objects)* abriter; **on the ~** *(fig)* aux frais de la maison; **~ arrest** *n* assignation *f* à résidence; **~boat** *n* bateau *m* (aménagé en habitation); **~bound** *adj* confiné(e) chez soi; **~breaking** *n* cambriolage *m* (avec effraction); **~hold** *n (persons)* famille *f*, maisonnée *f*; *(ADMIN etc)* ménage *m*; **~keeper** *n* gouvernante *f*; **~keeping** *n (work)* ménage *m*; **~keeping (money)** argent *m* du ménage; **~-warming (party)** *n* pendaison *f* de crémaillère; **~wife** *(irreg) n* ménagère *f*; femme *f* au foyer; **~work** *n* (travaux *mpl* du) ménage *m*

housing ['hauzɪŋ] *n* logement *m*; **~ development,** **~ estate** *n* lotissement *m*

hovel ['hɔvl] *n* taudis *m*

hover ['hɔvə'] *vi* planer; **~craft** *n* aéroglisseur *m*

how [hau] *adv* comment; **~ are you?** comment allez-vous?; **~ do you do?** bonjour; enchanté(e); **~ far is it to?** combien y a-t-il jusqu'à ...?; **~ long have you been here?** depuis combien de temps êtesvous là?; **~ lovely!** que *or* comme c'est joli!; **~ many/much?** combien?; **~ many people/much milk?** combien de gens/ lait?; **~ old are you?** quel âge avez-vous?

however [hau'ɛvə'] *adv* de quelque façon *or* manière que *+subj*; *(+adj)* quelque *or* si ... que *+subj*; *(in questions)* comment ♦ *conj* pourtant, cependant

howl [haul] *vi* hurler

H.P. *abbr* = **hire purchase**

h.p. *abbr* = **horsepower**

HQ *abbr* = **headquarters**

HTML *n abbr (= Hypertext Mark-up Language)* HTML

hub [hʌb] *n (of wheel)* moyeu *m*; *(fig)* centre *m*, foyer *m*; **~cap** *n* enjoliveur *m*

huddle ['hʌdl] *vi*: **to ~ together** se blottir les uns contre les autres

hue [hju:] *n* teinte *f*, nuance *f*

huff [hʌf] *n*: **in a ~** fâché(e)

hug [hʌg] *vt* serrer dans ses bras; *(shore, kerb)* serrer

huge [hju:dʒ] *adj* énorme, immense

hulk [hʌlk] *n (ship)* épave *f*; *(car, building)* carcasse *f*; *(person)* mastodonte *m*

hull [hʌl] *n* coque *f*

hullo [hə'ləu] *excl* = **hello**

hum [hʌm] *vt (tune)* fredonner ♦ *vi* fredonner; *(insect)* bourdonner; *(plane, tool)* vrombir

human ['hju:mən] *adj* humain(e) ♦ *n*: **~ being** être humain; **~e** [hju:'meɪn] *adj* humain(e), humanitaire; **~itarian** [hju:mænɪ'tɛərɪən] *adj* humanitaire; **~ity** [hju:-'mænɪtɪ] *n* humanité *f*

humble ['hʌmbl] *adj* humble, modeste ♦ *vt* humilier

humdrum ['hʌmdrʌm] *adj* monotone

humid ['hju:mɪd] *adj* humide

humiliate [hju:'mɪlɪeɪt] *vt* humilier; **humiliation** [hju:mɪlɪ'eɪʃən] *n* humiliation *f*

humorous ['hju:mərəs] *adj* humoristique;

(*person*) plein(e) d'humour

humour ['hju:mər] (*US* **humor**) *n* humour *m*; (*mood*) humeur *f* ♦ *vt* (*person*) faire plaisir à; se prêter aux caprices de

hump [hʌmp] *n* bosse *f*

hunch [hʌntʃ] *n* (*premonition*) intuition *f*; ~**back** *n* bossu(e); ~**ed** *adj* voûté(e)

hundred ['hʌndrəd] *num* cent; ~**s of** des centaines de; ~**weight** *n* (*BRIT*) 50.8 kg, 112 lb; (*US*) 45.3 kg, 100 lb

hung [hʌŋ] *pt, pp of* **hang**

Hungary ['hʌŋɡərɪ] *n* Hongrie *f*

hunger ['hʌŋɡər] *n* faim *f* ♦ *vi*: **to ~ for** avoir faim de, désirer ardemment

hungry ['hʌŋɡrɪ] *adj* affamé(e); (*keen*): ~ **for** avide de; **to be ~** avoir faim

hunk [hʌŋk] *n* (*of bread etc*) gros morceau

hunt [hʌnt] *vt* chasser; (*criminal*) pourchasser ♦ *vi* chasser; (*search*): **to ~ for** chercher (partout) ♦ *n* chasse *f*; ~**er** *n* chasseur *m*; ~**ing** *n* chasse *f*

hurdle ['hə:dl] *n* (*SPORT*) haie *f*; (*fig*) obstacle *m*

hurl [hə:l] *vt* lancer (avec violence); (*abuse, insults*) lancer

hurrah [hu'rɑ:] *excl* = **hooray**

hurray [hu'reɪ] *excl* = **hooray**

hurricane ['hʌrɪkən] *n* ouragan *m*

hurried ['hʌrɪd] *adj* pressé(e), précipité(e); (*work*) fait(e) à la hâte; ~**ly** *adv* précipitamment, à la hâte

hurry ['hʌrɪ] (*vb: also*: ~ **up**) *n* hâte *f*, précipitation *f* ♦ *vi* se presser, se dépêcher ♦ *vt* (*person*) faire presser, faire se dépêcher; (*work*) presser; **to be in a ~** être pressé(e); **to do sth in a ~** faire qch en vitesse; **to ~ in/out** entrer/sortir précipitamment

hurt [hə:t] (*pt, pp* **hurt**) *vt* (*cause pain to*) faire mal à; (*injure, fig*) blesser ♦ *vi* faire mal ♦ *adj* blessé(e); ~**ful** *adj* (*remark*) blessant(e)

hurtle ['hə:tl] *vi*: **to ~ past** passer en trombe; **to ~ down** dégringoler

husband ['hʌzbənd] *n* mari *m*

hush [hʌʃ] *n* calme *m*, silence *m* ♦ *vt* faire taire; ~! chut!; ~ **up** *vt* (*scandal*) étouffer

husk [hʌsk] *n* (*of wheat*) balle *f*; (*of rice,*

maize) enveloppe *f*

husky ['hʌskɪ] *adj* rauque ♦ *n* chien *m* esquimau *or* de traîneau

hustle ['hʌsl] *vt* pousser, bousculer ♦ *n*: ~ **and bustle** tourbillon *m* (d'activité)

hut [hʌt] *n* hutte *f*; (*shed*) cabane *f*

hutch [hʌtʃ] *n* clapier *m*

hyacinth ['haɪəsɪnθ] *n* jacinthe *f*

hydrant ['haɪdrənt] *n* (*also*: **fire ~**) bouche *f* d'incendie

hydraulic [haɪ'drɔːlɪk] *adj* hydraulique

hydroelectric ['haɪdrəʊ'lektrɪk] *adj* hydro-électrique

hydrofoil ['haɪdrəfɔɪl] *n* hydrofoil *m*

hydrogen ['haɪdrədʒən] *n* hydrogène *m*

hyena [haɪ'iːnə] *n* hyène *f*

hygiene ['haɪdʒiːn] *n* hygiène *f*; **hygienic** *adj* hygiénique

hymn [hɪm] *n* hymne *m*; cantique *m*

hype [haɪp] (*inf*) *n* battage *m* publicitaire

hypermarket ['haɪpəmɑːkɪt] (*BRIT*) *n* hypermarché *m*

hypertext ['haɪpətekst] *n* (*COMPUT*) hypertexte *m*

hyphen ['haɪfn] *n* trait *m* d'union

hypnotize ['hɪpnətaɪz] *vt* hypnotiser

hypocrisy [hɪ'pɒkrɪsɪ] *n* hypocrisie *f*; **hypocrite** ['hɪpəkrɪt] *n* hypocrite *m/f*; **hypocritical** *adj* hypocrite

hypothesis [haɪ'pɒθɪsɪs] (*pl* **hypotheses**) *n* hypothèse *f*

hysterical [hɪ'sterɪkl] *adj* hystérique; (*funny*) hilarant(e); ~ **laughter** fou rire *m*

hysterics [hɪ'sterɪks] *npl*: **to be in/have ~** (*anger, panic*) avoir une crise de nerfs; (*laughter*) attraper un fou rire

I, i

I [aɪ] *pron* je; (*before vowel*) j'; (*stressed*) moi

ice [aɪs] *n* glace *f*; (*on road*) verglas *m* ♦ *vt* (*cake*) glacer ♦ *vi* (*also*: ~ **over**, ~ **up**) geler; (*window*) se givrer; ~**berg** *n* iceberg *m*; ~**box** *n* (*US*) réfrigérateur *m*; (*BRIT*) compartiment *m* à glace; (*insulated box*) glacière *f*; ~ **cream** *n* glace *f*; ~ **cube** *n* glaçon *m*; **~d** *adj* glacé(e); **~ hockey** *n* hockey *m* sur glace; **Iceland** *n* Islande *f*; **~ lolly** *n* (*BRIT*) esquimau *m* (glace); **~ rink** *n* patinoire *f*; **~-skating** *n* patinage *m* (sur glace)

icicle ['aɪsɪkl] *n* glaçon *m* (*naturel*)

icing ['aɪsɪŋ] *n* (*CULIN*) glace *f*; **~ sugar** (*BRIT*) *n* sucre *m* glace

icon ['aɪkɔn] *n* (*COMPUT*) icône *f*

icy ['aɪsɪ] *adj* (*road*) verglacé(e); (*weather, temperature*) glacial(e)

I'd [aɪd] = **I would; I had**

idea [aɪ'dɪə] *n* idée *f*

ideal [aɪ'dɪəl] *n* idéal *m* ♦ *adj* idéal(e)

identical [aɪ'dɛntɪkl] *adj* identique

identification [aɪdɛntɪfɪ'keɪʃən] *n* identification *f*; **means of ~** pièce *f* d'identité

identify [aɪ'dɛntɪfaɪ] *vt* identifier

Identikit picture ® [aɪ'dɛntɪkɪt-] *n* portrait-robot *m*

identity [aɪ'dɛntɪtɪ] *n* identité *f*; **~ card** *n* carte *f* d'identité

ideology [aɪdɪ'ɔlədʒɪ] *n* idéologie *f*

idiom ['ɪdɪəm] *n* expression *f* idiomatique; (*style*) style *m*

idiosyncrasy [ɪdɪəu'sɪŋkrəsɪ] *n* (*of person*) particularité *f*, petite manie

idiot ['ɪdɪət] *n* idiot(e), imbécile *m/f*; **~ic** [ɪdɪ'ɔtɪk] *adj* idiot(e), bête, stupide

idle ['aɪdl] *adj* sans occupation, désœuvré(e); (*lazy*) oisif(-ive), paresseux(-euse); (*unemployed*) au chômage; (*question, pleasures*) vain(e), futile ♦ *vi* (*engine*) tourner au ralenti; **to lie ~** être arrêté(e), ne pas fonctionner

idol ['aɪdl] *n* idole *f*; **~ize** *vt* idolâtrer, adorer

i.e. *adv abbr* (= *id est*) c'est-à-dire

if [ɪf] *conj* si; **~ so** si c'est le cas; **~ not** sinon; **~ only** si seulement

ignite [ɪg'naɪt] *vt* mettre le feu à, enflammer ♦ *vi* s'enflammer; **ignition** *n* (*AUT*) allumage *m*; **to switch on/off the ignition** mettre/couper le contact; **ignition key** *n* clé *f* de contact

ignorant ['ɪgnərənt] *adj* ignorant(e); **to be ~ of** (*subject*) ne rien connaître à; (*events*) ne pas être au courant de

ignore [ɪg'nɔːʳ] *vt* ne tenir aucun compte de; (*person*) faire semblant de ne pas reconnaître, ignorer; (*fact*) méconnaître

ill [ɪl] *adj* (*sick*) malade; (*bad*) mauvais(e) ♦ *n* mal *m* ♦ *adv*: **to speak/think ~ of** dire/penser du mal de; **~s** *npl* (*misfortunes*) maux *mpl*, malheurs *mpl*; **to be taken ~** tomber malade; **~-advised** *adj* (*decision*) peu judicieux(-euse); (*person*) malavisé(e); **~-at-ease** *adj* mal à l'aise

I'll [aɪl] = **I will; I shall**

illegal [ɪ'liːgl] *adj* illégal(e)

illegible [ɪ'lɛdʒɪbl] *adj* illisible

illegitimate [ɪlɪ'dʒɪtɪmət] *adj* illégitime

ill-fated [ɪl'feɪtɪd] *adj* malheureux(-euse); (*day*) néfaste

ill feeling *n* ressentiment *m*, rancune *f*

illiterate [ɪ'lɪtərət] *adj* illettré(e)

ill: ~-mannered *adj* (*child*) mal élevé(e); **~ness** *n* maladie *f*; **~-treat** *vt* maltraiter

illuminate [ɪ'luːmɪneɪt] *vt* (*room, street*) éclairer; (*for special effect*) illuminer; **illumination** [ɪluːmɪ'neɪʃən] *n* éclairage *m*; illumination *f*

illusion [ɪ'luːʒən] *n* illusion *f*

illustrate ['ɪləstreɪt] *vt* illustrer; **illustration** [ɪlə'streɪʃən] *n* illustration *f*

ill will *n* malveillance *f*

I'm [aɪm] = **I am**

image ['ɪmɪdʒ] *n* image *f*; (*public face*) image de marque; **~ry** *n* images *fpl*

imaginary [ɪ'mædʒɪnərɪ] *adj* imaginaire

imagination [ɪmædʒɪ'neɪʃən] *n* imagination *f*

imaginative [ɪ'mædʒɪnətɪv] *adj* imaginatif(-ive); (*person*) plein(e) d'imagination

imagine [ɪ'mædʒɪn] *vt* imaginer, s'imaginer; (*suppose*) imaginer, supposer

imbalance [ɪm'bæləns] *n* déséquilibre *m*

imitate ['ɪmɪteɪt] *vt* imiter; **imitation** [ɪmɪ'teɪʃən] *n* imitation *f*

immaculate [ɪ'mækjulət] *adj* impeccable; (*REL*) immaculé(e)

immaterial [ɪmə'tɪərɪəl] *adj* sans importance, insignifiant(e)

immature [ɪmə'tjuəʳ] *adj* (*fruit*) (qui n'est)

pas mûr(e); (person) qui manque de maturité

immediate [ɪˈmiːdɪət] adj immédiat(e); **~ly** adv (at once) immédiatement; **~ly next to** juste à côté de

immense [ɪˈmɛns] adj immense; énorme

immerse [ɪˈmɜːs] vt immerger, plonger; **immersion heater** (BRIT) n chauffe-eau m électrique

immigrant [ˈɪmɪɡrənt] n immigrant(e); immigré(e); **immigration** [ɪmɪˈɡreɪʃən] n immigration f

imminent [ˈɪmɪnənt] adj imminent(e)

immoral [ɪˈmɒrl] adj immoral(e)

immortal [ɪˈmɔːtl] adj, n immortel(le)

immune [ɪˈmjuːn] adj: **~ (to)** immunisé(e) (contre); (fig) à l'abri de; **immunity** n immunité f

impact [ˈɪmpækt] n choc m, impact m; (fig) impact

impair [ɪmˈpɛər] vt détériorer, diminuer

impart [ɪmˈpɑːt] vt communiquer, transmettre; (flavour) donner

impartial [ɪmˈpɑːʃl] adj impartial(e)

impassable [ɪmˈpɑːsəbl] adj infranchissable; (road) impraticable

impassive [ɪmˈpæsɪv] adj impassible

impatience [ɪmˈpeɪʃəns] n impatience f

impatient [ɪmˈpeɪʃənt] adj impatient(e); **to get** or **grow ~** s'impatienter; **~ly** adv avec impatience

impeccable [ɪmˈpɛkəbl] adj impeccable, parfait(e)

impede [ɪmˈpiːd] vt gêner; **impediment** n obstacle m; (also: **speech impediment**) défaut m d'élocution

impending [ɪmˈpɛndɪŋ] adj imminent(e)

imperative [ɪmˈpɛrətɪv] adj (need) urgent(e), pressant(e); (tone) impérieux(-euse) ♦ n (LING) impératif m

imperfect [ɪmˈpɜːfɪkt] adj imparfait(e); (goods etc) défectueux(-euse)

imperial [ɪmˈpɪərɪəl] adj impérial(e); (BRIT: measure) légal(e)

impersonal [ɪmˈpɜːsənl] adj impersonnel(le)

impersonate [ɪmˈpɜːsəneɪt] vt se faire

passer pour; (THEATRE) imiter

impertinent [ɪmˈpɜːtɪnənt] adj impertinent(e), insolent(e)

impervious [ɪmˈpɜːvɪəs] adj (fig): **~ to** insensible à

impetuous [ɪmˈpɛtjuəs] adj impétueux(-euse), fougueux(-euse)

impetus [ˈɪmpətəs] n impulsion f; (of runner) élan m

impinge [ɪmˈpɪndʒ]: **to ~ on** vt fus (person) affecter, toucher; (rights) empiéter sur

implement [n ˈɪmplɪmənt, vb ˈɪmplɪment] n outil m, instrument m; (for cooking) ustensile m ♦ vt exécuter

implicit [ɪmˈplɪsɪt] adj implicite; (complete) absolu(e), sans réserve

imply [ɪmˈplaɪ] vt suggérer, laisser entendre; indiquer, supposer

impolite [ɪmpəˈlaɪt] adj impoli(e)

import [vb ɪmˈpɔːt, n ˈɪmpɔːt] vt importer ♦ n (COMM) importation f

importance [ɪmˈpɔːtns] n importance f

important [ɪmˈpɔːtənt] adj important(e)

importer [ɪmˈpɔːtər] n importateur(-trice)

impose [ɪmˈpəʊz] vt imposer ♦ vi: **to ~ on sb** abuser de la gentillesse de qn; **imposing** adj imposant(e), impressionnant(e); **imposition** [ɪmpəˈzɪʃən] n (of tax etc) imposition f; **to be an imposition on** (person) abuser de la gentillesse or la bonté de

impossible [ɪmˈpɒsɪbl] adj impossible

impotent [ˈɪmpətnt] adj impuissant(e)

impound [ɪmˈpaʊnd] vt confisquer, saisir

impoverished [ɪmˈpɒvərɪʃt] adj appauvri(e), pauvre

impractical [ɪmˈpræktɪkl] adj pas pratique; (person) qui manque d'esprit pratique

impregnable [ɪmˈprɛɡnəbl] adj (fortress) imprenable

impress [ɪmˈprɛs] vt impressionner, faire impression sur; (mark) imprimer, marquer; **to ~ sth on sb** faire bien comprendre qch à qn; **~ed** adj impressionné(e)

impression [ɪmˈprɛʃən] n impression f; (of stamp, seal) empreinte f; (imitation) imitation f; **to be under the ~ that** avoir l'impression que; ~ist n (ART) impressioniste m/f; (entertainer) imitateur(-trice) m/f

impressive [ɪmˈpresɪv] adj impressionnant(e)

imprint [ˈɪmprɪnt] n (outline) marque f, empreinte f

imprison [ɪmˈprɪzn] vt emprisonner, mettre en prison

improbable [ɪmˈprɔbəbl] adj improbable; (excuse) peu plausible

improper [ɪmˈprɔpə] adj (unsuitable) déplacé(e), de mauvais goût; indécent(e); (dishonest) malhonnête

improve [ɪmˈpruːv] vt améliorer ♦ vi s'améliorer; (pupil etc) faire des progrès; ~ment n amélioration f (in de); progrès m

improvise [ˈɪmprəvaɪz] vt, vi improviser

impudent [ˈɪmpjudnt] adj impudent(e)

impulse [ˈɪmpʌls] n impulsion f; on ~ impulsivement, sur un coup de tête; impulsive adj impulsif(-ive)

────────────
│ *KEYWORD* │
────────────

in [ɪn] prep 1 (indicating place, position) dans; **in the house/the fridge** dans la maison/ le frigo; **in the garden** dans le or au jardin; **in town** en ville; **in the country** à la campagne; **in school** à l'école; **in here/ there** ici/là

2 (with place names: of town, region, country): **in London** à Londres; **in England** en Angleterre; **in Japan** au Japon; **in the United States** aux États-Unis

3 (indicating time: during): **in spring** au printemps; **in summer** en été; **in May/ 1992** en mai/1992; **in the afternoon** (dans) l'après-midi; **at 4 o'clock in the afternoon** à 4 heures de l'après-midi

4 (indicating time: in the space of) en; (: future) dans; **I did it in 3 hours/days** je l'ai fait en 3 heures/jours; **I'll see you in 2 weeks** or **in 2 weeks' time** je te verrai dans 2 semaines

5 (indicating manner etc) à; **in a loud/soft voice** à voix haute/basse; **in pencil** au crayon; **in French** en français; **the boy in the blue shirt** le garçon à or avec la chemise bleue

6 (indicating circumstances): **in the sun** au soleil; **in the shade** à l'ombre; **in the rain** sous la pluie

7 (indicating mood, state): **in tears** en larmes; **in anger** sous le coup de la colère; **in despair** au désespoir; **in good condition** en bon état; **to live in luxury** vivre dans le luxe

8 (with ratios, numbers): **1 in 10 (households), 1 (household) in 10** 1 (ménage) sur 10; **20 pence in the pound** 20 pence par livre sterling; **they lined up in twos** ils se mirent en rangs (deux) par deux; **in hundreds** par centaines

9 (referring to people, works) chez; **the disease is common in children** c'est une maladie courante chez les enfants; **in (the works of) Dickens** chez Dickens, dans (l'œuvre de) Dickens

10 (indicating profession etc) dans; **to be in teaching** être dans l'enseignement

11 (after superlative) de; **the best pupil in the class** le meilleur élève de la classe

12 (with present participle): **in saying this** en disant ceci

♦ adv: **to be in** (person: at home, work) être là; (train, ship, plane) être arrivé(e); (in fashion) être à la mode; **to ask sb in** inviter qn à entrer; **to run/limp** etc **in** entrer en courant/boitant etc

♦ n: **the ins and outs (of)** (of proposal, situation etc) les tenants et aboutissants (de)

────────────

in. abbr = **inch**

inability [ɪnəˈbɪlɪtɪ] n incapacité f

inaccurate [ɪnˈækjurət] adj inexact(e); (person) qui manque de précision

inadequate [ɪnˈædɪkwət] adj insuffisant(e), inadéquat(e)

inadvertently [ɪnədˈvəːtntlɪ] adv par mégarde

inadvisable [ɪnədˈvaɪzəbl] adj (action) à déconseiller

inane [ɪˈneɪn] adj inepte, stupide

inanimate [ɪnˈænɪmət] adj inanimé(e)

inappropriate [ɪnə'prəuprɪət] *adj* inopportun(e), mal à propos; (*word, expression*) impropre

inarticulate [ɪnɑː'tɪkjulət] *adj* (*person*) qui s'exprime mal; (*speech*) indistinct(e)

inasmuch as [ɪnəz'mʌtʃ-] *adv* (*insofar as*) dans la mesure où; (*seeing that*) attendu que

inauguration [ɪnɔːgju'reɪʃən] *n* inauguration *f*; (*of president*) investiture *f*

inborn [ɪn'bɔːn] *adj* (*quality*) inné(e)

inbred [ɪn'brɛd] *adj* inné(e), naturel(le); (*family*) consanguin(e)

Inc. *abbr* = **incorporated**

incapable [ɪn'keɪpəbl] *adj* incapable

incapacitate [ɪnkə'pæsɪteɪt] *vt*: **to ~ sb from doing** rendre qn incapable de faire

incense [*n* 'ɪnsɛns, *vb* ɪn'sɛns] *n* encens *m* ♦ *vt* (*anger*) mettre en colère

incentive [ɪn'sɛntɪv] *n* encouragement *m*, raison *f* de se donner de la peine

incessant [ɪn'sɛsnt] *adj* incessant(e); ~**ly** *adv* sans cesse, constamment

inch [ɪntʃ] *n* pouce *m* (= 25 mm; 12 in a foot); **within an ~ of** à deux doigts de; **he didn't give an ~** (*fig*) il n'a pas voulu céder d'un pouce

incident ['ɪnsɪdnt] *n* incident *m*; ~**al** [ɪnsɪ'dɛntl] *adj* (*additional*) accessoire; ~**al to** qui accompagne; ~**ally** *adv* (*by the way*) à propos

inclination [ɪnklɪ'neɪʃən] *n* (*fig*) inclination *f*

incline [*n* 'ɪnklaɪn, *vb* ɪn'klaɪn] *n* pente *f* ♦ *vt* incliner ♦ *vi* (*surface*) s'incliner; **to be ~d to do** avoir tendance à faire

include [ɪn'kluːd] *vt* inclure, comprendre; **including** *prep* y compris; **inclusive** *adj* inclus(e), compris(e); **inclusive of tax** *etc* taxes *etc* comprises

income ['ɪnkʌm] *n* revenu *m*; ~ **tax** *n* impôt *m* sur le revenu

incoming ['ɪnkʌmɪŋ] *adj* qui arrive; (*president*) entrant(e); ~ **mail** courrier *m* du jour; ~ **tide** marée montante

incompetent [ɪn'kɔmpɪtnt] *adj* incompétent(e), incapable

incomplete [ɪnkəm'pliːt] *adj* incomplet(-ète)

incongruous [ɪn'kɔngruəs] *adj* incongru(e)

inconsiderate [ɪnkən'sɪdərət] *adj* (*person*) qui manque d'égards; (*action*) inconsidéré(e)

inconsistency [ɪnkən'sɪstənsɪ] *n* (*of actions etc*) inconséquence *f*; (*of work*) irrégularité *f*; (*of statement etc*) incohérence *f*

inconsistent [ɪnkən'sɪstnt] *adj* inconséquent(e); irrégulier(-ère); peu cohérent(e); ~ **with** incompatible avec

inconspicuous [ɪnkən'spɪkjuəs] *adj* qui passe inaperçu(e); (*colour, dress*) discret(-ète)

inconvenience [ɪnkən'viːnjəns] *n* inconvénient *m*; (*trouble*) dérangement *m* ♦ *vt* déranger

inconvenient [ɪnkən'viːnjənt] *adj* (*house*) malcommode; (*time, place*) mal choisi(e), qui ne convient pas; (*visitor*) importun(e)

incorporate [ɪn'kɔːpəreɪt] *vt* incorporer; (*contain*) contenir; ~**d company** (*US*) *n* ≃ société *f* anonyme

incorrect [ɪnkə'rɛkt] *adj* incorrect(e)

increase [*n* 'ɪnkriːs, *vb* ɪn'kriːs] *n* augmentation *f* ♦ *vi, vt* augmenter; **increasing** *adj* (*number*) croissant(e); **increasingly** *adv* de plus en plus

incredible [ɪn'krɛdɪbl] *adj* incroyable

incubator ['ɪnkjubeɪtə*r*] *n* (*for babies*) couveuse *f*

incumbent [ɪn'kʌmbənt] *n* (*president*) président *m* en exercice; (*REL*) titulaire *m/f* ♦ *adj*: **it is ~ on him to ...** il lui incombe or appartient de ...

incur [ɪn'kəː*r*] *vt* (*expenses*) encourir; (*anger, risk*) s'exposer à; (*debt*) contracter; (*loss*) subir

indebted [ɪn'dɛtɪd] *adj*: **to be ~ to sb (for)** être redevable à qn (de)

indecent [ɪn'diːsnt] *adj* indécent(e), inconvenant(e); ~ **assault** (*BRIT*) *n* attentat *m* à la pudeur; ~ **exposure** *n* outrage *m* (public) à la pudeur

indecisive [ɪndɪ'saɪsɪv] *adj* (*person*) indécis(e)

indeed [ɪn'di:d] *adv* vraiment; en effet; (*furthermore*) d'ailleurs; **yes ~!** certainement!

indefinitely [ɪn'dɛfɪnɪtlɪ] *adv* (*wait*) indéfiniment

indemnity [ɪn'dɛmnɪtɪ] *n* (*safeguard*) assurance *f*, garantie *f*; (*compensation*) indemnité *f*

independence [ɪndɪ'pɛndns] *n* indépendance *f*

Independence Day
---

i L'**Independence Day** *est la fête nationale aux États-Unis, le 4 juillet. Il commémore l'adoption de la déclaration d'Indépendance, en 1776, écrite par Thomas Jefferson et proclamant la séparation des 13 colonies américaines de la Grande-Bretagne.*

independent [ɪndɪ'pɛndnt] *adj* indépendant(e); (*school*) privé(e); (*radio*) libre

index ['ɪndɛks] *n* (*pl*: ~es: *in book*) index *m*; (: *in library etc*) catalogue *m*; (*pl*: *indices*: *ratio, sign*) indice *m*; ~ **card** *n* fiche *f*; ~ **finger** *n* index *m*; ~-**linked** *adj* indexé(e) (sur le coût de la vie *etc*)

India ['ɪndɪə] *n* Inde *f*; ~**n** *adj* indien(ne) ♦ *n* Indien(ne); **(American)** ~**n** Indien(ne) (d'Amérique); ~**n Ocean** *n* océan Indien

indicate ['ɪndɪkeɪt] *vt* indiquer; **indication** [ɪndɪ'keɪʃən] *n* indication *f*, signe *m*; **indicative** [ɪn'dɪkətɪv] *adj*: **indicative of** symptomatique de ♦ *n* (*LING*) indicatif *m*; **indicator** *n* (*sign*) indicateur *m*; (*AUT*) clignotant *m*

indices ['ɪndɪsi:z] *npl of* **index**

indictment [ɪn'daɪtmənt] *n* accusation *f*

indifferent [ɪn'dɪfrənt] *adj* indifférent(e); (*poor*) médiocre, quelconque

indigenous [ɪn'dɪdʒɪnəs] *adj* indigène

indigestion [ɪndɪ'dʒɛstʃən] *n* indigestion *f*, mauvaise digestion

indignant [ɪn'dɪgnənt] *adj*: ~ **(at sth / with sb)** indigné(e) (de qch/contre qn)

indignity [ɪn'dɪgnɪtɪ] *n* indignité *f*, affront

indirect [ɪndɪ'rɛkt] *adj* indirect(e)

indiscreet [ɪndɪs'kri:t] *adj* indiscret(-ète); (*rash*) imprudent(e)

indiscriminate [ɪndɪs'krɪmɪnət] *adj* (*person*) qui manque de discernement; (*killings*) commis(e) au hasard

indisputable [ɪndɪs'pju:təbl] *adj* incontestable, indiscutable

individual [ɪndɪ'vɪdjuəl] *n* individu *m* ♦ *adj* individuel(le); (*characteristic*) particulier(-ère), original(e)

indoctrination [ɪndɔktrɪ'neɪʃən] *n* endoctrinement *m*

Indonesia [ɪndə'ni:zɪə] *n* Indonésie *f*

indoor ['ɪndɔ:ʳ] *adj* (*plant*) d'appartement; (*swimming pool*) couvert(e); (*sport, games*) pratiqué(e) en salle; ~**s** *adv* à l'intérieur

induce [ɪn'dju:s] *vt* (*persuade*) persuader; (*bring about*) provoquer; ~**ment** *n* (*incentive*) récompense *f*; (*pej: bribe*) pot-de-vin *m*

indulge [ɪn'dʌldʒ] *vt* (*whim*) céder à, satisfaire; (*child*) gâter ♦ *vi*: **to ~ in sth** (*luxury*) se permettre qch; (*fantasies etc*) se livrer à qch; ~**nce** *n* fantaisie *f* (que l'on s'offre); (*leniency*) indulgence *f*; ~**nt** *adj* indulgent(e)

industrial [ɪn'dʌstrɪəl] *adj* industriel(le); (*injury*) du travail; ~ **action** *n* action revendicative; ~ **estate** (*BRIT*) *n* zone industrielle; ~**ist** *n* industriel *m*; ~ **park** (*US*) *n* = **industrial estate**

industrious [ɪn'dʌstrɪəs] *adj* travailleur(-euse)

industry ['ɪndəstrɪ] *n* industrie *f*; (*diligence*) zèle *m*, application *f*

inebriated [ɪ'ni:brɪeɪtɪd] *adj* ivre

inedible [ɪn'ɛdɪbl] *adj* immangeable; (*plant etc*) non comestible

ineffective [ɪnɪ'fɛktɪv], **ineffectual** [ɪnɪ'fɛktʃuəl] *adj* inefficace

inefficient [ɪnɪ'fɪʃənt] *adj* inefficace

inequality [ɪnɪ'kwɔlɪtɪ] *n* inégalité *f*

inescapable [ɪnɪ'skeɪpəbl] *adj* inéluctable, inévitable

inevitable [ɪn'ɛvɪtəbl] *adj* inévitable; **inevitably** *adv* inévitablement

inexpensive [ɪnɪk'spɛnsɪv] *adj* bon marché *inv*

inexperienced [ɪnɪk'spɪərɪənst] *adj* inexpérimenté(e)

infallible [ɪn'fælɪbl] *adj* infaillible

infamous ['ɪnfəməs] *adj* infâme, abominable

infancy ['ɪnfənsɪ] *n* petite enfance, bas âge

infant ['ɪnfənt] *n* (*baby*) nourrisson *m*; (*young child*) petit(e) enfant; ~ **school** (*BRIT*) *n* classes *fpl* préparatoires (*entre 5 et 7 ans*)

infatuated [ɪn'fætjueɪtɪd] *adj*: ~ **with** entiché(e) de; **infatuation** [ɪnfætju'eɪʃən] *n* engouement *m*

infect [ɪn'fɛkt] *vt* infecter, contaminer; ~**ion** *n* infection *f*; (*contagion*) contagion *f*; ~**ious** *adj* infectieux(-euse); (*also fig*) contagieux(-euse)

infer [ɪn'fəːʳ] *vt* conclure, déduire

inferior [ɪn'fɪərɪəʳ] *adj* inférieur(e); (*goods*) de qualité inférieure ♦ *n* inférieur(e); (*in rank*) subalterne *m/f*; ~**ity** [ɪnfɪərɪ'ɔrətɪ] *n* infériorité *f*

infertile [ɪn'fəːtaɪl] *adj* stérile

infighting ['ɪnfaɪtɪŋ] *n* querelles *fpl* internes

infinite ['ɪnfɪnɪt] *adj* infini(e)

infinitive [ɪn'fɪnɪtɪv] *n* infinitif *m*

infinity [ɪn'fɪnɪtɪ] *n* infinité *f*; (*also MATH*) infini *m*

infirmary [ɪn'fəːmərɪ] *n* (*hospital*) hôpital *m*

inflamed [ɪn'fleɪmd] *adj* enflammé(e)

inflammable [ɪn'flæməbl] (*BRIT*) *adj* inflammable

inflammation [ɪnflə'meɪʃən] *n* inflammation *f*

inflatable [ɪn'fleɪtəbl] *adj* gonflable

inflate [ɪn'fleɪt] *vt* (*tyre, balloon*) gonfler; (*price*) faire monter; **inflation** *n* (*ECON*) inflation *f*; **inflationary** *adj* inflationniste

inflict [ɪn'flɪkt] *vt*: **to ~ on** infliger à

influence ['ɪnfluəns] *n* influence *f* ♦ *vt* influencer; **under the ~ of alcohol** en état d'ébriété; **influential** [ɪnflu'ɛnʃl] *adj* influent(e)

influenza [ɪnflu'ɛnzə] *n* grippe *f*

influx ['ɪnflʌks] *n* afflux *m*

infomercial ['ɪnfəuməːʃl] (*US*) *n* (*for product*) publi-information *f*; (*POL*) émission où un candidat présente son programme électoral

inform [ɪn'fɔːm] *vt*: **to ~ sb (of)** informer *or* avertir qn (de) ♦ *vi*: **to ~ on sb** dénoncer qn

informal [ɪn'fɔːml] *adj* (*person, manner, party*) simple; (*visit, discussion*) dénué(e) de formalités; (*announcement, invitation*) non officiel(le); (*colloquial*) familier(-ère); ~**ity** [ɪnfɔː'mælɪtɪ] *n* simplicité *f*, absence *f* de cérémonie; caractère non officiel

informant [ɪn'fɔːmənt] *n* informateur(-trice)

information [ɪnfə'meɪʃən] *n* information *f*; renseignements *mpl*; (*knowledge*) connaissances *fpl*; **a piece of ~** un renseignement; ~ **desk** *n* accueil *m*; ~ **office** *n* bureau *m* de renseignements

informative [ɪn'fɔːmətɪv] *adj* instructif(-ive)

informer [ɪn'fɔːməʳ] *n* (*also*: **police ~**) indicateur(-trice)

infringe [ɪn'frɪndʒ] *vt* enfreindre ♦ *vi*: **to ~ on** empiéter sur; ~**ment** *n*: ~**ment (of)** infraction *f* (à)

infuriating [ɪn'fjuərɪeɪtɪŋ] *adj* exaspérant(e)

ingenious [ɪn'dʒiːnjəs] *adj* ingénieux(-euse); **ingenuity** [ɪndʒɪ'njuːɪtɪ] *n* ingéniosité *f*

ingenuous [ɪn'dʒɛnjuəs] *adj* naïf (naïve), ingénu(e)

ingot ['ɪŋgət] *n* lingot *m*

ingrained [ɪn'greɪnd] *adj* enraciné(e)

ingratiate [ɪn'greɪʃɪeɪt] *vt*: **to ~ o.s. with** s'insinuer dans les bonnes grâces de, se faire bien voir de

ingredient [ɪn'griːdɪənt] *n* ingrédient *m*; (*fig*) élément *m*

inhabit [ɪn'hæbɪt] *vt* habiter; ~**ant** *n* habitant(e)

inhale [ɪn'heɪl] *vt* respirer; (*smoke*) avaler ♦ *vi* aspirer; (*in smoking*) avaler la fumée

inherent [ɪn'hɪərənt] *adj*: ~ **(in** *or* **to)** inhérent(e) (à)

inherit [ɪnˈherɪt] *vt* hériter (de); ~**ance** *n* héritage *m*

inhibit [ɪnˈhɪbɪt] *vt* (*PSYCH*) inhiber; (*growth*) freiner; ~**ion** [ɪnhɪˈbɪʃən] *n* inhibition *f*

inhuman [ɪnˈhjuːmən] *adj* inhumain(e)

initial [ɪˈnɪʃl] *adj* initial(e) ♦ *n* initiale *f* ♦ *vt* parafer; ~**s** *npl* (*letters*) initiales *fpl*; (*as signature*) parafe *m*; ~**ly** *adv* initialement, au début

initiate [ɪˈnɪʃɪeɪt] *vt* (*start*) entreprendre, amorcer; (*entreprise*) lancer; (*person*) initier; **to ~ proceedings against sb** intenter une action à qn; **initiative** *n* initiative *f*

inject [ɪnˈdʒekt] *vt* injecter; (*person*): **to ~ sb with sth** faire une piqûre de qch à qn; ~**ion** *n* injection *f*, piqûre *f*

injure [ˈɪndʒəʳ] *vt* blesser; (*reputation etc*) compromettre; ~**d** *adj* blessé(e); **injury** *n* blessure *f*; ~ **time** *n* (*SPORT*) arrêts *mpl* de jeu

injustice [ɪnˈdʒʌstɪs] *n* injustice *f*

ink [ɪŋk] *n* encre *f*

inkling [ˈɪŋklɪŋ] *n*: **to have an/no ~ of** avoir une (vague) idée de/n'avoir aucune idée de

inlaid [ˈɪnleɪd] *adj* incrusté(e); (*table etc*) marqueté(e)

inland [*adj* ˈɪnlənd, *adv* ɪnˈlænd] *adj* intérieur(e) ♦ *adv* à l'intérieur, dans les terres; **Inland Revenue** (*BRIT*) *n* fisc *m*

in-laws [ˈɪnlɔːz] *npl* beaux-parents *mpl*; belle famille

inlet [ˈɪnlet] *n* (*GEO*) crique *f*

inmate [ˈɪnmeɪt] *n* (*in prison*) détenu(e); (*in asylum*) interné(e)

inn [ɪn] *n* auberge *f*

innate [ɪˈneɪt] *adj* inné(e)

inner [ˈɪnəʳ] *adj* intérieur(e); ~ **city** *n* centre *m* de zone urbaine; ~ **tube** *n* (*of tyre*) chambre *f* à air

innings [ˈɪnɪŋz] *n* (*CRICKET*) tour *m* de batte

innocent [ˈɪnəsnt] *adj* innocent(e)

innocuous [ɪˈnɔkjuəs] *adj* inoffensif(-ive)

innuendo [ɪnjuˈendəu] (*pl* ~**es**) *n* insinuation *f*, allusion (malveillante)

innumerable [ɪˈnjuːmrəbl] *adj* innombrable

inpatient [ˈɪnpeɪʃənt] *n* malade hospitalisé(e)

input [ˈɪnput] *n* (*resources*) ressources *fpl*; (*COMPUT*) entrée *f* (de données); (: *data*) données *fpl*

inquest [ˈɪnkwest] *n* enquête *f*; (**coroner's**) ~ enquête judiciaire

inquire [ɪnˈkwaɪəʳ] *vi* demander ♦ *vt* demander; **to ~ about** se renseigner sur; ~ **into** *vt fus* faire une enquête sur; **inquiry** *n* demande *f* de renseignements; (*investigation*) enquête *f*, investigation *f*; **inquiries** *npl*: **the inquiries** (*RAIL etc*) les renseignements; **inquiry** *or* **inquiries office** (*BRIT*) *n* bureau *m* des renseignements

inquisitive [ɪnˈkwɪzɪtɪv] *adj* curieux(-euse)

ins *abbr* = **inches**

insane [ɪnˈseɪn] *adj* fou (folle); (*MED*) aliéné(e); **insanity** [ɪnˈsænɪtɪ] *n* folie *f*; (*MED*) aliénation (mentale)

inscription [ɪnˈskrɪpʃən] *n* inscription *f*; (*in book*) dédicace *f*

inscrutable [ɪnˈskruːtəbl] *adj* impénétrable; (*comment*) obscur(e)

insect [ˈɪnsekt] *n* insecte *m*; ~**icide** [ɪnˈsektɪsaɪd] *n* insecticide *m*; ~ **repellent** *n* crème *f* anti-insecte

insecure [ɪnsɪˈkjuəʳ] *adj* peu solide; peu sûr(e); (*person*) anxieux(-euse)

insensitive [ɪnˈsensɪtɪv] *adj* insensible

insert [ɪnˈsəːt] *vt* insérer; ~**ion** *n* insertion *f*

in-service [ˈɪnˈsəːvɪs] *adj* (*training*) continu(e), en cours d'emploi; (*course*) de perfectionnement; de recyclage

inshore [ˈɪnˈʃɔːʳ] *adj* côtier(-ère) ♦ *adv* près de la côte; (*move*) vers la côte

inside [ˈɪnˈsaɪd] *n* intérieur *m* ♦ *adj* intérieur(e) ♦ *adv* à l'intérieur, dedans ♦ *prep* à l'intérieur de; (*of time*): ~ **10 minutes** en moins de 10 minutes; ~**s** *npl* (*inf*) intestins *mpl*; ~ **information** *n* renseignements obtenus à la source; ~ **lane** *n* (*AUT*: *in Britain*) voie *f* de gauche; (: *in US, Europe etc*) voie de droite; ~ **out** *adv* à l'envers; (*know*) à fond; ~**r dealing**, ~**r trading** *n* (*St Ex*) délit *m* d'initié

insight ['ɪnsaɪt] n perspicacité f; (glimpse, idea) aperçu m

insignificant [ɪnsɪg'nɪfɪkənt] adj insignifiant(e)

insincere [ɪnsɪn'sɪər] adj hypocrite

insinuate [ɪn'sɪnjueɪt] vt insinuer

insist [ɪn'sɪst] vi insister; **to ~ on doing** insister pour faire; **to ~ on sth** exiger qch; **to ~ that** insister pour que; (claim) maintenir or soutenir que; **~ent** adj insistant(e), pressant(e); (noise, action) ininterrompu(e)

insole ['ɪnsəul] n (removable) semelle intérieure

insolent ['ɪnsələnt] adj insolent(e)

insolvent [ɪn'sɔlvənt] adj insolvable

insomnia [ɪn'sɔmnɪə] n insomnie f

inspect [ɪn'spekt] vt inspecter; (ticket) contrôler; **~ion** n inspection f; contrôle m; **~or** n inspecteur(-trice); (BRIT: on buses, trains) contrôleur(-euse)

inspire [ɪn'spaɪər] vt inspirer

install [ɪn'stɔːl] vt installer; **~ation** [ɪnstə'leɪʃən] n installation f

instalment [ɪn'stɔːlmənt] (US **installment**) n acompte m, versement partiel; (of TV serial etc) épisode m; **in ~s** (pay) à tempérament; (receive) en plusieurs fois

instance ['ɪnstəns] n exemple m; **for ~** par exemple; **in the first ~** tout d'abord, en premier lieu

instant ['ɪnstənt] n instant m ♦ adj immédiat(e); (coffee, food) instantané(e), en poudre; **~ly** adv immédiatement, tout de suite

instead [ɪn'sted] adv au lieu de cela; **~ of** au lieu de; **~ of sb** à la place de qn

instep ['ɪnstep] n cou-de-pied m; (of shoe) cambrure f

instigate ['ɪnstɪgeɪt] vt (rebellion) fomenter, provoquer; (talks etc) promouvoir

instil [ɪn'stɪl] vt: **to ~ (into)** inculquer (à); (courage) insuffler (à)

instinct ['ɪnstɪŋkt] n instinct m

institute ['ɪnstɪtjuːt] n institut m ♦ vt instituer, établir; (inquiry) ouvrir; (proceedings) entamer

institution [ɪnstɪ'tjuːʃən] n institution f; (educational) établissement m (scolaire); (mental home) établissement (psychiatrique)

instruct [ɪn'strʌkt] vt: **to ~ sb in sth** enseigner qch à qn; **to ~ sb to do** charger qn or ordonner à qn de faire; **~ion** n instruction f; **~ions** npl (orders) directives fpl; **~ions (for use)** mode m d'emploi; **~or** n professeur m; (for skiing, driving) moniteur m

instrument ['ɪnstrumənt] n instrument m; **~al** [ɪnstru'mentl] adj: **to be ~al in** contribuer à; **~ panel** n tableau m de bord

insufficient [ɪnsə'fɪʃənt] adj insuffisant(e)

insular ['ɪnsjulər] adj (outlook) borné(e); (person) aux vues étroites

insulate ['ɪnsjuleɪt] vt isoler; (against sound) insonoriser; **insulation** [ɪnsju'leɪʃən] n isolation f; insonorisation f

insulin ['ɪnsjulɪn] n insuline f

insult [n 'ɪnsʌlt, vb ɪn'sʌlt] n insulte f, affront m ♦ vt insulter, faire affront à

insurance [ɪn'ʃuərəns] n assurance f; **fire/life ~** assurance-incendie/-vie; **~ policy** n police f d'assurance

insure [ɪn'ʃuər] vt assurer; **to ~ (o.s.) against** (fig) parer à

intact [ɪn'tækt] adj intact(e)

intake ['ɪnteɪk] n (of food, oxygen) consommation f; (BRIT: SCOL): **an ~ of 200 a year** 200 admissions fpl par an

integral ['ɪntɪgrəl] adj (part) intégrant(e)

integrate ['ɪntɪgreɪt] vt intégrer ♦ vi s'intégrer

intellect ['ɪntəlekt] n intelligence f; **~ual** [ɪntə'lektjuəl] adj, n intellectuel(le)

intelligence [ɪn'telɪdʒəns] n intelligence f; (MIL etc) informations fpl, renseignements mpl; **~ service** n services secrets; **intelligent** adj intelligent(e)

intend [ɪn'tend] vt (gift etc): **to ~ sth for** destiner qch à; **to ~ to do** avoir l'intention de faire

intense [ɪn'tens] adj intense; (person) véhément(e); **~ly** adv intensément; profondément

intensive [ɪn'tensɪv] *adj* intensif(-ive); **~ care unit** *n* service *m* de réanimation

intent [ɪn'tent] *n* intention *f* ♦ *adj* attentif(-ive); **to all ~s and purposes** en fait, pratiquement; **to be ~ on doing sth** être (bien) décidé à faire qch; **~ion** *n* intention *f*; **~ional** *adj* intentionnel(le), délibéré(e); **~ly** *adv* attentivement

interact [ɪntər'ækt] *vi* avoir une action réciproque; (*people*) communiquer; **~ive** *adj* (*COMPUT*) interactif(-ive)

interchange [*n* 'ɪntətʃeɪndʒ, *vb* ɪntə'tʃeɪndʒ] *n* (*exchange*) échange *m*; (*on motorway*) échangeur *m*; **~able** *adj* interchangeable

intercom ['ɪntəkəm] *n* interphone *m*

intercourse ['ɪntəkɔːs] *n* (*sexual*) rapports *mpl*

interest ['ɪntrɪst] *n* intérêt *m*; (*pastime*): **my main ~** ce qui m'intéresse le plus; (*COMM*) intérêts *mpl* ♦ *vt* intéresser; **to be ~ed in sth** s'intéresser à qch; **I am ~ed in going** ça m'intéresse d'y aller; **~ing** *adj* intéressant(e); **~ rate** *n* taux *m* d'intérêt

interface ['ɪntəfeɪs] *n* (*COMPUT*) interface *f*

interfere [ɪntə'fɪər] *vi*: **to ~ in** (*quarrel*) s'immiscer dans; (*other people's business*) se mêler de; **to ~ with** (*object*) toucher à; (*plans*) contrecarrer; (*duty*) être en conflit avec; **~nce** *n* (*in affairs*) ingérance *f*; (*RADIO, TV*) parasites *mpl*

interim ['ɪntərɪm] *adj* provisoire ♦ *n*: **in the ~** dans l'intérim, entre-temps

interior [ɪn'tɪərɪər] *n* intérieur *m* ♦ *adj* intérieur(e); (*minister, department*) de l'Intérieur; **~ designer** *n* styliste *m/f*, designer *m/f*

interjection [ɪntə'dʒekʃən] *n* (*interruption*) interruption *f*; (*LING*) interjection *f*

interlock [ɪntə'lɔk] *vi* s'enclencher

interlude ['ɪntəluːd] *n* intervalle *m*; (*THEATRE*) intermède *m*

intermediate [ɪntə'miːdɪət] *adj* intermédiaire; (*SCOL: course, level*) moyen(ne)

intermission [ɪntə'mɪʃən] *n* pause *f*; (*THEATRE, CINEMA*) entracte *m*

intern [*vb* ɪn'təːn, *n* 'ɪntəːn] *vt* interner ♦ *n*

(*US*) interne *m/f*

internal [ɪn'təːnl] *adj* interne; (*politics*) intérieur(e); **~ly** *adv*: **"not to be taken ~ly"** "pour usage externe"; **I~ Revenue Service** (*US*) *n* fisc *m*

international [ɪntə'næʃənl] *adj* international(e)

Internet ['ɪntənet] *n* Internet *m*; **~ café** *n* cybercafé *m*; **~ service provider** *n* fournisseur *m* d'accès à Internet

interplay ['ɪntəpleɪ] *n* effet *m* réciproque, interaction *f*

interpret [ɪn'təːprɪt] *vt* interpréter ♦ *vi* servir d'interprète; **~er** *n* interprète *m/f*

interrelated [ɪntərɪ'leɪtɪd] *adj* en corrélation, en rapport étroit

interrogate [ɪn'terəɡeɪt] *vt* interroger; (*suspect etc*) soumettre à un interrogatoire; **interrogation** [ɪnterəu'ɡeɪʃən] *n* interrogation *f*; interrogatoire *m*

interrupt [ɪntə'rʌpt] *vt, vi* interrompre

intersect [ɪntə'sekt] *vi* (*roads*) se croiser, se couper; **~ion** *n* (*of roads*) croisement *m*

intersperse [ɪntə'spəːs] *vt*: **to ~ with** parsemer de

intertwine [ɪntə'twaɪn] *vi* s'entrelacer

interval ['ɪntəvl] *n* intervalle *m*; (*BRIT: THEATRE*) entracte *m*; (: *SPORT*) mi-temps *f*; **at ~s** par intervalles

intervene [ɪntə'viːn] *vi* (*person*) intervenir; (*event*) survenir; (*time*) s'écouler (entre-temps); **intervention** *n* intervention *f*

interview ['ɪntəvjuː] *n* (*RADIO, TV etc*) interview *f*; (*for job*) entrevue *f* ♦ *vt* interviewer; avoir une entrevue avec; **~er** *n* (*RADIO, TV*) interviewer *m*

intestine [ɪn'testɪn] *n* intestin *m*

intimacy ['ɪntɪməsɪ] *n* intimité *f*

intimate [*adj* 'ɪntɪmət, *vb* 'ɪntɪmeɪt] *adj* intime; (*friendship*) profond(e); (*knowledge*) approfondi(e) ♦ *vt* (*hint*) suggérer, laisser entendre

into ['ɪntuː] *prep* dans; **~ pieces/French** en morceaux/français

intolerant [ɪn'tɔlərnt] *adj*: **~ (of)** intolérant(e) (de)

intoxicated [ɪn'tɔksɪkeɪtɪd] *adj* (*drunk*) ivre

intractable [ɪn'træktəbl] adj (child) indocile, insoumis(e); (problem) insoluble

intranet ['ɪntrənet] n intranet m

intransitive [ɪn'trænsɪtɪv] adj intransitif(-ive)

intravenous [ɪntrə'viːnəs] adj intraveineux(-euse)

in-tray ['ɪntreɪ] n courrier m "arrivée"

intricate ['ɪntrɪkət] adj complexe, compliqué(e)

intrigue [ɪn'triːg] n intrigue f ♦ vt intriguer; **intriguing** adj fascinant(e)

intrinsic [ɪn'trɪnsɪk] adj intrinsèque

introduce [ɪntrə'djuːs] vt introduire; (TV show, people to each other) présenter; **to ~ sb to** (pastime, technique) initier qn à; **introduction** n introduction f; (of person) présentation f; (to new experience) initiation f; **introductory** adj préliminaire, d'introduction; **introductory offer** n (COMM) offre f de lancement

intrude [ɪn'truːd] vi (person) être importun(e); **to ~ on** (conversation etc) s'immiscer dans; **~r** n intrus(e)

intuition [ɪntjuː'ɪʃən] n intuition f

inundate ['ɪnʌndeɪt] vt: **to ~ with** inonder de

invade [ɪn'veɪd] vt envahir

invalid [n 'ɪnvəlɪd, adj ɪn'vælɪd] n malade m/f; (with disability) invalide m/f ♦ adj (not valid) non valide or valable

invaluable [ɪn'væljuəbl] adj inestimable, inappréciable

invariably [ɪn'vεərɪəblɪ] adv invariablement; toujours

invent [ɪn'vent] vt inventer; **~ion** n invention f; **~ive** adj inventif(-ive); **~or** n inventeur(-trice)

inventory ['ɪnvəntrɪ] n inventaire m

invert [ɪn'vəːt] vt intervertir; (cup, object) retourner; **~ed commas** (BRIT) npl guillemets mpl

invest [ɪn'vest] vt investir ♦ vi: **to ~ in sth** placer son argent dans qch; (fig) s'offrir qch

investigate [ɪn'vestɪgeɪt] vt (crime etc) faire une enquête sur; **investigation**

[ɪnvestɪ'geɪʃən] n (of crime) enquête f

investment [ɪn'vestmənt] n investissement m, placement m

investor [ɪn'vestəʳ] n investisseur m; actionnaire m/f

invigilator [ɪn'vɪdʒɪleɪtəʳ] n surveillant(e)

invigorating [ɪn'vɪgəreɪtɪŋ] adj vivifiant(e); (fig) stimulant(e)

invisible [ɪn'vɪzɪbl] adj invisible

invitation [ɪnvɪ'teɪʃən] n invitation f

invite [ɪn'vaɪt] vt inviter; (opinions etc) demander; **inviting** adj engageant(e), attrayant(e)

invoice ['ɪnvɔɪs] n facture f

involuntary [ɪn'vɔləntrɪ] adj involontaire

involve [ɪn'vɔlv] vt (entail) entraîner, nécessiter; (concern) concerner; (associate): **to ~ sb (in)** impliquer qn (dans), mêler qn (à); faire participer qn (à); **~d** adj (complicated) complexe; **to be ~d in** participer à; **~ment** n: **~ment (in)** participation f (à); rôle m (dans); (enthusiasm) enthousiasme m (pour)

inward ['ɪnwəd] adj (thought, feeling) profond(e), intime; (movement) vers l'intérieur; **~(s)** adv vers l'intérieur

I/O abbr (COMPUT: = input/output) E/S

iodine ['aɪəudiːn] n iode m

iota [aɪ'əutə] n (fig) brin m, grain m

IOU n abbr (= I owe you) reconnaissance f de dette

IQ n abbr (= intelligence quotient) Q.I. m

IRA n abbr (= Irish Republican Army) IRA m

Iran [ɪ'rɑːn] n Iran m

Iraq [ɪ'rɑːk] n Irak m

irate [aɪ'reɪt] adj courroucé(e)

Ireland ['aɪələnd] n Irlande f

iris ['aɪrɪs] (pl **~es**) n iris m

Irish ['aɪrɪʃ] adj irlandais(e) ♦ npl: **the ~** les Irlandais; **~man** (irreg) n Irlandais m; **~ Sea** n mer f d'Irlande; **~woman** (irreg) n Irlandaise f

iron ['aɪən] n fer m; (for clothes) fer m à repasser ♦ cpd de or en fer; (fig) de fer ♦ vt (clothes) repasser; **~ out** vt (fig) aplanir; faire disparaître

ironic(al) [aɪ'rɔnɪk(l)] adj ironique

ironing [ˈaɪənɪŋ] *n* repassage *m*; **~ board** *n* planche *f* à repasser
ironmonger's (shop) [ˈaɪənmʌŋgəz-] *n* quincaillerie *f*
irony [ˈaɪrənɪ] *n* ironie *f*
irrational [ɪˈræʃənl] *adj* irrationnel(le)
irregular [ɪˈregjuləʳ] *adj* irrégulier(-ère); (*surface*) inégal(e)
irrelevant [ɪˈreləvənt] *adj* sans rapport, hors de propos
irresistible [ɪrɪˈzɪstɪbl] *adj* irrésistible
irrespective [ɪrɪˈspektɪv]: **~ of** *prep* sans tenir compte de
irresponsible [ɪrɪˈspɒnsɪbl] *adj* (*act*) irréfléchi(e); (*person*) irresponsable, inconscient(e)
irrigate [ˈɪrɪgeɪt] *vt* irriguer; **irrigation** [ɪrɪˈgeɪʃən] *n* irrigation *f*
irritate [ˈɪrɪteɪt] *vt* irriter
irritating *adj* irritant(e); **irritation** [ɪrɪˈteɪʃən] *n* irritation *f*
IRS (*US*) *n abbr* = **Internal Revenue Service**
is [ɪz] *vb see* **be**
Islam [ˈɪzlɑːm] *n* Islam *m*; **~ic** *adj* islamique; **~ic fundamentalists** intégristes *mpl* musulmans
island [ˈaɪlənd] *n* île *f*; **~er** *n* habitant(e) d'une île, insulaire *m/f*
isle [aɪl] *n* île *f*
isn't [ˈɪznt] = **is not**
isolate [ˈaɪsəleɪt] *vt* isoler; **~d** *adj* isolé(e); **isolation** *n* isolation *f*
ISP *n abbr* = **Internet Service Provider**
Israel [ˈɪzreɪl] *n* Israël *m*; **~i** [ɪzˈreɪlɪ] *adj* israélien(ne) ♦ *n* Israélien(ne)
issue [ˈɪʃjuː] *n* question *f*, problème *m*; (*of book*) publication *f*, parution *f*; (*of banknotes etc*) émission *f*; (*of newspaper etc*) numéro *m* ♦ *vt* (*rations, equipment*) distribuer; (*statement*) publier, faire; (*banknotes etc*) émettre, mettre en circulation; **at ~** en jeu, en cause; **to take ~ with sb (over)** exprimer son désaccord avec qn (sur); **to make an ~ of sth** faire une montagne de qch

⎡**KEYWORD**⎤

it [ɪt] *pron* **1** (*specific: subject*) il (elle); (*: direct object*) le (la, l'); (*: indirect object*) lui; **it's on the table** c'est *or* il (*or* elle) est sur la table; **about/from/of it** en; **I spoke to him about it** je lui en ai parlé; **what did you learn from it?** qu'est-ce que vous en avez retiré?; **I'm proud of it** j'en suis fier; **in/to it** y; **put the book in it** mettez-y le livre; **he agreed to it** il y a consenti; **did you go to it?** (*party, concert etc*) est-ce que vous y êtes allé(s)?
2 (*impersonal*) il; ce; **it's raining** il pleut; **it's Friday tomorrow** demain c'est vendredi *or* nous sommes vendredi; **it's 6 o'clock** il est 6 heures; **who is it? - it's me** qui est-ce? - c'est moi

Italian [ɪˈtæljən] *adj* italien(ne) ♦ *n* Italien(ne); (*LING*) italien *m*
italics [ɪˈtælɪks] *npl* italiques *fpl*
Italy [ˈɪtəlɪ] *n* Italie *f*
itch [ɪtʃ] *n* démangeaison *f* ♦ *vi* (*person*) éprouver des démangeaisons; (*part of body*) démanger; **I'm ~ing to do** l'envie me démange de faire; **~y** *adj* qui démange; **to be ~y** avoir des démangeaisons
it'd [ˈɪtd] = **it would**; **it had**
item [ˈaɪtəm] *n* article *m*; (*on agenda*) question *f*, point *m*; (*also:* **news ~**) nouvelle *f*; **~ize** *vt* détailler, faire une liste de
itinerary [aɪˈtɪnərərɪ] *n* itinéraire *m*
it'll [ˈɪtl] = **it will**; **it shall**
its [ɪts] *adj* son (sa), ses *pl*
it's [ɪts] = **it is**; **it has**
itself [ɪtˈself] *pron* (*reflexive*) se; (*emphatic*) lui-même (elle-même)
ITV *n abbr* (*BRIT: Independent Television*) chaîne privée
IUD *n abbr* (= *intra-uterine device*) DIU *m*, stérilet *m*
I've [aɪv] = **I have**
ivory [ˈaɪvərɪ] *n* ivoire *m*
ivy [ˈaɪvɪ] *n* lierre *m*

J, j

jab [dʒæb] *vt*: **to ~ sth into** enfoncer *or* planter qch dans ♦ *n* (*inf*: *injection*) piqûre *f*

jack [dʒæk] *n* (*AUT*) cric *m*; (*CARDS*) valet *m*; **~ up** *vt* soulever (au cric)

jackal ['dʒækl] *n* chacal *m*

jacket ['dʒækɪt] *n* veste *f*, veston *m*; (*of book*) jaquette *f*, couverture *f*; **~ potato** *n* pomme *f* de terre en robe des champs

jack: **~knife** *vi*: **the lorry ~knifed** la remorque (du camion) s'est mise en travers; **~ plug** *n* (*ELEC*) prise jack mâle *f*; **~pot** *n* gros lot

jaded ['dʒeɪdɪd] *adj* éreinté(e), fatigué(e)

jagged ['dʒægɪd] *adj* dentelé(e)

jail [dʒeɪl] *n* prison *f* ♦ *vt* emprisonner, mettre en prison

jam [dʒæm] *n* confiture *f*; (*also*: **traffic ~**) embouteillage *m* ♦ *vt* (*passage etc*) encombrer, obstruer; (*mechanism, drawer etc*) bloquer, coincer; (*RADIO*) brouiller ♦ *vi* se coincer, se bloquer; (*gun*) s'enrayer; **to be in a ~** (*inf*) être dans le pétrin; **to ~ sth into** entasser qch dans; enfoncer qch dans

Jamaica [dʒə'meɪkə] *n* Jamaïque *f*

jam: **~ jar** *n* pot *m* à confiture; **~med** *adj* (*window etc*) coincé(e); **~-packed** *adj*: **~-packed (with)** bourré(e) (de)

jangle ['dʒæŋgl] *vi* cliqueter

janitor ['dʒænɪtər] *n* concierge *m*

January ['dʒænjuərɪ] *n* janvier *m*

Japan [dʒə'pæn] *n* Japon *m*; **~ese** [dʒæpə'niːz] *adj* japonais(e) ♦ *n inv* Japonais(e); (*LING*) japonais *m*

jar [dʒɑːr] *n* (*stone, earthenware*) pot *m*; (*glass*) bocal *m* ♦ *vi* (*sound discordant*) produire un son grinçant *or* discordant; (*colours etc*) jurer

jargon ['dʒɑːgən] *n* jargon *m*

jaundice ['dʒɔːndɪs] *n* jaunisse *f*

javelin ['dʒævlɪn] *n* javelot *m*

jaw [dʒɔː] *n* mâchoire *f*

jay [dʒeɪ] *n* geai *m*; **~walker** *n* piéton indiscipliné

jazz [dʒæz] *n* jazz *m*; **~ up** *vt* animer, égayer

jealous ['dʒeləs] *adj* jaloux(-ouse); **~y** *n* jalousie *f*

jeans [dʒiːnz] *npl* jean *m*

jeer [dʒɪər] *vi*: **to ~ (at)** se moquer cruellement (de), railler

Jehovah's Witness [dʒɪ'həʊvəz-] *n* témoin *m* de Jéhovah

jelly ['dʒelɪ] *n* gelée *f*; **~fish** ['dʒelɪfɪʃ] *n* méduse *f*

jeopardy ['dʒepədɪ] *n*: **to be in ~** être en danger *or* péril

jerk [dʒɜːk] *n* secousse *f*; saccade *f*; sursaut *m*, spasme *m*; (*inf*: *idiot*) pauvre type *m* ♦ *vt* (*pull*) tirer brusquement ♦ *vi* (*vehicles*) cahoter

jersey ['dʒɜːzɪ] *n* (*pullover*) tricot *m*; (*fabric*) jersey *m*

Jesus ['dʒiːzəs] *n* Jésus

jet [dʒet] *n* (*gas, liquid*) jet *m*; (*AVIAT*) avion *m* à réaction, jet *m*; **~-black** *adj* (d'un noir) de jais; **~ engine** *n* moteur *m* à réaction; **~ lag** *n* (fatigue due au) décalage *m* horaire

jettison ['dʒetɪsn] *vt* jeter par-dessus bord

jetty ['dʒetɪ] *n* jetée *f*, digue *f*

Jew [dʒuː] *n* Juif *m*

jewel ['dʒuːəl] *n* bijou *m*, joyau *m*; (*in watch*) rubis *m*; **~ler** (*US* **jeweler**) *n* bijoutier(-ère), joaillier *m*; **~ler's (shop)** *n* bijouterie *f*, joaillerie *f*; **~lery** (*US* **jewelry**) *n* bijoux *mpl*

Jewess ['dʒuːɪs] *n* Juive *f*

Jewish ['dʒuːɪʃ] *adj* juif (juive)

jibe [dʒaɪb] *n* sarcasme *m*

jiffy ['dʒɪfɪ] (*inf*) *n*: **in a ~** en un clin d'œil

jigsaw ['dʒɪgsɔː] *n* (*also*: **~ puzzle**) puzzle *m*

jilt [dʒɪlt] *vt* laisser tomber, plaquer

jingle ['dʒɪŋgl] *n* (*for advert*) couplet *m* publicitaire ♦ *vi* cliqueter, tinter

jinx [dʒɪŋks] (*inf*) *n* (mauvais) sort *m*

jitters ['dʒɪtəz] (*inf*) *npl*: **to get the ~** (*inf*) avoir la trouille *or* la frousse

job [dʒɔb] *n* (*chore, task*) travail *m*, tâche *f*; (*employment*) emploi *m*, poste *m*, place *f*; **it's a good ~ that ...** c'est heureux *or* c'est une chance que ...; **just the ~!** (c'est) juste *or* exactement ce qu'il faut!; **~ centre** (*BRIT*) *n* agence *f* pour l'emploi; **~less** *adj* sans travail, au chômage

jockey ['dʒɔkɪ] *n* jockey *m* ♦ *vi*: **to ~ for position** manœuvrer pour être bien placé

jog [dʒɔg] *vt* secouer ♦ *vi* (*SPORT*) faire du jogging; **to ~ sb's memory** rafraîchir la mémoire de qn; **~ along** *vi* cheminer; trotter; **~ging** *n* jogging *m*

join [dʒɔɪn] *vt* (*put together*) unir, assembler; (*become member of*) s'inscrire à; (*meet*) rejoindre, retrouver; (*queue*) se joindre à ♦ *vi* (*roads, rivers*) se rejoindre, se rencontrer ♦ *n* raccord *m*; **~ in** *vi* se mettre de la partie, participer ♦ *vt fus* participer à, se mêler à; **~ up** *vi* (*meet*) se rejoindre; (*MIL*) s'engager

joiner ['dʒɔɪnəʳ] (*BRIT*) *n* menuisier *m*

joint [dʒɔɪnt] *n* (*TECH*) jointure *f*; joint *m*; (*ANAT*) articulation *f*, jointure; (*BRIT: CULIN*) rôti *m*; (*inf: place*) boîte *f*; (: *of cannabis*) joint *m* ♦ *adj* commun(e); **~ account** (*with bank etc*) compte joint

joke [dʒəuk] *n* plaisanterie *f*; (*also:* **practical ~**) farce *f* ♦ *vi* plaisanter; **to play a ~ on** jouer un tour à, faire une farce à; **~r** *n* (*CARDS*) joker *m*

jolly ['dʒɔlɪ] *adj* gai(e), enjoué(e); (*enjoyable*) amusant(e), plaisant(e) ♦ *adv* (*BRIT: inf*) rudement, drôlement

jolt [dʒəult] *n* cahot *m*, secousse *f*; (*shock*) choc *m* ♦ *vt* cahoter, secouer

Jordan ['dʒɔːdən] *n* (*country*) Jordanie *f*

jostle ['dʒɔsl] *vt* bousculer, pousser

jot [dʒɔt] *n*: **not one ~** pas un brin; **~ down** *vt* noter; **~ter** (*BRIT*) *n* cahier *m* (de brouillon); (*pad*) bloc-notes *m*

journal ['dʒɔːnl] *n* journal *m*; **~ism** *n* journalisme *m*; **~ist** *n* journaliste *m/f*

journey ['dʒɔːnɪ] *n* voyage *m*; (*distance covered*) trajet *m*

joy [dʒɔɪ] *n* joie *f*; **~ful** *adj* joyeux(-euse); **~rider** *n* personne qui fait une virée dans

une voiture volée; **~stick** *n* (*AVIAT, COMPUT*) manche *m* à balai

JP *n abbr* = **Justice of the Peace**

Jr *abbr* = **junior**

jubilant ['dʒuːbɪlnt] *adj* triomphant(e); réjoui(e)

judge [dʒʌdʒ] *n* juge *m* ♦ *vt* juger; **judg(e)ment** *n* jugement *m*

judicial [dʒuː'dɪʃl] *adj* judiciaire; **judiciary** *n* (*pouvoir m*) judiciaire *m*

judo ['dʒuːdəu] *n* judo *m*

jug [dʒʌg] *n* pot *m*, cruche *f*

juggernaut ['dʒʌgənɔːt] (*BRIT*) *n* (*huge truck*) énorme poids lourd

juggle ['dʒʌgl] *vi* jongler; **~r** *n* jongleur *m*

juice [dʒuːs] *n* jus *m*; **juicy** *adj* juteux(-euse)

jukebox ['dʒuːkbɔks] *n* juke-box *m*

July [dʒuːˈlaɪ] *n* juillet *m*

jumble ['dʒʌmbl] *n* fouillis *m* ♦ *vt* (*also:* **~ up**) mélanger, brouiller; **~ sale** (*BRIT*) *n* vente *f* de charité

---

jumble sale

🛈 Les **jumble sales** ont lieu dans les églises, salles de fêtes ou halls d'écoles, et l'on y vend des articles de toutes sortes, en général bon marché et surtout d'occasion, pour collecter des fonds pour une œuvre de charité, une école ou encore une église.

---

jumbo (jet) ['dʒʌmbəu-] *n* jumbo-jet *m*, gros porteur

jump [dʒʌmp] *vi* sauter, bondir; (*start*) sursauter; (*increase*) monter en flèche ♦ *vt* sauter, franchir ♦ *n* saut *m*, bond *m*; sursaut *m*; **to ~ the queue** (*BRIT*) passer avant son tour

jumper ['dʒʌmpəʳ] *n* (*BRIT: pullover*) pullover *m*; (*US: dress*) robe-chasuble *f*

jumper cables (*US*), **jump leads** (*BRIT*) *npl* câbles *mpl* de démarrage

jumpy ['dʒʌmpɪ] *adj* nerveux(-euse), agité(e)

Jun. *abbr* = **junior**

junction ['dʒʌŋkʃən] (*BRIT*) *n* (*of roads*) carrefour *m*; (*of rails*) embranchement *m*

juncture [ˈdʒʌŋktʃəʳ] *n*: **at this ~** à ce moment-là, sur ces entrefaites

June [dʒuːn] *n* juin *m*

jungle [ˈdʒʌŋgl] *n* jungle *f*

junior [ˈdʒuːnɪəʳ] *adj, n*: **he's ~ to me (by 2 years), he's my ~ (by 2 years)** il est mon cadet (de 2 ans), il est plus jeune que moi (de 2 ans); **he's ~ to me** (*seniority*) il est en dessous de moi (dans la hiérarchie), j'ai plus d'ancienneté que lui; **~ school** (*BRIT*) *n* ≃ école *f* primaire

junk [dʒʌŋk] *n* (*rubbish*) camelote *f*; (*cheap goods*) bric-à-brac *m inv*; **~ food** *n* aliments *mpl* sans grande valeur nutritive; **~ mail** *n* prospectus *mpl* (non sollicités); **~ shop** *n* (boutique *f* de) brocanteur *m*

Junr *abbr* = **junior**

juror [ˈdʒuərəʳ] *n* juré *m*

jury [ˈdʒuəri] *n* jury *m*

just [dʒʌst] *adj* juste ♦ *adv*: **he's ~ done it/left** il vient de le faire/partir; **~ right/ two o'clock** exactement *or* juste ce qu'il faut/deux heures; **she's ~ as clever as you** elle est tout aussi intelligente que vous; **it's ~ as well (that) …** heureusement que …; **~ as he was leaving** au moment *or* à l'instant précis où il partait; **~ before/enough/here** juste avant/ assez/ici; **it's ~ me/a mistake** ce n'est que moi/(rien) qu'une erreur; **~ missed/ caught** manqué/attrapé de justesse; **~ listen to this!** écoutez un peu ça!

justice [ˈdʒʌstɪs] *n* justice *f*; (*US: judge*) juge *m* de la Cour suprême; **J~ of the Peace** *n* juge *m* de paix

justify [ˈdʒʌstɪfaɪ] *vt* justifier

jut [dʒʌt] *vi* (*also*: **~ out**) dépasser, faire saillie

juvenile [ˈdʒuːvənaɪl] *adj* juvénile; (*court, books*) pour enfants ♦ *n* adolescent(e)

K, k

K *abbr* (= *one thousand*) K; (= *kilobyte*) Ko

kangaroo [kæŋgəˈruː] *n* kangourou *m*

karate [kəˈrɑːtɪ] *n* karaté *m*

kebab [kəˈbæb] *n* kébab *m*

keel [kiːl] *n* quille *f*; **on an even ~** (*fig*) à flot

keen [kiːn] *adj* (*eager*) plein(e) d'enthousiasme; . (*interest, desire, competition*) vif (vive); (*eye, intelligence*) pénétrant(e); (*edge*) effilé(e); **to be ~ to do** *or* **on doing sth** désirer vivement faire qch, tenir beaucoup à faire qch; **to be ~ on sth/sb** aimer beaucoup qch/qn

keep [kiːp] (*pt, pp* **kept**) *vt* (*retain, preserve*) garder; (*detain*) retenir; (*shop, accounts, diary, promise*) tenir; (*house*) avoir; (*support*) entretenir; (*chickens, bees etc*) élever ♦ *vi* (*remain*) rester; (*food*) se conserver ♦ *n* (*of castle*) donjon *m*; (*food etc*): **enough for his ~** assez pour (assurer) sa subsistance; (*inf*): **for ~s** pour de bon, pour toujours; **to ~ doing sth** ne pas arrêter de faire qch; **to ~ sb from doing** empêcher qn de faire *or* que qn ne fasse; **to ~ sb happy/a place tidy** faire que qn soit content/ qu'un endroit reste propre; **to ~ sth to o.s.** garder qch pour soi, tenir qch secret; **to ~ sth (back) from sb** cacher qch à qn; **to ~ time** (*clock*) être à l'heure, ne pas retarder; **well kept** bien entretenu(e); **~ on** *vi*: **to ~ on doing** continuer à faire; **don't ~ on about it!** arrête (d'en parler)!; **~ out** *vt* empêcher d'entrer; **"~ out"** "défense d'entrer"; **~ up** *vt* continuer, maintenir ♦ *vi*: **to ~ up with sb** (*in race etc*) aller aussi vite que qn; (*in work etc*) se maintenir au niveau de qn; **~er** *n* gardien(ne); **~-fit** *n* gymnastique *f* d'entretien; **~ing** *n* (*care*) garde *f*; **in ~ing with** en accord avec; **~sake** *n* souvenir *m*

kennel [ˈkɛnl] *n* niche *f*; **~s** *npl* (*boarding ~s*) chenil *m*

kerb [kəːb] (*BRIT*) *n* bordure *f* du trottoir

kernel [ˈkəːnl] *n* (*of nut*) amande *f*; (*fig*) noyau *m*

kettle [ˈkɛtl] *n* bouilloire *f*; ~**drum** *n* timbale *f*

key [kiː] *n* (*gen , MUS*) clé *f*; (*of piano, typewriter*) touche *f* ♦ *cpd* clé ♦ *vt* (*also:* ~ **in**) introduire (au clavier), saisir; ~**board** *n* clavier *m*; ~**ed up** *adj* (*person*) surexcité(e); ~**hole** *n* trou *m* de la serrure; ~**hole surgery** *n* chirurgie très minutieuse où l'incision est minimale; ~**note** *n* (*of speech*) note dominante; (*MUS*) tonique *f*; ~ **ring** *n* porte-clés *m*

khaki [ˈkɑːkɪ] *n* kaki *m*

kick [kɪk] *vt* donner un coup de pied à ♦ *vi* (*horse*) ruer ♦ *n* coup *m* de pied; (*thrill*): **he does it for ~s** il le fait parce que ça l'excite, il le fait pour le plaisir; **to ~ the habit** (*inf*) arrêter; ~ **off** *vi* (*SPORT*) donner le coup d'envoi

kid [kɪd] *n* (*inf: child*) gamin(e), gosse *m/f*; (*animal, leather*) chevreau *m* ♦ *vi* (*inf*) plaisanter, blaguer

kidnap [ˈkɪdnæp] *vt* enlever, kidnapper; ~**per** *n* ravisseur(-euse); ~**ping** *n* enlèvement *m*

kidney [ˈkɪdnɪ] *n* (*ANAT*) rein *m*; (*CULIN*) rognon *m*

kill [kɪl] *vt* tuer ♦ *n* mise *f* à mort; ~**er** *n* tueur(-euse); meurtrier(-ère); ~**ing** *n* meurtre *m*; (*of group of people*) tuerie *f*, massacre *m*; **to make a ~ing** (*inf*) réussir un beau coup (de filet); ~**joy** *n* rabat-joie *m/f*

kiln [kɪln] *n* four *m*

kilo [ˈkiːləu] *n* kilo *m*; ~**byte** *n* (*COMPUT*) kilo-octet *m*; ~**gram(me)** *n* kilogramme *m*; ~**metre** (*US* **kilometer**) *n* kilomètre *m*; ~**watt** *n* kilowatt *m*

kilt [kɪlt] *n* kilt *m*

kin [kɪn] *n* see **next**

kind [kaɪnd] *adj* gentil(le), aimable ♦ *n* sorte *f*, espèce *f*, genre *m*; **to be two of a ~** se ressembler; **in ~** (*COMM*) en nature

kindergarten [ˈkɪndəgɑːtn] *n* jardin *m* d'enfants

kind-hearted [kaɪndˈhɑːtɪd] *adj* bon (bonne)

kindle [ˈkɪndl] *vt* allumer, enflammer

kindly [ˈkaɪndlɪ] *adj* bienveillant(e), plein(e) de gentillesse ♦ *adv* avec bonté; **will you ~ ...!** auriez-vous la bonté *or* l'obligeance de ...?

kindness [ˈkaɪndnɪs] *n* bonté *f*, gentillesse *f*

king [kɪŋ] *n* roi *m*; ~**dom** *n* royaume *m*; ~**fisher** *n* martin-pêcheur *m*; ~**-size bed** *n* grand lit (*de 1,95 m de large*); ~**-size(d)** *adj* format géant *inv*; (*cigarettes*) long (longue)

kiosk [ˈkiːɔsk] *n* kiosque *m*; (*BRIT: TEL*) cabine *f* (téléphonique)

kipper [ˈkɪpəʳ] *n* hareng fumé et salé

kiss [kɪs] *n* baiser *m* ♦ *vt* embrasser; **to ~ (each other)** s'embrasser; ~ **of life** (*BRIT*) *n* bouche à bouche *m*

kit [kɪt] *n* équipement *m*, matériel *m*; (*set of tools etc*) trousse *f*; (*for assembly*) kit *m*

kitchen [ˈkɪtʃɪn] *n* cuisine *f*; ~ **sink** *n* évier *m*

kite [kaɪt] *n* (*toy*) cerf-volant *m*

kitten [ˈkɪtn] *n* chaton *m*, petit chat

kitty [ˈkɪtɪ] *n* (*money*) cagnotte *f*

km *abbr* = **kilometre**

knack [næk] *n*: **to have the ~ of doing** avoir le coup pour faire

knapsack [ˈnæpsæk] *n* musette *f*

knead [niːd] *vt* pétrir

knee [niː] *n* genou *m*; ~**cap** *n* rotule *f*

kneel [niːl] (*pt, pp* **knelt**) *vi* (*also:* ~ **down**) s'agenouiller

knew [njuː] *pt of* **know**

knickers [ˈnɪkəz] (*BRIT*) *npl* culotte *f* (de femme)

knife [naɪf] (*pl* **knives**) *n* couteau *m* ♦ *vt* poignarder, frapper d'un coup de couteau

knight [naɪt] *n* chevalier *m*; (*CHESS*) cavalier *m*; ~**hood** (*BRIT*) *n* (*title*): **to get a ~hood** être fait chevalier

knit [nɪt] *vt* tricoter ♦ *vi* tricoter; (*broken bones*) se ressouder; **to ~ one's brows** froncer les sourcils; ~**ting** *n* tricot *m*; ~**ting needle** *n* aiguille *f* à tricoter; ~**wear** *n* tricots *mpl*, lainages *mpl*

knives [naɪvz] *npl* of **knife**

knob [nɔb] *n* bouton *m*

knock [nɔk] *vt* frapper; *(bump into)* heurter; *(inf)* dénigrer ♦ *vi (at door etc)*: **to ~ at** *or* **on** frapper à ♦ *n* coup *m*; ~ **down** *vt* renverser; ~ **off** *vi (inf: finish)* s'arrêter (de travailler) ♦ *vt (from price)* faire un rabais de; *(inf: steal)* piquer; ~ **out** *vt* assommer; *(BOXING)* mettre k.-o.; *(defeat)* éliminer; ~ **over** *vt* renverser, faire tomber; **~er** *n (on door)* heurtoir *m*; **~out** *n (BOXING)* knockout *m*, K.-O. *m*; **~out competition** compétition *f* avec épreuves éliminatoires

knot [nɔt] *n (gen)* nœud *m* ♦ *vt* nouer

know [nəʊ] *(pt* **knew**, *pp* **known**) *vt* savoir; *(person, place)* connaître; **to ~ how to do** savoir (comment) faire; **to ~ how to swim** savoir nager; **to ~ about** *or* **of sth** être au courant de qch; **to ~ about** *or* **of sb** avoir entendu parler de qn; **~-all** *(pej)* *n* je-sais-tout *m/f*; **~-how** *n* savoir-faire *m*; **~ing** *adj (look etc)* entendu(e); **~ingly** *adv* sciemment; *(smile, look)* d'un air entendu

knowledge ['nɔlɪdʒ] *n* connaissance *f*; *(learning)* connaissances, savoir *m*; **~able** *adj* bien informé(e)

knuckle ['nʌkl] *n* articulation *f* (des doigts), jointure *f*

Koran [kɔ'rɑːn] *n* Coran *m*

Korea [kə'rɪə] *n* Corée *f*

kosher ['kəʊʃə*r*] *adj* kascher *inv*

Kosovo ['kɔsəvəʊ] *n* Kosovo *m*

L, l

L *abbr* (= *lake, large*) L; (= *left*) g; *(BRIT: AUT: learner)* signale un conducteur débutant

lab [læb] *n abbr* (= *laboratory*) labo *m*

label ['leɪbl] *n* étiquette *f* ♦ *vt* étiqueter

labor *etc* ['leɪbə*r*] *(US)* = **labour** *etc*

laboratory [lə'bɔrətəri] *n* laboratoire *m*

labour ['leɪbə*r*] *(US* **labor**) *n (work)* travail *m*; *(workforce)* main-d'œuvre *f* ♦ *vi*: **to ~ (at)** travailler dur (à), peiner (sur) ♦ *vt*: **to ~ a point** insister sur un point; **in ~** *(MED)* en travail, en train d'accoucher; **L~, the**

L~ party *(BRIT)* le parti travailliste, les travaillistes *mpl*; **~ed** ['leɪbəd] *adj (breathing)* pénible, difficile; **~er** *n* manœuvre *m*; **farm ~er** ouvrier *m* agricole

lace [leɪs] *n* dentelle *f*; *(of shoe etc)* lacet *m* ♦ *vt (shoe: also:* ~ **up**) lacer

lack [læk] *n* manque *m* ♦ *vt* manquer de; **through** *or* **for ~ of** faute de, par manque de; **to be ~ing** manquer, faire défaut; **to be ~ing in** manquer de

lacquer ['lækə*r*] *n* laque *f*

lad [læd] *n* garçon *m*, gars *m*

ladder ['lædə*r*] *n* échelle *f*; *(BRIT: in tights)* maille filée

laden ['leɪdn] *adj*: ~ **(with)** chargé(e) (de)

ladle ['leɪdl] *n* louche *f*

lady ['leɪdɪ] *n* dame *f*; *(in address)*: **ladies and gentlemen** Mesdames (et) Messieurs, **young ~** jeune fille *f*; *(married)* jeune femme *f*; **the ladies' (room)** les toilettes *fpl* (pour dames); **~bird** *(US* **ladybug**) *n* coccinelle *f*; **~like** *adj* distingué(e); **~ship** *n*: **your ~ship** Madame la comtesse/la baronne *etc*

lag [læg] *n* retard *m* ♦ *vi (also:* ~ **behind**) rester en arrière, traîner; *(fig)* rester en traîne ♦ *vt (pipes)* calorifuger

lager ['lɑːgə*r*] *n* bière blonde

lagoon [lə'guːn] *n* lagune *f*

laid [leɪd] *pt, pp* of **lay**; **~-back** *(inf)* *adj* relaxe, décontracté(e); ~ **up** *adj* alité(e)

lain [leɪn] *pp* of **lie**

lake [leɪk] *n* lac *m*

lamb [læm] *n* agneau *m*; ~ **chop** *n* côtelette *f* d'agneau

lame [leɪm] *adj* boiteux(-euse)

lament [lə'mɛnt] *n* lamentation *f* ♦ *vt* pleurer, se lamenter sur

laminated ['læmɪneɪtɪd] *adj* laminé(e); *(windscreen)* (en verre) feuilleté

lamp [læmp] *n* lampe *f*; **~post** *(BRIT)* *n* réverbère *m*; **~shade** *n* abat-jour *m inv*

land [lænd] *n (as opposed to sea)* terre *f* *(ferme)*; *(soil)* terre; terrain *m*; *(estate)* terre(s), domaine(s) *m(pl)*; *(country)* pays *m* ♦ *vi (AVIAT)* atterrir; *(fig)* (re)tomber ♦ *vt (passengers, goods)* débarquer; **to ~ sb**

with sth (*inf*) coller qch à qn; ~ **up** *vi* atterrir, (finir par) se retrouver; ~**fill** site *n* décharge *f*; ~**ing** *n* (*AVIAT*) atterrissage *m*; (*of staircase*) palier *m*; (*of troops*) débarquement *m*; ~**ing strip** *n* piste *f* d'atterrissage; ~**lady** *n* propriétaire *f*, logeuse *f*; (*of pub*) patronne *f*; ~**locked** *adj* sans littoral; ~**lord** *n* propriétaire *m*, logeur *m*; (*of pub etc*) patron *m*; ~**mark** *n* (point *m* de) repère *m*; **to be a ~mark** (*fig*) faire date *or* époque; ~**owner** *n* propriétaire foncier *or* terrien; ~**scape** *n* paysage *m*; ~**scape gardener** *n* jardinier(-ère) paysagiste; ~**slide** *n* (*GEO*) glissement *m* (de terrain); (*fig: POL*) raz-de-marée (électoral)

lane [leɪn] *n* (*in country*) chemin *m*; (*AUT*) voie *f*, file *f*; (*in race*) couloir *m*; **"get in ~"** (*AUT*) "mettez-vous dans *or* sur la bonne file"

language ['læŋgwɪdʒ] *n* langue *f*; (*way one speaks*) langage *m*; **bad ~** grossièretés *fpl*, langage grossier; ~ **laboratory** *n* laboratoire *m* de langues

lank [læŋk] *adj* (*hair*) raide et terne

lanky ['læŋkɪ] *adj* grand(e) et maigre, efflanqué(e)

lantern ['læntən] *n* lanterne *f*

lap [læp] *n* (*of track*) tour *m* (de piste); (*of body*): **in** *or* **on one's ~** sur les genoux ♦ *vt* (*also: ~ **up**) laper ♦ *vi* (*waves*) clapoter; ~ **up** *vt* (*fig*) accepter béatement, gober

lapel [lə'pel] *n* revers *m*

Lapland ['læplænd] *n* Laponie *f*

lapse [læps] *n* défaillance *f*; (*in behaviour*) écart *m* de conduite ♦ *vi* (*LAW*) cesser d'être en vigueur; (*contract*) expirer; **to ~ into bad habits** prendre de mauvaises habitudes; ~ **of time** laps *m* de temps, intervalle *m*

laptop (computer) ['læptɒp(-)] *n* portable *m*

larceny ['lɑːsənɪ] *n* vol *m*

larch [lɑːtʃ] *n* mélèze *m*

lard [lɑːd] *n* saindoux *m*

larder ['lɑːdər] *n* garde-manger *m inv*

large [lɑːdʒ] *adj* grand(e); (*person, animal*) gros(se); **at ~** (*free*) en liberté; (*generally*)

en général; *see also* **by**; ~**ly** *adv* en grande partie; (*principally*) surtout; ~**-scale** *adj* (*action*) d'envergure; (*map*) à grande échelle

lark [lɑːk] *n* (*bird*) alouette *f*; (*joke*) blague *f*, farce *f*

laryngitis [lærɪn'dʒaɪtɪs] *n* laryngite *f*

laser ['leɪzər] *n* laser *m*; ~ **printer** *n* imprimante *f* laser

lash [læʃ] *n* coup *m* de fouet; (*also: eyelash*) cil *m* ♦ *vt* fouetter; (*tie*) attacher; ~ **out** *vi*: **to ~ out** *or* **against** attaquer violemment

lass [læs] *n* (*BRIT*) (jeune) fille *f*

lasso [læˈsuː] *n* lasso *m*

last [lɑːst] *adj* dernier(-ère) ♦ *adv* en dernier; (*finally*) finalement ♦ *vi* durer; ~ **week** la semaine dernière; ~ **night** (*evening*) hier soir; (*night*) la nuit dernière; **at ~** enfin; ~ **but one** avant-dernier(-ère); ~**-ditch** *adj* (*attempt*) ultime, désespéré(e); ~**ing** *adj* durable; ~**ly** *adv* en dernier lieu, pour finir; ~**-minute** *adj* de dernière minute

latch [lætʃ] *n* loquet *m*

late [leɪt] *adj* (*not on time*) en retard; (*far on in day etc*) tardif(-ive); (*edition, delivery*) dernier(-ère); (*former*) ancien(ne) ♦ *adv* tard; (*behind time, schedule*) en retard; **of ~** dernièrement; **in ~ May** vers la fin (du mois) de mai, fin mai; **the ~ Mr X** feu M. X; ~**comer** *n* retardataire *m/f*; ~**ly** *adv* récemment; ~**r** *adj* (*date etc*) ultérieur(e); (*version etc*) plus récent(e) ♦ *adv* plus tard; ~**r on** plus tard; ~**st** *adj* tout(e) dernier(-ère); **at the ~st** au plus tard

lathe [leɪð] *n* tour *m*

lather ['lɑːðər] *n* mousse *f* (de savon) ♦ *vt* savonner

Latin ['lætɪn] *n* latin *m* ♦ *adj* latin(e); ~ **America** *n* Amérique latine; ~ **American** *adj* latino-américain(e)

latitude ['lætɪtjuːd] *n* latitude *f*

latter ['lætər] *adj* deuxième, dernier(-ère) ♦ *n*: **the ~** ce dernier, celui-ci; ~**ly** *adv* dernièrement, récemment

laudable ['lɔːdəbl] *adj* louable

laugh [lɑːf] *n* rire *m* ♦ *vi* rire; ~ **at** *vt fus* se moquer de; rire de; ~ **off** *vt* écarter par une plaisanterie *or* par une boutade; ~**able** *adj* risible, ridicule; ~**ing stock** *n*: **the ~ing stock of** la risée de; ~**ter** *n* rire *m*; rires *mpl*

launch [lɔːntʃ] *n* lancement *m*; (*motorboat*) vedette *f* ♦ *vt* lancer; ~ **into** *vt fus* se lancer dans

Launderette ® [lɔːnˈdrɛt] (*BRIT*), **Laundromat** ® [ˈlɔːndrəmæt] (*US*) *n* laverie *f* (automatique)

laundry [ˈlɔːndrɪ] *n* (*clothes*) linge *m*; (*business*) blanchisserie *f*; (*room*) buanderie *f*

laurel [ˈlɔrl] *n* laurier *m*

lava [ˈlɑːvə] *n* lave *f*

lavatory [ˈlævətərɪ] *n* toilettes *fpl*

lavender [ˈlævəndəʳ] *n* lavande *f*

lavish [ˈlævɪʃ] *adj* (*amount*) copieux(-euse); (*person*): ~ **with** prodigue de ♦ *vt*: **to ~ sth on sb** prodiguer qch à qn; (*money*) dépenser qch sans compter pour qn/qch

law [lɔː] *n* loi *f*; (*science*) droit *m*; ~-**abiding** *adj* respectueux(-euse) des lois; ~ **and order** *n* l'ordre public; ~ **court** *n* tribunal *m*, cour *f* de justice; ~**ful** *adj* légal(e); ~**less** *adj* (*action*) illégal(e)

lawn [lɔːn] *n* pelouse *f*; ~**mower** *n* tondeuse *f* à gazon; ~ **tennis** *n* tennis *m*

law school (*US*) *n* faculté *f* de droit

lawsuit [ˈlɔːsuːt] *n* procès *m*

lawyer [ˈlɔːjəʳ] *n* (*consultant, with company*) juriste *m*; (*for sales, wills etc*) notaire *m*; (*partner, in court*) avocat *m*

lax [læks] *adj* relâché(e)

laxative [ˈlæksətɪv] *n* laxatif *m*

lay [leɪ] (*pt, pp* **laid**) *pt of* **lie** ♦ *adj* laïque; (*not expert*) profane ♦ *vt* poser, mettre; (*eggs*) pondre; **to ~ the table** mettre la table; ~ **aside** *vt* mettre de côté; ~ **by** *vt* = **lay aside**; ~ **down** *vt* poser; **to ~ down the law** faire la loi; **to ~ down one's life** sacrifier sa vie; ~ **off** *vt* (*workers*) licencier; ~ **on** *vt* (*provide*) fournir; ~ **out** *vt* (*display*) disposer, étaler; ~**about** (*inf*) *n* fainéant(e); ~-**by** (*BRIT*) *n* aire *f* de stationnement (sur le bas-côté)

layer [ˈleɪəʳ] *n* couche *f*

layman [ˈleɪmən] (*irreg*) *n* profane *m*

layout [ˈleɪaut] *n* disposition *f*, plan *m*, agencement *m*; (*PRESS*) mise *f* en page

laze [leɪz] *vi* (*also*: ~ **about**) paresser

lazy [ˈleɪzɪ] *adj* paresseux(-euse)

lb *abbr* = **pound** (*weight*)

lead¹ [liːd] (*pt, pp* **led**) *n* (*distance, time ahead*) avance *f*; (*clue*) piste *f*; (*THEATRE*) rôle principal; (*ELEC*) fil *m*; (*for dog*) laisse *f* ♦ *vt* mener, conduire; (*be ~ of*) être à la tête de ♦ *vi* (*street etc*) mener, conduire; (*SPORT*) mener, être en tête; **in the ~** en tête; **to ~ the way** montrer le chemin; ~ **away** *vt* emmener; ~ **back** *vt*: **to ~ back to** ramener à; ~ **on** *vt* (*tease*) faire marcher; ~ **to** *vt fus* mener à; conduire à; ~ **up to** *vt fus* conduire à

lead² [lɛd] *n* (*metal*) plomb *m*; (*in pencil*) mine *f*; ~**ed petrol** *n* essence *f* au plomb; ~**en** *adj* (*sky, sea*) de plomb

leader [ˈliːdəʳ] *n* chef *m*; dirigeant(e), leader *m*; (*SPORT: in league*) leader; (*: in race*) coureur *m* de tête; ~**ship** *n* direction *f*; (*quality*) qualités *fpl* de chef

lead-free [ˈlɛdfriː] *adj* (*petrol*) sans plomb

leading [ˈliːdɪŋ] *adj* principal(e); de premier plan; (*in race*) de tête; ~ **lady** *n* (*THEATRE*) vedette (féminine); ~ **light** *n* (*person*) vedette *f*, sommité *f*; ~ **man** (*irreg*) *n* vedette (masculine)

lead singer [liːd-] *n* (*in pop group*) (chanteur *m*) vedette *f*

leaf [liːf] (*pl* **leaves**) *n* feuille *f* ♦ *vi*: **to ~ through** feuilleter; **to turn over a new ~** changer de conduite *or* d'existence

leaflet [ˈliːflɪt] *n* prospectus *m*, brochure *f*; (*POL, REL*) tract *m*

league [liːg] *n* ligue *f*; (*FOOTBALL*) championnat *m*; **to be in ~ with** avoir partie liée avec, être de mèche avec

leak [liːk] *n* fuite *f* ♦ *vi* (*pipe, liquid etc*) fuir; (*shoes*) prendre l'eau; (*ship*) faire eau ♦ *vt* (*information*) divulguer

lean [liːn] (*pt, pp* **leaned** *or* **leant**) *adj* maigre ♦ *vt*: **to ~ sth on sth** appuyer qch sur qch ♦ *vi* (*slope*) pencher; (*rest*): **to ~**

against s'appuyer contre; être appuyé(e) contre; **to ~ on** s'appuyer sur; **to ~ back/forward** se pencher en arrière/avant; **~ out** *vi* se pencher au dehors; **~ over** *vi* se pencher; **~ing** *n*: **~ing (towards)** tendance *f* (à), penchant *m* (pour); **~t** [lɛnt] *pt, pp of* **lean**

leap [liːp] (*pt, pp* **leaped** *or* **leapt**) *n* bond *m*, saut *m* ♦ *vi* bondir, sauter; **~frog** *n* saute-mouton *m*; **~t** [lɛpt] *pt, pp of* **leap**; **~ year** *n* année *f* bissextile

learn [ləːn] (*pt, pp* **learned** *or* **learnt**) *vt, vi* apprendre; **to ~ to do sth** apprendre à faire qch; **to ~ about sth** (*hear, read*) apprendre qch; **~ed** ['ləːnɪd] *adj* érudit(e), savant(e); **~er** (*BRIT*) *n* (*also*: **~er driver**) (conducteur(-trice)) débutant(e); **~ing** *n* (*knowledge*) savoir *m*; **~t** *pt, pp of* **learn**

lease [liːs] *n* bail *m* ♦ *vt* louer à bail

leash [liːʃ] *n* laisse *f*

least [liːst] *adj*: **the ~** (+*noun*) le (la) plus petit(e), le (la) moindre; (: *smallest amount of*) le moins de ♦ *adv* (+*verb*) le moins; (+*adj*): **the ~** le (la) moins; **at ~** au moins; (*or rather*) du moins; **not in the ~** pas le moins du monde

leather ['lɛðər] *n* cuir *m*

leave [liːv] (*pt, pp* **left**) *vt* laisser; (*go away from*) quitter; (*forget*) oublier ♦ *vi* partir, s'en aller ♦ *n* (*time off*) congé *m*; (*MIL also*: *consent*) permission *f*; **to be left** rester; **there's some milk left over** il reste du lait; **on ~** en permission; **~ behind** *vt* (*person, object*) laisser; (*forget*) oublier; **~ out** *vt* oublier, omettre; **~ of absence** *n* congé exceptionnel; (*MIL*) permission spéciale

leaves [liːvz] *npl of* **leaf**

Lebanon ['lɛbənən] *n* Liban *m*

lecherous ['lɛtʃərəs] (*pej*) *adj* lubrique

lecture ['lɛktʃər] *n* conférence *f*; (*SCOL*) cours *m* ♦ *vi* donner des cours; enseigner ♦ *vt* (*scold*) sermonner, réprimander; **to give a ~ on** faire une conférence sur; donner un cours sur; **~r** (*BRIT*) *n* (*at university*) professeur *m* (d'université)

led [lɛd] *pt, pp of* **lead**¹

ledge [lɛdʒ] *n* (*of window, on wall*) rebord *m*; (*of mountain*) saillie *f*, corniche *f*

ledger ['lɛdʒər] *n* (*COMM*) registre *m*, grand livre

leech [liːtʃ] *n* (*also fig*) sangsue *f*

leek [liːk] *n* poireau *m*

leer [liər] *vi*: **to ~ at sb** regarder qn d'un air mauvais *or* concupiscent

leeway ['liːweɪ] *n* (*fig*): **to have some ~** avoir une certaine liberté d'action

left [lɛft] *pt, pp of* **leave** ♦ *adj* (*not right*) gauche ♦ *n* gauche *f* ♦ *adv* à gauche; **on the ~, to the ~** à gauche; **the L~** (*POL*) la gauche; **~-handed** *adj* gaucher(-ère); **~-hand side** *n* gauche *f*; **~-luggage locker** *n* (casier *m* à) consigne *f* automatique; **~-luggage (office)** (*BRIT*) *n* consigne *f*; **~overs** *npl* restes *mpl*; **~-wing** *adj* (*POL*) de gauche

leg [lɛg] *n* jambe *f*; (*of animal*) patte *f*; (*of furniture*) pied *m*; (*CULIN: of chicken, pork*) cuisse *f*; (: *of lamb*) gigot *m*; (*of journey*) étape *f*; **1st/2nd ~** (*SPORT*) match *m* aller/retour

legacy ['lɛgəsɪ] *n* héritage *m*, legs *m*

legal ['liːgl] *adj* légal(e); **~ holiday** (*US*) *n* jour férié; **~ tender** *n* monnaie légale

legend ['lɛdʒənd] *n* légende *f*

leggings ['lɛgɪŋz] *npl* caleçon *m*

legible ['lɛdʒəbl] *adj* lisible

legislation [lɛdʒɪs'leɪʃən] *n* législation *f*; **legislature** ['lɛdʒɪslətʃər] *n* (*corps m*) législatif *m*

legitimate [lɪ'dʒɪtɪmət] *adj* légitime

leg-room ['lɛgruːm] *n* place *f* pour les jambes

leisure ['lɛʒər] *n* loisir *m*, temps *m* libre; loisirs *mpl*; **at ~** (tout) à loisir; à tête reposée; **~ centre** *n* centre *m* de loisirs; **~ly** *adj* tranquille; fait(e) sans se presser

lemon ['lɛmən] *n* citron *m*; **~ade** [lɛmə'neɪd] *n* limonade *f*; **~ tea** *n* thé *m* au citron

lend [lɛnd] (*pt, pp* **lent**) *vt*: **to ~ sth (to sb)** prêter qch (à qn)

length [lɛŋθ] *n* longueur *f*; (*section: of road, pipe etc*) morceau *m*, bout *m*; (*of time*) durée f; **at ~** (*at last*) enfin, à la fin; (*~ily*) longuement; **~en** vt allonger, prolonger ♦ vi s'allonger; **~ways** adv dans le sens de la longueur, en long; **~y** adj (très) long (longue)

lenient ['li:nɪənt] adj indulgent(e), clément(e)

lens [lɛnz] n lentille f; (*of spectacles*) verre m; (*of camera*) objectif m

Lent [lɛnt] n carême m

lent [lɛnt] pt, pp of **lend**

lentil ['lɛntɪl] n lentille f

Leo ['li:əʊ] n le Lion

leotard ['li:ətɑ:d] n maillot m (*de danseur etc*), collant m

leprosy ['lɛprəsɪ] n lèpre f

lesbian ['lɛzbɪən] n lesbienne f

less [lɛs] adj moins de ♦ pron, adv moins ♦ prep moins; **~ than that/you** moins que cela/vous; **~ than half** moins de la moitié; **~ than ever** moins que jamais; **~ and ~** de moins en moins; **the ~ he works ...** moins il travaille ...; **~en** vi diminuer, s'atténuer ♦ vt diminuer, réduire, atténuer; **~er** adj moindre; **to a ~er extent** à un degré moindre

lesson ['lɛsn] n leçon f; **to teach sb a ~** (*fig*) donner une bonne leçon à qn

let [lɛt] (*pt, pp* **let**) vt laisser; (*BRIT: lease*) louer; **to ~ sb do sth** laisser qn faire qch; **to ~ sb know sth** faire savoir qch à qn, prévenir qn de qch; **~'s go** allons-y; **~ him come** qu'il vienne; **"to ~"** "à louer"; **~ down** vt (*tyre*) dégonfler; (*person*) décevoir, faire faux bond à; **~ go** vi lâcher prise ♦ vt lâcher; **~ in** vt laisser entrer; (*visitor etc*) faire entrer; **~ off** vt (*culprit*) ne pas punir; (*firework etc*) faire partir; **~ on** (*inf*) vi dire; **~ out** vt laisser sortir; (*scream*) laisser échapper; **~ up** vi diminuer; (*cease*) s'arrêter

lethal ['li:θl] adj mortel(le), fatal(e)

letter ['lɛtə^r] n lettre f; **~ bomb** n lettre piégée; **~box** (*BRIT*) n boîte f aux or à lettres; **~ing** n lettres fpl; caractères mpl

lettuce ['lɛtɪs] n laitue f, salade f

let-up ['lɛtʌp] n répit m, arrêt m

leukaemia [lu:'ki:mɪə] (*US* **leukemia**) n leucémie f

level ['lɛvl] adj plat(e), plan(e), uni(e); horizontal(e) ♦ n niveau m ♦ vt niveler, aplanir; **to be ~ with** être au même niveau que; **to draw ~ with** (*person, vehicle*) arriver à la hauteur de; **"A" ~s** (*BRIT*) ≃ baccalauréat m; **"O" ~s** (*BRIT*) ≃ B.E.P.C.; **on the ~** (*fig: honest*) régulier(-ère); **~ off** vi (*prices etc*) se stabiliser; **~ out** vi = **level off**; **~ crossing** (*BRIT*) n passage m à niveau; **~-headed** adj équilibré(e)

lever ['li:və^r] n levier m; **~age** n: **~age (on** *or* **with)** prise f (sur)

levy ['lɛvɪ] n taxe f, impôt m ♦ vt prélever, imposer; percevoir

lewd [lu:d] adj obscène, lubrique

liability [laɪə'bɪlətɪ] n responsabilité f; (*handicap*) handicap m; **liabilities** npl (*on balance sheet*) passif m

liable ['laɪəbl] adj (*subject*): **~ to** sujet(te) à; passible de; (*responsible*): **~ (for)** responsable (de); (*likely*): **~ to do** susceptible de faire

liaise [li:'eɪz] vi: **to ~ (with)** assurer la liaison avec; **liaison** n liaison f

liar ['laɪə^r] n menteur(-euse)

libel ['laɪbl] n diffamation f; (*document*) écrit m diffamatoire ♦ vt diffamer

liberal ['lɪbərl] adj libéral(e); (*generous*): **~ with** prodigue de, généreux(-euse) avec; **the L~ Democrats** (*BRIT*) le parti libéral-démocrate

liberation [lɪbə'reɪʃən] n libération f

liberty ['lɪbətɪ] n liberté f; **to be at ~ to do** être libre de faire

Libra ['li:brə] n la Balance

librarian [laɪ'brɛərɪən] n bibliothécaire m/f

library ['laɪbrərɪ] n bibliothèque f

libretto [lɪ'brɛtəʊ] n livret m

Libya ['lɪbɪə] n Libye f

lice [laɪs] npl of **louse**

licence ['laɪsns] (*US* **license**) n autorisation f, permis m; (*RADIO, TV*) redevance f; **driving ~**, (*US*) **driver's license** permis m (de conduire); **~ number** n numéro m d'immatriculation; **~ plate** n plaque f minéra-

logique
license ['laɪsns] *n* (US) = **licence** ♦ *vt* donner une licence à; **~d** *adj* (car) muni(e) de la vignette; (to sell alcohol) patenté(e) pour la vente des spiritueux, qui a une licence de débit de boissons

lick [lɪk] *vt* lécher; (inf: defeat) écraser; **to ~ one's lips** (fig) se frotter les mains

licorice ['lɪkərɪs] (US) *n* = **liquorice**

lid [lɪd] *n* couvercle *m*; (eyelid) paupière *f*

lie [laɪ] (pt **lay**, pp **lain**) *vi* (rest) être étendu(e) or allongé(e) or couché(e); (in grave) être enterré(e), reposer; (be situated) se trouver, être; (be untruthful: pt, pp ~d) mentir ♦ *n* mensonge *m*; **to ~ low** (fig) se cacher; **~ about** *vi* traîner; **~ around** *vi* = **lie about**; **~-down** (BRIT) *n*: **to have a ~-down** s'allonger, se reposer; **~-in** (BRIT) *n*: **to have a ~-in** faire la grasse matinée

lieutenant [lef'tenənt, (US) luː'tenənt] *n* lieutenant *m*

life [laɪf] (pl **lives**) *n* vie *f*; **to come to ~** (fig) s'animer; **~ assurance** (BRIT) *n* = **life insurance**; **~belt** (BRIT) *n* bouée *f* de sauvetage; **~boat** *n* canot *m* or chaloupe *f* de sauvetage; **~buoy** *n* bouée *f* de sauvetage; **~guard** *n* surveillant *m* de baignade; **~ insurance** *n* assurance-vie *f*; **~ jacket** *n* gilet *m* or ceinture *f* de sauvetage; **~less** *adj* sans vie, inanimé(e); (dull) qui manque de vie or de vigueur; **~like** *adj* qui semble vrai(e) or vivant(e); (painting) réaliste; **~long** *adj* de toute une vie, de toujours; **~ preserver** (US) *n* = **lifebelt; life jacket; ~-saving** *n* sauvetage *m*; **~ sentence** *n* condamnation *f* à perpétuité; **~-size(d)** *adj* grandeur nature *inv*; **~ span** *n* (durée *f* de) vie *f*; **~style** *n* style *m* or mode *m* de vie; **~-support system** *n* (MED) respirateur artificiel; **~time** *n* vie *f*; **in his ~time** de son vivant

lift [lɪft] *vt* soulever, lever; (end) supprimer, lever ♦ *vi* (fog) se lever ♦ *n* (BRIT: elevator) ascenseur *m*; **to give sb a ~** (BRIT: AUT) emmener or prendre qn en voiture; **~-off** *n* décollage *m*

light [laɪt] (pt, pp **lit**) *n* lumière *f*; (lamp)

lampe *f*; (AUT: rear ~) feu *m*; (: headlight) phare *m*; (for cigarette etc): **have you got a ~?** avez-vous du feu? ♦ *vt* (candle, cigarette, fire) allumer; (room) éclairer ♦ *adj* (room, colour) clair(e); (not heavy) léger(-ère); (not strenuous) peu fatigant(e); **~s** *npl* (AUT: traffic ~s) feux *mpl*; **to come to ~** être dévoilé(e) or découvert(e); **~ up** *vi* (face) s'éclairer ♦ *vt* (illuminate) éclairer, illuminer; **~ bulb** *n* ampoule *f*; **~en** *vt* (make less heavy) alléger; **~er** *n* (also: **cigarette ~er**) briquet *m*; **~-headed** *adj* étourdi(e); (excited) grisé(e); **~-hearted** *adj* gai(e), joyeux(-euse), enjoué(e); **~house** *n* phare *m*; **~ing** *n* (on road) éclairage *m*; (in theatre) éclairages; **~ly** *adv* légèrement; **to get off ~ly** s'en tirer à bon compte; **~ness** *n* (in weight) légèreté *f*

lightning ['laɪtnɪŋ] *n* éclair *m*, foudre *f*; **~ conductor** (US **lightning rod**) *n* paratonnerre *m*

light pen *n* crayon *m* optique

lightweight ['laɪtweɪt] *adj* (suit) léger(-ère) ♦ *n* (BOXING) poids léger

like [laɪk] *vt* aimer (bien) ♦ *prep* comme ♦ *adj* semblable, pareil(le) ♦ *n*: **and the ~** et d'autres du même genre; **his ~s and dislikes** ses goûts *mpl* or préférences *fpl*; **I would ~, I'd ~** je voudrais, j'aimerais; **would you ~ a coffee?** voulez-vous du café?; **to be/look ~ sb/sth** ressembler à qn/qch; **what does it look ~?** de quoi est-ce que ça a l'air?; **what does it taste ~?** quel goût est-ce que ça a?; **that's just ~ him** c'est bien de lui, ça lui ressemble; **do it ~ this** fais-le comme ceci; **it's nothing ~ ...** ce n'est pas du tout comme ...; **~able** *adj* sympathique, agréable

likelihood ['laɪklɪhud] *n* probabilité *f*

likely ['laɪklɪ] *adj* probable; plausible; **he's ~ to leave** il va sûrement partir, il risque fort de partir; **not ~!** (inf) pas de danger!

likeness ['laɪknɪs] *n* ressemblance *f*; **that's a good ~** c'est très ressemblant

likewise ['laɪkwaɪz] *adv* de même, pareillement

liking ['laɪkɪŋ] n (for person) affection f; (for thing) penchant m, goût m

lilac ['laɪlək] n lilas m

lily ['lɪlɪ] n lis m; ~ **of the valley** n muguet m

limb [lɪm] n membre m

limber up ['lɪmbər-] vi se dégourdir, faire des exercices d'assouplissement

limbo ['lɪmbəu] n: **to be in ~** (fig) être tombé(e) dans l'oubli

lime [laɪm] n (tree) tilleul m; (fruit) lime f, citron vert; (GEO) chaux f

limelight ['laɪmlaɪt] n: **in the ~** (fig) en vedette, au premier plan

limerick ['lɪmərɪk] n poème m humoristique (de 5 vers)

limestone ['laɪmstəun] n pierre f à chaux; (GEO) calcaire m

limit ['lɪmɪt] n limite f ♦ vt limiter; **~ed** adj limité(e), restreint(e); **to be ~ed to** se limiter à, ne concerner que; **~ed (liability) company** (BRIT) n ≃ société f anonyme

limousine ['lɪməzi:n] n limousine f

limp [lɪmp] n: **to have a ~** boiter ♦ vi boiter ♦ adj mou (molle)

limpet ['lɪmpɪt] n patelle f

line [laɪn] n ligne f; (stroke) trait m; (wrinkle) ride f; (rope) corde f; (wire) fil m; (of poem) vers m; (row, series) rangée f; (of people) file f, queue f; (railway track) voie f; (COMM: series of goods) article(s) m(pl); (work) métier m, type m d'activité; (attitude, policy) position f ♦ vt (subj: trees, crowd) border; **in a ~** aligné(e); **in his ~ of business** dans sa partie, dans son rayon; **in ~ with** en accord avec; **to ~ (with)** (clothes) doubler (de); (box) garnir or tapisser (de); **~ up** vi s'aligner, se mettre en rang(s) ♦ vt aligner; (event) prévoir, préparer; **~d** adj (face) ridé(e), marqué(e); (paper) réglé(e)

linen ['lɪnɪn] n linge m (de maison); (cloth) lin m

liner ['laɪnər] n paquebot m (de ligne); (for bin) sac m à poubelle

linesman ['laɪnzmən] (irreg) n juge m de touche; (TENNIS) juge m de ligne

line-up ['laɪnʌp] n (US: queue) file f; (SPORT) (composition f de l')équipe f

linger ['lɪŋgər] vi s'attarder; traîner; (smell, tradition) persister

linguist ['lɪŋgwɪst] n: **to be a good ~** être doué(e) par les langues; **~ics** [lɪŋ'gwɪstɪks] n linguistique f

lining ['laɪnɪŋ] n doublure f

link [lɪŋk] n lien m, rapport m; (of a chain) maillon m ♦ vt relier, lier, unir; **~s** npl (GOLF) (terrain m de) golf m; **~ up** vt relier ♦ vi se rejoindre; s'associer

lino ['laɪnəu] n = **linoleum**

linoleum [lɪ'nəulɪəm] n linoléum m

lion ['laɪən] n lion m; **~ess** n lionne f

lip [lɪp] n lèvre f

liposuction ['lɪpəusʌkʃən] n liposuccion f

lip: **~-read** vi lire sur les lèvres; **~ salve** n pommade f rosat or pour les lèvres; **~ service** n: **to pay ~ service to sth** ne reconnaître le mérite de qch que pour la forme; **~stick** n rouge m à lèvres

liqueur [lɪ'kjuər] n liqueur f

liquid ['lɪkwɪd] adj liquide ♦ n liquide m; **~ize** vt (CULIN) passer au mixer; **~izer** n mixer m

liquor ['lɪkər] (US) n spiritueux m, alcool m

liquorice ['lɪkərɪs] (BRIT) n réglisse f

liquor store (US) n magasin m de vins et spiritueux

lisp [lɪsp] vi zézayer

list [lɪst] n liste f ♦ vt (write down) faire une or la liste de; (mention) énumérer; **~ed building** (BRIT) n monument classé

listen ['lɪsn] vi écouter; **to ~ to** écouter; **~er** n auditeur(-trice)

listless ['lɪstlɪs] adj indolent(e), apathique

lit [lɪt] pt, pp of **light**

liter ['li:tər] (US) n = **litre**

literacy ['lɪtərəsɪ] n degré m d'alphabétisation, fait m de savoir lire et écrire

literal ['lɪtərəl] adj littéral(e); **~ly** adv littéralement; (really) réellement

literary ['lɪtərərɪ] adj littéraire

literate ['lɪtərət] adj qui sait lire et écrire, instruit(e)

literature ['lɪtrɪtʃəʳ] *n* littérature *f*; (*brochures etc*) documentation *f*

lithe [laɪð] *adj* agile, souple

litigation [lɪtɪ'geɪʃən] *n* litige *m*; contentieux *m*

litre ['liːtəʳ] (*US* **liter**) *n* litre *m*

litter ['lɪtəʳ] *n* (*rubbish*) détritus *mpl*, ordures *fpl*; (*young animals*) portée *f*; ~ **bin** (*BRIT*) *n* boîte *f* à ordures, poubelle *f*; ~**ed** *adj*: ~**ed with** jonché(e) de, couvert(e) de

little ['lɪtl] *adj* (*small*) petit(e) ♦ *adv* peu; ~ **milk/time** peu de lait/temps; **a** ~ un peu (de); **a** ~ **bit** un peu; ~ **by** ~ petit à petit, peu à peu

live¹ [laɪv] *adj* (*animal*) vivant(e), en vie; (*wire*) sous tension; (*bullet, bomb*) non explosé(e); (*broadcast*) en direct; (*performance*) en public

live² [lɪv] *vi* vivre; (*reside*) vivre, habiter; ~ **down** *vt* faire oublier (avec le temps); ~ **on** *vt fus* (*food, salary*) vivre de; ~ **together** *vi* vivre ensemble, cohabiter; ~ **up to** *vt fus* se montrer à la hauteur de

livelihood ['laɪvlɪhud] *n* moyens *mpl* d'existence

lively ['laɪvlɪ] *adj* vif (vive), plein(e) d'entrain; (*place, book*) vivant(e)

liven up ['laɪvn-] *vt* animer ♦ *vi* s'animer

liver ['lɪvəʳ] *n* foie *m*

lives [laɪvz] *npl of* **life**

livestock ['laɪvstɔk] *n* bétail *m*, cheptel *m*

livid ['lɪvɪd] *adj* livide, blafard(e); (*inf: furious*) furieux(-euse), furibond(e)

living ['lɪvɪŋ] *adj* vivant(e), en vie ♦ *n*: **to earn** *or* **make a** ~ gagner sa vie; ~ **conditions** *npl* conditions *fpl* de vie; ~ **room** *n* salle *f* de séjour; ~ **standards** *npl* niveau *m* de vie; ~ **wage** *n* salaire *m* permettant de vivre (décemment)

lizard ['lɪzəd] *n* lézard *m*

load [ləud] *n* (*weight*) poids *m*; (*thing carried*) chargement *m*, charge *f* ♦ *vt* (*also:* ~ **up**): **to** ~ (**with**) charger (de); (*gun, camera*) charger (avec); (*COMPUT*) charger; **a** ~ **of**, ~**s of** (*fig*) un *or* des tas de, des masses de; **to talk a** ~ **of rubbish** dire des bêtises; ~**ed** *adj* (*question*) insidieux(-

euse); (*inf: rich*) bourré(e) de fric

loaf [ləuf] (*pl* **loaves**) *n* pain *m*, miche *f*

loan [ləun] *n* prêt *m* ♦ *vt* prêter; **on** ~ prêté(e), en prêt

loath [ləuθ] *adj*: **to be** ~ **to do** répugner à faire

loathe [ləuð] *vt* détester, avoir en horreur

loaves [ləuvz] *npl of* **loaf**

lobby ['lɔbɪ] *n* hall *m*, entrée *f*; (*POL*) groupe *m* de pression, lobby *m* ♦ *vt* faire pression sur

lobster ['lɔbstəʳ] *n* homard *m*

local ['ləukl] *adj* local(e) ♦ *n* (*BRIT: pub*) pub *m* *or* café *m* du coin; **the** ~**s** *npl* (*inhabitants*) les gens *mpl* du pays *or* du coin; ~ **anaesthetic** *n* anesthésie locale; ~ **authority** *n* collectivité locale, municipalité *f*; ~ **call** *n* communication urbaine; ~ **government** *n* administration locale *or* municipale; ~**ity** [ləu'kælɪtɪ] *n* région *f*, environs *mpl*; (*position*) lieu *m*

locate [ləu'keɪt] *vt* (*find*) trouver, repérer; (*situate*): **to be** ~**d in** être situé(e) à *or* en; **location** *n* emplacement *m*; **on location** (*CINEMA*) en extérieur

loch [lɔx] *n* lac *m*, loch *m*

lock [lɔk] *n* (*of door, box*) serrure *f*; (*of canal*) écluse *f*; (*of hair*) mèche *f*, boucle *f* ♦ *vt* (*with key*) fermer à clé ♦ *vi* (*door etc*) fermer à clé; (*wheels*) se bloquer; ~ **in** *vt* enfermer; ~ **out** *vt* enfermer dehors; (*deliberately*) mettre à la porte; ~ **up** *vt* (*person*) enfermer; (*house*) fermer à clé ♦ *vi* tout fermer (à clé)

locker ['lɔkəʳ] *n* casier *m*; (*in station*) consigne *f* automatique

locket ['lɔkɪt] *n* médaillon *m*

locksmith ['lɔksmɪθ] *n* serrurier *m*

lockup ['lɔkʌp] *n* (*prison*) prison *f*

locum ['ləukəm] *n* (*MED*) suppléant(e) (de médecin)

lodge [lɔdʒ] *n* pavillon *m* (de gardien); (*hunting* ~) pavillon de chasse ♦ *vi* (*person*): **to** ~ (**with**) être logé(e) (chez), être en pension (chez); (*bullet*) se loger ♦ *vt*: **to** ~ **a complaint** porter plainte; ~**r** *n* locataire *m/f*; (*with meals*) pensionnaire *m/f*;

lodgings *npl* chambre *f*; meublé *m*

loft [lɒft] *n* grenier *m*

lofty [ˈlɒftɪ] *adj* (*noble*) noble, élevé(e); (*haughty*) hautain(e)

log [lɒg] *n* (*of wood*) bûche *f*; (*book*) = **logbook** ♦ *vt* (*record*) noter; **~book** *n* (*NAUT*) livre *m* or journal *m* de bord; (*AVIAT*) carnet *m* de vol; (*of car*) ≃ carte grise

loggerheads [ˈlɒgəhedz] *npl*: **at ~ (with)** à couteaux tirés (avec)

logic [ˈlɒdʒɪk] *n* logique *f*; **~al** *adj* logique

log on *vi* (*COMPUT*) se connecter

log off *or* **out** *vi* (*COMPUT*) se déconnecter

loin [lɔɪn] *n* (*CULIN*) filet *m*, longe *f*

loiter [ˈlɔɪtəʳ] *vi* traîner

loll [lɒl] *vi* (*also:* **~ about**) se prélasser, fainéanter

lollipop [ˈlɒlɪpɒp] *n* sucette *f*; **~ man/lady** *n* (*BRIT*) voir encadré

---

lollipop men/ladies

*ⓘ Les **lollipop men/ladies** sont employés pour aider les enfants à traverser la rue à proximité des écoles à l'heure où ils entrent en classe et à la sortie. On les repère facilement à cause de leur long ciré blanc et ils portent une pancarte ronde pour faire signe aux automobilistes de s'arrêter. On les appelle ainsi car la forme circulaire de cette pancarte rappelle une sucette.*

---

lolly [ˈlɒlɪ] (*inf*) *n* (*lollipop*) sucette *f*; (*money*) fric *m*

London [ˈlʌndən] *n* Londres *m*; **~er** *n* Londonien(ne)

lone [ləun] *adj* solitaire

loneliness [ˈləunlɪnɪs] *n* solitude *f*, isolement *m*

lonely [ˈləunlɪ] *adj* seul(e); solitaire, isolé(e)

long [lɒŋ] *adj* long (longue) ♦ *adv* longtemps ♦ *vi*: **to ~ for sth** avoir très envie de qch; attendre qch avec impatience; **so** *or* **as ~ as** pourvu que; **don't be ~!** dépêchez-vous!; **how ~ is this river/course?** quelle est la longueur de ce fleuve/la durée de ce cours?; **6 metres ~** (long) de 6 mètres; **6 months ~** qui dure 6 mois, de 6 mois; **all night ~** toute la nuit; **he no ~er comes** il ne vient plus; **I can't stand it any ~er** je ne peux plus le supporter; **~ before/after** longtemps avant/après; **before ~** (*+future*) avant peu, dans peu de temps; (*+past*) peu de temps après; **at ~ last** enfin; **~-distance** *adj* (*call*) interurbain(e); **~er** [ˈlɒŋgəʳ] *adv* see **long**; **~hand** *n* écriture normale *or* courante; **~ing** *n* désir *m*, envie *f*, nostalgie *f*

longitude [ˈlɒngɪtjuːd] *n* longitude *f*

long: **~ jump** *n* saut *m* en longueur; **~-life** *adj* (*batteries etc*) longue durée *inv*; (*milk*) longue conservation; **~-lost** *adj* (*person*) perdu(e) de vue depuis longtemps; **~-range** *adj* à longue portée; **~-sighted** *adj* (*MED*) presbyte; **~-standing** *adj* de longue date; **~-suffering** *adj* empreint(e) d'une patience résignée; extrêmement patient(e); **~-term** *adj* à long terme; **~ wave** *n* grandes ondes; **~-winded** *adj* intarissable, interminable

loo [luː] (*BRIT: inf*) *n* W.-C. *mpl*, petit coin

look [luk] *vi* regarder; (*seem*) sembler, paraître, avoir l'air; (*building face*): **to ~ south/(out) onto the sea** donner au sud/sur la mer ♦ *n* regard *m*; (*appearance*) air *m*, allure *f*, aspect *m*; **~s** *npl* (*good ~s*) physique *m*, beauté *f*; **to have a ~** regarder; **~!** regardez!; **~ (here)!** (*annoyance*) écoutez!; **~ after** *vt fus* (*care for, deal with*) s'occuper de; **~ at** *vt fus* regarder; (*problem etc*) examiner; **~ back** *vi*: **to ~ back on** (*event etc*) évoquer, repenser à; **~ down on** *vt fus* (*fig*) regarder de haut, dédaigner; **~ for** *vt fus* chercher; **~ forward to** *vt fus* attendre avec impatience; **we ~ forward to hearing from you** (*in letter*) dans l'attente de vous lire; **~ into** *vt fus* examiner, étudier; **~ on** *vi* regarder (en spectateur); **~ out** *vi* (*beware*): **to ~ out (for)** prendre garde (à), faire attention (à); **~ out for** *vt fus* être à la recherche de; guetter; **~ round** *vi* regarder derrière soi, se retourner; **~ to** *vt fus* (*rely on*) compter sur; **~ up** *vi* lever les yeux; (*improve*) s'améliorer ♦ *vt* (*word, name*) chercher; **~ up to** *vt fus* avoir du respect pour ♦ *n* poste *m* de guet; (*person*) guetteur *m*; **to be on the ~ out (for)** guetter

loom [luːm] *vi* (*also:* **~ up**) surgir; (*approach: event etc*) être imminent(e); (*threaten*) menacer ♦ *n* (*for weaving*) métier *m* à tisser

loony ['luːnɪ] (*inf*) *adj, n* timbré(e), cinglé(e)

loop [luːp] *n* boucle *f*; **~hole** *n* (*fig*) porte *f* de sortie; échappatoire *f*

loose [luːs] *adj* (*knot, screw*) desserré(e); (*clothes*) ample, lâche; (*hair*) dénoué(e), épars(e); (*not firmly fixed*) pas solide; (*morals, discipline*) relâché(e) ♦ *n*: **on the ~** en liberté; **~ change** *n* petite monnaie; **~ chippings** *npl* (*on road*) gravillons *mpl*; **~ end** *n*: **to be at a ~ end** *or* (*US*) **at ~ ends** ne pas trop savoir quoi faire; **~ly** *adv* sans serrer; (*imprecisely*) approximativement; **~n** *vt* desserrer

loot [luːt] *n* (*inf: money*) pognon *m*, fric *m* ♦ *vt* piller

lopsided ['lɒp'saɪdɪd] *adj* de travers, asymétrique

lord [lɔːd] *n* seigneur *m*; **L~ Smith** lord Smith; **the L~** le Seigneur; **good L~!** mon Dieu!; **the (House of) L~s** (*BRIT*) la Chambre des lords; **my L~** = **your Lordship**; **L~ship** *n*: **your L~ship** Monsieur le comte/le baron/le juge; (*to bishop*) Monseigneur

lore [lɔːʳ] *n* tradition(s) *f(pl)*

lorry ['lɒrɪ] (*BRIT*) *n* camion *m*; **~ driver** (*BRIT*) *n* camionneur *m*, routier *m*

lose [luːz] (*pt, pp* **lost**) *vt, vi* perdre; **to ~ (time)** (*clock*) retarder; **to get lost** ♦ *vi* se perdre; **~r** *n* perdant(e)

loss [lɒs] *n* perte *f*; **to be at a ~** être perplexe *or* embarrassé(e)

lost [lɒst] *pt, pp of* **lose** ♦ *adj* perdu(e); **~ and found** (*US*), **~ property** *n* objets trouvés

lot [lɒt] *n* (*set*) lot *m*; **the ~** le tout; **a ~ (of)** beaucoup (de); **~s of** des tas de; **to**

draw ~s (for sth) tirer (qch) au sort

lotion ['ləʊʃən] *n* lotion *f*

lottery ['lɒtərɪ] *n* loterie *f*

loud [laʊd] *adj* bruyant(e), sonore; (*voice*) fort(e); (*support, condemnation*) vigoureux(-euse); (*gaudy*) voyant(e), tapageur(-euse) ♦ *adv* (*speak etc*) fort; **out ~** tout haut; **~-hailer** (*BRIT*) *n* porte-voix *m inv*; **~ly** *adv* fort, bruyamment; **~speaker** *n* haut-parleur *m*

lounge [laʊndʒ] *n* salon *m*; (*at airport*) salle *f*; (*BRIT: also:* **~ bar**) (salle de) café *m or* bar *m* ♦ *vi* (*also:* **~ about** *or* **around**) se prélasser, paresser; **~ suit** (*BRIT*) *n* complet *m*; (*on invitation*) "tenue de ville"

louse [laʊs] (*pl* **lice**) *n* pou *m*

lousy ['laʊzɪ] (*inf*) *adj* infect(e), moche; **I feel ~** je suis mal fichu(e)

lout [laʊt] *n* rustre *m*, butor *m*

lovable ['lʌvəbl] *adj* adorable; très sympathique

love [lʌv] *n* amour *m* ♦ *vt* aimer; (*caringly, kindly*) aimer beaucoup; **"~ (from) Anne"** "affectueusement, Anne"; **I ~ chocolate** j'adore le chocolat; **to be/fall in ~ with** être/tomber amoureux(-euse) de; **to make ~** faire l'amour; **"15 ~"** (*TENNIS*) "15 à rien *or* zéro"; **~ affair** *n* liaison (amoureuse); **~ life** *n* vie sentimentale

lovely ['lʌvlɪ] *adj* (très) joli(e), ravissant(e); (*delightful: person*) charmant(e); (*holiday etc*) (très) agréable

lover ['lʌvəʳ] *n* amant *m*; (*person in love*) amoureux(-euse); (*amateur*): **a ~ of** un amateur de; un(e) amoureux(-euse) de

loving ['lʌvɪŋ] *adj* affectueux(-euse), tendre

low [ləʊ] *adj* bas (basse); (*quality*) mauvais(e), inférieur(e); (*person: depressed*) déprimé(e); (: *ill*) bas (basse), affaibli(e) ♦ *adv* bas ♦ *n* (*METEOROLOGY*) dépression *f*; **to be ~ on** être à court de; **to feel ~** se sentir déprimé(e); **to reach an all-time ~** être au plus bas; **~-alcohol** *adj* peu alcoolisé(e); **~-calorie** *adj* hypocalorique; **~-cut** *adj* (*dress*) décolleté(e); **~er** *adj* inférieur(e) ♦ *vt* abaisser, baisser; **~er sixth** (*BRIT*) *n* (*SCOL*) première *f*; **~-fat** *adj* maigre; **~lands** *npl* (GEO) plaines *fpl*; **~ly** *adj* humble, modeste

loyal ['lɔɪəl] *adj* loyal(e), fidèle; **~ty** *n* loyauté *f*, fidélité *f*; **~ty card** *n* carte *f* de fidélité

lozenge ['lɔzɪndʒ] *n* (MED) pastille *f*

LP *n abbr* = **long-playing record**

L-plates ['elpleɪts] (BRIT) *npl* plaques *fpl* d'apprenti conducteur

---

> **L-plates**
>
> *Les* **L-plates** *sont des carrés blancs portant un "L" rouge que l'on met à l'avant et à l'arrière de sa voiture pour montrer qu'on n'a pas encore son permis de conduire. Jusqu'à l'obtention du permis, l'apprenti conducteur a un permis provisoire et n'a le droit de conduire que si un conducteur qualifié est assis à côté de lui. Il est interdit aux apprentis conducteurs de circuler sur les autoroutes, même s'ils sont accompagnés.*

Ltd *abbr* (= limited) ≃ S.A.

lubricant ['lu:brɪkənt] *n* lubrifiant *m*

lubricate ['lu:brɪkeɪt] *vt* lubrifier, graisser

luck [lʌk] *n* chance *f*; **bad ~** malchance *f*, malheur *m*; **bad** *or* **hard** *or* **tough ~!** pas de chance!; **good ~!** bonne chance!; **~ily** *adv* heureusement, par bonheur; **~y** *adj* (person) qui a de la chance; (coincidence, event) heureux(-euse); (object) porte-bonheur *inv*

ludicrous ['lu:dɪkrəs] *adj* ridicule, absurde

lug [lʌg] (inf) *vt* traîner, tirer

luggage ['lʌgɪdʒ] *n* bagages *mpl*; **~ rack** *n* (on car) galerie *f*

lukewarm ['lu:kwɔ:m] *adj* tiède

lull [lʌl] *n* accalmie *f*; (in conversation) pause *f* ♦ *vt*: **to ~ sb to sleep** bercer qn pour qu'il s'endorme; **to be ~ed into a false sense of security** s'endormir dans une fausse sécurité

lullaby ['lʌləbaɪ] *n* berceuse *f*

lumbago [lʌm'beɪgəu] *n* lumbago *m*

lumber ['lʌmbəʳ] *n* (wood) bois *m* de charpente; (junk) bric-à-brac *m inv*; **~jack** *n*

bûcheron *m*

luminous ['lu:mɪnəs] *adj* lumineux(-euse)

lump [lʌmp] *n* morceau *m*; (swelling) grosseur *f* ♦ *vt*: **to ~ together** réunir, mettre en tas; **~ sum** *n* somme globale *or* forfaitaire; **~y** *adj* (sauce) avec des grumeaux; (bed) défoncé(e), peu confortable

lunar ['lu:nəʳ] *adj* lunaire

lunatic ['lu:nətɪk] *adj* fou (folle), cinglé(e) (inf)

lunch [lʌntʃ] *n* déjeuner *m*

luncheon ['lʌntʃən] *n* déjeuner *m* (chic); **~ meat** *n* sorte de mortadelle; **~ voucher** (BRIT) *n* chèque-repas *m*

lung [lʌŋ] *n* poumon *m*

lunge [lʌndʒ] *vi* (also: **~ forward**) faire un mouvement brusque en avant; **to ~ at** envoyer *or* assener un coup à

lurch [lə:tʃ] *vi* vaciller, tituber ♦ *n* écart *m* brusque; **to leave sb in the ~** laisser qn se débrouiller *or* se dépêtrer tout(e) seul(e)

lure [luəʳ] *n* (attraction) attrait *m*, charme *m* ♦ *vt* attirer *or* persuader par la ruse

lurid ['luərɪd] *adj* affreux(-euse), atroce; (pej: colour, dress) criard(e)

lurk [lə:k] *vi* se tapir, se cacher

luscious ['lʌʃəs] *adj* succulent(e); appétissant(e)

lush [lʌʃ] *adj* luxuriant(e)

lust [lʌst] *n* (sexual) désir *m*; (fig): **~ for** soif *f* de; **~y** *adj* vigoureux(-euse), robuste

Luxembourg ['lʌksəmbə:g] *n* Luxembourg *m*

luxurious [lʌg'zjuərɪəs] *adj* luxueux(-euse)

luxury ['lʌkʃərɪ] *n* luxe *m* ♦ *cpd* de luxe

lying ['laɪɪŋ] *n* mensonge *m(pl)* ♦ *vb see* **lie**

lyrical ['lɪrɪkl] *adj* lyrique

lyrics ['lɪrɪks] *npl* (of song) paroles *fpl*

M, m

m. *abbr* = **metre**; **mile**; **million**

M.A. *abbr* = **Master of Arts**

mac [mæk] (*BRIT*) *n* imper(méable) *m*

macaroni [mækə'rəʊnɪ] *n* macaroni *mpl*

machine [mə'ʃiːn] *n* machine *f* ♦ *vt* (*TECH*) façonner à la machine; (*dress etc*) coudre à la machine; ~ **gun** *n* mitrailleuse *f*; ~ **language** *n* (*COMPUT*) langage-machine *m*; ~**ry** *n* machinerie *f*, machines *fpl*; (*fig*) mécanisme(s) *m(pl)*

mackerel ['mækrl] *n inv* maquereau *m*

mackintosh ['mækɪntɒʃ] (*BRIT*) *n* imperméable *m*

mad [mæd] *adj* fou (folle); (*foolish*) insensé(e); (*angry*) furieux(-euse); (*keen*): **to be ~ about** être fou (folle) de

madam ['mædəm] *n* madame *f*

madden ['mædn] *vt* exaspérer

made [meɪd] *pt*, *pp of* **make**

Madeira [mə'dɪərə] *n* (*GEO*) Madère *f*; (*wine*) madère *m*

made-to-measure ['meɪdtə'meʒə'] (*BRIT*) *adj* fait(e) sur mesure

madly ['mædlɪ] *adv* follement; ~ **in love** éperdument amoureux(-euse)

madman ['mædmən] (*irreg*) *n* fou *m*

madness ['mædnɪs] *n* folie *f*

magazine [mægə'ziːn] *n* (*PRESS*) magazine *m*, revue *f*; (*RADIO*, *TV: also*: ~ **programme**) magazine

maggot ['mægət] *n* ver *m*, asticot *m*

magic ['mædʒɪk] *n* magie *f* ♦ *adj* magique; ~**al** *adj* magique; (*experience*, *evening*) merveilleux(-euse); ~**ian** [mə'dʒɪʃən] *n* magicien(ne); (*conjurer*) prestidigitateur *m*

magistrate ['mædʒɪstreɪt] *n* magistrat *m*; juge *m*

magnet ['mægnɪt] *n* aimant *m*; ~**ic** [mæg'netɪk] *adj* magnétique

magnificent [mæg'nɪfɪsnt] *adj* superbe, magnifique; (*splendid*: *robe*, *building*) somptueux(-euse), magnifique

magnify ['mægnɪfaɪ] *vt* grossir; (*sound*) am-

plifier; ~**ing glass** *n* loupe *f*

magnitude ['mægnɪtjuːd] *n* ampleur *f*

magpie ['mægpaɪ] *n* pie *f*

mahogany [mə'hɒgənɪ] *n* acajou *m*

maid [meɪd] *n* bonne *f*; **old ~** (*pej*) vieille fille

maiden ['meɪdn] *n* jeune fille *f* ♦ *adj* (*aunt etc*) non mariée; (*speech*, *voyage*) inaugural(e); ~ **name** *n* nom *m* de jeune fille

mail [meɪl] *n* poste *f*; (*letters*) courrier *m* ♦ *vt* envoyer (par la poste); ~**box** (*US*) *n* boîte *f* aux lettres; ~**ing list** *n* liste *f* d'adresses; ~**-order** *n* vente *f or* achat *m* par correspondance

maim [meɪm] *vt* mutiler

main [meɪn] *adj* principal(e) ♦ *n*: **the ~(s)** ♦ *n(pl)* (*gas*, *water*) conduite principale, canalisation *f*; **the ~s** *npl* (*ELEC*) le secteur; **the ~ thing** l'essentiel; **in the ~** dans l'ensemble; ~**frame** *n* (*COMPUT*) (gros) ordinateur, unité centrale; ~**land** *n* continent *m*; ~**ly** *adv* principalement, surtout; ~ **road** *n* grand-route *f*; ~**stay** *n* (*fig*) pilier *m*; ~**stream** *n* courant principal

maintain [meɪn'teɪn] *vt* entretenir; (*continue*) maintenir; (*affirm*) soutenir; **maintenance** ['meɪntənəns] *n* entretien *m*; (*alimony*) pension *f* alimentaire

maize [meɪz] *n* maïs *m*

majestic [mə'dʒestɪk] *adj* majestueux(-euse)

majesty ['mædʒɪstɪ] *n* majesté *f*

major ['meɪdʒə'] *n* (*MIL*) commandant *m* ♦ *adj* (*important*) important(e); (*most important*) principal(e); (*MUS*) majeur(e)

Majorca [mə'jɔːkə] *n* Majorque *f*

majority [mə'dʒɒrɪtɪ] *n* majorité *f*

make [meɪk] (*pt*, *pp* **made**) *vt* faire; (*manufacture*) fabriquer; (*earn*) gagner; (*cause to be*): **to ~ sb sad** *etc* rendre qn triste *etc*; (*force*): **to ~ sb do sth** obliger qn à faire qch, faire faire qch à qn; (*equal*): **2 and 2 ~ 4** 2 et 2 font 4 ♦ *n* fabrication *f*; (*brand*) marque *f*; **to ~ a fool of sb** (*ridicule*) ridiculiser qn; (*trick*) avoir *or* duper qn; **to ~ a profit** faire un *or* des bénéfice(s); **to ~ a loss** essuyer une perte;

to ~ it (*arrive*) arriver; (*achieve sth*) parvenir à qch, réussir; **what time do you ~ it?** quelle heure avez-vous?; **to ~ do with** se contenter de; se débrouiller avec; **~ for** vt fus (*place*) se diriger vers; **~ out** vt (*write out: cheque*) faire; (*decipher*) déchiffrer; (*understand*) comprendre; (*see*) distinguer; **~ up** vt (*constitute*) constituer; (*invent*) inventer, imaginer; (*parcel, bed*) faire ♦ vi se réconcilier; (*with cosmetics*) se maquiller; **~ up for** vt fus compenser; **~-believe** n: **it's just ~-believe** (*game*) c'est pour faire semblant; (*invention*) c'est de l'invention pure; **~r** n fabricant m; **~shift** adj provisoire, improvisé(e); **~-up** n maquillage m

making ['meɪkɪŋ] n (*fig*): **in the ~** en formation *or* gestation; **to have the ~s of** (*actor, athlete etc*) avoir l'étoffe de

malaria [mə'lɛərɪə] n malaria f

Malaysia [mə'leɪzɪə] n Malaisie f

male [meɪl] n (*BIO*) mâle m ♦ adj mâle; (*sex, attitude*) masculin(e); (*child etc*) du sexe masculin

malevolent [mə'lɛvələnt] adj malveillant(e)

malfunction [mæl'fʌŋkʃən] n fonctionnement défectueux

malice ['mælɪs] n méchanceté f, malveillance f; **malicious** [mə'lɪʃəs] adj méchant(e), malveillant(e)

malignant [mə'lɪgnənt] adj (*MED*) malin(-igne)

mall [mɔːl] n (*also:* **shopping ~**) centre commercial

mallet ['mælɪt] n maillet m

malpractice [mæl'præktɪs] n faute professionnelle; négligence f

malt [mɔːlt] n malt m ♦ cpd (*also:* **~ whisky**) pur malt

Malta ['mɔːltə] n Malte f

mammal ['mæml] n mammifère m

mammoth ['mæməθ] n mammouth m ♦ adj géant(e), monstre

man [mæn] (*pl* **men**) n homme m ♦ vt (*NAUT: ship*) garnir d'hommes; (*MIL: gun*) servir; (*: post*) être de service à; (*machine*) assurer le fonctionnement de; **an old ~**

un vieillard; **~ and wife** mari et femme

manage ['mænɪdʒ] vi se débrouiller ♦ vt (*be in charge of*) s'occuper de; (*: business etc*) gérer; (*control: ship*) manier, manœuvrer; (*: person*) savoir s'y prendre avec; **to ~ to do** réussir à faire; **~able** adj (*task*) faisable; (*number*) raisonnable; **~ment** n gestion f, administration f, direction f; **~r** n directeur m; administrateur m; (*SPORT*) manager m; (*of artist*) impresario m; **~ress** [mænɪdʒə'rɛs] n directrice f; gérante f; **~rial** [mænɪ'dʒɪərɪəl] adj directorial(e); (*skills*) de cadre, de gestion; **managing director** n directeur général

mandarin ['mændərɪn] n (*also:* **~ orange**) mandarine f; (*person*) mandarin m

mandatory ['mændətərɪ] adj obligatoire

mane [meɪn] n crinière f

maneuver [mə'nuːvər] (*US*) vt, vi, n = **manoeuvre**

manfully ['mænfəlɪ] adv vaillamment

mangle ['mæŋgl] vt déchiqueter; mutiler

mango ['mæŋgəu] (*pl* **~es**) n mangue f

mangy ['meɪndʒɪ] adj galeux(-euse)

man: **~handle** vt malmener; **~hole** n trou m d'homme; **~hood** n âge m d'homme; virilité f; **~-hour** n heure f de main-d'œuvre; **~hunt** n (*POLICE*) chasse f à l'homme

mania ['meɪnɪə] n manie f; **~c** ['meɪnɪæk] n maniaque m/f; (*fig*) fou (folle) m/f; **manic** ['mænɪk] adj maniaque

manicure ['mænɪkjuər] n manucure f

manifest ['mænɪfɛst] vt manifester ♦ adj manifeste, évident(e); **~o** [mænɪ'fɛstəu] n manifeste m

manipulate [mə'nɪpjuleɪt] vt manipuler; (*system, situation*) exploiter

man: **~kind** [mæn'kaɪnd] n humanité f, genre humain; **~ly** adj viril(e); **~-made** adj artificiel(le); (*fibre*) synthétique

manner ['mænər] n manière f, façon f; (*behaviour*) attitude f, comportement m; (*sort*) **all ~ of** toutes sortes de; **~s** npl (*behaviour*) manières f; **~ism** n particularité f de langage (*or* de comportement), tic m

manoeuvre [mə'nuːvər] (*US* **maneuver**) vt

(*move*) manœuvrer; (*manipulate: person*) manipuler; (: *situation*) exploiter ♦ *vi* manœuvrer ♦ *n* manœuvre *f*

manor ['mænər] *n* (*also:* ~ **house**) manoir *m*

manpower ['mænpauər] *n* main-d'œuvre *f*

mansion ['mænʃən] *n* château *m*, manoir *m*

manslaughter ['mænslɔ:tər] *n* homicide *m* involontaire

mantelpiece ['mæntlpi:s] *n* cheminée *f*

manual ['mænjuəl] *adj* manuel(le) ♦ *n* manuel *m*

manufacture [mænju'fæktʃər] *vt* fabriquer ♦ *n* fabrication *f*; ~**r** *n* fabricant *m*

manure [mə'njuər] *n* fumier *m*

manuscript ['mænjuskrɪpt] *n* manuscrit *m*

many ['mɛnɪ] *adj* beaucoup de, de nombreux(-euses) ♦ *pron* beaucoup, un grand nombre; **a great** ~ un grand nombre (de); ~ **a ...** bien des ..., plus d'un(e) ...

map [mæp] *n* carte *f*; (*of town*) plan *m*; ~ **out** *vt* tracer; (*task*) planifier

maple ['meɪpl] *n* érable *m*

mar [mɑ:r] *vt* gâcher, gâter

marathon ['mærəθən] *n* marathon *m*

marble ['mɑ:bl] *n* marbre *m*; (*toy*) bille *f*

March [mɑ:tʃ] *n* mars *m*

march [mɑ:tʃ] *vi* marcher au pas; (*fig: protesters*) défiler ♦ *n* marche *f*; (*demonstration*) manifestation *f*

mare [mɛər] *n* jument *f*

margarine [mɑ:dʒə'ri:n] *n* margarine *f*

margin ['mɑ:dʒɪn] *n* marge *f*; ~**al** (**seat**) *n* (*POL*) siège disputé

marigold ['mærɪgəuld] *n* souci *m*

marijuana [mærɪ'wɑ:nə] *n* marijuana *f*

marina [mə'ri:nə] *n* (*harbour*) marina *f*

marine [mə'ri:n] *adj* marin(e) ♦ *n* fusilier marin; (*US*) marine *m*

marital ['mærɪtl] *adj* matrimonial(e); ~ **status** situation *f* de famille

marjoram ['mɑ:dʒərəm] *n* marjolaine *f*

mark [mɑ:k] *n* marque *f*; (*of skid etc*) trace *f*; (*BRIT: SCOL*) note *f*; (*currency*) mark *m* ♦ *vt* marquer; (*stain*) tacher; (*BRIT: SCOL*) no-

ter; corriger; **to** ~ **time** marquer le pas; ~**er** *n* (*sign*) jalon *m*; (*bookmark*) signet *m*

market ['mɑ:kɪt] *n* marché *m* ♦ *vt* (*COMM*) commercialiser; ~ **garden** (*BRIT*) *n* jardin maraîcher; ~**ing** *n* marketing *m*; ~**place** *n* place *f* du marché; (*COMM*) marché *m*; ~ **research** *n* étude *f* de marché

marksman ['mɑ:ksmən] (*irreg*) *n* tireur *m* d'élite

marmalade ['mɑ:məleɪd] *n* confiture *f* d'oranges

maroon [mə'ru:n] *vt*: **to be** ~**ed** être abandonné(e); (*fig*) être bloqué(e) ♦ *adj* bordeaux *inv*

marquee [mɑ:'ki:] *n* chapiteau *m*

marriage ['mærɪdʒ] *n* mariage *m*; ~ **certificate** *n* extrait *m* d'acte de mariage

married ['mærɪd] *adj* marié(e); (*life, love*) conjugal(e)

marrow ['mærəu] *n* moelle *f*; (*vegetable*) courge *f*

marry ['mærɪ] *vt* épouser, se marier avec; (*subj: father, priest etc*) marier ♦ *vi* (*also:* **get married**) se marier

Mars [mɑ:z] *n* (*planet*) Mars *f*

marsh [mɑ:ʃ] *n* marais *m*, marécage *m*

marshal ['mɑ:ʃl] *n* maréchal *m*; (*US: fire, police*) ≈ capitaine *m*; (*SPORT*) membre *m* du service d'ordre ♦ *vt* rassembler

marshy ['mɑ:ʃɪ] *adj* marécageux(-euse)

martyr ['mɑ:tər] *n* martyr(e); ~**dom** *n* martyre *m*

marvel ['mɑ:vl] *n* merveille *f* ♦ *vi*: **to** ~ (**at**) s'émerveiller (de); ~**lous** (*US* **marvelous**) *adj* merveilleux(-euse)

Marxist ['mɑ:ksɪst] *adj* marxiste ♦ *n* marxiste *m/f*

marzipan ['mɑ:zɪpæn] *n* pâte *f* d'amandes

mascara [mæs'kɑ:rə] *n* mascara *m*

masculine ['mæskjulɪn] *adj* masculin(e)

mash [mæʃ] *vt* écraser, réduire en purée; ~**ed potatoes** *npl* purée *f* de pommes de terre

mask [mɑ:sk] *n* masque *m* ♦ *vt* masquer

mason ['meɪsn] *n* (*also:* **stonemason**) maçon *m*; (*also:* **freemason**) franc-maçon *m*; ~**ry** *n* maçonnerie *f*

masquerade [mæskə'reɪd] *vi*: **to ~ as** se faire passer pour

mass [mæs] *n* multitude *f*, masse *f*; (*PHYSICS*) masse; (*REL*) messe *f* ♦ *cpd* (*communication*) de masse; (*unemployment*) massif(-ive) ♦ *vi* se masser; **the ~es** les masses; **~es of** des tas de

massacre ['mæsəkə^r] *n* massacre *m*

massage ['mæsɑ:ʒ] *n* massage *m* ♦ *vt* masser

massive ['mæsɪv] *adj* énorme, massif(-ive)

mass media *n inv* mass-media *mpl*

mass production *n* fabrication *f* en série

mast [mɑ:st] *n* mât *m*; (*RADIO*) pylône *m*

master ['mɑ:stə^r] *n* maître *m*; (*in secondary school*) professeur *m*; (*title for boys*): **M~ X** Monsieur X ♦ *vt* maîtriser; (*learn*) apprendre à fond; **~ly** *adj* magistral(e); **~mind** *n* esprit supérieur ♦ *vt* diriger, être le cerveau de; **M~ of Arts/Science** *n* ≈ maîtrise *f* (en lettres/sciences); **~piece** *n* chef-d'œuvre *m*; **~plan** *n* stratégie *f* d'ensemble; **~y** *n* maîtrise *f*; connaissance parfaite

mat [mæt] *n* petit tapis; (*also:* **doormat**) paillasson *m*; (*also:* **tablemat**) napperon *m* ♦ *adj* = **matt**

match [mætʃ] *n* allumette *f*; (*game*) match *m*, partie *f*; (*fig*) égal(e) ♦ *vt* (*also:* **~ up**) assortir; (*go well with*) aller bien avec, s'assortir à; (*equal*) égaler, valoir ♦ *vi* être assorti(e); **to be a good ~** être bien assorti(e); **~box** *n* boîte *f* d'allumettes; **~ing** *adj* assorti(e)

mate [meɪt] *n* (*inf*) copain (copine); (*animal*) partenaire *m/f*, mâle/femelle; (*in merchant navy*) second *m* ♦ *vi* s'accoupler

material [mə'tɪərɪəl] *n* (*substance*) matière *f*, matériau *m*; (*cloth*) tissu *m*, étoffe *f*; (*information, data*) données *fpl* ♦ *adj* matériel(le); (*relevant: evidence*) pertinent(e); **~s** *npl* (*equipment*) matériaux *mpl*

maternal [mə'tə:nl] *adj* maternel(le)

maternity [mə'tə:nɪtɪ] *n* maternité *f*; **~ dress** *n* robe *f* de grossesse; **~ hospital** *n* maternité *f*

mathematical [mæθə'mætɪkl] *adj* mathématique

mathematics [mæθə'mætɪks] *n* mathématiques *fpl*

maths [mæθs] (*US* **math**) *n* math(s) *fpl*

matinée ['mætɪneɪ] *n* matinée *f*

mating call *n* appel *m* du mâle

matrices ['meɪtrɪsi:z] *npl of* **matrix**

matriculation [mətrɪkju'leɪʃən] *n* inscription *f*

matrimonial [mætrɪ'məunɪəl] *adj* matrimonial(e), conjugal(e)

matrimony ['mætrɪmənɪ] *n* mariage *m*

matrix ['meɪtrɪks] (*pl* **matrices**) *n* matrice *f*

matron ['meɪtrən] *n* (*in hospital*) infirmière-chef *f*; (*in school*) infirmière *f*

mat(t) [mæt] *adj* mat(e)

matted ['mætɪd] *adj* emmêlé(e)

matter ['mætə^r] *n* question *f*; (*PHYSICS*) matière *f*; (*content*) contenu *m*, fond *m*; (*MED: pus*) pus *m* ♦ *vi* importer; **~s** *npl* (*affairs, situation*) la situation; **it doesn't ~** cela n'a pas d'importance; (*I don't mind*) cela ne fait rien; **what's the ~?** qu'est-ce qu'il y a?, qu'est-ce qui ne va pas?; **no ~ what** quoiqu'il arrive; **as a ~ of course** tout naturellement; **as a ~ of fact** en fait; **~-of-fact** *adj* terre à terre; (*voice*) neutre

mattress ['mætrɪs] *n* matelas *m*

mature [mə'tjuə^r] *adj* mûr(e); (*cheese*) fait(e); (*wine*) arrivé(e) à maturité ♦ *vi* (*person*) mûrir; (*wine, cheese*) se faire

maul [mɔ:l] *vt* lacérer

mauve [məuv] *adj* mauve

maximum ['mæksɪməm] (*pl* **maxima**) *adj* maximum ♦ *n* maximum *m*

May [meɪ] *n* mai *m*; **~ Day** *n* le Premier Mai; *see also* **mayday**

may [meɪ] (*conditional* **might**) *vi* (*indicating possibility*): **he ~ come** il se peut qu'il vienne; (*be allowed to*): **~ I smoke?** puis-je fumer?; (*wishes*): **~ God bless you!** (que) Dieu vous bénisse!; **you ~ as well go** à votre place, je partirais

maybe ['meɪbi:] *adv* peut-être; **~ he'll ...** peut-être qu'il ...

mayday ['meɪdeɪ] *n* SOS *m*

mayhem ['meɪhɛm] *n* grabuge *m*

mayonnaise [meɪə'neɪz] *n* mayonnaise *f*

mayor [mɛəʳ] *n* maire *m*; **~ess** *n* épouse *f* du maire

maze [meɪz] *n* labyrinthe *m*, dédale *m*

M.D. *n abbr* (= *Doctor of Medicine*) titre *universitaire*; = **managing director**

me [miː] *pron* me, m' +*vowel*; (*stressed, after prep*) moi; **he heard ~** il m'a entendu(e); **give ~ a book** donnez-moi un livre; **after ~** après moi

meadow ['mɛdəu] *n* prairie *f*, pré *m*

meagre ['miːgəʳ] (*US* **meager**) *adj* maigre

meal [miːl] *n* repas *m*; (*flour*) farine *f*; **~time** *n* l'heure *f* du repas

mean [miːn] (*pt, pp* **meant**) *adj* (*with money*) avare, radin(e); (*unkind*) méchant(e); (*shabby*) misérable; (*average*) moyen(ne) ♦ *vt* signifier, vouloir dire; (*refer to*) faire allusion à, parler de; (*intend*): **to ~ to do** avoir l'intention de faire ♦ *n* moyenne *f*; **~s** *npl* (*way, money*) moyens *mpl*; **by ~s of** par l'intermédiaire de; au moyen de; **by all ~s!** je vous en prie!; **to be ~t for sb/sth** être destiné(e) à qn/qch; **do you ~ it?** vous êtes sérieux?; **what do you ~?** que voulez-vous dire?

meander [mɪ'ændəʳ] *vi* faire des méandres

meaning ['miːnɪŋ] *n* signification *f*, sens *m*; **~ful** *adj* significatif(-ive); (*relationship, occasion*) important(e); **~less** *adj* dénué(e) de sens

meanness ['miːnnɪs] *n* (*with money*) avarice *f*; (*unkindness*) méchanceté *f*; (*shabbiness*) médiocrité *f*

meant [mɛnt] *pt, pp of* **mean**

meantime ['miːntaɪm] *adv* (*also:* **in the ~**) pendant ce temps

meanwhile ['miːnwaɪl] *adv* = **meantime**

measles ['miːzlz] *n* rougeole *f*

measure ['mɛʒəʳ] *vt, vi* mesurer ♦ *n* mesure *f*; (*ruler*) règle (graduée); **~ments** *npl* mesures *fpl*; **chest/hip ~ment(s)** tour *m* de poitrine/hanches

meat [miːt] *n* viande *f*; **~ball** *n* boulette *f* de viande

Mecca ['mɛkə] *n* La Mecque

mechanic [mɪ'kænɪk] *n* mécanicien *m*; **~al** *adj* mécanique; **~s** *n* (*PHYSICS*) mécanique *f* ♦ *npl* (*of reading, government etc*) mécanisme *m*

mechanism ['mɛkənɪzəm] *n* mécanisme *m*

medal ['mɛdl] *n* médaille *f*; **~lion** [mɪ'dælɪən] *n* médaillon *m*; **~list** (*US* **medalist**) *n* (*SPORT*) médaillé(e)

meddle ['mɛdl] *vi*: **to ~ in** se mêler de, s'occuper de; **to ~ with** toucher à

media ['miːdɪə] *npl* media *mpl*

mediaeval [mɛdɪ'iːvl] *adj* = **medieval**

median ['miːdɪən] (*US*) *n* (*also:* **~ strip**) bande médiane

mediate ['miːdɪeɪt] *vi* servir d'intermédiaire

Medicaid ® ['mɛdɪkeɪd] (*US*) *n* assistance médicale aux indigents

medical ['mɛdɪkl] *adj* médical(e) ♦ *n* visite médicale

Medicare ® ['mɛdɪkɛəʳ] (*US*) *n* assistance médicale aux personnes âgées

medication [mɛdɪ'keɪʃən] *n* (*drugs*) médicaments *mpl*

medicine ['mɛdsɪn] *n* médecine *f*; (*drug*) médicament *m*

medieval [mɛdɪ'iːvl] *adj* médiéval(e)

mediocre [miːdɪ'əukəʳ] *adj* médiocre

meditate ['mɛdɪteɪt] *vi* méditer

Mediterranean [mɛdɪtə'reɪnɪən] *adj* méditerranéen(ne); **the ~ (Sea)** la (mer) Méditerranée

medium ['miːdɪəm] (*pl* **media**) *adj* moyen(ne) ♦ *n* (*means*) moyen *m*; (*pl* **~s**: *person*) médium *m*; **the happy ~** le juste milieu; **~-sized** *adj* de taille moyenne; **~ wave** *n* ondes moyennes

medley ['mɛdlɪ] *n* mélange *m*; (*MUS*) potpourri *m*

meek [miːk] *adj* doux (douce), humble

meet [miːt] (*pt, pp* **met**) *vt* rencontrer; (*by arrangement*) retrouver, rejoindre; (*for the first time*) faire la connaissance de; (*go and fetch*): **I'll ~ you at the station** j'irai te chercher à la gare; (*opponent, danger*) faire face à; (*obligations*) satisfaire à ♦ *vi* (*friends*) se rencontrer, se retrouver; (*in* *session*) se réunir; (*join: lines, roads*) se rejoindre; **~ with** *vt* rencontrer; **~ing** *n* rencontre *f*; (*session: of club etc*) réunion *f*; (*POL*) meeting *m*; **she's at a ~ing** (*COMM*) elle est en conférence

mega ['mɛgə] (*inf*) *adv*: **he's ~ rich** il est hyper-riche; **~byte** *n* (*COMPUT*) mégaoctet *m*; **~phone** *n* porte-voix *m inv*

melancholy ['mɛlənkəlı] *n* mélancolie *f* ♦ *adj* mélancolique

mellow ['mɛləu] *adj* velouté(e); doux (douce); (*sound*) mélodieux(-euse) ♦ *vi* (*person*) s'adoucir

melody ['mɛlədı] *n* mélodie *f*

melon ['mɛlən] *n* melon *m*

melt [mɛlt] *vi* fondre ♦ *vt* faire fondre; (*metal*) fondre; **~ away** *vi* fondre complètement; **~ down** *vt* fondre; **~down** *n* fusion *f* (du cœur d'un réacteur nucléaire); **~ing pot** *n* (*fig*) creuset *m*

member ['mɛmbər] *n* membre *m*; **M~ of Parliament** (*BRIT*) député *m*; **M~ of the European Parliament** Eurodéputé *m*; **~ship** *n* adhésion *f*; statut *m* de membre; (*members*) membres *mpl*, adhérents *mpl*; **~ship card** *n* carte *f* de membre

memento [mə'mɛntəu] *n* souvenir *m*

memo ['mɛməu] *n* note *f* (de service)

memoirs ['mɛmwɑːz] *npl* mémoires *mpl*

memorandum [mɛmə'rændəm] (*pl* **memoranda**) *n* note *f* (de service)

memorial [mɪ'mɔːrɪəl] *n* mémorial *m* ♦ *adj* commémoratif(-ive)

memorize ['mɛmərɑɪz] *vt* apprendre par cœur; retenir

memory ['mɛmərɪ] *n* mémoire *f*; (*recollection*) souvenir *m*

men [mɛn] *npl of* **man**

menace ['mɛnɪs] *n* menace *f*; (*nuisance*) plaie *f* ♦ *vt* menacer; **menacing** *adj* menaçant(e)

mend [mɛnd] *vt* réparer; (*darn*) raccommoder, repriser ♦ *n*: **on the ~** en voie de guérison; **to ~ one's ways** s'amender; **~ing** *n* réparation *f*; (*clothes*) raccommodage *m*

menial ['miːnɪəl] *adj* subalterne

meningitis [mɛnɪn'dʒɑɪtɪs] *n* méningite *f*

menopause ['mɛnəupɔːz] *n* ménopause *f*

menstruation [mɛnstru'eɪʃən] *n* menstruation *f*

mental ['mɛntl] *adj* mental(e); **~ity** [mɛn'tælɪtɪ] *n* mentalité *f*

mention ['mɛnʃən] *n* mention *f* ♦ *vt* mentionner, faire mention de; **don't ~ it!** je vous en prie, il n'y a pas de quoi!

menu ['mɛnjuː] *n* (*set ~, COMPUT*) menu *m*; (*list of dishes*) carte *f*

MEP *n abbr* = **Member of the European Parliament**

mercenary ['məːsɪnərɪ] *adj* intéressé(e), mercenaire ♦ *n* mercenaire *m*

merchandise ['məːtʃəndɑɪz] *n* marchandises *fpl*

merchant ['məːtʃənt] *n* négociant *m*, marchand *m*; **~ bank** (*BRIT*) *n* banque *f* d'affaires; **~ navy** (*US* **merchant marine**) *n* marine marchande

merciful ['məːsɪful] *adj* miséricordieux(-euse), clément(e); **a ~ release** une délivrance

merciless ['məːsɪlɪs] *adj* impitoyable, sans pitié

mercury ['məːkjurɪ] *n* mercure *m*

mercy ['məːsɪ] *n* pitié *f*, indulgence *f*; (*REL*) miséricorde *f*; **at the ~ of** à la merci de

mere [mɪər] *adj* simple; (*chance*) pur(e); **a ~ two hours** seulement deux heures; **~ly** *adv* simplement, purement

merge [məːdʒ] *vt* unir ♦ *vi* (*colours, shapes, sounds*) se mêler; (*roads*) se joindre; (*COMM*) fusionner; **~r** *n* (*COMM*) fusion *f*

meringue [mə'ræŋ] *n* meringue *f*

merit ['mɛrɪt] *n* mérite *m*, valeur *f*

mermaid ['məːmeɪd] *n* sirène *f*

merry ['mɛrɪ] *adj* gai(e); **M~ Christmas!** Joyeux Noël!; **~-go-round** *n* manège *m*

mesh [mɛʃ] *n* maille *f*

mesmerize ['mɛzmərɑɪz] *vt* hypnotiser; fasciner

mess [mɛs] *n* désordre *m*, fouillis *m*, pagaille *f*; (*muddle: of situation*) gâchis *m*; (*dirt*) saleté *f*; (*MIL*) mess *m*, cantine *f*; **~ about** (*inf*) *vi* perdre son temps; **~ about**

with (*inf*) *vt fus* tripoter; **~ around** (*inf*) *vi* = **mess about**; **~ around with** *vt fus* = **mess about with**; **~ up** *vt* (*dirty*) salir; (*spoil*) gâcher

message ['mesɪdʒ] *n* message *m*; **messenger** ['mesɪndʒər] *n* messager *m*

Messrs ['mesəz] *abbr* (*on letters*) MM

messy ['mesɪ] *adj* sale; en désordre

met [met] *pt, pp of* **meet**

metal ['metl] *n* métal *m*; **~lic** [mɪ'tælɪk] *adj* métallique

meteorology [miːtɪə'rɔlədʒɪ] *n* météorologie *f*

meter ['miːtər] *n* (*instrument*) compteur *m*; (*also:* **parking ~**) parcomètre *m*; (*US: unit*) = **metre**

method ['meθəd] *n* méthode *f*; **~ical** [mɪ'θɔdɪkl] *adj* méthodique; **M~ist** *n* méthodiste *m/f*

meths [meθs] (*BRIT*), **methylated spirit** ['meθɪleɪtɪd-] (*BRIT*) *n* alcool *m* à brûler

metre ['miːtər] (*US* **meter**) *n* mètre *m*; **metric** ['metrɪk] *adj* métrique

metropolitan [metrə'pɔlɪtn] *adj* métropolitain(e); **the M~ Police** (*BRIT*) la police londonienne

mettle ['metl] *n*: **to be on one's ~** être d'attaque

mew [mjuː] *vi* (*cat*) miauler

mews [mjuːz] (*BRIT*) *n*: **~ cottage** cottage *m* aménagé dans une ancienne écurie

Mexico ['meksɪkəu] *n* Mexique *m*

miaow [miː'au] *vi* miauler

mice [maɪs] *npl of* **mouse**

micro ['maɪkrəu] *n* (*also:* **~computer**) micro-ordinateur *m*; **~chip** *n* puce *f*; **~phone** *n* microphone *m*; **~scope** *n* microscope *m*; **~wave** *n* (*also:* **~wave oven**) four *m* à micro-ondes

mid [mɪd] *adj*: **in ~ May** à la mi-mai; **~ afternoon** le milieu de l'après-midi; **in ~ air** en plein ciel; **~day** *n* midi *m*

middle ['mɪdl] *n* milieu *m*; (*waist*) taille *f* ♦ *adj* (*average*) moyen(ne); **in the ~ of the night** au milieu de la nuit; **~-aged** *adj* d'un certain âge; **M~ Ages** *npl*: **the M~ Ages** le moyen âge; **~-class**

adj ≈ bourgeois(e); **~ class(es)** *n(pl)*: **the ~ class(es)** ≈ les classes moyennes; **M~ East** *n* Proche-Orient *m*, Moyen-Orient *m*; **~man** (*irreg*) *n* intermédiaire *m*; **~ name** *n* deuxième nom *m*; **~-of-the-road** *adj* (*politician*) modéré(e); (*music*) neutre; **~weight** *n* (*BOXING*) poids moyen; **middling** *adj* moyen(ne)

midge [mɪdʒ] *n* moucheron *m*

midget ['mɪdʒɪt] *n* nain(e)

Midlands ['mɪdləndz] *npl* comtés du centre de l'Angleterre

midnight ['mɪdnaɪt] *n* minuit *m*

midriff ['mɪdrɪf] *n* estomac *m*, taille *f*

midst [mɪdst] *n*: **in the ~ of** au milieu de

midsummer [mɪd'sʌmər] *n* milieu *m* de l'été

midway [mɪd'weɪ] *adj, adv*: **~ (between)** à mi-chemin (entre); **~ through ...** au milieu de ..., en plein(e) ...

midweek [mɪd'wiːk] *adj* au milieu de la semaine

midwife ['mɪdwaɪf] (*pl* **midwives**) *n* sage-femme *f*

might [maɪt] *vb see* **may** ♦ *n* puissance *f*, force *f*; **~y** *adj* puissant(e)

migraine ['miːgreɪn] *n* migraine *f*

migrant ['maɪgrənt] *adj* (*bird*) migrateur(-trice); (*worker*) saisonnier(-ère)

migrate [maɪ'greɪt] *vi* émigrer

mike [maɪk] *n abbr* (= *microphone*) micro *m*

mild [maɪld] *adj* doux (douce); (*reproach, infection*) léger(-ère); (*illness*) bénin(-igne); (*interest*) modéré(e); (*taste*) peu relevé(e) ♦ *n* (*beer*) bière légère; **~ly** *adv* doucement; légèrement; **to put it ~ly** c'est le moins qu'on puisse dire

mile [maɪl] *n* mi(l)le *m* (= 1609 *m*); **~age** *n* distance *f* en milles; ≈ kilométrage *m*; **~ometer** [maɪ'lɔmɪtər] *n* compteur *m* (kilométrique); **~stone** *n* borne *f*; (*fig*) jalon *m*

militant ['mɪlɪtnt] *adj* militant(e)

military ['mɪlɪtərɪ] *adj* militaire

militia [mɪ'lɪʃə] *n* milice(s) *f(pl)*

milk [mɪlk] *n* lait *m* ♦ *vt* (*cow*) traire; (*fig: person*) dépouiller, plumer; (: *situation*) exploiter à fond; ~ **chocolate** n chocolat m au lait; **~man** (*irreg*) n laitier m; ~ **shake** n milk-shake m; **~y** adj (*drink*) au lait; (*colour*) laiteux(-euse); **M~y Way** n voie lactée

mill [mɪl] n moulin m; (*steel* ~) aciérie f; (*spinning* ~) filature f; (*flour* ~) minoterie f ♦ vt moudre, broyer ♦ vi (*also*: ~ **about**) grouiller; **~er** n meunier m

millennium bug [mɪˈlɛnɪəm-] n bogue m or bug m de l'an 2000

milligram(me) [ˈmɪlɪɡræm] n milligramme m

millimetre [ˈmɪlɪmiːtər] (US **millimeter**) n millimètre m

million [ˈmɪljən] n million m

milometer [maɪˈlɔmɪtər] n ≃ compteur m kilométrique

mime [maɪm] n mime m ♦ vt, vi mimer; **mimic** [ˈmɪmɪk] n imitateur(-trice) ♦ vt imiter, contrefaire

min. abbr = **minute(s)**; **minimum**

mince [mɪns] vt hacher ♦ n (*BRIT*: *CULIN*) viande hachée, hachis m; **~meat** n (*fruit*) hachis de fruits secs utilisé en pâtisserie; (*US*: *meat*) viande hachée, hachis; ~ **pie** n (*sweet*) sorte de tarte aux fruits secs; **~r** n hachoir m

mind [maɪnd] n esprit m ♦ vt (*attend to, look after*) s'occuper de; (*be careful*) faire attention à; (*object to*): **I don't ~ the noise** le bruit ne me dérange pas; **I don't ~ cela ne me dérange pas; it is on my ~** cela me préoccupe; **to my ~** à mon avis or sens; **to be out of one's ~** ne plus avoir toute sa raison; **to keep** or **bear sth in ~** tenir compte de qch; **to make up one's ~** se décider; ~ **you, ...** remarquez ...; **never ~** ça ne fait rien; (*don't worry*) ne vous en faites pas; **"~ the step"** "attention à la marche"; **~er** n (*child-minder*) gardienne f; (*inf*: *bodyguard*) ange gardien (*fig*); **~ful** adj: **~ful of** attentif(-ive) à, soucieux(-euse) de; **~less** adj irréfléchi(e); (*boring*: *job*) idiot(e)

mine[1] [maɪn] pron le (la) mien(ne), les miens (miennes) ♦ adj: **this book is ~** ce livre est à moi

mine[2] [maɪn] n mine f ♦ vt (*coal*) extraire; (*ship*) miner; **~field** n champ m de mines; (*fig*) situation (très délicate); **~r** n mineur m

mineral [ˈmɪnərəl] adj minéral(e) ♦ n minéral m; **~s** npl (*BRIT*: *soft drinks*) boissons gazeuses; ~ **water** n eau minérale

mingle [ˈmɪŋɡl] vi: **to ~ with** se mêler à

miniature [ˈmɪnətʃər] adj (en) miniature ♦ n miniature f

minibus [ˈmɪnɪbʌs] n minibus m

Minidisc ® [ˈmɪnɪdɪsk] n minidisque m, Minidisc ® m

minimal [ˈmɪnɪml] adj minime

minimize [ˈmɪnɪmaɪz] vt (*reduce*) réduire au minimum; (*play down*) minimiser

minimum [ˈmɪnɪməm] (*pl* **minima**) adj, n minimum m

mining [ˈmaɪnɪŋ] n exploitation minière

minister [ˈmɪnɪstər] n (*BRIT*: *POL*) ministre m; (*REL*) pasteur m ♦ vi: **to ~ to sb('s needs)** pourvoir aux besoins de qn; **~ial** [mɪnɪsˈtɪərɪəl] (*BRIT*) adj (*POL*) ministériel(le); **ministry** n (*BRIT*: *POL*) ministère m; (*REL*): **to go into the ministry** devenir pasteur

mink [mɪŋk] n vison m

minor [ˈmaɪnər] adj petit(e), de peu d'importance; (*MUS, poet, problem*) mineur(e) ♦ n (*LAW*) mineur(e)

minority [maɪˈnɔrɪtɪ] n minorité f

mint [mɪnt] n (*plant*) menthe f; (*sweet*) bonbon m à la menthe ♦ vt (*coins*) battre; **the (Royal) M~**, (*US*) **the (US) M~** ≃ l'Hôtel m de la Monnaie; **in ~ condition** à l'état de neuf

minus [ˈmaɪnəs] n (*also*: ~ **sign**) signe m moins ♦ prep moins

minute[1] [maɪˈnjuːt] adj minuscule; (*detail, search*) minutieux(-euse)

minute[2] [ˈmɪnɪt] n minute f; **~s** npl (*official record*) procès-verbal, compte rendu

miracle [ˈmɪrəkl] n miracle m

mirror [ˈmɪrər] n miroir m, glace f; (*in car*) rétroviseur m

mirth [məːθ] n gaieté f

misadventure [mɪsədˈvɛntʃər] n mésaventure f

misapprehension ['mɪsæprɪ'henʃən] *n* malentendu *m*, méprise *f*

misappropriate [mɪsə'prəuprɪeɪt] *vt* détourner

misbehave [mɪsbɪ'heɪv] *vi* mal se conduire

miscalculate [mɪs'kælkjuleɪt] *vt* mal calculer

miscarriage ['mɪskærɪdʒ] *n* (MED) fausse couche; **~ of justice** erreur *f* judiciaire

miscellaneous [mɪsɪ'leɪnɪəs] *adj* (items) divers(es); (selection) varié(e)

mischief ['mɪstʃɪf] *n* (naughtiness) sottises *fpl*; (fun) farce *f*; (playfulness) espièglerie *f*; (maliciousness) méchanceté *f*; **mischievous** ['mɪstʃɪvəs] *adj* (playful, naughty) coquin(e), espiègle

misconception ['mɪskən'sepʃən] *n* idée fausse

misconduct [mɪs'kɔndʌkt] *n* inconduite *f*; **professional ~** faute professionnelle

misdemeanour [mɪsdɪ'miːnəʳ] (US **misdemeanor**) *n* écart *m* de conduite; infraction *f*

miser ['maɪzəʳ] *n* avare *m/f*

miserable ['mɪzərəbl] *adj* (person, expression) malheureux(-euse); (conditions) misérable; (weather) maussade; (offer, donation) minable; (failure) pitoyable

miserly ['maɪzəlɪ] *adj* avare

misery ['mɪzərɪ] *n* (unhappiness) tristesse *f*; (pain) souffrances *fpl*; (wretchedness) misère *f*

misfire [mɪs'faɪəʳ] *vi* rater

misfit ['mɪsfɪt] *n* (person) inadapté(e)

misfortune [mɪs'fɔːtʃən] *n* malchance *f*, malheur *m*

misgiving [mɪs'gɪvɪŋ] *n* (apprehension) craintes *fpl*; **to have ~s about** avoir des doutes quant à

misguided [mɪs'gaɪdɪd] *adj* malavisé(e)

mishandle [mɪs'hændl] *vt* (mismanage) mal s'y prendre pour résoudre *or* résoudre *etc*

mishap ['mɪshæp] *n* mésaventure *f*

misinform [mɪsɪn'fɔːm] *vt* mal renseigner

misinterpret [mɪsɪn'tɜːprɪt] *vt* mal interpréter

misjudge [mɪs'dʒʌdʒ] *vt* méjuger

mislay [mɪs'leɪ] (irreg: like **lay**) *vt* égarer

mislead [mɪs'liːd] (irreg: like **lead**) *vt* induire en erreur; **~ing** *adj* trompeur(-euse)

mismanage [mɪs'mænɪdʒ] *vt* mal gérer

misplace [mɪs'pleɪs] *vt* égarer

misprint ['mɪsprɪnt] *n* faute *f* d'impression

Miss [mɪs] *n* Mademoiselle

miss [mɪs] *vt* (fail to get, attend or see) manquer, rater; (regret the absence of): **I ~ him/it** il/cela me manque ♦ *vi* manquer ♦ *n* (shot) coup manqué; **~ out** (BRIT) *vt* oublier

misshapen [mɪs'ʃeɪpən] *adj* difforme

missile ['mɪsaɪl] *n* (MIL) missile *m*; (object thrown) projectile *m*

missing ['mɪsɪŋ] *adj* manquant(e); (after escape, disaster: person) disparu(e); **to go ~** disparaître; **to be ~** avoir disparu

mission ['mɪʃən] *n* mission *f*; **~ary** ['mɪʃənrɪ] *n* missionnaire *m/f*; **~ statement** *n* déclaration *f* d'intention

mist [mɪst] *n* brume *f* ♦ *vi* (also: **~ over**: eyes) s'embuer; **~ over** *vi* (windows etc) s'embuer; **~ up** *vi* = **mist over**

mistake [mɪs'teɪk] (irreg: like **take**) *n* erreur *f*, faute *f* ♦ *vt* (meaning, remark) mal comprendre; se méprendre sur; **to make a ~** se tromper, faire une erreur; **by ~** par erreur, par inadvertance; **to ~ for** prendre pour; **~n** *pp of* **mistake** ♦ *adj* (idea etc) erroné(e); **to be ~n** faire erreur, se tromper

mister ['mɪstəʳ] (inf) *n* Monsieur *m*; see also **Mr**

mistletoe ['mɪsltəu] *n* gui *m*

mistook [mɪs'tuk] *pt of* **mistake**

mistress ['mɪstrɪs] *n* maîtresse *f*; (BRIT: in primary school) institutrice *f*; (: in secondary school) professeur *m*

mistrust [mɪs'trʌst] *vt* se méfier de

misty ['mɪstɪ] *adj* brumeux(-euse); (glasses, window) embué(e)

misunderstand [mɪsʌndə'stænd] (irreg) *vt*, *vi* mal comprendre; **~ing** *n* méprise *f*, malentendu *m*

misuse [*n* mɪs'juːs, *vb* mɪs'juːz] *n* mauvais

emploi; (of power) abus m ♦ vt mal employer; abuser de; ~ **of funds** détournement m de fonds

mitigate ['mɪtɪgeɪt] vt atténuer

mitt(en) ['mɪt(n)] n mitaine f; moufle f

mix [mɪks] vt mélanger; (sauce, drink etc) préparer ♦ vi se mélanger; (socialize): **he doesn't ~ well** il est peu sociable ♦ n mélange m; **to ~ with** (people) fréquenter; ~ **up** vt mélanger; (confuse) confondre; ~**ed** adj (feelings, reactions) contradictoire; (salad) mélangé(e); (school, marriage) mixte; ~**ed grill** n assortiment m de grillades; ~**ed-up** adj (confused) désorienté(e), embrouillé(e); ~**er** n (for food) batteur m, mixer m; (person): **he is a good ~er** il est très liant; ~**ture** n assortiment m, mélange m; (MED) préparation f; ~**-up** n confusion f

mm abbr (= millimetre) mm

moan [məun] n gémissement m ♦ vi gémir; (inf: complain): **to ~ (about)** se plaindre (de)

moat [məut] n fossé m, douves fpl

mob [mɒb] n foule f; (disorderly) cohue f ♦ vt assaillir

mobile ['məubaɪl] adj mobile ♦ n mobile m; ~ **home** n (grande) caravane f; ~ **phone** n téléphone portatif

mock [mɒk] vt ridiculiser; (laugh at) se moquer de ♦ adj faux (fausse); ~ **exam** examen blanc; ~**ery** n moquerie f, raillerie f; **to make a ~ery of** tourner en dérision; ~**-up** n maquette f

mod [mɒd] adj see **convenience**

mode [məud] n mode m

model ['mɒdl] n modèle m; (person: for fashion) mannequin m; (: for artist) modèle ♦ vt (with clay etc) modeler ♦ vi travailler comme mannequin ♦ adj (railway: toy) modèle réduit inv; (child, factory) modèle; **to ~ clothes** présenter des vêtements; **to ~ o.s. on** imiter

modem ['məudɛm] n (COMPUT) modem m

moderate [adj 'mɒdərət, vb 'mɒdəreɪt] adj modéré(e); (amount, change) peu important(e) ♦ vi se calmer ♦ vt modérer

modern ['mɒdən] adj moderne; ~**ize** vt moderniser

modest ['mɒdɪst] adj modeste; ~**y** n modestie f

modify ['mɒdɪfaɪ] vt modifier

mogul ['məugl] n (fig) nabab m

mohair ['məuhɛər] n mohair m

moist [mɔɪst] adj humide, moite; ~**en** vt humecter, mouiller légèrement; ~**ure** n humidité f; ~**urizer** n produit hydratant

molar ['məulər] n molaire f

molasses [mə'læsɪz] n mélasse f

mold [məuld] (US) n, vt = **mould**

mole [məul] n (animal, fig: spy) taupe f; (spot) grain m de beauté

molest [mə'lɛst] vt (harass) molester; (LAW: sexually) attenter à la pudeur de

mollycoddle ['mɒlɪkɒdl] vt chouchouter, couver

molt [məult] (US) vi = **moult**

molten ['məultən] adj fondu(e); (rock) en fusion

mom [mɒm] (US) n = **mum**

moment ['məumənt] n moment m, instant m; **at the ~** en ce moment; **at that ~** à ce moment-là; ~**ary** adj momentané(e), passager(-ère); ~**ous** [məu'mɛntəs] adj important(e), capital(e)

momentum [məu'mɛntəm] n élan m, vitesse acquise; (fig) dynamique f; **to gather ~** prendre de la vitesse

mommy ['mɒmɪ] (US) n maman f

Monaco ['mɒnəkəu] n Monaco m

monarch ['mɒnək] n monarque m; ~**y** n monarchie f

monastery ['mɒnəstərɪ] n monastère m

Monday ['mʌndɪ] n lundi m

monetary ['mʌnɪtərɪ] adj monétaire

money ['mʌnɪ] n argent m; **to make ~** gagner de l'argent; ~ **belt** n ceinture-portefeuille f; ~ **order** n mandat m; ~**-spinner** (inf) n mine f d'or (fig)

mongrel ['mʌŋgrəl] n (dog) bâtard m

monitor ['mɒnɪtər] n (TV, COMPUT) moniteur m ♦ vt contrôler; (broadcast) être à l'écoute de; (progress) suivre (de près)

monk [mʌŋk] n moine m

monkey ['mʌŋkɪ] *n* singe *m*; ~ **nut** (*BRIT*) *n* cacahuète *f*

monopoly [mə'nɔpəlɪ] *n* monopole *m*

monotone ['mɔnətəun] *n* ton *m* (*or* voix *f*) monocorde; **monotonous** [mə'nɔtənəs] *adj* monotone

monsoon [mɔn'su:n] *n* mousson *f*

monster ['mɔnstər] *n* monstre *m*; **monstrous** ['mɔnstrəs] *adj* monstrueux(-euse); (*huge*) gigantesque

month [mʌnθ] *n* mois *m*; ~**ly** *adj* mensuel(le) ♦ *adv* mensuellement

monument ['mɔnjumənt] *n* monument *m*

moo [mu:] *vi* meugler, beugler

mood [mu:d] *n* humeur *f*, disposition *f*; **to be in a good/bad** ~ être de bonne/ mauvaise humeur; ~**y** *adj* (*variable*) d'humeur changeante, lunatique; (*sullen*) morose, maussade

moon [mu:n] *n* lune *f*; ~**light** *n* clair *m* de lune; ~**lighting** *n* travail *m* au noir; ~**lit** *adj*: **a** ~**lit night** une nuit de lune

moor [muər] *n* lande *f* ♦ *vt* (*ship*) amarrer ♦ *vi* mouiller; ~**land** *n* lande *f*

moose [mu:s] *n inv* élan *m*

mop [mɔp] *n* balai *m* à laver; (*for dishes*) lavette *f* (à vaisselle) ♦ *vt* essuyer; ~ **of hair** tignasse *f*; ~ **up** *vt* éponger

mope [məup] *vi* avoir le cafard, se morfondre

moped ['məuped] *n* cyclomoteur *m*

moral ['mɔrl] *adj* moral(e) ♦ *n* morale *f*; ~**s** *npl* (*attitude, behaviour*) moralité *f*

morale [mɔ'rɑ:l] *n* moral *m*

morality [mə'rælɪtɪ] *n* moralité *f*

morass [mə'ræs] *n* marais *m*, marécage *m*

KEYWORD

more [mɔːr] *adj* **1** (*greater in number etc*) plus (de), davantage; **more people/work (than)** plus de gens/de travail (que)

2 (*additional*) encore (de); **do you want (some) more tea?** voulez-vous encore du thé?; **I have no** *or* **I don't have any more money** je n'ai plus d'argent; **it'll take a few more weeks** ça prendra encore quelques semaines

♦ *pron* plus, davantage; **more than 10** plus de 10; **it cost more than we expected** cela a coûté plus que prévu; **I want more** j'en veux plus *or* davantage; **is there any more?** est-ce qu'il en reste?; **there's no more** il n'y en a plus; **a little more** un peu plus; **many/much more** beaucoup plus, bien davantage

♦ *adv*: **more dangerous/easily (than)** plus dangereux/facilement (que); **more and more expensive** de plus en plus cher; **more or less** plus ou moins; **more than ever** plus que jamais

---

moreover [mɔː'rəuvər] *adv* de plus

morning ['mɔːnɪŋ] *n* matin *m*; matinée *f* ♦ *cpd* matinal(e); (*paper*) du matin; **in the** ~ le matin; **7 o'clock in the** ~ 7 heures du matin; ~ **sickness** *n* nausées matinales

Morocco [mə'rɔkəu] *n* Maroc *m*

moron ['mɔːrɔn] (*inf*) *n* idiot(e)

Morse [mɔːs] *n*: ~ **code** morse *m*

morsel ['mɔːsl] *n* bouchée *f*

mortar ['mɔːtər] *n* mortier *m*

mortgage ['mɔːgɪdʒ] *n* hypothèque *f*; (*loan*) prêt *m* (*or* crédit *m*) hypothécaire ♦ *vt* hypothéquer; ~ **company** (*US*) *n* société *f* de crédit immobilier

mortuary ['mɔːtjuərɪ] *n* morgue *f*

mosaic [məu'zeɪɪk] *n* mosaïque *f*

Moscow ['mɔskəu] *n* Moscou

Moslem ['mɔzləm] *adj, n* = **Muslim**

mosque [mɔsk] *n* mosquée *f*

mosquito [mɔs'ki:təu] (*pl* ~**es**) *n* moustique *m*

moss [mɔs] *n* mousse *f*

most [məust] *adj* la plupart de; le plus de ♦ *pron* la plupart ♦ *adv* le plus; (*very*) très, extrêmement; **the** ~ (*also:* + *adjective*) le plus; ~ **of** la plus grande partie de; ~ **of them** la plupart d'entre eux; **I saw (the)** ~ j'en ai vu la plupart; c'est moi qui en ai vu le plus; **at the (very)** ~ au plus; **to make the** ~ **of** profiter au maximum de; ~**ly** *adv* (*chiefly*) surtout; (*usually*) généralement

MOT *n abbr* (*BRIT: Ministry of Transport*):

the MOT (test) *la visite technique (annuelle) obligatoire des véhicules à moteur*

motel [məu'tel] *n* motel *m*

moth [mɔθ] *n* papillon *m* de nuit; (*in clothes*) mite *f*

mother ['mʌðəʳ] *n* mère *f* ♦ *vt* (*act as* ~ *to*) servir de mère à; (*pamper, protect*) materner; ~ **country** mère patrie; ~**hood** *n* maternité *f*; ~-**in-law** *n* belle-mère *f*; ~**ly** *adj* maternel(le); ~-**of-pearl** *n* nacre *f*; **M~'s Day** *n* fête *f* des Mères; ~-**to-be** *n* future maman; ~ **tongue** *n* langue maternelle

motion ['məuʃən] *n* mouvement *m*; (*gesture*) geste *m*; (*at meeting*) motion *f* ♦ *vt, vi*: **to** ~ **(to) sb to do** faire signe à qn de faire; ~**less** *adj* immobile, sans mouvement; ~ **picture** *n* film *m*

motivated ['məutɪveɪtɪd] *adj* motivé(e); **motivation** [məutɪ'veɪʃən] *n* motivation *f*

motive ['məutɪv] *n* motif *m*, mobile *m*

motley ['mɔtlɪ] *adj* hétéroclite

motor ['məutəʳ] *n* moteur *m*; (*BRIT: inf: vehicle*) auto *f* ♦ *cpd* (*industry, vehicle*) automobile; ~**bike** *n* moto *f*; ~**boat** *n* bateau *m* à moteur; ~**car** (*BRIT*) *n* automobile *f*; ~**cycle** *n* vélomoteur *m*; ~**cycle racing** *n* course *f* de motos; ~**cyclist** *n* motocycliste *m/f*; ~**ing** (*BRIT*) *n* tourisme *m* automobile; ~**ist** *n* automobiliste *m/f*; ~ **mechanic** *n* mécanicien *m* garagiste; ~ **racing** (*BRIT*) *n* course *f* automobile; ~**way** (*BRIT*) *n* autoroute *f*

mottled ['mɔtld] *adj* tacheté(e), marbré(e)

motto ['mɔtəu] (*pl* ~**es**) *n* devise *f*

mould [məuld] (*US* **mold**) *n* moule *m*; (*mildew*) moisissure *f* ♦ *vt* mouler, modeler; (*fig*) façonner; **mo(u)ldy** *adj* moisi(e); (*smell*) de moisi

moult [məult] (*US* **molt**) *vi* muer

mound [maund] *n* monticule *m*, tertre *m*; (*heap*) monceau *m*, tas *m*

mount [maunt] *n* mont *m*, montagne *f* ♦ *vt* monter ♦ *vi* (*inflation, tension*) augmenter; (*also:* ~ **up:** *problems etc*) s'accumuler; ~ **up** *vi* (*bills, costs, savings*) s'accumuler

mountain ['mauntɪn] *n* montagne *f* ♦ *cpd* de montagne; ~ **bike** *n* VTT *m*, vélo

tout-terrain; ~**eer** [mauntɪ'nɪəʳ] *n* alpiniste *m/f*; ~**eering** *n* alpinisme *m*; ~**ous** *adj* montagneux(-euse); ~ **rescue team** *n* équipe *f* de secours en montagne; ~**side** *n* flanc *m* or versant *m* de la montagne

mourn [mɔːn] *vt* pleurer ♦ *vi*: **to** ~ **(for)** (*person*) pleurer (la mort de); ~**er** *n* parent(e) *or* ami(e) du défunt; personne *f* en deuil; ~**ing** *n* deuil *m*; **in** ~**ing** en deuil

mouse [maus] (*pl* **mice**) *n* (*also COMPUT*) souris *f*; ~ **mat**, ~ **pad** (*COMPUT*) tapis *m* de souris; ~**trap** *n* souricière *f*

mousse [muːs] *n* mousse *f*

moustache [məsˈtaːʃ] (*US* **mustache**) *n* moustache(s) *f(pl)*

mousy ['mausɪ] *adj* (*hair*) d'un châtain terne

mouth [mauθ] (*pl* ~**s**) *n* bouche *f*; (*of dog, cat*) gueule *f*; (*of river*) embouchure *f*; (*of hole, cave*) ouverture *f*; ~**ful** *n* bouchée *f*; ~ **organ** *n* harmonica *m*; ~**piece** *n* (*of musical instrument*) embouchure *f*; (*spokesman*) porte-parole *m inv*; ~**wash** *n* eau *f* dentifrice; ~-**watering** *adj* qui met l'eau à la bouche

movable ['muːvəbl] *adj* mobile

move [muːv] *n* (~*ment*) mouvement *m*; (*in game*) coup *m*; (: *turn to play*) tour *m*; (*change: of house*) déménagement *m*; (: *of job*) changement *m* d'emploi ♦ *vt* déplacer, bouger; (*emotionally*) émouvoir; (*POL: resolution etc*) proposer; (*in game*) jouer ♦ *vi* (*gen*) bouger, remuer; (*traffic*) circuler; (*also:* ~ **house**) déménager; (*situation*) progresser; **that was a good** ~ bien joué!; **to get a** ~ **on** se dépêcher, se remuer; **to** ~ **sb to do sth** pousser *or* inciter qn à faire qch; ~ **about** *vi* (*fidget*) remuer; (*travel*) voyager, se déplacer; (*change residence, job*) ne pas rester au même endroit; ~ **along** *vi* se pousser; ~ **around** *vi* = **move about**; ~ **away** *vi* s'en aller; ~ **back** *vi* revenir, retourner; ~ **forward** *vi* avancer; ~ **in** *vi* (*to a house*) emménager; (*police, soldiers*) intervenir; ~ **on** *vi* se remettre en route; ~ **out** *vi* (*of house*) déménager; ~ **over** *vi* se pousser, se déplacer; **~ up** *vi* (*pupil*) passer dans la classe supérieure; (*employee*) avoir de l'avancement; **~able** *adj* = **movable**

movement ['muːvmənt] *n* mouvement *m*

movie ['muːvɪ] *n* film *m*; **the ~s** le cinéma

moving ['muːvɪŋ] *adj* en mouvement; (*emotional*) émouvant(e)

mow [məʊ] (*pt* **mowed**, *pp* **mowed** or **mown**) *vt* faucher; (*lawn*) tondre; **~ down** *vt* faucher; **~er** *n* (*also:* **lawn-mower**) tondeuse *f* à gazon

MP *n abbr* = **Member of Parliament**

MP3 *abbr:* **~ player** lecteur *m* MP3

mph *abbr* = **miles per hour**

Mr ['mɪstər] *n:* **~ Smith** Monsieur Smith, M. Smith

Mrs ['mɪsɪz] *n:* **~ Smith** Madame Smith, Mme Smith

Ms [mɪz] *n* (= *Miss or Mrs*): **~ Smith** Madame Smith, Mme Smith

MSc *abbr* = **Master of Science**

MSP *n abbr* = (*Member of the Scottish Parliament*) député *m* au Parlement écossais

much [mʌtʃ] *adj* beaucoup de ♦ *adv*, *n*, *pron* beaucoup; **how ~ is it?** combien est-ce que ça coûte?; **too ~** trop (de); **as ~ as** autant de

muck [mʌk] *n* (*dirt*) saleté *f*; **~ about** or **around** (*inf*) *vi* faire l'imbécile; **~ up** (*inf*) *vt* (*exam, interview*) se planter à (*fam*); **~y** *adj* (*très*) sale

mud [mʌd] *n* boue *f*

muddle ['mʌdl] *n* (*mess*) pagaille *f*, désordre *m*; (*mix-up*) confusion *f* ♦ *vt* (*also:* **~ up**) embrouiller; **~ through** *vi* se débrouiller

muddy ['mʌdɪ] *adj* boueux(-euse)

mudguard ['mʌdgɑːd] *n* garde-boue *m inv*

muesli ['mjuːzlɪ] *n* muesli *m*

muffle ['mʌfl] *vt* (*sound*) assourdir, étouffer; (*against cold*) emmitoufler; **~d** *adj* (*sound*) étouffé(e); **~r** (*US*) *n* (*AUT*) silencieux *m*

mug [mʌg] *n* (*cup*) grande tasse (*sans soucoupe*); (: *for beer*) chope *f*; (*inf: face*) bouille *f*; (: *fool*) poire *f* ♦ *vt* (*assault*) agresser; **~ger** *n* agresseur *m*; **~ging** *n* agression *f*

muggy ['mʌgɪ] *adj* lourd(e), moite

multi-level ['mʌltɪlevl] (*US*) *adj* = **multi-storey**

multiple ['mʌltɪpl] *adj* multiple ♦ *n* multiple *m*; **~ sclerosis** [-sklɪ'rəʊsɪs] *n* sclérose *f* en plaques

multiplex cinema ['mʌltɪpleks-] *n* cinéma *m* multisalles

multiplication [mʌltɪplɪ'keɪʃən] *n* multiplication *f*; **multiply** ['mʌltɪplaɪ] *vt* multiplier ♦ *vi* se multiplier

multistorey ['mʌltɪ'stɔːrɪ] (*BRIT*) *adj* (*building*) à étages; (*car park*) à étages or niveaux multiples ♦ *n* (*car park*) parking *m* à plusieurs étages

mum [mʌm] (*BRIT: inf*) *n* maman *f* ♦ *adj:* **to keep ~** ne pas souffler mot

mumble ['mʌmbl] *vt, vi* marmotter, marmonner

mummy ['mʌmɪ] *n* (*BRIT: mother*) maman *f*; (*embalmed*) momie *f*

mumps [mʌmps] *n* oreillons *mpl*

munch [mʌntʃ] *vt, vi* mâcher

mundane [mʌn'deɪn] *adj* banal(e), terre à terre *inv*

municipal [mjuː'nɪsɪpl] *adj* municipal(e)

murder ['mɜːdər] *n* meurtre *m*, assassinat *m* ♦ *vt* assassiner; **~er** *n* meurtrier *m*, assassin *m*; **~ous** *adj* meurtrier(-ère)

murky ['mɜːkɪ] *adj* sombre, ténébreux(-euse); (*water*) trouble

murmur ['mɜːmər] *n* murmure *m* ♦ *vt, vi* murmurer

muscle ['mʌsl] *n* muscle *m*; (*fig*) force *f*; **~ in** *vi* (*on territory*) envahir; (*on success*) exploiter; **muscular** ['mʌskjulər] *adj* musculaire; (*person, arm*) musclé(e)

muse [mjuːz] *vi* méditer, songer

museum [mjuː'zɪəm] *n* musée *m*

mushroom ['mʌʃrum] *n* champignon *m* ♦ *vi* pousser comme un champignon

music ['mjuːzɪk] *n* musique *f*; **~al** *adj* musical(e); (*person*) musicien(ne) ♦ *n* (*show*) comédie musicale; **~al instrument** *n* instrument *m* de musique; **~ centre** *n* chaîne compacte; ~ian [mju:'zɪʃən] n musicien(ne)

Muslim ['mʌzlɪm] adj, n musulman(e)

muslin ['mʌzlɪn] n mousseline f

mussel ['mʌsl] n moule f

must [mʌst] aux vb (obligation): **I ~ do it** je dois le faire, il faut que je le fasse; (probability): **he ~ be there by now** il doit y être maintenant, il y est probablement maintenant; (suggestion, invitation): **you ~ come and see me** il faut que vous veniez me voir; (indicating sth unwelcome): **why ~ he behave so badly?** qu'est-ce qui le pousse à se conduire si mal? ♦ n nécessité f, impératif m; **it's a ~** c'est indispensable

mustache ['mʌstæʃ] (US) n = **moustache**

mustard ['mʌstəd] n moutarde f

muster ['mʌstə'] vt rassembler

mustn't ['mʌsnt] = **must not**

mute [mju:t] adj muet(te); ~d adj (colour) sourd(e); (reaction) voilé(e)

mutiny ['mju:tɪnɪ] n mutinerie f ♦ vi se mutiner

mutter ['mʌtə'] vt, vi marmonner, marmotter

mutton ['mʌtn] n mouton m

mutual ['mju:tʃuəl] adj mutuel(le), réciproque; (benefit, interest) commun(e); ~ly adv mutuellement

muzzle ['mʌzl] n museau m; (protective device) muselière f; (of gun) gueule f ♦ vt museler

my [maɪ] adj mon (ma), mes pl; **~ house/ car/gloves** ma maison/mon auto/mes gants; **I've washed ~ hair/cut ~ finger** je me suis lavé les cheveux/coupé le doigt; ~self [maɪ'self] pron (reflexive) me; (emphatic) moi-même; (after prep) moi; see also **oneself**

mysterious [mɪs'tɪərɪəs] adj mystérieux(-euse)

mystery ['mɪstərɪ] n mystère m

mystify ['mɪstɪfaɪ] vt mystifier; (puzzle) ébahir

myth [mɪθ] n mythe m; ~ology [mɪ'θɒlədʒɪ] n mythologie f

N, n

n/a abbr = **not applicable**

naff [næf] (BRIT: inf) adj nul(le)

nag [næg] vt (scold) être toujours après, reprendre sans arrêt; ~ging adj (doubt, pain) persistant(e)

nail [neɪl] n (human) ongle m; (metal) clou m ♦ vt clouer; **to ~ sb down to a date/ price** contraindre qn à accepter or donner une date/un prix; ~brush n brosse f à ongles; ~file n lime f à ongles; ~ polish n vernis m à ongles; **~ polish remover** n dissolvant m; ~ scissors npl ciseaux mpl à ongles; ~ varnish (BRIT) n = **nail polish**

naïve [naɪ'i:v] adj naïf(-ïve)

naked ['neɪkɪd] adj nu(e)

name [neɪm] n nom m; (reputation) réputation f ♦ vt nommer; (identify: accomplice etc) citer; (price, date) fixer, donner; **by ~** par son nom; **in the ~ of** au nom de; **what's your ~?** comment vous appelezvous?; ~less adj sans nom; (witness, contributor) anonyme; ~ly adv à savoir; ~sake n homonyme m

nanny ['nænɪ] n bonne f d'enfants

nap [næp] n (sleep) (petit) somme ♦ vi: **to be caught ~ping** être pris à l'improviste or en défaut

nape [neɪp] n: **~ of the neck** nuque f

napkin ['næpkɪn] n serviette f (de table)

nappy ['næpɪ] (BRIT) n couche f (gen pl); ~ **rash** n: **to have ~ rash** avoir les fesses rouges

narcissus [nɑ:'sɪsəs] (pl **narcissi**) n narcisse m

narcotic [nɑ:'kɒtɪk] n (drug) stupéfiant m; (MED) narcotique m

narrative ['nærətɪv] n récit m

narrow ['nærəu] adj étroit(e); (fig) restreint(e), limité(e) ♦ vi (road) devenir plus étroit, se rétrécir; (gap, difference) se réduire; **to have a ~ escape** l'échapper belle; **to ~ sth down to** réduire qch à; ~ly adv:

he ~ly missed injury/the tree il a failli se blesser/rentrer dans l'arbre; **~-minded** *adj* à l'esprit étroit, borné(e); *(attitude)* borné

nasty ['nɑ:stɪ] *adj (person: malicious)* méchant(e); *(: rude)* très désagréable; *(smell)* dégoûtant(e); *(wound, situation, disease)* mauvais(e)

nation ['neɪʃən] *n* nation *f*

national ['næʃnl] *adj* national(e) ♦ *n (abroad)* ressortissant(e); *(when home)* national(e); **~ anthem** *n* hymne national; **~ dress** *n* costume national; **N~ Health Service** *(BRIT)* *n* service national de santé; ≃ Sécurité Sociale; **N~ Insurance** *(BRIT)* *n* ≃ Sécurité Sociale; **~ism** *n* nationalisme *m*; **~ist** *adj* nationaliste ♦ *n* nationaliste *m/f*; **~ity** [næʃə'nælɪtɪ] *n* nationalité *f*; **~ize** *vt* nationaliser; **~ly** *adv (as a nation)* du point de vue national; *(nationwide)* dans le pays entier; **~ park** *n* parc national

---
National Trust

ⓘ *Le* **National Trust** *est un organisme indépendant, à but non lucratif, dont la mission est de protéger et de mettre en valeur les monuments et les sites britanniques en raison de leur intérêt historique ou de leur beauté naturelle.*

---

nationwide ['neɪʃənwaɪd] *adj* s'étendant à l'ensemble du pays; *(problem)* à l'échelle du pays entier ♦ *adv* à travers *or* dans tout le pays

native ['neɪtɪv] *n* autochtone *m/f*, habitant(e) du pays ♦ *adj* du pays, indigène; *(country)* natal(e); *(ability)* inné(e); **a ~ of Russia** une personne originaire de Russie; **a ~ speaker of French** une personne de langue maternelle française; **N~ American** *n* Indien(ne) d'Amérique; **~ language** *n* langue maternelle

NATO ['neɪtəu] *n abbr (= North Atlantic Treaty Organization)* OTAN *f*

natural ['nætʃrəl] *adj* naturel(le); **~ gas** *n* gaz naturel; **~ist** *n* naturaliste *m/f*; **~ly** *adv* naturellement

nature ['neɪtʃər] *n* nature *f*; **by ~** par tempérament, de nature

naught [nɔ:t] *n* = **nought**

naughty ['nɔ:tɪ] *adj (child)* vilain(e), pas sage

nausea ['nɔ:sɪə] *n* nausée *f*

naval ['neɪvl] *adj* naval(e); **~ officer** *n* officier *m* de marine

nave [neɪv] *n* nef *f*

navel ['neɪvl] *n* nombril *m*

navigate ['nævɪgeɪt] *vt (steer)* diriger; *(plot course)* naviguer ♦ *vi* naviguer; **navigation** [nævɪ'geɪʃən] *n* navigation *f*

navvy ['nævɪ] *(BRIT)* *n* terrassier *m*

navy ['neɪvɪ] *n* marine *f*; **~(-blue)** *adj* bleu marine *inv*

Nazi ['nɑ:tsɪ] *n* Nazi(e)

NB *abbr (= nota bene)* NB

near [nɪər] *adj* proche ♦ *adv* près ♦ *prep (also: ~ to)* près de ♦ *vt* approcher de; **~by** [nɪə'baɪ] *adj* proche ♦ *adv* tout près, à proximité; **~ly** *adv* presque; **I ~ly fell** j'ai failli tomber; **~ miss** *n (AVIAT)* quasi-collision *f*; **that was a ~ miss** *(gen)* il s'en est fallu de peu; *(of shot)* c'est passé très près; **~side** *n (AUT: in Britain)* côté *m* gauche; *(: in US, Europe etc)* côté droit; **~-sighted** *adj* myope

neat [ni:t] *adj (person, work)* soigné(e); *(room etc)* bien tenu(e) *or* rangé(e); *(skilful)* habile; *(spirits)* pur(e); **~ly** *adv* avec soin *or* ordre; habilement

necessarily ['nesɪsrɪlɪ] *adv* nécessairement

necessary ['nesɪsrɪ] *adj* nécessaire; **necessity** [nɪ'sesɪtɪ] *n* nécessité *f*; *(thing needed)* chose nécessaire *or* essentielle; **necessities** *npl* nécessaire *m*

neck [nɛk] *n* cou *m*; *(of animal, garment)* encolure *f*; *(of bottle)* goulot *m* ♦ *vi (inf)* se peloter; **~ and ~** à égalité; **~lace** *n* collier *m*; **~line** *n* encolure *f*; **~tie** *n* cravate *f*

need [ni:d] *n* besoin *m* ♦ *vt* avoir besoin de; **to ~ to do** devoir faire; avoir besoin de faire; **you don't ~ to go** vous n'avez pas besoin *or* vous n'êtes pas obligé de partir

needle ['ni:dl] *n* aiguille *f* ♦ *vt* asticoter, tourmenter

needless ['ni:dlɪs] *adj* inutile

needlework ['ni:dlwə:k] *n* (*activity*) travaux *mpl* d'aiguille; (*object(s)*) ouvrage *m*

needn't ['ni:dnt] = **need not**

needy ['ni:dɪ] *adj* nécessiteux(-euse)

negative ['nɛgətɪv] *n* (PHOT, ELEC) négatif *m*; (LING) terme *m* de négation ♦ *adj* négatif(-ive); **~ equity** situation dans laquelle la valeur d'une maison est inférieure à celle de l'emprunt-logement contracté pour la payer

neglect [nɪ'glɛkt] *vt* négliger ♦ *n* (*of person, duty, garden*) le fait de négliger; (*state of ~*) abandon *m*; **~ed** *adj* négligé(e), à l'abandon

negligee ['nɛglɪʒeɪ] *n* déshabillé *m*

negotiate [nɪ'gəuʃɪeɪt] *vi, vt* négocier; **negotiation** [nɪgəuʃɪ'eɪʃən] *n* négociation *f*, pourparlers *mpl*

neigh [neɪ] *vi* hennir

neighbour ['neɪbə*r] (US **neighbor**) *n* voisin(e); **~hood** *n* (*place*) quartier *m*; (*people*) voisinage *m*; **~ing** *adj* voisin(e), avoisinant(e); **~ly** *adj* obligeant(e); (*action etc*) amical(e)

neither ['naɪðə*r] *adj, pron* aucun(e) (des deux), ni l'un(e) ni l'autre ♦ *conj*: **I didn't move and ~ did Claude** je n'ai pas bougé, (et) Claude non plus ♦ *adv*: **~ good nor bad** ni bon ni mauvais; **..., ~ did I refuse** ..., (et *or* mais) je n'ai pas non plus refusé

neon ['ni:ɔn] *n* néon *m*; **~ light** *n* lampe *f* au néon

nephew ['nɛvju:] *n* neveu *m*

nerve [nə:v] *n* nerf *m*; (*fig: courage*) sang-froid *m*, courage *m*; (: *impudence*) aplomb *m*, toupet *m*; **to have a fit of ~s** avoir le trac; **~-racking** *adj* angoissant(e)

nervous ['nə:vəs] *adj* nerveux(-euse); (*anxious*) inquiet(-ète), plein(e) d'appréhension; (*timid*) intimidé(e); **~ break-down** *n* dépression nerveuse

nest [nɛst] *n* nid *m* ♦ *vi* (se) nicher, faire son nid; **~ egg** *n* (*fig*) bas *m* de laine, magot *m*

nestle ['nɛsl] *vi* se blottir

net [nɛt] *n* filet *m*; **the Net** (INTERNET) le Net ♦ *adj* net(te) ♦ *vt* (*fish etc*) prendre au filet; (*profit*) rapporter; **~ball** *n* netball *m*

Netherlands ['nɛðələndz] *npl*: **the ~** les Pays-Bas *mpl*

nett [nɛt] *adj* = **net**

netting ['nɛtɪŋ] *n* (*for fence etc*) treillis *m*, grillage *m*

nettle ['nɛtl] *n* ortie *f*

network ['nɛtwə:k] *n* réseau *m*

neurotic [njuə'rɔtɪk] *adj* névrosé(e)

neuter ['nju:tə*r] *adj* neutre ♦ *vt* (*cat etc*) châtrer, couper

neutral ['nju:trəl] *adj* neutre ♦ *n* (AUT) point mort; **~ize** *vt* neutraliser

never ['nɛvə*r] *adv* (ne ...) jamais; **~ again** plus jamais; **~ in my life** jamais de ma vie; *see also* **mind**; **~-ending** *adj* interminable; **~theless** *adv* néanmoins, malgré tout

new [nju:] *adj* nouveau (nouvelle); (*brand ~*) neuf (neuve); **N~ Age** *n* New Age *m*; **~born** *adj* nouveau-né(e); **~comer** *n* nouveau venu/nouvelle venue *n*; **~-fangled** ['nju:'fæŋgld] (*pej*) *adj* ultramoderne (et farfelu(e)); **~-found** *adj* (*enthusiasm*) de fraîche date; (*friend*) nouveau (nouvelle); **~ly** *adv* nouvellement, récemment; **~lyweds** *npl* jeunes mariés *mpl*

news [nju:z] *n* nouvelle(s) *f(pl)*; (RADIO, TV) informations *fpl*, actualités *fpl*; **a piece of ~** une nouvelle; **~ agency** *n* agence *f* de presse; **~agent** (BRIT) *n* marchand *m* de journaux; **~caster** *n* présentateur(-trice); **~ flash** *n* flash *m* d'information; **~letter** *n* bulletin *m*; **~paper** *n* journal *m*; **~print** *n* papier *m* (de) journal; **~reader** *n* = **newscaster**; **~reel** *n* actualités (filmées); **~ stand** *n* kiosque *m* à journaux

newt [nju:t] *n* triton *m*

New Year *n* Nouvel An; **~'s Day** *n* le jour de l'An; **~'s Eve** *n* la Saint-Sylvestre

New Zealand [-'zi:lənd] *n* la Nouvelle-Zélande; **~er** *n* Néo-zélandais(e)

next [nɛkst] *adj* (*seat, room*) voisin(e), d'à côté; (*meeting, bus stop*) suivant(e); (*in time*) prochain(e) ♦ *adv* (*place*) à côté; (*time*) la fois suivante, la prochaine fois; (*afterwards*) ensuite; **the ~ day** le lendemain, le jour suivant or d'après; **~ year** l'année prochaine; **~ time** la prochaine fois; **~ to** à côté de; **~ to nothing** presque rien; **~, please!** (*at doctor's etc*) au suivant!; **~ door** *adv* à côté ♦ *adj* d'à côté; **~-of-kin** *n* parent *m* le plus proche

NHS *n abbr* = **National Health Service**

nib [nɪb] *n* (bec *m* de) plume *f*

nibble ['nɪbl] *vt* grignoter

nice [naɪs] *adj* (*pleasant, likeable*) agréable; (*pretty*) joli(e); (*kind*) gentil(le); **~ly** *adv* agréablement; joliment; gentiment

niceties ['naɪsɪtɪz] *npl* subtilités *fpl*

nick [nɪk] *n* (*indentation*) encoche *f*; (*wound*) entaille *f* ♦ *vt* (BRIT: *inf*) faucher, piquer; **in the ~ of time** juste à temps

nickel ['nɪkl] *n* nickel *m*; (US) pièce *f* de 5 cents

nickname ['nɪkneɪm] *n* surnom *m* ♦ *vt* surnommer

nicotine patch ['nɪkəti:n-] *n* timbre *m* anti-tabac, patch *m*

niece [ni:s] *n* nièce *f*

Nigeria [naɪ'dʒɪərɪə] *n* Nigéria *m or f*

niggling ['nɪglɪŋ] *adj* (*person*) tatillon(ne); (*detail*) insignifiant(e); (*doubts, injury*) persistant(e)

night [naɪt] *n* nuit *f*; (*evening*) soir *m*; **at ~** la nuit; **by ~** de nuit; **the ~ before last** avant-hier soir; **~cap** *n* boisson prise avant le coucher; **~ club** *n* boîte *f* de nuit; **~dress** *n* chemise *f* de nuit; **~fall** *n* tombée *f* de la nuit; **~gown** *n* chemise *f* de nuit; **~ie** ['naɪtɪ] *n* chemise *f* de nuit; **~ingale** ['naɪtɪŋgeɪl] *n* rossignol *m*; **~life** *n* vie *f* nocturne; **~ly** *adj* de chaque nuit or soir; (*by night*) nocturne ♦ *adv* chaque nuit or soir; **~mare** *n* cauchemar *m*; **~ porter** *n* gardien *m* de nuit, concierge *m* de service la nuit; **~ school** *n* cours *mpl* du soir; **~ shift** *n* équipe *f* de nuit; **~-time** *n* nuit *f*; **~ watchman** *n* veilleur *m* or gardien *m* de nuit

nil [nɪl] *n* rien *m*; (BRIT: SPORT) zéro *m*

Nile [naɪl] *n*: **the ~** le Nil

nimble ['nɪmbl] *adj* agile

nine [naɪn] *num* neuf; **~teen** ['naɪn'ti:n] *num* dix-neuf; **~ty** ['naɪntɪ] *num* quatre-vingt-dix; **ninth** [naɪnθ] *num* neuvième

nip [nɪp] *vt* pincer

nipple ['nɪpl] *n* (ANAT) mamelon *m*, bout *m* du sein

nitrogen ['naɪtrədʒən] *n* azote *m*

KEYWORD

no [nəu] (*pl* **noes**) *adv* (*opposite of "yes"*) non; **are you coming? - no (I'm not)** est-ce que vous venez? - non; **would you like some more? - no thank you** vous en voulez encore? - non merci
♦ *adj* (*not any*) pas de, aucun(e) (*used with "ne"*); **I have no money/books** je n'ai pas d'argent/de livres; **no student would have done it** aucun étudiant ne l'aurait fait; **"no smoking"** "défense de fumer"; **"no dogs"** "les chiens ne sont pas admis"
♦ *n* non *m*

nobility [nəu'bɪlɪtɪ] *n* noblesse *f*

noble ['nəubl] *adj* noble

nobody ['nəubədɪ] *pron* personne

nod [nɔd] *vi* faire un signe de tête (*affirmatif ou amical*); (*sleep*) somnoler ♦ *vt*: **to ~ one's head** faire un signe de (la) tête; (*in agreement*) faire signe que oui ♦ *n* signe *m* de (la) tête; **~ off** *vi* s'assoupir

noise [nɔɪz] *n* bruit *m*; **noisy** *adj* bruyant(e)

nominal ['nɔmɪnl] *adj* symbolique

nominate ['nɔmɪneɪt] *vt* (*propose*) proposer; (*appoint*) nommer; **nominee** [nɔmɪ'ni:] *n* candidat agréé; personne nommée

non... [nɔn] *prefix* non-; **~-alcoholic** *adj* non-alcoolisé(e); **~committal** *adj* évasif(-ive); **~descript** *adj* quelconque, indéfinissable

none [nʌn] *pron* aucun(e); **~ of you** aucun

d'entre vous, personne parmi vous; **I've ~ left** je n'en ai plus; **he's ~ the worse for it** il ne s'en porte pas plus mal

nonentity [nɔ'nentɪtɪ] n personne insignifiante

nonetheless ['nʌnðə'les] adv néanmoins

non-existent [nɔnɪg'zɪstənt] adj inexistant(e)

non-fiction [nɔn'fɪkʃən] n littérature f non-romanesque

nonplussed [nɔn'plʌst] adj perplexe

nonsense ['nɔnsəns] n absurdités fpl, idioties fpl; **~!** ne dites pas d'idioties!

non: **~-smoker** n non-fumeur m; **~- smoking** adj non-fumeur; **~-stick** adj qui n'attache pas; **~-stop** adj direct(e), sans arrêt (or escale) ♦ adv sans arrêt

noodles ['nu:dlz] npl nouilles fpl

nook [nuk] n: **~s and crannies** recoins mpl

noon [nu:n] n midi m

no one ['nəuwʌn] pron = **nobody**

noose [nu:s] n nœud coulant; (hangman's) corde f

nor [nɔ:r] conj = **neither** ♦ adv see **neither**

norm [nɔ:m] n norme f

normal adj normal(e); **~ly** ['nɔ:məlɪ] adv normalement

Normandy ['nɔ:məndɪ] n Normandie f

north [nɔ:θ] n nord m ♦ adj du nord, nord inv ♦ adv au or vers le nord; **N~ America** n Amérique f du Nord; **~-east** n nord-est m; **~erly** ['nɔ:ðəlɪ] adj du nord; **~ern** ['nɔ:ðən] adj du nord, septentrional(e); **N~ern Ireland** n Irlande f du Nord; **N~ Pole** n pôle m Nord; **N~ Sea** n mer f du Nord; **~ward(s)** adv vers le nord; **~-west** n nord-ouest m

Norway ['nɔ:weɪ] n Norvège f; **Norwegian** [nɔ:'wi:dʒən] adj norvégien(ne) ♦ n Norvégien(ne); (LING) norvégien m

nose [nəuz] n nez m; **~ about, around** vi fouiner or fureter (partout); **~bleed** n saignement m du nez; **~-dive** n (descente f en) piqué m; **~y** (inf) adj = **nosy**

nostalgia [nɔs'tældʒɪə] n nostalgie f

nostril ['nɔstrɪl] n narine f; (of horse) na-

seau m

nosy ['nəuzɪ] (inf) adj curieux(-euse)

not [nɔt] adv (ne ...) pas; **he is ~ or isn't here** il n'est pas ici; **you must ~ or you mustn't do that** tu ne dois pas faire ça; **it's too late, isn't it** or **is it ~?** c'est trop tard, n'est-ce pas?; **~ yet/now** pas encore/maintenant; **~ at all** pas du tout; see also **all**; **only**

notably ['nəutəblɪ] adv (particularly) en particulier; (markedly) spécialement

notary ['nəutərɪ] n notaire m

notch [nɔtʃ] n encoche f

note [nəut] n note f; (letter) mot m; (banknote) billet m ♦ vt (also: **~ down**) noter; (observe) constater; **~book** n carnet m; **~d** adj réputé(e); **~pad** n bloc-notes m; **~paper** n papier m à lettres

nothing ['nʌθɪŋ] n rien m; **he does ~** il ne fait rien; **~ new** rien de nouveau; **for ~** pour rien

notice ['nəutɪs] n (announcement, warning) avis m; (period of time) délai m; (resignation) démission f; (dismissal) congé m ♦ vt remarquer, s'apercevoir de; **to take ~ of** prêter attention à; **to bring sth to sb's ~** porter qch à la connaissance de qn; **at short ~** dans un délai très court; **until further ~** jusqu'à nouvel ordre; **to hand in one's ~** donner sa démission, démissionner; **~able** adj visible; **~ board** (BRIT) n panneau m d'affichage

notify ['nəutɪfaɪ] vt: **to ~ sth to sb** notifier qch à qn; **to ~ sb (of sth)** avertir qn (de qch)

notion ['nəuʃən] n idée f; (concept) notion f

notorious [nəu'tɔ:rɪəs] adj notoire (souvent en mal)

nought [nɔ:t] n zéro m

noun [naun] n nom m

nourish ['nʌrɪʃ] vt nourrir; **~ing** adj nourrissant(e); **~ment** n nourriture f

novel ['nɔvl] n roman m ♦ adj nouveau (nouvelle), original(e); **~ist** n romancier m; **~ty** n nouveauté f

November [nəu'vembər] n novembre m

now [nau] adv maintenant ♦ conj: **~ (that)**

maintenant que; **right ~** tout de suite; **by ~** à l'heure qu'il est; **just ~**: **that's the fashion just ~** c'est la mode en ce moment; **~ and then, ~ and again** de temps en temps; **from ~ on** dorénavant; **~adays** *adv* de nos jours

nowhere ['nəuwɛə'] *adv* nulle part

nozzle ['nɔzl] *n* (*of hose etc*) ajutage *m*; (*of vacuum cleaner*) suceur *m*

nuclear ['nju:klɪə'] *adj* nucléaire

nucleus ['nju:klɪəs] (*pl* **nuclei**) *n* noyau *m*

nude [nju:d] *adj* nu(e) ♦ *n* nu *m*; **in the ~** (tout(e)) nu(e)

nudge [nʌdʒ] *vt* donner un (petit) coup de coude à

nudist ['nju:dɪst] *n* nudiste *m/f*

nuisance ['nju:sns] *n*: **it's a ~** c'est (très) embêtant; **he's a ~** il est assommant or casse-pieds; **what a ~!** quelle barbe!

null [nʌl] *adj*: **~ and void** nul(le) et non avenu(e)

numb [nʌm] *adj* engourdi(e); (*with fear*) paralysé(e)

number ['nʌmbə'] *n* nombre *m*; (*numeral*) chiffre *m*; (*of house, bank account etc*) numéro *m* ♦ *vt* numéroter; (*amount to*) compter; **a ~ of** un certain nombre de; **they were seven in ~** ils étaient (au nombre de) sept; **to be ~ed among** compter parmi; **~ plate** *n* (*AUT*) plaque *f* minéralogique or d'immatriculation

numeral ['nju:mərəl] *n* chiffre *m*

numerate ['nju:mərɪt] (*BRIT*) *adj*: **to be ~** avoir des notions d'arithmétique

numerical [nju:'mɛrɪkl] *adj* numérique

numerous ['nju:mərəs] *adj* nombreux(-euse)

nun [nʌn] *n* religieuse *f*, sœur *f*

nurse [nə:s] *n* infirmière *f* ♦ *vt* (*patient, cold*) soigner

nursery ['nə:sərɪ] *n* (*room*) nursery *f*; (*institution*) crèche *f*; (*for plants*) pépinière *f*; **~ rhyme** *n* comptine *f*, chansonnette *f* pour enfants; **~ school** *n* école maternelle; **~ slope** *n* (*SKI*) piste *f* pour débutants

nursing ['nə:sɪŋ] *n* (*profession*) profession *f* d'infirmière; (*care*) soins *mpl*; **~ home** *n*

clinique *f*; maison *f* de convalescence

nut [nʌt] *n* (*of metal*) écrou *m*; (*fruit*) noix *f*; noisette *f*; cacahuète *f*; **~crackers** *npl* casse-noix *m inv*, casse-noisette(s) *m*

nutmeg ['nʌtmɛg] *n* (noix *f*) muscade *f*

nutritious [nju:'trɪʃəs] *adj* nutritif(-ive), nourrissant(e)

nuts [nʌts] (*inf*) *adj* dingue

nutshell ['nʌtʃɛl] *n*: **in a ~** en un mot

nutter ['nʌtə'] (*BRIT*: *inf*) *n*: **he's a complete ~** il est complètement cinglé

nylon ['naɪlɔn] *n* nylon *m* ♦ *adj* de or en nylon

O, o

oak [əuk] *n* chêne *m* ♦ *adj* de or en (bois de) chêne

OAP (*BRIT*) *n abbr* = **old-age pensioner**

oar [ɔ:'] *n* aviron *m*, rame *f*

oasis [əu'eɪsɪs] (*pl* **oases**) *n* oasis *f*

oath [əuθ] *n* serment *m*; (*swear word*) juron *m*; **under ~,** (*BRIT*) **on ~** sous serment

oatmeal ['əutmi:l] *n* flocons *mpl* d'avoine

oats [əuts] *n* avoine *f*

obedience [ə'bi:dɪəns] *n* obéissance *f*; **obedient** *adj* obéissant(e)

obey [ə'beɪ] *vt* obéir à; (*instructions*) se conformer à

obituary [ə'bɪtjuərɪ] *n* nécrologie *f*

object [*n* 'ɔbdʒɪkt, *vb* əb'dʒɛkt] *n* objet *m*; (*purpose*) but *m*, objet; (*LING*) complément *m* d'objet ♦ *vi*: **to ~ to** (*attitude*) désapprouver; (*proposal*) protester contre; **expense is no ~** l'argent n'est pas un problème; **he ~ed that ...** il a fait valoir or a objecté que ...; **I ~!** je proteste!; **~ion** [əb'dʒɛkʃən] *n* objection *f*; **~ionable** *adj* très désagréable; (*language*) choquant(e); **~ive** *n* objectif *m* ♦ *adj* objectif(-ive)

obligation [ɔblɪ'geɪʃən] *n* obligation *f*, devoir *m*; **without ~** sans engagement; **obligatory** [ə'blɪgətərɪ] *adj* obligatoire

oblige [ə'blaɪdʒ] *vt* (*force*): **to ~ sb to do** obliger or forcer qn à faire; (*do a favour*) rendre service à, obliger; **to be ~d to sb**

for sth être obligé(e) à qn de qch; **oblig-ing** *adj* obligeant(e), serviable

oblique [ə'bliːk] *adj* oblique; (*allusion*) indirect(e)

obliterate [ə'blɪtəreɪt] *vt* effacer

oblivion [ə'blɪvɪən] *n* oubli *m*; **oblivious** *adj*: **oblivious of** oublieux(-euse) de

oblong ['ɔblɔŋ] *adj* oblong (oblongue) ♦ *n* rectangle *m*

obnoxious [əb'nɔkʃəs] *adj* odieux(-euse); (*smell*) nauséabond(e)

oboe ['əubəu] *n* hautbois *m*

obscene [əb'siːn] *adj* obscène

obscure [əb'skjuər] *adj* obscur(e) ♦ *vt* obscurcir; (*hide: sun*) cacher

observant [əb'zəːvənt] *adj* observateur(-trice)

observation [ɔbzə'veɪʃən] *n* (*remark*) observation *f*; (*watching*) surveillance *f*

observatory [əb'zəːvətri] *n* observatoire *m*

observe [əb'zəːv] *vt* observer; (*remark*) faire observer *or* remarquer; **~r** *n* observateur(-trice)

obsess [əb'sɛs] *vt* obséder; **~ive** *adj* obsédant(e)

obsolete ['ɔbsəliːt] *adj* dépassé(e); démodé(e)

obstacle ['ɔbstəkl] *n* obstacle *m*; **~ race** *n* course *f* d'obstacles

obstinate ['ɔbstɪnɪt] *adj* obstiné(e)

obstruct [əb'strʌkt] *vt* (*block*) boucher, obstruer; (*hinder*) entraver

obtain [əb'teɪn] *vt* obtenir

obvious ['ɔbvɪəs] *adj* évident(e), manifeste; **~ly** *adv* manifestement; **~ly not!** bien sûr que non!

occasion [ə'keɪʒən] *n* occasion *f*; (*event*) événement *m*; **~al** *adj* pris(e) *or* fait(e) *etc* de temps en temps; occasionnel(le); **~ally** *adv* de temps en temps, quelquefois

occupation [ɔkju'peɪʃən] *n* occupation *f*; (*job*) métier *m*, profession *f*; **~al hazard** *n* risque *m* du métier

occupier ['ɔkjupaɪər] *n* occupant(e)

occupy ['ɔkjupaɪ] *vt* occuper; **to ~ o.s. in** *or* **with doing** s'occuper à faire

occur [ə'kəːr] *vi* (*event*) se produire; (*phe-nomenon, error*) se rencontrer; **to ~ to sb** venir à l'esprit de qn; **~rence** *n* (*exist-ence*) présence *f*, existence *f*; (*event*) cas *m*, fait *m*

ocean ['əuʃən] *n* océan *m*

o'clock [ə'klɔk] *adv*: **it is 5 ~** il est 5 heures

OCR *n abbr* = **optical character reader**; **optical character recognition**

October [ɔk'təubər] *n* octobre *m*

octopus ['ɔktəpəs] *n* pieuvre *f*

odd [ɔd] *adj* (*strange*) bizarre, curieux(-euse); (*number*) impair(e); (*not of a set*) dépareillé(e); **60-~** 60 et quelques; **at ~ times** de temps en temps; **the ~ one out** l'exception *f*; **~ity** *n* (*person*) excentrique *m/f*; (*thing*) curiosité *f*; **~-job man** *n* homme *m* à tout faire; **~ jobs** *npl* petits travaux divers; **~ly** *adv* bizarrement, curieusement; **~ments** *npl* (*COMM*) fins *fpl* de série; **~s** *npl* (*in betting*) cote *f*; **it makes no ~s** cela n'a pas d'importance; **at ~s** en désaccord; **~s and ends** de petites choses

odour ['əudər] (*US* **odor**) *n* odeur *f*

KEYWORD
---

of [ɔv, əv] *prep* **1** (*gen*) de; **a friend of ours** un de nos amis; **a boy of 10** un garçon de 10 ans; **that was kind of you** c'était gentil de votre part

2 (*expressing quantity, amount, dates etc*) de; **a kilo of flour** un kilo de farine; **how much of this do you need?** combien vous en faut-il?; **there were 3 of them** (*people*) ils étaient 3; (*objects*) il y en avait 3; **3 of us went** 3 d'entre nous y sont allé(e)s; **the 5th of July** le 5 juillet

3 (*from, out of*) en, de; **a statue of mar-ble** une statue de *or* en marbre; **made of wood** (fait) en bois

off [ɔf] *adj, adv* (*engine*) coupé(e); (*tap*) fer-mé(e); (*BRIT: food: bad*) mauvais(e); (: *milk: bad*) tourné(e); (*absent*) absent(e); (*can-celled*) annulé(e) ♦ *prep* de; sur; **to be ~** (*to leave*) partir, s'en aller; **to be ~ sick**

être absent pour cause de maladie; **a day ~** un jour de congé; **to have an ~ day** n'être pas en forme; **he had his coat ~** il avait enlevé son manteau; **10% ~** (*COMM*) 10% de rabais; **~ the coast** au large de la côte; **I'm ~ meat** je ne mange plus de viande, je n'aime plus la viande; **on the ~ chance** à tout hasard

offal ['ɔfl] *n* (*CULIN*) abats *mpl*

off-colour ['ɔf'kʌləʳ] (*BRIT*) *adj* (*ill*) malade, mal fichu(e)

offence [ə'fɛns] (*US* **offense**) *n* (*crime*) délit *m*, infraction *f*; **to take ~ at** se vexer de, s'offenser de

offend [ə'fɛnd] *vt* (*person*) offenser, blesser; **~er** *n* délinquant(e)

offense [ə'fɛns] (*US*) *n* = **offence**

offensive [ə'fɛnsɪv] *adj* offensant(e), choquant(e); (*smell etc*) très déplaisant(e); (*weapon*) offensif(-ive) ♦ *n* (*MIL*) offensive *f*

offer ['ɔfəʳ] *n* offre *f*, proposition *f* ♦ *vt* offrir, proposer; **"on ~"** (*COMM*) "en promotion"; **~ing** *n* offrande *f*

offhand [ɔf'hænd] *adj* désinvolte ♦ *adv* spontanément

office ['ɔfɪs] *n* (*place, room*) bureau *m*; (*position*) charge *f*, fonction *f*; **doctor's ~** (*US*) cabinet (médical); **to take ~** entrer en fonctions; **~ automation** *n* bureautique *f*; **~ block** (*US* **office building**) *n* immeuble *m* de bureaux; **~ hours** *npl* heures *fpl* de bureau; (*US: MED*) heures de consultation

officer ['ɔfɪsəʳ] *n* (*MIL etc*) officier *m*; (*also:* **police ~**) agent *m* (de police); (*of organization*) membre *m* du bureau directeur

office worker *n* employé(e) de bureau

official [ə'fɪʃl] *adj* officiel(le) ♦ *n* officiel *m*; (*civil servant*) fonctionnaire *m/f*; employé(e)

officiate [ə'fɪʃɪeɪt] *vi* (*REL*) officier; **to ~ at a marriage** célébrer un mariage

officious [ə'fɪʃəs] *adj* trop empressé(e)

offing ['ɔfɪŋ] *n*: **in the ~** (*fig*) en perspective

off: **~-licence** (*BRIT*) *n* (*shop*) débit *m* de vins et de spiritueux; **~-line** *adj, adv*

(*COMPUT*) (en mode) autonome; (: *switched off*) non connecté(e); **~-peak** *adj* aux heures creuses; (*electricity, heating, ticket*) au tarif heures creuses; **~-putting** (*BRIT*) *adj* (*remark*) rébarbatif(-ive); (*person*) rebutant(e), peu engageant(e); **~-road vehicle** *n* véhicule *m* tout-terrain; **~-season** *adj, adv* hors-saison *inv*; **~set** (*irreg*) *vt* (*counteract*) contrebalancer, compenser; **~shoot** *n* (*fig*) ramification *f*, antenne *f*; **~shore** *adj* (*breeze*) de terre; (*fishing*) côtier(-ère); **~side** *adj* (*SPORT*) hors jeu; (*AUT: in Britain*) de droite; (: *in US, Europe*) de gauche; **~spring** *n inv* progéniture *f*; **~stage** *adv* dans les coulisses; **~-the-peg** (*US* **off-the-rack**) *adv* en prêt-à-porter; **~-white** *adj* blanc cassé *inv*

off-licence

🛈 *Un* **off-licence** *est un magasin où l'on vend de l'alcool (à emporter) aux heures où les pubs sont fermés. On peut également y acheter des boissons non alcoolisées, des cigarettes, des chips, des bonbons, des chocolats etc.*

Oftel ['ɔftɛl] *n organisme qui supervise les télécommunications*

often ['ɔfn] *adv* souvent; **how ~ do you go?** vous y allez tous les combien?; **how ~ have you gone there?** vous y êtes allé combien de fois?

Ofwat ['ɔfwɔt] *n organisme qui surveille les activités des compagnies des eaux*

oh [əu] *excl* ô!, oh!, ah!

oil [ɔɪl] *n* huile *f*; (*petroleum*) pétrole *m*; (*for central heating*) mazout *m* ♦ *vt* (*machine*) graisser; **~can** *n* burette *f* de graissage; (*for storing*) bidon *m* à huile; **~field** *n* gisement *m* de pétrole; **~ filter** *n* (*AUT*) filtre *m* à huile; **~ painting** *n* peinture *f* à l'huile; **~ refinery** *n* raffinerie *f*; **~ rig** *n* derrick *m*; (*at sea*) plate-forme pétrolière; **~ slick** *n* nappe *f* de mazout; **~ tanker** *n* (*ship*) pétrolier *m*; (*truck*) camion-citerne *m*; **~ well** *n* puits *m* de pétrole; **~y** *adj* huileux(-euse); (*food*) gras(se)

ointment [ˈɔɪntmənt] *n* onguent *m*

O.K., okay [ˈəuˈkeɪ] *excl* d'accord! ♦ *adj* (*average*) pas mal ♦ *vt* approuver, donner son accord à; **is it ~?, are you ~?** ça va?

old [əuld] *adj* vieux (vieille); (*person*) vieux, âgé(e); (*former*) ancien(ne), vieux; **how ~ are you?** quel âge avez-vous?; **he's 10 years ~** il a 10 ans, il est âgé de 10 ans; **~er brother/sister** frère/sœur aîné(e); **~ age** vieillesse *f*; **~ age pensioner** (*BRIT*) *n* retraité(e); **~-fashioned** *adj* démodé(e); (*person*) vieux jeu *inv*

olive [ˈɔlɪv] *n* (*fruit*) olive *f*; (*tree*) olivier *m* ♦ *adj* (*also:* **~-green**) (vert) olive *inv*; **~ oil** *n* huile *f* d'olive

Olympic [əuˈlɪmpɪk] *adj* olympique; **the ~ Games, the ~s** les Jeux *mpl* olympiques

omelet(te) [ˈɔmlɪt] *n* omelette *f*

omen [ˈəumən] *n* présage *m*

ominous [ˈɔmɪnəs] *adj* menaçant(e), inquiétant(e); (*event*) de mauvais augure

omit [əuˈmɪt] *vt* omettre; **to ~ to do** omettre de faire

on [ɔn] *prep* **1** (*indicating position*) sur; **on the table** sur la table; **on the wall** sur le *or* au mur; **on the left** à gauche

2 (*indicating means, method, condition etc*): **on foot** à pied; **on the train/plane** (*be*) dans le train/l'avion; (*go*) en train/avion; **on the telephone/radio/television** au téléphone/à la radio/à la télévision; **to be on drugs** se droguer; **on holiday** en vacances

3 (*referring to time*): **on Friday** vendredi; **on Fridays** le vendredi; **on June 20th** le 20 juin; **a week on Friday** vendredi en huit; **on arrival** à l'arrivée; **on seeing this** en voyant cela

4 (*about, concerning*) sur, de; **a book on Balzac/physics** un livre sur Balzac/de physique

♦ *adv* **1** (*referring to dress, covering*): **to have one's coat on** avoir (mis) son manteau; **to put one's coat on** mettre son manteau; **what's she got on?** qu'est-ce qu'elle porte?; **screw the lid on tightly** vissez bien le couvercle

2 (*further, continuously*): **to walk** *etc* **on** continuer à marcher *etc*; **on and off** de temps à autre

♦ *adj* **1** (*in operation: machine*) en marche; (*: radio, TV, light*) allumé(e); (*: tap, gas*) ouvert(e); (*: brakes*) mis(e); **is the meeting still on?** (*not cancelled*) est-ce que la réunion a bien lieu?; (*in progress*) la réunion dure-t-elle encore?; **when is this film on?** quand passe ce film?

2 (*inf*): **that's not on!** (*not acceptable*) cela ne se fait pas!; (*not possible*) pas question!

once [wʌns] *adv* une fois; (*formerly*) autrefois ♦ *conj* une fois que; **~ he had left/it was done** une fois qu'il fut parti/que ce fut terminé; **at ~** tout de suite, immédiatement; (*simultaneously*) à la fois; **~ a week** une fois par semaine; **~ more** encore une fois; **~ and for all** une fois pour toutes; **~ upon a time** il y avait une fois, il était une fois

oncoming [ˈɔnkʌmɪŋ] *adj* (*traffic*) venant en sens inverse

one [wʌn] *num* un(e); **one hundred and fifty** cent cinquante; **one day** un jour

♦ *adj* **1** (*sole*) seul(e), unique; **the one book which** l'unique *or* le seul livre qui; **the one man who** le seul (homme) qui

2 (*same*) même; **they came in the one car** ils sont venus dans la même voiture

♦ *pron* **1**: **this one** celui-ci (celle-ci); **that one** celui-là (celle-là); **I've already got one/a red one** j'en ai déjà un(e)/un(e) rouge; **one by one** un(e) à *or* par un(e)

2: **one another** l'un(e) l'autre; **to look at one another** se regarder

3 (*impersonal*) on; **one never knows** on ne sait jamais; **to cut one's finger** se couper le doigt

one: **~-day excursion** (*US*) *n* billet *m* d'aller-retour (valable pour la journée);

~-man *adj* (*business*) dirigé(e) *etc* par un seul homme; **~-man band** *n* homme-orchestre *m*; **~-off** (*BRIT: inf*) *n* exemplaire *m* unique

oneself [wʌn'sɛlf] *pron* (*reflexive*) se; (*after prep*) soi(-même); (*emphatic*) soi-même; **to hurt ~** se faire mal; **to keep sth for ~** garder qch pour soi; **to talk to ~** se parler à soi-même

one: **~-sided** *adj* (*argument*) unilatéral; **~-to-~** *adj* (*relationship*) univoque; **~-way** *adj* (*street, traffic*) à sens unique

ongoing ['ɔngəʊɪŋ] *adj* en cours; (*relationship*) suivi(e)

onion ['ʌnjən] *n* oignon *m*

on-line ['ɔnlaɪn] *adj, adv* (*COMPUT*) en ligne; (: *switched on*) connecté(e)

onlooker ['ɔnlʊkəʳ] *n* spectateur(-trice)

only ['əʊnlɪ] *adv* seulement ♦ *adj* seul(e), unique ♦ *conj* seulement, mais; **an ~ child** un enfant unique; **not ~ ... but also** non seulement ... mais aussi

onset ['ɔnsɛt] *n* début *m*; (*of winter, old age*) approche *f*

onshore ['ɔnʃɔːʳ] *adj* (*wind*) du large

onslaught ['ɔnslɔːt] *n* attaque *f*, assaut *m*

onto ['ɔntu] *prep* = **on to**

onward(s) ['ɔnwəd(z)] *adv* (*move*) en avant; **from that time ~** à partir de ce moment

ooze [uːz] *vi* suinter

opaque [əʊ'peɪk] *adj* opaque

OPEC ['əʊpɛk] *n abbr* (= *Organization of Petroleum-Exporting Countries*) O.P.E.P. *f*

open ['əʊpn] *adj* ouvert(e); (*car*) découvert(e); (*road, view*) dégagé(e); (*meeting*) public(-ique); (*admiration*) manifeste ♦ *vt* ouvrir ♦ *vi* (*flower, eyes, door, debate*) s'ouvrir; (*shop, bank, museum*) ouvrir; (*book etc: commence*) commencer, débuter; **in the ~ (air)** en plein air; **~ on to** *vt fus* (*subj: room, door*) donner sur; **~ up** *vt* ouvrir; (*blocked road*) dégager ♦ *vi* s'ouvrir; **~ing** *n* ouverture *f*; (*opportunity*) occasion *f* ♦ *adj* (*remarks*) préliminaire; **~ing hours** *npl* heures *fpl* d'ouverture; **~ly** *adv* ouvertement; **~-minded** *adj* à l'esprit ouvert;

~-necked *adj* à col ouvert; **~-plan** *adj* sans cloisons

Open University
---

i *L'***Open University** *a été fondée en 1969. Ce type d'enseignement comprend des cours (certaines plages horaires sont réservées à cet effet à la télévision et à la radio), des devoirs qui sont envoyés par l'étudiant à son directeur ou sa directrice d'études, et un séjour obligatoire en université d'été. Il faut couvrir un certain nombre d'unités de valeur pendant une période de temps déterminée et obtenir la moyenne à un certain nombre d'entre elles pour recevoir le diplôme visé.*

---

opera ['ɔpərə] *n* opéra *m*; **~ singer** *n* chanteur(-euse) d'opéra

operate ['ɔpəreɪt] *vt* (*machine*) faire marcher, faire fonctionner ♦ *vi* fonctionner; (*MED*): **to ~ (on sb)** opérer (qn)

operatic [ɔpə'rætɪk] *adj* d'opéra

operating table *n* table *f* d'opération

operating theatre *n* salle *f* d'opération

operation [ɔpə'reɪʃən] *n* opération *f*; (*of machine*) fonctionnement *m*; **to be in ~** (*system, law*) être en vigueur; **to have an ~** (*MED*) se faire opérer

operative ['ɔpərətɪv] *adj* (*measure*) en vigueur

operator ['ɔpəreɪtəʳ] *n* (*of machine*) opérateur(-trice); (*TEL*) téléphoniste *m/f*

opinion [ə'pɪnjən] *n* opinion *f*, avis *m*; **in my ~** à mon avis; **~ated** *adj* aux idées bien arrêtées; **~ poll** *n* sondage *m* (d'opinion)

opponent [ə'pəʊnənt] *n* adversaire *m/f*

opportunity [ɔpə'tjuːnɪtɪ] *n* occasion *f*; **to take the ~ of doing** profiter de l'occasion pour faire; **en profiter pour faire**

oppose [ə'pəʊz] *vt* s'opposer à; **~d to** opposé(e) à; **as ~d to** par opposition à; **opposing** *adj* (*side*) opposé(e)

opposite ['ɔpəzɪt] *adj* opposé(e); (*house etc*) d'en face ♦ *adv* en face ♦ *prep* en face de ♦ *n* opposé *m*, contraire *m*; **the ~**

sex l'autre sexe, le sexe opposé; **opposition** [əpəˈzɪʃən] *n* opposition *f*

oppressive [əˈpresɪv] *adj* (*political regime*) oppressif(-ive); (*weather*) lourd(e); (*heat*) accablant(e)

opt [ɔpt] *vi*: **to ~ for** opter pour; **to ~ to do** choisir de faire; **~ out** *vi*: **to ~ out of** choisir de ne pas participer à *or* de ne pas faire

optical [ˈɔptɪkl] *adj* optique; (*instrument*) d'optique; **~ character recognition/reader** *n* lecture *f*/lecteur *m* optique

optician [ɔpˈtɪʃən] *n* opticien(ne)

optimist [ˈɔptɪmɪst] *n* optimiste *m/f*; **~ic** [ɔptɪˈmɪstɪk] *adj* optimiste

option [ˈɔpʃən] *n* choix *m*, option *f*; (*SCOL*) matière *f* à option; (*COMM*) option; **~al** *adj* facultatif(-ive); (*COMM*) en option

or [ɔːʳ] *conj* ou; (*with negative*): **he hasn't seen ~ heard anything** il n'a rien vu ni entendu; **~ else** sinon; ou bien

oral [ˈɔːrəl] *adj* oral(e) ♦ *n* oral *m*

orange [ˈɔrɪndʒ] *n* (*fruit*) orange *f* ♦ *adj* orange *inv*

orbit [ˈɔːbɪt] *n* orbite *f* ♦ *vt* graviter autour de; **~al** (*motorway*) *n* périphérique *m*

orchard [ˈɔːtʃəd] *n* verger *m*

orchestra [ˈɔːkɪstrə] *n* orchestre *m*; (*US: seating*) (fauteuils *mpl* d')orchestre

orchid [ˈɔːkɪd] *n* orchidée *f*

ordain [ɔːˈdeɪn] *vt* (*REL*) ordonner

ordeal [ɔːˈdiːl] *n* épreuve *f*

order [ˈɔːdəʳ] *n* ordre *m*; (*COMM*) commande *f* ♦ *vt* ordonner; (*COMM*) commander; **in ~** en ordre; (*document*) en règle; **in (working) ~** en état de marche; **out of ~** (*not in correct ~*) en désordre; (*not working*) en dérangement; **in ~ to do/that** pour faire/que +*sub*; **on ~** (*COMM*) en commande; **to ~ sb to do** ordonner à qn de faire; **~ form** *n* bon *m* de commande; **~ly** *n* (*MIL*) ordonnance *f*; (*MED*) garçon *m* de salle ♦ *adj* (*room*) en ordre; (*person*) qui a de l'ordre

ordinary [ˈɔːdnrɪ] *adj* ordinaire, normal(e); (*pej*) ordinaire, quelconque; **out of the ~** exceptionnel(le)

Ordnance Survey map [ˈɔːdnəns-] *n* ≃ carte *f* d'Etat-Major

ore [ɔːʳ] *n* minerai *m*

organ [ˈɔːgən] *n* organe *m*; (*MUS*) orgue *m*, orgues *fpl*; **~ic** [ɔːˈgænɪk] *adj* organique; (*food*) biologique

organization [ɔːgənaɪˈzeɪʃən] *n* organisation *f*

organize [ˈɔːgənaɪz] *vt* organiser; **~r** *n* organisateur(-trice)

orgasm [ˈɔːgæzəm] *n* orgasme *m*

Orient [ˈɔːrɪənt] *n*: **the ~** l'Orient *m*; **o~al** [ɔːrɪˈentl] *adj* oriental(e)

origin [ˈɔrɪdʒɪn] *n* origine *f*

original [əˈrɪdʒɪnl] *adj* original(e); (*earliest*) originel(le) ♦ *n* original *m*; **~ly** *adv* (*at first*) à l'origine

originate [əˈrɪdʒɪneɪt] *vi*: **to ~ from** (*person*) être originaire de; (*suggestion*) provenir de; **to ~ in** prendre naissance dans; avoir son origine dans

Orkney [ˈɔːknɪ] *n* (*also*: **the ~ Islands**) les Orcades *fpl*

ornament [ˈɔːnəmənt] *n* ornement *m*; (*trinket*) bibelot *m*; **~al** [ɔːnəˈmentl] *adj* décoratif(-ive); (*garden*) d'agrément

ornate [ɔːˈneɪt] *adj* très orné(e)

orphan [ˈɔːfn] *n* orphelin(e)

orthopaedic [ɔːθəˈpiːdɪk] (*US* **orthopedic**) *adj* orthopédique

ostensibly [ɔsˈtensɪblɪ] *adv* en apparence

ostentatious [ɔstenˈteɪʃəs] *adj* prétentieux(-euse)

ostracize [ˈɔstrəsaɪz] *vt* frapper d'ostracisme

ostrich [ˈɔstrɪtʃ] *n* autruche *f*

other [ˈʌðəʳ] *adj* autre ♦ *pron*: **the ~ (one)** l'autre; **~s** (*~ people*) d'autres; **~ than** autrement que; à part; **~wise** *adv*, *conj* autrement

otter [ˈɔtəʳ] *n* loutre *f*

ouch [autʃ] *excl* aïe!

ought [ɔːt] (*pt* **ought**) *aux vb*: **I ~ to do it** je devrais le faire, il faudrait que je le fasse; **this ~ to have been corrected** cela aurait dû être corrigé; **he ~ to win** il devrait gagner

ounce [auns] *n* once *f* (= 28.35g; 16 in a pound)

our ['auə^r] *adj* notre, nos *pl*; *see also* **my**; **~s** *pron* le (la) nôtre, les nôtres; *see also* **mine**[1]; **~selves** [auə'selvz] *pron pl* (*reflexive, after preposition*) nous; (*emphatic*) nous-mêmes; *see also* **oneself**

oust [aust] *vt* évincer

out [aut] *adv* dehors; (*published, not at home etc*) sorti(e); (*light, fire*) éteint(e); **~ here** ici; **~ there** là-bas; **he's ~** (*absent*) il est sorti; (*unconscious*) il est sans connaissance; **to be ~ in one's calculations** s'être trompé dans ses calculs; **to run/back etc ~** sortir en courant/en reculant *etc*; **~ loud** à haute voix; **~ of** (*~side*) en dehors de; (*because of: anger etc*) par; (*from among*): **~ of 10** sur 10; (*without*): **~ of petrol** sans essence, à court d'essence; **~ of order** (*machine*) en panne; (*TEL: line*) en dérangement; **~-and-~** *adj* (*liar, thief etc*) véritable; **~back** *n* (*in Australia*): **the ~back** l'intérieur *m*; **~board** *n* (*also:* **~board motor**) (moteur *m*) hors-bord *m*; **~break** *n* (*of war, disease*) début *m*; (*of violence*) éruption *f*; **~burst** *n* explosion *f*, accès *m*; **~cast** *n* exilé(e); (*socially*) paria *m*; **~come** *n* issue *f*, résultat *m*; **~crop** *n* (*of rock*) affleurement *m*; **~cry** *n* tollé (général); **~dated** *adj* démodé(e); **~do** (*irreg*) *vt* surpasser; **~door** *adj* de *or* en plein air; **~doors** *adv* dehors; au grand air

outer ['autə^r] *adj* extérieur(e); **~ space** *n* espace *m* cosmique

outfit ['autfit] *n* (*clothes*) tenue *f*

out: **~going** *adj* (*character*) ouvert(e), extraverti(e); (*departing*) sortant(e); **~goings** (*BRIT*) *npl* (*expenses*) dépenses *fpl*; **~grow** (*irreg*) *vt* (*clothes*) devenir trop grand(e) pour; **~house** *n* appentis *m*, remise *f*

outing ['autɪŋ] *n* sortie *f*; excursion *f*

out: **~law** *n* hors-la-loi *m inv* ♦ *vt* mettre hors-la-loi; **~lay** *n* dépenses *fpl*; (*investment*) mise *f* de fonds; **~let** *n* (*for liquid etc*) issue *f*, sortie *f*; (*US: ELEC*) prise *f* de courant; (*also: retail ~let*) point *m* de vente; **~line** *n* (*shape*) contour *m*; (*summary*) esquisse *f*, grandes lignes ♦ *vt* (*fig: theory, plan*) exposer à grands traits; **~live** *vt* survivre à; **~look** *n* perspective *f*; **~lying** *adj* écarté(e); **~moded** *adj* démodé(e); dépassé(e); **~number** *vt* surpasser en nombre; **~-of-date** *adj* (*passport*) périmé(e); (*theory etc*) dépassé(e); (*clothes etc*) démodé(e); **~-of-the-way** *adj* (*place*) loin de tout; **~patient** *n* malade *m/f* en consultation externe; **~post** *n* avant-poste *m*; **~put** *n* rendement *m*, production *f*; (*COMPUT*) sortie *f*

outrage ['autreɪdʒ] *n* (*anger*) indignation *f*; (*violent act*) atrocité *f*; (*scandal*) scandale *m* ♦ *vt* outrager; **~ous** [aut'reɪdʒəs] *adj* atroce; scandaleux(-euse)

outright [*adv* aut'raɪt, *adj* 'autraɪt] *adv* complètement; (*deny, refuse*) catégoriquement; (*ask*) carrément; (*kill*) sur le coup ♦ *adj* complet(-ète); catégorique

outset ['autset] *n* début *m*

outside [aut'saɪd] *n* extérieur *m* ♦ *adj* extérieur(e) ♦ *adv* (au) dehors, à l'extérieur ♦ *prep* hors de, à l'extérieur de; **at the ~** (*fig*) au plus *or* maximum; **~ lane** *n* (*AUT: in Britain*) voie *f* de droite; (: *in US, Europe*) voie *f* de gauche; **~ line** *n* (*TEL*) ligne extérieure; **~r** *n* (*stranger*) étranger(-ère)

out: **~size** ['autsaɪz] *adj* énorme; (*clothes*) grande taille *inv*; **~skirts** *npl* faubourgs *mpl*; **~spoken** *adj* très franc (franche); **~standing** *adj* remarquable, exceptionnel(le); (*unfinished*) en suspens; (*debt*) impayé(e); (*problem*) non réglé(e); **~stay** *vt*: **to ~stay one's welcome** abuser de l'hospitalité de son hôte; **~stretched** [aut'stretʃt] *adj* (*hand*) tendu(e); **~strip** [aut'strɪp] *vt* (*competitors, demand*) dépasser; **~ tray** *n* courrier *m* "départ"

outward ['autwəd] *adj* (*sign, appearances*) extérieur(e); (*journey*) (d')aller

outweigh [aut'weɪ] *vt* l'emporter sur

outwit [aut'wɪt] *vt* se montrer plus malin que

oval ['əuvl] *adj* ovale ♦ *n* ovale *m*

Oval Office

i *L'***Oval Office** *est le bureau personnel du président des États-Unis à la Maison-Blanche, ainsi appelé du fait de sa forme ovale. Par extension, ce terme désigne la présidence elle-même.*

---

ovary ['əuvəri] *n* ovaire *m*

oven ['ʌvn] *n* four *m*; **~proof** *adj* allant au four

over ['əuvər] *adv* (par-)dessus ♦ *adj* (*finished*) fini(e), terminé(e); (*too much*) en plus ♦ *prep* sur; par-dessus; (*above*) au-dessus de; (*on the other side of*) de l'autre côté de; (*more than*) plus de; (*during*) pendant; **~ here** ici; **~ there** là-bas; **all ~** (*everywhere*) partout, fini(e); **~ and ~ (again)** à plusieurs reprises; **~ and above** en plus de; **to ask sb ~** inviter qn (à passer)

overall [*adj, n* 'əuvərɔːl, *adv* əuvər'ɔːl] *adj* (*length, cost etc*) total(e); (*study*) d'ensemble ♦ *n* (*BRIT*) blouse *f* ♦ *adv* dans l'ensemble, en général; **~s** *npl* bleus *mpl* (de travail)

over: ~awe *vt* impressionner; **~balance** *vi* basculer; **~board** *adv* (*NAUT*) par-dessus bord; **~book** *vt* faire du surbooking; **~cast** *adj* couvert(e)

overcharge [əuvə'tʃɑːdʒ] *vt*: **to ~ sb for sth** faire payer qch trop cher à qn

overcoat ['əuvəkəut] *n* pardessus *m*

overcome [əuvə'kʌm] (*irreg*) *vt* (*defeat*) triompher de; (*difficulty*) surmonter

over: ~crowded *adj* bondé(e); **~do** (*irreg*) *vt* exagérer; (*overcook*) trop cuire; **to ~do it** (*work etc*) se surmener; **~dose** *n* dose excessive; **~draft** *n* découvert *m*; **~drawn** *adj* (*account*) à découvert; (*person*) dont le compte est à découvert; **~due** *adj* en retard; (*change, reform*) qui tarde; **~estimate** *vt* surestimer

overflow [əuvə'fləu] *vi* déborder ♦ *n* (*also*: **~ pipe**) tuyau *m* d'écoulement, trop-plein *m*

overgrown [əuvə'grəun] *adj* (*garden*) envahi(e) par la végétation

overhaul [*vb* əuvə'hɔːl, *n* 'əuvəhɔːl] *vt* réviser ♦ *n* révision *f*

overhead [*adv* əuvə'hed, *adj, n* 'əuvəhed] *adv* au-dessus ♦ *adj* aérien(ne); (*lighting*) vertical(e) ♦ *n* (*US*) = **overheads**; **~s** *npl* (*expenses*) frais généraux; **~ projector** *n* rétroprojecteur *m*

over: ~hear (*irreg*) *vt* entendre (par hasard); **~heat** *vi* (*engine*) chauffer; **~joyed** *adj*: **~joyed (at)** ravi(e) (de), enchanté(e) (de)

overland ['əuvəlænd] *adj, adv* par voie de terre

overlap [əuvə'læp] *vi* se chevaucher

over: ~leaf *adv* au verso; **~load** *vt* surcharger; **~look** *vt* (*have view of*) donner sur; (*miss: by mistake*) oublier; (*forgive*) fermer les yeux sur

overnight [*adv* əuvə'naɪt, *adj* 'əuvənaɪt] *adv* (*happen*) durant la nuit; (*fig*) soudain ♦ *adj* d'une (*or* de) nuit; **he stayed there ~** il y a passé la nuit

overpass ['əuvəpɑːs] *n* pont autoroutier

overpower [əuvə'pauər] *vt* vaincre; (*fig*) accabler; **~ing** *adj* (*heat, stench*) suffocant(e)

over: ~rate *vt* surestimer; **~ride** (*irreg*: *like* **ride**) *vt* (*order, objection*) passer outre à; **~riding** *adj* prépondérant(e); **~rule** *vt* (*decision*) annuler; (*claim*) rejeter; (*person*) rejeter l'avis de; **~run** (*irreg*: *like* **run**) *vt* (*country*) occuper; (*time limit*) dépasser

overseas [əuvə'siːz] *adv* outre-mer; (*abroad*) à l'étranger ♦ *adj* (*trade*) extérieur(e); (*visitor*) étranger(-ère)

overshadow [əuvə'ʃædəu] *vt* (*fig*) éclipser

oversight ['əuvəsaɪt] *n* omission *f*, oubli *m*

oversleep [əuvə'sliːp] (*irreg*) *vi* se réveiller (trop) tard

overstep [əuvə'step] *vt*: **to ~ the mark** dépasser la mesure

overt [əu'vəːt] *adj* non dissimulé(e)

overtake [əuvə'teɪk] (*irreg*) *vt* (*AUT*) dépasser, doubler

over: ~throw (*irreg*) *vt* (*government*) renverser; **~time** *n* heures *fpl* supplémentaires; **~tone** *n* (*also*: **~tones**) note *f*, sous-entendus *mpl*

overture ['əʊvətʃʊəʳ] *n* (*MUS, fig*) ouverture *f*

over: ~**turn** *vt* renverser ♦ *vi* se retourner; ~**weight** *adj* (*person*) trop gros(se); ~**whelm** *vt* (*subj: emotion*) accabler; (*enemy, opponent*) écraser; ~**whelming** *adj* (*victory, defeat*) écrasant(e); (*desire*) irrésistible

overwrought [əʊvəˈrɔːt] *adj* excédé(e)

owe [əʊ] *vt*: **to ~ sb sth, to ~ sth to sb** devoir qch à qn; **owing to** *prep* à cause de, en raison de

owl [aʊl] *n* hibou *m*

own [əʊn] *vt* posséder ♦ *adj* propre; **a room of my ~** une chambre à moi, ma propre chambre; **to get one's ~ back** prendre sa revanche; **on one's ~** tout(e) seul(e); ~ **up** *vi* avouer; ~**er** *n* propriétaire *m/f*; ~**ership** *n* possession *f*

ox [ɔks] (*pl* ~**en**) *n* bœuf *m*; ~**tail** *n*: ~**tail soup** soupe *f* à la queue de bœuf

oxygen ['ɔksɪdʒən] *n* oxygène *m*

oyster ['ɔɪstəʳ] *n* huître *f*

oz. *abbr* = **ounce(s)**

ozone ['əʊzəʊn] *n*: ~-**friendly** *adj* qui n'attaque pas *or* qui préserve la couche d'ozone; ~ **hole** *n* trou *m* d'ozone; ~ **layer** *n* couche *f* d'ozone

P, p

p *abbr* = **penny; pence**

PA *n abbr* = **personal assistant; public address system**

pa [pɑː] (*inf*) *n* papa *m*

p.a. *abbr* = **per annum**

pace [peɪs] *n* pas *m*; (*speed*) allure *f*; vitesse *f* ♦ *vi*: **to ~ up and down** faire les cent pas; **to keep ~ with** aller à la même vitesse que; ~**maker** *n* (*MED*) stimulateur *m* cardiaque; (*SPORT: also:* ~**setter**) meneur(-euse) de train

Pacific [pəˈsɪfɪk] *n*: **the ~ (Ocean)** le Pacifique, l'océan *m* Pacifique

pack [pæk] *n* (~*et, US: of cigarettes*) paquet *m*; (*of hounds*) meute *f*; (*of thieves etc*) bande *f*; (*back ~*) sac *m* à dos; (*of cards*) jeu *m* ♦ *vt* (*goods*) empaqueter, emballer; (*box*) remplir; (*cram*) entasser; **to ~ one's suitcase** faire sa valise; **to ~ (one's bags)** faire ses bagages; **to ~ sb off** to expédier qn à; ~ **it in!** laisse tomber!, écrase!

package ['pækɪdʒ] *n* paquet *m*; (*also:* ~ **deal**) forfait *m*; ~ **tour** *n* (*BRIT*) voyage organisé

packed *adj* (*crowded*) bondé(e); ~ **lunch** (*BRIT*) *n* repas froid

packet ['pækɪt] *n* paquet *m*

packing ['pækɪŋ] *n* emballage *m*; ~ **case** *n* caisse *f* (d'emballage)

pact [pækt] *n* pacte *m*; traité *m*

pad [pæd] *n* bloc(-notes) *m*; (*to prevent friction*) tampon *m*; (*inf: home*) piaule *f* ♦ *vt* rembourrer; ~**ding** *n* rembourrage *m*

paddle ['pædl] *n* (*oar*) pagaie *f*; (*US: for table tennis*) raquette *f* de ping-pong ♦ *vt*: **to ~ a canoe** *etc* pagayer ♦ *vi* barboter, faire trempette; **paddling pool** (*BRIT*) *n* petit bassin

paddock ['pædək] *n* enclos *m*; (*RACING*) paddock *m*

padlock ['pædlɔk] *n* cadenas *m*

paediatrics [piːdɪˈætrɪks] (*US* **pediatrics**) *n* pédiatrie *f*

pagan ['peɪgən] *adj, n* païen(ne)

page [peɪdʒ] *n* (*of book*) page *f*; (*also:* ~ **boy**) groom *m*, chasseur *m*; (*at wedding*) garçon *m* d'honneur ♦ *vt* (*in hotel etc*) (faire) appeler

pageant ['pædʒənt] *n* spectacle *m* historique; ~**ry** *n* apparat *m*, pompe *f*

pager ['peɪdʒəʳ], **paging device** *n* (*TEL*) récepteur *m* d'appels

paid [peɪd] *pt, pp* of **pay** ♦ *adj* (*work, official*) rémunéré(e); (*holiday*) payé(e); **to put ~ to** (*BRIT*) mettre fin à, régler

pail [peɪl] *n* seau *m*

pain [peɪn] *n* douleur *f*; **to be in ~** souffrir, avoir mal; **to take ~s to do** se donner du mal pour faire; ~**ed** *adj* peiné(e), chagrin(e); ~**ful** *adj* douloureux(-euse); (*fig*) difficile, pénible; ~**fully** *adv* (*fig: very*) terriblement; **~killer** n analgésique m; **~less** adj indolore; **~staking** ['peɪnzteɪkɪŋ] adj (person) soigneux(-euse); (work) soigné(e)

paint [peɪnt] n peinture f ♦ vt peindre; **to ~ the door blue** peindre la porte en bleu; **~brush** n pinceau m; **~er** n peintre m; **~ing** n peinture f; (picture) tableau m; **~work** n peinture f

pair [peəʳ] n (of shoes, gloves etc) paire f; (of people) couple m; **~ of scissors** (paire de) ciseaux mpl; **~ of trousers** pantalon m

pajamas [pə'dʒɑːməz] (US) npl pyjama(s) m(pl)

Pakistan [pɑːkɪ'stɑːn] n Pakistan m; **~i** adj pakistanais(e) ♦ n Pakistanais(e)

pal [pæl] (inf) n copain (copine)

palace ['pæləs] n palais m

palatable ['pælɪtəbl] adj bon (bonne), agréable au goût

palate ['pælɪt] n palais m (ANAT)

pale [peɪl] adj pâle ♦ n: **beyond the ~** (behaviour) inacceptable; **to grow ~** pâlir

Palestine ['pælɪstaɪn] n Palestine f; **Palestinian** [pælɪs'tɪnɪən] adj palestinien(ne) ♦ n Palestinien(ne)

palette ['pælɪt] n palette f

pall [pɔːl] n (of smoke) voile m ♦ vi devenir lassant(e)

pallet ['pælɪt] n (for goods) palette f

pallid ['pælɪd] adj blême

palm [pɑːm] n (of hand) paume f; (also: **~ tree**) palmier m ♦ vt: **to ~ sth off on sb** (inf) refiler qch à qn; **P~ Sunday** n le dimanche des Rameaux

paltry ['pɔːltrɪ] adj dérisoire

pamper ['pæmpəʳ] vt gâter, dorloter

pamphlet ['pæmflət] n brochure f

pan [pæn] n (also: **saucepan**) casserole f; (also: **frying ~**) poêle f; **~cake** n crêpe f

panda ['pændə] n panda m

pandemonium [pændɪ'məʊnɪəm] n tohubohu m

pander ['pændəʳ] vi: **to ~ to** flatter bassement; obéir servilement à

pane [peɪn] n carreau m, vitre f

panel ['pænl] n (of wood, cloth etc) panneau m; (RADIO, TV) experts mpl; (for interview, exams) jury m; **~ling** (US **paneling**) n boiseries fpl

pang [pæŋ] n: **~s of remorse/jealousy** áffres mpl du remords/de la jalousie; **~s of hunger/conscience** tiraillements mpl d'estomac/de la conscience

panic ['pænɪk] n panique f, affolement m ♦ vi s'affoler, paniquer; **~ky** adj (person) qui panique or s'affole facilement; **~stricken** adj affolé(e)

pansy ['pænzɪ] n (BOT) pensée f; (inf: pej) tapette f, pédé m

pant [pænt] vi haleter

panther ['pænθəʳ] n panthère f

panties ['pæntɪz] npl slip m

pantomime ['pæntəmaɪm] (BRIT) n spectacle m de Noël

---

pantomime

i Une **pantomime**, que l'on appelle également de façon familière "panto", est un genre de farce où le personnage principal est souvent un jeune garçon et où il y a toujours une **dame**, c'est-à-dire une vieille femme jouée par un homme, et un méchant. La plupart du temps, l'histoire est basée sur un conte de fées comme Cendrillon ou Le Chat botté, et le public est encouragé à participer en prévenant le héros d'un danger imminent. Ce genre de spectacle, qui s'adresse surtout aux enfants, vise également un public d'adultes au travers des nombreuses plaisanteries faisant allusion à des faits d'actualité.

---

pantry ['pæntrɪ] n garde-manger m inv

pants [pænts] npl (BRIT: woman's) slip m; (: man's) slip, caleçon m; (US: trousers) pantalon m

pantyhose ['pæntɪhəʊz] (US) npl collant m

paper ['peɪpəʳ] n papier m; (also: **wallpaper**) papier peint; (also: **newspaper**) journal m; (academic essay) article m; (exam) épreuve écrite ♦ adj en or de papier ♦ vt tapisser (de papier peint); **~s** npl (also: **identity ~s**) papiers (d'identité);

~back n livre m de poche; livre broché or non relié; ~ bag n sac m en papier; ~ clip n trombone m; ~ hankie n mouchoir m en papier; ~weight n presse-papiers m inv; ~work n papiers mpl; (pej) paperasserie f

par [pɑːʳ] n pair m; (GOLF) normale f du parcours; **on a ~ with** à égalité avec, au même niveau que

parachute ['pærəʃuːt] n parachute m

parade [pə'reɪd] n défilé m ♦ vt (fig) faire étalage de ♦ vi défiler

paradise ['pærədaɪs] n paradis m

paradox ['pærədɒks] n paradoxe m; ~ically [pærə'dɒksɪklɪ] adv paradoxalement

paraffin ['pærəfɪn] (BRIT) n (also: ~ oil) pétrole (lampant)

paragon ['pærəgən] n modèle m

paragraph ['pærəgrɑːf] n paragraphe m

parallel ['pærəlel] adj parallèle; (fig) semblable ♦ n (line) parallèle f; (fig, GEO) parallèle m

paralyse ['pærəlaɪz] (BRIT) vt paralyser; **paralysis** [pə'rælɪsɪs] n paralysie f; **paralyze** (US) vt = **paralyse**

paramount ['pærəmaunt] adj: **of ~ importance** de la plus haute or grande importance

paranoid ['pærənɔɪd] adj (PSYCH) paranoïaque

paraphernalia [pærəfə'neɪlɪə] n attirail m

parasol ['pærəsɒl] n ombrelle f; (over table) parasol m

paratrooper ['pærətruːpəʳ] n parachutiste m (soldat)

parcel ['pɑːsl] n paquet m, colis m ♦ vt (also: ~ **up**) empaqueter

parchment ['pɑːtʃmənt] n parchemin m

pardon ['pɑːdn] n pardon m; grâce f ♦ vt pardonner à; ~ **me!, I beg your ~!** pardon!, je suis désolé!; **(I beg your) ~?**, (US) ~ **me?** pardon?

parent ['pɛərənt] n père m or mère f; ~**s** npl parents mpl

Paris ['pærɪs] n Paris

parish ['pærɪʃ] n paroisse f; (BRIT: civil) ≃ commune f

Parisian [pə'rɪzɪən] adj parisien(ne) ♦ n Parisien(ne)

park [pɑːk] n parc m, jardin public ♦ vt garer ♦ vi se garer

parking ['pɑːkɪŋ] n stationnement m; **"no ~"** "stationnement interdit"; ~ **lot** (US) n parking m, parc m de stationnement; ~ **meter** n parcomètre m; ~ **ticket** n P.V. m

parliament ['pɑːləmənt] n parlement m; ~**ary** [pɑːlə'mɛntəri] adj parlementaire

parlour ['pɑːləʳ] (US **parlor**) n salon m

parochial [pə'rəukɪəl] (pej) adj à l'esprit de clocher

parole [pə'rəul] n: **on ~** en liberté conditionnelle

parrot ['pærət] n perroquet m

parry ['pærɪ] vt (blow) esquiver

parsley ['pɑːslɪ] n persil m

parsnip ['pɑːsnɪp] n panais m

parson ['pɑːsn] n ecclésiastique m; (Church of England) pasteur m

part [pɑːt] n partie f; (of machine) pièce f; (THEATRE etc) rôle m; (of serial) épisode m; (US: in hair) raie f ♦ adv = **partly** ♦ vt séparer ♦ vi (people) se séparer; (crowd) s'ouvrir; **to take ~ in** participer à, prendre part à; **to take sth in good ~** prendre qch du bon côté; **to take sb's ~** prendre le parti de qn, prendre parti pour qn; **for my ~** en ce qui me concerne; **for the most ~** dans la plupart des cas; ~ **with** vt fus se séparer de; ~ **exchange** (BRIT) n: **in ~ exchange** en reprise

partial ['pɑːʃl] adj (not complete) partiel(le); **to be ~ to** avoir un faible pour

participate [pɑː'tɪsɪpeɪt] vi: **to ~ (in)** participer (à), prendre part (à); **participation** [pɑːtɪsɪ'peɪʃən] n participation f

participle ['pɑːtɪsɪpl] n participe m

particle ['pɑːtɪkl] n particule f

particular [pə'tɪkjuləʳ] adj particulier(-ère); (special) spécial(e); (fussy) difficile; méticuleux(-euse); ~**s** npl (details) détails mpl; (personal) nom, adresse etc; **in ~** en particulier; ~**ly** adv particulièrement

parting ['pɑːtɪŋ] n séparation f; (BRIT: in

hair) raie f ♦ adj d'adieu

partisan [pɑːtɪ'zæn] n partisan(e) ♦ adj partisan(e); de parti

partition [pɑː'tɪʃən] n (wall) cloison f; (POL) partition f, division f

partly ['pɑːtlɪ] adv en partie, partiellement

partner ['pɑːtnə^r] n partenaire m/f; (in marriage) conjoint(e); (boyfriend, girlfriend) ami(e); (COMM) associé(e); (at dance) cavalier(-ère); ~**ship** n association f

partridge ['pɑːtrɪdʒ] n perdrix f

part-time ['pɑːt'taɪm] adj, adv à mi-temps, à temps partiel

party ['pɑːtɪ] n (POL) parti m; (group) groupe m; (LAW) partie f; (celebration) réception f; soirée f; fête f ♦ cpd (POL) de or du parti; ~ **dress** n robe habillée

pass [pɑːs] vt passer; (place) passer devant; (friend) croiser; (overtake) dépasser; (exam) être reçu(e) à, réussir; (approve) approuver, accepter ♦ vi passer; (SCOL) être reçu(e) or admis(e), réussir ♦ n (permit) laissez-passer m inv; carte f d'accès or d'abonnement; (in mountains) col m; (SPORT) passe f; (SCOL: also: ~ **mark**): **to get a ~** être reçu(e) (sans mention); **to make a ~ at sb** (inf) faire des avances à qn; ~ **away** vi mourir; ~ **by** vi passer ♦ vt négliger; ~ **on** vt (news, object) transmettre; (illness) passer; ~ **out** vi s'évanouir; ~ **up** vt (opportunity) laisser passer; ~**able** adj (road) praticable; (work) acceptable

passage ['pæsɪdʒ] n (also: ~**way**) couloir m; (gen, in book) passage m; (by boat) traversée f

passbook ['pɑːsbuk] n livret m

passenger ['pæsɪndʒə^r] n passager(-ère)

passer-by [pɑːsə'baɪ] (pl **~s-~**) n passant(e)

passing ['pɑːsɪŋ] adj (fig) passager(-ère); **in ~** en passant; ~ **place** n (AUT) aire f de croisement

passion ['pæʃən] n passion f; ~**ate** adj passionné(e)

passive ['pæsɪv] adj (also LING) passif(-ive); ~ **smoking** n tabagisme m passif

Passover ['pɑːsəuvə^r] n Pâque f (juive)

passport ['pɑːspɔːt] n passeport m; ~ **control** n contrôle m des passeports; ~ **office** n bureau m de délivrance des passeports

password ['pɑːswɜːd] n mot m de passe

past [pɑːst] prep (in front of) devant; (further than) au delà de, plus loin que; après; (later than) après ♦ adj passé(e); (president etc) ancien(ne) ♦ n passé m; **he's ~ forty** il a dépassé la quarantaine, il a plus de or passé quarante ans; **for the ~ few/3 days** depuis quelques/3 jours; ces derniers/3 derniers jours; **ten/quarter ~ eight** huit heures dix/un or et quart

pasta ['pæstə] n pâtes fpl

paste [peɪst] n pâte f; (meat ~) pâté m (à tartiner); (tomato ~) purée f, concentré m; (glue) colle f (de pâte) ♦ vt coller

pasteurized ['pæstʃəraɪzd] adj pasteurisé(e)

pastille [pæstɪl] n pastille f

pastime ['pɑːstaɪm] n passe-temps m inv

pastry ['peɪstrɪ] n pâte f; (cake) pâtisserie f

pasture ['pɑːstʃə^r] n pâturage m

pasty [n 'pæstɪ, adj 'peɪstɪ] n petit pâté (en croûte) ♦ adj (complexion) terreux(-euse)

pat [pæt] vt tapoter; (dog) caresser

patch [pætʃ] n (of material) pièce f; (eye ~) cache m; (spot) tache f; (on tyre) rustine f ♦ vt (clothes) rapiécer; **(to go through) a bad ~** (passer par) une période difficile; ~ **up** vt réparer (grossièrement); **to ~ up a quarrel** se raccommoder; ~**y** adj inégal(e); (incomplete) fragmentaire

pâté ['pæteɪ] n pâté m, terrine f

patent ['peɪtnt] n brevet m (d'invention) ♦ vt faire breveter ♦ adj patent(e), manifeste; ~ **leather** n cuir verni

paternal [pə'tɜːnl] adj paternel(le)

path [pɑːθ] n chemin m, sentier m; (in garden) allée f; (trajectory) trajectoire f

pathetic [pə'θetɪk] adj (pitiful) pitoyable; (very bad) lamentable, minable

pathological [pæθə'lɔdʒɪkl] adj pathologique

pathway ['pɑːθweɪ] n sentier m, passage

m

patience ['peɪʃns] *n* patience *f*; (*BRIT*: *CARDS*) réussite *f*

patient ['peɪʃnt] *n* malade *m/f*; (*of dentist etc*) patient(e) ♦ *adj* patient(e)

patio ['pætɪəu] *n* patio *m*

patriotic [pætrɪ'ɔtɪk] *adj* patriotique; (*person*) patriote

patrol [pə'trəul] *n* patrouille *f* ♦ *vt* patrouiller dans; **~ car** *n* voiture *f* de police; **~man** (*irreg*) (*US*) *n* agent *m* de police

patron ['peɪtrən] *n* (*in shop*) client(e); (*of charity*) patron(ne); **~ of the arts** mécène *m*; **~ize** ['pætrənaɪz] *vt* (*pej*) traiter avec condescendance; (*shop, club*) être (un) client *or* un habitué de

patter ['pætər] *n* crépitement *m*, tapotement *m*; (*sales talk*) boniment *m*

pattern ['pætən] *n* (*design*) motif *m*; (*SEWING*) patron *m*

pauper ['pɔ:pər] *n* indigent(e)

pause [pɔ:z] *n* pause *f*, arrêt *m* ♦ *vi* faire une pause, s'arrêter

pave [peɪv] *vt* paver, daller; **to ~ the way for** ouvrir la voie à

pavement ['peɪvmənt] (*BRIT*) *n* trottoir *m*

pavilion [pə'vɪlɪən] *n* pavillon *m*; tente *f*

paving ['peɪvɪŋ] *n* (*material*) pavé *m*, dalle *f*; **~ stone** *n* pavé *m*

paw [pɔ:] *n* patte *f*

pawn [pɔ:n] *n* (*CHESS, also fig*) pion *m* ♦ *vt* mettre en gage; **~broker** *n* prêteur *m* sur gages; **~shop** *n* mont-de-piété *m*

pay [peɪ] (*pt, pp* **paid**) *n* salaire *m*; paie *f* ♦ *vt* payer ♦ *vi* payer; (*be profitable*) être rentable; **to ~ attention (to)** prêter attention (à); **to ~ sb a visit** rendre visite à qn; **to ~ one's respects to sb** présenter ses respects à qn; **~ back** *vt* rembourser; **~ for** *vt fus* payer; **~ in** *vt* verser; **~ off** *vt* régler, acquitter; (*person*) rembourser ♦ *vi* (*scheme, decision*) se révéler payant(e); **~ up** *vt* (*money*) payer; **~able** *adj*: **~able to sb** (*cheque*) à l'ordre de qn; **~ee** [peɪ'i:] *n* bénéficiaire *m/f*; **~ envelope** (*US*) *n* = **pay packet**; **~ment** *n* paiement *m*; règlement *m*; **monthly ~ment** mensualité

f; **~ packet** (*BRIT*) *n* paie *f*; **~ phone** *n* cabine *f* téléphonique, téléphone public; **~roll** *n* registre *m* du personnel; **~ slip** (*BRIT*) *n* bulletin *m* de paie; **~ television** *n* chaînes *fpl* payantes

PC *n abbr* = **personal computer**

p.c. *abbr* = **per cent**

pea [pi:] *n* (petit) pois

peace [pi:s] *n* paix *f*; (*calm*) calme *m*, tranquillité *f*; **~ful** *adj* paisible, calme

peach [pi:tʃ] *n* pêche *f*

peacock ['pi:kɔk] *n* paon *m*

peak [pi:k] *n* (*mountain*) pic *m*, cime *f*; (*of cap*) visière *f*; (*fig: highest level*) maximum *m*; (: *of career, fame*) apogée *m*; **~ hours** *npl* heures *fpl* de pointe

peal [pi:l] *n* (*of bells*) carillon *m*; **~ of laughter** éclat *m* de rire

peanut ['pi:nʌt] *n* arachide *f*, cacahuète *f*; **~ butter** *n* beurre *m* de cacahuète

pear [pɛər] *n* poire *f*

pearl [pə:l] *n* perle *f*

peasant ['peznt] *n* paysan(ne)

peat [pi:t] *n* tourbe *f*

pebble ['pebl] *n* caillou *m*, galet *m*

peck [pek] *vt* (*also:* **~ at**) donner un coup de bec à ♦ *n* coup *m* de bec; (*kiss*) bise *f*; **~ing order** *n* ordre *m* des préséances; **~ish** (*BRIT: inf*) *adj*: **I feel ~ish** je mangerais bien quelque chose

peculiar [pɪ'kju:lɪər] *adj* étrange, bizarre, curieux(-euse); **~ to** particulier(-ère) à

pedal ['pedl] *n* pédale *f* ♦ *vi* pédaler

pedantic [pɪ'dæntɪk] *adj* pédant(e)

peddler ['pedlər] *n* (*of drugs*) revendeur(-euse)

pedestal ['pedəstl] *n* piédestal *m*

pedestrian [pɪ'destrɪən] *n* piéton *m*; **~ crossing** (*BRIT*) *n* passage clouté; **~ized** *adj*: **a ~ized street** une rue piétonne

pediatrics [pi:dɪ'ætrɪks] (*US*) *n* = **paediatrics**

pedigree ['pedɪgri:] *n* ascendance *f*; (*of animal*) pedigree *m* ♦ *cpd* (*animal*) de race

pee [pi:] (*inf*) *vi* faire pipi, pisser

peek [pi:k] *vi* jeter un coup d'œil (furtif)

peel [pi:l] *n* pelure *f*, épluchure *f*; (*of or-*

ange, lemon) écorce f ♦ *vt* peler, éplucher ♦ *vi (paint etc)* s'écailler; *(wallpaper)* se décoller; *(skin)* peler

peep [piːp] *n (BRIT: look)* coup d'œil furtif; *(sound)* pépiement *m* ♦ *vi (BRIT)* jeter un coup d'œil (furtif); **~ out** *(BRIT)* vi se montrer (furtivement); **~hole** *n* judas *m*

peer [pɪəʳ] *vi:* **to ~ at** regarder attentivement, scruter ♦ *n (noble)* pair *m*; *(equal)* pair, égal(e); **~age** ['pɪərɪdʒ] *n* pairie *f*

peeved [piːvd] *adj* irrité(e), fâché(e)

peg [pɛg] *n (for coat etc)* patère *f*; *(BRIT: also:* **clothes ~**) pince *f* à linge

Pekin(g)ese [piːkɪˈniːz] *n (dog)* pékinois *m*

pelican ['pɛlɪkən] *n* pélican *m*; **~ crossing** *(BRIT) n (AUT)* feu *m* à commande manuelle

pellet ['pɛlɪt] *n* boulette *f*; *(of lead)* plomb *m*

pelt [pɛlt] *vt:* **to ~ sb (with)** bombarder qn (de) ♦ *vi (rain)* tomber à seaux; *(inf: run)* courir à toutes jambes ♦ *n* peau *f*

pelvis ['pɛlvɪs] *n* bassin *m*

pen [pɛn] *n (for writing)* stylo *m*; *(for sheep)* parc *m*

penal ['piːnl] *adj* pénal(e); *(system, colony)* pénitentiaire; **~ize** ['piːnəlaɪz] *vt* pénaliser

penalty ['pɛnltɪ] *n* pénalité *f*; sanction *f*; *(fine)* amende *f*; *(SPORT)* pénalisation *f*; *(FOOTBALL)* penalty *m*; *(RUGBY)* pénalité *f*

penance ['pɛnəns] *n* pénitence *f*

pence [pɛns] *(BRIT) npl of* **penny**

pencil ['pɛnsl] *n* crayon *m*; **~ case** *n* trousse *f* (d'écolier); **~ sharpener** *n* taille-crayon(s) *m inv*

pendant ['pɛndnt] *n* pendentif *m*

pending ['pɛndɪŋ] *prep* en attendant ♦ *adj* en suspens

pendulum ['pɛndjuləm] *n (of clock)* balancier *m*

penetrate ['pɛnɪtreɪt] *vt* pénétrer dans; pénétrer

penfriend ['pɛnfrɛnd] *(BRIT) n* correspondant(e)

penguin ['pɛŋgwɪn] *n* pingouin *m*

penicillin [pɛnɪˈsɪlɪn] *n* pénicilline *f*

peninsula [pəˈnɪnsjulə] *n* péninsule *f*

penis ['piːnɪs] *n* pénis *m*, verge *f*

penitentiary [pɛnɪˈtɛnʃərɪ] *n* prison *f*

penknife ['pɛnnaɪf] *n* canif *m*

pen name *n* nom *m* de plume, pseudonyme *m*

penniless ['pɛnɪlɪs] *adj* sans le sou

penny ['pɛnɪ] *(pl* **pennies** *or (BRIT)* **pence)** *n* penny *m*

penpal ['pɛnpæl] *n* correspondant(e)

pension ['pɛnʃən] *n* pension *f*; *(from company)* retraite *f*; **~er** *(BRIT) n* retraité(e); **~ fund** *n* caisse *f* de pension; **~ plan** *n* plan *m* de retraite

Pentagon

ⓘ Le **Pentagon** est le nom donné aux bureaux du ministère de la Défense américain, situés à Arlington en Virginie, à cause de la forme pentagonale du bâtiment dans lequel ils se trouvent. Par extension, ce terme est également utilisé en parlant du ministère lui-même.

pentathlon [pɛnˈtæθlən] *n* pentathlon *m*

Pentecost ['pɛntɪkɔst] *n* Pentecôte *f*

penthouse ['pɛnthaus] *n* appartement *m* (de luxe) (en attique)

pent-up ['pɛntʌp] *adj (feelings)* refoulé(e)

penultimate [pɛˈnʌltɪmət] *adj* avant-dernier(-ère)

people ['piːpl] *npl* gens *mpl*; personnes *fpl*; *(inhabitants)* population *f*; *(POL)* peuple *m* ♦ *n (nation, race)* peuple *m*; **several ~ came** plusieurs personnes sont venues; **~ say that ...** on dit que ...

pep up ['pɛp-] *(inf)* vt remonter

pepper ['pɛpəʳ] *n* poivre *m*; *(vegetable)* poivron *m* ♦ *vt (fig):* **to ~ with** bombarder de; **~ mill** *n* moulin *m* à poivre; **~mint** *n (sweet)* pastille *f* de menthe

peptalk ['pɛptɔːk] *(inf) n* (petit) discours d'encouragement

per [pɜːʳ] *prep* par; **~ hour** *(miles etc)* à l'heure; *(fee)* (de) l'heure; **~ kilo** *etc* le kilo *etc*; **~ annum** par an; **~ capita** par personne, par habitant

perceive [pə'siːv] *vt* percevoir; (*notice*) remarquer, s'apercevoir de

per cent *adv* pour cent; **percentage** *n* pourcentage *m*

perception [pə'sɛpʃən] *n* perception *f*; (*insight*) perspicacité *f*

perceptive [pə'sɛptɪv] *adj* pénétrant(e); (*person*) perspicace

perch [pəːtʃ] *n* (*fish*) perche *f*; (*for bird*) perchoir *m* ♦ *vi*: **to ~ on** se percher sur

percolator ['pəːkəleɪtəʳ] *n* cafetière *f* (électrique)

percussion [pə'kʌʃən] *n* percussion *f*

perennial [pə'rɛnɪəl] *adj* perpétuel(le); (*BOT*) vivace

perfect [*adj*, *n* 'pəːfɪkt, *vb* pə'fɛkt] *adj* parfait(e) ♦ *n* (*also*: ~ **tense**) parfait *m* ♦ *vt* parfaire; mettre au point; **~ly** *adv* parfaitement

perforate ['pəːfəreɪt] *vt* perforer, percer; **perforation** [pəːfə'reɪʃən] *n* perforation *f*

perform [pə'fɔːm] *vt* (*carry out*) exécuter; (*concert etc*) jouer, donner ♦ *vi* jouer; **~ance** *n* représentation *f*, spectacle *m*; (*of an artist*) interprétation *f*; (*SPORT*) performance *f*; (*of car, engine*) fonctionnement *m*; (*of company, economy*) résultats *mpl*; **~er** *n* artiste *m/f*, interprète *m/f*

perfume ['pəːfjuːm] *n* parfum *m*

perhaps [pə'hæps] *adv* peut-être

peril ['pɛrɪl] *n* péril *m*

perimeter [pə'rɪmɪtəʳ] *n* périmètre *m*

period ['pɪərɪəd] *n* période *f*; (*of history*) époque *f*; (*SCOL*) cours *m*; (*full stop*) point *m*; (*MED*) règles *fpl* ♦ *adj* (*costume, furniture*) d'époque; **~ic(al)** [pɪərɪ'ɔdɪk(l)] *adj* périodique; **~ical** [pɪərɪ'ɔdɪkl] *n* périodique *m*

peripheral [pə'rɪfərəl] *adj* périphérique ♦ *n* (*COMPUT*) périphérique *m*

perish ['pɛrɪʃ] *vi* périr; (*decay*) se détériorer; **~able** *adj* périssable

perjury ['pəːdʒərɪ] *n* parjure *m*, faux serment

perk [pəːk] *n* avantage *m* accessoire, à-côté *m*; ~ **up** *vi* (*cheer up*) se ragaillardir; **~y** *adj* (*cheerful*) guilleret(te)

perm [pəːm] *n* (*for hair*) permanente *f*

permanent ['pəːmənənt] *adj* permanent(e)

permeate ['pəːmɪeɪt] *vi* s'infiltrer ♦ *vt* s'infiltrer dans; pénétrer

permissible [pə'mɪsɪbl] *adj* permis(e), acceptable

permission [pə'mɪʃən] *n* permission *f*, autorisation *f*

permissive [pə'mɪsɪv] *adj* tolérant(e), permissif(-ive)

permit [*n* 'pəːmɪt, *vb* pə'mɪt] *n* permis *m* ♦ *vt* permettre

perpendicular [pəːpən'dɪkjulaʳ] *adj* perpendiculaire

perplex [pə'plɛks] *vt* rendre perplexe

persecute ['pəːsɪkjuːt] *vt* persécuter

persevere [pəːsɪ'vɪəʳ] *vi* persévérer

Persian ['pəːʃən] *adj* persan(e) ♦ *n* (*LING*) persan *m*; **the ~ Gulf** le golfe Persique

persist [pə'sɪst] *vi*: **to ~ (in doing)** persister or s'obstiner (à faire); **~ent** *adj* persistant(e), tenace; **~ent vegetative state** état *m* végétatif persistant

person ['pəːsn] *n* personne *f*; **in ~** en personne; **~al** *adj* personnel(le); **~al assistant** *n* secrétaire privé(e); **~al column** *n* annonces personnelles; **~al computer** *n* ordinateur personnel; **~ality** [pəːsə'nælɪtɪ] *n* personnalité *f*; **~ally** *adv* personnellement; **to take sth ~ally** se sentir visé(e) (par qch); **~al organizer** *n* filofax ® *m*; **~al stereo** *n* Walkman ® *m*, baladeur *m*

personnel [pəːsə'nɛl] *n* personnel *m*

perspective [pə'spɛktɪv] *n* perspective *f*; **to get things into ~** faire la part des choses

Perspex ® ['pəːspɛks] *n* plexiglas ® *m*

perspiration [pəːspɪ'reɪʃən] *n* transpiration *f*

persuade [pə'sweɪd] *vt*: **to ~ sb to do sth** persuader qn de faire qch; **persuasion** [pə'sweɪʒən] *n* persuasion *f*; (*creed*) religion *f*

perverse [pə'vəːs] *adj* pervers(e); (*contrary*) contrariant(e); **pervert** [*n* 'pəːvəːt, *vb* pə'vəːt] *n* perverti(e) ♦ *vt* pervertir; (*words*) déformer

pessimist [ˈpɛsɪmɪst] *n* pessimiste *m/f*; ~**ic** [pɛsɪˈmɪstɪk] *adj* pessimiste

pest [pɛst] *n* animal *m* (*or* insecte *m*) nuisible; (*fig*) fléau *m*

pester [ˈpɛstər] *vt* importuner, harceler

pet [pɛt] *n* animal familier ♦ *cpd* (*favourite*) favori(te) ♦ *vt* (*stroke*) caresser, câliner; **teacher's** ~ chouchou *m* du professeur; ~ **hate** bête noire

petal [ˈpɛtl] *n* pétale *m*

peter out [ˈpiːtə-] *vi* (*stream, conversation*) tarir; (*meeting*) tourner court; (*road*) se perdre

petite [pəˈtiːt] *adj* menu(e)

petition [pəˈtɪʃən] *n* pétition *f*

petrified [ˈpɛtrɪfaɪd] *adj* (*fig*) mort(e) de peur

petrol [ˈpɛtrəl] (*BRIT*) *n* essence *f*; **four-star** ~ super *m*; ~ **can** *n* bidon *m* à essence

petroleum [pəˈtrəʊlɪəm] *n* pétrole *m*

petrol: ~ **pump** *n* pompe *f* à essence; ~ **station** (*BRIT*) *n* station-service *f*; ~ **tank** (*BRIT*) *n* réservoir *m* d'essence

petticoat [ˈpɛtɪkəʊt] *n* combinaison *f*

petty [ˈpɛtɪ] *adj* (*mean*) mesquin(e); (*unimportant*) insignifiant(e), sans importance; ~ **cash** *n* caisse *f* des dépenses courantes; ~ **officer** *n* second-maître *m*

petulant [ˈpɛtjʊlənt] *adj* boudeur(-euse), irritable

pew [pjuː] *n* banc *m* (d'église)

pewter [ˈpjuːtər] *n* étain *m*

phantom [ˈfæntəm] *n* fantôme *m*

pharmacy [ˈfɑːməsɪ] *n* pharmacie *f*

phase [feɪz] *n* phase *f* ♦ *vt*: **to** ~ **sth in/ out** introduire/supprimer qch progressivement

PhD *abbr* = **Doctor of Philosophy** ♦ *n abbr* (*title*) ≃ docteur *m* (en droit *or* lettres *etc*), ≃ doctorat *m*; (*person*) titulaire *m/f* d'un doctorat

pheasant [ˈfɛznt] *n* faisan *m*

phenomenon [fəˈnɔmɪnən] (*pl* **phenomena**) *n* phénomène *m*

philosophical [fɪləˈsɔfɪkl] *adj* philosophique

philosophy [fɪˈlɔsəfɪ] *n* philosophie *f*

phobia [ˈfəʊbjə] *n* phobie *f*

phone [fəʊn] *n* téléphone *m* ♦ *vt* téléphoner; **to be on the** ~ avoir le téléphone; (*be calling*) être au téléphone; ~ **back** *vt, vi* rappeler; ~ **up** *vt* téléphoner à ♦ *vi* téléphoner; ~ **bill** *n* facture *f* de téléphone; ~ **book** *n* annuaire *m*; ~ **booth**, ~ **box** (*BRIT*) *n* cabine *f* téléphonique; ~ **call** *n* coup *m* de fil *or* de téléphone; ~**card** *n* carte *f* de téléphone; ~**-in** (*BRIT*) *n* (*RADIO, TV*) programme *m* à ligne ouverte; ~ **number** *n* numéro *m* de téléphone

phonetics [fəˈnɛtɪks] *n* phonétique *f*

phoney [ˈfəʊnɪ] *adj* faux (fausse), factice; (*person*) pas franc (franche), poseur(-euse)

photo [ˈfəʊtəʊ] *n* photo *f*; ~**copier** *n* photocopieuse *f*; ~**copy** *n* photocopie *f* ♦ *vt* photocopier; ~**graph** *n* photographie *f* ♦ *vt* photographier; ~**grapher** [fəˈtɔɡrəfər] *n* photographe *m/f*; ~**graphy** [fəˈtɔɡrəfɪ] *n* photographie *f*

phrase [freɪz] *n* expression *f*; (*LING*) locution *f* ♦ *vt* exprimer; ~ **book** *n* recueil *m* d'expressions (*pour touristes*)

physical [ˈfɪzɪkl] *adj* physique; ~ **education** *n* éducation *f* physique; ~**ly** *adv* physiquement

physician [fɪˈzɪʃən] *n* médecin *m*

physicist [ˈfɪzɪsɪst] *n* physicien(ne)

physics [ˈfɪzɪks] *n* physique *f*

physiotherapist [fɪzɪəʊˈθɛrəpɪst] *n* kinésithérapeute *m/f*

physiotherapy [fɪzɪəʊˈθɛrəpɪ] *n* kinésithérapie *f*

physique [fɪˈziːk] *n* physique *m*; constitution *f*

pianist [ˈpiːənɪst] *n* pianiste *m/f*

piano [pɪˈænəʊ] *n* piano *m*

pick [pɪk] *n* (*tool: also:* ~**axe**) pic *m*, pioche *f* ♦ *vt* choisir; (*fruit etc*) cueillir; (*remove*) prendre; (*lock*) forcer; **take your** ~ faites votre choix; **the** ~ **of** le (la) meilleur(e) de; **to** ~ **one's nose** se mettre les doigts dans le nez; **to** ~ **one's teeth** se curer les dents; **to** ~ **a quarrel with sb** chercher noise à qn; ~ **at** *vt fus*: **to** ~ **at one's**

food manger du bout des dents, chipoter; **~ on** vt fus (*person*) harceler; **~ out** vt choisir; (*distinguish*) distinguer; **~ up** vi (*improve*) s'améliorer ♦ vt ramasser; (*collect*) passer prendre; (*AUT: give lift to*) prendre, emmener; (*learn*) apprendre; (*RADIO*) capter; **to ~ up speed** prendre de la vitesse; **to ~ o.s. up** se relever

picket ['pɪkɪt] n (*in strike*) piquet m de grève ♦ vt mettre un piquet de grève devant

pickle ['pɪkl] n (*also:* **~s**: *as condiment*) pickles mpl; *petits légumes macérés dans du vinaigre* ♦ vt conserver dans du vinaigre or dans de la saumure; **to be in a ~** (*mess*) être dans le pétrin

pickpocket ['pɪkpɔkɪt] n pickpocket m

pick-up ['pɪkʌp] n (*small truck*) pick-up m inv

picnic ['pɪknɪk] n pique-nique m

picture ['pɪktʃə'] n image f; (*painting*) peinture f, tableau m; (*etching*) gravure f; (*photograph*) photo(graphie) f; (*drawing*) dessin m; (*film*) film m; (*fig*) description f; tableau m ♦ vt se représenter; **the ~s** (*BRIT: inf*) le cinéma; **~ book** n livre m d'images

picturesque [pɪktʃə'rɛsk] adj pittoresque

pie [paɪ] n tourte f; (*of fruit*) tarte f; (*of meat*) pâté m en croûte

piece [piːs] n morceau m; (*item*): **a ~ of furniture / advice** un meuble/conseil ♦ vt: **to ~ together** rassembler; **to take to ~s** démonter; **~meal** adv (*irregularly*) au coup par coup; (*bit by bit*) par bouts; **~work** n travail m aux pièces

pie chart n graphique m circulaire, camembert m

pier [pɪə'] n jetée f

pierce [pɪəs] vt percer, transpercer; **~d** adj (*ears etc*) percé(e)

pig [pɪg] n cochon m, porc m

pigeon ['pɪdʒən] n pigeon m; **~hole** n casier m

piggy bank ['pɪgɪ-] n tirelire f

pig: ~headed adj entêté(e), têtu(e); **~let** n porcelet m, petit cochon m; **~skin** n peau

m de porc; **~sty** n porcherie f; **~tail** n natte f, tresse f

pike [paɪk] n (*fish*) brochet m

pilchard ['pɪltʃəd] n pilchard m (*sorte de sardine*)

pile [paɪl] n (*pillar, of books*) pile f; (*heap*) tas m; (*of carpet*) poils mpl ♦ vt (*also:* **~ up**) empiler, entasser ♦ vi (*also:* **~ up**) s'entasser, s'accumuler; **to ~ into** (*car*) s'entasser dans; **~s** npl hémorroïdes fpl; **~-up** n (*AUT*) télescopage m, collision f en série

pilfering ['pɪlfərɪŋ] n chapardage m

pilgrim ['pɪlgrɪm] n pèlerin m

pill [pɪl] n pilule f

pillage ['pɪlɪdʒ] vt piller

pillar ['pɪlə'] n pilier m; **~ box** (*BRIT*) n boîte f aux lettres (*publique*)

pillion ['pɪljən] n: **to ride ~** (*on motorcycle*) monter derrière

pillow ['pɪləu] n oreiller m; **~case** n taie f d'oreiller

pilot ['paɪlət] n pilote m ♦ cpd (*scheme etc*) pilote, expérimental(e) ♦ vt piloter; **~ light** n veilleuse f

pimp [pɪmp] n souteneur m, maquereau m

pimple ['pɪmpl] n bouton m

pin [pɪn] n épingle f; (*TECH*) cheville f ♦ vt épingler; **~s and needles** fourmis fpl; **to ~ sb down** (*fig*) obliger qn à répondre; **to ~ sth on sb** (*fig*) mettre qch sur le dos de qn

PIN [pɪn] n abbr (= *personal identification number*) numéro m d'identification personnel

pinafore ['pɪnəfɔː'] n tablier m

pinball ['pɪnbɔːl] n flipper m

pincers ['pɪnsəz] npl tenailles fpl; (*of crab etc*) pinces fpl

pinch [pɪntʃ] n (*of salt etc*) pincée f ♦ vt pincer; (*inf: steal*) piquer, chiper; **at a ~** à la rigueur

pincushion ['pɪnkuʃən] n pelote f à épingles

pine [paɪn] n (*also:* **~ tree**) pin m ♦ vi: **to ~ for** s'ennuyer de, désirer ardemment; **~ away** vi dépérir

pineapple ['paɪnæpl] *n* ananas *m*

ping [pɪŋ] *n* (*noise*) tintement *m*; **~-pong** ® *n* ping-pong ® *m*

pink [pɪŋk] *adj* rose ♦ *n* (*colour*) rose *m*; (*BOT*) œillet *m*, mignardise *f*

PIN (number) ['pɪn(-)] *n* code *m* confidentiel

pinpoint ['pɪnpɔɪnt] *vt* indiquer *or* localiser (avec précision); (*problem*) mettre le doigt sur

pint [paɪnt] *n* pinte *f* (*BRIT = 0.57l; US = 0.47l*); (*BRIT: inf*) ≃ demi *m*

pioneer [paɪə'nɪə*r*] *n* pionnier *m*

pious ['paɪəs] *adj* pieux(-euse)

pip [pɪp] *n* (*seed*) pépin *m*; **the ~s** *npl* (*BRIT: time signal on radio*) le(s) top(s) sonore(s)

pipe [paɪp] *n* tuyau *m*, conduite *f*; (*for smoking*) pipe *f* ♦ *vt* amener par tuyau; **~s** *npl* (*also:* **bagpipes**) cornemuse *f*; **~ cleaner** *n* cure-pipe *m*; **~ dream** *n* chimère *f*, château *m* en Espagne; **~line** *n* pipe-line *m*; **~r** *n* joueur(-euse) de cornemuse

piping ['paɪpɪŋ] *adv*: **~ hot** très chaud(e)

pique ['pi:k] *n* dépit *m*

pirate ['paɪərət] *n* pirate *m*; **~d** *adj* pirate

Pisces ['paɪsi:z] *n* les Poissons *mpl*

piss [pɪs] (*inf!*) *vi* pisser; **~ed** (*inf!*) *adj* (*drunk*) bourré(e)

pistol ['pɪstl] *n* pistolet *m*

piston ['pɪstən] *n* piston *m*

pit [pɪt] *n* trou *m*, fosse *f*; (*also:* **coal ~**) puits *m* de mine; (*quarry*) carrière *f* ♦ *vt*: **to ~ one's wits against sb** se mesurer à qn; **~s** *npl* (*AUT*) aire *f* de service

pitch [pɪtʃ] *n* (*MUS*) ton *m*; (*BRIT: SPORT*) terrain *m*; (*tar*) poix *f*; (*fig*) degré *m*; point *m* ♦ *vt* (*throw*) lancer ♦ *vi* (*fall*) tomber; **to ~ a tent** dresser une tente; **~-black** *adj* noir(e) (comme du cirage); **~ed battle** *n* bataille rangée

pitfall ['pɪtfɔ:l] *n* piège *m*

pith [pɪθ] *n* (*of orange etc*) intérieur *m* de l'écorce; **~y** *adj* piquant(e)

pitiful ['pɪtɪful] *adj* (*touching*) pitoyable

pitiless ['pɪtɪlɪs] *adj* impitoyable

pittance ['pɪtns] *n* salaire *m* de misère

pity ['pɪtɪ] *n* pitié *f* ♦ *vt* plaindre; **what a ~!** quel dommage!

pizza ['pi:tsə] *n* pizza *f*

placard ['plækɑ:d] *n* affiche *f*; (*in march*) pancarte *f*

placate [plə'keɪt] *vt* apaiser, calmer

place [pleɪs] *n* endroit *m*, lieu *m*; (*proper position, job, rank, seat*) place *f*; (*home*): **at/to his ~** chez lui ♦ *vt* (*object*) placer, mettre; (*identify*) situer; reconnaître; **to take ~** avoir lieu; **out of ~** (*not suitable*) déplacé(e), inopportun(e); **to change ~s with sb** changer de place avec qn; **in the first ~** d'abord, en premier

plague [pleɪg] *n* fléau *m*; (*MED*) peste *f* ♦ *vt* (*fig*) tourmenter

plaice [pleɪs] *n inv* carrelet *m*

plaid [plæd] *n* tissu écossais

plain [pleɪn] *adj* (*in one colour*) uni(e); (*simple*) simple; (*clear*) clair(e), évident(e); (*not handsome*) quelconque, ordinaire ♦ *adv* franchement, carrément ♦ *n* plaine *f*; **~ chocolate** *n* chocolat *m* à croquer; **~ clothes** *adj* (*police officer*) en civil; **~ly** *adv* clairement; (*frankly*) carrément, sans détours

plaintiff ['pleɪntɪf] *n* plaignant(e)

plait [plæt] *n* tresse *f*, natte *f*

plan [plæn] *n* plan *m*; (*scheme*) projet *m* ♦ *vt* (*think in advance*) projeter; (*prepare*) organiser; (*house*) dresser les plans de, concevoir ♦ *vi* faire des projets; **to ~ to do** prévoir de faire

plane [pleɪn] *n* (*AVIAT*) avion *m*; (*ART, MATH etc*) plan *m*; (*fig*) niveau *m*, plan; (*tool*) rabot *m*; (*also:* **~ tree**) platane *m* ♦ *vt* raboter

planet ['plænɪt] *n* planète *f*

plank [plæŋk] *n* planche *f*

planner ['plænə*r*] *n* planificateur(-trice); (*town ~*) urbaniste *m/f*

planning ['plænɪŋ] *n* planification *f*; **family ~** planning familial; **~ permission** *n* permis *m* de construire

plant [plɑ:nt] *n* plante *f*; (*machinery*) matériel *m*; (*factory*) usine *f* ♦ *vt* planter; (*bomb*) poser; (*microphone, incriminating evidence*) cacher

plaster ['plɑːstər] *n* plâtre *m*; (*also:* ~ **of Paris**) plâtre à mouler; (*BRIT: also:* **sticking** ~) pansement adhésif ♦ *vt* plâtrer; (*cover*): **to** ~ **with** couvrir de; ~ed (*inf*) *adj* soûl(e)

plastic ['plæstɪk] *n* plastique *m* ♦ *adj* (*made of* ~) en plastique; ~ **bag** *n* sac *m* en plastique

Plasticine ® ['plæstɪsiːn] *n* pâte *f* à modeler

plastic surgery *n* chirurgie *f* esthétique

plate [pleɪt] *n* (*dish*) assiette *f*; (*in book*) gravure *f*, planche *f*; (*dental* ~) dentier *m*

plateau ['plætəu] (*pl* ~**s** *or* ~**x**) *n* plateau *m*

plate glass *n* verre *m* (de vitrine)

platform ['plætfɔːm] *n* plate-forme *f*; (*at meeting*) tribune *f*; (*stage*) estrade *f*; (*RAIL*) quai *m*

platinum ['plætɪnəm] *n* platine *f*

platter ['plætər] *n* plat *m*

plausible ['plɔːzɪbl] *adj* plausible; (*person*) convaincant(e)

play [pleɪ] *n* (*THEATRE*) pièce *f* (de théâtre) ♦ *vt* (*game*) jouer à; (*team, opponent*) jouer contre; (*instrument*) jouer de; (*part, piece of music, note*) jouer; (*record etc*) passer ♦ *vi* jouer; **to** ~ **safe** ne prendre aucun risque; ~ **down** *vt* minimiser; ~ **up** *vi* (*cause trouble*) faire des siennes; ~**boy** *n* playboy *m*; ~**er** *n* joueur(-euse); (*THEATRE*) acteur(-trice); (*MUS*) musicien(ne); ~**ful** *adj* enjoué(e); ~**ground** *n* cour *f* de récréation; (*in park*) aire *f* de jeux; ~**group** *n* garderie *f*; ~**ing card** *n* carte *f* à jouer; ~**ing field** *n* terrain *m* de sport; ~**mate** *n* camarade *m/f*, copain (copine); ~**-off** *n* (*SPORT*) belle *f*; ~**pen** *n* parc *m* (pour bébé); ~**thing** *n* jouet *m*; ~**time** *n* récréation *f*; ~**wright** *n* dramaturge *m*

plc *abbr* (= *public limited company*) SARL *f*

plea [pliː] *n* (*request*) appel *m*; (*LAW*) défense *f*

plead [pliːd] *vt* plaider; (*give as excuse*) invoquer ♦ *vi* (*LAW*) plaider; (*beg*): **to** ~ **with sb** implorer qn

pleasant ['plɛznt] *adj* agréable; ~**ries** *npl* (*polite remarks*) civilités *fpl*

please [pliːz] *excl* s'il te (*or* vous) plaît ♦ *vt* plaire à ♦ *vi* plaire; (*think fit*): **do as you** ~ faites comme il vous plaira; ~ **yourself!** à ta (*or* votre) guise!; ~d *adj*: ~**d (with)** content(e) (de); ~**d to meet you** enchanté (de faire votre connaissance); **pleasing** *adj* plaisant(e), qui fait plaisir

pleasure ['plɛʒər] *n* plaisir *m*; **"it's a** ~**"** "je vous en prie"

pleat [pliːt] *n* pli *m*

pledge [plɛdʒ] *n* (*promise*) promesse *f* ♦ *vt* engager; promettre

plentiful ['plɛntɪful] *adj* abondant(e), copieux(-euse)

plenty ['plɛntɪ] *n*: ~ **of** beaucoup de; (bien) assez de

pliable ['plaɪəbl] *adj* flexible; (*person*) malléable

pliers ['plaɪəz] *npl* pinces *fpl*

plight [plaɪt] *n* situation *f* critique

plimsolls ['plɪmsəlz] (*BRIT*) *npl* chaussures *fpl* de tennis, tennis *mpl*

plinth [plɪnθ] *n* (*of statue*) socle *m*

P.L.O. *n abbr* (= *Palestine Liberation Organization*) OLP *f*

plod [plɒd] *vi* avancer péniblement; (*fig*) peiner

plonk [plɒŋk] (*inf*) *n* (*BRIT: wine*) pinard *m*, piquette *f* ♦ *vt*: **to** ~ **sth down** poser brusquement qch

plot [plɒt] *n* complot *m*, conspiration *f*; (*of story, play*) intrigue *f*; (*of land*) lot *m* de terrain, lopin *m* ♦ *vt* (*sb's downfall*) comploter; (*mark out*) pointer; relever, déterminer ♦ *vi* comploter

plough [plau] (*US* **plow**) *n* charrue *f* ♦ *vt* (*earth*) labourer; **to** ~ **money into** investir dans; ~ **through** *vt fus* (*snow etc*) avancer péniblement dans; ~**man's lunch** (*BRIT*) *n* assiette froide avec du pain, du fromage et des pickles

ploy [plɔɪ] *n* stratagème *m*

pluck [plʌk] *vt* (*fruit*) cueillir; (*musical instrument*) pincer; (*bird*) plumer; (*eyebrow*) épiler ♦ *n* courage *m*, cran *m*; **to** ~ **up courage** prendre son courage à deux mains

plug [plʌg] *n* (*ELEC*) prise *f* de courant; (*stopper*) bouchon *m*, bonde *f*; (*AUT: also:* **spark(ing) ~**) bougie *f* ♦ *vt* (*hole*) boucher; (*inf: advertise*) faire du battage pour; **~ in** *vt* (*ELEC*) brancher

plum [plʌm] *n* (*fruit*) prune *f* ♦ *cpd*: **~ job** (*inf*) travail *m* en or

plumb [plʌm] *vt*: **to ~ the depths** (*fig*) toucher le fond (du désespoir)

plumber [ˈplʌmər] *n* plombier *m*

plumbing [ˈplʌmɪŋ] *n* (*trade*) plomberie *f*; (*piping*) tuyauterie *f*

plummet [ˈplʌmɪt] *vi*: **to ~ (down)** plonger, dégringoler

plump [plʌmp] *adj* rondelet(te), dodu(e), bien en chair ♦ *vi*: **to ~ for** (*inf: choose*) se décider pour

plunder [ˈplʌndər] *n* pillage *m*; (*loot*) butin *m* ♦ *vt* piller

plunge [plʌndʒ] *n* plongeon *m*; (*fig*) chute *f* ♦ *vt* plonger ♦ *vi* (*dive*) plonger; (*fall*) tomber, dégringoler; **to take the ~** se jeter à l'eau; **plunging** [ˈplʌndʒɪŋ] *adj*: **plunging neckline** décolleté plongeant

pluperfect [pluːˈpəːfɪkt] *n* plus-que-parfait *m*

plural [ˈpluərl] *adj* pluriel(le) ♦ *n* pluriel *m*

plus [plʌs] *n* (*also:* **~ sign**) signe *m* plus ♦ *prep* plus; **ten/twenty ~** plus de dix/vingt

plush [plʌʃ] *adj* somptueux(-euse)

ply [plaɪ] *vt* (*a trade*) exercer ♦ *vi* (*ship*) faire la navette ♦ (*of wool, rope*) fil *m*, brin *m*; **to ~ sb with drink** donner continuellement à boire à qn; **to ~ sb with questions** presser qn de questions; **~wood** *n* contre-plaqué *m*

PM *abbr* = **Prime Minister**

p.m. *adv abbr* (= *post meridiem*) de l'après-midi

pneumatic drill [njuːˈmætɪk-] *n* marteau-piqueur *m*

pneumonia [njuːˈməunɪə] *n* pneumonie *f*

poach [pəutʃ] *vt* (*cook*) pocher; (*steal*) pêcher (*or* chasser) sans permis ♦ *vi* braconner; **~ed egg** *n* œuf poché; **~er** *n* braconnier *m*

P.O. box *n abbr* = **post office box**

pocket [ˈpɔkɪt] *n* poche *f* ♦ *vt* empocher; **to be out of ~** (*BRIT*) en être de sa poche; **~book** (*US*) *n* (*wallet*) portefeuille *m*; **~ calculator** *n* calculette *f*; **~ knife** *n* canif *m*; **~ money** *n* argent *m* de poche

pod [pɔd] *n* cosse *f*

podgy [ˈpɔdʒɪ] *adj* rondelet(te)

podiatrist [pɔˈdiːətrɪst] (*US*) *n* pédicure *m/f*, podologue *m/f*

poem [ˈpəuɪm] *n* poème *m*

poet [ˈpəuɪt] *n* poète *m*; **~ic** [pəuˈetɪk] *adj* poétique; **~ry** [ˈpəuɪtrɪ] *n* poésie *f*

poignant [ˈpɔɪnjənt] *adj* poignant(e); (*sharp*) vif (vive)

point [pɔɪnt] *n* point *m*; (*tip*) pointe *f*; (*in time*) moment *m*; (*in space*) endroit *m*; (*subject, idea*) point, sujet *m*; (*purpose*) sens *m*; (*ELEC*) prise *f*; (*also:* **decimal ~**): **2 ~ 3 (2.3)** 2 virgule 3 (2,3) ♦ *vt* (*show*) indiquer; (*gun etc*): **to ~ sth at** braquer *or* diriger qch sur ♦ *vi*: **to ~ at** montrer du doigt; **~s** *npl* (*AUT*) vis platinées; (*RAIL*) aiguillage *m*; **to be on the ~ of doing sth** être sur le point de faire qch; **to make a ~ of doing** ne pas manquer de faire; **to get the ~** comprendre, saisir; **to miss the ~** ne pas comprendre; **to come to the ~** en venir au fait; **there's no ~ (in doing)** cela ne sert à rien (de faire); **~ out** *vt* faire remarquer, souligner; **~ to** *vt fus* (*fig*) indiquer; **~-blank** *adv* (*fig*) catégoriquement; (*also:* **at ~-blank range**) à bout portant; **~ed** *adj* (*shape*) pointu(e); (*remark*) plein(e) de sous-entendus; **~er** *n* (*needle*) aiguille *f*; (*piece of advice*) conseil *m*; (*clue*) indice *m*; **~less** *adj* inutile, vain(e); **~ of view** *n* point *m* de vue

poise [pɔɪz] *n* (*composure*) calme *m*

poison [ˈpɔɪzn] *n* poison *m* ♦ *vt* empoisonner; **~ous** *adj* (*snake*) venimeux(-euse); (*plant*) vénéneux(-euse); (*fumes etc*) toxique

poke [pəuk] *vt* (*fire*) tisonner; (*jab with finger, stick etc*) piquer; pousser du doigt; (*put*): **to ~ sth in(to)** fourrer *or* enfoncer qch dans; **~ about** *vi* fureter; **~r** *n* tisonnier *m*; (*CARDS*) poker *m*

poky ['pəʊkɪ] *adj* exigu(ë)

Poland ['pəʊlənd] *n* Pologne *f*

polar ['pəʊlə^r] *adj* polaire; ~ **bear** *n* ours blanc

Pole [pəʊl] *n* Polonais(e)

pole [pəʊl] *n* poteau *m*; (*of wood*) mât *m*, perche *f*; (*GEO*) pôle *m*; ~ **bean** (*US*) *n* haricot *m* (à rames); ~ **vault** *n* saut *m* à la perche

police [pə'li:s] *npl* police *f* ♦ *vt* maintenir l'ordre dans; ~ **car** *n* voiture *f* de police; ~**man** (*irreg*) *n* agent *m* de police, policier *m*; ~ **station** *n* commissariat *m* de police; ~**woman** (*irreg*) *n* femme-agent *f*

policy ['pɒlɪsɪ] *n* politique *f*; (*also:* **insurance** ~) police *f* (d'assurance)

polio ['pəʊlɪəʊ] *n* polio *f*

Polish ['pəʊlɪʃ] *adj* polonais(e) ♦ *n* (*LING*) polonais *m*

polish ['pɒlɪʃ] *n* (*for shoes*) cirage *m*; (*for floor*) cire *f*, encaustique *f*; (*shine*) éclat *m*, poli *m*; (*fig: refinement*) raffinement *m* ♦ *vt* (*put ~ on shoes, wood*) cirer; (*make shiny*) astiquer, faire briller; ~ **off** (*inf*) *vt* (*food*) liquider; ~**ed** *adj* (*fig*) raffiné(e)

polite [pə'laɪt] *adj* poli(e); **in ~ society** dans la bonne société; ~**ly** *adv* poliment; ~**ness** *n* politesse *f*

political [pə'lɪtɪkl] *adj* politique; ~**ly correct** *adj* politiquement correct(e)

politician [pɒlɪ'tɪʃən] *n* homme *m*/femme *f* politique

politics ['pɒlɪtɪks] *npl* politique *f*

poll [pəʊl] *n* scrutin *m*, vote *m*; (*also:* **opinion** ~) sondage *m* (d'opinion) ♦ *vt* obtenir

pollen ['pɒlən] *n* pollen *m*

polling day ['pəʊlɪŋ-] (*BRIT*) *n* jour *m* des élections

polling station (*BRIT*) *n* bureau *m* de vote

pollute [pə'lu:t] *vt* polluer; **pollution** *n* pollution *f*

polo ['pəʊləʊ] *n* polo *m*; ~-**necked** *adj* à col roulé; ~ **shirt** *n* polo *m*

polyester [pɒlɪ'estə^r] *n* polyester *m*

polystyrene [pɒlɪ'staɪri:n] *n* polystyrène *m*

polythene ['pɒlɪθi:n] *n* polyéthylène *m*; ~ **bag** *n* sac *m* en plastique

pomegranate ['pɒmɪɡrænɪt] *n* grenade *f*

pomp [pɒmp] *n* pompe *f*, faste *f*, apparat *m*; ~**ous** *adj* pompeux(-euse)

pond [pɒnd] *n* étang *m*; mare *f*

ponder ['pɒndə^r] *vt* considérer, peser; ~**ous** *adj* pesant(e), lourd(e)

pong [pɒŋ] (*BRIT: inf*) *n* puanteur *f*

pony ['pəʊnɪ] *n* poney *m*; ~**tail** *n* queue *f* de cheval; ~ **trekking** (*BRIT*) *n* randonnée *f* à cheval

poodle ['pu:dl] *n* caniche *m*

pool [pu:l] *n* (*of rain*) flaque *f*; (*pond*) mare *f*; (*also:* **swimming** ~) piscine *f*; (*billiards*) poule *f* ♦ *vt* mettre en commun; ~**s** *npl* (*football ~s*) ≈ loto sportif

poor [pʊə^r] *adj* pauvre; (*mediocre*) médiocre, faible, mauvais(e) ♦ *npl*: **the** ~ les pauvres *mpl*; ~**ly** *adj* souffrant(e), malade ♦ *adv* mal; médiocrement

pop [pɒp] *n* (*MUS*) musique *f* pop; (*drink*) boisson gazeuse; (*US: inf: father*) papa *m*; (*noise*) bruit sec ♦ *vt* (*put*) mettre (rapidement) ♦ *vi* éclater; (*cork*) sauter; ~ **in** *vi* entrer en passant; ~ **out** *vi* sortir (brièvement); ~ **up** *vi* apparaître, surgir; ~**corn** *n* pop-corn *m*

pope [pəʊp] *n* pape *m*

poplar ['pɒplə^r] *n* peuplier *m*

popper ['pɒpə^r] (*BRIT: inf*) *n* bouton-pression *m*

poppy ['pɒpɪ] *n* coquelicot *m*; pavot *m*

Popsicle ® ['pɒpsɪkl] (*US*) *n* esquimau *m* (*glace*)

popular ['pɒpjʊlə^r] *adj* populaire; (*fashionable*) à la mode

population [pɒpjʊ'leɪʃən] *n* population *f*

porcelain ['pɔ:slɪn] *n* porcelaine *f*

porch [pɔ:tʃ] *n* porche *m*; (*US*) véranda *f*

porcupine ['pɔ:kjʊpaɪn] *n* porc-épic *m*

pore [pɔ:^r] *n* pore *m* ♦ *vi*: **to ~ over** s'absorber dans, être plongé(e) dans

pork [pɔ:k] *n* porc *m*

porn [pɔ:n] (*inf*) *adj*, *n* porno *m*

pornographic [pɔ:nə'ɡræfɪk] *adj* pornographique

pornography [pɔːˈnɔgrəfɪ] *n* pornographie *f*

porpoise [ˈpɔːpəs] *n* marsouin *m*

porridge [ˈpɔrɪdʒ] *n* porridge *m*

port [pɔːt] *n* (*harbour*) port *m*; (*NAUT: left side*) bâbord *m*; (*wine*) porto *m*; **~ of call** escale *f*

portable [ˈpɔːtəbl] *adj* portatif(-ive)

porter [ˈpɔːtəʳ] *n* (*for luggage*) porteur *m*; (*doorkeeper*) gardien(ne); portier *m*

portfolio [pɔːtˈfəʊlɪəu] *n* portefeuille *m*; (*of artist*) portfolio *m*

porthole [ˈpɔːthəul] *n* hublot *m*

portion [ˈpɔːʃən] *n* portion *f*, part *f*

portrait [ˈpɔːtreɪt] *n* portrait *m*

portray [pɔːˈtreɪ] *vt* faire le portrait de; (*in writing*) dépeindre, représenter; (*subj: actor*) jouer

Portugal [ˈpɔːtjugl] *n* Portugal *m*; **Portuguese** [pɔːtjuˈgiːz] *adj* portugais(e) ♦ *n inv* Portugais(e); (*LING*) portugais *m*

pose [pəuz] *n* pose *f* ♦ *vi* (*pretend*): **to ~ as** se poser en ♦ *vt* poser; (*problem*) créer

posh [pɔʃ] (*inf*) *adj* chic *inv*

position [pəˈzɪʃən] *n* position *f*; (*job*) situation *f* ♦ *vt* placer

positive [ˈpɔzɪtɪv] *adj* positif(-ive); (*certain*) sûr(e), certain(e); (*definite*) formel(le), catégorique

possess [pəˈzɛs] *vt* posséder; **~ion** *n* possession *f*

possibility [pɔsɪˈbɪlɪtɪ] *n* possibilité *f*; éventualité *f*

possible [ˈpɔsɪbl] *adj* possible; **as big as ~** aussi gros que possible; **possibly** *adv* (*perhaps*) peut-être; **if you possibly can** si cela vous est possible; **I cannot possibly come** il m'est impossible de venir

post [pəust] *n* poste *f*; (*BRIT: letters, delivery*) courrier *m*; (*job, situation, MIL*) poste *m*; (*pole*) poteau *m* ♦ *vt* (*BRIT: send by ~*) poster; (: *appoint*): **to ~ to** affecter à; **~age** *n* tarifs *mpl* d'affranchissement; **~al order** *n* mandat(-poste) *m*; **~box** (*BRIT*) *n* boîte *f* aux lettres; **~card** *n* carte postale; **~code** (*BRIT*) *n* code postal

poster [ˈpəustəʳ] *n* affiche *f*

poste restante [pəustˈrɛstãnt] (*BRIT*) *n* poste restante

postgraduate [ˈpəustˈgrædjuət] *n* ≈ étudiant(e) de troisième cycle

posthumous [ˈpɔstjuməs] *adj* posthume

postman [ˈpəustmən] (*irreg*) *n* facteur *m*

postmark [ˈpəustmɑːk] *n* cachet *m* (de la poste)

postmortem [pəustˈmɔːtəm] *n* autopsie *f*

post office *n* (*building*) poste *f*; (*organization*): **the P~ O~** les Postes; **~ box** *n* boîte postale

postpone [pəusˈpəun] *vt* remettre (à plus tard)

posture [ˈpɔstʃəʳ] *n* posture *f*; (*fig*) attitude *f*

postwar [pəustˈwɔːʳ] *adj* d'après-guerre

postwoman *n* factrice *f*

posy [ˈpəuzɪ] *n* petit bouquet

pot [pɔt] *n* pot *m*; (*for cooking*) marmite *f*; casserole *f*; (*teapot*) théière *f*; (*coffeepot*) cafetière *f*; (*inf: marijuana*) herbe *f* ♦ *vt* (*plant*) mettre en pot; **to go to ~** (*inf: work, performance*) aller à vau-l'eau

potato [pəˈteɪtəu] (*pl* **~es**) *n* pomme *f* de terre; **~ peeler** *n* épluche-légumes *m inv*

potent [ˈpəutnt] *adj* puissant(e); (*drink*) fort(e), très alcoolisé(e); (*man*) viril

potential [pəˈtɛnʃl] *adj* potentiel(le) ♦ *n* potentiel *m*

pothole [ˈpɔthəul] *n* (*in road*) nid *m* de poule; (*BRIT: underground*) gouffre *m*, caverne *f*; **potholing** (*BRIT*) *n*: **to go potholing** faire de la spéléologie

potluck [pɔtˈlʌk] *n*: **to take ~** tenter sa chance

pot plant *n* plante *f* d'appartement

potted [ˈpɔtɪd] *adj* (*food*) en conserve; (*plant*) en pot; (*abbreviated*) abrégé(e)

potter [ˈpɔtəʳ] *n* potier *m* ♦ *vi*: **to ~ around, ~ about** (*BRIT*) bricoler; **~y** *n* poterie *f*

potty [ˈpɔtɪ] *adj* (*inf: mad*) dingue ♦ *n* (*child's*) pot *m*

pouch [pautʃ] *n* (*ZOOL*) poche *f*; (*for tobacco*) blague *f*; (*for money*) bourse *f*

poultry ['pəʊltrɪ] n volaille f

pounce [paʊns] vi: **to ~ (on)** bondir (sur), sauter (sur)

pound [paʊnd] n (*unit of money*) livre f; (*unit of weight*) livre ♦ vt (*beat*) bourrer de coups, marteler; (*crush*) piler, pulvériser ♦ vi (*heart*) battre violemment, taper

pour [pɔːʳ] vt verser ♦ vi couler à flots; **to ~ (with rain)** pleuvoir à verse; **to ~ sb a drink** verser *or* servir à boire à qn; ~ **away** vt vider; ~ **in** vi (*people*) affluer, se précipiter; (*news, letters etc*) arriver en masse; ~ **off** vt = **pour away**; ~ **out** vi (*people*) sortir en masse ♦ vt vider; (*fig*) déverser; (*serve: a drink*) verser; ~**ing** ['pɔːrɪŋ] adj: ~**ing rain** pluie torrentielle

pout [paʊt] vi faire la moue

poverty ['pɒvətɪ] n pauvreté f, misère f; ~**-stricken** adj pauvre, déshérité(e)

powder ['paʊdəʳ] n poudre f ♦ vt: **to ~ one's face** se poudrer; ~ **compact** n poudrier m; ~**ed milk** n lait m en poudre; ~ **room** n toilettes fpl (pour dames)

power ['paʊəʳ] n (*strength*) puissance f, force f; (*ability, authority*) pouvoir m; (*of speech, thought*) faculté f; (ELEC) courant m; **to be in ~** (POL *etc*) être au pouvoir; ~ **cut** (BRIT) n coupure f de courant; ~**ed** adj: ~**ed by** actionné(e) par, fonctionnant à; ~ **failure** n panne f de courant; ~**ful** adj puissant(e); ~**less** adj impuissant(e); ~ **point** (BRIT) n prise f de courant; ~ **station** n centrale f électrique; ~ **struggle** n lutte f pour le pouvoir

p.p. abbr (= *per procurationem*): **p.p. J. Smith** pour M. J. Smith

PR n abbr = **public relations**

practical ['præktɪkl] adj pratique; ~**ity** [præktɪ'kælɪtɪ] (*no pl*) n (*of person*) sens m pratique; ~**ities** npl (*of situation*) aspect m pratique; ~ **joke** n farce f; ~**ly** adv (*almost*) pratiquement

practice ['præktɪs] n pratique f; (*of profession*) exercice m; (*at football etc*) entraînement m; (*business*) cabinet m ♦ vt, vi (US) = **practise**; **in ~** (*in reality*) en pratique; **out of ~** rouillé(e)

practise ['præktɪs] (US **practice**) vt (*musical instrument*) travailler; (*train for: sport*) s'entraîner à; (*a sport, religion*) pratiquer; (*profession*) exercer ♦ vi s'exercer, travailler; (*train*) s'entraîner; (*lawyer, doctor*) exercer; **practising** adj (*Christian etc*) pratiquant(e); (*lawyer*) en exercice

practitioner [præk'tɪʃənəʳ] n praticien(ne)

prairie ['prɛərɪ] n steppe f, prairie f

praise [preɪz] n éloge(s) m(pl), louange(s) f(pl) ♦ vt louer, faire l'éloge de; ~**worthy** adj digne d'éloges

pram [præm] (BRIT) n landau m, voiture f d'enfant

prance [prɑːns] vi (*also*: ~ **about**: *person*) se pavaner

prank [præŋk] n farce f

prawn [prɔːn] n crevette f (*rose*); ~ **cocktail** n cocktail m de crevettes

pray [preɪ] vi prier; ~**er** [prɛəʳ] n prière f

preach [priːtʃ] vt, vi prêcher

precaution [prɪ'kɔːʃən] n précaution f

precede [prɪ'siːd] vt précéder

precedent ['presɪdənt] n précédent m

preceding adj qui précède/précédait *etc*

precinct ['priːsɪŋkt] n (US) circonscription f, arrondissement m; ~**s** npl (*neighbourhood*) alentours mpl, environs mpl; **pedestrian ~** (BRIT) zone piétonnière *or* piétonne; **shopping ~** (BRIT) centre commercial

precious ['preʃəs] adj précieux(-euse)

precipitate [prɪ'sɪpɪteɪt] vt précipiter

precise [prɪ'saɪs] adj précis(e); ~**ly** adv précisément

precocious [prɪ'kəʊʃəs] adj précoce

precondition ['priːkən'dɪʃən] n condition f nécessaire

predecessor ['priːdɪsesəʳ] n prédécesseur m

predicament [prɪ'dɪkəmənt] n situation f difficile

predict [prɪ'dɪkt] vt prédire; ~**able** adj prévisible

predominantly [prɪ'dɒmɪnəntlɪ] adv en majeure partie; surtout

pre-empt [priː'emt] vt anticiper, devancer

preen [priːn] *vt*: **to ~ itself** (*bird*) se lisser les plumes; **to ~ o.s.** s'admirer

prefab ['priːfæb] *n* bâtiment préfabriqué

preface ['prefəs] *n* préface *f*

prefect ['priːfekt] (*BRIT*) *n* (*in school*) élève chargé(e) de certaines fonctions de discipline

prefer [prɪ'fəːʳ] *vt* préférer; **~ably** ['prefrəblɪ] *adv* de préférence; **~ence** ['prefrəns] *n* préférence *f*; **~ential** [prefə'renʃəl] *adj*: **~ential treatment** traitement *m* de faveur *or* préférentiel

prefix ['priːfɪks] *n* préfixe *m*

pregnancy ['pregnənsɪ] *n* grossesse *f*

pregnant ['pregnənt] *adj* enceinte; (*animal*) pleine

prehistoric ['priːhɪs'tɔrɪk] *adj* préhistorique

prejudice ['predʒudɪs] *n* préjugé *m*; **~d** *adj* (*person*) plein(e) de préjugés; (*in a matter*) partial(e)

premarital ['priː'mærɪtl] *adj* avant le mariage

premature ['premətʃuəʳ] *adj* prématuré(e)

premenstrual syndrome [priː'menstruəl-] *n* syndrome prémenstruel

premier ['premɪəʳ] *adj* premier(-ère), principal(e) ♦ *n* (*POL*) Premier ministre

première ['premɪeəʳ] *n* première *f*

Premier League *n* première division

premise ['premɪs] *n* prémisse *f*; **~s** *npl* (*building*) locaux *mpl*; **on the ~s** sur les lieux; sur place

premium ['priːmɪəm] *n* prime *f*; **to be at a ~** faire prime; **~ bond** (*BRIT*) *n* bon *m* à lot, obligation *f* à prime

premonition [premə'nɪʃən] *n* prémonition *f*

preoccupied [priː'ɔkjupaɪd] *adj* préoccupé(e)

prep [prep] *n* (*SCOL*) étude *f*

prepaid [priː'peɪd] *adj* payé(e) d'avance

preparation [prepə'reɪʃən] *n* préparation *f*; **~s** *npl* (*for trip, war*) préparatifs *mpl*

preparatory [prɪ'pærətərɪ] *adj* préliminaire; **~ school** (*BRIT*) *n* école primaire privée

prepare [prɪ'peəʳ] *vt* préparer ♦ *vi*: **to ~ for** se préparer à; **~d to** prêt(e) à

preposition [prepə'zɪʃən] *n* préposition *f*

preposterous [prɪ'pɔstərəs] *adj* absurde

prep school *n* = **preparatory school**

prerequisite [priː'rekwɪzɪt] *n* condition *f* préalable

Presbyterian [prezbɪ'tɪərɪən] *adj*, *n* presbytérien(ne) *m/f*

prescribe [prɪ'skraɪb] *vt* prescrire; **prescription** [prɪ'skrɪpʃən] *n* (*MED*) ordonnance *f*; (*: medicine*) médicament (obtenu sur ordonnance)

presence ['prezns] *n* présence *f*; **~ of mind** présence d'esprit

present [*adj, n* 'preznt, *vb* prɪ'zent] *adj* présent(e) ♦ *n* (*gift*) cadeau *m*; (*actuality*) présent *m* ♦ *vt* présenter; (*prize, medal*) remettre; (*give*): **to ~ sb with sth** *or* **sth to sb** offrir qch à qn; **to give sb a ~** offrir un cadeau à qn; **at ~** en ce moment; **~ation** [prezn'teɪʃən] *n* présentation *f*; (*ceremony*) remise *f* du cadeau (*or* de la médaille *etc*); **~-day** *adj* contemporain(e), actuel(le); **~er** *n* (*RADIO, TV*) présentateur(-trice); **~ly** *adv* (*with verb in past*) peu après; (*soon*) tout à l'heure, bientôt; (*at present*) en ce moment

preservative [prɪ'zəːvətɪv] *n* agent *m* de conservation

preserve [prɪ'zəːv] *vt* (*keep safe*) préserver, protéger; (*maintain*) conserver, garder; (*food*) mettre en conserve ♦ *n* (*often pl: jam*) confiture *f*

president ['prezɪdənt] *n* président(e); **~ial** [prezɪ'denʃl] *adj* présidentiel(le)

press [pres] *n* presse *f*; (*for wine*) pressoir *m* ♦ *vt* (*squeeze*) presser, serrer; (*push*) appuyer sur; (*clothes: iron*) repasser; (*put pressure on*) faire pression sur; (*insist*): **to ~ sth on sb** presser qn d'accepter qch ♦ *vi* appuyer, peser; **to ~ for sth** faire pression pour obtenir qch; **we are ~ed for time/ money** le temps/l'argent nous manque; **~ on** *vi* continuer; **~ conference** *n* conférence *f* de presse; **~ing** *adj* urgent(e), pressant(e); **~ stud** (*BRIT*) *n* bouton-pression *m*; **~-up** (*BRIT*) *n* traction *f*

pressure ['prɛʃəʳ] *n* pression *f*; (*stress*) tension *f*; **to put ~ on sb (to do)** faire pression sur qn (pour qu'il/elle fasse); **~ cooker** *n* cocotte-minute *f*; **~ gauge** *n* manomètre *m*; **~ group** *n* groupe *m* de pression

prestige [prɛs'tiːʒ] *n* prestige *m*; **prestigious** [prɛs'tɪdʒəs] *adj* prestigieux(-euse)

presumably [prɪ'zjuːməblɪ] *adv* vraisemblablement

presume [prɪ'zjuːm] *vt* présumer, supposer

pretence [prɪ'tɛns] (*US* **pretense**) *n* (*claim*) prétention *f*; **under false ~s** sous des prétextes fallacieux

pretend [prɪ'tɛnd] *vt* (*feign*) feindre, simuler ♦ *vi* faire semblant

pretext ['priːtɛkst] *n* prétexte *m*

pretty ['prɪtɪ] *adj* joli(e) ♦ *adv* assez

prevail [prɪ'veɪl] *vi* (*be usual*) avoir cours; (*win*) l'emporter, prévaloir; **~ing** *adj* dominant(e); **prevalent** ['prɛvələnt] *adj* répandu(e), courant(e)

prevent [prɪ'vɛnt] *vt*: **to ~ (from doing)** empêcher (de faire); **~ative** [prɪ'vɛntətɪv], **~ive** [prɪ'vɛntɪv] *adj* préventif(-ive)

preview ['priːvjuː] *n* (*of film etc*) avant-première *f*

previous ['priːvɪəs] *adj* précédent(e); antérieur(e); **~ly** *adv* précédemment, auparavant

prewar [priː'wɔːʳ] *adj* d'avant-guerre

prey [preɪ] *n* proie *f* ♦ *vi*: **to ~ on** s'attaquer à; **it was ~ing on his mind** cela le travaillait

price [praɪs] *n* prix *m* ♦ *vt* (*goods*) fixer le prix de; **~less** *adj* sans prix, inestimable; **~ list** *n* liste *f* des prix, tarif *m*

prick [prɪk] *n* piqûre *f* ♦ *vt* piquer; **to ~ up one's ears** dresser or tendre l'oreille

prickle ['prɪkl] *n* (*of plant*) épine *f*; (*sensation*) picotement *m*; **prickly** *adj* piquant(e), épineux(-euse); **prickly heat** *n* fièvre *f* miliaire

pride [praɪd] *n* orgueil *m*; fierté *f* ♦ *vt*: **to ~ o.s. on** se flatter de; s'enorgueillir de

priest [priːst] *n* prêtre *m*; **~hood** *n* prêtrise *f*, sacerdoce *m*

prim [prɪm] *adj* collet monté *inv*, guindé(e)

primarily ['praɪmərɪlɪ] *adv* principalement, essentiellement

primary ['praɪmərɪ] *adj* (*first in importance*) premier(-ère), primordial(e), principal(e) ♦ *n* (*US: election*) (élection *f*) primaire *f*; **~ school** (*BRIT*) *n* école primaire *f*

prime [praɪm] *adj* primordial(e), fondamental(e); (*excellent*) excellent(e) ♦ *n*: **in the ~ of life** dans la fleur de l'âge ♦ *vt* (*wood*) apprêter; (*fig*) mettre au courant; **P~ Minister** *n* Premier ministre *m*

primeval [praɪ'miːvəl] *adj* primitif(-ive); **~ forest** forêt *f* vierge

primitive ['prɪmɪtɪv] *adj* primitif(-ive)

primrose ['prɪmrəuz] *n* primevère *f*

primus (stove) ® ['praɪməs-] (*BRIT*) *n* réchaud *m* de camping

prince [prɪns] *n* prince *m*

princess [prɪn'sɛs] *n* princesse *f*

principal ['prɪnsɪpl] *adj* principal(e) ♦ *n* (*headmaster*) directeur(-trice), principal *m*

principle ['prɪnsɪpl] *n* principe *m*; **in/on ~** en/par principe

print [prɪnt] *n* (*mark*) empreinte *f*; (*letters*) caractères *mpl*; (*ART*) gravure *f*, estampe *f*; (: *photograph*) photo *f* ♦ *vt* imprimer; (*publish*) publier; (*write in block letters*) écrire en caractères d'imprimerie; **out of ~** épuisé(e); **~ed matter** *n* imprimé(s) *m(pl)*; **~er** *n* imprimeur *m*; (*machine*) imprimante *f*; **~ing** *n* impression *f*; **~-out** *n* copie *f* papier

prior ['praɪəʳ] *adj* antérieur(e), précédent(e); (*more important*) prioritaire ♦ *adv*: **~ to doing** avant de faire; **~ity** [praɪ'ɔrɪtɪ] *n* priorité *f*

prise [praɪz] *vt*: **to ~ open** forcer

prison ['prɪzn] *n* prison *f* ♦ *cpd* pénitentiaire; **~er** *n* prisonnier(-ère)

pristine ['prɪstiːn] *adj* parfait(e)

privacy ['prɪvəsɪ] *n* intimité *f*, solitude *f*

private ['praɪvɪt] *adj* privé(e); (*personal*) personnel(le); (*house, lesson*) particulier(-ère); (*quiet: place*) tranquille; (*reserved: per-*

son) secret(-ète) ♦ *n* soldat *m* de deuxième classe; **"~"** (*on envelope*) "personnelle"; **in ~** en privé; **~ detective** *n* détective privé; **~ enterprise** *n* l'entreprise privée; **~ property** *n* propriété privée; **privatize** *vt* privatiser

privet ['prɪvɪt] *n* troène *m*

privilege ['prɪvɪlɪdʒ] *n* privilège *m*

privy ['prɪvɪ] *adj*: **to be ~ to** être au courant de

prize [praɪz] *n* prix *m* ♦ *adj* (*example, idiot*) parfait(e); (*bull, novel*) primé(e) ♦ *vt* priser, faire grand cas de; **~-giving** *n* distribution *f* des prix; **~winner** *n* gagnant(e)

pro [prəʊ] *n* (*SPORT*) professionnel(le); **the ~s and cons** le pour et le contre

probability [prɒbə'bɪlɪtɪ] *n* probabilité *f*

probable ['prɒbəbl] *adj* probable; **probably** *adv* probablement

probation [prə'beɪʃən] *n*: **on ~** (*LAW*) en liberté surveillée, en sursis; (*employee*) à l'essai

probe [prəʊb] *n* (*MED, SPACE*) sonde *f*; (*enquiry*) enquête *f*, investigation *f* ♦ *vt* sonder, explorer

problem ['prɒbləm] *n* problème *m*

procedure [prə'siːdʒər] *n* (*ADMIN, LAW*) procédure *f*; (*method*) marche *f* à suivre, façon *f* de procéder

proceed [prə'siːd] *vi* continuer; (*go forward*) avancer; **to ~ (with)** continuer, poursuivre; **to ~ to do** se mettre à faire; **~ings** *npl* (*LAW*) poursuites *fpl*; (*meeting*) réunion *f*, séance *f*; **~s** ['prəʊsiːdz] *npl* produit *m*, recette *f*

process ['prəʊses] *n* processus *m*; (*method*) procédé *m* ♦ *vt* traiter; **~ing** *n* (*PHOT*) développement *m*; **~ion** [prə'seʃən] *n* défilé *m*, cortège *m*; (*REL*) procession *f*; **funeral ~ion** (*on foot*) cortège *m* funèbre; (*in cars*) convoi *m* mortuaire

proclaim [prə'kleɪm] *vt* déclarer, proclamer

procrastinate [prəʊ'kræstɪneɪt] *vi* faire traîner les choses, vouloir tout remettre au lendemain

procure [prə'kjʊər] *vt* obtenir

prod [prɒd] *vt* pousser

prodigal ['prɒdɪgl] *adj* prodigue

prodigy ['prɒdɪdʒɪ] *n* prodige *m*

produce [*n* 'prɒdjuːs, *vb* prə'djuːs] *n* (*AGR*) produits *mpl* ♦ *vt* produire; (*to show*) présenter; (*cause*) provoquer, causer; (*THEATRE*) monter, mettre en scène; **~r** *n* producteur *m*; (*THEATRE*) metteur *m* en scène

product ['prɒdʌkt] *n* produit *m*

production [prə'dʌkʃən] *n* production *f*; (*THEATRE*) mise *f* en scène; **~ line** *n* chaîne *f* (de fabrication)

productivity [prɒdʌk'tɪvɪtɪ] *n* productivité *f*

profession [prə'feʃən] *n* profession *f*; **~al** *n* professionnel(le) ♦ *adj* professionnel(le); (*work*) de professionnel; (*SPORT: play*) en professionnel; **she sings ~ally** c'est une chanteuse professionnelle; **I only know him ~ally** je n'ai avec lui que des relations de travail

professor [prə'fesər] *n* professeur *m* (*titulaire d'une chaire*)

proficiency [prə'fɪʃənsɪ] *n* compétence *f*, aptitude *f*

profile ['prəʊfaɪl] *n* profil *m*

profit ['prɒfɪt] *n* bénéfice *m*; profit *m* ♦ *vi*: **to ~ (by** *or* **from)** profiter (de); **~able** *adj* lucratif(-ive), rentable

profound [prə'faʊnd] *adj* profond(e)

profusely [prə'fjuːslɪ] *adv* abondamment; avec effusion

prognosis [prɒg'nəʊsɪs] (*pl* **prognoses**) *n* pronostic *m*

programme ['prəʊgræm] (*US* **program**) *n* programme *m*; (*RADIO, TV*) émission *f* ♦ *vt* programmer; **~r** (*US* **programer**) *n* programmeur(-euse); **programming** (*US* **programing**) *n* programmation *f*

progress [*n* 'prəʊgres, *vb* prə'gres] *n* progrès *m(pl)* ♦ *vi* progresser, avancer; **in ~** en cours; **~ive** [prə'gresɪv] *adj* progressif(-ive); (*person*) progressiste

prohibit [prə'hɪbɪt] *vt* interdire, défendre

project [*n* 'prɒdʒekt, *vb* prə'dʒekt] *n* (*plan*) projet *m*, plan *m*; (*venture*) opération *f*, entreprise *f*; (*research*) étude *f*, dossier *m*

♦ *vt* projeter ♦ *vi* faire saillie, s'avancer; ~**ion** *n* projection *f*; (*overhang*) saillie *f*; ~**or** *n* projecteur *m*

prolong [prə'lɒŋ] *vt* prolonger

prom [prɒm] *n abbr* = **promenade**; (*US: ball*) bal *m* d'étudiants

promenade [prɒmə'nɑːd] *n* (*by sea*) esplanade *f*, promenade *f*; ~ **concert** (*BRIT*) *n* concert *m* populaire (de musique classique)

---
promenade concert
---

*En Grande-Bretagne, un **promenade** **concert** (ou **prom**) est un concert de musique classique, ainsi appelé car, à l'origine, le public restait debout et se promenait au lieu de rester assis. De nos jours, une partie du public reste debout, mais il y a également des places assises (plus chères). Les Proms les plus connus sont les Proms londoniens. La dernière séance (the Last Night of the Proms) est un grand événement médiatique où se jouent des airs traditionnels et patriotiques. Aux États-Unis et au Canada, le **prom** ou **promenade** est un bal organisé par le lycée.*

prominent ['prɒmɪnənt] *adj* (*standing out*) proéminent(e); (*important*) important(e)

promiscuous [prə'mɪskjuəs] *adj* (*sexually*) de mœurs légères

promise ['prɒmɪs] *n* promesse *f* ♦ *vt, vi* promettre; **promising** *adj* prometteur(-euse)

promote [prə'məut] *vt* promouvoir; (*new product*) faire la promotion de; ~**r** *n* (*of event*) organisateur(-trice); (*of cause, idea*) promoteur(-trice); **promotion** *n* promotion *f*

prompt [prɒmpt] *adj* rapide ♦ *adv* (*punctually*) à l'heure ♦ *n* (*COMPUT*) message *m* (de guidage) ♦ *vt* provoquer; (*person*) inciter, pousser; (*THEATRE*) souffler (son rôle *or* ses répliques) à; ~**ly** *adv* rapidement, sans délai; ponctuellement

prone [prəun] *adj* (*lying*) couché(e) (face contre terre); ~ **to** enclin(e) à

prong [prɒŋ] *n* (*of fork*) dent *f*

pronoun ['prəunaun] *n* pronom *m*

pronounce [prə'nauns] *vt* prononcer; **pronunciation** [prənʌnsɪ'eɪʃən] *n* prononciation *f*

proof [pruːf] *n* preuve *f*; (*TYP*) épreuve *f* ♦ *adj*: ~ **against** à l'épreuve de

prop [prɒp] *n* support *m*, étai *m*; (*fig*) soutien *m* ♦ *vt* (*also*: ~ **up**) étayer, soutenir; (*lean*): **to ~ sth against** appuyer qch contre *or* à

propaganda [prɒpə'gændə] *n* propagande *f*

propel [prə'pɛl] *vt* propulser, faire avancer; ~**ler** *n* hélice *f*

propensity [prə'pɛnsɪtɪ] *n*: **a ~ for** *or* **to/to do** une propension à/à faire

proper ['prɒpə'] *adj* (*suited, right*) approprié(e), bon (bonne); (*seemly*) correct(e), convenable; (*authentic*) vrai(e), véritable; (*referring to place*): **the village ~** le village proprement dit; ~**ly** *adv* correctement, convenablement; ~ **noun** *n* nom *m* propre

property ['prɒpətɪ] *n* propriété *f*; (*things owned*) biens *mpl*; propriété(s) *f(pl)*; (*land*) terres *fpl*

prophecy ['prɒfɪsɪ] *n* prophétie *f*

prophesy ['prɒfɪsaɪ] *vt* prédire

prophet ['prɒfɪt] *n* prophète *m*

proportion [prə'pɔːʃən] *n* proportion *f*; (*share*) part *f*; partie *f*; ~**al**, ~**ate** *adj* proportionnel(le)

proposal [prə'pəuzl] *n* proposition *f*, offre *f*; (*plan*) projet *m*; (*of marriage*) demande *f* en mariage

propose [prə'pəuz] *vt* proposer, suggérer ♦ *vi* faire sa demande en mariage; **to ~ to do** avoir l'intention de faire; **proposition** [prɒpə'zɪʃən] *n* proposition *f*

proprietor [prə'praɪətə'] *n* propriétaire *m/f*

propriety [prə'praɪətɪ] *n* (*seemliness*) bienséance *f*, convenance *f*

prose [prəuz] *n* (*not poetry*) prose *f*

prosecute ['prɒsɪkjuːt] *vt* poursuivre; **prosecution** [prɒsɪ'kjuːʃən] *n* poursuites *fpl* judiciaires; (*accusing side*) partie plaignante; **prosecutor** n (*US: plaintiff*) plaignant(e); (*also:* **public prosecutor**) procureur m, ministère public

prospect [n 'prɔspekt, vb prə'spekt] n perspective f ♦ vt, vi prospecter; **~s** npl (*for work etc*) possibilités fpl d'avenir, débouchés mpl; **~ing** n (*for gold, oil etc*) prospection f; **~ive** adj (*possible*) éventuel(le); (*future*) futur(e)

prospectus [prə'spektəs] n prospectus m

prosperity [prɔ'speriti] n prospérité f

prostitute ['prɔstitjuːt] n prostitué(e)

protect [prə'tekt] vt protéger; **~ion** n protection f; **~ive** adj protecteur(-trice); (*clothing*) de protection

protein ['prəutiːn] n protéine f

protest [n 'prəutest, vb prə'test] n protestation f ♦ vi, vt: **to ~ (that)** protester (que)

Protestant ['prɔtistənt] adj, n protestant(e)

protester [prə'testər] n manifestant(e)

protracted [prə'træktid] adj prolongé(e)

protrude [prə'truːd] vi avancer, dépasser

proud [praud] adj fier(-ère); (*pej*) orgueilleux(-euse)

prove [pruːv] vt prouver, démontrer ♦ vi: **to ~ (to be) correct** etc s'avérer juste etc; **to ~ o.s.** montrer ce dont on est capable

proverb ['prɔvəːb] n proverbe m

provide [prə'vaid] vt fournir; **to ~ sb with sth** fournir qch à qn; **~ for** vt fus (*person*) subvenir aux besoins de; (*future event*) prévoir; **~d (that)** conj à condition que +sub; **providing** conj: **providing (that)** à condition que +sub

province ['prɔvins] n province f; (*fig*) domaine m; **provincial** [prə'vinʃəl] adj provincial(e)

provision [prə'viʒən] n (*supplying*) fourniture f; approvisionnement m; (*stipulation*) disposition f; **~s** npl (*food*) provisions fpl; **~al** adj provisoire

proviso [prə'vaizəu] n condition f

provocative [prə'vɔkətiv] adj provocateur(-trice), provocant(e)

provoke [prə'vəuk] vt provoquer

prowess ['prauis] n prouesse f

prowl [praul] vi (*also:* **~ about**, **~ around**) rôder ♦ n: **on the ~** à l'affût; **~er** n rôdeur(-euse)

proxy ['prɔksi] n procuration f

prudent ['pruːdnt] adj prudent(e)

prune [pruːn] n pruneau m ♦ vt élaguer

pry [prai] vi: **to ~ into** fourrer son nez dans

PS n abbr (= *postscript*) p.s.

psalm [sɑːm] n psaume m

pseudonym ['sjuːdənim] n pseudonyme m

psyche ['saiki] n psychisme m

psychiatrist [sai'kaiətrist] n psychiatre m/f

psychic ['saikik] adj (*also:* **~al**) (méta)psychique; (*person*) doué(e) d'un sixième sens

psychoanalyst [saikəu'ænəlist] n psychanalyste m/f

psychological [saikə'lɔdʒikl] adj psychologique

psychologist [sai'kɔlədʒist] n psychologue m/f

psychology [sai'kɔlədʒi] n psychologie f

PTO abbr (= *please turn over*) T.S.V.P.

pub [pʌb] n (*public house*) pub m

---

pub

ⓘ *Un* **pub** *comprend en général deux salles: l'une ("the lounge") est plutôt confortable, avec des fauteuils et des bancs capitonnés, tandis que l'autre ("the public bar") est simplement un bar où les consommations sont en général moins chères. Cette dernière est souvent aussi une salle de jeux, les jeux les plus courants étant les fléchettes, les dominos et le billard. Il y a parfois aussi une petite arrière-salle douillette appelée "the snug". Beaucoup de pubs servent maintenant des repas, surtout à l'heure du déjeuner, et c'est alors le seul moment où les enfants sont acceptés, à condition d'être accompagnés. Les pubs sont en général ouverts de 11 h à 23 h, mais cela peut varier selon leur licence; certains pubs ferment l'après-midi.*

---

public ['pʌblik] adj public(-ique) ♦ n public

m; **in ~** en public; **to make ~** rendre public; **~ address system** *n* (système *m* de) sonorisation *f*; hauts-parleurs *mpl*

publican ['pʌblɪkən] *n* patron *m* de pub

public: **~ company** *n* société *f* anonyme (*cotée en Bourse*); **~ convenience** (BRIT) *n* toilettes *fpl*; **~ holiday** *n* jour férié; **~ house** (BRIT) *n* pub *m*

publicity [pʌbˈlɪsɪtɪ] *n* publicité *f*

publicize ['pʌblɪsaɪz] *vt* faire connaître, rendre public(-ique)

public: **~ opinion** *n* opinion publique; **~ relations** *n* relations publiques; **~ school** (BRIT) école (secondaire) privée; (US) école publique; **~-spirited** *adj* qui fait preuve de civisme; **~ transport** *n* transports *mpl* en commun

publish ['pʌblɪʃ] *vt* publier; **~er** *n* éditeur *m*; **~ing** *n* édition *f*

pub lunch *n* repas *m* de bistrot

pucker ['pʌkər] *vt* plisser

pudding ['pudɪŋ] *n* pudding *m*; (BRIT: *sweet*) dessert *m*, entremets *m*; **black ~,** (US) **blood ~** boudin (noir)

puddle ['pʌdl] *n* flaque *f* (d'eau)

puff [pʌf] *n* bouffée *f* ♦ *vt*: **to ~ one's pipe** tirer sur sa pipe ♦ *vi* (*pant*) haleter; **~ out** *vt* (*fill with air*) gonfler; **~ pastry** (US **puff paste**) *n* pâte feuilletée; **~y** *adj* bouffi(e), boursouflé(e)

pull [pul] *n* (*tug*): **to give sth a ~** tirer sur qch ♦ *vt* tirer; (*trigger*) presser ♦ *vi* tirer; **to ~ to pieces** mettre en morceaux; **to ~ one's punches** ménager son adversaire; **to ~ one's weight** faire sa part (du travail); **to ~ o.s. together** se ressaisir; **to ~ sb's leg** (*fig*) faire marcher qn; **~ apart** *vt* (*break*) mettre en pièces, démantibuler; **~ down** *vt* (*house*) démolir; **~ in** *vi* (AUT) entrer; (RAIL) entrer en gare; **~ off** *vt* enlever, ôter; (*deal etc*) mener à bien, conclure; **~ out** *vi* démarrer, partir ♦ *vt* sortir; arracher; **~ over** *vi* (AUT) se ranger; **~ through** *vi* s'en sortir; **~ up** *vi* (*stop*) s'arrêter ♦ *vt* remonter; (*uproot*) déraciner, arracher

pulley ['pulɪ] *n* poulie *f*

pullover ['puləuvər] *n* pull-(over) *m*, tricot *m*

pulp [pʌlp] *n* (*of fruit*) pulpe *f*

pulpit ['pulpɪt] *n* chaire *f*

pulsate [pʌlˈseɪt] *vi* battre, palpiter; (*music*) vibrer

pulse [pʌls] *n* (*of blood*) pouls *m*; (*of heart*) battement *m*; (*of music, engine*) vibrations *fpl*; (BOT, CULIN) légume sec

pump [pʌmp] *n* pompe *f*; (*shoe*) escarpin *m* ♦ *vt* pomper; **~ up** *vt* gonfler

pumpkin ['pʌmpkɪn] *n* potiron *m*, citrouille *f*

pun [pʌn] *n* jeu *m* de mots, calembour *m*

punch [pʌntʃ] *n* (*blow*) coup *m* de poing; (*tool*) poinçon *m*; (*drink*) punch *m* ♦ *vt* (*hit*): **to ~ sb/sth** donner un coup de poing à qn/sur qch; **~line** *n* (*of joke*) conclusion *f*; **~-up** (BRIT: *inf*) *n* bagarre *f*

punctual ['pʌŋktjuəl] *adj* ponctuel(le)

punctuation [pʌŋktjuˈeɪʃən] *n* ponctuation *f*

puncture ['pʌŋktʃər] *n* crevaison *f*

pundit ['pʌndɪt] *n* individu *m* qui pontifie, pontife *m*

pungent ['pʌndʒənt] *adj* piquant(e), âcre

punish ['pʌnɪʃ] *vt* punir; **~ment** *n* punition *f*, châtiment *m*

punk [pʌŋk] *n* (*also*: **~ rocker**) punk *m/f*; (*also*: **~ rock**) le punk rock; (US: *inf*: *hoodlum*) voyou *m*

punt [pʌnt] *n* (*boat*) bachot *m*

punter ['pʌntər] (BRIT) *n* (*gambler*) parieur(-euse); (*inf*): **the ~s** le public

puny ['pjuːnɪ] *adj* chétif(-ive); (*effort*) piteux(-euse)

pup [pʌp] *n* chiot *m*

pupil ['pjuːpl] *n* (SCOL) élève *m/f*; (*of eye*) pupille *f*

puppet ['pʌpɪt] *n* marionnette *f*, pantin *m*

puppy ['pʌpɪ] *n* chiot *m*, jeune chien(ne)

purchase ['pɜːtʃɪs] *n* achat *m* ♦ *vt* acheter; **~r** *n* acheteur(-euse)

pure [pjuər] *adj* pur(e); **~ly** *adv* purement

purge [pɜːdʒ] *n* purge *f* ♦ *vt* purger

purple ['pɜːpl] *adj* violet(te); (*face*) cramoisi(e)

purpose ['pə:pəs] n intention f, but m; **on ~** exprès; **~ful** adj déterminé(e), résolu(e)

purr [pə:^r] vi ronronner

purse [pə:s] n (BRIT: for money) porte-monnaie m inv; (US: handbag) sac m à main ♦ vt serrer, pincer

purser n (NAUT) commissaire m du bord

pursue [pə'sju:] vt poursuivre; **pursuit** [pə'sju:t] n poursuite f; (occupation) occupation f, activité f

push [puʃ] n poussée f ♦ vt pousser; (button) appuyer sur; (product) faire de la publicité pour; (thrust): **to ~ sth (into)** enfoncer qch (dans) ♦ vi pousser; (demand): **to ~ for** exiger, demander avec insistance; **~ aside** vt écarter; **~ off** (inf) vi filer, ficher le camp; **~ on** vi (continue) continuer; **~ through** vi se frayer un chemin ♦ vt (measure) faire accepter; **~ up** vt (total, prices) faire monter; **~chair** (BRIT) n poussette f; **~er** n (drug pusher) revendeur(-euse) (de drogue), ravitailleur(-euse) (en drogue); **~over** (inf) n: **it's a ~over** c'est un jeu d'enfant; **~-up** (US) n traction f; **~y** (pej) adj arriviste

puss [pus], **pussy (cat)** ['pusi(kæt)] (inf) n minet m

put [put] (pt, pp **put**) vt mettre, poser, placer; (say) dire, exprimer; (a question) poser; (case, view) exposer, présenter; (estimate) estimer; **~ about** vt (rumour) faire courir; **~ across** vt (ideas etc) communiquer; **~ away** vt (store) ranger; **~ back** vt (replace) remettre, replacer; (postpone) remettre; (delay) retarder; **~ by** vt (money) mettre de côté, économiser; **~ down** vt (parcel etc) poser, déposer; (in writing) mettre par écrit, inscrire; (suppress: revolt etc) réprimer, faire cesser; (animal) abattre; (dog, cat) faire piquer; (attribute) attribuer; **~ forward** vt (ideas) avancer; **~ in** vt (gas, electricity) installer; (application, complaint) soumettre; (time, effort) consacrer; **~ off** vt (light etc) éteindre; (postpone) remettre à plus tard, ajourner; (discourage) dissuader; **~ on** vt (clothes, lipstick, record) mettre; (light etc) allumer; (play etc) monter; (food: cook) mettre à cuire or à chauffer; (gain): **to ~ on weight** prendre du poids, grossir; **to ~ the brakes on** freiner; **to ~ the kettle on** mettre l'eau à chauffer; **~ out** vt (take out) mettre dehors; (one's hand) tendre; (light etc) éteindre; (person: inconvenience) déranger, gêner; **~ through** vt (TEL: call) passer; (: person) mettre en communication; (plan) faire accepter; **~ up** vt (raise) lever, relever, remonter; (pin up) afficher; (hang) accrocher; (build) construire, ériger; (tent) monter; (umbrella) ouvrir; (increase) augmenter; (accommodate) loger; **~ up with** vt fus supporter

putt [pʌt] n coup roulé; **~ing green** n green m

putty ['pʌti] n mastic m

put-up ['putʌp] (BRIT) adj: **~-~ job** coup monté

puzzle ['pʌzl] n énigme f, mystère m; (jigsaw) puzzle m ♦ vt intriguer, rendre perplexe ♦ vi se creuser la tête; **~d** adj perplexe; **puzzling** adj déconcertant(e)

pyjamas [pə'dʒɑ:məz] (BRIT) npl pyjama(s) m(pl)

pylon ['paɪlən] n pylône m

pyramid ['pɪrəmɪd] n pyramide f

Pyrenees [pɪrə'ni:z] npl: **the ~** les Pyrénées fpl

Q, q

quack [kwæk] n (of duck) coin-coin m inv; (pej: doctor) charlatan m

quad [kwɔd] n abbr = **quadrangle**; **quadruplet**

quadrangle ['kwɔdræŋgl] n (courtyard) cour f

quadruple [kwɔ'dru:pl] vt, vi quadrupler; **~ts** npl quadruplés

quail [kweil] n (ZOOL) caille f ♦ vi: **to ~ at** or **before** reculer devant

quaint [kweint] adj bizarre; (house, village) au charme vieillot, pittoresque

quake [kweik] vi trembler

qualification [kwɔlɪfɪˈkeɪʃən] *n* (*often pl*: *degree etc*) diplôme *m*; (*training*) qualification(s) *f(pl)*, expérience *f*; (*ability*) compétence(s) *f(pl)*; (*limitation*) réserve *f*, restriction *f*

qualified [ˈkwɔlɪfaɪd] *adj* (*trained*) qualifié(e); (*professionally*) diplômé(e); (*fit, competent*) compétent(e), qualifié(e); (*limited*) conditionnel(le)

qualify [ˈkwɔlɪfaɪ] *vt* qualifier; (*modify*) atténuer, nuancer ♦ *vi*: **to ~ (as)** obtenir son diplôme (de); **to ~ (for)** remplir les conditions requises (pour); (*SPORT*) se qualifier (pour)

quality [ˈkwɔlɪtɪ] *n* qualité *f*; ~ **time** *n* moments privilégiés

quality (news)papers

i Les **quality (news)papers** (*ou la* **quality press**) englobent les journaux sérieux, quotidiens ou hebdomadaires, par opposition aux journaux populaires (**tabloid press**). Ces journaux visent un public qui souhaite des informations détaillées sur un éventail très vaste de sujets et qui est prêt à consacrer beaucoup de temps à leur lecture. Les quality newspapers sont en général de grand format.

qualm [kwɑːm] *n* doute *m*; scrupule *m*

quandary [ˈkwɔndrɪ] *n*: **in a ~** devant un dilemme, dans l'embarras

quantity [ˈkwɔntɪtɪ] *n* quantité *f*; ~ **surveyor** *n* métreur *m* vérificateur

quarantine [ˈkwɔrntiːn] *n* quarantaine *f*

quarrel [ˈkwɔrl] *n* querelle *f*, dispute *f* ♦ *vi* se disputer, se quereller

quarry [ˈkwɔrɪ] *n* (*for stone*) carrière *f*; (*animal*) proie *f*, gibier *m*

quart [kwɔːt] *n* ≈ litre *m*

quarter [ˈkwɔːtəʳ] *n* quart *m*; (*US: coin: 25 cents*) quart de dollar; (*of year*) trimestre *m*; (*district*) quartier *m* ♦ *vt* (*divide*) partager en quartiers or en quatre; ~**s** *npl* (*living ~*) logement *m*; (*MIL*) quartiers *mpl*, cantonnement *m*; **a ~ of an hour** un quart d'heure; ~ **final** *n* quart *m* de fina-

le; ~**ly** *adj* trimestriel(le) ♦ *adv* tous les trois mois

quartet(te) [kwɔːˈtet] *n* quatuor *m*; (*jazz players*) quartette *m*

quartz [kwɔːts] *n* quartz *m*

quash [kwɔʃ] *vt* (*verdict*) annuler

quaver [ˈkweɪvəʳ] *vi* trembler

quay [kiː] *n* (*also*: ~**side**) quai *m*

queasy [ˈkwiːzɪ] *adj*: **to feel ~** avoir mal au cœur

queen [kwiːn] *n* reine *f*; (*CARDS etc*) dame *f*; ~ **mother** *n* reine mère *f*

queer [kwɪəʳ] *adj* étrange, curieux(-euse); (*suspicious*) louche ♦ *n* (*inf!*) homosexuel *m*

quell [kwɛl] *vt* réprimer, étouffer

quench [kwɛntʃ] *vt*: **to ~ one's thirst** se désaltérer

query [ˈkwɪərɪ] *n* question *f* ♦ *vt* remettre en question, mettre en doute

quest [kwɛst] *n* recherche *f*, quête *f*

question [ˈkwɛstʃən] *n* question *f* ♦ *vt* (*person*) interroger; (*plan, idea*) remettre en question, mettre en doute; **beyond ~** sans aucun doute; **out of the ~** hors de question; ~**able** *adj* discutable; ~ **mark** *n* point *m* d'interrogation; ~**naire** [kwɛstʃəˈneəʳ] *n* questionnaire *m*

queue [kjuː] (*BRIT*) *n* queue *f*, file *f* ♦ *vi* (*also*: ~ **up**) faire la queue

quibble [ˈkwɪbl] *vi*: ~ (**about sth**) or (**over sth**) or (**with sth**) ergoter (sur qch)

quick [kwɪk] *adj* rapide; (*agile*) agile, vif (vive) ♦ *n*: **cut to the ~** (*fig*) touché(e) au vif; **be ~!** dépêche-toi!; ~**en** *vt* accélérer, presser ♦ *vi* s'accélérer, devenir plus rapide; ~**ly** *adv* vite, rapidement; ~**sand** *n* sables mouvants; ~**-witted** *adj* à l'esprit vif

quid [kwɪd] (*BRIT: inf*) *n, pl inv* livre *f*

quiet [ˈkwaɪət] *adj* tranquille, calme; (*voice*) bas(se); (*ceremony, colour*) discret(-ète) ♦ *n* tranquillité *f*, calme *m*; (*silence*) silence *m* ♦ *vt, vi* (*US*) = **quieten; keep ~!** tais-toi!; ~**en** *vi* (*also*: ~**en down**) se calmer, s'apaiser ♦ *vt* calmer, apaiser; ~**ly** *adv* tranquillement, calmement; (*silently*) silencieusement; **~ness** n tranquillité f, calme m; (silence) silence m

quilt [kwɪlt] n édredon m; (continental ~) couette f

quin [kwɪn] n abbr = **quintuplet**

quintuplets [kwɪn'tjuːplɪts] npl quintuplé(e)s

quip [kwɪp] n remarque piquante or spirituelle, pointe f

quirk [kwəːk] n bizarrerie f

quit [kwɪt] (pt, pp **quit** or **quitted**) vt quitter; (smoking, grumbling) arrêter de ♦ vi (give up) abandonner, renoncer; (resign) démissionner

quite [kwaɪt] adv (rather) assez, plutôt; (entirely) complètement, tout à fait; (following a negative = almost): **that's not ~ big enough** ce n'est pas tout à fait assez grand; **I ~ understand** je comprends très bien; **~ a few of them** un assez grand nombre d'entre eux; **~ (so)!** exactement!

quits [kwɪts] adj: **~ (with)** quitte (envers); **let's call it ~** restons-en là

quiver ['kwɪvə^r] vi trembler, frémir

quiz [kwɪz] n (game) jeu-concours m ♦ vt interroger; **~zical** adj narquois(e)

quota ['kwəutə] n quota m

quotation [kwəu'teɪʃən] n citation f; (estimate) devis m; **~ marks** npl guillemets mpl

quote [kwəut] n citation f; (estimate) devis m ♦ vt citer; (price) indiquer; **~s** npl guillemets mpl

R, r

rabbi ['ræbaɪ] n rabbin m

rabbit ['ræbɪt] n lapin m; **~ hutch** n clapier m

rabble ['ræbl] (pej) n populace f

rabies ['reɪbiːz] n rage f

RAC n abbr (BRIT) = **Royal Automobile Club**

rac(c)oon [rə'kuːn] n raton laveur m

race [reɪs] n (species) race f; (competition, rush) course f ♦ vt (horse) faire courir ♦ vi (compete) faire la course, courir; (hurry) al-ler à toute vitesse, courir; (engine) s'emballer; (pulse) augmenter; **~ car** (US) n = **racing car**; **~ car driver** (US) = **racing driver**; **~course** n champ m de courses; **~horse** n cheval m de course; **~r** n (bike) vélo m de course; **~track** n piste f

racial ['reɪʃl] adj racial(e)

racing ['reɪsɪŋ] n courses fpl; **~ car** (BRIT) n voiture f de course; **~ driver** (BRIT) n pilote m de course

racism ['reɪsɪzəm] n racisme m; **racist** adj raciste ♦ n raciste m/f

rack [ræk] n (for guns, tools) râtelier m; (also: **luggage ~**) porte-bagages m inv, filet m à bagages; (also: **roof ~**) galerie f; (dish ~) égouttoir m ♦ vt tourmenter; **to ~ one's brains** se creuser la cervelle

racket ['rækɪt] n (for tennis) raquette f; (noise) tapage m; vacarme m; (swindle) escroquerie f

racquet ['rækɪt] n raquette f

racy ['reɪsɪ] adj plein(e) de verve; (slightly indecent) osé(e)

radar ['reɪdɑː^r] n radar m

radial ['reɪdɪəl] adj (also: **~-ply**) à carcasse radiale

radiant ['reɪdɪənt] adj rayonnant(e)

radiate ['reɪdɪeɪt] vt (heat) émettre, dégager; (emotion) rayonner de ♦ vi (lines) rayonner; **radiation** [reɪdɪ'eɪʃən] n rayonnement m; (radioactive) radiation f; **radiator** ['reɪdɪeɪtə^r] n radiateur m

radical ['rædɪkl] adj radical(e)

radii ['reɪdɪaɪ] npl of **radius**

radio ['reɪdɪəu] n radio f ♦ vt appeler par radio; **on the ~** à la radio; **~active** ['reɪdɪəu'æktɪv] adj radioactif(-ive); **~ cassette** n radiocassette m; **~-controlled** adj téléguidé(e); **~ station** n station f de radio

radish ['rædɪʃ] n radis m

radius ['reɪdɪəs] n (pl **radii**) rayon m

RAF n abbr = **Royal Air Force**

raffle ['ræfl] n tombola f

raft [rɑːft] n (craft; also: **life ~**) radeau m

rafter ['rɑːftə^r] n chevron m

rag [ræg] n chiffon m; (pej: newspaper) feuille *f* de chou, torchon *m*; (*student ~*) *attractions organisées au profit d'œuvres de charité*; **~s** *npl* (*torn clothes etc*) haillons *mpl*; **~ doll** *n* poupée *f* de chiffon

rage [reɪdʒ] *n* (*fury*) rage *f*, fureur *f* ♦ *vi* (*person*) être fou (folle) de rage; (*storm*) faire rage, être déchaîné(e); **it's all the ~** cela fait fureur

ragged [ˈrægɪd] *adj* (*edge*) inégal(e); (*clothes*) en loques; (*appearance*) déguenillé(e)

raid [reɪd] *n* (*attack, also:* MIL) raid *m*; (*criminal*) hold-up *m inv*; (*by police*) descente *f*, rafle *f* ♦ *vt* faire un raid sur *or* un hold-up *or* une descente dans

rail [reɪl] *n* (*on stairs*) rampe *f*; (*on bridge, balcony*) balustrade *f*; (*of ship*) bastingage *m*; **~s** *npl* (*track*) rails *mpl*, voie ferrée; **by ~** par chemin de fer, en train; **~ing(s)** *n(pl)* grille *f*; **~road** (*US*), **~way** (*BRIT*) *n* (*track*) voie ferrée; (*company*) chemin *m* de fer; **~way line** (*BRIT*) *n* ligne *f* de chemin de fer; **~wayman** (*BRIT*) (*irreg*) *n* cheminot *m*; **~way station** (*BRIT*) *n* gare *f*

rain [reɪn] *n* pluie *f* ♦ *vi* pleuvoir; **in the ~** sous la pluie; **it's ~ing** il pleut; **~bow** *n* arc-en-ciel *m*; **~coat** *n* imperméable *m*; **~drop** *n* goutte *f* de pluie; **~fall** *n* chute *f* de pluie; (*measurement*) hauteur *f* des précipitations; **~forest** *n* forêt *f* tropicale humide; **~y** *adj* pluvieux(-euse)

raise [reɪz] *n* augmentation *f* ♦ *vt* (*lift*) lever; hausser; (*increase*) augmenter; (*morale*) remonter; (*standards*) améliorer; (*question, doubt*) provoquer, soulever; (*cattle, family*) élever; (*crop*) faire pousser; (*funds*) rassembler; (*loan*) obtenir; (*army*) lever; **to ~ one's voice** élever la voix

raisin [ˈreɪzn] *n* raisin sec

rake [reɪk] *n* (*tool*) râteau *m* ♦ *vt* ratisser

rally [ˈrælɪ] *n* (*POL etc*) meeting *m*, rassemblement *m*; (*AUT*) rallye *m*; (*TENNIS*) échange *m* ♦ *vt* (*support*) gagner ♦ *vi* (*sick person*) aller mieux; (*Stock Exchange*) reprendre; **~ round** *vt fus* venir en aide à

RAM [ræm] *n abbr* (= *random access memory*) mémoire vive

ram [ræm] *n* bélier *m* ♦ *vt* enfoncer; (*crash into*) emboutir; percuter

Ramadan [ˌræmədæn] *n* ramadan *m*

ramble [ˈræmbl] *n* randonnée *f* ♦ *vi* (*walk*) se promener, faire une randonnée; (*talk: also:* **~ on**) discourir, pérorer; **~r** *n* promeneur(-euse), randonneur(-euse); (*BOT*) rosier grimpant; **rambling** *adj* (*speech*) décousu(e); (*house*) plein(e) de coins et de recoins; (*BOT*) grimpant(e)

ramp [ræmp] *n* (*incline*) rampe *f*; dénivellation *f*; **on ~, off ~** (*US:* AUT) bretelle *f* d'accès

rampage [ræmˈpeɪdʒ] *n*: **to be on the ~** se déchaîner

rampant [ˈræmpənt] *adj* (*disease etc*) qui sévit

ram raiding [-ˌreɪdɪŋ] *n* pillage d'un magasin en enfonçant la vitrine avec une voiture

ramshackle [ˈræmʃækl] *adj* (*house*) délabré(e); (*car etc*) déglingué(e)

ran [ræn] *pt of* **run**

ranch [rɑːntʃ] *n* ranch *m*; **~er** *n* propriétaire *m* de ranch

rancid [ˈrænsɪd] *adj* rance

rancour [ˈræŋkər] (*US* **rancor**) *n* rancune *f*

random [ˈrændəm] *adj* fait(e) *or* établi(e) au hasard; (*MATH*) aléatoire ♦ *n*: **at ~** au hasard; **~ access** *n* (*COMPUT*) accès sélectif

randy [ˈrændɪ] (*BRIT: inf*) *adj* excité(e); lubrique

rang [ræŋ] *pt of* **ring**

range [reɪndʒ] *n* (*of mountains*) chaîne *f*; (*of missile, voice*) portée *f*; (*of products*) choix *m*, gamme *f*; (*MIL: also:* **shooting ~**) champ *m* de tir; (*indoor*) stand *m* de tir; (*also:* **kitchen ~**) fourneau *m* (de cuisine) ♦ *vt* (*place in a line*) mettre en rang, ranger ♦ *vi*: **to ~ from ... to** aller de ... à; **a ~ of** (*series of proposals etc*) divers(es)

ranger [ˈreɪndʒər] *n* garde forestier

rank [ræŋk] *n* rang *m*; (*MIL*) grade *m*; (*BRIT: also:* **taxi ~**) station *f* de taxis ♦ *vi*: **to ~ among** compter *or* se classer parmi ♦ *adj* (*stinking*) fétide, puant(e); **the ~ and file** (*fig*) la masse, la base

ransack ['rænsæk] *vt* fouiller (à fond); (*plunder*) piller

ransom ['rænsəm] *n* rançon *f*; **to hold to ~** (*fig*) exercer un chantage sur

rant [rænt] *vi* fulminer

rap [ræp] *vt* frapper sur *or* à; taper sur ♦ *n*: **~ music** rap *m*

rape [reɪp] *n* viol *m*; (*BOT*) colza *m* ♦ *vt* violer; **~(seed) oil** *n* huile *f* de colza

rapid ['ræpɪd] *adj* rapide; **~s** *npl* (*GEO*) rapides *mpl*

rapist ['reɪpɪst] *n* violeur *m*

rapport [ræ'pɔ:r] *n* entente *f*

rapturous ['ræptʃərəs] *adj* enthousiaste, frénétique

rare [rɛər] *adj* rare; (*CULIN: steak*) saignant(e)

raring ['rɛərɪŋ] *adj*: **~ to go** (*inf*) très impatient(e) de commencer

rascal ['rɑːskl] *n* vaurien *m*

rash [ræʃ] *adj* imprudent(e), irréfléchi(e) ♦ *n* (*MED*) rougeur *f*, éruption *f*; (*spate: of events*) série (noire)

rasher ['ræʃər] *n* fine tranche (de lard)

raspberry ['rɑːzbərɪ] *n* framboise *f*; **~ bush** *n* framboisier *m*

rasping ['rɑːspɪŋ] *adj*: **~ noise** grincement *m*

rat [ræt] *n* rat *m*

rate [reɪt] *n* taux *m*; (*speed*) vitesse *f*, rythme *m*; (*price*) tarif *m* ♦ *vt* classer; évaluer; **~s** *npl* (*BRIT: tax*) impôts locaux; (*fees*) tarifs *mpl*; **to ~ sb/sth as** considérer qn/ qch comme; **~able value** (*BRIT*) *n* valeur locative imposable; **~payer** ['reɪtpeɪər] (*BRIT*) *n* contribuable *m/f* (*payant les impôts locaux*)

rather ['rɑːðər] *adv* plutôt; **it's ~ expensive** c'est assez cher; (*too much*) c'est un peu cher; **there's ~ a lot** il y en a beaucoup; **I would** *or* **I'd ~ go** j'aimerais mieux *or* je préférerais partir

rating ['reɪtɪŋ] *n* (*assessment*) évaluation *f*; (*score*) classement *m*; **~s** *npl* (*RADIO, TV*) indice *m* d'écoute

ratio ['reɪʃɪəu] *n* proportion *f*

ration ['ræʃən] *n* (*gen pl*) ration(s) *f(pl)*

rational ['ræʃənl] *adj* raisonnable, sensé(e); (*solution, reasoning*) logique; **~e** [ræʃə'nɑːl] *n* raisonnement *m*; **~ize** *vt* rationaliser; (*conduct*) essayer d'expliquer *or* de motiver

rat race *n* foire *f* d'empoigne

rattle ['rætl] *n* (*of door, window*) battement *m*; (*of coins, chain*) cliquetis *m*; (*of train, engine*) bruit *m* de ferraille; (*object: for baby*) hochet *m* ♦ *vi* cliqueter; (*car, bus*): **to ~ along** rouler dans un bruit de ferraille ♦ *vt* agiter (bruyamment); (*unnerve*) décontenancer; **~snake** *n* serpent *m* à sonnettes

raucous ['rɔːkəs] *adj* rauque; (*noisy*) bruyant(e), tapageur(-euse)

rave [reɪv] *vi* (*in anger*) s'emporter; (*with enthusiasm*) s'extasier; (*MED*) délirer ♦ *n* (*BRIT: inf: party*) rave *f*, soirée *f* techno

raven ['reɪvən] *n* corbeau *m*

ravenous ['rævənəs] *adj* affamé(e)

ravine [rə'viːn] *n* ravin *m*

raving ['reɪvɪŋ] *adj*: **~ lunatic** ♦ *n* fou (folle) furieux(-euse)

ravishing ['rævɪʃɪŋ] *adj* enchanteur(-eresse)

raw [rɔː] *adj* (*uncooked*) cru(e); (*not processed*) brut(e); (*sore*) à vif, irrité(e); (*inexperienced*) inexpérimenté(e); (*weather, day*) froid(e) et humide; **~ deal** (*inf*) *n* sale coup *m*; **~ material** *n* matière première

ray [reɪ] *n* rayon *m*; **~ of hope** lueur *f* d'espoir

raze [reɪz] *vt* (*also: ~ to the ground*) raser, détruire

razor ['reɪzər] *n* rasoir *m*; **~ blade** *n* lame *f* de rasoir

Rd *abbr* = **road**

RE *n abbr* = **religious education**

re [riː] *prep* concernant

reach [riːtʃ] *n* portée *f*, atteinte *f*; (*of river etc*) étendue *f* ♦ *vt* atteindre; (*conclusion, decision*) parvenir à ♦ *vi* s'étendre, étendre le bras; **out of/within ~** hors de/à portée; **within ~ of the shops** pas trop loin des *or* à proximité des magasins; **~ out** *vt* tendre ♦ *vi*: **to ~ out (for)** allonger le bras (pour prendre)

react [riːˈækt] *vi* réagir; **~ion** *n* réaction *f*

reactor [riːˈæktəʳ] *n* réacteur *m*

read [riːd, *pt, pp* rɛd] (*pt, pp* **read**) *vi* lire ♦ *vt* lire; (*understand*) comprendre, interpréter; (*study*) étudier; (*meter*) relever; **~ out** *vt* lire à haute voix; **~able** *adj* facile or agréable à lire; (*writing*) lisible; **~er** *n* lecteur(-trice) *f*, (*BRIT: at university*) chargé(e) d'enseignement; **~ership** *n* (*of paper etc*) (nombre *m* de) lecteurs *mpl*

readily [ˈrɛdɪlɪ] *adv* volontiers, avec empressement; (*easily*) facilement

readiness [ˈrɛdɪnɪs] *n* empressement *m*; **in ~** (*prepared*) prêt(e)

reading [ˈriːdɪŋ] *n* lecture *f*; (*understanding*) interprétation *f*; (*on instrument*) indications *fpl*

ready [ˈrɛdɪ] *adj* prêt(e); (*willing*) prêt, disposé(e); (*available*) disponible ♦ *n*: **at the ~** (*MIL*) prêt à faire feu; **to get ~** se préparer ♦ *vt* préparer; **~-made** *adj* tout(e) fait(e); **~-to-wear** *adj* prêt(e) à porter

real [rɪəl] *adj* véritable; réel(le); **in ~ terms** dans la réalité; **~ estate** *n* biens fonciers or immobiliers; **~istic** [rɪəˈlɪstɪk] *adj* réaliste; **~ity** [riːˈælɪtɪ] *n* réalité *f*

realization [rɪəlaɪˈzeɪʃən] *n* (*awareness*) prise *f* de conscience; (*fulfilment; also: of asset*) réalisation *f*

realize [ˈrɪəlaɪz] *vt* (*understand*) se rendre compte de; (*a project, COMM: asset*) réaliser

really [ˈrɪəlɪ] *adv* vraiment; **~?** vraiment?, c'est vrai?

realm [rɛlm] *n* royaume *m*; (*fig*) domaine *m*

realtor ® [ˈrɪəltɔːʳ] (*US*) *n* agent immobilier

reap [riːp] *vt* moissonner; (*fig*) récolter

reappear [riːəˈpɪəʳ] *vi* réapparaître, reparaître

rear [rɪəʳ] *adj* de derrière, arrière *inv*; (*AUT: wheel etc*) arrière ♦ *n* arrière *m* ♦ *vt* (*cattle, family*) élever ♦ *vi* (*also:* **~ up**: *animal*) se cabrer; **~guard** *n* (*MIL*) arrière-garde *f*; **~-view mirror** *n* (*AUT*) rétroviseur *m*

reason [ˈriːzn] *n* raison *f* ♦ *vi*: **to ~ with sb** raisonner qn, faire entendre raison à qn; **to have ~ to think** avoir lieu de penser; **it stands to ~ that** il va sans dire que; **~able** *adj* raisonnable; (*not bad*) acceptable; **~ably** *adv* raisonnablement; **~ing** *n* raisonnement *m*

reassurance [riːəˈʃuərəns] *n* réconfort *m*; (*factual*) assurance *f*, garantie *f*

reassure [riːəˈʃuəʳ] *vt* rassurer

rebate [ˈriːbeɪt] *n* (*on tax etc*) dégrèvement *m*

rebel [*n* ˈrɛbl, *vb* rɪˈbɛl] *n* rebelle *m/f* ♦ *vi* se rebeller, se révolter; **~lious** [rɪˈbɛljəs] *adj* rebelle

rebound [*vb* rɪˈbaund, *n* ˈriːbaund] *vi* (*ball*) rebondir ♦ *n* rebond *m*; **to marry on the ~** se marier immédiatement après une déception amoureuse

rebuff [rɪˈbʌf] *n* rebuffade *f*

rebuke [rɪˈbjuːk] *vt* réprimander

rebut [rɪˈbʌt] *vt* réfuter

recall [*vb* rɪˈkɔːl, *n* ˈriːkɔl] *vt* rappeler; (*remember*) se rappeler, se souvenir de ♦ *n* rappel *m*; (*ability to remember*) mémoire *f*

recant [rɪˈkænt] *vi* se rétracter; (*REL*) abjurer

recap [ˈriːkæp], **recapitulate** [riːkəˈpɪtjuleɪt] *vt, vi* récapituler

rec'd *abbr* = **received**

recede [rɪˈsiːd] *vi* (*tide*) descendre; (*disappear*) disparaître peu à peu; (*memory, hope*) s'estomper; **receding** *adj* (*chin*) fuyant(e); **receding hairline** front dégarni

receipt [rɪˈsiːt] *n* (*document*) reçu *m*; (*for parcel etc*) accusé *m* de réception; (*act of receiving*) réception *f*; **~s** *npl* (*COMM*) recettes *fpl*

receive [rɪˈsiːv] *vt* recevoir; **~r** *n* (*TEL*) récepteur *m*, combiné *m*; (*RADIO*) récepteur *m*; (*of stolen goods*) receleur *m*; (*LAW*) administrateur *m* judiciaire

recent [ˈriːsnt] *adj* récent(e); **~ly** *adv* récemment

receptacle [rɪˈsɛptɪkl] *n* récipient *m*

reception [rɪˈsɛpʃən] *n* réception *f*; (*welcome*) accueil *m*, réception; **~ desk** *n* réception *f*; **~ist** *n* réceptionniste *m/f*

recess [rɪ'ses] n (in room) renfoncement m, alcôve f; (secret place) recoin m; (POL etc: holiday) vacances fpl
recession [rɪ'seʃən] n récession f
recipe ['resɪpɪ] n recette f
recipient [rɪ'sɪpɪənt] n (of payment) bénéficiaire m/f; (of letter) destinataire m/f
recital [rɪ'saɪtl] n récital m
recite [rɪ'saɪt] vt (poem) réciter
reckless ['rekləs] adj (driver etc) imprudent(e)
reckon ['rekən] vt (count) calculer, compter; (think): **I ~ that ...** je pense que ...; **~ on** vt fus compter sur, s'attendre à; **~ing** n compte m, calcul m; estimation f
reclaim [rɪ'kleɪm] vt (demand back) réclamer (le remboursement or la restitution de); (land: from sea) assécher; (waste materials) récupérer
recline [rɪ'klaɪn] vi être allongé(e) or étendu(e); **reclining** adj (seat) à dossier réglable
recluse [rɪ'kluːs] n reclus(e), ermite m
recognition [rekəg'nɪʃən] n reconnaissance f; **to gain ~** être reconnu(e); **transformed beyond ~** méconnaissable
recognizable ['rekəgnaɪzəbl] adj: **~ (by)** reconnaissable (à)
recognize ['rekəgnaɪz] vt: **to ~ (by/as)** reconnaître (à/comme étant)
recoil [vb rɪ'kɔɪl, n 'riːkɔɪl] vi (person): **to ~ (from doing/doing sth)** reculer (devant qch/l'idée de faire qch) ♦ n (of gun) recul m
recollect [rekə'lekt] vt se rappeler, se souvenir de; **~ion** n souvenir m
recommend [rekə'mend] vt recommander
reconcile ['rekənsaɪl] vt (two people) réconcilier; (two facts) concilier, accorder; **to ~ o.s. to** se résigner à
recondition [riːkən'dɪʃən] vt remettre à neuf; réviser entièrement
reconnoitre [rekə'nɔɪtər] (US **reconnoiter**) vt (MIL) reconnaître
reconsider [riːkən'sɪdər] vt reconsidérer
reconstruct [riːkən'strʌkt] vt (building) reconstruire; (crime, policy, system) reconsti-

tuer
record [n 'rekɔːd, vb rɪ'kɔːd] n rapport m, récit m; (of meeting etc) procès-verbal m; (register) registre m; (file) dossier m; (also: **criminal ~**) casier m judiciaire; (MUS: disc) disque m; (SPORT) record m; (COMPUT) article m ♦ vt (set down) noter; (MUS: song etc) enregistrer; **in ~ time** en un temps record inv; **off the ~** ♦ adj officieux(-euse) ♦ adv officieusement; **~ card** n (in file) fiche f; **~ed delivery** n (BRIT: POST): **~ed delivery letter** etc lettre etc recommandée; **~er** n (MUS) flûte f à bec; **~ holder** n (SPORT) détenteur(-trice) du record; **~ing** n (MUS) enregistrement m; **~ player** n tourne-disque m
recount [rɪ'kaunt] vt raconter
re-count ['riːkaunt] n (POL: of votes) deuxième compte m
recoup [rɪ'kuːp] vt: **to ~ one's losses** récupérer ce qu'on a perdu, se refaire
recourse [rɪ'kɔːs] n: **to have ~ to** avoir recours à
recover [rɪ'kʌvər] vt récupérer ♦ vi: **to ~ (from)** (illness) se rétablir (de); (from shock) se remettre (de); **~y** n récupération f; rétablissement m; (ECON) redressement m
recreation [rekrɪ'eɪʃən] n récréation f, détente f; **~al** adj pour la détente, récréatif(-ive)
recruit [rɪ'kruːt] n recrue f ♦ vt recruter
rectangle ['rektæŋgl] n rectangle m; **rectangular** [rek'tæŋgjulər] adj rectangulaire
rectify ['rektɪfaɪ] vt (error) rectifier, corriger
rector ['rektər] n (REL) pasteur m
recuperate [rɪ'kjuːpəreɪt] vi récupérer; (from illness) se rétablir
recur [rɪ'kɜːr] vi se reproduire, (symptoms) réapparaître; **~rence** n répétition f; réapparition f; **~rent** adj périodique, fréquent(e)
recycle [riː'saɪkl] vt recycler; **recycling** n recyclage m
red [red] n rouge m; (POL: pej) rouge m/f ♦ adj rouge; (hair) roux (rousse); **in the ~** (account) à découvert; (business) en déficit; **~ carpet treatment** n réception f en

grande pompe; **R~ Cross** *n* Croix-Rouge *f*; **~currant** *n* groseille *f* (rouge); **~den** *vt*, *vi* rougir

redecorate [ri:'dekəreɪt] *vi* (with wallpaper) retapisser; (with paint) refaire les peintures

redeem [rɪ'di:m] *vt* (debt) rembourser; (sth in pawn) dégager; (fig, also REL) racheter; **~ing** *adj* (feature) qui sauve, qui rachète (le reste)

redeploy [ri:dɪ'plɔɪ] *vt* (resources) réorganiser

red: ~-haired *adj* roux (rousse); **~-handed** *adj*: **to be caught ~-handed** être pris(e) en flagrant délit *or* la main dans le sac; **~head** *n* roux (rousse); **~ herring** *n* (fig) diversion *f*, fausse piste; **~-hot** *adj* chauffé(e) au rouge, brûlant(e)

redirect [ri:daɪ'rekt] *vt* (mail) faire suivre

red light *n*: **to go through a ~** (AUT) brûler un feu rouge; **red-light district** *n* quartier *m* des prostituées

redo [ri:'du:] (irreg) *vt* refaire

redress [rɪ'dres] *n* réparation *f* ♦ *vt* redresser

red: R~ Sea *n* mer Rouge *f*; **~skin** *n* Peau-Rouge *m/f*; **~ tape** *n* (fig) paperasserie (administrative)

reduce [rɪ'dju:s] *vt* réduire; (lower) abaisser; **"~ speed now"** (AUT) "ralentir"; **reduction** [rɪ'dʌkʃən] *n* réduction *f*; (discount) rabais *m*

redundancy [rɪ'dʌndənsɪ] (BRIT) *n* licenciement *m*, mise *f* au chômage

redundant [rɪ'dʌndnt] *adj* (BRIT: worker) mis(e) au chômage, licencié(e); (detail, object) superflu(e); **to be made ~** être licencié(e), être mis(e) au chômage

reed [ri:d] *n* (BOT) roseau *m*; (MUS: of clarinet etc) anche *f*

reef [ri:f] *n* (at sea) récif *m*, écueil *m*

reek [ri:k] *vi*: **to ~ (of)** puer, empester

reel [ri:l] *n* bobine *f*; (FISHING) moulinet *m*; (CINEMA) bande *f*; (dance) quadrille écossais ♦ *vi* (sway) chanceler; **~ in** *vt* (fish, line) ramener

ref [ref] (inf) *n* abbr (= referee) arbitre *m*

refectory [rɪ'fektərɪ] *n* réfectoire *m*

refer [rɪ'fə:r] *vt*: **to ~ sb to** (inquirer: for information, patient: to specialist) adresser qn à; (reader: to text) renvoyer qn à; (dispute, decision): **to ~ sth to** soumettre qch à ♦ *vi*: **~ to** (allude to) parler de, faire allusion à; (consult) se reporter à

referee [refə'ri:] *n* arbitre *m*; (BRIT: for job application) répondant(e)

reference ['refrəns] *n* référence *f*, renvoi *m*; (mention) allusion *f*, mention *f*; (for job application: letter) références, lettre *f* de recommandation; **with ~ to** (COMM: in letter) me référant à, suite à; **~ book** *n* ouvrage *m* de référence

refill [vb ri:'fɪl, n 'ri:fɪl] *vt* remplir à nouveau; (pen, lighter etc) recharger ♦ *n* (for pen etc) recharge *f*

refine [rɪ'faɪn] *vt* (sugar, oil) raffiner; (taste) affiner; (theory, idea) fignoler (inf); **~d** *adj* (person, taste) raffiné(e); **~ry** *n* raffinerie *f*

reflect [rɪ'flekt] *vt* (light, image) refléter, réfléter; (fig) refléter ♦ *vi* (think) réfléchir, méditer; **it ~s badly on him** cela le discrédite; **it ~s well on him** c'est tout à son honneur; **~ion** [rɪ'flekʃən] *n* réflexion *f*; (image) reflet *m*; (criticism): **~ion on** critique *f* de; atteinte *f* à; **on ~ion** réflexion faite

reflex ['ri:fleks] *adj* (LING) réfléxe *m*; **~ive** [rɪ'fleksɪv] *adj* (LING) réfléchi(e)

reform [rɪ'fɔ:m] *n* réforme *f* ♦ *vt* réformer; **~atory** [rɪ'fɔ:mətərɪ] (US) *n* ≃ centre *m* d'éducation surveillée

refrain [rɪ'freɪn] *vi*: **to ~ from doing** s'abstenir de faire ♦ *n* refrain *m*

refresh [rɪ'freʃ] *vt* rafraîchir; (subj: sleep) reposer; **~er course** (BRIT) *n* cours *m* de recyclage; **~ing** *adj* (drink) rafraîchissant(e); (sleep) réparateur(-trice); **~ments** *npl* rafraîchissements *mpl*

refrigerator [rɪ'frɪdʒəreɪtər] *n* réfrigérateur *m*, frigidaire ® *m*

refuel [ri:'fjuəl] *vi* se ravitailler en carburant

refuge ['refju:dʒ] *n* refuge *m*; **to take ~ in** se réfugier dans; **~e** [refju'dʒi:] *n* réfugié(e)

refund [n 'ri:fʌnd, vb rɪ'fʌnd] *n* remboursement *m* ♦ *vt* rembourser

refurbish [riːˈfəːbɪʃ] *vt* remettre à neuf

refusal [rɪˈfjuːzəl] *n* refus *m*; **to have first ~ on** avoir droit de préemption sur

refuse¹ [rɪˈfjuːz] *vt, vi* refuser

refuse² [ˈrɛfjuːs] *n* ordures *fpl*, détritus *mpl*; **~ collection** *n* ramassage *m* d'ordures

regain [rɪˈɡeɪn] *vt* regagner; retrouver

regal [ˈriːɡl] *adj* royal(e)

regard [rɪˈɡɑːd] *n* respect *m*, estime *f*, considération *f* ♦ *vt* considérer; **to give one's ~s to** faire ses amitiés à; **"with kindest ~s"** "bien amicalement"; **as ~s, with ~ to** = regarding; **~ing** *prep* en ce qui concerne; **~less** *adv* quand même; **~less of** sans se soucier de

régime [reɪˈʒiːm] *n* régime *m*

regiment [ˈrɛdʒɪmənt] *n* régiment *m*; **~al** [rɛdʒɪˈmɛntl] *adj* d'un *or* du régiment

region [ˈriːdʒən] *n* région *f*; **in the ~ of** (*fig*) aux alentours de; **~al** *adj* régional(e)

register [ˈrɛdʒɪstər] *n* registre *m*; (*also:* **electoral ~**) liste électorale ♦ *vt* enregistrer; (*birth, death*) déclarer; (*vehicle*) immatriculer; (*POST: letter*) envoyer en recommandé; (*subj: instrument*) marquer ♦ *vi* s'inscrire; (*at hotel*) signer le registre; (*make impression*) être (bien) compris(e); **~ed** *adj* (*letter, parcel*) recommandé(e); **~ed trademark** *n* marque déposée. **registrar** [ˈrɛdʒɪstrɑː] *n* officier *m* de l'état civil; **registration** [rɛdʒɪsˈtreɪʃən] *n* enregistrement *m*; (*BRIT: AUT: also:* **registration number**) numéro *m* d'immatriculation

registry [ˈrɛdʒɪstrɪ] *n* bureau *m* de l'enregistrement; **~ office** (*BRIT*) *n* bureau *m* de l'état civil; **to get married in a ~ office** ≃ se marier à la mairie

regret [rɪˈɡrɛt] *n* regret *m* ♦ *vt* regretter; **~fully** *adv* à *or* avec regret

regular [ˈrɛɡjulər] *adj* régulier(-ère); (*usual*) habituel(le); (*soldier*) de métier ♦ *n* (*client etc*) habitué(e); **~ly** *adv* régulièrement

regulate [ˈrɛɡjuleɪt] *vt* régler; **regulation** [rɛɡjuˈleɪʃən] *n* (*rule*) règlement *m*; (*adjust-*

ment) réglage *m*

rehabilitation [ˈriːəbɪlɪˈteɪʃən] *n* (*of offender*) réinsertion *f*; (*of addict*) réadaptation *f*

rehearsal [rɪˈhəːsəl] *n* répétition *f*

rehearse [rɪˈhəːs] *vt* répéter

reign [reɪn] *n* règne *m* ♦ *vi* régner

reimburse [riːɪmˈbəːs] *vt* rembourser

rein [reɪn] *n* (*for horse*) rêne *f*

reindeer [ˈreɪndɪər] *n, pl inv* renne *m*

reinforce [riːɪnˈfɔːs] *vt* renforcer; **~d concrete** *n* béton armé; **~ments** *npl* (*MIL*) renfort(s) *m(pl)*

reinstate [riːɪnˈsteɪt] *vt* rétablir, réintégrer

reject [*n* ˈriːdʒɛkt, *vb* rɪˈdʒɛkt] *n* (*COMM*) article *m* de rebut ♦ *vt* refuser; (*idea*) rejeter; **~ion** *n* rejet *m*, refus *m*

rejoice [rɪˈdʒɔɪs] *vi:* **to ~ (at** *or* **over)** se réjouir (de)

rejuvenate [rɪˈdʒuːvəneɪt] *vt* rajeunir

relapse [rɪˈlæps] *n* (*MED*) rechute *f*

relate [rɪˈleɪt] *vt* (*tell*) raconter; (*connect*) établir un rapport entre ♦ *vi:* **this ~s to** cela se rapporte à; **to ~ to sb** entretenir des rapports avec qn; **~d** *adj* apparenté(e); **relating to** *prep* concernant

relation [rɪˈleɪʃən] *n* (*person*) parent(e); (*link*) rapport *m*, lien *m*; **~ship** *n* rapport *m*, lien *m*; (*personal ties*) relations *fpl*, rapports; (*also:* **family ~ship**) lien de parenté

relative [ˈrɛlətɪv] *n* parent(e) ♦ *adj* relatif(-ive); **all her ~s** toute sa famille; **~ly** *adv* relativement

relax [rɪˈlæks] *vi* (*muscle*) se relâcher; (*person: unwind*) se détendre ♦ *vt* relâcher; (*mind, person*) détendre; **~ation** [riːlækˈseɪʃən] *n* relâchement *m*; (*of mind*) détente *f*, relaxation *f*; (*recreation*) détente, délassement *m*; **~ed** *adj* détendu(e); **~ing** *adj* délassant(e)

relay [*n* ˈriːleɪ, *vb* rɪˈleɪ] *n* (*SPORT*) course *f* de relais ♦ *vt* (*message*) retransmettre, relayer

release [rɪˈliːs] *n* (*from prison, obligation*) libération *f*; (*of gas etc*) émission *f*; (*of film etc*) sortie *f*; (*new recording*) disque *m* ♦ *vt* (*prisoner*) libérer; (*gas etc*) émettre, dégager; (*free: from wreckage etc*) dégager;

(*TECH: catch, spring etc*) faire jouer; (*book, film*) sortir; (*report, news*) rendre public, publier

relegate ['relɪgeɪt] vt reléguer; (*BRIT: SPORT*): **to be ~d** descendre dans une division inférieure

relent [rɪ'lent] vi se laisser fléchir; **~less** adj implacable; (*unceasing*) continuel(le)

relevant ['relɪvənt] adj (*question*) pertinent(e); (*fact*) significatif(-ive); (*information*) utile; **~ to** ayant rapport à, approprié à

reliable [rɪ'laɪəbl] adj (*person, firm*) sérieux(-euse), fiable; (*method, machine*) fiable; (*news, information*) sûr(e); **reliably** adv: **to be reliably informed** savoir de source sûre

reliance [rɪ'laɪəns] n: **~ (on)** (*person*) confiance f (en); (*drugs, promises*) besoin m (de), dépendance f (de)

relic ['relɪk] n (*REL*) relique f; (*of the past*) vestige m

relief [rɪ'liːf] n (*from pain, anxiety etc*) soulagement m; (*help, supplies*) secours m(pl); (*ART, GEO*) relief m

relieve [rɪ'liːv] vt (*pain, patient*) soulager; (*fear, worry*) dissiper; (*bring help*) secourir; (*take over from: gen*) relayer; (: *guard*) relever; **to ~ sb of sth** débarrasser qn de qch; **to ~ o.s.** se soulager

religion [rɪ'lɪdʒən] n religion f; **religious** adj religieux(-euse); (*book*) de piété

relinquish [rɪ'lɪŋkwɪʃ] vt abandonner; (*plan, habit*) renoncer à

relish ['relɪʃ] n (*CULIN*) condiment m; (*enjoyment*) délectation f ♦ vt (*food etc*) savourer; **to ~ doing** se délecter à faire

relocate [riːləʊ'keɪt] vt installer ailleurs ♦ vi déménager, s'installer ailleurs

reluctance [rɪ'lʌktəns] n répugnance f

reluctant [rɪ'lʌktənt] adj peu disposé(e), qui hésite; **~ly** adv à contrecœur

rely on [rɪ'laɪ-] vt fus (*be dependent*) dépendre de; (*trust*) compter sur

remain [rɪ'meɪn] vi rester; **~der** n reste m; **~ing** adj qui reste; **~s** npl restes mpl

remake ['riːmeɪk] n (*CINEMA*) remake m

remand [rɪ'mɑːnd] n: **on ~** en détention préventive ♦ vt: **to be ~ed in custody** être placé(e) en détention préventive

remark [rɪ'mɑːk] n remarque f, observation f ♦ vt (faire) remarquer, dire; **~able** adj remarquable; **~ably** adv remarquablement

remarry [riː'mærɪ] vi se remarier

remedial [rɪ'miːdɪəl] adj (*tuition, classes*) de rattrapage; **~ exercises** gymnastique corrective

remedy ['remədɪ] n: **~ (for)** remède m (contre or à) ♦ vt remédier à

remember [rɪ'membər] vt se rappeler, se souvenir de; (*send greetings*): **~ me to him** saluez-le de ma part; **remembrance** n souvenir m; mémoire f; **Remembrance Day** n le jour de l'Armistice

---

Remembrance Sunday

ⓘ Remembrance Sunday ou Remembrance Day *est le dimanche le plus proche du 11 novembre, jour où la Première Guerre mondiale a officiellement pris fin, et rend hommage aux victimes des deux guerres mondiales. À cette occasion, un silence de deux minutes est observé à 11 h, heure de la signature de l'armistice avec l'Allemagne en 1918; certains membres de la famille royale et du gouvernement déposent des gerbes de coquelicots au cénotaphe de Whitehall, et des couronnes sont placées sur les monuments aux morts dans toute la Grande-Bretagne; par ailleurs, les gens portent des coquelicots artificiels fabriqués et vendus par des membres de la légion britannique blessés au combat, au profit des blessés de guerre et de leur famille.*

---

remind [rɪ'maɪnd] vt: **to ~ sb of** rappeler à qn; **to ~ sb to do** faire penser à qn à faire, rappeler à qn qu'il doit faire; **~er** n (*souvenir*) souvenir m; (*letter*) rappel m

reminisce [remɪ'nɪs] vi: **to ~ (about)** évoquer ses souvenirs (de); **~nt** adj: **to be ~nt of** rappeler, faire penser à

remiss [rɪ'mɪs] *adj* négligent(e); **~ion** *n* (*of illness, sins*) rémission *f*; (*of debt, prison sentence*) remise *f*

remit [rɪ'mɪt] *vt* (*send: money*) envoyer; **~tance** *n* paiement *m*

remnant ['remnant] *n* reste *m*, restant *m*; (*of cloth*) coupon *m*; **~s** *npl* (COMM) fins *fpl* de série

remorse [rɪ'mɔ:s] *n* remords *m*; **~ful** *adj* plein(e) de remords; **~less** *adj* (*fig*) impitoyable

remote [rɪ'məut] *adj* éloigné(e), lointain(e); (*person*) distant(e); (*possibility*) vague; **~ control** *n* télécommande *f*; **~ly** *adv* au loin; (*slightly*) très vaguement

remould ['ri:məuld] (BRIT) *n* (*tyre*) pneu rechapé

removable [rɪ'mu:vəbl] *adj* (*detachable*) amovible

removal [rɪ'mu:vəl] *n* (*taking away*) enlèvement *m*; suppression *f*; (BRIT: *from house*) déménagement *m*; (*from office: dismissal*) renvoi *m*; (*of stain*) nettoyage *m*; (MED) ablation *f*; **~ van** (BRIT) *n* camion *m* de déménagement

remove [rɪ'mu:v] *vt* enlever, retirer; (*employee*) renvoyer; (*stain*) faire partir; (*abuse*) supprimer; (*doubt*) chasser

render ['rendəʳ] *vt* rendre; **~ing** *n* (MUS *etc*) interprétation *f*

rendezvous ['rɔndɪvu:] *n* rendez-vous *m inv*

renew [rɪ'nju:] *vt* renouveler; (*negotiations*) reprendre; (*acquaintance*) renouer; **~able** *adj* (*energy*) renouvelable; **~al** *n* renouvellement *m*; reprise *f*

renounce [rɪ'nauns] *vt* renoncer à

renovate ['renəveɪt] *vt* rénover; (*art work*) restaurer

renown [rɪ'naun] *n* renommée *f*; **~ed** *adj* renommé(e)

rent [rent] *n* loyer *m* ♦ *vt* louer; **~al** *n* (*for television, car*) (prix *m* de) location *f*

reorganize [ri:'ɔ:gənaɪz] *vt* réorganiser

rep [rep] *n* *abbr* = **representative**; **repertory**

repair [rɪ'pɛəʳ] *n* réparation *f* ♦ *vt* réparer;

in good/bad ~ en bon/mauvais état; **~ kit** *n* trousse *f* de réparation

repatriate [ri:'pætrɪeɪt] *vt* rapatrier

repay [ri:'peɪ] (*irreg*) *vt* (*money, creditor*) rembourser; (*sb's efforts*) récompenser; **~ment** *n* remboursement *m*

repeal [rɪ'pi:l] *n* (*of law*) abrogation *f* ♦ *vt* (*law*) abroger

repeat [rɪ'pi:t] *n* (RADIO, TV) reprise *f* ♦ *vt* répéter; (COMM: *order*) renouveler; (SCOL: *a class*) redoubler ♦ *vi* répéter; **~edly** *adv* souvent, à plusieurs reprises

repel [rɪ'pel] *vt* repousser; **~lent** *adj* repoussant(e) ♦ *n*: **insect ~lent** insectifuge *m*

repent [rɪ'pent] *vi*: **to ~ (of)** se repentir (de); **~ance** *n* repentir *m*

repertory ['repətərɪ] *n* (*also*: **~ theatre**) théâtre *m* de répertoire

repetition [repɪ'tɪʃən] *n* répétition *f*

repetitive [rɪ'petɪtɪv] *adj* (*movement, work*) répétitif(-ive); (*speech*) plein(e) de redites

replace [rɪ'pleɪs] *vt* (*put back*) remettre, replacer; (*take the place of*) remplacer; **~ment** *n* (*substitution*) remplacement *m*; (*person*) remplaçant(e)

replay ['ri:pleɪ] *n* (*of match*) match rejoué; (*of tape, film*) répétition *f*

replenish [rɪ'plenɪʃ] *vt* (*glass*) remplir (de nouveau); (*stock etc*) réapprovisionner

replica ['replɪkə] *n* réplique *f*, copie exacte

reply [rɪ'plaɪ] *n* réponse *f* ♦ *vi* répondre

report [rɪ'pɔ:t] *n* rapport *m*; (PRESS *etc*) reportage *m*; (BRIT: *also*: **school ~**) bulletin *m* (scolaire); (*of gun*) détonation *f* ♦ *vt* rapporter, faire un compte rendu de; (PRESS *etc*) faire un reportage sur; (*bring to notice: occurrence*) signaler ♦ *vi* (*make a ~*) faire un rapport (*or* un reportage); (*present o.s.*): **to ~ (to sb)** se présenter (chez qn); (*be responsible to*): **to ~ to sb** être sous les ordres de qn; **~ card** (US, SCOTTISH) *n* bulletin *m* scolaire; **~edly** *adv*: **she is ~edly living in ...** elle habiterait ...; **he ~edly told them to ...** il leur aurait ordonné de ...; **~er** *n* reporter *m*

repose [rɪ'pəuz] *n*: **in ~** en *or* au repos

represent [rɛprɪ'zɛnt] vt représenter; (view, belief) présenter, expliquer; (describe): **to ~ sth as** présenter or décrire qch comme; **~ation** [rɛprɪzɛn'teɪʃən] n représentation f; **~ations** npl (protest) démarche f; **~ative** [rɛprɪ'zɛntətɪv] n représentant(e); (US: POL) député m ♦ adj représentatif(-ive), caractéristique

repress [rɪ'prɛs] vt réprimer; **~ion** n répression f

reprieve [rɪ'priːv] n (LAW) grâce f; (fig) sursis m, délai m

reprisal [rɪ'praɪzl] n: **~s** ♦ npl représailles fpl

reproach [rɪ'prəʊtʃ] vt: **to ~ sb with sth** reprocher qch à qn; **~ful** adj de reproche

reproduce [riːprə'djuːs] vt reproduire ♦ vi se reproduire; **reproduction** [riːprə'dʌkʃən] n reproduction f

reproof [rɪ'pruːf] n reproche m

reptile ['rɛptaɪl] n reptile m

republic [rɪ'pʌblɪk] n république f; **~an** adj républicain(e)

repudiate [rɪ'pjuːdɪeɪt] vt répudier, rejeter

repulsive [rɪ'pʌlsɪv] adj repoussant(e), répulsif(-ive)

reputable ['rɛpjutəbl] adj de bonne réputation; (occupation) honorable

reputation [rɛpju'teɪʃən] n réputation f

reputed [rɪ'pjuːtɪd] adj (supposed) supposé(e); **~ly** adv d'après ce qu'on dit

request [rɪ'kwɛst] n demande f; (formal) requête f ♦ vt: **to ~ (of or from sb)** demander (à qn); **~ stop** (BRIT) n (for bus) arrêt facultatif

require [rɪ'kwaɪər] vt (need: subj: person) avoir besoin de; (: thing, situation) demander; (want) exiger; (order): **to ~ sb to do sth/sth of sb** exiger que qn fasse qch/qch de qn; **~ment** n exigence f; besoin m; condition requise

requisition [rɛkwɪ'zɪʃən] n: **~ (for)** demande f (de) ♦ vt (MIL) réquisitionner

rescue ['rɛskjuː] n (from accident) sauvetage m; (help) secours mpl ♦ vt sauver; **~ party** n équipe f de sauvetage; **~r** n sauveteur m

research [rɪ'səːtʃ] n recherche(s) f(pl) ♦ vt faire des recherches sur

resemblance [rɪ'zɛmbləns] n ressemblance f

resemble [rɪ'zɛmbl] vt ressembler à

resent [rɪ'zɛnt] vt être contrarié(e) par; **~ful** adj irrité(e), plein(e) de ressentiment; **~ment** n ressentiment m

reservation [rɛzə'veɪʃən] n (booking) réservation f; (doubt) réserve f; (for tribe) réserve; **to make a ~ (in a hotel/a restaurant/on a plane)** réserver or retenir une chambre/une table/une place

reserve [rɪ'zəːv] n réserve f; (SPORT) remplaçant(e) ♦ vt (seats etc) réserver, retenir; **~s** npl (MIL) réservistes mpl; **in ~** en réserve; **~d** adj réservé(e)

reshuffle [riː'ʃʌfl] n: **Cabinet ~** (POL) remaniement ministériel

residence ['rɛzɪdəns] n résidence f; **~ permit** (BRIT) n permis m de séjour

resident ['rɛzɪdənt] n résident(e) ♦ adj résidant(e); **~ial** [rɛzɪ'dɛnʃəl] adj résidentiel(le); (course) avec hébergement sur place; **~ial school** n internat m

residue ['rɛzɪdjuː] n reste m; (CHEM, PHYSICS) résidu m

resign [rɪ'zaɪn] vt (one's post) démissionner de ♦ vi démissionner; **to ~ o.s. to** se résigner à; **~ation** [rɛzɪg'neɪʃən] n (of post) démission f; (state of mind) résignation f; **~ed** adj résigné(e)

resilient [rɪ'zɪlɪənt] adj (material) élastique; (person) qui réagit, qui a du ressort

resist [rɪ'zɪst] vt résister à; **~ance** n résistance f

resit [riː'sɪt] vt (exam) repasser ♦ n deuxième session f (d'un examen)

resolution [rɛzə'luːʃən] n résolution f

resolve [rɪ'zɔlv] n résolution f ♦ vt (problem) résoudre ♦ vi: **to ~ to do** résoudre or décider de faire

resort [rɪ'zɔːt] n (seaside town) station f balnéaire; (ski ~) station de ski; (recourse) recours m ♦ vi: **to ~ to** avoir recours à; **in the last ~** en dernier ressort

resounding [rɪ'zaʊndɪŋ] adj retentissant(e)

resource [rɪˈsɔːs] n ressource f; **~s** npl (supplies, wealth etc) ressources; **~ful** adj ingénieux(-euse), débrouillard(e)

respect [rɪsˈpɛkt] n respect m ♦ vt respecter; **~s** npl (compliments) respects, hommages mpl; **with ~ to** en ce qui concerne; **in this ~** à cet égard; **~able** adj respectable; **~ful** adj respectueux(-euse); **~ively** adv respectivement

respite [ˈrɛspaɪt] n répit m

respond [rɪsˈpɔnd] vi répondre; (react) réagir; **response** n réponse f; réaction f

responsibility [rɪspɔnsɪˈbɪlɪtɪ] n responsabilité f

responsible [rɪsˈpɔnsɪbl] adj (liable): **~ (for)** responsable (de); (person) digne de confiance; (job) qui comporte des responsabilités

responsive [rɪsˈpɔnsɪv] adj qui réagit; (person) qui n'est pas réservé(e) or indifférent(e)

rest [rɛst] n repos m; (stop) arrêt m, pause f; (MUS) silence m; (support) support m, appui m; (remainder) reste m, restant m ♦ vi se reposer; (be supported): **to ~ on** appuyer or reposer sur; (remain) rester ♦ vt (lean): **to ~ sth on/against** appuyer qch sur/contre; **the ~ of them** les autres; **it ~s with him to ...** c'est à lui de ...

restaurant [ˈrɛstərɔn] n restaurant m; **~ car** (BRIT) n wagon-restaurant m

restful [ˈrɛstful] adj reposant(e)

restive [ˈrɛstɪv] adj agité(e), impatient(e); (horse) rétif(-ive)

restless [ˈrɛstlɪs] adj agité(e)

restoration [rɛstəˈreɪʃən] n restauration f; restitution f; rétablissement m

restore [rɪsˈtɔːʳ] vt (building) restaurer; (sth stolen) restituer; (peace, health) rétablir; **to ~ to** (former state) ramener à

restrain [rɪsˈtreɪn] vt contenir; (person): **to ~ (from doing)** retenir (de faire); **~ed** adj (style) sobre; (manner) mesuré(e); **~t** n (restriction) contrainte f; (moderation) retenue f

restrict [rɪsˈtrɪkt] vt restreindre, limiter; **~ion** n restriction f, limitation f

rest room (US) n toilettes fpl

result [rɪˈzʌlt] n résultat m ♦ vi: **to ~ in** aboutir à, se terminer par; **as a ~ of** à la suite de

resume [rɪˈzjuːm] vt, vi (work, journey) reprendre

résumé [ˈreɪzjuːmeɪ] n résumé m; (US) curriculum vitae m

resumption [rɪˈzʌmpʃən] n reprise f

resurgence [rɪˈsɜːdʒəns] n (of energy, activity) regain m

resurrection [rɛzəˈrɛkʃən] n résurrection f

resuscitate [rɪˈsʌsɪteɪt] vt (MED) réanimer

retail [ˈriːteɪl] adj de or au détail ♦ adv au détail; **~er** n détaillant(e); **~ price** n prix m de détail

retain [rɪˈteɪn] vt (keep) garder, conserver; **~er** n (fee) acompte m, provision f

retaliate [rɪˈtælɪeɪt] vi: **to ~ (against)** se venger (de); **retaliation** [rɪtælɪˈeɪʃən] n représailles fpl, vengeance f

retarded [rɪˈtɑːdɪd] adj retardé(e)

retch [rɛtʃ] vi avoir des haut-le-cœur

retentive [rɪˈtɛntɪv] adj: **~ memory** excellente mémoire

retina [ˈrɛtɪnə] n rétine f

retire [rɪˈtaɪəʳ] vi (give up work) prendre sa retraite; (withdraw) se retirer, partir; (go to bed) (aller) se coucher; **~d** adj (person) retraité(e); **~ment** n retraite f; **retiring** adj (shy) réservé(e); (leaving) sortant(e)

retort [rɪˈtɔːt] vi riposter

retrace [riːˈtreɪs] vt: **to ~ one's steps** revenir sur ses pas

retract [rɪˈtrækt] vt (statement, claws) rétracter; (undercarriage, aerial) rentrer, escamoter

retrain [riːˈtreɪn] vt (worker) recycler

retread [ˈriːtrɛd] n (tyre) pneu rechapé

retreat [rɪˈtriːt] n retraite f ♦ vi battre en retraite

retribution [rɛtrɪˈbjuːʃən] n châtiment m

retrieval [rɪˈtriːvəl] n (see vb) récupération f; réparation f

retrieve [rɪˈtriːv] vt (sth lost) récupérer; (situation, honour) sauver; (error, loss) réparer; ~r *n* chien *m* d'arrêt

retrospect ['retrəspekt] *n*: **in ~** rétrospectivement, après coup; **~ive** [retrə'spektɪv] *adj* rétrospectif(-ive); (*law*) rétroactif(-ive)

return [rɪ'tə:n] *n* (*going or coming back*) retour *m*; (*of sth stolen etc*) restitution *f*; (*FINANCE: from land, shares*) rendement *m*, rapport *m* ♦ *cpd* (*journey*) de retour; (*BRIT: ticket*) aller et retour; (*match*) retour ♦ *vi* (*come back*) revenir; (*go back*) retourner ♦ *vt* rendre; (*bring back*) rapporter; (*send back; also: ball*) renvoyer; (*put back*) remettre; (*POL: candidate*) élire; **~s** *npl* (*COMM*) recettes *fpl*; (*FINANCE*) bénéfices *mpl*; **in ~ (for)** en échange (de); **by ~ (of post)** par retour (du courrier); **many happy ~s (of the day)!** bon anniversaire!

reunion [riː'juːnɪən] *n* réunion *f*

reunite [riːjuː'naɪt] *vt* réunir

reuse [riː'juːz] *vt* réutiliser

rev [rev] *n abbr* (*AUT: = revolution*) tour *m* ♦ *vt* (*also:* **rev up**) emballer

revamp [riː'væmp] *vt* (*firm, system etc*) réorganiser

reveal [rɪ'viːl] *vt* (*make known*) révéler; (*display*) laisser voir; **~ing** *adj* révélateur(-trice); (*dress*) au décolleté généreux *or* suggestif

revel ['revl] *vi*: **to ~ in sth/in doing** se délecter de qch/à faire

revenge [rɪ'vendʒ] *n* vengeance *f*; **to take ~ on** (*enemy*) se venger sur

revenue ['revənjuː] *n* revenu *m*

reverberate [rɪ'vəːbəreɪt] *vi* (*sound*) retentir, se répercuter; (*fig: shock etc*) se propager

reverence ['revərəns] *n* vénération *f*, révérence *f*

Reverend ['revərənd] *adj* (*in titles*): **the ~ John Smith** (*Anglican*) le révérend John Smith; (*Catholic*) l'abbé (John) Smith; (*Protestant*) le pasteur (John) Smith

reversal [rɪ'vəːsl] *n* (*of opinion*) revirement *m*; (*of order*) renversement *m*; (*of direction*) changement *m*

reverse [rɪ'vəːs] *n* contraire *m*, opposé *m*; (*back*) dos *m*, envers *m*; (*of paper*) verso *m*; (*of coin; also:* setback) revers *m*; (*AUT: also:* **~ gear**) marche *f* arrière ♦ *adj* (*order, direction*) opposé(e), inverse ♦ *vt* (*order, position*) changer, inverser; (*direction, policy*) changer complètement de; (*decision*) annuler; (*roles*) renverser; (*car*) faire marche arrière avec ♦ *vi* (*BRIT: AUT*) faire marche arrière; **he ~d (the car) into a wall** il a embouti un mur en marche arrière; **~d charge call** (*BRIT*) *n* (*TEL*) communication *f* en PCV; **reversing lights** (*BRIT*) *npl* (*AUT*) feux *mpl* de marche arrière *or* de recul

revert [rɪ'vəːt] *vi*: **to ~ to** revenir à, retourner à

review [rɪ'vjuː] *n* revue *f*; (*of book, film*) critique *f*, compte rendu *m*; (*of situation, policy*) examen *m*, bilan *m* ♦ *vt* passer en revue; faire la critique de; examiner; **~er** *n* critique *m*

revise [rɪ'vaɪz] *vt* réviser, modifier; (*manuscript*) revoir, corriger ♦ *vi* (*study*) réviser; **revision** [rɪ'vɪʒən] *n* révision *f*

revival [rɪ'vaɪvl] *n* reprise *f*; (*recovery*) rétablissement *m*; (*of faith*) renouveau *m*

revive [rɪ'vaɪv] *vt* (*person*) ranimer; (*custom*) rétablir; (*economy*) relancer; (*hope, courage*) raviver, faire renaître; (*play*) reprendre ♦ *vi* (*person*) reprendre connaissance; (: *from ill health*) se rétablir; (*hope etc*) renaître; (*activity*) reprendre

revoke [rɪ'vəuk] *vt* révoquer; (*law*) abroger

revolt [rɪ'vəult] *n* révolte *f* ♦ *vi* se révolter, se rebeller ♦ *vt* révolter, dégoûter; **~ing** *adj* dégoûtant(e)

revolution [revə'luːʃən] *n* révolution *f*; (*of wheel etc*) tour *m*, révolution; **~ary** *adj* révolutionnaire ♦ *n* révolutionnaire *m/f*

revolve [rɪ'vɔlv] *vi* tourner

revolver [rɪ'vɔlvə*] *n* revolver *m*

revolving [rɪ'vɔlvɪŋ] *adj* tournant(e); (*chair*) pivotant(e); **~ door** *n* (*porte f à*) tambour *m*

revulsion [rɪ'vʌlʃən] *n* dégoût *m*, répugnance *f*

reward [rɪ'wɔːd] *n* récompense *f* ♦ *vt*: **to ~ (for)** récompenser (de); **~ing** *adj* (*fig*) qui (en) vaut la peine, gratifiant(e)

rewind [riː'waɪnd] (*irreg*) *vt* (*tape*) rembobiner

rewire [riː'waɪər] *vt* (*house*) refaire l'installation électrique de

rheumatism ['ruːmətɪzəm] *n* rhumatisme *m*

Rhine [raɪn] *n* Rhin *m*

rhinoceros [raɪ'nɔsərəs] *n* rhinocéros *m*

Rhone [rəun] *n* Rhône *m*

rhubarb ['ruːbɑːb] *n* rhubarbe *f*

rhyme [raɪm] *n* rime *f*; (*verse*) vers *mpl*

rhythm ['rɪðm] *n* rythme *m*

rib [rɪb] *n* (*ANAT*) côte *f*

ribbon ['rɪbən] *n* ruban *m*; **in ~s** (*torn*) en lambeaux

rice [raɪs] *n* riz *m*; **~ pudding** *n* riz au lait

rich [rɪtʃ] *adj* riche; (*gift, clothes*) somptueux(-euse) ♦ *npl*: **the ~** les riches *mpl*; **~es** *npl* richesses *fpl*; **~ly** *adv* richement; (*deserved, earned*) largement

rickets ['rɪkɪts] *n* rachitisme *m*

rid [rɪd] (*pt, pp* **rid**) *vt*: **to ~ sb of** débarrasser qn de; **to get ~ of** se débarrasser de

riddle ['rɪdl] *n* (*puzzle*) énigme *f* ♦ *vt*: **to be ~d with** être criblé(e) de; (*fig: guilt, corruption, doubts*) être en proie à

ride [raɪd] (*pt* **rode**, *pp* **ridden**) *n* promenade *f*, tour *m*; (*distance covered*) trajet *m* ♦ *vi* (*as sport*) monter (à cheval), faire du cheval; (*go somewhere: on horse, bicycle*) aller (à cheval *or* bicyclette *etc*); (*journey: on bicycle, motorcycle, bus*) rouler ♦ *vt* (*a certain horse*) monter; (*distance*) parcourir, faire; **to take sb for a ~** (*fig*) faire marcher qn; **to ~ a horse/bicycle** monter à cheval/à bicyclette; **~r** *n* cavalier(-ère); (*in race*) jockey *m*; (*on bicycle*) cycliste *m/f*; (*on motorcycle*) motocycliste *m/f*

ridge [rɪdʒ] *n* (*of roof, mountain*) arête *f*; (*of hill*) faîte *m*; (*on object*) strie *f*

ridicule ['rɪdɪkjuːl] *n* ridicule *m*; dérision *f*

ridiculous [rɪ'dɪkjuləs] *adj* ridicule

riding ['raɪdɪŋ] *n* équitation *f*; **~ school** *n* manège *m*, école *f* d'équitation

rife [raɪf] *adj* répandu(e); **~ with** abondant(e) en, plein(e) de

riffraff ['rɪfræf] *n* racaille *f*

rifle ['raɪfl] *n* fusil *m* (à canon rayé) ♦ *vt* vider, dévaliser; **~ through** *vt* (*belongings*) fouiller; (*papers*) feuilleter; **~ range** *n* champ *m* de tir; (*at fair*) stand *m* de tir

rift [rɪft] *n* fente *f*, fissure *f*; (*fig: disagreement*) désaccord *m*

rig [rɪg] *n* (*also:* **oil ~**: *at sea*) plate-forme pétrolière ♦ *vt* (*election etc*) truquer; **~ out** (*BRIT*) *vt*: **to ~ out as/in** habiller en/de; **~ up** *vt* arranger, faire avec des moyens de fortune; **~ging** *n* (*NAUT*) gréement *m*

right [raɪt] *adj* (*correctly chosen: answer, road etc*) bon (bonne); (*true*) juste, exact(e); (*suitable*) approprié(e), convenable; (*just*) juste, équitable; (*morally good*) bien *inv*; (*not left*) droit(e) ♦ *n* (*what is morally ~*) bien *m*; (*title, claim*) droit *m*; (*not left*) droite *f* ♦ *adv* (*answer*) correctement, juste; (*treat*) bien, comme il faut; (*not on the left*) à droite ♦ *vt* redresser ♦ *n* (*what is right*) droit(e) ♦ *n* bon!; **to be ~** (*person*) avoir raison; (*answer*) être juste *or* correct(e); (*clock*) à l'heure (juste); **by ~s** en toute justice; **on the ~** à droite; **to be in the ~** avoir raison; **~ now** en ce moment même; tout de suite; **~ in the middle** en plein milieu; **~ away** immédiatement; **~ angle** *n* (*MATH*) angle droit; **~eous** ['raɪtʃəs] *adj* droit(e), vertueux(-euse); (*anger*) justifié(e) ♦ *n* (*what is morally ~*) droit *m* de passage; (*AUT*) priorité *f*; **~-wing** *adj* (*POL*) de droite

rigid ['rɪdʒɪd] *adj* rigide; (*principle, control*) strict(e)

rigmarole ['rɪgmərəul] *n* comédie *f*

rigorous ['rɪgərəs] *adj* rigoureux(-euse)

rile [raɪl] *vt* agacer

rim [rɪm] *n* bord *m*; (*of spectacles*) monture *f*; (*of wheel*) jante *f*

rind [raɪnd] *n* (*of bacon*) couenne *f*; (*of lemon etc*) écorce *f*, zeste *m*; (*of cheese*) croûte *f*

ring [rɪŋ] (*pt* **rang**, *pp* **rung**) *n* anneau *m*;

(*on finger*) bague f; (*also:* **wedding ~**) alliance f; (*of people, objects*) cercle m; (*of spies*) réseau m; (*of smoke etc*) rond m; (*arena*) piste f, arène f; (*for boxing*) ring m; (*sound of bell*) sonnerie f ♦ vi (*telephone, bell*) sonner; (*person: by telephone*) téléphoner; (*also:* **~ out**: *voice, words*) retentir; (*ears*) bourdonner ♦ vt (BRIT: TEL: *also:* **~ up**) téléphoner à, appeler; (*bell*) faire sonner; **to ~ the bell** sonner; **to give sb a ~** (BRIT: TEL) appeler qn; **~ back** (BRIT) vt, vi (TEL) rappeler; **~ off** (BRIT) vi (TEL) raccrocher; **~ up** (BRIT) vt (TEL) appeler; **~ binder** n classeur m à anneaux; **~ing** ['rɪŋɪŋ] n (*of telephone*) sonnerie f; (*of bell*) tintement m; (*in ears*) bourdonnement m; **~ing tone** (BRIT) n (TEL) sonnerie f; **~leader** n (*of gang*) chef m, meneur m; **~lets** npl anglaises fpl; **~ road** (BRIT) n route f de ceinture; (*motorway*) périphérique m; **~tone** n sonnerie f (*de téléphone portable*)

rink [rɪŋk] n (*also:* **ice ~**) patinoire f

rinse [rɪns] vt rincer

riot ['raɪət] n émeute f; (*of flowers, colour*) profusion f ♦ vi faire une émeute, manifester avec violence; **to run ~** se déchaîner; **~ous** adj (*mob, assembly*) séditieux(-euse), déchaîné(e); (*living, behaviour*) débauché(e); (*party*) très animé(e); (*welcome*) délirant(e)

rip [rɪp] n déchirure f ♦ vt déchirer ♦ vi se déchirer; **~cord** n poignée f d'ouverture

ripe [raɪp] adj (*fruit*) mûr(e); (*cheese*) fait(e); **~n** vt mûrir ♦ vi mûrir

rip-off (*inf*) n: **it's a ~~!** c'est de l'arnaque!

ripple ['rɪpl] n ondulation f; (*of applause, laughter*) cascade f ♦ vi onduler

rise [raɪz] (*pt* **rose**, *pp* **risen**) n (*slope*) côte f, pente f; (*hill*) hauteur f; (*increase: in wages:* BRIT) augmentation f; (: *in prices, temperature*) hausse f, augmentation f; (*fig: to power etc*) ascension f ♦ vi s'élever, monter; (*prices, numbers*) augmenter; (*waters*) monter; (*sun; person: from chair, bed*) se lever; (*also:* **~ up**: *tower, building*) s'élever;

(: *rebel*) se révolter; se rebeller; (*in rank*) s'élever; **to give ~ to** donner lieu à; **to ~ to the occasion** se montrer à la hauteur; **~r** n: **to be an early ~r** être matinal(e); **rising** adj (*number, prices*) en hausse; (*tide*) montant(e); (*sun, moon*) levant(e)

risk [rɪsk] n risque m ♦ vt risquer; **at ~** en danger; **at one's own ~** à ses risques et périls; **~y** adj risqué(e)

rite [raɪt] n rite m; **last ~s** derniers sacrements

ritual ['rɪtjuəl] adj rituel(le) ♦ n rituel m

rival ['raɪvl] adj, n rival(e); (*in business*) concurrent(e) ♦ vt (*match*) égaler; **~ry** ['raɪvlrɪ] n rivalité f, concurrence f

river ['rɪvə^r] n rivière f; (*major, also fig*) fleuve m ♦ cpd (*port, traffic*) fluvial(e); **up/down ~** en amont/aval; **~bank** n rive f, berge f; **~bed** n lit m (de rivière/fleuve)

rivet ['rɪvɪt] n rivet m ♦ vt (*fig*) river, fixer

Riviera [rɪvɪ'eərə] n: **the (French) ~** la Côte d'Azur; **the Italian ~** la Riviera (italienne)

road [rəud] n route f; (*in town*) rue f; (*fig*) chemin, voie f; **major/minor ~** route principale *or* à priorité/voie secondaire; **~ accident** n accident m de la circulation; **~block** n barrage routier; **~hog** n chauffard m; **~ map** n carte routière; **~ rage** n comportement très agressif de certains usagers de la route; **~ safety** n sécurité routière; **~side** n bord m de la route, bas-côté m; **~ sign** n panneau m de signalisation; **~way** n chaussée f; **~ works** npl travaux mpl (de réfection des routes); **~worthy** adj en bon état de marche

roam [rəum] vi errer, vagabonder

roar [rɔː^r] n rugissement m; (*of crowd*) hurlements mpl; (*of vehicle, thunder, storm*) grondement m ♦ vi rugir; hurler; gronder; **to ~ with laughter** éclater de rire; **to do a ~ing trade** faire des affaires d'or

roast [rəust] n rôti m ♦ vt (faire) rôtir; (*coffee*) griller, torréfier; **~ beef** n rôti m de bœuf, rosbif m

rob [rɔb] vt (*person*) voler; (*bank*) dévaliser; **to ~ sb of sth** voler *or* dérober qch à qn;

(*fig: deprive*) priver qn de qch; **~ber** *n* bandit *m*, voleur *m*; **~bery** *n* vol *m*

robe [rəub] *n* (*for ceremony etc*) robe *f*; (*also:* **bathrobe**) peignoir *m*; (*US*) couverture *f*

robin [ˈrɔbɪn] *n* rouge-gorge *m*

robot [ˈrəubɔt] *n* robot *m*

robust [rəuˈbʌst] *adj* robuste; (*material, appetite*) solide

rock [rɔk] *n* (*substance*) roche *f*, roc *m*; (*boulder*) rocher *m*; (*US: small stone*) caillou *m*; (*BRIT: sweet*) ≈ sucre *m* d'orge ♦ *vt* (*swing gently: cradle*) balancer; (*: child*) bercer; (*shake*) ébranler, secouer ♦ *vi* (*se*) balancer; être ébranlé(e) *or* secoué(e); **on the ~s** (*drink*) avec des glaçons; (*marriage etc*) en train de craquer; **~ and roll** *n* rock (and roll) *m*, rock'n'roll *m*; **~-bottom** *adj* (*fig: prices*) sacrifié(e); **~ery** *n* (jardin *m* de) rocaille *f*

rocket [ˈrɔkɪt] *n* fusée *f*; (*MIL*) fusée, roquette *f*

rocking chair *n* fauteuil *m* à bascule

rocking horse *n* cheval *m* à bascule

rocky [ˈrɔkɪ] *adj* (*hill*) rocheux(-euse); (*path*) rocailleux(-euse)

rod [rɔd] *n* (*wooden*) baguette *f*; (*metallic*) tringle *f*; (*TECH*) tige *f*; (*also:* **fishing ~**) canne *f* à pêche

rode [rəud] *pt of* **ride**

rodent [ˈrəudnt] *n* rongeur *m*

rodeo [ˈrəudɪəu] (*US*) *n* rodéo *m*

roe [rəu] *n* (*species: also:* **~ deer**) chevreuil *m*; (*of fish: also:* **hard ~**) œufs *mpl* de poisson; **soft ~** laitance *f*

rogue [rəug] *n* coquin(e)

role [rəul] *n* rôle *m*; **~ play** *n* jeu *m* de rôle

roll [rəul] *n* rouleau *m*; (*of banknotes*) liasse *f*; (*also:* **bread ~**) petit pain; (*register*) liste *f*; (*sound: of drums etc*) roulement *m* ♦ *vt* rouler; (*also:* **~ up:** *string*) enrouler; (*: sleeves*) retrousser; (*also:* **~ out:** *pastry*) étendre au rouleau, abaisser ♦ *vi* rouler; **~ about** *vi* rouler ça et là; (*person*) se rouler par terre; **~ around** *vi* = **roll about**; **~ by** *vi* (*time*) s'écouler, passer; **~ over** *vi* se

retourner; **~ up** *vi* (*inf: arrive*) arriver, s'amener ♦ *vt* rouler; **~ call** *n* appel *m*; **~er** *n* rouleau *m*; (*wheel*) roulette *f*; (*for road*) rouleau compresseur; **~er blade** *n* patin *m* en ligne; **~er coaster** *n* montagnes *fpl* russes; **~er skates** *npl* patins *mpl* à roulettes; **~er skating** *n* patin *m* à roulettes; **~ing** *adj* (*landscape*) onduleux(-euse); **~ing pin** *n* rouleau *m* à pâtisserie; **~ing stock** *n* (*RAIL*) matériel roulant

ROM [rɔm] *n abbr* (= *read only memory*) mémoire morte

Roman [ˈrəumən] *adj* romain(e); **~ Catholic** *adj, n* catholique *m/f*

romance [rəˈmæns] *n* (*love affair*) idylle *f*; (*charm*) poésie *f*; (*novel*) roman *m* à l'eau de rose

Romania [rəuˈmeɪnɪə] *n* Roumanie *f*; **~n** *adj* roumain(e) ♦ *n* Roumain(e); (*LING*) roumain *m*

Roman numeral *n* chiffre romain

romantic [rəˈmæntɪk] *adj* romantique; sentimental(e)

Rome [rəum] *n* Rome

romp [rɔmp] *n* jeux bruyants ♦ *vi* (*also:* **~ about**) s'ébattre, jouer bruyamment; **~ers** *npl* barboteuse *f*

roof [ru:f] (*pl* **~s**) *n* toit *m* ♦ *vt* couvrir (d'un toit); **the ~ of the mouth** la voûte du palais; **~ing** *n* toiture *f*; **~ rack** *n* (*AUT*) galerie *f*

rook [ruk] *n* (*bird*) freux *m*; (*CHESS*) tour *f*

room [ru:m] *n* (*in house*) pièce *f*; (*also:* **bedroom**) chambre *f* (à coucher); (*in school etc*) salle *f*; (*space*) place *f*; **~s** *npl* (*lodging*) meublé *m*; **"~s to let"** (*BRIT*) *or* **"~s for rent"** (*US*) "chambres à louer"; **single/double ~** chambre pour une personne/deux personnes; **there is ~ for improvement** cela laisse à désirer; **~ing house** (*US*) *n* maison *f* or immeuble *m* de rapport; **~mate** *n* camarade *m/f* de chambre; **~ service** *n* service *m* des chambres (*dans un hôtel*); **~y** *adj* spacieux(-euse); (*garment*) ample

roost [ru:st] *vi* se jucher

rooster [ˈru:stər] *n* (*esp US*) coq *m*

root [ruːt] *n* (BOT, MATH) racine *f*; (*fig: of problem*) origine *f*, fond *m* ♦ *vi* (*plant*) s'enraciner; ~ **about** *vi* (*fig*) fouiller; ~ **for** *vt fus* encourager, applaudir; ~ **out** *vt* (*find*) dénicher

rope [rəʊp] *n* corde *f*; (NAUT) cordage *m* ♦ *vt* (*tie up or together*) attacher; (*climbers: also: ~ together*) encorder; (*area: ~ off*) interdire l'accès de; (: *divide off*) séparer, **to know the ~s** (*fig*) être au courant, connaître les ficelles; ~ **in** *vt* (*fig: person*) embringuer

rosary ['rəʊzərɪ] *n* chapelet *m*

rose [rəʊz] *pt of* **rise** ♦ *n* rose *f*; (*also: ~bush*) rosier *m*; (*on watering can*) pomme *f*

rosé ['rəʊzeɪ] *n* rosé *m*

rosebud ['rəʊzbʌd] *n* bouton *m* de rose

rosemary ['rəʊzmərɪ] *n* romarin *m*

roster ['rɒstəʳ] *n*: **duty ~** tableau *m* de service

rostrum ['rɒstrəm] *n* tribune *f* (*pour un orateur etc*)

rosy ['rəʊzɪ] *adj* rose; **a ~ future** un bel avenir

rot [rɒt] *n* (*decay*) pourriture *f*; (*fig: pej*) idioties *fpl* ♦ *vt, vi* pourrir

rota ['rəʊtə] *n* liste *f*, tableau *m* de service; **on a ~ basis** par roulement

rotary ['rəʊtərɪ] *adj* rotatif(-ive)

rotate [rəʊ'teɪt] *vt* (*revolve*) faire tourner; (*change round: jobs*) faire à tour de rôle ♦ *vi* (*revolve*) tourner; **rotating** *adj* (*movement*) tournant(e)

rotten ['rɒtn] *adj* (*decayed*) pourri(e); (*dishonest*) corrompu(e); (*inf: bad*) mauvais(e), moche; **to feel ~** (*ill*) être mal fichu(e)

rotund [rəʊ'tʌnd] *adj* (*person*) rondelet(te)

rough [rʌf] *adj* (*cloth, skin*) rêche, rugueux(-euse); (*terrain*) accidenté(e); (*path*) rocailleux(-euse); (*voice*) rauque, rude; (*person, manner: coarse*) rude, fruste; (: *violent*) brutal(e); (*district, weather*) mauvais(e); (*sea*) houleux(-euse); (*plan etc*) ébauché(e); (*guess*) approximatif(-ive) ♦ *n* (GOLF) rough *m* ♦ *vt*: **to ~ it** vivre à la dure; **to sleep ~** (BRIT) coucher à la dure;

~**age** *n* fibres *fpl* alimentaires; ~-**and-ready** *adj* rudimentaire; ~ **copy** ~ **draft** *n* brouillon *m*; ~**ly** *adv* (*handle*) rudement, brutalement; (*speak*) avec brusquerie; (*make*) grossièrement; (*approximately*) à peu près, en gros

roulette [ruː'let] *n* roulette *f*

Roumania [ruː'meɪnɪə] *n* = **Romania**

round [raʊnd] *adj* rond(e) ♦ *n* (BRIT: of toast) tranche *f*; (*duty: of policeman, milkman etc*) tournée *f*; (: *of doctor*) visites *fpl*; (*game: of cards, in competition*) partie *f*; (BOXING) round *m*; (*of talks*) série *f* ♦ *vt* (*corner*) tourner ♦ *prep* autour de ♦ *adv*: **all ~** tout autour; **the long way ~** (par) le chemin le plus long; **all the year ~** toute l'année; **it's just ~ the corner** (*fig*) c'est tout près; ~ **the clock** 24 heures sur 24; **to go ~ to sb's (house)** aller chez qn; **go ~ the back** passez par derrière; **enough to go ~** assez pour tout le monde; ~ **of ammunition** cartouche *f*; ~ **of applause** ban *m*, applaudissements *mpl*; ~ **of drinks** tournée *f*; ~ **of sandwiches** sandwich *m*; ~ **off** *vt* (*speech etc*) terminer; ~ **up** *vt* rassembler; (*criminals*) effectuer une rafle de; (*price, figure*) arrondir (au chiffre supérieur); ~**about** *n* (BRIT: AUT) rond-point *m* (à sens giratoire); (: *at fair*) manège *m* (de chevaux de bois) ♦ *adj* (*route, means*) détourné(e); ~**ers** *n* (*game*) sorte de baseball; ~**ly** *adv* (*fig*) tout net, carrément; ~ **trip** *n* (*voyage m*) aller et retour *m*; ~**up** *n* rassemblement *m*; (*of criminals*) rafle *f*

rouse [raʊz] *vt* (*wake up*) réveiller; (*stir up*) susciter; provoquer; éveiller; **rousing** *adj* (*welcome*) enthousiaste

route [ruːt] *n* itinéraire *m*; (*of bus*) parcours *m*; (*of trade, shipping*) route *f*

routine [ruː'tiːn] *adj* (*work*) ordinaire, courant(e); (*procedure*) d'usage ♦ *n* (*habits*) habitudes *fpl*; (*pej*) train-train *m*; (THEATRE) numéro *m*

rove [rəʊv] *vt* (*area, streets*) errer dans

row¹ [rəʊ] *n* (*line*) rangée *f*; (*of people, seats, KNITTING*) rang *m*; (*behind one an-*

other: of cars, people) file *f* ♦ *vi (in boat)* ramer; *(as sport)* faire de l'aviron ♦ *vt (boat)* faire aller à la rame *or* à l'aviron; **in a ~** *(fig)* d'affilée

row² [rau] *n (noise)* vacarme *m; (dispute)* dispute *f*, querelle *f; (scolding)* réprimande *f*, savon *m* ♦ *vi* se disputer, se quereller

rowboat ['rəubəut] *(US) n* canot *m* (à rames)

rowdy ['raudɪ] *adj* chahuteur(-euse); *(occasion)* tapageur(-euse)

rowing ['rəuɪŋ] *n* canotage *m; (as sport)* aviron *m;* ~ **boat** *(BRIT) n* canot *m* (à rames)

royal ['rɔɪəl] *adj* royal(e); **R~ Air Force** *(BRIT) n* armée de l'air britannique; **~ty** *n (royal persons)* (membres *mpl* de la) famille royale; *(payment: to author)* droits *mpl* d'auteur; *(: to inventor)* royalties *fpl*

rpm *abbr (AUT)* (= *revolutions per minute*) tr/mn

RSVP *abbr* (= *répondez s'il vous plaît*) R.S.V.P.

Rt Hon. *abbr (BRIT: Right Honourable)* titre donné aux députés de la Chambre des communes

rub [rʌb] *vt* frotter; frictionner; *(hands)* se frotter ♦ *n (with cloth)* coup *m* chiffon *or* de torchon; **to give sth a ~** donner un coup de chiffon *or* de torchon à; **to ~ sb up** *(BRIT)* **or to ~ sb** *(US)* **the wrong way** prendre à rebrousse-poil; ~ **off** *vi* partir; ~ **off on** *vt fus* déteindre sur; ~ **out** *vt* effacer

rubber ['rʌbər] *n* caoutchouc *m; (BRIT: eraser)* gomme *f* (à effacer); ~ **band** *n* élastique *m;* ~ **plant** *n* caoutchouc *m (plante verte)*

rubbish ['rʌbɪʃ] *n (from household)* ordures *fpl; (fig: pej)* camelote *f; (: nonsense)* bêtises *fpl*, idioties *fpl;* ~ **bin** *(BRIT) n* poubelle *f;* ~ **dump** *n* décharge publique, dépotoir *m*

rubble ['rʌbl] *n* décombres *mpl; (smaller)* gravats *mpl; (CONSTR)* blocage *m*

ruby ['ru:bɪ] *n* rubis *m*

rucksack ['rʌksæk] *n* sac *m* à dos

rudder ['rʌdər] *n* gouvernail *m*

ruddy ['rʌdɪ] *adj (face)* coloré(e); *(inf: damned)* sacré(e), fichu(e)

rude [ru:d] *adj (impolite)* impoli(e); *(coarse)* grossier(-ère); *(shocking)* indécent(e), inconvenant(e)

ruffle ['rʌfl] *vt (hair)* ébouriffer; *(clothes)* chiffonner; *(fig: person)*: **to get ~d** s'énerver

rug [rʌg] *n* petit tapis; *(BRIT: blanket)* couverture *f*

rugby ['rʌgbɪ] *n (also: ~ football)* rugby *m*

rugged ['rʌgɪd] *adj (landscape)* accidenté(e); *(features, character)* rude

ruin ['ru:ɪn] *n* ruine *f* ♦ *vt* ruiner; *(spoil, clothes)* abîmer; *(event)* gâcher; **~s** *npl (of building)* ruine(s)

rule [ru:l] *n* règle *f; (regulation)* règlement *m; (government)* autorité *f*, gouvernement *m* ♦ *vt (country)* gouverner; *(person)* dominer ♦ *vi* commander; *(LAW)* statuer; **as a ~** normalement, en règle générale; ~ **out** *vt* exclure; **~d** *adj (paper)* réglé(e); **~r** *n (sovereign)* souverain(e); *(for measuring)* règle *f;* **ruling** *adj (party)* au pouvoir; *(class)* dirigeant(e) ♦ *n (LAW)* décision *f*

rum [rʌm] *n* rhum *m*

Rumania [ru:'meɪnɪə] *n* = **Romania**

rumble ['rʌmbl] *vi* gronder; *(stomach, pipe)* gargouiller

rummage ['rʌmɪdʒ] *vi* fouiller

rumour ['ru:mər] *(US* **rumor***) n* rumeur *f*, bruit *m* (qui court) ♦ *vt:* **it is ~ed that** le bruit court que

rump [rʌmp] *n (of animal)* croupe *f; (inf: of person)* postérieur *m;* ~ **steak** *n* rumsteck *m*

rumpus ['rʌmpəs] *(inf) n* tapage *m*, chahut *m*

run [rʌn] *(pt* **ran***, pp* **run***) n (fast pace)* pas *m* de) course *f; (outing)* tour *m or* promenade *f (en voiture); (distance travelled)* parcours *m*, trajet *m; (series)* suite *f*, série *f; (THEATRE)* série de représentations; *(SKI)* piste *f; (CRICKET, BASEBALL)* point *m; (in tights, stockings)* maille filée, échelle *f* ♦ *vt (operate: business)* diriger; *(: competition,* *course*) organiser; (: *hotel, house*) tenir; (*race*) participer à; (COMPUT) exécuter; (*to pass: hand, finger*) passer; (*water, bath*) faire couler; (PRESS: *feature*) publier ♦ *vi* courir; (*flee*) s'enfuir; (*work: machine, factory*) marcher; (*bus, train*) circuler; (*continue: play*) se jouer; (: *contract*) être valide; (*flow: river, bath; nose*) couler; (*colours, washing*) déteindre; (*in election*) être candidat, se présenter; **to go for a ~** faire un peu de course à pied; **there was a ~ on ...** (*meat, tickets*) les gens se sont rués sur ...; **in the long ~** à longue échéance; à la longue; **en fin de** compte; **on the ~** en fuite; **I'll ~ you to the station** je vais vous emmener *or* conduire à la gare; **to ~ a risk** courir un risque; ~ **about** *vi* (*children*) courir çà et là; ~ **across** *vt fus* (*find*) trouver par hasard; ~ **around** *vi* = **run about**; ~ **away** *vi* s'enfuir; ~ **down** *vt* (*production*) réduire progressivement; (*factory*) réduire progressivement la production de; (AUT) renverser; (*criticize*) critiquer, dénigrer; **to be ~ down** (*person: tired*) être fatigué(e) *or* à plat; ~ **in** (BRIT) *vt* (*car*) roder; ~ **into** *vt fus* (*meet: person*) rencontrer par hasard; (*trouble*) se heurter à; (*collide with*) heurter; ~ **off** *vi* s'enfuir ♦ *vt* (*water*) laisser s'écouler; (*copies*) tirer; ~ **out** *vi* (*person*) sortir en courant; (*liquid*) couler; (*lease*) expirer; (*money*) être épuisé(e); ~ **out of** *vt fus* se trouver à court de; ~ **over** *vt* (AUT) écraser ♦ *vt fus* (*revise*) revoir, reprendre; ~ **through** *vt fus* (*recapitulate*) reprendre; (*play*) répéter; ~ **up** *vt*: **to ~ up against** (*difficulties*) se heurter à; **to ~ up a debt** s'endetter; **~away** *adj* (*horse*) emballé(e); (*truck*) fou (folle); (*person*) fugitif(-ive); (*teenager*) fugueur(-euse)

rung [rʌŋ] *pp of* **ring** ♦ *n* (*of ladder*) barreau *m*

runner ['rʌnər] *n* (*in race: person*) coureur(-euse); (: *horse*) partant *m*; (*on sledge*) patin *m*; (*for drawer etc*) coulisseau *m*; ~ **bean** (BRIT) *n* haricot *m* (à rames); **~-up** *n* second(e)

running ['rʌnɪŋ] *n* course *f*; (*of business, organization*) gestion *f*, direction *f* ♦ *adj* (*water*) courant(e); **to be in/out of the ~ for sth** être/ne pas être sur les rangs pour qch; **6 days ~** 6 jours de suite; ~ **commentary** *n* commentaire détaillé; ~ **costs** *npl* frais *mpl* d'exploitation

runny ['rʌnɪ] *adj* qui coule

run-of-the-mill ['rʌnəvðə'mɪl] *adj* ordinaire, banal(e)

runt [rʌnt] *n* avorton *m*

run-up ['rʌnʌp] *n*: **~~ to sth** (*election etc*) période *f* précédant qch

runway ['rʌnweɪ] *n* (AVIAT) piste *f*

rupture ['rʌptʃər] *n* (MED) hernie *f*

rural ['ruərl] *adj* rural(e)

rush [rʌʃ] *n* (*hurry*) hâte *f*, précipitation *f*; (*of crowd*, COMM: *sudden demand*) ruée *f*; (*current*) flot *m*; (*of emotion*) vague *f*; (BOT) jonc *m* ♦ *vt* (*hurry*) transporter *or* envoyer d'urgence ♦ *vi* se précipiter; ~ **hour** *n* heures *fpl* de pointe

rusk [rʌsk] *n* biscotte *f*

Russia ['rʌʃə] *n* Russie *f*; **~n** *adj* russe ♦ *n* Russe *m/f*; (LING) russe *m*

rust [rʌst] *n* rouille *f* ♦ *vi* rouiller

rustic ['rʌstɪk] *adj* rustique

rustle ['rʌsl] *vi* bruire, produire un bruissement ♦ *vt* froisser

rustproof ['rʌstpruːf] *adj* inoxydable

rusty ['rʌstɪ] *adj* rouillé(e)

rut [rʌt] *n* ornière *f*; (ZOOL) rut *m*; **to be in a ~** suivre l'ornière, s'encroûter

ruthless ['ruːθlɪs] *adj* sans pitié, impitoyable

rye [raɪ] *n* seigle *m*

S, s

Sabbath ['sæbəθ] *n* (*Jewish*) sabbat *m*; (*Christian*) dimanche *m*

sabotage ['sæbətɑːʒ] *n* sabotage *m* ♦ *vt* saboter

saccharin(e) ['sækərɪn] *n* saccharine *f*

sachet ['sæʃeɪ] *n* sachet *m*

sack [sæk] *n* (*bag*) sac *m* ♦ *vt* (*dismiss*) renvoyer, mettre à la porte; (*plunder*) piller, mettre à sac; **to get the ~** être renvoyé(e), être mis(e) à la porte; **~ing** *n* (*material*) toile *f* à sac; (*dismissal*) renvoi *m*

sacrament ['sækrəmənt] *n* sacrement *m*

sacred ['seɪkrɪd] *adj* sacré(e)

sacrifice ['sækrɪfaɪs] *n* sacrifice *m* ♦ *vt* sacrifier

sad [sæd] *adj* triste; (*deplorable*) triste, fâcheux(-euse)

saddle ['sædl] *n* selle *f* ♦ *vt* (*horse*) seller; **to be ~d with sth** (*inf*) avoir qch sur les bras; **~bag** *n* sacoche *f*

sadistic [sə'dɪstɪk] *adj* sadique

sadly ['sædlɪ] *adv* tristement; (*unfortunately*) malheureusement; (*seriously*) fort

sadness ['sædnɪs] *n* tristesse *f*

s.a.e. *n abbr* = **stamped addressed envelope**

safe [seɪf] *adj* (*out of danger*) hors de danger, en sécurité; (*not dangerous*) sans danger; (*cautious*) prudent(e); (*sure: bet etc*) assuré(e) ♦ *n* coffre-fort *m*; **~ from** à l'abri de; **~ and sound** sain(e) et sauf (sauve); **(just) to be on the ~ side** pour plus de sûreté, par précaution; **~ journey!** bon voyage!; **~-conduct** *n* sauf-conduit *m*; **~-deposit** *n* (*vault*) dépôt *m* de coffres-forts; (*box*) coffre-fort *m*; **~guard** *n* sauvegarde *f*, protection *f* ♦ *vt* sauvegarder, protéger; **~keeping** *n* bonne garde; **~ly** *adv* (*assume, say*) sans risque d'erreur; (*drive, arrive*) sans accident; **~ sex** *n* rapports *mpl* sexuels sans risque

safety ['seɪftɪ] *n* sécurité *f*; **~ belt** *n* ceinture *f* de sécurité; **~ pin** *n* épingle *f* de sûreté *or* de nourrice; **~ valve** *n* soupape *f* de sûreté

sag [sæg] *vi* s'affaisser; (*hem, breasts*) pendre

sage [seɪdʒ] *n* (*herb*) sauge *f*; (*person*) sage *m*

Sagittarius [sædʒɪ'tɛərɪəs] *n* le Sagittaire

Sahara [sə'hɑːrə] *n*: **the ~ (Desert)** le (désert du) Sahara

said [sɛd] *pt, pp of* **say**

sail [seɪl] *n* (*on boat*) voile *f*; (*trip*): **to go**

for a ~ faire un tour en bateau ♦ *vt* (*boat*) manœuvrer, piloter ♦ *vi* (*travel: ship*) avancer, naviguer; (*set off*) partir, prendre la mer; (*SPORT*) faire de la voile; **they ~ed into Le Havre** ils sont entrés dans le port du Havre; **~ through** *vi, vt fus* (*fig*) réussir haut la main; **~boat** (*US*) *n* bateau *m* à voiles, voilier *m*; **~ing** *n* (*SPORT*) voile *f*; **to go ~ing** faire de la voile; **~ing boat** *n* bateau *m* à voiles, voilier *m*; **~ing ship** *n* grand voilier *m*; **~or** *n* marin *m*, matelot *m*

saint [seɪnt] *n*: saint(e)

sake [seɪk] *n*: **for the ~ of** pour (l'amour de), dans l'intérêt de; par égard pour

salad ['sæləd] *n* salade *f*; **~ bowl** *n* saladier *m*; **~ cream** (*BRIT*) *n* (sorte *f* de) mayonnaise *f*; **~ dressing** *n* vinaigrette *f*

salami [sə'lɑːmɪ] *n* salami *m*

salary ['sælərɪ] *n* salaire *m*

sale [seɪl] *n* vente *f*; (*at reduced prices*) soldes *mpl*; **"for ~"** "à vendre"; **on ~** en vente; **on ~ or return** vendu(e) avec faculté de retour; **~room** *n* salle *f* des ventes; **~s assistant** (*US* **sales clerk**) *n* vendeur(-euse); **~sman** (*irreg*) *n* vendeur *m*; (*representative*) représentant *m*; **~s rep** *n* (*COMM*) représentant(e) *m/f*; **~swoman** (*irreg*) *n* vendeuse *f*; (*representative*) représentante *f*

salmon ['sæmən] *n inv* saumon *m*

salon ['sælɔn] *n* salon *m*

saloon [sə'luːn] *n* (*US*) bar *m*; (*BRIT: AUT*) berline *f*; (*ship's lounge*) salon *m*

salt [sɔːlt] *n* sel *m* ♦ *vt* saler; **~ cellar** *n* salière *f*; **~water** *adj* de mer; **~y** *adj* salé(e)

salute [sə'luːt] *n* salut *m* ♦ *vt* saluer

salvage ['sælvɪdʒ] *n* (*saving*) sauvetage *m*; (*things saved*) biens sauvés *or* récupérés ♦ *vt* sauver, récupérer

salvation [sæl'veɪʃən] *n* salut *m*; **S~ Army** *n* armée *f* du Salut

same [seɪm] *adj* même ♦ *pron*: **the ~** (la) même, les mêmes; **the ~ book as** le même livre que; **at the ~ time** en même temps; **all** *or* **just the ~** tout de même, quand même; **to do the ~** faire de même, en faire autant; **to do the ~ as sb** faire comme qn; **the ~ to you!** à vous de même!; (*after insult*) toi-même!

sample ['sɑːmpl] *n* échantillon *m*; (*blood*) prélèvement *m* ♦ *vt* (*food, wine*) goûter

sanction ['sæŋkʃən] *n* approbation *f*, sanction *f*

sanctity ['sæŋktɪtɪ] *n* sainteté *f*, caractère sacré

sanctuary ['sæŋktjuərɪ] *n* (*holy place*) sanctuaire *m*; (*refuge*) asile *m*; (*for wild life*) réserve *f*

sand [sænd] *n* sable *m* ♦ *vt* (*furniture: also:* **~ down**) poncer

sandal ['sændl] *n* sandale *f*

sand: **~box** (*US*) *n* tas *m* de sable; **~castle** *n* château *m* de sable; **~paper** *n* papier *m* de verre; **~pit** (*BRIT*) *n* (*for children*) tas *m* de sable; **~stone** *n* grès *m*

sandwich ['sændwɪtʃ] *n* sandwich *m*; **cheese/ham ~** sandwich au fromage/jambon; **~ course** (*BRIT*) *n* cours *m* de formation professionnelle

sandy ['sændɪ] *adj* sablonneux(-euse); (*colour*) sable *inv*, blond roux *inv*

sane [seɪn] *adj* (*person*) sain(e) d'esprit; (*outlook*) sensé(e), sain(e)

sang [sæŋ] *pt of* **sing**

sanitary ['sænɪtərɪ] *adj* (*system, arrangements*) sanitaire; (*clean*) hygiénique; **~ towel** (*US* **sanitary napkin**) *n* serviette *f* hygiénique

sanitation [sænɪ'teɪʃən] *n* (*in house*) installations *fpl* sanitaires; (*in town*) système *m* sanitaire; **~ department** (*US*) *n* service *m* de voirie

sanity ['sænɪtɪ] *n* santé mentale; (*common sense*) bon sens

sank [sæŋk] *pt of* **sink**

Santa Claus [sæntə'klɔːz] *n* le père Noël

sap [sæp] *n* (*of plants*) sève *f* ♦ *vt* (*strength*) saper, miner

sapling ['sæplɪŋ] *n* jeune arbre *m*

sapphire ['sæfaɪə*r*] *n* saphir *m*

sarcasm ['sɑːkæzm] *n* sarcasme *m*, raillerie *f*; **sarcastic** [sɑː'kæstɪk] *adj* sarcastique

sardine [sɑː'diːn] *n* sardine *f*

Sardinia [sɑː'dɪnɪə] *n* Sardaigne *f*

sash [sæʃ] *n* écharpe *f*

sat [sæt] *pt, pp of* **sit**

satchel ['sætʃl] *n* cartable *m*

satellite ['sætəlaɪt] *n* satellite *m*; **~ dish** *n* antenne *f* parabolique; **~ television** *n* télévision *f* par câble

satin ['sætɪn] *n* satin *m* ♦ *adj* en *or* de satin, satiné(e)

satire ['sætaɪə*r*] *n* satire *f*

satisfaction [sætɪs'fækʃən] *n* satisfaction *f*

satisfactory [sætɪs'fæktərɪ] *adj* satisfaisant(e)

satisfied ['sætɪsfaɪd] *adj* satisfait(e)

satisfy ['sætɪsfaɪ] *vt* satisfaire, contenter; (*convince*) convaincre, persuader; **~ing** *adj* satisfaisant(e)

Saturday ['sætədɪ] *n* samedi *m*

sauce [sɔːs] *n* sauce *f*; **~pan** *n* casserole *f*

saucer ['sɔːsə*r*] *n* soucoupe *f*

Saudi ['saʊdɪ]: **~ Arabia** *n* Arabie Saoudite; **~ (Arabian)** *adj* saoudien(ne)

sauna ['sɔːnə] *n* sauna *m*

saunter ['sɔːntə*r*] *vi*: **to ~ along/in/out** *etc* marcher/entrer/sortir *etc* d'un pas nonchalant

sausage ['sɒsɪdʒ] *n* saucisse *f*; (*cold meat*) saucisson *m*; **~ roll** *n* ≈ friand *m*

savage ['sævɪdʒ] *adj* (*cruel, fierce*) brutal(e), féroce; (*primitive*) primitif(-ive), sauvage ♦ *n* sauvage *m/f*

save [seɪv] *vt* (*person, belongings*) sauver; (*money*) mettre de côté, économiser; (*time*) (faire) gagner; (*keep*) garder; (*COMPUT*) sauvegarder; (*SPORT: stop*) arrêter; (*avoid: trouble*) éviter ♦ *vi* (*also:* **~ up**) mettre de l'argent de côté ♦ *n* (*SPORT*) arrêt *m* (du ballon) ♦ *prep* sauf, à l'exception de

saving ['seɪvɪŋ] *n* économie *f* ♦ *adj*: **the ~ grace of sth** ce qui rachète qch; **~s** *npl* (*money saved*) économies *fpl*; **~s account** *n* compte *m* d'épargne; **~s bank** *n* caisse *f* d'épargne

saviour ['seɪvjə*r*] (*US* **savior**) *n* sauveur *m*

savour ['seɪvə*r*] (*US* **savor**) *vt* savourer; **~y** (*US* **savory**) *adj* (*dish: not sweet*) salé(e)

saw [sɔ:] (*pt* **sawed**, *pp* **sawed** *or* **sawn**) *vt* scier ♦ *n* (*tool*) scie *f* ♦ *pt of* **see**; **~dust** *n* sciure *f*; **~mill** *n* scierie *f*; **~n-off** *adj*: **~n-off shotgun** carabine *f* à canon scié

sax [sæks] (*inf*) *n* saxo *m*

saxophone ['sæksəfəun] *n* saxophone *m*

say [seɪ] (*pt*, *pp* **said**) *n*: **to have one's ~** dire ce qu'on a à dire ♦ *vt* dire; **to have a** *or* **some ~ in sth** avoir voix au chapitre; **could you ~ that again?** pourriez-vous répéter ce que vous venez de dire?; **that goes without ~ing** cela va sans dire, cela va de soi; **~ing** *n* dicton *m*, proverbe *m*

scab [skæb] *n* croûte *f*; (*pej*) jaune *m*

scaffold ['skæfəld] *n* échafaud *m*; **~ing** *n* échafaudage *m*

scald [skɔ:ld] *n* brûlure *f* ♦ *vt* ébouillanter

scale [skeɪl] *n* (*of fish*) écaille *f*; (*MUS*) gamme *f*; (*of ruler, thermometer etc*) graduation *f*, échelle (graduée); (*of salaries, fees etc*) barème *m*; (*of map, also size, extent*) échelle ♦ *vt* (*mountain*) escalader; **~s** *npl* (*for weighing*) balance *f*; (*also*: **bathroom ~**) pèse-personne *m inv*; **on a large ~** sur une grande échelle, en grand; **~ of charges** tableau *m* des tarifs; **~ down** *vt* réduire

scallop ['skɔləp] *n* coquille *f* Saint-Jacques; (*SEWING*) feston *m*

scalp [skælp] *n* cuir chevelu ♦ *vt* scalper

scampi ['skæmpɪ] *npl* langoustines (frites), scampi *mpl*

scan [skæn] *vt* scruter, examiner; (*glance at quickly*) parcourir; (*TV, RADAR*) balayer ♦ *n* (*MED*) scanographie *f*

scandal ['skændl] *n* scandale *m*; (*gossip*) ragots *mpl*

Scandinavia [skændɪ'neɪvɪə] *n* Scandinavie *f*; **~n** *adj* scandinave

scant [skænt] *adj* insuffisant(e); **~y** ['skæntɪ] *adj* peu abondant(e), insuffisant(e); (*underwear*) minuscule

scapegoat ['skeɪpgəut] *n* bouc *m* émissaire

scar [skɑː] *n* cicatrice *f* ♦ *vt* marquer (d'une cicatrice)

scarce [skeəs] *adj* rare, peu abondant(e);

to make o.s. ~ (*inf*) se sauver; **~ly** *adv* à peine; **scarcity** *n* manque *m*, pénurie *f*

scare [skeəʳ] *n* peur *f*, panique *f* ♦ *vt* effrayer, faire peur à; **to ~ sb stiff** faire une peur bleue à qn; **bomb ~** alerte *f* à la bombe; **~ away**; **~ off** *vt* = **scare away**; **~crow** *n* épouvantail *m*; **~d** *adj*: **to be ~d** avoir peur

scarf [skɑːf] (*pl* **~s** *or* **scarves**) *n* (*long*) écharpe *f*; (*square*) foulard *m*

scarlet ['skɑːlɪt] *adj* écarlate; **~ fever** *n* scarlatine *f*

scary ['skeərɪ] (*inf*) *adj* effrayant(e)

scathing ['skeɪðɪŋ] *adj* cinglant(e), acerbe

scatter ['skætəʳ] *vt* éparpiller, répandre; (*crowd*) disperser ♦ *vi* se disperser; **~brained** *adj* écervelé(e), étourdi(e)

scavenger ['skævəndʒəʳ] *n* (*person: in bins etc*) pilleur *m* de poubelles

scene [siːn] *n* scène *f*; (*of crime, accident*) lieu(x) *m(pl)*; (*sight, view*) spectacle *m*, vue *f*; **~ry** ['siːnərɪ] *n* (*THEATRE*) décor(s) *m(pl)*; (*landscape*) paysage *m*; **scenic** *adj* (*picturesque*) offrant de beaux paysages *or* panoramas

scent [sent] *n* parfum *m*, odeur *f*; (*track*) piste *f*

sceptical ['skeptɪkl] (*US* **skeptical**) *adj* sceptique

schedule ['ʃedjuːl, (*US*) 'skedjuːl] *n* programme *m*, plan *m*; (*of trains*) horaire *m*; (*of prices etc*) barème *m*, tarif *m* ♦ *vt* prévoir; **on ~** à l'heure (prévue); à la date prévue; **to be ahead of/behind ~** avoir de l'avance/du retard; **~d flight** *n* vol régulier

scheme [skiːm] *n* plan *m*, projet *m*; (*dishonest plan, plot*) complot *m*, combine *f*; (*arrangement*) arrangement *m*, classification *f*; (*pension ~ etc*) régime *m* ♦ *vi* comploter, manigancer; **scheming** *adj* rusé(e), intrigant(e) ♦ *n* manigances *fpl*, intrigues *fpl*

scholar ['skɔləʳ] *n* érudit(e); (*pupil*) boursier(-ère); **~ship** *n* (*knowledge*) érudition *f*; (*grant*) bourse *f* (d'études)

school [skuːl] *n* école *f*; (*secondary ~*) collège *m*, lycée *m*; (*US: university*) université *f*; (*in university*) faculté *f* ♦ *cpd* scolaire; **~book** *n* livre *m* scolaire *or* de classe; **~boy** *n* écolier *m*; collégien *m*, lycéen *m*; **~children** *npl* écoliers *mpl*; collégiens *mpl*, lycéens *mpl*; **~girl** *n* écolière *f*; collégienne *f*, lycéenne *f*; **~ing** *n* instruction *f*, études *fpl*; **~master** *n* professeur *m*; **~mistress** *n* professeur *m*; **~teacher** *n* instituteur(-trice); professeur *m*

science ['saɪəns] *n* science *f*; **~ fiction** *n* science-fiction *f*; **scientific** [saɪən'tɪfɪk] *adj* scientifique; **scientist** *n* scientifique *m/f*; (*eminent*) savant *m*

scissors ['sɪzəz] *npl* ciseaux *mpl*

scoff [skɒf] *vt* (*BRIT: inf: eat*) avaler, bouffer ♦ *vi*: **to ~ (at)** (*mock*) se moquer (de)

scold [skəʊld] *vt* gronder

scone [skɒn] *n* sorte de petit pain rond au lait

scoop [skuːp] *n* pelle *f* (à main); (*for ice cream*) boule *f* à glace; (*PRESS*) scoop *m*; **~ out** *vt* évider, creuser; **~ up** *vt* ramasser

scooter ['skuːtəʳ] *n* (*also: motor ~*) scooter *m*; (*toy*) trottinette *f*

scope [skəʊp] *n* (*capacity: of plan, undertaking*) portée *f*, envergure *f*; (: *of person*) compétence *f*, capacités *fpl*; (*opportunity*) possibilités *fpl*; **within the ~ of** dans les limites de

scorch [skɔːtʃ] *vt* (*clothes*) brûler (légèrement), roussir; (*earth, grass*) dessécher, brûler

score [skɔːʳ] *n* score *m*, décompte *m* des points; (*MUS*) partition *f*; (*twenty*) vingt ♦ *vt* (*goal, point*) marquer; (*success*) remporter ♦ *vi* marquer un but; (*keep ~*) compter les points; **~s of** (*very many*) beaucoup de, un tas de (*fam*); **on that ~** sur ce chapitre, à cet égard; **to ~ 6 out of 10** obtenir 6 sur 10; **~ out** *vt* rayer, barrer, biffer; **~board** *n* tableau *m*

scorn [skɔːn] *n* mépris *m*, dédain *m*

Scorpio ['skɔːpɪəʊ] *n* le Scorpion

Scot [skɒt] *n* Écossais(e)

Scotch [skɒtʃ] *n* whisky *m*, scotch *m*

scot-free ['skɒt'friː] *adv*: **to get off ~-~** s'en tirer sans être puni(e)

Scotland ['skɒtlənd] *n* Écosse *f*; **Scots** *adj* écossais(e); **Scotsman** (*irreg*) *n* Écossais; **Scotswoman** (*irreg*) *n* Écossaise *f*; **Scottish** *adj* écossais(e); **Scottish Parliament** *n* Parlement *m* écossais

scoundrel ['skaʊndrl] *n* vaurien *m*

scour ['skaʊəʳ] *vt* (*search*) battre, parcourir

scout [skaʊt] *n* (*MIL*) éclaireur *m*; (*also: boy ~*) scout *m*; **girl ~** (*US*) guide *f*; **~ around** *vi* explorer, chercher

scowl [skaʊl] *vi* se renfrogner, avoir l'air maussade; **to ~ at** regarder de travers

scrabble ['skræbl] *vi* (*also: ~ around: search*) chercher à tâtons; (*claw*): **to ~ (at)** gratter ♦ *n*: **S~** ® Scrabble ® *m*

scram [skræm] (*inf*) *vi* ficher le camp

scramble ['skræmbl] *n* (*rush*) bousculade *f*, ruée *f* ♦ *vi*: **to ~ up/down** grimper/descendre tant bien que mal; **to ~ out** sortir *or* descendre à toute vitesse; **to ~ through** se frayer un passage (à travers); **to ~ for** se bousculer *or* se disputer pour (avoir); **~d eggs** *npl* œufs brouillés

scrap [skræp] *n* bout *m*, morceau *m*; (*fight*) bagarre *f*; (*also: ~ iron*) ferraille *f* ♦ *vt* jeter, mettre au rebut; (*fig*) abandonner, laisser tomber ♦ *vi* (*fight*) se bagarrer; **~s** *npl* (*waste*) déchets *mpl*; **~book** *n* album *m*; **~ dealer** *n* marchand *m* de ferraille

scrape [skreɪp] *vt, vi* gratter, racler ♦ *n*: **to get into a ~** s'attirer des ennuis; **to ~ through** réussir de justesse; **to ~ together** *vt* (*money*) racler ses fonds de tiroir pour réunir

scrap: **~ heap** *n*: **on the ~ heap** (*fig*) au rancart *or* rebut; **~ merchant** (*BRIT*) *n* marchand *m* de ferraille; **~ paper** *n* papier *m* brouillon

scratch [skrætʃ] *n* égratignure *f*, rayure *f*; éraflure *f*; (*from claw*) coup *m* de griffe ♦ *cpd*: **~ team** équipe de fortune *or* improvisée ♦ *vt* (*rub*) (se) gratter; (*record*) rayer; (*paint etc*) érafler; (*with claw, nail*) griffer

♦ *vi* (se) gratter; **to start from ~** partir de zéro; **to be up to ~** être à la hauteur

scrawl [skrɔːl] *vi* gribouiller

scrawny ['skrɔːnɪ] *adj* décharné(e)

scream [skriːm] *n* cri perçant, hurlement *m* ♦ *vi* crier, hurler

screech [skriːtʃ] *vi* hurler; (*tyres*) crisser; (*brakes*) grincer

screen [skriːn] *n* écran *m*; (*in room*) paravent *m*; (*fig*) écran, rideau *m* ♦ *vt* (*conceal*) masquer, cacher; (*from the wind etc*) abriter, protéger; (*film*) projeter; (*candidates etc*) filtrer; ~**ing** *n* (MED) test *m* (*or* tests) de dépistage; ~**play** *n* scénario *m*

screw [skruː] *n* vis *f* ♦ *vt* visser; ~ **up** *vt* (*paper etc*) froisser; **to ~ up one's eyes** plisser les yeux; ~**driver** *n* tournevis *m*

scribble ['skrɪbl] *vt, vi* gribouiller, griffonner

script [skrɪpt] *n* (CINEMA *etc*) scénario *m*, texte *m*; (*system of writing*) (écriture *f*) script *m*

Scripture(s) ['skrɪptʃə^r(-əz)] *n(pl)* (*Christian*) Écriture sainte (*other religions*) écritures saintes

scroll [skrəʊl] *n* rouleau *m*

scrounge [skraʊndʒ] (*inf*) *vt*: **to ~ sth off** *or* **from sb** taper qn de qch; ~**r** (*inf*) *n* parasite *m*

scrub [skrʌb] *n* (*land*) broussailles *fpl* ♦ *vt* (*floor*) nettoyer à la brosse; (*pan*) récurer; (*washing*) frotter; (*inf: cancel*) annuler

scruff [skrʌf] *n*: **by the ~ of the neck** par la peau du cou

scruffy ['skrʌfɪ] *adj* débraillé(e)

scrum(mage) ['skrʌm(ɪdʒ)] *n* (RUGBY) mêlée *f*

scruple ['skruːpl] *n* scrupule *m*

scrutiny ['skruːtɪnɪ] *n* examen minutieux

scuff [skʌf] *vt* érafler

scuffle ['skʌfl] *n* échauffourée *f*, rixe *f*

sculptor ['skʌlptə^r] *n* sculpteur *m*

sculpture ['skʌlptʃə^r] *n* sculpture *f*

scum [skʌm] *n* écume *f*, mousse *f*; (*pej: people*) rebut *m*, lie *f*

scurry ['skʌrɪ] *vi* filer à toute allure; **to ~ off** détaler, se sauver

scuttle ['skʌtl] *n* (*also:* **coal ~**) seau *m* (à charbon) ♦ *vt* (*ship*) saborder ♦ *vi* (*scamper*): **to ~ away** *or* **off** détaler

scythe [saɪð] *n* faux *f*

SDP *n abbr* = **Social Democratic Party**

sea [siː] *n* mer *f* ♦ *cpd* marin(e), de (la) mer; **by ~** (*travel*) par mer, en bateau; **on the ~** (*boat*) en mer; (*town*) au bord de la mer; **to be all at ~** (*fig*) nager complètement; **out to ~** au large; **(out) at ~** en mer; ~**board** *n* côte *f*; ~**food** *n* fruits *mpl* de mer; ~**front** *n* bord *m* de mer; ~**going** *adj* (*ship*) de mer; ~**gull** *n* mouette *f*

seal [siːl] *n* (*animal*) phoque *m*; (*stamp*) sceau *m*, cachet *m* ♦ *vt* sceller; (*envelope*) coller; (: *with* ~) cacheter; ~ **off** *vt* (*forbid entry to*) interdire l'accès de

sea level *n* niveau *m* de la mer

sea lion *n* otarie *f*

seam [siːm] *n* couture *f*; (*of coal*) veine *f*, filon *m*

seaman ['siːmən] (*irreg*) *n* marin *m*

seance ['seɪɒns] *n* séance *f* de spiritisme

seaplane ['siːpleɪn] *n* hydravion *m*

search [sɜːtʃ] *n* (*for person, thing,* COMPUT) recherche(s) *f(pl)*; (LAW: *at sb's home*) perquisition *f* ♦ *vt* fouiller; (*examine*) examiner minutieusement; scruter ♦ *vi*: **to ~ for** chercher; **in ~ of** à la recherche de; ~ **through** *vt fus* fouiller; ~ **engine** *n* (COMPUT) moteur *m* de recherche; ~**ing** *adj* pénétrant(e); ~**light** *n* projecteur *m*; ~ **party** *n* expédition *f* de secours; ~ **warrant** *n* mandat *m* de perquisition

sea: ~**shore** *n* rivage *m*, plage *f*, bord *m* de (la) mer; ~**sick** *adj*: **to be ~sick** avoir le mal de mer; ~**side** *n* bord *m* de la mer; ~**side resort** *n* station *f* balnéaire

season ['siːzn] *n* saison *f* ♦ *vt* assaisonner, relever; **to be in/out of ~** être/ne pas être de saison; ~**al** *adj* (*work*) saisonnier(ère); ~**ed** *adj* (*fig*) expérimenté(e); ~ **ticket** *n* carte *f* d'abonnement

seat [siːt] *n* siège *m*; (*in bus, train: place*) place *f*; (*buttocks*) postérieur *m*; (*of trousers*) fond *m* ♦ *vt* faire asseoir, placer;

(have room for) avoir des places assises pour, pouvoir accueillir; ~ **belt** *n* ceinture *f* de sécurité

sea: ~ **water** *n* eau *f* de mer; **~weed** *n* algues *fpl*; **~worthy** *adj* en état de naviguer

sec. *abbr* = **second(s)**

secluded [sɪ'klu:dɪd] *adj* retiré(e), à l'écart

seclusion [sɪ'klu:ʒən] *n* solitude *f*

second¹ [sɪ'kɒnd] *(BRIT)* *vt (employee)* affecter provisoirement

second² ['sɛkənd] *adj* deuxième, second(e) ♦ *adv (in race etc)* en seconde position ♦ *n (unit of time)* seconde *f*; *(AUT: ~ gear)* seconde; *(COMM: imperfect)* article *m* de second choix; *(BRIT: UNIV)* licence *f* avec mention ♦ *vt (motion)* appuyer; **~ary** *adj* secondaire; **~ary school** *n* collège *m*, lycée *m*; **~-class** *adj* de deuxième classe; *(RAIL)* de seconde (classe); *(POST)* au tarif réduit; *(pej)* de qualité inférieure ♦ *adv (RAIL)* en seconde; *(POST)* au tarif réduit; **~hand** *adj* d'occasion, de seconde main; ~ **hand** *n (on clock)* trotteuse *f*; **~ly** *adv* deuxièmement; **~ment** [sɪ'kɒndmənt] *(BRIT)* *n* détachement *m*; **~-rate** *adj* de deuxième ordre, de qualité inférieure; ~ **thoughts** *npl* doutes *mpl*; **on ~ thoughts** *or (US)* **thought** à la réflexion

secrecy ['si:krəsɪ] *n* secret *m*

secret ['si:krɪt] *adj* secret(-ète) ♦ *n* secret *m*; **in ~** en secret, secrètement, en cachette

secretary ['sɛkrətərɪ] *n* secrétaire *m/f*; *(COMM)* secrétaire général; **S~ of State (for)** *(BRIT: POL)* ministre *m* (de)

secretive ['si:krətɪv] *adj* dissimulé(e)

secretly ['si:krɪtlɪ] *adv* en secret, secrètement

sectarian [sɛk'tɛərɪən] *adj* sectaire

section ['sɛkʃən] *n* section *f*; *(of document)* section, article *m*, paragraphe *m*; *(cut)* coupe *f*

sector ['sɛktər] *n* secteur *m*

secular ['sɛkjulər] *adj* profane; laïque; séculier(-ère)

secure [sɪ'kjuər] *adj (free from anxiety)* sans

inquiétude, sécurisé(e); *(firmly fixed)* solide, bien attaché(e) *(or* fermé(e) *etc)*; *(in safe place)* en lieu sûr, en sûreté ♦ *vt (fix)* fixer, attacher; *(get)* obtenir, se procurer

security [sɪ'kjuərɪtɪ] *n* sécurité *f*, mesures *fpl* de sécurité; *(for loan)* caution *f*, garantie *f*; ~ **guard** *n* garde chargé de la sécurité; *(when transporting money)* convoyeur *m* de fonds

sedate [sɪ'deɪt] *adj* calme; posé(e) ♦ *vt (MED)* donner des sédatifs à

sedative ['sɛdɪtɪv] *n* calmant *m*, sédatif *m*

seduce [sɪ'dju:s] *vt* séduire; **seduction** [sɪ'dʌkʃən] *n* séduction *f*; **seductive** *adj* séduisant(e); *(smile)* séducteur(-trice); *(fig: offer)* alléchant(e)

see [si:] *(pt* **saw**, *pp* **seen)** *vt* voir; *(accompany)*: **to ~ sb to the door** reconduire *or* raccompagner qn jusqu'à la porte ♦ *vi* voir ♦ *n* évêché *m*; **to ~ that** *(ensure)* veiller à ce que +*sub*, faire en sorte que +*sub*, s'assurer que; ~ **you soon!** à bientôt!; ~ **about** *vt fus* s'occuper de; ~ **off** *vt* accompagner (à la gare *or* à l'aéroport *etc)*; ~ **through** *vt* mener à bonne fin ♦ *vt fus* voir clair dans; ~ **to** *vt fus* s'occuper de, se charger de

seed [si:d] *n* graine *f*; *(sperm)* semence *f*; *(fig)* germe *m*; *(TENNIS etc)* tête *f* de série; **to go to ~** monter en graine; *(fig)* se laisser aller; **~ling** *n* jeune plant *m*, semis *m*; **~y** *adj (shabby)* minable, miteux(-euse)

seeing ['si:ɪŋ] *conj:* ~ **(that)** vu que, étant donné que

seek [si:k] *(pt, pp* **sought)** *vt* chercher, rechercher

seem [si:m] *vi* sembler, paraître; **there ~s to be ...** il semble qu'il y a ...; on dirait qu'il y a ...; **~ingly** *adv* apparemment

seen [si:n] *pp* of **see**

seep [si:p] *vi* suinter, filtrer

seesaw ['si:sɔ:] *n* (jeu *m* de) bascule *f*

seethe [si:ð] *vi* être en effervescence; **to ~ with anger** bouillir de colère

see-through ['si:θru:] *adj* transparent(e)

segment ['sɛgmənt] *n* segment *m*; *(of orange)* quartier *m*

segregate ['segrigeit] vt séparer, isoler

seize [si:z] vt saisir, attraper; (*take posses-sion of*) s'emparer de; (*opportunity*) saisir; ~ **up** vi (*TECH*) se gripper; ~ (**up**)**on** vt fus saisir, sauter sur

seizure ['si:ʒər] n (*MED*) crise f, attaque f; (*of power*) prise f

seldom ['seldəm] adv rarement

select [si'lekt] adj choisi(e), d'élite ♦ vt sé-lectionner, choisir; ~**ion** n sélection f, choix m

self [self] (*pl* **selves**) n: **the ~** le moi inv ♦ prefix auto-; ~-**assured** adj sûr(e) de soi; ~-**catering** (*BRIT*) adj avec cuisine, où l'on peut faire sa cuisine; ~-**centred** (*US* **self-centered**) adj égocentrique; ~-**confidence** n confiance f en soi; ~-**conscious** adj timide, qui manque d'as-surance; ~-**contained** (*BRIT*) adj (*flat*) avec entrée particulière, indépendant(e); ~-**control** n maîtrise f de soi; ~-**defence** (*US* **self-defense**) n autodéfense f; (*LAW*) légitime défense f; ~-**discipline** n disci-pline personnelle; ~-**employed** adj qui travaille à son compte; ~-**evident** adj: **to be ~-evident** être évident(e), aller de soi; ~-**governing** adj autonome; ~-**indulgent** adj qui ne se refuse rien; ~-**interest** n intérêt personnel; ~**ish** adj égoïste; ~**ishness** n égoïsme m; ~**less** adj désintéressé(e); ~-**pity** n apitoiement m sur soi-même; ~-**possessed** adj assu-ré(e); ~-**preservation** n instinct m de conservation; ~-**respect** n respect m de soi, amour-propre m; ~-**righteous** adj suffisant(e); ~-**sacrifice** n abnégation f; ~-**satisfied** adj content(e) de soi, suffi-sant(e); ~-**service** adj libre-service, self-service; ~-**sufficient** adj autosuffisant(e); (*person: independent*) indépendant(e); ~-**taught** adj (*artist, pianist*) qui a appris par lui-même

sell [sel] (*pt, pp* **sold**) vt vendre ♦ vi se vendre; **to ~ at** or **for 10 F** se vendre 10 F; ~ **off** vt liquider; ~ **out** vi: **to ~ out (of sth)** (*use up stock*) vendre tout son stock (de qch); **the tickets are all sold out** il ne reste plus de billets; ~-**by date** n date f limite de vente; ~**er** n vendeur(-euse), marchand(e); ~**ing price** n prix m de vente

Sellotape ® ['seləuteip] (*BRIT*) n papier m collant, scotch ® m

selves [selvz] npl of **self**

semblance ['sembləns] n semblant m

semen ['si:mən] n sperme m

semester [si'mestər] (*esp US*) n semestre m

semi ['semi] prefix semi-, demi-; à demi, à moitié; ~**circle** n demi-cercle m; ~**colon** n point-virgule m; ~**detached (house)** (*BRIT*) n maison jumelée or jumelle; ~**final** n demi-finale f

seminar ['seminɑ:r] n séminaire m; ~**y** n (*REL: for priests*) séminaire m

semiskilled [semi'skild] adj: ~ **worker** ouvrier(-ère) spécialisé(e)

semi-skimmed milk [semi'skimd-] n lait m demi-écrémé

senate ['senit] n sénat m; **senator** n sé-nateur m

send [send] (*pt, pp* **sent**) vt envoyer; ~ **away** vt (*letter, goods*) envoyer, expédier; (*unwelcome visitor*) renvoyer; ~ **away for** vt fus commander par correspondance, se faire envoyer; ~ **back** vt renvoyer; ~ **for** vt fus envoyer chercher; faire venir; ~ **off** vt (*goods*) envoyer, expédier; (*BRIT: SPORT: player*) expulser or renvoyer du terrain; ~ **out** vt (*invitation*) envoyer (par la poste); (*light, heat, signal*) émettre; ~ **up** vt faire monter; (*BRIT: parody*) mettre en boîte, pa-rodier; ~**er** n expéditeur(-trice); ~-**off** n: **a good ~-off** des adieux chaleureux

senior ['si:niər] adj (*high-ranking*) de haut niveau; (*of higher rank*): **to be ~ to sb** être le supérieur de qn ♦ n (*older*): **she is 15 years his ~** elle est son aînée de 15 ans, elle est plus âgée que lui de 15 ans; ~ **citizen** n personne âgée; ~**ity** [si:ni'ɔriti] n (*in service*) ancienneté f

sensation [sen'seifən] n sensation f; ~**al** adj qui fait sensation; (*marvellous*) sensa-tionnel(le)

sense [sens] n sens m; (*feeling*) sentiment

m; (*meaning*) sens, signification *f*; (*wisdom*) bon sens ♦ *vt* sentir, pressentir; **it makes ~** c'est logique; **~less** *adj* insensé(e), stupide; (*unconscious*) sans connaissance

sensible ['sensibl] *adj* sensé(e), raisonnable; sage

sensitive ['sensitiv] *adj* sensible

sensual ['sensjuəl] *adj* sensuel(le)

sensuous ['sensjuəs] *adj* voluptueux(-euse), sensuel(le)

sent [sent] *pt, pp of* **send**

sentence ['sentns] *n* (LING) phrase *f*; (LAW: *judgment*) condamnation *f*, sentence *f*; (: *punishment*) peine *f* ♦ *vt*: **to ~ sb to death/to 5 years in prison** condamner qn à mort/à 5 ans de prison

sentiment ['sentimənt] *n* sentiment *m*; (*opinion*) opinion *f*, avis *m*; **~al** [senti'mentl] *adj* sentimental(e)

sentry ['sentri] *n* sentinelle *f*

separate [*adj* 'seprit, *vb* 'sepəreit] *adj* séparé(e), indépendant(e), différent(e) ♦ *vt* séparer; (*make a distinction between*) distinguer ♦ *vi* se séparer; **~ly** *adv* séparément; **~s** *npl* (*clothes*) coordonnés *mpl*; **separation** [sepə'reifən] *n* séparation *f*

September [sep'tembə'] *n* septembre *m*

septic ['septik] *adj* (*wound*) infecté(e); **~ tank** *n* fosse *f* septique

sequel ['si:kwl] *n* conséquence *f*; séquelles *fpl*; (*of story*) suite *f*

sequence ['si:kwəns] *n* ordre *m*, suite *f*; (*film ~*) séquence *f*; (*dance ~*) numéro *m*

sequin ['si:kwin] *n* paillette *f*

Serbia ['sə:biə] *n* Serbie *f*

serene [sɪ'ri:n] *adj* serein(e), calme, paisible

sergeant ['sɑ:dʒənt] *n* sergent *m*; (POLICE) brigadier *m*

serial ['siəriəl] *n* feuilleton *m*; **~ killer** *n* meurtrier *m* tuant en série; **~ number** *n* numéro *m* de série

series ['siəriz] *n inv* série *f*; (PUBLISHING) collection *f*

serious ['siəriəs] *adj* sérieux(-euse); (*illness*) grave; **~ly** *adv* sérieusement; (*hurt*) gravement

sermon ['sə:mən] *n* sermon *m*

serrated [sɪ'reitid] *adj* en dents de scie

servant ['sə:vənt] *n* domestique *m/f*; (*fig*) serviteur/servante

serve [sə:v] *vt* (*employer etc*) servir, être au service de; (*purpose*) servir à; (*customer, food, meal*) servir; (*subj: train*) desservir; (*apprenticeship*) faire, accomplir; (*prison term*) purger ♦ *vi* servir; (*be useful*): **to ~ as/for/to do** servir de/à/à faire ♦ *n* (TENNIS) service *m*; **it ~s him right** c'est bien fait pour lui; **~ out, ~ up** *vt* (*food*) servir

service ['sə:vis] *n* service *m*; (AUT: *maintenance*) révision *f* ♦ *vt* (*car, washing machine*) réviser; **the S~s** les forces armées; **to be of ~ to sb** rendre service à qn; **15% ~ included** service 15% compris; **~ not included** service non compris; **~able** *adj* pratique, commode; **~ area** *n* (*on motorway*) aire *f* de services; **~ charge** (BRIT) *n* service *m*; **~man** (*irreg*) *n* militaire *m*; **~ station** *n* station-service *f*

serviette [sə:vi'et] (BRIT) *n* serviette *f* (de table)

session ['sefən] *n* séance *f*

set [set] (*pt, pp* **set**) *n* série *f*, assortiment *m*; (*of tools etc*) jeu *m*; (RADIO, TV) poste *m*; (TENNIS) set *m*; (*group of people*) cercle *m*, milieu *m*; (THEATRE: *stage*) scène *f*; (: *scenery*) décor *m*; (MATH) ensemble *m*; (HAIRDRESSING) mise *f* en plis ♦ *adj* (*fixed*) fixe, déterminé(e); (*ready*) prêt(e) ♦ *vt* (*place*) poser, placer; (*fix, establish*) fixer; (: *record*) établir; (*adjust*) régler; (*decide: rules etc*) fixer, choisir; (*task*) donner; (*exam*) composer ♦ *vi* (*sun*) se coucher; (*jam, jelly, concrete*) prendre; (*bone*) se ressouder; **to be ~ on doing** être résolu à faire; **to ~ the table** mettre la table; **to ~ (to music)** mettre en musique; **to ~ on fire** mettre le feu à; **to ~ free** libérer; **to ~ sth going** déclencher qch; **to ~ sail** prendre la mer; **~ about** *vt fus* (*task*) entreprendre, se mettre à; **~ aside** *vt* mettre de côté; (*time*) garder; **~ back** *vt* (*in time*): **to ~ back (by)** retarder (de); (*cost*): **to ~ sb back £5** coûter 5 livres à qn; **~ off** *vi* se mettre en route, partir ♦ vt (bomb) faire exploser; (cause to start) déclencher; (show up well) mettre en valeur, faire valoir; ~ **out** vi se mettre en route, partir ♦ vt (arrange) disposer; (arguments) présenter, exposer; **to ~ out to do** entreprendre de faire, avoir pour but or intention de faire; ~ **up** vt (organization) fonder, créer; ~**back** n (hitch) revers m, contretemps m; ~ **menu** n menu m

settee [sɛ'ti:] n canapé m

setting ['sɛtɪŋ] n cadre m; (of jewel) monture f; (position: of controls) réglage m

settle ['sɛtl] vt (argument, matter, account) régler; (problem) résoudre; (MED: calm) calmer ♦ vi (bird, dust etc) se poser; (also: ~ **down**) s'installer, se fixer; (calm down) se calmer; **to ~ for sth** accepter qch, se contenter de qch; **to ~ on sth** opter or se décider pour qch; ~ **in** vi s'installer; ~ **up** vi: **to ~ up with sb** régler (ce que l'on doit à) qn; ~**ment** n (payment) règlement m; (agreement) accord m; (village etc) établissement m; hameau m; ~**r** n colon m

setup ['sɛtʌp] n (arrangement) manière f dont les choses sont organisées; (situation) situation f

seven ['sɛvn] num sept; ~**teen** num dix-sept; ~**th** num septième; ~**ty** num soixante-dix

sever ['sɛvər] vt couper, trancher; (relations) rompre

several ['sɛvrəl] adj, pron plusieurs m/fpl; ~ **of us** plusieurs d'entre nous

severance ['sɛvərəns] n (of relations) rupture f; ~ **pay** n indemnité f de licenciement

severe [sɪ'vɪər] adj (stern) sévère, strict(e); (serious) grave, sérieux(-euse); (plain) sévère, austère; **severity** [sɪ'vɛrɪtɪ] n sévérité f; gravité f; rigueur f

sew [səu] (pt **sewed**, pp **sewn**) vt, vi coudre; ~ **up** vt (re)coudre

sewage ['su:ɪdʒ] n vidange(s) f(pl)

sewer ['su:ər] n égout m

sewing ['səuɪŋ] n couture f; (item(s)) ouvrage m; ~ **machine** n machine f à coudre

sewn [səun] pp of **sew**

sex [sɛks] n sexe m; **to have ~ with** avoir des rapports (sexuels) avec; ~**ism** n sexisme m; ~**ist** adj sexiste; ~**ual** ['sɛksjuəl] adj sexuel(le); ~**uality** [sɛksju'ælɪtɪ] n sexualité f; ~**y** adj sexy inv

shabby ['ʃæbɪ] adj miteux(-euse); (behaviour) mesquin(e), méprisable

shack [ʃæk] n cabane f, hutte f

shackles ['ʃæklz] npl chaînes fpl, entraves fpl

shade [ʃeɪd] n ombre f; (for lamp) abat-jour m inv; (of colour) nuance f, ton m ♦ vt abriter du soleil, ombrager; **in the ~** à l'ombre; **a ~ too large/more** un tout petit peu trop grand(e)/plus

shadow ['ʃædəu] n ombre f ♦ vt (follow) filer; ~ **cabinet** (BRIT) n (POL) cabinet parallèle formé par l'Opposition; ~**y** adj ombragé(e); (dim) vague, indistinct(e)

shady ['ʃeɪdɪ] adj ombragé(e); (fig: dishonest) louche, véreux(-euse)

shaft [ʃɑ:ft] n (of arrow, spear) hampe f; (AUT, TECH) arbre m; (of mine) puits m; (of lift) cage f; (of light) rayon m, trait m

shaggy ['ʃægɪ] adj hirsute; en broussaille

shake [ʃeɪk] (pt **shook**, pp **shaken**) vt secouer; (bottle, cocktail) agiter; (house, confidence) ébranler ♦ vi trembler; **to ~ one's head** (in refusal) dire or faire non de la tête; (in dismay) secouer la tête; **to ~ hands with sb** serrer la main à qn; ~ **off** vt secouer; (pursuer) se débarrasser de; ~ **up** vt secouer; ~**n** pp of **shake**; **shaky** adj (hand, voice) tremblant(e); (building) branlant(e), peu solide

shall [ʃæl] aux vb: **I ~ go** j'irai; ~ **I open the door?** j'ouvre la porte?; **I'll get the coffee, ~ I?** je vais chercher le café, d'accord?

shallow ['ʃæləu] adj peu profond(e); (fig) superficiel(le)

sham [ʃæm] n frime f ♦ vt simuler

shambles ['ʃæmblz] n (muddle) confusion f, pagaïe f, fouillis m

shame [ʃeɪm] n honte f ♦ vt faire honte à;

it is a ~ (that/to do) c'est dommage (que +*sub*/de faire); **what a ~!** quel dommage!; **~ful** *adj* honteux(-euse), scandaleux(-euse); **~less** *adj* éhonté(e), effronté(e).

shampoo [ʃæm'puː] *n* shampooing *m* ♦ *vt* faire un shampooing à; **~ and set** *n* shampooing *m* (et) mise *f* en plis

shamrock ['ʃæmrɔk] *n* trèfle *m* (*emblème de l'Irlande*)

shandy ['ʃændɪ] *n* bière panachée

shan't [ʃɑːnt] = **shall not**

shanty town ['ʃæntɪ-] *n* bidonville *m*

shape [ʃeɪp] *n* forme *f* ♦ *vt* façonner, modeler; (*sb's ideas*) former; (*sb's life*) déterminer ♦ *vi* (*also: ~ up: events*) prendre tournure; (: *person*) faire des progrès, s'en sortir; **to take ~** prendre forme *or* tournure; **-~d** *suffix*: **heart-~d** en forme de cœur; **~less** *adj* informe, sans forme; **~ly** *adj* bien proportionné(e), beau (belle)

share [ʃɛəʳ] *n* part *f*; (*COMM*) action *f* ♦ *vt* partager; (*have in common*) avoir en commun; **~ out** *vi* partager; **~holder** *n* actionnaire *m/f*

shark [ʃɑːk] *n* requin *m*

sharp [ʃɑːp] *adj* (*razor, knife*) tranchant(e), bien aiguisé(e); (*point, voice*) aigu(-guë); (*nose, chin*) pointu(e); (*outline, increase*) net(te); (*cold, pain*) vif (vive); (*taste*) piquant(e), âcre; (*MUS*) dièse; (*person: quick-witted*) vif (vive), éveillé(e); (: *unscrupulous*) malhonnête ♦ *n* (*MUS*) dièse *m* ♦ *adv* (*precisely*): **at 2 o'clock ~** à 2 heures pile *or* précises; **~en** *vt* aiguiser; (*pencil*) tailler; **~ener** *n* (*also:* **pencil ~ener**) taille-crayon(s) *m inv*; **~-eyed** *adj* à qui rien n'échappe; **~ly** *adv* (*turn, stop*) brusquement; (*stand out*) nettement; (*criticize, retort*) sèchement, vertement

shatter ['ʃætəʳ] *vt* briser; (*fig: upset*) bouleverser; (: *ruin*) briser, ruiner ♦ *vi* voler en éclats, se briser

shave [ʃeɪv] *vt* raser ♦ *vi* se raser ♦ *n*: **to have a ~** se raser; **~r** *n* (*also:* **electric ~r**) rasoir *m* électrique

shaving ['ʃeɪvɪŋ] (*action*) rasage *m*; **~s** *npl*

(*of wood etc*) copeaux *mpl*; **~ brush** *n* blaireau *m*; **~ cream** *n* crème *f* à raser; **~ foam** *n* mousse *f* à raser

shawl [ʃɔːl] *n* châle *m*

she [ʃiː] *pron* elle ♦ *prefix*: **~-cat** chatte *f*; **~-elephant** éléphant *m* femelle

sheaf [ʃiːf] (*pl* **sheaves**) *n* gerbe *f*; (*of papers*) liasse *f*

shear [ʃɪəʳ] (*pt* **sheared**, *pp* **shorn**) *vt* (*sheep*) tondre; **~s** *npl* (*for hedge*) cisaille(s) *f(pl)*

sheath [ʃiːθ] *n* gaine *f*, fourreau *m*, étui *m*; (*contraceptive*) préservatif *m*

shed [ʃed] (*pt, pp* **shed**) *n* remise *f*, resserre *f* ♦ *vt* perdre; (*tears*) verser, répandre; (*workers*) congédier

she'd [ʃiːd] = **she had; she would**

sheen [ʃiːn] *n* lustre *m*

sheep [ʃiːp] *n inv* mouton *m*; **~dog** *n* chien *m* de berger; **~skin** *n* peau *f* de mouton

sheer [ʃɪəʳ] *adj* (*utter*) pur(e), pur et simple; (*steep*) à pic, abrupt(e); (*almost transparent*) extrêmement fin(e) ♦ *adv* à pic, abruptement

sheet [ʃiːt] *n* (*on bed*) drap *m*; (*of paper*) feuille *f*; (*of glass, metal etc*) feuille, plaque *f*

sheik(h) [ʃeɪk] *n* cheik *m*

shelf [ʃelf] (*pl* **shelves**) *n* étagère *f*, rayon *m*

shell [ʃel] *n* (*on beach*) coquillage *m*; (*of egg, nut etc*) coquille *f*; (*explosive*) obus *m*; (*of building*) carcasse *f* ♦ *vt* (*peas*) écosser; (*MIL*) bombarder (d'obus)

she'll [ʃiːl] = **she will; she shall**

shellfish ['ʃelfɪʃ] *n inv* (*crab etc*) crustacé *m*; (*scallop etc*) coquillage *m* ♦ *npl* (*as food*) fruits *mpl* de mer

shell suit *n* survêtement *m* (*en synthétique froissé*)

shelter ['ʃeltəʳ] *n* abri *m*, refuge *m* ♦ *vt* abriter, protéger; (*give lodging to*) donner asile à ♦ *vi* s'abriter, se mettre à l'abri; **~ed housing** *n* foyers *mpl* (*pour personnes âgées ou handicapées*)

shelve [ʃelv] *vt* (*fig*) mettre en suspens *or*

en sommeil; ~s *npl* of **shelf**

shepherd ['ʃepəd] *n* berger *m* ♦ *vt* (*guide*) guider, escorter; ~'s **pie** (*BRIT*) *n* ≃ hachis *m* Parmentier

sheriff ['ʃerɪf] (*US*) *n* shérif *m*

sherry ['ʃerɪ] *n* xérès *m*, sherry *m*

she's [ʃiːz] = **she is**; **she has**

Shetland ['ʃetlənd] *n* (*also*: **the ~ Islands**) les îles *fpl* Shetland

shield [ʃiːld] *n* bouclier *m*; (*protection*) écran *m* de protection ♦ *vt*: **to ~ (from)** protéger (de *or* contre)

shift [ʃɪft] *n* (*change*) changement *m*; (*work period*) période *f* de travail; (*of workers*) équipe *f*, poste *m* ♦ *vt* déplacer, changer de place; (*remove*) enlever ♦ *vi* changer de place, bouger; ~ **work** *n* travail *m* en équipe *or* par relais *or* par roulement; ~**y** *adj* sournois(e); (*eyes*) fuyant(e)

shimmer ['ʃɪmər] *vi* miroiter, chatoyer

shin [ʃɪn] *n* tibia *m*

shine [ʃaɪn] (*pt, pp* **shone**) *n* éclat *m*, brillant *m* ♦ *vi* briller ♦ *vt* (*torch etc*): **to ~ on** braquer sur; (*polish: pt, pp* ~**d**) faire briller *or* reluire

shingle ['ʃɪŋgl] *n* (*on beach*) galets *mpl*; ~**s** *n* (*MED*) zona *m*

shiny ['ʃaɪnɪ] *adj* brillant(e)

ship [ʃɪp] *n* bateau *m*; (*large*) navire *m* ♦ *vt* transporter (par mer); (*send*) expédier (par mer); ~**building** *n* construction navale; ~**ment** *n* cargaison *f*; ~**ping** *n* (*ships*) navires *mpl*; (*the industry*) industrie navale; (*transport*) transport *m*; ~**wreck** *n* (*ship*) épave *f*; (*event*) naufrage *m* ♦ *vt*: **to be ~wrecked** faire naufrage; ~**yard** *n* chantier naval

shire ['ʃaɪər] (*BRIT*) *n* comté *m*

shirt [ʃəːt] *n* (*man's*) chemise *f*; (*woman's*) chemisier *m*; **in (one's) ~ sleeves** en bras de chemise

shit [ʃɪt] (*infl*) *n, excl* merde *f* (!)

shiver ['ʃɪvər] *n* frisson *m* ♦ *vi* frissonner

shoal [ʃəul] *n* (*of fish*) banc *m*; (*fig: also*: ~**s**) masse *f*, foule *f*

shock [ʃɔk] *n* choc *m*; (*ELEC*) secousse *f*; (*MED*) commotion *f*, choc ♦ *vt* (*offend*)

choquer, scandaliser; (*upset*) bouleverser; ~ **absorber** *n* amortisseur *m*; ~**ing** *adj* (*scandalizing*) choquant(e), scandaleux(-euse); (*appalling*) épouvantable

shoddy ['ʃɔdɪ] *adj* de mauvaise qualité, mal fait(e)

shoe [ʃuː] (*pt, pp* **shod**) *n* chaussure *f*, soulier *m*; (*also*: **horseshoe**) fer *m* à cheval ♦ *vt* (*horse*) ferrer; ~**lace** *n* lacet *m* (de soulier); ~ **polish** *n* cirage *m*; ~ **shop** *n* magasin *m* de chaussures; ~**string** *n* (*fig*): **on a ~string** avec un budget dérisoire

shone [ʃɔn] *pt, pp* of **shine**

shook [ʃuk] *pt* of **shake**

shoot [ʃuːt] (*pt, pp* **shot**) *n* (*on branch, seedling*) pousse *f* ♦ *vt* (*game*) chasser; tirer; abattre; (*person*) blesser (*or* tuer) d'un coup de fusil (*or* de revolver); (*execute*) fusiller; (*arrow*) tirer; (*gun*) tirer un coup de; (*film*) tourner ♦ *vi* (*with gun, bow*): **to ~ (at)** tirer (sur); (*FOOTBALL*) shooter, tirer; ~ **down** *vt* (*plane*) abattre; ~ **in** *vi* entrer comme une flèche; ~ **out** *vi* sortir comme une flèche; ~ **up** *vi* (*fig*) monter en flèche; ~**ing** *n* (*shots*) coups *mpl* de feu, fusillade *f*; (*HUNTING*) chasse *f*; ~**ing star** *n* étoile filante

shop [ʃɔp] *n* magasin *m*; (*workshop*) atelier *m* ♦ *vi* (*also*: **go ~ping**) faire ses courses *or* ses achats; ~ **assistant** (*BRIT*) *n* vendeur(-euse); ~ **floor** (*BRIT*) *n* (*INDUSTRY: fig*) ouvriers *mpl*; ~**keeper** *n* commerçant(e); ~**lifting** *n* vol *m* à l'étalage; ~**per** *n* personne *f* qui fait ses courses, acheteur(-euse); ~**ping** *n* (*goods*) achats *mpl*, provisions *fpl*; ~**ping bag** *n* sac *m* (à provisions); ~**ping centre** (*US* **shopping center**) *n* centre commercial; ~**soiled** *adj* défraîchi(e), qui a fait la vitrine; ~ **steward** (*BRIT*) *n* (*INDUSTRY*) délégué(e) syndical(e); ~ **window** *n* vitrine *f*

shore [ʃɔːr] *n* (*of sea, lake*) rivage *m*, rive *f* ♦ *vt*: **to ~ (up)** étayer; **on ~** à terre

shorn [ʃɔːn] *pp* of **shear**

short [ʃɔːt] *adj* (*not long*) court(e); (*soon finished*) court, bref (brève); (*person, step*) petit(e); (*curt*) brusque, sec (sèche); (*insufficient*) insuffisant(e); **to be/run ~ of sth** être à court de *or* manquer de qch; **in ~** bref; en bref; **~ of doing …** à moins de faire …; **everything ~ of** tout sauf; **it is ~ for** c'est l'abréviation *or* le diminutif de; **to cut ~** (*speech, visit*) abréger, écourter; **to fall ~ of** ne pas être à la hauteur de; **to run ~ of** arriver à court de, venir à manquer de; **to stop ~** s'arrêter net; **to stop ~ of** ne pas aller jusqu'à; **~age** *n* manque *m*, pénurie *f*; **~bread** *n* ≃ sablé *m*; **~-change** *vt* ne pas rendre assez à; **~-circuit** *n* court-circuit *m*; **~coming** *n* défaut *m*; **~(crust) pastry** (*BRIT*) *n* pâte brisée; **~cut** *n* raccourci *m*; **~en** *vt* raccourcir; (*text, visit*) abréger; **~fall** *n* déficit *m*; **~hand** (*BRIT*) *n* sténo(graphie) *f*; **~hand typist** (*BRIT*) *n* sténodactylo *m/f*; **~list** (*BRIT*) *n* (*for job*) liste *f* des candidats sélectionnés; **~ly** *adv* bientôt, sous peu; **~ notice** *n*: **at ~ notice** au dernier moment; **~s** *npl*: **(a pair of) ~s** un short; **~-sighted** *adj* (*BRIT*) myope; (*fig*) qui manque de clairvoyance; **~-staffed** *adj* à court de personnel; **~-stay** *adj* (*car park*) de courte durée; **~ story** *n* nouvelle *f*; **~-tempered** *adj* qui s'emporte facilement; **~-term** *adj* (*effect*) à court terme; **~ wave** *n* (*RADIO*) ondes courtes

shot [ʃɔt] *pt, pp* of **shoot** ♦ *n* coup *m* (de feu); (*try*) coup, essai *m*; (*injection*) piqûre *f*; (*PHOT*) photo *f*; **he's a good/poor ~** il tire bien/mal; **like a ~** comme une flèche; (*very readily*) sans hésiter; **~gun** *n* fusil *m* de chasse

should [ʃud] *aux vb*: **I ~ go now** je devrais partir maintenant; **he ~ be there now** il devrait être arrivé maintenant; **I ~ go if I were you** si j'étais vous, j'irais; **I ~ like to** j'aimerais bien, volontiers

shoulder ['ʃəuldəʳ] *n* épaule *f* ♦ *vt* (*fig*) endosser, se charger de; **~ bag** *n* sac *m* à bandoulière; **~ blade** *n* omoplate *f*

shouldn't ['ʃudnt] = **should not**

shout [ʃaut] *n* cri *m* ♦ *vt* crier ♦ *vi* (*also: ~ out*) crier, pousser des cris; **~ down** *vt*

huer; **~ing** *n* cris *mpl*

shove [ʃʌv] *vt* pousser; (*inf: put*): **to ~ sth in** fourrer *or* ficher qch dans; **~ off** (*inf*) *vi* ficher le camp

shovel ['ʃʌvl] *n* pelle *f*

show [ʃəu] (*pt* **showed**, *pp* **shown**) *n* (*of emotion*) manifestation *f*, démonstration *f*; (*semblance*) semblant *m*, apparence *f*; (*exhibition*) exposition *f*, salon *m*; (*THEATRE, TV*) spectacle *m* ♦ *vt* montrer; (*film*) donner; (*courage etc*) faire preuve de, manifester; (*exhibit*) exposer ♦ *vi* se voir, être visible; **for ~** pour l'effet; **on ~** (*exhibits etc*) exposé(e); **to ~** (*person*) faire entrer; **~ off** *vi* (*pej*) crâner ♦ *vt* (*display*) faire valoir; **~ out** *vt* (*person*) reconduire (jusqu'à la porte); **~ up** *vi* (*stand out*) ressortir; (*inf: turn up*) se montrer ♦ *vt* (*flaw*) faire ressortir; **~ business** *n* le monde du spectacle; **~down** *n* épreuve *f* de force

shower ['ʃauəʳ] *n* (*rain*) averse *f*; (*of stones etc*) pluie *f*, grêle *f*; (*~bath*) douche *f* ♦ *vi* prendre une douche, se doucher ♦ *vt*: **to ~ sb with** (*gifts etc*) combler qn de; **to have** *or* **take a ~** prendre une douche; **~proof** *adj* imperméabilisé(e)

showing ['ʃəuɪŋ] *n* (*of film*) projection *f*

show jumping *n* concours *m* hippique

shown [ʃəun] *pp* of **show**

show: ~-off (*inf*) *n* (*person*) crâneur(-euse), m'as-tu-vu(e); **~piece** *n* (*of exhibition*) trésor *m*; **~room** *n* magasin *m* *or* salle *f* d'exposition

shrank [ʃræŋk] *pt* of **shrink**

shrapnel ['ʃræpnl] *n* éclats *mpl* d'obus

shred [ʃred] *n* (*gen pl*) lambeau *m*, petit morceau ♦ *vt* mettre en lambeaux, déchirer; (*CULIN: grate*) râper; (: *lettuce etc*) couper en lanières; **~der** *n* (*for vegetables*) râpeur *m*; (*for documents*) déchiqueteuse *f*

shrewd [ʃru:d] *adj* astucieux(-euse), perspicace; (*businessman*) habile

shriek [ʃri:k] *vi* hurler, crier

shrill [ʃrɪl] *adj* perçant(e), aigu(-guë), strident(e)

shrimp [ʃrɪmp] *n* crevette *f*

shrine [ʃraɪn] *n* (*place*) lieu *m* de

pèlerinage

shrink [ʃrɪŋk] (*pt* **shrank**, *pp* **shrunk**) *vi* rétrécir; (*fig*) se réduire, diminuer; (*move: also:* ~ **away**) reculer ♦ *vt* (*wool*) (faire) rétrécir ♦ *n* (*inf: pej*) psychiatre *m/f*, psy *m/f*; **to** ~ **from** (**doing**) **sth** reculer devant (la pensée de faire) qch; ~**wrap** *vt* emballer sous film plastique

shrivel [ʃrɪvl] *vt* (*also:* ~ **up**) ratatiner, flétrir ♦ *vi* se ratatiner, se flétrir

shroud [ʃraud] *n* linceul *m* ♦ *vt*: ~**ed in mystery** enveloppé(e) de mystère

Shrove Tuesday [ʃrəuv-] *n* (le) Mardi gras

shrub *n* arbuste *m*; ~**bery** *n* massif *m* d'arbustes

shrug [ʃrʌg] *vt, vi*: **to** ~ (**one's shoulders**) hausser les épaules; ~ **off** *vt* faire fi de

shrunk [ʃrʌŋk] *pp of* **shrink**

shudder [ʃʌdər] *vi* frissonner, frémir

shuffle [ʃʌfl] *vt* (*cards*) battre; **to** ~ (**one's feet**) traîner les pieds

shun [ʃʌn] *vt* éviter, fuir

shunt [ʃʌnt] *vt* (*RAIL*) aiguiller

shut [ʃʌt] (*pt, pp* **shut**) *vt* fermer ♦ *vi* (se) fermer; ~ **down** *vt, vi* fermer définitivement; ~ **off** *vt* couper, arrêter; ~ **up** *vi* (*inf: keep quiet*) se taire ♦ *vt* (*close*) fermer; (*silence*) faire taire; ~**ter** *n* volet *m*; (*PHOT*) obturateur *m*

shuttle [ʃʌtl] *n* navette *f*; (*also:* ~ **service**) (service *m* de) navette *f*; ~**cock** *n* volant *m* (*de badminton*); ~ **diplomacy** *n* navettes *fpl* diplomatiques

shy [ʃaɪ] *adj* timide

Siberia [saɪˈbɪərɪə] *n* Sibérie *f*

Sicily [ˈsɪsɪlɪ] *n* Sicile *f*

sick [sɪk] *adj* (*ill*) malade; (*vomiting*): **to be** ~ vomir; (*humour*) noir(e), macabre; **to feel** ~ avoir envie de vomir, avoir mal au cœur; **to be** ~ **of** (*fig*) en avoir assez de; ~ **bay** *n* infirmerie *f*; ~**en** *vt* écœurer; ~**ening** *adj* (*fig*) écœurant(e), dégoûtant(e)

sickle [ˈsɪkl] *n* faucille *f*

sick: ~ **leave** *n* congé *m* de maladie; ~**ly** *adj* maladif(-ive), souffreteux(-euse); (*causing nausea*) écœurant(e); ~**ness** *n* mala-

die *f*; (*vomiting*) vomissement(s) *m(pl)*; ~ **note** *n* (*from parents*) mot *m* d'absence; (*from doctor*) certificat médical; ~ **pay** *n* indemnité *f* de maladie

side [saɪd] *n* côté *m*; (*of lake, road*) bord *m*; (*team*) camp *m*, équipe *f* ♦ *adj* (*door, entrance*) latéral(e) ♦ *vi*: **to** ~ **with sb** prendre le parti de qn, se ranger du côté de qn; **by the** ~ **of** au bord de; ~ **by** ~ côte à côte; **from** ~ **to** ~ d'un côté à l'autre; **to take** ~**s** (**with**) prendre parti (pour); ~**board** *n* buffet *m*; ~**boards** (*BRIT*), ~**burns** *npl* (*whiskers*) pattes *fpl*; ~ **drum** *n* tambour plat; ~ **effect** *n* effet *m* secondaire; ~**light** *n* (*AUT*) veilleuse *f*; ~**line** *n* (*SPORT*) (ligne *f* de) touche *f*; (*fig*) travail *m* secondaire; ~**long** *adj* oblique; ~**show** *n* attraction *f*; ~**step** *vt* (*fig*) éluder; ~ **street** *n* (petite) rue transversale; ~**track** *vt* (*fig*) faire dévier de son sujet; ~**walk** (*US*) *n* trottoir *m*; ~**ways** *adv* de côté

siding [ˈsaɪdɪŋ] *n* (*RAIL*) voie *f* de garage

siege [siːdʒ] *n* siège *m*

sieve [sɪv] *n* tamis *m*, passoire *f*

sift [sɪft] *vt* (*fig: also:* ~ **through**) passer en revue; (*lit: flour etc*) passer au tamis

sigh [saɪ] *n* soupir *m* ♦ *vi* soupirer, pousser un soupir

sight [saɪt] *n* (*faculty*) vue *f*; (*spectacle*) spectacle *m*; (*on gun*) mire *f* ♦ *vt* apercevoir; **in** ~ visible; **out of** ~ hors de vue; ~**seeing** *n* tourisme *m*; **to go** ~**seeing** faire du tourisme

sign [saɪn] *n* signe *m*; (*with hand etc*) signe, geste *m*; (*notice*) panneau *m*, écriteau *m* ♦ *vt* signer; ~ **on** *vi* (*as unemployed*) s'inscrire au chômage; (*for course*) s'inscrire ♦ *vt* (*employee*) embaucher; ~ **over** *vt*: **to** ~ **sth over to sb** céder qch par écrit à qn; ~ **up** *vt* engager ♦ *vi* (*MIL*) s'engager; (*for course*) s'inscrire

signal [ˈsɪgnl] *n* signal *m* ♦ *vi* (*AUT*) mettre son clignotant ♦ *vt* (*person*) faire signe à; (*message*) communiquer par signaux; ~**man** (*irreg*) *n* (*RAIL*) aiguilleur *m*

signature [ˈsɪgnətʃər] *n* signature *f*; ~

tune *n* indicatif musical

signet ring ['sɪgnət-] *n* chevalière *f*

significance [sɪg'nɪfɪkəns] *n* signification *f*; importance *f*

significant [sɪg'nɪfɪkənt] *adj* significatif(-ive); (*important*) important(e), considérable

sign language *n* langage *m* per signes

signpost *n* poteau indicateur

silence ['saɪləns] *n* silence *m* ♦ *vt* faire taire, réduire au silence; ~**r** *n* (*on gun, BRIT: AUT*) silencieux *m*

silent ['saɪlənt] *adj* silencieux(-euse); (*film*) muet(te); **to remain ~** garder le silence, ne rien dire; ~ **partner** *n* (*COMM*) bailleur *m* de fonds, commanditaire *m*

silhouette [sɪlu:'ɛt] *n* silhouette *f*

silicon chip ['sɪlɪkən-] *n* puce *f* électronique

silk [sɪlk] *n* soie *f* ♦ *cpd* de *or* en soie; ~**y** *adj* soyeux(-euse)

silly ['sɪlɪ] *adj* stupide, sot(te), bête

silt [sɪlt] *n* vase *f*; limon *m*

silver ['sɪlvər] *n* argent *m*; (*money*) monnaie *f* (en pièces d'argent); (*also: ~ware*) argenterie *f* ♦ *adj* d'argent, en argent; ~ **paper** (*BRIT*) *n* papier *m* d'argent *or* d'étain; ~**-plated** *adj* plaqué(e) argent *inv*; ~**smith** *n* orfèvre *m/f*; ~**y** *adj* argenté(e)

similar ['sɪmɪlər] *adj*: ~ **(to)** semblable (à); ~**ly** *adv* de la même façon, de même

simmer ['sɪmər] *vi* cuire à feu doux, mijoter

simple ['sɪmpl] *adj* simple; **simplicity** [sɪm'plɪsɪtɪ] *n* simplicité *f*; **simply** *adv* (*without fuss*) avec simplicité

simultaneous [sɪməl'teɪnɪəs] *adj* simultané(e)

sin [sɪn] *n* péché *m* ♦ *vi* pécher

since [sɪns] *adv*, *prep* depuis ♦ *conj* (*time*) depuis que; (*because*) puisque, étant donné que, comme; ~ **then, ever ~** depuis ce moment-là

sincere [sɪn'sɪər] *adj* sincère; ~**ly** *adv* see **yours**; **sincerity** [sɪn'serɪtɪ] *n* sincérité *f*

sinew ['sɪnjuː] *n* tendon *m*

sing [sɪŋ] (*pt* **sang**, *pp* **sung**) *vt*, *vi* chanter

Singapore [sɪŋgə'pɔːr] *n* Singapour *m*

singe [sɪndʒ] *vt* brûler légèrement; (*clothes*) roussir

singer ['sɪŋər] *n* chanteur(-euse)

singing ['sɪŋɪŋ] *n* chant *m*

single ['sɪŋgl] *adj* seul(e), unique; (*unmarried*) célibataire; (*not double*) simple ♦ *n* (*BRIT: also: ~ ticket*) aller *m* (simple); (*record*) 45 tours *m*; ~ **out** *vt* choisir; (*distinguish*) distinguer; ~ **bed** *n* lit *m* d'une personne; ~**-breasted** *adj* droit(e); ~ **file** *n*: **in ~ file** en file indienne; ~**-handed** *adv* tout(e) seul(e), sans (aucune) aide; ~**-minded** *adj* résolu(e), tenace; ~ **parent** *n* parent *m* unique; ~ **room** *n* chambre *f* à un lit *or* pour une personne; ~**s** *n* (*TENNIS*) simple *m*; ~**-track road** *n* route *f* à voie unique; **singly** *adv* séparément

singular ['sɪŋgjulər] *adj* singulier(-ère), étrange; (*outstanding*) remarquable; (*LING*) (au) singulier, du singulier ♦ *n* singulier *m*

sinister ['sɪnɪstər] *adj* sinistre

sink [sɪŋk] (*pt* **sank**, *pp* **sunk**) *n* évier *m* ♦ *vt* (*ship*) (faire) couler, faire sombrer; (*foundations*) creuser ♦ *vi* couler, sombrer; (*ground etc*) s'affaisser; (*also: ~ back, ~ down*) s'affaisser, se laisser retomber; **to ~ sth into** enfoncer qch dans; **my heart sank** j'ai complètement perdu courage; ~ **in** *vi* (*fig*) pénétrer, être compris(e)

sinner ['sɪnər] *n* pécheur(-eresse)

sinus ['saɪnəs] *n* sinus *m inv*

sip [sɪp] *n* gorgée *f* ♦ *vt* boire à petites gorgées

siphon ['saɪfən] *n* siphon *m*; ~ **off** *vt* siphonner; (*money: illegally*) détourner

sir [sər] *n* monsieur *m*; **S~ John Smith** sir John Smith; **yes ~** oui, Monsieur

siren ['saɪərn] *n* sirène *f*

sirloin ['səːlɔɪn] *n* (*also: ~ steak*) aloyau *m*

sissy ['sɪsɪ] (*inf*) *n* (*coward*) poule mouillée

sister ['sɪstər] *n* sœur *f*; (*nun*) religieuse *f*, sœur; (*BRIT: nurse*) infirmière *f* en chef; ~**-in-law** *n* belle-sœur *f*

sit [sɪt] (*pt*, *pp* **sat**) *vi* s'asseoir; (*be ~ting*) être assis(e); (*assembly*) être en séance, siéger; (*for painter*) poser ♦ *vt* (*exam*) passer, se présenter à; ~ **down** *vi* s'asseoir; ~ **in on** *vt fus* assister à; ~ **up** *vi* s'asseoir; (*straight*) se redresser; (*not go to bed*) rester debout, ne pas se coucher

sitcom ['sɪtkɔm] *n abbr* (= situation comedy) comédie *f* de situation

site [saɪt] *n* emplacement *m*, site *m*; (*also:* **building ~**) chantier *m* ♦ *vt* placer

sit-in ['sɪtɪn] *n* (*demonstration*) sit-in *m inv*, occupation *f* (de locaux)

sitting ['sɪtɪŋ] *n* (*of assembly etc*) séance *f*; (*in canteen*) service *m*; ~ **room** *n* salon *m*

situated ['sɪtjueɪtɪd] *adj* situé(e)

situation [sɪtju'eɪʃən] *n* situation *f*; **"~s vacant"** (*BRIT*) "offres d'emploi"

six [sɪks] *num* six; **~teen** *num* seize; **~th** *num* sixième; **~ty** *num* soixante

size [saɪz] *n* taille *f*; dimensions *fpl*; (*of clothing*) taille *f*; (*of shoes*) pointure *f*; (*fig*) ampleur *f*; (*glue*) colle *f*; ~ **up** *vt* juger, jauger; **~able** *adj* assez grand(e); assez important(e)

sizzle ['sɪzl] *vi* grésiller

skate [skeɪt] *n* patin *m*; (*fish: pl inv*) raie *f* ♦ *vi* patiner; **~board** *n* skateboard *m*, planche *f* à roulettes; **~boarding** *n* skateboard *m*; **~r** *n* patineur(-euse); **skating** *n* patinage *m*; **skating rink** *n* patinoire *f*

skeleton ['skɛlɪtn] *n* squelette *m*; (*outline*) schéma *m*; ~ **staff** *n* effectifs réduits

skeptical ['skɛptɪkl] (*US*) *adj* = **sceptical**

sketch [skɛtʃ] *n* (*drawing*) croquis *m*, esquisse *f*; (*THEATRE*) sketch *m*, saynète *f* ♦ *vt* esquisser, faire un croquis *or* une esquisse de; ~ **book** *n* carnet *m* à dessin; **~y** *adj* incomplet(-ète), fragmentaire

skewer ['skju:ə*r*] *n* brochette *f*

ski [ski:] *n* ski *m* ♦ *vi* skier, faire du ski; ~ **boot** *n* chaussure *f* de ski

skid [skɪd] *vi* déraper

ski: ~**er** *n* skieur(-euse); ~**ing** *n* ski *m*; ~ **jump** *n* saut *m* à skis

skilful ['skɪlful] (*US* **skillful**) *adj* habile, adroit(e)

ski lift *n* remonte-pente *m inv*

skill [skɪl] *n* habileté *f*, adresse *f*, talent *m*;

(*requiring training: gen pl*) compétences *fpl*; **~ed** *adj* habile, adroit(e); (*worker*) qualifié(e)

skim [skɪm] *vt* (*milk*) écrémer; (*glide over*) raser, effleurer ♦ *vi*: **to ~ through** (*fig*) parcourir; **~med milk** *n* lait écrémé

skimp [skɪmp] *vt* (*also:* ~ **on**: *work*) bâcler, faire à la va-vite; (: *cloth etc*) lésiner sur; **~y** *adj* (*skirt*) étriqué(e)

skin [skɪn] *n* peau *f* ♦ *vt* (*fruit etc*) éplucher; (*animal*) écorcher; **~ cancer** *n* cancer *m* de la peau; **~-deep** *adj* superficiel(le); **~-diving** *n* plongée sous-marine; **~head** *n* skinhead *m/f*; **~ny** *adj* maigre, maigrichon(ne); **~tight** *adj* (*jeans etc*) moulant(e), ajusté(e)

skip [skɪp] *n* petit bond *or* saut *m*; (*BRIT: container*) benne *f* ♦ *vi* gambader, sautiller; (*with rope*) sauter à la corde ♦ *vt* sauter

ski pass *n* forfait-skieur(s) *m*

ski pole *n* bâton *m* de ski

skipper ['skɪpə*r*] *n* capitaine *m*; (*in race*) skipper *m*

skipping rope ['skɪpɪŋ-] (*BRIT*) *n* corde *f* à sauter

skirmish ['skə:mɪʃ] *n* escarmouche *f*, accrochage *m*

skirt [skə:t] *n* jupe *f* ♦ *vt* longer, contourner; **~ing board** (*BRIT*) *n* plinthe *f*

ski: ~ **slope** *n* piste *f* de ski; ~ **suit** *n* combinaison *f* (de ski); ~ **tow** *n* remonte-pente *m inv*

skittle ['skɪtl] *n* quille *f*; **~s** *n* (*game*) (jeu *m* de) quilles *fpl*

skive [skaɪv] (*BRIT: inf*) *vi* tirer au flanc

skull [skʌl] *n* crâne *m*

skunk [skʌŋk] *n* mouffette *f*

sky [skaɪ] *n* ciel *m*; **~light** *n* lucarne *f*; **~scraper** *n* gratte-ciel *m inv*

slab [slæb] *n* (*of stone*) dalle *f*; (*of food*) grosse tranche

slack [slæk] *adj* (*loose*) lâche, desserré(e); (*slow*) stagnant(e); (*careless*) négligent(e), peu sérieux(-euse) *or* consciencieux(-euse); **~s** *npl* (*trousers*) pantalon *m*; **~en** *vi* ralentir, diminuer ♦ *vt* (*speed*) réduire; (*grip*) relâcher; (*clothing*) desserrer

slag heap [slæg-] *n* crassier *m*

slag off (*BRIT: inf*) *vt* dire du mal de

slam [slæm] *vt* (*door*) (faire) claquer; (*throw*) jeter violemment, flanquer (*fam*); (*criticize*) démolir ♦ *vi* claquer

slander ['slɑːndəʳ] *n* calomnie *f*; diffamation *f*

slang [slæŋ] *n* argot *m*

slant [slɑːnt] *n* inclinaison *f*; (*fig*) angle *m*, point *m* de vue; **~ed** *adj* = **slanting**; **~ing** *adj* en pente, incliné(e); **~ing eyes** yeux bridés

slap [slæp] *n* claque *f*, gifle *f*; tape *f* ♦ *vt* donner une claque *or* une gifle *or* une tape à; (*paint*) appliquer rapidement ♦ *adv* (*directly*) tout droit, en plein; **~dash** *adj* fait(e) sans soin *or* à la va-vite; (*person*) insouciant(e), négligent(e); **~stick** *n* (*comedy*) grosse farce, style *m* tarte à la crème; **~-up** (*BRIT*) *adj*: **a ~-up meal** un repas extra *or* fameux

slash [slæʃ] *vt* entailler, taillader; (*fig: prices*) casser

slat [slæt] *n* latte *f*, lame *f*

slate [sleɪt] *n* ardoise *f* ♦ *vt* (*fig: criticize*) éreinter, démolir

slaughter ['slɔːtəʳ] *n* carnage *m*, massacre *m* ♦ *vt* (*animal*) abattre; (*people*) massacrer; **~house** *n* abattoir *m*

slave [sleɪv] *n* esclave *m/f* ♦ *vi* (*also: ~ away*) trimer, travailler comme un forçat; **~ry** *n* esclavage *m*

slay [sleɪ] (*pt* **slew**, *pp* **slain**) *vt* tuer

sleazy ['sliːzɪ] *adj* miteux(-euse), minable

sledge [slɛdʒ] *n* luge *f* ♦ *vi*: **to go sledging** faire de la luge

sledgehammer *n* marteau *m* de forgeron

sleek [sliːk] *adj* (*hair, fur etc*) brillant(e), lisse; (*car, boat etc*) aux lignes pures *or* élégantes

sleep [sliːp] (*pt, pp* **slept**) *n* sommeil *m* ♦ *vi* dormir; (*spend night*) dormir, coucher; **to go to ~** s'endormir; **~ around** *vi* coucher à droite et à gauche; **~ in** *vi* (*oversleep*) se réveiller trop tard; **~er** (*BRIT*) *n*

(*RAIL: train*) train-couchettes *m*; (: *berth*) couchette *f*; **~ing bag** *n* sac *m* de couchage; **~ing car** *n* (*RAIL*) wagon-lit *m*, voiture-lit *f*; **~ing partner** (*BRIT*) *n* = **silent partner**; **~ing pill** *n* somnifère *m*; **~less** *adj*: **a ~less night** une nuit blanche; **~walker** *n* somnambule *m/f*; **~y** *adj* qui a sommeil, endormi(e)

sleet [sliːt] *n* neige fondue

sleeve [sliːv] *n* manche *f*; (*of record*) pochette *f*

sleigh [sleɪ] *n* traîneau *m*

sleight [slaɪt] *n*: **~ of hand** tour *m* de passe-passe

slender ['slɛndəʳ] *adj* svelte, mince; (*fig*) faible, ténu(e)

slept [slɛpt] *pt, pp of* **sleep**

slew [sluː] *vi* (*also: ~ around*) virer, pivoter ♦ *pt of* **slay**

slice [slaɪs] *n* tranche *f*; (*round*) rondelle *f*; (*utensil*) spatule *f*, truelle *f* ♦ *vt* couper en tranches (*or* en rondelles)

slick [slɪk] *adj* (*skilful*) brillant(e) (en apparence); (*salesman*) qui a du bagout ♦ *n* (*also: oil ~*) nappe *f* de pétrole, marée noire

slide [slaɪd] (*pt, pp* **slid**) *n* (*in playground*) toboggan *m*; (*PHOT*) diapositive *f*; (*BRIT: also: hair ~*) barrette *f*; (*in prices*) chute *f*, baisse *f* ♦ *vt* (faire) glisser ♦ *vi* glisser; **sliding** *adj* (*door*) coulissant(e); **sliding scale** *n* échelle *f* mobile

slight [slaɪt] *adj* (*slim*) mince, menu(e); (*frail*) frêle; (*trivial*) faible, insignifiant(e); (*small*) petit(e), léger(-ère) (*before n*) ♦ *n* offense *f*, affront *m*; **not in the ~est** pas le moins du monde, pas du tout; **~ly** *adv* légèrement, un peu

slim [slɪm] *adj* mince ♦ *vi* maigrir; (*diet*) suivre un régime amaigrissant

slime [slaɪm] *n* (*mud*) vase *f*; (*other substance*) substance visqueuse

slimming ['slɪmɪŋ] *adj* (*diet, pills*) amaigrissant(e); (*foodstuff*) qui ne fait pas grossir

sling [slɪŋ] (*pt, pp* **slung**) *n* (*MED*) écharpe *f*; (*for baby*) porte-bébé *m*; (*weapon*) fronde *f*, lance-pierre *m* ♦ *vt* lancer, jeter

slip [slɪp] n faux pas; (mistake) erreur f; étourderie f; bévue f; (underskirt) combinaison f; (of paper) petite feuille, fiche f ♦ vt (slide) glisser ♦ vi glisser; (decline) baisser; (move smoothly): **to ~ into/out of** se glisser or se faufiler dans/hors de; **to ~ sth on/off** enfiler/enlever qch; **to give sb the ~** fausser compagnie à qn; **a ~ of the tongue** un lapsus; **~ in** vt glisser ♦ vi (errors) s'y glisser; **~ out** vi sortir; **~ up** vi faire une erreur, gaffer; **~ped disc** n déplacement m de vertèbre

slipper [ˈslɪpəʳ] n pantoufle f

slippery [ˈslɪpərɪ] adj glissant(e)

slip: **~ road** (BRIT) n (to motorway) bretelle f d'accès; **~-up** n bévue f; **~way** n cale f (de construction or de lancement)

slit [slɪt] (pt, pp **slit**) n fente f; (cut) incision f ♦ vt fendre; couper; inciser

slither [ˈslɪðəʳ] vi glisser; (snake) onduler

sliver [ˈslɪvəʳ] n (of glass, wood) éclat m; (of cheese etc) petit morceau, fine tranche

slob [slɔb] (inf) n rustaud(e)

slog [slɔg] (BRIT) vi travailler très dur ♦ n gros effort; tâche fastidieuse

slogan [ˈsləugən] n slogan m

slope [sləup] n pente f, côte f; (side of mountain) versant m; (slant) inclinaison f ♦ vi: **to ~ down** être or descendre en pente; **to ~ up** monter; **sloping** adj en pente; (writing) penché(e)

sloppy [ˈslɔpɪ] adj (work) peu soigné(e), bâclé(e); (appearance) négligé(e), débraillé(e)

slot [slɔt] n fente f ♦ vt: **to ~ sth into** encastrer or insérer qch dans

sloth [sləuθ] n (laziness) paresse f

slouch [slautʃ] vi avoir le dos rond, être voûté(e)

slovenly [ˈslʌvənlɪ] adj sale, débraillé(e); (work) négligé(e)

slow [sləu] adj lent(e); (watch): **to be ~** retarder ♦ adv lentement ♦ vt, vi (also: **~ down**, **~ up**) ralentir; **"~"** (road sign) "ralentir"; **~ly** adv lentement; **~ motion** n: **in ~ motion** au ralenti

sludge [slʌdʒ] n boue f

slug [slʌg] n limace f; (bullet) balle f

sluggish [ˈslʌgɪʃ] adj (person) mou (molle), lent(e); (stream, engine, trading) lent

sluice [sluːs] n (also: **~ gate**) vanne f

slum [slʌm] n (house) taudis m

slump [slʌmp] n baisse soudaine, effondrement m; (ECON) crise f ♦ vi s'effondrer, s'affaisser

slung [slʌŋ] pt, pp of **sling**

slur [sləːʳ] n (fig: smear): **~ (on)** atteinte f (à); insinuation f (contre) ♦ vt mal articuler

slush [slʌʃ] n neige fondue

slut [slʌt] (pej) n souillon f

sly [slaɪ] adj (person) rusé(e); (smile, expression, remark) sournois(e)

smack [smæk] n (slap) tape f; (on face) gifle f ♦ vt donner une tape à; (on face) gifler; (on bottom) donner la fessée à ♦ vi: **to ~ of** avoir des relents de, sentir

small [smɔːl] adj petit(e); **~ ads** (BRIT) npl petites annonces; **~ change** n petite or menue monnaie; **~holder** (BRIT) n petit cultivateur; **~ hours** npl: **in the ~ hours** au petit matin; **~pox** n variole f; **~ talk** n menus propos

smart [smɑːt] adj (neat, fashionable) élégant(e), chic inv; (clever) intelligent(e), astucieux(-euse), futé(e); (quick) rapide, vif (vive), prompt(e) ♦ vi faire mal, brûler; (fig) être piqué(e) au vif; **~ card** n carte f à puce; **~en up** vi devenir plus élégant(e), se faire beau (belle) ♦ vt rendre plus élégant(e)

smash [smæʃ] n (also: **~-up**) collision f, accident m; (also: **~ hit**) succès foudroyant ♦ vt casser, briser, fracasser; (opponent) écraser; (SPORT: record) pulvériser ♦ vi se briser, se fracasser; s'écraser; **~ing** (inf) adj formidable

smattering [ˈsmætərɪŋ] n: **a ~ of** quelques notions de

smear [smɪəʳ] n tache f, salissure f; trace f; (MED) frottis m ♦ vt enduire; (make dirty) salir; **~ campaign** n campagne f de diffamation

smell [smɛl] (*pt, pp* **smelt** *or* **smelled**) *n* odeur f; (*sense*) odorat m ♦ *vt* sentir ♦ *vi* (*food etc*): **to ~ (of)** sentir (de); (*pej*) sentir mauvais; **~y** *adj* qui sent mauvais, malodorant(e)

smile [smaɪl] *n* sourire m ♦ *vi* sourire

smirk [smɔːk] *n* petit sourire suffisant *or* affecté

smock [smɔk] *n* blouse f

smog [smɔg] *n* brouillard mêlé de fumée, smog m

smoke [sməuk] *n* fumée f ♦ *vt, vi* fumer; **~d** *adj* (*bacon, glass*) fumé(e); **~r** *n* (*person*) fumeur(-euse); (*RAIL*) wagon m fumeurs; **~ screen** *n* rideau m *or* écran m de fumée; (*fig*) paravent m; **smoking** *n* tabagisme m; **"no smoking"** (*sign*) "défense de fumer"; **to give up smoking** arrêter de fumer; **smoking compartment** (*US* **smoking car**) *n* wagon m fumeurs; **smoky** *adj* enfumé(e); (*taste*) fumé(e)

smolder ['sməuldər] (*US*) *vi* = **smoulder**

smooth [smuːð] *adj* lisse; (*sauce*) onctueux(-euse); (*flavour, whisky*) moelleux(-euse); (*movement*) régulier(-ère), sans à-coups *or* heurts; (*pej: person*) doucereux(-euse), mielleux(-euse) ♦ *vt* (*also: ~ out: skirt, paper*) lisser, défroisser; (: *creases, difficulties*) faire disparaître

smother ['smʌðər] *vt* étouffer

smoulder ['sməuldər] (*US* **smolder**) *vi* couver

smudge [smʌdʒ] *n* tache f, bavure f ♦ *vt* salir, maculer

smug [smʌg] *adj* suffisant(e)

smuggle ['smʌgl] *vt* passer en contrebande *or* en fraude; **~r** *n* contrebandier(-ère); **smuggling** *n* contrebande f

smutty ['smʌtɪ] *adj* (*fig*) grossier(-ère), obscène

snack [snæk] *n* casse-croûte m *inv*; **~ bar** *n* snack(-bar) m

snag [snæg] *n* inconvénient m, difficulté f

snail [sneɪl] *n* escargot m

snake [sneɪk] *n* serpent m

snap [snæp] *n* (*sound*) claquement m, bruit sec; (*photograph*) photo f, instantané m ♦ *adj* subit(e); fait(e) sans réflexion ♦ *vt* (*break*) casser net; (*fingers*) faire claquer ♦ *vi* se casser net *or* avec un bruit sec; (*speak sharply*) parler d'un ton brusque; **to ~ shut** se refermer brusquement; **~ at** *vt fus* (*subj: dog*) essayer de mordre; **~ off** *vi* (*break*) casser net; **~ up** *vt* sauter sur, saisir; **~py** (*inf*) *adj* prompt(e); (*slogan*) qui a du punch; **make it ~py!** grouille-toi!, et que ça saute!; **~shot** *n* photo f, instantané m

snare [snɛər] *n* piège m

snarl [snɑːl] *vi* gronder

snatch [snætʃ] *n* (*small amount*): **~es of** des fragments mpl *or* bribes fpl de ♦ *vt* saisir (*d'un geste vif*); (*steal*) voler

sneak [sniːk] *vi*: **to ~ in/out** entrer/sortir furtivement *or* à la dérobée ♦ *n* (*inf: pej: informer*) faux jeton; **to ~ up on sb** s'approcher de qn sans faire de bruit; **~ers** *npl* tennis mpl, baskets mpl

sneer [snɪər] *vi* ricaner; **to ~ at** traiter avec mépris

sneeze [sniːz] *vi* éternuer

sniff [snɪf] *vi* renifler ♦ *vt* renifler, flairer; (*glue, drugs*) sniffer, respirer

snigger ['snɪgər] *vi* ricaner; pouffer de rire

snip [snɪp] *n* (*cut*) petit coup; (*BRIT: inf: bargain*) (bonne) occasion *or* affaire f ♦ *vt* couper

sniper ['snaɪpər] *n* tireur embusqué

snippet ['snɪpɪt] *n* bribe(s) f(pl)

snob [snɔb] *n* snob m/f; **~bish** *adj* snob *inv*

snooker ['snuːkər] *n* sorte de jeu de billard

snoop [snuːp] *vi*: **to ~ about** fureter

snooze [snuːz] *n* petit somme ♦ *vi* faire un petit somme

snore [snɔːr] *vi* ronfler

snorkel ['snɔːkl] *n* (*of swimmer*) tuba m

snort [snɔːt] *vi* grogner; (*horse*) renâcler

snout [snaut] *n* museau m

snow [snəu] *n* neige f ♦ *vi* neiger; **~ball** *n* boule f de neige; **~bound** *adj* enneigé(e), bloqué(e) par la neige; **~drift** *n* congère f; **~drop** *n* perce-neige m *or* f; **~fall** *n* chute f de neige; **~flake** *n* flocon m de neige; **~man** (*irreg*) *n* bonhomme *m* de neige; **~plough** (*US* **snowplow**) *n* chasse-neige *m inv*; **~shoe** *n* raquette *f* (*pour la neige*); **~storm** *n* tempête *f* de neige

snub [snʌb] *vt* repousser, snober ♦ *n* rebuffade *f*; **~-nosed** *adj* au nez retroussé

snuff [snʌf] *n* tabac *m* à priser

snug [snʌg] *adj* douillet(te), confortable; (*person*) bien au chaud

snuggle ['snʌgl] *vi*: **to ~ up to sb** se serrer *or* se blottir contre qn

⌐▔▔▔▔▔▔▔▔▔▔▔¬
│ KEYWORD │
└▁▁▁▁▁▁▁▁▁▁▁▁┘

so [səu] *adv* **1** (*thus, likewise*) ainsi; **if so** si oui; **so do** *or* **have I** moi aussi; **it's 5 o'clock – so it is!** il est 5 heures – en effet! *or* c'est vrai!; **I hope/think so** je l'espère/le crois; **so far** jusqu'ici, jusqu'à maintenant; (*in past*) jusque-là

2 (*in comparisons etc: to such a degree*) si, tellement; **so big (that)** si *or* tellement grand (que); **she's not so clever as her brother** elle n'est pas aussi intelligente que son frère

3: so much

♦ *adj, adv* tant (de); **I've got so much work** j'ai tant de travail; **I love you so much** je vous aime tant; **so many** tant (de)

4 (*phrases*): **10 or so** à peu près *or* environ 10; **so long!** (*inf: goodbye*) au revoir!, à un de ces jours!

♦ *conj* **1** (*expressing purpose*): **so as to do** pour faire, afin de faire; **so (that)** pour que *or* afin que +*sub*

2 (*expressing result*) donc, par conséquent; **so that** si bien que, de (telle) sorte que

soak [səuk] *vt* faire tremper; (*drench*) tremper ♦ *vi* tremper; **~ in** *vi* être absorbé(e); **~ up** *vt* absorber; **~ing** *adj* trempé(e)

soap [səup] *n* savon *m*; **~flakes** *npl* paillettes *fpl* de savon; **~ opera** *n* feuilleton télévisé; **~ powder** *n* lessive *f*; **~y** *adj* savonneux(-euse)

soar [sɔːʳ] *vi* monter (en flèche), s'élancer; (*building*) s'élancer

sob [sɔb] *n* sanglot *m* ♦ *vi* sangloter

sober ['səubəʳ] *adj* qui n'est pas (*or* plus) ivre; (*serious*) sérieux(-euse), sensé(e); (*colour, style*) sobre, discret(-ète); **~ up** *vt* dessoûler (*inf*) ♦ *vi* dessoûler (*inf*)

so-called ['səu'kɔːld] *adj* soi-disant *inv*

soccer ['sɔkəʳ] *n* football *m*

social ['səuʃl] *adj* social(e); (*sociable*) sociable ♦ *n* (petite) fête; **~ club** *n* amicale *f*, foyer *m*; **~ism** *n* socialisme *m*; **~ist** *adj* socialiste ♦ *n* socialiste *m/f*; **~ize** *vi*: **to ~ize (with)** lier connaissance (avec); parler (avec); **~ security** (*BRIT*) *n* aide sociale; **~ work** *n* assistance sociale, travail social; **~ worker** *n* assistant(e) social(e)

society [sə'saɪətɪ] *n* société *f*; (*club*) société, association *f*; (*also:* **high ~**) (haute) société, grand monde

sociology [səusɪ'ɔlədʒɪ] *n* sociologie *f*

sock [sɔk] *n* chaussette *f*

socket ['sɔkɪt] *n* cavité *f*; (*BRIT: ELEC: also:* **wall ~**) prise *f* de courant

sod [sɔd] *n* (*of earth*) motte *f*; (*BRIT: inf!*) con *m* (!); salaud *m* (!)

soda ['səudə] *n* (*CHEM*) soude *f*; (*also:* **~ water**) eau *f* de Seltz; (*US: also:* **~ pop**) soda *m*

sofa ['səufə] *n* sofa *m*, canapé *m*

soft [sɔft] *adj* (*not rough*) doux (douce); (*not hard*) doux; mou (molle); (*not loud*) doux, léger(-ère); (*kind*) gentil(le); **~ drink** *n* boisson non alcoolisée; **~en** *vt* (r)amollir; (*fig*) adoucir; atténuer ♦ *vi* se ramollir; s'adoucir; s'atténuer; **~ly** *adv* doucement; gentiment; **~ness** *n* douceur *f*; **~ware** *n* (*COMPUT*) logiciel *m*, software *m*

soggy ['sɔgɪ] *adj* trempé(e); détrempé(e)

soil [sɔɪl] *n* (*earth*) sol *m*, terre *f* ♦ *vt* salir; (*fig*) souiller

solar ['səuləʳ] *adj* solaire; **~ panel** *n* panneau *m* solaire; **~ power** *n* énergie solaire

sold [səuld] *pt, pp of* **sell**

solder ['səuldəʳ] *vt* souder (*au fil à souder*) ♦ *n* soudure *f*

soldier [ˈsəuldʒəʳ] *n* soldat *m*, militaire *m*

sole [səul] *n* (*of foot*) plante *f*; (*of shoe*) semelle *f*; (*fish: pl inv*) sole *f* ♦ *adj* seul(e), unique

solemn [ˈsɔləm] *adj* solennel(le); (*person*) sérieux(-euse), grave

sole trader *n* (COMM) chef *m* d'entreprise individuelle

solicit [səˈlɪsɪt] *vt* (*request*) solliciter ♦ *vi* (*prostitute*) racoler

solicitor [səˈlɪsɪtəʳ] *n* (*for wills etc*) ≈ notaire *m*; (*in court*) ≈ avocat *m*

solid [ˈsɔlɪd] *adj* solide; (*not hollow*) plein(e), compact(e), massif(-ive); (*entire*): **3 ~ hours** 3 heures entières ♦ *n* solide *m*

solidarity [sɔlɪˈdærɪtɪ] *n* solidarité *f*

solitary [ˈsɔlɪtərɪ] *adj* solitaire; **~ confinement** *n* (LAW) isolement *m*

solo [ˈsəuləu] *n* solo *m* ♦ *adv* (*fly*) en solitaire; **~ist** *n* soliste *m/f*

soluble [ˈsɔljubl] *adj* soluble

solution [səˈluːʃən] *n* solution *f*

solve [sɔlv] *vt* résoudre

solvent [ˈsɔlvənt] *adj* (COMM) solvable ♦ *n* (CHEM) (dis)solvant *m*

KEYWORD

some [sʌm] *adj* **1** (*a certain amount or number of*): **some tea/water/ice cream** du thé/de l'eau/de la glace; **some children/apples** des enfants/pommes

2 (*certain: in contrasts*): **some people say that ...** il y a des gens qui disent que ...; **some films were excellent, but most ...** certains films étaient excellents, mais la plupart ...

3 (*unspecified*): **some woman was asking for you** il y avait une dame qui vous demandait; **he was asking for some book (or other)** il demandait un livre quelconque; **some day** un de ces jours; **some day next week** un jour la semaine prochaine

♦ *pron* **1** (*a certain number*) quelques-un(e)s, certain(e)s; **I've got some** (*books etc*) j'en ai (quelques-uns); **some (of them) have been sold** certains ont été vendus

2 (*a certain amount*) un peu; **I've got some** (*money, milk*) j'en ai (un peu)

♦ *adv*: **some 10 people** quelque 10 personnes, 10 personnes environ

---

some: **~body** [ˈsʌmbədɪ] *pron* = **someone**; **~how** *adv* d'une façon ou d'une autre; (*for some reason*) pour une raison ou une autre; **~one** *pron* quelqu'un; **~place** (*US*) *adv* = **somewhere**

somersault [ˈsʌməsɔːlt] *n* culbute *f*, saut périlleux ♦ *vi* faire la culbute *or* un saut périlleux; (*car*) faire le tonneau

some: **~thing** *pron* quelque chose; **~thing interesting** quelque chose d'intéressant; **~time** *adv* (*in future*) un de ces jours, un jour ou l'autre; (*in past*): **~time last month** au cours du mois dernier; **~times** *adv* quelquefois, parfois; **~what** *adv* quelque peu, un peu; **~where** *adv* quelque part

son [sʌn] *n* fils *m*

song [sɔŋ] *n* chanson *f*; (*of bird*) chant *m*

son-in-law [ˈsʌnɪnlɔː] *n* gendre *m*, beau-fils *m*

soon [suːn] *adv* bientôt; (*early*) tôt; **~ afterwards** peu après; *see also* **as**; **~er** *adv* (*time*) plus tôt; (*preference*): **I would ~er do** j'aimerais autant *or* je préférerais faire; **~er or later** tôt ou tard

soot [sut] *n* suie *f*

soothe [suːð] *vt* calmer, apaiser

sophisticated [səˈfɪstɪkeɪtɪd] *adj* raffiné(e); sophistiqué(e); (*machinery*) hautement perfectionné(e), très complexe

sophomore [ˈsɔfəmɔːʳ] (*US*) *n* étudiant(e) de seconde année

sopping [ˈsɔpɪŋ] *adj* (*also:* **~ wet**) complètement trempé(e)

soppy [ˈsɔpɪ] (*pej*) *adj* sentimental(e)

soprano [səˈprɑːnəu] *n* (*singer*) soprano *m/f*

sorcerer [ˈsɔːsərəʳ] *n* sorcier *m*

sore [sɔːʳ] *adj* (*painful*) douloureux(-euse), sensible ♦ *n* plaie *f*; **~ly** [ˈsɔːlɪ] *adv* (*tempted*) fortement

sorrow [ˈsɔrəu] *n* peine *f*, chagrin *m*

sorry ['sɒrɪ] *adj* désolé(e); (*condition, excuse*) triste, déplorable; **~!** pardon!, excusez-moi!; **~?** pardon?; **to feel ~ for sb** plaindre qn

sort [sɔ:t] *n* genre *m*, espèce *f*, sorte *f* ♦ *vt* (*also:* **~ out**) trier; classer; ranger; (: *problems*) résoudre, régler; **~ing office** ['sɔ:tɪŋ-] *n* bureau *m* de tri

SOS *n* S.O.S. *m*

so-so ['səʊsəʊ] *adv* comme ci comme ça

sought [sɔ:t] *pt, pp of* **seek**

soul [səʊl] *n* âme *f*; **~ful** ['səʊlful] *adj* sentimental(e); (*eyes*) expressif(-ive)

sound [saʊnd] *adj* (*healthy*) en bonne santé, sain(e); (*safe, not damaged*) solide, en bon état; (*reliable, not superficial*) sérieux(-euse), solide; (*sensible*) sensé(e) ♦ *adv*: **~ asleep** profondément endormi(e) ♦ *n* son *m*; bruit *m*; (GEO) détroit *m*, bras *m* de mer ♦ *vt* (*alarm*) sonner ♦ *vi* sonner, retentir; (*fig: seem*) sembler (être); **to ~ like** ressembler à; **~ out** *vt* sonder; **~ barrier** *n* mur *m* du son; **~ bite** *n* phrase *f* toute faite (*pour être citée dans les médias*); **~ effects** *npl* bruitage *m*; **~ly** *adv* (*sleep*) profondément; (*beat*) complètement, à plate couture; **~proof** *adj* insonorisé(e); **~track** *n* (*of film*) bande *f* sonore

soup [su:p] *n* soupe *f*, potage *m*; **~ plate** *n* assiette creuse *or* à soupe; **~spoon** *n* cuiller *f* à soupe

sour ['saʊər] *adj* aigre; **it's ~ grapes** (*fig*) c'est du dépit

source [sɔ:s] *n* source *f*

south [saʊθ] *n* sud *m* ♦ *adj* sud *inv*, du sud ♦ *adv* au sud, vers le sud; **S~ Africa** *n* Afrique *f* du Sud; **S~ African** *adj* sud-africain(e) ♦ *n* Sud-Africain(e); **S~ America** *n* Amérique *f* du Sud; **S~ American** *adj* sud-américain(e) ♦ *n* Sud-Américain(e); **~-east** *n* sud-est *m*; **~erly** ['sʌðəlɪ] *adj* du sud; au sud; **~ern** ['sʌðən] *adj* (du) sud; méridional(e); **S~ Pole** *n* Pôle *m* Sud; **S~ Wales** *n* sud *m* du Pays de Galles; **~ward(s)** *adv* vers le sud; **~-west** *n* sud-ouest *m*

souvenir [su:və'nɪər] *n* (*objet*) souvenir *m*

sovereign ['sɒvrɪn] *n* souverain(e)

soviet ['səʊvɪət] *adj* soviétique; **the S~ Union** l'Union *f* soviétique

sow[1] [saʊ] *n* truie *f*

sow[2] [saʊ] (*pt* **sowed**, *pp* **sown**) *vt* semer

sown [səʊn] *pp of* **sow**[2]

soya ['sɔɪə] (*US* **soy**) *n*: **~ bean** graine *f* de soja; **soy(a) sauce** sauce *f* au soja

spa [spa:] *n* (*town*) station thermale; (*US: also:* **health ~**) établissement *m* de cure de rajeunissement *etc*

space [speɪs] *n* espace *m*; (*room*) place *f*; espace; (*length of time*) laps *m* de temps ♦ *cpd* spatial(e) ♦ *vt* (*also:* **~ out**) espacer; **~craft** *n* engin spatial; **~man** (*irreg*) *n* astronaute *m*, cosmonaute *m*; **~ship** *n* = **spacecraft**; **spacing** *n* espacement *m*; **spacious** ['speɪʃəs] *adj* spacieux(-euse), grand(e)

spade [speɪd] *n* (*tool*) bêche *f*, pelle *f*; (*child's*) pelle; **~s** *npl* (CARDS) pique *m*

Spain [speɪn] *n* Espagne *f*

span [spæn] *n* (*of bird, plane*) envergure *f*; (*of arch*) portée *f*; (*in time*) espace *m* de temps, durée *f* ♦ *vt* enjamber, franchir; (*fig*) couvrir, embrasser

Spaniard ['spænjəd] *n* Espagnol(e)

spaniel ['spænjəl] *n* épagneul *m*

Spanish ['spænɪʃ] *adj* espagnol(e) ♦ *n* (LING) espagnol *m*; **the ~** *npl* les Espagnols *mpl*

spank [spæŋk] *vt* donner une fessée à

spanner ['spænər] (BRIT) *n* clé *f* (de mécanicien)

spare [spɛər] *adj* de réserve, de rechange; (*surplus*) de *or* en trop, de reste ♦ *n* (*part*) pièce *f* de rechange, pièce détachée ♦ *vt* (*do without*) se passer de; (*afford to give*) donner, accorder; (*refrain from hurting*) épargner; **to ~** (*surplus*) en surplus, de trop; **~ part** *n* pièce *f* de rechange, pièce détachée; **~ time** *n* moments *mpl* de loisir, temps *m* libre; **~ wheel** *n* (AUT) roue *f* de secours; **sparingly** *adv* avec modération

spark [spa:k] *n* étincelle *f*; **~(ing) plug** *n* bougie *f*

sparkle ['spɑːkl] n scintillement m, éclat m
♦ vi étinceler, scintiller; **sparkling** adj
(wine) mousseux(-euse), pétillant(e); (water) pétillant(e); (fig: conversation, performance) étincelant(e), pétillant(e)

sparrow ['spærəu] n moineau m

sparse [spɑːs] adj clairsemé(e)

spartan ['spɑːtən] adj (fig) spartiate

spasm ['spæzəm] n (MED) spasme m;
~**odic** [spæz'mɔdɪk] adj (fig) intermittent(e)

spastic ['spæstɪk] n handicapé(e) moteur

spat [spæt] pt, pp of **spit**

spate [speɪt] n (fig): **a ~ of** une avalanche
or un torrent de

spawn [spɔːn] vi frayer ♦ n frai m

speak [spiːk] (pt **spoke**, pp **spoken**) vt
parler; (truth) dire ♦ vi parler; (make a
speech) prendre la parole; **to ~ to sb/of**
or **about sth** parler à qn/de qch; **~ up!**
parle plus fort!; ~**er** n (in public) orateur
m; (also: **loudspeaker**) haut-parleur m;
the S~er (BRIT: POL) le président de la
chambre des Communes; (US: POL) le président de la chambre des Représentants

spear [spɪəʳ] n lance f ♦ vt transpercer;
~**head** vt (attack etc) mener

spec [spɛk] (inf) n: **on ~** à tout hasard

special ['spɛʃl] adj spécial(e); ~**ist** n spécialiste m/f; ~**ity** [spɛʃɪ'ælɪtɪ] n spécialité f;
~**ize** vi: **to ~ize (in)** se spécialiser (dans);
~**ly** adv spécialement, particulièrement;
~**ty** (esp US) n = **speciality**

species ['spiːʃiːz] n inv espèce f

specific [spə'sɪfɪk] adj précis(e);
particulier(-ère); (BOT, CHEM etc) spécifique;
~**ally** adv expressément, explicitement;
~**ation** [spɛsɪfɪ'keɪʃən] n (TECH) spécification f; (requirement) stipulation f

specimen ['spɛsɪmən] n spécimen m,
échantillon m; (of blood) prélèvement m

speck [spɛk] n petite tache, petit point;
(particle) grain m

speckled ['spɛkld] adj tacheté(e), moucheté(e)

specs [spɛks] (inf) npl lunettes fpl

spectacle ['spɛktəkl] n spectacle m; ~**s**
npl (glasses) lunettes fpl; **spectacular**
[spɛk'tækjuləʳ] adj spectaculaire

spectator [spɛk'teɪtəʳ] n spectateur(-trice)

spectrum ['spɛktrəm] (pl **spectra**) n spectre m

speculation [spɛkju'leɪʃən] n spéculation f

speech [spiːtʃ] n (faculty) parole f; (talk)
discours m, allocution f; (manner of speaking) façon f de parler, langage m; (enunciation) élocution f; ~**less** adj muet(te)

speed [spiːd] n vitesse f; (promptness) rapidité f ♦ vi: **to ~ along/past** etc aller/
passer etc à toute vitesse or allure; **at full**
or **top ~** à toute vitesse or allure; ~ **up** vi
aller plus vite, accélérer ♦ vt accélérer;
~**boat** n vedette f, hors-bord m inv; ~**ily**
adv rapidement, promptement; ~**ing** n
(AUT) excès m de vitesse; ~ **limit** n limitation f de vitesse, vitesse maximale permise; ~**ometer** [spɪ'dɔmɪtəʳ] n compteur m
(de vitesse); ~**way** n (SPORT: also: ~**way**
racing) épreuve(s) f(pl) de vitesse de motos; ~**y** adj rapide, prompt(e)

spell [spɛl] (pt, pp **spelt** or **spelled**) n
(also: **magic ~**) sortilège m, charme m;
(period of time) (courte) période f ♦ vt (in
writing) écrire, orthographier; (aloud) épeler; (fig) signifier; **to cast a ~ on sb** jeter
un sort à qn; **he can't ~** il fait des fautes
d'orthographe; ~**bound** adj envoûté(e),
subjugué(e); ~**ing** n orthographe f

spend [spɛnd] (pt, pp **spent**) vt (money)
dépenser; (time, life) passer; consacrer;
~**thrift** n dépensier(-ère)

sperm [spɜːm] n sperme m

sphere [sfɪəʳ] n sphère f

spice [spaɪs] n épice f; **spicy** adj épicé(e),
relevé(e), (fig) piquant(e)

spider ['spaɪdəʳ] n araignée f

spike [spaɪk] n pointe f; (BOT) épi m

spill [spɪl] (pt, pp **spilt** or **spilled**) vt renverser; répandre ♦ vi se répandre; ~ **over**
vi déborder

spin [spɪn] (pt **spun** or **span**, pp **spun**) n
(revolution of wheel) tour m; (AVIAT) (chute
f en) vrille f; (trip in car) petit tour, balade
f ♦ vt (wool etc) filer; (wheel) faire tourner

♦ *vi* filer; (*turn*) tourner, tournoyer

spinach ['spɪnɪtʃ] *n* épinard *m*; (*as food*) épinards

spinal ['spaɪnl] *adj* vertébral(e), spinal(e); ~ **cord** *n* moelle épinière

spin doctor *n personne employée pour présenter un parti politique sous un jour favorable*

spin-dryer [spɪn'draɪə^r] (*BRIT*) *n* essoreuse *f*

spine [spaɪn] *n* colonne vertébrale; (*thorn*) épine *f*; ~**less** *adj* (*fig*) mou (molle)

spinning ['spɪnɪŋ] *n* (*of thread*) filature *f*; ~ **top** *n* toupie *f*

spin-off ['spɪnɔf] *n* avantage inattendu; sous-produit *m*

spinster ['spɪnstə^r] *n* célibataire *f*; vieille fille (*péj*)

spiral ['spaɪərl] *n* spirale *f* ♦ *vi* (*fig*) monter en flèche; ~ **staircase** *n* escalier *m* en colimaçon

spire ['spaɪə^r] *n* flèche *f*, aiguille *f*

spirit ['spɪrɪt] *n* esprit *m*; (*mood*) état *m* d'esprit; (*courage*) courage *m*, énergie *f*; ~**s** *npl* (*drink*) spiritueux *mpl*, alcool *m*; **in good** ~**s** de bonne humeur; ~**ed** *adj* vif (vive), fougueux(-euse), plein(e) d'allant; ~**ual** *adj* spirituel(le); (*religious*) religieux(-euse)

spit [spɪt] (*pt*, *pp* **spat**) *n* (*for roasting*) broche *f*; (*saliva*) salive *f* ♦ *vi* cracher; (*sound*) crépiter

spite [spaɪt] *n* rancune *f*, dépit *m* ♦ *vt* contrarier, vexer; **in** ~ **of** en dépit de, malgré; ~**ful** *adj* méchant(e), malveillant(e)

spittle ['spɪtl] *n* salive *f*; (*of animal*) bave *f*; (*spat out*) crachat *m*

splash [splæʃ] *n* (*sound*) plouf *m*; (*of colour*) tache *f* ♦ *vt* éclabousser ♦ *vi* (*also*: ~ **about**) barboter, patauger

spleen [spliːn] *n* (*ANAT*) rate *f*

splendid ['splendɪd] *adj* splendide, superbe, magnifique

splint [splɪnt] *n* attelle *f*, éclisse *f*

splinter ['splɪntə^r] *n* (*wood*) écharde *f*; (*glass*) éclat *m* ♦ *vi* se briser, se fendre

split [splɪt] (*pt*, *pp* **split**) *n* fente *f*, déchiru-

re *f*; (*fig*: *POL*) scission *f* ♦ *vt* diviser; (*work, profits*) partager, répartir ♦ *vi* (*divide*) se diviser; ~ **up** *vi* (*couple*) se séparer, rompre; (*meeting*) se disperser

spoil [spɔɪl] (*pt*, *pp* **spoilt** or **spoiled**) *vt* (*damage*) abîmer; (*mar*) gâcher; (*child*) gâter; ~**s** *npl* butin *m*; (*fig*: *profits*) bénéfices *npl*; ~**sport** *n* trouble-fête *m*, rabatjoie *m*

spoke [spəuk] *pt of* **speak** ♦ *n* (*of wheel*) rayon *m*

spoken ['spəukn] *pp of* **speak**

spokesman ['spəuksmən], **spokeswoman** ['spəukswumən] (*irreg*) *n* porte-parole *m inv*

sponge [spʌndʒ] *n* éponge *f*; (*also*: ~ **cake**) ≃ biscuit *m* de Savoie ♦ *vt* éponger ♦ *vi*: **to** ~ **off** or **on** vivre aux crochets de; ~ **bag** (*BRIT*) *n* trousse *f* de toilette

sponsor ['spɔnsə^r] *n* (*RADIO, TV, SPORT*) sponsor *m*; (*for application*) parrain *m*, marraine *f*; (*BRIT*: *for fund-raising event*) donateur(-trice) ♦ *vt* sponsoriser; parrainer; faire un don à; ~**ship** *n* sponsoring *m*; parrainage *m*; dons *mpl*

spontaneous [spɔn'teɪnɪəs] *adj* spontané(e)

spooky ['spuːkɪ] (*inf*) *adj* qui donne la chair de poule

spool [spuːl] *n* bobine *f*

spoon [spuːn] *n* cuiller *f*; ~**-feed** *vt* nourrir à la cuiller; (*fig*) mâcher le travail à; ~**ful** *n* cuillerée *f*

sport [spɔːt] *n* sport *m*; (*person*) chic type (*fille*) ♦ *vt* arborer; ~**ing** *adj* sportif(-ive); **to give sb a** ~**ing chance** donner sa chance à qn; ~ **jacket** (*US*) *n* = **sports jacket**; ~**s car** *n* voiture *f* de sport; ~**s jacket** (*BRIT*) *n* veste *f* de sport; ~**sman** (*irreg*) *n* sportif *m*; ~**smanship** *n* esprit sportif, sportivité *f*; ~**swear** *n* vêtements *mpl* de sport; ~**swoman** (*irreg*) *n* sportive *f*; ~**y** *adj* sportif(-ive)

spot [spɔt] *n* tache *f*; (*dot*: *on pattern*) pois *m*; (*pimple*) bouton *m*; (*place*) endroit *m*, coin *m*; (*RADIO, TV*: *in programme*: *for person*) numéro *m*; (: *for activity*) rubrique *f*;

(*small amount*): **a ~ of** un peu de ♦ *vt* (*notice*) apercevoir, repérer; **on the ~** sur place, sur les lieux; (*immediately*) sur-le-champ; (*in difficulty*) dans l'embarras; **~ check** *n* sondage *m*, vérification ponctuelle; **~less** *adj* immaculé(e); **~light** *n* projecteur *m*; **~ted** *adj* (*fabric*) à pois; **~ty** *adj* (*face, person*) boutonneux(-euse)

spouse [spauz] *n* époux (épouse)

spout [spaut] *n* (*of jug*) bec *m*; (*of pipe*) orifice *m* ♦ *vi* jaillir

sprain [sprein] *n* entorse *f*, foulure *f* ♦ *vt*: **to ~ one's ankle** *etc* se fouler *or* se tordre la cheville *etc*

sprang [spræŋ] *pt of* **spring**

sprawl [sprɔːl] *vi* s'étaler

spray [sprei] *n* jet *m* (en fines gouttelettes); (*from sea*) embruns *mpl*, vaporisateur *m*; (*for garden*) pulvérisateur *m*; (*aerosol*) bombe *f*; (*of flowers*) petit bouquet *m* ♦ *vt* vaporiser, pulvériser; (*crops*) traiter

spread [spred] (*pt, pp* **spread**) *n* (*distribution*) répartition *f*; (*CULIN*) pâte *f* à tartiner; (*inf: meal*) festin *m* ♦ *vt* étendre, étaler; répandre; (*wealth, workload*) distribuer ♦ *vi* (*disease, news*) se propager; (*also:* **~ out**: *stain*) s'étaler; **~ out** (*people*) se disperser; **~-eagled** *adj* étendu(e) bras et jambes écartés; **~sheet** *n* (*COMPUT*) tableur *m*

spree [spriː] *n*: **to go on a ~** faire la fête

sprightly ['spraitli] *adj* alerte

spring [sprɪŋ] (*pt* **sprang**, *pp* **sprung**) *n* (*leap*) bond *m*, saut *m*; (*coiled metal*) ressort *m*; (*season*) printemps *m*; (*of water*) source *f* ♦ *vi* (*leap*) bondir, sauter; **in ~** au printemps; **to ~ from** provenir de; **~ up** *vi* (*problem*) se présenter, surgir; (*plant, buildings*) surgir de terre; **~board** *n* tremplin *m*; **~-clean(ing)** *n* grand nettoyage de printemps; **~time** *n* printemps *m*

sprinkle ['sprɪŋkl] *vt*: **to ~ water** *etc* **on, ~ with water** *etc* asperger d'eau *etc*; **to ~ sugar** *etc* **on, ~ with sugar** *etc* saupoudrer de sucre *etc*; **~r** *n* (*for lawn*) arroseur *m*; (*to put out fire*) diffuseur *m* d'extincteur automatique d'incendie

sprint [sprint] *n* sprint *m* ♦ *vi* courir à toute vitesse; (*SPORT*) sprinter; **~er** *n* sprinteur(-euse)

sprout [spraut] *vi* germer, pousser; **~s** *npl* (*also:* **Brussels ~s**) choux *mpl* de Bruxelles

spruce [spruːs] *n inv* épicéa *m* ♦ *adj* net(te), pimpant(e)

sprung [sprʌŋ] *pp of* **spring**

spun [spʌn] *pt, pp of* **spin**

spur [spəːr] *n* éperon *m*; (*fig*) aiguillon *m* ♦ *vt* (*also:* **~ on**) éperonner; aiguillonner; **on the ~ of the moment** sous l'impulsion du moment

spurious ['spjuəriəs] *adj* faux (fausse)

spurn [spəːn] *vt* repousser avec mépris

spurt [spəːt] *n* (*of blood*) jaillissement *m*; (*of energy*) regain *m*, sursaut *m* ♦ *vi* jaillir, gicler

spy [spai] *n* espion(ne) ♦ *vi*: **to ~ on** espionner, épier; (*see*) apercevoir; **~ing** *n* espionnage *m*

sq. *abbr* = **square**

squabble ['skwɔbl] *vi* se chamailler

squad [skwɔd] *n* (*MIL, POLICE*) escouade *f*, groupe *m*; (*FOOTBALL*) contingent *m*

squadron ['skwɔdrn] *n* (*MIL*) escadron *m*; (*AVIAT, NAUT*) escadrille *f*

squalid ['skwɔlid] *adj* sordide

squall [skwɔːl] *n* rafale *f*, bourrasque *f*

squalor ['skwɔləʳ] *n* conditions *fpl* sordides

squander ['skwɔndəʳ] *vt* gaspiller, dilapider

square [skweəʳ] *n* carré *m*; (*in town*) place *f* ♦ *adj* carré(e); (*inf: ideas, tastes*) vieux jeu *inv* ♦ *vt* (*arrange*) régler; arranger; (*MATH*) élever au carré ♦ *vi* (*reconcile*) concilier; **all ~** quitte; à égalité; **a ~ meal** un repas convenable; **2 metres ~** (de) 2 mètres sur 2; **2 ~ metres** 2 mètres carrés; **~ly** *adv* carrément

squash [skwɔʃ] *n* (*BRIT: drink*): **lemon/orange ~** citronnade *f*/orangeade *f*; (*US: marrow*) courge *f*; (*SPORT*) squash *m* ♦ *vt* écraser

squat [skwɔt] *adj* petit(e) et épais(se), ramassé(e) ♦ *vi* (*also:* **~ down**) s'accroupir;

~ter *n* squatter *m*

squeak [skwi:k] *vi* grincer, crier; (*mouse*) pousser un petit cri

squeal [skwi:l] *vi* pousser un *or* des cri(s) aigu(s) *or* perçant(s); (*brakes*) grincer

squeamish ['skwi:mɪʃ] *adj* facilement dégoûté(e)

squeeze [skwi:z] *n* pression *f*; (ECON) restrictions *fpl* de crédit ♦ *vt* presser; (*hand, arm*) serrer; **~ out** *vt* exprimer

squelch [skwɛltʃ] *vi* faire un bruit de succion

squid [skwɪd] *n* calmar *m*

squiggle ['skwɪgl] *n* gribouillis *m*

squint [skwɪnt] *vi* loucher ♦ *n*: **he has a ~** il louche, il souffre de strabisme

squirm [skwə:m] *vi* se tortiller

squirrel ['skwɪrəl] *n* écureuil *m*

squirt [skwə:t] *vi* jaillir, gicler

Sr *abbr* = **senior**

St *abbr* = **saint; street**

stab [stæb] *n* (*with knife etc*) coup *m* (de couteau *etc*); (*of pain*) lancée *f*; (*inf: try*): **to have a ~ at (doing) sth** s'essayer à (faire) qch ♦ *vt* poignarder

stable ['steɪbl] *n* écurie *f* ♦ *adj* stable

stack [stæk] *n* tas *m*, pile *f* ♦ *vt* (*also: ~ up*) empiler, entasser

stadium ['steɪdɪəm] (*pl* **stadia** *or* **~s**) *n* stade *m*

staff [stɑ:f] *n* (*workforce*) personnel *m*; (BRIT: SCOL) professeurs *mpl* ♦ *vt* pourvoir en personnel

stag [stæg] *n* cerf *m*

stage [steɪdʒ] *n* scène *f*; (*platform*) estrade *f* ♦ *n* (*point*) étape *f*, stade *m*; (*profession*): **the ~** le théâtre ♦ *vt* (*play*) monter, mettre en scène; (*demonstration*) organiser; **in ~s** par étapes, par degrés; **~coach** *n* diligence *f*; **~ manager** *n* régisseur *m*

stagger ['stægər] *vi* chanceler, tituber ♦ *vt* (*person: amaze*) stupéfier; (*hours, holidays*) étaler, échelonner; **~ing** *adj* (*amazing*) stupéfiant(e), renversant(e)

stagnate [stæg'neɪt] *vi* stagner, croupir

stag party *n* enterrement *m* de vie de garçon

staid [steɪd] *adj* posé(e), rassis(e)

stain [steɪn] *n* tache *f*; (*colouring*) colorant *m* ♦ *vt* tacher; (*wood*) teindre; **~ed glass window** *n* vitrail *m*; **~less steel** *n* acier *m* inoxydable, inox *m*; **~ remover** *n* détachant *m*

stair [steər] *n* (*step*) marche *f*; **~s** *npl* (*flight of steps*) escalier *m*; **~case, ~way** *n* escalier *m*

stake [steɪk] *n* pieu *m*, poteau *m*; (BETTING) enjeu *m*; (COMM: *interest*) intérêts *mpl* ♦ *vt* risquer, jouer; **to be at ~** être en jeu; **to ~ one's claim (to)** revendiquer

stale [steɪl] *adj* (*bread*) rassis(e); (*food*) pas frais (fraîche); (*beer*) éventé(e); (*smell*) de renfermé; (*air*) confiné(e)

stalemate ['steɪlmeɪt] *n* (CHESS) pat *m*; (*fig*) impasse *f*

stalk [stɔ:k] *n* tige *f* ♦ *vt* traquer ♦ *vi*: **to ~ out/off** sortir/partir d'un air digne

stall [stɔ:l] *n* (BRIT: *in street, market etc*) éventaire *m*, étal *m*; (*in stable*) stalle *f* ♦ *vt* (AUT) caler; (*delay*) retarder ♦ *vi* (AUT) caler; (*fig*) essayer de gagner du temps; **~s** *npl* (BRIT: *in cinema, theatre*) orchestre *m*

stallion ['stæljən] *n* étalon *m* (*cheval*)

stamina ['stæmɪnə] *n* résistance *f*, endurance *f*

stammer ['stæmər] *n* bégaiement *m* ♦ *vi* bégayer

stamp [stæmp] *n* timbre *m*; (*rubber ~*) tampon *m*; (*mark, also fig*) empreinte *f* ♦ *vi* (*also: ~ one's foot*) taper du pied ♦ *vt* (*letter*) timbrer; (*with rubber ~*) tamponner; **~ album** *n* album *m* de timbres(-poste); **~ collecting** *n* philatélie *f*

stampede [stæm'pi:d] *n* ruée *f*

stance [stæns] *n* position *f*

stand [stænd] (*pt, pp* **stood**) *n* (*position*) position *f*; (*for taxis*) station *f* (de taxis); (*music ~*) pupitre *m* à musique; (COMM) étalage *m*, stand *m*; (SPORT: *also:* **~s**) tribune *f* ♦ *vi* être *or* se tenir (debout); (*rise*) se lever, se mettre debout; (*be placed*) se trouver; (*remain: offer etc*) rester valable; (BRIT: *in election*) être candidat(e), se présenter ♦ *vt* (*place*) mettre, poser; (*tolerate,* *withstand*) supporter; (*treat, invite to*) offrir, payer; **to make** *or* **take a ~** prendre position; **to ~ at** (*score, value etc*) être de; **to ~ for parliament** (*BRIT*) se présenter aux élections législatives; **~ by** *vi* (*be ready*) se tenir prêt(e) ♦ *vt fus* (*opinion*) s'en tenir à; (*person*) ne pas abandonner, soutenir; **~ down** *vi* (*withdraw*) se retirer; **~ for** *vt fus* (*signify*) représenter, signifier; (*tolerate*) supporter, tolérer; **~ in for** *vt fus* remplacer; **~ out** *vi* (*be prominent*) ressortir; **~ up** *vi* (*rise*) se lever, se mettre debout; **~ up for** *vt fus* défendre; **~ up to** *vt fus* tenir tête à, résister à

standard ['stændəd] *n* (*level*) niveau (voulu); (*norm*) norme *f*, étalon *m*; (*criterion*) critère *m*; (*flag*) étendard *m* ♦ *adj* (*size etc*) ordinaire, normal(e); courant(e); (*text*) de base; **~s** *npl* (*morals*) morale *f*, principes *mpl*; **~ lamp** (*BRIT*) *n* lampadaire *m*; **~ of living** *n* niveau *m* de vie

stand-by ['stændbaɪ] *n* remplaçant(e); **to be on ~~** se tenir prêt(e) (à intervenir); être de garde; **~~ ticket** *n* (*AVIAT*) billet *m* stand-by

stand-in ['stændɪn] *n* remplaçant(e)

standing ['stændɪŋ] *adj* debout *inv*; (*permanent*) permanent(e) ♦ *n* réputation *f*, rang *m*, standing *m*; **of many years'** ~ qui dure *or* existe depuis longtemps; **~ joke** *n* vieux sujet de plaisanterie; **~ order** (*BRIT*) *n* (*at bank*) virement *m* automatique, prélèvement *m* bancaire; **~ room** *n* places *fpl* debout

standpoint ['stændpɔɪnt] *n* point *m* de vue

standstill ['stændstɪl] *n*: **at a ~** paralysé(e); **to come to a ~** s'immobiliser, s'arrêter

stank [stæŋk] *pt of* **stink**

staple ['steɪpl] *n* (*for papers*) agrafe *f* ♦ *adj* (*food etc*) de base ♦ *vt* agrafer; **~r** *n* agrafeuse *f*

star [stɑːʳ] *n* étoile *f*; (*celebrity*) vedette *f* ♦ *vi*: **to ~ (in)** être la vedette (de) ♦ *vt* (*CINEMA etc*) avoir pour vedette; **the ~s** *npl* l'horoscope *m*

starboard ['stɑːbəd] *n* tribord *m*

starch [stɑːtʃ] *n* amidon *m*; (*in food*) fécule *f*

stardom ['stɑːdəm] *n* célébrité *f*

stare [steəʳ] *n* regard *m* fixe ♦ *vi*: **to ~ at** regarder fixement

starfish ['stɑːfɪʃ] *n* étoile *f* de mer

stark [stɑːk] *adj* (*bleak*) désolé(e), morne ♦ *adv*: **~ naked** complètement nu(e)

starling ['stɑːlɪŋ] *n* étourneau *m*

starry ['stɑːrɪ] *adj* étoilé(e); **~-eyed** *adj* (*innocent*) ingénu(e)

start [stɑːt] *n* commencement *m*, début *m*; (*of race*) départ *m*; (*sudden movement*) sursaut *m*; (*advantage*) avance *f*, avantage *m* ♦ *vt* commencer; (*found*) créer; (*engine*) mettre en marche ♦ *vi* partir, se mettre en route; (*jump*) sursauter; **to ~ doing** *or* **to do sth** se mettre à faire qch; **~ off** *vi* commencer; (*leave*) partir; **~ up** *vi* commencer; (*car*) démarrer ♦ *vt* (*business*) créer; (*car*) mettre en marche; **~er** *n* (*AUT*) démarreur *m*; (*SPORT: official*) starter *m*; (*BRIT: CULIN*) entrée *f*; **~ing point** *n* point *m* de départ

startle ['stɑːtl] *vt* faire sursauter; donner un choc à; **startling** *adj* (*news*) surprenant(e)

starvation [stɑːˈveɪʃən] *n* faim *f*, famine *f*

starve [stɑːv] *vi* mourir de faim; être affamé(e) ♦ *vt* affamer

state [steɪt] *n* état *m*; (*POL*) État ♦ *vt* déclarer, affirmer; **the S~s** *npl* (*America*) les États-Unis *mpl*; **to be in a ~** être dans tous ses états; **~ly** *adj* majestueux(-euse), imposant(e); **~ly home** *n* château *m*; **~ment** *n* déclaration *f*; **~sman** (*irreg*) *n* homme *m* d'État

static ['stætɪk] *n* (*RADIO, TV*) parasites *mpl* ♦ *adj* statique

station ['steɪʃən] *n* gare *f*; (*police ~*) poste *m* de police ♦ *vt* placer, poster

stationary ['steɪʃnərɪ] *adj* à l'arrêt, immobile

stationer ['steɪʃənəʳ] *n* papetier(-ère); **~'s (shop)** *n* papeterie *f*; **~y** *n* papier *m* à lettres, petit matériel de bureau

stationmaster ['steɪʃənmɑːstər] *n* (*RAIL*) chef *m* de gare

station wagon (*US*) *n* break *m*

statistic *n* statistique *f*; **~s** [stə'tɪstɪks] *n* (*science*) statistique *f*

statue ['stætjuː] *n* statue *f*

status ['steɪtəs] *n* position *f*, situation *f*; (*official*) statut *m*; (*prestige*) prestige *m*; **~ symbol** *n* signe extérieur de richesse

statute ['stætjuːt] *n* loi *f*, statut *m*; **statutory** *adj* statutaire, prévu(e) par un article de loi

staunch [stɔːntʃ] *adj* sûr(e), loyal(e)

stay [steɪ] *n* (*period of time*) séjour *m* ♦ *vi* rester; (*reside*) loger; (*spend some time*) séjourner; **to ~ put** ne pas bouger; **to ~ with friends** loger chez des amis; **to ~ the night** passer la nuit; **~ behind** *vi* rester en arrière; **~ in** *vi* (*at home*) rester à la maison; **~ on** *vi* rester; **~ out** *vi* (*of house*) ne pas rentrer; **~ up** *vi* (*at night*) ne pas se coucher; **~ing power** *n* endurance *f*

stead [sted] *n*: **in sb's ~** à la place de qn; **to stand sb in good ~** être très utile à qn

steadfast ['stedfɑːst] *adj* ferme, résolu(e)

steadily ['stedɪlɪ] *adv* (*regularly*) progressivement; (*firmly*) fermement; (*: walk*) d'un pas ferme; (*fixedly: look*) sans détourner les yeux

steady ['stedɪ] *adj* stable, solide, ferme; (*regular*) constant(e), régulier(-ère); (*person*) calme, pondéré(e) ♦ *vt* stabiliser; (*nerves*) calmer; **a ~ boyfriend** un petit ami

steak [steɪk] *n* (*beef*) bifteck *m*, steak *m*; (*fish, pork*) tranche *f*

steal [stiːl] (*pt* **stole**, *pp* **stolen**) *vt* voler ♦ *vi* voler; (*move secretly*) se faufiler, se déplacer furtivement

stealth [stelθ] *n*: **by ~** furtivement

steam [stiːm] *n* vapeur *f* ♦ *vt* (*CULIN*) cuire à la vapeur ♦ *vi* fumer; **~ engine** *n* locomotive *f* à vapeur; **~er** *n* (*bateau m* à) vapeur *m*; **~ship** *n* = **steamer**; **~y** *adj* embué(e), humide

steel [stiːl] *n* acier *m* ♦ *adj* d'acier;

~works *n* aciérie *f*

steep [stiːp] *adj* raide, escarpé(e); (*price*) excessif(-ive)

steeple ['stiːpl] *n* clocher *m*

steer [stɪər] *vt* diriger; (*boat*) gouverner; (*person*) guider, conduire ♦ *vi* tenir le gouvernail; **~ing** *n* (*AUT*) conduite *f*; **~ing wheel** *n* volant *m*

stem [stem] *n* (*of plant*) tige *f*; (*of glass*) pied *m* ♦ *vt* contenir, arrêter, juguler; **~ from** *vt fus* provenir de, découler de

stench [stentʃ] *n* puanteur *f*

stencil ['stensl] *n* stencil *m*; (*pattern used*) pochoir *m* ♦ *vt* polycopier

stenographer [ste'nɔgrəfər] (*US*) *n* sténographe *m/f*

step [step] *n* pas *m*; (*stair*) marche *f*; (*action*) mesure *f*, disposition *f* ♦ *vi*: **to ~ forward/back** faire un pas en avant/arrière, avancer/reculer; **~s** *npl* (*BRIT*) = **stepladder**; **to be in/out of ~ (with)** (*fig*) aller dans le sens (de)/être déphasé(e) (par rapport à); **~ down** *vi* (*fig*) se retirer, se désister; **~ up** *vt* augmenter; intensifier; **~brother** *n* demi-frère *m*; **~daughter** *n* belle-fille *f*; **~father** *n* beau-père *m*; **~ladder** (*BRIT*) *n* escabeau *m*; **~mother** *n* belle-mère *f*; **~ping stone** *n* pierre *f* de gué; (*fig*) tremplin *m*; **~sister** *n* demi-sœur *f*; **~son** *n* beau-fils *m*

stereo ['steriəu] *n* (*sound*) stéréo *f*; (*hi-fi*) chaîne *f* stéréo *inv* ♦ *adj* (*also:* **~phonic**) stéréo(phonique)

sterile ['steraɪl] *adj* stérile; **sterilize** ['sterɪlaɪz] *vt* stériliser

sterling ['stɜːlɪŋ] *adj* (*silver*) de bon aloi, fin(e) ♦ *n* (*ECON*) livres *fpl* sterling *inv*; **a pound ~** une livre sterling

stern [stɜːn] *adj* sévère ♦ *n* (*NAUT*) arrière *m*, poupe *f*

stew [stjuː] *n* ragoût *m* ♦ *vt*, *vi* cuire (à la casserole)

steward ['stjuːəd] *n* (*on ship, plane, train*) steward *m*; **~ess** *n* hôtesse *f* (de l'air)

stick [stɪk] (*pt*, *pp* **stuck**) *n* bâton *m*; (*walking ~*) canne *f* ♦ *vt* (*glue*) coller; (*inf: put*) mettre, fourrer; (*: tolerate*) supporter;

(*thrust*): **to ~ sth into** planter *or* enfoncer qch dans ♦ *vi* (*become attached*) rester collé(e) *or* fixé(e); (*be unmoveable*: *wheels etc*) se bloquer; (*remain*) rester; **~ out** *vi* dépasser, sortir; **~ up** *vi* = **stick out**; **~ up for** *vt fus* défendre; **~er** *n* auto-collant *m*; **~ing plaster** *n* sparadrap *m*, pansement adhésif

stick-up ['stɪkʌp] (*inf*) *n* braquage *m*, hold-up *m inv*

sticky ['stɪkɪ] *adj* poisseux(-euse); (*label*) adhésif(-ive); (*situation*) délicat(e)

stiff [stɪf] *adj* raide; rigide; dur(e); (*difficult*) difficile, ardu(e); (*cold*) froid(e), distant(e); (*strong, high*) fort(e), élevé(e) ♦ *adv*: **to be bored / scared / frozen ~** s'ennuyer à mort/être mort(e) de peur/froid; **~en** *vi* se raidir; **~ neck** *n* torticolis *m*

stifle ['staɪfl] *vt* étouffer, réprimer

stigma ['stɪgmə] *n* stigmate *m*

stile [staɪl] *n* échalier *m*

stiletto [stɪ'letəu] (*BRIT*) *n* (*also*: **~ heel**) talon *m* aiguille

still [stɪl] *adj* immobile ♦ *adv* (*up to this time*) encore, toujours; (*even*) encore; (*nonetheless*) quand même, tout de même; **~born** *adj* mort-né(e); **~ life** *n* nature morte

stilt [stɪlt] *n* (*for walking on*) échasse *f*; (*pile*) pilotis *m*

stilted ['stɪltɪd] *adj* guindé(e), emprunté(e)

stimulate ['stɪmjuleɪt] *vt* stimuler

stimuli ['stɪmjulaɪ] *npl of* **stimulus**

stimulus ['stɪmjuləs] (*pl* **stimuli**) *n* stimulant *m*; (*BIOL, PSYCH*) stimulus *m*

sting [stɪŋ] (*pt, pp* **stung**) *n* piqûre *f*; (*organ*) dard *m* ♦ *vt, vi* piquer

stingy ['stɪndʒɪ] *adj* avare, pingre

stink [stɪŋk] (*pt* **stank**, *pp* **stunk**) *n* puanteur *f* ♦ *vi* puer, empester; **~ing** (*inf*) *adj* (*fig*) infect(e), vache; **a ~ing ...** un(e) foutu(e) ...

stint [stɪnt] *n* part *f* de travail ♦ *vi*: **to ~ on** lésiner sur, être chiche de

stir [stɜːʳ] *n* agitation *f*, sensation *f* ♦ *vt* remuer ♦ *vi* remuer, bouger; **~ up** *vt* (*trouble*) fomenter, provoquer

stirrup ['stɪrəp] *n* étrier *m*

stitch [stɪtʃ] *n* (*SEWING*) point *m*; (*KNITTING*) maille *f*; (*MED*) point de suture; (*pain*) point de côté ♦ *vt* coudre, piquer; (*MED*) suturer

stoat [stəut] *n* hermine *f* (*avec son pelage d'été*)

stock [stɔk] *n* réserve *f*, provision *f*; (*COMM*) stock *m*; (*AGR*) cheptel *m*, bétail *m*; (*CULIN*) bouillon *m*; (*descent, origin*) souche *f*; (*FINANCE*) valeurs *fpl*, titres *mpl* ♦ *adj* (*fig: reply etc*) classique ♦ *vt* (*have in* ~) avoir, vendre; **~s and shares** valeurs (mobilières), titres; **in/out of ~** en stock *or* en magasin/épuisé(e); **to take ~ of** (*fig*) faire le point de; **~ up** *vi*: **to ~ up (with)** s'approvisionner (en); **~broker** *n* agent *m* de change; **~ cube** *n* bouillon-cube *m*; **~ exchange** *n* Bourse *f*

stocking ['stɔkɪŋ] *n* bas *m*

stock: **~ market** *n* Bourse *f*, marché financier; **~pile** *n* stock *m*, réserve *f* ♦ *vt* stocker, accumuler; **~taking** (*BRIT*) *n* (*COMM*) inventaire *m*

stocky ['stɔkɪ] *adj* trapu(e), râblé(e)

stodgy ['stɔdʒɪ] *adj* bourratif(-ive), lourd(e)

stoke [stəuk] *vt* (*fire*) garnir, entretenir; (*boiler*) chauffer

stole [stəul] *pt of* **steal** ♦ *n* étole *f*

stolen ['stəuln] *pp of* **steal**

stomach ['stʌmək] *n* estomac *m*; (*abdomen*) ventre *m* ♦ *vt* digérer, supporter; **~ache** *n* mal m à l'estomac *or* au ventre

stone [stəun] *n* pierre *f*; (*pebble*) caillou *m*, galet *m*; (*in fruit*) noyau *m*; (*MED*) calcul *m*; (*BRIT: weight*) 6,348 kg ♦ *adj* de *or* en pierre ♦ *vt* (*person*) lancer des pierres sur, lapider; **~-cold** *adj* complètement froid(e); **~-deaf** *adj* sourd(e) comme un pot; **~work** *n* maçonnerie *f*

stood [stud] *pt, pp of* **stand**

stool [stuːl] *n* tabouret *m*

stoop [stuːp] *vi* (*also*: **have a ~**) être voûté(e); (*also*: **~ down**: *bend*) se baisser

stop [stɔp] *n* arrêt *m*; halte *f*; (*in punctuation*: *also*: **full ~**) point *m* ♦ *vt* arrêter, bloquer; (*break off*) interrompre; (*also*: **put a**

~ to) mettre fin à ♦ vi s'arrêter; (*rain, noise etc*) cesser, s'arrêter; **to ~ doing sth** cesser *or* arrêter de faire qch; **~ dead** vi s'arrêter net; **~ off** vi faire une courte halte; **~ up** vt (*hole*) boucher; **~gap** n (*person*) bouche-trou m; (*measure*) mesure f intérimaire; **~over** n halte f; (*AVIAT*) escale f; **~page** n (*strike*) arrêt de travail; (*blockage*) obstruction f; **~per** n bouchon m; **~ press** n nouvelles fpl de dernière heure; **~watch** n chronomètre m

storage ['stɔ:rɪdʒ] n entreposage m; **~ heater** n radiateur m électrique par accumulation

store [stɔ:r] n (*stock*) provision f, réserve f; (*depot*) entrepôt m; (*BRIT: large shop*) grand magasin; (*US*) magasin m ♦ vt emmagasiner; (*information*) enregistrer; **~s** npl (*food*) provisions f; **in ~**, en réserve; **~ up** vt mettre en réserve, accumuler; **~room** n réserve f, magasin m

storey ['stɔ:rɪ] (*US* **story**) n étage m

stork [stɔ:k] n cigogne f

storm [stɔ:m] n tempête f; (*thunderstorm*) orage m ♦ vi (*fig*) fulminer ♦ vt prendre d'assaut; **~y** adj orageux(-euse)

story ['stɔ:rɪ] n histoire m; récit m; (*US*) = **storey**; **~book** n livre m d'histoires *or* de contes

stout [staʊt] adj solide; (*fat*) gros(se), corpulent(e) ♦ n bière brune

stove [stəʊv] n (*for cooking*) fourneau m; (*: small*) réchaud m; (*for heating*) poêle m

stow [stəʊ] vt (*also: ~ away*) ranger; **~away** n passager(-ère) clandestin(e)

straddle ['strædl] vt enjamber, être à cheval sur

straggle ['strægl] vi être (*or* marcher) en désordre

straight [streɪt] adj droit(e); (*hair*) raide; (*frank*) honnête, franc (franche); (*simple*) simple ♦ adv (tout) droit; (*drink*) sec, sans eau; **to put** *or* **get ~** (*fig*) mettre au clair; **~ away, ~ off** (*at once*) tout de suite; **~en** vt ajuster; (*bed*) arranger; **~en out** vt (*fig*) débrouiller; **~-faced** adj impassible; **~forward** adj simple; (*honest*) direct(e)

strain [streɪn] n tension f; pression f; (*physical*) effort m; (*mental*) tension (nerveuse); (*breed*) race f ♦ vt (*stretch: resources etc*) mettre à rude épreuve, grever; (*hurt: back etc*) se faire mal à; (*vegetables*) égoutter; **~s** npl (*MUS*) accords mpl, accents mpl; **back ~** tour m de rein; **~ed** adj (*muscle*) froissé(e); (*laugh etc*) forcé(e), contraint(e); (*relations*) tendu(e); **~er** n passoire f

strait [streɪt] n (*GEO*) détroit m; **~s** npl: **to be in dire ~s** avoir de sérieux ennuis (d'argent); **~jacket** n camisole f de force; **~-laced** [streɪt'leɪst] adj collet monté *inv*

strand [strænd] n (*of thread*) fil m, brin m; (*of rope*) toron m; (*of hair*) mèche f; **~ed** adj en rade, en plan

strange [streɪndʒ] adj (*not known*) inconnu(e); (*odd*) étrange, bizarre; **~ly** adv étrangement, bizarrement; *see also* **enough**; **~r** n inconnu(e); (*from another area*) étranger(-ère)

strangle ['stræŋgl] vt étrangler; **~hold** n (*fig*) emprise totale, mainmise f

strap [stræp] n lanière f, courroie f, sangle f; (*of slip, dress*) bretelle f; **~py** adj (*dress*) à bretelles; (*sandals*) à lanières

strategic [strə'ti:dʒɪk] adj stratégique; **strategy** ['strætɪdʒɪ] n stratégie f

straw [strɔ:] n paille f; **that's the last ~!** ça, c'est le comble!

strawberry ['strɔ:bərɪ] n fraise f

stray [streɪ] adj (*animal*) perdu(e), errant(e); (*scattered*) isolé(e) ♦ vi s'égarer; **~ bullet** n balle perdue

streak [stri:k] n bande f, filet m; (*in hair*) raie f ♦ vt zébrer, strier ♦ vi: **to ~ past** passer à toute allure

stream [stri:m] n (*brook*) ruisseau m; (*current*) courant m, flot m; (*of people*) défilé ininterrompu, flot ♦ vt (*SCOL*) répartir par niveau ♦ vi ruisseler; **to ~ in/out** entrer/ sortir à flots

streamer ['stri:mər] n serpentin m; (*banner*) banderole f

streamlined ['stri:mlaɪnd] adj aérodynamique; (*fig*) rationalisé(e)

street [stri:t] n rue f; **~car** (*US*) n tramway

m; ~ **lamp** *n* réverbère *m*; ~ **plan** *n* plan *m* (des rues); ~**wise** (*inf*) *adj* futé(e), réaliste

strength [strεŋθ] *n* force *f*; (*of girder, knot etc*) solidité *f*; ~**en** *vt* (*muscle etc*) fortifier; (*nation, case etc*) renforcer; (*building, ECON*) consolider

strenuous ['strεnjuəs] *adj* vigoureux(-euse), énergique

stress [strεs] *n* (*force, pressure*) pression *f*; (*mental strain*) tension (nerveuse), stress *m*; (*accent*) accent *m* ♦ *vt* insister sur, souligner

stretch [strεtʃ] *n* (*of sand etc*) étendue *f* ♦ *vi* s'étirer; (*extend*): **to ~ to** *or* **as far as** s'étendre jusqu'à ♦ *vt* tendre, étirer; (*fig*) pousser (au maximum); ~ **out** *vi* s'étendre ♦ *vt* (*arm etc*) allonger, tendre; (*spread*) étendre

stretcher ['strεtʃər] *n* brancard *m*, civière *f*

stretchy ['strεtʃɪ] *adj* élastique

strewn [struːn] *adj*: ~ **with** jonché(e) de

stricken ['strɪkən] *adj* (*person*) très éprouvé(e); (*city, industry etc*) dévasté(e); ~ **with** (*disease etc*) frappé(e) *or* atteint(e) de

strict [strɪkt] *adj* strict(e)

stride [straɪd] (*pt* **strode**, *pp* **stridden**) *n* grand pas *m*, enjambée *f* ♦ *vi* marcher à grands pas

strife [straɪf] *n* conflit *m*, dissensions *fpl*

strike [straɪk] (*pt, pp* **struck**) *n* grève *f*; (*of oil etc*) découverte *f*; (*attack*) raid *m* ♦ *vt* frapper; (*oil etc*) trouver, découvrir; (*deal*) conclure ♦ *vi* faire grève; (*attack*) attaquer; (*clock*) sonner; **on ~** (*workers*) en grève; **to ~ a match** frotter une allumette; ~ **down** *vt* terrasser; ~ **up** *vt* (*MUS*) se mettre à jouer; **to ~ up a friendship with** se lier d'amitié avec; **to ~ up a conversation (with)** engager une conversation (avec); ~**r** *n* gréviste *m/f*; (*SPORT*) buteur *m*; **striking** *adj* frappant(e), saisissant(e); (*attractive*) éblouissant(e)

string [strɪŋ] (*pt, pp* **strung**) *n* ficelle *f*; (*row: of beads*) rang *m*; (: *of onions*) chapelet *m*; (*MUS*) corde *f* ♦ *vt*: **to ~ out** échelonner; **the ~s** *npl* (*MUS*) les instruments

mpl à cordes; **to ~ together** enchaîner; **to pull ~s** (*fig*) faire jouer le piston; ~**(ed) instrument** *n* (*MUS*) instrument *m* à cordes

stringent ['strɪndʒənt] *adj* rigoureux(-euse)

strip [strɪp] *n* bande *f* ♦ *vt* (*undress*) déshabiller; (*paint*) décaper; (*also*: ~ **down**: *machine*) démonter ♦ *vi* se déshabiller; ~ **cartoon** *n* bande dessinée

stripe [straɪp] *n* raie *f*, rayure *f*; (*MIL*) galon *m*; ~**d** *adj* rayé(e), à rayures

strip: ~ **lighting** (*BRIT*) *n* éclairage *m* au néon *or* fluorescent; ~**per** *n* stripteaseur(-euse) *f*; ~ **search** *n* fouille corporelle (*en faisant se déshabiller la personne*) ♦ *vt*: **he was ~ searched** on l'a fait se déshabiller et soumis à une fouille corporelle

stripy ['straɪpɪ] *adj* rayé(e)

strive [straɪv] (*pt* **strove**, *pp* **striven**) *vi*: **to ~ to do/for sth** s'efforcer de faire/d'obtenir qch

strode [strəud] *pt of* **stride**

stroke [strəuk] *n* coup *m*; (*SWIMMING*) nage *f*; (*MED*) attaque *f* ♦ *vt* caresser; **at a ~** d'un (seul) coup

stroll [strəul] *n* petite promenade ♦ *vi* flâner, se promener nonchalamment; ~**er** (*US*) *n* (*pushchair*) poussette *f*

strong [strɔŋ] *adj* fort(e); vigoureux(-euse); (*heart, nerves*) solide; **they are 50 ~** ils sont au nombre de 50; ~**hold** *n* bastion *m*; ~**ly** *adv* fortement, avec force; vigoureusement; solidement; ~**room** *n* chambre forte

strove [strəuv] *pt of* **strive**

struck [strʌk] *pt, pp of* **strike**

structural ['strʌktʃrəl] *adj* structural(e); (*CONSTR*: *defect*) de construction; (*damage*) affectant les parties portantes

structure ['strʌktʃər] *n* structure *f*; (*building*) construction *f*

struggle ['strʌgl] *n* lutte *f* ♦ *vi* lutter, se battre

strum [strʌm] *vt* (*guitar*) jouer (en sourdine) de

strung [strʌŋ] *pt, pp of* **string**

strut [strʌt] n étai m, support m ♦ vi se pavaner

stub [stʌb] n (of cigarette) bout m, mégot m; (of cheque etc) talon m ♦ vt: **to ~ one's toe** se cogner le doigt de pied; **~ out** vt écraser

stubble ['stʌbl] n chaume m; (on chin) barbe f de plusieurs jours

stubborn ['stʌbən] adj têtu(e), obstiné(e), opiniâtre

stuck [stʌk] pt, pp of **stick** ♦ adj (jammed) bloqué(e), coincé(e); **~-up** (inf) adj prétentieux(-euse)

stud [stʌd] n (on boots etc) clou m; (on collar) bouton m de col; (earring) petite boucle d'oreille; (of horses: also: **~ farm**) écurie f, haras m; (also: **~ horse**) étalon m ♦ vt (fig): **~ded with** parsemé(e) or criblé(e) de

student ['stju:dənt] n étudiant(e) ♦ adj estudiantin(e); d'étudiant; **~ driver** (US) n (conducteur(-trice)) débutant(e)

studio ['stju:dɪəu] n studio m, atelier m; (TV etc) studio

studious ['stju:dɪəs] adj studieux(-euse), appliqué(e); (attention) soutenu(e); **~ly** adv (carefully) soigneusement

study ['stʌdɪ] n étude f; (room) bureau m ♦ vt étudier; (examine) examiner ♦ vi étudier, faire ses études

stuff [stʌf] n chose(s) f(pl); affaires fpl, trucs mpl; (substance) substance f ♦ vt rembourrer; (CULIN) farcir; (inf: push) fourrer; **~ing** n bourre f, rembourrage m; (CULIN) farce f; **~y** adj (room) mal ventilé(e) or aéré(e); (ideas) vieux jeu inv

stumble ['stʌmbl] vi trébucher; **to ~ across** or **on** (fig) tomber sur; **stumbling block** n pierre f d'achoppement

stump [stʌmp] n souche f; (of limb) moignon m ♦ vt: **to be ~ed** sécher, ne pas savoir que répondre

stun [stʌn] vt étourdir; (fig) abasourdir

stung [stʌŋ] pt, pp of **sting**

stunk [stʌŋk] pp of **stink**

stunned [stʌnd] adj sidéré(e)

stunning ['stʌnɪŋ] adj (news etc) stupéfiant(e); (girl etc) éblouissant(e)

stunt [stʌnt] n (in film) cascade f, acrobatie f; (publicity ~) truc m publicitaire ♦ vt retarder, arrêter; **~man** ['stʌntmæn] (irreg) n cascadeur m

stupendous [stju:'pendəs] adj prodigieux(-euse), fantastique

stupid ['stju:pɪd] adj stupide, bête; **~ity** [stju:'pɪdɪtɪ] n stupidité f, bêtise f

sturdy ['stə:dɪ] adj robuste; solide

stutter ['stʌtəʳ] vi bégayer

sty [staɪ] n (for pigs) porcherie f

stye [staɪ] n (MED) orgelet m

style [staɪl] n style m; (distinction) allure f, cachet m, style; **stylish** adj élégant(e), chic inv

stylus ['staɪləs] (pl **styli** or **~es**) n (of record player) pointe f de lecture

suave [swɑ:v] adj doucereux(-euse), onctueux(-euse)

sub... [sʌb] prefix sub..., sous-; **~conscious** adj subconscient(e); **~contract** vt sous-traiter

subdue [səb'dju:] vt subjuguer, soumettre; **~d** adj (light) tamisé(e); (person) qui a perdu de son entrain

subject [n 'sʌbdʒɪkt, vb səb'dʒɛkt] n sujet m; (SCOL) matière f ♦ vt: **to ~ to** soumettre à; exposer à; **to be ~ to** (law) être soumis(e) à; (disease) être sujet(te) à; **~ive** [səb'dʒɛktɪv] adj subjectif(-ive); **~ matter** n (content) contenu m

sublet [sʌb'lɛt] vt sous-louer

submarine [sʌbmə'ri:n] n sous-marin m

submerge [səb'mə:dʒ] vt submerger ♦ vi plonger

submission [səb'mɪʃən] n soumission f; **submissive** adj soumis(e)

submit [səb'mɪt] vt soumettre ♦ vi se soumettre

subnormal [sʌb'nɔ:ml] adj au-dessous de la normale

subordinate [sə'bɔ:dɪnət] adj subalterne ♦ n subordonné(e) de

subpoena [səb'pi:nə] n (LAW) citation f, assignation f

subscribe [səb'skraɪb] vi cotiser; **to ~ to**

(*opinion, fund*) souscrire à; (*newspaper*) s'abonner à; être abonné(e) à; ~r *n* (*to periodical, telephone*) abonné(e); **subscription** [səbˈskrɪpʃən] *n* (*to magazine etc*) abonnement *m*

subsequent [ˈsʌbsɪkwənt] *adj* ultérieur(e), suivant(e); consécutif(-ive); ~**ly** *adv* par la suite

subside [səbˈsaɪd] *vi* (*flood*) baisser; (*wind, feelings*) tomber; ~**nce** [səbˈsaɪdns] *n* affaissement *m*

subsidiary [səbˈsɪdɪərɪ] *adj* subsidiaire; accessoire ♦ *n* filiale *f*

subsidize [ˈsʌbsɪdaɪz] *vt* subventionner; **subsidy** [ˈsʌbsɪdɪ] *n* subvention *f*

substance [ˈsʌbstəns] *n* substance *f*

substantial [səbˈstænʃl] *adj* substantiel(le); (*fig*) important(e); ~**ly** *adv* considérablement; (*in essence*) en grande partie

substantiate [səbˈstænʃɪeɪt] *vt* étayer, fournir des preuves à l'appui de

substitute [ˈsʌbstɪtjuːt] *n* (*person*) remplaçant(e); (*thing*) succédané *m* ♦ *vt*: **to ~ sth/sb for** substituer qch/qn à, remplacer par qch/qn

subterranean [sʌbtəˈreɪnɪən] *adj* souterrain(e)

subtitle [ˈsʌbtaɪtl] *n* (*CINEMA, TV*) sous-titre *m*; ~**d** *adj* sous-titré(e)

subtle [ˈsʌtl] *adj* subtil(e)

subtotal [sʌbˈtəʊtl] *n* total partiel

subtract [səbˈtrækt] *vt* soustraire, retrancher; ~**ion** *n* soustraction *f*

suburb [ˈsʌbəːb] *n* faubourg *m*; **the ~s** *npl* la banlieue; ~**an** [səˈbəːbən] *adj* de banlieue, suburbain(e); ~**ia** [səˈbəːbɪə] *n* la banlieue

subway [ˈsʌbweɪ] *n* (*US: railway*) métro *m*; (*BRIT: underpass*) passage souterrain

succeed [səkˈsiːd] *vi* réussir ♦ *vt* succéder à; **to ~ in doing** réussir à faire; ~**ing** *adj* (*following*) suivant(e)

success [səkˈses] *n* succès *m*; réussite *f*; ~**ful** *adj* (*venture*) couronné(e) de succès; **to be ~ful (in doing)** réussir (à faire); ~**fully** *adv* avec succès

succession [səkˈseʃən] *n* succession *f*; **3**

days in ~ 3 jours de suite

successive [səkˈsesɪv] *adj* successif(-ive); consécutif(-ive)

such [sʌtʃ] *adj* tel (telle); (*of that kind*): ~ **a book** un livre de ce genre, un livre pareil, un tel livre; (*so much*): ~ **courage** un tel courage ♦ *adv* si; ~ **books** des livres de ce genre, des livres pareils, de tels livres; ~ **a long trip** un si long voyage; ~ **a lot of** tellement *or* tant de; ~ **as** (*like*) tel que, comme; **as** ~ en tant que tel, à proprement parler; ~-**and**-~ *adj* tel ou tel

suck [sʌk] *vt* sucer; (*breast, bottle*) téter; ~**er** *n* ventouse *f*; (*inf*) poire *f*

suction [ˈsʌkʃən] *n* succion *f*

sudden [ˈsʌdn] *adj* soudain(e), subit(e); **all of a ~** soudain, tout à coup; ~**ly** *adv* brusquement, tout à coup, soudain

suds [sʌdz] *npl* eau savonneuse

sue [suː] *vt* poursuivre en justice, intenter un procès à

suede [sweɪd] *n* daim *m*

suet [ˈsuːɪt] *n* graisse *f* de rognon

suffer [ˈsʌfə*] *vt* souffrir, subir; (*bear*) tolérer, supporter ♦ *vi* souffrir; ~**er** *n* (*MED*) malade *m/f*; ~**ing** *n* souffrance(s) *f(pl)*

sufficient [səˈfɪʃənt] *adj* suffisant(e); ~ **money** suffisamment d'argent; ~**ly** *adv* suffisamment, assez

suffocate [ˈsʌfəkeɪt] *vi* suffoquer; étouffer

sugar [ˈʃugə*] *n* sucre *m* ♦ *vt* sucrer; ~ **beet** *n* betterave sucrière; ~ **cane** *n* canne *f* à sucre

suggest [səˈdʒest] *vt* suggérer, proposer; (*indicate*) dénoter; ~**ion** *n* suggestion *f*

suicide [ˈsuɪsaɪd] *n* suicide *m*; *see also* **commit**; ~ **bomber** *n* kamikaze *m/f*; ~ **bombing** *n* attentat suicide *m*

suit [suːt] *n* (*man's*) costume *m*, complet *m*; (*woman's*) tailleur *m*, ensemble *m*; (*LAW*) poursuite *f(pl)*, procès *m*; (*CARDS*) couleur *f* ♦ *vt* aller à; convenir à; (*adapt*): **to ~ sth to** adapter *or* approprier qch à; **well ~ed** (*matched*) faits l'un pour l'autre, très bien assortis; ~**able** *adj* qui convient; approprié(e); ~**ably** *adv* comme il se doit (*or se devait etc*), convenablement

suitcase ['su:tkeɪs] *n* valise *f*

suite [swi:t] *n* (*of rooms, also MUS*) suite *f*; (*furniture*): **bedroom / dining room ~** (ensemble *m* de) chambre *f* à coucher/salle *f* à manger

suitor ['su:tər] *n* soupirant *m*, prétendant *m*

sulfur ['sʌlfər] (*US*) *n* = **sulphur**

sulk [sʌlk] *vi* bouder; **~y** *adj* boudeur(-euse), maussade

sullen ['sʌlən] *adj* renfrogné(e), maussade

sulphur ['sʌlfər] (*US* **sulfur**) *n* soufre *m*

sultana [sʌl'tɑ:nə] *n* (*CULIN*) raisin (sec) de Smyrne

sultry ['sʌltrɪ] *adj* étouffant(e)

sum [sʌm] *n* somme *f*; (*SCOL etc*) calcul *m*; **~ up** *vt*, *vi* résumer

summarize ['sʌməraɪz] *vt* résumer

summary ['sʌmərɪ] *n* résumé *m*

summer ['sʌmər] *n* été *m* ♦ *adj* d'été, estival(e); **~house** *n* (*in garden*) pavillon *m*; **~time** *n* été *m*; **~ time** *n* (*by clock*) heure *f* d'été

summit ['sʌmɪt] *n* sommet *m*

summon ['sʌmən] *vt* appeler, convoquer; **~ up** *vt* rassembler, faire appel à; **~s** *n* citation *f*, assignation *f*

sun [sʌn] *n* soleil *m*; **in the ~** au soleil; **~bathe** *vi* prendre un bain de soleil; **~block** *n* écran *m* total; **~burn** *n* coup *m* de soleil; **~burned**, **~burnt** *adj* (*tanned*) bronzé(e)

Sunday ['sʌndɪ] *n* dimanche *m*; **~ school** *n* ≈ catéchisme *m*

sundial ['sʌndaɪəl] *n* cadran *m* solaire

sundown ['sʌndaun] *n* coucher *m* du (*or* de) soleil

sundries ['sʌndrɪz] *npl* articles divers

sundry ['sʌndrɪ] *adj* divers(e), différent(e) ♦ *n*: **all and ~** tout le monde, n'importe qui

sunflower ['sʌnflauər] *n* tournesol *m*

sung [sʌŋ] *pp of* **sing**

sunglasses ['sʌnglɑ:sɪz] *npl* lunettes *fpl* de soleil

sunk [sʌŋk] *pp of* **sink**

sun: **~light** *n* (lumière *f* du) soleil *m*; **~lit**
adj ensoleillé(e); **~ny** *adj* ensoleillé(e); **~rise** *n* lever *m* du (*or* de) soleil; **~ roof** *n* (*AUT*) toit ouvrant; **~screen** *n* crème *f* solaire; **~set** *n* coucher *m* du (*or* de) soleil; **~shade** *n* (*over table*) parasol *m*; **~shine** *n* (lumière *f* du) soleil *m*; **~stroke** *n* insolation *f*; **~tan** *n* bronzage *m*; **~tan lotion** *n* lotion *f or* lait *m* solaire; **~tan oil** *n* huile *f* solaire

super ['su:pər] (*inf*) *adj* formidable

superannuation [su:pərænju'eɪʃən] *n* (*contribution*) cotisations *fpl* pour la pension

superb [su:'pə:b] *adj* superbe, magnifique

supercilious [su:pə'sɪlɪəs] *adj* hautain(e), dédaigneux(-euse)

superficial [su:pə'fɪʃəl] *adj* superficiel(le)

superimpose ['su:pərɪm'pəuz] *vt* superposer

superintendent [su:pərɪn'tendənt] *n* directeur(-trice); (*POLICE*) ≈ commissaire *m*

superior [su'pɪərɪər], *adj*, *n* supérieur(e); **~ity** [supɪərɪ'ɒrɪtɪ] *n* supériorité *f*

superlative [su'pə:lətɪv] *n* (*LING*) superlatif *m*

superman ['su:pəmæn] (*irreg*) *n* surhomme *m*

supermarket ['su:pəmɑ:kɪt] *n* supermarché *m*

supernatural [su:pə'nætʃərəl] *adj* surnaturel(le)

superpower ['su:pəpauər] *n* (*POL*) superpuissance *f*

supersede [su:pə'si:d] *vt* remplacer, supplanter

superstitious [su:pə'stɪʃəs] *adj* superstitieux(-euse)

supervise ['su:pəvaɪz] *vt* surveiller; diriger; **supervision** [su:pə'vɪʒən] *n* surveillance *f*; contrôle *m*; **supervisor** *n* surveillant(e); (*in shop*) chef *m* de rayon

supper ['sʌpər] *n* dîner *m*; (*late*) souper *m*

supple ['sʌpl] *adj* souple

supplement [*n* 'sʌplɪmənt, *vb* sʌplɪ'mɛnt] *n* supplément *m* ♦ *vt* compléter; **~ary** [sʌplɪ'mɛntərɪ] *adj* supplémentaire; **~ary benefit** (*BRIT*) *n* allocation *f* (supplémentaire) d'aide sociale

supplier [sə'plaɪəʳ] *n* fournisseur *m*

supply [sə'plaɪ] *vt* (*provide*) fournir; (*equip*): **to ~ (with)** approvisionner *or* ravitailler (en); fournir (en) ♦ *n* provision *f*, réserve *f*; (~*ing*) approvisionnement *m*; **supplies** *npl* (*food*) vivres *mpl*; (*MIL*) subsistances *fpl*; **~ teacher** (*BRIT*) *n* suppléant(e)

support [sə'pɔ:t] *n* (*moral, financial etc*) soutien *m*, appui *m*; (*TECH*) support *m*, soutien ♦ *vt* soutenir, supporter; (*financially*) subvenir aux besoins de; (*uphold*) être pour, être partisan de, appuyer; **~er** *n* (*POL etc*) partisan(e); (*SPORT*) supporter *m*

suppose [sə'pəuz] *vt* supposer; imaginer; **to be ~d to do** être censé(e) faire; **~dly** [sə'pəuzɪdlɪ] *adv* soi-disant; **supposing** *conj* si, à supposer que +*sub*

suppress [sə'pres] *vt* (*revolt*) réprimer; (*information*) supprimer; (*yawn*) étouffer; (*feelings*) refouler

supreme [su'pri:m] *adj* suprême

surcharge ['sɜ:tʃɑ:dʒ] *n* surcharge *f*

sure [ʃuəʳ] *adj* sûr(e); (*definite, convinced*) sûr, certain(e); **~! (**of course**) bien sûr!; ~ enough** effectivement; **to make ~ of sth** s'assurer de *or* vérifier qch; **to make ~ that** s'assurer *or* vérifier que; **~ly** *adv* sûrement; certainement

surf [sɜ:f] *n* (*waves*) ressac *m*

surface ['sɜ:fɪs] *n* surface *f* ♦ *vt* (*road*) poser un revêtement sur ♦ *vi* remonter à la surface; faire surface; **~ mail** *n* courrier *m* par voie de terre (*or* maritime)

surfboard ['sɜ:fbɔ:d] *n* planche *f* de surf

surfeit ['sɜ:fɪt] *n*: **a ~ of** un excès de; une indigestion de

surfing ['sɜ:fɪŋ] *n* surf *m*

surge [sɜ:dʒ] *n* vague *f*, montée *f* ♦ *vi* déferler

surgeon ['sɜ:dʒən] *n* chirurgien *m*

surgery ['sɜ:dʒərɪ] *n* chirurgie *f*; (*BRIT: room*) cabinet *m* (de consultation); (*: also:* **~ hours**) heures *fpl* de consultation

surgical ['sɜ:dʒɪkl] *adj* chirurgical(e); **~ spirit** (*BRIT*) *n* alcool *m* à 90°

surname ['sɜ:neɪm] *n* nom *m* de famille

surplus ['sɜ:pləs] *n* surplus *m*, excédent *m* ♦ *adj* en surplus, de trop; (*COMM*) excédentaire

surprise [sə'praɪz] *n* surprise *f*; (*astonishment*) étonnement *m* ♦ *vt* surprendre; (*astonish*) étonner; **surprising** *adj* surprenant(e), étonnant(e); **surprisingly** *adv* (*easy, helpful*) étonnamment

surrender [sə'rendəʳ] *n* reddition *f*, capitulation *f* ♦ *vi* se rendre, capituler

surreptitious [sʌrəp'tɪʃəs] *adj* subreptice, furtif(-ive)

surrogate ['sʌrəgɪt] *n* substitut *m*; **~ mother** *n* mère porteuse *or* de substitution

surround [sə'raund] *vt* entourer; (*MIL etc*) encercler; **~ing** *adj* environnant(e); **~ings** *npl* environs *mpl*, alentours *mpl*

surveillance [sɜ:'veɪləns] *n* surveillance *f*

survey [*n* 'sɜ:veɪ, *vb* sɜ:'veɪ] *n* enquête *f*, étude *f*; (*in housebuying etc*) inspection *f*, (*rapport m d'*)expertise *f*; (*of land*) levé *m* ♦ *vt* enquêter sur; inspecter; (*look at*) embrasser du regard; **~or** *n* (*of house*) expert *m*; (*of land*) (arpenteur *m*) géomètre *m*

survival [sə'vaɪvl] *n* survie *f*; (*relic*) vestige *m*

survive [sə'vaɪv] *vi* survivre; (*custom etc*) subsister ♦ *vt* survivre à; **survivor** *n* survivant(e); (*fig*) battant(e)

susceptible [sə'septəbl] *adj*: **~ (to)** sensible (à); (*disease*) prédisposé(e) (à)

suspect [*adj, n* 'sʌspekt, *vb* səs'pekt] *adj, n* suspect(e) ♦ *vt* soupçonner, suspecter

suspend [səs'pend] *vt* suspendre; **~ed sentence** *n* condamnation *f* avec sursis; **~er belt** *n* porte-jarretelles *m inv*; **~ers** *npl* (*BRIT*) jarretelles *fpl*; (*US*) bretelles *fpl*

suspense [səs'pens] *n* attente *f*, incertitude *f*; (*in film etc*) suspense *m*

suspension [səs'penʃən] *n* suspension *f*; (*of driving licence*) retrait *m* provisoire; **~ bridge** *n* pont suspendu

suspicion [səs'pɪʃən] *n* soupçon(s) *m(pl)*; **suspicious** *adj* (*suspecting*) soupçonneux(-euse), méfiant(e); (*causing suspicion*) suspect(e)

sustain [səs'teɪn] vt soutenir; (food etc) nourrir, donner des forces à; (suffer) subir; recevoir; **~able** adj (development, growth etc) viable; **~ed** adj (effort) soutenu(e), prolongé(e); **sustenance** ['sʌstɪnəns] n nourriture f; (money) moyens mpl de subsistance

swab [swɔb] n (MED) tampon m

swagger ['swægəʳ] vi plastronner

swallow ['swɔləu] n (bird) hirondelle f ♦ vt avaler; **~ up** vt engloutir

swam [swæm] pt of **swim**

swamp [swɔmp] n marais m, marécage m ♦ vt submerger

swan [swɔn] n cygne m

swap [swɔp] vt: to **~ (for)** échanger (contre), troquer (contre)

swarm [swɔːm] n essaim m ♦ vi fourmiller, grouiller

swastika ['swɔstɪkə] n croix gammée

swat [swɔt] vt écraser

sway [sweɪ] vi se balancer, osciller ♦ vt (influence) influencer

swear [sweəʳ] (pt swore, pp sworn) vt, vi jurer; **~word** n juron m, gros mot

sweat [swɛt] n sueur f, transpiration f ♦ vi suer

sweater ['swɛtəʳ] n tricot m, pull m

sweaty ['swɛtɪ] adj en sueur, moite or mouillé(e) de sueur

Swede [swiːd] n Suédois(e)

swede [swiːd] (BRIT) n rutabaga m

Sweden ['swiːdn] n Suède f; **Swedish** adj suédois(e) ♦ n (LING) suédois m

sweep [swiːp] (pt, pp swept) n (also: **chimney ~**) ramoneur m ♦ vt balayer; (subj: current) emporter; **~ away** vt balayer; entraîner; emporter; **~ past** vi passer majestueusement or rapidement; **~ up** vt, vi balayer; **~ing** adj (gesture) large; circulaire; **a ~ing statement** une généralisation hâtive

sweet [swiːt] n (candy) bonbon m; (BRIT: pudding) dessert m ♦ adj doux (douce); (not savoury) sucré(e); (fig: kind) gentil(le); (baby) mignon(ne); **~corn** ['swiːtkɔːn] n maïs m; **~en** vt adoucir; (with sugar) su-

crer; **~heart** n amoureux(-euse); **~ness** n goût sucré; douceur f; **~ pea** n pois m de senteur

swell [swɛl] (pt swelled, pp swollen or swelled) n (of sea) houle f ♦ adj (US: inf: excellent) chouette ♦ vi grossir, augmenter; (sound) s'enfler; (MED) enfler; **~ing** n (MED) enflure f; (lump) grosseur f

sweltering ['swɛltərɪŋ] adj étouffant(e), oppressant(e)

swept [swɛpt] pt, pp of **sweep**

swerve [swəːv] vi faire une embardée or un écart; dévier

swift [swɪft] n (bird) martinet m ♦ adj rapide, prompt(e)

swig [swɪg] (inf) n (drink) lampée f

swill [swɪl] vt (also: **~ out, ~ down**) laver à grande eau

swim [swɪm] (pt swam, pp swum) n: to **go for a ~** aller nager or se baigner ♦ vi nager; (SPORT) faire de la natation; (head, room) tourner ♦ vt traverser (à la nage); (a length) faire (à la nage); **~mer** n nageur(-euse); **~ming** n natation f; **~ming cap** n bonnet m de bain; **~ming costume** (BRIT) n maillot m (de bain); **~ming pool** n piscine f; **~ming trunks** npl caleçon m or slip m de bain; **~suit** n maillot m (de bain)

swindle ['swɪndl] n escroquerie f

swine [swaɪn] (inf!) n inv salaud m (!)

swing [swɪŋ] (pt, pp swung) n balançoire f; (movement) balancement m, oscillations fpl; (change: in opinion etc) revirement m ♦ vt balancer, faire osciller; (also: **~ round**) tourner, faire virer ♦ vi se balancer, osciller; (also: **~ round**) virer, tourner; **to be in full ~** battre son plein; **~ bridge** n pont tournant; **~ door** (US **swinging door**) n porte battante

swingeing ['swɪndʒɪŋ] (BRIT) adj écrasant(e); (cuts etc) considérable

swipe [swaɪp] (inf) vt (steal) piquer

swirl [swəːl] vi tourbillonner, tournoyer

Swiss [swɪs] adj suisse ♦ n inv Suisse m/f

switch [swɪtʃ] n (for light, radio etc) bouton m; (change) changement m, revirement m

♦ *vt* changer; **~ off** *vt* éteindre; (*engine*) arrêter; **~ on** *vt* allumer; (*engine, machine*) mettre en marche; **~board** *n* (*TEL*) standard *m*

Switzerland ['swɪtsələnd] *n* Suisse *f*

swivel ['swɪvl] *vi* (*also:* **~ round**) pivoter, tourner

swollen ['swəulən] *pp of* **swell**

swoon [swu:n] *vi* se pâmer

swoop [swu:p] *n* (*by police*) descente *f* ♦ *vi* (*also:* **~ down**) descendre en piqué, piquer

swop [swɔp] *vt* = **swap**

sword [sɔ:d] *n* épée *f*; **~fish** *n* espadon *m*

swore [swɔ:ʳ] *pt of* **swear**

sworn [swɔ:n] *pp of* **swear** ♦ *adj* (*statement, evidence*) donné(e) sous serment

swot [swɔt] *vi* bûcher, potasser

swum [swʌm] *pp of* **swim**

swung [swʌŋ] *pt, pp of* **swing**

syllable ['sɪləbl] *n* syllabe *f*

syllabus ['sɪləbəs] *n* programme *m*

symbol ['sɪmbl] *n* symbole *m*

symmetry ['sɪmɪtrɪ] *n* symétrie *f*

sympathetic [sɪmpə'θetɪk] *adj* compatissant(e); bienveillant(e), compréhensif(-ive); (*likeable*) sympathique; **~ towards** bien disposé(e) envers

sympathize ['sɪmpəθaɪz] *vi*: **to ~ with sb** plaindre qn; (*in grief*) s'associer à la douleur de qn; **to ~ with sth** comprendre qch; **~r** *n* (*POL*) sympathisant(e)

sympathy ['sɪmpəθɪ] *n* (*pity*) compassion *f*; **sympathies** *npl* (*support*) soutien *m*; **left-wing** *etc* **sympathies** penchants *mpl* à gauche *etc*; **in ~ with** (*strike*) en *or* par solidarité avec; **with our deepest ~** en vous priant d'accepter nos sincères condoléances

symphony ['sɪmfənɪ] *n* symphonie *f*

symptom ['sɪmptəm] *n* symptôme *m*; indice *m*

syndicate ['sɪndɪkɪt] *n* syndicat *m*, coopérative *f*

synopsis [sɪ'nɔpsɪs] (*pl* **synopses**) *n* résumé *m*

synthetic [sɪn'θetɪk] *adj* synthétique

syphon ['saɪfən] *n, vb* = **siphon**

Syria ['sɪrɪə] *n* Syrie *f*

syringe [sɪ'rɪndʒ] *n* seringue *f*

syrup ['sɪrəp] *n* sirop *m*; (*also:* **golden ~**) mélasse raffinée

system ['sɪstəm] *n* système *m*; (*ANAT*) organisme *m*; **~atic** [sɪstə'mætɪk] *adj* systématique; méthodique; **~ disk** *n* (*COMPUT*) disque *m* système; **~s analyst** *n* analyste fonctionnel(le)

T, t

ta [tɑ:] (*BRIT: inf*) *excl* merci!

tab [tæb] *n* (*label*) étiquette *f*; (*on drinks can etc*) languette *f*; **to keep ~s on** (*fig*) surveiller

tabby ['tæbɪ] *n* (*also:* **~ cat**) chat(te) tigré(e)

table ['teɪbl] *n* table *f* ♦ *vt* (*BRIT: motion etc*) présenter; **to lay** *or* **set the ~** mettre le couvert *or* la table; **~cloth** *n* nappe *f*; **~ d'hôte** [tɑ:bl'dəut] *adj* (*meal*) à prix fixe; **~ lamp** *n* lampe *f* de table; **~mat** *n* (*for plate*) napperon *m*, set *m*; (*for hot dish*) dessous-de-plat *m inv*; **~ of contents** *n* table *f* des matières; **~spoon** *n* cuiller *f* de service; (*also:* **~spoonful: as measurement**) cuillerée *f* à soupe

tablet ['tæblɪt] *n* (*MED*) comprimé *m*

table tennis *n* ping-pong ℞ *m*, tennis *m* de table

table wine *n* vin *m* de table

tabloid ['tæblɔɪd] *n* quotidien *m* populaire

┌─────────────────┐
│ **tabloid press** │
└─────────────────┘

> *Le terme* **tabloid press** *désigne les journaux populaires de demi-format où l'on trouve beaucoup de photos et qui adoptent un style très concis. Ce type de journaux vise des lecteurs s'intéressant aux faits divers ayant un parfum de scandale; voir* **quality (news)papers**.

tack [tæk] *n* (*nail*) petit clou ♦ *vt* clouer; (*fig*) direction *f*; (*BRIT: stitch*) faufiler ♦ *vi* tirer un or des bord(s)

tackle ['tækl] n matériel m, équipement m; (for lifting) appareil m de levage; (RUGBY) plaquage m ♦ vt (difficulty, animal, burglar etc) s'attaquer à; (person: challenge) s'expliquer avec; (RUGBY) plaquer

tacky ['tæki] adj collant(e); (pej: of poor quality) miteux(-euse)

tact [tækt] n tact m; ~**ful** adj plein(e) de tact

tactical ['tæktɪkl] adj tactique

tactics ['tæktɪks] npl tactique f

tactless ['tæktlɪs] adj qui manque de tact

tadpole ['tædpəʊl] n têtard m

tag [tæg] n étiquette f; ~ **along** vi suivre

tail [teɪl] n queue f; (of shirt) pan m ♦ vt (follow) suivre, filer; ~**s** npl habit m; ~ **away**, ~ **off** vi (in size, quality etc) baisser peu à peu; ~**back** (BRIT) n (AUT) bouchon m; ~ **end** n bout m, fin f; ~**gate** n (AUT) hayon m arrière

tailor ['teɪlər] n tailleur m; ~**ing** n (cut) coupe f; ~-**made** adj fait(e) sur mesure; (fig) conçu(e) spécialement

tailwind ['teɪlwɪnd] n vent m arrière inv

tainted ['teɪntɪd] adj (food) gâté(e); (water, air) infecté(e); (fig) souillé(e)

take [teɪk] (pt **took**, pp **taken**) vt prendre; (gain: prize) remporter; (require: effort, courage) demander; (tolerate) accepter, supporter; (hold: passengers etc) contenir; (accompany) emmener, accompagner; (bring, carry) apporter, emporter; (exam) passer, se présenter à; **to ~ sth from** (drawer etc) prendre qch dans; (person) prendre qch à; **I ~ it that ...** je suppose que ...; ~ **after** vt fus ressembler à; ~ **apart** vt démonter; ~ **away** vt enlever; (carry off) emporter; ~ **back** vt (return) rendre, rapporter; (one's words) retirer; ~ **down** vt (building) démolir; (letter etc) prendre, écrire; ~ **in** vt (deceive) tromper, rouler; (understand) comprendre, saisir; (include) comprendre, inclure; (lodger) prendre; ~ **off** vi (AVIAT) décoller ♦ vt (go away) s'en aller; (remove) enlever; ~ **on** vt (work) accepter, se charger de; (employee) prendre, embaucher;

(opponent) accepter de se battre contre; ~ **out** vt (invite) emmener, sortir; (remove) enlever; **to ~ sth out of sth** (drawer, pocket etc) prendre qch dans qch; ~ **over** vt (business) reprendre ♦ vi: **to ~ over from sb** prendre la relève de qn; ~ **to** vt fus (person) se prendre d'amitié pour; (thing) prendre goût à; ~ **up** vt (activity) se mettre à; (dress) raccourcir; (occupy: time, space) prendre, occuper; **to ~ sb up on an offer** accepter la proposition de qn; ~**away** (BRIT) adj (food) à emporter ♦ n (shop, restaurant) café m qui vend de plats à emporter; ~**off** n (AVIAT) décollage m; ~**over** n (COMM) rachat m; **takings** npl (COMM) recette f

talc [tælk] n (also: ~**um powder**) talc m

tale [teɪl] n (story) conte m, histoire f; (account) récit m; **to tell ~s** (fig) rapporter

talent ['tælnt] n talent m, don m; ~**ed** adj doué(e), plein(e) de talent

talk [tɔːk] n (a speech) causerie f, exposé m; (conversation) discussion f, entretien m; (gossip) racontars mpl ♦ vi parler; ~**s** npl (POL etc) entretiens mpl; **to ~ about** parler de; **to ~ sb into/out of doing** persuader qn de faire/ne pas faire; **to ~ shop** parler métier or affaires; ~ **over** vt discuter (de); ~**ative** adj bavard(e); ~ **show** n causerie (télévisée or radiodiffusée)

tall [tɔːl] adj (person) grand(e); (building, tree) haut(e); **to be 6 feet ~** ≃ mesurer 1 mètre 80; ~ **story** n histoire f invraisemblable

tally ['tælɪ] n compte m ♦ vi: **to ~ (with)** correspondre (à)

talon ['tælən] n griffe f; (of eagle) serre f

tame [teɪm] adj apprivoisé(e); (fig: story, style) insipide

tamper ['tæmpər] vi: **to ~ with** toucher à

tampon ['tæmpɔn] n tampon m (hygiénique or périodique)

tan [tæn] n (also: **suntan**) bronzage m ♦ vt, vi bronzer ♦ adj (colour) brun roux inv

tang [tæŋ] n odeur (or saveur) piquante

tangent ['tændʒənt] n (MATH) tangente f; **to go off at a ~** (fig) changer de sujet

tangerine [tændʒəˈriːn] n mandarine f

tangle [ˈtæŋgl] n enchevêtrement m; **to get in(to) a ~** s'embrouiller

tank [tæŋk] n (water ~) réservoir m; (for fish) aquarium m; (MIL) char m d'assaut, tank m

tanker [ˈtæŋkəʳ] n (ship) pétrolier m, tanker m; (truck) camion-citerne m

tantalizing [ˈtæntəlaɪzɪŋ] adj (smell) extrêmement appétissant(e); (offer) terriblement tentant(e)

tantamount [ˈtæntəmaunt] adj: **~ to** qui équivaut à

tantrum [ˈtæntrəm] n accès m de colère

tap [tæp] n (on sink etc) robinet m; (gentle blow) petite tape ♦ vt frapper or taper légèrement; (resources) exploiter, utiliser; (telephone) mettre sur écoute; **on ~** (fig: resources) disponible; **~-dancing** n claquettes fpl

tape [teɪp] n ruban m; (also: **magnetic ~**) bande f (magnétique); (cassette) cassette f; (sticky) scotch m ♦ vt (record) enregistrer; (stick with ~) coller avec du scotch; **~ deck** n platine f d'enregistrement; **~ measure** n mètre m à ruban

taper [ˈteɪpəʳ] vi s'effiler

tape recorder n magnétophone m

tapestry [ˈtæpɪstrɪ] n tapisserie f

tar [tɑː] n goudron m

target [ˈtɑːgɪt] n cible f; (fig) objectif m

tariff [ˈtærɪf] n (COMM) tarif m; (taxes) tarif douanier

tarmac [ˈtɑːmæk] n (BRIT: on road) macadam m; (AVIAT) piste f

tarnish [ˈtɑːnɪʃ] vt ternir

tarpaulin [tɑːˈpɔːlɪn] n bâche (goudronnée)

tarragon [ˈtærəgən] n estragon m

tart [tɑːt] n (CULIN) tarte f; (BRIT: inf: prostitute) putain f ♦ adj (flavour) âpre, aigrelet(te); **~ up** (BRIT: inf) vt (object) retaper; **to ~ o.s. up** se faire beau (belle), s'attifer (pej)

tartan [ˈtɑːtn] n tartan m ♦ adj écossais(e)

tartar [ˈtɑːtəʳ] n (on teeth) tartre m; **~(e) sauce** n sauce f tartare

task [tɑːsk] n tâche f; **to take sb to ~** prendre qn à partie; **~ force** n (MIL, POLICE) détachement spécial

tassel [ˈtæsl] n gland m; pompon m

taste [teɪst] n goût m; (fig: glimpse, idea) idée f, aperçu m ♦ vt goûter ♦ vi: **to ~ of** or **like** (fish etc) avoir le or un goût de; **you can ~ the garlic (in it)** on sent bien l'ail; **can I have a ~ of this wine?** puis-je goûter un peu de ce vin?; **in good/bad ~** de bon/mauvais goût; **~ful** adj de bon goût; **~less** adj (food) fade; (remark) de mauvais goût; **tasty** adj savoureux(-euse), délicieux(-euse)

tatters [ˈtætəz] npl: **in ~** en lambeaux

tattoo [təˈtuː] n tatouage m; (spectacle) parade f militaire ♦ vt tatouer

tatty [ˈtætɪ] (BRIT: inf) adj (clothes) frippé(e); (shop, area) délabré(e)

taught [tɔːt] pt, pp of **teach**

taunt [tɔːnt] n raillerie f ♦ vt railler

Taurus [ˈtɔːrəs] n le Taureau

taut [tɔːt] adj tendu(e)

tax [tæks] n (on goods etc) taxe f; (on income) impôts mpl, contributions fpl ♦ vt taxer; imposer; (fig: patience etc) mettre à l'épreuve; **~able** adj (income) imposable; **~ation** [tækˈseɪʃən] n taxation f; impôts mpl, contributions fpl; **~ avoidance** n dégrèvement fiscal; **~ disc** n (AUT) vignette f (automobile); **~ evasion** n fraude fiscale; **~-free** adj exempt(e) d'impôts

taxi [ˈtæksɪ] n taxi m ♦ vi (AVIAT) rouler (lentement) au sol; **~ driver** n chauffeur m de taxi; **~ rank** n (BRIT) station f de taxis; **~ stand** n = **taxi rank**

tax: ~ payer n contribuable m/f; **~ relief** n dégrèvement fiscal; **~ return** n déclaration f d'impôts or de revenus

TB n abbr = **tuberculosis**

tea [tiː] n thé m; (BRIT: snack: for children) goûter m; **high ~** collation combinant goûter et dîner; **~ bag** n sachet m de thé; **~ break** n (BRIT) pause-thé f

teach [tiːtʃ] (pt, pp **taught**) vt: **to ~ sb sth, ~ sth to sb** apprendre qch à qn; (in school etc) enseigner qch à qn ♦ vi enseigner; ~er n (in secondary school) professeur m; (in primary school) instituteur(-trice); ~ing n enseignement m

tea: ~ cloth n torchon m; ~ cosy n cloche f à thé; ~cup n tasse f à thé

teak [tiːk] n teck m

tea leaves npl feuilles fpl de thé

team [tiːm] n équipe f; (of animals) attelage m; ~work n travail m d'équipe

teapot ['tiːpɔt] n théière f

tear¹ [tɛəʳ] (pt tore, pp torn) n déchirure f ♦ vt déchirer ♦ vi se déchirer; ~ along vi (rush) aller à toute vitesse; ~ up vt (sheet of paper etc) déchirer, mettre en morceaux or pièces

tear² [tɪəʳ] n larme f; in ~s en larmes; ~ful adj larmoyant(e); ~ gas n gaz m lacrymogène

tearoom ['tiːruːm] n salon m de thé

tease [tiːz] vt taquiner; (unkindly) tourmenter

tea set n service m à thé

teaspoon ['tiːspuːn] n petite cuiller; (also: ~ful: as measurement) ≈ cuillerée f à café

teat [tiːt] n tétine f

teatime ['tiːtaɪm] n l'heure f du thé

tea towel (BRIT) n torchon m (à vaisselle)

technical ['teknɪkl] adj technique; ~ity [tεknɪ'kælɪtɪ] n (detail) détail m technique; (point of law) vice m de forme; ~ly adv techniquement; (strictly speaking) en théorie

technician [tεk'nɪʃən] n technicien(ne)

technique [tεk'niːk] n technique f

techno ['tεknəʊ] n (music) techno f

technological [tεknə'lɔdʒɪkl] adj technologique

technology [tεk'nɔlədʒɪ] n technologie f

teddy (bear) ['tεdɪ(-)] n ours m en peluche

tedious ['tiːdɪəs] adj fastidieux(-euse)

teem [tiːm] vi: to ~ (with) grouiller (de); it is ~ing (with rain) il pleut à torrents

teenage ['tiːneɪdʒ] adj (fashions etc) pour jeunes, pour adolescents; (children) adolescent(e); ~r n adolescent(e)

teens [tiːnz] npl: to be in one's ~ être adolescent(e)

tee-shirt ['tiːʃəːt] n = T-shirt

teeter ['tiːtəʳ] vi chanceler, vaciller

teeth [tiːθ] npl of tooth

teethe [tiːð] vi percer ses dents

teething troubles npl (fig) difficultés initiales

teetotal ['tiː'təʊtl] adj (person) qui ne boit jamais d'alcool

tele: ~communications npl télécommunications fpl; ~conferencing n téléconférence(s) f(pl); ~gram n télégramme m; ~graph n télégraphe m; ~graph pole n poteau m télégraphique

telephone ['tεlɪfəʊn] n téléphone m ♦ vt (person) téléphoner à; (message) téléphoner; on the ~ au téléphone; to be on the ~ (BRIT: have a ~) avoir le téléphone; ~ booth, ~ box (BRIT) n cabine f téléphonique; ~ call n coup m de téléphone, appel m téléphonique; ~ directory n annuaire m (du téléphone); ~ number n numéro m de téléphone; telephonist [tə'lεfənɪst] (BRIT) n téléphoniste m/f

telesales ['tεlɪseɪlz] n télévente f

telescope ['tεlɪskəʊp] n télescope m

television ['tεlɪvɪʒən] n télévision f; on ~ à la télévision; ~ set n (poste f de) télévision m

telex ['tεlεks] n télex m

tell [tεl] (pt, pp told) vt dire; (relate: story) raconter; (distinguish): to ~ sth from distinguer qch de ♦ vi (talk): to ~ (of) parler (de); (have effect) se faire sentir, se voir; to ~ sb to do dire à qn de faire; ~ off vt réprimander, gronder; ~er n (in bank) caissier(-ère); ~ing adj (remark, detail) révélateur(-trice); ~tale adj (sign) éloquent(e), révélateur(-trice)

telly ['tεlɪ] (BRIT: inf) n abbr (= television) télé f

temp [tεmp] n abbr (= temporary) (secrétaire f) intérimaire f

temper ['tεmpəʳ] n (nature) caractère m; (mood) humeur f; (fit of anger) colère f ♦ vt (moderate) tempérer, adoucir; to be

in a ~ être en colère; **to lose one's ~** se mettre en colère

temperament ['tɛmprəmənt] *n* (*nature*) tempérament *m*; **~al** [tɛmprə'mɛntl] *adj* capricieux(-euse)

temperate ['tɛmprət] *adj* (*climate, country*) tempéré(e)

temperature ['tɛmprətʃər] *n* température *f*; **to have** *or* **run a ~** avoir de la fièvre

temple ['tɛmpl] *n* (*building*) temple *m*; (*ANAT*) tempe *f*

temporary ['tɛmpərərɪ] *adj* temporaire, provisoire; (*job, worker*) temporaire

tempt [tɛmpt] *vt* tenter; **to ~ sb into doing** persuader qn de faire; **~ation** [tɛmp'teɪʃən] *n* tentation *f*; **~ing** *adj* tentant(e)

ten [tɛn] *num* dix

tenacity [tə'næsɪtɪ] *n* ténacité *f*

tenancy ['tɛnənsɪ] *n* location *f*; état *m* de locataire

tenant ['tɛnənt] *n* locataire *m/f*

tend [tɛnd] *vt* s'occuper de ♦ *vi*: **to ~ to do** avoir tendance à faire; **~ency** ['tɛndənsɪ] *n* tendance *f*

tender ['tɛndər] *adj* tendre; (*delicate*) délicat(e); (*sore*) sensible ♦ *n* (*COMM: offer*) soumission *f* ♦ *vt* offrir

tenement ['tɛnəmənt] *n* immeuble *m*

tennis ['tɛnɪs] *n* tennis *m*; **~ ball** *n* balle *f* de tennis; **~ court** *n* (court *m* de) tennis; **~ player** *n* joueur(-euse) de tennis; **~ racket** *n* raquette *f* de tennis; **~ shoes** *npl* (chaussures *fpl* de) tennis *mpl*

tenor ['tɛnər] *n* (*MUS*) ténor *m*

tenpin bowling ['tɛnpɪn-] (*BRIT*) *n* bowling *m* (à dix quilles)

tense [tɛns] *adj* tendu(e) ♦ *n* (*LING*) temps *m*

tension ['tɛnʃən] *n* tension *f*

tent [tɛnt] *n* tente *f*

tentative ['tɛntətɪv] *adj* timide, hésitant(e); (*conclusion*) provisoire

tenterhooks ['tɛntəhuks] *npl*: **on ~** sur des charbons ardents

tenth [tɛnθ] *num* dixième

tent peg *n* piquet *m* de tente

tent pole *n* montant *m* de tente

tenuous ['tɛnjuəs] *adj* ténu(e)

tenure ['tɛnjuər] *n* (*of property*) bail *m*; (*of job*) période *f* de jouissance

tepid ['tɛpɪd] *adj* tiède

term [tə:m] *n* terme *m*; (*SCOL*) trimestre *m* ♦ *vt* appeler; **~s** *npl* (*conditions*) conditions *fpl*; (*COMM*) tarif *m*; **in the short/long ~** à court/long terme; **to come to ~s with** (*problem*) faire face à

terminal ['tə:mɪnl] *adj* (*disease*) dans sa phase terminale; (*patient*) incurable ♦ *n* (*ELEC*) borne *f*; (*for oil, ore etc, COMPUT*) terminal *m*; (*also:* **air ~**) aérogare *f*; (*BRIT: also:* **coach ~**) gare routière; **~ly** *adv*: **to be ~ly ill** être condamné(e)

terminate ['tə:mɪneɪt] *vt* mettre fin à; (*pregnancy*) interrompre

termini ['tə:mɪnaɪ] *npl of* **terminus**

terminus ['tə:mɪnəs] (*pl* **termini**) *n* terminus *m inv*

terrace ['tɛrəs] *n* terrasse *f*; (*BRIT: row of houses*) rangée *f* de maisons (*attenantes*); **the ~s** *npl* (*BRIT: SPORT*) les gradins *mpl*; **~d** *adj* (*garden*) en terrasses

terracotta ['tɛrə'kɔtə] *n* terre cuite

terrain [tɛ'reɪn] *n* terrain *m* (*sol*)

terrible ['tɛrɪbl] *adj* terrible, atroce; (*weather, conditions*) affreux(-euse), épouvantable; **terribly** *adv* terriblement; (*very badly*) affreusement mal

terrier ['tɛrɪər] *n* terrier *m* (*chien*)

terrific [tə'rɪfɪk] *adj* fantastique, incroyable, terrible; (*wonderful*) formidable, sensationnel(le)

terrify ['tɛrɪfaɪ] *vt* terrifier

territory ['tɛrɪtərɪ] *n* territoire *m*

terror ['tɛrər] *n* terreur *f*; **~ism** *n* terrorisme *m*; **~ist** *n* terroriste *m/f*

test [tɛst] *n* (*trial, check*) essai *m*; (*of courage etc*) épreuve *f*; (*MED*) examen *m*; (*CHEM*) analyse *f*; (*SCOL*) interrogation *f*; (*also:* **driving ~**) (examen du) permis *m* de conduire ♦ *vt* essayer; mettre à l'épreuve; examiner; analyser; faire subir une interrogation à

testament ['tɛstəmənt] *n* testament *m*;

the Old/New T~ l'Ancien/le Nouveau Testament

testicle ['tɛstɪkl] *n* testicule *m*

testify ['tɛstɪfaɪ] *vi* (*LAW*) témoigner, déposer; **to ~ to sth** attester qch

testimony ['tɛstɪmənɪ] *n* témoignage *m*; (*proof*) **to be (a) ~ to** être la preuve de

test match *n* (*CRICKET, RUGBY*) match international

test tube *n* éprouvette *f*

tetanus ['tɛtənəs] *n* tétanos *m*

tether ['tɛðəʳ] *vt* attacher ♦ *n*: **at the end of one's ~** à bout (de patience)

text [tɛkst] *n* texte *m*; SMS ♦ *vt*: **to text sb** envoyer un SMS à qn **~book** *n* manuel *m*

texture ['tɛkstʃəʳ] *n* texture *f*; (*of skin, paper etc*) grain *m*

Thailand ['taɪlænd] *n* Thaïlande *f*

Thames [tɛmz] *n*: **the ~** la Tamise

than [ðæn, ðən] *conj* que; (*with numerals*): **more ~ 10/once** plus de 10/d'une fois; **I have more/less ~ you** j'en ai plus/moins que toi; **she has more apples ~ pears** elle a plus de pommes que de poires

thank [θæŋk] *vt* remercier, dire merci à; **~s** *npl* (*gratitude*) remerciements *mpl* ♦ *excl* merci!; **~ you (very much)** merci (beaucoup); **~s to** grâce à; **~ God!** Dieu merci!; **~ful** *adj*: **~ful (for)** reconnaissant(e) (de); **~less** *adj* ingrat(e); **T~sgiving (Day)** *n* jour *m* d'action de grâce (*fête américaine*)

Thanksgiving Day

i **Thanksgiving Day** est un jour de congé aux États-Unis, le quatrième jeudi du mois de novembre, commémorant la bonne récolte que les Pèlerins venus de Grande-Bretagne ont eue en 1621; traditionnellement, c'est un jour où l'on remerciait Dieu et où l'on organisait un grand festin. Une fête semblable a lieu au Canada le deuxième lundi d'octobre.

KEYWORD

that [ðæt] *adj* (*demonstrative: pl those*) ce, cet +*vowel or h mute*, cette *f*; **that man/woman/book** cet homme/cette femme/ce livre; (*not "this"*) cet homme-là/cette femme-là/ce livre-là; **that one** celui-là (celle-là)

♦ *pron* 1 (*demonstrative: pl those*) ce; (*not "this one"*) cela, ça; **who's that?** qui est-ce?; **what's that?** qu'est-ce que c'est?; **is that you?** c'est toi?; **I prefer this to that** je préfère ceci à cela *or* ça; **that's what he said** c'est ce qu'il a dit; **that is (to say)** c'est-à-dire, à savoir

2 (*relative: subject*) qui; (: *object*) que; (: *indirect*) lequel (laquelle), lesquels (lesquelles) *pl*; **the book that I read** le livre que j'ai lu; **the books that are in the library** les livres qui sont dans la bibliothèque; **all that I have** tout ce que j'ai; **the box that I put it in** la boîte dans laquelle je l'ai mis; **the people that I spoke to** les gens auxquels *or* à qui j'ai parlé

3 (*relative: of time*) où; **the day that he came** le jour où il est venu

♦ *conj* que; **he thought that I was ill** il pensait que j'étais malade

♦ *adv* (*demonstrative*): **I can't work that much** je ne peux pas travailler autant que cela; **I didn't know it was that bad** je ne savais pas que c'était si *or* aussi mauvais; **it's about that high** c'est à peu près de cette hauteur

thatched [θætʃt] *adj* (*roof*) de chaume; **~ cottage** chaumière *f*

thaw [θɔː] *n* dégel *m* ♦ *vi* (*ice*) fondre; (*food*) dégeler ♦ *vt* (*food: also: ~ out*) (faire) dégeler

KEYWORD

the [ðiː, ðə] *def art* 1 (*gen*) le, la *f*, l' +*vowel or h mute*, les *pl*; **the boy/girl/ink** le garçon/la fille/l'encre; **the children** les enfants; **the history of the world** l'histoire du monde; **give it to the postman** donne-le au facteur; **to play the piano/flute** jouer du piano/de la flûte; **the rich and the poor** les riches et les pauvres

2 (*in titles*): **Elizabeth the First** Elisabeth première; **Peter the Great** Pierre le Grand
3 (*in comparisons*): **the more he works, the more he earns** plus il travaille, plus il gagne de l'argent

theatre ['θɪətər] *n* théâtre *m*; (*also*: **lecture ~**) amphi(théâtre) *m*; (*MED: also*: **operating ~**) salle *f* d'opération; **~-goer** *n* habitué(e) du théâtre; **theatrical** [θɪ'ætrɪkl] *adj* théâtral(e)
theft [θeft] *n* vol *m* (*larcin*)
their [ðɛər] *adj* leur; (*pl*) leurs; *see also* **my**; **~s** *pron* le (la) leur; (*pl*) les leurs; *see also* **mine**[1]
them [ðem, ðəm] *pron* (*direct*) les; (*indirect*) leur; (*stressed, after prep*) eux (elles); *see also* **me**
theme [θiːm] *n* thème *m*; **~ park** *n* parc *m* (d'attraction) à thème; **~ song** *n* chanson principale
themselves [ðəm'sɛlvz] *pl pron* (*reflexive*) se; (*emphatic, after prep*) eux-mêmes (elles-mêmes); *see also* **oneself**
then [ðen] *adv* (*at that time*) alors, à ce moment-là; (*next*) puis, ensuite; (*and also*) et puis ♦ *conj* (*therefore*) alors, dans ce cas ♦ *adj*: **the ~ president** le président d'alors *or* de l'époque; **by ~** (*past*) à ce moment-là; (*future*) d'ici là; **from ~ on** dès lors
theology [θɪ'ɒlədʒɪ] *n* théologie *f*
theoretical [θɪə'rɛtɪkl] *adj* théorique
theory ['θɪərɪ] *n* théorie *f*
therapy ['θɛrəpɪ] *n* thérapie *f*

⸺ KEYWORD ⸺

there [ðɛər] *adv* 1: **there is, there are** il y a; **there are 3 of them** (*people, things*) il y en a 3; **there has been an accident** il y a eu un accident
2 (*referring to place*) là, là-bas; **it's there** c'est là(-bas); **in/on/up/down there** là-dedans/là-dessus/là-haut/en bas; **he went there on Friday** il y est allé vendredi; **I want that book there** je veux ce livre-là; **there he is!** le voilà!

3: **there, there** (*esp to child*) allons, allons!

there: **~abouts** *adv* (*place*) par là, près de là; (*amount*) environ, à peu près; **~after** *adv* par la suite; **~by** *adv* ainsi; **~fore** *adv* donc, par conséquent; **~'s** = **there is**; **there has**
thermal ['θɜːml] *adj* (*springs*) thermal(e); (*underwear*) en thermolactyl ®; (*COMPUT: paper*) thermosensible; (: *printer*) thermique
thermometer [θə'mɒmɪtər] *n* thermomètre *m*
Thermos ® ['θɜːməs] *n* (*also*: **~ flask**) thermos ® *m or f inv*
thermostat ['θɜːməustæt] *n* thermostat *m*
thesaurus [θɪ'sɔːrəs] *n* dictionnaire *m* des synonymes
these [ðiːz] *pl adj* ces; (*not "those"*): **~ books** ces livres-ci ♦ *pl pron* ceux-ci (celles-ci)
thesis ['θiːsɪs] (*pl* **theses**) *n* thèse *f*
they [ðeɪ] *pl pron* ils (elles); (*stressed*) eux (elles); **~ say that ...** (*it is said that*) on dit que ...; **~'d** = **they had**; **they would**; **~'ll** = **they shall**; **they will**; **~'re** = **they are**; **~'ve** = **they have**
thick [θɪk] *adj* épais(se); (*stupid*) bête, borné(e) ♦ *n*: **in the ~ of** au beau milieu de, en plein cœur de; **it's 20 cm ~** il/elle a 20 cm d'épaisseur; **~en** *vi* s'épaissir ♦ *vt* (*sauce etc*) épaissir; **~ness** *n* épaisseur *f*; **~set** *adj* trapu(e), costaud(e)
thief [θiːf] (*pl* **thieves**) *n* voleur(-euse)
thigh [θaɪ] *n* cuisse *f*
thimble ['θɪmbl] *n* dé *m* (à coudre)
thin [θɪn] *adj* mince; (*skinny*) maigre; (*soup, sauce*) peu épais(se), clair(e); (*hair, crowd*) clairsemé(e) ♦ *vt*: **to ~ (down)** (*sauce, paint*) délayer
thing [θɪŋ] *n* chose *f*; (*object*) objet *m*; (*contraption*) truc *m*; (*mania*): **to have a ~ about** être obsédé(e) par; **~s** *npl* (*belongings*) affaires *fpl*; **poor ~!** le (la) pauvre!; **the best ~ would be to** le mieux serait de; **how are ~s?** comment ça va?
think [θɪŋk] (*pt, pp* **thought**) *vi* penser, ré-

fléchir; (*believe*) penser ♦ *vt* (*imagine*) imaginer; **what did you ~ of them?** qu'avez-vous pensé d'eux?; **to ~ about sth/sb** penser à qch/qn; **I'll ~ about it** je vais y réfléchir; **to ~ of doing** avoir l'idée de faire; **I ~ so/not** je crois *or* pense que oui/non; **to ~ well of** avoir une haute opinion de; **~ over** *vt* bien réfléchir à; **~ up** *vt* inventer, trouver; **~ tank** *n* groupe *m* de réflexion

thinly [ˈθɪnlɪ] *adv* (*cut*) en fines tranches; (*spread*) en une couche mince

third [θɜːd] *num* troisième ♦ *n* (*fraction*) tiers *m*; (*AUT*) troisième (vitesse) *f*; (*BRIT: SCOL: degree*) ≃ licence *f* sans mention; **~ly** *adv* troisièmement; **~ party insurance** (*BRIT*) *n* assurance *f* au tiers; **~-rate** *adj* de qualité médiocre; **the T~ World** *n* le tiers monde

thirst [θɜːst] *n* soif *f*; **~y** *adj* (*person*) qui a soif, assoiffé(e); (*work*) qui donne soif; **to be ~y** avoir soif

thirteen [θɜːˈtiːn] *num* treize

thirty [ˈθɜːtɪ] *num* trente

this [ðɪs] *adj* (*demonstrative: pl these*) ce, cet +*vowel or h mute*, cette *f*; **this man/woman/book** cet homme/cette femme/ce livre; (*not "that"*) cet homme-ci/cette femme-ci/ce livre-ci; **this one** celui-ci (celle-ci)

♦ *pron* (*demonstrative: pl these*) ce; (*not "that one"*) celui-ci (celle-ci), ceci; **who's this?** qui est-ce?; **what's this?** qu'est-ce que c'est?; **I prefer this to that** je préfère ceci à cela; **this is what he said** voici ce qu'il a dit; **this is Mr Brown** (*in introductions*) je vous présente Mr Brown; (*in photo*) c'est Mr Brown; (*on telephone*) ici Mr Brown

♦ *adv* (*demonstrative*): **it was about this big** c'était à peu près de cette grandeur *or* grand comme ça; **I didn't know it was this bad** je ne savais pas que c'était si *or* aussi mauvais

thistle [ˈθɪsl] *n* chardon *m*

thorn [θɔːn] *n* épine *f*

thorough [ˈθʌrə] *adj* (*search*) minutieux(-euse); (*knowledge, research*) approfondi(e); (*work, person*) consciencieux(-euse); (*cleaning*) à fond; **~bred** *n* (*horse*) pur-sang *m inv*; **~fare** *n* route *f*; **"no ~fare"** "passage interdit"; **~ly** *adv* minutieusement; en profondeur; à fond; (*very*) tout à fait

those [ðəuz] *pl adj* ces; (*not "these"*): **~ books** ces livres-là ♦ *pl pron* ceux-là (celles-là)

though [ðəu] *conj* bien que +*sub*, quoique +*sub* ♦ *adv* pourtant

thought [θɔːt] *pt, pp of* **think** ♦ *n* pensée *f*; (*idea*) idée *f*; (*opinion*) avis *m*; **~ful** *adj* (*deep in thought*) pensif(-ive); (*serious*) réfléchi(e); (*considerate*) prévenant(e); **~less** *adj* étourdi(e); qui manque de considération

thousand [ˈθauzənd] *num* mille; **two ~** deux mille; **~s of** des milliers de; **~th** *num* millième

thrash [θræʃ] *vt* rouer de coups; donner une correction à; (*defeat*) battre à plate couture; **~ about, ~ around** *vi* se débattre; **~ out** *vt* débattre de

thread [θrɛd] *n* fil *m*; (*TECH*) pas *m*, filetage *m* ♦ *vt* (*needle*) enfiler; **~bare** *adj* râpé(e), élimé(e)

threat [θrɛt] *n* menace *f*; **~en** *vi* menacer ♦ *vt*: **to ~en sb with sth/to do** menacer qn de qch/de faire

three [θriː] *num* trois; **~-dimensional** *adj* à trois dimensions; **~-piece suit** *n* complet *m* (avec gilet); **~-piece suite** *n* salon *m* comprenant un canapé et deux fauteuils assortis; **~-ply** *adj* (*wool*) trois fils *inv*

threshold [ˈθrɛʃhəuld] *n* seuil *m*

threw [θruː] *pt of* **throw**

thrifty [ˈθrɪftɪ] *adj* économe

thrill [θrɪl] *n* (*excitement*) émotion *f*, sensation forte; (*shudder*) frisson *m* ♦ *vt* (*audience*) électriser; **to be ~ed** (*with gift etc*) être ravi(e); **~er** *n* film *m* (*or* roman *m or* pièce *f*) à suspense; **~ing** *adj* saisissant(e), palpitant(e)

thrive [θraɪv] (*pt, pp* **thrived**) *vi* pousser, se développer; (*business*) prospérer; **he ~s on it** cela lui réussit; **thriving** *adj* (*business, community*) prospère

throat [θrəut] *n* gorge *f*; **to have a sore ~** avoir mal à la gorge

throb [θrɔb] *vi* (*heart*) palpiter; (*engine*) vibrer; **my head is ~bing** j'ai des élancements dans la tête

throes [θrəuz] *npl*: **in the ~ of** au beau milieu de

throne [θrəun] *n* trône *m*

throng ['θrɔŋ] *n* foule *f* ♦ *vt* se presser dans

throttle ['θrɔtl] *n* (*AUT*) accélérateur *m* ♦ *vt* étrangler

through [θru:] *prep* à travers; (*time*) pendant, durant; (*by means of*) par, par l'intermédiaire de; (*owing to*) à cause de ♦ *adj* (*ticket, train, passage*) direct(e) ♦ *adv* à travers; **to put sb ~ to sb** (*BRIT: TEL*) passer qn à qn; **to be ~** (*BRIT: TEL*) avoir la communication; (*esp US: have finished*) avoir fini; **to be ~ with sb** (*relationship*) avoir rompu avec qn; **"no ~ road"** (*BRIT*) "impasse"; **~out** *prep* (*place*) partout dans; (*time*) durant tout(e) le (la) ♦ *adv* partout

throw [θrəu] (*pt* **threw**, *pp* **thrown**) *n* jet *m*; (*SPORT*) lancer *m* ♦ *vt* lancer, jeter; (*SPORT*) lancer; (*rider*) désarçonner; (*fig*) déconcentrer; **to ~ a party** donner une réception; **~ away** *vt* jeter; **~ off** *vt* se débarrasser de; **~ out** *vt* jeter; (*reject*) rejeter; (*person*) mettre à la porte; **~ up** *vi* vomir; **~away** *adj* à jeter; (*remark*) fait(e) en passant; **~-in** *n* (*SPORT*) remise *f* en jeu

thru [θru:] (*US*) = **through**

thrush [θrʌʃ] *n* (*bird*) grive *f*

thrust [θrʌst] (*pt, pp* **thrust**) *n* (*TECH*) poussée *f* ♦ *vt* pousser brusquement; (*push in*) enfoncer

thud [θʌd] *n* bruit sourd

thug [θʌg] *n* voyou *m*

thumb [θʌm] *n* (*ANAT*) pouce *m* ♦ *vt*: **to ~ a lift** faire de l'auto-stop, arrêter une voi-

ture; **~ through** *vt* (*book*) feuilleter; **~tack** (*US*) *n* punaise *f* (*clou*)

thump [θʌmp] *n* grand coup; (*sound*) bruit sourd ♦ *vt* cogner sur ♦ *vi* cogner, battre fort

thunder ['θʌndər] *n* tonnerre *m* ♦ *vi* tonner; (*train etc*): **to ~ past** passer dans un grondement *or* un bruit de tonnerre; **~bolt** *n* foudre *f*; **~clap** *n* coup *m* de tonnerre; **~storm** *n* orage *m*; **~y** *adj* orageux(-euse)

Thursday ['θɜ:zdɪ] *n* jeudi *m*

thus [ðʌs] *adv* ainsi

thwart [θwɔ:t] *vt* contrecarrer

thyme [taɪm] *n* thym *m*

tiara [tɪ'ɑ:rə] *n* diadème *m*

tick [tɪk] *n* (*sound: of clock*) tic-tac *m*; (*mark*) coche *f*; (*ZOOL*) tique *f*; (*BRIT: inf*): **in a ~** dans une seconde ♦ *vi* faire tic-tac ♦ *vt* (*item on list*) cocher; **~ off** *vt* (*item on list*) cocher; (*person*) réprimander, attraper; **~ over** *vi* (*engine*) tourner au ralenti; (*fig*) aller *or* marcher doucettement

ticket ['tɪkɪt] *n* billet *m*; (*for bus, tube*) ticket *m*; (*in shop: on goods*) étiquette *f*; (*for library*) carte *f*; (*parking ~*) papillon *m*, p.-v. *m*; **~ collector** *n*; **~ inspector** *n* contrôleur(-euse); **~ office** *n* guichet *m*, bureau *m* de vente des billets

tickle ['tɪkl] *vt, vi* chatouiller; **ticklish** *adj* (*person*) chatouilleux(-euse); (*problem*) épineux(-euse)

tidal ['taɪdl] *adj* (*force*) de la marée; (*estuary*) à marée; **~ wave** *n* raz-de-marée *m inv*

tidbit ['tɪdbɪt] (*US*) *n* = **titbit**

tiddlywinks ['tɪdlɪwɪŋks] *n* jeu *m* de puce

tide [taɪd] *n* marée *f*; (*fig: of events*) cours *m* ♦ *vt*: **to ~ sb over** dépanner qn; **high/low ~** marée haute/basse

tidy ['taɪdɪ] *adj* (*room*) bien rangé(e); (*dress, work*) net(te), soigné(e); (*person*) ordonné(e), qui a de l'ordre ♦ *vt* (*also:* **~ up**) ranger

tie [taɪ] *n* (*string etc*) cordon *m*; (*BRIT: also:* **necktie**) cravate *f*; (*fig: link*) lien *m*; (*SPORT: draw*) égalité *f* de points; match nul ♦ vt (parcel) attacher; (ribbon, shoe-laces) nouer ♦ vi (SPORT) faire match nul; finir à égalité de points; **to ~ sth in a bow** faire un nœud à or avec qch; **to ~ a knot in sth** faire un nœud à qch; ~ **down** vt (fig): **to ~ sb down (to)** contraindre qn (à accepter); **to be ~d down** (by relationship) se fixer; ~ **up** vt (parcel) ficeler; (dog, boat) attacher; (prisoner) ligoter; (arrangements) conclure; **to be ~d up** (busy) être pris(e) or occupé(e)

tier [tɪər] n gradin m; (of cake) étage m

tiger [ˈtaɪgər] n tigre m

tight [taɪt] adj (rope) tendu(e), raide; (clothes) étroit(e), très juste; (budget, pro-gramme, bend) serré(e); (control) strict(e), sévère; (inf: drunk) ivre, rond(e) ♦ adv (squeeze) hermétiquement, bien; ~**en** vt (rope) tendre; (screw) resser-rer; (control) renforcer ♦ vi se tendre, se resserrer; ~**fisted** adj avare; ~**ly** adv (grasp) bien, très fort; ~**rope** n corde f raide; ~**s** (BRIT) npl collant m

tile [taɪl] n (on roof) tuile f; (on wall or floor) carreau m; ~**d** adj en tuiles; carrelé(e)

till [tɪl] n caisse (enregistreuse) ♦ vt (land) cultiver ♦ prep, conj = **until**

tiller [ˈtɪlər] n (NAUT) barre f (du gouver-nail)

tilt [tɪlt] vt pencher, incliner ♦ vi pencher, être incliné(e)

timber [ˈtɪmbər] n (material) bois m (de construction); (trees) arbres mpl

time [taɪm] n temps m; (epoch: often pl) époque f, temps; (by clock) heure f; (mo-ment) moment m; (occasion, also MATH) fois f; (MUS) mesure f ♦ vt (race) chrono-métrer; (programme) minuter; (visit) fixer; (remark etc) choisir le moment de; **a long ~** un long moment, longtemps; **for the ~ being** pour le moment; **4 at a ~** 4 à la fois; **from ~ to ~** de temps en temps; **at ~s** parfois; **in ~** (soon enough) à temps; (after some ~) avec le temps, à la longue; (MUS) en mesure; **in a week's ~** dans une semaine; **in no ~** en un rien de temps; **any ~** n'importe quand; **on ~** à

l'heure; **5 ~s 5** 5 fois 5; **what ~ is it?** quelle heure est-il?; **to have a good ~** bien s'amuser; ~ **bomb** n bombe f à re-tardement; ~ **lag** (BRIT) n décalage m; (in travel) décalage horaire; ~**less** adj éter-nel(le); ~**ly** adj opportun(e); ~ **off** n temps m libre; ~**r** n (TECH) minuteur m; (in kitchen) compte-minutes m inv; ~**scale** n délais mpl; ~-**share** n maison f/appartement m en multipropriété; ~ **switch** (BRIT) n minuteur m; (for lighting) minuterie f; ~**table** n (RAIL) (indicateur m) horaire m; (SCOL) emploi m du temps; ~ **zone** n fuseau m horaire

timid [ˈtɪmɪd] adj timide; (easily scared) peureux(-euse)

timing [ˈtaɪmɪŋ] n minutage m; chronomé-trage m; **the ~ of his resignation** le mo-ment choisi pour sa démission

timpani [ˈtɪmpəni] npl timbales fpl

tin [tɪn] n étain m; (also: ~ **plate**) fer-blanc m; (BRIT: can) boîte f (de conserve); (for storage) boîte f; ~**foil** n papier m d'étain or aluminium

tinge [tɪndʒ] n nuance f ♦ vt: ~**d with** tein-té(e) de

tingle [ˈtɪŋgl] vi picoter; (person) avoir des picotements

tinker [ˈtɪŋkər] n (gipsy) romanichel m; ~ **with** vt fus bricoler, rafistoler

tinkle [ˈtɪŋkl] vi tinter

tinned [tɪnd] (BRIT) adj (food) en boîte, en conserve

tin opener (BRIT) n ouvre-boîte(s) m

tinsel [ˈtɪnsl] n guirlandes fpl de Noël (ar-gentées)

tint [tɪnt] n teinte f; (for hair) shampooing colorant; ~**ed** adj (hair) teint(e); (specta-cles, glass) teinté(e)

tiny [ˈtaɪni] adj minuscule

tip [tɪp] n (end) bout m; (gratuity) pourboire m; (BRIT: for rubbish) décharge f; (advice) tuyau m ♦ vt (waiter) donner un pourboi-re à; (tilt) incliner; (overturn: also: ~ **over**) renverser; (empty: ~ **out**) déverser; ~-**off** n (hint) tuyau m; ~**ped** (BRIT) adj (cigarette) (à bout) filtre inv

tipsy ['tɪpsɪ] (*inf*) *adj* un peu ivre, éméché(e)

tiptoe ['tɪptəu] *n*: **on ~** sur la pointe des pieds

tiptop [tɪp'tɔp] *adj*: **in ~ condition** en excellent état

tire ['taɪər] *n* (*US*) = **tyre ♦** *vt* fatiguer **♦** *vi* se fatiguer; **~d** *adj* fatigué(e); **to be ~d of** en avoir assez de, être las (lasse) de; **~less** *adj* (*person*) infatigable; (*efforts*) inlassable; **~some** *adj* ennuyeux(-euse); **tiring** *adj* fatigant(e)

tissue ['tɪʃuː] *n* tissu *m*; (*paper handkerchief*) mouchoir *m* en papier, kleenex ® *m*; **~ paper** *n* papier *m* de soie

tit [tɪt] *n* (*bird*) mésange *f*; **to give ~ for tat** rendre la pareille

titbit ['tɪtbɪt] *n* (*food*) friandise *f*; (*news*) potin *m*

title ['taɪtl] *n* titre *m*; **~ deed** *n* (*LAW*) titre (constitutif) de propriété; **~ role** *n* rôle principal

TM *abbr* = **trademark**

KEYWORD

to [tuː, tə] *prep* **1** (*direction*) à; **to go to France/Portugal/London/school** aller en France/au Portugal/à Londres/à l'école; **to go to Claude's/the doctor's** aller chez Claude/le docteur; **the road to Edinburgh** la route d'Édimbourg

2 (*as far as*) (jusqu')à; **to count to 10** compter jusqu'à 10; **from 40 to 50 people** de 40 à 50 personnes

3 (*with expressions of time*): **a quarter to 5** 5 heures moins le quart; **it's twenty to 3** il est 3 heures moins vingt

4 (*for, of*) de; **the key to the front door** la clé de la porte d'entrée; **a letter to his wife** une lettre (adressée) à sa femme

5 (*expressing indirect object*) à; **to give sth to sb** donner qch à qn; **to talk to sb** parler à qn

6 (*in relation to*) à; **3 goals to 2** 3 (buts) à 2; **30 miles to the gallon** 9,4 litres aux cent (km)

7 (*purpose, result*): **to come to sb's aid** venir au secours de qn, porter secours à qn; **to sentence sb to death** condamner qn à mort; **to my surprise** à ma grande surprise

♦ with *vb* **1** (*simple infinitive*): **to go/eat** aller/manger

2 (*following another vb*): **to want/try/start to do** vouloir/essayer de/commencer à faire

3 (*with vb omitted*): **I don't want to** je ne veux pas

4 (*purpose, result*) pour; **I did it to help you** je l'ai fait pour vous aider

5 (*equivalent to relative clause*): **I have things to do** j'ai des choses à faire; **the main thing is to try** l'important est d'essayer

6 (*after adjective etc*): **ready to go** prêt(e) à partir; **too old/young to ...** trop vieux/jeune pour ...

♦ *adv*: **push/pull the door to** tirez/poussez la porte

toad [təud] *n* crapaud *m*

toadstool ['təudstuːl] *n* champignon (vénéneux)

toast [təust] *n* (*CULIN*) pain grillé, toast *m*; (*drink, speech*) toast **♦** *vt* (*CULIN*) faire griller; (*drink to*) porter un toast à; **~er** *n* grille-pain *m inv*

tobacco [tə'bækəu] *n* tabac *m*; **~nist** *n* marchand(e) de tabac; **~nist's (shop)** *n* (bureau *m* de) tabac *m*

toboggan [tə'bɔgən] *n* toboggan *m*; (*child's*) luge *f* **♦** *vi*: **to go ~ing** faire de la luge

today [tə'deɪ] *adv* (*also fig*) aujourd'hui **♦** *n* aujourd'hui *m*

toddler ['tɔdlər] *n* enfant *m/f* qui commence à marcher, bambin *m*

toe [təu] *n* doigt *m* de pied, orteil *m*; (*of shoe*) bout *m* **♦** *vt*: **to ~ the line** (*fig*) obéir, se conformer; **~nail** *n* ongle *m* du pied

toffee ['tɔfɪ] *n* caramel *m*; **~ apple** (*BRIT*) *n* pomme caramélisée

together [tə'geðər] *adv* ensemble; (*at same*

time) en même temps; **~ with** avec

toil [tɔɪl] *n* dur travail, labeur *m* ♦ *vi* peiner

toilet ['tɔɪlət] *n* (*BRIT: lavatory*) toilettes *fpl* ♦ *cpd* (*accessories etc*) de toilette; **~ bag** *n* nécessaire *m* de toilette; **~ paper** *n* papier *m* hygiénique; **~ries** *npl* articles *mpl* de toilette; **~ roll** *n* rouleau *m* de papier hygiénique

token ['təukən] *n* (*sign*) marque *f*, témoignage *m*; (*metal disc*) jeton *m* ♦ *adj* (*strike, payment etc*) symbolique; **book/record ~** (*BRIT*) chèque-livre/-disque *m*; **gift ~** bon-cadeau *m*

told [təuld] *pt, pp of* **tell**

tolerable ['tɔlərəbl] *adj* (*bearable*) tolérable; (*fairly good*) passable

tolerant ['tɔlərnt] *adj*: **~ (of)** tolérant(e) (à l'égard de)

tolerate ['tɔləreɪt] *vt* supporter, tolérer

toll [təul] *n* (*tax, charge*) péage *m* ♦ *vi* (*bell*) sonner; **the accident ~ on the roads** le nombre des victimes de la route

tomato [tə'mɑːtəu] (*pl* **~es**) *n* tomate *f*

tomb [tuːm] *n* tombe *f*

tomboy ['tɔmbɔɪ] *n* garçon manqué

tombstone ['tuːmstəun] *n* pierre tombale

tomcat ['tɔmkæt] *n* matou *m*

tomorrow [tə'mɔrəu] *adv n* demain ♦ *n* demain *m*; **the day after ~** après-demain; **~ morning** demain matin

ton [tʌn] *n* tonne *f* (*BRIT = 1016kg; US = 907kg*), (*metric*) tonne (*= 1000 kg*); **~s of** (*inf*) des tas de

tone [təun] *n* ton *m* ♦ *vi* (*also: ~ in*) s'harmoniser; **~ down** *vt* (*colour, criticism*) adoucir; (*sound*) baisser; **~ up** *vt* (*muscles*) tonifier; **~-deaf** *adj* qui n'a pas d'oreille

tongs [tɔŋz] *npl* (*for coal*) pincettes *fpl*; (*for hair*) fer *m* à friser

tongue [tʌŋ] *n* langue *f*; **~ in cheek** ironiquement; **~-tied** *adj* (*fig*) muet(te); **~ twister** *n* phrase *f* très difficile à prononcer

tonic ['tɔnɪk] *n* (*MED*) tonique *m*; (*also: ~ water*) tonic *m*, Schweppes ® *m*

tonight [tə'naɪt] *adv, n* cette nuit; (*this evening*) ce soir

tonsil ['tɔnsl] *n* amygdale *f*; **~litis** [tɔnsɪ'laɪtɪs] *n* angine *f*

too [tuː] *adv* (*excessively*) trop; (*also*) aussi; **~ much** *adv* trop ♦ *adj* trop de; **~ many** trop de; **~ bad!** tant pis!

took [tuk] *pt of* **take**

tool [tuːl] *n* outil *m*; **~ box** *n* boîte *f* à outils

toot [tuːt] *n* (*of car horn*) coup *m* de klaxon; (*of whistle*) coup de sifflet ♦ *vi* (*with car horn*) klaxonner

tooth [tuːθ] (*pl* **teeth**) *n* (*ANAT, TECH*) dent *f*; **~ache** *n* mal *m* de dents; **~brush** *n* brosse *f* à dents; **~paste** *n* (pâte *f*) dentifrice *m*; **~pick** *n* cure-dent *m*

top [tɔp] *n* (*of mountain, head*) sommet *m*; (*of page, ladder, garment*) haut *m*; (*of box, cupboard, table*) dessus *m*; (*lid: of box, jar*) couvercle *m*; (: *of bottle*) bouchon *m*; (*toy*) toupie *f* ♦ *adj* du haut; (*in rank*) premier(-ère); (*best*) meilleur(e) ♦ *vt* (*exceed*) dépasser; (*be first in*) être en tête de; **on ~ of** sur; (*in addition to*) en plus de; **from ~ to bottom** de fond en comble; **~ up** (*US* **~ off**) *vt* (*bottle*) remplir; (*salary*) compléter; **~ floor** *n* dernier étage; **~ hat** *n* haut-de-forme *m*; **~-heavy** *adj* (*object*) trop lourd(e) du haut

topic ['tɔpɪk] *n* sujet *m*, thème *m*; **~al** *adj* d'actualité

top: ~less *adj* (*bather etc*) aux seins nus; **~-level** *adj* (*talks*) au plus haut niveau; **~most** *adj* le (la) plus haut(e)

topple ['tɔpl] *vt* renverser, faire tomber ♦ *vi* basculer; tomber

top-secret ['tɔp'siːkrɪt] *adj* top secret(-ète)

topsy-turvy ['tɔpsɪ'tɜːvɪ] *adj, adv* sens dessus dessous

torch [tɔːtʃ] *n* torche *f*; (*BRIT: electric*) lampe *f* de poche

tore [tɔːr] *pt of* **tear**[1]

torment [*n* 'tɔːmɛnt, *vb* tɔː'mɛnt] *n* tourment *m* ♦ *vt* tourmenter; (*fig: annoy*) harceler

torn [tɔːn] *pp of* **tear**[1]

tornado [tɔː'neɪdəu] (*pl* **~es**) *n* tornade *f*

torpedo [tɔː'piːdəu] (*pl* **~es**) *n* torpille *f*

torrent ['tɔrnt] *n* torrent *m*; **~ial** [tɔ'rɛnʃl] *adj* torrentiel(le)

tortoise ['tɔːtəs] *n* tortue *f*; **~shell** *adj* en écaille

torture ['tɔːtʃər] *n* torture *f* ♦ *vt* torturer

Tory ['tɔːrɪ] (BRIT: POL) *adj*, *n* tory (*m/f*), conservateur(-trice)

toss [tɔs] *vt* lancer, jeter; (*pancake*) faire sauter; (*head*) rejeter en arrière; **to ~ a coin** jouer à pile ou face; **to ~ up for sth** jouer qch à pile ou face; **to ~ and turn** (*in bed*) se tourner et se retourner

tot [tɔt] *n* (BRIT: *drink*) petit verre; (*child*) bambin *m*

total ['təutl] *adj* total(e) ♦ *n* total *m* ♦ *vt* (*add up*) faire le total de, additionner; (*amount to*) s'élever à; **~ly** *adv* totalement

totter ['tɔtər] *vi* chanceler

touch [tʌtʃ] *n* contact *m*, toucher *m*; (*sense, also skill: of pianist etc*) toucher ♦ *vt* toucher; (*tamper with*) toucher à; **a ~ of** (*fig*) un petit peu de; une touche de; **to get in ~ with** prendre contact avec; **to lose ~** (*friends*) se perdre de vue; **~ on** *vt fus* (*topic*) effleurer, aborder; **~ up** *vt* (*paint*) retoucher; **~-and-go** *adj* incertain(e); **~down** *n* atterrissage *m*; (*on sea*) amerrissage *m*; (US: FOOTBALL) touché-en-but *m*; **~ed** *adj* (*moved*) touché(e); **~ing** *adj* touchant(e), attendrissant(e); **~line** *n* (SPORT) (ligne *f* de) touche *f*; **~y** *adj* (*person*) susceptible

tough [tʌf] *adj* dur(e); (*resistant*) résistant(e), solide; (*meat*) dur, coriace; (*firm*) inflexible; (*task*) dur, pénible; **~en** *vt* (*character*) endurcir; (*glass etc*) renforcer

toupee ['tuːpeɪ] *n* postiche *m*

tour ['tuər] *n* voyage *m*; (*also:* **package ~**) voyage organisé; (*of town, museum*) tour *m*, visite *f*; (*by artist*) tournée *f* ♦ *vt* visiter; **~ guide** *n* (*person*) guide *m/f*

tourism ['tuərɪzm] *n* tourisme *m*

tourist ['tuərɪst] *n* touriste *m/f* ♦ *cpd* touristique; **~ office** *n* syndicat *m* d'initiative

tournament ['tuənəmənt] *n* tournoi *m*

tousled ['tauzld] *adj* (*hair*) ébouriffé(e)

tout [taut] *vi*: **to ~ for** essayer de raccro-

cher, racoler ♦ *n* (*also:* **ticket ~**) revendeur *m* de billets

tow [təu] *vt* remorquer; (*caravan, trailer*) tracter; **"on ~"** (BRIT) or **"in ~"** (US) (AUT) "véhicule en remorque"

toward(s) [tə'wɔːd(z)] *prep* vers; (*of attitude*) envers, à l'égard de; (*of purpose*) pour

towel ['tauəl] *n* serviette *f* (de toilette); **~ling** *n* (*fabric*) tissu éponge *m*; **~ rail** (US **towel rack**) *n* porte-serviettes *m inv*

tower ['tauər] *n* tour *f*; **~ block** (BRIT) *n* tour *f* (d'habitation); **~ing** *adj* très haut(e), imposant(e)

town [taun] *n* ville *f*; **to go to ~** aller en ville; (*fig*) y mettre le paquet; **~ centre** *n* centre *m* de la ville, centre-ville *m*; **~ council** *n* conseil municipal; **~ hall** *n* ≈ mairie *f*; **~ plan** *n* plan *m* de ville; **~ planning** *n* urbanisme *m*

towrope ['təurəup] *n* (câble *m* de) remorque *f*

tow truck (US) *n* dépanneuse *f*

toy [tɔɪ] *n* jouet *m*; **~ with** *vt fus* jouer avec; (*idea*) caresser

trace [treɪs] *n* trace *f* ♦ *vt* (*draw*) tracer, dessiner; (*follow*) suivre la trace de; (*locate*) retrouver; **tracing paper** *n* papier-calque *m*

track [træk] *n* (*mark*) trace *f*; (*path: gen*) chemin *m*, piste *f*; (: *of bullet etc*) trajectoire *f*; (: *of suspect, animal*) piste *f*; (RAIL) voie ferrée, rails *mpl*; (*on tape, SPORT*) piste *f*; (*on record*) plage *f* ♦ *vt* suivre la trace or la piste de; **to keep ~ of** suivre; **~ down** *vt* (*prey*) trouver et capturer; (*sth lost*) finir par retrouver; **~suit** *n* survêtement *m*

tract [trækt] *n* (*of land*) étendue *f*

traction ['trækʃən] *n* traction *f*; (MED): **in ~** en extension

tractor ['træktər] *n* tracteur *m*

trade [treɪd] *n* commerce *m* ♦ *vi* faire du commerce ♦ *vt* (*exchange*): **to ~ sth (for sth)** échanger qch (contre qch); **~ in** *vt* (*old car etc*) faire reprendre; **~ fair** *n* foire(-exposition) commerciale; **~-in price** *n* prix *m* à la reprise; **~mark** *n* marque *f* de fabrique; **~**

name *n* nom *m* de marque; **~r** *n* commerçant(e), négociant(e); **~sman** (*irreg*) *n* (*shopkeeper*) commerçant; **~ union** *n* syndicat *m*; **~ unionist** *n* syndicaliste *m/f*

tradition [trəˈdɪʃən] *n* tradition *f*; **~al** *adj* traditionnel(le)

traffic [ˈtræfɪk] *n* trafic *m*; (*cars*) circulation *f* ♦ *vi*: **to ~ in** (*pej: liquor, drugs*) faire le trafic de; **~ calming** *n* ralentissement *m* de la circulation; **~ circle** (*US*) *n* rond-point *m*; **~ jam** *n* embouteillage *m*; **~ lights** *npl* feux *mpl* (de signalisation); **~ warden** *n* contractuel(le)

tragedy [ˈtrædʒədɪ] *n* tragédie *f*

tragic [ˈtrædʒɪk] *adj* tragique

trail [treɪl] *n* (*tracks*) trace *f*, piste *f*; (*path*) chemin *m*, piste; (*of smoke etc*) traînée *f* ♦ *vt* traîner, tirer; (*follow*) suivre ♦ *vi* traîner; (*in game, contest*) être en retard; **~ behind** *vi* traîner, être à la traîne; **~er** *n* (*AUT*) remorque *f*; (*US*) caravane *f*; (*CINEMA*) bande-annonce *f*; **~er truck** (*US*) *n* (camion *m*) semi-remorque *m*

train [treɪn] *n* train *m*; (*in underground*) rame *f*; (*of dress*) traîne *f* ♦ *vt* (*apprentice, doctor etc*) former; (*sportsman*) entraîner; (*dog*) dresser; (*memory*) exercer; (*point: gun etc*): **to ~ sth on** braquer qch sur ♦ *vi* suivre une formation; (*SPORT*) s'entraîner; **one's ~ of thought** le fil de sa pensée; **~ed** *adj* qualifié(e), qui a reçu une formation; (*animal*) dressé(e); **~ee** [treɪˈniː] *n* stagiaire *m/f*; (*in trade*) apprenti(e); **~er** *n* (*SPORT: coach*) entraîneur(-euse); (: *shoe*) chaussure *f* de sport; (*of dogs etc*) dresseur(-euse); **~ing** *n* formation *f*; entraînement *m*; **in ~ing** (*SPORT*) à l'entraînement; (*fit*) en forme; **~ing college** *n* école professionnelle; (*for teachers*) ≈ école normale; **~ing shoes** *npl* chaussures *fpl* de sport

trait [treɪt] *n* trait *m* (de caractère)

traitor [ˈtreɪtəʳ] *n* traître *m*

tram [træm] (*BRIT*) *n* (*also*: **~car**) tram(way) *m*

tramp [træmp] *n* (*person*) vagabond(e), clochard(e); (*inf: pej: woman*): **to be a ~** être coureuse ♦ *vi* marcher d'un pas lourd

trample [ˈtræmpl] *vt*: **to ~ (underfoot)** piétiner

trampoline [ˈtræmpəliːn] *n* trampoline *m*

tranquil [ˈtræŋkwɪl] *adj* tranquille; **~lizer** (*US* **tranquilizer**) *n* (*MED*) tranquillisant *m*

transact [trænˈzækt] *vt* (*business*) traiter; **~ion** *n* transaction *f*

transatlantic [ˈtrænzətˈlæntɪk] *adj* transatlantique

transfer [*n* ˈtrænsfəʳ, *vb* trænsˈfəːʳ] *n* (*gen, also SPORT*) transfert *m*; (*POL: of power*) passation *f*; (*picture, design*) décalcomanie *f*; (: *stick-on*) autocollant *m* ♦ *vt* transférer; passer; **to ~ the charges** (*BRIT: TEL*) téléphoner en P.C.V.; **~ desk** *n* (*AVIAT*) guichet *m* de transit

transform [trænsˈfɔːm] *vt* transformer

transfusion [trænsˈfjuːʒən] *n* transfusion *f*

transient [ˈtrænzɪənt] *adj* transitoire, éphémère

transistor [trænˈzɪstəʳ] *n* (**~ radio**) transistor *m*

transit [ˈtrænzɪt] *n*: **in ~** en transit

transitive [ˈtrænzɪtɪv] *adj* (*LING*) transitif(-ive)

transit lounge *n* salle *f* de transit

translate [trænzˈleɪt] *vt* traduire; **translation** *n* traduction *f*; **translator** *n* traducteur(-trice)

transmission [trænzˈmɪʃən] *n* transmission *f*

transmit [trænzˈmɪt] *vt* transmettre; (*RADIO, TV*) émettre

transparency [trænsˈpɛərnsɪ] *n* (*of glass etc*) transparence *f*; (*BRIT: PHOT*) diapositive *f*

transparent [trænsˈpærnt] *adj* transparent(e)

transpire [trænsˈpaɪəʳ] *vi* (*turn out*): **it ~d that ...** on a appris que ...; (*happen*) arriver

transplant [*vb* trænsˈplɑːnt, *n* ˈtrænsplɑːnt] *vt* transplanter; (*seedlings*) repiquer ♦ *n* (*MED*) transplantation *f*

transport [*n* ˈtrænspɔːt, *vb* trænsˈpɔːt] *n*

transport *m*; (*car*) moyen *m* de transport, voiture *f* ♦ *vt* transporter; **~ation** ['trænspɔ:'teɪʃən] *n* transport *m*; (*means of transportation*) moyen *m* de transport; **~ café** (*BRIT*) *n* ≈ restaurant *m* de routiers

trap [træp] *n* (*snare, trick*) piège *m*; (*carriage*) cabriolet *m* ♦ *vt* prendre au piège; (*confine*) coincer; **~ door** *n* trappe *f*

trapeze [trə'pi:z] *n* trapèze *m*

trappings ['træpɪŋz] *npl* ornements *mpl*; attributs *mpl*

trash [træʃ] (*pej*) *n* (*goods*) camelote *f*; (*nonsense*) sottises *fpl*; **~ can** (*US*) *n* poubelle *f*; **~y** (*inf*) *adj* de camelote; (*novel*) de quatre sous

trauma ['trɔ:mə] *n* traumatisme *m*; **~tic** [trɔ:'mætɪk] *adj* traumatisant(e)

travel ['trævl] *n* voyage(s) *m(pl)* ♦ *vi* voyager; (*news, sound*) se propager ♦ *vt* (*distance*) parcourir; **~ agency** *n* agence *f* de voyages; **~ agent** *n* agent *m* de voyages; **~ler** (*US* **traveler**) *n* voyageur(-euse); **~ler's cheque** (*US* **traveler's check**) *n* chèque *m* de voyage; **~ling** (*US* **traveling**) *n* voyage(s) *m(pl)*; **~ sickness** *n* mal *m* de la route (*or* de mer *or* de l'air)

trawler ['trɔ:lər] *n* chalutier *m*

tray [treɪ] *n* (*for carrying*) plateau *m*; (*on desk*) corbeille *f*

treacherous ['tretʃərəs] *adj* (*person, look*) traître(-esse); (*ground, tide*) dont il faut se méfier

treacle ['tri:kl] *n* mélasse *f*

tread [trɛd] (*pt* **trod**, *pp* **trodden**) *n* pas *m*; (*sound*) bruit *m* de pas; (*of tyre*) chape *f*, bande *f* de roulement ♦ *vi* marcher; **~ on** *vt fus* marcher sur

treason ['tri:zn] *n* trahison *f*

treasure ['trɛʒər] *n* trésor *m* ♦ *vt* (*value*) tenir beaucoup à; **~r** *n* trésorier(-ère); **treasury** *n*: **the Treasury**, (*US*) **the Treasury Department** le ministère des Finances

treat [tri:t] *n* petit cadeau, petite surprise ♦ *vt* traiter; **to ~ sb to sth** offrir qch à qn

treatment *n* traitement *m*

treaty ['tri:tɪ] *n* traité *m*

treble ['trɛbl] *adj* triple ♦ *vt, vi* tripler; **~ clef** *n* (*MUS*) clé *f* de sol

tree [tri:] *n* arbre *m*

trek [trɛk] *n* (*long*) voyage; (*on foot*) (longue) marche, tirée *f*

tremble ['trɛmbl] *vi* trembler

tremendous [trɪ'mɛndəs] *adj* (*enormous*) énorme, fantastique; (*excellent*) formidable

tremor ['trɛmər] *n* tremblement *m*; (*also*: **earth ~**) secousse *f* sismique

trench [trɛntʃ] *n* tranchée *f*

trend [trɛnd] *n* (*tendency*) tendance *f*; (*of events*) cours *m*; (*fashion*) mode *f*; **~y** *adj* (*idea, person*) dans le vent; (*clothes*) dernier cri *inv*

trespass ['trɛspəs] *vi*: **to ~ on** s'introduire sans permission dans; **"no ~ing"** "propriété privée", "défense d'entrer"

trestle ['trɛsl] *n* tréteau *m*

trial ['traɪəl] *n* (*LAW*) procès *m*, jugement *m*; (*test: of machine etc*) essai *m*; **~s** *npl* (*unpleasant experiences*) épreuves *fpl*; **to be on ~** (*LAW*) passer en jugement; **by ~ and error** par tâtonnements; **~ period** *n* période *f* d'essai

triangle ['traɪæŋgl] *n* (*MATH, MUS*) triangle *m*; **triangular** [traɪˈæŋgjulər] *adj* triangulaire

tribe [traɪb] *n* tribu *f*; **~sman** (*irreg*) *n* membre *m* d'une tribu

tribunal [traɪ'bju:nl] *n* tribunal *m*

tributary ['trɪbjutərɪ] *n* (*river*) affluent *m*

tribute ['trɪbju:t] *n* tribut *m*, hommage *m*; **to pay ~ to** rendre hommage à

trick [trɪk] *n* (*magic ~*) tour *m*; (*joke, prank*) tour, farce *f*; (*skill, knack*) astuce *f*, truc *m*; (*CARDS*) levée *f* ♦ *vt* attraper, rouler; **to play a ~ on sb** jouer un tour à qn; **that should do the ~** ça devrait faire l'affaire; **~ery** *n* ruse *f*

trickle ['trɪkl] *n* (*of water etc*) filet *m* ♦ *vi* couler en un filet *or* goutte à goutte

tricky ['trɪkɪ] *adj* difficile, délicat(e)

tricycle ['traɪsɪkl] *n* tricycle *m*

trifle ['traɪfl] *n* bagatelle *f*; (*CULIN*) ≈ diplomate *m* ♦ *adv*: **a ~ long** un peu long;

trifling *adj* insignifiant(e)
trigger ['trɪgə*r*] *n* (*of gun*) gâchette *f*; ~ **off**
vt déclencher
trim [trɪm] *adj* (*house, garden*) bien tenu(e); (*figure*) svelte ♦ *n* (*haircut etc*) légère coupe; (*on car*) garnitures *fpl* ♦ *vt* (*cut*) couper légèrement; (*NAUT: a sail*) gréer; (*decorate*): **to ~ (with)** décorer (de); ~**mings** *npl* (*CULIN*) garniture *f*
trinket ['trɪŋkɪt] *n* bibelot *m*; (*piece of jewellery*) colifichet *m*
trip [trɪp] *n* voyage *m*; (*excursion*) excursion *f*; (*stumble*) faux pas ♦ *vi* faire un faux pas, trébucher; **on a ~** en voyage; ~ **up** *vi* trébucher ♦ *vt* faire un croc-en-jambe à
tripe [traɪp] *n* (*CULIN*) tripes *fpl*; (*pej: rubbish*) idioties *fpl*
triple ['trɪpl] *adj* triple; ~**ts** *npl* triplés(-ées); **triplicate** ['trɪplɪkət] *n*: **in triplicate** en trois exemplaires
tripod ['traɪpɔd] *n* trépied *m*
trite [traɪt] (*pej*) *adj* banal(e)
triumph ['traɪʌmf] *n* triomphe *m* ♦ *vi*: **to ~ (over)** triompher (de)
trivia ['trɪvɪə] (*pej*) *npl* futilités *fpl*; ~**l** *adj* insignifiant(e); (*commonplace*) banal(e)
trod [trɔd] *pt of* **tread**; ~**den** *pp of* **tread**
trolley ['trɔlɪ] *n* chariot *m*
trombone [trɔm'bəun] *n* trombone *m*
troop [tru:p] *n* bande *f*, groupe *m* ♦ *vi*: ~ **in/out** entrer/sortir en groupe; ~**s** *npl* (*MIL*) troupes *fpl*; (*: men*) hommes *mpl*, soldats *mpl*; ~**ing the colour** (*BRIT*) *n* (*ceremony*) le salut au drapeau
trophy ['trəufɪ] *n* trophée *m*
tropic ['trɔpɪk] *n* tropique *m*; ~**al** *adj* tropical(e)
trot [trɔt] *n* trot *m* ♦ *vi* trotter; **on the ~** (*BRIT: fig*) d'affilée
trouble ['trʌbl] *n* difficulté(s) *f(pl)*, problème(s) *m(pl)*; (*worry*) ennuis *mpl*, soucis *mpl*; (*bother, effort*) peine *f*; (*POL*) troubles *mpl*; (*MED*): **stomach** *etc* ~ troubles gastriques *etc* ♦ *vt* (*disturb*) déranger, gêner; (*worry*) inquiéter ♦ *vi*: **to ~ to do** prendre la peine de faire; ~**s** *npl* (*POL etc*) troubles *mpl*; (*personal*) ennuis, soucis; **to be in ~**

avoir des ennuis; (*ship, climber etc*) être en difficulté; **what's the ~?** qu'est-ce qui ne va pas?; ~**d** *adj* (*person*) inquiet(-ète); (*epoch, life*) agité(e); ~**maker** *n* élément perturbateur, fauteur *m* de troubles; ~**shooter** *n* (*in conflict*) médiateur *m*; ~**some** *adj* (*child*) fatigant(e), difficile; (*cough etc*) gênant(e)
trough [trɔf] *n* (*also:* **drinking ~**) abreuvoir *m*; (*also:* **feeding ~**) auge *f*; (*depression*) creux *m*
trousers ['trauzəz] *npl* pantalon *m*; **short ~** culottes courtes
trout [traut] *n inv* truite *f*
trowel ['trauəl] *n* truelle *f*; (*garden tool*) déplantoir *m*
truant ['truənt] (*BRIT*) *n*: **to play ~** faire l'école buissonnière
truce [tru:s] *n* trêve *f*
truck [trʌk] *n* camion *m*; (*RAIL*) wagon *m* à plate-forme; ~ **driver** *n* camionneur *m*; ~ **farm** (*US*) *n* jardin maraîcher
true [tru:] *adj* vrai(e); (*accurate*) exact(e); (*genuine*) vrai, véritable; (*faithful*) fidèle; **to come ~** se réaliser
truffle ['trʌfl] *n* truffe *f*
truly ['tru:lɪ] *adv* vraiment, réellement; (*truthfully*) sans mentir; *see also* **yours**
trump [trʌmp] *n* (*also:* ~ **card**) atout *m*
trumpet ['trʌmpɪt] *n* trompette *f*
truncheon ['trʌntʃən] (*BRIT*) *n* bâton *m* (d'agent de police); matraque *f*
trundle ['trʌndl] *vt, vi*: **to ~ along** rouler lentement (et bruyamment)
trunk [trʌŋk] *n* (*of tree, person*) tronc *m*; (*of elephant*) trompe *f*; (*case*) malle *f*; (*US: AUT*) coffre *m*; ~**s** *npl* (*also:* **swimming ~s**) maillot *m* or slip *m* de bain
truss [trʌs] *vt*: **to ~ (up)** ligoter
trust [trʌst] *n* confiance *f*; (*responsibility*) charge *f*; (*LAW*) fidéicommis *m* ♦ *vt* (*rely on*) avoir confiance en; (*hope*) espérer; (*entrust*): **to ~ sth to sb** confier qch à qn; **to take sth on ~** accepter qch les yeux fermés; ~**ed** *adj* en qui l'on a confiance; ~**ee** [trʌs'ti:] *n* (*LAW*) fidéicommissaire *m/f*; (*of school etc*) administrateur(-trice); ~**ful,**

~ing *adj* confiant(e); ~worthy *adj* digne de confiance

truth [tru:θ] *n* vérité *f*; ~ful *adj* (*person*) qui dit la vérité; (*answer*) sincère

try [traɪ] *n* essai *m*, tentative *f*; (*RUGBY*) essai ♦ *vt* (*attempt*) essayer, tenter; (*test: sth new: also: ~ out*) essayer, tester; (*LAW: person*) juger; (*strain*) éprouver ♦ *vi* essayer; **to have a ~** essayer; **to ~ to do** essayer de faire; (*seek*) chercher à faire; ~ **on** *vt* (*clothes*) essayer; ~ing *adj* pénible

T-shirt ['ti:ʃə:t] *n* tee-shirt *m*

T-square ['ti:skwɛəʳ] *n* équerre *f* en T, té *m*

tub [tʌb] *n* cuve *f*; (*for washing clothes*) baquet *m*; (*bath*) baignoire *f*

tubby ['tʌbɪ] *adj* rondelet(te)

tube [tju:b] *n* tube *m*; (*BRIT: underground*) métro *m*; (*for tyre*) chambre *f* à air

tuberculosis [tjubə:kju'ləusɪs] *n* tuberculose *f*

TUC *n abbr* (*BRIT: Trades Union Congress*) *confédération des syndicats britanniques*

tuck [tʌk] *vt* (*put*) mettre; ~ **away** *vt* cacher, ranger; ~ **in** *vt* rentrer; (*child*) border ♦ *vi* (*eat*) manger (de bon appétit); ~ **up** *vt* (*child*) border; ~ **shop** (*BRIT*) *n* boutique *f* à provisions (*dans une école*)

Tuesday ['tju:zdɪ] *n* mardi *m*

tuft [tʌft] *n* touffe *f*

tug [tʌg] *n* (*ship*) remorqueur *m* ♦ *vt* tirer (sur); ~**-of-war** *n* lutte *f* à la corde; (*fig*) lutte acharnée

tuition [tju:'ɪʃən] *n* (*BRIT*) leçons *fpl*; (: *private ~*) cours particuliers; (*US: school fees*) frais *mpl* de scolarité

tulip ['tju:lɪp] *n* tulipe *f*

tumble ['tʌmbl] *n* (*fall*) chute *f*, culbute *f* ♦ *vi* tomber, dégringoler; **to ~ to sth** (*inf*) réaliser qch; ~**down** *adj* délabré(e); ~ **dryer** (*BRIT*) *n* séchoir *m* à air chaud

tumbler ['tʌmbləʳ] *n* (*glass*) verre (droit), gobelet *m*

tummy ['tʌmɪ] *n* (*inf*) ventre *m*; ~ **upset** *n* maux *mpl* de ventre

tumour ['tju:məʳ] (*US* **tumor**) *n* tumeur *f*

tuna ['tju:nə] *n inv* (*also: ~ fish*) thon *m*

tune [tju:n] *n* (*melody*) air *m* ♦ *vt* (*MUS*) accorder; (*RADIO, TV, AUT*) régler; **to be in/ out of ~** (*instrument*) être accordé/ désaccordé; (*singer*) chanter juste/faux; **to be in/out of ~ with** (*fig*) être en accord/ désaccord avec; ~ **in** *vi* (*RADIO, TV*): **to ~ in (to)** se mettre à l'écoute (de); ~ **up** *vi* (*musician*) accorder son instrument; ~ful *adj* mélodieux(-euse); ~r *n*: **piano ~r** accordeur *m* (de pianos)

tunic ['tju:nɪk] *n* tunique *f*

Tunisia [tju:'nɪzɪə] *n* Tunisie *f*

tunnel ['tʌnl] *n* tunnel *m*; (*in mine*) galerie *f* ♦ *vi* percer un tunnel

turbulence ['tə:bjuləns] *n* (*AVIAT*) turbulence *f*

tureen [tə'ri:n] *n* (*for soup*) soupière *f*; (*for vegetables*) légumier *m*

turf [tə:f] *n* gazon *m*; (*clod*) motte *f* (de gazon) ♦ *vt* gazonner; ~ **out** (*inf*) *vt* (*person*) jeter dehors

Turk [tə:k] *n* Turc (Turque)

Turkey ['tə:kɪ] *n* Turquie *f*

turkey ['tə:kɪ] *n* dindon *m*, dinde *f*

Turkish ['tə:kɪʃ] *adj* turc (turque) ♦ *n* (*LING*) turc *m*

turmoil ['tə:mɔɪl] *n* trouble *m*, bouleversement *m*; **in ~** en émoi, en effervescence

turn [tə:n] *n* tour *m*; (*in road*) tournant *m*; (*of mind, events*) tournure *f*; (*performance*) numéro *m*; (*MED*) crise *f*, attaque *f* ♦ *vt* tourner; (*collar, steak*) retourner; (*change*): **to ~ sth into** changer qch en ♦ *vi* (*object, wind, milk*) tourner; (*person: look back*) se (re)tourner; (*reverse direction*) faire demi-tour; (*become*) devenir; (*age*) atteindre; **to ~ into** se changer en; **a good ~** un service; **it gave me quite a ~** ça m'a fait un coup; **"no left ~"** (*AUT*) "défense de tourner à gauche"; **it's your ~** c'est à vous (votre) tour; **in ~** à son tour; à tour de rôle; **to take ~s (at)** se relayer (pour *or* à); ~ **away** *vi* se détourner ♦ *vt* (*applicants*) refuser; ~ **back** *vi* revenir, faire demi-tour ♦ *vt* (*person, vehicle*) faire faire demi-tour à; (*clock*) reculer; ~ **down** *vt* (*refuse*) rejeter, refuser; (*reduce*) baisser; (*fold*) rabattre; ~ **in** vi (inf: go to bed) aller se coucher ♦ vt (fold) rentrer; ~ **off** vi (from road) tourner ♦ vt (light, radio etc) éteindre; (tap) fermer; (engine) arrêter; ~ **on** vt (light, radio etc) allumer; (tap) ouvrir; (engine) mettre en marche; ~ **out** vt (light, gas) éteindre; (produce) produire ♦ vi (voters, troops etc) se présenter; **to ~ out to be ...** s'avérer ...; se révéler ...; ~ **over** vi (person) se retourner ♦ vt (object) retourner; (page) tourner; ~ **round** vi faire demi-tour; (rotate) tourner; ~ **up** vi (person) arriver, se pointer (inf); (lost object) être retrouvé(e) ♦ vt (collar) remonter; (radio, heater) mettre plus fort; ~**ing** n (in road) tournant m; ~**ing point** n (fig) tournant m, moment décisif

turnip ['tə:nɪp] n navet m

turn: ~**out** n (of voters) taux m de participation; ~**over** n (COMM: amount of money) chiffre m d'affaires; (: of goods) roulement m; (of staff) renouvellement m, changement m; ~**pike** (US) n autoroute f à péage; ~**stile** n tourniquet m (d'entrée); ~**table** n (on record player) platine f; ~**up** (BRIT) n (on trousers) revers m

turpentine ['tə:pəntaɪn] n (also: **turps**) (essence f de) térébenthine f

turquoise ['tə:kwɔɪz] n (stone) turquoise f ♦ adj turquoise inv

turret ['tʌrɪt] n tourelle f

turtle ['tə:tl] n tortue marine or d'eau douce; ~**neck (sweater)** n (BRIT) pullover m à col montant; (US) pullover à col roulé

tusk [tʌsk] n défense f

tutor ['tju:tə*] n (in college) directeur(-trice) d'études; (private teacher) précepteur(-trice); ~**ial** [tju:'tɔ:rɪəl] n (SCOL) (séance f de) travaux mpl pratiques

tuxedo [tʌk'si:dəu] (US) n smoking m

TV n abbr (= television) télé f

twang [twæŋ] n (of instrument) son vibrant; (of voice) ton nasillard

tweed [twi:d] n tweed m

tweezers ['twi:zəz] npl pince f à épiler

twelfth [twelfθ] num douzième

twelve [twelv] num douze; **at ~** (o'clock) à midi; (midnight) à minuit

twentieth ['twentɪɪθ] num vingtième

twenty ['twentɪ] num vingt

twice [twaɪs] adv deux fois; ~ **as much** deux fois plus

twiddle ['twɪdl] vt, vi: **to ~ (with) sth** tripoter qch; **to ~ one's thumbs** (fig) se tourner les pouces

twig [twɪg] n brindille f ♦ vi (inf) piger

twilight ['twaɪlaɪt] n crépuscule m

twin [twɪn] adj, n jumeau(-elle) ♦ vt jumeler; ~**(-bedded) room** n chambre f à deux lits; ~ **beds** npl lits jumeaux

twine [twaɪn] n ficelle f ♦ vi (plant) s'enrouler

twinge [twɪndʒ] n (of pain) élancement m; **a ~ of conscience** un certain remords; **a ~ of regret** un pincement au cœur

twinkle ['twɪŋkl] vi scintiller; (eyes) pétiller

twirl [twə:l] vt faire tournoyer ♦ vi tournoyer

twist [twɪst] n torsion f, tour m; (in road) virage m; (in wire, flex) tortillon m; (in story) coup m de théâtre ♦ vt tordre; (weave) entortiller; (roll around) enrouler; (fig) déformer ♦ vi (road, river) serpenter

twit [twɪt] (inf) n crétin(e)

twitch [twɪtʃ] n (pull) coup sec, saccade f; (nervous) tic m ♦ vi se convulser; avoir un tic

two [tu:] num deux; **to put ~ and ~ together** (fig) faire le rapprochement; ~**door** adj (AUT) à deux portes; ~**faced** (pej) adj (person) faux (fausse); ~**fold** adv: **to increase ~fold** doubler; ~**piece (suit)** n (man's) costume m (deux-pièces); (woman's) (tailleur m) deux-pièces m inv; ~**piece (swimsuit)** n (maillot m de bain) deux-pièces m inv; ~**some** n (people) couple m; ~**way** adj (traffic) dans les deux sens

tycoon [taɪ'ku:n] n: **(business) ~** gros homme d'affaires

type [taɪp] n (category) type m, genre m, espèce f; (model, example) type m, modèle m; (TYP) type, caractère m ♦ vt (letter etc) taper (à la machine); ~**cast** adj (actor) condamné(e) à toujours jouer le même rôle; **~face** *n* (*TYP*) œil *m* de caractère; **~script** *n* texte dactylographié; **~writer** *n* machine *f* à écrire; **~written** *adj* dactylographié(e)

typhoid ['taɪfɔɪd] *n* typhoïde *f*

typical ['tɪpɪkl] *adj* typique, caractéristique

typing ['taɪpɪŋ] *n* dactylo(graphie) *f*

typist ['taɪpɪst] *n* dactylo *m/f*

tyrant ['taɪərnt] *n* tyran *m*

tyre ['taɪər] (*US* **tire**) *n* pneu *m*; **~ pressure** *n* pression *f* (de gonflage)

U, u

U-bend ['juːbɛnd] *n* (*in pipe*) coude *m*

ubiquitous [juːˈbɪkwɪtəs] *adj* omniprésent(e)

udder ['ʌdər] *n* pis *m*, mamelle *f*

UFO ['juːfəʊ] *n abbr* (= *unidentified flying object*) OVNI *m*

Uganda [juːˈgændə] *n* Ouganda *m*

ugh [əːh] *excl* pouah!

ugly ['ʌglɪ] *adj* laid(e), vilain(e); (*situation*) inquiétant(e)

UHT *abbr* (= *ultra heat treated*): **UHT milk** lait *m* UHT *or* longue conservation

UK *n abbr* = **United Kingdom**

ulcer ['ʌlsər] *n* ulcère *m*; (*also: mouth ~*) aphte *f*

Ulster ['ʌlstər] *n* Ulster *m*; (*inf: Northern Ireland*) Irlande *f* du Nord

ulterior [ʌlˈtɪərɪər] *adj*: **~ motive** arrière-pensée *f*

ultimate ['ʌltɪmət] *adj* ultime, final(e); (*authority*) suprême; **~ly** *adv* (*at last*) en fin de compte; (*fundamentally*) finalement

ultrasound ['ʌltrəsaund] *n* ultrason *m*

umbilical cord [ʌmˈbɪlɪkl-] *n* cordon ombilical

umbrella [ʌmˈbrɛlə] *n* parapluie *m*; (*for sun*) parasol *m*

umpire ['ʌmpaɪər] *n* arbitre *m*

umpteen [ʌmpˈtiːn] *adj* je ne sais combien de; **~th** *adj*: **for the ~th time** pour la nième fois

UN *n abbr* = **United Nations**

unable [ʌnˈeɪbl] *adj*: **to be ~ to** ne pas pouvoir, être dans l'impossibilité de; (*incapable*) être incapable de

unacceptable [ʌnəkˈsɛptəbl] *adj* (*behaviour*) inadmissible; (*price, proposal*) inacceptable

unaccompanied [ʌnəˈkʌmpənɪd] *adj* (*child, lady*) non accompagné(e); (*song*) sans accompagnement

unaccustomed [ʌnəˈkʌstəmd] *adj*: **to be ~ to sth** ne pas avoir l'habitude de qch

unanimous [juːˈnænɪməs] *adj* unanime; **~ly** *adv* à l'unanimité

unarmed [ʌnˈɑːmd] *adj* (*without a weapon*) non armé(e); (*combat*) sans armes

unattached [ʌnəˈtætʃt] *adj* libre, sans attaches; (*part*) non attaché(e), indépendant(e)

unattended [ʌnəˈtɛndɪd] *adj* (*car, child, luggage*) sans surveillance

unattractive [ʌnəˈtræktɪv] *adj* peu attrayant(e); (*character*) peu sympathique

unauthorized [ʌnˈɔːθəraɪzd] *adj* non autorisé(e), sans autorisation

unavoidable [ʌnəˈvɔɪdəbl] *adj* inévitable

unaware [ʌnəˈwɛər] *adj*: **to be ~ of** ignorer, être inconscient(e) de; **~s** *adv* à l'improviste, au dépourvu

unbalanced [ʌnˈbælənst] *adj* déséquilibré(e); (*report*) peu objectif(-ive)

unbearable [ʌnˈbɛərəbl] *adj* insupportable

unbeatable [ʌnˈbiːtəbl] *adj* imbattable

unbeknown(st) [ʌnbɪˈnəʊn(st)] *adv*: **~ to me/Peter** à mon insu/l'insu de Peter

unbelievable [ʌnbɪˈliːvəbl] *adj* incroyable

unbend [ʌnˈbɛnd] (*irreg*) *vi* se détendre ♦ *vt* (*wire*) redresser, détordre

unbiased [ʌnˈbaɪəst] *adj* impartial(e)

unborn [ʌnˈbɔːn] *adj* à naître, qui n'est pas encore né(e)

unbreakable [ʌnˈbreɪkəbl] *adj* incassable

unbroken [ʌnˈbrəʊkən] *adj* intact(e); (*fig*) continu(e), ininterrompu(e)

unbutton [ʌnˈbʌtn] *vt* déboutonner

uncalled-for [ʌnˈkɔːldfɔːr] *adj* déplacé(e), injustifié(e)

uncanny [ʌnˈkænɪ] *adj* étrange, troublant(e)

unceremonious [ʌnserɪˈməʊnɪəs] *adj* (*abrupt, rude*) brusque

uncertain [ʌnˈsɜːtn] *adj* incertain(e); (*hesitant*) hésitant(e); **in no ~ terms** sans équivoque possible; **~ty** *n* incertitude *f*, doute(s) *m(pl)*

uncivilized [ʌnˈsɪvɪlaɪzd] *adj* (*gen*) non civilisé(e); (*fig: behaviour etc*) barbare; (*hour*) indu(e)

uncle [ˈʌŋkl] *n* oncle *m*

uncomfortable [ʌnˈkʌmfətəbl] *adj* inconfortable, peu confortable; (*uneasy*) mal à l'aise, gêné(e); (*situation*) désagréable

uncommon [ʌnˈkɒmən] *adj* rare, singulier(-ère), peu commun(e)

uncompromising [ʌnˈkɒmprəmaɪzɪŋ] *adj* intransigeant(e), inflexible

unconcerned [ʌnkənˈsɜːnd] *adj*: **to be ~ (about)** ne pas s'inquiéter (de)

unconditional [ʌnkənˈdɪʃənl] *adj* sans conditions

unconscious [ʌnˈkɒnʃəs] *adj* sans connaissance, évanoui(e); (*unaware*): **~ of** inconscient(e) de ♦ *n*: **the ~** l'inconscient *m*; **~ly** *adv* inconsciemment

uncontrollable [ʌnkənˈtrəʊləbl] *adj* indiscipliné(e); (*temper, laughter*) irrépressible

unconventional [ʌnkənˈvenʃənl] *adj* peu conventionnel(le)

uncouth [ʌnˈkuːθ] *adj* grossier(-ère), fruste

uncover [ʌnˈkʌvər] *vt* découvrir

undecided [ʌndɪˈsaɪdɪd] *adj* indécis(e), irrésolu(e)

under [ˈʌndər] *prep* sous; (*less than*) (de) moins de; au-dessous de; (*according to*) selon, en vertu de ♦ *adv* au-dessous; en dessous; **~ there** là-dessous; **~ repair** en (cours de) réparation; **~age** *adj* (*person*) qui n'a pas l'âge réglementaire; **~carriage** *n* (*AVIAT*) train *m* d'atterrissage; **~charge** *vt* ne pas faire payer assez à; **~coat** *n* (*paint*) couche *f* de fond; **~cover** *adj* secret(-ète), clandestin(e); **~current** *n* courant *or* sentiment sous-jacent;

~dog *n* opprimé *m*; **~done** *adj* (*CULIN*) saignant(e); (*pej*) pas assez cuit(e); **~estimate** *vt* sous-estimer; **~fed** *adj* sous-alimenté(e); **~foot** *adv* sous les pieds; **~go** (*irreg*) *vt* subir; (*treatment*) suivre; **~graduate** *n* étudiant(e) (qui prépare la licence); **~ground** *n* (*BRIT: railway*) métro *m*; (*POL*) clandestinité *f* ♦ *adj* souterrain(e); (*fig*) clandestin(e) ♦ *adv* dans la clandestinité, clandestinement; **~growth** *n* broussailles *fpl*, sous-bois *m*; **~hand(ed)** *adj* (*fig: behaviour, method etc*) en dessous; **~lie** (*irreg*) *vt* être à la base de; **~line** *vt* souligner; **~mine** *vt* saper, miner; **~neath** *adv* (en) dessous ♦ *prep* sous, au-dessous de; **~paid** *adj* sous-payé(e); **~pants** *npl* caleçon *m*, slip *m*; **~pass** (*BRIT*) *n* passage souterrain; (*on motorway*) passage inférieur; **~privileged** *adj* défavorisé(e), économiquement faible; **~rate** *vt* sous-estimer; **~shirt** (*US*) *n* tricot *m* de corps; **~shorts** (*US*) *npl* caleçon *m*, slip *m*; **~side** *n* dessous *m*; **~skirt** (*BRIT*) *n* jupon *m*

understand [ʌndəˈstænd] (*irreg: like* **stand**) *vt, vi* comprendre; **I ~ that ...** je me suis laissé dire que ...; je crois comprendre que ...; **~able** *adj* compréhensible; **~ing** *adj* compréhensif(-ive) ♦ *n* compréhension *f*; (*agreement*) accord *m*

understatement [ˈʌndəsteɪtmənt] *n*: **that's an ~** c'est (bien) peu dire, le terme est faible

understood [ʌndəˈstʊd] *pt, pp of* **understand** ♦ *adj* entendu(e); (*implied*) sous-entendu(e)

understudy [ˈʌndəstʌdɪ] *n* doublure *f*

undertake [ʌndəˈteɪk] (*irreg*) *vt* entreprendre; se charger de; **to ~ to do sth** s'engager à faire qch

undertaker [ˈʌndəteɪkər] *n* entrepreneur *m* des pompes funèbres, croque-mort *m*

undertaking [ˈʌndəteɪkɪŋ] *n* entreprise *f*; (*promise*) promesse *f*

under: **~tone** *n*: **in an ~tone** à mi-voix; **~water** *adv* sous l'eau ♦ *adj* sous-marin(e); **~wear** *n* sous-vêtements *mpl*;

(*women's only*) dessous *mpl*; **~world** *n* (*of crime*) milieu *m*, pègre *f*; **~write** *n* (*INSURANCE*) assureur *m*

undies ['ʌndɪz] (*inf*) *npl* dessous *mpl*, lingerie *f*

undiplomatic ['ʌndɪplə'mætɪk] *adj* peu diplomatique

undo [ʌn'du:] (*irreg*) *vt* défaire; **~ing** *n* ruine *f*, perte *f*

undoubted [ʌn'dautɪd] *adj* indubitable, certain(e); **~ly** *adv* sans aucun doute

undress [ʌn'drɛs] *vi* se déshabiller

undue [ʌn'dju:] *adj* indu(e), excessif(-ive)

undulating ['ʌndjuleɪtɪŋ] *adj* ondoyant(e), onduleux(-euse)

unduly [ʌn'dju:lɪ] *adv* trop, excessivement

unearth [ʌn'ə:θ] *vt* déterrer; (*fig*) dénicher

unearthly [ʌn'ə:θlɪ] *adj* (*hour*) indu(e), impossible

uneasy [ʌn'i:zɪ] *adj* mal à l'aise, gêné(e); (*worried*) inquiet(-ète); (*feeling*) désagréable; (*peace, truce*) fragile

uneconomic(al) ['ʌni:kə'nɔmɪk(l)] *adj* peu économique

uneducated [ʌn'ɛdjukeɪtɪd] *adj* (*person*) sans instruction

unemployed [ʌnɪm'plɔɪd] *adj* sans travail, en *or* au chômage ♦ *n*: **the ~** les chômeurs *mpl*; **unemployment** *n* chômage *m*

unending [ʌn'ɛndɪŋ] *adj* interminable, sans fin

unerring [ʌn'ə:rɪŋ] *adj* infaillible, sûr(e)

uneven [ʌn'i:vn] *adj* inégal(e); (*quality, work*) irrégulier(-ère)

unexpected [ʌnɪks'pɛktɪd] *adj* inattendu(e), imprévu(e); **~ly** [ʌnɪks'pɛktɪdlɪ] *adv* (*arrive*) à l'improviste; (*succeed*) contre toute attente

unfailing [ʌn'feɪlɪŋ] *adj* inépuisable; (*remedy*) infaillible

unfair [ʌn'fɛəʳ] *adj*: **~ (to)** injuste (envers)

unfaithful [ʌn'feɪθful] *adj* infidèle

unfamiliar [ʌn'fəmɪlɪəʳ] *adj* étrange, inconnu(e); **to be ~ with** mal connaître

unfashionable [ʌn'fæʃnəbl] *adj* (*clothes*) démodé(e); (*place*) peu chic *inv*

unfasten [ʌn'fɑ:sn] *vt* défaire; détacher; (*open*) ouvrir

unfavourable [ʌn'feɪvrəbl] (*US* **unfavorable**) *adj* défavorable

unfeeling [ʌn'fi:lɪŋ] *adj* insensible, dur(e)

unfinished [ʌn'fɪnɪʃt] *adj* inachevé(e)

unfit [ʌn'fɪt] *adj* en mauvaise santé; pas en forme; (*incompetent*): **~ (for)** impropre (à); (*work, service*) inapte (à)

unfold [ʌn'fəuld] *vt* déplier ♦ *vi* se dérouler

unforeseen ['ʌnfɔ:'si:n] *adj* imprévu(e)

unforgettable [ʌnfə'gɛtəbl] *adj* inoubliable

unfortunate [ʌn'fɔ:tʃənət] *adj* malheureux(-euse); (*event, remark*) malencontreux(-euse); **~ly** *adv* malheureusement

unfounded [ʌn'faundɪd] *adj* sans fondement

unfriendly [ʌn'frɛndlɪ] *adj* inamical(e), peu aimable

ungainly [ʌn'geɪnlɪ] *adj* gauche, dégingandé(e)

ungodly [ʌn'gɔdlɪ] *adj* (*hour*) indu(e)

ungrateful [ʌn'greɪtful] *adj* ingrat(e)

unhappiness [ʌn'hæpɪnɪs] *n* tristesse *f*, peine *f*

unhappy [ʌn'hæpɪ] *adj* triste, malheureux(-euse); **~ about** *or* **with** (*arrangements etc*) mécontent(e) de, peu satisfait(e) de

unharmed [ʌn'hɑ:md] *adj* indemne, sain(e) et sauf (sauve)

UNHCR *n abbr* (= *United Nations High Commission for refugees*) HCR *m*

unhealthy [ʌn'hɛlθɪ] *adj* malsain(e); (*person*) maladif(-ive)

unheard-of [ʌn'hə:dɔv] *adj* inouï(e), sans précédent

unhurt [ʌn'hə:t] *adj* indemne

unidentified [ʌnaɪ'dɛntɪfaɪd] *adj* non identifié(e); *see also* **UFO**

uniform ['ju:nɪfɔ:m] *n* uniforme *m* ♦ *adj* uniforme

uninhabited [ʌnɪn'hæbɪtɪd] *adj* inhabité(e)

unintentional [ʌnɪn'tɛnʃənəl] *adj* involontaire

union ['ju:njən] n union f; (also: **trade ~**) syndicat m ♦ cpd du syndicat, syndical(e); U~ **Jack** n drapeau du Royaume-Uni

unique [ju:'ni:k] adj unique

UNISON ['ju:nɪsn] n grand syndicat des services publics en Grande-Bretagne

unison ['ju:nɪsn] n: **in ~** (sing) à l'unisson; (say) en chœur

unit ['ju:nɪt] n unité f; (section: of furniture etc) élément m, bloc m; **kitchen ~** élément de cuisine

unite [ju:'naɪt] vt unir ♦ vi s'unir; ~**d** adj uni(e); unifié(e); (effort) conjugué(e); U~**d Kingdom** n Royaume-Uni m; U~**d Nations (Organization)** n (Organisation f des) Nations unies; U~**d States (of America)** n États-Unis mpl

unit trust (BRIT) n fonds commun de placement

unity ['ju:nɪtɪ] n unité f

universal [ju:nɪ'və:sl] adj universel(le)

universe ['ju:nɪvə:s] n univers m

university [ju:nɪ'və:sɪtɪ] n université f

unjust [ʌn'dʒʌst] adj injuste

unkempt [ʌn'kempt] adj négligé(e), débraillé(e); (hair) mal peigné(e)

unkind [ʌn'kaɪnd] adj peu gentil(le), méchant(e)

unknown [ʌn'nəʊn] adj inconnu(e)

unlawful [ʌn'lɔ:ful] adj illégal(e)

unleaded ['ʌn'ledɪd] adj (petrol, fuel) sans plomb

unleash [ʌn'li:ʃ] vt (fig) déchaîner, déclencher

unless [ʌn'les] conj: **~ he leaves** à moins qu'il ne parte

unlike [ʌn'laɪk] adj dissemblable, différent(e) ♦ prep contrairement à

unlikely [ʌn'laɪklɪ] adj (happening) improbable; (explanation) invraisemblable

unlimited [ʌn'lɪmɪtɪd] adj illimité(e)

unlisted ['ʌn'lɪstɪd] (US) adj (TEL) sur la liste rouge

unload [ʌn'ləʊd] vt décharger

unlock [ʌn'lɔk] vt ouvrir

unlucky [ʌn'lʌkɪ] adj (person) malchanceux(-euse); (object, number) qui porte malheur; **to be ~** (person) ne pas avoir de chance

unmarried [ʌn'mærɪd] adj célibataire

unmistak(e)able [ʌnmɪs'teɪkəbl] adj indubitable; qu'on ne peut pas ne pas reconnaître

unmitigated [ʌn'mɪtɪgeɪtɪd] adj non mitigé(e), absolu(e), pur(e)

unnatural [ʌn'nætʃrəl] adj non naturel(le); (habit) contre nature

unnecessary [ʌn'nesəsərɪ] adj inutile, superflu(e)

unnoticed [ʌn'nəʊtɪst] adj: **(to go** or **pass) ~** (passer) inaperçu(e)

UNO n abbr = **United Nations Organization**

unobtainable [ʌnəb'teɪnəbl] adj impossible à obtenir

unobtrusive [ʌnəb'tru:sɪv] adj discret(-ète)

unofficial [ʌnə'fɪʃl] adj (news) officieux(-euse); (strike) sauvage

unorthodox [ʌn'ɔ:θədɔks] adj peu orthodoxe; (REL) hétérodoxe

unpack [ʌn'pæk] vi défaire sa valise ♦ vt (suitcase) défaire; (belongings) déballer

unpalatable [ʌn'pælətəbl] adj (meal) mauvais(e); (truth) désagréable (à entendre)

unparalleled [ʌn'pærəleld] adj incomparable, sans égal

unpleasant [ʌn'pleznt] adj déplaisant(e), désagréable

unplug [ʌn'plʌg] vt débrancher

unpopular [ʌn'pɔpjulər] adj impopulaire

unprecedented [ʌn'presɪdəntɪd] adj sans précédent

unpredictable [ʌnprɪ'dɪktəbl] adj imprévisible

unprofessional [ʌnprə'feʃənl] adj: **~ conduct** manquement m aux devoirs de la profession

UNPROFOR n abbr (= United Nations Protection Force) FORPRONU f

unqualified [ʌn'kwɔlɪfaɪd] adj (teacher) non diplômé(e), sans titres; (success, disaster) sans réserve, total(e)

unquestionably [ʌn'kwestʃənəblɪ] adv incontestablement

unravel [ʌnˈrævl] *vt* démêler

unreal [ʌnˈrɪəl] *adj* irréel(le); (*extraordinary*) incroyable

unrealistic [ˈʌnrɪəˈlɪstɪk] *adj* irréaliste; peu réaliste

unreasonable [ʌnˈriːznəbl] *adj* qui n'est pas raisonnable

unrelated [ʌnrɪˈleɪtɪd] *adj* sans rapport; sans lien de parenté

unreliable [ʌnrɪˈlaɪəbl] *adj* sur qui (*or* quoi) on ne peut pas compter, peu fiable

unremitting [ʌnrɪˈmɪtɪŋ] *adj* inlassable, infatigable, acharné(e)

unreservedly [ʌnrɪˈzɜːvɪdlɪ] *adv* sans réserve

unrest [ʌnˈrest] *n* agitation *f*, troubles *mpl*

unroll [ʌnˈrəʊl] *vt* dérouler

unruly [ʌnˈruːlɪ] *adj* indiscipliné(e)

unsafe [ʌnˈseɪf] *adj* (*in danger*) en danger; (*journey, car*) dangereux(-euse)

unsaid [ʌnˈsed] *adj*: **to leave sth ~** passer qch sous silence

unsatisfactory [ˈʌnsætɪsˈfæktərɪ] *adj* peu satisfaisant(e)

unsavoury [ʌnˈseɪvərɪ] (*US* **unsavory**) *adj* (*fig*) peu recommandable

unscathed [ʌnˈskeɪðd] *adj* indemne

unscrew [ʌnˈskruː] *vt* dévisser

unscrupulous [ʌnˈskruːpjʊləs] *adj* sans scrupules

unsettled [ʌnˈsetld] *adj* perturbé(e); instable

unshaven [ʌnˈʃeɪvn] *adj* non *or* mal rasé(e)

unsightly [ʌnˈsaɪtlɪ] *adj* disgracieux(-euse), laid(e)

unskilled [ʌnˈskɪld] *adj*: **~ worker** manœuvre *m*

unspeakable [ʌnˈspiːkəbl] *adj* indicible; (*awful*) innommable

unstable [ʌnˈsteɪbl] *adj* instable

unsteady [ʌnˈstedɪ] *adj* mal assuré(e), chancelant(e), instable

unstuck [ʌnˈstʌk] *adj*: **to come ~** se décoller; (*plan*) tomber à l'eau

unsuccessful [ʌnsəkˈsesful] *adj* (*attempt*) infructueux(-euse), vain(e); (*writer, proposal*) qui n'a pas de succès; **to be ~** (*in attempting sth*) ne pas réussir; ne pas avoir de succès; (*application*) ne pas être retenu(e)

unsuitable [ʌnˈsuːtəbl] *adj* qui ne convient pas, peu approprié(e); inopportun(e)

unsure [ʌnˈʃʊər] *adj* pas sûr(e); **to be ~ of o.s.** manquer de confiance en soi

unsuspecting [ʌnsəsˈpektɪŋ] *adj* qui ne se doute de rien

unsympathetic [ˈʌnsɪmpəˈθetɪk] *adj* (*person*) antipathique; (*attitude*) peu compatissant(e)

untapped [ʌnˈtæpt] *adj* (*resources*) inexploité(e)

unthinkable [ʌnˈθɪŋkəbl] *adj* impensable, inconcevable

untidy [ʌnˈtaɪdɪ] *adj* (*room*) en désordre; (*appearance, person*) débraillé(e); (*person: in character*) sans ordre, désordonné

untie [ʌnˈtaɪ] *vt* (*knot, parcel*) défaire; (*prisoner, dog*) détacher

until [ənˈtɪl] *prep* jusqu'à; (*after negative*) avant ♦ *conj* jusqu'à ce que +*sub*; (*in past, after negative*) avant que +*sub*; **~ he comes** jusqu'à ce qu'il vienne, jusqu'à son arrivée; **~ now** jusqu'à présent, jusqu'ici; **~ then** jusque-là

untimely [ʌnˈtaɪmlɪ] *adj* inopportun(e); (*death*) prématuré(e)

untold [ʌnˈtəʊld] *adj* (*story*) jamais raconté(e); (*wealth*) incalculable; (*joy, suffering*) indescriptible

untoward [ʌntəˈwɔːd] *adj* fâcheux(-euse), malencontreux(-euse)

unused[1] [ʌnˈjuːzd] *adj* (*clothes*) neuf (neuve)

unused[2] [ʌnˈjuːst] *adj*: **to be ~ to sth/to doing sth** ne pas avoir l'habitude de qch/de faire qch

unusual [ʌnˈjuːʒʊəl] *adj* insolite, exceptionnel(le), rare

unveil [ʌnˈveɪl] *vt* dévoiler

unwanted [ʌnˈwɒntɪd] *adj* (*child, pregnancy*) non désiré(e); (*clothes etc*) à donner

unwelcome [ʌnˈwɛlkəm] *adj* importun(e); (*news*) fâcheux(-euse)

unwell [ʌnˈwɛl] *adj* souffrant(e); **to feel ~** ne pas se sentir bien

unwieldy [ʌnˈwiːldɪ] *adj* (*object*) difficile à manier; (*system*) lourd(e)

unwilling [ʌnˈwɪlɪŋ] *adj*: **to be ~ to do** ne pas vouloir faire; **~ly** *adv* à contrecœur, contre son gré

unwind [ʌnˈwaɪnd] (*irreg*) *vt* dérouler ♦ *vi* (*relax*) se détendre

unwise [ʌnˈwaɪz] *adj* irréfléchi(e), imprudent(e)

unwitting [ʌnˈwɪtɪŋ] *adj* involontaire

unworkable [ʌnˈwəːkəbl] *adj* (*plan*) impraticable

unworthy [ʌnˈwəːðɪ] *adj* indigne

unwrap [ʌnˈræp] *vt* défaire; ouvrir

unwritten [ʌnˈrɪtn] *adj* (*agreement*) tacite

KEYWORD

up [ʌp] *prep*: **he went up the stairs/the hill** il a monté l'escalier/la colline; **the cat was up a tree** le chat était dans un arbre; **they live further up the street** ils habitent plus haut dans la rue

♦ *adv* 1 (*upwards, higher*): **up in the sky/the mountains** (là-haut) dans le ciel/les montagnes; **put it a bit higher up** mettez-le un peu plus haut; **up there** là-haut; **up above** au-dessus

2: **to be up** (*out of bed*) être levé(e); (*prices*) avoir augmenté *or* monté

3: **up to** (*as far as*) jusqu'à; **up to now** jusqu'à présent

4: **to be up to** (*depending on*): **it's up to you** c'est à vous de décider; (*equal to*): **he's not up to it** (*job, task etc*) il n'en est pas capable; (*inf: be doing*): **what is he up to?** qu'est-ce qu'il peut bien faire?

♦ *n*: **ups and downs** hauts et bas *mpl*

up-and-coming [ʌpəndˈkʌmɪŋ] *adj* plein(e) d'avenir *or* de promesses

upbringing [ˈʌpbrɪŋɪŋ] *n* éducation *f*

update [ʌpˈdeɪt] *vt* mettre à jour

upgrade [ʌpˈɡreɪd] *vt* (*house*) moderniser; (*job*) revaloriser; (*employee*) promouvoir

upheaval [ʌpˈhiːvl] *n* bouleversement *m*; branle-bas *m*

uphill [ʌpˈhɪl] *adj* qui monte; (*fig: task*) difficile, pénible ♦ *adv* (*face, look*) en amont; **to go ~** monter

uphold [ʌpˈhəʊld] (*irreg*) *vt* (*law, decision*) maintenir

upholstery [ʌpˈhəʊlstərɪ] *n* rembourrage *m*; (*cover*) tissu *m* d'ameublement; (*of car*) garniture *f*

upkeep [ˈʌpkiːp] *n* entretien *m*

upon [əˈpɒn] *prep* sur

upper [ˈʌpər] *adj* supérieur(e); du dessus ♦ *n* (*of shoe*) empeigne *f*; **~-class** *adj* de la haute société, aristocratique; **~ hand** *n*: **to have the ~ hand** avoir le dessus; **~most** *adj* le (la) plus haut(e); **what was ~most in my mind** ce à quoi je pensais surtout; **~ sixth** *n* terminale *f*

upright [ˈʌpraɪt] *adj* droit(e); vertical(e); (*fig*) droit, honnête

uprising [ˈʌpraɪzɪŋ] *n* soulèvement *m*, insurrection *f*

uproar [ˈʌprɔːr] *n* tumulte *m*; (*protests*) tempête *f* de protestations

uproot [ʌpˈruːt] *vt* déraciner

upset [*n* ˈʌpsɛt, *vb, adj* ʌpˈsɛt] (*irreg: like* **set**) *n* bouleversement *m*; (*stomach ~*) indigestion *f* ♦ *vt* (*glass etc*) renverser; (*plan*) déranger; (*person: offend*) contrarier; (: *grieve*) faire de la peine à; bouleverser ♦ *adj* contrarié(e); peiné(e); (*stomach*) dérangé(e)

upshot [ˈʌpʃɔt] *n* résultat *m*

upside-down [ʌpsaɪdˈdaʊn] *adv* à l'envers; **to turn ~ ~** mettre sens dessus dessous

upstairs [ʌpˈstɛəz] *adv* en haut ♦ *adj* (*room*) du dessus, d'en haut ♦ *n*: **the ~** l'étage *m*

upstart [ˈʌpstɑːt] (*pej*) *n* parvenu(e)

upstream [ʌpˈstriːm] *adv* en amont

uptake [ˈʌpteɪk] *n*: **to be quick/slow on the ~** comprendre vite/être lent à comprendre

uptight [ʌpˈtaɪt] (*inf*) *adj* très tendu(e), crispé(e)

up-to-date [ˈʌptəˈdeɪt] *adj* moderne; (*information*) très récent(e)

upturn [ˈʌptəːn] *n* (*in luck*) retournement *m*; (*COMM: in market*) hausse *f*

upward [ˈʌpwəd] *adj* ascendant(e); vers le haut; **~(s)** *adv* vers le haut; **~(s) of 200** 200 et plus

urban [ˈəːbən] *adj* urbain(e); **~ clearway** *n* rue *f* à stationnement einterdit

urbane [əːˈbeɪn] *adj* urbain(e), courtois(e)

urchin [ˈəːtʃɪn] *n* polisson *m*

urge [əːdʒ] *n* besoin *m*; envie *f*; forte envie, désir *m* ♦ *vt*: **to ~ sb to do** exhorter qn à faire, pousser qn à faire; recommander vivement à qn de faire

urgency [ˈəːdʒənsɪ] *n* urgence *f*; (*of tone*) insistance *f*

urgent [ˈəːdʒənt] *adj* urgent(e); (*tone*) insistant(e), pressant(e)

urinal [ˈjuərɪnl] *n* urinoir *m*

urine [ˈjuərɪn] *n* urine *f*

urn [əːn] *n* urne *f*; (*also:* **tea ~**) fontaine *f* à thé

US *n abbr* = **United States**

us [ʌs] *pron* nous; *see also* **me**

USA *n abbr* = **United States of America**

use [*n* juːs, *vb* juːz] *n* emploi *m*, utilisation *f*; usage *m*; (*~fulness*) utilité *f* ♦ *vt* se servir de, utiliser, employer; **in ~** en usage; **out of ~** hors d'usage; **to be of ~** servir, être utile; **it's no ~** ça ne sert à rien; **she ~d to do it** elle le faisait (autrefois), elle avait coutume de le faire; **~d to: to be ~d to** avoir l'habitude de, être habitué(e) à; **~ up** *vt* finir, épuiser; consommer; **~d** [juːzd] *adj* (*car*) d'occasion; **~ful** [ˈjuːsful] *adj* utile; **~fulness** *n* utilité *f*; **~less** [ˈjuːslɪs] *adj* inutile; (*person: hopeless*) nul(le); **~r** [ˈjuːzəʳ] *n* utilisateur(-trice), usager *m*; **~r-friendly** *adj* (*computer*) convivial(e), facile d'emploi

usher [ˈʌʃəʳ] *n* (*at wedding ceremony*) placeur *m*; **~ette** [ʌʃəˈrɛt] *n* (*in cinema*) ouvreuse *f*

usual [ˈjuːʒuəl] *adj* habituel(le); **as ~** comme d'habitude; **~ly** [ˈjuːʒuəlɪ] *adv*

d'habitude, d'ordinaire

utensil [juːˈtɛnsl] *n* ustensile *m*

uterus [ˈjuːtərəs] *n* utérus *m*

utility [juːˈtɪlɪtɪ] *n* utilité *f*; (*also:* **public ~**) service public; **~ room** *n* buanderie *f*

utmost [ˈʌtməust] *adj* extrême, le (la) plus grand(e) ♦ *n*: **to do one's ~** faire tout son possible

utter [ˈʌtəʳ] *adj* total(e), complet(-ète) ♦ *vt* (*words*) prononcer, proférer; (*sounds*) émettre; **~ance** *n* paroles *fpl*; **~ly** *adv* complètement, totalement

U-turn [ˈjuːˈtəːn] *n* demi-tour *m*

V, v

v. *abbr* = **verse**; **versus**; **volt**; (= *vide*) voir

vacancy [ˈveɪkənsɪ] *n* (*BRIT: job*) poste vacant; (*room*) chambre *f* disponible; **"no vacancies"** "complet"

vacant [ˈveɪkənt] *adj* (*seat etc*) libre, disponible; (*expression*) distrait(e)

vacate [vəˈkeɪt] *vt* quitter

vacation [vəˈkeɪʃən] *n* vacances *fpl*

vaccinate [ˈvæksɪneɪt] *vt* vacciner

vacuum [ˈvækjum] *n* vide *m*; **~ cleaner** *n* aspirateur *m*; **~-packed** *adj* emballé(e) sous vide

vagina [vəˈdʒaɪnə] *n* vagin *m*

vagrant [ˈveɪɡrənt] *n* vagabond(e)

vague [veɪɡ] *adj* vague, imprécis(e); (*blurred: photo, outline*) flou(e); **~ly** *adv* vaguement

vain [veɪn] *adj* (*useless*) vain(e); (*conceited*) vaniteux(-euse); **in ~** en vain

valentine [ˈvæləntaɪn] *n* (*also:* **~ card**) carte *f* de la Saint-Valentin; (*person*) bien-aimé(e) (*le jour de la Saint-Valentin*); **V~'s day** *n* Saint-Valentin *f*

valiant [ˈvælɪənt] *adj* vaillant(e)

valid [ˈvælɪd] *adj* valable; (*document*) valable, valide

valley [ˈvælɪ] *n* vallée *f*

valour [ˈvæləʳ] (*US* **valor**) *n* courage *m*

valuable [ˈvæljuəbl] *adj* (*jewel*) de valeur; (*time, help*) précieux(-euse); **~s** *npl* objets *mpl* de valeur

valuation [vælju'eɪʃən] *n* (*price*) estimation *f*; (*quality*) appréciation *f*

value ['vælju:] *n* valeur *f* ♦ *vt* (*fix price*) évaluer, expertiser; (*appreciate*) apprécier; ~ **added tax** (*BRIT*) *n* taxe *f* à la valeur ajoutée; ~d *adj* (*person*) estimé(e); (*advice*) précieux(-euse)

valve [vælv] *n* (*in machine*) soupape *f*, valve *f*; (*MED*) valve, valvule *f*

van [væn] *n* (*AUT*) camionnette *f*

vandal ['vændl] *n* vandale *m/f*; ~ism *n* vandalisme *m*; ~ize *vt* saccager

vanguard ['vænɡɑːd] *n* (*fig*): **in the ~ of** à l'avant-garde de

vanilla [vəˈnɪlə] *n* vanille *f*

vanish ['vænɪʃ] *vi* disparaître

vanity ['vænɪtɪ] *n* vanité *f*

vantage point ['vɑːntɪdʒ-] *n* bonne position

vapour ['veɪpəʳ] (*US* **vapor**) *n* vapeur *f*; (*on window*) buée *f*

variable ['vɛərɪəbl] *adj* variable; (*mood*) changeant(e)

variance ['vɛərɪəns] *n*: **to be at ~ (with)** être en désaccord (avec); (*facts*) être en contradiction (avec)

varicose ['værɪkəus] *adj*: ~ **veins** varices *fpl*

varied ['vɛərɪd] *adj* varié(e), divers(e)

variety [vəˈraɪətɪ] *n* variété *f*; (*quantity*) nombre *m*, quantité *f*; ~ **show** *n* (*spectacle m* de) variétés *fpl*

various ['vɛərɪəs] *adj* divers(e), différent(e); (*several*) divers, plusieurs

varnish ['vɑːnɪʃ] *n* vernis *m* ♦ *vt* vernir

vary ['vɛərɪ] *vt*, *vi* varier, changer

vase [vɑːz] *n* vase *m*

Vaseline ® ['væsɪliːn] *n* vaseline *f*

vast [vɑːst] *adj* vaste, immense; (*amount*, *success*) énorme

VAT [væt] *n abbr* (= value added tax) TVA *f*

vat [væt] *n* cuve *f*

vault [vɔːlt] *n* (*of roof*) voûte *f*; (*tomb*) caveau *m*; (*in bank*) salle *f* des coffres; chambre forte ♦ *vt* (*also*: ~ **over**) sauter (d'un bond)

vaunted ['vɔːntɪd] *adj*: **much-~** tant vanté(e)

VCR *n abbr* = **video cassette recorder**

VD *n abbr* = **venereal disease**

VDU *n abbr* = **visual display unit**

veal [viːl] *n* veau *m*

veer [vɪəʳ] *vi* tourner; virer

vegan ['viːɡən] *n* végétalien(ne)

vegeburger ['vedʒɪbəːɡəʳ] *n* burger végétarien

vegetable ['vedʒtəbl] *n* légume *m* ♦ *adj* végétal(e)

vegetarian [vedʒɪˈtɛərɪən] *adj*, *n* végétarien(ne)

vehement ['viːɪmənt] *adj* violent(e), impétueux(-euse); (*impassioned*) ardent(e)

vehicle ['viːɪkl] *n* véhicule *m*

veil [veɪl] *n* voile *m*

vein [veɪn] *n* veine *f*; (*on leaf*) nervure *f*

velocity [vɪˈlɔsɪtɪ] *n* vitesse *f*

velvet ['velvɪt] *n* velours *m*

vending machine ['vendɪŋ-] *n* distributeur *m* automatique

veneer [vəˈnɪəʳ] *n* (*on furniture*) placage *m*; (*fig*) vernis *m*

venereal [vɪˈnɪərɪəl] *adj*: ~ **disease** maladie vénérienne

Venetian blind [vɪˈniːʃən-] *n* store vénitien

vengeance ['vendʒəns] *n* vengeance *f*; **with a ~** (*fig*) vraiment, pour de bon

venison ['venɪsn] *n* venaison *f*

venom ['venəm] *n* venin *m*

vent [vent] *n* conduit *m* d'aération; (*in dress*, *jacket*) fente *f* ♦ *vt* (*fig*: *one's feelings*) donner libre cours à

ventilator ['ventɪleɪtəʳ] *n* ventilateur *m*

ventriloquist [venˈtrɪləkwɪst] *n* ventriloque *m/f*

venture ['ventʃəʳ] *n* entreprise *f* ♦ *vt* risquer, hasarder ♦ *vi* s'aventurer, se risquer

venue ['venjuː] *n* lieu *m*

verb [vəːb] *n* verbe *m*; ~al *adj* verbal(e); (*translation*) littéral(e)

verbatim [vəːˈbeɪtɪm] *adj*, *adv* mot pour mot

verdict ['vəːdɪkt] *n* verdict *m*

verge [vəːdʒ] n (BRIT) bord m, bas-côté m; **"soft ~s"** (BRIT: AUT) "accotement non stabilisé"; **on the ~ of doing** sur le point de faire; **~ on** vt fus approcher de

verify ['vɛrɪfaɪ] vt vérifier; (confirm) confirmer

vermin ['vəːmɪn] npl animaux mpl nuisibles; (insects) vermine f

vermouth ['vəːməθ] n vermouth m

versatile ['vəːsətaɪl] adj polyvalent(e)

verse [vəːs] n (poetry) vers mpl; (stanza) strophe f; (in Bible) verset m

version ['vəːʃən] n version f

versus ['vəːsəs] prep contre

vertical ['vəːtɪkl] adj vertical(e) ♦ n verticale f

vertigo ['vəːtɪgəu] n vertige m

verve [vəːv] n brio m, enthousiasme m

very ['vɛrɪ] adv très ♦ adj: **the ~ book which** le livre même que; **the ~ last** le tout dernier; **at the ~ least** tout au moins; **~ much** beaucoup

vessel ['vɛsl] n (ANAT, NAUT) vaisseau m; (container) récipient m

vest [vɛst] n (BRIT) tricot m de corps; (US: waistcoat) gilet m

vested interest n (COMM) droits acquis

vet [vɛt] n abbr (BRIT: veterinary surgeon) vétérinaire m/f ♦ vt examiner soigneusement

veteran ['vɛtərn] n vétéran m; (also: **war ~**) ancien combattant

veterinary surgeon ['vɛtrɪnərɪ-] (BRIT), **veterinarian** [vɛtrɪ'nɛərɪən] (US) n vétérinaire m/f

veto ['viːtəu] (pl **~es**) n veto m ♦ vt opposer son veto à

vex [vɛks] vt fâcher, contrarier; **~ed** adj (question) controversé(e)

via ['vaɪə] prep par, via

viable ['vaɪəbl] adj viable

vibrate [vaɪ'breɪt] vi vibrer

vicar ['vɪkər] n pasteur m (de l'Église anglicane); **~age** n presbytère m

vicarious [vɪ'kɛərɪəs] adj indirect(e)

vice [vaɪs] n (evil) vice m; (TECH) étau m

vice- [vaɪs] prefix vice-

vice squad n ≃ brigade mondaine

vice versa ['vaɪsɪ'vəːsə] adv vice versa

vicinity [vɪ'sɪnɪtɪ] n environs mpl, alentours mpl

vicious ['vɪʃəs] adj (remark) cruel(le), méchant(e); (blow) brutal(e); (dog) méchant(e), dangereux(-euse); (horse) vicieux(-euse); **~ circle** n cercle vicieux

victim ['vɪktɪm] n victime f

victor ['vɪktər] n vainqueur m

Victorian [vɪk'tɔːrɪən] adj victorien(ne)

victory ['vɪktərɪ] n victoire f

video ['vɪdɪəu] cpd vidéo inv ♦ n (~ film) vidéo f; (also: **~ cassette**) vidéocassette f; (also: **~ cassette recorder**) magnétoscope m; **~ tape** n bande f vidéo inv; (cassette) vidéocassette f; **~ wall** n mur m d'images vidéo

vie [vaɪ] vi: **to ~ with** rivaliser avec

Vienna [vɪ'ɛnə] n Vienne

Vietnam ['vjɛt'næm] n Viêt-Nam m, Vietnam m; **~ese** [vjɛtnə'miːz] adj vietnamien(ne) ♦ n inv Vietnamien(ne); (LING) vietnamien m

view [vjuː] n vue f; (opinion) avis m, vue ♦ vt voir, regarder; (situation) considérer; (house) visiter; **in full ~ of** sous les yeux de; **in ~ of the weather/the fact that** étant donné le temps/que; **in my ~** à mon avis; **~er** n (TV) téléspectateur(-trice); **~finder** n viseur m; **~point** n point m de vue

vigorous ['vɪgərəs] adj vigoureux(-euse)

vile [vaɪl] adj (action) vil(e); (smell, food) abominable; (temper) massacrant(e)

villa ['vɪlə] n villa f

village ['vɪlɪdʒ] n village m; **~r** n villageois(e)

villain ['vɪlən] n (scoundrel) scélérat m; (BRIT: criminal) bandit m; (in novel etc) traître m

vindicate ['vɪndɪkeɪt] vt (person) innocenter; (action) justifier

vindictive [vɪn'dɪktɪv] adj vindicatif(-ive), rancunier(-ère)

vine [vaɪn] n vigne f; (climbing plant) plante grimpante

vinegar ['vɪnɪgər] n vinaigre m
vineyard ['vɪnjɑːd] n vignoble m
vintage ['vɪntɪdʒ] n (year) année f, millésime m; ~ **car** n voiture f d'époque; ~ **wine** n vin m de grand cru
viola [vɪ'əʊlə] n (MUS) alto m
violate ['vaɪəleɪt] vt violer
violence ['vaɪələns] n violence f
violent ['vaɪələnt] adj violent(e)
violet ['vaɪələt] adj violet(te) ♦ n (colour) violet m; (plant) violette f
violin [vaɪə'lɪn] n violon m; ~**ist** [vaɪə'lɪnɪst] n violoniste m/f
VIP n abbr (= very important person) V.I.P. m
virgin ['vɜːdʒɪn] n vierge f ♦ adj vierge
Virgo ['vɜːgəʊ] n la Vierge
virile ['vɪraɪl] adj viril(e)
virtually ['vɜːtjʊəlɪ] adv (almost) pratiquement
virtual reality ['vɜːtjʊəl-] n (COMPUT) réalité virtuelle
virtue ['vɜːtjuː] n vertu f; (advantage) mérite m, avantage m; **by ~ of** en vertu or en raison de; **virtuous** adj vertueux(-euse)
virus ['vaɪərəs] n (COMPUT) virus m
visa ['viːzə] n visa m
visibility [vɪzɪ'bɪlɪtɪ] n visibilité f
visible ['vɪzəbl] adj visible
vision ['vɪʒən] n (sight) vue f, vision f; (foresight, in dream) vision
visit ['vɪzɪt] n visite f; (stay) séjour m ♦ vt (person) rendre visite à; (place) visiter; ~**ing hours** npl (in hospital etc) heures fpl de visite; ~**or** n visiteur(-euse); (to one's house) visite f, invité(e); ~**or centre** n hall m or centre m d'accueil
visor ['vaɪzər] n visière f
vista ['vɪstə] n vue f
visual ['vɪzjʊəl] adj visuel(le); ~ **aid** n support visuel; ~ **display unit** n console f de visualisation, visuel m; ~**ize** vt se représenter, s'imaginer; ~**ly-impaired** adj malvoyant(e)
vital ['vaɪtl] adj vital(e); (person) plein(e) d'entrain; ~**ly** adv (important) absolument; ~ **statistics** npl (fig) mensurations fpl

vitamin ['vɪtəmɪn] n vitamine f
vivacious [vɪ'veɪʃəs] adj animé(e), qui a de la vivacité
vivid ['vɪvɪd] adj (account) vivant(e); (light, imagination) vif (vive); ~**ly** adv (describe) d'une manière vivante; (remember) de façon précise
V-neck ['viːnɛk] n décolleté m en V
vocabulary [vəʊ'kæbjʊlərɪ] n vocabulaire m
vocal ['vəʊkl] adj vocal(e); (articulate) qui sait s'exprimer; ~ **cords** npl cordes vocales
vocation [vəʊ'keɪʃən] n vocation f; ~**al** adj professionnel(le)
vociferous [və'sɪfərəs] adj bruyant(e)
vodka ['vɔdkə] n vodka f
vogue [vəʊg] n: **in** ~ en vogue f
voice [vɔɪs] n voix f ♦ vt (opinion) exprimer, formuler; ~ **mail** n (system) messagerie f vocale; (device) boîte f vocale
void [vɔɪd] n vide m ♦ adj nul(le); ~ **of** vide de, dépourvu(e) de
volatile ['vɔlətaɪl] adj volatil(e); (person) versatile; (situation) explosif(-ive)
volcano [vɔl'keɪnəʊ] (pl ~**es**) n volcan m
volition [və'lɪʃən] n: **of one's own** ~ de son propre gré
volley ['vɔlɪ] n (of gunfire) salve f; (of stones etc) grêle f, volée f; (of questions) multitude f, série f; (TENNIS etc) volée f; ~**ball** n volley(-ball) m
volt [vəʊlt] n volt m; ~**age** n tension f, voltage m
volume ['vɔljuːm] n volume m
voluntarily ['vɔləntrɪlɪ] adv volontairement
voluntary ['vɔləntərɪ] adj volontaire; (unpaid) bénévole
volunteer [vɔlən'tɪər] n volontaire m/f ♦ vi (MIL) s'engager comme volontaire; **to** ~ **to do** se proposer pour faire
vomit ['vɔmɪt] vt, vi vomir
vote [vəʊt] n vote m, suffrage m; (cast) voix f, vote; (franchise) droit m de vote ♦ vt (elect): **to be ~d chairman** etc être élu président etc; (propose): **to** ~ **that** proposer que ♦ vi voter; ~ **of thanks** discours

m de remerciement; ~**r** *n* électeur(-trice); **voting** *n* scrutin *m*, vote *m*

voucher ['vautʃər] *n* (*for meal, petrol, gift*) bon *m*

vouch for ['vautʃ-] *vt fus* se porter garant de

vow [vau] *n* vœu *m*, serment *m* ♦ *vi* jurer

vowel ['vauəl] *n* voyelle *f*

voyage ['vɔɪdʒ] *n* voyage *m* par mer, traversée *f*; (*by spacecraft*) voyage

vulgar ['vʌlgər] *adj* vulgaire

vulnerable ['vʌlnərəbl] *adj* vulnérable

vulture ['vʌltʃər] *n* vautour *m*

W, w

wad [wɔd] *n* (*of cotton wool, paper*) tampon *m*; (*of banknotes etc*) liasse *f*

waddle ['wɔdl] *vi* se dandiner

wade [weɪd] *vi*: **to ~ through** marcher dans, patauger dans; (*fig: book*) s'évertuer à lire

wafer ['weɪfər] *n* (*CULIN*) gaufrette *f*

waffle ['wɔfl] *n* (*CULIN*) gaufre *f*; (*inf*) verbiage *m*, remplissage *m* ♦ *vi* parler pour ne rien dire, faire du remplissage

waft [wɔft] *vt* porter ♦ *vi* flotter

wag [wæg] *vt* agiter, remuer ♦ *vi* remuer

wage [weɪdʒ] *n* (*also:* ~**s**) salaire *m*, paye *f* ♦ *vt*: **to ~ war** faire la guerre; ~ **earner** *n* salarié(e); ~ **packet** *n* (enveloppe *f* de) paye *f*

wager ['weɪdʒər] *n* pari *m*

wag(g)on ['wægən] *n* (*horse-drawn*) chariot *m*; (*BRIT: RAIL*) wagon *m* (de marchandises)

wail [weɪl] *vi* gémir; (*siren*) hurler

waist [weɪst] *n* taille *f*; ~**coat** (*BRIT*) *n* gilet *m*; ~**line** *n* (tour *m* de) taille *f*

wait [weɪt] *n* attente *f* ♦ *vi* attendre; **to keep sb ~ing** faire attendre qn; **to ~ for** attendre; **I can't ~ to ...** (*fig*) je meurs d'envie de ...; ~ **behind** *vi* rester (à attendre); ~ **on** *vt fus* servir; ~**er** *n* garçon *m* (de café), serveur *m*; ~**ing** *n*: **"no ~ing"** (*BRIT: AUT*) "stationnement inter-

dit"; ~**ing list** *n* liste *f* d'attente; ~**ing room** *n* salle *f* d'attente; ~**ress** *n* serveuse *f*

waive [weɪv] *vt* renoncer à, abandonner

wake [weɪk] (*pt* **woke, waked**, *pp* **woken, waked**) *vt* (*also:* ~ **up**) réveiller ♦ *vi* (*also:* ~ **up**) se réveiller ♦ *n* (*for dead person*) veillée *f* mortuaire; (*NAUT*) sillage *m*

Wales [weɪlz] *n* pays *m* de Galles; **the Prince of ~** le prince de Galles

walk [wɔːk] *n* promenade *f*; (*short*) petit tour; (*gait*) démarche *f*; (*path*) chemin *m*; (*in park etc*) allée *f* ♦ *vi* marcher; (*for pleasure, exercise*) se promener ♦ *vt* (*distance*) faire à pied; (*dog*) promener; **10 minutes' ~ from** à 10 minutes à pied de; **from all ~s of life** de toutes conditions sociales; ~ **out** *vi* (*audience*) sortir, quitter la salle; (*workers*) se mettre en grève; ~ **out on** (*inf*) *vt fus* quitter, plaquer; ~**er** *n* (*person*) marcheur(-euse); ~**ie-talkie** *n* talkie-walkie *m*; ~**ing** *n* marche *f* à pied; ~**ing shoes** *npl* chaussures *fpl* de marche; ~**ing stick** *n* canne *f*; **W~man** ® *n* Walkman ® *m*; ~**out** *n* (*of workers*) grève-surprise *f*; ~**over** (*inf*) *n* victoire *f* or examen *m* etc facile; ~**way** *n* promenade *f*

wall [wɔːl] *n* mur *m*; (*of tunnel, cave etc*) paroi *m*; ~**ed** *adj* (*city*) fortifié(e); (*garden*) entouré(e) d'un mur, clos(e)

wallet ['wɔlɪt] *n* portefeuille *m*

wallflower ['wɔːlflauər] *n* giroflée *f*; **to be a ~** (*fig*) faire tapisserie

wallow ['wɔləu] *vi* se vautrer

wallpaper ['wɔːlpeɪpər] *n* papier peint ♦ *vt* tapisser

walnut ['wɔːlnʌt] *n* noix *f*; (*tree, wood*) noyer *m*

walrus ['wɔːlrəs] (*pl* ~ *or* ~**es**) *n* morse *m*

waltz [wɔːlts] *n* valse *f* ♦ *vi* valser

wand [wɔnd] *n* (*also:* **magic ~**) baguette *f* (magique)

wander ['wɔndər] *vi* (*person*) errer; (*thoughts*) vagabonder, errer ♦ *vt* errer dans

wane [weɪn] *vi* (*moon*) décroître; (*reputa-*

tion) décliner

wangle ['wæŋgl] (*BRIT: inf*) *vt* se débrouiller pour avoir; carotter

want [wɒnt] *vt* vouloir; (*need*) avoir besoin de ♦ *n*: **for ~ of** par manque de, faute de; **~s** *npl* besoins *mpl*; **to ~ to do** vouloir faire; **to ~ sb to do** vouloir que qn fasse; **~ed** *adj* (*criminal*) recherché(e) par la police; **"cook ~ed"** "on recherche un cuisinier"; **~ing** *adj*: **to be found ~ing** ne pas être à la hauteur

war [wɔːr] *n* guerre *f*; **to make ~ (on)** faire la guerre (à)

ward [wɔːd] *n* (*in hospital*) salle *f*; (*POL*) canton *m*; (*LAW: child*) pupille *m/f*; **~ off** *vt* (*attack, enemy*) repousser, éviter

warden ['wɔːdn] *n* gardien(ne); (*BRIT: of institution*) directeur(-trice); (: *also*: **traffic ~**) contractuel(le); (*of youth hostel*) père *m* or mère *f* aubergiste

warder ['wɔːdər] (*BRIT*) *n* gardien *m* de prison

wardrobe ['wɔːdrəub] *n* (*cupboard*) armoire *f*; (*clothes*) garde-robe *f*; (*THEATRE*) costumes *mpl*

warehouse ['weəhaus] *n* entrepôt *m*

wares [weəz] *npl* marchandises *fpl*

warfare ['wɔːfeər] *n* guerre *f*

warhead ['wɔːhed] *n* (*MIL*) ogive *f*

warily ['weərɪlɪ] *adv* avec prudence

warm [wɔːm] *adj* chaud(e); (*thanks, welcome, applause, person*) chaleureux(-euse); **it's ~** il fait chaud; **I'm ~** j'ai chaud; **~ up** *vi* (*person, room*) se réchauffer; (*water*) chauffer; (*athlete*) s'échauffer ♦ *vt* (*food*) (faire) réchauffer, (faire) chauffer; (*engine*) faire chauffer; **~-hearted** *adj* affectueux(-euse); **~ly** *adv* chaudement, chaleureusement; **~th** *n* chaleur *f*

warn [wɔːn] *vt* avertir, prévenir; **to ~ sb (not) to do** conseiller à qn de (ne pas) faire; **~ing** *n* avertissement *m*; (*notice*) avis *m*; (*signal*) avertisseur *m*; **~ing light** *n* avertisseur lumineux; **~ing triangle** *n* (*AUT*) triangle *m* de présignalisation

warp [wɔːp] *vi* (*wood*) travailler, se déformer ♦ *vt* (*fig: character*) pervertir

warrant ['wɒrnt] *n* (*guarantee*) garantie *f*; (*LAW: to arrest*) mandat *m* d'arrêt; (: *to search*) mandat de perquisition; **~y** *n* garantie *f*

warren ['wɒrən] *n* (*of rabbits*) terrier *m*; (*fig: of streets etc*) dédale *m*

warrior ['wɒrɪər] *n* guerrier(-ère)

Warsaw ['wɔːsɔː] *n* Varsovie

warship ['wɔːʃɪp] *n* navire *m* de guerre

wart [wɔːt] *n* verrue *f*

wartime ['wɔːtaɪm] *n*: **in ~** en temps de guerre

wary ['weərɪ] *adj* prudent(e)

was [wɒz] *pt of* **be**

wash [wɒʃ] *vt* laver ♦ *vi* se laver; (*sea*): **to ~ over/against sth** inonder/baigner qch ♦ *n* (*clothes*) lessive *f*; (*~ing programme*) lavage *m*; (*of ship*) sillage *m*; **to have a ~** se laver, faire sa toilette; **to give sth a ~** laver qch; **~ away** *vt* (*stain*) enlever au lavage; (*subj: river etc*) emporter; **~ off** *vi* partir au lavage; **~ up** *vi* (*BRIT*) faire la vaisselle; (*US*) se débarbouiller; **~able** *adj* lavable; **~basin** (*US* **washbowl**) *n* lavabo *m*; **~cloth** (*US*) *n* gant *m* de toilette; **~er** *n* (*TECH*) rondelle *f*, joint *m*; **~ing** *n* (*dirty*) linge *m*; (*clean*) lessive *f*; **~ing machine** *n* machine *f* à laver; **~ing powder** (*BRIT*) *n* lessive *f* (en poudre); **~ing-up** *n* vaisselle *f*; **~ing-up liquid** *n* produit *m* pour la vaisselle; **~-out** (*inf*) *n* désastre *m*; **~room** (*US*) *n* toilettes *fpl*

wasn't ['wɒznt] = **was not**

wasp [wɒsp] *n* guêpe *f*

wastage ['weɪstɪdʒ] *n* gaspillage *m*; (*in manufacturing, transport etc*) pertes *fpl*, déchets *mpl*; **natural ~** départs naturels

waste [weɪst] *n* gaspillage *m*; (*of time*) perte *f*; (*rubbish*) déchets *mpl*; (*also*: **household ~**) ordures *fpl* ♦ *adj* (*land, ground*: *in city*) à l'abandon; (*leftover*): **~ material** déchets *mpl* ♦ *vt* gaspiller; (*time, opportunity*) perdre; **~s** *npl* (*area*) étendue *f* désertique; **~ away** *vi* dépérir; **~ disposal unit** (*BRIT*) *n* broyeur *m* d'ordures; **~ful** *adj* gaspilleur(-euse); (*process*) peu économique; **~ ground** (*BRIT*) *n* terrain *m* vague;

~**paper basket** *n* corbeille *f* à papier

watch [wɔtʃ] *n* montre *f*; (*act of ~ing*) surveillance *f*; guet *m*; (MIL: *guards*) garde *f*; (NAUT: *guards, spell of duty*) quart *m* ♦ *vt* (*look at*) observer; (: *match, programme, TV*) regarder; (*spy on, guard*) surveiller; (*be careful with*) faire attention à ♦ *vi* regarder; (*keep guard*) monter la garde; ~ **out** *vi* faire attention; ~**dog** *n* chien *m* de garde; (*fig*) gardien(ne); ~**ful** *adj* attentif(-ive), vigilant(e); ~**maker** *n* horloger(-ère); ~**man** (*irreg*) *n see* **night**; ~**strap** *n* bracelet *m* de montre

water ['wɔːtəʳ] *n* eau *f* ♦ *vt* (*plant, garden*) arroser ♦ *vi* (*eyes*) larmoyer; (*mouth*): **it makes my mouth** ~ j'en ai l'eau à la bouche; **in British** ~**s** dans les eaux territoriales britanniques; ~ **down** *vt* (*milk*) couper d'eau; (*fig: story*) édulcorer; ~**colour** (US **watercolor**) *n* aquarelle *f*; ~**cress** *n* cresson *m* (de fontaine); ~**fall** *n* chute *f* d'eau; ~ **heater** *n* chauffe-eau *m*; ~**ing can** *n* arrosoir *m*; ~ **lily** *n* nénuphar *m*; ~**line** *n* (NAUT) ligne *f* de flottaison; ~**logged** *adj* (*ground*) détrempé(e); ~ **main** *n* canalisation *f* d'eau; ~**melon** *n* pastèque *f*; ~**proof** *adj* imperméable; ~**shed** *n* (GEO) ligne *f* de partage des eaux; (*fig*) moment *m* critique, point décisif; ~-**skiing** *n* ski *m* nautique; ~**tight** *adj* étanche; ~**way** *n* cours *m* d'eau navigable; ~**works** *n* (*building*) station *f* hydraulique; ~**y** *adj* (*coffee, soup*) trop faible; (*eyes*) humide, larmoyant(e)

watt [wɔt] *n* watt *m*

wave [weɪv] *n* vague *f*; (*of hand*) geste *m*, signe *m*; (RADIO) onde *f*; (*in hair*) ondulation *f* ♦ *vi* faire signe de la main; (*flag*) flotter au vent; (*grass*) ondoyer ♦ *vt* (*handkerchief*) agiter; (*stick*) brandir; ~**length** *n* longueur *f* d'ondes

waver ['weɪvəʳ] *vi* vaciller; (*voice*) trembler; (*person*) hésiter

wavy ['weɪvɪ] *adj* (*hair, surface*) ondulé(e); (*line*) onduleux(-euse)

wax [wæks] *n* cire *f*; (*for skis*) fart *m* ♦ *vt* cirer; (*car*) lustrer; (*skis*) farter ♦ *vi* (*moon*) croître; ~**works** *npl* personnages *mpl* de cire ♦ *n* musée *m* de cire

way [weɪ] *n* chemin *m*, voie *f*; (*distance*) distance *f*; (*direction*) chemin, direction *f*; (*manner*) façon *f*, manière *f*; (*habit*) habitude *f*, façon; **which** ~? - **this** ~ par où? - par ici; **on the** ~ (*en route*) en route; **to be on one's** ~ être en route; **to go out of one's** ~ **to do** (*fig*) se donner du mal pour faire; **to be in the** ~ bloquer le passage; (*fig*) gêner; **to lose one's** ~ perdre son chemin; **under** ~ en cours; **in a** ~ dans un sens; **in some** ~**s** à certains égards; **by the** ~ ... à propos ...; **"~ in"** (BRIT) "entrée"; **"~ out"** (BRIT) "sortie"; **the** ~ **back** le chemin du retour; **"give** ~**"** (BRIT: AUT) "cédez le passage"; ~**lay** (*irreg*) *vt* attaquer

wayward ['weɪwəd] *adj* capricieux(-euse), entêté(e)

W.C. *n abbr* w.c. *mpl*, waters *mpl*

we [wiː] *pl pron* nous

weak [wiːk] *adj* faible; (*health*) fragile; (*beam etc*) peu solide; ~**en** *vi* faiblir, décliner ♦ *vt* affaiblir; ~**ling** *n* (*physically*) gringalet *m*; (*morally etc*) faible *m/f*; ~**ness** *n* faiblesse *f*; (*fault*) point *m* faible; **to have a** ~**ness for** avoir un faible pour

wealth [welθ] *n* (*money, resources*) richesse(s) *f(pl)*; (*of details*) profusion *f*; ~**y** *adj* riche

wean [wiːn] *vt* sevrer

weapon ['wepən] *n* arme *f*

wear [wɛəʳ] (*pt* **wore**, *pp* **worn**) *n* (*use*) usage *m*; (*deterioration through use*) usure *f*; (*clothing*): **sports/babywear** vêtements *mpl* de sport/pour bébés ♦ *vt* (*clothes*) porter; (*put on*) mettre; (*damage: through use*) user ♦ *vi* (*last*) faire de l'usage; (*rub etc through*) s'user; **town/evening** ~ tenue *f* de ville/soirée; ~ **away** *vt* user, ronger ♦ *vi* (*inscription*) s'effacer; ~ **down** *vt* user; (*strength, person*) épuiser; ~ **off** *vi* disparaître; ~ **out** *vt* user; (*person, strength*) épuiser; ~ **and tear** *n* usure *f*

weary ['wɪərɪ] *adj* (*tired*) épuisé(e); (*dispirited*) las (lasse), abattu(e) ♦ *vi*: **to** ~ **of** se lasser de

weasel ['wiːzl] *n* (*ZOOL*) belette *f*

weather ['wɛðəʳ] *n* temps *m* ♦ *vt* (*tempest, crisis*) essuyer, réchapper à; survivre à; **under the ~** (*fig: ill*) mal fichu(e); **~-beaten** *adj* (*person*) hâlé(e); (*building*) dégradé(e) par les intempéries; **~cock** *n* girouette *f*; **~ forecast** *n* prévisions *fpl* météorologiques, météo *f*; **~ man** (*irreg*) (*inf*) *n* météorologue *m*; **~ vane** *n* = **weathercock**

weave [wiːv] (*pt* **wove**, *pp* **woven**) *vt* (*cloth*) tisser; (*basket*) tresser; **~r** *n* tisserand(e)

web [wɛb] *n* (*of spider*) toile *f*; (*on foot*) palmure *f*; (*fabric, also fig*) tissu *m*; **the (World Wide) W~** le Web

website ['wɛbsaɪt] *n* (*COMPUT*) site *m* Web

wed [wɛd] (*pt, pp* **wedded**) *vt* épouser ♦ *vi* se marier

we'd [wiːd] = **we had**; **we would**

wedding ['wɛdɪŋ] *n* mariage *m*; **silver/golden ~ (anniversary)** noces *fpl* d'argent/d'or; **~ day** *n* jour *m* du mariage; **~ dress** *n* robe *f* de mariée; **~ ring** *n* alliance *f*

wedge [wɛdʒ] *n* (*of wood etc*) coin *m*, cale *f*; (*of cake*) part *f* ♦ *vt* (*pack tightly*) enfoncer

Wednesday ['wɛdnzdɪ] *n* mercredi *m*

wee [wiː] (*SCOTTISH*) *adj* (*tout(e)*) petit(e)

weed [wiːd] *n* mauvaise herbe ♦ *vt* désherber; **~killer** *n* désherbant *m*; **~y** *adj* (*man*) gringalet

week [wiːk] *n* semaine *f*; **a ~ today/on Friday** aujourd'hui/vendredi en huit; **~day** *n* jour *m* de semaine; (*COMM*) jour ouvrable; **~end** *n* week-end *m*; **~ly** *adv* une fois par semaine, chaque semaine ♦ *adj* hebdomadaire ♦ *n* hebdomadaire *m*

weep [wiːp] (*pt, pp* **wept**) *vi* (*person*) pleurer; **~ing willow** *n* saule pleureur

weigh [weɪ] *vt, vi* peser; **to ~ anchor** lever l'ancre; **~ down** *vt* (*person, animal*) écraser; (*fig: with worry*) accabler; **~ up** *vt* examiner

weight [weɪt] *n* poids *m*; **to lose/put on ~** maigrir/grossir; **~ing** *n* (*allowance*) indemnité *f*, allocation *f*; **~lifter** *n* haltérophile *m*; **~lifting** *n* haltérophilie *f*; **~y** *adj* lourd(e); (*important*) de poids, important(e)

weir [wɪəʳ] *n* barrage *m*

weird [wɪəd] *adj* bizarre

welcome ['wɛlkəm] *adj* bienvenu(e) ♦ *n* accueil *m* ♦ *vt* accueillir; (*also: bid ~*) souhaiter la bienvenue à; (*be glad of*) se réjouir de; **thank you - you're ~!** merci - de rien *or* il n'y a pas de quoi!

welder ['wɛldəʳ] *n* soudeur(-euse)

welfare ['wɛlfɛəʳ] *n* (*well-being*) bien-être *m*; (*social aid*) assistance sociale; **~ state** *n* État-providence *m*

well [wɛl] *n* puits *m* ♦ *adv* bien ♦ *adj*: **to be ~** aller bien ♦ *excl* eh bien!; (*relief also*) bon!; (*resignation*) enfin!; **as ~** aussi, également; **as ~ as** en plus de; **~ done!** bravo!; **get ~ soon** remets-toi vite!; **to do ~** bien réussir; (*business*) prospérer; **~ up** *vi* monter

we'll [wiːl] = **we will**; **we shall**

well: **~-behaved** *adj* sage, obéissant(e); **~-being** *n* bien-être *m*; **~-built** *adj* (*person*) bien bâti(e); **~-deserved** *adj* (*bien*) mérité(e); **~-dressed** *adj* bien habillé(e); **~-heeled** (*inf*) *adj* (*wealthy*) nanti(e)

wellingtons ['wɛlɪŋtənz] *npl* (*also: wellington boots*) bottes *fpl* de caoutchouc

well: **~-known** *adj* (*person*) connu(e); **~-mannered** *adj* bien élevé(e); **~-meaning** *adj* bien intentionné(e); **~-off** *adj* aisé(e); **~-read** *adj* cultivé(e); **~-to-do** *adj* aisé(e); **~-wishers** *npl* amis *mpl* et admirateurs *mpl*; (*friends*) amis *mpl*

Welsh [wɛlʃ] *adj* gallois(e) ♦ *n* (*LING*) gallois *m*; **the ~** *npl* (*people*) les Gallois *mpl*; **~ Assembly** *n* Parlement *m* gallois; **~man** (*irreg*) *n* Gallois *m*; **~woman** (*irreg*) *n* Galloise *f*

went [wɛnt] *pt of* **go**

wept [wɛpt] *pt, pp of* **weep**

were [wəːʳ] *pt of* **be**

we're [wɪəʳ] = **we are**

weren't [wəːnt] = **were not**

west [wɛst] *n* ouest *m* ♦ *adj* ouest *inv*, de *or* à l'ouest ♦ *adv* à *or* vers l'ouest; **the W~** l'Occident *m*, l'Ouest; **the W~ Coun-**

try (*BRIT*) ♦ *n* le sud-ouest de l'Angleterre; **~erly** *adj* (*wind*) d'ouest; (*point*) à l'ouest; **~ern** *adj* occidental(e), de *or* à l'ouest ♦ *n* (*CINEMA*) western *m*; **W~ Indian** *adj* antillais(e) ♦ *n* Antillais(e); **W~ Indies** *npl* Antilles *fpl*; **~ward(s)** *adv* vers l'ouest

wet [wɛt] *adj* mouillé(e); (*damp*) humide; (*soaked*) trempé(e); (*rainy*) pluvieux(-euse) ♦ *n* (*BRIT*: *POL*) modéré *m* du parti conservateur; **to get ~** se mouiller; **"~ paint"** "attention peinture fraîche"; **~ suit** *n* combinaison *f* de plongée

we've [wi:v] = **we have**

whack [wæk] *vt* donner un grand coup à

whale [weɪl] *n* (*ZOOL*) baleine *f*

wharf [wɔ:f] (*pl* **wharves**) *n* quai *m*

KEYWORD
---

what [wɔt] *adj* quel(le); **what size is he?** quelle taille fait-il?; **what colour is it?** de quelle couleur est-ce?; **what books do you need?** quels livres vous faut-il?; **what a mess!** quel désordre!
♦ *pron* **1** (*interrogatory*) que, *prep* +quoi; **what are you doing?** que faites-vous?, qu'est-ce que vous faites?; **what is happening?** qu'est-ce qui se passe?, que se passe-t-il?; **what are you talking about?** de quoi parlez-vous?; **what is it called?** comment est-ce que ça s'appelle?; **what about me?** et moi?; **what about doing ...?** et si on faisait ...?
2 (*relative*: *subject*) ce qui; (: *direct object*) ce que; (: *indirect object*) ce +*prep* +quoi, ce dont; **I saw what you did/was on the table** j'ai vu ce que vous avez fait/ce qui était sur la table; **tell me what you remember** dites-moi ce dont vous vous souvenez
♦ *excl* (*disbelieving*) quoi!, comment!

whatever [wɔt'ɛvər] *adj*: **~ book** quel que soit le livre que (*or* qui) +*sub*; n'importe quel livre ♦ *pron*: **do ~ is necessary** faites (tout) ce qui est nécessaire; **~ happens** quoi qu'il arrive; **no reason ~** pas

la moindre raison; **nothing ~** rien du tout

whatsoever [wɔtsəu'ɛvər] *adj* = **whatever**

wheat [wi:t] *n* blé *m*, froment *m*

wheedle [wi:dl] *vt*: **to ~ sb into doing sth** cajoler *or* enjôler qn pour qu'il fasse qch; **to ~ sth out of sb** obtenir qch de qn par des cajoleries

wheel [wi:l] *n* roue *f*; (*also*: **steering ~**) volant *m*; (*NAUT*) gouvernail *m* ♦ *vt* (*pram etc*) pousser ♦ *vi* (*birds*) tournoyer; (*also*: **~ round**: *person*) virevolter; **~barrow** *n* brouette *f*; **~chair** *n* fauteuil roulant; **~ clamp** *n* (*AUT*) sabot *m* (de Denver)

wheeze [wi:z] *vi* respirer bruyamment

KEYWORD
---

when [wɛn] *adv* quand; **when did he go?** quand est-ce qu'il est parti?
♦ *conj* **1** (*at, during, after the time that*) quand, lorsque; **she was reading when I came in** elle lisait quand *or* lorsque je suis entré
2 (*on, at which*): **on the day when I met him** le jour où je l'ai rencontré
3 (*whereas*) alors que; **I thought I was wrong when in fact I was right** j'ai cru que j'avais tort alors qu'en fait j'avais raison

---

whenever [wɛn'ɛvər] *adv* quand donc ♦ *conj* quand; (*every time that*) chaque fois que

where [wɛər] *adv, conj* où; **this is ~** c'est là que; **~abouts** [wɛərəbauts] *adv* où donc ♦ *n*: **nobody knows his ~abouts** personne ne sait où il se trouve; **~as** [wɛər'æz] *conj* alors que; **~by** *adv* par lequel (*or* laquelle *etc*); **~ver** [wɛər'ɛvər] *adv* où donc ♦ *conj* où que +*sub*; **~withal** [wɛərwiðɔ:l] *n* moyens *mpl*

whether [wɛðər] *conj* si; **I don't know ~ to accept or not** je ne sais pas si je dois accepter ou non; **it's doubtful ~** il est peu probable que +*sub*; **~ you go or not** que vous y alliez ou non

which [wɪtʃ] *adj* (*interrogative: direct, indirect*) quel(le); **which picture do you want?** quel tableau voulez-vous?; **which one?** lequel (laquelle)?; **in which case** auquel cas
♦ *pron* **1** (*interrogative*) lequel (laquelle), lesquels (lesquelles) *pl*; **I don't mind which** peu importe lequel; **which (of these) are yours?** lesquels sont à vous?; **tell me which you want** dites-moi lesquels *or* ceux que vous voulez
2 (*relative: subject*) qui; (*: object*) que, *prep* +lequel (laquelle); **the apple which you ate/which is on the table** la pomme que vous avez mangée/qui est sur la table; **the chair on which you are sitting** la chaise sur laquelle vous êtes assis; **the book of which you spoke** le livre dont vous avez parlé; **he knew, which is true/I feared** il le savait, ce qui est vrai/ce que je craignais; **after which** après quoi

whichever [wɪtʃ'evər] *adj*: **take ~ book you prefer** prenez le livre que vous préférez, peu importe lequel; **~ book you take** quel que soit le livre que vous preniez
while [waɪl] *n* moment *m* ♦ *conj* pendant que; (*as long as*) tant que; (*whereas*) alors que; bien que +*sub*; **for a ~** pendant quelque temps; **~ away** *vt* (*time*) (faire) passer
whim [wɪm] *n* caprice *m*
whimper ['wɪmpər] *vi* geindre
whimsical ['wɪmzɪkəl] *adj* (*person*) capricieux(-euse); (*look, story*) étrange
whine [waɪn] *vi* gémir, geindre
whip [wɪp] *n* fouet *m*; (*for riding*) cravache *f*; (*POL: person*) chef de file assurant la discipline dans son groupe parlementaire ♦ *vt* fouetter; (*eggs*) battre; (*move quickly*) enlever/sortir brusquement; **~ped cream** *n* crème fouettée; **~-round** (*BRIT*) *n* collecte *f*
whirl [wəːl] *vi* tourbillonner; (*dancers*) tour-

noyer ♦ *vt* faire tourbillonner; faire tournoyer; **~pool** *n* tourbillon *m*; **~wind** *n* tornade *f*
whirr [wəːr] *vi* (*motor etc*) ronronner; (*: louder*) vrombir
whisk [wɪsk] *n* (*CULIN*) fouet *m* ♦ *vt* fouetter; (*eggs*) battre; **to ~ sb away** *or* **off** emmener qn rapidement
whiskers ['wɪskəz] *npl* (*of animal*) moustaches *fpl*; (*of man*) favoris *mpl*
whisky ['wɪskɪ] (*IRELAND, US* **whiskey**) *n* whisky *m*
whisper ['wɪspər] *vt, vi* chuchoter
whistle ['wɪsl] *n* (*sound*) sifflement *m*; (*object*) sifflet *m* ♦ *vi* siffler
white [waɪt] *adj* blanc (blanche); (*with fear*) blême ♦ *n* blanc *m*; (*person*) blanc (blanche); **~ coffee** (*BRIT*) *n* café *m* au lait, (*café*) crème *m*; **~-collar worker** *n* employé(e) de bureau; **~ elephant** *n* (*fig*) objet dispendieux et superflu; **~ lie** *n* pieux mensonge; **~ paper** *n* (*POL*) livre blanc; **~wash** *vt* blanchir à la chaux; (*fig*) blanchir ♦ *n* (*paint*) blanc *m* de chaux
whiting ['waɪtɪŋ] *n inv* (*fish*) merlan *m*
Whitsun ['wɪtsn] *n* la Pentecôte
whizz [wɪz] *vi*: **to ~ past** *or* **by** passer à toute vitesse; **~ kid** (*inf*) *n* petit prodige
who [huː] *pron* qui; **~dunit** [huː'dʌnɪt] (*inf*) *n* roman policier
whoever [huː'evər] *pron*: **~ finds it** celui (celle) qui le trouve(, qui que ce soit), quiconque le trouve; **ask ~ you like** demandez à qui vous voulez; **~ he marries** quelle que soit la personne qu'il épouse; **~ told you that?** qui a bien pu vous dire ça?
whole [həʊl] *adj* (*complete*) entier(-ère), tout(e); (*not broken*) intact(e), complet(-ète) ♦ *n* (*all*): **the ~ of** la totalité de, tout(e) le (la); (*entire unit*) tout *m*; **the ~ of the town** la ville tout entière; **on the ~, as a ~** dans l'ensemble; **~food(s)** *n(pl)* aliments complets; **~hearted** *adj* sans réserve(s); **~meal** (*BRIT*) *adj* (*bread, flour*) complet(-ète); **~sale** *n* (*vente f en*) gros *m* ♦ *adj* (*price*) de gros; (*destruction*)

whom → will

systématique ♦ *adv* en gros; ~**saler** *n* grossiste *m/f*; ~**some** *adj* sain(e); ~**wheat** *adj* = **wholemeal**; **wholly** [ˈhəʊlɪ] *adv* entièrement, tout à fait

KEYWORD

whom [huːm] *pron* 1 (*interrogative*) qui; **whom did you see?** qui avez-vous vu?; **to whom did you give it?** à qui l'avez-vous donné?

2 (*relative*) que, *prep* +qui; **the man whom I saw/to whom I spoke** l'homme que j'ai vu/à qui j'ai parlé

whooping cough [ˈhuːpɪŋ-] *n* coqueluche *f*

whore [hɔːʳ] (*inf: pej*) *n* putain *f*

KEYWORD

whose [huːz] *adj* 1 (*possessive: interrogative*): **whose book is this?** à qui est ce livre?; **whose pencil have you taken?** à qui est le crayon que vous avez pris?, c'est le crayon de qui que vous avez pris?; **whose daughter are you?** de qui êtes-vous la fille?

2 (*possessive: relative*): **the man whose son you rescued** l'homme dont *or* de qui vous avez sauvé le fils; **the girl whose sister you were speaking to** la fille à la sœur de qui *or* de laquelle vous parliez; **the woman whose car was stolen** la femme dont la voiture a été volée

♦ *pron* à qui; **whose is this?** à qui est ceci?; **I know whose it is** je sais à qui c'est

why [waɪ] *adv* pourquoi ♦ *excl* eh bien!, tiens!; **the reason ~** la raison pour laquelle; **tell me ~** dites-moi pourquoi; **~ not?** pourquoi pas?

wicked [ˈwɪkɪd] *adj* mauvais(e), méchant(e); (*crime*) pervers(e); (*mischievous*) malicieux(-euse)

wicket [ˈwɪkɪt] *n* (CRICKET) guichet *m*; terrain *m* (*entre les deux guichets*)

wide [waɪd] *adj* large; (*area, knowledge*) vaste, très étendu(e); (*choice*) grand(e) ♦ *adv*: **to open ~** ouvrir tout grand; **to shoot ~** tirer à côté; ~**awake** *adj* bien éveillé(e); ~**ly** *adv* (*differing*) radicalement; (*spaced*) sur une grande étendue; (*believed*) généralement; (*travel*) beaucoup; ~**n** *vt* élargir ♦ *vi* s'élargir; ~ **open** *adj* grand(e) ouvert(e); ~**spread** *adj* (*belief etc*) très répandu(e)

widow [ˈwɪdəʊ] *n* veuve *f*; ~**ed** *adj* veuf (veuve); ~**er** *n* veuf *m*

width [wɪdθ] *n* largeur *f*

wield [wiːld] *vt* (*sword*) manier; (*power*) exercer

wife [waɪf] (*pl* **wives**) *n* femme *f*, épouse *f*

wig [wɪg] *n* perruque *f*

wiggle [ˈwɪgl] *vt* agiter, remuer

wild [waɪld] *adj* sauvage; (*sea*) déchaîné(e); (*idea, life*) fou (folle); (*behaviour*) extravagant(e), déchaîné(e); **to make a ~ guess** émettre une hypothèse à tout hasard; ~**erness** [ˈwɪldənɪs] *n* désert *m*, région *f* sauvage; ~**life** *n* (*animals*) faune *f*; ~**ly** *adv* (*behave*) de manière déchaînée; (*applaud*) frénétiquement; (*hit, guess*) au hasard; (*happy*) follement; ~**s** *npl* (*remote area*) régions *fpl* sauvages

wilful [ˈwɪlful] (US **willful**) *adj* (*person*) obstiné(e); (*action*) délibéré(e)

KEYWORD

will [wɪl] (*vt: pt, pp* **willed**) *aux vb* 1 (*forming future tense*): **I will finish it tomorrow** je le finirai demain; **I will have finished it by tomorrow** je l'aurai fini d'ici demain; **will you do it? - yes I will/no I won't** le ferez-vous? - oui/non

2 (*in conjectures, predictions*): **he will** *or* **he'll be there by now** il doit être arrivé à l'heure qu'il est; **that will be the postman** ça doit être le facteur

3 (*in commands, requests, offers*): **will you be quiet!** voulez-vous bien vous taire!; **will you help me?** est-ce que vous pouvez m'aider?; **will you have a cup of tea?** voulez-vous une tasse de thé?; **I won't put up with it!** je ne le tolérerai

pas!

♦ *vt*: **to will sb to do** souhaiter ardemment que qn fasse; **he willed himself to go on** par un suprême effort de volonté, il continua

♦ *n* volonté *f*; testament *m*

willing ['wɪlɪŋ] *adj* de bonne volonté, serviable; **he's ~ to do it** il est disposé à le faire, il veut bien le faire; **~ly** *adv* volontiers; **~ness** *n* bonne volonté

willow ['wɪləu] *n* saule *m*

willpower ['wɪl'pauər] *n* volonté *f*

willy-nilly ['wɪlɪ'nɪlɪ] *adv* bon gré mal gré

wilt [wɪlt] *vi* dépérir; (*flower*) se faner

win [wɪn] (*pt, pp* **won**) *n* (*in sports etc*) victoire *f* ♦ *vt* gagner; (*prize*) remporter; (*popularity*) acquérir ♦ *vi* gagner; ~ **over** *vt* convaincre; ~ **round** (*BRIT*) *vt* = **win over**

wince [wɪns] *vi* tressaillir

winch [wɪntʃ] *n* treuil *m*

wind[1] [wɪnd] *n* (*also MED*) vent *m*; (*breath*) souffle *m* ♦ *vt* (*take breath*) couper le souffle à

wind[2] [waɪnd] (*pt, pp* **wound**) *vt* enrouler; (*wrap*) envelopper; (*clock, toy*) remonter ♦ *vi* (*road, river*) serpenter; ~ **up** *vt* (*clock*) remonter; (*debate*) terminer, clôturer

windfall ['wɪndfɔːl] *n* coup *m* de chance

winding ['waɪndɪŋ] *adj* (*road*) sinueux(-euse); (*staircase*) tournant(e)

wind instrument [wɪnd-] *n* (*MUS*) instrument *m* à vent

windmill ['wɪndmɪl] *n* moulin *m* à vent

window ['wɪndəu] *n* fenêtre *f*; (*in car, train, also: ~ pane*) vitre *f*; (*in shop etc*) vitrine *f*; ~ **box** *n* jardinière *f*; ~ **cleaner** *n* (*person*) laveur(-euse) de vitres; ~ **ledge** *n* rebord *m* de la fenêtre; ~ **pane** *n* vitre *f*, carreau *m*; **~-shopping** *n*: **to go ~-shopping** faire du lèche-vitrines; **~sill** ['wɪndəusɪl] *n* (*inside*) appui *m* de la fenêtre; (*outside*) rebord *m* de la fenêtre

windpipe ['wɪndpaɪp] *n* trachée *f*

wind power [wɪnd-] *n* énergie éolienne

windscreen ['wɪndskriːn] *n* pare-brise *m inv*; ~ **washer** *n* lave-glace *m inv*; ~

wiper *n* essuie-glace *m inv*

windshield ['wɪndʃiːld] (*US*) *n* = **windscreen**

windswept ['wɪndswept] *adj* balayé(e) par le vent; (*person*) ébouriffé(e)

windy ['wɪndɪ] *adj* venteux(-euse); **it's ~** il y a du vent

wine [waɪn] *n* vin *m*; ~ **bar** *n* bar *m* à vin; ~ **cellar** *n* cave *f* à vin; ~ **glass** *n* verre *m* à vin; ~ **list** *n* carte *f* des vins; ~ **waiter** *n* sommelier *m*

wing [wɪŋ] *n* aile *f*; **~s** *npl* (*THEATRE*) coulisses *fpl*; **~er** *n* (*SPORT*) ailier *m*

wink [wɪŋk] *n* clin *m* d'œil ♦ *vi* faire un clin d'œil; (*blink*) cligner des yeux

winner ['wɪnər] *n* gagnant(e)

winning ['wɪnɪŋ] *adj* (*team*) gagnant(e); (*goal*) décisif(-ive); **~s** *npl* gains *mpl*

winter ['wɪntər] *n* hiver *m*; **in ~** en hiver; ~ **sports** *npl* sports *mpl* d'hiver; **wintry** *adj* hivernal(e)

wipe [waɪp] *n*: **to give sth a ~** donner un coup de torchon/de chiffon/d'éponge à qch ♦ *vt* essuyer; (*erase: tape*) effacer; ~ **off** *vt* enlever; ~ **out** *vt* (*debt*) éteindre, amortir; (*memory*) effacer; (*destroy*) anéantir; ~ **up** *vt* essuyer

wire ['waɪər] *n* fil *m* (de fer); (*ELEC*) fil électrique; (*TEL*) télégramme *m* ♦ *vt* (*house*) faire l'installation électrique de; (*also:* ~ **up**) brancher; (*person: send telegram to*) télégraphier à; **~less** (*BRIT*) *n* poste *m* de radio; **wiring** *n* installation *f* électrique; **wiry** *adj* noueux(-euse), nerveux(-euse); (*hair*) dru(e)

wisdom ['wɪzdəm] *n* sagesse *f*; (*of action*) prudence *f*; ~ **tooth** *n* dent *f* de sagesse

wise [waɪz] *adj* sage, prudent(e); (*remark*) judicieux(-euse) ♦ *suffix*: **...wise**: **time-wise** *etc* en ce qui concerne le temps *etc*

wish [wɪʃ] *n* (*desire*) désir *m*; (*specific desire*) souhait *m*, vœu *m* ♦ *vt* souhaiter, désirer, vouloir; **best ~es** (*on birthday etc*) meilleurs vœux; **with best ~es** (*in letter*) bien amicalement; **to ~ sb goodbye** dire au revoir à qn; **he ~ed me well** il m'a souhaité bonne chance; **to ~ to do/sb to do**

désirer *or* vouloir faire/que qn fasse; **to ~ for** souhaiter; **~ful** *adj*: **it's ~ful thinking** c'est prendre ses désirs pour des réalités

wistful ['wɪstful] *adj* mélancolique

wit [wɪt] *n* (*gen pl*) intelligence *f*, esprit *m*; (*presence of mind*) présence *f* d'esprit; (*wittiness*) esprit; (*person*) homme/femme d'esprit

witch [wɪtʃ] *n* sorcière *f*; **~craft** *n* sorcellerie *f*

KEYWORD

---

with [wɪð, wɪθ] *prep* **1** (*in the company of*) avec; (*at the home of*) chez; **we stayed with friends** nous avons logé chez des amis; **I'll be with you in a minute** je suis à vous dans un instant

2 (*descriptive*): **a room with a view** une chambre avec vue; **the man with the grey hat/blue eyes** l'homme au chapeau gris/aux yeux bleus

3 (*indicating manner, means, cause*): **with tears in her eyes** les larmes aux yeux; **to walk with a stick** marcher avec une canne; **red with anger** rouge de colère; **to shake with fear** trembler de peur; **to fill sth with water** remplir qch d'eau

4: **I'm with you** (*I understand*) je vous suis; **to be with it** (*inf*: *up-to-date*) être dans le vent

---

withdraw [wɪθ'drɔː] (*irreg*) *vt* retirer ♦ *vi* se retirer; **~al** *n* retrait *m*; **~al symptoms** *npl* (*MED*): **to have ~al symptoms** être en état de manque; **~n** *adj* (*person*) renfermé(e)

wither ['wɪðəʳ] *vi* (*plant*) se faner

withhold [wɪθ'həuld] (*irreg*) *vt* (*money*) retenir; **to ~ (from)** (*information*) cacher (à); (*permission*) refuser (à)

within [wɪð'ɪn] *prep* à l'intérieur de ♦ *adv* à l'intérieur; **~ his reach** à sa portée; **~ sight of** en vue de; **~ a kilometre of** à moins d'un kilomètre de; **~ the week** avant la fin de la semaine

without [wɪð'aut] *prep* sans; **~ a coat** sans manteau; **~ speaking** sans parler; **to go ~**

sth se passer de qch

withstand [wɪθ'stænd] (*irreg*) *vt* résister à

witness ['wɪtnɪs] *n* (*person*) témoin *m* ♦ *vt* (*event*) être témoin de; (*document*) attester l'authenticité de; **to bear ~ (to)** (*fig*) attester; **~ box** (*US* **witness stand**) *n* barre *f* des témoins

witty ['wɪtɪ] *adj* spirituel(le), plein(e) d'esprit

wives [waɪvz] *npl* of **wife**

wizard ['wɪzəd] *n* magicien *m*

wk *abbr* = **week**

wobble ['wɒbl] *vi* trembler; (*chair*) branler

woe [wəu] *n* malheur *m*

woke [wəuk] *pt* of **wake**; **~n** *pp* of **wake**

wolf [wulf] (*pl* **wolves**) *n* loup *m*

woman ['wumən] (*pl* **women**) *n* femme *f*; **~ doctor** *n* femme *f* médecin; **~ly** *adj* féminin(e)

womb [wuːm] *n* (*ANAT*) utérus *m*

women ['wɪmɪn] *npl* of **woman**; **~'s lib** (*inf*) *n* MLF *m*; **W~'s (Liberation) Movement** *n* mouvement *m* de libération de la femme

won [wʌn] *pt, pp* of **win**

wonder ['wʌndəʳ] *n* merveille *f*, miracle *m*; (*feeling*) émerveillement *m* ♦ *vi*: **to ~ whether/why** se demander si/pourquoi; **to ~ at** (*marvel*) s'émerveiller de; **to ~ about** songer à; **it's no ~ (that)** il n'est pas étonnant (que +*sub*); **~ful** *adj* merveilleux(-euse)

won't [wəunt] = **will not**

wood [wud] *n* (*timber, forest*) bois *m*; **~ carving** *n* sculpture *f* en *or* sur bois; **~ed** *adj* boisé(e); **~en** *adj* en bois; (*fig*) raide; inexpressif(-ive); **~pecker** *n* pic *m* (*oiseau*); **~wind** *n* (*MUS*): **the ~wind** les bois *mpl*; **~work** *n* menuiserie *f*; **~worm** *n* ver *m* du bois

wool [wul] *n* laine *f*; **to pull the ~ over sb's eyes** (*fig*) en faire accroire à qn; **~len** (*US* **woolen**) *adj* de *or* en laine; (*industry*) lainier(-ère); **~lens** *npl* (*clothes*) lainages *mpl*; **~ly** (*US* **wooly**) *adj* laineux(-euse); (*fig: ideas*) confus(e)

word [wəːd] *n* mot *m*; (*promise*) parole *f*;

(*news*) nouvelles *fpl* ♦ *vt* rédiger, formuler; **in other ~s** en d'autres termes; **to break/keep one's ~** manquer à sa parole/tenir parole; **~ing** *n* termes *mpl*; libellé *m*; **~ processing** *n* traitement *m* de texte; **~ processor** *n* machine *f* de traitement de texte

wore [wɔːʳ] *pt of* **wear**

work [wəːk] *n* travail *m*; (*ART, LITERATURE*) œuvre *f* ♦ *vi* travailler; (*mechanism*) marcher, fonctionner; (*plan etc*) marcher; (*medicine*) agir ♦ *vt* (*clay, wood etc*) travailler; (*mine etc*) exploiter; (*machine*) faire marcher *or* fonctionner; (*miracles, wonders etc*) faire; **to be out of ~** être sans emploi; **~ loose** se défaire, se desserrer; **~ on** *vt fus* travailler à; (*influence*) (essayer d')influencer; **~ out** *vi* (*plans etc*) marcher ♦ *vt* (*problem*) résoudre; (*plan*) élaborer; **it ~s out at £100** ça fait 100 livres; **~ up** *vt*: **to get ~ed up** se mettre dans tous ses états; **~able** *adj* (*solution*) réalisable; **~aholic** [wəːkəˈhɔlɪk] *n* bourreau *m* de travail; **~er** *n* travailleur(-euse), ouvrier(-ère); **~ experience** *n* stage *m*; **~force** *n* main-d'œuvre *f*; **~ing class** *n* classe ouvrière; **~ing-class** *adj* ouvrier(-ère); **~ing order** *n*: **in ~ing order** en état de marche; **~man** (*irreg*) *n* ouvrier *m*; **~manship** (*skill*) *n* métier *m*, habileté *f*; **~s** *n* (*BRIT: factory*) usine *f* ♦ *npl* (*of clock, machine*) mécanisme *m*; **~ sheet** *n* (*COMPUT*) feuille *f* de programmation; **~shop** *n* atelier *m*; **~ station** *n* poste *m* de travail; **~-to-rule** (*BRIT*) *n* grève *f* du zèle

world [wəːld] *n* monde *m* ♦ *cpd* (*champion*) du monde; (*power, war*) mondial(e); **to think the ~ of sb** (*fig*) ne jurer que par qn; **~ly** *adj* de ce monde; (*knowledgeable*) qui a l'expérience du monde; **~wide** *adj* universel(le); **W~-Wide Web** *n* Web *m*

worm [wəːm] *n* ver *m*

worn [wɔːn] *pp of* **wear** ♦ *adj* usé(e); **~-out** *adj* (*object*) complètement usé(e); (*person*) épuisé(e)

worried [ˈwʌrɪd] *adj* inquiet(-ète)

worry [ˈwʌrɪ] *n* souci *m* ♦ *vt* inquiéter ♦ *vi* s'inquiéter, se faire du souci

worse [wəːs] *adj* pire, plus mauvais(e) ♦ *adv* plus mal ♦ *n* pire *m*; **a change for the ~** une détérioration; **~ off** *adj* moins à l'aise financièrement; (*fig*): **you'll be ~ off this way** ça ira moins bien de cette façon

worship [ˈwəːʃɪp] *n* culte *m* ♦ *vt* (*God*) rendre un culte à; (*person*) adorer; **Your W~** (*BRIT: to mayor*) Monsieur le maire; (*: to judge*) Monsieur le juge

worst [wəːst] *adj* le (la) pire, le (la) plus mauvais(e) ♦ *adv* le plus mal ♦ *n* pire *m*; **at ~** au pis aller

worth [wəːθ] *n* valeur *f* ♦ *adj*: **to be ~** valoir; **it's ~ it** cela en vaut la peine, ça vaut la peine; **it is ~ one's while (to do)** on gagne à (faire); **~less** *adj* qui ne vaut rien; **~while** *adj* (*activity, cause*) utile, louable

worthy [ˈwəːðɪ] *adj* (*person*) digne; (*motive*) louable; **~ of** digne de

KEYWORD

would [wud] *aux vb* **1** (*conditional tense*): **if you asked him he would do it** si vous le lui demandiez, il le ferait; **if you had asked him he would have done it** si vous le lui aviez demandé, il l'aurait fait

2 (*in offers, invitations, requests*): **would you like a biscuit?** voulez-vous un biscuit?; **would you close the door please?** voulez-vous fermer la porte, s'il vous plaît?

3 (*in indirect speech*): **I said I would do it** j'ai dit que je le ferais

4 (*emphatic*): **it WOULD have to snow today!** naturellement il neige aujourd'hui! *or* il fallait qu'il neige aujourd'hui!

5 (*insistence*): **she wouldn't do it** elle n'a pas voulu *or* elle a refusé de le faire

6 (*conjecture*): **it would have been midnight** il devait être minuit

7 (*indicating habit*): **he would go there on Mondays** il y allait le lundi

would-be [ˈwudbiː] (*pej*) *adj* soi-disant

wouldn't ['wudnt] = **would not**
wound[1] [wu:nd] *n* blessure *f* ♦ *vt* blesser
wound[2] [waund] *pt, pp* of **wind**[2]
wove [wəuv] *pt* of **weave**; **~n** *pp* of **weave**
wrap [ræp] *vt* (*also:* **~ up**) envelopper, emballer; (*wind*) enrouler; **~per** *n* (*BRIT: of book*) couverture *f*; (*on chocolate*) emballage *m*, papier *m*; **~ping paper** *n* papier *m* d'emballage; (*for gift*) papier cadeau
wreak [ri:k] *vt*: **to ~ havoc (on)** avoir un effet désastreux (sur)
wreath [ri:θ] (*pl* **~s**) *n* couronne *f*
wreck [rɛk] *n* (*ship*) épave *f*; (*vehicle*) véhicule accidenté; (*pej: person*) loque humaine ♦ *vt* démolir; (*fig*) briser, ruiner; **~age** *n* débris *mpl*; (*of building*) décombres *mpl*; (*of ship*) épave *f*
wren [rɛn] *n* (*ZOOL*) roitelet *m*
wrench [rɛntʃ] *n* (*TECH*) clé *f* (à écrous); (*tug*) violent mouvement de torsion; (*fig*) déchirement *m* ♦ *vt* tirer violemment sur, tordre; **to ~ sth from** arracher qch à *or* de
wrestle ['rɛsl] *vi*: **to ~ (with sb)** lutter (avec qn); **~r** *n* lutteur(-euse); **wrestling** *n* lutte *f*; (*also:* **all-in wrestling**) catch *m*, lutte *f* libre
wretched ['rɛtʃɪd] *adj* misérable; (*inf*) maudit(e)
wriggle ['rɪgl] *vi* (*also:* **~ about**) se tortiller
wring [rɪŋ] (*pt, pp* **wrung**) *vt* tordre; (*wet clothes*) essorer; (*fig*): **to ~ sth out of sb** arracher qch à qn
wrinkle ['rɪŋkl] *n* (*on skin*) ride *f*; (*on paper etc*) pli *m* ♦ *vt* plisser ♦ *vi* se plisser; **~d** *adj* (*skin, face*) ridé(e)
wrist [rɪst] *n* poignet *m*; **~watch** *n* montre-bracelet *f*
writ [rɪt] *n* acte *m* judiciaire
write [raɪt] (*pt* **wrote**, *pp* **written**) *vt, vi* écrire; (*prescription*) rédiger; **~ down** *vt* noter; (*put in writing*) mettre par écrit; **~ off** *vt* (*debt*) passer aux profits et pertes; (*project*) mettre une croix sur; **~ out** *vt* écrire; **~ up** *vt* rédiger; **~-off** *n* perte totale; **~r** *n* auteur *m*, écrivain *m*
writhe [raɪð] *vi* se tordre

writing ['raɪtɪŋ] *n* écriture *f*; (*of author*) œuvres *fpl*; **in ~** par écrit; **~ paper** *n* papier *m* à lettres
wrong [rɒŋ] *adj* (*incorrect*) faux (fausse); (*morally*) mauvais(e); (*wicked*) mal; (*unfair*) injuste ♦ *adv* mal ♦ *n* tort *m* ♦ *vt* faire du tort à, léser; **you are ~ to do it** tu as tort de le faire; **you are ~ about that, you've got it ~** tu te trompes; **what's ~?** qu'est-ce qui ne va pas?; **you've got the ~ number** vous vous êtes trompé de numéro; **to go ~** (*person*) se tromper; (*plan*) mal tourner; (*machine*) tomber en panne; **to be in the ~** avoir tort; **~ful** *adj* injustifié(e); **~ly** *adv* mal, incorrectement; **~ side** *n* (*of material*) envers *m*
wrote [rəut] *pt* of **write**
wrought iron [rəut-] *n* fer forgé
wrung [rʌŋ] *pt, pp* of **wring**
wt. *abbr* = **weight**
WWW *n abbr* (= *World Wide Web*): **the ~** le Web

X, x

Xmas ['ɛksməs] *n abbr* = **Christmas**
X-ray ['ɛksreɪ] *n* (*ray*) rayon *m* X; (*photo*) radio(graphie) *f*
xylophone ['zaɪləfəun] *n* xylophone *m*

Y, y

yacht [jɒt] *n* yacht *m*; voilier *m*; **~ing** *n* yachting *m*, navigation *f* de plaisance; **~sman** (*irreg*) *n* plaisancier *m*
Yank [jæŋk], **Yankee** ['jæŋkɪ] (*pej*) *n* Amerloque *m/f*
yap [jæp] *vi* (*dog*) japper
yard [jɑːd] *n* (*of house etc*) cour *f*; (*measure*) yard *m* (= 91,4 *cm*); **~stick** *n* (*fig*) mesure *f*, critères *mpl*
yarn [jɑːn] *n* fil *m*; (*tale*) longue histoire
yawn [jɔːn] *n* bâillement *m* ♦ *vi* bâiller; **~ing** *adj* (*gap*) béant(e)
yd. *abbr* = **yard(s)**

yeah [jɛə] (*inf*) *adv* ouais

year [jɪəʳ] *n* an *m*, année *f*; **to be 8 ~s old** avoir 8 ans; **an eight-~-old child** un enfant de huit ans; **~ly** *adj* annuel(le) ♦ *adv* annuellement

yearn [jə:n] *vi*: **to ~ for sth** aspirer à qch, languir après qch

yeast [ji:st] *n* levure *f*

yell [jɛl] *vi* hurler

yellow [ˈjɛləu] *adj* jaune

yelp [jɛlp] *vi* japper; glapir

yes [jɛs] *adv* oui; (*answering negative question*) si ♦ *n* oui *m*; **to say/answer ~** dire/répondre oui

yesterday [ˈjɛstədɪ] *adv* hier ♦ *n* hier *m*; **~ morning/evening** hier matin/soir; **all day ~** toute la journée d'hier

yet [jɛt] *adv* encore; déjà ♦ *conj* pourtant, néanmoins; **it is not finished ~** ce n'est pas encore fini *or* toujours pas fini; **the best ~** le meilleur jusqu'ici *or* jusque-là; **as ~** jusqu'ici, encore

yew [ju:] *n* if *m*

yield [ji:ld] *n* production *f*, rendement *m*; rapport *m* ♦ *vt* produire, rendre, rapporter; (*surrender*) céder ♦ *vi* céder; (*US: AUT*) céder la priorité

YMCA *n abbr* (= *Young Men's Christian Association*) YMCA *m*

yob [jɔb] (*BRIT: inf*) *n* loubar(d) *m*

yoghourt [ˈjəugət] *n* yaourt *m*

yog(h)urt [ˈjəugət] *n* = **yoghourt**

yoke [jəuk] *n* joug *m*

yolk [jəuk] *n* jaune *m* (d'œuf)

KEYWORD

you [ju:] *pron* **1** (*subject*) tu; (*polite form*) vous; (*plural*) vous; **you French enjoy your food** vous autres Français, vous aimez bien manger; **you and I will go** toi et moi *or* vous et moi, nous irons

2 (*object: direct, indirect*) te, t' +*vowel*, vous; **I know you** je te *or* vous connais; **I gave it to you** je vous l'ai donné, je te l'ai donné

3 (*stressed*) toi; vous; **I told YOU to do it** c'est à toi *or* vous que j'ai dit de le faire

4 (*after prep, in comparisons*) toi; vous; **it's for you** c'est pour toi *or* vous; **she's younger than you** elle est plus jeune que toi *or* vous

5 (*impersonal: one*) on; **fresh air does you good** l'air frais fait du bien; **you never know** on ne sait jamais

---

you'd [ju:d] = **you had**; **you would**

you'll [ju:l] = **you will**; **you shall**

young [jʌŋ] *adj* jeune ♦ *npl* (*of animal*) petits *mpl*; (*people*): **the ~** les jeunes, la jeunesse; **~er** [jʌŋgəʳ] *adj* (*brother etc*) cadet(te); **~ster** *n* jeune *m* (garçon *m*); (*child*) enfant *m/f*

your [jɔ:ʳ] *adj* ton (ta), tes *pl*; (*polite form, pl*) votre, vos *pl*; *see also* **my**

you're [juəʳ] = **you are**

yours [jɔ:z] *pron* le (la) tien(ne), les tiens (tiennes); (*polite form, pl*) le (la) vôtre, les vôtres; **~ sincerely/faithfully/truly** veuillez agréer l'expression de mes sentiments les meilleurs; *see also* **mine**[1]

yourself [jɔ:ˈsɛlf] *pron* (*reflexive*) te; (: *polite form*) vous; (*after prep*) toi; vous; (*emphatic*) toi-même; vous-même; *see also* **oneself**; **yourselves** *pl pron* vous; (*emphatic*) vous-mêmes

youth [ju:θ] *n* jeunesse *f*; (*young man: pl* **~s**) jeune homme *m*; **~ club** *n* centre *m* de jeunes; **~ful** *adj* jeune; (*enthusiasm*) de jeunesse, juvénile; **~ hostel** *n* auberge *f* de jeunesse

you've [ju:v] = **you have**

YTS *n abbr* (*BRIT: Youth Training Scheme*) ≃ TUC *m*

Yugoslav [ˈju:gəuslɑ:v] *adj* yougoslave ♦ *n* Yougoslave *m/f*

Yugoslavia [ˈju:gəuˈslɑ:vɪə] *n* Yougoslavie *f*

yuppie [ˈjʌpɪ] (*inf*) *n* yuppie *m/f*

YWCA *n abbr* (= *Young Women's Christian Association*) YWCA *m*

Z, z

zany ['zeɪnɪ] *adj* farfelu(e), loufoque

zap [zæp] *vt* (*COMPUT*) effacer

zeal [zi:l] *n* zèle *m*, ferveur *f*; empressement *m*

zebra ['zi:brə] *n* zèbre *m*; ~ **crossing** (*BRIT*) *n* passage clouté *or* pour piétons

zero ['zɪərəu] *n* zéro *m*

zest [zest] *n* entrain *m*, élan *m*; (*of orange*) zeste *m*

zigzag ['zɪgzæg] *n* zigzag *m*

Zimbabwe [zɪm'bɑ:bwɪ] *n* Zimbabwe *m*

Zimmer frame ['zɪmə-] *n* déambulateur *m*

zinc [zɪŋk] *n* zinc *m*

zip [zɪp] *n* fermeture *f* éclair ® ♦ *vt* (*also:* ~ **up**) fermer avec une fermeture éclair ®; ~ **code** (*US*) *n* code postal; ~**per** (*US*) *n* = **zip**

zit [zɪt] (*inf*) *n* bouton *m*

zodiac ['zəudɪæk] *n* zodiaque *m*

zone [zəun] *n* zone *f*

zoo [zu:] *n* zoo *m*

zoom [zu:m] *vi*: **to ~ past** passer en trombe; ~ **lens** *n* zoom *m*

zucchini [zu:'ki:nɪ] (*US*) *n(pl)* courgette(s) *f(pl)*

LE DICTIONNAIRE ET LA GRAMMAIRE

Bien qu'un dictionnaire ne puisse jamais remplacer une grammaire détaillée, il fournit néanmoins un grand nombre de renseignements grammaticaux. Le Robert & Collins Mini présente les indications grammaticales de la façon suivante:

Les catégories grammaticales

Elles sont données en italique immédiatement après la transcription phonétique des entrées. La liste des abréviations se trouve pages xi et xii.

Les changements de catégorie grammaticale au sein d'un article – par exemple, d'adjectif à adverbe, ou de nom à verbe intransitif à verbe transitif – sont indiqués au moyen de losanges – comme pour le mot français "large" et l'anglais "act".

Les adverbes

La règle générale pour former les adverbes en anglais est d'ajouter "-ly" à l'adjectif ou à sa racine. Ainsi:

bad > badly

gentle > gently

La terminaison en "-ly" est souvent l'équivalent du français "-ment":

slowly – lentement

slyly – sournoisement

Il faut toutefois faire attention car certains mots en "-ly" sont des adjectifs et non des adverbes. Par exemple: "friendly", "likely", "ugly", "silly". Ces mots ne peuvent pas être utilisés en tant qu'adverbes. Il faut donc bien vérifier la catégorie grammaticale du mot que vous voulez utiliser.

Les adverbes figurent soit dans les articles des adjectifs correspondants s'ils suivent ces adjectifs dans l'ordre alphabétique ("fortunately"), soit comme entrées à part entière s'ils précèdent alphabétiquement l'adjectif ("happily"). Si leur usage est moins fréquent, ils n'apparaissent pas du tout. Vous pouvez cependant les traduire facilement en français d'après la traduction de l'adjectif correspondant.

Le pluriel des noms en anglais

Normalement, on forme le pluriel des noms anglais en ajoutant un "-s" au singulier.

cat > cats

Le pluriel des noms qui finissent en "-o" est formé en ajoutant "-es" au singulier.

Tous les pluriels irréguliers sont donnés entre parenthèses et en caractères gras immédiatement après la transcription phonétique (v. "tomato").

Certains noms ont un pluriel irrégulier, comme "knife" et "man" en regard. Ces pluriels irréguliers apparaissent également en tant qu'entrées à part entière dans le texte et renvoient au singulier (v. "knives" et "men").

Les verbes irréguliers

Les verbes irréguliers sont clairement signalés dans ce dictionnaire: les formes du prétérit (*pt*) et du participe passé (*pp*) sont données en caractères gras entre parenthèses immédiatement après la transcription phonétique de l'entrée. Voir les verbes "to teach" et "to swim".

Par ailleurs les formes du prétérit et du participe passé des verbes irréguliers apparaissent elles-mêmes comme des entrées à part entière dans le dictionnaire et renvoient à l'infinitif du verbe. Voir "taught", "swam" et "swum".

De plus, vous avez la possibilité de vous référer rapidement à la liste des verbes irréguliers anglais pages 587 et 588 vers la fin de votre dictionnaire.

Enfin, pour ce qui est des verbes réguliers, vous remarquerez que leur prétérit et leur participe passé ne sont pas donnés. Ceci est dû au fait que ces formes ne présentent aucun problème puisqu'on ajoute toujours "-ed" à l'infinitif pour les obtenir (ou bien "-d" si l'infinitif se termine par la voyelle "-e").

		prétérit		**participe passé**
exemples:	to help	– helped	–	helped
	to love	– loved	–	loved

THE DICTIONARY AND GRAMMAR

While it is true that a dictionary can never be a substitute for a detailed grammar it nevertheless provides a great deal of grammatical information. If you know how to extract this information you will be able to use French more accurately both in speech and in writing.

The Collins French Dictionary presents grammatical information as follows.

Parts of speech

Parts of speech are given in italics immediately after the phonetic spellings of headwords. Abbreviated forms are used. Abbreviations can be checked on pages xi and xii.

Changes in parts of speech within an entry – for example, from adjective to adverb to noun, or from noun to intransitive verb to transitive verb – are indicated by means of lozenges - ♦ - as with the French 'large' and the English 'act'.

Genders of French nouns

The gender of each noun in the French-English section of the dictionary is indicated in the following way:

> *nm* = nom masculin
>
> *nf* = nom féminin

You will occasionally see *nm/f* beside an entry. This indicates that a noun – 'concierge', for example – can be either masculine or feminine.

Feminine and *irregular* plural forms of nouns are shown, as with 'chercheur' and 'cheval': the ending which follows the entry is substituted, so that 'chercheur' becomes 'chercheuse' in the feminine, and 'cheval' becomes 'chevaux' in the plural.

In the English-French section of the dictionary, the gender immediately follows the noun translation, as with 'grass'. Where a noun can be either masculine or feminine, this is shown by '*m/f*' if the form of the noun does not change, or by the bracketed feminine ending if it does change, as with 'graduate'.

So many things depend on your knowing the correct gender of a French noun – whether you use 'il' or 'elle' to translate 'it'; the way you spell and pronounce certain adjectives; the changes you make to past participles, etc. If you are in any doubt as to the gender of a noun, it is always best to check it in your dictionary.

Adjectives

Adjectives are given in both their masculine and feminine forms, where these are different. The usual rule is to add an '-e' to the masculine form to make an adjective feminine, as with 'noir'.

In the English-French section, an adjective's feminine form or ending appears immediately after it in brackets, as with 'soft'.

Some adjectives have identical masculine and feminine forms. Where this occurs, there is no 'e' beside the basic masculine form.

Many French adjectives, however, do not follow the regular pattern. Where an adjective has an irregular feminine or plural form, this information is clearly provided in your dictionary, usually with the irregular form being given in full. Consider the entries for 'net' and 'sec'.

Adverbs

The normal 'rule' for forming adverbs in French is to add '-ment' to the feminine form of the adjective. Thus:

> lent > lente > lentement

The '-ment' ending is often the equivalent of the English '-ly':

> lentement   – slowly
> sournoisement – slyly

Adjectives ending in '-ant' and '-ent' are slightly different:

> courant > couramment
> prudent > prudemment

In your dictionary some adverbs appear as a separate entry; others appear as subentries of adjective headwords; while others do not feature in the dictionary at all. Compare 'heureusement', 'froidement' and 'sournoisement'.

Where an adverb does not appear, this is usually because it is not a particularly common one. However, you should be able to work out a translation from the adjective once you have found that in the dictionary.

Information about verbs

A major problem facing language learners is that the form of a verb will change according to the subject and/or the tense being used. A typical French verb can take many different forms – too many to list in a dictionary entry.

Yet, although verbs are listed in your dictionary in their infinitive forms only, this does not mean that the dictionary is of limited value when it comes to handling the verb system of the French language. On the contrary, it contains much valuable information.

First of all, your dictionary will help you with the meanings of unfamiliar verbs. If you came across the word 'remplit' in a text and looked it up in your dictionary you wouldn't find it. You must deduce that it is part of a verb and look for the infinitive form. Thus you will see that 'remplit' is a form of the verb 'remplir'. You now have the basic meaning of the word you are concerned with – something to do with the English verb 'fill' – and this should be enough to help you understand the text you are reading.

It is usually an easy task to make the connection between the form of a verb and the infinitive. For example, 'remplissent', 'remplira', 'remplissons' and 'rempli' are all recognisable as parts of the infinitive 'remplir'. However, sometimes it is less obvious – for example, 'voyons', 'verrai' and 'vu' are all parts of 'voir'. The only real solution to this problem is to learn the various forms of the main French regular and irregular verbs.

And this is the second source of help offered by your dictionary. The verb tables on pages 585 to 586 of the Collins French Dictionary provide a summary of some of the main forms of the main tenses of regular and irregular verbs. Consider the verb 'voir' below where the following information is given:

1	voyant	–	Present Participle
2	vu	–	Past Participle
3	vois, voyons, voient	–	Present Tense forms
4	voyais	–	1st Person Singular of the Imperfect Tense
5	verrai	–	1st Person Singular of the Future Tense
7	voie	–	1st Person Singular of the Present Subjunctive

The regular '-er' verb 'parler' is presented in greater detail. The main tenses and the different endings are given in full. This information can be transferred and applied to all verbs in the list. In addition, the main parts of the most common irregular verbs are listed in the body of the dictionary.

PARLER

1 parlant
2 parlé
3 parle, parles, parle, parlons, parlez, parlent
4 parlais, parlais, parlait, parlions, parliez, parlaient
5 parlerai, parleras, parlera, parlerons, parlerez, parleront
6 parlerais, parlerais, parlerait, parlerions, parleriez, parleraient
7 parle, parles, parle, parlons, parliez, parlent *impératif* parle!, parlez!

In order to make maximum use of the information contained in these pages, a good working knowledge of the various rules affecting French verbs is required. You will acquire this in the course of your French studies and your Collins dictionary will serve as a useful 'aide-mémoire'. If you happen to forget how to form the second person singular form of the Future Tense of 'voir' there will be no need to panic — your dictionary contains the information!

FRENCH VERB FORMS

1 Participe présent *2* Participe passé *3* Présent *4* Imparfait *5* Futur *6* Conditionnel *7* Subjonctif présent

acquérir *1* acquérant *2* acquis *3* acquiers, acquérons, acquièrent *4* acquérais *5* acquerrai *7* acquière

ALLER *1* allant *2* allé *3* vais, vas, va, allons, allez, vont *4* allais *5* irai *6* irais *7* aille

asseoir *1* asseyant *2* assis *3* assieds, asseyons, asseyez, asseyent *4* asseyais *5* assiérai *7* asseye

atteindre *1* atteignant *2* atteint *3* atteins, atteignons *4* atteignais *7* atteigne

AVOIR *1* ayant *2* eu *3* ai, as, a, avons, avez, ont *4* avais *5* aurai *6* aurais *7* aie, aies, ait, ayons, ayez, aient

battre *1* battant *2* battu *3* bats, bat, battons *4* battais *7* batte

boire *1* buvant *2* bu *3* bois, buvons, boivent *4* buvais *7* boive

bouillir *1* bouillant *2* bouilli *3* bous, bouillons *4* bouillais *7* bouille

conclure *1* concluant *2* conclu *3* conclus, concluons *4* concluais *7* conclue

conduire *1* conduisant *2* conduit *3* conduis, conduisons *4* conduisais *7* conduise

connaître *1* connaissant *2* connu *3* connais, connaît, connaissons *4* connaissais *7* connaisse

coudre *1* cousant *2* cousu *3* couds, cousons, cousez, cousent *4* cousais *7* couse

courir *1* courant *2* couru *3* cours, courons *4* courais *5* courrai *7* coure

couvrir *1* couvrant *2* couvert *3* couvre, couvrons *4* couvrais *7* couvre

craindre *1* craignant *2* craint *3* crains, craignons *4* craignais *7* craigne

croire *1* croyant *2* cru *3* crois, croyons, croient *4* croyais *7* croie

croître *1* croissant *2* crû, crue, crus, crues *3* croîs, croissons *4* croissais *7* croisse

cueillir *1* cueillant *2* cueilli *3* cueille, cueillons *4* cueillais *5* cueillerai *7* cueille

devoir *1* devant *2* dû, due, dus, dues *3* dois, devons, doivent *4* devais *5* devrai *7* doive

dire *1* disant *2* dit *3* dis, disons, dites, disent *4* disais *7* dise

dormir *1* dormant *2* dormi *3* dors, dormons *4* dormais *7* dorme

écrire *1* écrivant *2* écrit *3* écris, écrivons *4* écrivais *7* écrive

ÊTRE *1* étant *2* été *3* suis, es, est, sommes, êtes, sont *4* étais *5* serai *6* serais *7* sois, sois, soit, soyons, soyez, soient

FAIRE *1* faisant *2* fait *3* fais, fais, fait, faisons, faites, font *4* faisais *5* ferai *6* ferais *7* fasse

falloir *2* fallu *3* faut *4* fallait *5* faudra *7* faille

FINIR *1* finissant *2* fini *3* finis, finis, finit, finissons, finissez, finissent *4* finissais *5* finirai *6* finirais *7* finisse

fuir *1* fuyant *2* fui *3* fuis, fuyons, fuient *4* fuyais *7* fuie

joindre *1* joignant *2* joint *3* joins, joignons *4* joignais *7* joigne

lire *1* lisant *2* lu *3* lis, lisons *4* lisais *7* lise

luire *1* luisant *2* lui *3* luis, luisons *4* luisais *7* luise

maudire *1* maudissant *2* maudit *3* maudis, maudissons *4* maudissait *7* maudisse

mentir *1* mentant *2* menti *3* mens, mentons *4* mentais *7* mente

mettre *1* mettant *2* mis *3* mets, mettons *4* mettais *7* mette

mourir *1* mourant *2* mort *3* meurs, mourons, meurent *4* mourais *5* mourrai *7* meure

naître *1* naissant *2* né *3* nais, naît, naissons *4* naissais *7* naisse

offrir *1* offrant *2* offert *3* offre, offrons *4* offrais *7* offre

PARLER *1* parlant *2* parlé *3* parle, parles, parle, parlons, parlez, parlent *4* parlais, parlais, parlait, parlions, parliez, parlaient *5* parlerai, parleras, parlera, parlerons, parlerez, parleront *6* parlerais, parlerais, parlerait, parlerions, parleriez, parleraient *7* parle, parles, parle, parlions, parliez, parlent *impératif* parle, parlez

partir *1* partant *2* parti *3* pars, partons *4* partais *7* parte

plaire *1* plaisant *2* plu *3* plais, plaît, plaisons *4* plaisais *7* plaise

pleuvoir *1* pleuvant *2* plu *3* pleut, pleuvent *4* pleuvait *5* pleuvra *7* pleuve

pourvoir *1* pourvoyant *2* pourvu *3* pourvois, pourvoyons, pourvoient *4* pourvoyais *7* pourvoie

pouvoir *1* pouvant *2* pu *3* peux, peut, pouvons, peuvent *4* pouvais *5* pourrai *7* puisse

prendre *1* prenant *2* pris *3* prends, prenons, prennent *4* prenais *7* prenne

prévoir *comme* voir *5* prévoirai

RECEVOIR *1* recevant *2* reçu *3* reçois, reçois,

reçoit, recevons, recevez, reçoivent *4* recevais *5* recevrai *6* recevrais *7* reçoive

RENDRE *1* rendant *2* rendu *3* rends, rends, rend, rendons, rendez, rendent *4* rendais *5* rendrai *6* rendrais *7* rende

résoudre *1* résolvant *2* résolu *3* résous, résout, résolvons *4* résolvais *7* résolve

rire *1* riant *2* ri *3* ris, rions *4* riais *7* rie

savoir *1* sachant *2* su *3* sais, savons, savent *4* savais *5* saurai *7* sache *impératif* sache, sachons, sachez

servir *1* servant *2* servi *3* sers, servons *4* servais *7* serve

sortir *1* sortant *2* sorti *3* sors, sortons *4* sortais *7* sorte

souffrir *1* souffrant *2* souffert *3* souffre, souffrons *4* souffrais *7* souffre

suffire *1* suffisant *2* suffi *3* suffis, suffisons *4* suffisais *7* suffise

suivre *1* suivant *2* suivi *3* suis, suivons *4* suivais *7* suive

taire *1* taisant *2* tu *3* tais, taisons *4* taisais *7* taise

tenir *1* tenant *2* tenu *3* tiens, tenons, tiennent *4* tenais *5* tiendrai *7* tienne

vaincre *1* vainquant *2* vaincu *3* vaincs, vainc, vainquons *4* vainquais *7* vainque

valoir *1* valant *2* valu *3* vaux, vaut, valons *4* valais *5* vaudrai *7* vaille

venir *1* venant *2* venu *3* viens, venons, viennent *4* venais *5* viendrai *7* vienne

vivre *1* vivant *2* vécu *3* vis, vivons *4* vivais *7* vive

voir *1* voyant *2* vu *3* vois, voyons, voient *4* voyais *5* verrai *7* voie

vouloir *1* voulant *2* voulu *3* veux, veut, voulons, veulent *4* voulais *5* voudrai *7* veuille *impératif* veuillez

LE VERBE ANGLAIS

present	pt	pp	present	pt	pp
arise	arose	arisen	fall	fell	fallen
awake	awoke	awoken	feed	fed	fed
be (am, is, are; being)	was, were	been	feel	felt	felt
			fight	fought	fought
bear	bore	born(e)	find	found	found
beat	beat	beaten	flee	fled	fled
become	became	become	fling	flung	flung
begin	began	begun	fly (flies)	flew	flown
behold	beheld	beheld	forbid	forbade	forbidden
bend	bent	bent	forecast	forecast	forecast
beseech	besought	besought	forego	forewent	foregone
beset	beset	beset	foresee	foresaw	foreseen
bet	bet, betted	bet, betted	foretell	foretold	foretold
bid	bid, bade	bid, bidden	forget	forgot	forgotten
bind	bound	bound	forgive	forgave	forgiven
bite	bit	bitten	forsake	forsook	forsaken
bleed	bled	bled	freeze	froze	frozen
blow	blew	blown	get	got	got, (US) gotten
break	broke	broken			
breed	bred	bred	give	gave	given
bring	brought	brought	go (goes)	went	gone
build	built	built	grind	ground	ground
burn	burnt, burned	burnt, burned	grow	grew	grown
			hang	hung, hanged	hung, hanged
burst	burst	burst			
buy	bought	bought	have (has; having)	had	had
can	could	(been able)			
cast	cast	cast	hear	heard	heard
catch	caught	caught	hide	hid	hidden
choose	chose	chosen	hit	hit	hit
cling	clung	clung	hold	held	held
come	came	come	hurt	hurt	hurt
cost	cost	cost	keep	kept	kept
creep	crept	crept	kneel	knelt, kneeled	knelt, kneeled
cut	cut	cut			
deal	dealt	dealt	know	knew	known
dig	dug	dug	lay	laid	laid
do (3rd person: he/she/it does)	did	done	lead	led	led
			lean	leant, leaned	leant, leaned
draw	drew	drawn	leap	leapt, leaped	leapt, leaped
dream	dreamed, dreamt	dreamed, dreamt	learn	learnt, learned	learnt, learned
drink	drank	drunk			
drive	drove	driven	leave	left	left
dwell	dwelt	dwelt	lend	lent	lent
eat	ate	eaten	let	let	let

present	pt	pp	present	pt	pp
lie (lying)	lay	lain	speed	sped, speeded	sped, speeded
light	lit, lighted	lit, lighted	spell	spelt, spelled	spelt, spelled
lose	lost	lost			
make	made	made	spend	spent	spent
may	might	—	spill	spilt, spilled	spilt, spilled
mean	meant	meant			
meet	met	met	spin	spun	spun
mistake	mistook	mistaken	spit	spat	spat
mow	mowed	mown, mowed	split	split	split
must	(had to)	(had to)	spoil	spoiled, spoilt	spoiled, spoilt
pay	paid	paid			
put	put	put	spread	spread	spread
quit	quit, quitted	quit, quitted	spring	sprang	sprung
			stand	stood	stood
read	read	read	steal	stole	stolen
rid	rid	rid	stick	stuck	stuck
ride	rode	ridden	sting	stung	stung
ring	rang	rung	stink	stank	stunk
rise	rose	risen	stride	strode	stridden
run	ran	run	strike	struck	struck, stricken
saw	sawed	sawn			
say	said	said	strive	strove	striven
see	saw	seen	swear	swore	sworn
seek	sought	sought	sweep	swept	swept
sell	sold	sold	swell	swelled	swollen, swelled
send	sent	sent			
set	set	set	swim	swam	swum
shake	shook	shaken	swing	swung	swung
shall	should	—	take	took	taken
shear	sheared	shorn, sheared	teach	taught	taught
shed	shed	shed	tear	tore	torn
shine	shone	shone	tell	told	told
shoot	shot	shot	think	thought	thought
show	showed	shown	throw	threw	thrown
shrink	shrank	shrunk	thrust	thrust	thrust
shut	shut	shut	tread	trod	trodden
sing	sang	sung	wake	woke	woken
sink	sank	sunk	waylay	waylaid	waylaid
sit	sat	sat	wear	wore	worn
slay	slew	slain	weave	wove, weaved	woven, weaved
sleep	slept	slept			
slide	slid	slid	wed	wedded, wed	wedded, wed
sling	slung	slung			
slit	slit	slit	weep	wept	wept
smell	smelt, smelled	smelt, smelled	win	won	won
			wind	wound	wound
sow	sowed	sown, sowed	wring	wrung	wrung
speak	spoke	spoken	write	wrote	written

LES NOMBRES

NUMBERS

un(une)	1	one
deux	2	two
trois	3	three
quatre	4	four
cinq	5	five
six	6	six
sept	7	seven
huit	8	eight
neuf	9	nine
dix	10	ten
onze	11	eleven
douze	12	twelve
treize	13	thirteen
quatorze	14	fourteen
quinze	15	fifteen
seize	16	sixteen
dix-sept	17	seventeen
dix-huit	18	eighteen
dix-neuf	19	nineteen
vingt	20	twenty
vingt et un(une)	21	twenty-one
vingt-deux	22	twenty-two
trente	30	thirty
quarante	40	forty
cinquante	50	fifty
soixante	60	sixty
soixante-dix	70	seventy
soixante et onze	71	seventy-one
soixante-douze	72	seventy-two
quatre-vingts	80	eighty
quatre-vingt-un(-une)	81	eighty-one
quatre-vingt-dix	90	ninety
quatre-vingt-onze	91	ninety-one
cent	100	a hundred
cent un(une)	101	a hundred and one
trois cents	300	three hundred
trois cent un(une)	301	three hundred and one
mille	1 000	a thousand
un million	1 000 000	a million

premier (première), 1er	first, 1st
deuxième, 2e or 2ème	second, 2nd
troisième, 3e or 3ème	third, 3rd
quatrième	fourth, 4th
cinquième	fifth, 5th
sixième	sixth, 6th
septième	seventh

LES NOMBRES

huitième
neuvième
dixième
onzième
douzième
treizième
quatorzième
quinzième
seizième
dix-septième
dix-huitième
dix-neuvième
vingtième
vingt-et-unième
vingt-deuxième
trentième
centième
cent-unième
millième

Les Fractions etc

un demi
un tiers
deux tiers
un quart
un cinquième
zéro virgule cinq, 0,5
trois virgule quatre, 3,4
dix pour cent
cent pour cent

Exemples

il habite au dix
c'est au chapitre sept
à la page sept
il habite au septième (étage)
il est arrivé (le) septième
une part d'un septième
échelle au vingt-cinq millième

NUMBERS

eighth
ninth
tenth
eleventh
twelfth
thirteenth
fourteenth
fifteenth
sixteenth
seventeenth
eighteenth
nineteenth
twentieth
twenty-first
twenty-second
thirtieth
hundredth
hundred-and-first
thousandth

Fractions etc

a half
a third
two thirds
a quarter
a fifth
(nought) point five, 0.5
three point four, 3.4
ten per cent
a hundred per cent

Examples

he lives at number 10
it's in chapter 7
on page 7
he lives on the 7th floor
he came in 7th
a share of one seventh
scale one to twenty-five
thousand

L'HEURE

THE TIME

quelle heure est-il?

what time is it?

il est ...

it's ...

minuit	midnight
une heure (du matin)	one o'clock (in the morning), one (a.m.)
une heure cinq	five past one
une heure dix	ten past one
une heure et quart	a quarter past one, one fifteen
une heure vingt-cinq	twenty-five past one, one twenty-five
une heure et demie, une heure trente	half past one, one thirty
une heure trente-cinq, deux heures moins vingt-cinq	twenty-five to two, one thirty-five
deux heures moins vingt, une heure quarante	twenty to two, one forty
deux heures moins le quart, une heure quarante-cinq	a quarter to two, one forty-five
deux heures moins dix, une heure cinquante	ten to two, one fifty
midi	twelve o'clock, midday, noon
deux heures (de l'après-midi)	two o'clock (in the afternoon), two (p.m.)
sept heures (du soir)	seven o'clock (in the evening), seven (p.m.)

à quelle heure?

at what time?

à minuit	at midnight
à sept heures	at seven o'clock
dans vingt minutes	in twenty minutes
il y a quinze minutes	fifteen minutes ago